Fundamentals of Marketing

NINTH CANADIAN EDITION

MONTROSE S. SOMMERS
Ryerson Polytechnic University

JAMES G. BARNES
Memorial University of Newfoundland

McGraw-Hill Ryerson

Toronto   Montréal   Boston   Burr Ridge, IL   Dubuque, IA   Madison, WI   New York
San Francisco   St. Louis   Bangkok   Bogotá   Caracas   Kuala Lumpur   Lisbon   London   Madrid
Mexico City   Milan   New Delhi   Santiago   Seoul   Singapore   Sydney   Taipei

McGraw-Hill Ryerson Limited
A Subsidiary of The McGraw-Hill Companies

FUNDAMENTALS OF MARKETING
Ninth Canadian Edition

ISBN 0-07-087252-X

1 2 3 4 5 6 7 8 9 0   TCP   0 9 8 7 6 5 4 3 2 1

VICE-PRESIDENT AND EDITORIAL DIRECTOR: Pat Ferrier
SPONSORING EDITOR: Lenore Gray-Spence
DEVELOPMENTAL EDITOR: Elke Price
SUPERVISING EDITOR: Alissa Messner
PERMISSIONS EDITOR: Alison Derry
COPY EDITOR: Erin Moore
SENIOR MARKETING MANAGER: Jeff MacLean
PRODUCTION SUPERVISOR: Nicla Dattolico
INTERIOR & COVER DESIGN: Dianna Little
COVER IMAGE: Artville
ELECTRONIC PAGE MAKE-UP: Heather Brunton/ArtPlus Limited
PRINTER: Transcontinental Printing Group

Canadian Cataloguing in Publication Data

Sommers, Montrose S., 1933-
    Fundamentals of marketing

9th Canadian ed.

Includes bibliographical references and index.

ISBN 0-07-087252-X

1. Marketing.   2. Marketing in Canada.   I. Barnes, James G.   II. Title.

HF5415.S745 2001   658.8   C00-932648-0

To Annie and Michael and with
a goodbye to Jesse, our dear old friend

M.S.S.

To Jennifer, Stephanie, and Karen

J.G.B.

About the Authors

Montrose Sommers is Adjunct Professor in the School of Business Management of Ryerson Polytechnic University. He received his B. Comm. from the University of British Columbia, his M.B.A. from Northwestern University and his D.B.A. from the University of Colorado. Dr. Sommers has been a consultant to private- and public-sector organizations involved in petroleum marketing, financial services, telecommunications, various retailing specializations, marketing research, and advertising. His teaching background is extensive; he has worked with Bachelor, Master, and Ph.D. students at the Universities of British Columbia, Texas, Hawaii, Toronto, Guelph, York, Nairobi in Kenya, Witwatersrand in South Africa, Huazhong and Tianjin in China, and the LSE in Great Britain. Dr. Sommers has also served on the editorial boards of the *Journal of Marketing*, the *Journal of International Management and Organizations*, and the *Journal of the Service Industries*.

Jim Barnes is Professor of Marketing at Memorial University of Newfoundland. Dr. Barnes received his B. Comm. and B.A. degrees from Memorial, his M.B.A. from the Harvard Business School, and his Ph.D. from the University of Toronto. He has been a member of the faculty at Memorial University since 1968, and served as Dean from 1978 to 1988. He has been a visiting professor at Queen's University, the University of Bath (England), University College Dublin (Ireland), Université de Reims (France), and Macquarie University (Australia). He is co-founder and Executive Vice-President of Bristol Group, a full-service marketing communications and information firm with four offices in Canada. He serves as consultant to many national and international companies and regularly delivers seminars and lectures on marketing-related subjects in many countries. In 1997, Dr. Barnes received the national Leaders in Management Education award from *The Financial Post*. He was elected a Fellow of the Professional Marketing Research Society of Canada in 1999. He serves on the Editorial Boards of the *International Journal of Bank Marketing* and *The International Journal of Customer Relationship Management*. His most recent book, *Secrets of Customer Relationship Management: It's All About How You Make Them Feel*, was published in 2001 by McGraw-Hill.

Contents in Brief

Contents

List of Cases

Preface

The Ninth Edition of *Fundamentals of Marketing* retains the fundamental concepts of managerial marketing presented in a highly readable fashion that has been a hallmark of this book since its beginning. To that foundation, Sommers and Barnes have added new structure and substance that seamlessly integrate electronic technology and emerging concepts and practices, creating an effective learning tool for today's student.

To The Student

Ask yourself the question: "What does marketing have to do with me?" We think the answer is: "A lot more than you would think!" When you finish reading this book, we know you will agree.

Marketing is an integral part of all of our lives. A surprising amount of time is taken up by our efforts to market something — our ideas, our skills, our experiences, ourselves — to others. And, of course, others spend a lot of time marketing to us. Whether you are a student, a small business owner, a lawyer, a professor, or an accountant doesn't make any difference, you are engaged in marketing. The challenge is to do it well and that requires an understanding of what marketing is and how to perform it.

But there is more to modern marketing, the new marketing, than learning what it involves. Much of the excitement of marketing is created by the context in which it occurs. The most obvious example today is the field of communications. How has a greater access to faster computers, the Internet, MP3 technology, Napster and its successors, affected your life? Consider the other extraordinary changes in communication technology and multiply all of that by the changes in other areas, such as in manufacturing, transportation, entertainment, financial services, and agriculture. Add to this the continuing rapid globalization that the new communication technology enables. Evidence of the rate of technological change and the shrinking of distances is all around us. We are faced with new challenges, large and small, domestic and international, and they seem to come at us almost daily. But every change, every challenge, from whatever the source, creates new marketing opportunities.

What does this mean for marketers? In some respects their jobs won't change. They will still decide what products and services to offer, set prices they think customers will consider to be good value for their money, provide products where customers can conveniently find them, and design promotional information to inform and persuade buyers. But the challenges they face and the tools they have available will change. In today's highly dynamic environment, marketing and other managers will be faced with more new situations than ever before. They will have access to more information and information sources than did their predecessors — much more of it Web-based. They will have to learn how to separate the essential from the interesting and how to use it effectively. They will have more strategic alternatives from which to select, but the cost of selecting the wrong one will be greater. They will be pursuing smaller market segments with products that have shorter lives. They will face a changing mix of competitors. In short, marketers will be operating in a faster-paced, higher-risk, and more technically complex environment.

What does this mean for you? Your career is beginning during a time of unprecedented challenge and change. You could translate this into success. To make the most of this opportunity, you need an understanding of contemporary marketing and how it works in the dynamic world of today. The objective of this new edition of *Fundamentals of Marketing* is to help you gain that understanding.

Special Features of the Ninth Edition

Since 1971, when it was first published, *Fundamentals of Marketing* has been a leader — easy and enjoyable to read, practical and comprehensive in its content and orientation, full of current topical information, and examples and illustrations of marketing as it is "best practiced" in Canada and around the world by leading Canadian and Canadian-based global firms, large and small. This ninth edition not only continues this tradition, but also meets the challenges we face in our ever-changing environment.

We present marketing as a total system of business actions carried out by managers in individual organizations in the context of the larger economy and society as a whole. Regardless of whether managers are employed by a business or nonprofit organization, are providers of goods or services, or are doing business domestically or globally, they need to understand certain fundamentals of marketing.

We share those fundamentals with you through the framework of the marketing management process. An organization first sets objectives, taking into consideration the environmental forces and competitors that influence its efforts. The managers then select target markets and build a marketing program to achieve those objectives. The four elements integrated by managers in designing a marketing program — product, price, distribution, and promotion — are at the heart of marketing as is working through people for successful implementation of marketing programs. Finally, an organization evaluates its performance and makes adjustments to its marketing strategy.

To help you understand and appreciate the new marketing and the marketing management process, we have not only provided clear explanations but also many real-life current examples. Each chapter opens with a real marketing story that illustrates the basic content of the material that follows. In addition to the text explanations, there are many current, real-life examples and illustrations of large and small Canadian firms in the form of boxed inserts called Marketing At Work Files. These files illustrate how firms actually implement the ideas you are studying in the Canadian and the global marketplace. While we have provided much more information on Internet marketing and the dot.com world, we have highlighted the importance of people and their contribution to the development and delivery of marketing programs.

Now, turn to Chapter 1 and start discovering that marketing is much more than you thought!

To The Instructor

What's New and Improved

◆ *Complete integration of the Internet, multimedia, and the "New Marketing" throughout.*

- The inclusion of numerous chapter openers, Marketing at Work Files and text illustrations, and examples of Internet and dot.com marketing activity; much of it linked to Canadian and other companies with which students will be familiar and which are relevant to them.

- Numerous Web site references are placed throughout the text material. These references direct students to companies and other sites that provide more information or allow the students to explore topics in greater detail. Some cases also require a review of selected Web sites.
- There are selected Web-based end of chapter problems and questions as well as video cases with supporting Internet resources.
- Increased emphasis throughout the book on the new view of marketing, focusing on current applications of service quality, customer retention, and customer relationships.
- A focus on really understanding the customer and his/her needs as the essence of marketing.

◆ *Major realignment and integration of text material, resulting in a book consisting of 21 chapters instead of 24 in previous editions.*

- International marketing, in keeping with globalization, is fully integrated throughout, with emphasis on consumer behaviour, business to business marketing, and channels of distribution.
- The discussion of marketing communications has been restructured to highlight the integrated marketing communications approach (IMC).
- Not-for-profit marketing has been reallocated and distributed throughout the book.
- The basic pricing coverage has been simplified and made more accessible to students with less emphasis on the "economics" of pricing and more on practical applications.

◆ *Relevance and readability enhanced with major emphasis on rapid student involvement in material and easy follow-through reading.*

- The major focus on chapter opening material dealing with situations, companies, and illustrations which are easily recognized by and of interest to your students.
- Descriptive chapter openings, text, and Marketing At Work Files are written in familiar and comfortable language to further enhance our reputation as a "fun text to read."
- A return to four-colour hardcover with careful page set-up and design for easy reading with changes of pace in presentation form and convenient use in terms of locating materials, structure of presentations, and centrality of discussions.

Revising a successful book is a delicate process. It is essential that new developments and material be incorporated into a revised edition and the presentation be lively and engaging. At the same time, many of the features that have been eminently successful over time should be retained. We have worked hard to maintain this balance by updating, and revising the book while preserving the organization. This book has always been noted by students as an enjoyable "fun" book to read compared with others. It has been noted by instructors as being well structured, comprehensive, and containing more Canadian perspectives, information, illustrations and examples than others.

The book is divided into seven parts to reflect the marketing management process.

◆ *Part One: The Field of Marketing and Its Dynamic Environment* Serves as an introduction and includes chapters on the marketing environment and strategic marketing planning.

◆ *Part Two: Target Markets* Devoted to the analysis and selection of consumer and business target markets. It also includes a detailed treatment of the very important strategic concepts of market segmentation and positioning, and the collection and use of market information.

◆ *Part Three: Products and Services* Topics related to the product are discussed with separate chapters on product planning and development, product mix strategies, and branding and packaging. There is also a special chapter on the marketing and delivery of services.

◆ *Part Four: Price* The choice of a price and the adjustments made are handled in a price determination and a pricing policies and strategies chapter.

◆ *Part Five: Distribution* The nature of channels of distribution and their management, the wholesaling and logistics operations, and retailing institutions and their dynamics and management are discussed in separate chapters.

◆ *Part Six: Marketing Communications* Chapters in this part cover effective communication to markets with a focus on the nature of promotional programs, personal selling and its management, and the management of advertising, sales promotion, and public relations.

◆ *Part Seven: Managing the Marketing Effort* This concluding part presents discussions on issues associated with successful marketing implementation, the performance of marketing, and presents our view of future developments.

Pedagogical Support

Chapter Opening Vignettes

Each chapter begins with a contemporary case vignette that introduces some of the concepts, strategies, and techniques covered in the chapter. Subjects of the vignettes include Molson Canadian "I Am" — marketing campaign, Tim Hortons — services marketing and customer relationships, MP3 and Napster — pricing, and Famous Players — retailing markets and institutions.

Marketing at Work Files

The majority of the Marketing at Work Files are new and illustrate new developments and successful implementations by recognizable companies. Over sixty-five MAWs are included in this edition. Examples include Would You Like Fries with Your Pokemon?, Canadian Net and Shopping Behaviour, eh!, B2B Builds New Market in the Great Web Bazaar, and Coke Charges More For Same Fizz.

Cases

Six of the seven parts end with at least three cases. There are 19 part-ending cases. Thirteen of these cases are new to this edition and six have been retained and revised. All deal with familiar firms facing significant marketing challenges. Each case is designed to be realistic, yet the focus is on a specific aspect of marketing to prevent the beginning student from being overwhelmed by the complexity common to many marketing problems. Of the thirteen new cases, three are Video Cases. Two of these Video Cases are tied

 to a video segment from the popular CBC *Venture* program. The other is from the CBC *Marketplace* program. Some of the part-ending cases are Modrobes, GlobalStudent.com, and Toys "R" Us.

Summary/Key Terms/Assignments

Every chapter concludes with a chapter summary, a list of key terms and concepts with chapter page references, and two types of assignments. The first is a set of eight to ten Questions and Problems designed to help students discover how to analyze issues and make applications based on the chapter discussion. The second type of assignment is called Hands-On Marketing. These assignments require the students to get out of the classroom and interact with customers or marketers as well as make use of the Internet.

Teaching and Learning Support

For the Instructor

INSTRUCTOR'S RESOURCE The new Instructor's Resource CD-ROM for *Fundamentals of Marketing* contains the Instructor's Manual, PowerPoint® slides, Test Bank, and Lecture Launchers.

- **Instructor's Manual** by Sommers, Barnes, and Peter Dunne. Peter worked closely with the authors throughout this revision. The Instructor's Manual uses a fresh approach that is based on the practical needs of instructors who want to help the students learn in the way that works best for the students. The goal is to help students learn more effectively by providing instructors with strategy suggestions (such as World Wide Web activities, group work, and case studies) to encourage learning in the context of an Introductory Marketing course. Case solutions for the text cases are also provided.

- **PowerPoint®** This software includes a set of over 300 slides. The slides include point-form summaries of key concepts discussed in the text.

- **Test Bank** The test bank comprises multiple choice and true/false questions, as well as caselettes — short, current case descriptions with accompanying multiple choice questions. The 2,200 questions in the test bank are coded to identify the type — concept, definition, or application.

- **Lecture Launchers** The lecture launchers, which are also in PowerPoint® format, provide an overview of the key points in the chapters.

VIDEO CASES AND VIDEO GUIDE This collection of video cases correspond with selected companies profiled in the part-ending cases. They feature a variety of organizations and marketing topics. Suggestions for their use are provided in the video guide.

TRANSPARENCY ACETATES A comprehensive colour transparency program is available to enhance lectures and class discussions.

For the Student

STUDY GUIDE by R. David Nowell. This useful study guide provides guidelines for analyzing marketing cases, chapter goals, chapter summaries, key terms and concepts, self-test questions (true-false, multiple choice, matching, and sentence completion), problems and applications questions, and interesting real world cases and articles related to chapter concepts. The Study Guide contains 95 percent new one-page cases and 75 percent new activities with answers provided in the Instructor's Manual.

ONLINE LEARNING CENTRE   Students and instructors can visit this Web site to gain access to a variety of aides and support, including student quiz questions with e-mail feature, interactive Flash-based chapter concept illustrations with exercises, interactive glossary, learning objectives, downloadable interactive Marketing Math tutorial and instructor's materials, Web links, cases, and video exercises.

Visit www.mcgrawhill.ca/college/sommers today.

Acknowledgements

Through nine editions of this book, many people have made important contributions. These include students, colleagues, clients, marketing managers in Canadian firms, and instructors at many universities and colleges. All have provided insights and commentary on the Canadian marketing scene and the teaching and learning of marketing. We sincerely thank them for their advice, thoughtfulness, and support.

We wish to acknowledge in particular those research and editorial assistants who contributed to the essential research and material preparation process necessary for this revision. Peter Dunne, in St. John's, has provided editorial and material preparation assistance in a most exemplary fashion. We are thankful for his skill and diligence and pleased that he has also worked with us on the Instructor's Manual.

Special research assistance was provided by Paymon Teymouri of Ryerson Polytechnic University in Toronto, and Jennifer Barnes authored many of the Marketing at Work Files. We are also indebted to the business and other executives who allowed us to write cases on their companies or organizations.

Another group that was instrumental in the preparation of this book was the group of reviewers used by our publisher. These include the following colleagues: Neil Beattie, Sheridan College; Diane Gauvin, Dawson College; Pat Kolodziejski, Mohawk College; Keith Murray, Langara College; Beth Pett, Niagara College; Diana Serafini, Dawson College; Ian Spencer, St. Francis Xavier University; Gail Tibbo, Douglas College; and Wayne Carlson, Southern Alberta Institute of Technology. They provided much useful insight and commentary and we would like to thank each of them. One colleague in particular requires special mention — David Nowell of Sheridan College. In addition to reviewing the manuscript, David made a significant contribution in the preparation of the supplementary materials for this edition of the text.

Finally, we would like to acknowledge with much appreciation the support and cooperation we receive from the staff of McGraw-Hill Ryerson. We are particularly grateful to Lenore Gray, who worked with us before, and is our Sponsoring Editor for this edition. She kept both her team and us focussed on the task. And in addition, she was fun to work with. We owe special thanks to Elke Price, Project Editor, Alison Derry, Photo Reseacher, Alissa Messner, Production Editor, and Erin Moore, Copy Editor who provided important assistance and information and helped us ensure that this edition will meet the goals and objectives of all those involved.

Montrose S. Sommers
James G. Barnes

McGraw-Hill Ryerson **Online Learning Centre**

O L C

McGraw-Hill Ryerson offers you an online resource that combines the best content with the flexibility and power of the Internet. Organized by chapter, the SOMMERS Online Learning Centre (OLC) offers the following features to enhance your learning and understanding of Fundamentals of Marketing.

- Online Quiz Questions
- Web Resources
- Online Glossary
- Internet Application Exercises
- Interactive Exercises

By connecting to the "real world" through the OLC, you will enjoy a dynamic and rich source of current information that will help you get more from your course and improve your chances for success, both in the course and in the future.

For the Instructor

DOWNLOADABLE SUPPLEMENTS

All the key supplements are available, password-protected for instant access!

ONLINE RESOURCES

McGraw-Hill Ryerson offers various online resource tools such as lecture notes and key figures to help you get the latest news and information for immediate use in class.

PAGEOUT

Create your own course Web page for free, quickly and easily. Your professionally designed Web site links directly to OLC material, allows you to post a class syllabus, offers an online gradebook, and much more! Visit www.pageout.net

A New Way to Deliver

For the Student

ONLINE QUIZ QUESTIONS

Do you understand the material? You'll know after taking an Online Quiz! Try the Multiple Choice questions for each chapter. They're auto-graded with feedback and you have the option to send results directly to faculty.

WEB RESOURCES

This section links you to various Web sites, including all Web Resources from the text.

INTERNET APPLICATION QUESTIONS

Test your Internet savvy with these online, skill-based exercises linked to companies featured in the text.

ONLINE GLOSSARY

All definitions in the text are included in the searchable glossary.

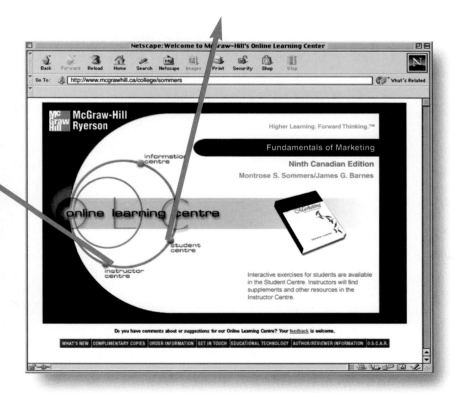

Your Internet companion to the most exciting educational tools on the Web!

The Online Learning Centre can be found at:
www.mcgrawhill.ca/college/sommers

EDUCATIONAL CONTEN

Part one

The Field of Marketing and Its Dynamic Environment

An overview of the new marketing, the rapidly changing marketing environment, and the essentials of strategic planning in marketing

*M*arketing is dynamic, challenging, and rewarding. Sometimes it may be frustrating. But it is never dull! Welcome to the part of the business or organization where everything comes together and finally happens — the place where ideas, planning, and execution get the acid test of market acceptance or rejection.

Chapter 1 explains the new view of marketing, how marketing continues to develop, and its importance to society and you personally. Chapter 2 discusses the environmental forces that shape a marketing program. Then, Chapter 3 discusses the management process in marketing and introduces the basic elements of strategic marketing planning.

Chapter One

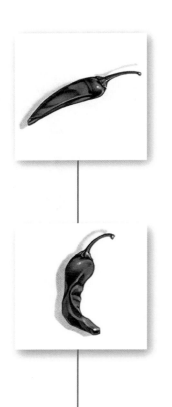

The Field of Marketing

"What is marketing?" Chapter 1 answers this question — and the answer may surprise you. After studying this chapter, you should have an understanding of:

◆ The relationship between exchange and marketing.

◆ How marketing applies to business and nonbusiness situations.

◆ The evolution of marketing.

◆ Services and relationship marketing.

◆ An understanding of the factors that drive customer satisfaction.

◆ The difference between selling and marketing.

◆ The marketing concept.

◆ The impact of quality, service, and ethics in modern marketing.

◆ Marketing's role in the global economy, in Canada's economy, in an individual organization, and in your life.

Canada.com: The Canadian Portal to the Information Highway

As the new millennium began, record numbers of Canadian consumers began to see the merits of Internet shopping. This was especially the case during the last holiday season of the twentieth century. Canada.com (www.canada. com) was a hit with on-line shoppers during this time, posting a 167 percent increase in traffic in December 1999 over the same time the previous year. Surprisingly, the most popular category for the holiday season was clothing.

Since clothing had previously been regarded as a "high touch" product that would not sell particularly well through the Internet, this represented a significant milestone in e-retail. Those products that were initially accepted and enjoyed high webonomic success followed clothing: computers, books, music, travel, and toys. Such success may be attributed to the quality Canadian retailers that

have been collected under the Canada. com banner. These include HMV.com, Roots Canada, Club Monaco, Holt Renfrew, chapters.ca, Onvia.com, toyboutique.com, and Peachtree.

The way that Canadians shop had begun to be transformed as Canadian retailers recognized the value of establishing an online presence. This was further facilitated through the organization of sites such as Canada.com that create full-service portals

to the Internet to fill a variety of consumer needs, causing them to return repeatedly to the same site thereby fostering an ongoing relationship with the service provider.

Created by Southam, Inc. (as in the newspapers), the Canada.com site has created a "web community" through provision of free e-mail, personalized homepage settings, career postings, online shopping, and news. There is national, international, business, sports, and entertainment news. As well, there is weather for the country, horoscopes, TV listings, contests, and results of provincial and regional lotteries. If you're a betting person, there are also tips on how to play the lottery and select the most common winning numbers.

The next evolutionary stage in shopping may be considered the online auction — and yes, this is also available — Click-abid (www.clickabid.com) allows the shopper to

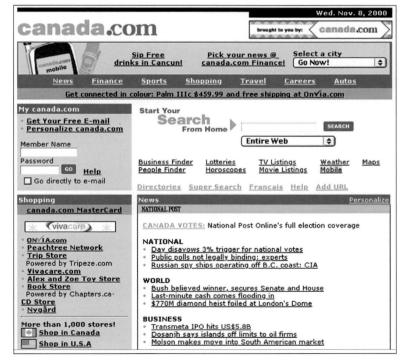

participate in silent auctions on everything from classic cars to that hard-to-find Beanie Baby to complete your collection. There are also charity auctions.

The Canada.com site also provides a general WWW search engine and links to top-rated Canadian sites. This wide variety of informational, personal, and entertainment options has created an address on the Web that provides a range of free services to the consumer. At the same time, it provides marketing opportunities to many Canadian retailers through the development of an ongoing online relationship as the site becomes a personal resource to the Web surfer. Canada.com receives, on average, 42 million page views per month from over 2.3 million users.

Nature and Scope of Marketing

The provision of these services by Canada.com, with the ability to customize the site to each customer's needs, helps to build a relationship with customers while "capturing" a market for those retailers that pay Canada.com to be represented on this site.

Let's step back and look at marketing in more general terms. Marketing exists in many forms — we participate in various aspects of the marketing process every time we buy a pair of jeans or get a haircut. You probably have had a job that included dealing with customers. But did you realize that you also engage in a form of marketing when you vote in a provincial election, donate to the Canadian Cancer Society, and prepare your resume? At the heart of each of these forms of marketing is the concept of **exchange**. Marketing can be perceived as a part of every activity within any organization. Each of these activities should be orchestrated to increasing long-term "customer" satisfaction.

exchange
The voluntary act of providing a person or organization something of value in order to acquire something else of value in return.

Exchange as the Focus

Marketing is happening any time one social unit (person or organization) strives to exchange something of value with another social unit. In this broad sense, marketing consists of activities designed to generate and facilitate exchanges intended to satisfy human needs or wants. It is important to keep in mind — and we will return to this point many times in this book — that customer needs exist at a number of different levels. Customers not only need the products that they buy, they need the function that the product will perform. They also need what having that product or service makes it possible for them to do. It is often observed that a family when dealing with a bank does not *need* a mortgage; what they really need is a home. The mortgage makes home ownership possible. Customers also *need* good service, and they *need* to be made to feel important and respected.

Exchange is one of a number of ways in which a person can satisfy a want. If you *want* a pair of slacks, you could sew them, you could borrow them from a friend, you could trade a Tragically Hip T-shirt for them, or you can offer something of value (money, in most cases) to another person who will voluntarily exchange the slacks for what you offer. It is only the last approach that we call an exchange, in the sense that marketing is taking place.

The following conditions must exist for a marketing exchange to take place:

◆ Two or more social units — people or organizations — must be involved, and each must have wants to be satisfied. If you are totally self-sufficient in some area, there is no need for an exchange.

◆ The parties must be involved voluntarily (although some argue that a situation in which consumers deal with monopolies, such as electric utilities or public transit systems, violates this condition — this is not so, as these organizations must engage in marketing too).

◆ Each party must have something of perceived value to contribute in the exchange, and each must believe that it will benefit from the exchange. In the case of resume preparation, for example, the items of value are desirable employee skills and attributes for one side of the exchange and the prospect of gainful employment for the other party.

◆ The parties must communicate with each other. This information exchange can take many forms and may even be through a third party, but without communication there can be no exchange.

These exchange conditions introduce a number of terms that deserve some elaboration. First, there are the parties involved in the exchange. On one side of the exchange is the marketer. **Marketers** take the initiative in trying to stimulate and facilitate exchanges. They develop marketing plans and programs, and implement them in the hope of creating an exchange that can be repeated over time. A college or university that is recruiting students, the United Way soliciting donors, MuchMusic (www.muchmusic. com) appealing to viewers, and Air Canada (www.aircanada.ca) seeking passengers are all marketers looking to communicate with potential customers.

On the other side of the exchange is the **market**, made up of people or organizations to whom marketing programs are directed and who will play a key role in the acceptance or rejection of a marketer's offer. Markets are made up of *customers* — any person or group with whom an individual or organizational marketer has an existing or potential exchange relationship. Examples of markets include employees, clients, passengers, patrons, donors, students, taxpayers, and patients.

The people who constitute a market play a number of roles. First, there is the *decision-maker*, the individual or organizational unit that has the authority to commit to an exchange. Then there is the *consumer*, the one who actually uses or consumes the product or service. Another role is that of *purchaser*, the party who actually carries out the exchange. Finally, there are *influencers*, who affect the decisions of others because of their expertise, position, or power. These definitions are not simply semantic distinctions. These roles are very important in determining how marketers carry out their marketing programs, what information they direct to whom, what appeals are likely to work for different people in the process.

Let's illustrate the roles that various individuals (and others) play in the exchange process. In recent years there has been a great deal of investment by pet food manufacturers in the development of specialized nutritional formulations. These were aimed at fortifying teeth, bones, and coat. These also addressed the pet's nutritional requirements at various life stages. As these products were often significantly more expensive for the consumer to buy, few retail outlets carried the products and few of their customers (*decision-makers* and *purchasers*) bought them when available. It was not until such formulations were recommended and endorsed by professional associations and veterinarians (*influencers*) that this market expanded significantly. The marketing problem for this industry was: What should the marketing effort look like when trying to influence purchase at the retail and individual level? This example is unique in that the opinion of the actual *consumer* of this product is not targeted through marketing efforts. The cats and dogs who are the ultimate consumers only get to voice their opinion at the food dish.

marketer
Any person or organization that desires to make exchanges.

market
People or organizations with wants to satisfy, money to spend, and the willingness to spend it.

This consumer is neither decision-maker nor purchaser.

An organization's markets include more than the customers for its primary product. For example, in addition to appealing to the students who "consume" an education and the parents who frequently pay for some or all of it, a university or college directs its marketing to local and provincial officials in order to secure resources. Also, it is directed to people living near the university who are affected by its activities, to alumni and businesses who support various university programs, and the pool of prospective employees. A firm's markets also includes government regulatory agencies, environmentalists, and its shareholders.

Marketers, while keeping in mind the various roles in the marketplace, must keep in mind that their principal task is to offer customers a product or service that will produce satisfaction. Marketing is the process of satisfying customer *needs* and *wants* through an exchange process. In describing exchanges, we use the terms needs and wants interchangeably because marketing is relevant to both. Technically, needs can be viewed in a strict physiological sense (food, clothing, and shelter), and everything else can be defined as a want. However, from a customer's perspective, the distinction is not clear. For example, many people consider a television set or a computer to be a necessity. We also must remember that customer needs extend well beyond the actual product or service being offered.

Beyond the fulfilment of the core need, there are "higher order" elements that must be considered in the marketing of most products and services. Are the support services and systems sufficient? This refers to delivery and billing systems, hours of service, and staffing levels. Does the provider get the core product and support services right? This means getting the product right, defect free, and delivered to the customer in a timely fashion. Was the interaction between the service provider and the customer satisfactory? This refers to the interface between the two parties, whether it is face-to-face or technology-based. At this level, the marketer is dealing with emotional components of the exchange. Do the customers feel that they were treated with respect and that their patronage is appreciated? Essentially, how does the company make its customers *feel*?

product

A set of tangible attributes, including packaging, colour, price, quality, and brand, plus the services and reputation of the seller. A product may be a good, service, place, person, or idea.

Finally, the objective of the exchange or what is being marketed is referred to generically as the **product**. It can be a tangible, physical product, a service, an idea, a person, or a place. A box of corn flakes is a tangible product; accounting advice is an example of a service; an advertising slogan sold by an ad agency represents an idea; an individual who applies for a job is marketing a person; and a provincial government trying to attract tourism is an example of marketing a place as the product. All of these products can and are marketed, as we shall see. Beyond the obvious examples of products, exchanges also involve more subtle components, such as an employee showing a strong interest in the customer's well being. The expression of interest can add an element to the process that takes it beyond the simple purchase of a product. The exchange then includes more emotional dimensions.

THE CONCEPT OF RELATIONSHIP IN EXCHANGE When two people or organizations are voluntarily involved in an exchange situation, are communicating with each other, and are contributing something of value to the exchange and thereby mutually satisfying needs or wants, a **relationship** can develop. Some people refer to transient interactions as relationships. Generally, however, relationships are of a more long-term nature and involve many exchanges and interactions over a number of years. At the level of relationships between customers and suppliers, more emotional exchanges occur. These are characterized by feelings of attachment or closeness, loyalty and trust. Think about companies with which you and your family have been doing business for many years. These may be with small firms like the neighbourhood drugstore or auto repair shop. Your family probably keeps going back again and again because they know the owner and are made to feel welcome.

The longer such an exchange relationship lasts, the more likely it is to be of special value to those taking part in it. Buyers and sellers understand each other better; they better understand the value of what they are exchanging and how their needs are being satisfied, and they are able to communicate more easily.

How does a drugstore forge customer relationships and become "everything you want in a drugstore"? Shoppers Drug Mart (www.shoppersdrugmart.ca) believes it can do this by talking to customers one-on-one and by inviting its customers to drop by for special occasions. So far, it sounds like a relationship.

Pharmacists have always been sought out by customers to provide relatively personal advice — Shoppers Drug Mart is seeking to evolve this tradition to a modern form. The drugstore has, in the past, courted the seniors market with its monthly discount day, providing refreshments and entertainment. They have developed the Healthwatch® system to profile customers' medical histories and medications in an effort to become a "partner" in the customer's healthcare. Recent print and television ads have asked customers to come in and ask about diseases or illnesses that have high incidence rates among certain groups, so they can learn of the warning signs. Also, to come in and visit the pharmacist if they have been diagnosed. They have also held screening and information clinics in an effort to demonstrate concern for the health of their customers. Print and television advertisements present direct statements asking that people become more active in investigating their own health with the help of SDM. Advertisements are done in a personal and familiar tone and indicate that SDM will be there to assist.

Applications of Marketing

This book focuses on the activities carried out by individuals and organizations to facilitate mutually beneficial exchanges and develop marketing relationships. The organizations may be business firms in the conventional sense of the word, or they may be nonbusiness, or not-for-profit, organizations, such as a hospital, a university, a Big Brothers/Big Sisters organization, a church, a police department, or a museum. Both groups — business and nonbusiness — face the same basic marketing problems and can make use of the same marketing ideas. And it is the people in organizations, in their own businesses and even in their personal lives, who apply marketing ideas not only inside and outside their firms but also in such personal situations as when applying for a job.

Our definition of marketing — applicable in businesses, not-for-profit organizations, and personal situations — is as follows:

marketing
A total system of business activities designed to plan, price, promote, and distribute want-satisfying products to target markets in order to achieve organizational objectives.

Marketing is a total system of business activities designed to plan, price, promote, and distribute want-satisfying products, services, and ideas to target markets in order to achieve the objectives of both the consumer and the organization.

Marketing is:	
a system:	for business activities
designed to:	plan, price, promote, and distribute
something of value:	want-satisfying products, services, and ideas in the context of a valuable relationship
for the benefit of:	the target market — present and potential household consumers or business users
to achieve:	satisfaction of the needs and objectives of both consumers and the firm or organization.

This definition has some significant implications when marketing is properly applied:

◆ It is a systems definition, which means that it should be understood and applied by everyone in an organization.

◆ The entire system of business or organizational activities must be customer-oriented and focus on the quality of the customer relationship — customers' needs and wants must be recognized and satisfied effectively. The ultimate objective of marketing is to achieve customer satisfaction.

◆ The marketing program starts with an idea for a product or service and does not end until the customer's wants are completely satisfied, which may be some time after an exchange is made. This also suggests that the process of customer satisfaction is an ongoing one, and does not end when the sale is made.

◆ An organization's marketing program, generally termed the *marketing mix*, usually consists of four co-ordinated elements:

1. a product or service assortment,

2. a pricing structure,

3. distribution systems and channels, and

4. promotional activities.

Marketers have recently begun to express the view that although getting the components of the marketing mix right is important or even necessary, this may not be sufficient to guarantee customer satisfaction. In other words, as marketers have begun to pay more attention to the application of the marketing concept to marketing in service organizations and to the development of long-term customer relationships, they have realized that other factors, such as how customers are treated and the physical facilities of the company, are important in influencing customer satisfaction.

Marketing at Work 1 – 1

Would You Like Fries with Your Pokémon?

In the age of the value-driven consumer, fast food retailers must compete fiercely on the basis of price, quantity, quality, and customer service.

For an extra 49¢ your order can be upgraded to the "Supersize" version at McDonald's, KFC has introduced home delivery and "Toonie Tuesdays," and Wendy's has a constant menu of value-priced items for 99¢ or $1.39. But the real battle for "value" is being fought and won based on who has the best TOY!

There is an expectation on the part of consumers that they will get something extra for their hard-earned money. Toys provide the incentive needed for fast food retailers to entice customers through their front doors. Determining whose front door to walk through, however, is no longer a brand decision based on the food, but rather on the "treat of the week."

Fast food retailers today are earning a lot of their brand awareness from the toy they flog. Hence the evolution of the promotion. It is no longer enough to offer a two-dimensional plastic hand puppet, or a lick-and-stick tattoo featuring the Hamburglar. Today's toys have to be the latest and greatest, which is why fast food retailers are partnering with blockbuster movies such as *Toy Story* and *Star Wars* as well as with the makers of Beanie Babies.

Rem Langan, VP, National Director of Marketing at McDonald's cites two ingredients needed to get the promotion right. Something unique, of high quality and value. And the addition of a branded name. He says that this winning combination gives consumers an opportunity to feel this is something they couldn't buy anywhere else, or if they could that it would cost them more.

Source: Adapted from Astrid Van Den Broek, "Pester's Paradise," *Marketing Magazine*, November 8, 1999, p. 13.

&volution of Marketing

The foundations of marketing in Canada were laid in pioneer times when settlers began trading among themselves and with various groups of Native peoples thereby developing various exchange and barter relationships. Since then, marketing has evolved through three successive stages of development: production orientation, sales orientation, and marketing orientation. Following from the last stage, marketing is now focusing more on the processes involved in providing service and developing marketing relationships.

The three stages through which marketing has evolved reflect not only development over time, but also states of mind. Although many firms have progressed to the third stage and beyond, the orientation of some firms and some individuals is still in the second or even the first stage, as shown in Figure 1-1.

Production-Orientation Stage

production-orientation stage
The first stage in the evolution of marketing management, in which the basic assumption is that making a good product will ensure business success.

Firms in the **production-orientation stage**, typically manufacturers, focused on increasing output while assuming that customers would seek out and buy reasonably priced and well-made products. Executives in production and engineering shaped the firm's planning. The function of the sales department was simply to sell the company's output at a price set by production and finance executives. The primary focus in business at this stage was to produce large quantities of goods and produce them efficiently. Finding customers was viewed as a relatively minor function. This focus on the production of physical goods was common during the first half of the 20th century, although some firms still think this way today — "if we make it, surely they will want to buy it."

Sales-Orientation Stage

As the economy grew in North America it became clear that the main problem was no longer to produce or grow enough, but rather to sell the output. Just making a better product brought no assurance of market success. Firms started to realize that the sale

FIGURE 1-1
The Three Stages of Marketing Evolution

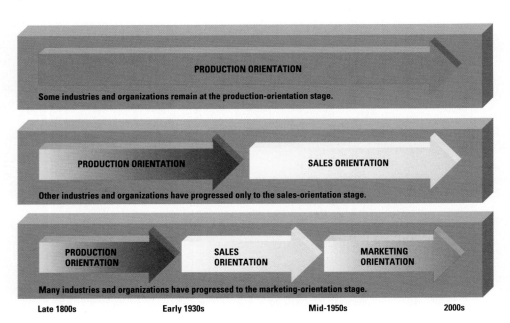

PRODUCTION ORIENTATION

Some industries and organizations remain at the production-orientation stage.

PRODUCTION ORIENTATION   SALES ORIENTATION

Other industries and organizations have progressed only to the sales-orientation stage.

PRODUCTION ORIENTATION   SALES ORIENTATION   MARKETING ORIENTATION

Many industries and organizations have progressed to the marketing-orientation stage.

Late 1800s   Early 1930s   Mid-1950s   2000s

sales-orientation stage
The second stage in the evolution of marketing management, in which the emphasis is on selling whatever the organization produces.

of products required substantial promotional effort. Thus began a period — the **sales-orientation stage** — when selling activities and sales executives gained new respect and responsibility from company management. It was also during this period that selling acquired much of its bad reputation, as "hard sell" approaches and shady sales tactics evolved. The sales stage was common until the 1950s, when the marketing era began to emerge. The emphasis on sales is still a feature of the operations of many companies, particularly in a business-to-business context.

Marketing-Orientation Stage

After World War II there was an enormous pent-up demand for consumer goods. Manufacturers produced large quantities of goods that were quickly purchased. However, the postwar surge in consumer spending slowed down as supply caught up with demand, and many firms found they had excess production capacity. In an attempt to stimulate sales, firms reverted to the aggressive promotional and sales activities of the sales-orientation era. However, this time consumers were less willing to be persuaded and had more selection. Experience and the mass media produced more knowledgeable consumers and new technologies provided a wider variety of goods and greater choices.

marketing-orientation stage
The third stage in the evolution of marketing management, in which a company focuses on the needs of its customers and carries out a broad range of marketing activities.

Thus the evolution of marketing continued. Many companies recognized that to put idle capacity to work they had to produce what consumers wanted. In the **marketing-orientation stage**, companies identify what customers want and tailor all the activities of the firm to satisfy those needs as efficiently as possible. The objective of marketing-oriented companies became to satisfy the customer.

In this third stage, firms are marketing rather than merely selling. Tasks that were once associated with other business functions become the responsibility of the top marketing executive, typically the marketing manager or vice-president of marketing. For instance, inventory control, warehousing, and some aspects of product planning are turned over to the head of marketing as a way of serving customers better. For a firm to be most effective, the top marketing executive must be involved at the beginning of a production cycle as well as at the end. In addition, marketing must be included in both short-term and long-term company planning.

For a firm's marketing to be effective, its top executive must have a favourable attitude toward marketing. Philip Knight, chairman and CEO of Nike (www.nike.com), makes this point: "For years we thought of ourselves as a production-oriented company, meaning we put all our emphasis on designing and manufacturing the product. But now we understand that the most important thing we do is market the product."[1]

It is not necessary for marketing executives to hold the top positions in a company or for the president of a firm to have come up through the marketing department. But it is necessary for the CEO to understand the importance of marketing, that is, to be *marketing-oriented* and to focus on putting in place programs and systems that will contribute to satisfying the customer in the long term. The processes must be customer-focused, meaning the customer's wants and needs are central to their design.

Many business firms and not-for-profit organizations are in this third stage in the evolution of marketing. Others may recognize the importance of a marketing orientation but have difficulty implementing it, for at least two reasons. First, implementation requires accepting the notion that the wants and needs of customers, not the desires of management, direct the organization. A leading business publication puts it this way: "Instead of choosing from what you have to offer, the new consumer tells you what he wants."[2]

TABLE 1-1 What Business Are You In?

Company	Production-Oriented Answer	Marketing-Oriented Answer
Bell Canada	We operate a telephone company.	We provide multiple forms of reliable, efficient, and inexpensive communications services.
Esso	We produce oil and gasoline products.	We provide various types of safe and cost-effective energy.
Visa Canada	We provide credit cards.	We facilitate the purchase of products and services and the transfer of funds.
Canadian National	We run a railway.	We offer a transportation and materials-handling system.
Levi Strauss	We make blue jeans.	We offer comfort, fashion, and durability in wearing apparel.
Kodak	We make cameras and film.	We help preserve beautiful memories.
Bombardier Inc.	We make planes.	We provide innovative ways of transporting people quickly and safely.
Rogers AT&T	We provide cell phones.	We enable people to communicate freely, from practically anywhere in the world.
Pegasus Intelligence	We design CAD/CAM software.	We allow companies to reach a superior level in the optimization and business processes.
National Hockey League	We provide hockey games.	We create and promote events that are an excellent means of family entertainment.

Placing customers first affects the way an organization describes what it does. Table 1-1 shows how some well-known organizations might define their businesses under a production orientation and how differently the business would be defined using a marketing orientation.

In some situations, an organization may be viewed as not needing to be marketing-oriented to prosper. A monopoly service provider, such as a provincial power utility, is virtually guaranteed to have customers. In such a situation, management is often more concerned with low-cost, efficient production. Nevertheless, the customer's satisfaction should remain the primary concern. In recent years in the telecommunications industry, former monopolies such as Bell Canada began to face competition from companies such as AT&T Canada, Sprint Canada, and cable television operators. Canada is now experiencing the deregulation of electrical utility service with multiple providers beginning service in Ontario in November 2000. Again, large provincial monopolies are facing new direct competition in a newly deregulated arena. Unless they prepare to develop service and customer-focused work environments, they will suffer huge losses in the open market.

In some instances, potential customers consider a product or service to be so superior or so desirable that they will seek it out. In such situations, the need for marketing may not be obvious, especially if one considers marketing to imply the need to sell the product or service. This may be the case when you line up for hours to buy tickets to a rock concert. But, even in these cases, if a company does not get its customer service right, customers will not continue to buy. An important lesson at this stage is that a great product and an attractive price are not enough to guarantee long-term customer satisfaction and long-term success for the firm or organization.

Marketing at Work 1-2

Water, Water Everywhere . . . But What Company to Drink?

Wondering how to make a splash at your next store opening, corporate retreat, product launch, or quench your thirst for an increase in your brand awareness? All you may need is a bottle of water.

Last year Canadians spent millions of dollars on bottled water. No longer the domain of Perrier and Evian, it seems that anyone and everyone can have their own brand of bottled water. Private Reserve Water, of Langley B.C., has capitalized on Canadians' thirst and earns revenues in excess of one million dollars a year bottling more than 100,000 litres of water each month. Its clients include Clearnet Communications, Holiday Inn Express, and Deloitte & Touche. Bottles of water are produced in three sizes, 500 ml, 1 L, and 1.5 L, with the appropriate company logo.

Three years ago, two B.C. businessmen saw an untapped niche in the growing bottled water industry. Today, 80 percent of its business is in private label packaging. The company has two main customer segments: restaurants, hotels, and other food and beverage operations who want to provide their customers with a self-branded product; and corporations that dis-

tribute self-branded bottles of water as promotional items. One of its clients, Clearnet Communications, has integrated bottled water into its marketing campaign by giving away Clearnet branded bottles of water at its retail stores across Canada as support for its slogan "Try us, we're refreshing and new."

Source: Adapted from Norma Ramage, "Private-label H₂0," *Marketing Magazine*, October 11, 1999, p. 3.

Differences Between Marketing and Selling Orientations

As marketing has evolved from a sales orientation to a marketing orientation, the terms *marketing* and *selling* are often used interchangeably. Some people think they are synonymous, but there are vast differences between the two activities. The basic difference is that selling is oriented to what is available and to the organization's needs, while marketing is oriented to the customer's needs and to how a product and service mix can satisfy them. These differences are highlighted in Table 1-2.

TABLE 1-2 Focus on Selling and Marketing

Selling Orientation	Marketing Orientation
Emphasis is on the product.	Emphasis is on satisfying customers' needs.
Company first makes the product and then figures out how to sell it.	Company first determines customers' wants and needs and then figures out how to make and deliver a product to satisfy those wants and needs.
Management is sales-volume oriented.	Management is profit oriented.
Focus is short-term: sell the product, meet the sales quota.	Focus is longer-term: create long-term customer value and repeat business.
Planning is short-run oriented, in terms of today's products and markets.	Planning is long-run oriented, in terms of new products, and markets, tomorrow's markets, and future growth.
Stresses needs of seller.	Stresses needs and wants of buyers.

Services

The Canadian economy, like that of most of the developed world, has experienced a major shift from goods production to service production over the last twenty-five years. The growth of service industries has resulted in an increased focus on the requirement to meet customers' needs through providing efficient, effective, and high-quality service. We can think of services as falling into two categories: first, as an intangible product to be sold, such as a cleaning service; second, as the service accompanying the sale of most tangible products. For example, a consumer who buys a refrigerator may require it to be delivered; the delivery of the product is a service provided by the retailer.

Marketers have become very conscious of the fact that consumers are demanding more and better services. To meet the requirements for customer satisfaction, marketers must think about how services are provided and what component parts make up a service. It is useful to distinguish between core elements and non-core features. For example, a traveller who checks into a hotel is purchasing a room for the night — that is the core product. However, the hotel guest expects that certain things will be included with the purchase of the room that go beyond the provision of a place to spend the night. The hotel usually will be expected to allow the customer to reserve the room. Upon arrival, the customer will check in. There are certain processes involved in completing the check-in which the customer expects will run smoothly and efficiently. Once the guest is shown to the room, there is an expectation of cleanliness, pleasant decor, and amenities such as bath supplies, water glasses, and laundry bags. The temperature of the room must allow the guest to be comfortable. If the individual calls for room service or valet service, there is an expectation that it will be provided in a timely, competent, and courteous manner. In interactions with hotel staff, the customer has certain expectations about the appropriate way for staff to respond. The employees involved in the exchange must be able to interact so that the customer receives the right amount of service to meet his or her needs and wants. This interaction may lead to relationship development between the customer and the employees or the business. If the interaction is not handled satisfactorily, the customer may experience negative feelings about it and the company. Often these feelings arise from brief comments made by unthinking or inappropriately trained staff.

drivers of customer satisfaction
Factors that contribute to customer satisfaction.

The above example includes five levels of factors that contribute to customer satisfaction, which we can call **drivers of customer satisfaction**.[3] Figure 1-2 illustrates these five levels. The core is the basic product or service provided by the organization. Generally, we tend to think of tangible products as the core because they are easy to visualize, but a service may be the core offering. In the hotel example, the core product is the room, the bed, and the bathroom. These aspects of the product are the most basic things being offered to the customer. When customers evaluate service, they require that the hotel gets at least the core product right.

FIGURE 1-2
Factors That Drive Customer Satisfaction

- Emotional Elements of the Interaction
- Interaction with the Firm and its Employees
- Technical Performance
- Processes and Support
- Core

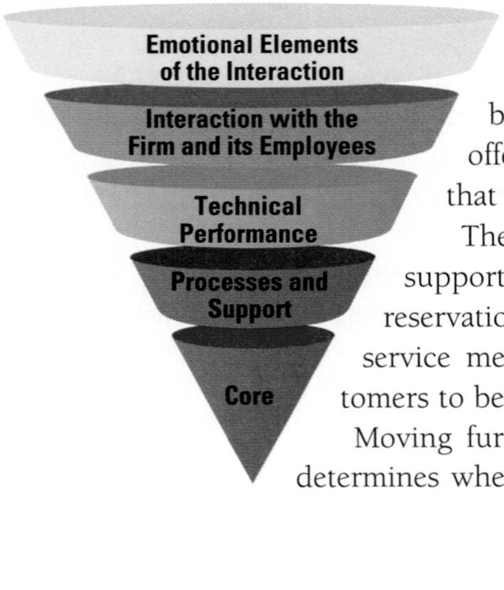

The second level in the drivers of customer satisfaction model is that of support services and systems. It includes such things, in our example, as reservation services, billing systems, convenience of hotel location, and room service menu. Failing to provide satisfactory support services can cause customers to be dissatisfied and not return.

Moving further up the model, the third level is technical performance, which determines whether the service provider gets the core product and support services right. The emphasis is on meeting the expectations of the customer. Is the hotel room clean and ready when the guest arrives? Customer dissatisfaction will result from a failure to meet customer expectations that things will go smoothly and as promised.

The fourth level of the model concerns the customer's interaction with the organization and its employees. This level can involve both face-to-face interaction and the interaction that occurs through technology-based contact over the telephone or through e-mail or the Internet. Satisfaction, at this level, is determined by whether or not the service provider makes it easy for customers to do business with it. Are customers treated with respect? Is the staff efficient, pleasant, helpful, and courteous? Understanding this level of customer satisfaction indicates that a firm has thought beyond the provision of the core product and service and is focused on the delivery of service at the point where the company meets the customer.

Finally, service marketers must think beyond the basic elements of the interaction with customers to consider the sometimes-subtle messages that firms send to customers. These messages may create either positive or negative feelings toward the company. Essentially, this level is concerned with emotional considerations (i.e., how the customer *feels* about the exchange). Often a customer's satisfaction or dissatisfaction has nothing to do with the quality of the core product or service or with how it is provided to the customer. Business may be lost because of some comment from a staff member or some other "little thing" that goes wrong and that may not even be noticed by staff.

Relationship Marketing

relationship marketing
An attempt by a sales person or company to develop a deeper, longer-lasting relationship built on trust with key customers — usually larger accounts.

As marketers began to think about the elements of satisfaction involved in the provision of services to consumers, a new awareness of the value of relationships in marketing began to emerge. The concept of **relationship marketing** involves building personal, long-term bonds with customers. Many of the factors discussed in relation to the fourth and fifth levels of the drivers of customer satisfaction in Figure 1-2 contribute to the development of relationships in marketing exchanges. This new emphasis on relations and relationship marketing is a further step in the development of a market orientation. Identifying the needs of customers and satisfying them can be profitable, but establishing a connection with customers so that the organization is regularly relied on for products and services is much more valuable. Such a relationship, which involves being more like a partner than simply a participant in an exchange, only occurs if a sense of closeness, trust, and commitment is established between buyer and seller. While many factors affect the development of a strong relationship marketing program, two major factors are (1) the provision of quality products and services, and (2) the conducting of marketing relationships within a trusting and ethical framework.

marketing concept
A philosophy of doing business that emphasizes customer orientation and co-ordination of marketing activities in order to achieve the organization's performance objectives.

The Marketing Concept

The evolution of marketing thinking from an emphasis on production to a focus on relationships has led to successive steps in the development of a philosophy of doing business. Called the **marketing concept**, this philosophy emphasizes customer orientation and the co-ordination of marketing activities to achieve the mutual long-term objectives of both the customer and the organization. Although customer satisfaction is important, this focus will work only if it is accomplished at the same time that the organization's objectives are being met. The needs of both parties in the marketing exchange must be met simultaneously.

Long-term customer satisfaction leads to the retention of customers and generates substantial profits.[4] It is more profitable for firms to keep customers than to be constantly seeking new ones.[5] Developing satisfied customers is therefore an important way to meet the organization's performance objectives.

Nature and Rationale

The marketing concept is based on three beliefs that are illustrated in Figure 1-3:

◆ All planning and operations should be *customer oriented*. Every department and employee should be focused on contributing to the satisfaction of customers' needs. At potato-chip producer Frito-Lay, engineers developed a simulated human mouth to measure the jaw effort needed to crunch a chip. By comparing taste-preference results with test results from the simulated mouth, researchers found that four pounds per square inch (2 kg per 2.5 cm²) of oral pressure is the ideal level of crunchiness. Now all chips are tested to meet this standard. As a company executive pointed out, "We have to be perfect; after all, no one really needs a potato chip."[6]

◆ All marketing activities in an organization should be *co-ordinated*. Marketing efforts (product and service planning, pricing, distribution, promotion, and customer service) should be designed and combined in a coherent, consistent way, and one executive should have overall authority and responsibility for the complete set of marketing activities. Other employees who work in different organizational functions should be made aware of their roles in supporting a marketing orientation for the organization.

◆ Customer-oriented, coordinated marketing is essential to achieve the *organization's performance objectives* while at the same time meeting the customer's needs. The primary objective for a business is typically a profitable sales volume. In not-for-profit organizations, the objective might be to increase the number of people served or the variety of services offered. Advancing technology has enabled many companies to become very conscious of the requirement for customer-oriented coordinated approaches to marketing. To better meet the needs of business travellers, some companies are marrying cellular telephones with tracking technologies to create location-based e-commerce. For example, a business person on a trip to Paris may receive a beep and a message on his mobile phone advising him that he is only a few blocks from a specialty wine store. The phone has been programmed to tell this wine connoisseur when he is close to an opportunity to add a rare wine to his collection.[7]

FIGURE 1-3
Components and
Outcomes of the
Marketing Concept

New Focal Points in the Marketing Concept

All ideas and concepts evolve and become more refined, and the marketing concept is no exception.

THE SOCIETAL MARKETING CONCEPT As the marketing concept has become widely accepted by many organizations, it has also come under fire. Critics have charged that it ignores social responsibility — although it may lead to an organization achieving its goals, it may at the same time encourage actions that conflict with society's best interests.

From one point of view, these charges are true. A firm may totally satisfy its customers (and in the process achieve a hefty profit), while also adversely affecting society. To illustrate, a pulp and paper mill in British Columbia may be supplying its customers in the newspaper industry with the right product at a reasonable price, but in doing so may be polluting the air and water near its B.C. mill.

However, this need not be the case. A firm's social responsibility can be quite compatible with the marketing concept. Compatibility depends on two things: how broadly a firm perceives its marketing goals, and how long it is willing to wait to achieve those goals. A firm that sufficiently extends the breadth and time dimensions of its marketing goals to fulfil its social responsibility is practising the **societal marketing concept**.

When a company extends the marketing concept's *breadth*, it recognizes that its market includes not only the buyers of its products but also anyone directly affected by its operations. In our example, the pulp and paper mill has several "customer" groups to satisfy (1) the buyers of the pulp and paper, (2) the consumers of the air and water that contain impurities given off by the mill, and (3) the recreational users of the local river and bay where the mill releases its waste matter.

Extending the *time* dimension of its marketing goals means that a firm should take a long-term view of customer satisfaction and performance objectives, rather than concentrating only on tomorrow. For a company to prosper in the long run, it must satisfy its customers' social needs as well as their economic needs.

The marketing concept and a company's social responsibility are compatible if management strives over the long run to (1) satisfy the wants of the customers who buy their products and services, (2) meet the societal needs of others affected by the firm's activities, and (3) achieve the company's performance objectives. The challenge of balancing these three often-conflicting goals frequently places marketers in ethical predicaments. The issue of ethics deserves our consideration.

societal marketing concept
A revised version of the marketing concept under which a company recognizes that it should be concerned about not only the buyers of a firm's product but also other people directly affected by the firm's operations and not only with tomorrow but also with the long term.

Trust, Ethics, and Marketing Relationships

The task of marketers is to "deliver a standard of living" to customers. To accomplish this goal, marketers have a variety of tools at their disposal. Broadly speaking, these tools include the design of a product or service, the price at which it is offered, the message used to describe it, the channel through which it is made available, and the level of service provided to customers. And, of course, what is of utmost importance is the manner in which these tools are used.

Marketers are also responsible to a variety of groups. Certainly their customers depend on them to provide good products and services at reasonable prices. Their employers expect them to generate sales and profits; suppliers and distributors look to them for their continued business, and society expects them to be responsible citizens. The potential for the misuse of marketing tools and the frequently divergent interests of the groups dependent on the marketer create a wide variety of ethical challenges.

What Is Ethical Behaviour?

The professional association for North American marketers, the American Marketing Association, has formulated the code of ethics presented in Table 1-3. A discussion of the philosophical underpinnings of ethics is beyond the scope of this book.[8] However, it is safe to say that there is considerable disagreement about what constitutes ethical conduct. Ethics vary from society to society. For example, bribery, though repugnant in many societies, is an accepted and even necessary aspect of business behaviour in some parts of the world. For our purposes, it is sufficient to say that **ethics** are the rules we play by, the standards of behaviour generally accepted by a society. Some of these standards are found in the various provincial and company consumer and human rights codes. One is more likely to find them in company ethics codes, but most likely of all to find them in individual codes of conduct.

ethics
The rules and standards of moral behaviour that are generally accepted by a society.

Instilling an Ethical Orientation

Organizations are not ignoring ethical issues. A growing number are holding ethics workshops and setting up ethics committees. However, as long as there are conflicting goals and opportunities for people to make judgments, ethical failures will occur. To relieve some of the pressure on employees faced with ethical challenges and perhaps reduce the frequency and severity of ethical problems, organizations have taken several steps.

One dimension of creating an ethical environment is to make sure that the performance demands on employees are reasonable. People faced with unrealistic quotas and deadlines are much more likely to cut corners to accomplish their objectives.

Another important facet of an ethical orientation is communicating clearly the organization's standards. Hewlett-Packard, for example, makes sure that all employees are completely familiar with its extensive code of conduct. To remind employees of the importance of ethical behaviour, Texas Instruments includes a weekly column on ethics in its international electronic news service. Included in the column are answers to specific issues raised by employees.

To help employees deal with ethical issues, some companies employ a full-time ethics officer or ombudsman. This high-level executive gives advice to senior management and responds to the complaints and questions of employees at all levels.

TABLE 1-3   Code of Ethics for Members of the American Marketing Association

As a member of the American Marketing Association, I recognize the significance of my professional conduct and my responsibility to society and the other members of my profession:

1. By acknowledging my accountability to the organization for which I work.
2. By pledging my efforts to assure that all presentations of goods, services, and concepts be made honestly and clearly.
3. By striving to improve marketing knowledge and practice in order to better serve society.
4. By supporting free consumer choice in circumstances that are legal and consistent with generally accepted community standards.
5. By pledging to use the highest professional standards in my work and in my competitive activity.
6. By acknowledging the right of the American Marketing Association, through established procedure, to withdraw my membership if I am found to be in violation of ethical standards of professional conduct.

Source: American Marketing Association.

Marketing at Work 1-3

Benetton Ads Make Shock Waves

Most are familiar with Benetton's approach to advertising which is both challenging and startling in its social commentary. A few years ago one Benetton ad featuring a black stallion mounting a white mare, while another featured a man with AIDS looking suspiciously Christ-like on his deathbed. These controversial ads have generated more profile for Benetton than they could ever achieve from paid media. But do they know where to draw the line? It is one thing to make ads which express a point of view and are designed to generate talk-value, but quite another when they are intended only to cause offence.

The latest series of Benetton ads feature Jerome Sheets, Bobby Lee Harris, Leroy Orange, and Jerome Mallett — all convicted murderers on Death Row in Missouri who are awaiting the electric chair. What was Benetton trying to say in their advertising by featuring these men? What were the criminals themselves hoping to achieve by appearing in the ads?

Were they perhaps hoping to change the minds of the 70 percent of Americans who support death by execution?

Benetton claims that the ads were intended to encourage debate on capital punishment, and that the campaign has been reported on in newspapers and on TV stations around the world. No doubt they accomplished their goal of stirring things up, but what does it say about the company itself? Does Benetton have any sense of social responsibility? How do the families of the victims feel, having seen the ads that can't help but sensationalize the vicious crimes that took the lives of their loved ones?

If Benetton can create ads which do double duty by expressing a point of view and making people think, in addition to selling more clothes, that's commendable. But maybe it's time to pull the plug on advertising that has the sole purpose of creating offence.

Source: Adapted from David Chilton, "Benetton's Crime," *Marketing Magazine*, February 28, 2000, p. 38.

Organizations are also taking greater care to reward ethical performance. It is important for employees to see that success is the result of admirable behaviour, not questionable practices.

The Benefits of Ethical Behaviour: Consumer Trust

One could argue that ethical behaviour should in itself be rewarding. However, there are tangible benefits as well. Successful long-term businesses are built on successful relationships with suppliers, customers, employees, and other groups. The strength of a relationship is largely a function of the amount of trust the parties have in each other. Unethical or socially irresponsible behaviour on the part of a company undermines trust and destroys closeness in a relationship. The *Report on Business* magazine conducts an annual poll of Canada's business leaders on the subject of Canada's Most Respected Corporations. The CEOs of more than one thousand companies were asked to rate Canadian corporations on factors such as corporate social responsibility, human resources management, product and service quality, and innovation, as well as financial performance and long-term investment value. Among those companies listed in the top twenty-five were Nortel Networks, Bombardier, BCE, the Royal Bank of Canada, and TD Bank. Conducting one's business in an ethical and socially responsible manner is a highly significant issue in business today, and the building of trust results in profitable marketing relationships.[9]

Advertising that builds relationships and appeals to people's emotions.

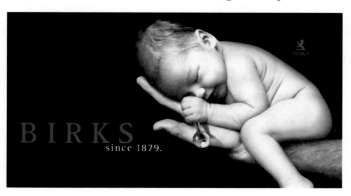

Quality and the Marketing Relationship

Quality has always been important to consumers. The success of Maytag's long-running "lonely repair-man" television commercials is a good indication of this. The campaign, which communicates the dependability of Maytag service and appliances, started on Canadian radio in the 1960s and continues to be used on television today. Rather than focusing on quality, many businesses chose in the past to maximize output through mass production and minimize prices through cost controls. The objective was to have an "acceptable" level of quality, which meant being as good as the competition. This strategy was successful as long as quality remained fairly constant across competitors.

Some would argue that some North American managers allowed themselves to become complacent about quality, convincing themselves that even minor product and service improvements would raise costs dramatically and thus make a firm uncompetitive. Meanwhile, new state-of-the-art manufacturing techniques were adopted by overseas firms who then added quality as a key ingredient of their strategies. We know from the success of foreign firms in automobiles, electronics, and computer hardware that a commitment to quality has many benefits. Thus, the improvement of technical quality has become a high priority for North American and European firms over the past twenty-five years or so, with the result that consumers today generally receive excellent quality in the products that they buy.

What Is Quality?

One definition of quality is the absence of variation in products and services. That doesn't mean that a Chevrolet should perform as well as a Lexus, or that the service at a Holiday Inn should be the same as the service at a Four Seasons hotel or resort. What it does mean is that a product or service should consistently deliver what it was designed to deliver, without variation from one experience to another. Thus, every Chevrolet model or every Holiday Inn service category should provide consumers with an identical experience. A series of "quality experiences" is a foundation for a quality relationship.

The most obvious application of variance control is in manufacturing. Variance control in service provision, while possible, is more difficult to achieve. Most manufacturers have had quality control departments for many years. However, the title "quality control" was misleading because it was limited to inspecting finished products in order to prevent defective ones from leaving the plant. But meeting specifications in production did not ensure quality if the product was poorly designed or if it was improperly serviced after it was sold. Thus, the real indication of **quality** is how well a product meets the product and service expectations of the customer, not of the production department.

Organizations also learned that quality control cannot be delegated to one department — it must permeate the organization and be every employee's responsibility. This is known as **total quality management**, which has as its goals:

quality
How well a product or service meets the expectations of the customer.

total quality management (TQM)
A philosophy as well as specific procedures, policies, and practices that commit an organization to continuous quality improvement in all of its activities.

◆ Better, more appealing, and less variable product and service quality.

◆ Quicker and less variable responses from design all the way to delivery.

◆ Greater flexibility in responding to customers' needs, both before and after the sale.

◆ Lower costs as a result of quality improvements, reductions in reworking, proper service performance, and waste elimination.[10]

For marketers, the best measure of quality is repeated customer satisfaction. In a competitive environment, the ultimate indication of satisfaction is whether the customer returns to buy the product or service a second, third, or fourth time and forms a long-term relationship with the provider. However, a firm can't assume that its marketing decisions are correct and wait for repeat purchases to confirm or reject those judgments. Instead, managers realize that satisfaction is determined by the extent to which a product or service meets or exceeds a customer's expectations. Therefore, marketers must do two things:

1. Ensure that all marketing activities, such as the price of a product, the claims made for it in advertising, and the places in which it is sold, contribute to creating reasonable customer expectations.

2. Eliminate variations in customers' experiences in purchasing and consuming the product. For example, not only should every new Honda Civic or Compaq notebook computer provide the same level of performance, but every customer interaction with a dealer or service person should be appropriately consistent, without surprises, and aid in creating trust.

INSTILLING QUALITY As managers have become more concerned about quality, a variety of quality-improvement programs have been developed. Though the programs have some differences, they typically involve:

◆ Studying competitors and noncompetitors to identify the highest standards of performance in such areas as delivery delays, eliminating defects, and training for product operations. This process is called *benchmarking*.

◆ Management and employees working closely together in an atmosphere of trust and co-operation to improve production and customer contact performance.

◆ All employees making a commitment to constantly search for better ways of performing their functions and improving their relationships with customers.

◆ Forming partnerships with suppliers and customers so that their inputs for improvement can be incorporated into the firm's internal operations and external contacts.

◆ Measuring product and service quality and the resulting customer satisfaction.

SERVICE QUALITY Measuring, or defining, the quality of service provided by a firm or organization is considerably more difficult than it is in the case of a physical product. The difficulty stems from those very same differences that distinguish products and services. It is important however that service organizations pay close and constant attention to the quality of service they are providing to their customers. The quality of service should be both of a high and consistent level. But how does an organization achieve this?

Service firms must establish a program within the organization to monitor and fix quality problems. Such a program, in fact, should become part of the corporate culture. Such a program would set standards of service and performance for all members of the organization. How these are to be measured must also be clearly defined and communicated. Such measurement must take place regularly. Once a firm determines the level of service that is appropriate for that organization, it must be sure that this can be delivered consistently.

Reporting service quality issues must be made easy for both customers and employees. There must also be a system to address these issues when they arise, correct them, and follow-up to determine the success of the proscribed solution. Aside from monitoring the system for potential improvement, there should also be a service recovery program that can detect and address disgruntled customers that may not return or speak ill of the organization. Such customers should be actively pursued in an effort to correct the negative experience. Successful recovery in such instances can create a very loyal and valuable customer while eliminating the chance that this consumer will discourage other potential customers.

Importance of Marketing

Coca-Cola is sold in virtually every country in the world. Japanese cars continue to be popular in North America, more so in Canada than in the United States. Consumers choose from numerous brands of personal computers and foods. Many students from your school obtained good jobs following graduation last year. Effective marketing is the common denominator in these situations. And, as these examples suggest, marketing plays a major role in the global economy, in Canada, and in any individual organization. It also has significance for you personally — in business, in your personal life, and certainly in your role as a consumer.

In the Global Economy

Today, Canadian firms face competition from all over the world. Canadians have become accustomed to well-known brands that originate in and are manufactured in many other countries. We live in a global economy where products, services, and marketing ideas in one part of the world influence people and businesses in many other parts. The phenomenal growth of the Internet has simply accelerated and enhanced the power of globalization.

Although we don't yet know all the results of dramatic increases in global competition, one thing is certain: We live in a global economy. Most nations today — regardless of their degree of economic development or political philosophy — recognize the importance of marketing beyond their own borders. Indeed, economic growth in the less developed nations of the world depends greatly on their ability to design effective marketing systems that will produce global customers for their raw materials and industrial output.

In the Canadian System

Aggressive, effective marketing practices have contributed to the high standard of living in Canada. Today we have the continued efficiency of mass marketing — extensive and rapid communication with customers through a wide variety of media and a distribution system that makes products readily available — combined with production processes that make more products available with increased value. At the same time, we have growing mass customization, combined with more personally focused databases and innovative personal media, providing products that are continually becoming closely tailored to individual needs. As a result, we enjoy things that once were considered luxuries and in many countries are still available only to people earning high incomes. Producing products and services of high quality has become relatively easy; the real challenge has been marketing them.

EMPLOYMENT AND COSTS We can get an idea of the significance of marketing in the Canadian economy by looking at how many of us are employed in some way in marketing and at how much of what we spend covers the cost of marketing. Between one-fourth and one-third of the Canadian labour force is engaged in marketing activities. This figure includes employees in retailing, wholesaling, transportation, warehousing, and communications industries, as well as people who work in marketing departments in manufacturing, agriculture, mining, and service industries. Furthermore, over the past century, jobs in marketing have increased at a much more rapid rate than have jobs in production, reflecting marketing's expanded role in the economy.

On average, about fifty cents of each dollar consumers spend goes to cover marketing costs. The money pays for designing the products to meet our needs, making them readily available when and where we want them, and informing us about their benefits and features. These activities add want-satisfying ability, or what is called *utility*, to products.

value
The quantitative measure of the worth of a product to attract other products in exchange.

utility
The attribute in an item that makes it capable of satisfying human wants.

CREATING CUSTOMER VALUE A customer purchases a product or service because it provides satisfaction. The quality that makes a product capable of satisfying wants is its value or utility. Marketing creates much of a product's **value** or **utility**. The concept of value is an important one in marketing because marketers must be aware of what will be valued by customers. The addition of value to what marketers offer to customers and the ways in which marketers treat customers through the purchase and post-purchase processes add value to the customer's experience, thereby contributing to the creation of satisfaction. "Marketing at Work" File 1-4 illustrates how firms and organizations are able to add value for their customers.

In Organizations

Marketing considerations should be an integral part of all short-range and long-range planning in any company. Here's why:

◆ The success of any business comes from satisfying the needs and wants of its customers, which is the social and economic basis for the existence of all organizations.

◆ Although many activities are essential to a company's growth, **marketing is the only activity that produces revenue directly**. (This is sometimes overlooked by the production managers who use these revenues and the finance executives who manage them.) When managers are internally focused, products are designed by designers, manufactured by manufacturing people, priced by accounting staff, and then given to sales managers to sell. This approach generally won't work in today's environment of intense competition and constant change. Just building a good product will not result in sales.

Recent statistics report that only one in five new small ventures make it past their tenth birthday. The study shows that to become ten years old, businesses must focus on the basics of product quality and customer satisfaction. Once the business moves beyond the basics, innovation and employee training appear to add greatly to business growth. Technological innovation without the basics does not guarantee survival.[11]

SERVICE MARKETERS Canada has gone from being primarily a manufacturing economy to becoming a more service-oriented economy. Services are now much more important than goods as the object of a transaction; examples are transportation, tourism, communications, entertainment, education, financial services, health care, and a host of professional services. Services probably will be even more important in the economy of the 21st century than they have been in the recent past.

Marketing at Work 1-4

Rollerblade Marketing Creates Six Types of Value or Utility

Consider this example. A marketer came up with the idea for a new product that combined the concept of a single blade from ice skates and the wheels of roller skates: the in-line skate. To produce the product, a company called Rollerblade Ltd. was established in Montreal. But Rollerblades in Montreal in April are of little value to a person in Vancouver who wants to buy a pair for a Christmas present. So the in-line skates must be transported to the West Coast (and hundreds of other places) and placed in stores near potential customers. Then, potential buyers must be informed about the product's existence and benefits through various forms of promotion. Let's see what kinds of value or utility have been created in this process:

- **Form utility** is associated primarily with production — the physical or chemical changes that make a product more valuable. When lumber is made into furniture, form utility is created. This is production, not marketing. However, marketing research may aid in decisions about product design, colour, quantities produced, or some other aspect of a product. For in-line skates, as with most other products, marketing is involved in developing the concept, designing the appearance, and selecting the materials and colours. All these things contribute to the product's form utility.
- **Place utility** exists when a product is readily accessible to potential customers. Rollerblades in Montreal are of little value to customers in other parts of the country, so moving the product to a store near the customer adds to its value.

- **Time utility** means having a product available when you want it. In the case of Rollerblades, customers like having a selection of skates in stores so that they can shop at their convenience. Having a product available when we want it is very convenient, but it means that the retailer must anticipate our desires and maintain an inventory. Thus, there are costs involved in providing time utility.
- **Information utility** is created by informing prospective buyers that a product exists. Unless you know a product exists and where you can get it, the product has no value. Advertising that describes in-line skates, or a sales person answering a customer's questions about the durability of Rollerblades, creates information utility. **Image utility** is a special type of information utility. It is the emotional or psychological value that a person attaches to a product or brand because of its reputation or social standing. Image utility ordinarily is associated with prestige or high-status products such as designer clothes, expensive foreign automobiles, and certain residential neighbourhoods.
- **Possession utility** is created when ownership is transferred to the buyer. Rollerblades in a store's window or on a shelf don't provide customers with any satisfaction. To consume and enjoy the product, a transaction must take place. This occurs when you exchange your money for a pair of the skates.
- **Satisfaction utility** is created when the customer is pleased with the product or service and it meets the individual's expectations. If the customer is satisfied, value is created in the organization. The customer is more likely to repurchase from that organization, promote the products offered by Rollerblades Ltd. through word of mouth, and generate increased revenue for the firm.

NOT-FOR-PROFIT MARKETERS During the 1990s, many not-for-profit organizations realized that they needed effective marketing programs to counteract difficult economic times, shrinking government subsidies, and a decrease in charitable contributions. Charities with falling donations, service clubs with declining memberships, and symphony orchestras playing to vacant seats all began to understand that marketing was essential to help them turn their situations around.

Today political organizations, museums, and even churches — all organizations that formerly rejected any thought of marketing — are embracing it as a means of growth and, for some, survival. This trend is likely to accelerate for two reasons:

◆   Increasing competition among not-for-profit organizations. For example, the competition among colleges and universities for students interested in specialized programs is intensifying as the number of young people of college age declines, and the search for donors has become more intense as the number of charities has increased.

◆ Not-for-profit organizations need to improve their images and gain greater acceptance among donors, government agencies, news media, and, of course, consumers, all of which collectively determine an organization's success.

In Your Life

Okay, so marketing is important globally, in our economy, and in an individual organization. But what's in it for you? Why should you study marketing? There are a number of reasons:

◆ Marketing pervades our daily activities. Consider how many marketers view you as part of their market. With people like you in mind, firms such as Nike, Loblaw, Air Canada, MuchMusic, and Tim Hortons have designed their products and services, set prices, created advertisements, and chosen the best methods of making their products and services available to you. They have devised customer service strategies and developed programs to ensure that you come back to do business with them in the future. In response, you watch television commercials, buy various items from different retail stores or through the Internet, and sometimes complain about prices or the quality of service you receive. Marketing occupies a large part of your daily life. If you doubt this, just imagine for a moment what it would be like if there were no marketing institutions — no retail stores to buy from and no advertising to give you information, for example.

◆ Studying marketing will make you a better-informed consumer. You'll understand more about what underlies a seller's pricing and how brand names are selected, as well as the role of promotion and distribution.

◆ Lastly, marketing probably relates, directly or indirectly, to your career aspirations. If you are thinking about studying more marketing courses and considering employment in a marketing position, you can develop a feel for what marketing managers do. If you're planning a career in accounting, finance, or another business field, you can learn how marketing affects managerial decision-making in these areas. Finally, if you are thinking about a career in a nonbusiness field such as health care, government, music, theatre, or education, you will learn how to use marketing in these organizations. When you become serious about a job search, all the marketing ideas and tools will be of great help to you in defining potential employer groups and their interests and clarifying how you can present yourself to them.

Summary

The foundation of marketing is exchange within the context of a successful marketing relationship. One party provides to another party something of value in return for something else of value. In a broad sense, marketing consists of all activities designed to generate or facilitate an exchange intended to satisfy human needs.

Business firms and not-for-profit organizations engage in marketing. Products marketed include goods as well as services, ideas, people, and places. Marketing activities are targeted at markets, consisting of product purchasers as well as the individuals and groups that influence the success of an organization.

In a business context, marketing is a total system of business activities designed to plan, price, promote, and distribute want-satisfying products to target markets in order to achieve consumer and organizational objectives. The main difference between marketing and selling is that, in selling, the emphasis is on the product; in marketing, the emphasis is on meeting customers' wants and needs.

Marketing's evolution in Canada has gone through three stages. It began with a production orientation, passed through a sales orientation, and is now in the marketing orientation. In this third stage, a company's efforts are focused on identifying and satisfying customers' needs in order to establish effective marketing relationships.

Some organizations remain at the first or second stage, not progressing to the marketing-orientation stage, because they have monopoly power or because their products are in such great demand. Other firms have difficulty implementing a marketing orientation.

The service industries have provided opportunities for marketers to explore in depth the process of interaction that occurs between the buyer and the seller. To meet customer needs, it is usually necessary to go beyond providing core products. Customers demand a great deal more that can be considered as the five levels of the factors that drive customer satisfaction. Failure to provide satisfaction at any one of these levels can lead to lost customers and lost revenue.

A business philosophy called the marketing concept has evolved in marketing. According to the marketing concept, a firm is best able to achieve its performance objectives by adopting a customer orientation and co-ordinating all its marketing activities. Relationship marketing helps to build long-term customer relationships based on getting to know customers and understanding their needs in order to provide quality and service within a trusting and ethical framework.

Marketing is practised today in all modern nations, regardless of their political philosophy. As international competition has heated up, increasing attention has been paid to marketing. Between one-quarter and one-third of the work force is involved in marketing, and about one-half of consumer spending covers the cost of marketing. Marketing creates form, information, place, time, and possession utilities.

Depending on circumstances, marketing can be vital to an organization's success. In recent years numerous service firms and not-for-profit organizations have found marketing to be necessary and worthwhile. Marketing also can be useful to individual students, particularly in reference to career opportunities.

Key Terms and Concepts

Exchange 4	Production-orientation stage 10	Societal marketing concept 17
Marketers 5	Sales-orientation stage 11	Ethics 18
Market 5	Marketing-orientation stage 11	Quality 20
Product 7	Drivers of customer satisfaction 14	Total quality management 20
Relationship 7	Relationship marketing 15	Value/utility 23
Marketing 8	Marketing concept 15	

Questions and Problems

1. Explain the concept of an exchange, including the conditions that must exist for an exchange to take place, and give an example of an exchange that does not involve money.

2. Name some companies that you feel are still in the production or sales stage in the evolution of marketing. Explain why you chose each of them. Why do you feel they are at this stage and why have they not become more marketing-oriented?

3. Explain the five levels in the model of the drivers of customer satisfaction. Discuss how each level can influence the customer and generate satisfaction or dissatisfaction.

4. "The marketing concept does not imply that marketing executives will run the firm. The concept requires only that whoever is in top management be marketing-oriented." Give examples of how a production manager, a vice-president of finance, or a personnel manager can be marketing-oriented.

5. For each of the following organizations, describe what is being marketed.

    a. Toronto Raptors professional basketball team.

b. Canadian Airline Pilots Association labour union.

c. Professor teaching a first-year chemistry course.

d. Police department in your city.

6. One way of explaining the value or utility provided by marketing is to consider how we would live if there were no marketing facilities. Describe some of the ways in which your daily activities would be affected if there were no retail stores or advertising.

7. Name two service firms that, in your opinion, do a good marketing job. Then name some that do a poor marketing job. Explain your reasoning in each case.

Hands-On Marketing

1. Select a restaurant, hotel, dry cleaner, or other service company near your school; think about how it operates, if possible observe the operation, and interview a manager and some customers to identify: (a) what is being exchanged; and (b) whether the company is production-, sales-, or marketing-oriented.

2. Find out from a business in your community what changes or additions it has made during the last year to keep customers satisfied. Categorize the changes by the six types of utility discussed in this chapter ("Marketing at Work" File 1-4). Based on your conversation, what value or utility dimension has the greatest potential for improving customer relationships in the future?

Chapter Two

The Changing Marketing Environment

After studying this chapter, you should have an understanding of:

◆ The concept of monitoring a firm's environment (environmental scanning).

◆ How external environmental forces such as demography, economic and competitive conditions, social and cultural forces, technology, and political and legal systems can influence a company's marketing program.

◆ How external forces such as suppliers and intermediaries that are specific to a firm can influence its marketing program.

◆ How the nonmarketing resources and departments within a firm can influence the ways in which it practises marketing.

Another Chapter in the Bookselling Saga...

As markets and consumers change, it is important that retailers and other marketers change with the times to remain competitive. It is even better if one anticipates these changes and leads the marketplace, thereby taking advantage of these changes and turning them to their own advantage.

This is what has happened in the Canadian book industry, propelling Chapters, Inc. (www.chaptersinc.com) into a leadership position as a fierce competitor in the international marketplace.[1] The Canadian book market was estimated to be approximately $2 billion in 2000. Per capita, 35 to 54-year-olds purchase more books than other age groups. Also, this segment of the market is expected to grow by 20 percent by 2010. What does this mean to Canadian booksellers? Growth means change — change requires a quick response in order to be prepared for a new market environment. Chapters, Inc. has remained in front and has shaped changes in the market.

As the parent company of 316 bookstores, and with six thousand employees across the country, Chapters, Inc. is known to consumers as Coles, SmithBooks, The World's Largest Bookstore, Chapters, and on the Internet as Chapters.ca (www.chapters.ca).[2]

Responding to the tastes and trends of this group, management has transformed the Chapters organization into a dominant entity in the Canadian retail scene, with a more upscale, book boutique image in its Chapters superstores, more traditional bookstores in Coles and SmithBooks, and the dominant e-tailing site in the country. Aside from a wide selection of books, music, DVDs, software, educational aids, etc., the atmosphere in the Chapters superstores is deliberately different, with much greater attention paid attention to décor.

Except for the obvious differences in size and inventory, Chapters superstores behave in some ways like the local bookseller, or at least try to emulate an atmosphere that is as comfortable — cozy nooks to try on a book before bringing it home, a hot cup of coffee, etc. Stores feature readings, art exhibitions, musical performances, and books by local authors are prominently featured. The "traditional" stores in the Chapters chain — Coles and SmithBooks — carry many of the same titles, and hardcover new releases are carried at a regular 25 percent savings.

Not to stop there, Chapters has continually responded to changes in the marketplace and set out upon its Internet retailing journey in October 1998. As consumer markets became global, so did this bookseller's neighbourhood with the creation of Chapters Online (www.chapters.ca). With over 2.5 million book titles, over 4.6 million CD titles, and over 28,000 DVD titles in its virtual catalogue, Chapters has customers in the United States, Japan, South Africa, and New Zealand. Seeing that the Internet represents a medium that would persevere and that theirs was a product that would sell through such a medium, the company moved rapidly into the new arena. While many customers have been skittish about security concerns online — Chapters has countered with a credit card guarantee covering liabilities up to $50 (credit card companies cover amounts over this when fraud is involved). Chapters Online has removed the one big concern of many consumers regarding e-retail.

Chapters offers its online and offline customers a "loyalty program" that promises special savings, promotions, and points for regular customers. The Chapters Web site provides book reviews from the company and from site visitors, links to related information, sampling with sound, text, and video clips, and a customer database that updates customers regarding new books that may be of particular interest to them. An extensive network of affiliates whose sites are linked to the Chapters site further enhances the company's Internet presence. This includes retailing through a second site that carries online news from *The Globe and Mail.* By offering a range of features that appeal to book customers, and keeping these features current, the company has maintained the lion's share of the Canadian book market. Chapters, Inc. also has established a publishing division, Prospero Books, to publish books for distribution through Chapters outlets, and its own wholesaling arm, Pegasus, to handle distribution from publishers to Chapters retail stores and to others.

As this literature-bullish segment of the market embraces the conveniences offered by technology, Chapters is optimistic about moving into the next evolution in publishing — the e-book. The e-book enables the immediate downloading of a book from the Internet, so that it can then be read on a portable, hand-held reading device. The company is eager to get a jump on other Canadian retailers and plans to give consumers free trials of the e-book. This will include *Coles Notes* for students — trying to lock in a new generation.[3]

The strategic changes being made by Chapters, Inc. and other organizations are the result of environmental monitoring, a practice that many companies are adopting in order to stay on top of the changing world in which they operate. Environmental forces influence the way in which a company does its marketing. Some of these forces are external to the company, while others come from within. There isn't much that management can do about controlling the external forces that influence the marketplace, competition and the needs and preferences of customers. At most, it can monitor them and respond in a manner to capitalize on opportunities and reduce threats. Generally, management can control internal forces. An organization must manage its marketing program within its combined external and internal environments.

Environmental Monitoring

environmental monitoring
The process of gathering information regarding a company's external environment, analyzing it, and forecasting the impact of whatever trends the analysis suggests.

Environmental monitoring, also called environmental scanning, is the process of (1) gathering information regarding a company's external environment, (2) analyzing it, and (3) forecasting the impact of the trends suggested by the analysis.

Today, much environmental discussion concerns the state of the *physical* environment — air quality, water pollution, the disposal of solid waste, and the conservation of natural resources. However, the term environment is used in a much broader sense in this chapter.

An organization operates within an external environment that it generally cannot control. At the same time, there are marketing and nonmarketing resources within the organization that generally can be controlled by its management group.

There are two levels of external forces:

◆ Macro influences (so called because they affect all firms) include demographics, economic conditions, technological development, culture, and the legal system.

◆ Micro influences (so called because they affect a particular firm) consist of suppliers, customers, and the channels such as wholesalers and retailers through which the company sells its products and services. Micro influences, while external, are closely related to a specific company and are part of its total marketing system.

Successful marketing depends largely on a company's ability to manage its marketing programs within its environment. To do this, a firm's marketing executives must determine what makes up the firm's environment and then monitor it in a systematic, ongoing fashion. These marketing managers must be alert to identify trends in the firm's environment that could represent opportunities or problems for their organization. And they must be able to respond to these trends with the resources they can control.

External Macroenvironment

The following six interrelated macroenvironmental forces have a considerable effect on any organization's marketing system. Yet they are, for the most part, not controllable by management (see Figure 2-1).

◆ Demography.

◆ Economic conditions.

◆ Competition.

◆ Social and cultural forces.

◆ Technology.

◆ Political and legal forces.

demography
The statistical study of human population and its distribution.

Note that these forces are *largely*, but not *totally*, uncontrollable by management. A company must be able to manage its external environment to some extent. For example, through corporate and industry lobbying in Ottawa or provincial capitals, a company may have some influence on the political and legal forces in its environment. In addition, new-product research and development that is on the leading edge of technological innovation can influence a firm's competitive position. In fact, one company's technology may be the external environmental force of technology that is affecting other organizations.

If there is one similarity in the six environmental factors, it is that they are all subject to considerable change, and at different rates. Also, an important point from a marketing perspective is that not all markets or all consumers are affected by these changes in the same way. For example, some consumers cope with difficult economic times better than others do; some people are more adept at using the latest technological innovations; some accept new ideas and new ways of doing things much more readily than others do. The result is an extremely complex marketplace that is influenced by external factors that the marketer cannot influence but must understand and appreciate. The following section examines each of the six major environmental forces.

FIGURE 2-1
External Macroenvironment of a Company's Marketing Program
Six largely uncontrollable external forces influence an organization's marketing activities.

Demography

Demography is the statistical study of human population and its distribution. It is especially important to marketing executives, because people make up markets. People who have similar demographic characteristics such as age, geographic location, or income level often share other relevant characteristics, creating a potential segment, or market, for a particular product or service. Demography will be discussed in greater detail in the section on markets; at this point, we shall mention just a couple of examples of how demographic factors influence marketing systems.

One of the most significant demographic factors that Canadian marketers are addressing today is the phenomenon of the baby boomers — that segment of the population born between 1946 and 1966, the twenty years following World War II.[4] What is special about this population segment is the fact that there are so many of them. Canada produced more than 400,000 new Canadians in each year of the baby boom, and the number peaked in 1959 at 479,000. In the first of the baby boom years, 1946, 19 percent more babies were born than was the case a year earlier. During several of these years the birthrate reached 120 per thousand women, compared with 44.4 per thousand women in 1997.[5] Canada's demographics are unique because that so-called "baby boomer" segment of the population is larger in Canada than in any other country. Because this segment is so large and believed to share consumption patterns, some marketers believe that buying patterns can be significantly influenced by it. The implications of so many people in a particular age range are important to consider when marketing a product or service in Canada.

Some media are taking direct aim at the teen market.

The baby boom segment is passing through its middle years (late 30s to 50s). The aging of the baby boom generation is beginning to bring changes in "middle-aged" values, tastes, and concerns. When their children have grown, they will indulge themselves with well-earned vacations and luxury cars instead of a family minivan. The older boomers are also entering the stage where they are more likely to inherit sums from their aging parents and other relatives as they pass on. More wealth will be inherited by this generation than at any other time in the past. Their expanding waistlines will bring a boom in larger-sized jeans and more conservative casual clothing. As they forsake their city and suburban residences for cottage country, the price of recreational property will rise. Their interest in healthy living will continue into their 50s and 60s, resulting in a renewed emphasis on sensible eating and less active sports such as curling, golf, and bowling.

But it is not just the baby boomers who represent a lucrative and challenging target segment. Their children, now in their late teens and early 20s — a group often referred to as Generation X — also constitute an attractive age segment. Because there were so many babies born between 1946 and 1966, they produced lots of children, even though they had fewer children per family. This generation, which is facing the challenge of entering the work force in circumstances less attractive than the situation their parents faced, tends to react differently to conventional approaches to marketing.[6]

Such attention has begun to be paid to this group that a number of terms have been coined to distinguish, and focus upon, different subgroups such as echo, nexus, 'tweens, generation Y. Youth magazines such as *Watch* (aimed at the 14–18 group) and *Bang* (for the 9–13 segment) have been developed and made available through larger junior high and high schools in Canada, reaching a market of up to 1.7 million young Canadians. Frequent advertisers include Airwalk, Coca-Cola, Levi's, MuchMusic, Paramount Pictures, Salomon, Sony Playstation, and Virgin Music, among others. The entertainment and reading preferences of this younger generation of Canadians produce opportunities for new media, such as *Watch*, that represent a potential threat for established media such as daily newspapers, as we can see in "Marketing at Work" File 2-1.

Marketing at Work 2-1

The Net Threat

When was the last time you read a newspaper? This morning, yesterday, last week? For most Canadians, newspapers are the primary source for news, weather, sports and entertainment information. For most "adult" Canadians, that is.

Today's youth market, teens and tweens, is much more likely to log on for information than pick up a newspaper. The reason: simply because the Internet is more familiar, accessible, and relevant to this group than the traditional daily paper.

According to the Canadian Newspaper Association, people start forming their news-gathering habits in their early teens, and these habits continue throughout their lives. This insight threatens the future of broadsheets and tabloids alike that have traditionally cornered the market on up-to-date information.

Some newspaper are going online where the young would-be readers are, but these sites are merely a synopsis of the printed version as opposed to something new and relevant for the youth market. Other Canadian dailies have taken the threat from the Net more seriously and are actively targeting their future customers with dedicated sections that provide stories and information of interest to young people. The *Halifax*

Chronicle Herald runs a section called YouthPress every Thursday, and the *Toronto Star* recently revamped its teen section, *boom!*, that runs on Tuesdays. Even pretweens are not being ignored as the *Toronto Star* and *National Post* both have pages devoted to children aged five to eight.

In addition to editorial efforts, newspapers are trying their brand awareness with teens and tweens through cross promotions. *The Vancouver Sun* and the *Province*, for example, are sponsors of the Science World — an interactive science centre in Vancouver for children and young adults, and the *National Post* runs contests for tickets to movie premieres and pop concerts.

So are newspapers' efforts paying off? One of the best indicators of the value of a demographic segment to a newspaper is whether advertisers use it as a vehicle to reach that target. To date this does not appear to be the case. Advertisers do not seem convinced that newspapers are the best way to reach the youth market when there are other media that reach them more effectively and efficiently such as the Internet.

Source: Adapted from Kristy Thorne, "Getting Into the Habit," *Marketing Magazine*, February 7, 2000, p. 24.

Another population segment undergoing major change is the seniors market. In the mid-1980s, for the first time in history, the number of people aged 65 and older surpassed the number of teenagers — and this gap is widening considerably. Prominent Canadian demographer David Foot breaks this market down into three groups: young seniors (65–74), mid-seniors (75–84), and senior seniors (85 and up). The most senior of the groups is the segment that is growing the most rapidly because these individuals were born in a time of strong population growth. Foot, a professor of Economics, who believes that demography is the most powerful tool for understanding the past and forecasting the future, refers to this period as the "grey interlude" where the population distribution is dominated by older Canadians.[7]

It would be incorrect to assume that all seniors have the same interests and wants from the marketplace. They come from many backgrounds and span a wide range of age categories. Many new products and services are being offered and developed for seniors in all of the categories identified by David Foot. The cruise ship industry, for instance, has benefited greatly from the young seniors group, and upscale retirement homes or communities are of interest to the mid-seniors. The oldest age group is the group of lowest affluence, and many in this category tend to be interested in affordable retirement services and products.[8]

A further demographic change relates to the growing market segment consisting of single people. Today, almost 25 percent of Canadian households are made up of people who live alone. An increasing percentage of these single-person households contain older people, mostly women, who have been widowed. Many of these single, older consumers are healthy and lead active lives, and they represent an attractive target market for travel and tour companies, among others.

The marketing implications of this demographic segment are almost limitless. The frozen-food industry caters to this market with high-quality frozen entrées in a wide variety of menu offerings, many of which involve single servings. Automobile manufacturers and banks recognize the increased buying power of single women and have developed marketing programs and services specifically for this segment. Homebuilders are designing homes, condominium units, and housing developments with older singles in mind, while tour companies regularly offer bus tour vacations and cruises for this increasingly affluent group.

The increasing buying power of women in general has also created changes in how firms market their products. With 40 percent of cars now purchased by women, auto manufacturers have developed marketing programs directed at women, after gaining an understanding that women approach car purchasing differently from men and that this must be reflected in marketing efforts. For example, while Ford held 23 percent of the Canadian auto market in 1998, less than 15 percent of their sales were to women. Ford responded in unique ways such as sponsoring the CIBC Run for the Cure and advertising on popular "women's" Web sites. The company also created an all-female design team to redesign the Windstar minivan and incorporated this into their advertising campaign for the vehicle. Other newly enlightened businesses that have traditionally run male-oriented advertising campaigns include Home Depot, Marriott Hotels, and Toronto-based Mr. Lube.[9]

While demographics are crucial in determining the existence and size of potential markets, there are many other factors that contribute to the success of marketing efforts. These will be discussed throughout the chapter.

Economic Conditions

economic environment
A set of factors, including the business cycle, inflation, and interest rates, that affect the marketing activities of an organization.

People alone do not make a market. They must have money to spend and be willing to spend it. Consequently, the **economic environment** is a significant force that affects the marketing system of just about any organization. A marketing system is affected especially by such economic considerations as the current stage of the business cycle, inflation, and interest rates.

STAGE OF THE BUSINESS CYCLE Marketing executives should understand what stage of the **business cycle** the economy currently is in, because this cycle has a large impact on a company's marketing system. The traditional business cycle goes through four stages: prosperity, recession, depression, and recovery. However, various economic strategies have been adopted by the federal government; these strategies have averted the depression stage in Canada and other developed countries for more than sixty years. Consequently, today we think of a three-stage business cycle: prosperity, recession, and recovery.

business cycle
The three recurring stages in an economy, typically prosperity, recession, and recovery.

A company usually operates its marketing system quite differently during each stage. Prosperity is characterized typically as a period of economic growth. During this stage, organizations tend to expand their marketing programs as they add new products and enter new markets. A recession, on the other hand, involves higher rates of unemployment and reduced consumer spending and typically is a period of retrenchment for consumers and businesses. People can become discouraged, scared, and angry. These feelings affect their buying behaviour, which, in turn, has major implications for the marketing programs in countless firms.

Recovery finds the economy moving from recession to prosperity: The marketers' challenge is determining how quickly prosperity will return and to what level. As the unemployment rate declines and disposable income increases, companies expand their marketing efforts to improve sales and profits.

inflation
A rise in the prices of goods and services.

INFLATION **Inflation** is a rise in price levels. When prices rise at a faster rate than personal income, there is a decline in consumer buying power. During the late 1970s and early 1980s, Canada experienced a relatively high inflation rate of 10 to 15 percent. Although inflation rates declined to just over 2 percent by 2000, economic growth has been accompanied by a fear that higher rates of inflation may return.[10] This spectre continues to influence government policies, consumer psychology, and the marketing programs of business.

Inflation presents some real challenges in the management of a marketing program, especially in the area of pricing and cost control. Consumers are adversely affected as their buying power declines. At the same time, they may overspend today for fear that prices will be higher tomorrow.

interest rates
The percentage amounts either charged to lend money or paid to acquire money.

INTEREST RATES **Interest rates** are another external economic factor influencing marketing programs. When interest rates are high, for example, consumers tend to hold back on long-term purchases such as housing. Higher rates mean it is more expensive to borrow money. Whether consumers think that interest rates will increase or decline also affects consumer purchases. Marketers sometimes offer below-market interest rates (a form of price cut) as a promotional device to increase business. Auto manufacturers have used this tactic extensively in recent years.

UNEMPLOYMENT RATES   One of the most important indicators of the strength of an economy is the percentage of people who are employed and the percentage looking for work. During a strong economic growth period, unemployment rates are generally lower. At other times, and in certain parts of Canada, unemployment is higher. This affects greatly the amount of disposable income that consumers have to spend on products and services and is of considerable interest to marketers.

A marketer must pay considerable attention to the condition of the economy in which his or her company is operating. Purchasers of certain products and services may react quickly to changes or expected changes in economic conditions. The marketer must be ready to respond with changes in the marketing program.

Competition

A company's competitive environment is a major influence in shaping its marketing system. Any executives worth their salt should be constantly gathering intelligence and otherwise monitoring all aspects of their competitors' marketing activities. Expanded trade with other countries means that Canadian firms will have to pay greater attention to foreign competition and, with the movement toward global free trade, increasingly find opportunities for Canadian products and services in foreign markets.

The North American Free Trade Agreement (NAFTA), for example, has expanded the Canadian business environment to include the United States and Mexico. In some cases, this shift in the environment has resulted in Canadian businesses having to deal with significantly increased competition. One such situation occurred with the entry into Canada of large American retailers such as Home Depot and Wal-Mart, which prompted Canadian retailers to mount a defensive strategy. Two aspects of competition we shall consider briefly here are the types of competition and the competitive market structure in which the companies may be operating.

A firm generally faces competition from three sources:

◆ *Direct brand competition and store competition* from marketers of similar and directly competing products and services. Air Canada currently holds a monopoly on many domestic routes, but must still compete with KLM, British Airways, United Airlines, Cathay Pacific, and other foreign carriers on international routes. Bauer competes with Micron, Lange, and CCM in the skate business. Cooper competes with overseas companies such as Karhu and Koho for the Canadian hockey stick business. Domestic retailers face competition from international retailers such as Wal-Mart, and IKEA. Even charitable organizations such as the Canadian Cancer Society, the Heart and Stroke Foundation of Canada, and the Salvation Army compete for donations and for the time of canvassers and volunteers.

◆ *Substitute products* that satisfy the same basic need. For example, vinyl records have disappeared in the face of competition first from tape cassettes and then from compact discs. Local courier companies and Canada Post have seen a portion of their business taken away by the business use of fax machines and increasingly by e-mail. Many conventional delivery services are threatened by the use of electronic delivery systems. Future developments will see the sale of downloadable music and books. The use of mail services and long-distance telephone calling is being challenged by e-mail, and even business air travel may be under threat from the teleconferencing and video conferencing services offered by telephone companies. Many department stores and clothing retailers are realizing that their competition is coming not only from other stores down the street or in the same town, but from Internet retailers such as L. L. Bean, Lands' End and J. Crew, many of which are headquartered in other countries. This competition has increased sharply with the growing popularity of Internet shopping. Technology has increased the number of competitors substantially for most any product or service available.

A historic change in the marketing environment of provincial utility providers has placed these firms in a position that they have never before faced. Deregulation in some industries has created the need for these companies to actively market and solicit customers for their core products. For the first time in this country telecommunications and electrical utilities have been opened up to competitive forces, ending their former monopolies.

◆ In the third type of competition — more general in nature — *every company or organization* is competing for the consumer's limited buying power. In this regard, the competition faced by a marketer of tennis racquets may come from other companies that are marketing jeans or shoes, or from a car repair bill, or a weekend ski holiday. Competition for discretionary spending is one of the greatest challenges for marketers.

On the international scene, two fairly recent developments in the competitive environment have created important challenges for Canadian marketers. One is the creation of blocs of nations around the world that have combined into free-trade zones, thereby allowing a less restricted flow of products and services across international borders. The unification of the European Community has created one such bloc, while NAFTA has linked Canada, the United States, and Mexico in an economic union. In Europe such agreements have gone so far as to introduce a common currency across most countries — the euro.

The second development involves the radical change from a government-controlled system to a relatively free market economy in many countries, particularly in Eastern Europe and the countries of the former Soviet Union. Prices have been decontrolled and government subsidies removed on many products in Poland, Russia, and Estonia, for example. In addition, some major companies and industries, formerly 100 percent government-owned, have been sold to private interests.

Social and Cultural Forces

The task facing marketing executives is becoming more complex because cultural patterns — lifestyles, social values, and beliefs — are changing much more quickly than they used to. Here are a few changes in **social and cultural forces** that have significant marketing implications.

social and cultural forces
A set of factors, including lifestyles, social values, and beliefs, that affect the marketing activities of an organization.

CHANGING VALUES — EMPHASIS ON QUALITY OF LIFE Our emphasis today is increasingly on the quality of life rather than merely on the quality of goods and services. The theme is "Not more — but better." We seek value, durability, comfort, and safety in the products and services we buy.

Looking ahead, we will worry more about education, health, and the environment, and less about keeping up with the neighbours in automobiles, clothing, and homes. Our growing concern for the physical environment and our discontent with pollution and resource waste are leading to significant changes in our lifestyles. And when our lifestyles change, marketing is affected.

Marketing at Work 2-2

AD Nauseam

It is referred to by some in the ad biz as "ambient advertising." It is a new type of out-of-home advertising that is popping up everywhere due to numerous start-up companies offering unique venues for companies' messages. Through these new media, marketers are able to get their brand name in front of consumers one last time before the purchase decision is made, capitalize on a clutter-free environment, or speak to consumers during periods of downtime throughout their day.

Floorgraphics Inc., of Princeton, New Jersey, installs full-colour two by three-foot/60 by 90-cm self-adhesive billboards on the floors of supermarkets, drugstores, and mass merchandisers. The company claims that these floor ads deliver a 25 to 27 percent increase in sales for their clients. This is almost the same increase that an instant-coupon machine delivers, but without having to sacrifice margins. Campbell Soup Co. used this new medium to support its SpaghettiOs product by affixing a trail of Hansel and Gretel-like SpagettiO decals leading to the main ad at the foot of the shelf display.

Parkad Media Ltd., of Toronto, Ontario, capitalizes on dingy and clutter-free parking garages by installing back-lit posters on their walls in office towers and shopping malls. The company cites high visibility, a captive audience, as well as the ability to target upscale consumers as advantages of this new medium. Boom-Ad Advertising Systems Ltd., also of Toronto, leverages parking lots as well, but uses gate arms to place advertising at more than 350 parking lots across Canada.

For those that pump their own gas, the downtime while the tank is being filled will be empty no more thanks to Fillboards and the Pump Radio Network. Fillboards, created by Alvern Inc. in Houston, Texas, are three by five-inch/76 by 127-mm ads that sit on top of a pump nozzle. Even more enterprising is the Pump Radio Network, produced by Advanced Information Systems LLC, Midland, Michigan, that attaches a battery-operated Fuelling Talker to the pump nozzle and airs four 20-second and two 10-second ads while the gasoline flows. These media can be persuasive vehicles to encourage consumers to visit the gas station convenience store, or even to frequent neighbouring businesses.

What's next, advertising in the loo? Well, yes.

Companies requiring a very captive audience must look no further, thanks to NewAd Media of Toronto, Ontario. NewAd is installing moving, talking, "Video Boards" in washrooms of restaurants and bars, allowing companies to run commercials while consumers are in the establishment. When a patron approaches the sign a sensor is activated triggering the ad which is stored on a CD-ROM. The signs are typically placed above urinals in the gents and next to the mirrors in the ladies.

Source: Adapted from John Grossman, "UPSTARTS Nontraditional Ads," *Inc.*, March 2000, pp. 23–26; John Heinzl, "Firm parks billboards underground," *The Globe and Mail*, April 7, 2000, p. M1; and John Heinzl, "NewAd Flushes out new ad space," *The Globe and Mail*, April 11, 2000, p. B5.

This change in values among Canadians is evident in a number of areas, as consumers reject the accumulation of assets that was in vogue fifteen or twenty years ago in favour of a return to products that reflect the values of the past. An important influence on the changing values of which Canadian marketers should be aware is the effect of the large number of recent immigrants on shaping values in certain parts of the country. Each immigrant group brings with it a unique set of values shaped by the culture of its home country. One group of authors has identified the following as characteristic of many of the immigrant groups who have recently made Canada their home:

◆ A high degree of control by family elders over purchasing power and buying decisions.

◆ A suspicion of government and government-sponsored programs.

◆ An aversion to the use of credit cards and to the accumulation of debt.

◆ A focus on household and family goals, including securing a job, home ownership, and education for the children.

81% of Chinese pay cash when they buy a car

Consider the Chinese market in your drive for success !
The *Vancouver Chinese Media Index 1998*, compiled by ACNielsen•DJC Research, confirms its substantial purchasing power.

For instance, did you know that-

- 71% of Chinese drivers bought new cars instead of used cars

- 73% of Chinese households are equipped with a PC, compared with just 36% of average Canadian households

- 87% of Chinese households have an automobile, compared with 72% of average Canadian **Households**

- 57% of Chinese households own a cellular phone, compared with only 19% of average Canadian households

- One in every seven people in the Vancouver Census Metropolitan Area is Chinese*

The *Vancouver Chinese Media Index 1998* tells you all this and much more. It's your essential tool for in-depth information on the Chinese profile and preferred media in Vancouver.

The research confirms once again that Fairchild Television is the number one preferred Chinese media. Every week, our programming reaches approximately 50% of the total Chinese-Canadian audience. As Canada's only national Chinese television network, Fairchild Television is the primary source of news, information and entertainment for many Chinese Canadians.

*According to the **1999** Census

新 時 代 電 視
FAIRCHILD TELEVISION

The Only National Chinese Television Network

Other media are targeting lucrative ethnic audiences.

Such values lead to recurrent patterns of behaviour among these consumers, which marketers must consider when plotting marketing strategy to appeal to them.[11] For example, almost one million Canadians report that they are Chinese by their ethnic origin; 80 percent of these Chinese-Canadians live in Ontario and British Columbia, making them a very attractive market segment with their own unique buying patterns and behaviour (see www.ftv.com). One effort to target this important segment is reflected in the advertisement for a national Chinese television network presented on this page.

ROLE OF MEN AND WOMEN One of the most dramatic shifts in our culture has been the changing role of women. What is especially significant is the erosion of stereotypes regarding male-female roles in families, jobs, recreation, and product use.

The evolving roles of women have many implications for marketers. Well over one-half of the women in Canada are working outside the home today. This has changed some traditional buying patterns in households. Long gone are the days when women were the sole buyers of groceries and household items and men were the purchasers of hardware and car maintenance. The entry of women into the work force on a mass scale has increased the requirement for day-care facilities and the usage of time-saving appliances and food products. People working outside the home buy different clothing than do those working at home. The sharing of family responsibility is a characteristic of most modern Canadian families, to the point where many employers have begun to extend programs to men that had been available only for women, including paternity leave, pregnancy-education programs, and parenting seminars.

ATTITUDES TOWARD PHYSICAL FITNESS AND EATING In recent years, an increased interest in health and physical fitness seems generally to have cut across most demographic and economic segments of our society. Participation in physical fitness activities from aerobics to yoga is on the increase. Stores supplying activity products and service organizations catering to this trend have multiplied. Public facilities (bicycle paths, hiking trails, jogging paths, and playgrounds) have been improved.

Paralleling the physical fitness phenomenon, significant changes are occurring in the eating patterns of Canadians. We are becoming more sensitive to the relationship between our diet and major killing diseases such as heart disease and cancer. Consequently, there is a growing interest in weight-control eating, in foods low in salt, food additives, and cholesterol, and in foods high in vitamins, minerals, and fibre content. Health foods now occupy large sections in many supermarkets. Over the past twenty years, per capita consumption of chicken in Canada has increased by more than 35 percent, while the consumption of fish has increased by almost 50 percent. School cafeterias, once considered havens of junk food, have dramatically changed their menus to meet the needs of ethnic groups and the many teenagers who have become vegetarians. According to the Toronto Board of Education, there has been a shift to pasta and salads. Sales of hamburgers have dropped off dramatically.[12] Campbell's has developed a line of soups that feature reduced fat and/or reduced sodium (salt) content for health-conscious consumers.

Current debate regarding health and eating centres around genetically modified organisms/foods (GMOs). Concern for the unknown future health effects has created a backlash in the U.K. where supermarkets advertise the fact that they do not carry such products. When the world's largest french-fry manufacturer, New Brunswick's McCain Foods, announced in 1999 that they would not purchase GMOs for french-fry production the tide began to turn in Canada. Early in 2000, several groups protested, boycotted supermarkets, and circulated information about what branded products contained GMOs in an attempt to pressure manufacturers and retailers. McCain's anticipated public concern and had correctly decided that the public relations cost was not worth it and sought crops from sources other than their usual suppliers.

EMPHASIS ON SERVICE QUALITY As consumers have become more confident of their rights and the power they wield in the marketplace, they have become increasingly demanding about the manner in which they are treated by business. Although companies have long appreciated that they must produce quality products to compete effectively for the consumer's loyalty, most are now beginning to realize that quality is equally important in service delivery.

Quality in services is not easily defined because it depends on the expectations of the customer. Each individual brings to a service encounter his or her own concept of what constitutes quality. The concept is based on personal experiences and individual likes and dislikes. Much work has been done by marketers on how to measure quality in service industries. Unlike manufacturing, where standards can be objectively set on the basis of stress factors, safety features, and size, among others, services cannot be as easily standardized.

With the growth in the service economy, the quality of service delivery and the level of customer expectations is becoming more of an issue. More people are spending money on services, and more services are available to them. Consumers are also more sophisticated than ever before, they travel more, and they are more able to discern quality and dictate what they want and don't want.

Decisions to purchase at certain stores or stay at specific hotels are made not only on the basis of tangible products, the decor of the room, or the quality of food in the restaurant (although these are important), but on the much more intangible factor of the level and quality of the service provided. It is the customer's *perception* regarding these that will greatly influence the decision made. Customers now regularly tell businesses that they want to be treated as though their business is welcomed and appreciated. The best companies have responded with sophisticated programs to measure the satisfaction of customers and with other programs designed to deliver a higher level of service quality.

CONCERN FOR THE ENVIRONMENT Possibly one of the most important forces that will influence Canadian business and marketing in the coming years is Canadians' concern for the physical environment. As we have seen the damage done to the quality of water, air, and the land during the past century, there has been a collective outpouring of support for programs and products that allow us to take action to protect the environment. Such concern has elevated this to an industry onto itself that relies heavily on marketing and lobbying efforts.

Consequently, governments have moved to control the emissions of automobiles and factories; food manufacturers package products in less wasteful and more biodegradable packages; and municipalities across the country have established recycling programs in which many householders and most businesses participate. Supermarket chains stock many products labelled "environmentally friendly," meaning that their packages and ingredients are not harmful to the environment. The result is a major movement driven by the changing values of consumers, who are concerned about air and water pollution, acid rain, holes in the ozone layer, the destruction of forests, over-fishing, and the disposal of chemicals and solid waste. The environmental movement is a global concern, as consumers in most countries of the world have adopted similar attitudes.

Within Canada, concern for the environment is a major factor. In a global survey conducted in twenty-four countries, three-quarters of Canadians felt that protecting the environment was more important than promoting economic growth. In this regard, Canada was tied for second place among all the countries surveyed.[13]

This has several implications for business:

◆ As many as 50 percent of consumers in the future are expected to make purchases on the basis of environmental factors.

◆ McDonald's and other fast-food retailers have replaced their polystyrene containers with cardboard and paper containers.

◆ Companies such as The Body Shop have successfully positioned themselves on the basis of their concern for the environment and other social issues.

◆ A number of cosmetics manufacturers have begun to offer products packaged in recyclable containers and developed without testing on animals.

◆ Many consumers are altering their purchase behaviour significantly as they look for products that do not contain harsh or unnecessary chemicals.

Marketing at Work 2-3

Will that be Debit or Credit?

Canadians are passionate about plastic, preferring to use debit and credit cards to pay for their purchases rather than cash and cheques. However, customers' payment preferences have not always been met as not all merchants are equipped to process electronic payments. This has not been as great a barrier for credit cards since merchants could dust off their manual imprinter, but making payment with a debit card has been an impossibility.

Many merchants have not been able to accept debit cards for payment of goods or services due to the mobile nature of their business. Debit transactions have traditionally been processed using electronic point-of-sale devices that require land-based telephone lines. This has meant that cab drivers, contractors, and the entire sector of home delivery services have been locked out of the growing debit frenzy.

Soft Tracks Enterprises Ltd., a small Vancouver-area company, has provided a solution — a wireless point-of-sale device that allows consumers to swipe their debit and credit cards just about anywhere. The devices retail for $2000 per unit, a cost that Soft Tracks believes will be quickly offset by the extra revenue generated by being able to accept debit and credit card payments.

The upside of this new wireless device is the removal of barriers to payment for merchants and greater convenience and flexibility for consumers. The potential pitfalls include service interruptions due to the cellular-based technology and consumers' security concerns that are inherent in any new payment technology.

Only time will tell how consumers will respond to wireless debit and credit card payments, but if the adoption of ATMs and debit cards at point-of-sale are leading indicators, it should prove to be a roaring success.

Source: Adapted from Ann Gibbon, "Selling Points," *The Globe and Mail*, March 23, 2000, pp. T1, T2.

◆   The success of products such as downloadable books, magazines, and music may be enhanced as they do not require production of excess inventories or packaging.

DESIRE FOR CONVENIENCE   As an outgrowth of the increase in discretionary purchasing power and the importance of time, there has been a continuing increase in consumers' desire for convenience. We want products ready and easy to use, and convenient credit plans to pay for them. We want these products packaged in a variety of sizes, quantities, and forms. We want stores located close by and open at virtually all hours.

Every major phase of a company's marketing program is affected by this craving for convenience. Product planning is influenced by the need for customer convenience in packaging, quantity, and selection. Pricing policies must be established in conformity with the demand for credit and with the costs of providing the various kinds of convenience. Distribution policies must provide for convenient locations and hours of business. As a result, Canada's banks have placed thousands of automated banking machines in various locations in cities and towns across Canada, so that their customers now have access to banking services in off-premise locations and at any time of the day or night. Banks also offer telephone banking and banking by the Internet where bills can be paid by phone or online, transfers can be made, account information accessed, as well as application for loans or mortgages. With new advances in the development of "smart cards," banks will soon offer customers access to cash without their ever having to enter a bank.

Another example of business responding to the consumer's desire for convenience is the increasing use of catalogues to order products. Even people who live in major cities and who have access to a wide variety of retail stores find it less time-consuming and more convenient to shop from catalogues. These catalogue retailers make shopping from home as easy as possible through the use of toll-free 1-800/888/877, etc., telephone numbers, their acceptance of major credit cards, and relatively risk-free shopping through generous exchange and refund policies. This has also proliferated on the Internet, sometimes including free shipping and discounts to encourage first-time users.

The advances in the availability and efficiency of the Internet are a major change that is creating considerable convenience for the consumer. Information on product and service quality and availability can be easily accessed through the World Wide Web. Companies are also making it increasingly easy for products to be purchased directly on the Internet. It is estimated that retailing on the Internet in Canada will reach US$70 billion by 2003 (www.e-com.ic.gc.ca).[14]

IMPULSE BUYING Partly as a result of attractive in-store displays, much retail purchasing involves impulse buying — purchasing done without much advance planning. A shopper may go to the grocery store with a mental note to buy meat and bread. In the store, he may also select some fresh peaches because they look appealing or are priced attractively. Another shopper, seeing facial tissues on the shelf, may be reminded that she is running low and may buy two boxes. These are impulse purchases.

A key point to understand is that some impulse buying is done on a very rational basis. Self-service, open-display selling has brought about a marketing situation wherein planning may be postponed until the buyer reaches the retail outlet. Because of the trend toward impulse buying, emphasis must be placed on promotional programs designed to get people into a store. Displays must be appealing because the manufacturer's package must serve as a silent salesperson.

Even nonstore retailers, who sell their products through vending machines, catalogues, and home demonstration parties, must be mindful of the phenomenon of impulse shopping. Again they make their offerings as attractive as possible and facilitate the process by offering free delivery, free catalogues, credit, and toll-free telephone numbers.

Technology

technology
The science of practical or industrial art.

Technology has a tremendous impact on our lifestyles, consumption patterns, and economic well-being. Just think of the effect of major technological developments such as the airplane, plastics, television, computers, antibiotics, lasers, and compact discs. Except perhaps for the airplane, all these technologies reached the large-scale marketing stage only in your lifetime or your parents' lifetime. Think about how your life in the future might be affected by cures for the common cold, the development of energy sources to replace fossil fuels, low-cost methods for making ocean water drinkable, or even commercial travel to outer space.

Consider for a moment some of the dramatic technological breakthroughs expanding our horizons as we started the new millennium. The role of robotics undoubtedly will expand considerably. Robots are now used extensively in manufacturing, space exploration, and satellite maintenance.

At the heart of a robot's operating mechanism is a miniature electronic computer system, which leads us into another technological breakthrough area — miniature electronic products. It's hard to grasp the fantastic possibilities in this field. Then there is the awesome potential of the superconductor, a means of transmitting electrical energy with virtually no resistance. Further developments in fibre optics, the Internet, high-definition television, digital transmission, and CD-ROM technology will open vistas of communication that were not possible even five years ago.

The advancement of CD-ROM technology is changing the way we buy books, videos, and records. New developments in digitizing have led to the creation of the digital versatile disc (DVD), which enables the storage of multimedia formats. DVDs have established a technology that will enable us to buy recordings that combine text, graphics, sound, video, and music on a single disc that is available for use when the individual consumer wants it. Such digital technology will establish a new high standard in home entertainment and information storage and retrieval.

The Internet has seen rapid development in the last few years. Virtually every home and office in Canada is becoming linked through interactive telephone lines, thereby allowing families to shop and do their banking from their living room and to order video movies from a catalogue for instant viewing. In Canada a number of direct-to-home satellite services have been approved by the CRTC. These innovative approaches to TV viewing are bypassing earlier technologies and offering consumers opportunities not previously considered. In another area, travel plans to practically any location can now be made by directly accessing airline Internet home pages and destination marketing sites.

Technological development is not only changing the lives of consumers, it is also changing the way companies do business. Any firm in today's marketplace must be able to integrate electronic communications and marketing with other forms of customer contact. Though Internet commerce is still experiencing some drawbacks (such as guaranteed security for credit card users), more and more companies are marketing through this interactive medium. Internally, companies are engaging in projects that are undertaken by "virtual" teams — groups formed through e-mail communications who may never meet face to face. Linking the core technologies of the Internet with the company's own needs, intranets, or private corporate networks is resulting in more effective internal communications, distribution, and retrieval and updating of information.[15]

Major technological breakthroughs have a threefold impact on marketing:

◆ To start entirely new industries, such as computers, robots, lasers, fax machines, and microwave ovens have done, and as the Internet, CD-ROM and its heir-apparent the DVD-ROM, as well as other digital technologies, will do in the future.

◆ To alter radically or virtually destroy existing industries. Television had a significant impact on movies and radio when it was introduced in the 1950s. Compact discs have eliminated vinyl records and threaten cassette tapes. Fax machines have cut into the conventional mail business of Canada Post, which now offers its own courier and electronic mail services. Sensors imbedded in toll highways, such as the 407 north of Toronto, record cars as they pass over them and bill their owners for the tolls they have used, thereby eliminating toll booths and speeding up traffic.[16] Movie companies in the United States are sending movies to theatres directly from the studio through digital transmission over the telephone lines, thereby eliminating traditional distribution channels and companies.

◆ To stimulate other markets and industries not related to the new technology. New home appliances and entertainment products have certainly altered the pattern of time use within the home and outside. Cable television, the VCR, CD players, video games, computer games, and microwave ovens have revolutionized the ways consumers use their time. This development has also led to new industries providing entertainment products and food products that are used with these new devices and that were not available a few years ago.

There is virtually no aspect of our lives that is not being affected in a significant way by new technology. In 1999, over 40 percent of Canadians were accessing the World Wide Web.[17] This number will continue to rise. Banks are offering their customers the use of debit cards, PC banking, and smart cards, which allow shoppers to pay bills or buy products by a direct debit to their bank accounts. Interactive technology is the tone of the new age. The Internet allows consumers not only to receive messages, as the old media did, but to respond to them. According to Sympatico, a Canadian Internet service, Internet marketing and shopping is the direction for the future. Marketers can provide customers with as much information as they feel is necessary, or they can give customers an opportunity to provide information about themselves. The medium makes one-to-one communication possible.[18] With new advances in multimedia such as in-home shopping that uses cable, telephone, and Internet connections, technology is opening up whole new vistas for marketers.

Despite the advances that have been made, technology is often a mixed blessing. A new technology may improve our lives in one area while creating environmental and social problems in other areas. The automobile makes life great in some ways, but it also creates traffic jams and air pollution. Television provides a built-in baby-sitter, but it also can have an adverse effect on family discussions and on children's reading habits. The Internet provides virtually unlimited access to information, but that material must be organized and catalogued to be useful. It is ironic that technology is strongly criticized for creating problems (air pollution, for example), but at the same time it is expected to solve these problems.

Political and Legal Forces

political and legal forces
The influence stemming both from legislation and from policies established by government agencies.

To an increasing extent, every company's conduct is influenced by **political and legal forces** in society. Legislation at all levels exercises more influence on the marketing activities of an organization than on any other phase of its operations. The political-legal influences on marketing can be grouped into six categories. In each, the influence stems both from legislation and from policies established by the maze of government agencies.

1. *General monetary and fiscal policies.* Marketing systems obviously are affected by the level of government spending, the money supply, and tax legislation.

2. *Our legislative framework and codes and policies set by government agencies.* Human rights codes and programs to reduce unemployment fall into this category. Also included is legislation controlling the environment. For example, marketers in the direct-mail business are coming under increasing attack for what some consumers feel is the waste involved in flyers and mailing pieces that arrive unsolicited in their mailboxes, much of which ends up in the garbage unread. Legislators are being pressured by environmental groups to pass legislation regulating the sending of such mail.

3. *Social legislation.* Governments often pass legislation that is intended to protect members of society. A ban on smoking in airplanes, mandatory seat belt use, and the prohibition of cigarette advertising are examples of this type of legislation.

4. *Government relationships with individual industries.* Here we find subsidies in agriculture, shipbuilding, passenger rail transportation, culture, and other industries. Tariffs and import quotas also affect specific industries. Throughout the 1990s, governments in Canada and in many other countries moved to reduce the extent to which they are involved in the operation of businesses. Many have sold government-owned corporations to the private sector. There has been a major move toward deregulation, as industries such as banking, airlines, trucking, telecommunications, and broadcasting have been freed to a greater extent from regulations imposed by government. Deregulation of electrical utilities also began in 2000. Through subsidies and tariff protection, Canadian governments have been involved in such traditional industries as the production of agricultural products. Some of these industries have been threatened with the removal of that protection as industries are deregulated throughout the world and as tariff barriers are removed. Such barriers will continue to fall as the movement toward freedom in international trade expands and as such government involvement in industry is seen to be an impediment to free trade.

5. *Legislation specifically related to marketing.* Marketing executives do not have to be lawyers. But they should know something about these laws, especially the major ones — why they were passed, what their main provisions are, and the current ground rules set by the courts and government agencies for administering these laws.

   The federal department Industry Canada, through its Consumer Products, Marketing Practices, and Competition Policy divisions, administers much of the legislation included in categories 3 and 4 above. Table 2-1 contains examples of the legislation administered by that department that is relevant for marketers. In addition, many other pieces of legislation relating to such topics as food products and advertising are administered by other departments of the federal government. We shall discuss these laws and regulations at the appropriate places throughout this book.

6. *The provision of information and the purchase of products.* This sixth area of government influence in marketing is quite different from the other five. Instead of telling marketing executives what they must do or cannot do — instead of legislation and regulations — the government is clearly helping them. The federal government, through Statistics Canada, is the largest source of secondary marketing information in the country, and the government is the largest single buyer of products and services in the country.

$\mathcal{E}$xternal Microenvironment

Three environmental forces that are external, but are a part of a company's marketing system, are that firm's market, its suppliers, and its marketing intermediaries. Although they are generally uncontrollable, these external forces can be influenced more than the macro forces can. A marketing organization, for example, may be able to exert pressure on its suppliers or intermediaries. And, through its advertising, a firm should have some influence on its market (see Figure 2-2).

FIGURE 2-2
External Microenvironment of a Company's Marketing Program

TABLE 2-1	**Marketing-Related Legislation Administered by Industry Canada**	
• Bankruptcy and Insolvency Act	• National Research Council Act
• Boards of Trade Act	• Natural Sciences and Engineering Research Council Act
• Business Development Bank of Canada Act	• Patent Act
• Canada Business Corporations Act	• Precious Metals Marketing Act
• Canada Co-operative Associations Act	• Public Servants Inventions Act
• Canada Corporations Act	• Radiocommunication Act
• Canadian Space Agency Act	• Small Business Investment Grants Act
• Companies' Creditors Arrangement Act	• Small Business Loans Act
• Competition Act	• Social Sciences and Humanities Research Council Act
• Competition Tribunal Act	• Standards Council of Canada Act
• Consumer Packaging and Labelling Act	• Statistics Act
• Copyright Act	• Telecommunications Act
• Department of Industry Act	• Textile Labelling Act
• Electricity and Gas Inspection Act	• Timber Marketing Act
• Industrial Design Act	• Trademarks Act
• Integrated Circuit Topography Act	• Weights and Measures Act
• Investment Canada Act	• Winding-up Act
• Lobbyists Registration Act	

The Market

The market really is what marketing is all about — how to reach it and serve it profitably and in a socially responsible manner. The market should be the focus of all marketing decisions in an organization. But just what is a market? A market may be defined as a place where buyers and sellers meet, goods or services are offered for sale, and transfers of ownership occur. A market may also be defined as the demand made by a certain group of potential buyers for a good or service. For instance, there is a farm market for petroleum products.

These definitions are not sufficiently precise to be useful to us here. For business purposes we define a **market** as people or organizations with wants (needs) to satisfy, money to spend, and the willingness to spend it. Thus, in the market demand for any given product or service, there are three factors to consider:

market
People or organizations with wants to satisfy, money to spend, and the willingness to spend it.

◆ People or organizations with wants (needs).

◆ Their purchasing power.

◆ Their buying behaviour.

When we say "needs," we mean what the dictionary says it means: the lack of anything that is required, desired, or useful. We do not limit needs to the physiological requirements of food, clothing, and shelter essential for survival. In our discussions about marketing, the words *needs* and *wants* are used synonymously and interchangeably.

Suppliers

You can't sell a product if you can't first make it or buy it. That's why the people or firms who supply the goods or services that we need to produce what we sell are critical to

Marketing at Work 2-4

Clubbing for Good Reviews

Book clubs are just one of the special-interest groups that Universal Films of Canada has targeted for its new film releases. Book clubs however are not a well-defined target market as they can include any number of people, are geographically diverse, and cover a broad range of ages. One of the biggest barriers associated with these groups is their informality which makes them extremely difficult to reach. Nonetheless, Universal Films felt they represented a group of consumers who could help to create a good buzz for their film *Snow Falling on Cedars* since the book of the same name was such a literary fiction success.

Jamie Raskin, production coordinator at Universal Films, began by talking to people he knew who were members of book clubs, and they in turn passed along other names. The studio was able to track down a dozen or so book clubs in Vancouver and Toronto and sent them preview passes for the soon-to-be-released film. Passes were also sent to a select number of members of Chapters' and Indigo's loyalty programs. In total, approximately one thousand passes were distributed.

Raskin believes the return for their efforts is high quality word-of-mouth as book club members are most often well-educated, well-read, and influential. This idea of targeting special-interest groups has moved beyond book clubs at Universal. For *The Hurricane*, the story of a wrongfully imprisoned boxer, the studio invited social justice groups, including Amnesty International, to preview the film.

Source: Adapted from Astrid Van Den Broek, "Book clubs used in movie marketing," *Marketing Magazine*, January 17, 2000, p. 4.

suppliers
The people or firms that supply the goods or services that an organization needs to produce what it sells.

our marketing success. And that's why we consider a firm's **suppliers** as part of its marketing system. Marketing executives often are not concerned enough with the supply side of the marketing system. But they do become very concerned when shortages occur. Shortages make clear the need for co-operative relationships with suppliers.

Marketing Intermediaries

marketing intermediary
An independent business organization that directly aids in the flow of products between a marketing organization and its markets.

Marketing intermediaries are independent business organizations that directly aid in the flow of goods and services between a marketing organization and its markets. There are two types of intermediaries: (1) the firms we call middlemen or intermediaries[19] — wholesalers and retailers; and (2) various facilitating organizations that provide such services as transportation, warehousing, and financing that are needed to complete exchanges between buyers and sellers. These intermediaries operate between a company and its markets and between a company and its suppliers. Thus they are part of what we call channels of distribution. In some cases it may be more efficient for a company to take a "do-it-yourself" approach and not use marketing intermediaries. A producer can deal directly with its suppliers or sell directly to its customers and do its own shipping, financing, and so on. But marketing intermediaries are specialists in their respective fields. They often do a better job at a lower cost than the marketing organization can do by itself.

Organization's Internal Environment

An organization's marketing system is also shaped by internal forces that are controllable by management (see Figure 2-3). These internal influences include a firm's production, financial, and personnel activities. If Procter & Gamble is considering the manufacture of a new brand of soap, for example, it must determine whether existing production facilities and expertise can be used. If the new product requires a new plant or machinery, financial capability enters the picture.

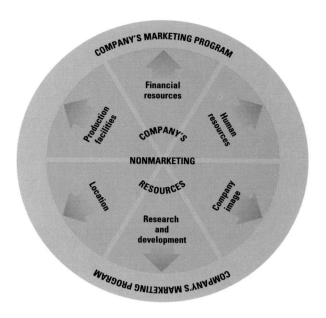

FIGURE 2-3 Internal Environment Affecting a Company's Marketing Activities
A company's internal non-marketing resources influence and support its marketing program.

Other nonmarketing forces are the company's location, its research and development (R&D) strength, and the overall image the firm projects to the public. Plant location often determines the geographic limits of a company's market, particularly if transportation costs are high or its products are perishable. The R&D factor may determine whether a company will lead or follow in its industry.

Another thing to consider in a firm's internal environment is the need to co-ordinate its marketing and nonmarketing activities. Sometimes this can be difficult because of conflicts in goals and executive personalities. Production people, for example, like to see long production runs of standardized items. However, marketing executives may want a variety of models, sizes, and colours to satisfy different market segments. Financial executives typically want tighter credit and expense limits than the marketing people feel are necessary to be competitive.

Figure 2-4 shows how all environmental forces combine to shape an organization's marketing program. Within the framework of these constraints, management should develop a marketing program to provide want-satisfaction to its markets. The strategic planning of marketing programs is the topic of the next chapter. Permeating the planning and operation of a marketing program is a company's marketing information system — a key marketing subsystem intended to aid management in solving its problems and making decisions. Chapter 8 is devoted to the subjects of marketing research and a company's flow of information.

The Internal Market

Marketing may be thought of as having its roots within the firm or organization. Products and services are produced by people — the employees. These employees form different departments and functions within the organization. These work together to produce an output — some sort of tangible or intangible product for the marketplace. These employees may be considered to be an internal market and the organization an internal marketplace.

In today's global marketplace we exist in an increasingly service-oriented economy. The nature of doing business is changing and efficient and tailored customer service has come to be recognized as the root to success in this environment for both service and manufacturing sectors.[20]

When you see that organizations are made of people and not just their end products, and that the efforts of these people ultimately dictate the quality, dependability, and productivity, you realize that every firm has a service component within it. That makes these people a critical resource in the success of the organization.

Traditionally labelled as nonmarketing resources, as in Figure 2-3, the production facilities, company image, R&D, and human resources do actually shape and affect the ulti-

FIGURE 2-4

A Company's Complete Marketing Environment
A framework of internal resources operate within a set of external forces.

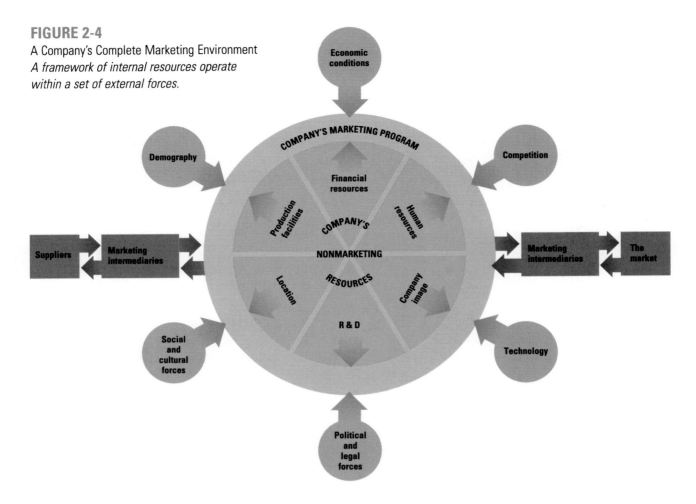

mate success of the firm's traditional marketing efforts. In fact, it is difficult to isolate any of these variables as they all combine to create the working and production environment. Consider the contributions of each:

◆ Research and Development — provides advances in both product features and production procedures.

◆ Production facilities — determines the level of productivity and quality. Improvements increase efficiency and cost-effectiveness.

◆ Financial resources — determines the level of staffing, training, materials, and production facilities.

◆ Human Resources — determines selection and training of appropriate personnel. The more effective this function, the better the working environment, decreasing employee turnover. Also, increased employee satisfaction, loyalty, and quality thereby increasing product/service quality, productivity, and cost effectiveness.

◆ Image — Superior production, quality, employees, service, etc., all contribute to the image of the organization. This attracts customers, a wider pool of potential employees as well as other businesses/suppliers that seek to do business and be associated with the organization.

Therefore, those components of the firm labelled marketing and nonmarketing resources should not, in practice, be considered in isolation from each other. They all contribute directly or indirectly to the success of the marketing operations of the company.

Summary

Various environmental forces influence an organization's marketing activities. Some are external to the firm and are largely uncontrollable by the organization. Other forces are within the firm and are generally controllable by management. A company manages its marketing system within this external and internal environment. To start with, management should set up a system for environmental monitoring — the process of gathering and evaluating environmental information.

Six broad variables constitute the external environment that generally cannot be controlled by an organization. Demographic conditions are one of these macro influences. Another is economic conditions such as the business cycle, inflation, and interest rates. Management must be aware of the various types of competition and the competitive structure within which a given firm operates. Social and cultural forces, including cultural changes, are another factor with which to contend. Technology and political and legal forces round out the group of external macroenvironmental influences.

Another set of environmental factors — suppliers, marketing intermediaries, and the market itself — is also external to the firm. But these elements are part of the firm's marketing system and can be controlled to some extent by the firm. At the same time, a set of nonmarketing resources within the firm — production facilities, personnel, finance, location, research and development, and company image — influences its marketing system. These variables generally are controllable by senior management outside the marketing area.

Key Terms and Concepts

Environmental monitoring 30
Demography 31
Economic environment 35
Business cycle 35
Inflation 35
Interest rates 35
Social and cultural forces 37
Technology 43
Political and legal forces 45
Market 47
Suppliers 48
Marketing intermediaries 48

Questions and Problems

1. It is predicted that university and college enrolments will decline during the next several years. What marketing measures should your school take to respond to this forecast?

2. For each of the following products and services, give some examples of how its marketing program is likely to differ during periods of prosperity as contrasted with periods of recession.

    a. McCain's Pizza Pockets.

    b. Palm Pilot.

    c. Adidas running shoes.

    d. Caribbean vacations.

3. If interest rates are high, how is the situation likely to affect the market for the following products?

    a.   Roots sweatshirts.

    b.   Building materials.

    c.   CD-ROMs.

    d.   Day-care programs.

4. Explain the three types of competition faced by a company. What marketing strategies or programs would you recommend to meet each type?

5. Give some examples of how the changing attitudes of Canadians toward the environment and their changing food consumption patterns have been reflected in the marketing programs of various companies.

6. What are some of the marketing implications of the increasing public interest in health and physical fitness?

7. What should be the role of marketing in treating the following major social problems?

    a.   Air pollution.

    b.   The depletion of irreplaceable resources.

    c.   Seasonal unemployment.

8. Using examples other than those in this chapter, explain how a firm's marketing system can be influenced by the environmental factor of technology and particularly by the Internet.

9. Give some examples of the effects of marketing legislation in your own buying, recreation, and other everyday activities. Do you believe these laws are effective? If not, what changes would you recommend?

10. Explain how each of the following resources within a company might influence that company's marketing program. How could each be a source(s) of advantage and/or disadvantage?

    a.   Plant location.

    b.   Company image.

    c.   Financial resources.

    d.   Personnel capability.

11. Specify some internal environmental forces affecting the marketing program of:

    a.   Shoppers Drug Mart.

    b.   Your school.

    c.   A local restaurant.

    d.   Air Canada.

12. Explain how or under what conditions a company might exert some control over its suppliers and intermediaries in its marketing program.

13. What policies or efforts could an organization develop to improve marketing efforts within the organization? How would these measures improve the organization's final output or product?

Hands-On Marketing

1. Identify two controversial social-cultural issues in the community where your school is located, and explain their impact on firms that market in the community.

2. After interviewing some consumers and/or business people in your community, identify two products or companies (national or local) that you think are doing very well in their treatment of or interaction with the physical environment. Identify two that you think are doing a poor job.

Chapter Three

Strategic Marketing Planning

In this chapter we'll examine how a company plans its total marketing program. After studying this chapter, you should have an understanding of:

- ◆ The nature and scope of planning and how it fits within the management process.

- ◆ Similarities and differences among mission, objectives, strategies, and tactics.

- ◆ The essential difference between strategic company planning and strategic marketing planning.

- ◆ The steps involved in strategic marketing planning.

- ◆ The purpose and contents of an annual marketing plan.

- ◆ How planning models can be useful aids in developing a marketing program.

A Marketing Strategy that's "Ford Tough"

The automobile market in Canada has pretty much reached its absolute size. Autos are a widely accepted product, all its uses have been exploited, and most people wish to have one — we no longer have to be convinced of the merits of the horseless carriage.

Yet this market continues to change while not varying, to any significant degree, in size. Ford Canada, like any other firm, is seeking market growth and increased sales. Where can a firm expect this to come from? That's easy — steal it from the competition! To remain competitive in the automotive industry, to keep or gain market share, it is very important to respond to changing conditions in the marketplace. Changes in age demographics, tastes, social trends, and the state of the economy will all influence what customers look for in your product. As such, these trends must be incorporated into the strategic planning and goal-setting of a firm.

It is estimated that 80 percent of consumer spending in Canada is controlled by women, and that 70 percent of these women generally ignore campaigns aimed toward them because of the predominantly male mindset from which they originate. Auto marketers have begun to realize that there is more potential here and that the methods previously utilized must be re-evaluated. Ford Canada is one organization that has realigned its strategic goals with female

granddaughter
cousin
niece
daughter
aunt
grandmother
sister
mother
wife

The reasons we're asking you to run are all relative.

One way or another, Breast Cancer may affect someone that's close to you.
So as a national sponsor, Ford is encouraging everyone to get out there on Sunday, October 1st
to support the CIBC Run for the Cure, raising funds for Breast Cancer Research.
1·800·387·9816

Ford

Ford Motor Company of Canada, Limited
www.ford.ca

market growth as the ultimate destination.

As one of two "Big Three" auto makers in Canada led by women, one may not think that marketing toward women would be a challenge — in fact, what difference does it make when you are selling cars? Quite a big difference it seems. With approximately 23 percent of the Canadian market, less than 15 percent of Ford sales are to females. Women generally make many decisions based upon a different set of criteria than the average male. This, of course, is not news to any female reading this — why should car buying decisions be any different? This point is critical because women constitute 40 percent of car purchases in a marketplace that has largely ignored them.

Ford has made increasing sales to women consumers a stated objective in the strategic direction of the organization. This mission has been formalized, and given structure, through the development of the Women's Marketing Department. Through researching how women shop for big-ticket items, a number of different tactical programs have been designed to attract female buyers. Among the differences that have been found: women do more research (six to nine months to less than three by men), often stress value over absolute price, and do not respond to high-pressure sales tactics as do men. Female consumers often want a dialogue and relationship with a brand. They appreciate products that "take a stand" and have community involvement. If the brand is aligned with self-interests they buy and remain loyal customers. Women, more than men, rely upon word of mouth with regard to product and service experiences. Loyal, and satisfied, female consumers can be seen as marketing missionaries for future sales.

The company, perhaps best known for its "Ford Tough" truck image and early muscle cars such as the Mustang, understandably may not strike a chord of identification with women consumers. Tactical efforts to change this impression include modified promotional efforts, dealership changes, and product evaluation.

To garner the attention of female consumers, Ford has begun sponsorship of the CIBC *Run for the Cure*. The Internet has also served as a timely tool in these efforts. The desire to research car purchases without any pressure establishes the first strands of a relationship with potential female con-

sumers. Community involvement, a family focus, as well as a focus on value are all features of the company's online magazine. There are links to Young Drivers as well as a feature to send electronic greeting cards to friends and family. Ford has also placed links to their Web site to related sites that have high female traffic thus allowing the company a higher level of awareness among female surfers.

Product design has also been affected by this change in strategic direction. The Windstar minivan has been redesigned by a female design team to reflect the modern family's requirements — a point proudly demonstrated in ads for the vehicle. The new 2000 Cougar was designed to ensure appeal to the average female car purchaser's desire for value in a reliable vehicle that is aesthetically appealing. The sporty coupe has been designed keeping in mind that women's earnings still average less than three-quarters of what men earn. Also, less is typically spent on second vehicles, which still tend to be relegated to the female driver. Even such apparently small features such as manually operated driver's seat height adjustment on the new 2000 Focus also reflect this change in thinking.

Traditional advertising has also been adapted. The advertisement for the 2001 F-150 Supercrew four-door pick-up series

features a team of firefighters including women members. In Alberta, where trucks account for 83 percent of sales, new car spots have been designed with feedback from Ford's Women's Advisory Council. One features sentimental music while a single young woman views the Ford Escort and suddenly begins daydreaming about her future. The spot ends with the tagline "Something to Believe in." Another features the sportier ZX2 sneaking out of a dealership late at night for a rendezvous with a sportscar to the tune of "Fever." These spots are intended to attract women as well as younger shoppers.

Finally, dealerships are becoming more "female friendly" by employing greater numbers of females in relevant positions. Cleaner bathrooms and available play areas also make locations more user-friendly. Courses have also been designed such as "Service — Responding to a Women's Perspective" and "Selling to Women."

The *Pit Pass* program that allows potential buyers to compare Ford with competitive models outside the dealership setting now features *Women's Days*. On these special days vehicles such as the super duty F-series trucks and its competitors are not on location, instead, stress is put on products such as the Cougar, Mustang, Windstar, and their competitors.[1]

It is easy to see how changes in the marketplace, including competition, cause firms to step back and evaluate their current practices and products. It is also clear that the development of strategies, tactics, and plans and their implementation is what large and small organizations, chains and independents alike, can do to respond to actual and anticipated changes in their markets. In Chapter 1 we discussed the marketing component of marketing management; now we discuss the management component.

Planning as Part of Management

The management process, as applied to marketing, consists basically of (1) planning a marketing program, (2) implementing it, and (3) evaluating its performance. This process is illustrated in Figure 3-1.

FIGURE 3-1
The Management
Process in Marketing

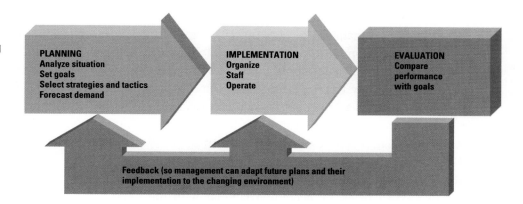

FIGURE 3-1
The Management
Process in Marketing

The planning stage includes setting goals and designing strategies and tactics to reach these goals. The implementation stage entails forming and staffing the marketing organization and directing the actual operation of the organization according to the plan. The evaluation stage consists of analyzing past performance in relation to organizational goals. This third stage indicates the interrelated, continuing nature of the management process. That is, the results of this stage of the management process are used in planning goals and strategies for future periods. And the cycle continues.

The Nature of Planning

"If you don't know where you're going, any road will get you there." The point of this axiom is that all organizations need both general and specific plans to be successful. Management first should decide what it intends to accomplish as a total organization and then develop a strategic plan to achieve these results. On the basis of this overall plan, each department within the organization should determine what its own plans will be. Of course, the role of marketing in these plans needs to be considered.

If planning is so important, exactly what is it? Quite simply, planning is deciding now what we are going to do later, including how and when we are going to do it. Without a plan, we cannot get things done effectively and efficiently, because we don't know what needs to be done or how to do it. In **strategic planning**, managers match an organization's resources with its market opportunities over the long run.

The fact that strategic planning has a long-run perspective does not mean that plans can be developed or executed in a casual manner. Many years ago the term **strategic window** was suggested to describe the limited amount of time in which a firm's resources can actually be made available to take advantage of a particular market opportunity.[2] Typically, the window is open only temporarily. Thus a firm must be able to move rapidly and decisively when a strategic window opens. Microsoft Systems (www.microsoft.com) did just that when the World Wide Web component of the Internet grew explosively. Almost overnight, there were thousands, and then millions, of Web sites — locations on the Internet that provide information and/or sell products. Internet users were faced with the task of having to sort through many sites on the Web in order to find the specific material they were looking for. Microsoft quickly capitalized upon its easy-to-use Windows operating system by bundling it with its own browser software. Through very aggressive business and negotiation practices Microsoft had contractually guaranteed that this software was factory installed on the majority of PCs produced. So aggressive was this practice that in April 2000 a federal judge in the United

strategic planning
The managerial process of matching a firm's resources with its market opportunities over the long run.

strategic window
The limited amount of time in which a firm's resources are available to take advantage of a marketing opportunity.

States ruled that the company had violated antitrust and competition laws by attempting to maintain a monopoly in computer operating systems and dominate the Web browser market. Similar charges followed in Europe. Quick and aggressive action had caused Microsoft to rise to being one of the most valuable companies in the world, while any delay in capitalizing upon the company's strengths would have seen this opportunity pass as other companies gained a foothold in the browser market. While most such windows of opportunity are brief, never has a rapid response been so crucial as it is in the new technology-based industries.

Key Planning Concepts

We'll begin by becoming familiar with the basic terms used in discussing marketing management, especially the planning phase.

mission
The statement that indicates the boundaries of an organization's activities.

MISSION An organization's **mission** states what customers it serves, what needs it satisfies, and what types of products it offers. A mission statement indicates the boundaries of an organization's activities. A mission statement should be neither both too broad and vague, nor too narrow and specific. To say that a firm's mission is "to benefit Canadian consumers" is too vague; to state that its purpose is "to make tennis balls" is too narrow. Neither statement outlines meaningful benefits for customers or provides much guidance to management. Unless the firm's purpose is clear to executives and other levels of management, strategic planning will likely result in disagreement and confusion.

Traditionally, companies stated their missions in production-oriented terms, such as "We make furnaces" (or telephones or tennis racquets). Today, firms following the marketing concept express their mission in customer-oriented terms. Executives should think about the wants they are satisfying and the benefits they are providing. Thus, instead of "We produce snowmobiles, ATVs and small watercraft," Canada's Bombardier Inc.'s mission statement should be "We provide safe, comfortable travel for wherever our customer wants, or needs, to go." Similarly, many of the available Internet search engine companies should not think "We provide lists of cyberaddresses" but that "We help users find what they require as quickly as possible." Recall that Table 1-1 illustrated different ways of stating a company's mission. A more customer-oriented statement will facilitate asking questions, the answers to which will result in product and process improvements.

objective
A desired outcome.

OBJECTIVES AND GOALS We treat objectives and goals as synonyms. An **objective** is simply a desired outcome. Effective planning must begin with a set of objectives that are to be achieved by carrying out plans. To be worthwhile and workable, objectives should be:

◆ Clear and specific.

◆ Stated in writing.

◆ Ambitious, but realistic.

◆ Consistent with one another.

◆ Quantitatively measurable wherever possible.

◆ Tied to a particular time period.

Consider these examples:

Weak (too general)	Workable
Increase our market share.	Increase our market share to 25 percent next year from its present 20 percent level.
Improve our company's public image.	Receive favourable recognition awards next year from at least three consumer or environmental groups.

strategy
A broad plan of action by which an organization intends to reach its objective(s).

STRATEGIES AND TACTICS The term *strategy* originally applied to the art of military leadership. In business, a **strategy** is a broad plan of action by which an organization intends to reach its objectives. In marketing, the relationship between objectives and strategies may be illustrated as follows:

Objectives	Possible Strategies
Increase sales next year by 8 percent over this year's figure.	1. Intensify marketing efforts in domestic markets.
	2. Expand into foreign markets.
	3. Increase customer retention by reducing account closings by 10 percent.

Two organizations might have the same objective but use different strategies to reach it. For example, two firms both might aim to increase their market shares by 20 percent over the next three years. To do that, one firm might intensify its efforts in household markets, while the other might concentrate on expanding into institutional markets (e.g., food-service organizations). Conversely, two organizations might have different objectives but select the same strategy to reach them.

tactic
An operational means by which a strategy is to be implemented or activated.

A **tactic** is a means by which a strategy is implemented. A tactic is a more specific, detailed course of action than is a strategy. Also, tactics generally cover shorter time periods than strategies. Here's an illustration:

Strategy	Tactics
Direct our promotion to males aged 25–40.	1. Advertise in magazines read by this group of people.
	2. Advertise on television programs watched by this group.
Increase revenue from existing customers.	3. Redesign the customer information system.
	4. Create a loyalty program for light and medium users.
	5. Retrain account analysts and service personnel.

To be effective, a tactic must coincide with, and support, the strategy to which it is related.

Scope of Planning

Planning may cover long or short periods. Strategic planning is usually long-range, covering three, five, ten, or (infrequently) twenty-five years. It requires the participation of top management and often involves a planning staff.

Long-range planning deals with company-wide issues such as expanding or contracting production, markets, and product lines. For example, all firms in the North American auto industry must look ahead to, say, 2005 to identify key markets, plan new products, and update production technologies. As technology advances affecting all manufacturing and service industries, planning cycles have continued to decrease. New automobiles once typically took five years from planning to production. Now this can be achieved in less than three years. Technology has allowed industries to be more responsive to customer wants while increasing competition has forced them to. In technology-based industries, long-range planning may mean only months as new advancements alter the entire structure upon which products, or industries, are based. In many technology-based industries the failure to frequently revisit and revise strategic plans may result in not just a deterioration in the firm's competitive position, but may also result in quickly putting the company out of business.

Short-range planning traditionally covered one year or less and is the responsibility of middle and lower-level managers. It focuses on such issues as determining which target markets will receive special attention and what the marketing mix will be. Looking again at the auto industry, Ford annually decides which target markets it will concentrate on and whether its marketing mixes for each of these markets should be changed. Naturally, short-range plans must be compatible with the organization's long-range plans.

Marketing at Work 3-1

Burger King Canada Answers Key Questions

Did you know that there were 1,024 possible ways to order a Whopper? How many different ways have you tried? It takes planning to be able to do that!

Burger King Canada is a part of the global operations of the Burger King Corporaton, second only to MacDonald's in size, operates more than 10,700 restaurants (more than 92 percent owned by independent franchisees) in over fifty-five countries and territories. In Canada, Burger King operates across the country and is more evenly spread than its competitors who have regional concentrations. Here is how Burger King Canada approaches the questions of mission, objectives, strategies, and tactics.

CONCEPT	QUESTION	BURGER KING ANSWERS
Mission	What business are we in?	Convenience food: Whopper and fries.
Objectives	What do we want to accomplish?	Growth through expansion.
Strategies	In general terms, how are we going to get the job done?	Increase outlets from 240 to 500 in five years by targeting underdeveloped markets
Tactics	In specific terms, how are we going to get the job done now? What are we going to do on a daily basis?	Acquire new sites in Alberta and the Maritimes; campuses, hospitals, partnerships with retailers, gas stations.

As a result of pursuing the stated mission, objectives, strategies and tactics, Burger King has now increased the number of outlets it operates to about 335 and is concentrating on underdeveloped markets in Edmonton, Calgary, Montreal, and Quebec City. It has moved up from fourth place in market share to second place (behind MacDonald's 51 percent) with 11 percent, ahead of Harvey's and A&W. But, in the final analysis, as George Michel, president of Burger King Canada, has said: "You can have all the strategies and the best marketing plan in the world, but if the execution at the restaurant level is not there, then you're going to miss."

Source: Adapted from Mikala Folb, "BK Targets West, Maritimes for Growth," *Marketing Magazine*, January 27, 1997, p. 3 and reprinted with permission and Zena Olijnyk, "Chains beef up for burger battle," *National Post*, July 24, 2000, p. C1, C3.

Planning the marketing strategies in a firm should be conducted on three different levels:

◆ *Strategic company planning.* At this level, management defines an organization's mission, sets long-range goals, and formulates broad strategies to achieve these goals. These company-wide goals and strategies then become the framework for planning in the firm's different functional areas, such as production, finance, human resources, research and development, and marketing.

◆ *Strategic marketing planning.* The top marketing executives set goals and strategies for an organization's marketing effort. Strategic marketing planning should be co-ordinated with company-wide planning.

◆ *Annual marketing planning.* Short-term plans should be prepared for a firm's major functions. Covering a specific period, usually one year, the annual marketing plan is based on the firm's strategic marketing planning.

Strategic Company Planning

Strategic company planning consists of four essential steps:

strategic company planning
The level of planning that consists of (1) defining the organization's mission, (2) setting organizational objectives, (3) evaluating the firm's strategic business units, and (4) selecting appropriate strategies so as to achieve the organization's objectives.

1. Defining the organizational mission.
2. Analyzing the situation.
3. Setting organizational objectives.
4. Selecting strategies to achieve these objectives.

The process is shown in the top part of Figure 3-2.

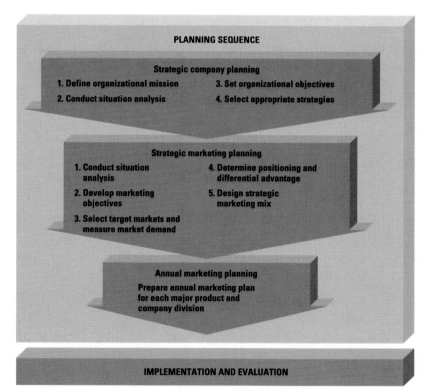

FIGURE 3-2
Three Levels of
Organizational Planning

situation analysis
The stage in a marketing research study that involves obtaining information about the company and its business environment by means of library research and extensive interviewing of company officials.

organizational strategies
Broad, basic plans of action by which an organization intends to achieve its goals and fulfil its mission. These plans are for (1) the total organization in a small, single-product company or (2) each SBU in a large multiproduct or multibusiness organization.

The first step, defining the organizational mission, influences all subsequent planning. For some firms, this step requires only reviewing the existing mission statement and confirming that it is still suitable. Still, this straightforward step is too often ignored.

The second step, conducting a **situation analysis**, is vital because strategic planning is influenced by many factors beyond and within an organization. By situation analysis, we simply mean gathering and studying information pertaining to one or more specified aspect of an organization. We'll talk more about conducting a situation analysis in an upcoming section.

The third step in strategic company planning requires management to decide on a set of objectives to guide the organization in fulfilling its mission. Objectives also provide standards for evaluating an organization's performance.

Such an objective provides a means of measurement throughout the process, such as gaining a 10-percent market share within five years. By this point in its strategic planning, the organization has determined where it wants to go. The fourth step, selecting appropriate strategies, indicates how the firm is going to get there. **Organizational strategies** represent broad plans of action by which an organization intends to achieve its goals and fulfil its mission. Strategies are selected either for the entire company, if it is small and has only a single product, or for each division, if the company is large and has multiple products or units.

Do companies actually engage in this kind of planning and then prepare a written plan? According to one survey, almost 70 percent of firms have strategic plans in place; among them, nearly 90 percent believe their strategic plans have been effective.[3] Interestingly, a larger proportion of younger firms (one to ten years old) than older firms have formal strategic plans.

Strategic Marketing Planning

After conducting strategic planning for the organization as a whole, management needs to lay plans for each major functional area, such as marketing or production. Of course, planning for each function should be guided by the organization-wide mission and objectives.

strategic marketing planning
The level of planning that consists of (1) conducting a situation analysis, (2) determining marketing objectives, (3) selecting target markets and measuring the market, and (4) designing a strategic marketing mix.

Strategic marketing planning is a five-step process:

1. Conduct a situation analysis.

2. Develop marketing objectives.

3. Determine positioning and differential advantage.

4. Select target markets and measure market demand.

5. Design a strategic marketing mix.

These five steps are shown in the middle of Figure 3-2. Each step is discussed below.

Situation Analysis

The first step in strategic marketing planning, situation analysis, involves analyzing where the company's marketing program has been, how it has been doing, and what it is likely to face in the years ahead. Doing this enables management to determine if it's necessary to revise the old plans or devise new ones to achieve the company's objectives.

Situation analysis normally covers external environmental forces and internal non-marketing resources, discussed in Chapter 2. A situation analysis also considers the groups of consumers served by the company, the strategies used to satisfy them, and key measures of marketing performance.

As the basis for planning decisions, situation analysis is critical. But it can be costly, time-consuming, and frustrating. For example, it's usually difficult to extract timely, accurate information from the "mountains" of data compiled during a situation analysis. Moreover, some valuable information, such as sales or market-share figures for competitors, is often unavailable.

SWOT assessment
Identifying and evaluating an organization's most significant strengths, weaknesses, opportunities, and threats.

As part of a situation analysis, many organizations perform a **SWOT assessment**. In this activity, a firm identifies and evaluates its most significant Strengths, Weaknesses, Opportunities, and Threats. To fulfil its mission, an organization needs to capitalize on its key strengths, overcome or alleviate its major weaknesses, avoid significant threats, and take advantage of the most promising opportunities.

We're referring to strengths and weaknesses in an organization's own capabilities. For example, prior to the financial difficulties leading to Eaton's final closure in 1999, the company's strength was its large size, which gave it — among other things — clout in dealing with suppliers. However, weaknesses included its frequent merchandising changes and its comparatively high operating expenses. High inventories and outstanding debts left the company in a vulnerable position. International retailer Wal-Mart (www.wal-mart.com) also has this strength, however it has used it to control its suppliers such that a very efficient inventory supply system has been developed whereby almost no excess inventory is carried.

Opportunities and threats often originate outside the organization. These fall under little control of the organization. For example, an opportunity identified by Wal-Mart when expanding into Canada was the large number of metropolitan areas in which it could open its highly efficient stores. But an unknown threat was the competition that could come from such firms as Zellers (www.hbc.com/zellers/) and Canadian Tire (www.canadiantire.com). Both stores possess strong Canadian identities and a long-standing presence in Canadian shopping centres. In the Canadian marketplace there has recently been some return to patriotic purchase considerations guided by a healthy suspicion of U.S. superstores that are "wiping out the little guys."[4] Zellers has tried to position itself as "Truly Canadian" even spawning an in-house product-line of the same name.[5]

Another factor that may have been underestimated by the U.S. super-retailer is the long-standing and very successful loyalty programs of these stores. Zellers is now into its second-generation program — Generation Z.[6] Canadian Tire money, around for decades, is so popular from coast to coast that it is often joked as being the second Canadian currency. Canadian Tire is now planning to add a cyber component to the currency program.[7] These points serve as potential threats to Wal-Mart while being strengths for the Canadian retailers. According to a recent study, mergers have resulted in a concentration of retailers in this country, but Canadian-owned retail remains very strong.[8]

Marketing Objectives

The next step in strategic marketing planning is to determine marketing objectives. Marketing goals should be closely related to company-wide goals and strategies. In fact, a company strategy often translates into a marketing goal. For example, to reach an organizational objective of a 20 percent return on investment next year, one organizational strategy might be to reduce marketing costs by 15 percent. This company strategy would become a marketing goal. In turn, converting all salespeople from salaried compensation to a commission basis might be one of the marketing strategies adopted to achieve this marketing goal.

We already know that strategic planning involves matching an organization's resources with its market opportunities. With this in mind, each objective should be assigned a priority based on its urgency and potential impact on the marketing area and, in turn, the organization. Then resources should be allocated in line with these priorities.[9]

Positioning and Differential Advantage

The third step in strategic marketing planning actually involves two complementary decisions: how to position a product in the marketplace, and how to distinguish it from competitors. **Positioning** refers to a product's image in relation to directly competitive products as well as other products marketed by the same company.[10] For example, given rising health consciousness among many consumers, manufacturers of mayonnaise, corn oil, and other food products recognized the need to introduce products that would be perceived as more wholesome.[11] CPC International is trying to position its Hellmann's Dijonnaise, which combines no-fat mustard with mayonnaise ingredients (but no egg yolks), as a healthful and tasty product. Buckley's Cough syrup (www.buckleys.com), long famous for its horrible taste (what can you expect from pine needles!), has positioned itself based on the dreaded taste — "it tastes awful…and it works." It has been a memorable approach, and successful. The company has distinguished itself with humour that has successfully convinced consumers that it must work! Buckley's is trying to win over U.S and international markets with the same approach. This included a contest in the National Enquirer asking users to send photos showing their worst post-Buckley's facial expressions.[12] This is a rare example of how a common strategy can work across international markets.

positioning
A company's strategies and actions related to favourably distinguishing itself and its products from competitors in the minds (and hearts) of selected groups of consumers.

Buckley's links "awful taste" to effectiveness and makes it work as a differential advantage.

Funny, people never complain about the effectiveness of Buckley's.

(The taste on the other hand.)

What else would you expect from ingredients like Pine Needle Oil, Camphor and Canada Balsam? But, if you can get past the taste, nothing works faster or more effectively to get rid of nasty coughs due to colds as Buckley's. Good luck.

Buckley's Mixture.
It tastes awful. And it works.

Available at all RITE AID stores and Jewel OSCO, OSCO drug, Sav-On-Drug and other fine pharmacies. 1-800-434-1034 www.buckleys.com

differential advantage
Any feature of an organization or brand perceived by customers to be desirable and different from the competition.

differential disadvantage
Any feature of an organization or brand perceived by customers to be undesirable and similar to the competition.

market
People or organizations with wants to satisfy, money to spend, and the willingness to spend it.

target market
A group of customers (people or organizations) at whom a seller aims its marketing effort.

marketing mix
A combination of the four elements — product, pricing structure, distribution system, and promotional activities — that comprise a company's marketing program. Many marketers now consider service and the "people" side of marketing to be a fifth component of the marketing mix, especially in the marketing of services.

After the product is positioned, a viable differential advantage has to be identified. **Differential advantage** refers to any feature of an organization or brand perceived by customers to be desirable and different from those of the competition.[13] At the same time, a company has to avoid a differential disadvantage for its product. Consider Apple Computers (www.apple.com): For many years, the Macintosh's user friendliness (based on its unique operating system) represented a strong differential for the brand and allowed Apple to sell the computer at a premium price. Then, when Microsoft (www.microsoft.com) introduced its Windows 95 operating system, which provided a very similar form of user friendliness, this advantage disappeared and Apple was faced with **differential disadvantages** stemming from both its operating system and its pricing strategies. Apple has since been forced into many product and marketing changes in the search for new differential advantages. This has resulted in a new product focus and pricing strategy. Apple is once again known for its distinctive appearance – but this time it comes from its zany translucent colours and design. The new iMac PC design is credited with saving the company.[14]

Target Markets and Market Demand

Selecting target markets is the fourth step in marketing planning. A **market** consists of people or organizations with needs to satisfy, money to spend, and the willingness to spend it. For example, many people need transportation and are willing to pay for it. However, this large group is made up of a number of segments (that is, parts of markets) with various transportation needs. One segment may want low-cost, efficient transportation, while another may prefer luxury and privacy. Air Canada segments the air travel market by offering economy, business, and first-class travel, with each class offering a different service bundle ranging from checking-in privileges to different seat widths, and, of course, at very different prices. This is not very different from auto manufacturers, as already discussed, offering products ranging from heavy-duty trucks to luxury cars and economical compact cars.

Ordinarily it is impractical for a firm to satisfy every segment that has different needs. Instead, a company targets its efforts at one or more of these segments. Thus a **target market** refers to a group of people or organizations at which a firm directs a marketing program. Designing the actual product is a part of that marketing effort.

Target markets must be selected on the basis of opportunities. In a new company, management should analyze markets in detail to identify potential target markets. In an existing firm, management should routinely examine any changes in the characteristics of its target markets and alternative markets. A firm must forecast demand, that is, sales, in each market. The results of sales or demand forecasting will determine whether the firm's targets are worth pursuing or whether alternatives need to be identified. We'll consider demand forecasting in Chapter 5.

Marketing Mix

Next, management must design a **marketing mix** — the combination of a product or service, how it is distributed and promoted, and its price. Traditionally, the marketing mix has been considered in terms of four elements that together must satisfy the needs of the organization's target markets and, at the same time, achieve its marketing objectives. In recent years, as marketers have turned their thinking more toward marketing in service organizations and to the service elements that must accompany the sale and marketing of any product or service, some have expanded their view of the marketing mix to include the essential element of customer service. This refers to the way in which the customer is treated not only by marketing personnel, but by all employees and by the company itself. Let's consider the elements of the expanded marketing mix and some of the concepts and strategies you'll learn about in later chapters:

◆ *Product.* Strategies are needed for managing existing products over time, adding new ones, and dropping failed products. Strategic decisions must also be made regarding service levels, branding, packaging, and other product features such as warranties.

◆ *Price.* Necessary strategies pertain to the locations of customers, price flexibility, related items within a product line, and terms of sale. Also, pricing strategies for entering a market, especially with a new product, must be designed.

◆ *Distribution.* Here, strategies involve the management of the channel(s) by which ownership of products is transferred from producer to customer and, in many cases, the system(s) by which goods are moved from the place where they are produced to the place where they are purchased by the final customer. Strategies applicable to intermediaries, such as wholesalers and retailers, must be designed.

◆ *Marketing communications.* Strategies are needed to combine individual methods such as advertising, personal selling, and sales promotion into a co-ordinated campaign. In addition, these strategies must be adjusted as a product moves from the early stages to the later stages of its life. Strategic decisions must also be made regarding each individual method of marketing communications.

◆ *Customer service.* This component of the marketing mix deals with how the customer is handled as he or she deals with the firm or organization. Marketers must develop strategies concerning how customer service is to be delivered, what level of service is needed to allow the company to compete, and what level of service it can afford to provide to customers.

The elements of the marketing mix are interrelated; decisions in one area often affect actions in another. To illustrate, the design of a marketing mix is certainly affected by whether a firm chooses to compete on the basis of price, service, or on one or more other elements. When a firm relies on price as its primary competitive tool, the other elements must be designed to support aggressive pricing. For example, the promotional campaign likely will be built around a theme of "low, low prices." In nonprice competition, however, product, distribution, customer and service strategies, and/or promotion strategies come to the forefront. For instance, the product and supporting services must have features worthy of a higher price, and marketing communications must create a high-quality image for the product.

Each marketing-mix element contains countless variables. An organization may market one product or many, and these products may be related or unrelated to each other. The product may be distributed through wholesalers, to retailers without the benefit of wholesalers, or even directly to final customers. Ultimately, from the multitude of variables, management must select a combination of elements that will satisfy target markets and achieve organizational and marketing goals.

✒ *Annual Marketing Plan*

Besides strategic planning for several years into the future, more specific, shorter-term planning is also vital. Thus, strategic marketing planning in an organization leads to the

annual marketing plan
A written document that details the planned marketing activities for the given business unit or product for the given year.

preparation of an annual marketing plan, as shown in the bottom part of Figure 3-2. An **annual marketing plan** is the master blueprint for a year's marketing activity for a specified organizational division or major product. Note that it is a written document.

A separate plan normally should be prepared for each major product and company division. Sometimes, depending on a company's circumstances, separate plans are developed for key brands and important target markets.[15] As the name implies, an annual marketing plan usually covers one year. However, there are exceptions. For instance, because of the seasonal nature of some products or markets, it is advisable to prepare plans for shorter time periods. In the fashion clothing industry, plans are made for each season, lasting just several months.

Purposes and Responsibilities

An annual marketing plan serves several purposes:

◆ It summarizes the marketing strategies and tactics that will be used to achieve specified objectives in the upcoming year. Thus it becomes the "what-to-do" document that guides executives and other employees involved in marketing.

◆ The plan also focuses on "how to do it," pointing to what needs to be done with respect to the other steps in the management process, primarily implementation. The detail of implementation provides important basic information that gives direction to the evaluation of the marketing program.

◆ Moreover, the plan outlines who is responsible for which activities, when the activities are to be carried out, and how much time and money can be spent.

The executive responsible for the division or product covered by the plan typically prepares it. All or part of the task may be delegated to subordinates.

Preparation of an annual marketing plan may begin nine months or more before the start of the period covered by the plan. Early work includes necessary research and arranging other information sources. The bulk of the work occurs one to three months prior to the plan's starting date. The last steps are to have the plan reviewed and approved by upper management. Some revision may be necessary before final approval is granted. The final version of the plan, or relevant parts of it, should be shared with all employees who will be involved in implementing the agreed-upon strategies and tactics. The failure to have a plan understood and accepted by those implementing it both within and outside of the organization threatens both service quality and the quality of the market relationships ultimately established. Since an annual plan contains confidential information, it should not be distributed too widely.

Recommended Contents

The exact contents of an annual marketing plan should be determined by an organization's circumstances. For example, a firm in an intensely competitive industry would assess its competitors in a separate section. A firm in another industry would present this assessment as part of the situation analysis. Similarly, some organizations include alternative (or contingency) plans; others don't. An example of a contingency plan is the set of steps the firm will take if a competitor introduces a new product, as is rumoured.

Annual marketing planning follows a sequence similar to strategic marketing planning. However, annual planning has a shorter time frame and is more specific, both with respect

TABLE 3–1   Contents of an Annual Marketing Plan

1. *Executive Summary.* In this one- or two-page section, the thrust of the plan is described and explained. It is intended for executives who desire an overview of the plan but need not be knowledgeable about the details.

2. *Situation Analysis.* Essentially, the marketing program for the strategic business unit (SBU) or product covered by the plan is examined within the context of pertinent past, present, and future conditions. It is vital that a reliable assessment of human resource needs and capabilities be part of the analysis. Much of this section might be derived from the results of strategic marketing planning. Additional information of particular relevance to a one-year planning period may be included in this section.

3. *Objectives.* The objectives in an annual plan are more specific than those produced by strategic marketing planning. However, annual objectives must help achieve organizational goals and strategic marketing goals.

4. *Strategies.* As in strategic marketing planning, the strategies in an annual plan should indicate which target markets are going to be satisfied through a combination of product, price, distribution, and promotion.

5. *Tactics.* Specific activities, sometimes called action plans, are devised for carrying out each major strategy included in the preceding section. For ease of understanding, strategies and tactics may be covered together. Tactics specifically answer the question of what is to be done, who will do it, and how the tasks will be accomplished. The who and the how tend to show that a plan is actually implementable, given the finances in section 6.

6. *Financial Schedules.* This section normally includes three kinds of financial information: projected sales, expenses, and profits in what's called a pro-forma financial statement; and the amounts of resources dedicated to different activities in one or more budgets.

7. *Timetable.* This section, often including a diagram, answers the question of when various marketing activities will be carried out during the upcoming year.

8. *Evaluation Procedures.* This section addresses the questions of what, who, how, and when connected with measuring performance against goals, both during and at the end of the year. The results of evaluations during the year may lead to adjustments in the plan's strategies and/or tactics or even in the objectives to be achieved.

to the issues addressed and to the plans laid. Still, as shown in Table 3-1, the major sections of an annual marketing plan are similar to the steps in strategic marketing planning.

In an annual marketing plan, more attention can be devoted to tactical details than is feasible in other levels of planning. As an example, strategic marketing planning might stress personal selling within the marketing mix. If so, the annual plan might recommend increased college or university recruiting as a source of additional salespeople.

Also note that an annual marketing plan relates to all three steps of the management process, not just planning. That is, sections 5 through 7 in Table 3-1 deal with implementation, and section 8 is concerned with evaluation. We will return to implementation when we discuss the various components of the marketing mix in the chapters that follow.

Selected Planning Models

A number of frameworks or tools — we'll call them *models* — have been designed to assist with strategic planning. Most of these models can be used with both strategic company planning and strategic marketing planning. In this section, we briefly discuss several planning models that have received ample attention in recent years. First, however, you need to be familiar with a form of organization, the strategic business unit (SBU), that pertains to these planning models.

Strategic Business Units

Most large and medium-sized companies, and even some smaller firms, consist of multiple units and produce numerous products. In such diversified firms, company-wide planning cannot serve as an effective guide for executives who oversee the organization's various divisions. Bombardier Inc. (http://www.bombardier.com), a company probably best known to most Canadians as the manufacturer of Ski-Doo® snowmobiles, provides a good example. The mission, objectives, and strategies of the divisions within the motorized consumer products group (which includes the Sea-Doo®/Ski-Doo® Division) are — and must be — quite different from those that guide marketing and other activities in its aerospace group (where the strategic business units include Canadair (http://www.canadair.com) and De Havilland, manufacturers of airplanes) and its transportation equipment group, where the strategic business units are involved in the manufacture of subway and railway cars, shuttle-train cars for the tunnel under the English Channel, and PeopleMover Transportation systems.

Consequently, for more effective planning and operations, a multi-business or multi-product organization should be divided according to its major markets or products. Each such entity is called a **strategic business unit** (SBU). Each SBU may be a major product or service division in an organization, a geographic organization such as an international or country division, a group of related products, or even a single major product or brand that is marketed globally.

To be identified as an SBU, an entity should:

◆ Be a separately identifiable business.

◆ Have a distinct mission.

◆ Have its own competitors.

◆ Have its own executive group with profit responsibility.

The trick in setting up SBUs in an organization is to arrive at the optimum number. Too many can bog down the top management in details associated with planning, operating, and reporting. Too few SBUs can result in each one covering too broad an area for managerial planning. Of course, most companies have fewer SBUs than Bombardier.

Let's now consider two of many different planning models: the **Boston Consulting Group** matrix and the product-market growth matrix.

The Boston Consulting Group Matrix

Developed by a management consulting firm, the Boston Consulting Group (BCG) matrix (www.bcg.com) dates back almost thirty years.[16] Using this model, an organization classifies each of its SBUs (and, sometimes, its major products) according to two factors: its market share relative to competitors, and the growth rate of the industry in which the SBU operates. When the factors are divided simply into high and low categories, a 2 by 2 grid is created, as displayed in Figure 3-3.

In turn, the four quadrants in the grid represent distinct categories of SBUs or major products. The categories differ with respect not only to market share and industry growth rate but also to cash needs and appropriate strategies.

strategic business unit (SBU)
A separate division for a major product or market in a multiproduct or multibusiness organization.

Boston Consulting Group (BCG) matrix
A strategic planning model that classifies strategic business units or major products according to market shares and growth rates.

FIGURE 3-3
The Boston Consulting Group (BCG) Matrix

COMPANY'S MARKET SHARE

High   Low

INDUSTRY GROWTH RATE

High

Stars   Question marks

Low

Cash cows   Dogs

Marketing at Work 3-2

From Newspaper To Electronic Information Powerhouse

Thomson newspapers started business in 1934 with the purchase of *The Daily Press* in Timmins, Ontario. Today, with the exception of the flagship newspaper *The Globe and Mail*, The Thomson Corporation is putting five dailies in Canada and more than 130 other newspapers in the U.S. on the auction block for as much as $2.5 billion U.S. Since 1934, newspapers formed the backbone of this sprawling empire, and they are still profitable. In fact, the time for the sale could not be better because advertising sales are booming — thanks to the dot. com company rush to gain consumer attention. What then could be wrong with keeping these papers?

Over time, Thomson expanded beyond its newspaper business. The $6 billion conglomerate includes: Thomson Financial, which owns a host of specialized financial publications and databases; the West Group, a legal publishing business, and Thomson Learning, a rapidly growing provider of educational software and other education related products and services. These company units are in newly emerging and rapidly growing new markets. By comparison, the Thomson's newspaper holdings, although profitable, appeared too small and regionally focused. A careful situation analysis demonstrated to management that high market growth and much higher profitability was available in the newly emerging information markets, where Thomson already had a solid foothold.

The auctioning of the newspaper assets is inevitable given Thomson's strategic refocus. The new Thomson goal was to become a global electronic information and solutions business. Those strategic business units of the conglomerate that could contribute to this goal were to be nurtured, those that were peripheral to achieving it were to be sold so that their proceeds would be available to nurture potential stars.

The Globe and Mail was originally not to be sold but later 50 percent was. Its brand strength is national, not local, and it has within the Globe organization a number of strategic units that are important in pursuing the stated goal. A key asset of *The Globe* is the *Report on Business* magazine which not only generates a lot of revenue but also already has a number of new media offspring. *ROB TV*, or the TV station owned by *The Globe*, provides financial news over cable and satellite. *The Globe* also operates a number of Web sites including *globemegawheel.com* and *globeinvestor.com*. Plans for other Web sites, leveraging the Globe brand, are being formulated so as to complete a solid roster of valuable Internet properties.

This strategic refocus should reshape Thomson's geographically dispersed and regionally focused newpaper operation into a centralized yet global organization which focuses on the emerging information markets.

Source: Adapted from Brian Milner and Susanne Craig, "Thomson Takes Aim At Web in Divesting Newspapers," *The Globe and Mail Internet Edition*, Feb. 16, 2000.

---

stars
According to the Boston Consulting Group matrix, strategic business units that are characterized by high market shares and high industry growth rates.

cash cows
According to the Boston Consulting Group matrix, strategic business units that are characterized by high market shares and do business in mature industries (those with low growth rates).

question marks
Strategic business units characterized by low market shares but high industry growth rates.

◆ **Stars**. High market shares and high industry growth rates typify SBUs in this category. However, an SBU that falls into this category poses a challenge for companies because it requires lots of cash to remain competitive in growing markets. Aggressive marketing strategies are imperative for stars to maintain or even build market share. Microsoft's Windows (www.microsoft.com) software package and 3Com's Palm "digital personal assistant" (www.3com.com) exemplify this category.

◆ **Cash cows**. These SBUs have high market shares and do business in mature industries (those with low growth rates). When an industry's growth diminishes, stars move into this category. Because most of their customers have been with them for some time and are still loyal, a cash cow's marketing costs are not high. Consequently, it generates more cash than can be reinvested profitably in its own operations. As a result, cash cows can be "milked" to support the firm's other SBUs that need more resources. Marketing strategies for cash cows seek to defend market share, largely by reinforcing customer loyalty. As examples, consider Bausch & Lomb's sunglasses (such as its Ray-Ban brand (www.rayban.com)) and Campbell's canned soups.

◆ **Question marks** (sometimes called *problem children*). SBUs characterized by low market shares but high industry growth rates fit in this category. A question mark has not achieved a strong foothold in an expanding but highly competitive market. The question surrounding this type of SBU is whether it can gain adequate market share and be profitable. If management answers "no," then the SBU should be divested or liquidated. If management instead answers "yes," the firm must come up with the cash to build market share — more cash than the typical question mark generates from its own profits. Appropriate marketing strategies for question marks focus on creating an impact in the market by displaying a strong differential advantage and, thereby, building customer support. When Walt Disney tried to compete with popular general interest portals such as Yahoo! (www.yahoo.com), it was unable to attract sufficient traffic causing a strategic change to focus the URL as an entertainment and leisure portal.[17]

dogs
According to the Boston Consulting Group matrix, strategic business units that are characterized by low market shares and operate in industries with low growth rates.

◆ **Dogs**. These SBUs have low market shares and operate in industries with low growth rates. A company normally would be unwise to invest substantial funds in SBUs in this category. Marketing strategies for dogs are intended to maximize any potential profits by minimizing expenditures or to promote a differential advantage to build market share. The company can instead say "Enough's enough!" and divest or liquidate an SBU that's a dog. This is what Chrysler did in the late nineties when it ceased operation of their Eagle division which included the Talon and Vista. This represented the first time in over thirty years that an American auto-maker retired an entire brand line. It did salvage the associated Jeep product line, promoting its popularity in the growing sport utility segment of the auto market. By utilizing only small cosmetic changes of appearance of these vehicles, the company could minimize costs associated with factory retooling that comes with vehicle redesign.

Ordinarily, one firm cannot affect the growth rate for an entire industry. An exception might be the leading firm in a fairly new industry. If growth rate cannot be influenced, companies must turn their attention to the other factor in the BCG matrix, market share. Hence, marketing strategies based on the BCG matrix tend to concentrate on building or maintaining market share, depending on which of the four SBU categories is involved. Various strategies require differing amounts of cash, which means that management must continually allocate the firm's limited resources (notably cash) to separate marketing endeavours.

In the financial arena, an investor needs a balanced portfolio with respect to risks and potential returns. Similarly, a company should seek a balanced portfolio of SBUs. Certainly, cash cows are indispensable. Stars and question marks are integral to a balanced portfolio, because products in growing markets determine a firm's long-term performance. While dogs are undesirable, it is rare that a company doesn't have at least one. Thus, the portfolios of most organizations with numerous SBUs or major products include a mix of stars, cash cows, question marks, and dogs.

product-market growth matrix
A planning model that consists of four alternative growth strategies, based on whether an organization will be selling its present products or new products to its present markets or new markets.

Product-Market Growth Matrix

Most organizations' statements of mission and objectives focus on growth — that is, a desire to increase revenues and profits. In seeking growth, a company must consider both its markets and its products. Then it has to decide whether to continue doing what it is now doing — only do it better — or establish new ventures. The **product-market growth matrix**, first proposed by Igor Ansoff, depicts these options. Essentially, as shown in Figure 3-4, there are four product-market growth strategies:[18]

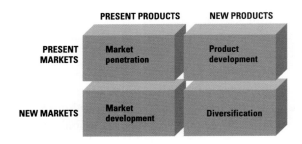

FIGURE 3-4
Product-Market Growth Matrix

market penetration
A product-market growth strategy in which a company tries to sell more of its present products to its present markets.

market development
A product-market growth strategy in which a company continues to sell its present products, but to a new market.

Diversification into new products and markets can be risky. The risk is reduced if the same customer uses both product lines.

◆ **Market penetration.** A company tries to sell more of its present products to its present markets. Supporting tactics might include greater spending on advertising, targeted mailings, or telemarketing. A company can try to become a single source of supply by offering preferential treatment to customers who will concentrate all their purchases with it. Examples of this include insurance companies that will provide increasingly higher discounts the more policies you carry with them. Banks will also negotiate reduced service charges, or free services, as clients increase the number of products or value of holdings with that institution giving a new dimension to the idea of bulk buying.

◆ **Market development.** A firm continues to sell its present products, but to a new market. Frequently, firms turn to exporting to new foreign markets or to developing their own foreign organizations. A combined domestic and foreign approach to market development is when Canadian ski resort operators make efforts to attract families and tourists from the U.S. and Europe. Skiing is most popular among 18–24-year-olds and during the winter, therefore, this age segment has been the primary market for such facilities. In an effort to attract older consumers and families, facilities such as Mont Tremblant in Quebec have added more entertainment venues, more upscale dining and accommodations, and off-season attractions stressing the unique Québécois culture of the area.[19]

◆ **Product development.** This strategy calls for a company to develop new products to sell to its existing markets. To remain competitive, Panasonic (www.panasonic.com) and Sony (www.sony.com) have to develop and introduce new products continuously in order to keep "Just Slightly Ahead of Our Time." While DVD players quickly decrease in price and flood the marketplace, these companies have already introduced a second-generation of portable models to the marketplace. Resembling a small laptop, the DVD player comes with its own flip-up screen. Competition keeps such firms competing to make their products lighter, provide greater picture resolution, and last longer between battery charges.

◆ **Diversification.** A company develops new products to sell to new markets. This strategy is risky because it doesn't rely on either the company's successful products or its position in established markets. Sometimes it works, but sometimes it doesn't. Cow's Inc. (www.cows.ca) started as a local P.E.I.-based ice cream vendor. In fact, in the beginning, Cow's only ice cream flavour was vanilla. Now, it has several stores across Canada with a multitude of flavours and an extensive merchandising line available in-store and through mail order featuring the Holstein cow that is the company symbol. What does really good ice cream have in common with T-shirts, sweatshirts, stationery items, and other clothing? Nothing really, unless you count the success of both product lines.[20]

As market conditions change over time, a company may shift product-market growth strategies. For example, when its present market is fully saturated, a company may have no choice other than to pursue new markets within Canada, nearby American states, or Asian countries.

Marketing at Work 3-3

Diversification Through Strategic Alliances

Sometimes, instead of outspending your competitor, and no matter how challenging and gratifying it might be to outsmart them, the most efficient and effective way to compete is to partner with them to form an alliance. A recent three-way strategic alliance between Alliance/Atlantis Communications, Famous Players, and Galaxy Entertainment, appears to fulfil all of the objectives of the product-market growth matrix sought by each of the above. To further illustrate this remarkable execution, a bit of profiling of each player in the deal would help:

Alliance/Atlantis → An internationally renowned Canadian production shop which produces a variety of products from TV series to art-house films. They also exhibit their films but are limited to the urban audiences because of the repertory theatre nature of their film division's outlets.

Famous Players → A large scale distributor of mainstream films and operator of 102 movie theatres across Canada. Famous focuses on the market side and is in constant need of new film in order to fill the seats in their theatres.

Galaxy Entertainment Inc → A Toronto-based company which buys run-down cinemas in small towns and renovates them into flashy multi-screen complexes.

Now look at the opportunities for each party and the strategies by which they can be achieved:

Alliance/Atlantis → Opportunity: expand to new markets and export unique product beyond their current urban audience base. Strategy: Use Famous Players and Galaxy Entertainment as vehicles to increase penetraton in current markets and help develop new ones

Famous Players → Opportunity: increase position in existing markets and expand to new ones. Strategy: develop new markets by adding the Galaxy screens and capitalizing on the popularity and mainstream nature of movies it distributes as well as broadening its menu by including Alliance/Atlantis' films.

Galaxy Entertainment → Opportunity: increase penetration in existing markets in small towns with unfulfilled demand. Strategy: offer more popular movies from Famous Players with mainstream appeal to increase traffic and broaden its offerings with the introduction of unique films from Alliance Atlantis.

The three companies are staring at each other's resources with envy. Galaxy cannot easily pursue a strategy to establish movie theatres across the street from Famous Players as they would most certainly be expensive. Alliance/Atlantis can't bank on being the single source of attraction in small-city markets alone. Famous Players would have to spend a great deal in order to expand and reach new markets, thus capitalizing on Galaxy's already in place and renovated outlets is very attractive.

Source: Adapted from Susan Heinrich, "Alliance Atlantis & Famous Players Take Stake in Theatre Firm," *The National Post, Internet Edition*, Feb. 18, 2000.

Assessment of the Planning Models

Each of these planning models has been praised and criticized. While each is somewhat distinctive, all share some common weaknesses and strengths.

The primary weakness is probably oversimplification. Each model bases its assessment of market opportunities and subsequent decisions on only two or three key factors. Another weakness is the possibility of placing an SBU on a grid or choosing a strategy without relevant, reliable information. For example, the extent to which market share is critical to a product's profitability is still debated. A third possible weakness is that the results from one of the models might be used to contradict or substitute for the critical business judgments made by line managers (such as a marketing vice-president).

However, these models also possess noteworthy strengths. Most notable is straightforward classification. That is, each model permits an organization to examine its entire portfolio of SBUs or major products in relation to criteria that influence business performance. A second strength is that the models can pinpoint attractive business opportunities and suggest ventures to avoid. They encourage the careful, consistent assessment of opportunities, allocation of resources, and formulation of strategies. Without planning models, these activities might be haphazard — for example, using one set of criteria this month and, with no good reason, another set next month.

Overall, these and other planning models can help management in allocating resources and in developing sound business and marketing strategies. Of course, any planning model should supplement, rather than substitute for, managers' judgments and decisions.

Summary

The management process consists of planning, implementation, and evaluation. Planning is deciding now what we are going to do later, including when and how we are going to do it. Planning provides direction to an organization. Strategic planning is intended to match an organization's resources with its market opportunities over the long run.

In any organization, there should be three levels of planning: strategic company planning, strategic marketing planning, and annual marketing planning. In strategic company planning, management defines the organization's mission, assesses its operating environment, sets long-range goals, and formulates broad strategies to achieve the goals. This level of planning guides planning in different functional areas, including marketing.

Strategic marketing planning entails five steps: conduct a situation analysis; develop objectives; determine positioning and differential advantage; select target markets and measure market demand; and design a marketing mix. Based on strategic marketing plans, an annual marketing plan lays out a year's marketing activities for each major product and division of an organization. An annual plan includes tactics as well as strategies and should be specific about the people involved — the who and how of implementation. It is typically prepared by the executive responsible for the division or product.

Management can rely on either or both of the models discussed for assistance with strategic planning: the Boston Consulting Group matrix and Ansoff's product-market growth matrix. A planning model helps management see how best to allocate its resources and to select effective marketing strategies.

Key Terms and Concepts

Strategic planning 57	Positioning 64	Stars 70
Strategic window 57	Differential advantage 65	Cash cows 70
Mission 58	Differential disadvantage 65	Question marks 70
Objective 58	Market 65	Dogs 71
Strategy 59	Target market 65	Product-market growth matrix 71
Tactic 59	Marketing mix 65	Market penetration 72
Strategic company planning 61	Annual marketing plan 67	Market development 72
Situation analysis 62	Strategic business unit (SBU) 69	Product development 72
Organizational strategies 62	Boston Consulting Group (BCG)	Diversification 72
Strategic marketing planning 62	matrix 69	
SWOT assessment 63		

Questions and Problems

1. In light of the considerations that led Ford Canada to develop a strategy around the female car buyer, can you think of other smaller groups, based upon any type of demographic distinction(s) that an automaker could target? What is the strategic approach(es) you would recommend?

2. Should a small firm (either a manufacturer, a retailer, or an online enterprise) engage in formal strategic planning? Why or why not?

3. Considering the impact of changing technology in technology-based industries, should firms involved in these follow the same guidelines and timeframe for strategic planning as traditional organizations? Explain.

4. Using a customer-oriented approach (benefits provided or wants satisfied), answer the question "What business are we in?" for each of the following companies:

   a. Holiday Inn.

   b. Tim Hortons.

   c. Dell computers.

5. In the situation-analysis step of strategic marketing planning, what specific external environmental factors should be analyzed by a manufacturer of equipment used for backpacking in the wilderness?

6. If you were the vice-president of marketing for Canada 3000, a major charter airline, which planning model would you find most useful? Why?

7. "The European Union (EU) which seeks the economic unification of Europe means absolute chaos for Canadian firms trying to market to consumers in these countries. For a number of years, the situation will be so dynamic that executives should not waste their time on formal strategic planning related to European markets." Do you agree with this statement? Support your position.

8. Use an example to explain the concept of a strategic business unit.

9. Keeping in mind the characteristics that are described for each in the text, can you name an organization that would fit under each quadrant of the BCG matrix?

Hands-On Marketing

1. Go to your school's library and obtain a copy of an annual report for a major corporation. Based on your examination of the year-end review, which of the following product-market growth strategies is being used by this company: market penetration, market development, product development, and/or diversification?

2. Talk with a marketing executive at a local firm. Based on the information you obtain, determine the differential advantage or disadvantage of the firm's primary product or service. Indicate how the advantage could be strengthened or the disadvantage alleviated.

3. Go to the Gap Web site (www.gapinc.com) and, by reviewing the content of "About Us" and "Our Business," determine the Gap's objectives.

Case 1-1

NIKE, INC.
The Race to Stay Ahead in an Evolving Global Marketplace

In a multi-billion dollar market like athletic footwear where the purchase motive ranges from function to fashion, there is bound to be a lot of competition. And there is, there really is! With such high stakes, a firm today must always be on top of trends in areas as varied as the different sports, changing pastimes and activities, and emerging fashion trends. It is a marketplace where promotion and image have often come to be as functional and important as the actual product.

As many readers probably assume, Nike has been the leader in athletic footwear for quite a while — almost twenty years in fact. It dominates the category with about a 40 percent market share. Nike has been named one of the one hundred most powerful corporate brands of the century. In 1999, *Popular Mechanics* awarded the Gauntlet running shoe a design and engineering award, *Business Week* named the Air Zoom M9 soccer boot one of the best products of the year. Also, the Nike Triax 300 sport watch received an IDEA design of the decade award from the Industrial Design Society of America. It would seem that things have been pretty sweet up to this point. However, despite a long series of successes, the company currently faces stiff challenges.

The Starting Line
In the 60s, there were few choices when buying athletic footwear. The top ones are still around today — Converse All-Stars and Keds. Of course they aren't as popular as they used to be now that we have athletic shoes for every activity we engage in. There were some specialized shoes available — for football or track — by Adidas or Puma.

Physical fitness became a "movement" during the 70s as health clubs, fitness studios, and running (it was called jogging back then) became more and more popular. This created a large market of 20 and 30 somethings ripe for the picking. And like any other trend, there was also those wannabes who wanted to convey the sporting image. Therein was born the athletic shoe as fashion statement. By the end of the 80s, 90 percent of the North American population owned a pair, and over 70 percent bought a new pair each year.

Doing It
Phil Knight and his former track coach formed Blue Ribbon Sports in 1964 with the objective of providing competitive athletes with quality shoes. This originally involved importing a Japanese product, Tiger Brand. Believing that they could develop something better, they changed directions and formed Nike, named for the Greek goddess of victory.

In the beginning there was very little marketing (looking at the company today, it's hard to believe!). They began by convincing top American distance runners and coaches to try their products. They had created a product that the "pros" liked and sales grew. It didn't hurt that in the U.S. marathon trials for the 1972 Olympics four of the top seven finishers were wearing the new products — a point that the company quickly publicized, and sales continued to grow. During the late 70s, sales and profits grew at a rate of 75 percent per year. Retail markets were changing, however, as by the early 80s about 80 percent of this footwear was purchased for non-athletic purposes.

Change: Threat, Opportunity, and Fad
In the 1980s the aerobics craze took off, something Nike did not take as a very significant change in the landscape. When the company finally realized that this was more than a fad it did finally produce a shoe for

aerobics. It was highly functional, but not very attractive. Although these errors in judgment may seem to be minor aberrations, they indicate more serious problems.

The company had fallen out of touch with the market, and had therefore missed significant changes; an entirely new functional category of shoe and the fact that many purchases were motivated aside from just function. Much of this footwear was now bought for non-athletic purposes and the company had failed to consider these motives. Firms such as Reebok and L.A. Gear had greatly benefited from Nike's miscalculations and had developed significant market share. By the mid-80s Nike's market share had dropped from 50 percent to only 22 percent.

The company had learned that function was just part of the overall marketing process required in the still-evolving market. Characteristics of image, style, and appearance were developing increasing importance. It was at this point that Nike realized it needed to become more marketing-oriented. One of the company's first moves under this new strategy was to sign Michael Jordan to endorse basketball shoes, a significant component of the company's total sales. It was here that Nike advertising began its pattern of emphasizing fashion and lifestyle as part of the product offering. Likewise, the "Just Do It" campaign had wide appeal, supporting each person's desire to improve, regardless of his or her actual level or ability.

Swoosh!

The 90s moved at breakneck speed for the company as it expanded into, well, everything. The Nike swoosh was put on apparel, equipment, and accessories. At the same time, the company continued to develop an ever-wider assortment of specialty athletic shoes. The company now produces everything from golf clubs to snowboards, with all the apparel and accessories required for each sport or market sector.

Promotion also became a specialty of the company during this time. Aside from a seemingly endless stream of celebrity endorsements, the company became a sponsor of professional and collegiate teams. They also began sponsorship of anything from soccer matches to golf tournaments. The Nike swoosh was everywhere — the symbol alone became enough to relay the product message. The Nike symbol has been rated as one of the best-known corporate symbols of all time. By 1997, sales exceeded US$9.2 billion.

It was during this time that Nike fine-tuned its aggressive advertising and marketing tactics. They may be largely responsible for what is now referred to as guerilla marketing. Although the company today spends a great deal of money sponsoring events, the company has managed to garner a great deal of the goodwill that sponsorship generates without actually being a sponsor. This has been done by running heavy ad campaigns throughout events it hadn't paid to sponsor, such as the Olympics. In fact, many believe that Nike was a sponsor of the 1998 Winter Olympics — they were not. Although, it did step in to become a sponsor for the 2000 Games in Sydney at the last moment when a rival athletic equipment manufacturer backed out. This generated a great deal of positive attention and public relations for the company.

Success and its Price

The return to glory of the company and its forward momentum into more and more product areas drew a great deal of attention from many areas. Great corporate success brings with it the attention of the public and the inherent risk that any misstep will receive the same attention and publicity as any success of the company. In fact, it often draws greater attention and harsher criticism. Events combined to create such problems for the company toward the end of the 90s.

Nike, like some other international manufacturers, operates many factories in third world countries. These countries are quite undeveloped by most standards and the standard of living does not even compare to that of North America. Although the company compensated workers accordingly with the economic development of those areas, a number of activist groups targeted the company for human-rights violations and poor treatment of these workers. Wages in these labour markets are low and working conditions are generally poor. Protesters felt that a wealthy company such as Nike should treat workers better and that they were taking advantage of the conditions in these countries. Initially, the company defended their policies as they followed all local labour regulations including those regarding child labour. Later the company acknowledged that operators who had been contracted to run these operations may have mistreated employees and allowed working conditions to deteriorate.

At the product-development level, the trend for extreme sports and activities was long ignored by Nike, not unlike the aerobic oversight in the 80s. The company was left unprepared for the full force impact of sports such as snowboarding and mountain-biking. These have become popular lifestyle and fashion trends that Nike has only recently devoted its attention towards. Another fashion trend that has affected shoe sales has been that of the move towards casual shoes and hiking boots for everyday wear by all age groups. Nike continues to dominate the category, but all similar manufacturers have been affected by this trend. Athletic shoes as a proportion of all shoe sales has declined substantially.

In a segment where it emphasized innovation, the company has gone a long time without introducing meaningful changes that they can market to the consumer. At the same time Nike continues to increase the variety of styles and prices. The company designs as many as 350 styles each year, yet the last meaningful innovation consumers can recall is the air cushions that first arrived in stores in 1987. At the same time the company has increased their product lines far, far beyond running shoes and apparel. They have shown up in almost every sport — sometimes with a well-publicized blunder! This has had some impact on its goal to be a sports equipment leader. Let's see, there was the ultra-light hockey stick that split apart, the synthetic baseball glove that nobody would use, and of course the in-line skates with the wheels that disintegrated. Often, such product blunders attract more attention and leave more lasting memories then a well-executed product.

During all of this, salaries paid to high-powered celebrities received greater attention than did the actual endorsements they performed. These amounts grew more and more outrageous as the public began to question the salaries of sports figures in light of their public and personal behaviour, such as the negative publicity surrounding athletic strikes. Many feel that an individual receiving over $100 million in endorsements is not actually earning this money and that such people should do more for society. Tiger Woods, for example, is reported to have received over $60 million in a five-year deal from Nike. The initial Tiger golf apparel line by Nike, with shirts priced between $65 and $80, has so far performed quite poorly.

The Fallout

These events have resulted in a drop in sales through the late 90s as well as a drop in the value of Nike stock. The company finally acknowledged it had become overconfident and complacent, and that problems existed. As a result, there were a number of measures taken from the creation of new divisions, to redesigning distribution systems, and restructuring promotional efforts.

Phil Knight and Nike management have become immersed in efforts to alter the culture within the company and focused on how the marketing function is performed within the company.

A new unit was developed and located separately from the main footwear operation, designed for non-traditional sports — ACG (for All Conditions Gear). These products are branded distinctively and include footwear, apparel, and equipment for extreme sports. The separation, providing its own staff, etc., indicates a new start, signalling that things would not be business as usual.

The company has responded to the increased participation of women in sports, particularly team sports. This has included lining up more endorsements from female athletes. With the increasing popularity of soccer, Nike has taken the lead in product development in footwear for female players. These players had often been wearing ill-fitting men's footwear to play. Capitalizing on the company's technical strengths, Nike carefully studied the needs of female players and discovered that many fundamental alterations were required. Mia Hamm was signed to endorse the products that were developed.

Nike determined that the bad publicity regarding overseas factories could not be overcome. The company would have to concede to the perceptions of North American consumers. Although conditions were typical for these areas and the company was not violating local regulations, cultural differences and trends of social responsibility strongly outweighed any business argument that could be made. The company's first response of deflecting responsibility was altered to that of internalization and a commitment to improve conditions in those countries. The company has taken the position that they are responsible to see that these workers are treated better. A vice president of social responsibility was hired, and a staff of ninety-five was soon in place.

The company has insisted on better working conditions in its plants, stricter policies to ensure workers get appropriate wages, and more overseeing of subcontractors' operations. The company has also allowed some independent monitoring of these conditions.

To hasten the process of turning bad into good publicity it has widely publicized these changes. To improve its image on this front the company has also started a literacy program for workers in Indonesia. The University of Arizona, a harsh critic of Nike on this issue, was invited to send students to tour overseas factories — all expenses to be taken care of by Nike and guarantees that reports by the students would be posted on the Nike Web site. Nike also participates in an alliance that includes Reebok and Adidas that funds schooling in these areas.

Nike is also the first large apparel company to disclose the names and sites of its overseas factories, a significant concession to the anti-sweatshop movement among college students. Many student groups praised Nike for this action.

Advertising has become focused less on big dollar endorsement deals and celebrity power, and has moved toward the product and relating to the values of the audience. Celebrities are, or course, still used but it has become less about — look at who we have now! To continue reaching young consumers, the company has placed great focus on developing its Web presence. Nike has been slow to adapt to the Internet, and until recently there has been mostly brand communication and investor information on the Net, with little product presence.

The company's Web site is becoming a successful marketing tool to communicate the firm's new positioning, and to showcase all of its products. The development of Nike iD has even enabled consumers to personalize Nike shoes. Indeed, Nike has thus given consumers the ability to customize their own Nike marketing campaign with the likes of the Nike Movie Maker, enabling visitors to edit online commercials.

The company has made the unprecedented move of forming an alliance with sports e-tailer Fogdog Sports (www.fogdog.com). Although facing growing competition, Fogdog's success thus far has been through emphasizing product selection and service instead of low prices. Up to this point Nike had obstructed online-only retailers from carrying its brand.

TV promotions for the Web site include cliffhanger ads that encourage viewers to visit the site. Here they can view alternative endings (www.whatever.nike.com). The creative director for the spots believes that the approach takes a thirty-second experience and turns it into a fifteen- or twenty-minute experience — or longer! The consumer receives a very strong selling message by the time the experience is over.

Although Nike is now frequently an official event sponsor, guerilla tactics are still employed such as during the 1999 New York Marathon. The company placed representatives with Nike signage along the route during the race, drawing criticism from organizers. Nike is no longer a sponsor of the event.

Today's youth, paradoxically, want to follow trends and at the same time express their individuality. The Nike Swoosh is everywhere — from snowboards to gramp's golfing hat. This can be a problem for these consumers. As such, the company is using the symbol a little more discerningly.

Still Doing It?

The world's largest shoe manufacturer had earnings of US$427.7 million for fiscal 1999. It announced in early 2000 that it would miss earnings forecasts for 2000 and 2001 as consumer demand slows. Investors pummeled the company's stock, causing it to plunge 18 percent. The stock was still recovering from when it bottomed out in 1998.

Can Nike regain ground lost? Can the past be recaptured? In an industry suffering from a proliferation of product and brands, the category seems to have finally hit the mature stage in its life cycle where promotion may play a major role in determining who will continue to be successful in the future. Considering it was once said that Nike had stopped selling shoes and began selling cool — given the company's knack for promotion, it could be in a worse position under such circumstances.

Pertinent Web Sites

www.nike.com
www.whatever.nike.com
www.fogdog.com

Questions

1. Discuss the marketing potential for Nike with regard to the external macroenvironmental factors discussed in Chapter 2 of the text.

2. What problems, challenges, or opportunities exist for manufacturers participating in this product category?

3. How can components of the internal environment be employed to help Nike meet changes in the market environment?

4. Taking into account one of the challenges facing the future market potential of Nike athletic footwear products, briefly outline appropriate responses following the five strategic planning steps outlined in Chapter 3.

5. How would you describe the positioning of Nike in the market? What advantages and disadvantages does the company/brand possess? How can the company capitalize on any advantages that you have identified?

6. Considering that Nike, Inc. has largely explored all four options of the Product-Market Growth Matrix, is there anything else that the company can do?

Sources: Patricia Sellers, "Big, Hairy, Audacious Goals Don't Work," *Fortune*, April 3, 2000, pp. 39–40, 44; Wayne Friedman, "Nike Picks up the Pace to Harness Web," *Advertising Age*, March 6, 2000, p. S4; Terry Lefton, "Nike, Others no Shoes in Atlanta," *Brandweek*, February 21, 2000; Louise Lee, "Take Our Swoosh, Please," *Business Week*, February 21, 2000, p. 128; Louise Lee, "Can Nike Still Do It?" *Business Week*, February 21, 2000, pp. 120–128; Eleftheria Parpis, "Weiden and Kennedy Nike Ads Bring the Net and TV Closer," *Adweek*, February 14, 2000, pp. 23–24; James Pilcher, "Extreme Sports Dominate Gear Market," *Associated Press Online*, February 11, 2000, www.ap.org; Leslie Kaufman, "Cooling Customer Demand for Athletic Shoes Shrinks Nike's Profit," *New York Times*, February 9, 2000, p. C1; Lee Gomes, "Nike Forecasts Disappointing Sales as Outlets for Sneakers Dwindle," *Wall Street Journal*, February 9, 2000, p. B10; Mark Hyman, "Fogdog is Eager to Fetch," *Business Week*, November 29, 1999, p. 173; Pila Martinez, "Nike Asks UA Protesters to Tour Overseas Shoe Factories," The Arizona Daily Star, November 7, 1999, p. B4; Constance Hays, "Nike's Enthusiastic New Campaign Draws Criticism From New York Marathon Officials," *New York Times*, November 1, 1999, p. C12; Steven Greenhouse, "Nike Identifies Plants Abroad Making Goods for Universities," *New York Times*, October 8, 1999, p. C1; Julie Schmit, "Nike's Image Problem After Global Outcry, Company Makes Strides to Improve," *USA Today*, October 4, 1999, p. 1B.

Case 1-2

McDONALD'S
You Have to Keep Experimenting

"I don't know what we'll be serving in the year 2000, but we'll be serving more of it than anybody." Ray Kroc, founder

When McDonald's opened its doors in 1955, the "fast food" industry was an uncomplicated business. The company, like most others, began with a simple "recipe" — basic hamburgers, fries, soft drinks, clean facilities, reasonable prices, and fast service – that was it! It is from this that the Golden Arches have grown into a symbol now recognized across the globe. It may appear that there isn't much more to it today. You know some burgers, chicken nuggets and french-fries — not exactly rocket science.

Actually, you would be wrong if you made such an assumption. Surviving in today's fast food industry and successfully managing operations around the globe is about a lot more than just serving hot burgers from attractive restaurants. In this league, it's as much about promotion, marketing, distribution, pricing, quality, consistency, and new product introduction as it is in any other retail business. It may not be rocket science, but considering the time, research, and resources involved in making these decisions it isn't that far from it!

McDonald's operated for many years in a relatively unchanging environment — people seemed to gobble up what the restaurant offered and the corporation continued to grow. Eventually, however, any company that continues to operate the same way will find themselves eventually out of synch with the marketplace either with their operations or their product line — perhaps both. As such, companies must monitor their surrounding environments and evolve.

By the mid-90s McDonald's was one such company that had found itself with a series of imminent problems. At a time in North America when increasingly more was being spent on food consumption outside of the home, McDonald's was actually experiencing a decline in sales and market share. By this time the brand had a stagnant product line, a marketing strategy that lacked focus, and franchisees that were growing increasingly unhappy with the organization. While these events were brewing domestically, the company was busy expanding its international operations, which now includes restaurants in almost 120 countries around the globe. This expansion process has continued to provide a host of challenges.

McDonald's may, however, be starting to address these challenges face-on and move in a new direction under the leadership of Jack Greenberg. He became CEO in 1998 and has begun to implement changes that *maybe* are beginning to yield positive results for the chain in North America.

Where's the Beef?

Despite the fact that McDonald's frequently seems to be adding new items to its menu, the company has not had a really successful new product in about fifteen years since it introduced Chicken McNuggets. There have been new products like the Arch Deluxe, McLean, pasta, pizza, fajitas, and the Big Extra to name a few of the more memorable, but they have failed to strike just the right chord with hungry consumers. In this same period however, Burger King has had half a dozen successful new products added to its menu. As well, consumer taste ranking for McDonald's had slipped, reaching 87th of 91 restaurants in the *Restaurants and Institutions* survey of 1998. Clearly Ronald McDonald was no longer the king of fast food.

Once the industry innovator, the company was now scrambling to copy Burger King. It found itself trying to introduce burgers to compete with the Whopper and even changing its food preparation process to become similar to what Burger King has always employed. Instead of batch processing whereby food is "processed" in quantity and kept warm in heated bins until ordered and served, McDonald's introduced "Made for You" which meant each order was now prepared only when an order was received. This encouraged customers to place customized orders, improved the freshness and taste of the product, and also helped to reduce waste.

Over the past decade the company has continued to try to develop menu items that appeal to adult tastes. Research shows that busy families today dine out more frequently, and a considerable portion of this business is going to more "restaurant" style outlets as opposed to fast food style locations. McDonald's has also recognized that parents will often purchase meals for their children (such as the Happy Meal) without actually purchasing food for themselves. The company has tinkered with healthier food products and altered fat levels in products without any great sales success. It is, however, continuing to test salads and vegetable burgers. Recently they have introduced the McSalad Shaker — salad in a convenient covered cup.

The new breakfast bagel sandwiches have had, thus far, favourable reviews. McDonald's holds the leadership position in the breakfast category and focused a special advertising campaign in early 2000 on strengthening its breakfast trade.

The company has, of late, also been acquiring new restaurant concepts and brand extensions. For the first time, the company has invested in other restaurant chains. It has bought Donatos, a small pizza chain, as well as Boston Market after it went into Chapter 11 bankruptcy proceedings. It has also acquired a stake in Chipotle Mexican Grill and Food.com. McDonald's stake in Food.com reveals a multibrand online strategy as the site offers visitors takeout or delivery options available in their surrounding area by specifying where they are located.

The ailing 850-outlet Boston Market chain will be studied to see which units should be converted to McDonald's, fledgling Chipotle Mexican Grill, and Donatos Pizza restaurant formats.

Distribution

For several years the company has very aggressively pursued international expansion. The company has spared little expense in this pursuit. They have adapted menus to almost every culture and opened outlets in countries where fast-food markets did not exist and where much of the population would seemingly not be able to afford such a "luxury."

The chain's domestic expansion plans included stepping up from two hundred new outlets in the U.S. in 1991 and 1992 to more than nineteen hundred new outlets in 1994 and 1995. U.S. franchise owners were not pleased to say the least. These owner/operators felt that the chain was starting to cannibalize sales from existing locations. When sales figures were analyzed showing that a trend of declining sales existed at these locations, a backlash by these franchisees occurred.

Increasing frustration caused these restaurant owners to form a consortium (Consortium Members, Inc.) in order to be able to influence the plans of McDonald's management. Clearly, the domestic market was saturated. Overall sales had increased, but this was at the expense of individual outlets. In 1998 only forty-nine new locations opened and about two hundred unprofitable outlets were closed.

It would appear that Greenberg is making an effort to listen to owner/operators. Such a management approach worked well for McDonald's in the past considering that many ideas for the chain's most successful products have come from this very source. This includes the Big Mac, Egg McMuffin, Hot Apple Pie, and most recently the McFlurry ice-cream dessert.

Greenberg has reorganized some of the infrastructure in order to facilitate the information and idea sharing process. The company has been split into five geographic divisions with each division's management having more decision-making power. This has thinned out management levels and bureaucracy, enabling corporate McDonald's to be more responsive and local divisions to be more autonomous.

Technology has long been a problem for the chain. This is now being addressed as technology is now being developed as a business driver. Thus far this has included a new computerized drive-through order system complete with customer order screens to improve speed and accuracy. Also, the testing of digitized menu systems that allow customers to touch what they want, feed in their money, and have their meals handed to them.

Burger King has also devoted a renewed focus on distribution and product testing. Chains such as McDonald's and Burger King use corporate-owned stores for testing new products and format changes. In the U.S., Burger King owns about 5.5 percent of its outlets while McDonald's has corporate ownership of approximately 15 percent of outlets. Burger King plans, over the next few years, to increase the number of these outlets in order to increase testing efforts for everything from architectural design to new products directed at ethnic groups.

McDonald's has also recognized the diversity of the North American population, receiving praise at a White House ceremony recognizing its many minority economic empowerment efforts. The chain currently has franchise organizations to support several minority franchisee groups, including African-American suppliers, Hispanics, Asians, and women. Such associations work to introduce more of the ethnic group into the supply chain, improve marketing efforts by tailoring them to ethnic groups, and expanding involvement in community service programs, such as feeding the hungry and reading to children. Others in the industry have tried similar programs but have not had the success that McDonald's has achieved.

Pricing

As with other products, pricing has at times become an issue with the chain's products. In what seemed a brilliant promotion with the right elements of nostalgia, value, and self-promotion, in 1997 McDonald's offered the Big Mac for 55 cents representing the year the chain was founded. It was confusing however as this price was available only with the purchase of fries and a drink. Otherwise it was regular price. Franchisees were concerned the promotion would be unprofitable and were reluctant to participate. Within several weeks of announcing the discount, sales were actually down 6 percent compared to the previous year. During this time, Burger King offered its Whopper for 99 cents — and widely advertised "no strings attached." McDonald's eventually dropped the promotion. McDonald's has continued to offer time restricted and tie-in specials. Burger King has continued to play off of these promotions from its "Have it Your Way" campaign to its "Break the Rules" ad campaign where it parodied frustrated Mickey D employees trying to memorize discount policies and the day of the week so they know what's on special.

Since the disappointing Big Mac promotion, McDonald's has increasingly come to rely on marketing research as well as franchisee input to make pricing decisions. And, as in other areas, it has allowed some autonomy at the regional level for outlets to offer discounts. This has allowed the chain as a whole to be more responsive to local competition when necessary. The chain continues, however, to offer national time-of-day and day-of-the-week specials on particular items. These specials are also offered simultaneously with other promotions.

Promotion

Today, people rushing to McDonald's restaurants might be just as likely to be looking for toys as they are for food. In fact, the size of a new series of toys often dictates how often a child "needs" to have a Happy Meal. The chain has an exclusive deal to offer toys that tie in with many of Disney's children's movies. As well, there have been a stream of Barbie, Hot Wheels, and Teenie Beanie Baby toys. The inclusion of Beanies in Happy Meal promotions has been found to increase sales significantly for that period. It's not hard to see why McDonald's remains a favourite with young children (and some adults!). The adult market, in general, still remains a challenge for the company and it continues to research menu items geared toward increasing sales to this group.

McDonald's remains the most recognized brand in the world, reported to be even better known than Coca-Cola. The American market receives a $600 million advertising budget, which has recently seen the amount allocated to local spending increased from 25 percent to 50 percent. All ads, however, bear the national slogan.

The national slogan, of course, changes from time to time. But it generally is something a little relationship-based — remembering the good times, the past, reflecting how McDonald's is a part of growing up. For a while in the mid-90s it was the nostalgic "My McDonalds" but this didn't do anything to stimulate sales and the chain moved advertising firms and slogans. Next it was "Did Somebody Say McDonald's?" In 2000 the chain tried, "We Love to See You Smile." Although the national slogan is used for all efforts, some believe that the McDonald's brand is being watered down by the use of regional campaigns.

Swallowing the Foreign Market

Although it would seem that the chain has appeared in some unlikely locations across the globe, international revenues account for about 50 percent of sales and about 60 percent of its total profits. McDonald's locations now number about 25,000 in almost 120 countries. International expansion has clearly been successful — it has been achieved through reapplying its original and simple recipe for success — quality, service, in a pleasant environment. It is a recipe that works, but like all dishes, many will tire of it eventually and the recipe will require a little spicing up from time to time.

There has been the start of some concerns in some foreign markets, however, as after several years of substantial growth there has been a slow down in sales. Such has happened in Brazil where the chain has responded by discounting price, but has continued to expand in that market. Brazil, in fact, has served as an excellent source of market research for the chain's international operations. Cultures vary and the markets into which the chain has expanded run the gamut of social, religious, economic, and ethnic varieties. The values of a society will greatly influence what its citizens eat and on what they will spend their disposable resources. This country serves to demonstrate such challenges that could not naturally be anticipated. For example, the custom of early afternoon siestas so common in Brazil plays havoc with lunchtime trade. As well, Brazilians traditionally eat breakfast only at home. The economy in Brazil is very precarious, leaving many citizens reluctant to spend their disposable resources on the American confabulation called "fast food."

Delivering the McDonald's experience in some of these far-flung countries can be an expensive endeavour and profit margins suffer as a result. In fact, only eight countries account for 80 percent of the chain's international earnings. McDonald's may have already reached the point of saturation in some of these countries and with prime locations becoming scarcer, the chain has begun to venture into economically underdeveloped countries.

What's Next?

The purchase of new restaurant brands is just one of a three-pronged growth strategy led by the chain's new brand-extension executive. The company wants to expand and develop several lines of McDonald's-brand consumer goods. Snacks and other packaged goods, as well as a line of McDonald's books and videos are currently under consideration. The initial thrust of this strategy will be overseas; German consumers can already purchase McDonald's-brand ketchup. Finally, the company has decided it needs to focus on improving burger sales. This last part of the strategic plan would seem to go without saying for a company that has risen to fame on the buns of a hamburger. Can the introduction of such a diversified strategy indicate that the McDonald's restaurant brand has gone as far as it can be taken with its 25,000 outlets around the globe?

Despite all of these events, the chain still accounts for as much as 80 percent of the fast food market in some countries and about 40 percent of the domestic market. Despite this, reported earnings for 1999 were below expected projections, causing stock price to fall. The beginning of 2000, however, saw small sales' increases domestically and in markets in France, Italy, Spain, and the Asia/Pacific region. As the world's largest restaurant company with a reported net income of US$450.9 million in the first quarter of 2000, it can be appreciated that Ray Kroc certainly couldn't have anticipated some of the menu items in some of its far-flung markets, but he certainly hit the mark when he predicted the chain would be serving more of it than anyone else.

Pertinent Web Sites

www.mcdonalds.com

www.food.com

Questions

1. Is McDonald's doing a good job of identifying the needs of various stakeholders? Who are the key stakeholders?

2. McDonald's has developed a business strategy containing "diversified" interests. Why would the company do this? Could this benefit the McDonald's restaurant brand?

3. Should the chain continue to devote so much attention to the international market? How should it proceed?

4. How should the chain adapt its marketing strategies for the international marketplace?

5. Is there anything particularly different about the Canadian market that would cause McDonald's to use a different marketing strategy in Canada than it does in the United States?

Sources: Jennifer Ordonez, "McDonald's Reports 12% Increase in Net on Sales Strength, Recovery Overseas," The *Wall Street Journal*, April 21, 2000, p. B8; Kate MacArthur, "Burger Giants Dig Up Dinos for Summer Movie Tie-ins," *Advertising Age*, April 17, 2000, pp. 3, 20; Jennifer Ordonez, "Will Big Mac Find New Sizzle in Shoes, Videos?" The *Wall Street Journal*, April 14, 2000, p. B1; Michael Arndt, "Did Somebody Say McBurrito?" *Business Week*, April 10, 2000, pp. 166–170; Alan Liddle, "McD's Stake in Food.com Reveals Multibrand Online Strategy," *Nation's Restaurant News*, March 27, 2000, pp. 39, 44; Amy Zuber, "Minority Franchisees Prosper With Help From McD Support Groups," *Nation's Restaurant News*, February 14, 2000, pp. 26, 30; Brad Gamble & Richard Sandor, "McDonald's Answer to the Morning Daze: A Creative way to Sell Breakfast to the Time-pressed," *Marketing Magazine*, January 31, 2000, p. 31; "Menu's New Magic," *Restaurant Business*, January 1, 2000, pp. 67–68; Jennifer Ordonez, "McDonald's Appoints Chief Executive of International as President," *The Wall Street Journal*, December 3, 1999, p. B10; Andrew Edgecliffe-Johnson, "McDonald's Buys Small Slice of US Pizza Market," *Financial Times*, May 7, 1999, p. 19; David Leonhardt, "Getting off Their McButts," *Business Week*, February 12, 1999, pp. 84, 88; Louise Kramer, "More Nimble McDonald's Is Getting Back on Track," *Advertising Age*, January 18, 1999, p. 6; Kevin Helliker & Richard Gibson, "The New Chief Is Ordering Up Changes at McDonald's," *The Wall Street Journal*, August 24, 1998, p. B1; Richard Gibson & Matt Moffett, "Why You Won't Find Any Egg McMuffins for Breakfast in Brazil," *The Wall Street Journal*, October 23, 1997, pp. A1, A12; Shelly Branch, "What's Eating McDonald's?" *Fortune*, October 13, 1997, pp. 122–125; Richard Gibson, "Burger Wars Sizzle as McDonald's Clones the Whopper," *The Wall Street Journal*, September 17, 1997, p. B1; Greg Burns, "Fast-Food Fight," *Business Week*, June 2, 1997, pp. 34–36; Richard Gibson, "Big Price Cut at McDonald's Seems a McFlop," *The Wall Street Journal*, May 9, 1997, pp. B1, B2.

Case 1-3

SPIN MASTER TOYS, INC.

In the industry they call it "magic," the ability to make kids say "Cool" or "Neat," or perhaps more importantly "I gotta have one!" And the Air Hog Sky Shark air pressure plane has it in spades, or more accurately in aces — high flying aces!

The story of Spin Master Toys Inc. could be a case study in how to bring a new product to market with all of the inherent challenges and glitches that happen along the way to market — including when the product refuses to work! — and initially that's just what happened! It is also a story of an almost religious belief in the power of public relations, and how it can turn a good idea into magic. It's what happens when innovation meets marketing savvy.

It's actually the story of a little purple and yellow foam plane that became one of the biggest hits of the 1998 holiday season, receiving stellar reviews and flying out of stores faster than new stock could be delivered. The first air-powered toy of its kind, it launched the small company into big markets and big distribution deals. The partners' style of marketing and promotion has opened many doors for the company and has cleared the runway for its introduction of follow-up products into desirable retail locations. It would appear that Spin Master Toys might be on to something, considering its string of successes in an industry where nine out of ten new products fail.

Grassroots Beginnings

It was fate that the three partners responsible for the success of Air Hogs would become business partners. Their families had moved to Toronto from South Africa and the boys first met at Camp Northland a couple of years after arriving in Canada. Eventually, each of the future partners ended up at the University of Western Ontario. Initially, Anton Rabie and Ronnen Harary began working together while still at school producing and marketing a university poster called Campus Faces in 1991. Just days after graduation they were joined in business by Ben Varadi. All in their early twenties and with $10,000 in capital, the young entrepreneurs set about developing their first product. It began in 1994 when they began manufacturing Earth Buddies — little grassy scalped guys based on the popular Chia Pet model. Essentially a stocking, a little sawdust, and some grass seed. They felt the environmental cachet of the product would be a nice fit with the image espoused by Roots Canada Ltd. and approached the company. They began test marketing at Roots stores, and soon mega-retailer K-Mart was placing large orders. In short, Earth Buddies was a hit, eventually selling over three million units — that is an awful lot of stockings and sawdust!

Also in 1994, the partners developed Devil Sticks, a three-rod juggling game that in 1995 became the #1 non-promoted toy in Canada. It was at this time that the company began to break into U.S. distribution and adopted the name Spin Master Toys, Inc. — a name that has proven to be appropriate in more ways than one.

The company has always focused on demonstrations, point-of-sale displays, unique public relations, and developing relationships. It seemed an appropriate way to gain attention in a marketplace dominated by giant manufacturers. In the early days when an advertising budget was nothing more than a pipe dream it was all the partners had to work with. The Earth Buddy was promoted in-store by placing a bald buddy next to another with a full head of luxurious green "hair" which seemed to communicate all that needed to be said about the product. For the Devil Sticks, college students were hired in different regions of the country to travel around demonstrating the game.

Four years later the partners found themselves on greener pastures. Well, actually it was a golf course in Arizona and Spin Master was filming a commercial for its latest product — the Air Hog. This would be the first toy airplane to run on compressed air rather than gas or a rubber band. This would be a breakthrough in the industry and the partners had their fingers crossed that it would actually work as they anticipated. The product was in pre-production and, until the planes were mass-produced, the partners had only theories to cling to about what the Sky Shark would actually do once in the hands of children (or whomever).

In fact, that day the plane they were using wouldn't work very well and repeatedly bailed after only a couple of yards. They managed to get the commercial shot without actually faking the performance of the product — a strict no-no in toy commercials! But the company also didn't change its expectations of the product — they would make sure it did perform as originally planned before it went to market. They felt it was too late to turn back as they had invested two and a half years and half a million dollars to develop the concept. Eventually, the Air Hog would take to the skies successfully.

The three partners took a risk, and the gamble paid off. The air pressure toy plane flew off shelves quicker than they could be restocked during the 1998 holiday season. At Cdn$49.99 the pre-assembled plane came with the needed pump, an instructional video and a toll-free number to speak to Captain Air Hog for advice and flying tips. Testing showed that only 40 percent of children could assemble and get the plane to perform as desired, compared to 100 percent success for those who saw the video. The toll-free number averaged about eighty calls a day from kids eager for flying tips and to tell stories about their successful flights to the captain. The partners often spend time answering these calls and listening to what these children had to say about the product. Such input has even led to the modification and reinforced wing structure of the current Air Hog models.

Initially, small and independent retailers formed most of the distribution network for Spin Master Toys, Inc. but increasing media attention about the product began to attract the attention of major specialty toy stores across North America and even further. Aside from developing close relationships with distribution network members, the company has also successfully focused on developing ties with the media. One promotion included sending out "press kits" — these were shaped like suitcases and contained the Air Hog equipment, Air Hog plane ticket, single-serving size bag of peanuts and a motion-sickness bag. The promotion was a success with many members of the press in Canada and the United States writing favourably about the product.

"Air" Apparent

How could such a buzz in the toy market come from a product as simple as a toy airplane? Although not a new toy concept and not based upon any new type of technology, this relatively low-tech entry into the market created a new product class in this category. The Air Hog is the first ever air-powered model airplane. Just pump it up and the Air Hog's precision designed (and patented) engine will fly over ninety metres — the length of a football field — at altitudes of up to thirty metres. But never mind the company's hype, it does actually work, and it actually performs as advertised. The Air Hog airplane has filled the wide gap between cardboard planes that sell for a couple of bucks and may work a couple of times and the motorized model planes that sell for a couple of hundred dollars.

The original Air Hogs sold for $49.99 and, powered by only air pressure, the one-horsepower motor sends the plane dipping and gliding with a realistic engine sound even though no batteries are used.

How Could They Have Been So Wrong?

Major toy manufacturers such as Mattel and Hasbro had rejected the toy's design before Spin Master Toys took it on and developed the product from beginning to end. It was a bonafide hit for the 1998 holiday season. *Time* magazine put it with the Furby, Teletubbies, and Lego Mindstorms as the hottest toys for the year. *Popular Science* put it on its "Best of What's New" cover, trumpeting it as one of the year's top 100 achievements in science and technology. It even made it onto the *Today* show in a pre-Christmas "Gadget Guru" segment as well as getting airplay on *Live! With Regis and Kathie Lee*. Oh yes, it also tripled Spin Master's revenue in one year to $36 million. At a time when interactive toys are becoming increasingly popular with children and parents, the Air Hog seemed to have struck a popular balance between skill and entertainment value.

It is curious to think how two of the biggest players in the industry would not touch the concept, and a third company optioned the idea but later decided to pass on it leaving the product available for the three eager partners. What did the partners see that seasoned experts failed to? Or perhaps the question should be — what do these partners have that these larger companies lack?

By early 1999, the partners had turned an entrepreneurial partnership into a global company with an entire line of air-pressure toys: several planes (Avenger, Renegade), cars (Road Rippers), and a top-secret weapon, the Hydro Vector Rocket, which had not yet been publicly announced and was not yet ready for production. Although it wasn't fully tested, major U.S. retailers such as Toys 'R' Us were anxious to get a peek at whatever the next Spin Master product would be. In fact, when the water rocket did reach stores, it sold fifty thousands units in its first month.

The company now felt it was ready to take on big time retailers throughout North America although they were already having problems maintaining enough supply to existing customers. Battling growing demand and growing pains, major retailers such as Toys 'R' Us have expressed interest in forging partnerships but can the fledgling company keep up in the big time? Other U.S. retailers that have begun to carry the company's products include specialty retailers KB Kids, Mastermind, Noodle Kidoodle, and Zany Brainy.

Still Flying High

The company has just developed a new line of finger bikes similar in concept to fingerboards. They have all the moving parts and are based on real bikes currently in production. Each features moving pedals, working brakes, and markings to match the full-sized bike models. Like fingerboards, kids can perform extreme stunts riding the bike with their fingers. There are twenty-eight Flick Trix bikes in the collection, each modeled after the coolest bikes in the business from Diamond Back to Mongoose to Redline. Each model sells for just under $10.

The company's Web site profiles all the bikes and accessories, provides tips, action downloads, extreme videos, and BMX links. Early indications are that these will also be successful. The company has also developed E-chargers — the smallest motorized flying planes ever. They run on four AA batteries and charge in only ten seconds. The Web site is set up to sell all these products directly to consumers.

Copyright © 2000. This case was prepared by Peter A. Dunne as a basis for class discussion and is not intended to reflect either an effective or an ineffective handling of problems facing management.

Pertinent Web Site

www.spinmaster.com

Questions

1. What types of marketing efforts were successfully employed by Spin Master Toys? Why is the use of such tools particularly important/beneficial to a company of this size and experience in the marketplace?

2. What types of environmental factors have the potential to affect the continued success of this toy company?

3. Why have these three young entrepreneurs been successful with each of the products they have decided to develop, considering the high failure rate in this industry?

4. The partners have developed a pattern of utilizing promotion and publicity when introducing their products to the marketplace. What recommendations would you make for promoting their latest additions to the product line?

Sources: Spin Master Toys, Inc. home page, July 20, 2000, wwwspinmaster.com; CBC *Venture*, "High Flyers," Episode #739, February 15, 2000, or see www.cbc.ca/business/programs/venture; David North, Cool Rules, *Canadian Business*, December 31, 1999, p. 132; Patricia Chisholm, In Search of the Hot Toy, *Maclean's*, December 14, 1999, p. 62; "In Hot Pursuit of Cool: The Toronto-Based Creators of Popular Air Hogs are Gambling that Tiny Bicycles Will Fly, too, this Christmas," *Toronto Star*, December 6, 1999, pp. E1, E5; Carolyn Blackman, *Canadian Jewish News*, December 2, 1999, p. 48; Kara Kuryllowicz, "Air Hogs," The Sequel?, *Profit: The Magazine for Canadian Entrepreneurs*, September, 1999, p. 10; Shawna Cohen, "Spin Master Lifts Off With Air Hog," *Marketing Magazine*, December 14, 1998, p. 8; Shawna Steinberg & Joe Chidley, "Fun For The Money," *Canadian Business*, December 11, 1998, pp. 45–52;

Target Markets

An analysis of the people and organizations who buy, why they buy, and how they buy

In Part Two, we discuss the selection of an organization's intended customers — its target market. Chapter 4 examines the concept of market segmentation as it relates to the selection of target markets, and we discuss several approaches to the segmentation of markets. In Chapter 5, we explore the strategic concept of positioning as a means to ensure that a company's offerings appeal to its target segments. We also discuss the important topic of forecasting. Chapter 6 is devoted to consumer buying behaviour and the buying process involved in the purchase of products and services. In Chapter 7, we examine in detail the business-to-business market, thereby reminding ourselves that there is a massive market that many end consumers rarely see — the one that involves businesses marketing to businesses and other organizations. Finally, Chapter 8 covers marketing research and marketing information systems, the means whereby marketers learn about their markets and the target consumers and customers who comprise them.

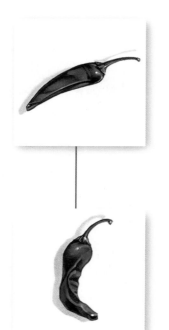

Chapter Four

Foundations for Market Segmentation

After studying this chapter, you should have an understanding of:

◆ The fundamental principles behind target market identification and selection.

◆ The concept of market segmentation — its meaning, benefits, limitations, and situations where it finds greatest use.

◆ The difference between ultimate consumer markets and business markets.

◆ The principal bases for segmenting consumer markets.

◆ Segmentation of the market through examination of the distribution and composition of the population of Canada.

◆ Segmentation of the market through examination of consumer groups on the basis of income distribution and spending patterns.

Stretching Limits with Stretch Denim

One of the most competitive markets targeting today's youth is the jeans industry. With almost 540 million pairs produced annually in North America, getting denim to the checkout counters is not always an easy task. Success means getting many of those denims on the hips of teenagers and young adults through the use of hip advertising that develops a "personality" for the brand, creating image appeal for certain market segments.

One of the more daring marketing efforts has come from Parasuco Jeans of Montreal (www.parasuco.com). Offering its products in Canada, the United States, Italy and Japan. The company annually sells about 2 million pairs of jeans and another half million denim jackets, tops, and skirts. Parasuco has added two new apparel lines to its already profitable jeans line – the Parasuco Collection and Rebel-i. The Collection is for the young career woman who wants to look sexy and feminine, yet serious. Rebel-i is a line of European influenced streetwear.

Founded in 1975, the company moved into the U.S. market in 1988 where their stretch jeans and un-American-sounding name attracted a large Latino following. Approximately 70 percent of the company's sales are now in the U.S. with approximately 75 percent of these to black and Hispanic consumers. According to Salvatore Parasuco, the company's president, the company's original decision was to target the multicultural market by featuring visible minorities in their print ads instead of the "usual blond bombshells." However, with the addition of the two new clothing lines and changing consumer attitudes, their advertising strategy has shifted to keep abreast of the times. In keeping with the new cross-over market where increasing numbers of Caucasians, Hispanic and Black consumers listen to the same music, wear the same styles and are loyal to the same brands, Parasuco's advertising approach was altered to reflect this new appeal. Whereas the models used in print advertising are still culturally diverse the themes are more of intergration and less stress is placed on the differences.

The ads, in the past, have often featured models in suggestive positions and have elicited angry calls from people who think they border on pornography. "The ads are sexy, meaning cool or hip," explains Parasuco. "We're edgier than the competition and it shows in our advertising. People expect to find something different from Parasuco and we are prepared to pay for it." This edge has not been lost with the new campaign approach, although it has been refined and is more subtle than previous campaigns. According to the top U.S. vendor, the logo on the product has become a status symbol in black and Hispanic markets and is now crossing over into the other market demographics, as well. In fact, many celebrities are now opting to wear Parasuco jeans because of their fit, cut and overall style.[1]

Did denim desire **democracy?**

To continue growth, Parasuco has begun opening its own retail outlets. In Montreal, changing rooms have clear glass doors that cloud over upon the flick of a switch, hiding the occupant. Television ads are urban and contemporary as if they were filmed in any North American city. These advertisements are run on channels such as MuchMusic, Musique Plus, MTV, and Black Entertainment TV in order to increase the likelihood of being seen by consumer groups that comprise the bulk of Parasuco's customer base. This year the consumer base was expanded to include Italy and Japan where Parasuco jeans are fast becoming a very hot commodity. In Milan the jeans are being sold alongside Gucci and Versace for quadruple the price of which they are sold in North America. In Japan, Parasuco has fit in perfectly with the Japanese fixation on North American fashions and styles.

What segment of the market is the company trying to target? And why bother? Aren't jeans, well, just jeans? Apparently not according to the buying trend of this brand. Clearly jeans companies are interested in younger segments of the market as they wear these products most often — but it is a product that is consumed across a wide range of ages or over 500 million pairs wouldn't be produced each year in North America. So who is buying these jeans? Who is wearing these jeans? Why? What factors are taken into consideration when making such purchases? Why does a consumer choose one brand of jeans over another?

Once we deal with such questions, it should be obvious who the primary target market(s) are for a marketer's products. This example serves to introduce a number of very important topics in marketing: the selection of a target market segment; the fact that the target segment should be characterized on the basis of a number of factors, only some of which may be demographic; and the need to position a product so that it appeals to the target segment.

$\mathscr{S}$electing A Target Market

market
People or organizations with wants to satisfy, money to spend, and the willingness to spend it.

target market
A group of customers (people or organizations) at whom a seller aims its marketing effort.

In Chapter 1 we defined a **market** as people or organizations with (1) wants (needs) to satisfy, (2) money to spend, and (3) the willingness to spend it. A **target market** is a group of customers (people or firms) at whom the seller specifically aims its marketing efforts. The careful selection and accurate definition and identification of target markets are essential for the development of an effective marketing program. One of the fundamental principles underlying the practice of market segmentation is that most companies and brands can no longer aspire to be "all things to all people." Doing this ensures that the brand will actually mean very little to those looking for specific, and different, characteristics.

This is especially so with the changes taking place in the competitive environment. Companies in most industries today are faced with new competition from many sources. Not only is the global nature of marketing creating new competitors from other countries, but customers are now able to buy products from companies with which they would never have dealt a few years ago. With access to the Internet, customers in Canada can access products from companies all over the world. The e-commerce environment fragments a market by exposing customers to companies they have never heard of before. With this fragmentation of the marketplace and the increased level of competition from local, domestic, and international competitors, most marketers practise a strategy of carving out of the mass market a manageable target group of consumers upon which they will concentrate.

Firms select a target group (or groups) that, after conducting customer research, they believe will purchase their product(s) or service(s). Often, products are specifically designed for a particular group. Lever Pond's targets 18 to 34 year-old Canadians with its marketing for Degree anti-perspirant,[2] while Banff Ice Vodka hopes primarily to reach male Canadians from the legal drinking age to 30 years of age with an active lifestyle.[3] G.I. Energy Drinks of Montreal focuses on its core 16 to 24 year-old target group in large Canadian cities by maintaining a presence on the rave scene with its Guru beverage.[4]

Panasonic is aiming at 15 to 35-year-olds with its Shockwave and Rebel portable audio products.[5] While Sony goes for the 18 to 24-year-olds with the ESP2 discman campaign.[6]

Guidelines in Market Selection

Sony targets young adults with a sports theme.

Four general guidelines govern the selection of target markets. The first is that target markets should be compatible with the organization's goals and image. A firm marketing high-priced personal computers should not sell through discount chain stores in an effort to reach a mass market.

A second guideline — consistent with our definition of strategic planning — is to match the market opportunity with the company's resources. In many ways this is what Parasuco Jeans has done to achieve sales growth. The company's products clearly appeal to particular groups of youths. Instead of attempting to modify products and market to a wider group within Canada, the company maintained their distinctive styling (and advertising image) that was their trademark and spread into large metropolitan U.S. markets where large numbers of these groups of customers reside. This has also led to expansion into sophisticated fashion markets of Europe and the Far East.

Over the long run, a business must generate a profit if it is to survive. This translates into what is perhaps an obvious market selection guideline. That is, an organization should consciously seek markets that will generate sufficient sales volume at a low enough cost to result in a profit. Surprisingly, companies often have overlooked the profit factor in their quest for high-volume markets. The goal was sales volume alone, not *profitable* sales volume.

Finally, a company ordinarily should seek a market wherein the number of competitors and their size are such that the new entrant is able to compete effectively. An organization should not enter a market that is already saturated with competition unless it has some overriding competitive advantage that will enable it to take customers from existing firms.

Market Opportunity Analysis

Theoretically a market opportunity exists at any time and at any place where there is a person or an organization with an unfilled need or want. Such opportunities exist, for example, when there are significant changes in a population's age demographics as discussed throughout this text. As the population ages, there will be more age-relevant products and services needed, as well as increased opportunities for entrepreneurial firms to create and develop new products and services for an older customer group.

Realistically, of course, a company's market opportunity does have restrictions. Thus, selecting a target market requires an appraisal of market opportunities available to the organization. A market opportunity analysis begins with a study of the environmental forces (as discussed in Chapter 2) that affect a firm's marketing program. Then the organization must analyze the three components of a market — people or organizations, their buying power, and their willingness to spend. Analysis of the "people" component involves a study of the geographic distribution and demographic composition of the population. The second component is analyzed through the distribution of consumer income and consumer expenditure patterns. Finally, to determine consumers' "willingness to spend," management must study consumer-buying behaviour. Population and buying power are discussed more fully later in this chapter. Buying behaviour is covered in Chapter 6.

Target-Market Strategy: Aggregation or Segmentation

In defining the market or markets it will sell to, an organization has its choice of two approaches. In one, the total market is viewed as a single unit — as one mass, aggregate market. This approach leads to the strategy of market aggregation. In the other approach, the total market is seen as many smaller, more homogeneous segments. This approach leads to the strategy of market segmentation, in which one or more segments are selected as the top target market(s). Deciding which **target-market strategy** to adopt is a key in selecting target markets. We shall discuss market aggregation and segmentation in more detail in Chapter 5.

Measuring Selected Markets

When selecting target markets, a company should make quantitative estimates of the potential sales volume of the market for its product or service. This process requires estimating, first, the total industry potential for the company's product in the target market or among the target segment and, second, the share of this total market that can be achieved. It is essential that management also prepare a realistic sales forecast, usually for a one-year period. The existence of a group large enough to target is not a guarantee of equivalent sales. Consumers must become aware of your product or service, be able to obtain it, and they must choose it over your competitors' offerings and other alternative purchases.

A sales forecast is an important foundation for budgeting and short-term operational planning in all departments — marketing, production, and finance. Sales forecasting will be discussed in more detail in Chapter 5, after we build a better knowledge of market segmentation.

⟡ Nature of Market Segmentation

The total market for most types of products is too varied — too heterogeneous — to be considered a single, uniform entity. To speak of the market for vitamin pills or electric razors or education is to ignore the fact that the total market for each product or service consists of sub-markets that differ significantly from one another. This lack of uniformity may be traced to differences in buying habits, in ways in which the product or service is used, in motives for buying, or in other factors. Market segmentation takes these differences into account.

Not all consumers want to wear the same type of clothing, use the same shampoo, or participate in the same recreational activities. Nor do all business firms want to buy the same kind of computers or delivery trucks. At the same time, a marketer usually cannot afford to tailor-make a different product or service for every single customer (although there are companies today that are doing just that by delivering custom-made products on order to individual customers). Consequently, market segmentation is the strategy that most marketers adopt as a compromise between the extremes of one product or service for all and a different one for each customer. A major element in a company's success is its ability to select the most effective location on this segmentation spectrum between the two extremes. In other words, this means to find the blend of product customization and mass appeal that will produce the greatest sales potential for the firm.

What Is Market Segmentation?

Market segmentation is the process of dividing the total heterogeneous market for a product or service into several segments, each of which tends to be homogeneous in all significant aspects. Management selects one or more of these market segments as the organization's target market. A separate marketing program and approach is developed for each segment or group of segments in this target market.

Benefits of Market Segmentation

Market segmentation is a customer-oriented philosophy and thus is consistent with the marketing concept. We first identify the needs of customers within a sub-market (segment) and then develop an approach to marketing that will satisfy those needs.

By tailoring marketing programs to individual market segments, management can do a better marketing job and make more efficient use of marketing resources. A small firm with limited resources might compete very effectively in one or two market segments, whereas the same firm would be buried if it aimed for the total market. By employing the strategy of market segmentation, a company can design products and services that really match market demands. Advertising media can be used more effectively because promotional messages — and the media chosen to present them — can be aimed specifically toward each segment of the market. Some of the most successful marketers are small or medium-sized firms that have decided to concentrate on a small number of market segments and to gain a strong market position and disproportionate market share in these segments. This relates to the principle of niche marketing, which will be discussed in greater detail in Chapter 5.

Even very large companies with the resources to engage in mass marketing supported by expensive national advertising campaigns are now abandoning mass marketing strategies. Instead, these companies have accepted market segmentation as a more effective strategy to reach the fractured fragments that once constituted a mass, homogeneous market. Procter & Gamble's (www.pg.com) marketing program nicely illustrates these changing conditions. Once the epitome of a mass marketer with innovative but utilitarian products, P&G advertised heavily on network television. But today it's a different ball game. Fewer people are at home during the day to watch television. Those who spend time in front of the television may be watching programs, viewing videos or a film or program that was recorded a day or two earlier, or playing video games. Video game manufacturers have found advantage in this by selling product placement within the actual video games. Brands such as Coca-Cola and Tommy Hilfiger can be seen on background billboards within the context of the game much like they can be seen at sponsored sporting events or highway billboards.

Even if potential consumers are watching TV, they may be tuned to any one of up to one hundred channels. As such, any given channel has a smaller potential audience and with such a variety of programming to choose from, many viewers spend much of their time "surfing" from channel to channel during commercial periods, using their remote-control devices.

Faced with this fragmentation of the television audience, Procter & Gamble has developed a variety of marketing campaigns, each designed to appeal to a different target market segment. The company now offers six varieties of its market-leading Tide detergent, each targeted to consumers with different needs and reasons for buying laundry detergent. Within its line of hand and bath soaps, P&G offers Ivory, Zest, Coast, Safeguard,

Camay, and Oil of Olay. Many of these brands come in different sizes for sink and tub, various colours to match bathroom decor, and different forms — bar soaps, body wash, and liquid soap in pump dispensers. Procter & Gamble, by offering such a wide range of options to the consumer, is competing in a soap market that is segmented by skin type (oily versus dry; normal versus sensitive), fragrance, aesthetics, the desire for convenience, economy, and the primary benefit sought (clean hands or a pleasant, deodorized fragrance). It is clear that all consumers buy soap for cleansing, but they also expect other benefits from the soap they use. Hence, many segments exist.

Advances in technology have made market segmentation easier for companies in many industries as they have created efficiencies by permitting the targeting of specific segments. For example, many companies regularly collect data on their customers and their purchasing patterns. Data can be collected that offer specific information on individuals or groups of individuals. Telephone companies, for example, can identify the types of services used by individuals or groups of people, and can assess that information in relation to demographics or other individual characteristics. Firms that utilize the Internet can easily gather consumer information from visitors, track customer purchasing, and develop electronic mailing lists. This provides a much more targeted list than is possible in most traditional direct mail campaigns.

When companies maintain data bases on purchasing behaviour, it is possible to target products and brands to customers who have certain characteristics, buying patterns and needs. Such targeting of products and services to specific segments or even to specific customers through the use of databases makes marketing much more cost-effective than was ever possible in the past.

Marketing at Work 4-1

Unravelling the Web

Surfers, Bargainers, and Sportsters may sound like groups of people on vacation in California, but they are actually the names given to three of the six segments of active Internet users identified by McKinsey and Media Metrix, the leader in Internet and digital media audience measurement.

The novelty of the Internet has worn thin for many companies. Their feelings have turned from excitement surrounding the launch to concern about the bottom line, and they are now looking to recoup their significant investment in this new channel. To do this, marketers must match their online strategies to the needs of their target customers, or risk attracting unprofitable visitors to their Web sites and alienating the profitable ones.

To learn more about those online McKinsey and Media Metrix analyzed the actual online behaviour of a sample of the most active online users among the Media Metrix U.S. panel of fifty thousand users. Their findings revealed six segments of online users: Simplifiers, Surfers, Bargainers, Connectors, Routiners, and Sportsters.

For companies looking to sell products online, Simplifiers are the most attractive customers, but may also be the most challenging to serve. Users in this segment access the Internet to simplify their lives, consequently they don't spend much time online and demand superior end-to-end convenience. For this group the site must be simple — pop-up windows and too many chat rooms may drive them away as the site will appear too complicated. Ease of access and use is critical as users need to be convinced that doing their business online is easier or faster than in the physical world. Meeting the needs of this segment is not an easy task, but companies that do it well will be rewarded as Simplifiers account for half of all online transactions.

Surfers are only 8 percent of active Internet users, but spend far more time online than any other segment. To maintain interest and encourage repeat visits, companies need to offer cutting-edge design, constant updates, a strong online brand, and an assortment of products and services that users in this segment would be interested in purchasing. If the first few pages of the site are successful in getting Surfers to stay, marketers must then maximize advertising opportunities which encourage transactions. This group requires a big effort but has the potential to yield big rewards.

It should come as no surprise that Bargainers use the Internet to search for deals. They spend a little less time online than the average user and account for 52 percent of all visits to eBay. Other online favourites include uBid.com, price-line.com, and Quote.com. In order for a site to gain repeat visits from Bargainers it must appeal to them on rational and emotional levels — it must satisfy their need for competitive pricing while providing the excitement inherent in the quest for a good deal as well as a sense of community.

Connectors are relative novices on the Internet and thus have not formed distinct Internet habits. This group is still looking for reasons to use the Internet and is unclear about what is available online and what has value. Currently they use the Internet primarily to connect with other people through chat rooms or by e-mail. Marketers must focus on shaping Connectors' Internet habits so that they become members of a more attractive segment such as Simplifiers. Because of their inexperience online, Connectors are likely to be guided to relevant sites by strong offline brands they know

and trust. Regardless of the strength of the brand offline, however, once online the site must be as accessible as possible for first-time users, and should clearly communicate its purpose and value to the user.

Routiners and Sportsters are similar in that both groups use the Internet as a source of information. Routiners typically visit news and financial sites and expect superior and exclusive content delivered in a timely and insightful manner. Conversely, Sportsters are more interested in sports and entertainment sites. They expect the sites they visit to be fresh, colourful, and interactive. Marketers have historically liked sites visited by these segments because of the high traffic volumes, but are now challenged to make these users' visits generate revenue.

Given that Internet profitability is dependent on repeat customer purchases and higher transaction sizes, targeting one of these segments is likely to prove more successful than trying to appeal to everyone. Over time, advances in technology will provide the ability to personalize content by user which will enable marketers to show different pages and products to different user segments.

Segment	Hours active/ month	Unique domains accessed/ month	Pages accessed/ month	Percent buying
Simplifiers	7.1	62	1,021	87
Surfers	30.2	224	4,852	71
Bargainers	8.3	43	1,295	64
Connectors	5.7	54	791	42
Routiners	8.2	32	624	50
Sportsters	7.1	47	1,023	51
Average	9.8	74	1,398	61

Source: "All Visitors Are Not Created Equal," *McKinsey Marketing Practice*, 2000.

Limitations of Market Segmentation

Although market segmentation can provide a lot of marketing benefits to an organization, this strategy also has some drawbacks with respect to costs and market coverage. In the first place, market segmentation can be an expensive proposition in both the production and marketing of products and services. In production, it obviously is less expensive to produce mass quantities of one model and one colour than to produce a variety of models, colours, and sizes. Similarly, offering a variety of services costs more than providing only one.

Segmentation increases marketing expenses in several ways. Total inventory costs go up because adequate inventories of each style, colour, and the like must be maintained.

Advertising costs go up because different ads may be required for each market segment. Or some segments may be too small for the seller to make effective use of television or another advertising medium. Administrative expenses go up when management must plan and implement several different programs.

But this is a narrow view of the "costs" of segmentation. In fact, while it may appear that it costs more to engage in a segmentation strategy, the more appropriate view is that these additional "costs" actually represent an investment in a much more efficient and effective approach to marketing. Not to engage in a segmentation approach results in much lost effort in that many people are reached through advertising and other marketing efforts who are not at all interested in the product or service. A segmentation strategy increases the likelihood that the marketing effort reaches those who are most likely to be interested in buying.

Conditions for Effective Segmentation

Ideally, management's goal should be to segment markets in such a way that each segment responds in a homogeneous way to a given marketing program. Three **conditions for effective segmentation** will help management move toward this goal.

◆ The basis for segmenting — that is, the characteristics used to categorize customers — must be measurable, and the data must be accessible. The "desire for ecologically compatible products" may be a characteristic that is useful in segmenting the market for a given product, but data on this characteristic may not be readily accessible or easily quantified. Vancouver-based *NUVO* magazine recently decided being ridiculously wealthy was a good enough criterion by itself to be a target segment for their new magazine. *NUVO* was created in 1998 to fill a neglected niche in the Canadian market. Its targeted readers are those with private and public interest in food, wine, travel, recreation, the arts, fashion, entrepreneurship, and the lives of individuals of achievement — all of which make up what the magazine calls "reflections of the good life." Thus it provides a cost-efficient vehicle for advertisers to reach affluent Canadians with discretionary income.[7]

◆ The market segment itself should be accessible through existing marketing institutions — distribution channels, advertising media, company sales force — with a minimum of cost and waste. To aid marketers in this regard some national magazines, such as Maclean's (www.macleans.ca) and Chatelaine (www.chatelaine.com), publish separate geographical editions. This allows an advertiser to run an ad aimed at, say, a Western segment of the market, without having to pay for exposure in other, non-target areas. International marketers such as Coca-Cola often use regional campaigns to supplement global campaigns and to shore up weaknesses in local markets. For Winter 2000, Coke aired distinctly Canadian TV spots featuring teenage boys playing hockey on a frozen pond. As if that weren't Canadiana at its finest — before they begin to play a young girl belts out the national anthem as the two teams stand at attention on the ice. Through such advertisements Coke is attempting to be more responsive to consumers at a local level.[8]

◆ Each segment should be large enough to be profitable. In concept, management could treat each single customer as a separate segment. (This situation may be normal in business markets, as when Canadair (www.canadair.ca) markets passenger

Some marketers target a very high-end segment. NUVO, with a circulation of 35,000, targets achievers. Advertising and editorial design are co-ordinated.

airplanes to commercial airlines or when the Royal Bank of Canada makes a loan to a company planning to export to Europe.) But in segmenting a consumer market, a firm must not develop too broad an array of styles, colours, sizes, and prices. Usually the diseconomies of scale in production and inventory will put reasonable limits on this type of over-segmentation. In 1999, Levi-Strauss & Co. (Canada) cancelled its Personal Pairs program that allowed women to order custom-made jeans for an extra ten dollars. The core market for jeans, women aged 14 to 19, wanted increased personalization that was not feasible to offer with features such as zippers and button-fly closures.[9]

From a customer-oriented perspective, the ideal method for segmenting a market is on the basis of customers' desired benefits. Certainly, using benefits to segment a market is consistent with the idea that a company should be marketing benefits and not simply the physical characteristics of a product. After all, a carpenter wants a smooth surface (benefit), not sandpaper (the product). However, in many cases the benefits desired by customers do not meet the first condition described above. That is, they are not easily measured, because customers are unwilling or unable to reveal them. For example, what benefits do people derive from clothing that has the designer's label on the outside? Conversely, why do others refuse to wear such clothing?

Even when benefits are identified, possibly in focus-group studies, it is difficult to determine how widely they exist in the market. As a result, a variety of indirect indicators of benefits are often used to describe segments. These indicators, such as age, are not the reason customers buy, but they are easily measured characteristics that people seeking the same benefit frequently have in common. For example, middle-aged people are more likely to read *Canadian Business* than are teenagers, not because they are middle aged but because the content of the magazine is more directly relevant to their lives. Marketers of *Canadian Business* find it easier to measure age than relevance, so age becomes a segmentation variable for them. Several of these commonly used, indirect bases for segmentation are discussed next.

Bases for Market Segmentation — Ultimate Consumers and Business Users

A company can segment its market in many different ways, and the bases for segmentation vary from one product category to another. At the top of the list, however, is the division of the entire potential market into two broad categories: ultimate consumers and business users.

ultimate consumers
People who buy products for their personal, nonbusiness use.

The sole criterion for placement in one of these categories is the customer's reason for buying. **Ultimate consumers** buy goods or services for their own personal or household use. They are satisfying strictly non-business wants, and they constitute the "consumer market."

business user
An organization that buys goods or services to resell, use in its own business, or make other products.

Business users are business, industrial, or institutional organizations that buy goods or services to use in their own businesses or to make other products. A manufacturer that buys chemicals with which to make fertilizer is a business user of these chemicals. Farmers who buy the fertilizer to use in commercial farming are business users of the fertilizer. (If homeowners buy fertilizer to use on their yards, they are ultimate consumers because they buy it for personal, non-business use.) Supermarkets, museums, and paper manufacturers that buy the service of a chartered accountant are business users of this service. Business users constitute the "business market," which is discussed in greater detail in Chapter 7.

The segmentation of all markets into two groups — consumer and business — is extremely significant from a marketing point of view because the two markets buy differently. Consequently the composition of a seller's marketing mix — products and services, distribution, pricing, and promotion — will depend on whether it is directed toward the consumer market or the business market.

Bases for Consumer Market Segmentation

Dividing the total market into consumer and business segments is a worthwhile start toward useful segmentation, but it still leaves too broad and heterogeneous a grouping for most products. We need to identify some of the bases commonly used to segment these two markets further. As shown in Table 4-1, the following characteristics may provide **bases for segmenting the consumer market**:

◆ Geographic.

◆ Demographic.

◆ Psychographic.

◆ Behaviour toward product or service (product/service-related bases).

Marketing managers should be particularly aware of trends taking place in the demographic, psychographic, and behavioural characteristics of the markets in which they are operating. For example, if the population of Victoria is increasing because of a large number of people moving there to retire, this has obvious implications for businesses that operate in and around Victoria. Similarly, a company should be interested in knowing if the customers it has been serving are gradually reducing their usage of its product and using more of an indirectly competing product. This is precisely what has been happening in the beer market in Canada in recent years, as per capita consumption of the product has been declining gradually and as consumers have switched to consuming more wine and nonalcoholic drinks. Most industry representatives will agree that this change in consumption patterns is largely a result of the fact that the percentage of the Canadian population in the heavier beer-drinking age group has been declining in recent years as the "baby-boom" generation moved into their thirties and fourties and began drinking a lot more wine and less beer. This has led to price wars among brewers and a proliferation of large-scale promotional efforts ranging from free T-shirts to private concerts by popular performers.

The key word that marketers should keep in mind when examining such trends or changes in consumption and other segmentation variables is *implications*. The marketer should always look into the implications of such change and should be seeking information to guide an appropriate response to the market. Vancouver-based Clearly Canadian (www.clearly.ca) experienced a 15 percent drop in sales of its sparkling water in 1999 in a category that grew by 12 to 14 percent that same year. What does this mean

TABLE 4–1 Segmentation Bases for Consumer Markets

Segmentation Basis	Examples of Typical Market Segments
Geographic	
Region	Atlantic provinces; Quebec; Ontario; Prairie provinces; British Columbia: census regions.
City or CMA size	Under 25,000; 25,000 to 100,000; 100,000 to 250,000; 250,000 to 500,000; 500,000 to 1,000,000; over 1,000,000.
Urban–rural	Urban; rural; suburban; farm.
Climate and topography	Mountainous; seacoast; rainy; cold and snowy; etc.
Demographic	
Age	Under 6, 6–12, 13–19, 20–34, 35–49, 50–64, 65 and over.
Gender	Male, female.
Family life cycle	Young single; young married; no children; etc.
Family size	Single, couple, 3–5, 6 or more.
Education	Grade school only, high school graduate, college graduate.
Occupation	Professional, manager, clerical worker, skilled worker, salesperson, student, homemaker, unemployed.
Religion	Protestant, Catholic, Jewish, other.
Ethnic background	White; Black; Asian. British; French; Chinese; German; Ukrainian, Italian; Indian; etc.
Income	Under $10,000; $10,000–$25,000; $25,000–$35,000; $35,000–$50,000; over $50,000.
Psychographic	
Social class	Upper class, upper middle, lower middle, upper lower, etc.
Personality	Ambitious, self-confident, aggressive, introverted, extroverted, sociable, etc.
Lifestyle	Conservative, liberal, health and fitness oriented, adventuresome.
Value perception	Kinds of value the customer finds most attractive.
Relationships	Close, more close, less close, trusting, personal, distant.
Behaviour Toward Product or Service (or Product/Service-Related Bases)	
Benefits desired	Examples vary widely, depending upon product or service: appliance: cost, quality, life, repairs. aerobics class: fitness, appearance, health, fellowship. toothpaste: no cavities, plaque control, bright teeth. hairdressing: image, style, price, self-confidence.
Usage rate	Nonuser, light user, heavy user.
Loyalty/brand recognition	More or less loyal to particular companies and brands.

about the product? What should a firm do? Extensive market research told the company that consumers wanted a newer product that offered more value and diet flavours. The product had become "yesterday's news" — so the company changed the packaging, including the colours, increased the size and introduced new diet varieties. By careful evaluation and responses the company was able to revitalize the brand.[10] Such examples demonstrate the importance of environmental scanning as discussed in Chapter 2.

In using the bases outlined in Table 4-1 to segment markets, we should bear in mind two points. First, buying behaviour is rarely traceable to only one of these segmentation factors. Including variables from several bases develops useful segmentation. To illustrate, the market for a product rarely consists of all people living in British Columbia or all people over age sixty-five. Instead, the segment is more likely to be described through a combination of these variables. Thus a market segment for notebook computers might be travelling businesspersons, earning above average income, who are well-educated and

A clear need for a new brand image.

over thirty. As another example, one clothing manufacturer's target market might be affluent young women (income, age, gender).

The other point to observe is the interrelationships among these factors, especially among the demographic factors. For instance, age and life-cycle stage typically are related. Income depends to some degree on age, life-cycle stage, education, and occupation.

We shall discuss the two most commonly used bases for segmentation — geographic and demographic — in this chapter, leaving to Chapter 5 a detailed discussion of the more complex bases for market segmentation.

Geographic Segmentation

Subdivisions in the geographical distribution and demographic composition of the population are widely used bases for segmenting consumer markets. The reason for this is simply that consumer wants and product usage often are related to one or more of these subcategories. Geographic and demographic groupings also meet the conditions for effective segmentation — they are measurable, accessible, and large enough. Let's consider how the geographic distribution of population may serve as a segmentation basis.

Total Population

A logical place to start is with an analysis of total population. The rapid growth in population that was experienced during the baby boom years from 1945 to the early 1960s has slowed down to the point that Canada now has a declining population growth rate with a 1.14 fertility rate. By 1999 the Canadian population reached 30.4 million. The current low birth rate is expected to continue, so projections for total population indicate slow population growth for the next two decades reaching 33.4 million by 2011 and just over 36 million anticipated by 2026. Potentially, the population may actually begin to decrease in this country after that point.[11]

Other factors, such as the flow of inhabitants into and out of a country also influence total population size. Currently in Canada there are concerns regarding outward movement of educated, high-income potential professionals to the United States (the so-called "brain drain"), and controversy surrounding immigration policies. Another trend of interest includes Canada's increasingly aging population.

Marketing at Work 4-2

Malls Offer Free Foot Rubs to Loyal Shoppers

Reward programs are not a new phenomenon in the retail world, as many stores offer their customers points, discounts, or special privileges in an effort to ensure repeat business. Plagued with crowded parking lots and faced with the increasing popularity of Internet shopping, and the revitalization of many downtown shopping areas, malls are now jumping on the loyalty bandwagon.

Shoppers will now be invited to join a new membership program at Cadillac Fairview malls across the country. Members will be able to deposit their kids at children's learning areas for drama classes or an archeological dig while they shop undisturbed, or visit an "oasis" café to watch TV, listen to a CD, enjoy a drink or even receive a free foot rub.

The Canadian mall owner is aiming to increase the average spend per customer visit by introducing a customer satisfaction program intended to keep shoppers in its malls longer — shoppers who average less than 12 minutes per visit spend approximately $250 a month, while those who average an hour per visit spend $900 a month.

This program is the first major initiative to stem from two years of intense customer research that had a strong emphasis on psychographic segmentation and profiling.

Following thousands of exit interviews and dozens of focus groups with shoppers, coupled with behavioural analyses and geodemographic overlays, Cadillac Fairview categorized each of its forty malls into one of six profiles. The Toronto Eaton Centre and Pacific Centre in Vancouver are considered Urban Premiere properties, while malls that are predominantly located in upscale suburban areas are classified as Family centres. The remaining profiles include Francophone, Destination, Mature Lifestyle, and Community.

Dominick Bovalino, Cadillac Fairview's vice-president of marketing and corporate communications, thought it best not to paint all visitors to its properties with the same brush and believes relationships must be based on consumer attributes, centre attributes, and market attributes. So with the profiling work now completed, Cadillac Fairview will tailor its marketing programs to meet the needs of specific mall clusters.

Source: Adapted from Craig Saunders, "Cadillac Fairview rolls out the spoils," *Strategy,* May 8, 2000, p. 1.

The total market is so large and diverse that it must be analyzed in segments. Significant shifts are occurring in regional and urban-rural population distribution patterns. Market differences traceable to differences in age, gender, household arrangements, lifestyles, and ethnic backgrounds pose real challenges for marketing executives.

Regional Distribution

Figure 4-1 shows the distribution of the Canadian population in 1998 and its projected growth to 2016 by province. The biggest markets and the largest urban areas are located in Central Canada, where Ontario and Quebec together accounted for 62 percent of the Canadian population in 1999. The greatest rate of population *growth* during the late 1990s has occurred in Ontario and Western Canada, particularly in Alberta, where the population increased by 8.3 percent from 1995 to 1999.

The **regional distribution** of population is important to marketers, because people within a particular geographic region broadly tend to share the same values, attitudes, and style preferences. However, significant differences do exist among the various regions, because of differences in climate, social customs, and other factors. Ontario is a more urbanized province and represents the greatest concentration of people in Canada, especially in the corridor between Oshawa and Niagara Falls. This market is attractive to many marketers because of its sheer size and the diversity of consumers living there. On the other hand, the Atlantic region and the Prairie Provinces are characterized by a much more relaxed and rural lifestyle, which suggests a demand for different types of products and services. People in the West appear to be more relaxed and less formal than Eastern Canadians, and they spend more time outdoors. As this Western Canadian market grows, there will be a growth in demand for products associated with an outdoors lifestyle from clothing to leisure activities.

Urban, Rural, and Suburban Distribution

For many years in Canada there has been both a relative and an absolute decline in the farm population, and this decline in the rural market is expected to continue. The declining farm population has led some people to underestimate the importance of rural markets. However, both as an industrial market for farm machinery and other resource industry equipment and supplies, and as a consumer market with increased buying power and more urban sophistication, the rural market is still a major one. Sociological patterns (such as average family size and local customs) among rural people differ significantly from those of city dwellers. These patterns, affected by the **urban–suburban–rural distribution** of populations, have considerable influence on buying behaviour. Per capita consumption of cosmetics and other beauty aids, for example, is much lower in farm and rural markets than in city markets. At the same time it is higher in certain *geographical* regions, such as in areas of Quebec.

Census Metropolitan Areas

Census Metropolitan Area (CMA)
The major population centres of Canada as defined by Statistics Canada; generally containing population centres of 100,000 or more.

As the rural population has shrunk, the urban and suburban population has expanded. In recognition of the growing urbanization of the Canadian market, some years ago the federal government established the concept of a **Census Metropolitan Area** (CMA) as a geographic market-data measurement unit. A CMA is defined by Statistics Canada as the main labour market of a continuous built-up area having a population of 100,000 or more. Table 4-2 indicates the growth in the population of the twenty-five CMAs in Canada from 1986 to 1999. By 1999, these twenty-five areas accounted for almost 63 percent of the total population of Canada, and this percentage is expected to continue

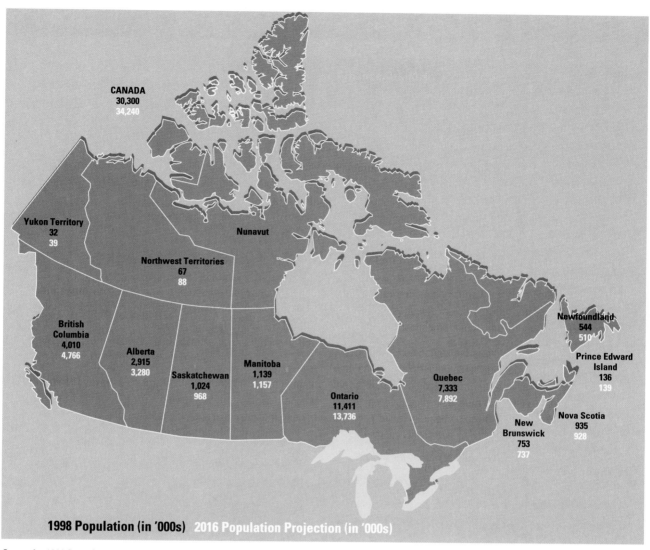

1998 Population (in '000s)   2016 Population Projection (in '000s)

Source for 1998 Data: Statistics Canada. Annual Demographic Statistics, 1998, catalogue number 91-213. Source for projected figures: *Market Research Handbook, 1995*, cat. no. 63-224, pp. 576–77. The projections of provincial population figures to 2016 are based on a series of assumptions: that the birth rate continues at approximately the level that pertained at the end of the 1980s (approximately 1.67 births per woman), and that the level of immigration is approximately 200,000 per year. Life expectancy is expected to increase to 77.2 years for men and 84.0 years for women by 2016.

Note: The 1998 population figures shown for the Northwest Territories include the territory now known as Nunavut (created on April 1, 1999)

FIGURE 4-1

Provincial Distribution of Canadian Population, 1998, and Projected Growth to 2016 (thousands)

to increase. This is especially so as immigration to Canada increases and as most immigrants settle in urban areas. Obviously, these census metropolitan areas represent attractive, geographically concentrated market targets with considerable sales potential.

In several places in Canada, the metropolitan areas have expanded to the point that there is no rural space between them. This joining of metropolitan areas has been called "interurbia." Where two or more city markets once existed, today there is a single market. For example, there is virtually no space between Quebec City and Niagara Falls that is not part of a major urban area.

Suburban Growth

As the metropolitan areas have been growing, something else has been going on within them. The central cities are growing very slowly, and in some cases the older established

TABLE 4-2 Census Metropolitan Areas Population, 1986, 1991, and 1999 (thousands)

	1986	1991	1999
Calgary, Alberta	671.3	754.0	933.7
Chicoutimi-Jonquière, Quebec	158.5	160.9	162.3
Edmonton, Alberta	785.5	839.9	929.1
Halifax, Nova Scotia	296.0	320.5	389.6
Hamilton, Ontario	557.0	599.7	665.2
Kitchener, Ontario	311.2	356.4	415.0
London, Ontario	342.3	381.5	418.7
Montreal, Quebec	2,921.4	3,127.2	3,438.5
Oshawa, Ontario	203.5	250.1	292.9
Ottawa–Hull, Ontario–Quebec	819.3	920.8	1,065.0
Quebec City, Quebec	603.3	645.5	668.1
Regina, Saskatchewan	186.5	191.6	199.2
St. Catharines–Niagara Falls, Ontario	343.3	364.5	389.6
St. John's, Newfoundland	161.9	171.8	174.5
Saint John, New Brunswick	121.3	124.9	127.2
Saskatoon, Saskatchewan	200.7	210.0	231.4
Sherbrooke, Quebec	130.0	139.1	153.1
Sudbury, Ontario	148.9	157.6	160.4
Thunder Bay, Ontario	122.2	124.4	126.6
Toronto, Ontario	3,427.2	3,893.0	4,680.3
Trois-Rivières, Quebec	128.9	136.3	141.8
Vancouver, British Columbia	1,380.7	1,602.5	2,016.6
Victoria, British Columbia	255.5	287.8	316.2
Windsor, Ontario	254.0	262.0	300.0
Winnipeg, Manitoba	625.3	652.3	677.6

Source: Statistics Canada, CANSIM matrices 9248–9249

parts of the cities are actually losing population. The real growth is occurring in the fringe areas of the central cities or in the suburbs outside these cities. For the past forty years, one of the most significant social and economic trends in Canada has been the shift of population to the suburbs. As middle-income families have moved to the suburbs, the economic, racial, and ethnic composition of many central cities (especially their core areas) has changed considerably, thus changing the nature of the markets in these areas.

The growth of the suburban population has some striking marketing implications. Since a great percentage of suburban people live in single-family residences, there is a vastly expanded market for lawn mowers, lawn furniture, home furnishings, and home repair supplies and equipment. Suburbanites are more likely to want two cars than are city dwellers. They are inclined to spend more leisure time at home, so there is a bigger market for home entertainment and recreation items.

As the new millennium began, marketing professionals observed the development of two possible counter-trends. One was the movement from the suburbs back to the central cities by older people whose children are grown. Rather than contend with commuting, home maintenance, and other suburban challenges, older people were moving to new apartments located nearer to downtown facilities. And it is not just older people who are returning to the downtown areas. In many Canadian cities, young professional families are locating close to their downtown places of work, preferring to renovate an older home rather than contend with commuting and other perceived shortcomings of suburban living.

The other reversal is that there has been an increase in the rural population near larger cities. Although the rural population of Canada has increased very little in recent years, most of that growth occurred in close proximity to the large census metropolitan areas. This growth has been brought about, not only because some people wish to live in a more rural setting, but also because of rising real estate prices in and near many Canadian cities. Some of the growth that has been experienced in the population of census metropolitan areas as shown in Table 4-2 has occurred because some of the areas around these CMAs have been incorporated into the cities.

In recent years, geographic segmentation has become much more refined through the use of **geodemographic clustering**, a process that uses census and other statistical data to cluster postal code areas into similar groups or segments. By examining such data, a marketer can identify groups of postal code areas that have similar patterns of education, income, household size, age, housing, occupation, and other factors. Thus, companies can make their direct marketing efforts much more efficient by targeting their advertising to homes located in postal code areas that best reflect the characteristics of the target markets they wish to reach. Such an approach is also useful for making efficient decisions on new store locations, to determine the best products and brands to offer in specific stores, and to direct mail-order catalogues with appropriate merchandise featured.[12]

> **geodemographic clustering**
> The use of statistical population data along with information on where people live, usually obtained from postal code data, to identify clusters of consumers or households with similar characteristics.

Demographic Segmentation

The most common basis for the **demographic segmentation** of consumer markets is some demographic category such as age, gender, family life-cycle stage, income distribution, education, occupation, or ethnic origin.

Age Groups

Analyzing the consumer market by age groups is a useful exercise in the marketing of many products and services. Age is one of the most fundamental bases for demographically segmenting markets, as we can see from the large number of products and services directed at seniors, children, teens, young adults, and so on. But marketers must be aware of the changing nature of the age mix of the Canadian population. Looking ahead again to the year 2016, we see an aging population that is not growing very quickly. In 1993, for example, there were almost 3.9 million people in Canada aged between 10 and 19. By 2001, this age group will have become slightly larger at 4.2 million; but by 2016, there will be only 3.7 million Canadians in this age bracket, assuming the birth rate remains at the present level. On the other hand, in 1986, there were only 2.7 million Canadians aged 65 and older. By 1993, this age bracket contained 3.3 million; by 2011, this group will increase in number to 4.8 million and to 5.6 million by 2016.[13]

The youth market (roughly aged 5 to 13) carries a three-way market impact. First, these children can influence parental purchases. Second, millions of dollars are spent on this group by their parents. Third, these children make purchases of goods and services for their own use and satisfaction, and the volume of these purchases increases as the children get older. Promotional programs are often geared to this market segment. Manufacturers of breakfast cereals, snack foods, and toys often advertise on television programs that are directed at children — except on the CBC television network, which prohibits advertising on children's programs.[14]

In an attempt to attract more of the family leisure-travel market, Air Canada and other airlines offer special children's menus, board games, books, colouring materials, cockpit visits, and play areas at major Canadian airports. Air Canada states that it believes children have a great influence on their parents when decisions are being made as to which airline to use. Air Canada management calls it "pester power." Keeping children entertained, they hope, will also create "relax power" for parents and for other passengers. This represents a good example of marketing to children by an organization whose target market is principally adults, but which is clearly interested in meeting family needs in the short term and in building brand loyalty to expand its market in the future.[15]

Zellers has expanded its Club Z to include membership for children. Generation Z allows children to accumulate the same number of points on purchases as their parents. These points can be used to get rewards from a 747 flight simulation to the latest boom box. This is an opportunity to cement relationships with moms while appealing to the next generation of consumers.[16] The Calgary Stampeders have attempted to make football an affordable family activity — as well as reducing prices, adding cash and prize giveaways, children get special attention. There is face-painting, Sony Playstations, an autograph tent and "high-fives" from the players before each game.[17] Swiss Chalet is redesigning their restaurants to attract customers typically "challenged by the dining-room style." More open concept kitchens and drive-thru locations are hoped to attract the tween and teen market as well as those families with children under ten.[18]

The teenage market is also recognized as an important one, yet many companies find it difficult to reach. The mistake might be in attempting to lump all teenagers together. Certainly, the 13–16 age group is very different from the 17–20 age bracket. Yet marketers must understand the teenage market because of the size of the segment and because its members have a great deal of money to spend.

Among young adults, postsecondary students are an excellent example of a segment that spends money. One author estimates that the amount is between $2 billion and $5 billion. A Montreal-based company has focused on this group in Ontario and Quebec with the Camplus loyalty card. With special discounts and rebates exclusively for these under-30 consumers, the company has developed a powerful database of all the services, products, and information about this group. Companies that agree to participate with the program gain access to a valuable market as well as market information gathered from electronic profiles. Students can provide this information regarding their activities in order to receive articles relevant to their lives. Participating firms, therefore, gain important market data as well as the opportunity to establish loyalty among a young clientele with the hope of claiming them for life.[19]

Because the size of this young-adult segment will decline in coming years, Canada's universities are aggressively competing for students by taking new strategic approaches to recruiting and introducing advertising and marketing campaigns, new scholarships, integrated student services, and enrolment management systems.[20]

In the 1990s the early-middle-age population segment (aged 35 to 50) was an especially large and lucrative market. These people are the products of the post-World War II baby boom and were the rebels of the 1960s and 1970s. They also were a very big and profitable teenage and young-adult market for many companies during those years. Now, as they move into middle age in the late 1990s, they are reaching their high-earning years.

Typically, their values and lifestyles are far different from those of the people of the same age category in previous generations. Already, companies are adjusting to these changing demographics. While toothpaste manufacturers like Procter & Gamble and Colgate-Palmolive capitalized on concern about cavity prevention in children's teeth in the 1950s and 1960s, thirty-five or more years later they are producing toothpaste to fight tartar — an adult dental problem. This generation, with more dual-income families and fewer children, have more money to spend on themselves. As a result, they are a prime market for products that promise convenience and for home and garden services.

The aging baby-boom generation makes an attractive market segment for a number of other reasons. Many are seeing their children graduate from college and university and have likely paid off the mortgage on the family home. Suddenly, they have a lot more disposable money to spend on themselves and on indulging their new grandchildren. Coupled with the fact that this age group has reached this stage in their family life cycle is the fact that, as a result of the recession that gripped Canada in the early 1990s, many have opted to take early retirement from their jobs. As a result, many have a lot of leisure time on their hands. Consequently, this age group makes an attractive target for vacation travel, entertainment, recreation, smaller homes and condominiums, and long-term investments intended to finance a long retirement. This group may be "aging," but this should not be confused with being old. Those born in the peak of the boom will not reach 65 until 2026. Many of these consumers want to shop at their neighbourhood bakery, butcher shop, or clothing boutiques where staff know their names, their likes and dislikes and as such the specialty retailer is on the comeback trail.[21]

At the older end of the age spectrum are two market segments that should not be overlooked. One is the group of people in their fifties and early sixties. This mature market is large and financially well off. Its members are at the peak of their earning power and typically no longer have financial responsibility for their children. Thus, this segment is a good target for marketers of high-priced, high-quality products and services.

The other older age group is made up of people over 65 — a segment that is growing both absolutely and as a percentage of the total population. Manufacturers and intermediaries alike are beginning to recognize that people in this age group are logical prospects for small, low-cost housing units, cruises and foreign tours, health products, and cosmetics developed especially for older people. Many firms are also developing promotional programs to appeal to this group because their purchasing power is surprisingly high. Also, the shopping behaviour of the over-65 market typically is different from that found in other age segments. On a per capita basis, seniors are increasing their spending faster than average in areas such as health care, entertainment, recreation, gifts, and charitable contributions. In this latter category, seniors give more dollars than the average Canadian, making them an attractive market segment for charities and religious groups.

This is a rapidly growing market segment that is spanning new products and presenting opportunities for marketers. One food company, Dinner Date Inc., of Scarborough, Ontario, specializes in meals for the elderly. The company partners with a number of organizations in local areas providing services to this target group. Sage and Co. operate a mail-order business providing gadgets for seniors. Items such as special gardening tools, leisure clothing, jar openers for arthritic hands, and other specially designed kitchen aids are made available to this population segment.[22]

We should not fall into the trap, however, of assuming that all older seniors are inactive or financially disadvantaged. Research shows that Canadians aged 75 and older are generally in good health, and an increasing percentage are living alone and enjoying an active life.

Gender

Gender is an obvious basis for consumer market analysis. Many products are made for use by members of one gender, not both. In many product categories — automobiles, for example — women and men typically look for different product benefits. **Market segmentation by gender** is also useful because either men only or women only have traditionally purchased many products.

However, some of these traditional buying patterns are breaking down, and marketers certainly should be alert to changes involving their products and services. According to Statistics Canada, 57.4 percent of women are participating in the Canadian workforce. The entry of women into the work force has occurred in great numbers since the 1970s. Though participation rates have levelled off in recent years, women now account for almost 47 percent of the Canadian work force in the 15 to 44 age bracket. These facts are significant for marketers. Working women share more values with working men than they do with housewives, and young women share more values with young men than with older women. Not only are the lifestyle and buying behaviour of women in the labour force quite different from those of women who do not work outside their homes, but many of those women are members of households where their spouses also are employed, thereby producing Canadian households with considerable buying power.[23]

Marketing at Work 4-3

52 Percent of the Population is *Not* a Niche

Women represent the third-largest economy in the world and control more than US$14 trillion in wealth, yet are still considered by many marketers to be a niche, not dissimilar from ethnic and other specialty markets.

Women constitute 52 percent of the world's population — clearly not a niche market. Why then aren't companies salivating over the huge potential of marketing their products to women instead of merely paying lip service to this huge and expanding market?

According to Marti Barletta, a Chicago-based marketing consultant, most attempts at marketing to women fail to live up to their potential due to a lack of proper market segmentation. All women are not exactly alike — stay-at-home mothers, working women, and retirees have very different needs and concerns.

Industries such as packaged goods, fashion, and cosmetics, which have traditionally been female-driven, have learned to speak to women on their terms. However, the financial services, automobile, and computer industries are much slower off the mark — especially considering that women

already purchase 50 percent of the computers sold in the U.S. and 65 percent of the new cars, and by 2010 will control wealth valued at more than US$22 trillion.

Companies have to walk a fine line when marketing to women as both women and men will be suspicious of a product marketed as a "women's product." Men won't buy anything they consider "girlie" and women will assume it to be inferior to the men's version of the product. The key is to understand how women view and use the product and to appeal to them on attitudinal and behavioural levels as opposed to purely demographics.

Two companies that appear to be doing it right are Apple Computer and Trimark Mutual Funds. Trimark focuses on how women can benefit from mutual funds at different stages in their lives, as opposed to emphasizing the performance value of the company's own mutual fund products. Apple's success has nothing to do with the pretty colours that its new iMac personal computer comes in, rather that the marketing materials that accompany the colourful PCs focus on its ease of use.

Source: Adapted from John Gray, "Expert says stop the lip service and start marketing to women," *Strategy*, February 15, 1999, p. 7.

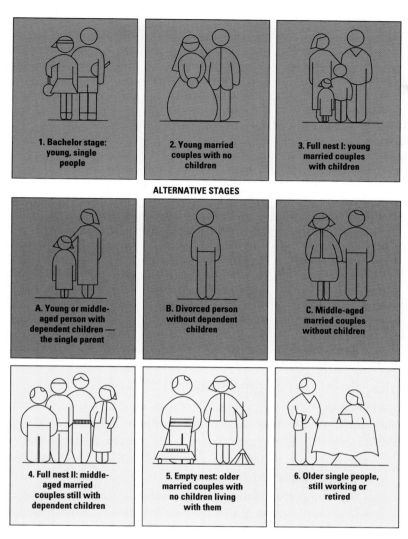

FIGURE 4-2
The Family Life Cycle

family life cycle
The series of life stages that a family goes through, starting with young single people and progressing through married stages with young and then older children, and ending with older married and single people.

Family Life Cycle

Frequently the main factor accounting for differences in consumption patterns between two people of the same age and sex is that they are in different life-cycle stages. The concept of the **family life cycle** implies that there are several distinct stages in the life of an ordinary family. The traditional six-stage family cycle is shown in Figure 4-2, along with three alternative stages that reflect significant changes from traditional patterns. In addition to the family configurations represented in Figure 4-2, numerous other examples exist, from same-sex marriages to families with shared child custody to co-habitation arrangements between mixed-sex groups. Lifestyles that do not reflect the traditional norm are often more the rule than the exception. We can think of life-cycle position, in any of its various patterns, as a major determinant of buyer behaviour and thus it can be a useful basis for segmenting consumer markets.[24]

A young couple with two children (the full-nest stage) has quite different needs from those of a couple in their mid-fifties whose children no longer live at home (the empty-nest stage). A single-parent family (divorced, widowed, or never married) with dependent children faces social and economic problems quite different from those of a two-parent family. Young married couples with no children typically devote large shares of their income to clothing, autos, and recreation. When children start arriving, expenditure patterns shift as many young families buy and furnish a home. Families with teenagers find larger portions of the budget going for food, clothing, and educational needs. One of the most rapidly growing segments among the Canadian population is the singles. In 1961, only 9.3 percent of Canadian households consisted of just one person — a single. By 1996, thirty-five years later, almost 24 percent of Canadian homes had only a single occupant, although the percentage of people living alone differs considerably from province to province. In Manitoba, for example, 27 percent of the households have only a single occupant, while the corresponding percentage in Newfoundland is only 14.5 percent. The total number of one-person households is increasing at a much faster rate than that of family units. Among the reasons for this increase in the number of one-person households are:

◆ The growing number of working women.

◆ People marrying at a later age.

◆ The reduced tendency for single people to live with their parens.

◆ A rising divorce rate.

The impact that single people of both sexes have on the market is demonstrated by such things as apartments for singles, social clubs for singles, and special tours, cruises, and eating places seeking the patronage of singles. Even in the mundane field of grocery products the growing singles market (including the divorced and widowed) is causing changes by retailers and food manufacturers.

Singles in the 25 to 39 age bracket are especially attractive to marketers because they are such a large group. Compared with the population as a whole, this singles group is:

◆ More affluent.

◆ More mobile.

◆ More experimental and less conventional.

◆ More fashion- and appearance-conscious.

◆ More active in leisure pursuits.

◆ More sensitive to social status.

Other Demographic Bases for Segmentation

The market for some consumer products is influenced by such factors as education, occupation, religion, and ethnic origin. With an increasing number of people attaining higher levels of **education**, for example, we can expect to see (1) changes in product preferences and (2) buyers with more discriminating taste and higher incomes. **Occupation** may be a more meaningful criterion than income in segmenting some markets. Truck drivers or auto mechanics may earn as much as young retailing executives or college professors. But the buying patterns of the first two are different from those of the second two because of attitudes, interests, and other lifestyle factors.

For some products, it is useful to analyze the population on the basis of **religion** or **ethnic origin**. The most important distinction in Canada is between the two founding races. French–English differences are fundamental to doing business in Canada and will be dealt with in greater detail in Chapter 6. Marketers have known for some time that certain products such as instant coffee and tomato juice sell much better in Quebec.

In larger Canadian cities, the cultural diversity of the population creates an increasing marketing opportunity for companies that specialize in products and services directed toward a particular ethnic community. In Toronto, for example, almost half the population was born outside Canada. Persons of Italian heritage represent almost 5 percent of the population in Ontario and more than 8 percent in Toronto. Almost 8 percent of the population of Alberta have German roots, as do almost 13 percent of people in Saskatchewan. Almost 7 percent of the people of Manitoba are Ukrainian Canadians.

In certain areas of the country, such as around Kitchener-Waterloo, Ontario, with its large German-Canadian population, and in many of the larger cities, ethnic groups represent a viable target market segment for certain specialty products and services. The large number of recent immigrants from Hong Kong and other Asian countries has transformed some neighbourhoods in some cities, as did immigrants from Portugal, Italy, and the Caribbean before them.

The Chinese community is one of the fastest-growing ethnic groups in Canada. The importance of this market segment to the Toronto business community is reflected in the fact that the market is served by three Chinese-language daily newspapers, two of which have been published since the late 1970s. Two popular magazines — *Maclean's* and *Toronto Life* — have also launched Chinese-language editions.[25] T&T Supermarkets, in Vancouver, caters to the burgeoning Asian market, which is estimated to make up more than 25 percent of the Lower Mainland population in British Columbia.[26]

Consumer Income and its Distribution

People alone do not make a market; they must have money to spend. Consequently, **consumer income**, its distribution, and how it is spent are essential factors in any quantitative market analysis.

Nature and Scope of Income

What is income? There are so many different concepts of income that it is good to review some definitions. The following outline is actually a "word equation" that shows how the several concepts are related.

National income: Total income from all sources, including employee compensation, corporate profits, and other income.

Less: Corporate profits, and pension and social program contributions.

Plus: Dividends, government transfer payments to persons, and net interest paid by government.

Equals:

Personal income: All forms of income received by persons and unincorporated businesses; including wages, salaries, and supplementary labour income; military pay and allowances; net income of non-farm business including rent; net income of farm operators from farm production; interest, dividends, and miscellaneous investment income; and transfer payment income from government, corporations, and nonresidents.

Less: All personal federal, provincial, and municipal taxes.

Equals:

Personal disposable income: Personal income less personal direct taxes and other current transfers to government from persons; represents the amount available for personal consumption expenditure and savings.

Less: (1) Essential expenditures for food, clothing, household utilities, and local transportation and (2) fixed expenditures for rent, mortgage payments, insurance, and instalment debt payments.

Equals:

Discretionary purchasing power: The amount of disposable personal income that is available after fixed commitments (debt repayments, rent) and essential household needs are taken care of. Compared with disposable personal income, discretionary purchasing power is a better (more sensitive) indicator of consumers' ability to spend for nonessentials.

In addition, we hear the terms "money income," "real income," and "psychic income." **Money income** is the amount a person receives in actual cash or cheques for wages, salaries, rent, interest, and dividends. **Real income** is what the money income will buy in goods and services; it is purchasing power. If a person's money income rises 5 percent in one year but the cost of purchases increases 2 percent on average, then real income increases by only 3 percent. **Psychic income** is an intangible, but highly important, income factor related to comfortable climate, a satisfying neighbourhood, enjoyment of one's job, and so on. Some people prefer to take less real income so they can live in a part of the country that features a fine climate — greater psychic income.

As measured by income, the Canadian economy has grown dramatically in recent years. With the exception of recessions in the early 1980s and early 1990s, the economy has enjoyed almost uninterrupted growth since the end of World War II. Personal disposable income, which stood at $159 billion in 1978 and at $237 billion in 1981, had jumped to $466 billion by 1991 and $511 billion by 1995. In the fifteen years from 1980 to 1995, per capita personal disposable income increased from $9,545 to $17,262. in 1996 this dropped slightly to $17,131. Discretionary purchasing power has, therefore, increased considerably during the past fifteen years or so. In light of the fact that inflation has been at very low levels in Canada in recent years, the improvement in consumer buying power is impressive.

Income Distribution

To get full value from an analysis of income, we should study the variations and trends in the distribution of income among regions and among population segments. Regional income data are especially helpful in pinpointing the particular market to which a firm wishes to appeal. Income data on cities and even on areas within cities may indicate the best locations for shopping centres and suburban branches of downtown stores.

A genuine income revolution has occurred in Canada over the past thirty years or so. During the second half of the twentieth century, the pattern of **income distribution** was dramatically altered (see Table 4-3). There has been a tremendous growth in the middle- and upper-income segments, and a corresponding decrease in the percentage of low-income groups.

The purchasing power of the average Canadian family is expected to continue to increase over the next ten years. We will see the effects of higher personal incomes and higher participation rates in the labour force. It is very likely that more than half of all Canadian families will have a total annual income in excess of $55,000 by the year 2016. This anticipated increase in the number of affluent households is the result of several factors. These include (1) the large growth in the number of people in the prime earning years 25 to 45, (2) the increase in dual-income families, and (3) the wider distribution of inherited wealth. We will still have low-income families. However, there will be fewer below the poverty line, even though that level (by government definition) is moving up, in recognition of both inflation and a society that is generally better able to provide its members with a reasonable income.

Marketing Significance of Income Data

The declining percentage of families in the poverty bracket, coupled with the sharp increases in the upper-income groups, presages an explosive growth in discretionary purchasing power. And, as discretionary income increases, so too does the demand for items that once were considered luxuries.

TABLE 4-3	Percentage Distribution of Families by Income Groups in Canada, Annual Income 1985, 1990, and 1997		
Income Group	**1985**	**1990**	**1997**
Less than $10,000	5.5	2.7	2.5
$10,000 to $14,999	8.4	4.3	3.7
$15,000 to $19,999	9.3	6.8	5.1
$20,000 to $24,999	8.8	7.0	6.8
$25,000 to $29,999	9.3	6.5	6.2
$30,000 to $34,999	9.7	7.2	6.8
$35,000 to $39,999	9.3	7.1	6.7
$40,000 to $44,999	8.0	7.5	6.0
$45,000 to $49,999	6.8	6.9	5.7
$50,000 to $59,999	10.2	11.2	11.6
$60,000 to $69,999	6.1	8.4	10.1
$70,000 and over	8.5	17.7	28.7

Source: Statistics Canada, *Income Distribution by Size in Canada*, cat. no. 13-207, 1997, pp. 62-63.

The middle-income market is a big and growing market, and it has forced many changes in marketing strategy. Many stores that once appealed to low-income groups have traded up to the huge middle-income market. These stores are upgrading the quality of the products they carry and are offering additional services.

In spite of the considerable increase in disposable income in the past thirty years, many households are still in the low-income bracket or find their higher incomes inadequate to fulfil all their wants. Furthermore, many customers are willing to forgo services in order to get lower prices. One consequence of this market feature has been the development of self-service retail outlets, discount houses, and the more recent superstores. These include those operated by furniture and appliance retailers like The Brick Warehouse in Ontario and Western Canada and by specialists in electronic sound equipment such as Future Shop.

Earlier in this chapter we noted the dramatic increase in the number of working women. This demographic factor also has had a tremendous impact on family income levels. The increase in two-income families has significant marketing and sociological implications. Dual incomes generally enable a family to offset the effects of inflation. But, more than that, two incomes often enable a family to buy within a short time the things their parents worked for years to acquire.

Consumer Expenditure Patterns

How consumers' income is spent is a major market determinant for most products and services. Consequently, marketers need to study **consumer spending patterns** as well as the distribution of consumer income. Marketers also should be aware of the significant shifts in family spending patterns that have occurred over the past two or three decades. Energy costs, inflation, and heavy consumer debt loads have had a major impact on our spending patterns. As examples, let's consider just a few of the changes in spending patterns that have occurred since the 1960s. Over that time span, families have increased the percentage of their total expenditures going for housing, health, and utilities. Spending (as a percentage of total) has decreased for food, beverage, clothing, and home expenses (except utilities).

Marketing at Work 4-4

Segmenting by Colour Preference?

The last time you bought an article of clothing or a school binder or knapsack, did you spend a great deal of time choosing the colour? When it comes to things such as clothes, most people are very particular about colour. Psychologists tell us that colour can produce physiological reactions such as increased blood pressure and heart rate changes. Red can make people very assertive, while purple can calm and settle people down.

The significance of colour is not lost on marketers. They are very interested in how colour influences your buying behaviour. The Cooper Marketing Group of Oak Park, Ill., working in conjunction with Market Facts of Arlington Heights, Ill., has developed colour or lifestyle segmentation, which is a system to segment customers according to the importance of colour in their buying decisions. They have identified three colour personalities:

Colour-Forward Consumers — like to be the first to try a new or daring colour and are willing to pay more for a product in a fashionable colour. They tend to be women under 30 or over 50, or men under 30, city dwellers, impulse buyers, and people who make less than $35,000 per year.

Colour-Prudent Consumers — wait for a colour to gain acceptance before they adopt it. They put quality ahead of colour when choosing products. They tend to be women aged 30 to 50, careful shoppers, and people who make more than $50,000 per year.

Colour-Loyal Consumers — prefer safe colours such as blue or grey rather than fashionable colours. They tend to be men over 60, suburban or rural, dislike shopping, and fall anywhere on the income spectrum.

In the fashion business a season's colours are worked out two years in advance. A new colour usually appears first in fashion and then moves into home furnishings and home decor. In a study of colour preferences conducted by the Pantone Color Institute of New Jersey, blue was found to be a preferred colour, with green on the rise in popularity. Young adults favoured bright and deep colours, while those over 45 favoured pastels and candy colours.

Source: Adapted from Jo Marney, "Coloring Consumer Purchasing Patterns," *Marketing Magazine*, September 16, 1996, p. 24.

But expenditure patterns are not the same for all families. These patterns vary considerably, depending on family income, life-cycle stage, and other factors.

Relation to Stage of Family Life Cycle

Consumer expenditure patterns are influenced by the consumer's stage in the life cycle. There are striking contrasts in spending patterns between, say, people in the full-nest stage, with very young children, and people in the empty-nest stage. Table 4-4 summarizes the behavioural influences and the spending patterns for families in each stage of the cycle. (This table expands the number of stages shown earlier in Figure 4-2.) Young married couples with no children typically devote large shares of their income to clothing, automobiles, and recreation. When children start arriving, expenditure patterns shift as many young families buy and furnish a home. Families with teenagers find larger portions of the budget going for food, clothing, and educational needs. Families in the empty-nest stage, especially when the head of the family is still in the labour force, are attractive to marketers. Typically, these families have more discretionary buying power.

Relation to Income Distribution

The pattern of consumer expenditures is influenced significantly by the income level of the household. For example, as we can see in Table 4-5, families with incomes in the range of $15,000 to $19,999 spend an average of 17.7 percent of their expenditures on

TABLE 4-4 Behaviour Influences and Buying Patterns, by Family Life-Cycle Stage

Bachelor stage: young single people not living at home	Newly married couples; young, no children	Full nest I; youngest child under 6	Full nest II; youngest child 6 or over	Full nest III; older married couples with dependent children
Few financial burdens.	Better off financially than they will be in near future.	Home purchasing at peak.	Financial position better.	Financial position still better.
Fashion opinion leader.	Highest purchase rate and highest average purchase of durables.	Liquid assets low.	In many cases, both spouses work outside the home.	In many cases, both spouses work outside the home.
Recreation-oriented.		In some cases, both spouses work outside the home.	Less influenced by advertising.	Some children get jobs.
Buy: basic kitchen equipment, basic furniture, cars, equipment for the mating game, vacations.	Buy: cars, refrigerators, stoves, sensible and durable furniture, vacations.	Dissatisfied with financial position and amount of money saved.	Buy larger-sized packages, multiple-unit deals.	Hard to influence with advertising.
		Interested in new products.	Buy: many foods, cleaning materials, bicycles, music lessons, pianos.	High average purchase of durables.
		Like advertised products.		Buy: new, more tasteful furniture, auto travel, non-necessary appliances, boats, dental services, magazines.
		Buy: washers, dryers, TV sets, baby food, chest rubs and cough medicine, vitamins, dolls, wagons, sleds, skates.		

Empty nest I; older married couples, no children living with them, head in labour force	Empty nest II; older married couples, no children living at home, head retired	Solitary survivor, in labour force	Solitary survivor, retired	
Home ownership at peak.	Drastic cut in income	Income still good but likely to sell home.	Same medical and product needs as other retired group; drastic cut in income.	
Most satisfied with financial position and money saved.	Keep home.		Special need for attention, affection, and security.	
Interested in travel, recreation, self-education.	Buy: medical appliances, medical care, products that aid health, sleep, and digestion.			
Make gifts and contributions.				
Not interested in new products.				
Buy: vacations, luxuries, home improvements.				

Source: William D. Wells and George Gubar, "Life Cycle Concept in Marketing Research," *Journal of Marketing Research*, November 1966, p. 362. Reprinted with permission from the American Marketing Association.

food. This percentage drops to 13.4 percent for those with annual incomes between $35,000 and $39,999, and to only 8.2 percent for those with incomes above $90,000 per annum. These and other findings from the analysis of Statistics Canada data suggest the type of information that marketers might obtain from analyzing spending patterns by income groups. Some additional generalizations from such data are summarized below.

◆ There is a high degree of uniformity in the expenditure patterns of middle-class spending units. As we shall note in Chapter 6, however, social-class structure is often a more meaningful criterion for determining expenditure patterns.

◆ For each product category, there is a considerable absolute increase in dollars spent as income rises (or, more correctly, as we compare one income group with a higher income group). In other words, people in a given income bracket spend significantly more dollars in each product category than do those in lower brackets. However, the lower-income households devote a larger percentage of their total expenditures to some product categories, such as food. Marketers are probably more concerned with the total dollars available from each income group than with the percentage share of total expenditures.

◆ In each successively higher income group, the amount spent for food declines as a percentage of total expenditures.

◆ The percentage of expenditures devoted to housing, household operation, and utilities totals approximately 24 percent. This varies from almost 36 percent for consumers with incomes between $15,000 and $20,000 to less than 20 percent for those whose family incomes are more than $90,000 annually.

◆ Dramatic differences are observed across income groups in their actual dollar expenditures on recreation. Whereas a family in the lower-income bracket may spend as little as $500 annually, the higher-income family will spend as much as $5,000.

◆ The percentage spent on clothing remains fairly constant across income groups, ranging between 4 percent and 5 percent. Dollar expenditures, however, range from $500 to well over $5,000 annually.

◆ A major difference between low-income and higher-income Canadian families lies in the percentage of their total income that goes to government in the form of taxes. Whereas a family whose total income is in the top 10 percent in Canada may pay well over 30 percent of total personal income in taxes, lower-income families may pay no tax at all.

◆ Major differences in expenditure patterns are also found when the Canadian population is examined across geographic regions. This is related in part to income differences, but also is caused to a degree by the differences in the cost of certain items in different areas of the country. For example, the average family in Montreal spends 13.0 percent of total expenditures on food, while a family in Halifax spends only 11.3 percent. On the other hand, a family in Victoria will spend 18.2 percent of its total expenditures on housing, as compared with only 16.0 percent in St. John's, Newfoundland.

Generalizations such as these provide a broad background against which marketing executives can analyze the market for their particular product or service. People with needs to satisfy and money to spend, however, must be willing to spend before a market can be said to exist. Consequently, Chapter 6 looks into consumer motivation and buying behaviour — the "willingness-to-buy" factor in our definition of a market.

Expenditure Category	Family Income $15,000–$19,999	$35,000–$39,999	$90,000 and over
Food	17.7%	13.4%	8.2%
Shelter	29.4	21.9	15.4
Household operation	6.4	5.2	4.0
Household furnishings and equipment	2.9	2.9	2.6
Clothing	4.8	4.7	4.3
Transportation	11.8	12.0	11.0
Health care	3.4	3.0	1.7
Personal care	1.9	1.5	1.1
Recreation	4.9	5.7	5.6
Reading materials and other printed matter	0.7	0.6	0.5
Education	1.4	1.3	1.5
Tobacco products and alcoholic beverages	3.4	2.7	1.5
Miscellaneous	1.6	1.6	1.6
Gifts and contributions	2.6	2.8	2.7
Personal taxes	4.4	14.6	32.2

TABLE 4-5 Detailed Family Expenditure by Selected Family Income Categories, All Families and Unattached Individuals, 1997

Source: Statistics Canada, *Market Research Handbook*, cat. no. 63-224, 1999, pp. 66-67.

Summary

A sound marketing program starts with the identification and analysis of target markets for whatever an organization is selling. A market consists of people or organizations with needs or wants, money to spend, and the willingness to spend it. There are some general guidelines to follow when selecting target markets.

Some form of market segmentation is the strategy that most marketers adopt as a compromise between the extremes of an aggregate, undifferentiated market and a different product tailor-made for each customer. Market segmentation is the process of dividing the total heterogeneous market into several homogeneous segments. A separate marketing program is developed for each segment that the seller selects as a target market. Market segmentation is a customer-oriented philosophy that is consistent with the marketing concept.

Market segmentation enables a company to make more efficient use of its marketing resources. Also, this strategy allows a small company to compete effectively in one or two segments. The main drawback of market segmentation is that it requires higher production and marketing costs than does a one-product, mass-market strategy. The requirements for effective segmentation are that (1) the bases for segmentation be measurable with accessible data; (2) the segments themselves be accessible to existing marketing institutions; and (3) the segments be large enough to be potentially profitable.

The total market may be divided into two broad segments: ultimate consumers and business users. The four major bases that may be used for further segmenting the consumer market are: (1) geographic — the distribution of population; (2) demographic — the composition of population such as age, gender, and income distribution; (3) psychographic — personality traits and lifestyles; and (4) product-related — product benefits desired and product usage rates.

In the consumer market, the makeup of the population – its distribution and composition — has a major effect on target-market selection. For some products it is useful to analyze population on a regional basis. Another useful division is by urban, suburban, and rural segments. In this context, the bulk of the population is concentrated in metropolitan areas. Moreover, these areas are expanding and joining together in several parts of the country.

The major age groups of the population make up another significant basis for market analysis — young adults, teenagers, the over-65 group, and so on. The stage of the family life cycle influences the market for many products. Other demographic bases for market analysis include education, occupation, religion, and ethnic origin.

Consumer income — especially disposable income and discretionary income — is a meaningful measure of buying power and market potential. The distribution of income affects the markets for many products. Income distribution has shifted considerably during the past twenty-five years. Today, a much greater percentage of families are in the over $90,000 bracket and a much smaller percentage earn under $30,000. A family's income level and life cycle are, in part, determinants of its spending patterns.

Key Terms and Concepts

Market 92	Urban–suburban–rural	Ethnic origin 112
Target market 92	distribution 104	Consumer income 113
Target-market strategy 94	Census Metropolitan Area (CMA) 104	National income 113
Market segmentation 95	Geodemographic clustering 107	Personal income 113
Conditions for effective	Demographic segmentation 107	Personal disposable income 113
segmentation 98	Market segmentation by	Discretionary purchasing power 113
Ultimate consumers 99	gender 110	Money income 114
Business users 99	Family life cycle 111	Real income 114
Bases for segmenting the consumer	Education 112	Psychic income 114
market 100	Occupation 112	Income distribution 114
Regional distribution 104	Religion 112	Consumer spending patterns 115

Questions and Problems

1. Outline some reasons why a company might adopt a strategy of market segmentation.

2. What benefits can a company expect to gain from segmenting its market?

3. Cite some regional differences in product preferences caused by factors other than climate.

4. Give several examples of products whose market demand would be particularly affected by each of the following population factors:

   a. Regional distribution.

   b. Marital status.

   c. Gender.

   d. Age.

   e. Urban–suburban–rural distribution.

5. List three of the major population trends noted in this chapter (for instance, a growing segment of the population is over 65 years of age). Then carefully explain how each of the following types of retail stores might be affected by each of the trends.

   a. Supermarket.

   b. Sporting goods store.

   c. Drugstore.

   d. Restaurant.

6. In which stage of the life cycle are families likely to be the best prospects for each of the following products or services?

   a. Braces on teeth.

   b. Suntan lotion.

   c.   Second car in the family.

   d.   Vitamin pills.

   e.   Refrigerators.

   f.   Life insurance.

   g.   Aerobics classes.

   h.   Fourteen-day Caribbean cruise.

7. In what ways has the rise in disposable personal income since 1960 influenced the marketing programs of a typical department store? A supermarket?

8. Give examples of products whose demand is substantially influenced by changes in discretionary purchasing power.

9. Using the demographic and income segmentation bases discussed in this chapter, describe the segment likely to be the best market for:

   a.   Skis.

   b.   Good French wines.

   c.   Power hand tools.

   d.   Birthday cards.

   e.   Gas barbecues.

10. Describe what you believe to be the demographic characteristics of heavy users of:

   a.   Dog food.

   b.   Ready-to-eat cereal.

   c.   CD players.

   d.   The Internet.

11. Suppose you are marketing automobiles. How is your marketing mix likely to differ when marketing to each of the following market segments?

   a.   High school students.

   b.   Retired teachers.

   c.   Blue-collar workers.

   d.   Mothers.

   e.   Young single adults.

12. Why should a marketer of children's clothing be interested in expenditure patterns on this product category across income levels and across provinces and cities? Consult Statistics Canada data to identify whether major differences exist in expenditures on children's clothing by these categories of consumers.

Hands-On Marketing

1. Interview three friends or acquaintances who all own running shoes, but who are from different demographic groups (for example, different education, age, or gender). Using demographic characteristics only, describe in as much detail as possible the market segment each of your friends represents. Is yours a very complete segment picture? Why?

2. Consider three retailers or three restaurants in your home town or the town or city in which your university or college is located, and describe in as much detail as possible the target market segment each of the stores or restaurants is serving.

Chapter Five

Segmentation, Positioning, and Forecasting

In this chapter, we continue our discussion of market segmentation and introduce the important strategic concept of positioning. Positioning involves occupying a position in the minds of consumers by creating an image that distinguishes a brand or store or company from the competition.

We conclude the chapter with a detailed discussion of forecasting, the last stage in the marketer's quest for target markets. To do an effective job of targeting, the marketer must not only know the characteristics of the segments, but also must be aware of their buying potential. After studying this chapter, you should have an understanding of:

◆ How to approach the segmentation of markets from a lifestyle or product-related perspective.

◆ How to deal with a number of different segments.

◆ The importance of positioning a brand or company to appeal to target market segments.

◆ Niche marketing and other positioning strategies to appeal to different consumers or segments.

◆ The importance of being able to forecast market demand and the market potential of each target segment.

I Am......A Great Marketing Campaign

Well, it has now been proven. You can bottle national pride. And the company that is doing it is Molson Breweries (www.molson.com). Molson began the millennium with a campaign that rolled across the country as it received thunderous applause and even standing ovations in movie theatres while selling Molson Canadian beer by the truckload. The latest instalment to the "I am Canadian" campaign featured an average Canadian "Joe" standing in front of a screen flashing images of Canada — Parliament Hill, beavers, and all that other Great White North stuff, while our friend Joe rails on about igloos, dogsleds, and toques. Joe's mission was to dispel those nasty misperceptions Americans have about their northern neighbours, you and me.

Joe explains he is neither a lumberjack, nor a fur trader. That he has a Prime Minister and not a president, that it's "zed," not "zee," and the differences between "about" and "aboot," policing and peacekeeping. As his voice strains he declares his belief in diversity, not assimilation and that he can proudly sew his country's flag on his backpack. As the music and his voice reach a crescendo, he declares with beaming pride — "*I am Canadian*" to whooping cheers.

While originally designed to target the 19–25 year-old market segment that Molson research states is becoming more

"overt" in their Canadian pride, the campaign struck a loud and strong chord across all groups. Inundated with e-mails, phone calls, and letters of praise, the company quickly exhausted its supply of video-cassettes for Canucks wanting to send the advertisement to their American clients and customers. Over two thousand Canadian-pride testimonials were posted by visitors to a special Web site within the first two weeks (www.iam.com). Live performances of the advertisement were staged at several hockey games, causing fans to be whipped into a frenzy before it was over. Sports bar owners reported similar responses when the spots came on TV monitors in their establishments, reporting that people got "pretty hyped." So hyped, in fact, that many even said the words along with the actor.[1]

This example reflects the main topics to be discussed in Chapter 5. We see how Molson has segmented the market for beer, not merely on demographics, but on the lifestyles and psychological makeup of prospective buyers. The result is an effective positioning of Molson Canadian products in the minds of consumers. The positioning ensures that the brand appeals to certain types of consumers and is distinct from other brands of beers. The added bonus turned out to be that this "in your face" flag-waving tirade struck favourable responses across the country. It did, however, bruise a few sensitive Americans to find out that their neighbour to the north is "the best part of North America."

Psychological Segmentation

Demographic data are used to segment markets because these data are related to behaviour and are relatively easy to gather. However, demographics are not in themselves the causes of behaviour. Consumers don't buy windsurfing equipment because they are young. They buy it because they enjoy an active, outdoor lifestyle, and it so happens that such people are also typically younger. Thus, demographics often correlate with behaviour, but they do not explain it.

Marketers have gone beyond demographic attributes in an effort to better understand why consumers behave as they do. They now engage in **psychological segmentation**, which involves examining attributes such as personality and lifestyles. When demographics and psychological attributes are combined, richer descriptions of segments are produced.

personality
An individual's pattern of traits that influences behavioural responses.

PERSONALITY CHARACTERISTICS An individual's **personality characteristics** are usually described in terms of traits that influence behaviour. Theoretically, they would seem to be a good basis for segmenting markets. Experience tells us that compulsive people buy differently from cautious consumers, and quiet introverts do not buy the same things nor in the same way as gregarious, outgoing people. However, personality characteristics pose problems that limit their usefulness in practical market segmentation. First, the presence and strength of these characteristics in the population are virtually impossible to measure. For example, how many people in Canada could be classified as outgoing? Another problem is associated with the accessibility condition of segmentation. There is no advertising medium that provides unique access to a particular personality type. That is, television reaches introverts as well as extroverts, aggressive people as well as timid people. So one of the major goals of segmentation, to avoid wasted marketing effort, is not likely to be accomplished using personality as a basis for market segmentation.

Nevertheless, many firms tailor their advertising messages to appeal to certain personality traits. Even though the importance of the personality dimension in a particular decision may be unmeasurable, the seller believes that it does play an influential role. Thus we see products and services advertised to consumers who are "on the way up," or are "people with taste," or who "want to break away from the crowd."

lifestyle
A person's activities, interests, and opinions.

LIFESTYLES The term **lifestyle** is a broad concept that sometimes overlaps personality characteristics. Being cautious, skeptical, ambitious, a workaholic, a copycat—are these personality or lifestyle traits? Lifestyles relate to your activities, interests, and opinions. They reflect how you spend your time, what books you read, which television programs, specialty channels, or DVDs you watch, where you surf on the Internet, where you spend your leisure time and your money, as well as what your beliefs are on various social, economic, and political issues.

There is no commonly accepted terminology of lifestyle categories for segmenting markets. Nevertheless, people's lifestyles undoubtedly affect their choice of products and their brand preferences. Marketers are well aware of this and often attempt to segment their markets on a lifestyle basis.

As consumer tastes and lifestyles have changed in recent years, most companies have had to make adjustments in their products and services to ensure that they remained attractive to their target customers. One company that has taken an aggressive approach in the retail industry is Nike (www.nike.com). Back in the 1980s, the advertising of this company set out to define the meaning of "cool" for millions of teenagers. Today, Nike is continuing to capture lifestyle images with the introduction of Nike Towns — single-brand stores — set up to reflect and represent the brand's desire to appear action-oriented and "with it." These stores are decorated in cyber-age video glyphs with screens showing athletes continuously in motion giving visitors the complete brand experience. This "experiential" chain of shops is directly targeted at the young, athletic consumer who responds positively to the electronic age.[2]

Launched in 1994, Banff Ice Vodka sales have grown by double-digit rates for the last five years. Quite a task considering that distilled spirits have had flat or declining numbers in recent years. It is now internationally recognized, having received awards for both its packaging and the product inside. After all, who better than Canadians to know how to make things from ice?[3] (See "Marketing at Work" File 5-1.)

Although it is a valuable marketing tool, lifestyle segmentation has some of the same serious limitations ascribed to segmentation based on personality characteristics. It is very difficult to measure accurately the size of lifestyle segments in order to determine

Marketing at Work 5-1

A Smooth Beverage With a Rough Edge

Banff Ice, launched in 1994, is one of the most successful Canadian-made vodkas introduced in the last decade. The brand experienced double-digit growth each year since its introduction and has received awards for both the packaging and the product. How the brand was being positioned and communicated to consumers, however, still needed some attention.

The company had always leveraged its geographic origins in its advertising by showing the snow-capped Rocky Mountains that are typically associated with the Banff region. The tagline "The world is turning to ice" linked the visuals in the advertising to the trend in the beverage alcohol category created by product introductions such as ice beer and ice wine. Other ads focused on the cold-filtered, triple-distillation process used in making the product and used the tagline "The Ultimate in Smoothness."

Although these features were important to consumers, research showed that the images portrayed in the advertising were not relevant and even alienated some. Consumers wanted the brand to have a personality that reflected their lives, or at least what they perceived their lives to be like.

The target group was identified as male, legal drinking age through 30, with an active lifestyle and an attitude. The new campaign therefore had to reflect the history and features of Banff Ice while being young, contemporary, edgy, and having a sense of humour.

The new campaign mirrored the product's origin and smoothness portrayed in the first campaign, but with an edge. The ads used illustrations from the 1920s to showcase the product's retro side and the new tagline "Smooth Vodka from a Rough Place" to highlight its contemporary positioning, humour and edginess. The ads appeared in urban weeklies such as *Now* in Toronto, the *Georgia Strait* in Vancouver and *Fast Forward* in Calgary, as well as in *Shift* magazine and restroom advertising.

The result was an ad campaign that people noticed and remembered. This translated into a more widely recognized brand for Banff Ice and share and volume growth throughout 1999.

Source: Adapted from Jan Field, "Ice With Edge," *Marketing Magazine*, February, 7, 2000, p. 17.

Smooth, yet rough.

their viability. Another problem that may affect the marketer's ability to deal with specific lifestyle segments relates to their accessibility. Although certain of the mass media (particularly magazines and television) offer options that appeal to particular lifestyle groups, such options for advertising may be out of the cost range of many smaller companies, making it difficult for them to reach their lifestyle targets in a cost-effective manner.

psychographics
A concept in consumer behaviour that describes consumers in terms of a combination of psychological and sociological influences.

PSYCHOGRAPHICS   The term **psychographics** was coined to describe a wide variety of psychological and behavioural descriptions of a market. The development of psychographics evolved from attempts by marketers to find measures more directly related to purchase and consumption than demographics.

Values are one such descriptor. According to psychologists, values are a reflection of our needs adjusted for the realities of the world in which we live. Research at the Survey Research Center at the University of Michigan has identified nine basic values that relate to purchase behaviour. The nine, which they call the **List of Values (LOV)**, are:[4]

◆   Self-respect.

◆   Self-fulfilment.

◆   Security.

◆   Sense of belonging.

◆   Excitement.

◆   Sense of accomplishment.

◆   Fun and enjoyment in life.

◆   Being well-respected.

◆   Having warm relationships.

While most people view all these values as desirable, their relative importance differs among people and their importance changes over a person's life. For example, people who value fun and enjoyment especially like skiing, dancing, bicycling, and backpacking, and people who value warm relationships give gifts for no particular reason. Thus, the relative strength of values could be the basis for segmenting a market.

Probably the best-known psychographic segmentation tool is VALS, developed in 1978 by the research firm SRI International (www.sri.com) and redesigned in 1990 as VALS2.[5] The **VALS** system was developed from a large study that divided adults into nine segments based on similarities in their values (beliefs, desires, and prejudices), attitudes, and their lifestyles — hence, the VALS acronym.

Relationship Segmentation

With the increased attention being paid to customer relationships in marketing, many companies are focusing on segmenting their customer base in terms of the kind of relationship their customers currently have with a company or the kind of relationship they would like to have. In recent years, many progressive companies have come to realize that the long-term future of their operations is very much linked to the extent to which they are able to develop appropriate relationships with customers. Those customers that perceive a relationship to exist are more likely to remain customers, more likely to spend more money with the company, and to refer other customers.

But not all customers want the same kind of relationship. While some want to feel very close to a company and to develop something approaching a friendship with a company and its employees, others will be content with a more distant and business-like relationship. Similarly, some customers want to hear from a company frequently with information about new products and services or simply to be asked if there is anything they need. Others simply don't want to hear from a company very often. Their view is that the company simply has to be there when needed; they don't want what they would consider "in-your-face" service.

It is extremely important, if a company intends to practise relationship marketing, that it develops appropriate relationships with customers so that their satisfaction is increased and they remain loyal customers. To do so requires a detailed understanding of the type of relationship that customers will find satisfying and a strategy to deliver different kinds of relationships with different segments of customers.

Behavioural Segmentation

behavioural segmentation
Market segmentation based on consumers' product-related behaviour, typically the benefits desired from a product and the rate at which the consumer uses the product.

Some marketers regularly attempt to segment their markets on the basis of product-related behaviour — they utilize **behavioural segmentation**. This section briefly considers two of these bases for segmentation: the benefits desired from a product, and the rate at which the consumer uses the product.

BENEFITS DESIRED Russell Haley is credited with drawing attention to the notion of benefit segmentation when he described a hypothetical division of the toothpaste market based on the **benefits desired**. The segment names, the benefits sought by each segment, and the likely preferred brands were:

◆ Sensories: flavour and appearance — Colgate or Stripe.

◆ Sociables: brightness of teeth — Macleans or Ultra Brite.

◆ Worriers: decay prevention — Crest.

◆ Independents: low price — any brand on sale.[6]

If Haley were to prepare a similar division today, he might include "plaque control" as a fifth benefit segment. As the marketplace became newly aware of the problem of plaque this certainly must have given the "worriers" something new to be concerned about, sending them into a panic to select a new toothpaste!

Two things determine the effectiveness of benefit segmentation. First, the specific benefits consumers are seeking must be identified. This typically involves several research steps, beginning with the identification of all possible benefits related to a particular product or behaviour through brainstorming, observing consumers, and listening to focus groups. Then, more focus groups are conducted to screen out unlikely or unrealistic benefits and to amplify and clarify the remaining possibilities. Finally, large-scale surveys are conducted to determine how important the benefits are and how many consumers seek each one.

To illustrate, the ExxonMobil Corporation (www.exxon.mobil.com) conducted a market segmentation study of gasoline buyers to determine how to design its gasoline stations. The study identified five primary segments. Contrary to conventional wisdom, only one, accounting for about 20 percent of the buyers, consisted of price shoppers. To attract the four more profitable non-price segments, Mobil has begun offering things that appeal to them — quick service with features such as Speedpass® that enables customers to be identified and billed by waving a special key-chain across the pump. This personal ID is linked to a credit card for payment. Also emphasized are nicer snack foods, a personal touch, privileges for regular customers and cleaner facilities.[7]

A second task, once the marketer has identified the various benefits that are to be used to segment the overall market, is to develop detailed **profiles** of each of the market segments that has been identified. The purpose of the profiling exercise is to develop as detailed an overview as possible of the consumers who make up each of the segments of interest, in terms of their demographic, psychographic, and lifestyle characteristics. The main premise behind this profiling is, the better we know the customers in each of the segments we plan to target, the more likely it is that we can put together an integrated marketing program that they will find attractive. This will, therefore, lead them to buy our products or services, and will keep them coming back to do business with us in the future. We indicated earlier that "accessibility" is a requirement for successful segmentation. Only by knowing as much as we can about our target customers can we possibly know how to reach them with our marketing messages.

Another approach to benefit segmentation that has become popular in the last twenty years is segmenting the market based on the occasions that customers would associate with the use of the product or service. There are numerous examples of this type of segmentation. With the ability of the Internet to bring markets to vendors through their use of search engines, this has proliferated as profitable markets can be found for extremely specialized services and products that would not otherwise have been affordable to access a customer base.

Special occasions, such as the rental of a limousine for graduation or a wedding is familiar to most of us. Many restaurants and hotels cater to special occasions by offering special entertainment and all-inclusive rates. Some companies have grown up around meeting special-occasion needs. One such example is The Artful Cookie in St. Catharines,

Ontario. This company specializes in preparing floral-like cookie arrangements, wrapped and presented as flower arrangements. It offers a variety of "bouquets" specifically designed for holidays, anniversaries, and special occasions.[8] In the true entrepreneurial spirit, The Alibi Agency (www.alibi.co.uk) will provide customers with assistance in arranging their illicit encounters. According to its Web site, the agency "can help protect your loved ones from undue anxiety and help ensure the stability of a long-term relationship and financial security by offering secure and professional handling of alibis." Such handling includes phony invitations to corporate events, telephone answering service to provide a choice of alibi background settings, and a buying service that ensures that gifts for the paramour do not appear on credit card statements. The company says it is helping not just philanderers, but their families as well.[9]

usage rate

The rate at which people use or consume a product.

USAGE RATE Another product-related basis for market segmentation is **usage rate** — the rate at which people use or consume a product. Thus we can have categories for nonusers, light users, medium users, and heavy users. Normally a company is most interested in the heavy users of its product. The 50 percent of the people who are the "heavy half" of the users of a product typically account for 80 to 90 percent of the total purchases of a given product or service.

That is not to say that this percentage applies precisely in all product or service categories. Rather, it is the principle that is important. Typically, a company can identify a number of different segments among its target customers. Among these segments, there are usually one or two that contain disproportionately heavier consumers of the product or service. For example, one segment may contain only 15 percent of customers, but these customers may account for 24 percent of all purchases of the company's product. Another segment may have a comparatively smaller number of consumers, accounting possibly for only 8 percent of potential customers, but their consumption patterns may be such that they account for 20 percent of all sales of the product or service. These segments, because they include such heavy consumers, represent important target segments. In such circumstances, most companies would prefer to be the market leader among the heavy users, rather than targeting their marketing efforts at customers who use relatively little of the product.

For example, Heinz's share of the ketchup market has declined as cheaper producers and private-label brands have captured more of this market. To win back customers, Heinz is going after the heavy half of ketchup users — children and teenagers — with a $50 million worldwide advertising campaign. The goals are to build a distinctive personality for Heinz Ketchup and increase usage by providing new ways to use the product. A Web site, Planet Ketchup (www.ketchup.wonderland.org), has also been launched describing some unusual uses in its "sin book." The site is also intended to present a very positive image of the Heinz brand.[10]

The remarkable feature of usage patterns is that they seem to be fairly constant across industries and over time. In most of the situations a marketer might encounter, there are bound to be heavy-user and light-user segments. Thus this segmentation base becomes an effective predictor of future buying behaviour.

Sometimes the target market is the nonuser or light user, and the objective is to woo this customer into a higher-use category. Or light users may constitute an attractive niche for a marketer simply because they are being ignored by other firms that are targeting heavy users. Once the characteristics of these light users have been identified, management can

Marketing at Work 5-2

Kids? Parents? You Have to Reach Both!

When advertising a kid-oriented product who should marketers be talking to? Opinions differ on this point. If the advertising appeals to the end-user, the kids, it risks alienating the purchaser, the parents, and thus won't ever make it into the kids' hands. Alternatively, if the parents like the advertising, that just might be enough to turn the kids off.

Nathalie Rivard, co-founder of Toronto-based youth marketing agency Caktus Communications, says that if kids are the primary customer they must be spoken to in their own language. In some cases this involves extreme imagery or gross-out humour, as used in TV ads for Playland and Pillsbury Pizza Pops, that has the potential to turn some grown-ups off. However, if the approach is softened, or elements that appeal to adults are dialed up, the outcome will probably be a combination that speaks to neither group effectively.

Marketers can also go so far in trying to appeal to kids that they form a barrier of resistance with parents. The key to preventing this according to Susan Mandryk, vice-president of marketing for YTV, is to exercise a modicum of adult judgment. Focus on the primary target, but keep the tone and content of the message within the boundaries that parents feel is acceptable.

This is exactly the approach that Nabisco Canada took in designing the packaging for its Snak Paks — individual-sized packages of Ritz Bits and Teddy Grahams which are targeted to kids under 15. The graphics on the package are designed to appeal to kids, but they found clever ways of incorporating the information that concerns parents. Hence the flash on the package which reads "Made with real cheese."

Most parents generally realize that their kids are consumers too, and can therefore accept that marketers want to make products available to them. They can live with advertising directed at their children as long as it isn't blatant — "Hey kids, go harass your parents to buy this for you."

Source: Adapted from David Todd, "Striking the right balance," *Strategy*, July 5, 1999, p. 17.

---

go to them directly with an introductory low-price offer. Or a marketer might increase usage rates by promoting (1) new uses for a product (baking soda as a deodorant); (2) new times for uses (off-season vacations); or (3) multiple packaging (a 12-pack of soft drinks).

Target-Market Strategies

Let's assume that a company has segmented the total market for its product. Now management is in a position to select one or more segments to which it will target its marketing efforts. The company can follow one of three **target-market strategies**: market aggregation, single-segment concentration, or multiple-segment targeting, as illustrated in Figure 5-1. To evaluate the strategies, management must determine the market potential of each segment that it has identified. But before a strategy is chosen, the potential of the identified segments must be determined. This calls for establishing some guidelines for target-market selection.

Guidelines in Selecting a Target Market

Four guidelines govern how to determine which segments should be the target markets. The first is that target markets should be compatible with the organization's goals and image. One business that is keenly aware of this guideline is Toronto-based Holt Renfrew & Co. (www.holtrenfrew.com) who plans to use its advertising and emphasize its private-label fashions as part of an extensive facelift for the eleven-store chain. In recent years, the older Holt Renfrew stores have undergone renovations to remove the memories of being your "parents' store." As a beacon of high-end fashion, the clothing retailer is attempting to attract younger consumers by increasing private-label offerings varying

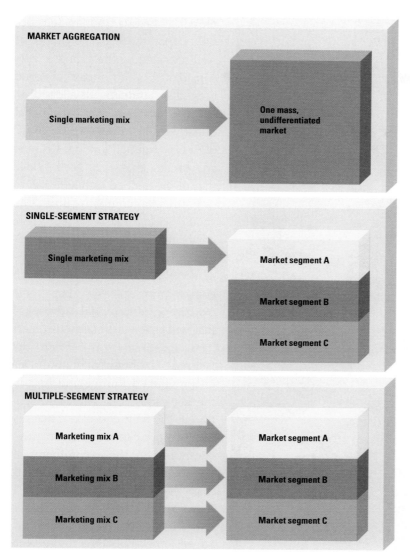

FIGURE 5-1
The Three Target-Market Strategies

from make-up to casual daywear. This has included redesigning the cosmetics department into an open concept design, allowing customers access to the products. Also, to attract existing and new customers alike, the store will utilize more frequent and targeted direct mail throughout the year. The company has also teamed up with successful e-retailers to offer exclusive discounts to tech-savvy customers through the Internet.[11]

A second guideline — consistent with our definition of strategic planning — is to match the market opportunity represented in the target markets with the company's resources. In examining new product opportunities, 3M considered many options but chose the do-it-yourself home improvement market because of the marketing economies that could be achieved. The firm's name was already well known to consumers, and the products could be sold through many of the retail outlets already selling 3M products. Thus, entering this market was much less expensive than entering a market in which 3M was inexperienced. Gerber Products Co. (www.gerber.com) has launched a line of baby products including shampoo, powder, rash ointment, and vitamin drops. Gerber has high expectations for the line as the company has very strong brand recognition. The company began producing baby food in 1928 and currently controls 75 percent of the market.[12] This means that the company has deeply penetrated the distribution channels for such products and therefore wields great power with retailers. These factors mean ease of distribution and consumers eager to try Gerber products.

Over the long run, a business must generate a profit to survive. This rather obvious statement translates into our third market-selection guideline. That is, an organization should seek markets that will generate sufficient sales volume at a low enough cost to result in a profit. Surprisingly, companies often have overlooked profit in their quest for high-volume markets. Their mistake is going after sales volume, not profitable sales volume. Companies that target the higher-yield customer must offer products or services that are perceived by the customer to have value. In some instances a combination of approaches may be beneficial. Tropicana Canada clearly has a product that can be marketed to all segments, however the company has also identified the Canadian Chinese community as a high potential consumer segment. Through research, Tropicana has discovered that Chinese immigrants to Canada who have arrived over the past ten years have a higher

一同樣精彩！	

Tropicana PURE PREMIUM
橙汁之極品

縱然名稱不同　　本質卻同樣優秀出眾
Tropicana 橙汁，源自鮮橙，味道至真至純——橙汁與鮮橙，同樣精彩！

Tropicana PURE PREMIUM
NOT FROM CONCENTRATE

Segmentation by association: oranges for luck

propensity to buy fresh orange juice rather than frozen. The orange is well regarded by the Chinese, who consider it a harbinger of good luck. The company developed an effective advertising program that quickly built awareness and usage of their product among Chinese consumers that was well above that of the general public.[13]

Fourth, a company ordinarily should seek a market where there are the fewest and smallest competitors. A company should not enter a market that is already saturated with competition unless it has some overriding differential advantage that will enable it to take customers from existing firms. When the Häagen-Dazs brand of premium ice cream entered Europe and Asia in the late 1980s, it had little competition at the high end of the market. Because per capita ice cream consumption on these continents is well below that of North America, many viewed the prospects of a high-priced brand in a low-usage market as not very attractive. However, Häagen-Dazs, now with sales well over $500 million, proved the doubters wrong. It wasn't that consumers disliked ice cream; rather, many simply had not been exposed to a high-quality version. By getting to the market first, Häagen-Dazs now has a significant advantage over later entrants.[14] The brand name has developed the strength to allow the company to expand into other, similar high-priced offerings such as frozen yogurt and individual-serving frozen confection "treats."

These are only guidelines. A marketer still has to decide how many segments to pursue as its target market, as we will see next.

Market Aggregation

market aggregation
A strategy whereby an organization treats its total market as a unit — as one mass market whose parts are considered to be alike in all major respects.

By adopting a strategy of **market aggregation**, also known as a mass-market or an undifferentiated-market strategy, an organization treats its total market as a single unit. This unit is one mass, aggregate market whose parts are considered to be alike in all major respects. Management then develops a single marketing program to reach as many customers as possible in this aggregate market. That is, the company develops a single product or service for this mass audience; it develops one pricing structure and one distribution system for its product; and it uses a single promotional program aimed at the entire market.

When is an organization likely to adopt the strategy of market aggregation? Generally when a large group of customers in the total market tends to have the same perception of the product's want-satisfying benefits. Firms that are marketing a non-differentiated, staple product such as gasoline, salt, or sugar often adopt this strategy. In the eyes of many people, sugar is sugar, regardless of the brand. All brands of table salt are pretty much alike, and one unleaded gasoline is about the same as another.

Basically, market aggregation is a production-oriented strategy. It enables a company to maximize its economies of scale in production, physical distribution, and promotion. Producing and marketing one product for one market means longer production runs at lower unit costs. Inventory costs are minimized when there is no (or a very limited) variety of colours and sizes of products. Warehousing and transportation efforts are most efficient when one product is going to one market.

Market aggregation will work only as long as the seller's single marketing mix continues to satisfy enough customers to meet the company's sales and profit expectations. The strategy of market aggregation typically is accompanied by the strategy of product or service differentiation in a company's marketing program. **Product or service differentiation** is the strategy by which one firm attempts to distinguish its product from competitive brands offered to the same aggregate market. By differentiating its product or service, an organization hopes to create the impression that what it offers is better than the competitors' brands. The seller also hopes to engage in non-price competition and thus avoid or minimize the threat of price competition.

A seller implements this strategy either (1) by changing some feature of the product (for example, packaging, colour, or label design, or, in the case of a service, staff image, decor of the establishment, or amount of attention); (2) by using a promotional appeal that features a differentiating benefit; or (3) by using advertising and other promotional strategies to create a differentiating image for the brand, product, or service. The new wave of non-alcoholic beverages splashing into the Canadian beverage market labelled as anything from "energy drink," "power drink," "health beverage," or "herbal cocktail" are distinguishing themselves on cooler shelves with bold names and sleek containers bearing funky graphics and flavour names. This is to position themselves away from traditional soft drinks and bottled waters.[15] Jumbo Video guarantees that the featured "new release" movies will be available when you come to the store and it is that promise that anchors its advertising spots. The popular search engine, Yahoo!, has become a part of the lexicon with "do you Yahoo?" and its irreverent ad images. Vancouver-based Science World decided to go for gross to attract its target segment. It bet correctly that kids would want to come and see its "Grossology" exhibit if marketed correctly — with burping pinball machines and a climbing wall replicating human skin (warts and pimples included) how could they go wrong? Demand was so great that they ended up building a third copy of the exhibit.[16]

Despite the similarity in their products, we know that oil companies do not practise market aggregation. Although the gasoline and many other products that each of them sells are virtually indistinguishable across brands, the major oil companies engage in a number of marketing practices that are intended to attract customers and dispel the impression that they are all alike. Petro-Canada, for example, positions itself as the only true Canadian oil company by showing how it has the only head office located in Canada — it does this, of course, during a blinding snow blizzard in which we can only see blowing snow, but this only emphasizes the point through humour. Sunoco stresses the

product or service differentiation
The strategy in which one firm promotes the features of its product or service over competitors' brands offered to the same market.

high-octane levels of its premium gasoline, indicating that it offers the highest octane rating in the industry, thereby positioning its brands squarely for owners of performance cars. In Western Canada, Mohawk positions itself as an environmentally-friendly oil company, while in the East, Irving Oil portrays itself as a local, down-home firm. In British Columbia, Chevron positions itself as a technologically advanced retailer, offering its customers access to instant payment at the pumps via credit cards. On the other hand, Imperial Oil (Esso) has chosen in recent years to compete for customers on the basis of the service offered at its retail outlets. Reflecting on the factors that affect customer satisfaction that were presented in Chapter 1, we realize that Sunoco is concentrating on differentiating its core product, gasoline. Chevron is differentiating itself by making payment more convenient for its customers, while the others are differentiating their entire company, or their brands, by appealing to customers' higher-order needs.

Differentiation is an important strategy in any situation where there is little difference across the offerings of various companies, or where the consumer is unable to understand or appreciate the differences that do exist. Increasingly, companies are turning to service to differentiate their products and even their companies. With so many products now being perceived by consumers to be quite similar, companies that can offer the best service to their customers are getting the business. In many industries, the highly competitive marketplace brought about by the recession of the early 1990s has forced companies to compete on the basis of service, thereby attempting to set themselves apart from their competitors.[17] British Airways has used this strategy successfully over the past few years. Despite the stiff competition in the airline business, British Airways has consistently outperformed its competitors. According to the former CEO of British Airways, Sir Colin Marshall, an element of the travelling public is willing to pay a slight premium for superior service. One of the things offered by this company is free lounge services to Concorde, First Class, Club World, and Club Europe customers. In addition, it seeks to make all customers feel that they are special by treating them individually in a caring manner. The company uses the phrase "Nothing too small, nothing too big" to let customers know it is looking after their individual needs while simultaneously providing a global service.[18]

Single-Segment Strategy

single-segment concentration strategy
The selection of one homogeneous segment from within a total market to be the target market.

A **single-segment concentration strategy** involves selecting as the target market one homogeneous segment from within the total market. One marketing mix is then developed to reach this single segment. A small company may want to concentrate on a single market segment rather than to take on many competitors in a broad market. One example of this is Lavender Expressions, a Calgary-based greeting card manufacturer. This company is differentiated from other such manufacturers because it develops cards for the gay and lesbian community. The company focuses its products to meet the needs and interests of people who are differentiated by lifestyle. The cards are distributed through specialty shops in forty-eight cities throughout North America.[19]

Modrobes (pronounced "mode robes") clothing provide another example of targeting a very specific target group. Modrobes Saldebus Lounge Clothing Inc. (www.modrobes.com) targets the student population that prefer a casual, baggy, and sort-of retro look. It started with a product Steve "Sal" Debus created for an entrepreneurship project at Brock University in St. Catharines. He thought students needed "exam pants" — something in which you could eat, sleep, get up the next day and go to class in — they were stain-resistant, needed no ironing and dried in ten minutes. Modrobes started in the student

Just the most comfortable ever.

market because it allowed the company to concentrate on a core audience. With a very small marketing budget the company was able to individually sell and service its product line with benefits like a money back guarantee if they were not the most comfortable pants the student had ever owned. The product benefits of the "exam pants'" low maintenance, stain resistant, quick dry, wrinkle resistant and hip styling appealed to the student market but traditional retail outlets did not cater to such a small and geographically widespread segment of the marketplace. By setting up miniature sales booths at universities and colleges across the country, Modrobes was able to reach their customers directly. The advantages of this type of marketing allowed the company to keep in close contact with its customers and out of the sights of much larger companies with larger marketing budgets.

Although, today Modrobes clothing is available in outlets across Canada, the company still concentrates its marketing on small segments of the market and through company-owned Concepts Shops in Toronto and Vancouver. With edgy slogans like "I want you in my pants," Modrobes promotes at concerts, raves, sports events, and campuses and advertises in youth niche magazines such as *Vice* and *Tribe*. The founder/designer Sal Debus still keeps a close handle on how Modrobes are advertised and wants to remain close to their "original market" for product development and trends.[20]

This focused strategy enables a company to penetrate one small market in depth and to acquire a reputation as a specialist or an expert in this limited market. Young consumers that appreciate Modrobes clothing feel that the company "gets them." A company can enter such a market with limited resources, and as long as the single segment remains a small market, large competitors are likely to leave the single-segment specialist alone. However, if the small market shows signs of becoming a large market, bigger companies may well jump in. This is exactly what happened in the market for herbal and specialty teas.

Prior to the 1980s, rose-hip, chamomile, Earl Grey, and similar specialty teas were sold primarily in health-food stores and specialty shops and were available from only a small number of manufacturers and importers. With changing consumer tastes and preferences during the past ten years or so, specialty teas have become more popular. The growth of the herbal and specialty segment was such that new tea companies entered this expanding corner of the market, including some major competitors such as Tetley and Lipton. Changes in the ethnic make-up of the population also caused these companies to import teas such as Yellow Label Tea, which is very popular in Hong Kong and Japan. Such teas have also become popular with non-ethnic markets in Canada.[21] Success of these specialty teas has also spread to the iced tea market where companies such as AriZona have marketed a line of iced green teas in a variety of flavours such as Mandarin Orange and Asia Plum. These are widely available in store coolers alongside soft drinks and bottled waters.

The big risk and limitation to a single-segment strategy is that the marketing firm has all its eggs in one basket. If that single segment declines in market potential, the seller can suffer considerably. Also, a seller with a strong name and reputation in one segment may find it difficult to expand into another segment.

The strategy of not concentrating the entire marketing effort on a single segment is also reflected in other industries. Toyota, Nissan, and Honda have traded their lines up to compete with the higher-priced models of BMW and Mercedes: Toyota with its Lexus line, Nissan with Infiniti, and Honda with its Acura. While, in the meantime, BMW and Mercedes-Benz have focused in recent years on developing models under $40,000. Nike, the massive apparel producer, has slid into snowboarding with the introduction of its own snowboard line featuring a half-pipe, an all-mountain, a speed board, and a lower-priced general board. They also produce bindings and a flexible liner-less boot.[22]

Multiple-Segment Strategy

multiple-segment strategy
A strategy that involves two or more groups of potential customers selected as target markets.

Under a **multiple-segment strategy**, two or more different groups of prospective customers are identified as target markets. A separate marketing mix is developed to reach each segment. A marketer of personal computers, for example, may identify three distinct market segments — university and college students, small businesses, and a home market — and then design a different marketing mix to reach each segment. Apple Computer

Inc. has followed this approach in its recent release of the Emate 300. This computer is designed for students and sells for under US$1,000. It is a stripped-down portable machine, easy to use, with few of the features needed in the corporate or consumer markets. In segmenting the automobile market, General Motors originally developed separate marketing programs for each of its five brands of passenger cars. Likewise, the company had different marketing programs for its Chevrolet and GMC trucks. The five divisions — Chevrolet, Buick, Pontiac, Oldsmobile, and Cadillac — essentially tried to reach the total market for automobiles on a segmented basis. This segmentation has been further enhanced with the addition of the Geo and Saturn brands, each of which is targeted at a different segment than are the five established brands or makes offered by General Motors. The distinction across the various GM brands has diminished over the years, however, as models offered by Chevrolet, Buick, and the others overlap in price, appearance, and features. As a result, the target markets for the brands are no longer clearly defined, and GM brands find themselves increasingly competing with one another.

In a multiple-segment strategy, a seller frequently develops a different version of the basic product for each segment. However, market segmentation can also be accomplished with no change in the product, but rather with separate distribution channels or promotional appeals, each tailored to a given market segment. Wrigley's, for example, targets smokers by promoting chewing gum as an alternative in situations where smoking is unwelcome. Air Wair, the company that markets and distributes Doc Martens footwear (www.drmartens.com), is starting to target an older market segment. To do so, it first made sure that the retailers were aware of how its products can be sold to this segment and encouraged them to carry a broader line. The company also developed a travelling shoeshine booth to feature at charity events across the country. Along with a shine, visitors can view a range of Doc Martens products.[23] The company still features its classic lines, but also has developed products for contemporary business dressing for both men and women. Also, there are sandals and casual all-terrain lines, as well as a children's line. This has allowed the company to continue providing "alternative" footwear choices for existing consumers as they enter different life stages.

 # Positioning

positioning

A company's strategies and actions related to favourably distinguishing itself and its products from competitors in the minds (and hearts) of selected groups of consumers.

The concept of market **positioning** is closely related to segmentation; a marketer must determine how the company's brands or stores or image are perceived by the public in general and more particularly by the segment of the market that has been selected as the principal target. As part of a company's marketing strategy, decisions must be made concerning how the company and its brands are to be portrayed to convey the correct image to the target segment. Positioning, therefore, relates to the use of various marketing techniques and marketing-mix variables to create the image or perception that will best fit with what the company wishes to be known for.

A company may develop a positioning strategy for a particular brand or group of brands, for a retail store or chain, or for the company itself. The process involves answering questions such as: Who are the target-market segments for this brand or store or company? On what basis do we wish to appeal to this segment? What do we want people to think of when they hear our name? What should our brand stand for; what should we mean to people? How do we wish to be seen to be different from our competitors or from other brands or companies in the market? In dealing with questions such as these,

ON WATER OR LAND, ROGER PENSKE HAS
A SPECIAL APPRECIATION OF THINGS MECHANICAL.

INCLUDING HIS YACHT-MASTER.

Roger Penske's passion for brilliant machines extends from engines for sports cars to luxury yachts. It's also reflected in the marvel of engineering he wears on his wrist, the Rolex Yacht-Master.

ROLEX

Rolex Yacht-Master Officially Certified Swiss Chronometer.
For the name and location of an Official Rolex Jeweler near you, please call 1-800-36ROLEX. Rolex, ⑧, Oyster Perpetual and Yacht-Master are trademarks. www.rolex.com

Rolex has always had its positioning correct.

the company is really asking: What position do we wish to occupy in this market?

The company's positioning strategy may be applied at the brand level, at the level of the retail store, or for entire companies. Sun-Rype Products, the largest fruit-products maker in Western Canada, positions its brand as healthy and fresh, with products produced in Canada from Canadian fruit. The company has a line of snack foods, chilled juices and drinks, fortified juices, and 100 percent juices. When this company recently entered the competitive juice market it did so by building on its healthy approach already established in snack foods.[24] Another juice product, this one for those of legal drinking age, is from Toronto-based Corby Distilleries. After extensive research among bartenders and consumers, the new line of coolers dubbed Shocktales is aimed at the entry-level drinker with flavours such as the cranberry infused Broken Down Golf Cart, the Blue Lagoon (vodka with orange and pineapple juices), and the Zombie (rum and pineapple juice). With cooler market growth reaching 150 percent in the last five years, Shocktales is trying to sweeten the way for new drinkers into the market.[25]

Another food company that has successfully positioned itself to compete is New York Fries. This product is sold as a premium fry product. Some people even refer to the product as "designer fries." This company is marketing quality fries described as "with the potato skins on to ensure protein is retained." Though the fries are higher priced, they are purchased because the product is perceived to be distinctive. The brand has developed a "personality" or "image" through its tongue-in-cheek marketing efforts such as its campaign to support the ethical treatment of potatoes. Positioning has also been bolstered by its presence in many of the newly-themed movie megaplexes across the country. The extra value created by this positioning seems to work, as avid buyers of New York Fries are prepared to pay more.[26]

Positioning, therefore, is a strategy for locating a brand or store in the consumer's mind, with respect to its rating on certain dimensions or attributes that the consumer considers important. It involves staking out a place in the collective perception of consumers in which the brand or store or company can establish an image that will be appropriate for certain segments of the market. This image is created through the effective use of marketing-mix variables, including advertising, product design, pricing, packaging, store decor, and level of service.

The creation of the appropriate image may be approached in a combination of ways. In the first place, a firm may wish to occupy a position in a market in relation to that occupied by competitors. It may choose a position that is distinct from that occupied by a competitor or may choose to challenge a competitor directly, thereby trying to occupy roughly the same position. On the other hand, the positioning strategy may be developed so as to position the brand or firm through the creation of an image tailored to the characteristics, preferences, attitudes, and feelings of a particular segment of the market. This approach is dependent on the company having selected certain target segments. The image of the product, brand, or store is then tailored to appeal to those segments.

Finally, a brand or company may be positioned on the basis of its inherent characteristics. In other words, the marketing staff of the company would have to decide what the brand or retailer is to be known for and set about creating the appropriate image. Such an approach deals implicitly with positioning against competition and meeting the needs of particular segments, but is often undertaken in response to the identification of a market gap, where no company has established a dominant position. Bell Canada and the other long-established telephone companies in Canada have chosen to position themselves to some extent on the basis of their inherent characteristics. In competing against their major long-distance competitors, AT&T Canada and Sprint Canada, both of whom are subsidiaries of American companies, the Canadian firms compete as full-service telecommunications providers and "local" companies. Both points of which are claims that should be important to their customers and which cannot be made by the competition.

Positioning Maps

One of the easiest ways to get a feel for the concept of positioning is to examine products, brands, or stores as they are arrayed on a **positioning map**. Such maps are developed through marketing research, which explores the image that consumers have of the various brands or stores in the market and rates each competing brand or store on a series of attributes. In such research, consumers are typically asked to identify the elements of the purchase situation and the product or store attributes that are important in influencing the purchase decision. Once these attributes and elements have been identified, research is undertaken to determine which are most important in influencing the consumer to select one brand over another. Finally, consumers are asked to rate the competing brands or stores in the market on each of the important dimensions or attributes. Such research data allow the researcher to present the brands or stores of interest in a map similar to that shown in Figure 5-2.

The lengths of the lines (or vectors) indicate the relative importance of the attributes, and the position of a brand relative to a vector indicates how closely the brand is associated with the attribute. For example, Calvin Klein jeans are perceived as more expensive than Gap jeans but not as comfortable, while Wranglers are seen as durable but low in status. This map suggests that brands offering comfort and durability at a reasonable price would have little competition from these other brands. Thus, it might be an attractive option.

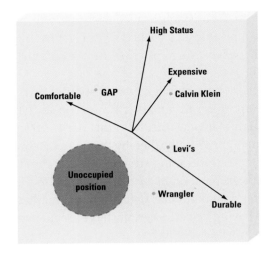

FIGURE 5-2
Perceptual Map of
Jeans Brands

Positioning maps allow the marketer to see where its brand is perceived to lie in the market in comparison with competing brands, how the brand is rated on various attributes, and where the brand lies in relation to the various identified segments. Typically, a number of brands that are perceived to have similar characteristics are clustered together in close proximity to those large segments of the market that have considerable buying power. Other brands occupy positions in the market where they are seen to appeal to different segments and to display different characteristics.

One benefit of examining perceptual market maps is that the marketer can identify how its brand or store is perceived by consumers in comparison with other competitors. Such examination often leads to a decision to reposition a brand, a topic covered later in this chapter. Also, the examination of market maps may lead to the identification of market gaps — positions in the market that are not now filled by existing brands or stores and where untapped market demand may be said to exist. One of the most interesting industries for which to prepare a market map is the restaurant business in any medium-sized to large city. There are usually enough restaurants and residents are sufficiently familiar with many of them that they can rate them on various dimensions, such as price, atmosphere, menu selection, value for money, speed of service, target-market group, and so on. Once such data are collected, a positioning map may be prepared that will identify those restaurants perceived by consumers to be located close to one another and that, therefore, are competing directly with one another. At the same time, it is likely that certain parts of the map will be "empty," suggesting that no restaurants occupy those positions and, therefore, reflecting a gap in the local restaurant market.

Niche Marketing

Some marketers may stake out "niche" positions for their brands; they create an image that is quite distinct and intended to appeal to a fairly narrow segment of the market. Within the Canadian beer market, for example, brands such as Schooner and Celtique, import beers such as Heineken, Guinness, and Corona, and the "handmade" brands are considered to be "niche" brands, while mainstream brands such as Molson Canadian and Labatt's Blue are positioned to appeal to much larger segments. Niche brands generally are not positioned to meet major competitors head-on, but rather to be leaders in a very narrow area of the market. Smaller companies often successfully carve out a niche for themselves. To continue with our beer examples, successful microbrewers such as Upper Canada Brewing, McAuslan Brewing (www.mcauslan.com), Sleeman's, Red Rock, and Granville Island Brewery are really niche marketers; they are satisfied with occupying a relatively small position in a very large market by catering to the tastes and preferences of consumers who want something different.

Sleeman's marketing strategy has enjoyed considerable success with their "chatty" commercials featuring John Sleeman talking informally about his company. The company has conveyed an image of a homespun cottage-industry operation. Brasserie McAuslan of Montreal has brewed an image of good corporate citizenship through community involvement and sponsorship. This has included tie-in promotions with bookstores, the Montreal International Film Festival, on-screen ads in art-house theatres and other ven-

Most micro-brewers stake out niche positions.

niche marketing
A strategy in which goods and services are tailored to meet the needs of small market segments.

ues in synch with their micro-niche market of sophisticated, better-educated-than-average consumers.[27]

Niche marketing is generally a successful strategy for smaller companies that do not have the financial and other resources generally available to large companies. In the travel business, for example, many travel agencies are seeking ways to set themselves apart from their competitors by specializing in narrow parts of the market. As travel has become more complex and travellers more demanding, some travel agencies have found it impossible to serve all segments equally well. Consequently, some become niche players, specializing in cruises, business travel, the ethnic market, or adventure travel. Bestway Tours and Safaris sells tours of South Asia, Central Asia, and the Middle East. It concentrates on providing tours to the least-visited locations on the globe and specializes in ecology and generally soft-adventure experiences. Tourism operators also choose to specialize in the products they provide. For example, Selkirk Tangiers (www.selkirk-tangiers.com) is a company located in the interior of British Columbia that offers only helicopter skiing. The Royal Garden Riverside in Bangkok, Thailand, is owned by the Marriott chain. This hotel is designed to serve the upscale business traveller who wishes to entertain and develop business connections in that country.[28]

Large organizations often target small market niches. For example, the Toronto Dominion Bank (www.tdbank.ca) has developed a service it calls "TD Aboriginal Banking Services." The outlets that deliver the service are located across Canada and are set up to serve clients of the First Nations.[29] To be successful in positioning itself as a niche player in the market, a company or the managers of a niche brand must have identified a segment of the market that is not now being served adequately by the brands and companies that are in the market; that segment must have sufficient potential buying power to warrant the development of a marketing program; it must be sufficiently small that larger companies are unlikely to retaliate if the niche brand is successful; and the niche marketer must have detailed knowledge of the characteristics of the members of the segment and their needs and preferences.

Marketing at Work 5-3

What Shall We Call This One?

Does your cell phone have a name? Is it Mike? Does your personal communication service (PCS) provider have a name? Is it named after that lovable pooch, Fido? It's difficult to imagine that cell phone manufacturers or cellular service providers would try to market their products through market aggregation. After all, what difference really exists between these phones? Sure they come in different colours, but after a while you just get a new one anyway. And how do you give personality to airtime?

Although cell phones have pretty much become a commodity (and almost disposable) product, cellular manufacturers have engaged in a number of marketing practices to attract customers, give their product a little "personality" and dispel the impression that all cell phones are alike. As demand continues to grow, along with different providers and technologies, research shows that consumers have become increasingly indifferent to brands of cell phones.

Nokia decided their marketing challenge was to make the features of their phones relevant to the increasingly diverse user base while customizing the look of the products available. The advertising focused on the notion that Nokia cellular phones complemented one's individuality. This was achieved by leveraging product features in the context of user individuality. The product line is also well known for its varied selection of colours and styles. Mike cellular phones have come to be seen as the perfect communication tool for people who work in groups. As this reputation for being on-the-road and in-the-trenches limited its attractiveness to certain segments, the company decided to target additional consumers such as the more sophisticated white collar professionals by positioning Mike as the ultimate "toy for boys" and the cool tool for power players and tech junkies.

Clearnet PCS, who also brings us Mike, was a late entry into the competitive wireless market in Canada and decided to differentiate itself by positioning Clearnet as the affordable, user-friendly service provider. The objective was to remove

the complexities and perceived barriers to going wireless. This was meant to attract consumers just entering the marketplace and those frustrated with other providers. Montreal-based Microcell Solutions had a similar, but more creative approach to positioning consumer-friendly and loyal service provision with the introduction of Fido. The bilingual term certainly suggests loyalty, obedience, and cozy thoughts of man's best friend as capitalized upon in Microcell's ads for the service. So popular has the service become in Quebec that people are commonly heard saying, "Call me on my Fido." The imagery of Fido is certainly more heart-warming and friendly, with greater associative value for the brand, than Clearnet's little green gecko or Cantel's hairy ape.

Source: Adapted from "From Billy Graham to Durex Condoms," *Strategy*, December 7, 1998, p. B32. Also, Danny Kucharsky, "A Doggone Great Brand," *Marketing Magazine Online*, December 20/27, 1999, www.marketingmag.ca.

One author has suggested that a company should follow four steps in implementing a successful niche marketing strategy.[30]

1. *Identify an appropriate niche* through marketing research that will identify segments of the market that are not being well served by existing brands or where competition is not intense.

2. *Exploit the niche* by determining the likelihood of competitive retaliation and the length of time the company will enjoy a competitive advantage.

3. *Expand the niche* by meeting changing needs of the market segment, expanding the customer base, and making more effective use of marketing variables.

4. *Defend the niche* by continuing to meet the needs of segment members through improving the product and offering better service or lower prices.

Positioning Strategies

positioning
A company's strategies and actions related to favourably distinguishing itself and its products from competitors in the minds (and hearts) of selected groups of consumers.

Once a company has determined its market segmentation objectives and has identified the segments toward which its brands are to be targeted, it may adopt a number of **positioning strategies** to accomplish its objectives.

1. *Take on the competition head-on:* By deciding to challenge the market leader or to target large segments of the market with a broad appeal, a marketer is saying, "Our brand is as good as or better than the leader." Such a strategy is exemplified in the so-called "cola wars," in which Pepsi-Cola and Coca-Cola have been fighting for market leadership by attempting to create the widest appeal to attract as many consumers as possible.

2. *Occupy a gap in the market:* A number of companies have moved to fill a gap in a market by positioning a brand to appeal to a certain segment of consumers or to take advantage of the disappearance of a competitor. For example, Michelin differentiates its tires from those of competitors by emphasizing safety.

3. *Set a brand apart from the competition:* Often a company will decide to employ a strategy that says, "Our brand is not like all the others; this is why you should buy ours." This involves positioning a brand or store so as to avoid head-to-head competition with market leaders or with brands that have an established image or reputation and a secure market share. Small communications companies in the technology sector operating in Canada are avoiding competing with the large giants such as Bell Canada and AT&T. CBCI Telecom in Montreal is concentrating on serving the needs of universities and health-care organizations. It is developing a specialization in these areas rather than fighting with the large companies for overall market share.[31]

4. *Occupy position of leadership:* Some companies that are clearly market leaders are not particularly interested in positioning themselves against the competition, but rather are likely to stake out a position as clear market leader, known to be ahead of the pack and leader in such areas as product quality, service to customers, profitability, innovations, or technology. Companies such as Loblaw, Northern Telecom, and the Royal Bank of Canada tend to be regarded by many consumers as market leaders whose market franchise is so large and well established that competitors often try to emulate them and to position themselves against them.

5. *Position to appeal to lifestyle segments:* Often a company will position itself to appeal to certain segments of the market that are defined not only by demographic characteristics but also by their lifestyles. For example, there are two equally large segments of Porsche buyers with quite different lifestyles and reasons for buying the car. One group is driven by power and control. Called "top guns" at Porsche, they buy the car to be noticed. Another group, the "proud patrons," view a Porsche as a reward for hard work. To them, owning the car is an end in itself. They don't need the acknowledgment of others to derive satisfaction from a Porsche. Clearly, an ad that would appeal to the top guns could easily alienate the proud patrons.[32]

Repositioning

Repositioning is a variation of a positioning strategy that involves changing the market position of a brand or store in response to changes taking place in the broader market environment. The need to reposition a brand or retail store may result from one of three market conditions. First, management may identify a gap in the market that may be filled by altering the image of the store or brand — that is, changing the position it occupies in the minds of consumers. For example, a retailer in a local market may realize that the average age of its customer base is increasing and may decide to reposition the store to have greater appeal to a older market segment.

Second, repositioning may be required by an increase in competitive activity. For example, Canada's retail industry has suffered considerable upheaval with the entry of new U.S. competitors. Birks, of Montreal (www.birks.com), attempted to reposition itself to include in its target market more mid-range shoppers. This, however, was not a successful venture and Birks has once again put a laser-sharp focus on the high-end jewellery market. There are fewer categories of products, a greater depth of inventory, and product exclusivity. An increased emphasis has been placed on staff training and compensation. Service has also been bolstered with a new private corporate shopping service and online ordering. By the end of 2002 all stores should have completed lavish renovations that are expected to cost $30 million.[33] Pharma Plus, a Toronto-based drug store, is undergoing a makeover involving a new store image. This company is positioning itself as a store that focuses on the core product categories of pharmacy, over-the-counter drugs, health and beauty aids, and baby care. This firm is finding it difficult to compete in non-pharmacy items because of the increased number of low-priced chains, such as Wal-Mart (www.wal-mart.com), who can undercut conventional drugstores in these product categories.[34] Zellers (www.hbc.com/zellers/) has responded to Wal-Mart by renewing focus on its loyalty program and by introducing "best-value" format stores that offer convenience through smaller store sizes located in densely-populated areas, offering fewer SKUs then regular outlets, and "awesome deals" not possible from large chain stores.[35]

Harry Rosen Inc. (www.harryrosen.com), known for its selection of professional business-wear has had to respond to changes in the workplace that began with casual Fridays and has spread through the week. Rosen has continued to provide traditional formal apparel, even celebrating it in a campaign featuring what well-known Canadians will be attired in for particular occasions, but they have also adapted by repositioning themselves as a source for fashionable casual business wear. To achieve a congruent position in the casual business-wear market they have developed a guide to dressing casually. These efforts have has been well integrated with their repositioning efforts to appeal to a younger demographic.[36]

Third, it may be necessary to reposition a brand or store in response to a change in the demographic characteristics or attitudes or values of the target consumer market. Packaged-food producers have addressed these trends in recent years as a result of significant changes in eating habits. High-fat foods are no longer appealing to mass markets. This is becoming particularly evident now that labels must carry information on package contents, and customers can easily determine the contents in the supermarket. Heinz, RJR Nabisco, Kraft, and other major packaged-food suppliers are creating new products such as Life-Savers Delites, Budget Gourmet, and Snack Wells to respond to these changing consumer tastes and values.[37]

Another change has been in the demand for "convenience" foods or "meal solutions." This has led manufacturers and supermarkets to alter their product offerings. Manufacturers have increased the number of meal "kits" they offer including prepared frozen main courses that require only cooking or to have added a certain amount of the consumer's meat of choice. The "deli" sections of supermarkets have expanded to offer consumers greater selections of Home Meal Replacements (HMR). An HMR is any frozen or fresh meal prepared in-store for immediate consumption at home.[38] This includes items as varied as salad-in-a-bag to prepared entrees bought by the kilogram to individual meal packages that have main and side dishes pre-selected.

forecasting market demand
The estimating of the sale of a product during a defined future period.

Forecasting Market Demand

As the final step in selecting its target markets, a company should forecast the market demand for its product or service. **Forecasting market demand** is estimating the sale of a product during some defined future period. Forecasting is done to make various kinds of predictions. For example, a forecast can refer to an entire industry (such as apparel), to one firm's product line (Levi casual wear), or to an individual brand (Levi 501 jeans). Thus, for a forecast to be understood, it is important to make very clear what it describes.

market factor
An item or element that (1) exists in a market, (2) may be measured quantitatively, and (3) is related to the demand for a good or service.

market index
A market factor expressed as a percentage, or in another quantitative form, relative to some base figure.

market potential
The total sales volume that all organizations selling a product during a stated time period in a specific market could expect to achieve under ideal conditions.

sales potential
The portion of market potential, applying only to one company's brand of a product, that a specific company could expect to achieve under ideal conditions.

sales forecast
An estimate of likely sales for one company's brand of a product during a stated time period in a specific market and assuming the use of a predetermined marketing plan.

Basic Forecasting Terms

This section defines some terms so that the discussion will be easier to follow.

MARKET FACTOR AND MARKET INDEX A **market factor** is an item or element that (1) exists in a market, (2) is measurable, and (3) is related to the demand for a product in a known way. To illustrate, the "number of cars three years old and older" is a market factor related to the demand for replacement tires that can be sold. A market index is simply a market factor expressed as a percentage or some other quantitative form. To illustrate, one market factor is "households owning appliance X"; in 2000, the **market index** for this factor was 142 (relative to 1980 equals 100). An index may also be composed on multiple market factors, such as the number of cars three years old and older, population, and disposable personal income.

MARKET POTENTIAL AND SALES POTENTIAL **Market potential** is the total sales volume that all organizations selling a product during a stated period of time in a specific market could expect to achieve under ideal conditions. **Sales potential** (synonymous with market share) is the portion of market potential that a specific company could expect to achieve under ideal circumstances. For example, market potential applies to all refrigerators, but sales potential refers only to a single brand of refrigerators (such as Whirlpool).

With either of these measures of potential, the market may encompass whatever group or area interests the forecaster. It could be the world, one country, or a smaller market defined by income or some other basis. For example, we may speak of the market potential for refrigerators in the Atlantic Provinces.

SALES FORECAST A **sales forecast** is an estimate of probable sales for one company's brand of a product during a stated period in a specific market. Like measures of market potential, a sales forecast can be expressed in dollars or product units.

Marketing at Work 5-4

Cybershoppers are Not Just Busy People

Peachtree Network Inc. planned to spend almost a million dollars in 2000 urging non-cybershoppers to buy their groceries online. The Montreal-based online grocery portal currently operates in sixteen markets across Canada and the U.S. but wants to broaden its user base beyond "Web-heads."

Online grocers have been struggling to capture a significant share of the offline grocery market, so Peachtree has been placing a heavy emphasis on customer research to better understand its potential user base. The goal is to learn who shops online and why, so that the company can grab a bigger chunk of Canada's $55 billion grocery market.

Peachtree traditionally segmented the market into three groups: busy people, people with mobility difficulties, and nerds. After delving into the minds and lives of the "busy people" just a little, Peachtree quickly realized that its division of the market was still very broad. For example, they discovered that people in Vancouver are more likely to shop online for positive reasons like being able to spend more time with their kids. Conversely, Torontonians are more likely to shop online to avoid negatives such as long lineups or their cars being dinged in the crowded parking lots.

Peachtree is now undertaking a lifestyle segmentation project so that it can speak knowledgeably and meaningfully to each potential user group. It further plans to adjust its advertising campaign in each market to reflect its unique differences.

Source: Adapted from Craig Saunders, "Peachtree invests in brand-building," *Strategy*, March 27, 2000, p. 1.

THE SALES FORECAST AND THE MARKETING PLAN The marketing goals and broad strategies — the core of a marketing plan — must be established before a sales forecast is made. That is, the sales forecast depends on these predetermined goals and strategies. Certainly, different sales forecasts will result, depending on whether the marketing goal is (1) to liquidate an excess inventory of product A or (2) to expand the firm's market share by aggressive advertising.

However, once the sales forecast is prepared, it does become the key controlling factor in all operational planning throughout the company. The scheduling of all production resources and facilities, such as setting labour needs and purchasing supplies and materials, depends on the sales forecast.

Methods of Forecasting Demand

Following are some commonly used methods of forecasting demand.

MARKET-FACTOR ANALYSIS In many situations, future demand for a product is related to the behaviour of certain market factors. When this is true, we can forecast future sales by studying the behaviour of these market factors. Basically, **market-factor analysis** entails determining what these factors are and then measuring their relationship to sales activity. Successful identification of the relevant factors is crucial.

market-factor analysis
A sales forecasting method based on the assumption that future demand for a product is related to the behaviour of certain market factors.

DIRECT DERIVATION Let's illustrate the use of this relatively simple method to estimate market potential. Suppose that a manufacturer of automobile tires wants to know the market potential for replacement tires in Canada in 2002. The primary market factor is the number of automobiles on the road. The first step is to estimate how many cars are likely prospects for new tires. Assume (1) that the seller's studies show that the average car is driven about 16,000 km a year and (2) that the average driver gets about 45,000 km from a set of four tires. This means that all cars that become three years old during 2002 can be considered a part of the potential market for replacement tires during that year. The seller can obtain a reasonably accurate count of the number of cars sold in 1999 from provincial licensing offices. (These are the cars that will become three years old in 2002.) In addition, the seller can determine how many cars will become six, nine, or twelve years old in 2002. (These ages are multiples of three. That is, a six-year-old car presumably would be ready for its second set of replacement tires.) The number of cars in these age brackets times four (tires per car) should give a fair approximation of the market potential for replacement tires in 2002. We are, of course, dealing in *averages*. Not all drivers will get 45,000 km from a set of tires, and not all cars will be driven exactly 16,000 km per year.

CORRELATION ANALYSIS This technique is a mathematical refinement of the direct-derivation method. When correlation analysis is used, the degree of association between potential sales of the product and the market factor is taken into account. In effect, a correlation analysis measures, on a scale of 0 to 1, the variations between two series of data. Consequently, this method can be used only when a lengthy sales history of the industry or firm is available, as well as a history of the market factor. For example, the data series might be the number of dogs registered in Penticton, B.C., each year from 1981 to 2001, and the sales of canned dog food in Penticton in the corresponding years.

Correlation analysis gives a more exact estimate of market demand, provided that the method is applied correctly. In direct derivation, the correlation measure is implicitly assumed to be 1.00. But rarely does this perfect association exist between a market factor and the sales of a product. Correlation analysis therefore takes the past history into account in predicting the future. It also allows a researcher to incorporate more than one factor into the formula.

This method is somewhat more sophisticated than others. It requires a good deal of data and assumes that market conditions will remain the same. Today, in some sectors this cannot be safely assumed.

survey of buyer intentions
A form of sales forecasting in which a firm asks a sample of current or potential customers how much of a particular product they would buy at a given price during a specified future time period.

SURVEYS OF BUYER INTENTIONS Another commonly used method of forecasting is to survey a sample of potential customers. These people are asked how much of the stated product or service they would buy or use at a given price during a specified future time period. Some firms maintain consumer panels on a continuing basis to act as a sounding board for new-product ideas, prices, and other features.

A major problem is that of selecting the sample of potential buyers. For many consumer products, a very large, and thus very costly, sample would be needed. As well, it is one thing for a consumer to state an intention to buy, however it is another for him or her to actually follow through.

Surveys of buyer intentions are probably most effective when (1) there are relatively few buyers; (2) these buyers are willing to express their buying intentions; and (3) their past record shows that their follow-up actions are consistent with their stated intentions.

test marketing
A marketing research technique in which a firm markets its product in a limited geographic area, measures the sales, and then — from this sample — projects (a) the company's sales over a larger area and/or (b) consumers' response to a strategy before committing to a major marketing effort.

TEST MARKETING In using this technique, firms market their products in a carefully selected, limited geographic area. Then, from this sample the companies project sales potential (market share) over a larger area. **Test marketing** is frequently used in deciding whether sufficient sales potential exists for a new product. The technique also serves as a basis for evaluating various product features and alternative marketing strategies.

The outstanding benefit of test marketing is that it can identify how many people actually buy the product, instead of only how many say they intend to buy. If a company can afford the time and money for this method and can run a valid test, this is the best way of measuring the potential for its product.

Test marketing is expensive in time and money. Great care is needed to control the test-marketing experiment. A competitor, learning that a company is test marketing, is usually adept at "jamming" the experiment. That is, by unusual promotional or other marketing efforts, a competitor can create an artificial situation that distorts test results. To avoid such test-market "wars," some companies use simulations of test markets. In effect, these marketers are conducting a test market in a laboratory, rather than in the field.[39]

past-sales and trend analysis
A method of sales forecasting that applies a flat percentage increase to the volume achieved last year, or to the average volume of the past few years, to predict future volume.

PAST SALES AND TREND ANALYSIS   A favourite method of forecasting is to base the estimate entirely on **past sales**. This technique is simple, inexpensive, and easy to apply. For a firm operating in a stable market, where its market share has remained constant for a period of years, past sales alone might be used to predict future volume. On balance, however, the method is highly unreliable. **Trend analysis** is a variation of forecasting based on past sales, but it is a bit more complicated. It involves either (1) a long-run projection of the sales trend, usually computed by statistical techniques, or (2) a short-run projection (forecasting for only a few months ahead) based upon a seasonal index of sales. The statistical sophistication of long-run trend analysis does not really remove the inherent weakness of basing future estimates only on past sales activity. Short-run trend analysis may be acceptable if the firm's sales follow a reliable seasonal pattern.

sales force composite
A method of forecasting sales that consists of collecting from all sales-people and intermediaries an estimate of sales in their territories during the forecasting period.

SALES-FORCE COMPOSITE   This is a buildup method that may be used to forecast sales or to estimate market potential. As used in sales forecasting, the **sales-force composite** method consists of collecting from all salespeople and intermediaries an estimate of sales in their territories during the forecasting period. The total (the composite) of these separate estimates is the company's sales forecast. This method can be used advantageously if the firm has competent, high-calibre salespeople. It is also useful for firms selling to a market composed of relatively few, but large, customers. Thus, this method would be more applicable to sales of large electrical generators than small general-use motors.

The sales-force composite method takes advantage of the salespeople's specialized knowledge of their own market and helps them understand how their sales quotas are determined.

executive judgment
A method of sales forecasting that consists of obtaining opinions regarding future sales volume from one or more executives.

EXECUTIVE JUDGMENT   This method covers a wide range of possibilities. Basically, it consists of obtaining opinions regarding future sales volume from one or more executives. If these are really informed opinions, based on valid measures such as market-factor analysis, then the **executive judgment** is useful and desirable. Certainly all the previously discussed forecasting methods should be tempered with sound executive judgment. On the other hand, forecasting by executive opinion alone is risky. In some instances, such opinions are simply intuition or guesswork.

Summary

One of the most important lessons to be learned concerning the use of market segmentation as a marketing strategy is to get beyond the rather simplistic geographic and demographic bases for segmenting a market. Many marketers today are successful in segmenting markets on psychographic and product-usage bases, which involve targeting products and services at groups of consumers based on their personality and lifestyle characteristics and on why they select a product, how much of it they use, or how often they buy it.

A marketer can choose from three alternative segmentation strategies when selecting a target market: market aggregation, single-segment concentration, or multiple segmentation. Market aggregation involves using one marketing mix to reach a mass, undifferentiated market. In single-segment concentration, a company still uses only one marketing mix, but it is directed at only one segment of the total market. The third alternative involves selecting two or more segments and then developing a separate marketing mix to reach each one.

The concept of market positioning involves developing a position for a product, brand, retail store, or company in the minds of the members of the target segment or even in the minds of the general public. In essence, it involves management asking what they want the brand or store to be known for, as compared with the customer's image of the competition; what do they want consumers to think of when they hear the brand or store name? The task of creating the right position or image for a brand or store is accomplished through strategic use of the marketing mix variables.

One of the most effective ways to determine the current position that a brand or store occupies in the consumer's mind is to develop a positioning map based on research into consumer perceptions of the various competitors in the market. Such maps may be used to identify gaps in the market, to determine whether there exists a niche toward which a brand may be directed, and to identify a need to reposition a brand for some other reason.

A company may take a number of approaches to position a brand, a retail store, or the company itself in the minds of target consumers: (1) it may decide to meet competitors head on; (2) it may reposition a brand to occupy a gap in the market; (3) it may decide to distance a brand from its main competitors; (4) it may stake out a position as the market leader; or (5) it may position a brand to appeal to certain lifestyle segments. Often a decision is made to reposition a brand or store because of changes that have taken place within the market environment. Decisions to reposition may result from the identification of a market gap, an increase in competitive activity, or a decision to respond to changing consumer demographics, attitudes, and values.

Before deciding on a target market, the company should forecast the demand in the total market and in each segment under consideration. Demand forecasting involves measuring the industry's market potential, then determining the company's sales potential (market share), and finally preparing a sales forecast. The sales forecast is the foundation of all budgeting and operational planning in all major departments of a company. There are several major methods available for forecasting market demand.

Key Terms and Concepts

Psychological segmentation 124

Personality characteristics 124

Lifestyle 124

Psychographics 126

List of Values (LOV) 126

VALS 127

Behavioural segmentation 127

Benefits desired 127

Profiles 128

Usage rate 129

Target-market strategies 130

Market aggregation 132

Product or service differentiation 133

Single-segment concentration strategy 134

Multiple-segment strategy 136

Positioning 137

Positioning map 139

Niche marketing 141

Positioning strategies 143

Repositioning 144

Forecasting market demand 145

Market factor and market index 145

Market potential and sales potential 145

Sales forecast 145

Market-factor analysis 146

Surveys of buyer intentions 147

Test marketing 147

Past sales and trend analysis 148

Sales-force composite 148

Executive judgment 148

Questions and Problems

1. Consult back issues of your local newspaper and a number of consumer magazines to identify examples of companies that are positioning their brands to appeal to target lifestyle segments of the consumer market. Identify examples of other brands that are targeted at consumers on the basis of product usage.

2. Explain the similarities and differences between a single-segment and a multiple-segment target-market strategy.

3. How might the following organizations implement the strategy of market segmentation?
   a. Dell Computers.
   b. Canadian Red Cross.
   c. Vancouver Aquarium.
   d. Upper Canada Brewing Company.

4. Assume that a company has developed a new type of portable headphone-type cassette player in the general product category of a Sony Walkman. Which of the three target-market strategies should this company adopt?

5. What positioning strategy has each of the following marketers chosen?
   a. Mark's Work Wearhouse.
   b. Your provincial liquor board or corporation.
   c. IKEA furniture stores.
   d. Colgate toothpaste.
   e. Toronto Dominion Bank.
   f. Oh Henry! chocolate bar.

6. Identify a number of brands, retailers, or restaurants with which you are familiar that have chosen to occupy a niche in the market. How would you describe the niche each occupies? Why do you feel each has chosen this niche?

7. Why would a company decide that one of its brands needs to be repositioned? What market conditions are likely to lead to a decision to reposition a brand or company? Can you think of any brands or stores with which you are familiar that have recently been repositioned? What were their original positions? How would you describe the new position each occupies in the market? How was the repositioning accomplished in each case?

8. Carefully distinguish between market potential and a sales forecast, using examples of consumer or business-to-business products.

9. What are some logical market factors that you might use in estimating the market potential for each of the following products?
   a. Central home air conditioners.
   b. Symphony tickets.
   c. Golf clubs.
   d. A visit to Canada's Wonderland.
   e. Safety goggles.

10. How would you determine the market potential for a textbook written for the introductory course in marketing?

11. Explain the direct-derivation method of sales forecasting, using a product example other than automobile tires. How does this forecasting method differ from the correlation-analysis method?

12. What are some of the problems a researcher faces when using the test-market method for determining market potential or sales potential?

Hands-On Marketing

1. Identify a number of brands of breakfast cereal (both hot and cold) available in supermarkets in your town or city, and indicate how each of the brands is differentiated and how each is positioned to appeal to a specific segment of the market.

2. Prepare a positioning map of the restaurants in the area around your college or university. On what dimensions should the restaurants be positioned? What gaps in the market have you identified?

Chapter Six

Social and Psychological Influences on Buyer Behaviour

In Chapters 4 and 5, our discussions of market segmentation and positioning focused on the target market. In this chapter, we consider the consumer's willingness to buy as determined by information sources, social environment, psychological forces, and situational factors.

After studying this chapter, you should have an understanding of:

◆ The process consumers go through in making purchasing decisions.

◆ The importance of commercial and social information sources in buying decisions.

◆ The influence of culture, subcultures, and social class characteristics on buying behaviour.

◆ The direct impact of reference groups on buying behaviour.

◆ Family and household buying behaviour.

◆ The roles of motivation, perception, learning, personality, and attitudes in shaping consumer behaviour.

◆ The importance of situational factors in buying.

Bugaboos: Function or Fashion?

Why aren't all sunglasses the same? — They all go in the same place and serve the same function! But they don't really, do they? Sunglasses don't really have that much to do with UV protection — today, they provide for us an opportunity to express ourselves and our individuality. Or for others it's a look that says my friends and I have the same kinds of glasses or have a certain image — cool! Today's styles allow people to do this in an on your face, in your face sort of way.

How else could Bugaboos Eyewear, named for the famous B.C. mountain range, successfully carry their extreme styled UV protection under six different brands each reflecting its own image and personality? (www.bugaboos.com). Lines such as Hardcore, Diva, Why, Ryders, Area Unlimited, and kidz are each designed to appeal to a different consumer sensibility.

Sunglasses have long been a fashion accessory but in recent years have become especially popular in youth and young adult markets as "extreme"

accessories for extreme fashions and sport activities.

As we said, cool shades are still cool — and the young, irreverent image portrayed in Bugaboos marketing hits all the psychological and social cues to appeal to

IS YOUR DAUGHTER HOME?

today's youth markets, as well as those who still wish they were. Marketing elements combine to manipulate the social and psychological makeup of the consumer to identify with the images and people presented. The situations are similar to, or represent, what the target segment desires. The image of the company and the activities in which it involves itself represent a lifestyle desirable to the target consumer.

The *Ryders Eyewear* line has an image which relies on its advertising and sponsorship of all types of bike sports, water sports and beach volleyball. There is also a small golf line, a sport increasing in popularity among younger demographics in North America. Clearly, such images will appeal to young extreme bikers and boarders as they attempt to *be* the images they see portrayed and be a part of the cool crowd. The "technical features" of the glasses represent the product as cutting edge and serve to offer a value proposition that justifies paying a few extra dollars for the product.

The ladies line of *Diva* sunglasses offers a "chic yet sporty feel," "funky and modern with retro flair" suitable to wear all year round. The *Diva* images will attract the female segment wishing to demonstrate the same flair for UV protection as the guys. *Hardcore* products are aimed at mountain sports such as boarding and for street wear. *Area Unlimited* gears itself to the "café culture" lifestyle, while *Why* sunglasses are fashion oriented for the older in this segment with special attention to technical features and "vibes that beat to an emerging global rhythm."

Each with a distinct personality, the different Bugaboos lines are sure to appeal to some segment of trendy young consumers. With distinctive brand labels, these become the insignia of the identity that has come to be represented in the consumer's mind by that pair of sunglasses. Image and style elements are important in influencing consumers to purchase nonessential goods such as this. Marketers such as Nike, and Sony have successfully demonstrated this for the past several years.[1]

As this discussion of consumer influence illustrates, marketing has become more complicated. The reasons are simple. Consumers have become more sophisticated and demanding, the domestic and international marketplaces have become more competitive and more technologically complex, and the full impact of e-commerce is unpredictable at this time. However, our understanding of consumer buying behaviour continues to improve. But there is still much more to learn. And because marketing success largely depends on the ability to anticipate what buyers will do, in this chapter we examine the challenging topic of consumer buying behaviour. First we develop an overview by describing the buying-decision process. Next we consider the sources of information used by consumers — without information there are no decisions. We then describe the various social and group forces in society that influence decision-making and the psychological characteristics of the individual that affect the decision process in buying. In the final section, our focus shifts to the significant role that situational factors play in buying decisions.

FIGURE 6-1

The Consumer Buying-Decision Process and the Factors That Influence It

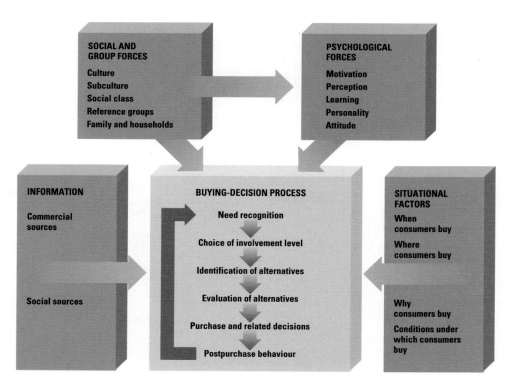

Figure 6-1 brings all the dimensions of buying behaviour together in a model that provides the structure for our discussion. The model features a six-stage **buying-decision process** influenced by four primary forces.

The Buying-Decision Process

buying-decision process
The series of logical stages a prospective purchaser goes through when faced with a buying problem. The stages differ for consumers and organizations.

To deal with the marketing environment — whether on the ground or in cyberspace — and to make purchases, consumers must engage in a decision process. The process, which divides nicely into six stages, can be thought of as a problem-solving approach. When faced with a buying problem ("I'm bored. How do I satisfy my need for entertainment?"), the consumer goes through a series of logical stages to arrive at a decision. As shown in the centre of Figure 6-1, the stages are:

1. **Need recognition:** The consumer is moved to action by a need.

2. **Choice of an involvement level:** The consumer decides how much time and effort to invest in satisfying the need and thus the energy devoted to the remaining stages of the problem-solving process.

3. **Identification of alternatives:** The consumer collects information about products, services, and brands.

4. **Evaluation of alternatives:** The consumer weighs the pros and cons of the alternatives identified.

5. **Purchase and related decisions:** The consumer decides to buy or not to buy.

6. **Postpurchase behaviour:** The consumer seeks reassurance that the choice made was the correct one, experiences the product or service in use, and, the marketer hopes, becomes satisfied and is prepared to engage in the process again as the need arises.

Though this model is a useful starting point for examining purchase decisions, the process is not always as straightforward as it may appear. Consider these possible variations:

◆ The consumer can withdraw from the purchase process at any stage prior to the actual purchase. If, for example, the need diminishes, or no satisfactory alternatives are available, or the search is not worth the effort, the process may come to an abrupt end.

◆ It is not uncommon for some stages to be skipped. All six stages are likely to be followed only in certain buying situations — for instance, when buying high-priced, infrequently purchased items. However, for frequently purchased, familiar products, purchasing is usually routine. The aroused need is often satisfied by repurchasing a familiar brand, and the third and fourth stages are bypassed.

◆ The stages are not generally of the same length. When a mechanic tells you that your car's engine needs an overhaul, it may take only a moment to recognize the need for a new car. However, picking out and evaluating the alternative models may go on for weeks.

◆ Some stages may be performed consciously in certain purchase situations and subconsciously in others. For example, we don't consciously calculate for every purchase the amount of time and effort we will put into reaching a decision. Yet the fact that we spend more time on some purchases and less on others indicates that level of involvement is part of the process.

In the following discussion we use this six-stage process. However, the stages may have to be adjusted to fit the circumstances of a particular purchase situation. Also, what a consumer wants at the end of the process is satisfaction, and that doesn't necessarily mean a simple exchange. As we have observed in Chapter 1, there are many aspects of the interaction between buyers and sellers that can affect satisfaction levels.

1. Recognition of an Unsatisfied Need

The process begins when an unsatisfied need creates tension or discomfort for the consumer. This condition may arise internally (for example, a person feels hungry). Or the need may be dormant until it is aroused by an external stimulus, such as a TV advertisement, a jiggling banner ad on a Web page, or the sight of some product being used or worn by someone passing by. Another possible source of tension is dissatisfaction with a product currently being used. Perhaps the item is worn out, or you are just tired of wearing that same old jacket or pair of sneakers.

While hunger represents an actual physiological need that we all possess, the term "need" in this marketing context is used to refer to both needs and wants of consumers — such as that new pair of sunglasses you simply *need* to buy!

Once a need has been recognized, consumers often become aware of conflicting or competing uses for their scarce resources of time and money. Our desire to fulfill all these "needs" must be balanced with a sense of practicality and the fact that we never have enough money (and probably never will!) to satisfy all our wants as consumers. It is the existence of this "conflict" that forces consumers into some form of decision-making process.

Let's say a student is considering purchasing a personal computer for school, but for the same amount of money she could buy a great portable stereo, new CDs, and still have money left over. On the other hand, by spending all her money on a basic model PC she could do assignments and download class notes from home. Also, she could access entertainment on the Web including pre-release music clips before they are available in the stores. She must resolve these conflicts before proceeding. Otherwise the buying process stops.

high involvement
A purchase decision that involves all six stages of the buying decision process.

low involvement
A purchase decision in which the consumer moves directly from need recognition to purchase, skipping the stages in between.

2. Choice of an Involvement Level

Very early in the process the consumer consciously or subconsciously decides how much effort to exert in satisfying a need. Sometimes when a need arises, a consumer is dissatisfied with the quantity or quality of information about the purchase situation and decides to actively collect and evaluate more. These are **high-involvement** purchases that usually entail all six stages of the buying-decision process. If, on the other hand, a consumer is comfortable with the information and alternatives readily available, the purchase situation is viewed as **low involvement**. In such a case, the buyers will likely skip directly from need recognition to the purchase, ignoring the stages in-between.

Some of the major differences in consumer behaviour in high- and low-involvement situations are shown in the chart below.

Behaviour	High Involvement	Low Involvement
Time invested	Large amount	Small amount
Information search	Active	Little or none
Response to information	Critically evaluate	Ignore or accept without evaluation
Brand evaluations	Clear and distinct	Vague and general
Likelihood of brand loyalty developing	High	Low
Interaction with sales/service persons	Committed and demanding	Nominal but sensitive

Though it is somewhat risky to generalize because consumers differ, involvement tends to be greater under any of the following conditions:

◆ The consumer lacks information about the purchase. It may be a new class of product, or the first time the consumer has sought this product or service.

◆ The product or its benefits are viewed as important. Such a product may be heavily relied upon each day, or involve safety issues.

◆ The practical or social consequence of making a bad decision is perceived as high. What if it is poor quality, has outdated technology, or just isn't considered a "hip" brand?

◆ The quality of the interaction is high; taking part in the process itself is enjoyable.

Thus most buying decisions for relatively low-priced products that have close substitutes would be low-involvement. Typical examples are the majority of items sold in supermarkets, variety stores, and hardware stores. However, for a wealthy person the purchase of a car could be a low-involvement experience, while for a person with a high need for social acceptance, purchasing toothpaste might be highly involving. Such a consumer may look for assurances of whiter teeth and fresher breath. It is important to remember that involvement must be viewed from the perspective of the consumer, not the product.

The advent of the Internet as a source of product/purchase information may result in an increasingly higher level of time and involvement in otherwise lower involvement decisions. Where once existed a clearer trade-off between time and effort expended in gathering more or better data for a more informed decision, now the time and involvement trade-off has changed. With less time and effort than in the past, and the use of a good search engine, or a clutch of them simultaneously, one can collect a lot of very useful product and purchase information. But it is also true that the ease with which information (on anything and everything!) can be gathered — without stepping out of the house — can draw the consumer into increased search time. This complicates the seemingly clear distinction presented in the previous chart regarding involvement levels. In actuality, the distinction would lie more with consumer differences than with the type of purchase.

With Web page links and product and service reviews offering a variety of brand, technical, dealer location, and cost and price information, Web surfing has become as popular as traditional channel surfing during TV commercials. As this "browsing" grows as a new form of entertainment, potential has developed for online (click companies) and combination ("clicks and bricks," or "click and mortar" companies) retailers if they can establish a site that can stand out and grab the viewer's double-click attention span.

impulse buying
Low-involvement purchases made with little or no advance planning.

Impulse buying, or purchasing with little or no advance planning, is an important form of low-involvement decision-making. A shopper who goes to the grocery store with only the intention of buying vegetables and bread and on noticing a display of peaches at an attractive price decides to buy some engages in impulse buying. This form of purchasing behaviour is crucial in the grocery industry and must be taken into account when designing grocery shopping on the Internet (for example, www.peachtree.ca). It seems that a good proportion of purchasing on the Internet — current surveys estimate 25 percent — is unplanned or impulse buying.

Self-service, open-display retailing has conditioned shoppers to postpone planning and engage in more impulse buying. Because of the growth of this type of low-involvement purchasing, greater emphasis must be placed on promotional programs to get shoppers into a store or to visit a large-scale portal, or large scale virtual mall site (for example, www.norstarmall.ca). Displays, graphics, and packages must be made appealing because they serve as silent salespeople. Chapters Online (www.chapters.ca) capitalized on the visceral enjoyment Canadians take in scratch lottery tickets by offering prizes including a new car and shopping sprees in just such a promotion. By moving their mouse over a virtual scratch-and-win card, visitors could instantly win coupons, shopping sprees, and 3Com Palm Connected Organizers, and then enter to win a 2000 Ford Focus.[2]

Unless a retailer has a physical store location as well as a Web address, then issues arise with many products with regard to touching and feeling the product. People are touchy and feely creatures and it's a big part of many shopping experiences. It is this that has slowed the acceptance of purchasing some items over the Internet.[3] La Senza, the Montreal-based lingerie company (www.lasenza.com), whose products' touch and feel are of the utmost importance to its consumers, incorporated into their cyber-stores the ability to zoom in on products to assess the fit, cut, and fabric of the garment. An added bonus of the cyber-stores is that many who are uncomfortable shopping for such products in the traditional La Senza stores can visit the click store in complete privacy. Another Canadian lingerie click company has designed its site such that visitors can watch how the clothes move as they are modeled down a runway. Soon a variety of models with different body types will be available for such online demonstrations.[4]

3. Identification of Alternatives

Once a need has been recognized and the level of involvement is determined, the consumer must next identify the alternatives capable of satisfying the need. First, alternative products and then alternative brands are identified. Product and brand identification may range from a simple internal, or memory, scan of previous experiences to an extensive external search of the physical or cyber environment. Consider this example. Suppose a couple decides not to cook but to have an already-prepared item for their evening meal. Identifying alternatives might entail checking the freezer to see if any frozen dinners are on hand, examining the newspaper for specials or discount coupons, and recalling a radio advertisement that described a new restaurant. Alternatively, they may log on to a local event/entertainment portal and check out what places are recommended in their area (for example, www.restaurant.ca).

The search for alternatives is influenced by:

◆ How much information the consumer already has from past experiences and other sources.

◆ The consumer's confidence in that information.

◆ The expected benefit or value of additional information or, put another way, what the additional information is worth in terms of the effort, time, or money required to obtain it.

4. Evaluation of Alternatives

Once all the reasonable alternatives have been identified, the consumer must evaluate them before making a decision. The evaluation involves establishing some criteria against which each alternative is compared. In the preceding meal example, the decision-maker may have a single criterion ("How quickly can we sit down to eat?") or several criteria (speed, taste, nutrition, and price). When multiple criteria are involved, they typically do not carry equal weight. For example, preparation time might be more important than nutrition.

The criteria that consumers use in the evaluation result from their past experience and feelings toward various brands, as well as the opinions of family members, friends, or even experts. More and more often people are including the Internet in their pool of available resources. There are news and discussion groups that are highly specialized pertaining to almost any product or service imaginable. There is no shortage of people wanting to express their opinions as evidenced by the Epinions Web site (www.epinions.com) where people can share their experiences and views on anything from brands of bowling balls to ski vacations and operating systems. Used car salesmen jokes may also become a thing of the past as shoppers can now know for sure if there was only that one owner — you know, that little old lady who only drove it to church! With CarFax (www.carfax.com), used car histories can be retrieved with the help of the Instant Lemon Check.

In some situations, differences in the criteria applied or the relative importance that different consumers place on them are what can determine market segments.

Because experience is often limited or dated and information from sources such as advertising or friends can be biased, evaluations can be factually incorrect. That is, a consumer may believe that the price of brand A is higher than that of brand B, when in fact the opposite is true. Marketers monitor consumers to determine what choice criteria they use, to identify any changes that may be taking place in their criteria, and to correct any damaging misperceptions.

5. Purchase and Related Decisions

After searching and evaluating, the consumer must decide whether to buy. Thus the first outcome is the decision to purchase or not to purchase the alternative evaluated as most desirable. If the decision is to buy, a series of related decisions must be made regarding features, where and when to make the actual purchase, how to take delivery or possession, the method of payment, and other issues. So the decision to make a purchase is really the beginning of an entirely new series of decisions that may be as time-consuming and difficult as the initial one. Alert marketers recognize that the outcome of these additional decisions affects satisfaction, so they find ways to help consumers make them as efficiently as possible. For example, car dealers have speeded up loan approval, reduced decision-making by offering a small number of set option packages, and made delivery of the car a "mini-ceremony" to make the customer feel important. Saturn salespeople often gather around with balloons as new owners drive the car out of the showroom themselves. One Calgary Honda dealer insists that new owners have their picture taken with their new cars so a calendar can be made and sent to the customer. People may feel a little foolish about changing their minds after that!

patronage buying motives
The reasons why a consumer chooses to shop at a certain store.

Selecting a source from which to make a purchase is one of the buying decisions. Sources can be as varied as Internet sites or manufacturers' outlets. The most common source is a retail store, and the reasons a consumer chooses to shop at a retail store or a cyberspace or electronic store are called **patronage buying motives**. People want to feel comfortable when they shop. This may mean that they want the assurance of being around people like themselves and in an environment that reflects their values or that they can trust, or that they want the convenience, lack of pressure, and anonymity of an electronic store.

Patronage motives can range from something as simple as convenience when you want a soft drink, to something more complex, such as the atmosphere of a restaurant.

Some common patronage motives are:

◆ Location or access convenience.

◆ Merchandise assortment.

◆ Service speed.

◆ Services offered.

◆ Merchandise accessibility — either physically or in cyberspace.

◆ Appearance of the premises or Web site.

◆ Confidence in the firm or supplier.

◆ Quality of staff.

◆ Prices.

◆ Mix of other customers.

◆ Reliability of products and level of service.

◆ Reputation for after sales delivery and service.

Like the criteria consumers use to choose products and brands, their patronage motives will vary depending on the purchase situation. Successful retailers and Internet firms (e-tailers, e-commerce firms, etc. — common usage of a single term has yet to occur) evaluate their target customers carefully and design their stores and/or cyber presence accordingly. A manufacturer, in turn, selects physical or electronic retailers with the patronage characteristics that complement its product and appeal to the desired target market. Tourist destinations market their attraction based on the factors that target segments want in a vacation.

Patronage motives for e-shopping are as important as those traditional shopping — but in a slightly modified form. The "look" of the site matters, as it gives an impression of the style and image of the "brand." It also gives consumers confidence as does clear evidence of security, privacy, and clearly displayed delivery policies and prices. Accessibility through easy convenient site navigation and text links ensure that consumers will stay the course and hit the order submit button. If shoppers are frustrated by the quality of the experience as they fill their cyber carts — they can simply walk away leaving their carts in the aisle. This is not so easy to do in the brick environment. A handy "trick" of cyber retailers that use log-in IDs is that of keeping those items in the shopping cart upon return visits with a reminder that something is in your cart. In a store you may see a book on a shelf and say — perhaps I'll come back for it — but it never crosses your mind again. But if it gets as far as the cart with e-retailers, you'll be reminded until you remove it.

5. Postpurchase Behaviour

What a consumer learns from going through the buying process has an influence on how he or she will behave the next time the same need arises. If the consumer's expectations for all aspects of the process are met, consumer satisfaction results. The consumer will feel that he or she has received fair value. If the consumer's expectations have been more than met, then satisfaction is even greater and the consumer feels that superior value has been received. From the marketer's viewpoint, for both these cases, and in varying degrees, the foundation for a long-term customer relationship has been established.

By completing the buying process, by having gathered information, evaluated alternatives, and arrived at a decision, the consumer has acquired additional knowledge about the product and various brands. Furthermore, new opinions and beliefs have been formed and old ones have been revised. The appreciation of product benefits, the service that was provided, the quality of the interaction between the buyer and seller or service person, the post purchase service — all of these can then be fed back, as is indicated by an arrow in Figure 6-1, from the **postpurchase behaviour** stage of the buying-decision process model to the next need-recognition stage. In other words, a consumer who has experienced a high degree of satisfaction in a purchase situation will be prepared to repeat the process with the same marketer for the same product or service. Otherwise, this alternative may well be eliminated from any future purchase considerations.

Something else often occurs following a purchase. Have you ever gone through a careful decision process for a major purchase (say, a stereo, video game system, or an expensive item of clothing), selected what you thought was the best alternative, but then had doubts about your choice after the purchase? Have you asked yourself if maybe you should have bought the other one you were considering? What you were experiencing is post-purchase **cognitive dissonance** — a state of anxiety brought on by the difficulty of choosing from among several alternatives. Unfortunately for marketers, dissonance is quite common; and, if the anxiety is not relieved, the consumer may be unhappy with the chosen product even if it performs adequately!

Post-purchase cognitive dissonance occurs when each of the alternatives seriously considered by the consumer has both attractive and unattractive features. For example, in purchasing the stereo system, the equipment selected may be the most expensive (unattractive), but provides superior sound (attractive). The brand of system not chosen is popular among your friends (attractive), but has a very limited service warranty (unattractive). After the purchase is made, the unattractive features of the product purchased grow in importance in the consumer's mind, as do the attractive features offered by the rejected alternatives. As a result, we begin to doubt the wisdom of the choice and experience anxiety over the decision.

Dissonance typically increases: (1) the higher the dollar value or perceived risk of the purchase; (2) the greater the similarity between the item selected and item(s) rejected; and (3) the greater the importance of the purchase decision to the consumer. Thus buying a new colour laser printer creates more dissonance than buying the paper for it.

Consumers try to reduce their post-purchase anxieties. They avoid information (such as ads for the rejected products) that is likely to increase the dissonance. And they seek out information that supports their decision, even to the extreme of reading ads for a product after it has been purchased. Also, prior to the purchase, putting more effort into evaluating alternatives can increase a consumer's confidence and reduce dissonance.

Some useful generalizations can be developed from the theory of cognitive dissonance. For example, anything sellers can do in their advertising, personal selling or other communications activity to reassure buyers — say, by stressing the number of satisfied owners — will reduce dissonance. Also, the quality of a seller's follow-up and post sale service programs can be significant factors in reducing dissonance. Online marketers have a particularly good opportunity to reassure buyers since they have easy access to all the customer information they need and can communicate supportive information or direct buyers to supportive Web sites and chat rooms as well as favourable product reviews.

postpurchase behaviour
Efforts by the consumer to reduce the anxiety often accompanying purchase decisions.

cognitive dissonance
The anxiety created by the fact that in most purchases the alternative selected has some negative features and the alternatives not selected have some positive features.

Marketing at Work 6-1

Canadian Net and Shopping Behaviour, eh!

What!!! Only 18 percent of Canadian online users actually purchased something. Wait, let's look at more results from a number of net research studies.

Canadians are technically capable: About 60 percent of all Canadians have at least one computer; 38 percent use the Internet compared with 25 percent of Australians and Americans — 15 percent in the U.K. and Germany, 11 percent in France. When it comes to gender, 48 percent of Canadian males and 34 percent of females use the Internet compared with 30 percent and 21 percent in the U.S. and 20 percent and 9 percent in Germany.

Internet usage: How long online — 30 percent of home users spend at least ten hours a week; 75 percent of home users say that they use the net for shopping or as a source of information about products so there is active participation. Canadians have the world's highest rate of online banking — 17 percent, the same proportion as in Sweden but much higher than the 13 percent for the U.S. Most home users use dial-up connections. Females spend about eight hours per week online compared with 10 for males.

At work, 58 percent of users also log on to either buy something or gather information about products or services but they spend almost twice as much time on line. At work users typically have faster broad band Internet connections.

Ways in which online time is spent: Over 90 percent use email, more than two thirds get news and do research/education followed by obtaining financial services and information, seeking automobile information, playing games, and obtaining medical services and information.

Buying behaviour: Banking services aside, American adults are the world's leading online buyers, 31 percent have recently purchased something compared with 21 percent of Swedish adults, 19 percent of Swiss followed by 18 percent of

Canadians. Overall, 40 percent of all Internet users have made at least one purchase with 25 percent of these being unplanned. The typical American buyer spent US$828 during the first three months of 2000 with US$720 for the typical Canadian buyer. The 16 percent of Canadians who buy online most often are the home based Internet shoppers who have been online for more than four years.

Motivation: Peer group pressure, word of mouth, advertising, curiosity, convenience, time management, comfort, and the pleasure and fun of random surfing.

Lifestyle: Canadian Web shoppers, like those in other countries, tend to be affluent, young, and well educated. Of those who purchased online last year, 65 percent had a household income of over Cdn$100,000. Nearly 50 percent of those who purchased more than five items are between 18 and 34 years old, 47 percent have university degrees, 71 percent have a credit card, they travel a good deal, and take part in many active leisure activities. In general, Internet users who are not e-shoppers have similar demographics and life styles as do e-shoppers — they are directionally the same but not as pronounced.

Special issues: New Internet users are overwhelmingly concerned about personal security and privacy and are not easily reassured by technically based promises. Canadians are willing to trust pan-Canadian institutions such as banks and phone companies. In the U.S., surfers are prepared to share personal information in exchange for better service and more personalized treatment by having the Web site "remember" their personal details and past purchases in order to improve service as well as make shopping more convenient. Web site privacy policies and statements are viewed as important.

Source: Adapted from the Pollara Survey: "E-commerce in Canada," as reported on the Canoe.ca Web site, March 15, 2000; *Cyberatlas: The Webmarketers Guide to Online Facts,* cyberatlas.internet.com, April 5, 2000; Katherine Macklem, "Canadians lead parade with Internet banking," *Financial Post,* April 11, 2000, p. C9.

With this background on the buying-decision process, we can examine what influences buying behaviour. We'll begin with the sources and types of information used by consumers.

Information and Purchase Decisions

Consumers must find out what products and services are available, what brands offer what features and benefits, what services are available to support the purchase, who sells them at what prices, where they can be purchased, and what kind of follow-up is likely.

Without this market information there wouldn't be a decision process because there would not be any decisions to make.

What are some of the sources and types of information that exist in the buying environment? As shown in Figure 6-1, two information sources — the commercial environment and the social environment — influence the buying-decision process. As already discussed, the Internet has revolutionized access to this information and made possible greater quantities than would ever have been gathered manually. The **commercial information** environment consists of all marketing organizations and individuals that attempt to communicate with consumers. It includes manufacturers, retailers, advertisers, e-commerce Web site sponsors, and salespeople whenever any of them are engaged in efforts to inform or persuade.

The other source is the **social information** environment, made up of family, friends, and acquaintances that directly or indirectly provide information about products. If you think for a moment about how often your conversation with friends at the coffee shop or with cyber-pals in a chat room deals with purchases you are considering or those you have made, you will begin to appreciate the marketing significance of these social sources. Also, it is interesting to note that people will report negative experiences with products and services to more people than they will relay their positive experiences.

Advertising is the most common type of commercial information. Other commercial sources are direct sales efforts by store clerks, telemarketing, and direct mail and e-mail to consumers' homes and computers, as well as consumers' physical involvement with products (examining packages, trial product use, and sampling). More and more consumers are obtaining important information they need about products and services through the Internet. Both in e-commerce and e-business (business-to-business marketing), one of the first sources of information on products, services, and prospective suppliers is their Web sites.

The most important kind of social information is word-of-mouth communication, in which two or more people simply have a conversation about a product or service. The proliferation of product review sites and special topic discussion groups/chat rooms on the Internet has enhanced this effect. Other social sources include the observations of others using products and exposure to products in the homes of others.

When all the different types of information are taken into consideration, it becomes apparent that there is enormous competition for the consumer's attention. It has been estimated that the typical adult is exposed to about three hundred ad messages a day, or almost ten thousand per month.[5] With the increasing ad content within the context of the Internet this is sure to be considerably higher for those that surf on a regular basis. Coincidentally, the consumer's mind has to be a marvelously efficient machine to sort and process this barrage of information. To understand how the consumer functions, we will begin by examining the social and group forces that influence the individual's psychological makeup and also play a role in specific buying decisions.

Social and Group Forces

The way we think, believe, and act is determined to a great extent by social forces and groups. In addition, our individual buying decisions — including our needs, the alternatives we consider, and the way in which we evaluate them — are affected by the social forces that surround us. To reflect this dual impact, the arrows in Figure 6-1 extend from

---

commercial information environment
All marketing organizations and individuals that directly or indirectly communicate with consumers.

social information environment
Family, friends, and acquaintances who directly or indirectly provide information about products.

the social and group forces in two directions: to the psychological makeup of the individual and to the buying-decision process. Our description begins with culture, the force with the most indirect impact, and moves to the force with the most direct impact, the household.

Definition of Culture and Cultural Influence

culture
A complex of symbols and artifacts created by a given society and handed down from generation to generation as determinants and regulators of human behaviour.

A **culture** is the complex of symbols and artifacts created by a given society and handed down from generation to generation as determinants and regulators of human behaviour. The symbols may be intangible (attitudes, beliefs, values, languages, religions) or tangible (tools, housing, products, works of art). A culture implies a totally learned and "handed-down" way of life. It does not include instinctive acts. However, standards for performing instinctive biological acts (eating, eliminating body wastes, and sexual relationships) can be culturally established. Thus everybody gets hungry, but what people eat and how they act to satisfy the hunger drive will vary among cultures.

Actually, much of our behaviour is culturally determined. Our sociocultural institutions (family, schools, churches, and languages) provide behavioural guidelines. Years ago, Clyde Kluckhohn observed: "Culture . . . regulates our lives at every turn. From the moment we are born until we die there is constant conscious and unconscious pressure upon us to follow certain types of behaviour that other men have created for us."[6] People living in a culture share a whole set of similarities and beliefs — and these often differ from those originating in other cultures.

When a culture is relatively homogeneous, as in Japan, using cultural factors in analyzing for marketing purposes can be very effective. As well, within a given culture, say Canada, for those goods and services where the cultural characteristics of consumers have no effect, it is suitable to use the notion of "homogeneity of the market." For example, if all Canadians, regardless of where they live and whatever their ethnicity, believe equally in the need for efficiency, then goods and services that are presented with efficiency claims would be equally acceptable. But if there is less homogeneity in terms of values and way of life or lifestyle, culture is not as effective a guide for marketing managers as is subculture.

Many Canadian Cultures

sub-culture
Groups that exhibit characteristic behaviour patterns sufficient to distinguish them from other groups within the same culture.

Compared with many other countries, Canada is a culturally complex society. Marketers need to understand the concept of **sub-cultures** and analyze them as potentially profitable market segments. Any time there is a culture as heterogeneous as ours, there are bound to be significant sub-cultures based upon factors such as race, nationality, religion, geographic location, age, and urban–rural distribution. Some of these were recognized in Chapter 4, when we analyzed the demographic market factors. Ethnicity, for example, is a cultural factor that has significant marketing implications. Concentrations of Middle or Eastern Europeans in the Prairies provide a market for some products that would go unnoticed in Italian or Chinese sections of Toronto, Montreal, or Vancouver.

The cultural diversity of the Canadian market has taken on increased importance for some companies in recent years. Not too long ago, most companies ignored ethnic and linguistically based segmentation. However, as groups grew in size, as immigration continued, French-English differences became emphasized, and marketplace competition escalated, segmentation became accepted as a viable marketing strategy. Besides the large French Canadian population, there are also large communities of Italian, Chinese, German, and Portuguese in this country. Although many that have come to Canada have been here as long as fifty years, language loyalty continues to remain high indicating the pervasive influence of original cultures within Canada's cultural mosaic.[7]

The most obvious marketing efforts to reach ethnic market segments are found in major markets such as Toronto, Vancouver, and Montreal. In Toronto, for example, Fairchild Radio reaches 24 percent of the Chinese population while CHIN reaches 11 percent. The CFMT television system in Ontario (www.ultimatetv.com/tv/ca) boasts the number one Cantonese language newscast in Ontario with a 71 percent weekly reach. CFMT also broadcasts Armenian, Filipino, Greek, Iranian, Japanese, Korean, Macedonian, Maltese, Polish, Russian, South Asian, and Ukrainian productions. The company also proposes to begin LMTV — a multicultural and multilingual television station to serve the lower mainland and Victoria in British Columbia.

Television and newspapers are available to the Chinese communities in Vancouver, Toronto, Montreal, and elsewhere. Toronto's Spanish-language *El Popular* is targeted at the area's 250,000 Spanish speakers and is distributed from Quebec to British Columbia. Edmonton's Aboriginal Media Services sells airtime for its native radio station as well as advertising space in its seventy native newspapers. These and similar media represent attractive advertising outlets for companies who wish to reach growing subcultural and linguistic market segments. These include national and international brands beside those firms with products with specific ethnic appeal.

The sharpest cultural differences of concern to marketers are portrayed in the attitudinal and behavioural differences between English- and French-speaking communities on a country-wide basis, including Acadian markets. As indicated in Chapter 4, marketing to French-speaking Canada involves considerably more than a cursory acknowledgment of ethnic and linguistic differences.

The Québécois Market

While French Canada is technically, and politically for some, a subculture, its sheer size, homogeneity, main geographic location, purchasing power, and social and political orientation makes it a cultural rather than a sub-cultural market — at least outside of Montreal. No other ethnic or non-English-speaking linguistic group comes close to comprising 14 percent of the Canadian population (in total, approximately 31 percent of the population speak French),[8] relatively highly concentrated in one geographic area, and with a long-established and fully developed set of cultural, social, artistic, and legal institutions. Quebec consumers consistently exhibit consumption patterns unlike those in the rest of Canada. A number of studies have found that when demographics are either matched or controlled for, consumption differences exist between Quebecers and other Canadians and that these differences are attributable to cultural factors — values and lifestyle preferences. Common examples of such generalized consumption differences are:[9]

◆ A better acceptance in Quebec of premium-priced products such as premium-grade gasoline and liquors.

◆ Willingness to pay higher prices for convenience items.

◆ A greater popularity in Quebec of coupons and premiums.

◆ A greater per capita expenditure in Quebec on clothing, personal care items, tobacco, wine, and beer. But there is a lower consumption of "hard" liquor although stronger brands of beer are preferred.

- A greater per capita consumption of soft drinks (regular, not diet), maple sugar, molasses, candy, and presweetened cereals in Quebec than in the rest of Canada. Lottery tickets as well.

- Much higher consumption rates for instant and decaffeinated coffee in Quebec.

- More time spent with television and radio in Quebec than in the rest of the country.

- Quebec women show different patterns of cosmetics use including more perfumes and toilet water, as well as hair colouring.

- Quebec consumers are wary of new products, often waiting for them to prove themselves before purchasing them.

- A difference in banking and financial practices resulting from the popularity of credit unions (caisse populaires). There is also a trend away from the use of credit and credit cards.

- Consumers exhibit brand loyalty, but are susceptible to special offers and sale prices. These consumers link price to perceived value.

The Impact of Cultural Differences on Marketing

The fact that French Canada as well as the various ethnic minority communities in Canada represent distinctively different markets requires marketers who wish to be successful in, say, the Quebec market, to develop unique marketing programs for the segment. There must be an appreciation of the fact that certain products will not be successful in French Canada simply because they are not appropriate to the French Canadian culture and lifestyle. In other cases, products that are successful in English Canada must be marketed differently in French Canada because French Canadians have a different perception of these products, their importance, and the way in which they are used. It may be necessary for companies to develop new products or appropriate variations of existing products specifically for the Quebec market. Similarly, the retail buying behaviour of residents of that province may necessitate the use of different channels of distribution. Residents spend a greater amount on personal grooming and fashion items resulting in a greater preference for specialty boutiques than in the rest of the country. As a result, distribution of such products may be more successful through smaller, specialized retail outlets than through department store formats.

A similar, but not the same, case can be made for the various ethnic-minority and linguistically based markets in our country. Because most of these communities are so much smaller in both scale and purchasing power than Francophone Quebec, the scope for and amount of marketing program adaptation that is feasible for firms to engage in is frequently limited to advertising in the appropriate language and using, where possible, culturally acceptable themes. While the large Asian population represents a most attractive ethnic market, there are intricacies that must be considered. Within this large group, there are differences in origin that amount to significant differences. This group is comprised of people from Hong Kong, Taiwan, and China; the first speaking Cantonese and the two latter speaking Mandarin. Within the Chinese community, the words used may differ according to place of origin, and of course differences in expressions and puns exist. Common understanding of illustrations, copy, and message must be insured. There is also the possibility of insult through stereotyping. Burger King faced language concerns head-on with their "Now we're speaking the same language" campaign in which they chose Cantonese as it is the most common dialect in the Canadian Chinese community.[10] Special attention was taken, as Cantonese is quite complex when sung. It is very important to use the correct tones and colloquialisms. Colours are even important in such advertising. White flowers, for example, are a sign of death in this culture and may have been used in the background of advertisements — the point being you must know the target culture or risk such errors.

Differences exist even between Canada and the United States. While there are many common product-usage patterns between the two countries, differences exist which national and international marketers must recognize in order to maximize their chances for success.[11]

There is a growing appreciation of the significance of ethnic markets in some parts of Canada and marketers are placing more emphasis in this area. The Asian communities in Toronto and Vancouver, for example, are becoming prominent targets. The Bay recently redesigned its outlet in Richmond, B.C., to attract Asian shoppers.[12] *Maclean's* and *Toronto Life* offered Chinese-language editions of their magazines but could not maintain them profitably because of lack of circulation and advertising revenues and were forced to stop publishing after a trial period. Some companies exploring this market through magazine advertising include General Motors, Visa, Cathay Pacific, Toronto Dominion Bank, and Canon. White Spot restaurants, many Vancouver financial institutions, jewellers, and clothiers are advertising in *Mehfil*, an English-language publication aimed at the South Asian market.[13] The Ford Canada Web site can be viewed in English, French, or Chinese text (www.ford.ca). This is wise marketing considering 85 percent of metropolitan Chinese community members own automobiles, 86 percent own home computers, 71 percent buy new over used, and 81 percent pay cash when buying a car.[14]

Entrepreneurs in these metropolitan areas have catered specifically to ethnic needs. We have numerous examples of ethnic foods such as Italian, Ukrainian, Chinese, or Indian, which were originally imported or produced and distributed exclusively for ethnic communities but which have become more widely available in the Canadian market at large. Every supermarket has them on display, and Loblaw makes a practice of continually adding more prepared ethnic foods to their offerings.

Reference Group Influences

Consumers' perceptions and buying behaviour are also influenced by the reference groups to which they belong. These groups include the large social classes and smaller reference groups. The smallest, yet usually the strongest, social-group influence is a person's family. For teens and young adults, peer group relationships can be more important and influential when it comes to food, clothing, entertainment, and a host of related consumption decisions. For young girls shopping is still a top leisure activity that they share with their core group experimenting with different styles.

The elusive 12 to 24 year-old demographic has become such a hot focus in marketing that it has become a specialty in marketing whereby surrounding themselves with the trappings of teen culture, trend-spotters hope to anticipate new trends before they pass right by.

Influence of Social Class

social class
A division of society based on education, occupation, and type of residential neighbourhood.

People's buying behaviour is often influenced by the class to which they belong, or to which they aspire, simply because they have values, beliefs, and lifestyles that are characteristic of a **social class**. This occurs whether they are conscious of class notions or not — and frequently, they are not. The idea of a social-class structure and the terms upper, middle, and lower class may be repugnant to many Canadians. However, using class concepts does provide a useful way to look at a market. Therefore, it is another useful basis for segmenting consumer markets.

A social-class structure currently useful to marketing managers is one developed by Richard Coleman and Lee Rainwater, two respected researchers in social-class theory. The placement of people in this structure is determined primarily by such variables as education, occupation, and type of neighbourhood of residence. Originally consisting of five strata, the authors later developed a condensed model with three main levels, yet within these, it is the subcategories that still are useful for this type of segmentation. It is the original model we will discuss in this chapter.[15]

Note that "amount of income" is not one of the placement criteria. There may be a general relationship between amount of income and social class – people in the upper classes usually have higher incomes than people in the lower classes. But within each social class there typically is a wide range of incomes. Also, the same amount of income may be earned by families in different social classes. The relevant question for marketers is — How does class affect the use of income?

For purposes of marketing planning and analysis, marketing executives and researchers often divide the total consumer market into five social classes. These classes and their characteristics are summarized below. The percentages are only approximations and may vary from one city or region to another, but fairly represent the general distribution of wealth in North America.

SOCIAL CLASSES AND THEIR CHARACTERISTICS   The **upper class**, about 2 percent of the population, includes two groups: (1) the socially prominent "old families" of inherited wealth and (2) the "new rich" of the corporate executives, owners of large businesses, and wealthy professionals. They live in large homes in the best neighbourhoods and display a sense of social responsibility. They buy expensive products and services, but they do not conspicuously display their purchases. They patronize exclusive shops.

The **upper-middle class**, about 12 percent of the population, is composed of moderately successful business and professional people and owners of medium-sized companies. They are well educated, have a strong drive for success, and want their children to do well. Their purchases are more conspicuous than those in the upper class. This class buys status symbols that show their success, yet are socially acceptable. They live well, belong to private clubs, and support the arts and various social causes.

The **lower-middle class**, about 32 percent of the population, consists of the white-collar workers — office workers, most salespeople, teachers, technicians, and small-business owners. The **upper-lower class**, about 38 percent of the population, is the blue-collar "working class" of factory workers, semi-skilled workers, and service people. Because these two groups together represent the mass market and thus are so important to most marketers, the attitudes, beliefs, and lifestyles they exhibit are the focus for much marketing research.

The **lower-lower class**, about 16 percent of the population, is composed of unskilled workers, the chronically unemployed, unassimilated immigrants, and people frequently on welfare. They typically are poorly educated, with low incomes, and live in substandard houses and neighbourhoods. They tend to live for the present and often do not purchase wisely. The public tends to differentiate (within this class) between the "working poor" and the "welfare poor."

MARKETING SIGNIFICANCE OF SOCIAL CLASSES Now let's summarize the basic conclusions from social-class research that are highly significant for marketing:

◆ A social-class system can be observed whether people are aware of it or not. Such systems can be found in every society. There are substantial differences between classes regarding their buying behaviour.

◆ Differences in beliefs, attitudes, and orientations exist among the classes. Thus the classes respond differently to a seller's marketing program.

◆ For many products, class membership is a better predictor of buyer behaviour than is income.

This last point — the relative importance of income versus social class — has generated considerable controversy. There is an old saying that "a rich man is just a poor man with money — and that, given the same amount of money, a poor man would behave exactly like a rich man." Studies of social-class structure have proved that this statement simply is not true. Two people, each earning the same income but belonging to different social classes, will have quite different buying patterns. They will shop at different stores, expect different treatment from sales and service people, and buy different products and even different brands. Also, when a family's income increases because more family members get a job, this increase almost never results in a change in the family's social class.

Influence of Small Reference Groups

Consumer behaviour is influenced by the small groups to which consumers belong or aspire to belong. These groups may include family, sports clubs or teams, church groups, or a circle of close friends from school, work, or the neighbourhood. Each of these groups has its own standards of behaviour that serve as guides or "frames of reference" for actual or aspiring members. A person may agree with all the ideas of the group or only some of them. Also, a person does not have to belong to a group to be influenced by it. Actual and potential **reference groups** operate to influence a person's attitudes, values, and behaviour.

reference group
A group of people who influence a person's attitudes, values, and behaviour.

Studies have shown that personal advice in face-to-face reference groups is much more effective in influencing buying behaviour than is advertising in newspapers, television, or other mass media. That is, in selecting products or changing brands, we are more likely to be influenced by advice, comments, or word-of-mouth from satisfied (or dissatisfied) customers in our reference group. This is true especially when we consider the speaker to be knowledgeable regarding the particular product or service or concerning the problem a product or service is designed to address. There is a growing awareness of the importance and influence that Internet based reference groups or special interest communities have on those who spend a good deal of time in online conversations with individuals as well as in chat rooms — either in giving opinions or monitoring them. Notoriously popular among today's tween generation (between child and teenager at 9 to 14 years), online groups and chat rooms make tweens feel empowered. The experience allows their creativity to roam wild, and unleashes their imagination as they role-play while communicating with faceless individuals at the other end.[16]

Advertisers are relying on reference group influence when they use celebrity spokespersons. Professional athletes, musicians, models, and actors can influence people who would like to be associated with them in some way or who admire them. Recent examples include Mia Hamm and Michael Jordan for Nike, Buffy the Vampire Slayer's Sarah Michelle Gellar

What would you do with an extra 8 hours?

Introducing New TYLENOL® Arthritis Pain. Golf, walk, garden. With time comes the freedom to enjoy life. But for millions of Canadians, it can also bring the early signs of Osteoarthritis. Thats why weve created TYLENOL® Arthritis Pain. To help relieve the pain of arthritis. With its patented bi-layer caplet, the first layer offers almost immediate relief. While the second layer provides time-released relief for up to 8 hours. And its Easy-to-Open cap is commended by The Arthritis Society. All so you can continue doing what you love. Day in and day out.

Easy-to-Open cap commended by The Arthritis Society. For more information contact us at 1 800-321-1433 or www.arthritis.ca

Do you think Wayne Gretzky's presence helps Tylenol?

innovators
The first group — a venturesome group — of people to adopt something new (good, service).

opinion leader
The member of a reference group who is the information source and who influences the decision-making of others in the group.

household
A single person, a family, or any group of unrelated persons who occupy a housing unit.

for Maybelline, Jennifer Love Hewitt for Neutrogena, Shania Twain for Covergirl cosmetics, Wayne Gretzky for Tylenol, or Martha Stewart for any of her own product lines. Her assurance on a product is accepted on anything from housewares to gardening supplies. A variation on this is actually supplying professional organizations with your products like Bauer Inc., for example, as part of its parent company Nike's sponsorship deal with the International Ice Hockey Federation, dressed the Canada hockey team in Bauer uniforms and equipment.[17]

Reference-group influence in marketing is not limited to well-known personalities. Any group whose qualities a person admires can act as a reference. The physically fit, the environmentally conscious, and the professionally successful have all served as reference groups in advertisements. Another useful reference group factor pertains to the flow of information between and within groups — it tends be flow horizontally from group to group on a similar social level rather than trickle down from high-status to lower-status groups.[18]

The proven role of small groups as behaviour determinants, plus the concept of horizontal information flow, suggests that a marketer is faced with two key problems. The first is to identify the relevant reference group likely to influence a consumer in a given buying situation. The second is to identify and communicate with two key people in the group — the **innovator** (early buyer) and the influential person (**opinion leader**). Every group has a leader — a taste-maker, or opinion leader — who influences the decision-making of others in the group. The key is for marketers to convince that person of the value of their products or services. The opinion leader in one group may be an opinion follower in another. A person who is influential in matters concerning food, because of a special interest or skill in that area, may follow the opinions of another when it comes to buying gardening equipment, software, or home office equipment.

Family and Household Influence

A **family** is commonly viewed as a group of two or more people related by blood, marriage, adoption, or common practice, living together in a household. During their lives many people will belong to at least two families — the one into which they are born and the one they form at marriage. The birth family primarily determines core values and attitudes. The marriage family, in contrast, has a more direct influence on specific purchases. For example, family size is important in the purchase of a car.

A **household** is a broader concept than a family. It consists of a single person, a family, or any group of unrelated persons who occupy a housing unit. Thus an unmarried homeowner, college students sharing an off-campus apartment, and cohabiting couples are examples of households.

Since households are not necessarily comprised of a couple with children, sensitivity to household structure is important in designing marketing strategy. It affects such dimensions as product type and form (semi-processed or prepared gourmet meals for singles or busy working couples), product size (how large a serving for older couples, how large a refrigerator or microwave oven), and the design of advertising (Who shall be depicted in a TV ad: a traditional family or a couple? What kind of couple?).

In addition to the direct, immediate impact households have on the purchasing behaviour of members, it is also interesting to consider the buying behaviour of the household as a unit. Who does the buying for a household? Marketers should treat this question as five separate ones, because each may call for different strategies:

◆ Who influences the buying decision?

◆ Who makes the buying decision?

◆ Who makes the actual purchase?

◆ Who uses the product or service?

◆ Who follows up on service and performance concerns?

Different household members may assume these various roles, or one individual may play several roles in a particular purchase. In families, for many years the stay-at-home female household head did most of the day-to-day buying. However, these days, this behaviour has changed since such a high proportion of married women are in the work force and men have assumed greater household responsibility.

Teenagers and young children are important decision-makers in family buying, as well as actual shoppers. Canadian teenagers could represent a $10 billion plus market by the year 2005. According to a study by YTV, the more than 2.3 million Canadian "tweens" who are between kids and teenagers have $1.1 billion in disposable income to spend.[19] This certainly is enough to warrant the attention of many manufacturers. Even very young children influence buying decisions today because they watch TV advertising and ask for products when they shop with their parents. Children are also making their way onto the Internet and "window shopping" — there have yet to be reports of them making massive use of parent' credit cards on an unauthorized basis. The power this market holds is evidenced by recent changes in retail offerings aimed at this group.

Ch!ckaboom is a clothing store for girls 5 to 14 years of age. Girls can shop, fiddle with accessories, or hang out in a place all their own. The stores database tracks birthdays, so these customers can receive cards with gift certificates. There are also theme days and activities to entertain such as Valentine's Day and Halloween parties. Other retailers have also focused on this segment of little girls who are in control of mom's credit cards. Le Chateau and La Senza also have developed product lines and marketing for this segment. Le Chateau anticipates that they will develop these lines into free-standing stores in the near future.[20]

When children aren't influencing the process, purchasing decisions are often made jointly by husband and wife. Young couples are much more likely to make buying decisions on a joint basis than older couples are. Apparently the longer a couple live together, the more they feel they can trust each other's judgment.

Knowing which family member is likely to make the purchase decision will influence a firm's entire marketing mix. If children are the key decision-makers, as is often the case with breakfast cereals, then a manufacturer will produce something that tastes good to children, design the package with youngsters in mind, and advertise on Saturday morning cartoon shows. Even sedate and wholesome products such as milk can have added appeal with a packaging makeover. Canada's four major dairies have in recent years all launched loudly packaged single serving milkshakes and flavoured milks whose cool design, advertising, and convenience aim for strong teen appeal. Such strategies are employed regardless of who actually makes the purchase and who else (besides the children) in the household might eat cereal.

 ## *Psychological Factors*

In discussing the psychological component of consumer behaviour, we continue to use the model in Figure 6-1. One or more motives within a person activates goal-oriented behaviour. One such behaviour is perception — the collection and processing of information. Other important psychological activities are learning and attitude formation. We then consider the roles that personality and self-concept play in buying decisions. These psychological variables help to shape a person's lifestyle and values. The term **psychographics** is used in marketing as a synonym for those variables that include lifestyle and values.

psychographics
A concept in consumer behaviour that describes consumers in terms of a combination of psychological and sociological influences.

Motivation — The Starting Point

To understand why consumers behave as they do, we must first ask why a person acts at all. The answer is, "Because he or she experiences a need." All behaviour starts with a recognized need. Security, social acceptance, and prestige are examples of needs. Thus, a **motive** is a need sufficiently stimulated to move an individual to seek satisfaction.

motive
A need sufficiently stimulated that an individual is moved to seek satisfaction.

We have many dormant needs that do not activate behaviour because they are not sufficiently intense. Hunger strong enough to cause us to search for food and fear great enough to motivate a search for security are examples of aroused needs that become motives for behaviour.

Identifying the motive(s) for behaviour can range from simple to unexplainable. To illustrate, buying motives may be grouped in three different levels, depending on consumers' awareness of them and their willingness to divulge them. At one level, buyers recognize, and are quite willing to talk about, their motives for buying certain products or services. At a second level, they are aware of their reasons for buying but will not admit them to others. A man may buy a luxury car because he feels it adds to his social position in the neighbourhood. Or a woman may buy expensive golf clubs to keep up with her peer group. But when questioned about their motives, they offer other reasons that they think will be more socially acceptable. The most difficult motives to uncover are those at the third level, where even the buyers themselves cannot explain the real factors motivating their buying actions.

To further complicate our understanding, a purchase is often the result of multiple motives. Moreover, various motives may conflict with one another. In buying a jacket, a young man may want to (1) please himself, (2) please his girlfriend, (3) be considered fashion savvy among his friends, and (4) strive for value. To accomplish all these objectives in one purchase is truly a difficult assignment. Also a person's buying behaviour changes because of changes in income, lifestyle, and other factors. Finally, identical behaviour by several people may result from quite different motives, and different behaviour by the same person at various times may result from the same motive.

CLASSIFICATION OF MOTIVES Psychologists generally agree that motives can be grouped in two broad categories:

◆ Needs aroused from physiological states of tension (such as the need for sleep).

◆ Needs aroused from psychological states of tension (such as the needs for affection and self-respect).

Maslow's hierarchy of needs
A needs structure consisting of five levels and organized according to the order in which people seek need gratification.

A refinement of these two sets is Maslow's hierarchy of five levels of needs, arrayed in the order in which people appear to seek to gratify them.[21] **Maslow's hierarchy of needs**, shown in Figure 6-2, recognizes that a normal person is most likely to be working toward need satisfaction on several levels at the same time and that rarely are all needs on a given level fully satisfied. However, the hierarchy indicates that the majority of needs on a particular level must be reasonably well satisfied before a person is motivated at the next higher level.

In their attempts to market products or communicate with particular segments, marketers often must go beyond a general classification like Maslow's to understand the specific motives underlying behaviour. For example, to observe that a consumer on a shopping trip may be satisfying physiological and social needs because he or she purchases food and talks to friends in the store may be useful, but often more detail is required. Much more needs to be done, however, to identify marketing-specific motives and to measure their strengths.

A recently proposed model suggests that all behavior is determined by fifteen fundamental motives, and that individual differences are the result of varying priorities and intensities among these motives.[22] These motives are: curiosity, food, honour, rejection, sex, physical exercise, order, independence, power, citizenship, pain avoidance, prestige, family, social contact, and vengeance. Appealing to a relevant motive in marketing efforts will thus garner the attention of some group of consumers. The curiosity motive is what appears to drive many to surf the Web not just to see what is out there but to gather information on a myriad of topics of interest as well as for shopping and product comparison information.

perception
Collecting and processing information from the environment in order to give meaning to the world around us.

Perception

A motive is an aroused need. It, in turn, activates behaviour intended to satisfy the aroused need. One form that behaviour takes is collecting and processing information from the environment, a process known as **perception**. We constantly receive, organize, and assign meaning to stimuli detected by our five senses. In this way, we interpret or give meaning to the world around us. Perception plays a major role in the alternative-identification stage of the buying-decision process.

What we perceive — the meaning we give something sensed — depends on the object and our experiences. In an instant, the mind is capable of receiving information, comparing it with a huge store of images in memory, and providing an interpretation.

Though important, visual stimuli are just one factor in perception. Consumers make use of all five senses. Scents, for example, are powerful behaviour triggers. Who can resist the aroma of popcorn in a theatre or of fresh cookies in a bakery? As with all perception, memory plays a large part with aromas. A recent study of common odours that evoke pleasant childhood memories found that older consumers identified natural smells of horses, flowers, and hay. However, younger subjects associated pleasant recollections with the scent of Play-Doh and even jet fuel! Marketers are using this type of information to associate odours with products and shopping environments to create positive perceptions.

FIGURE 6-2
Maslow's Hierarchy of Needs

Every day we come in contact with an enormous number of marketing stimuli. However, a process of selectivity limits our perceptions. As an illustration, consider that:

◆ We pay attention by exception. That is, of all the marketing stimuli our senses are exposed to, only those with the power to capture and hold our attention have the potential of being perceived. This phenomenon is called **selective attention**.

◆ We may alter information that is inconsistent with our beliefs and attitudes. Thus someone may say, "Despite the evidence, I don't believe smoking will be hazardous to my health." This is **selective distortion**.

◆ We retain only part of what we have selectively perceived. We may read an ad but later forget it. This is known as **selective retention**.

There are many communication implications in this selectivity process. For example, to grasp and hold attention, an ad must be involving enough to stimulate the consumer to seek more information. If the ad is too familiar, it will be ignored. On the other hand, if it is too complex, the ad will be judged not worth the time and effort to understand it. Thus, the goal is a mildly ambiguous first impression that heightens the consumer's interest.

Selective distortion tells us that marketers cannot assume that a message, even if it is factually correct, will necessarily be accepted as fact by consumers. In designing a message, the distance between the audience's current belief and the position proposed by the message must be considered. If the distance is large, a moderate claim may be more believable than a dramatic claim and therefore more effective in moving consumers in the desired direction.

Even messages received undistorted are still subject to selective retention. Consequently ads are repeated many times. The hope is that numerous exposures will etch the message into the recipient's memory. This partially explains why a firm with very familiar products, such as Wrigley's, spends over $100 million a year in Canada and the United States to reinforce its brand name. Such practices are intended to cause top-of-mind awareness. In other words, your particular brand will be the first brand thought of when buying gum occurs to the consumer.

Learning

Learning may be defined as changes in behaviour resulting from previous experiences. Thus it excludes behaviour that is attributable to instinct, such as breathing, or temporary states, such as hunger or fatigue. The ability to interpret and predict the consumer's learning process enhances our understanding of buying behaviour, since learning plays a role at every stage of the buying-decision process. No simple learning theory has emerged as universally workable and acceptable. However, the one with the most direct application to marketing strategy is the stimulus-response theory.[23]

According to **stimulus-response theory**, learning occurs as a person (1) responds to some stimulus and (2) is rewarded with need satisfaction for a correct response or penalized for an incorrect one. When the same correct response is repeated in reaction to the same stimulus, a behaviour pattern or learning is established.

Once a habitual behaviour pattern has been established, it replaces conscious, wilful behaviour. This is the same as saying that a consumer, having been satisfied or more than satisfied, continues a relationship with the seller. The task for competitors is to find a way, by arousing need in a different way or once need has been aroused, to break into the process and cause the consumer to pay attention to other information.

selective attention
The process that limits our perceptions such that, of all the marketing stimuli our senses are exposed to, only those able to capture and hold our attention have the potential of being perceived.

selective distortion
The process of mentally altering information that is inconsistent with one's own beliefs or attitudes.

selective retention
The process of retaining in memory some portion of what is perceived.

learning
Changes in behaviour resulting from previous experiences.

stimulus-response theory
The theory that learning occurs as a person responds to some stimuli and is rewarded with need satisfaction for a correct response or penalized for an incorrect one.

Marketing at Work 6-2

Images of Canada: How Foreign Consumers Perceive Canadian Imports

When Canadian consumer goods marketers move from a domestic to an international strategy, they run into the contradiction that consumers around the world are both the same and different. But they should know all about this, after all, Canada is a place of many sub-cultures, each with its own perceptions, attitudes and other learned experiences — all, to varying degrees, culturally based. And we should keep in mind the fact that while perceptions do not necessarily change easily, first hand experience is one of the best ways of getting them to change.

We should expect, therefore, to deal with the fact that consumers in the U.S., Germany, Japan or anywhere else for that matter, have some interesting learned stereotypes and perceptions about Canada and Canadian products and brands. International marketers have to know what these perceptions are so that they can try and position products and brands in useful terms. In the language of international marketing, this is called the "country of origin" problem.

A general appreciation of the acceptance of foreign consumer products can be found in the results of a nineteen-country survey, with twenty thousand participants, conducted by the Gallup Organization for Bozell Worldwide Inc., an international advertising agency. The survey measured perceptions about the quality of both imported and domestic goods. Interviewing was done by telephone in developed countries and face-to-face in less developed ones. Among the twenty thousand participants, the percentage who rated each of the following country's manufactured products as excellent or very good were:

	Percent		Percent
Japan	41.2	Spain	10.0
Germany	35.1	China	8.2
United States	34.9	Taiwan	7.6
Britain	21.2	South Korea	7.2
France	20.8	Russia	5.3
Canada	17.9	Mexico	4.6
Italy	16.6	Brazil	4.4

If we look at self-centredness — how the inhabitants of each country rated their own manufactures — we find that 69 percent of Japanese rated their products as very good to excellent; Canadians came next with 60 percent for domestic goods, 41 percent for Japanese, and 34 percent for American — smug, eh! American consumers rated Japanese products ahead of their own; the British prefer German imports; the Chinese are happier with anything foreign, led by Japan; 40 percent of French consumers rated their own highly, tied with German goods at 40 percent; 43 percent of Germans rated their own highly but had little regard for anyone else's.

If we look at cutting edge industries such as technology and health care, the U.S. is seen as the No. 1 supplier according to 54 percent of respondents from around the world. For computer equipment alone, a huge 80 percent of Japanese felt the U.S. was the best supplier while only 44 percent of Canadians agreed.

Perhaps things are different for food products. Into the perceived inhospitable German market comes a special Canadian food promotion. Upscale KaDeWe, a German department store chain, featured 160 Canadian food products in its fine-foods section, replete with two red-coated Mounties (hard to find at home) and a group of Blackfoot people from Alberta. You should know that among many Germans, there is a great interest in Canada's "Wild West." Maple syrup, smoked salmon, Robin Hood cookie mixes, Dare cookies, Bite Lite potato snacks, jams, mint jellies, and Upper Canada beer (which meets Germany's stringent purity regulations) all sold very well, and some items ran out of stock. The Canadian government, which helped put this show together, used it as a rehearsal for its next promotion of sixty Canadian foods in one hundred Karlstadt department stores across Germany.

The image of Canada in Japan is one of being clean, pure, natural, and trustworthy. So it is not a surprise when C.E. Jameson vitamins, produced in Windsor, Ontario, and represented in Japan by Oriex, a drugstore and food chain with 2,300 outlets, are advertised using a poster depicting sparkling glacial lakes and snow-covered Rocky Mountain peaks beneath the Canadian flag. "This product is imported from Canada, home of forests and lakes," reads the Japanese copy.

Well, international consumer goods marketing *is* different from domestic marketing.

Source: Adapted in part from Alan Freeman, "Canadian Food Finds an Upmarket Niche," *The Globe and Mail*, January 28, 1997, p. B13; Brian Miller, "Survey Finds Pride in Canadian Products High," *The Globe and Mail*, December 4, 1996, p. B8; Barrie McKenna, "Canada's Image Used to Sell Vitamins," *The Globe and Mail*, May 6, 1997, p. B19; and Kathleen Macklem, "Anti-Americanism Stops in the Shops," *The Financial Post*, April 13, 2000, pp. A1–A2.

Marketers have taught consumers to respond to certain cues:

◆ End-of-aisle displays in supermarkets suggest that an item is on sale.

◆ Sale signs in store windows suggest that bargains can be found inside.

◆ Large type in newspaper grocery ads suggests that featured items are particularly good bargains.

But the sad fact for marketers is that what is learned can be unlearned, and effective competitors search the decision-making process and the detail of each stage to find ways of disrupting habitual learned behaviour. Of course, the consumer adds to a marketer's frustration by seeking variety, by finding oneself short of time or money and thus prepared to behave differently, or by facing an empty shelf where one expects to find a favourite brand.

Personality

The study of human personality has given rise to many, sometimes widely divergent, schools of psychological thought. As a result, attempts to inventory and classify personality traits have produced a variety of different structures. In this discussion, **personality** is defined broadly as an individual's pattern of traits that influence behavioural responses. We speak of people as being self-confident, aggressive, shy, domineering, dynamic, secure, introverted, flexible, or friendly and as being influenced (but not controlled) by these personality traits in their responses to situations.

It is generally agreed that personality traits do influence consumers' perceptions and buying behaviour. However, there is considerable disagreement about the nature of this relationship, that is, about how personality influences behaviour. Although we know that people's personalities often are reflected in the clothes they wear, the cars they drive (or whether they use a bike or motorcycle instead of a car), and the restaurants they eat in, we have not been successful in predicting behaviour from particular personality traits. The reason is simple: Many things besides personality enter into the consumer buying-decision process.

THE SELF-CONCEPT Your **self-concept**, or self-image, is the way you see yourself. At the same time, it is the picture you think others have of you. Social psychologists distinguish between (1) the **actual self-concept** (the way you really see yourself) and (2) the **ideal self-concept** (the way you want to be seen or would like to see yourself). To some extent, the self-concept theory is a reflection of other psychological and sociological dimensions already discussed. A person's self-concept is influenced, for instance, by innate and learned physiological and psychological needs. It is conditioned also by economic factors, demographic factors, and social-group influences.

Studies of purchases show that people generally prefer brands and products that are compatible with their self-concept. There are mixed reports concerning the degree of influence of the actual and ideal self-concepts on brand and product preferences. Some researchers contend that consumption preferences correspond to a person's actual self-concept. Others hold that the ideal self-concept is dominant in consumers' choices.

Perhaps there is no consensus here because in real life we often switch back and forth between our actual and our ideal self-concepts. A middle-aged man may buy some comfortable, but not fashionable, clothing to wear at home on a weekend, where he is reflecting his actual self-concept. Then later he buys some expensive, high-fashion exercise

personality
An individual's pattern of traits that influences behavioural responses.

self-concept
A person's self-image.

actual self
The way you really see yourself. To be distinguished from *ideal self.*

ideal self
The way you want to be seen or would like to see yourself. To be distinguished from *actual self.*

clothing, envisioning himself (ideal self-concept) as a young, active, upwardly mobile guy. This same fellow may drive his old, beat-up minivan for his weekend errands (actual self-concept). But he'll drive his new, European sports sedan to work, where he wants to project a different (ideal) self-concept.[24]

The various self-concept frames of reference can be used to design marketing research projects as well as help to organize approaches to interviewing consumers and analyzing research results. The self- and/or ideal self-concept frames of reference can be used in advertisements as a before-and-after approach as well as by sales and service personnel in determining customer problems, needs, and aspirations.

Attitudes

attitude

A learned predisposition to respond to an object or class of objects in a consistently favourable or unfavourable way.

Attitude is traditionally defined as a learned predisposition to respond to an object or class of objects in a consistently favourable or unfavourable way. In our model of the buying-decision process, attitudes play a major role in the evaluation of alternatives. Numerous studies have reported a relationship between consumers' attitudes and their buying behaviour regarding both types of products and services selected and brands chosen. Surely, then, it is in a marketer's best interest to understand how attitudes are formed, the functions they perform, and how they can be changed.

All attitudes have the following characteristics in common:

◆ Attitudes are learned. The information individuals acquire through their direct experiences with a product or an idea, indirect experiences (such as reading about a product in *Canadian Living* or on the Internet), and interactions with individuals in their social groups all contribute to the formation of attitudes. For example, the opinions expressed by a good friend about diet foods plus the consumer's favourable or unfavourable experience as a result of using diet foods will contribute to an attitude toward diet foods in general.

◆ Attitudes have an object. By definition, we can hold attitudes only toward something. The object can be general (professional sports) or specific (Toronto Blue Jays); it can be abstract (college life) or concrete (the computer lab). In attempting to determine consumers' attitudes it is very important to define carefully the object of the attitude because a person might have a favourable attitude toward the general concept (exercise) but a negative attitude toward a specific dimension (jogging).

◆ Attitudes have direction and intensity. Our attitudes are either favourable or unfavourable toward the object. They cannot be neutral. In addition, they have a strength. For example, you may mildly like this textbook or you may like it very much (we hope!). This factor is important for marketers because strongly held attitudes are difficult to change.

◆ Finally, attitudes are arranged in structures that tend to be stable and generalizable. Once formed, attitudes usually endure, and the longer they are held, the more resistant to change they become. People also have a tendency to generalize attitudes. For instance, if a person is treated well by a salesperson in a particular store, there is a tendency to form a favourable attitude toward the entire store.

A consumer's attitudes do not always predict purchase behaviour. A person may hold very favourable attitudes toward a product but not buy it because of some inhibiting factor. Typical inhibitors are not having enough money or discovering your preferred product or brand has been replaced by a new model or is out of stock when the purchase must be made. Under such circumstances, purchase behaviour may even contradict attitudes.

As the preceding discussion suggests, it is extremely difficult to change strongly held attitudes. Moderately held or weakly held attitudes are much more amenable to change. Marketers need to know what consumer attitudes are to many aspects of their products, services, personnel, and advertisements, as well as the strength of such attitudes. Only then can they determine the bases for either satisfaction or dissatisfaction and where their relationships with consumers are vulnerable. When a marketer is faced with strongly held negative or unfavourable attitudes, it has two options. The first is to try to change the attitude to be compatible with the product. The second is to change the product, or more likely its image, to match attitudes. Ordinarily it is much easier to change the product image than to change consumers' strongly held attitudes.

Nevertheless, in many situations, attitudes have been changed. Consider how negative attitudes have changed in favour of trucks and sports utility vehicles or air bags, how positive attitudes have changed about tobacco products, how yellow tennis balls or off-season vacations have been accepted.

Values and Lifestyles

lifestyle
A person's activities, interests, and opinions.

One of the most valuable ways of looking at a market and its potential involves consideration of consumer **lifestyles and values**. Marketers now develop marketing programs based not only on how old their customers are or where they live, but also on how they spend their leisure time, what type of movies they like to watch, and what things they consider important in their lives. This is an integral part of the concept of market segmentation, which we discussed in Chapters 4 and 5. Essentially, the Canadian market is made up of many types of people. Once we can identify how these various groups think and live, we can do a better job of developing products, services, advertising, and other marketing techniques to appeal to them.

The field of psychographic research was developed in the 1960s and initially examined consumer activities, interests, and opinions. Further developments of this approach have been the use of a program known as VALS (Values, Attitudes, and Lifestyle), which was developed at the Stanford Research Institute and is discussed in Chapter 5. VALS research involved the study of thousands of consumers and measures their opinions, interests, attitudes, values, beliefs, and activities in a variety of different areas. Today, psychographic research is considered by many in marketing to have transcended the demographic categories of age, gender, religion, social class, and ethnicity. Michael Adams, president of Environics Research Ltd., has produced the social-value "tribes" of Canada (see the accompanying box), which presents the three major generational divisions that exist in Canada: the Elders, the Boomers, and the GenXers. Everyone in the country fits into one of these three on the basis of age alone. Each of these generational groups is further subdivided pyschographically, resulting in thumbnail sketches for the twelve social value tribes of Canada. Each sketch provides a quick review of the group size, age distribution, geographic location, common motivation factors, social values, catchphrases, and, finally, heroes or icons. Locate yourself, your parents, friends, employers, or potential employers in these groups. The social-value tribes classification provides marketers with a quick, comprehensive, and integrated multivariate view of the basic segmentation of the country. This kind of information signals who is interested in what kinds of products and services, their location, their preferred information themes, their orientations to product claims, and the kinds of information contexts they would likely attend.

The Social-Value "Tribes" of Canada

In the book *Sex in the Snow*, author and pollster Michael Adams proposes that Canadians can be segmented into one of twelve social-value tribes. Initially, Adams divides the Canadian population into three sections: Elders, Boomers, and GenXers. Each of these three categories can be further divided by distinguishing the fundamental motivators, key values, words of advice, and icons of each of the twelve groups. Take a look at the categories below to determine where you fall in Michael Adams' social tribes!

The Elders (aged 50+)

Rational Traditionalists
(54 percent of Elders)
Financial independence, stability, and security are the fundamental motivators of this population group. Some of their key values include primacy of reason, deferred gratification, duty, and guilt. A rational traditionalist could be heard saying "Better safe than sorry," "A woman's place is in the home," or "A bird in the hand is worth two in the bush." These Canadians would idolize individuals such as Sir Winston Churchill, 50's TV character Ward Cleaver, and Franklin D. Roosevelt.

Extroverted Traditionalists
(26 percent of Elders)
This category includes a higher than average proportion of women and individuals from the Maritimes and Quebec. Their fundamental motivators include social status, institutions, and traditional communities. Religion, family, fear, and respect for tradition and institutions are highly valued, and words of wisdom would include epitaphs such as "Duty above all else," "A woman's work is never done," and "A penny saved is a penny earned." Icons of the Extroverted Traditionalists would include Mother Teresa and Jesus Christ.

Cosmopolitan Modernists
(20 percent of Elders)
The category of Cosmopolitan Modernists includes a higher than average proportion of individuals who are from British Columbia, are over fifty, and possess postsecondary education. Traditional institutions and experience seeking are the fundamental motivators of this group, and they place high value on things such as education, innovation, and a global perspective. Cosmopolitan Modernists believe that people should "take time to smell the roses" and that "the world is their oyster." Icons of this group include author Pierre Berton and former Prime Minister Pierre Trudeau.

The Boomers (aged 35–54)

Autonomous Rebels
(25 percent of Boomers)
This category of the boomers have fundamental motivators that include personal autonomy and self-fulfilment. They place a high value on freedom and individuality and are sceptical about traditional institutions. Words of advice from an individual in the Autonomous Rebel category could be: "To each his own," "Knowledge is power," or "I did it my way." Icons include Bill and Hillary Clinton, John Lennon, and Scully and Mulder from *The X-Files*.

Anxious Communicators
(20 percent of Boomers)
Traditional communities, institutions, and social status are considered the fundamental motivators of this social tribe. They value family, community, respect, and fear. The Anxious Communicators believe that "Wisdom comes with age" and "The children are our future." The icons of this category would include individuals such as Oprah Winfrey, Martha Stewart, and Ann Landers.

Disengaged Darwinists
(41 percent of Boomers)
This is the largest group within the Boomers category. It includes a higher proportion of men and blue-collar workers who are motivated by financial independence, stability, and security. Key values of the Disengaged Darwinists are fear and nostalgia for the past. Advice from this group would include "Look out for number one" and "Every man for himself." Icons include Chuck Norris and David Frum.

GenXers (aged 15–29)

Aimless Dependents
(27 percent of GenXers)
This section of GenXers crave the financial independence, security, and stability that their parents, members of the boomers, possessed. Their key

The Social-Value "Tribes" of Canada continued

values include a desire for independence and fear. Words of wisdom from this group would include: "What's the point," "I couldn't care less," and "What's the system going to do for me?" The icons for this group include Eric Lindros, Courtney Love, and the Smashing Pumpkins.

Thrill-Seeking Materialists
(25 percent of GenXers)
The fundamental motivators of Thrill-Seeking Materialists include traditional communities, social status, and experience seeking. Their key values include the desire for money, material possessions, respect, and admiration. Words of advice from this group would be "Live dangerously" and "Money is power." Icons of the Thrill-Seeking Materialists are Pamela Anderson Lee and Calvin Klein.

New Aquarians
(13 percent of GenXers)
This group is characterized by their desire for new experiences and new communities. They believe in hedonism, ecologism, and egalitarianism. Advice from the New Aquarians could include "There is no being, only becoming" and "Unity is diversity."

Their icons include Tori Amos, Sarah McLachlan, and William Gibson.

Autonomous Post-Materialists
(20 percent of GenXers)
The fundamental motivators of this group of GenXers are personal autonomy and self-fulfilment, and their key values include freedom and respect for human rights. In the mind of an Autonomous Post-Materialist, words to live by would include "It's my life," "Image is nothing," and "There is more to life than money." Icons of this group include Dennis Rodman, Bart Simpson, and Ashley MacIsaac.

Social Hedonists
(15 percent of GenXers)
This group of GenXers seeks new experiences and new communications. They value immediate gratification, sexual permissiveness, and hedonism. They advise people, "Party hard," "If you look good you feel good," and "Don't worry, be happy." The icons of this group include Janet Jackson and Chris Shepard.

Source: Adapted from Michael Adams, "The Demise of Demography," *The Globe and Mail*, January 18, 1997, p. D5, and based on *Sex in the Snow: Canadian Social Values at the End of the Millennium* (Toronto: Penguin Canada, 1997).

Situational Influences

situational influences
Temporary forces, associated with the immediate purchase environment, that affect behaviour.

After all is said and done, the situations in which we find ourselves play a large part in determining how we actually behave. Students, for example, act differently in a classroom than they do in their favourite coffee shop. The same holds true of buying behaviour. You might get your hair cut because of an upcoming job interview. On vacation you might buy a souvenir that seems very strange when you get home. For a close friend's wedding gift, you might buy a fancier brand of small appliance than you would buy for yourself. These are all examples of **situational influences**, temporary forces associated with the immediate purchase environment that affect behaviour. Situational influence tends to be less significant when the consumer is very loyal to a brand and when the consumer is highly involved in the purchase. However, it often plays a major role in buying decisions. The five categories of situational influences are explained next.

When Consumers Buy — The Time Dimension

Marketers should be able to answer at least two time-related questions about consumer buying: Is it influenced by the season, week, day, or hour? What impact do past and present events have on the purchase decision?

The time dimension of buying has implications for promotion scheduling. Promotional messages must reach consumers when they are in a decision-making frame of mind. Marketers also adjust prices in an attempt to even out demand. For instance, supermarkets may offer double coupons on Wednesdays, usually a slow business day. If seasonal buying patterns exist, marketers can sometimes extend the buying season. There is obviously (or so you'd think) little opportunity to extend the buying season for Easter bunnies or Christmas ornaments, although some "Christmas" stores operate year round. Hallmark (www.hallmark.com/), known for its greeting cards, also has an ornament division. They have created ornament markets that did not exist before. Halloween, Easter, Valentine's Day, St. Patrick's Day now all have their own collectible ornaments. Hallmark's popular dated Christmas ornaments known for appreciating in value over time "debut" each July and is therefore available for gift giving over several months. Hallmark has developed a reputation as a gift of quality and supports their collectible markets through sponsorship of local collector groups and events.

Even the traditional season for vacations has been shifted to such an extent that winter and other "off-season" or "shoulder-season" vacations are now quite popular.

The second question concerns the impact of past or future events. For example, the length of time since you last went out to dinner at a nice restaurant may influence a decision on where to go tonight. Or the significance of an upcoming event, such as a vacation trip to a resort area, could result in a greater than normal amount of clothing purchases. Marketers need to know enough about the targeted consumers to anticipate the effects of these past and future events.

Dual-income boomers are finding it difficult to make time in their busy schedules to prepare meals at home, yet they can afford to take the family out to eat at a restaurant that offers something more in terms of quality than do the mainstream fast-food outlets such as McDonald's, Burger King, and Harvey's. Rather than standing in long lines for burgers and fries, these families are heading for restaurants that offer a wider menu selection, table service, and a family atmosphere. As a result, there is currently considerable growth in the sector of the restaurant business labelled family restaurants, which include Swiss Chalet, White Spot, and Golden Griddle, and in the slightly more pricey casual-dining sector, where we find East Side Mario's, Jack Astor's, and such regional chains as Milestone's.[25]

The growth and popularity of fast-food restaurants, quick-oil-change outlets, highly specialized Web sites, and catalogue retailers are marketers' responses to consumers' time pressures. Dual-income households, job activity (including business trips and travel time to and from work), and mandatory leisure-time activities (such as car pooling children to social and sports events) leave little time for relaxed shopping. The results are measurable. In 1988 the average consumer spent ninety minutes on a mall-shopping trip. The figure today has fallen below sixty-five minutes. To help consumers conserve time, marketers are making large and small changes. For example, some photo-processing operations return developed prints by mail, e-mail, or send them to their customer's Web site to save time and effort.

Since Internet based marketers are open for business twenty-four hours a day, whether they are of the pure "click" or "click and brick" variety, time of buying can and is being changed. And it

Are you and your friends comfortable eating at Swiss Chalet? Is the service quick enough? Who else eats there?

will continue to change as more people gain more confidence in buying on the Internet and using the leisure times available to them, which is not normally traditional shopping times, to conduct searches and engage in transactions. This will eventually have an impact on the business hours of physical establishments.

Where Consumers Buy — The Physical and Social Surroundings

Physical surroundings are the features of a situation that are apparent to the senses, such as lighting, smells, weather, and sounds. Think of the importance of atmosphere in a restaurant or the sense of excitement and action created by the sights and sounds in a gambling casino. Music can be an important element in a store's strategy. Colours, smells, and sounds can all be engineered to control the consumer's retail experience and attempt to influence their behaviour.

The social surroundings are the number, mix, and actions of other people at the purchase site. You probably would not go into a strange restaurant that has an empty parking lot. And in a crowded store with other customers waiting, you will probably ask the clerk fewer questions and spend less time comparing products.

Surroundings also impact experiences on the Internet. The ease with which product information can be obtained and orders can be made in the virtual surroundings will decide if a site will be considered for future purchases. The Internet also places greater control in consumers' hands. Wherever the purchase is made, consumers can now arm themselves with huge quantities of technical and pricing information that allows greater leverage when making unfamiliar and/or large purchases. This knowledge combined with information regarding actual and virtual locations to buy a product help prevent a consumer from being taken advantage of, or simply making uninformed purchasing decisions.

How Consumers Buy — The Terms and Conditions of the Purchase

How consumers buy refers to the terms and conditions of sale as well as the transaction-related activities that buyers are willing to perform. Many more retailers sell on credit today than just a few years ago. Not only do consumers use credit for instalment purchases (to buy things today with future income), but many now use credit for convenience. The ability to use Visa or MasterCard to make a wide variety of purchases while not carrying cash is an attractive option to many consumers as is use of the debit card. Another recent development is the increase in purchases made by mail, phone, and Internet. The growth of catalogue distribution, telephone/mail-order, and e-commerce has enabled consumers to buy everything from food to a new house without setting foot outside the door.

Many firms now make products and services available only through cyberspace. Maple Square, Sympatico's Canadian Internet directory, for example, offers a listing of hundreds of companies in all areas ranging from private investigative services to accounting services to kitchen appliances.[26]

Finally, the trend toward one-stop shopping with the increasing pressures on our time has encouraged traditional retailers to add unrelated items to their basic mix of products. Consider, for example, the wide variety of goods found in what we call a drugstore. Many Shoppers Drug Mart locations, for example, carry many household cleaning supplies and grocery items. E-tailers attempt to design and develop Web sites which carry more and more items. Amazon. com continues to add product lines to what was originally a "books only" Internet site.

Marketers have also experimented with transferring functions or activities to consumers. What were once called "service stations" are now called "gas stations" because you pump your own gas and wash your own windshield. These retailers have also added value through offering grocery items as well as franchise food services such as McDonald's and Pizza Hut counters. Consumers have shown a willingness to assemble products, bag their own groceries, and buy in bulk quantities — all in exchange for lower prices. Banks have succeeded in getting customers to complete many of their own transactions through ATMs and telephone and PC banking. This has escalated from performing your own withdrawals to purchasing savings instruments and processing much of your own home mortgage.

Why Consumers Buy — The Objective of the Purchase

The intent of or reason for a purchase affects the choices made. We are likely to behave very differently if we are buying a product for a gift rather than buying the same product for our personal use. When purchasing a wristwatch, a consumer may be most interested in one that will provide accurate time at a reasonable price. However, the appearance of a watch bought as a graduation present can be very important. Occasions often represent reasons why consumers make purchases and can influence the type of purchase made. Commemorating wedding anniversaries, for example, can be the objective for jewellery purchases and dinner arrangements.

A marketer must understand the consumer's objective in buying the product or service in order to design an effective marketing mix. For example, the failure of most watchmakers to appeal to the functional, non-gift watch market is what allowed Timex to be so successful with its reasonably priced product.

Conditions Under Which Consumers Buy — States and Moods

Sometimes consumers are in a temporary state that influences their buying decisions. When you are ill or rushed, you may be unwilling to wait in line or to take the time or care that a particular purchase deserves. Moods can also influence purchases. Feelings such as anger or excitement can result in purchases that otherwise would not have been made. In the exciting atmosphere of a rock concert, for example, you might pay more for a commemorative T-shirt than you would under normal circumstances. Salespeople must be trained to recognize consumers' moods and adjust their presentations accordingly.

Marketers must also monitor long-term situational influences. The optimistic consumers of the 1980s were free-spending and apparently carefree. Household debt grew 50 percent faster than disposable income during the decade as the baby boom generation acquired cars, homes, and household possessions. However, the recession that rocked the economy at the end of the 1980s produced many changes. It created more conservative buyers who save more, avoid debt, and purchase more carefully. As we started the new millennium, consumers of all ages were more sophisticated and demanding than in any previous times. Greater education and access to information is largely responsible for these changes, along with lessons from the 80s. Though it is difficult to predict if changes such as these in consumer psychology are temporary or permanent, they have important implications for virtually all marketers.

When a particular situational influence becomes widely accepted and strongly embedded (such as shopping on particular days of the week), overcoming it can be difficult. The marketer may have to carry out an extensive campaign with no guarantee of success.

Scheduling shopping and banking is now, of course, no longer an issue to the computer-savvy. The information superhighway allows the consumer to perform many such errands without having to concern themselves with traffic, parking, line-ups, getting the children to bed, or other daily pressures. On the Internet you quickly arrive at your destination of choice, and you can do it in your robe and slippers. This will certainly cause many to be in a better mood when shopping. The down side is that this form of shopping doesn't deliver the same instant gratification as provided by walking out of the store with your new purchase. So while many routine purchases, window-shopping, information seeking and banking may go the way of cyberspace, how successful will other consumer goods fair in this marketplace?

Summary

The buying behaviour of ultimate consumers can be examined using a five-part model: the buying-decision process, information, social and group forces, psychological forces, and situational factors.

The buying-decision process is composed of six stages consumers go through in making purchases. The stages are need recognition, choice of an involvement level, identification of alternatives, evaluation of alternatives, purchase and related decisions, and postpurchase behaviour.

Information fuels the buying-decision process. Without it, there would be no decisions. There are two categories of information sources: commercial and social. Commercial sources include advertising, personal selling, selling by phone or Internet, and personal involvement with a product. Word of mouth, observation, and experience with a product owned by someone else are social sources.

Social and group forces are composed of culture, sub-culture, social class, reference groups, family, and households. Culture has the broadest and most general influence on buying behaviour, while a person's household has the most immediate impact. Social and group forces have a direct impact on individual purchase decisions as well as a person's psychological makeup.

Psychological forces that affect buying decisions are motivation, perception, learning, personality, and attitudes. All behaviour is motivated by some aroused need. Perception is the way we interpret the world around us and is subject to three types of selectivity: attention, distortion, and retention. Learning is a change in behaviour as a result of experience. Continued reinforcement leads to habitual buying and brand loyalty.

Personality is the sum of an individual's traits that influence behavioural responses. Personality patterns predispose consumers to certain types of information, product features, and interactions. The self-concept is related to personality. Because purchasing and consumption are very expressive actions, they communicate to the world our actual and ideal self-concepts.

Attitudes are learned predispositions to respond to an object or class of objects in a consistent fashion. Besides being learned, all attitudes are directed toward an object, have direction and intensity, and tend to be stable and generalizable. Strongly held attitudes are difficult to change.

Situational influences deal with when, where, how, and why consumers buy, and with the consumer's personal condition at the time of purchase. Situational influences are often so powerful that they can override all of the other forces in the buying-decision process.

Key Terms and Concepts

Buying-decision process 155
High involvement 156
Low involvement 156
Impulse buying 157
Patronage buying motives 159
Postpurchase behaviour 161
Cognitive dissonance 161
Commercial information 163
Social information 163
Culture 164

Sub-culture 164
Social class 167
Upper class 168
Upper-middle class 168
Lower-middle class 168
Upper-lower class 168
Lower-lower class 168
Reference groups 169
Innovator 170
Opinion leader 170

Family and household 170
Psychographics 172
Motive 172
Maslow's hierarchy of needs 173
Perception 173
Selective attention 174
Selective distortion 174
Selective retention 174
Learning 174
Stimulus-response theory 174

Personality 176
Self-concept 176
Actual self-concept 176
Ideal self-concept 176
Attitude 177
Lifestyles and values 178
Situational influences 180

Questions and Problems

1. When might the purchase of a colour television be a low-involvement decision?

2. When a consumer's experience with a product equals her or his expectations for the product, the person is satisfied. Is there any disadvantage to a marketer whose product causes consumers' experience to greatly exceed expectations?

3. From a consumer-behaviour perspective, why is it incorrect to view the European Union or the countries of Asia as single markets?

4. Explain why reference-group influence would affect the choice of the product, the brand, or neither for the following items:

   a. Bath soap.

   b. Auto tune-up.

   c. Haircut.

   d. Laptop computer.

5. What roles would you expect a couple and their young child to play in the purchase of the following items?

   a. Nintendo.

   b. Choice of a fast-food outlet for dinner.

   c. Personal computer.

   d. Lawn-care service.

6. Explain how self-concept might come into play in the purchase of the following products:

   a. Eyeglasses.

   b. New suit.

   c. Eye-shadow.

   d. College education.

7. What situational influences might affect a family's choice of a motel in a strange town while on a vacation?

8. List three products/services for which usage would not be greatly affected by cultural or ethnic differences. List three that would be so affected by such differences. Explain how.

9. How could you go about assessing your product for its appeal to different cultures or subcultures within or outside of your own country? In other words, how do you find a market for your product?

Hands-On Marketing

1. Interview the manager of a store that sells big-ticket items (furniture, appliances, electronic equipment) about what methods, if any, the store uses to reinforce purchase decisions and reduce the cognitive dissonance of its customers. What additional methods can you suggest?

2. Have a friend describe a high-involvement purchase that he or she recently made. Show how each of the six stages described in this chapter are reflected in the description. Identify the primary social influences that played a part in the decision.

Chapter Seven

The Business Market

In many ways business markets are similar to the consumer markets we have been examining, but there are also important differences. After studying this chapter, in addition to being able to describe how business markets differ from consumer markets, you should have an understanding of:

◆ The nature and scope of the business market.

◆ The components of the business market.

◆ The characteristics of business market demand.

◆ The determinants of business market demand.

◆ The buying motives, buying processes, and buying patterns in business markets.

Nortel Asks Business — And The Rest of Us: What Do You Want The Internet To Be?

*W*hile consumer goods marketing, and the Internet component of it is an "in your face" activity, the real Internet action, and the real money, is behind the scenes — taking place *between* businesses. In early 2000, approximately 80 percent of Internet sales were transacted in the business to business market or e-business. While in the past, business to business marketing (also called B2B marketing) was not very visible, now, in the high-tech information age, we are becoming much more aware of it because more firms in the business market advertise in consumer and general media in a fashion similar to that engaged in by consumer goods firms. These companies have begun marketing toward their target markets and broader publics by capitalizing upon traditional consumer marketing styles to capture a place — an image — in the minds of business decision-makers, influencers, users, and more general audiences. This is often done through aligning their marketing efforts with the visions, goals, and directions of the firm and its employees and investors.

Take Nortel Networks, Canada's biggest high-technology provider as well as a major global competitor (www.nortelnet works.com). Nortel supplies Internet hardware and infrastructure equipment — the plumbing of the Internet. It is also a major "business solutions provider." Nortel has mounted, in Canada and other countries, advertising and promotional programs with the theme: "What Do You Want the Internet To Be?" The company is asking Canadians (and citizens around the world) what they want this new technology to be for them — personally and professionally. It is appealing to all markets by showing how this technology can and will play an important part in each of our lives. The same theme is utilized

in recruitment ads with the hope of "selling" the firm to potential employees. Print and media ads foster the idea of entering the Internet era together with Nortel showing the way, navigating a safe and beneficial voyage. Rival IBM is employing a similar campaign, injected with humour.

The nature of these new "virtual" business solutions has enabled a change in the approaches taken to many aspects of B2B marketing. New is a "feel good" approach with a soft side not commonly seen in this competitive arena. Television advertisements feature music that appeals to the nostalgic sensibilities of many viewers who are of a relevant age in this marketplace. Nortel's Internet presence goes beyond the usual generic presentation of its varied product lines, it also features downloadable video and audio advertisements. Visitors to the Nortel Web site can reply to that promotional question and have an opportunity to be selected to appear in future advertisements in this campaign. Also, visitors may write about an individual they feel should be featured in the "Your Hero" segment. As well, there are features on socially conscious personalities such as Elton John, founder of the AIDS Foundation.

The Nortel Networks message to business, and all others watching, is that we are all entering a new era of communications, collaboration, and commerce. "Created by Nortel and its customers, it touches everyone and everything." From the wired to the wireless, Nortel poses a question based on limitless possibility — What do you want the Internet to be?[1]

The Nature and Scope of the Business Market

The **business market** consists of all **business users** — organizations that buy goods and services for one of the following purposes:

◆ *To make other goods and services.* Campbell's Soups buys fresh vegetables for its Leamington, Ontario plant; Bombardier (www.bombardier.com) in Montreal and its other Canadian and worldwide locations buys a great variety of different materials to make products as varied as their Ski-Doos® snowmobiles, Sea-Doos® personal watercraft, ATVs (the Traxter), as well as regional jets. ATI Technologies in Toronto, makers of high speed graphics cards for computers, also buys parts and components for its manufacturing processes from a large variety of domestic and global sources.

◆ *To resell to other business users or to consumers.* Loblaw buys canned tuna fish from South America and Asia to sell across Canada; Western Pipe buys lawn sprinkler equipment and supplies from Canadian, American and other offshore manufacturers and resells them to sprinkler contractors in the West. Private-label brands are usually purchased from brand name manufacturers and then relabelled by grocery and department stores. This ranges from food items to major appliances and automobiles. Brand names can also matter for component parts. Most computer producers utilize the Intel Pentium processor (www.intel.com), going so far to label this tiny part on the outside of the finished product ("intel inside"). This is not a part they produced, but merely bought for assembly.

A complex parts and materials supply chain has to be put in place before these ski-doos can be parked.

◆ *To conduct the organization's operations.* The University of Calgary buys office supplies and electronic office equipment for use in the registrar's office; Winnipeg's St. Boniface General Hospital buys supplies to use in its operating rooms; Canadian Tire buys software to coordinate and manage its inventory system across the country. Even firms we all patronize have large business clients — after all, they too must buy electrical and phone utilities. Imagine the power bill for a clothing factory, or the phone bill for a regional call centre! Also, companies such as Purolator buy fleets of vans and trucks each year from the same auto companies where we buy our cars and SUVs.

business marketing
The marketing of goods and services to business users.

In the business market we deal with both consumer products and business products. **Business marketing**, then, is the marketing of goods and services to business users, in contrast to ultimate, or end, consumers.

Because the business market is largely unknown to the average consumer, we underrate its significance. It is huge when measured by total sales volume and the number of firms involved. About 50 percent of all manufactured products are sold to the business market. In addition, about 80 percent of all farm products and virtually all forest, sea, and mineral products are business goods. All these goods are sold to firms for further processing.

The magnitude and complexity of the business market are also evident from the many transactions required to produce and market a product. Consider, for example, the business marketing transactions and total sales volume involved in getting those thick-soled, leather hi-top boots to their teenage and young adult end-users. First, cattle are sold through one or two intermediaries before reaching a meatpacker. Then the hides are sold to a tanner, who in turn sells the leather to a specialized footwear manufacturer. The shoe manufacturer may sell the finished boots to a wholesaler, who markets them to select retail stores. Finally, they are then available to you, the end consumer. At least five transactions are involved here and each sale but the last one is a business to business market transaction. Each of the B2B transactions can be made in a market that operates for that type of transaction. We are usually only aware and familiar with the ultimate market, the retailer to consumer transaction at the consumer market level.

In addition, the footwear manufacturer buys metal eyelets, laces, thread, glue, heels and soles, zippers for some footwear, as well as polishes and dyes. Consider something as simple as the bootlaces. Other industrial firms must first buy the raw cotton and then spin, weave, dye, and cut it so that it becomes shoestring material. All the manufacturers involved have factories and offices with furniture, machinery, furnaces, lights, computer hardware and software, and maintenance equipment and supplies required to run them — and these also are business goods that have to be produced and marketed. Imagine, then, the number of transactions that have occurred from the cattle and cotton fields to the footwear you are now wearing. In short, hundreds of business products and business marketing activities may come into play before almost any product — consumer good or business good — reaches its final destination.

The magnitude and complexity of the business market loom even larger when we consider all the business services involved throughout our "simple" footwear example. Each firm engaged in any stage of the production process probably uses outside accountants, computer systems designers, and law firms. Several of the producers may use advertising agencies. All of these companies will use the services of various financial institutions.

Every retail store and wholesaling establishment is a business user. Every bus company, airline, and railway is part of this market. So is every hotel, restaurant, bank, insurance company, software provider, hospital, theatre, and school. In all, there are close to half a million business users in Canada. While this is far short of the approximately thirty million consumers, the total sales volume in the business market far surpasses total sales to consumers.

Components of the Business Market

Traditionally, business markets were referred to as industrial markets. This caused many people to think that the term referred only to approximately forty thousand Canadian manufacturing firms. These firms alone have an estimated shipment value in excess of $450 billion.[2] But as you can see from our discussion so far, the business market is a lot more than that. Certainly manufacturers constitute a major portion of the business market, but there are also five other components: agriculture, resellers, government agencies, service companies, and not-for-profit organizations. Although they are often underrated or overlooked because of the heavy attention devoted to manufacturing, each is a significant part of the business market. And it must be kept in mind that some of Canada's most important and fastest growing business markets are outside Canada — in the United States and many other countries.

The Agriculture Market

The worldwide income from the sale of Canadian agricultural products gives farmers, as a group, the purchasing power that makes them a highly attractive market. Moreover, world population forecasts and food shortages in many countries undoubtedly will keep pressure on farmers to increase their output. Companies hoping to sell to the farm market must analyze it carefully and be aware of significant trends. The proportion of farmers in the total population and the number of farms have been decreasing and probably will continue to decline. Counterbalancing this has been an increase in large corporate or "business" types of farms. Even the remaining "family farms" are expanding in order to survive. Farming is becoming more automated and mechanized. This means, of course, that capital investment in farming is increasing. **Agribusiness** — farming, food processing, and other large-scale farming-related businesses — is big business in every sense of the word.

agribusiness
The business side of farming. Usually involves large, highly mechanized farming operations.

Agriculture is a modern industry. Like other business executives, farmers are looking for better ways to increase their productivity, cut their expenses, and manage their cash flows. Technology is an important part of the process. For example, one large business farmer has developed a sensor and remote steering system that guides a tractor between the rows in a field to avoid destroying any crops. Caterpillar Equipment, in order to service large equipment in remote locations has a satellite that can monitor onboard systems, detect equipment wear, and perform diagnostic tests automatically shipping replacement parts within hours so they will arrive before they are required.

As farmers become fewer and larger, marketing to them effectively requires carefully designed strategies. For example, some large fertilizer producers have salespeople who visit individual farms. There, working with the farmer, the sales rep analyzes the soil and crops to determine exactly what fertilizer mix is best for the particular farm. Based on the analysis, the manufacturer prepares the appropriate blend of ingredients as a special order.

The Reseller Market

reseller market
Wholesaling and retailing intermediaries that buy products for resale to other business users or to consumers. A segment of the business market.

Intermediaries in the Canadian marketing system — a few hundred thousand wholesalers, retailers, and other organizations — constitute the **reseller market**. The basic activity of resellers — unlike that of any other business market segment — is buying products from supplier organizations and reselling these items in essentially the same form to the resellers' customers. In economic terms, resellers create time, place, and possession utilities, rather than form utility.

Resellers also buy many goods and services for use in operating their businesses — items such as office supplies and information and communication equipment, warehouses, materials-handling equipment, legal services, computer-system design services, electrical services, and janitorial supplies. In these buying activities, resellers are essentially no different from manufacturers, financial institutions, or any other segment of the business market.

It is their role as *buyers for resale* that differentiates resellers and attracts special marketing attention from their suppliers. To resell an item, you must please your customer. These people must decide what products will be popular or useful to those comprising their market(s). Usually it is more difficult to determine what will please an outside customer than to find out what will satisfy someone within your own organization. For example, an airline that decides to design new jackets for its flight crews for use in foul weather conditions. The airline can carefully study the conditions under which the uniforms will be worn and work closely with the people who will be wearing the uniforms to get their views. As a result, the airline should be able to select an all-weather jacket that will be lightweight and safe to wear when working, will be easy to clean, and reasonably acceptable to the employees. Contrast that with retailers trying, each year, to anticipate what outerwear to purchase and place on their shelves. What will the next trend be — short or long, function or fashion, and what about colours and fabrics? In both cases, clothing is being purchased, but the opportunity for interaction with the users, and the variety of uses and purposes differ greatly between groups and especially within the latter consumer group. This makes buying for resale for the "anonymous" consumer market more difficult and much more risky.

Buying for resale, especially in a large reseller's organization, can be a complex procedure. For a supermarket chain such as Sobey's, Loblaw, or Safeway, a buying committee made up of experts on market demand, trends, supply, and prices frequently does buying. This is needed as hundreds of products may be proposed to these stores each week for consideration, up to ten thousands each year.[3] Department stores may retain resident buyers — independent buying agencies — located in Toronto, London, Hong Kong, or other major market centres to be in constant touch with the latest fashion developments.

disintermediation
The replacement of some traditional intermediaries in a process due to the growth of Internet-based sales.

Resellers, also called "middlemen" or "intermediaries," are the business marketers most directly affected by the new competition of electronic commerce. The growth of Internet-based selling is contributing to the replacement of some traditional intermediaries in a process that has become so commonplace it has a name — **disintermediation**. Only resellers that can create the utility, or specific value, required by their business buyers will continue to prosper.

The Government Market

The large government market includes federal, provincial, territorial, Aboriginal, and municipal governments, as well as various Crown agencies and corporations that spend

The federal government's tendering Web site is operated on an "outsource" basis by Cebra.

millions of dollars worth each year buying for institutions such as schools, offices, hospitals, and military bases. At the federal level, Public Works and Government Services Canada purchases in excess of $170 billion worth of goods and services annually for other government units.[4] The largest "consumers" among these are Public Works and Government Services Canada and The Department of National Defence. Collectively, however, the other levels of governments listed are even more important markets than the federal government. There is even a magazine devoted to the business of public sector procurement at all levels called *Summit* (www.prospectus.com/summit).

Government procurement processes are different from those in the private sector of the business market. A unique feature of government buying is the competitive bidding system. Much government procurement is done on a bid basis and a growing amount of it is now taking place online. That is, the government agency advertises both off and online for bids using a format that states specifications for the intended purchase — any size of firm can usually bid as individual contracts vary greatly in size across departments. The agency must accept the lowest bid that meets these specifications. Contracts Canada (www.contractscanada.gc.ca) is the interdepartmental program to simplify access and improve awareness of federal government purchasing. Also, the Canada Business Services Centre provides information regarding provincial and federal programs as well as opportunities for bidding on government contracts (www.info.ic.gc.cbsc/). The electronic tendering service utilized by the federal government is MERX (www.merx.cebra.com), operated by Cebra, Inc., a member of the Bank of Montreal group of companies.

The top suppliers to the government of Canada include many familiar names such as Spar Aerospace, Imperial Oil Partnership, General Motors of Canada Ltd., AT&T of Canada, Dell Computer Corporation, IBM Canada Ltd., Petro Canada, Shell Canada Products Ltd., and Xerox Canada Ltd.[5]

A glance at an issue of the *Weekly Bulletin of Business Opportunities*, a government publication that lists business opportunities with the government, provides some idea of the size of this market. The potential is sufficiently attractive that some firms concentrate almost exclusively on government markets.

Despite the opportunities, many companies make no effort to sell to the government, because they are intimidated by the red tape. There is no question that dealing with the government to any significant extent usually requires specialized marketing techniques and information. Some firms, such as Spar Aerospace and Bombardier, have established special departments to deal with government markets. Also, information and guidelines are available from Supply and Services Canada on the proper procedures for doing business with the government.

Currently, government procurement is in a state of flux as a result of both budget cuts and downsizing. Some spending is being completely eliminated, as some services are no longer offered by government agencies. Also, more attention is being paid to the "make-or-buy" decision within government departments and there are more decisions to "outsource" or buy services. Also, Canadians are demanding better service and more accountability from governments. This is creating a trend toward partnerships with the private sector, particularly industry, producer, and consumer organizations. The result is a demand for entirely new categories of services provided by the private sector. In this environment, successful vendors will be those that quickly switch from order takers to proactive salespersons.[6]

The Services Market

Currently, firms that produce services greatly outnumber firms that produce goods. That is, there are more service firms than the total of all manufacturers, mining companies, construction firms, and enterprises engaged in farming, forestry, and fishing. The **services market** includes all transportation carriers and public utilities, communications firms, and the many financial, insurance, legal, and real estate firms. This market also includes organizations that produce and sell such diverse services as rental housing, recreation and entertainment, repairs, health care, personal care, and business services.

Service firms constitute a huge market that buys goods and other services. Four Seasons Hotels, for example, buy blankets and sheets from textile manufacturers. Hospitals in Canada and abroad buy supplies from Baxter Healthcare. These and other service firms buy legal, advertising, accounting, information technology equipment and systems, and consulting advice from other service marketers. The importance to Canadian marketers of the services market is dealt with in greater detail in Chapter 12.

The "Nonbusiness" Business Market

nonbusiness market
Such diverse institutions as churches, colleges and universities, museums, hospitals and other health institutions, political parties, labour unions, and charitable organizations.

In recent years, we have been giving some long-overdue marketing attention to the multi-million-dollar market made up of so-called nonbusiness, or not-for-profit, organizations. The **nonbusiness market** includes such diverse institutions as churches, colleges and universities, museums, hospitals and other health institutions, political parties, labour unions, and charitable organizations. Actually, each of these so-called nonbusiness organizations is a business organization. However, our society (and the institutions themselves) in the past did not perceive a museum or a hospital as being a business. Many people today still feel uncomfortable thinking of their church, school, or political party as a business organization. Nevertheless, these organizations do virtually all the things that any business does — offer and consume products or services, collect money, make investments, hire employees — and therefore require professional management.

Not-for-profit organizations also conduct marketing campaigns — albeit under a different name — in an effort to attract millions of dollars in contributions. In turn, they spend millions of dollars buying goods and services to run their operations.

The International Dimension

Since Canada exports over $180 billion or nearly 30 percent of its gross domestic product, and since a major portion of this export trade is conducted on a business-to-business basis, the international market, comprised of the same components as those that exist within Canada, is a vibrant collection of foreign-based business markets. The value of international B2B commerce may be expected to rise as the Internet continues to be a favoured tool for these buyers. While the total value of goods and services exchanged online by businesses was about US$131 billion in 1999, estimates for its value by 2003 vary from US$1 – US$1.5 trillion indicating an annual growth rate of 90+ percent.[7] Such uncertainty comes from the inability to accurately predict how quickly vendors, buyers, and product classes will adapt to the medium. One thing is for sure, growth will be phenomenal and Canadian vendors will be looking for their share.

The Internet has become invaluable for making international contacts even if a site does no more than list products/services and contact information. Even sites providing only traditional contact by snail mail or telephone will still turn up in Web-search results.[8] However, many transactions will continue to require face to face contact negotiations to reach completion. We wish to underscore here that marketing to businesses based abroad, whether in the United States, Japan, the United Kingdom, or the Gulf states, requires even more work on developing relationships than one would expect. This is the case because, whether one is dealing with a foreign subsidiary of a Canadian firm or with foreign firms, the cross-cultural dynamics of negotiation and relationship building cannot be taken for granted. Canadian marketers doing business abroad must become familiar with the values, customs, symbols, and standard practices and expectations of their foreign-based buyers, who include the individuals with whom one must negotiate as well as the firms that they represent. "Marketing at Work" File 7-1 provides a sample of what marketers doing business abroad can expect.

Characteristics of Business Market Demand

Four demand characteristics differentiate the business market from the consumer market: Demand is derived, demand tends to be inelastic, demand is widely fluctuating, and the market is well informed.

Demand Is Derived

The demand for a business product or service is derived from the demand for the consumer products in which that business product is used. Thus the demand for steel or plastics depends partially on consumer demand for automobiles and refrigerators, but it also depends on the demand for computer graphics boards, butter, hockey pads and equipment, mobile telephones, and portable DVD players. This is because the tools, machines, and other equipment needed to make these items are made of steel and plastic. Consequently, as the demand for hockey equipment increases, Bauer Sporting Goods may require more sewing machines and computers — each requiring plastic and steel.

There are two significant marketing implications of the fact that business market demand is a derived demand. First, to estimate the demand for a product, a business marketer must be very familiar with how it is used. This is fairly easy for a company like Pratt & Whitney, a maker of jet engines. But what about the manufacturer of rubber O-rings (doughnut-shaped rings of all sizes that are used to seal connections)? Considerable research may be necessary to identify uses, users, and potential new opportunities.

Second, the producer of a business product may engage in marketing efforts to encourage the sale of its buyers' products. For example, Intel consistently advertises to consumers, urging them when buying computers to ask specifically for products made with an Intel processor. Similarly, the NutraSweet Company (www.nutrasweet.com) ran a consumer advertising campaign designed to build consumer loyalty for products sweetened with NutraSweet. The idea, of course, is that increases in consumer demand will, in turn, trigger increases in derived demand for these business products. Likewise, BASF Canada, Inc. (http://www.basf.com) run TV advertisements for several consumer products — the catch being they don't produce any of them! BASF products we are told,

Marketing at Work 7-1

Developing Relationships and Negotiating in Global Business Markets

In doing business around the world, executives have found that economic and political environments are major factors in determining success or failure. But what have they learned about the styles of their international business counterparts? Consider these tips on what marketers going abroad can expect:

- In Germany, executives are thorough, systematic, well prepared, and quite rigid. They tend to be assertive, even intimidating, and not very willing to compromise. They are especially punctual and prize efficiency and directness. It is important to be the same. Germans may appear "stiff" socially and it is important to carefully select small talk and humour. During introductions, it is important to greet any women first and to wait for them to extend their hand before extending yours.

- In France, managers may insist that negotiations be conducted in French. Because they consider speaking to be an art, the French dislike being interrupted. Lengthy lunches with lots of wine are more likely to affect the negotiating skills of North Americans than French executives, who are used to such meals. The French are formal with strangers, therefore dress appropriately for business and never use first names without invitation to do so.

- In England, the style is friendly and easygoing. Executives are more likely to be underprepared than overprepared. They are flexible and open to initiatives. However, their kindly posture can be misleading, and they can become very stubborn if they sense a lack of respect.

- In Mexico, personal relationships are very important, so face-to-face contact is a must. Unlike in Canada, the rule is to socialize first and work later. To rush business matters when they are offering their hospitality may be seen as insulting. Mexicans are very ego-involved in business decisions, so concessions that make the decision-maker look good are important. They are quite flexible when it comes to trade-offs, but it is often best to negotiate with them in private, one-on-one conversations rather than in front of others.

- In China, small courtesies and follow-up gifts are important in establishing friendship. Being meticulous in preparation and consistent in presentations is crucial because the Chinese are very thorough. Decision-making cannot be rushed, so business arrangements often take a long time. Again, social engagements will precede business discussions. Most negotiations will involve the government, as there are many joint ventures and state enterprises. Also, distribution is tightly controlled and resistant to outside business involvement.

- In Japan, executives often consider the long-term relationship with a business contact to be as important as the immediate negotiations, so negotiators should keep the future as well as the present in mind. First impressions are crucial. Introductions and exchange of business cards is very ceremonial in this culture as order of presentation and business cards are tightly linked to who they are and their rank. Nonverbal communication, smiling, laughing, and eye contact all provide important communication cues in this culture. Because decisions often involve more people and more levels of management than in Canada, meetings tend to be large. Decision-making is thorough and will take time as each detail is analyzed carefully. The Japanese avoid saying no directly. As a result, any answer other than a definite yes may, in fact, be a no. It is crucial to get "concrete" guarantees. If circumstances change after an agreement is reached, the Japanese assume the right to renegotiate.

- In Russia, the tone of negotiations will be very bureaucratic and the red tape will be extensive. Decision-makers must be prepared for many delays. It is likely that managers will have interesting interpretations of Western or free-market concepts and will require detailed explanations of costs and pricing strategies. The price of a mistake is very large, so a manager's job or even career may be at stake in the negotiations.

Source: Sergey Frank, "Global Negotiating: Vive Les Differences!" *Sales & Marketing Management*, May 1992, pp. 65–69. Reprinted with permission of Sales & Marketing Management; Brian Banks, "English Too," *Canadian Business*, January, 1995, pp. 20–35; and Business Culture, www.business culture.com, March 2000.

however, make all these products better. To name only a few of their products, there are chemicals, fibres, coatings, plastics, urethanes, and polystyrenes. Therefore, they don't make the all-weather coat, they make it more weather resistant. And they don't make the skis, they make them faster. Such consumer products are also then labelled with the BASF branding. You can see the company's logo dangling on tags from garments and equipment in any sports store in the country.

Demand Is Inelastic

Another characteristic of the business market is that the demand for business products does not change easily because of price fluctuations. In economic terms, this refers to an item's price elasticity — how responsive demand is to a change in the price of a product. (To review some economics, price elasticity is explained early in Chapter 13.)

The demand for many business products is relatively inelastic, which means that the demand for a product responds very little to changes in its price. If the price of a business product such as velcro fastening materials should suddenly rise or fall considerably, how much effect would it have on retail prices at a store such as Vancouver-based Mountain Equipment Co-op (MEC)? MEC (www.mec.ca) uses these materials in their jackets, pants, vests, and knapsacks. In fact, it is used in some degree in most of their apparel. Therefore, this could mean a significant increase in their purchasing cost for this item. However, because the fasteners are such a small part of the jacket, pant, or knapsack the price increase would not likely change the retail price noticeably. As a result, Canadians would still flock to the stores and phones and demand for these MEC products would not change. This would be likewise for all other velcro buyers meaning that a price change in either direction would not alter demand for the business product.

The demand for business products is inelastic because ordinarily the cost of a single part or material is a small portion of the total cost of the finished product. The cost of the chemicals in a can of paint is a small part of the price a consumer pays for paint. The cost of the enamel paint on a refrigerator is a small part of its retail price. Even the cost of expensive capital equipment, such as a robot used in assembling automobiles, when spread over the tens of thousands of units it helps produce, becomes a very small part of the final price of each one. As a result, when the price of the business product changes, there is very little change in the price of the related consumer products.

From a marketing point of view, there are three factors that can moderate the lack of price sensitivity in business demand.

◆ Price changes must occur throughout an entire industry, not in a single firm. An industry-wide cut in the price of steel belts used in tires will have little effect on the price of tires and therefore little effect on the demand for automobile tires. Consequently, it will cause little shift in the total demand for steel belts. The pricing policy of an individual firm, however, can substantially alter the demand for its products. If one supplier cuts the price of its steel belts significantly, the drop in price may draw a great deal of business away from competitors. Thus, in the short run, the demand faced by a single firm may be quite elastic. However, any advantage will likely be temporary, because competitors will almost certainly retaliate in some way to recapture their lost business.

◆ The second marketing factor that can affect the lack of sensitivity to price changes is time. Much of our discussion here applies to short-term situations. Over the long run, the demand for a given industrial product is more variable or elastic. If the price of cloth for women's suits rises, there probably will be no immediate change in the price of the finished garment. However, continued increases in the cost of materials could very well be reflected in a rise in suit prices for next year. This rise could then influence the demand for suits, and thus for cloth, a year or more hence. If the materials have a restricted number of uses, and the end-products experience less consumer demand, then demand for components will also be reduced. This can be the case for technology-based items as new competitive innovations enter the market-place. For example, imagine how little demand there is currently for beta-format components of VCRs now that the beta format is technologically dead.

◆ The third factor is the relative importance of a specific business product in the cost of the finished good. We may generalize to this extent:

The greater the cost of a business product as a percentage of the total price of the finished good, the greater the elasticity of demand for this business product.

Demand Is Widely Fluctuating

Although the demand for business goods does not change much in response to price changes, it does respond to other factors. In fact, market demand for most classes of business goods fluctuates considerably more than the demand for consumer products. The demand for installations — major plant equipment, factories, and so on — is especially subject to change. Substantial fluctuations also exist in the market for accessory equipment — office furniture and machinery, delivery trucks, and similar products. These tend to accentuate the swings in the demand for business raw materials and fabricating parts. We can see this very clearly when declines in demand in the construction and auto industries affect suppliers of lumber, steel, plastics and other materials and parts.

The demand for these types of goods fluctuates quite a bit with the ups and downs of normal business cycles. A major reason for these fluctuations is that individual businesses are very concerned about having a shortage of inventory when consumer demand increases or being caught with excess inventory if consumer demand declines. Thus they tend to overreact to signals from the economy, building inventories when they see signs of growth in the economy and working inventories down when the signs suggest a slowdown. When the actions of all the individual firms are combined, the effect on their suppliers is widely fluctuating demand. This is known as the *acceleration principle*. One exception to this generalization is found in agricultural products intended for processing. Because people have to eat, there is a reasonably consistent demand for animals intended for meat products, for fruits and vegetables that will be canned or frozen, and for grains and dairy products used in cereals and baked goods.

Fluctuations in the demand for business products can influence all aspects of a marketing program. In product planning, fluctuations in demand may stimulate a firm to diversify into other products to ease production and marketing problems. Changes within the industry, competition, and technology may also cause concerns. For example, in the last few years, IBM has retreated in a major way from main frame computer manufacturing and marketing, it abandoned the further development of a proprietary operating system that competed with Microsoft, and it withdrew from a number of personal computer product lines. On the other hand, it expanded its operations greatly in many areas of digitally based consulting services with a major emphasis on B2B Internet system design and problem solving.

Buyers Are Well Informed

Typically, business buyers are better informed about what they are buying than are ultimate consumers. They know more about the relative merits of alternative sources of supply and competitive products for three reasons. First, there are relatively few alternatives for a business buyer to consider. Consumers typically have many more brands and sellers from which to choose than do business buyers. Consider, for example, how many options you would have in purchasing a TV set. However, in most business situations a buyer has only a few firms that offer the particular combination of product features and service desired. Second, the responsibility of a buyer in an organization is ordinarily limited to a few products. Unlike a consumer who buys many different things, a purchasing agent's job is to be very knowledgeable about a narrowly defined set of products. Third, for most consumer purchases, an error is only a minor inconvenience. However, in business buying, the cost of a mistake can easily be tens of thousands of dollars or even the decision-maker's job!

This need for a large amount of up-to-date information has significant marketing implications. Manufacturers and marketers of business products place a much greater emphasis on product information and personal contact to communicate than do firms that market consumer products. Business sales and service people must be carefully selected, properly trained, and adequately compensated. They must give informative and effective presentations and furnish satisfactory service to potential buyers both before and after a sale is made. Sales executives are devoting increased effort to the assignment of specialized salespeople to key accounts to ensure that they are compatible with business buyers.

These sales reps often form relationships with their client firms, often customizing products and/or using input for future improvements. Regular contact is maintained to ensure relationship strength. This is increasingly important as the Internet makes searching for information and finding the availability of additional suppliers, current information and new products easier than ever before. The ease with which this information can be obtained may be a threat to vendors unless they develop and maintain client relationships.

Pharmaceutical representatives, for example, often arrange to visit medical offices during lunch to bring information regarding a new product. They will also bring lunch for the office. These companies may also sponsor brunch or luncheon seminars afterwards providing tickets for that evening at a local entertainment venue. Taken to extremes, these activities have been a cause of concern. Incidents of giving gifts to institutional buyers such as large dollar-value items or trips have sometimes been interpreted as a form of "bribery." This has led some organizations to put in place policies restricting "gifts" from potential vendors.[9]

Determinants of Business Market Demand

To analyze a consumer market, a marketer would study the distribution of population and various demographics such as income, and then try to determine the consumers' buying motives and habits. A firm selling to the business market can use essentially the same type of analysis. The factors affecting the market for business products are the number of potential business users and their purchasing power, buying motives, and buying habits. In the following discussion we'll identify several basic differences between consumer markets and business markets.

Number and Types of Business Users
The business market contains relatively few buying units compared with the consumer market. There are approximately a half million business users, with about forty thousand of these being manufacturing establishments. In contrast, there are about thirty million consumers divided among more than nine million households. The business market will

seem even more limited to most companies because they sell to only a segment of the total market. A firm selling to meat-processing plants, for example, would have about forty-five potential customer plants. If you were interested in providing services to battery manufacturers, you would find about twenty-five companies as basic prospects. Consequently, marketing executives must try to pinpoint their market carefully by type of industry and geographic location. A firm marketing hard-rock mining equipment is not interested in the total business market, nor even in all firms engaged in mining and quarrying.

One very useful source of information that was used is the **Standard Industrial Classification (SIC)** system which enables a company to identify relatively small segments of its business market. All types of businesses in Canada had been divided into groups, as follows:

1. Agriculture.
2. Forestry.
3. Fishing and trapping.
4. Mines, quarries, and oil wells.
5. Manufacturing industries (twenty major groups).
6. Construction industry.
7. Transportation, communication, and other utilities.
8. Trade.
9. Finance, insurance, and real estate.
10. Community, business, and personal service industries (eight major groups).
11. Public administration and defence.
12. Industry unspecified or undefined.

A separate number was assigned to each major industry within each of the above groups; then, three- and four-digit classification numbers used to subdivide each major category into finer segments. To illustrate, in division 5 (manufacturing), major group 4 (leather) contains:

SIC code	Industrial group
172	Leather tanneries
174	Shoe factories
175	Leather-glove factories
179	Luggage, handbag, and small leather-goods manufacturers

With the development of an international economy and the emergence of new high-technology industries, the SIC system has begun to show its 50+ age. A new system has been jointly adopted by Canada, the United States, and Mexico. This is the **North American Industry Classification System (NAICS)**. The structure is similar, but with a greater number of industry sectors (there are twenty), providing a more detailed and contemporary classification scheme. These are divided into 96 three-digit sub-sectors, 313 four-digit industry groups, and 1,170 five- and six-digit industries. Table 7-1 lists the

Standard Industrial Classification (SIC) system
A coding system developed by the federal government that groups firms into similar types of businesses and thus enables a company to identify and analyze small segments of its market.

North American Industry Classification System (NAICS)
Coding system similar to the SIC, but has 20 rather than 10 industry sectors, to provide a more detailed and contemporary classification scheme.

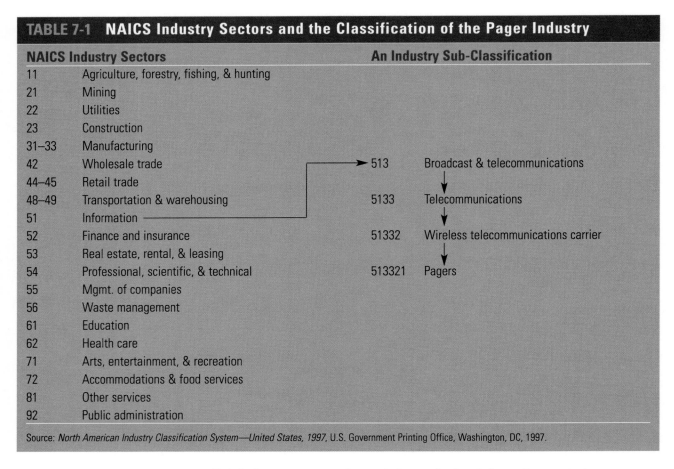

TABLE 7-1 **NAICS Industry Sectors and the Classification of the Pager Industry**

NAICS Industry Sectors		An Industry Sub-Classification	
11	Agriculture, forestry, fishing, & hunting		
21	Mining		
22	Utilities		
23	Construction		
31–33	Manufacturing		
42	Wholesale trade	513	Broadcast & telecommunications
44–45	Retail trade		
48–49	Transportation & warehousing	5133	Telecommunications
51	Information		
52	Finance and insurance	51332	Wireless telecommunications carrier
53	Real estate, rental, & leasing		
54	Professional, scientific, & technical	513321	Pagers
55	Mgmt. of companies		
56	Waste management		
61	Education		
62	Health care		
71	Arts, entertainment, & recreation		
72	Accommodations & food services		
81	Other services		
92	Public administration		

Source: *North American Industry Classification System—United States, 1997*, U.S. Government Printing Office, Washington, DC, 1997.

NAICS two-digit industry sector codes and shows the breakdown for one industry, pagers — a segment of the wireless telecommunication industry within the information sector.

SIZE OF BUSINESS USERS Although the market may be limited in the total number of buyers, it is large in purchasing power. As one might expect, business users range in size from very small companies with fewer than five employees to firms with staff numbering more than a thousand. A relatively small percentage of firms account for the greatest share of the value added by a given industry. For example, Statistics Canada data on the manufacturing sector in Canada indicate that slightly more than 1 percent of manufacturing firms — those with five hundred or more employees — account for approximately 40 percent of the total value added by manufacturing and for more than 30 percent of the total employment in manufacturing. The firms with fewer than fifty employees, while accounting for more than 80 percent of all manufacturing establishments, produce less than 15 percent of the value added by manufacturing.

The marketing significance in these facts is that buying power in the business market is highly concentrated in relatively few firms. This market concentration has considerable influence on a seller's policies regarding its channels of distribution. Intermediaries are not as essential as in the consumer market.

REGIONAL CONCENTRATION OF BUSINESS USERS There is substantial regional concentration in many of the major industries and among business users as a whole. A firm selling products usable in oil fields will find the bulk of its market in Alberta, the

Northwest Territories, offshore Newfoundland, and the United States and abroad. Rubber-products manufacturers are located mostly in Ontario, shoes are produced chiefly in Quebec, and most of the nation's garment manufacturers are located in southern Ontario and Quebec. There is a similar regional concentration in the farm market.

Although a large part of a firm's market may be concentrated in limited geographic areas, a good portion may lie outside these areas. Consequently, a distribution policy must be developed that will enable a firm to deal directly with the concentrated market and also to employ intermediaries (or a company sales force at great expense) to reach the outlying markets.

VERTICAL AND HORIZONTAL BUSINESS MARKETS For effective marketing planning, a company should know whether the market for its products is vertical or horizontal. If a firm's product is usable by virtually all firms in only one or two industries, it has a **vertical business market**. For example, some precision instruments are intended only for the marine market, but every boatbuilder or shipbuilder is a potential customer. If the product is usable by many industries, then it is said to have a broad or **horizontal business market**. Business supplies, such as Esso lubricating oils and greases and Canadian General Electric small motors, may be sold to a wide variety of industries.

A company's marketing program ordinarily is influenced by whether its markets are vertical or horizontal. In a vertical market, a product can be tailor-made to meet the specific needs of one industry. However, the industry must buy enough to support this specialization. In addition, advertising and personal selling and servicing can be directed more effectively in vertical markets. In a horizontal market, a product is developed as an all-purpose item, to reach a larger market. However, because of the larger potential market, the product is likely to face more competition.

Buying Power of Business Users

Another determinant of business market demand is the purchasing power of business users. This can be measured either by the expenditures of business users or by their sales volume. Many times, however, such information is not available or is very difficult to estimate. In such cases, it is more feasible to use an **activity indicator of buying power** — that is, some market factor that is related to income generation and expenditures. Sometimes an activity indicator is a combined indicator of purchasing power and the number of business users. Following are examples of activity indicators that might be used to estimate the purchasing power of business users.

MEASURES OF MANUFACTURING ACTIVITY Firms selling to manufacturers might use as market indicators such factors as the number of employees, the number of plants, or the dollar value added by manufacturing. One firm selling work gloves used the number of employees in manufacturing establishments to determine the relative value of various geographic markets. Another company that sold a product that controls stream pollution used two indicators: (1) the number of firms processing wood products (paper mills, plywood mills, and so forth) and (2) the manufacturing value added by these firms.

MEASURES OF MINING ACTIVITY The number of mines operating, the volume of their output, and the dollar value of the product as it leaves the mine all may indicate the purchasing power of mines. This information can be used by any firm marketing industrial products to mine operators.

activity indicator of buying power
A market factor that is related to income generation and expenditures.

MEASURES OF AGRICULTURAL ACTIVITY A company marketing fertilizer or agricultural equipment can estimate the buying power of its farm market by studying such indicators as cash farm income, acreage planted, or crop yields. The chemical producer that sells to a fertilizer manufacturer might study the same indices, because the demand for chemicals in this case is derived from the demand for fertilizer.

MEASURES OF CONSTRUCTION ACTIVITY If a firm is marketing building materials, such as lumber, brick, gypsum products, or builders' hardware, its market is dependent on construction activity. This may be indicated by the number and value of building permits issued or by the number of construction starts by type of housing (single-family residence, apartment, or commercial).

Business Buying Behaviour

Business buying behaviour, like consumer buying behaviour, is initiated when an aroused need (a motive) is recognized. This leads to goal-oriented activity designed to satisfy the need. Once again, marketers must try to determine what motivates the buyer, and then understand the buying process and buying patterns of business organizations in their markets.

The Importance of Business Buying

Business buying or purchasing, formerly a relatively minor function in most firms, is now an activity that top management is very much interested in. Once viewed as an isolated activity that focused primarily on searching out low prices, purchasing has become an important part of overall strategy for at least three reasons:

◆ Companies are making less and buying more. For example, 93 percent of the cost of an Apple computer is purchased content, and for all manufacturers, purchased content is over 50 percent of their final products. Managing all these supply relationships is time-consuming and therefore also consumes additional financial resources. While low price is important, savings can also be found through reducing the number of suppliers and maintaining those providing dependable quality service and products. Honda, at one time, had different suppliers producing mirrors for the inside and outside of their cars. Very happy with the relationship and working style of the Donnelly Corporation in their agreement to supply interior mirrors, the car company asked that this supplier develop exterior mirrors to supply for their cars thereby reducing their supplier list by one. This trend can be found across this industry as there may be up to 2000 supply relationships to manage in automobile manufacturing.

◆ Firms are under intense quality and time pressures. To reduce costs and improve efficiency, firms no longer buy and hold inventories of parts and supplies. Instead, they demand that raw materials and components that meet specifications be delivered "just in time" (JIT) to go into the production process. To take advantage of this, Canadian Auto Manufacturer Magna establishes its facilities near its main clients — the Big 3 auto producers. This ensures that inventories can be kept at a minimum yet fluctuations in demand will be met with guaranteed on-time delivery. This is achieved through computerized data interchange systems that link suppliers to their JIT clients.[10] To ensure quality, companies such as Xerox, will require suppliers to be

FIGURE 7-1

The Business Buying-Decision Process and the Factors that Influence It.

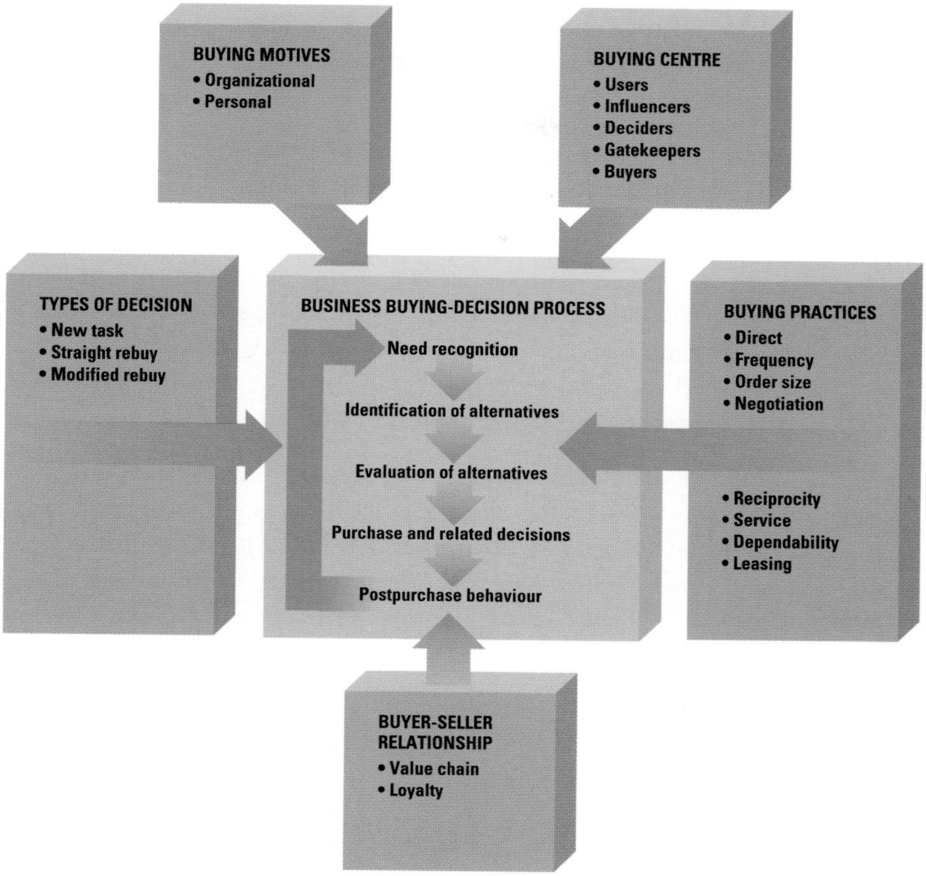

BUYING MOTIVES
- Organizational
- Personal

BUYING CENTRE
- Users
- Influencers
- Deciders
- Gatekeepers
- Buyers

TYPES OF DECISION
- New task
- Straight rebuy
- Modified rebuy

BUSINESS BUYING-DECISION PROCESS

Need recognition

Identification of alternatives

Evaluation of alternatives

Purchase and related decisions

Postpurchase behaviour

BUYING PRACTICES
- Direct
- Frequency
- Order size
- Negotiation

- Reciprocity
- Service
- Dependability
- Leasing

BUYER-SELLER RELATIONSHIP
- Value chain
- Loyalty

ISI 9000 certified. Certification means that a supplier has undergone an audit that ensures a quality management and quality assurance systems are operating within the firm and meet the international standards of this certification. Further, Xerox requires that the potential supplier pass another survey of their own design and complete additional quality training and evaluation.[11]

◆ To get what they need, firms are concentrating their purchases with fewer suppliers and developing long-term "partnering" relationships. This level of involvement extends beyond a purchase to include such things as working together to develop new products and providing financial support.[12] For example, at the Chrysler Design Centre, the headquarters for the Chrysler Corporation, there are at least thirty offices set up at any time for the full-time use of personnel that instead of being Chrysler employees actually work for various suppliers. By becoming a part of the operation these people create greater value by participating in development, maintenance, inventory, ordering and solution generation processes.

Buying-Decision Process in Business

The buying-decision process in business markets is a sequence of five stages similar to the ones followed by consumers, as discussed in the preceding chapter. Not every purchase involves all five steps. Straight-rebuy purchases usually are low-involvement situations for the buyer, so purchasers typically skip some stages. But a new-task purchase of an expensive product or service is likely to be a high-involvement, total-stage buying decision.

To illustrate the process, let's assume that Montreal-based Culinar, Inc., makers of Vachon, Jos Louis, and May West snack cakes, is considering a fat substitute in a special line of baked goods:

◆ *Need recognition.* Culinar's marketing executives are sensitive to the concerns of consumers about fat in their diets. The opportunity to produce a line of high-quality, good-tasting baked goods without fat is very attractive, but finding the right substitute is the challenge.

◆ *Identification of alternatives.* The marketing staff draws up a list of product-performance specifications for the fat-free baked goods — attractive appearance, special features, good taste, and reasonable cost. Then the purchasing department identifies the alternative brands and supply sources of fat substitutes that generally meet these specifications.

◆ *Evaluation of alternatives.* The production, research, and purchasing people jointly evaluate both the alternative products and sources of supply. They discover that some brands cannot withstand high temperatures, there are differences in how well they simulate the taste and texture of fat, and some have not received final approval from federal health authorities. The complete evaluation considers such factors as product performance, appearance, and price, as well as the suppliers' abilities to meet delivery schedules and provide consistent quality.

The well-trained buyer is an increasingly valuable member of the management team.

◆ *Purchase decision.* Based on the evaluation, the buyer decides on a specific brand and supplier. Next, the purchasing department negotiates the contract. Since large sums are involved, the contract will likely include many details. For example, if Culinar feels confident about the supplier, the contract relationship might go beyond price and delivery schedules. This could include the low-fat producer gaining access, through electronic data interchange (EDI) to production, quality control, shelf life, and product movement data so as to be able to provide a higher degree of accuracy in product delivery and better targeted service. A more effective schedule can help ensure a consistently fresher product perhaps leading to higher product sales. In such a situation, a long-term relationship appears to be in the baking, um, we mean making.

Marketing at Work 7-2

Building Continuing B2B Dialogues

Truly living up to the tagline "Solutions for a Small Planet," in February 2000 IBM conducted a three-week sales conference entitled "eForum2000" involving 2,500 IBM employees and business partners from more than ninety countries. The conference was held in cyberspace, where travel, accommodation, hospitality and food costs are either very low or non-existent. Its purpose was to demonstrate the technical prowess of IBM and showcase one of its publicized "Solutions for a Small Planet." The conference profiled 1999 successes, communicated key messages and strategies for 2000, educated IBM, supplier, and customer teams about IBM solutions and IBM supplier needs. The conference also demonstrated that the approach can significantly lower expenses, reach a higher number of people, and increase and deepen B2B contacts and discussions. This is achieved by taking them out of the hectic three-day standard conference format, which too easily becomes expensive, tiring, and frequently not a productive use of time, resources, or a useful venue for extended discussions.

Compared to the year before, IBM was able to more than triple the number of participants. Since there were no travel and hotel costs, they were able to stage the conference over a three-week period as opposed to the hurried three-day period. Presentations from keynote speakers were uploaded to a secure Web site, and remarks recorded over the telephone with the option of erasing and re-recording them if one was not happy with the delivery. Unlike real-time speeches, delegates could pause and review the remarks of the speaker, and even spread the remarks over a number of days for further analysis. Just as with a real-world meeting space, a virtual meeting space can hold a variety of materials, including collections of documents or other business data (presentations, multimedia, database-access links, Web sites, selections from the collaborative meeting record, and so on) from an intranet or on the Web. Leaders and participants can add new materials any time.

And what about the participants?? Well, they could become a member of this B2B community without catching a plane. All they needed was a PC and a telephone to plug it into at any time of the day or night, wherever they happened to be — looking after business. And they watch, listen, replay, download, peruse, join in, chat and .....!!

Source: Adapted from Don Tapscott, "IBM Saves Cash with Meeting in Cyberspace," *The National Post*, February 12, 2000

◆ *Postpurchase behaviour.* Culinar, Inc. continues to evaluate the performances of the fat substitute and the selected supplier to ensure that both meet expectations. Continued dealings will depend on this performance evaluation and on how well the supplier handles the total interaction process. Success with this product line would increase the likelihood of future projects between the two firms.

In the following sections, we explore several differences between consumer buying behaviour and the business buying behaviour reflected in the Culinar scenario.

Buying Motives of Business Users

buying motive
The reason why a person buys a specific product or shops at a specific store.

One view of **buying motives** is that business purchases are methodical and structured. Business buying motives, for the most part, are presumed to be practical and unemotional. Business buyers are assumed to be motivated to achieve the optimal combination of price, quality, and service in the products they buy. An alternative view is that business buyers are human and thus their business decisions are influenced by their attitudes, perceptions, and values. In fact, many salespeople would maintain that business buyers seem to be motivated more toward personal goals than organizational goals, and the two are often in conflict.

As is usual in such cases, the truth is actually somewhere in between. Business buyers have two goals — to further their company's position (in profits, in acceptance by customers) and to protect or improve their position in their firms (self-interest). Sometimes these goals are mutually consistent. For example, the firm's highest priority may be to reduce costs, and the buyer knows that he or she will be rewarded for negotiating a low price. Obviously the more consistent the goals are, the better for both the organization and the individual, and the easier it is to make buying decisions.

However, there are often significant areas where the buyer's goals do not coincide with those of the firm, as when the firm insists on dealing with the lowest-price supplier, but the buyer has developed a good relationship with another supplier and doesn't want to change. In these cases a seller must appeal to the buyer both on a rational "what's good for the firm" basis and on a self-interest "what's in it for me" basis. Promotional appeals directed to the buyer's self-interest are particularly useful when two or more competing sellers are offering essentially the same products, prices, and post-sale services.[13]

Types of Buying Situations

In Chapter 6 we observed that consumer purchases can range from routine to complex buying decisions. Similarly, the buying situations in business organizations vary widely in their complexity, number of people involved, and time required. In organizational buying behaviour there are three classes of business buying situations. The three **buy classes** are new-task buying, straight rebuy, and modified rebuy.

new-task buying
In the business market, a purchasing situation in which a company for the first time considers buying a given item.

◆ **New-task buy.** This is the most difficult and complex buying situation because it is a first-time purchase of a major product. Typically more people are involved in new-task buying than in the other two situations because the risk is great. Information needs are high and the evaluation of alternatives is difficult because the decision-makers have little experience with the product. Sellers have the challenge of finding out the buyer's needs and communicating the product's ability to provide satisfaction. A hospital's first-time purchase of laser surgical equipment or a company buying robots for a factory (or buying the factory itself) are new-task buying conditions. In these situations, firms with established relationships could work with buyers to help them define the buying task and suggest solutions because they are trusted. Potential suppliers must provide information and aid in the buying task in a form that engenders trust and allows them to begin the task of establishing a relationship.

straight rebuy
In the business market, a routine purchase with minimal information needs.

◆ **Straight rebuy.** This is a routine, low-involvement purchase with minimal information needs and no great consideration of alternatives. The buyer's extensive experience with the seller has been satisfactory, so there is no incentive to search. An example is the repeat purchase of steering wheels by Freightliner, a truck manufacturer. These buying decisions are made in the purchasing department, usually from a predetermined list of acceptable suppliers. Suppliers who are not on this list may have difficulty getting in to make a sales presentation to the buyer. But as more buyers gain experience making use of the Internet to both gather product and service information and actually buy online, the predetermined list is easily expanded by asking for bids from a broader base of suppliers.

modified rebuy
In the business market, a purchasing situation between a new task and a straight rebuy in terms of time required, information needed, and alternatives considered.

◆ **Modified rebuy.** This buying situation is somewhere between the other two in time and people involved, information needed, and alternatives considered. In selecting diesel engines for the trucks it manufactures, Freightliner considers Cummins and Caterpillar products, among others. However, because these engine makers frequently introduce new design and performance features, Freightliner evaluates each on a regular basis. Close relationships are common in situations where modified rebuys are frequent and, of course, should work to benefit both buyer and seller.

Multiple Buying Influences — The Buying Centre

multiple buying influences

A situation in which a purchasing decision is influenced by more than one person in the buyer's organization.

One of the biggest challenges in B2B marketing is to determine which individuals in the organization play the various buying roles. That is, who influences the buying decision, who determines product specifications, and who makes the buying decision? In the business market, these activities typically involve several people. In other words, there are **multiple buying influences**, particularly in medium-sized and large firms. Even in small companies where the owner-managers make all major decisions, knowledgeable employees are usually consulted before certain purchases are made.

buying centre

All of the people in an organization who participate in the buying-decision process.

Understanding the concept of a **buying centre** is helpful in identifying the multiple buying influences and understanding the buying process in business organizations. A buying centre may be defined as all the individuals or groups involved in making a decision to purchase. Thus a buying centre includes the people who play any of the following roles:

users

The people in a buying centre who actually use a particular product.

◆ **Users.** The people who actually use the business product — perhaps a secretary, an executive, a production-line employee, or a truck driver.

◆ **Influencers.** The people who set the specifications and aspects of buying decisions because of their technical expertise, their organizational position, or even their political power in the firm.

influencers

The people in a buying centre who set the specifications and aspects of buying decisions because of their technical expertise, financial position, or political power in the organization.

◆ **Deciders.** The people who make the actual buying decision regarding the business product and the supplier. A purchasing agent may be the decider in a straight-rebuy situation. But someone in top management may make the decision regarding whether to buy an expensive computer.

◆ **Gatekeepers.** The people who control the flow of purchasing information within the organization as well as between the firm and potential vendors. These people may be purchasing agents, secretaries, receptionists, or technical personnel.

deciders

The people in a buying centre who make the actual buying decision regarding a product and/or supplier.

◆ **Buyers.** The people who interact with the suppliers, arrange the terms of sale, and process the actual purchase orders. Typically this is the purchasing department's role. But again, if the purchase is an expensive, complex new buy, the buyer's role may be occupied by someone in top management.

gatekeepers

The people in a buying centre who control the flow of purchasing information within the organization and between the buying firm and potential vendors.

Several people in an organization may play the same role: There may be several users of the product. Or the same person may occupy more than one role: A secretary may be a user, an influencer, and a gatekeeper in the purchase of office equipment.

The size and composition of a buying centre will vary among business organizations. In one study, the average size of buying centres ranged from 2.7 to 5.1 persons.[14] Within a given organization, the size and makeup of the buying centre will vary depending on the product's cost, the complexity of the decision, and the stage of the buying process. The buying centre for a straight rebuy of office supplies will be quite different from the centre handling the purchase of a building or a fleet of trucks.

buyers

The people in a buying centre who select the suppliers, arrange the terms of sale, and process the actual purchase orders.

The variety of people involved in any business-buying situation, plus the differences among companies, present real challenges to salespeople. As they try to determine "who's on first" — that is, determine who does what in a buying situation — sales reps often call on the wrong executives. Even knowing who the decision-makers are at a certain time is not enough, because these people may be very difficult to reach, and people move into and out of the buying centre as the purchase proceeds through the decision process. This, in part, explains why a salesperson typically has only a few major accounts.

Certainly the challenges presented in the business buying-decision process should suggest the importance of co-ordinating the selling activities of the business marketer with the buying needs of the purchasing organization.

Buying Patterns of Business Users

Buying behaviour in the business market differs significantly from consumer behaviour in several ways. These differences stem from the products, markets, and buyer-seller relationships in business markets.

DIRECT PURCHASE   In the consumer market, consumers rarely buy directly from the producer except in the case of services. In the business market, however, direct purchase by the business user from the producer is quite common, even for goods. This is true especially when the order is large and the buyer needs much technical assistance. Computer-chip makers deal directly with personal computer manufacturers because the chip technology is changing so rapidly. From a seller's point of view, direct sale in the business market is reasonable, especially when there are relatively few potential buyers, when they are big, or when they are geographically concentrated. With phone, fax, and the Internet readily available, smaller sellers can both concentrate their efforts and work to expand their reach into markets that in the past were too expensive to serve at an appropriate level.

NATURE OF THE RELATIONSHIP   Many business marketers take a broad view of exchanges. Rather than focus only on the immediate customer, they approach marketing as a value chain. That is, they consider the roles of suppliers, producers, distributors, and end users to see how each contributes value to the final product. This perspective leads to recognition of the importance of all the parties involved in successfully bringing a product to market and an emphasis on building and maintaining relationships. For example, Apple Computer, which once relied exclusively on dealers, recognized that many of its larger customers needed specialized service. To satisfy this segment of the market and maintain strong ties to these key customers, the firm now has its own sales force calling directly on large accounts. However, many of the orders taken by the sales force are contracted out to dealers to ensure that they are protected.[15] A key factor in establishing and maintaining relationships is the seller working to build confidence and trust.

FREQUENCY OF PURCHASE   In the business market, firms buy certain products very infrequently. Large installations are purchased only once in many years. Small parts and materials to be used in the manufacture of a product may be ordered on long-term contracts, so that a selling opportunity exists as seldom as once a year. Even standard operating supplies, such as office supplies or cleaning products may be bought only once a month.

Because of this buying pattern, a great burden is placed on the personal-selling programs of business sellers. The sales force must call on potential customers often enough to provide the first-hand information that other media, such as a Web site, e-mail, or fax cannot effectively provide and to know when a customer is considering a purchase.

SIZE OF ORDER   The average business order is considerably larger than its counterpart in the consumer market. This fact, coupled with the infrequency of purchase, highlights the importance of each sale in the business market. A salesperson losing the sale of a pair of shoes to a consumer is not nearly as devastating as Canadair losing the sale of ten airplanes.

Marketing at Work 7-3

B2B Builds New Markets in the Great Web Bazaar

The most successful electronic commerce business models tend to be business-to-business ones. This should be no surprise, since business transactions are worth at least ten times as much as consumer sales. Few realized how quickly stodgy business firms would convert to electronic business, but, after all, many if not most business transactions are actually done at a distance, by fax, phone, mail, or private electronic links. Moving these processes to the Internet reduces transaction costs, speeds them up, and makes them easier to conduct.

One of the earliest and most impressive examples of business marketing and purchasing on the Internet came from innovating and benchmark-setting General Electric. The Electric Services Information Division had established a Trading Process Network (TPN), a Web site where, in 1997, GE did US$1 billion worth of business with about 1,400 of its suppliers — a value greater than all consumer electronic commerce at the time. In 2000 GE will buy more than US$7 billion in products and services through this medium. GE had designed software that lets its purchasers specify from whom they want bids and what sort of information a bid should include. The software manages the bids that come back, eliminates high bidders, handles further bidding rounds, and notifies the bidders of results of the process. Selected suppliers were notified and got an online form on which to complete necessary details.

Results: The length of the bidding process in the Lighting Division had been cut in half, from twenty-one days to ten. Purchasing officers now approach more suppliers because it is so easy to do. The increased bidding competition has lowered the cost of goods by 5 to 20 percent; it is now much easier to include foreign suppliers in the process, and 15 percent of orders have gone abroad. GE's size results in pulling small and medium-sized suppliers into electronic commerce, where they did not operate before, and they are able to increase their efficiency, sharpen prices, and improve service at a low cost, sometimes for just the price of a Web page. These suppliers have then broadened their market reach beyond GE with a more sophisticated use of the Internet. Some 1,400 other manufacturers have since joined TPN to enhance their buying practices including firms such as 3M and Hewlett-Packard.

Since its inception, the GE model has been emulated, improved upon, and extended. Cisco and Oracle, both hi-tech Internet supply companies, have transferred almost all of their purchasing, and most of their sales, to the Internet. Both Ford and General Motors, who each have thousands of suppliers, have recently transferred all their purchasing to the Web. As two icons of the Old Economy, this was seen as a yielding to pressures of the New Economy as these firms quickly became e-commerce's most potent players.

It was believed that this move solidified online B2B and delivered e-commerce into the business mainstream. The number of suppliers affected had to bring huge changes as thousands of companies had to improve and upgrade their technological abilities to participate. And participate they must in order to remain competitive. GM announced that all of its suppliers must move quickly to upgrade their IT systems as they will require all transactions to be conducted online by the end of 2001.

General Motors launched its TradeXchange Web site in December 1999 with 108 companies participating in a single auction to supply the company with metal stamping processes. There was also US$500,000 in purchase orders in the first week from catalogues on the site that list 200,000 items. Ford's *AutoXchange* was launched in early 2000 with similar results. Suppliers will also be able to use the sites to make their purchases and sell excess inventories. Revenues from the fees AutoXchange alone will charge suppliers that use the network are expected to reach US$500 million by the end of 2001 and hit US$5 billion by 2005.

Source: Adapted from Christopher Anderson, "A Survey of Electronic Commerce: In Search of the Perfect Market," *The Economist*, May 10, 1997, pp. 3, 16–17; John Parker, "Online Procurement Expected to Reshape the Automotive Industry," *Traffic World*, December 6, 1999, p. 19; "GM and Ford Look to the Web for Purchasing," *Industrial Distribution*, December 1999, pp. 23–24; and *The Economist*, Online Edition, "Survey of Commerce," February 26, March 4, and April 1, 2000.

LENGTH OF NEGOTIATION PERIOD The period of negotiation in a business sale is usually much longer than in a consumer transaction. General Electric, for example, negotiated over a five-year period before completing the purchase of a $9.5 million Cray supercomputer to aid in managing operations and research activities in Canada and the United States. Some reasons for extended negotiations are:

◆ Several executives participate in the buying decision.

◆ The sale involves a large amount of money.

◆ The business product is made to order, and considerable discussion is required to establish the specifications.

RECIPROCITY ARRANGEMENTS A highly controversial business buying practice is reciprocity, the policy of "I'll buy from you if you'll buy from me." Reciprocity was common among firms marketing homogeneous basic business products (oil, steel, rubber, paper products, and chemicals).

There has been a significant decline in, but not an elimination of, reciprocity. This decline has occurred for two reasons, one legal and the other economic. The Competition Act applies to reciprocity when the practice is similar to price discrimination. A firm can buy from a customer, but it must be able to prove that it is not given any special privileges regarding price, quality, or service that are not made available to competing buyers.

From an economic point of view, reciprocity may not make sense because the price, quality, or service offered by the seller may not be competitive. In addition, when a firm fails to pursue objectives that maximize profits, the morale of both the sales force and the purchasing department may suffer.

Reciprocity is an area in which firms run into problems in doing business overseas. In many parts of the world, it is taken for granted that if I buy your product, you will buy mine.

DEMAND FOR SERVICE The user's desire for excellent service is a strong business buying motive that may determine buying patterns. Frequently a firm's only differentiating feature is its service, because the product itself is so standardized that it can be purchased from any number of companies. Consider the choice of suppliers to provide elevators for a major office building or hotel. The installation of the elevators is no more important than keeping them operating safely and efficiently. Consequently, in its marketing efforts a firm such as Otis emphasizes its maintenance service as much as its products.

Sellers must be ready to furnish a continuous service program, not just before or just after a sale. For example, suppliers such as Kraft General Foods conduct a careful analysis of a supermarket's customers and sales performance and then suggest a product assortment and layout for the store's dairy department. In the case of office copiers, manufacturers train the buyers' office staffs in the use of the equipment, and after the machines have been installed, offer other services, such as repairs by specially trained technicians.

DEPENDABILITY OF SUPPLY Another business buying pattern is the user's insistence on an adequate quantity of uniform-quality products. Variations in the quality of materials going into finished products can cause considerable trouble for manufacturers. They may be faced with costly disruptions in their production processes if the imperfections exceed quality control limits. The right quantities at the right time are as important as the right quality. A work stoppage caused by an insufficient supply of materials is just as costly as one caused by inferior quality of materials. In one study of problems faced by purchasing agents for smaller manufacturers, the problem most often reported was the failure of sellers to deliver on schedule.

The emphasis on total quality management (TQM) has increased the significance of dependability. Now that it has been established that firms can operate with virtually zero defects, buyers expect a very high standard of performance.

LEASING INSTEAD OF BUYING A growing tendency among firms in the business market is leasing business goods instead of buying them. In the past this practice was limited to large equipment, such as large computers, packaging equipment, and heavy construction equipment. Industrial firms are now expanding leasing arrangements to include delivery trucks, automobiles used by salespeople, machine tools, and items such as software site licences that are generally less expensive than major installations.

Leasing has several merits for the lessor — the firm providing the equipment:

◆ Total net income — the income after charging off repairs and maintenance expenses — is often higher than it would be if the equipment were sold.

◆ The lessor's market may be expanded to include users who could not afford to buy the product, especially for large equipment.

◆ Leasing offers an effective method of getting users to try a new product. They may be more willing to rent a product than to buy it. If they are not satisfied, their expenditure is limited to a few monthly payments.

From the lessee's — or customer's — point of view, the benefits of leasing are:

◆ Leasing allows users to retain their investment capital for other purposes.

◆ Firms can enter a new business with less capital outlay than would be necessary if they had to buy equipment.

◆ Leased products are usually repaired and maintained by lessors, eliminating one headache associated with ownership.

◆ Leasing is particularly attractive to firms that need equipment seasonally or sporadically, such as food canning or construction.

Bases for Business Market Segmentation

Several of the bases used to segment the consumer market can also be used to segment the broad business market. For example, we can segment business markets on a geographical basis. Several industries are geographically concentrated, so any firm selling to these industries could nicely use this segmentation basis. Sellers also can segment on product-related bases such as usage rate or benefits desired.[16]

Let's look at three of the bases that are used solely for segmenting business markets — type of customer, size of customer, and type of buying situation.

Type of Customer

Any firm that sells to customers in a variety of business markets may want to segment this market on the basis of customer types. We discussed the SIC and NAIC codes as a very useful tool for identifying business and institutional target markets. A firm selling display cases or store fixtures to the retail market, for example, might start out with potential customers included in the two-digit code number 61 for shoe, apparel, fabric, and yarn industries — retail (under SIC). Then the three-digit code 612 identifies potential customers in the retail clothing business. Finally, the four-digit code 6121 pinpoints men's clothing specialty stores.

A firm selling janitorial supplies or small electric motors would have a broad potential market among many different industries. Management in this firm could segment its market by type of customer and then perhaps decide to sell to firms in only a limited number of these segments.

Size of Customer

In this situation, size can be measured by such factors as sales volume, number of production facilities, or number of sales offices. Many business-to-business marketers divide their potential market into large and small accounts, using separate distribution channels to reach each segment. The large-volume accounts, for example, may be sold to directly by the company's sales force. But to reach the smaller accounts, the seller may use a telemarketing or Internet approach or a manufacturers' agent or some other form of intermediary.

Type of Buying Situation

Earlier in this chapter, we discussed the three types of buying classes — new buy, modified rebuy, and straight rebuy. We also recognized in that discussion that a new buy is significantly different from a straight rebuy in several important respects. Consequently, a business seller might well segment its market into these three buy-class categories. Or the seller could at least set up two segments by combining new buy and modified rebuy into one segment. Then different marketing programs would be developed to reach each of these two or three segments.[17]

Summary

The business market consists of organizations that buy goods and services to produce other goods and services, to resell to other business users or consumers, or to conduct the organization's operations. It is an extremely large and complex market, spanning a wide variety of business users that buy a broad array of business goods and services. Besides manufacturing, the business market includes the agriculture, reseller, government, services, not-for-profit, and international markets.

Business market demand generally is derived, inelastic, and widely fluctuating. Business buyers usually are well informed about what they are buying. Business market demand is analyzed by evaluating the number and kinds of business users and their buying power.

Business buying, or purchasing, has taken on greater strategic importance because organizations are buying more and making less, under intense time and quality pressures, and developing long-term partnering relationships with suppliers.

Business buying motives are focused on achieving a firm's objectives, but the business buyer's self-interest must also be considered.

The buying-decision process in business markets may involve as many as five stages: need recognition, identification of alternatives, evaluation of alternatives, purchase decision, and post-purchase behaviour. The actual number of stages in a given purchase decision depends largely on the buying situation, whether new-task buy, straight rebuy, or modified rebuy.

The concept of a buying centre reflects the multiple buying influences in business purchasing decisions. In a typical buying centre are people playing the roles of users, influencers, deciders, gatekeepers, and buyers.

Buying patterns (habits) of business users often are quite different from patterns in the consumer market. In the business market, direct purchases (without intermediaries) are more common, purchases are made less frequently, and orders are larger. The negotiation period usually is longer, and reciprocity arrangements can exist. The demand for service is greater, and the dependability of supply is more critical. Finally, leasing (rather than product ownership) is quite common in business marketing.

Three segmentation bases that are used solely for segmenting the business market are customer type, customer size, and type of buying situation.

Key Terms and Concepts

Business market 188

Business users 188

Business marketing 189

Agribusiness 190

Reseller market 191

Disintermediation 191

Services market 193

Nonbusiness market 193

Standard Industrial Classification (SIC) 199

North American Industry Classification System (NAICS) 199

Vertical business market 201

Horizontal business market 201

Activity indicator of buying power 201

Buying motives 205

Buy classes 206

New-task buy 206

Straight rebuy 206

Modified rebuy 206

Multiple buying influences (buying centre) 207

Users 207

Influencers 207

Deciders 207

Gatekeepers 207

Buyers 207

Questions and Problems

1. What are some marketing implications of the fact that the demand for business goods:

   a. fluctuates widely?

   b. is inelastic?

   c. is derived?

2. What are the marketing implications for a seller of the fact that business customers are geographically concentrated and limited in number?

3. What differences would you expect to find between the marketing strategies of a company that sells to horizontal business markets and those of a company that sells to vertical business markets?

4. A manufacturer has been selling specialized software to a large oil company in Norway. In which of the three buy classes would you place this buyer-seller relationship? Is there any aspect of the relationship that is likely to fall into the straight-rebuy category?

5. Explain how the five stages in the buying-decision process might be applied in the following buying situations:

   a. New-task buying of a conveyor belt for a soft-drink bottling plant.

   b. Straight rebuying of maintenance services for that conveyor belt.

   c. Modified rebuy of advertising agency services for a hotel chain.

6. How would you go about determining who influences the buying decisions of business users?

7. Steelcase, IBM, Xerox, and other manufacturers of office equipment make a substantial proportion of their sales directly to business users. At the same time, wholesalers of office equipment are thriving. Are these two market situations inconsistent? Explain.

Hands-On Marketing

1. Find an ad for a business product or service that is directed toward the business market and another ad for the same product that is directed toward consumers (such as an ad for leasing fleets of Chevrolets and an ad for Chevrolet aimed at consumers). Discuss the buying motives appealed to in the ads.

2. Interview a purchasing agent about buying a product that would qualify as a modified rebuy. Draw a diagram that shows the purchasing agent's perceptions of: (a) the stages of the decision process; (b) who was in the buying centre at each stage of the decision process; and (c) what role(s) each person played at each stage of the process. Comment on how this diagram might be useful to a salesperson representing the product in question.

Chapter Eight

Marketing Research and Information

The management of any business or organization, whether a major automobile manufacturer, an auto dealership, or an art gallery, requires one fundamental input in order to achieve success in a competitive marketplace: accurate and timely information. To be effective, marketing managers need current information about the markets they are trying to reach, the macro-environment that affects their particular industry, and the internal and external factors that affect their specific market. We're about to see where this information can be obtained and how to use it. After studying this chapter, you should have an understanding of:

◆ What marketing research is and the role it plays in improving marketing decision-making.

◆ The systems that have been developed to increase the usefulness of data.

◆ The appropriate way to conduct a marketing research project.

◆ What kinds of organizations do marketing research.

◆ Recent changes in how marketing research is conducted in Canadian organizations.

Watch Out! The Tweens have, like, really landed!

*H*ow do young consumers, say, like, pre-teens make, like, totally cool purchase decisions?

With limited consumer experience, few if any major purchase decisions to make, and yet influencing about $1.5 billion in purchases — what *are* they thinking? How do they form their decisions, and what information do they use to get there?

With these answers far from being obvious, marketers have become increasingly determined to get into the minds of this consumer group determined not to let anyone in! Besides, once they realize their secrets are out — they're likely to only change their minds again. And once they know you're trying to get to them and impress them, they are no longer impressed! Once you're seen as *trying* to be cool — that's when they see right through you.

Rooted in demographics, the pre-teen group of Canadian consumers represents the bulk of the boomers' offspring. These 9 to 14 year-olds currently number almost 2.5 million in Canada. Research also shows that there will be another surge in

this age bracket in another few years. With all this market potential, researchers need to develop a means to find out what this powerful group wants — not an easy task as already discussed. Just one indication of the attention this group has been getting is that The Institute for International Research, the world's largest conference organization, has begun to offer conferences dealing exclusively on how to sell to this segment. Call them what you want — the echo boom, boomlet, mini-boom, *whatever*! The tweens are here and they have no problems with making their presence known!

While we all could express some insight into purchases made by these

youths, let's face it, it would really be an anecdote about a younger sibling or their friends — not really the stuff you'd want to gamble millions on, is it? The influence and reach that these guys have into their parents' pocketbooks is astounding and can only be really determined with sound, thorough market research.

There are companies that specialize in market research dealing with tweens, but perhaps one of the best sources is YTV — yes, the TV station whose tagline is "you rule" recognizing who's really in charge and who doesn't even pretend to strive for quality programming. A marketing machine, YTV has performed extensive marketing research to discover where tween money comes from, how they spend it, and how they help mom and dad spend theirs as well. Tweens receive money as gifts on birthdays and holidays, regular allowances, back-to-school money, and occasional jobs. In two-income households they often wind up with more resources as parents try to make up for quality time by providing for more of their "wants." Their tastes have a major impact on family purchases. Out of every ten in this segment, nine influence purchases of their own clothes and footwear, eight for games, toys, snack foods, and restaurants the family enjoys, and believe it or not three out of ten actually influence car purchases. YTV's tween information, gathered from its primarily tween-aged audience, is so hot that the network charges a whooping $1,700 per copy for the whole report.

Although difficult to pin down, tweens are a desirable target market for reasons other than the $1.5 billion we already discussed. Indications are that they are being raised in relatively affluent households that are increasingly brand-conscious. They themselves are very brand savvy — knowing current brands in all sorts of categories and they aren't afraid to express recommendations using the logic that the "cool" brand is the criterion for purchase — if we could just understand how it gets to be "cool"! They themselves tend to be brand loyal and are still open to introduction to branded products. Research shows as teens age they become more resistant and suspicious of whatever appears to be recommended by adults. This could represent a win-win for a brand! Hook them early — get them on your side now to buy now — and keep them buying.

Tweens are skeptical, however, so getting them may be difficult. They are media-savvy and well informed. They are highly transitional — they are neither child nor teenager. They are in a rush to grow up and perceive themselves as a few years older than they really are. They want to be like teenagers, but seek to be unconventional in their style. Ambiguity and contradiction prevail — they want to be different, just like everybody else. So don't treat them like children, but, ah, you can't really treat them like adults either! They are not like their parents — despite the popularity of what adults see as retro trends, they are not big on nostalgia.

They are deeply socialized at this age, are not articulate about their choices, and are passionate about trends — they either love or hate it, there's seldom anything in between. They are wired, with over half having Internet access in their homes. They are the only real surfers as research indicates that online time tapers off once they begin junior high. Believe it or not, they are serious about school! They know the world changes quickly and school is important for the future. Eighty-three percent report this with seven out of ten already reporting they plan to go to university.

If an advertiser wants to reach this elusive segment as well as teens, young adults, fringe dwellers like artists, musicians, night-clubbers — the people who, for the most part are ground zero for novel styles and ideas that will wash out into the mainstream — there's a lot they need to know. Some retailers are even moving in the other direction and targeting the fashion-conscious as young as five with retail environments that encourage these young consumers to hang, fiddle, sample, and shop to their little hearts' content.[1]

And you can't just ignore these segments. Levi Strauss & Co. thought they could and decided to hold steady in a product market where legs were getting wider, waistlines droopier, and everything was getting baggier. The company's market share dropped considerably, as Levi's became, to young people, the jeans of their parents. In other words, they were old! To reconnect with young consumers they introduced new styles, but were late comers to the marketplace. The spring 2000 line was launched with an ad campaign geared toward the 15 to 24 year-old set who are fans of shows like *Buffy the Vampire Slayer* and *The X-Files*, featuring mutant felines capturing young, hip humans to steal their Levis. Time will tell if Levi's will recover from their error in judgment of underestimating the influence of the younger market segments.[2]

How do you approach such ambitious goals? Who tells you how to do it? How do you find out what is happening out there? Such information and wisdom is neither common sense nor guesswork. Marketing research is the starting point.

Need for Marketing Research

Management in any organization needs information — and lots of it — about potential markets and environmental forces in order to develop successful strategic marketing plans and to respond to changes in the marketplace. More than ever before, a mass of data is available both from external sources and from within a firm. The challenge is how to transform the raw data into information and how to use it effectively. To see how to do this, we will begin by briefly discussing why organizations need information and why they need to do research. Then we will focus our attention on how organizations manage their research efforts.

Today, many forces dictate that every organization have access to timely information. Consider some of these factors and their relationship to information management:

◆ *Competitive pressure.* To be competitive, companies must develop and market new products and services more quickly and effectively than ever before. Pressures continue to increase as the Internet continues to eliminate geographic borders, drawing new competitors from around the globe. Also, new ways of marketing to consumers demands that companies know their customers as well as possible. Those companies that know their customers best have a distinct advantage when it comes to marketing to them.

◆ *Expanding markets.* Marketing activity is becoming increasingly complex and broader in scope as more firms operate in both domestic and foreign markets. Again, this trend has been accelerated by the growth of the new economy, blurring distinctions between the two markets. Today it doesn't matter where a company is located. If it is doing business on the Internet, it is competing globally.

◆ *Cost of a mistake.* Introducing and marketing a new product or service is enormously expensive. A failure can cause severe — even fatal — damage to a firm. Even making modifications to existing products is a risky business. Knowing what to change and when so as to ensure that a product remains competitive are decisions that should not be made without input from customers.

◆ *Growing customer expectations.* The lack of timely, adequate information about a problem that consumers are having with some aspect of an organization's marketing program can result in lost business. Greater competition has allowed consumers to become more demanding and selective. To prosper, a firm must know what the customer expects and meet those expectations.

◆ *Increased market complexity.* The marketplace that most companies and organizations are facing today is far more complex than it was in the past; as a result, managers must be as well informed as possible, armed with information in which they can have complete confidence.

Managers in a wide variety of organizations are called on a regular basis to make important marketing decisions. It is probably a self-evident fact that the best decisions are based upon the best available information. Before embarking upon marketing decisions relating to new product introduction, changes in the customer service program, the launch of an advertising campaign, or a program to target new customer segments, the marketing manager needs information. In most organizations, the necessary information is not generally available and must be obtained from some external sources. This is where marketing research comes in. The information obtained through research guides strategic decision-making. However, in order for the marketing manager to have complete confidence in the information, the research must be conducted professionally and in accordance with certain standards that will ensure that bias is minimized and that the results accurately reflect the situation the manager is facing. Marketing research is viewed by many managers as insurance that will help them succeed.[3]

marketing research
The process of specifying, assembling, and analyzing information used to identify and define marketing opportunities and problems; generate, refine, and evaluate marketing actions; monitor marketing performance; and improve understanding of marketing as a process.

What Is Marketing Research?

Marketing research includes all the activities that enable an organization to obtain the information it needs to make decisions about its marketing mix, and its present or potential customers and consumers. More specifically, marketing research involves the development, interpretation, and communication of decision-oriented information to be used in the strategic marketing process. Businesses and other organizations spend millions of dollars each year obtaining information to improve the quality of decision-making. Obviously, research is an important part of marketing!

To understand what modern marketing research is and what it does, we must keep in mind that:

◆ It plays a role in all three phases of the management process in marketing: planning, implementation, and evaluation.

◆ It is more than just collecting data.

◆ It recognizes the researcher's responsibility to develop information that will be useful to managers.[4]

Scope of Marketing Research Activities

The scope of marketing research activities that are typically practised by larger companies in particular is reflected in Table 8-1. These results indicate the percentage of Canadian companies that engaged in each of these types of research at the time this research was conducted.[5] Some of the results are particularly interesting and reflect the activities and interests of businesses. For example, approximately 90 percent of companies indicated that they monitor market share and market trends, and close to 80 percent analyze profits and costs, and perform market and sales forecasts. The relatively small percentage engaged in plant location studies and channel performance research probably reflects the fact that many companies are not engaged in the manufacture and distribution of physical products. It is encouraging to see that a very large percentage of the companies who responded to the study indicated that they are carrying out research in the areas of service quality and customer satisfaction. Possibly surprising is the fact that only 20.9 percent of respondents indicated that they are conducting export or international research.

Much of the marketing research conducted by Canadian business tends to be done in or on behalf of larger companies. Among companies with annual sales in excess of $5 million, 50 percent have an organized marketing research department, and an additional 28 percent have at least one person with responsibility for marketing research. Typically in these companies, marketing research departments are quite small, averaging 3.8 employees, including researchers and support staff. The small size reflects the fact that most companies have the actual marketing research studies conducted on their behalf by outside marketing research specialists. The staff of the marketing research departments in most cases carries out studies of the economy and industry trends and will supervise the purchase of specialized research services from outside suppliers.

In addition to the research studies conducted by a company's own marketing research department or on its behalf by an external research supplier, there are two other sources that are also important in providing the marketing information needed by managers:

◆ The marketing information system, which provides a continuous, scheduled flow of standardized reports to managers.

◆ The decision support system, which permits managers to interact directly with data through personal computers to answer specific questions.

TABLE 8-1 Selected Marketing Research Activities of Larger Canadian Companies

Subject Areas Examined	% doing
Business/Economic and Corporate Research	
Industry/market characteristics and trends	91.5
Market share analyses	89.7
Corporate image research	72.3
Quality/Satisfaction Research	
Customer satisfaction research	81.6
Customer profiling and segmentation research	74.1
Service quality research	70.9
Product quality research	68.4
Pricing Research	
Profit analysis	80.9
Demand Analysis Research	
Market potential	77.0
Sales potential	74.5
Sales forecasts	77.0
Cost analysis	76.2
Product Research	
Concept development/testing	66.3
Competitive product studies	52.5
Testing existing products	50.0
Test marketing	45.4
Distribution Research	
Plant/warehouse location studies	38.7
Channel performance studies	31.6
Advertising and Promotion Research	
Copy testing	52.5
Sales force compensation studies	51.4
Media research	48.9
Public image studies	47.9
Advertising post-testing	42.9
Buyer Behaviour Research	
Market segmentation research	56.4
Brand awareness research	48.2
Brand image/attitudes	47.5
Purchase intentions research	46.5

Source: Unpublished background data from the project reported in Eva E. Kiess-Moser and James G. Barnes, "Emerging Trends in Marketing Research: The Link with Customer Satisfaction," Ottawa: The Conference Board of Canada, Report 82-92, 1992. Reproduced with permission from The Conference Board of Canada.

Marketing Information Systems

marketing information system (MkIS)
An ongoing organized set of procedures and methods designed to generate, analyze, disseminate, store, and retrieve information for use in making marketing decisions.

In recent years, firms have come to rely on the increasing power and sophistication of computerized information systems to assist in the compilation and analysis of a sea of potentially useful marketing information. Out of this capability developed the **marketing information system (MkIS)** — an ongoing, organized procedure to generate, analyze, disseminate, store, and retrieve information for use in making marketing decisions. This internally-coordinated activity provides continuous, scheduled, or on-demand standardized reports through its ability to collect, store, and manipulate massive volumes of data. The MkIS has become even more important in recent years as many companies have access to data that are captured automatically every time a customer buys something or interacts with the company in some other way.

The ideal MkIS:

◆ Analyzes data using statistical analysis and mathematical models that represent the real world.

◆ Generates regular reports and recurring studies as needed.

◆ Integrates old and new data to provide information updates and identify trends.

Designing an MkIS

To build an MkIS, marketing managers must identify what information will help them make better decisions. Working with researchers and systems analysts, managers then determine whether the data needed are available within the organization (for example, in the daily reports made by salespeople or cost data from the accounting department or in customer records) or must be obtained from outside sources. Then it must be decided how the data should be organized, the form in which it should be reported, and the schedule according to which it will be delivered. For example, the manager at Procter & Gamble who is responsible for Tide wants to know the retail sales of all detergent brands by geographic area on a monthly basis. The same manager may want quarterly reports on the prices which competitors are charging and how much advertising they are doing.

Less frequently, possibly once a year, this manager needs to know about developments in the marketplace such as demographic changes that might affect sales of Tide in the long term. In addition to these (and probably other) regular reports, the manager may periodically request special reports that can be compiled from existing data. For example, the Tide manager may want to see what share of the total market each detergent brand had by quarter over the last five years and a projection of how each is likely to perform over the next three years.

A well-designed MkIS can provide a continuous flow of this type of information to support management decision-making. The storage and retrieval capability of an MkIS allows a wide variety of data to be collected and used. With this capability, managers can continually monitor the performance of products, markets, salespeople, and other marketing units.

An MkIS is of obvious value in a large company, where information for management is likely to get lost or distorted as it becomes widely dispersed. However, experience shows that even relatively simple information systems can upgrade management's decision-making in small and medium-sized firms.

FIGURE 8-1

The Structure of a Marketing Information System

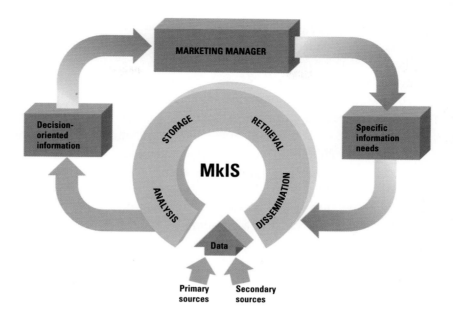

How well an MkIS functions depends on three factors:

◆ The nature and quality of the data available.

◆ The ways in which the data are processed to provide usable information.

◆ The ability of the operators of the MkIS and the managers who use the output to work together.

MkIS Limitations

When an MkIS doesn't do what management expects it to do, there are several possible explanations:

◆ It is not always obvious what information is needed on a regular basis to make better decisions. Some managers are comfortable using their experience and intuition and may find that information produced by an MkIS is "interesting" but not necessarily useful. Thus, an MkIS can produce exactly what has been requested, but the results may not improve decisions because the managers have not identified what will be of greatest value to them.

◆ Gathering, organizing, and storing data and disseminating reports customized to the needs of many managers can be extremely expensive. Beyond the cost of operating an MkIS, there is the need to keep it updated as more sophisticated data become available and managers recognize new and different information needs.

◆ Possibly most important, an MkIS is not well suited to the solution of unanticipated problems. The biggest challenges managers face are situations in which a decision must be made quickly, without all the details clearly defined, nor the implications of the options known. Under these conditions, standard reports produced according to predetermined schedules are unlikely to be of much value.

The features of an MkIS — a focus on preplanned, structured reports and centralized control over the information by computer specialists — resulted from the skills required to operate computers. Organizations were forced to depend on highly trained programmers working on large computers to produce the information requested by managers from the MkIS.[6] This is no longer the situation as a great deal of the information now available in MkIS files is automatically "captured" when a customer interacts with the business.

New customer relationship technologies allow the integration of sales, marketing and customer service applications operating from a common database and offer easier-to-use Web interfaces, more robust functionality, and simpler integration with back-office systems. Such solutions are becoming less expensive, more effective, and quicker to deploy. Sales-force automation applications also enable companies to shorten sales cycles, increase customer face-to-face time, guide the sales process, and promote team selling.[7] Less computer expertise is required but more marketing expertise may be required to make effective use of such applications.

Low-cost laptops and software packages, along with a reduced need for operational expertise, have enabled many small and medium sized firms to join the ranks of marketing personnel armed with high technology tools for marketing.

The ease of access and the proliferation of data have led to another concern. It has become quite easy to generate reports, but generating meaningful reports that have validity and that the firm can act upon, is not always what results. It has become easy to weigh management down with a lot of interesting but meaningless data. This is especially the case in larger firms with many types of data being measured by more and more powerful applications. It is important that a focused approach is taken to wade through the available combinations and calculations to deliver effective information that management can act upon. New technologies have also assisted with the action component of marketing decisions with the development of decision support system packages.

Marketing Decision Support Systems

decision support system (DSS)
A procedure that allows a manager to interact with data and methods of analysis to gather, analyze, and interpret information.

A decision support system (DSS) is a sophisticated management tool that allows a manager to interact with data and methods of analysis to gather, analyze, and interpret information. Like an MkIS, the heart of a DSS is data — different types of data from a wide variety of sources. Typically, there are data describing customers, competitors, economic and social trends, and the organization's performance. Also like an MkIS, the DSS has methods for analyzing data. These methods range from simple procedures such as computing ratios or graphs to sophisticated statistical techniques and mathematical models. Where the methods differ is in the extent to which they permit managers to interact directly with the data. As already mentioned, applications for customer relationship management allow user-friendly access for account and service representatives by access through their own personal computer terminals allowing them to retrieve data, examine relationships, and even produce reports to meet their specific needs. This interactive capability allows managers to react to what they see in a set of data by asking questions and getting immediate answers. The simplified application of new information technology to sales, marketing and customer service aids in strengthening customer relationships. Figure 8-2 depicts the relationships in a DSS.

Consider this example. Midway through the year, a manager wants to compare actual sales of a product with what was forecast. Sitting down at her computer, she calls up the monthly forecasts and the actual sales figures. Discovering that sales fell slightly below the forecast in the most recent month, she commands the system to provide similar data

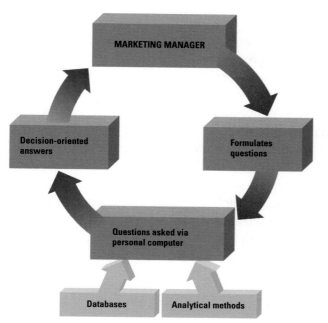

FIGURE 8-2
The Structure of a
Decision Support
System

for the company's other products. Finding that the other products are on target, she concludes that there may be a problem with the product in question. Next, she asks the system to break down the total sales figure by geographic areas and discovers that the poor sales results occurred in only two of seven regions. Suspecting competitive activity, she then compares advertising levels and prices of her product and those of competitors in the markets where sales forecasts were achieved and where they weren't. Finding nothing out of the ordinary, she decides to examine distribution levels for the sales regions. Requesting data on the size and types of retail outlets over time, she finds that in the two regions where sales have slipped there has been a slow but steady decline in the type of small, independent retailers that account for a significant portion of the product's sales. Thus, her strategy is to investigate the use of alternative outlets for selling the product in these problem regions. Notice that, with an adequate DSS, this entire task was done in a short time by simply asking for information, analyzing it, and moving on to another question suggested by the analysis.

The DSS adds speed and flexibility to the MkIS by making the manager an active part of the research process. The increased use of desktop and laptop computers, "user-friendly" software, and the ability to link computer systems at different locations (networking) have greatly enhanced the potential of DSS.

Databases

database
A set of related data
that is organized,
stored, and updated
in a computer.

An MkIS or a DSS uses data from a variety of sources both within the organization and from outside suppliers. These data are organized, stored, and updated in a computer in what is called a **database**. Often a database will contain separate data modules on such topics as customers, competitors, industry trends, and environmental changes.

Internally, data come from the sales force, marketing, manufacturing, and accounting departments. One of the most lucrative sources of customer data, for example, already exists within customer accounts and billing files in many companies. Some organizations, such as banks and telephone companies, maintain such detailed accounts that they know precisely what a customer has purchased. Some users of databases have begun using their data for predictive modelling, which seeks to determine which customers would be interested in a particular type of product or service. For example, by scanning its database of credit card customers for individuals who have used their card to purchase a computer in the past year, a bank could develop an excellent list of customers who would likely be interested in online banking and investment services.[8]

data warehouse
A collection of data from
a variety of internal and
external sources,
compiled by a firm for
use in conducting
transactions.

Some organizations move beyond databases to create large and complex data repositories. These are called **data warehouses**. They are enormous collections of data from a variety of internal and external sources compiled by a firm that is conducting transactions with millions of customers. For example, large companies such as banks, telephone companies, and credit card companies maintain massive data warehouses that maintain data files on each customer, including detailed records of each and every transaction, right down to each use of the credit card, each ATM transaction and each telephone call.[9]

Data warehouses can be analyzed in the same way as databases, searching for predetermined patterns in the data. But, due to their size it would be a slow and cumbersome process. Therefore, more advanced statistical and artificial-intelligence techniques are utilized for such processes. Referred to as **data mining**, these techniques have the capability to identify patterns and meaningful relationships in masses of data that would be overlooked or unrecognizable to researchers.[10] MCI, for example, is especially concerned about losing long-distance customers that have the greatest revenue-generating potential. Ideally, the firm would like to identify attributes of buyers and the range of values on those attributes that would be effective indicators of an imminent switch to another supplier. Evaluating its 140 million service subscribers, each with as many as ten thousand data points that include everything from income to calling habits in MCI's data warehouse, would perhaps take years with traditional methods. With data mining techniques, however, MCI was able to develop twenty-two detailed profiles of customers on the verge of switching carriers. The firm, in response, then developed specially tailored programs aimed to meet the concerns of each group (profile).[11]

One of the most successful users of customer databases in Canada is Zellers (www.hbc.com/zellers), which operates three hundred stores across Canada and now accounts for one-quarter of all discount department store sales in the country. Zellers introduced its Club Z customer loyalty program in 1986 and its companion program, Generation Z, for children in 1999. Club Z has over 10.5 million members, reaching an incredible 70 percent of all Canadian households. Club members earn one hundred points for every dollar spent at Zellers and can redeem their points for gifts from the Club Z catalogue. Today, Club Z rewards about 1.5 million members annually when they select gifts from the program catalogue. But the greatest value of Club Z and Generation Z to Zellers is the household information that the "clubs" provide, as well as information provided on every item purchased by Club Z members. Douglas Ajram, general manager, loyalty and direct marketing, observed, "We use our database to paint a picture of our customers, what they like about us, and what kind of merchandise they are interested in."[12] Many companies such as Zellers are using internally generated data to establish databases on their customers. The way in which a company analyzes and combines the data from such databases will determine their usefulness in planning and implementing marketing strategy.

The development and selling of mailing lists and databases is normal business practice, and an industry sector has evolved to rent computerized lists of potential customers who have certain characteristics and spending habits. A number of Canadian mailing list brokers rent more than two thousand lists to marketers wishing to target certain types of potential customers. These brokers do not sell the names and data on their lists but will rent them for one-time use to clients who wish to target direct-mail materials. Most brokers will want to approve samples of the material to be mailed before supplying the names.[13] There is growing pressure on mailing-list brokers and on users of databases generally to ensure that the information they have at their disposal is used in an ethical and responsible manner. Because of the availability of such computer-based data, there are many situations in which the privacy of consumers may be violated and information misused.[14]

Research has allowed marketers to move from undifferentiated, mass marketing to focusing on well-defined market segments. It is now suggested that through the manage-

data mining
Method used to identify patterns and meaningful relationships in masses of data that would be unrecognizable to researchers.

Kids flock to become part of Zellers' Generation Z.

ment of databases, marketers will be able to reach the ultimate level of segmentation — the individual. For example, Chapters Online (www.chapters.ca) greets returning visitors by name, makes recommendations and special offers based on previous purchases, and can hold items in your "shopping basket" between visits while you are deciding whether or not to buy. Online retailers have the ability to monitor and log which site pages were visited and for how long. Also what site you came from when you came to their site. This data can be used to prepare special offers to a market of one — especially if you join their mailing list. How a Web site is able to do this will be discussed later in the chapter.

Scanners and Single-Source Data

The data used by researchers and managers in databases and data warehouses are gathered from many sources. Internally, data can come from the sales force, marketing, manufacturing, and accounting departments. Externally, information can be obtained from hundreds of research suppliers. Computer systems are able to gather information from retail checkout systems to assess how well specific coupons work in specific neighbourhoods and which in-store displays are most effective in generating sales.

retail scanners
The electronic devices at retail checkouts that read the bar code on each item.

Perhaps the most important data source for databases is the **retail scanner**, the electronic device at retail checkouts that read bar codes located on each product that is purchased. Originally, these were meant simply to speed-up the process and reduce errors in supermarkets. With unique bar codes on each item indicating price information, prices did not need to be memorized, checked, and no keying errors could be made entering the price. However, it was soon discovered that this could also be used to improve decisions regarding inventory control and the allotment of shelf space for products.[15]

Many stores, grocery and department stores included, quickly discovered once again how to extend the use of this technology as a marketing tool and quickly developed what we all know as frequent shopper or loyalty programs. Some benefit or convenience is offered to a consumer for carrying a store's program card and allowing it to be "swiped" at the time of purchase. To receive the card the customer has provided some personal

Marketing at Work 8-1

Database Marketing Suits Harry

Although quick to notice what's hot on the runway each season, fashion retailers have been slow to take note of what consumers want, buy, and need. Database marketing isn't new to many retail sectors, but it is still in its infancy among Canada's clothiers.

Some retailers such as Tabi International, Sporting Life, and Fairweather are starting to dabble in database marketing while others like Harry Rosen Inc. have had tremendous success with database initiatives.

By learning who the customer is, including what he buys, his size, how often he shops, and how much he spends, Harry Rosen is able to achieve a sense of customer intimacy or insight into what the customer really wants.

Harry's system is quite simple. When a customer pays with a credit card, he is asked for his postal code. This information is merged with the customer name, already obtained from the credit card, and a street address pops up on the screen. The salesperson then asks for the customer's street number and the information gathering is complete. Any time that customer shops at any Harry Rosen store across Canada his purchase information will be saved in the system.

By using information contained in the database, Harry's employees are empowered to form more familiar customer relationships. For example, when Harry Rosen receives its fall line for Zegna, employees can access the database to pull customers who buy Zegna merchandise but who haven't been in the store for a few months. They can then call these customers and discuss what they liked about the Zegna products that they purchased in the past and tell them what is now in stock for fall.

The database is also used to isolate the names of customers who have made major purchases; a salesperson then phones them thirty days later to ensure that the customers are satisfied. The company also uses its database to send its "Harry" magalogue to its best customers; and to customize invitations for parties or promotional events.

The combination of individual customer knowledge, personalized invitations, and follow-up calls creates a powerful marketing tool. So powerful in fact that depending on the season, Harry Rosen attributes about 70 percent of its sales to its direct marketing initiatives.

Source: Adapted from Mikala Folb, "Where Data is in Fashion," *Marketing Magazine*, August 16, 1999, p. 20.

---

information that the store retains in a data file. This system enables the store to combine data stored on the card about household demographics and lifestyle with the shopper's scanned purchases. The store is then able to relate product choices to household characteristics and plan product assortment and store layouts to maximize sales potential. According to NCR, a manufacturer of such scanning systems, there are thousands of retailers electronically collecting customer data across North America, and the number is growing rapidly.[16]

Knowing what customers buy is even more important if a firm knows what advertising they have been exposed to. In many countries, research companies such as A.C. Nielsen have developed consumer household panels to create databases of information on advertising exposure and retail purchases. A representative sample of households agree to have their television viewing monitored by an electronic device known as a people meter and to have their purchases recorded when they buy groceries at scanner-equipped retail stores. Demographic information is obtained from each household when its members agree to be part of the scanner panel. The result is that household demographics can be correlated to television advertising exposure and product purchases. The result is called **single-source data** because exposure to television advertising and product purchases can be traced to individual households, providing a single source for both types of data.[17]

single-source data
A data-gathering method in which exposure to television advertising and product purchases can be traced to individual households.

Marketing Research Projects

Before the advent of computers and the development of marketing information systems and decision support systems, much of what was called marketing research consisted of nonrecurring projects to answer specific management questions. Projects, some that are nonrecurring and others that are repeated periodically, are still a major part of marketing research. The results of a research project may be used to enable management to reach a particular decision. They could also become part of a database to be used in an MkIS or DSS. Examples of marketing research projects are described briefly in Table 8-2. According to a study of the use of marketing research in Canadian businesses, the most common projects are studies of industry and market trends and market share analyses (see Table 8-1, earlier in this chapter).

Most marketing research projects follow the procedure outlined in Figure 8-3. Let's examine what goes into conducting a marketing research project.

FIGURE 8-3

Marketing Research Procedure

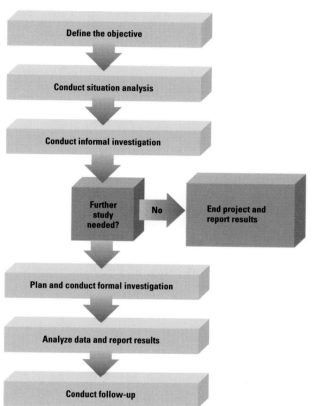

Define the Objective

Researchers need a clear idea of what they are trying to learn — the objective of the project. Usually the objective is to solve a problem, but this is not always so. Often the objective is to define the problem. Sometimes it's simply to determine if there is a problem. To illustrate, a manufacturer of commercial air-conditioning equipment had been enjoying a steady increase in sales volume over a period of years. Management decided to conduct a sales analysis. This research project uncovered the fact that, although the company's volume had been increasing, its share of the market had declined because the industry was growing even faster. In this instance, marketing research uncovered a problem that management did not know existed. After specifying the objective, the researcher is ready for the next step — the situation analysis.

TABLE 8-2	**Typical Marketing Research Projects**
Project	**Objective**
Concept test	To determine if a new product idea is attractive to potential customers, or to determine how targeted customers will respond to advertising concepts.
Copy test	To determine if the intended message in an advertisement is being communicated effectively.
Price responsiveness	To gauge the effect a price change would have on sales of a brand.
Market-share analysis	To determine a firm's proportion of the total sales of a product or service and whether that share is increasing or declining.
Segmentation studies	To identify distinct groups within the total market for a particular product or service, so that these groups may be targeted with specific marketing programs.
Customer satisfaction studies	To monitor how customers feel about an organization and its products or services, and with how they are treated by the company.

situation analysis
The stage in a marketing research study that involves obtaining information about the company and its business environment by means of library research and extensive interviewing of company officials.

secondary research data
Information already gathered by somebody else for some other purpose.

hypothesis
A tentative supposition or a possible solution to a problem.

Conduct a Situation Analysis

Next, the researchers try to get a "feel" for the situation surrounding the problem. They analyze the company, its market, its competition, and the industry in general. The **situation analysis** is a background investigation that helps in refining the research problem. It involves obtaining information about the company and its business environment by means of library research and extensive interviewing of company officials. This process generally relies upon the use of **secondary research**, meaning that the data already exist in some other form, often available from outside organizations such as Statistics Canada or trade associations.

In the situation analysis, researchers also try to refine the problem definition and develop hypotheses for testing. A research **hypothesis** is a tentative supposition that if proven would suggest a possible solution to a problem. Some examples of testable hypotheses are:

◆ Sales of grocery items are significantly greater when they are placed on end-of-aisle displays than when only they are located in their normal aisle positions.

◆ Sales of Nintendo Gameboy units will experience a sharp increase following each introduction of a new Pokemon game cartridge.

◆ Bank customers who use automatic banking machines and telephone banking services will accept and adopt PC-based banking systems once they have become aware of their availability.

◆ Sales will increase for cosmetic manufacturers using popular celebrity endorsements by stars such as Sarah Michelle Gellar, Jennifer Lopez, or Jennifer Love Hewitt.

◆ Demand for MP3 players will increase proportionally to the increasing availability of downloadable sampling via the Internet.

◆ Consumers in rural areas of Canada are more inclined to buy locally produced products and services than are those living in larger centres.

The project then turns to generating data that can be used to test the correctness of the hypotheses.

Conduct an Informal Investigation

informal investigation
The gathering of preliminary data from people inside and outside the company.

Having gotten a feel for the problem, the researchers are now ready to collect some preliminary data from the marketplace. This **informal investigation** consists of gathering readily available information from people inside and outside the company — intermediaries, competitors, advertising agencies, and consumers.

The informal investigation is a critical step in a research project because it will determine whether further study is necessary. Decisions can frequently be made with information gathered in the informal investigation. For example, a company considering opening sales offices for its computer software support service in Western Canada might first talk with representatives of trade associations representing the personal computer industry and with officials of companies that supply computers and software. Before contacting any prospective clients for their new service, the company would be interested in getting a "feel" for the market and for the extent to which demand for software support is being satisfied. The conclusion at this stage may be that the market is large enough to warrant further investigation. The company's representatives might then meet with office managers or information systems managers of prospective clients in cities such as Edmonton, Calgary, and Vancouver to discuss informally their needs for software support, where they are currently buying the service, and what they would look for in a new entrant into the market.

Much valuable information is obtained through an informal market investigation. The company not only will learn a great deal about the market it proposes to enter, but it will also determine whether further study is needed. A decision on the main problem can often be made with information gathered at the informal investigation stage.

Plan and Conduct a Formal Investigation

If the project warrants continued investigation, the researcher must determine what additional information is needed and how to gather it.

primary data
Original data gathered specifically for the project at hand.

secondary data
Information already gathered by somebody else for some other purpose.

syndicated data
Research information that is purchased from a research supplier on a shared-cost basis by a number of clients.

SELECT SOURCES OF INFORMATION Primary data, secondary data, or both can be used in an investigation. **Primary data** are original data gathered specifically for the project at hand. **Secondary data** have already been gathered for some other purpose. For example, when researchers conduct personal interviews, have individuals complete questionnaires, or answer questions on the telephone, they are collecting primary data. When they get information from Statistics Canada or from the local chamber of commerce, they are using a secondary source.

One of the biggest mistakes made in marketing research is to collect primary data before exhausting the information available in secondary sources. Ordinarily, secondary information can be gathered much faster and at far less expense than can primary data.

Syndicated data represent a third source of information that is a hybrid between primary and secondary data. Syndicated data are collected by a research supplier and may be purchased from that supplier by a number of clients, some of whom may be in direct competition with one another. The most common form of syndicated data involves the collection of data on a regular basis from an established sample or panel of consumers or retail stores. Clients subscribe to the reports, which are produced by the research company and essentially share the cost of collecting the data from the large sample. Although syndicated research does not provide privileged information to a single company, it does allow companies to obtain information on a shared-cost basis.

SOURCES OF SECONDARY AND SYNDICATED DATA Several excellent sources of secondary information and syndicated data are available to marketers and marketing researchers in Canada. A detailed review of the main sources of secondary and syndicated data in this country may be found in a number of Canadian marketing research textbooks. See Table 8-3 for an overview of key secondary resources for conducting marketing research in Canada.

SOURCES OF PRIMARY DATA After exhausting all the available secondary sources considered pertinent, researchers may still lack sufficient data. If so, they must turn to primary sources and gather or purchase the information. In a company's research project, for instance, a researcher may interview the firm's salespeople, wholesalers or retailers, or customers to obtain the market information needed.

TABLE 8-3 Key Sources of Secondary Research

Internal Sources

Internal sources include annual reports, profit and loss statements, sales figures, balance sheets, and prior research conducted by the organization. Research should begin within the company's own files and records, as well as that of the parent company if one exists.

Directories, Guides and Indexes

Business Periodical Index

Canadian Business Index

Canadian Periodical Index

Canadian Statistics Index

Canadian Trade Index

Directory of Association in Canada

Fraser's Canadian Trade Directory

Predicasts Index

Scott's Directories

Standards Periodical Directory

Ulrich's International Periodicals Directory

Selected Periodicals, Newspapers, etc.

Advertising Age

Adweek

Business Horizons

Canadian Business

Canadian Consumer

Canadian Markets

Forbes

Fortune

Harvard Business Review

Journal of Advertising

Journal of Consumer Research

Journal of the Academy of Marketing Science

Journal of Marketing

Journal of Marketing Research

Journal of Retailing

Marketing Magazine

Marketing News

Sales and Marketing Management

Strategy: The Canadian Marketing Report

The Globe and Mail

The Globe and Mail Report on Business Magazine

The National Post

The Financial Post Magazine

The Wall Street Journal

Selected Statistics Canada Publications

Annual Retail Trade

Canadian Economic Observer

Family Expenditure Guide

Market Research Handbook

Statistics Canada is also on the WWW at www.statcan.ca. Industry Canada also provides statistical information regarding various industries at www.stategis.ic.gc.ca. Additional information may also be available from specific government departments that can be linked through www.canada.gc.ca. Provincial government Web sites may also contain required information.

For Canadian companies researching international business opportunities; www.dfait-maeci.gc.ca, department of foreign affairs and international trade. Also, www.bdc.ca, the Business Development Bank of Canada.

Selected Trade Resources

A.C. Nielsen

Compusearch

Conference Board of Canada

Dun & Bradstreet

Equifax Canada

Find/SVP

Gale Research

Maclean-Hunter Research Bureau

MMRI (Simmons Market Research Bureau)

Predicasts International

PMB (Print Measurement Bureau)

R.L. Polk

Selected Databases

ABI/Inform (Proquest)

CANSIM (Statistics Canada)

CBCA (Canadian Business & Current Affairs)

Dialog

Dow Jones

Infoglobe

Infomart

Lexis-Nexis

PsycINFO

The Source

Wilson's Business Abstracts

Online Search Options

Canadian Corporate Newsnet at www.cdn-news.com/
Canada Newswire at www.newswire.ca/

General purpose Internet search engines such as Lycos, Excite, or Yahoo! also provide marketers with additional information on special topics. The most recent publication of *The Canadian Internet Directory* can also facilitate the search for more reputable Canadian Web sites.

DETERMINE HOW TO GATHER PRIMARY DATA There are four widely used methods of gathering primary data: survey, qualitative research, observation, and experimentation. Normally all four are not used on the same project, although more than one may be. Because each method has strengths and weaknesses, the choice of which to use depends on the nature of the problem, but it will also be influenced by how much time and money are available for the project.

survey method

A method of gathering data by interviewing a limited number of people (a sample) in person or by telephone or mail.

SURVEY METHOD A **survey** consists of gathering data by interviewing people or by having them complete a questionnaire of some form. What distinguishes a survey from qualitative research (which will be discussed later in this chapter) is that, in a survey, the information is usually collected from a fairly large sample of customers, generally several hundred or more, and the results are entered into computer files for analysis. Consequently, the results of survey research are generally considered **quantitative** in nature because they involve statistical analysis. The advantage of a survey is that information is firsthand. In fact, it may be the only way to determine the opinions or buying intentions of a group.

Quantitative research is favoured by most organizations as it provides "concrete" numbers on which to base decisions. As discussed, the development of new information systems has allowed the "gentrification" of statistical techniques. That is, they have come into the mainstream as more and more powerful applications have enabled non-academics to use more and more powerful statistical analysis to make sense of the confusing array of data patterns before them.[18]

Inherent in the survey method are certain limitations. There are opportunities for error in the construction of the survey questionnaire and in the data collection process. Moreover, surveys can be very expensive, and they do take some time to complete. Other possible weaknesses are that potential respondents sometimes refuse to participate, and the ones who do respond often cannot or will not give accurate answers.

personal interview

A face-to-face method of gathering data in a survey.

Survey data collection is usually done by the researcher either in person, by telephone, by mail, or through the Internet to be returned via e-mail. **Personal interviews** are more flexible than the other types because interviewers can probe more deeply if an answer is incomplete. Ordinarily it is possible to obtain more information by personal interview than by telephone or mail. Also the interviewer, by observation, can obtain data regarding the respondents' socioeconomic status — their home, neighbourhood, and apparent standard of living.

mall-intercept interview

Personal interview conducted in a shopping centre mall.

Rising costs and other problems associated with door-to-door interviewing have prompted many marketing researchers to survey people in central locations, typically regional shopping centres. This technique is called the **mall intercept** method of interviewing. By interviewing people as they pass through a shopping mall, the interviewer is better able to encounter large numbers of people, as the urban mall has essentially become the "main street" of North America. Although data collection is made somewhat easier by this method, the researcher is less confident that he or she is obtaining a representative sample of the population of interest. In such a situation, the ability to access large numbers of people at relatively low cost outweighs concerns about the representativeness of the sample.[19]

telephone survey

A method of gathering data in a survey by interviewing people over the telephone.

In a **telephone survey**, the respondent is contacted by telephone, and the interview is completed at that time. Participants in telephone surveys are generally selected at random from telephone directories or by random dialing of telephone numbers. In the case where a company wishes to obtain information from its own customers, generally the researchers will have available a list from which those to be called may be selected at random. Telephone surveys can usually be conducted more rapidly and at less cost than either face-to-face interviews or mail surveys. Since a number of interviewers can make many calls from a few central points, this method is quite easy to administer. Computer-assisted techniques have broadened the scope of telephone interviewing. These techniques involve automated random-number dialing and a facility for the interviewer to record the respondent's answers directly into the computer as they are received. This technology speeds up the entry and processing of data and the production of reports.

A telephone survey can be timely. For instance, people may be asked whether they are watching television at the moment and, if so, the name of the program and the advertiser. One limitation of the telephone survey is that interviews cannot be too long, although telephone interviews that take up to thirty minutes to complete are not uncommon. In fact, one of the myths of telephone interviewing is that the questionnaire must be very short, because participants will not be willing to stay on the line for more than a minute or so. This is simply not so, as many Canadians appear quite co-operative in participating in telephone surveys that take five to ten minutes to complete. What is making it more difficult to conduct telephone survey research is that progressively fewer people are at home, and those who are at home are becoming more difficult to reach. Although there appears to be no dramatic increase in the frequency of unlisted numbers, more and more people are installing telephone answering machines or subscribing to services such as voice mail and call display. Many people who have such devices or services are using them to screen incoming calls, forcing callers to leave messages, or are electing not to answer the call if they do not recognize the number or name displayed. The result is that telephone interviewers are unable to reach an increasing percentage of the population, thereby making telephone interviewing more costly and resulting in more biased samples.

Once again, new technology is developing a means to counteract the impact of these developments. Bias will always exist in that certain people will never participate in this information gathering, however random-digit dialing CD-ROM technology significantly cuts the costs of lists obtained from commercial sampling companies and the increased costs of the decreasing contact rates. Further, unlisted numbers can potentially fall within generated samples and reduced costs permit increased samples to be generated. Studies have found that this process maintains the external validity of the procedure while increasing cost-effectiveness.[20]

Telephone surveys have been used successfully to reach professionals and executives at work. When preceded by a letter introducing the study and a short call to make an appointment for the actual interview, these surveys can elicit a very high co-operation rate.

Collecting marketing research information through **mail surveys** involves mailing a questionnaire to potential respondents and having them return the completed form by mail. Since no interviewers are used, this type of survey is not hampered by interviewer bias or problems connected with the management of interviewers. Mailed questionnaires are more economical than personal interviews and are particularly useful in national surveys. If the respondents remain anonymous, they are more likely to give true answers because they are not biased by the presence of an interviewer.

A major problem with mail surveys is the compilation of a good mailing list, especially for a broad-scale survey. If the sample can be drawn from a limited list, such as property taxpayers in a certain province, region, or municipality, or subscribers to a certain magazine, the list presents no problem. Another significant limitation concerns the reliability of the questionnaires returned. The researchers have no control over who actually completes the questionnaire or how it is done. For example, a survey may be addressed to an adult male member of the household but because he is unavailable or not interested, his teenage daughter "helps out" by completing it. In addition, because there is no personal contact with the respondents, it is impossible to judge how much care and thought went into providing the answers.

Still another limitation is that there is usually a low response rate to a mail survey. It is not uncommon to receive completed replies from only 10 to 15 percent of those contacted. This is particularly important because if the respondents have characteristics that differentiate them from non-respondents on certain dimensions of the survey, the results will be biased. Techniques for improving mail response rates have been the subject of hundreds of experiments.[21] Some of these include making the subject matter of the survey as interesting as possible, offering incentives to the participant to encourage involvement, and guaranteeing anonymity to encourage participation. In the case of mailed questionnaires, a higher response rate can be obtained by paying for return postage and by sending a reminder note or card, or even a second questionnaire, within a week or so of mailing the original.

Because of the lack of control over the process, increased postal rates, low response rates, and the time needed to mail out questionnaires and to receive the completed ones, most marketing researchers are using far fewer mail surveys than was the case several years ago.

INTERNET RESEARCH Increasingly, the Internet is being used to collect survey data. According to American Demographics "Almost every form of market research has been tried online, from the simplest demographic surveys to the most complex focus groups."[22] Questionnaires can be posted on a firm's Web site or e-mailed to a sample of individuals. Speed and cost are the two most obvious advantages of this approach. Transmission is electronic, providing speed and significant personnel and material savings. Perseus Development Corporation, a company that specializes in electronic research services and survey development software, says a five-minute survey to one hundred people would cost $550 conducted by phone (including telephone costs, interviewers, and data entry), $500 by mail (including printing, postage, and data entry), and a mere $55 by Internet (including creation, delivery, and conversion of data).

The disadvantages of **Internet research** are similar to those of traditional mail methods. Clearly, the risk of bias is large, as the general population is not well represented when you consider the limited group that can be reached through the Internet. Although use of the Internet is expanding rapidly, at the time of writing this book, only slightly more than 50 percent of adult Canadians were users of the Internet. It is also often not possible to verify the identity of the respondent, quality lists of potential participants are difficult to find, and it is difficult to provide effective incentives. This new medium brings with it a new manifestation of bias. Reliability of data is a concern as people have the tendency to "reinvent" themselves online. As many as 50 percent of high school kids lie about their identity online, and 33 percent of university students will as well. Adults aren't much better, misrepresenting themselves 25 percent of the time. While validity scales are built into almost all surveys to ensure consistency of responses, this is still a major concern with the use of this medium for research. To combat incentives and honesty, online marketers

Marketing at Work 8-2

Surveys Say . . . Brown

UPS was finding it increasingly difficult to get customers and prospective customers to pay attention to their advertising and even more difficult to get them to make a move to UPS based on their advertising. They audited the courier business in Canada to find that not only is it extremely competitive, but it is a very low-interest category, with customers only switching when they experience a problem with their current courier.

UPS began the exercise of revamping its advertising by examining its brand equities. They found an overwhelming presence of the colour brown. On one hand it meant that the company was perceived as being down to earth and trusted, but on the other it yielded descriptors such as traditional, old-fashioned, and boring. UPS then embarked on a process dubbed the "APL Method" to develop a new strategic positioning for the company. Expertise, insight, and knowledge of the company was provided by key UPS personnel, including representatives from their advertising agency, which was combined with feedback from customers of UPS and its competition.

Customers were asked to create their ideal courier. In addition to trust, they revealed that they wanted solutions tailored to their needs that are backed by world-class technology. The advertising agency went to work and developed a TV, radio, and print campaign with the primary take-away that UPS's innovative and solution-oriented approach allows them to adapt to every customer's individual needs. This message is also summarized in the new UPS tagline "Moving at the speed of your business."

Although the campaign is still quite new, qualitative and quantitative research shows that it is having a positive impact on UPS's image, particularly with competitive courier users. The research also reveals higher scores for the company on brand awareness and consideration. Customers too are using different adjectives to describe UPS. Gone are boring and old-fashioned; they have been replaced by dynamic and contemporary.

Source: Adapted from Rob Pashko, "No More Yawns," *Marketing Magazine,* January 31, 2000, p. 34.

---

sweeten the pot with offers of electronic coupons, instant online shopping coupons, contests, and sweepstakes. As such, respondents are required to submit personal information such as e-mail and mailing addresses. As the Internet becomes a more universally used medium, there is no doubt the use of online surveys will intensify.[23]

QUALITATIVE RESEARCH   When research is intended to probe more deeply into the opinions and attitudes of people interviewed, different techniques are required. Qualitative research usually employs much smaller samples and interviews people in greater depth and for as long as ninety minutes or two hours. The two most widely used qualitative research techniques are the individual depth interview and the focus group interview.[24]

The **individual depth interview** is used in situations where the marketing researcher wishes to probe the consumer's thoughts concerning his or her purchase and use of a certain product or service. It is conducted in an individual rather than a group format often because the topics to be discussed are sensitive ones or because the people are difficult to reach and would be unlikely to attend a focus group session. For example, the individual depth interview is often used to interview business executives and professionals. Such interviews will generally take one hour or more to complete and range over a number of topics. The interviewer usually conducts the interview using a prepared interview guide.

In the case of the **focus group interview**, approximately eight to ten people are "recruited" to participate. They are usually selected to meet certain criteria relating to demographic characteristics, the use of a particular brand, frequent visits to certain vacation destinations, or similar criteria of interest to the researcher and client. The focus group interviewer or moderator orchestrates the discussion using a fairly loosely struc-

Focus groups provide marketers with valuable insights.

tured interview guide, rather than the more structured questionnaire of the typical face-to-face interview or telephone survey. Many interesting and enlightening findings are revealed through focus group interviews, which have become one of the most widely used techniques in marketing research.

Because these are qualitative marketing research techniques, their results are completely non-quantifiable; typically no statistics are generated and research reports contain few if any numbers. They do produce valuable insights into how consumers feel about certain concepts and why they make decisions as they do. The principal use of the focus group interview, for example, is to allow the marketer to really understand why customers are buying one brand over another, why this bar of soap and not that one, why this locally owned fitness centre and not the national chain. The research explores what customers like and dislike about each, and what would have to happen for them to switch to the alternative.

The typical focus group interview will involve a group of eight to ten individuals who have been invited to spend ninety minutes or more discussing a certain topic with a discussion leader or moderator. Participants are invited to attend and are usually paid as much as $40 or more. Focus groups are, by definition, loosely structured and are intended to provide marketers with insights that they simply cannot obtain through the more structured answers provided by survey research. Occasionally, marketing researchers will use the focus group technique to learn more about how consumers think about certain product or service categories or approach certain purchase decisions. They are then in a better position to design larger research surveys that may involve several hundred interviews with consumers.

Online focus groups have also been utilized — this would seem only natural with the proliferation of chat rooms on the Internet. It would seem, sometimes, that the Internet was created for chatting. A focus group would be like a focused chat room with a moderator. These have been criticized, however, as lacking the in-depth emotional information obtained from body language or tone of voice. In cyber groups, such expression is limited to the use of "smiley faces" and typing in capital letters.[25]

It is important to realize that qualitative and quantitative approaches to marketing research are not usually competing for the researcher's attention. Rarely will a marketing researcher be in a position where he or she will have to decide whether to use a survey or a series of focus group interviews. The approaches are used for quite different purposes, and each is appropriate in certain situations. Generally, qualitative techniques such as focus group interviews will be used where the researcher wants to explore certain subjects in great depth or where he or she is carrying out exploratory research on a topic about which the client knows very little.

observational method
Gathering data by observing personally or mechanically the actions of a person.

OBSERVATIONAL METHOD In the **observational method**, the data are collected by observing some action of the respondent. No interviews are involved, although an interview may be used as a follow-up to get additional information. For example, if customers are observed buying beer in cans instead of bottles, they may be asked why they prefer that form of packaging to the other. We should not adopt a too restricted view of what constitutes observational research. We can include any form of research that involves the automatic capture of information, where the customer or consumer is being observed by a machine or by technology rather than by another person. In each case, the information is often being collected without the customer's knowledge, which may raise ethical issues concerning this form of research.

In using this approach, researchers may collect information by personal or mechanical observation. In one form of **personal observation**, the researcher may pose as a customer in a store. This technique is often referred to as "mystery shopping" and is useful in getting information about the calibre of the salespeople or in determining what brands they promote. One example of **mechanical observation** that is often presented is the use of an electric cord stretched across a highway to count the number of cars that pass during a certain time period. Technology has advanced so rapidly that data are now captured by technology in many different settings. Builders of highways now imbed sensors in the surface of the road to not only count but to identify the vehicles that pass over them. Whenever we use ABMs at a bank we enable the bank to capture lots of information. The scanners that speed up the process of checking through our groceries at supermarkets also are automatically collecting information about what was purchased. If your supermarket also has a frequent-shopper club, the system uses the list of items purchased to update your personal data file. The resulting databases that most large retail firms and others now maintain on their customers are a direct result of data captured through such technology-based observation.

Retailers also find that watching the customer is a valuable way to gauge reactions and attitudes toward store displays and merchandise. Video recording consumer reactions has also provided valuable input. Urban Outfitters (www.urbn.com), the specialty clothing and accessory store, likes to use observation as a market research tool. They don't plan to find out what customers are saying, but rather what they are doing. They videotape and photograph customers in their stores. Managers are then able to determine what customers are wearing and this helps them make quick merchandise decisions.[26]

Marketers have even found a way to keep an eye on us when we are surfing the Internet. Through the use of "cookies," inactive data files are placed on a visitor's computer hard drive when you visit a particular Web site. The cookie records the visitor's activity while connected to the site — which pages were visited, how long was spent in what area, the links used, and from which site the visitor came from. The cookie allows the visitor to be identified and as such welcomed back on his or her next visit. Information on all purchases is also stored, allowing offers to be made on products based on past purchases.[27] Through the use of cookies, Amazon.com tracks the purchases of 4.5 million customers and offers suggestions about titles they might enjoy based upon previous selections.[28]

The observation method has several merits. It can be highly accurate. Often it removes all doubt about what the consumer does in a given situation. The consumers are usually unaware that they are being observed, so presumably they act in their usual fashion.

The observation technique reduces interviewer bias. However, the technique is limited in its application. Observation tells what happened, but it cannot tell why. It cannot delve into motives, attitudes, or opinions.

To overcome the biases inherent in the survey method, some firms are using sophisticated observational techniques that involve a combination of cable TV, electronic scanners in supermarkets, and computers. For example, some marketing research companies in Canada and the United States have established "scanner panels." Selected households are invited to participate in a program that involves recording electronically every TV commercial watched in participants' homes; every purchase the participants make in supermarkets equipped with checkout scanners is electronically recorded. With this observational method, researchers can measure which products members of the households are buying and determine which TV commercials they have seen. It provides an improved link between advertising and purchase that allows for more accurate measurement of the kinds of advertising that work and that don't work.

The A.C. Nielsen Company and the BBM Bureau of Measurement (www.bbm.ca) have installed such monitoring devices in more than two thousand Canadian homes. These devices record electronically on a regular basis the channel being watched. Information is also provided on each member of the household that participate in the panel. BBM has recently incorporated what they call PictureMatching™ technology into its PeopleMeter measurement system to provide more accurate data collection. Digital frequencies may carry as many as eight signals creating difficulty in accurate channel labelling. BBM's PictureMatching™ circumvents this by periodically "sampling" the actual video image on each participating TV screen. This time-stamped sample is then matched against all programming available at that time. Tested through 1998, the system will be launched throughout Canada by the end of 2001. It will make available daily, online audience reports and superior PC-based software that will let broadcasters and agencies analyze data in ways they never have before.

experimental method
A method of gathering primary data in which the researcher is able to observe the results of changing one variable in a situation while holding all others constant.

EXPERIMENTAL METHOD An **experiment** is a method of gathering primary data in which the researcher is able to observe the result of changing one variable in a situation while holding all others constant. Experiments are conducted in laboratory settings and in the field. In marketing research, the word laboratory is used to describe an environment over which the researcher has complete control during the experiment.

Consider the following example. A Vancouver film producer wished to determine whether Canadian films would be rented more frequently from video stores if they were identified as being Canadian. To assess this issue, he set up an experiment with ten Vancouver-area video stores in which he supplied them with a stock of Canadian videos to put on their shelves. In three stores, the tapes were mixed in with the other videos. In three stores, the Canadian films were separated on their own rack and identified as such; the remaining four stores, known as the promotional group, put the Canadian tapes in their own section, stuck little bar signs on each cassette, and promoted them with stickers and posters. Rentals were tracked over six months. The results indicated that people rented more Canadian videos when they were identified as such, and 45 percent more when they were promoted. These results, incidentally, contravene conventional wisdom that Canadians are not interested in films made in this country. As such, the information gained is of great interest to the Canadian film industry.[29]

Laboratory experiments can be used to test virtually any component of marketing strategy. However, it is important to recognize that the setting is unnatural and that consumers' responses may be biased by the situation.

An experiment carried out in the field, that is, under actual market conditions, is called **test marketing**. It is similar to a laboratory experiment but is conducted under more realistic conditions. The researcher therefore has less control. In test marketing, the researcher duplicates real market conditions in a small geographic area to measure consumers' responses to a strategy before committing itself to a major marketing effort. Test marketing may be undertaken to forecast sales or to evaluate different marketing mixes. Test marketing methodology is also used to evaluate pricing strategies, to obtain feedback on aspects of an advertisement, or to establish the effectiveness of an advertising campaign in influencing buying behaviour. Advertising testing is sometimes done by running two versions of the same advertisement and assessing changes in purchasing behaviour relative to each area.

The advantage of field experiments over laboratory experiments is their realism. However, there are several disadvantages. Test marketing is expensive (spending $500,000 or more to complete the test is not uncommon), time-consuming (nine to twelve months is normal), and impossible to keep secret from competitors (who may intentionally disrupt the test by temporarily changing their marketing programs). Another problem is the researcher's inability to control the situation. For example, a company that is test marketing a new product may encounter a certain amount of publicity while the product is in the test market, simply because of the innovativeness of the product. Although such publicity would normally be considered a good thing, when faced with it in a test market situation, the marketer is not sure about the extent to which it has distorted the sales results. In other words, what volume of sales resulted from the product and the regular marketing efforts of the company (what was actually being tested), and what resulted from the publicity that was generated?

Because of its inherent limitations, the use of traditional test marketing declined as faster, less expensive alternatives were developed. One of these alternatives is the **simulated test market**, in which a sample of consumers is shown ads for the product being tested as well as for other products. The subjects are then allowed to "shop" in a test facility that resembles a small grocery store. Follow-up interviews may be conducted immediately and also after the products have been used to better understand the consumers' behaviour. The entire set of data goes into a statistical model, and sales for the product are forecast.

The potential benefits of simulated test marketing include:

◆ Lower costs than a traditional test market.

◆ Results in as little as eight weeks.

◆ A test can be kept secret.

test marketing
A marketing research technique in which a firm markets its product in a limited geographic area, measures the sales, and then — from this sample — projects (a) the company's sales over a larger area and/or (b) consumers' response to a strategy before committing to a major marketing effort.

simulated test market
A confidential variation of test marketing in which consumers are shown advertising for a product and then are allowed to "shop" in a test store in order to measure their reactions to the advertising, the product, or both.

The drawbacks are:

◆ Questionable accuracy for unique, new products.

◆ Application limited to traditional packaged goods.

◆ Inability to predict the response of competitors or retailers.

◆ Inability to test changes in marketing variables like packaging or distribution because of the simulation's short duration.[30]

Simulated test marketing has not replaced traditional test markets because of these limitations. In fact, the two methods are often used together, with the simulation results used to make marketing mix modifications before beginning the traditional test market.

PREPARE FORMS FOR GATHERING DATA Whether interviewing or observing subjects, or when having respondents complete questionnaires on their own, as in the case of a mail survey, researchers use a questionnaire or form on which there are instructions and spaces to record answers or responses. It is not easy to design a data-gathering form that elicits precisely the information needed. When conducting surveys, researchers use questionnaires that are fairly structured and generally provide a number of responses, asking respondents or interviewers to check the most appropriate response or to write in an answer. When conducting focus group interviews or depth interviews, researchers use interview guides that are much less structured and that ensure that the interviewer raises all of the topics that must be covered during the interview.

Depending on whether questionnaires or interview guides are being used, different considerations apply. If the researcher is to obtain qualitative information through focus groups or depth interviews, no computer-based statistical analysis can be performed. The interpretation of these results is quite subjective and will consist of conclusions drawn from the comments made by participants during the interviews. On the other hand, if the researcher chooses to obtain quantitative data, usually through survey research, such information will lend itself quite readily to statistical analysis. In this latter case, care must be taken in ensuring that the questions asked will prove useful to the researcher and the marketing manager who has ordered the research.

The following represent some factors that must be considered when designing forms for the collection of research data:

◆ *Question wording.* If a question is misunderstood, the data it produces are worthless. Questions should be written with the potential respondent in mind. Vocabulary, reading level, and familiarity with jargon all must be considered. A common wording error is to inadvertently include two questions in one. For example, the question "How would you evaluate the speed and efficiency of our service?" followed by a rating scale that ranges from "poor" to "excellent" is likely to cause problems. Some respondents may see the service as fast, which is good, but with too many mistakes, which is bad.

◆ *Response format.* Questions asked in survey research are generally either designed for check-mark responses (such as yes-no, multiple choice, agree-disagree scales) or open-ended replies. Open-ended questions are more often associated with depth interviews and are easier to prepare and frequently produce richer answers, but they require more effort from the respondent and therefore lower the level of co-operation.

In addition, in a mail survey it is often difficult to read and interpret open-ended responses. Open-ended questions are used most often in personal or telephone interviews, where the interviewer can probe for explanations and additional details.

◆ *Questionnaire layout.* The normal procedure when constructing a questionnaire for use in a survey is to begin with easier and general questions and move to the more difficult, complicated, and specific questions. To understand behaviour, researchers must sometimes ask questions about possibly sensitive topics (for example, personal hygiene) or private matters (age, income). These questions are normally placed closer to the end of a questionnaire.

◆ *Pretesting.* All questionnaires should be pretested on a small group of respondents who are similar to the intended sample. Pretesting is designed to identify problems in the design of the questionnaire and to allow for corrections and refinements to be made prior to the actual study.

Many books have been written on questionnaire design. Extreme care and skill are needed to produce a questionnaire that maximizes the likelihood of getting a response while minimizing bias, misunderstanding, and respondent irritation.

PLAN THE SAMPLE   It is, of course, not necessary to survey or observe every person who could shed light on a research problem. It is sufficient to collect data from a sample if its reactions are expected to be representative of the entire group. We all employ sampling in our everyday activities. Often we base our opinion of a person on only one or two conversations. And we taste food before taking a larger quantity. The key in these personal examples and in marketing research is whether the sample provides accurate information.

The fundamental idea underlying sampling is that a small number of items — a **sample** — if properly selected from a larger number of items — a **population** — will have the same characteristics and in about the same proportion as the larger number. Obtaining reliable data with this method requires the right technique in selecting the sample.

Improper sampling is a source of error in many studies. One firm, for example, selected a sample of calls from all the calls made to its 1-800 number and used the information to make generalizations about its customers. Would you be comfortable saying that these callers are a **representative sample** of all the firm's customers or even all the dissatisfied ones?[31] Many hotels and restaurants use comment cards to obtain feedback from customers. The danger in generalizing from this information relates to the issue of who completes comment cards. The sample is self-selected and as such has built-in biases. Though numerous sampling techniques are used, only samples that are representative of the population of interest are appropriate for making generalizations from a sample to the population. A **random sample** is selected in such a way that every member of the population has a known probability of being included. In fact, unless the researcher has available a list of all members of the population, it is virtually impossible to select a random sample. As a result, marketing researchers will generally attempt to select a sample that is as representative of the population as possible.

Most of the samples used in survey research would be considered convenience samples. These are quite common in marketing research for two reasons. First, random samples are very difficult to get. Even though the researcher may select the subjects in a random fashion, there is no guarantee that all of those who are selected will participate.

random sample
A sample that is selected in such a way that every unit in the defined universe has an equal chance of being selected.

convenience sample
A sample that is selected in a nonrandom way such that every member of the universe does not have an equal chance of being included.

Some will be unavailable and others will refuse to co-operate. As a result, researchers often resort to carefully designed **convenience samples** that reflect the characteristics of the population as closely as possible. Second, not all research is done with the objective of generalizing to a population. Sometimes the company is interested in interviewing customers who visit a certain store or who telephone for service. In these cases, a convenience sample may be representative of the overall population. For example, if we want to assess whether regular users of a shopping centre are favourably disposed to the idea of installing lockers, then a convenience sample may be appropriate for this situation.

A common question regarding sampling is: How large should a sample be? With random sampling methods, a sample must be large enough to be truly representative of the population. Thus the size will depend on the diversity of characteristics of the population. All basic statistics books contain general formulas for calculating sample size. It is not, however, a simple matter to determine the appropriate size of a sample. The choice of sample size is normally made after consideration of a wide variety of factors. The researcher must determine whether there are natural groupings in the population, if the research objectives will require an investigation of whether one factor is associated with another, and the budget available to conduct the research.

COLLECT DATA Collecting primary data by interviewing, observation, or distributing questionnaires through the mail is often the weakest link in the research process. Ordinarily, in all other steps, it's possible to ensure accuracy. However, the fruits of these labours may be lost if the data gatherers are inadequately trained or supervised. Data collectors need to understand the importance of maintaining the integrity of the data collection methods. In other words, if it has been decided that they need to interview every third person entering a store, and this is how the sample is being selected, they cannot decide to interview the first twenty people because it is more convenient. Such interference with methodology can significantly bias the results. Data collectors need to be given, in their training, a basic understanding of research methodologies so that they can relate to the importance of the procedures used and why they must be observed as they are designed.

Motivating data collectors is often difficult, because they frequently are part-time workers doing what is often a monotonous task. As a result, many problems may crop up at this point. For instance, poorly trained interviewers may fail to establish rapport with respondents or may change the wording of questions. In extreme cases, there have even been instances where interviewers have attempted to fake the responses!

Analyze the Data and Present a Report

The value of research is determined by its results. Since data cannot speak for themselves, analysis and interpretation are key components of any project. Data analysis software packages have made it possible for researchers to tabulate and process masses of data quickly and inexpensively. This tool can be abused, however. Managers have little use for reams of computer output. Researchers must be able to identify pivotal relationships, spot trends, and find patterns — that's what transforms data into useful information. Proper coding of information assists in this process. Coding enables the researcher to determine how he or she wishes the data to be presented to ensure efficiency of interpretation. Qualitative data, such as the results of focus groups and depth interviews, are more time consuming and more difficult to analyze than quantitative data. It is very important to have clearly articulated the research objectives at the beginning of the project.

Knowing clearly what questions the research is designed to address makes it much easier to determine what the results are saying. Sometimes trends or patterns will develop that are not expected or anticipated in the planning stages. Good researchers must be able to interpret these findings relative to the research objectives.

The end product of the investigation is the researcher's conclusions and recommendations. Most projects require a written report, often accompanied by an oral presentation to management. Here communication skill becomes a factor. Not only must researchers be able to write and speak effectively, they must adopt the perspective of the manager in presenting research results.

Conduct Follow-up

Researchers should follow up their studies to determine whether their results and recommendations are being used. Management may choose not to use a study's findings for several reasons. The problem that generated the research may have been mis-defined, become less urgent, or even have disappeared. Or the research may have been completed too late to be useful. Without a follow-up, the researcher has no way of knowing if the project was on target and met management's needs or if it fell short, and an important source of information for improving research in the future would be ignored.

By this point you have probably realized that doing good research is not easy. It takes a well-designed set of objectives with a research methodology suitable to address these objectives. Unfortunately, research is not always done well. When interpreting research information, you should assess the methods used and be careful not to make generalizations that are not substantiated.

Who Does Marketing Research?

Marketing research can be done by a firm's own personnel or by outside researchers. Sometimes a job is divided, with company personnel doing parts of a project and using a research specialist for such tasks as collecting data or developing approaches for the analysis of data.

Within the Company

Separate marketing research departments exist primarily in larger companies and are usually quite small. The marketing research department may consist of only a single manager or may be as large as four or five professionals in large consumer-products companies. In most of these situations, the marketing research department rarely conducts research utilizing its own staff, but rather contracts the work out to suppliers outside the company. The primary role of the marketing research department, therefore, is to organize, monitor, and co-ordinate marketing research, which may be done by a number of different suppliers across the country. The manager of the marketing research department reports either to the chief marketing executive or directly to top management. The researchers who staff this department must be well versed in company procedures and know what information is already available within the company. They must also be familiar with the relative strengths and weaknesses of potential marketing research suppliers.

Outside the Company

A sign of the growth in the use of marketing research is the fact that there are now a great many companies across the country from which a marketing manager may seek help in mar-

Marketing at Work 8-3

Freedom: Prohibition or Privilege?

There are many ways researchers try to tap consumers' covert thoughts on behalf of their clients — role playing, observational research, focus groups — but none so fantastical as Clotaire Rapaille's "archetype research." Rapaille's technique seeks to uncover the characteristics that generate the choices we make. To do so he foregoes the typical question of asking what people want and replaces it with why.

Rapaille describes his work as a type of physics — trying to discover the cultural structure of people's minds. While working with autistic children he was baffled by the fact that quite smart children had such difficulty learning language. It is now commonly accepted in linguistic theory that autistic persons lack an emotional life, and it is emotion which keeps meaning alive in our minds. Rapaille then proposed that these subliminal emotions occupy a place between each individual's unconscious and the collective unconscious of the entire human race. It is this "cultural unconscious" which is closely associated with language and therefore differs from country to country.

According to Rapaille, the first time we experience something we make an imprint, and when we do we create a mental highway. We make use of these highways all the time and they become unconscious. To discover these secret codes or imprints Rapaille uses a technique similar to dream analysis. He foregoes straightforward questions aimed at the cortex — the seat of intellect, and directs his questions to the reptilian part of the brain — the home of smells, violence, sex, and other primal emotions. At the end of a day-long process involving word association games, meditation, and story telling, Rapaille collects the participants' stories and if he sees repetition in the narrative knows that he has found an archetypal association.

This process may seem a little hokey to the more traditional market researcher, but nearly fifty Fortune 100 companies disagree, having realized successful marketing campaigns as a result of Rapaille's insight into consumers' emotional connections with their product or service.

One such company is Disney. When the Magic Kingdom opened its gates in Paris, Europeans hated it, and Euro Disney lost US$1 million a day. Rapaille explained the lack of success as a difference in how Americans and Europeans define freedom. He explained that freedom exists on an axis and that there is a second element that counter-balances it. To Americans this element is prohibition — they experience tension all the time. Disney's Magical Kingdom celebrates their cultural concept of liberty while imposing harsh limitations — no smoking, no pets allowed in restaurants, and no drinking.

To Europeans these limitations were insulting. In France the counter-balance to freedom is privilege. The major changes to Euro Disney now include little islands of privilege — special areas for smoking, dogs, and drinking. The amusement park now operates at a profit and is one of Paris' most popular tourist destinations.

Source: Adapted from Jack Hitt, "Does the Smell of Coffee Brewing Remind You of Your Mother," *The New York Times*, May 7, 2000, p. 71.

keting research problems. There exist in Canada today well over one hundred companies that operate in the field of marketing research. When a marketing manager requires information on Canadian marketing research suppliers, a number of sources exist that may be consulted in order to obtain a list of potential suppliers. One listing of such suppliers is *The Directory of Canadian Marketing Research Organizations* (www.pmrs/~apmrs.com), produced by the Professional Marketing Research Society. This directory provides detailed information on those companies that operate in Canada in marketing research and related fields.

There are more than thirty full-service marketing research companies in Canada. These companies include such firms as the Creative Research International (www.crii.com), Canadian Facts (www.cfgroup.ca), Market Facts of Canada, and Thompson Lightstone. They provide a full range of marketing research services, from the design of a research study to the submission of a final report. In addition to the full-service marketing research companies, there are in Canada dozens of smaller firms that operate in various specialized areas of marketing research. These companies are usually small and may specialize by geographic region, by industry, or by service performed. Some concentrate in either consumer or industrial research or carry out studies that involve the application of specialized techniques. Other companies provide specialized marketing research services, such as the analysis of survey data. Some marketing research is also conducted in Canada by advertising agencies and management consulting firms.

Competitive Intelligence

A research area that is only recently receiving widespread, serious attention is **competitive intelligence (CI)**. In countries like Japan firms have made a science out of watching and learning from their rivals. We are not talking about industrial espionage, but legal and ethical information gathering about existing and potential competitors. CI experts will tell you that 90 perecent to 95 percent of the information that will help firms is available through public sources — the rest a good CI practitioner can fill in with his or her analytical skills.

CI is not quite the same as market research, although the two share many commonalties. Market research generally provides detailed information on specific markets and segments based on strict methodologies. CI, on the other hand, is much more like assembling a puzzle. It involves piecing together data from a variety of unique sources to answer key questions about other organizations — what are their upcoming plans? Expansion? New product lines? Price cuts?[32]

CI involves gathering and analyzing available public information about the activities and plans of competitors. This may come from a variety of internal and external sources. The most common are databases created and sold by research firms. The simplest of these may be collections of newspaper and magazine clippings on industries or companies. There are thousands of these database services available today.

Another source of research information on competitors is government reports from local, national and foreign government agencies. The primary internal source is employees, particularly salespeople. These are the people in the trenches talking to others in the industry and meeting with customers each day. Sometimes these customers are also customers of the competition. Sometimes these employees will shop the competitor to assess retail operations and price levels. Or buy a competitor's product to examine and test it. The competition can be one of your best marketing tools.

One of the newest tools for CI is, of course, the Internet. Frequently, information contained on Web sites will include price lists, distributors and suppliers, new-product information, etc. Firms boasting of their R&D projects will often list publications and other research papers published by their researchers that can be obtained in the public domain. These may provide insight into what that company is working on.

competitive intelligence (CI)
The process of gathering and analyzing publicly available information about the activities and plans of competitors.

Privacy and Ethical Issues

A topic such as competitive intelligence logically leads us into the murky issues of privacy and research ethics. This has received attention as public concerns become heightened as consumers express increasing worry over what happens to their personal information once they cross the information highway.

In 2000, Bill C-6, the Personal Information Protection and Electronics Document Act, was passed into law to go into effect January 2001. This new privacy law is intended to make consumers feel more comfortable about how their personal information is being used. The legislation applies to all federally regulated industries, including transportation, financial services, and telecommunications, and to any inter-provincial transfer of personal information — for even the simplest information exchange such as the use of an address for a mailing label. The provinces have until 2004 to develop their own privacy laws, with the exception of Quebec, which already has one.

As of January 1, 2001, companies require the consent of an individual to collect information, to use information, to transfer information, and for use of the information for other than the original purpose for which it was collected. Marketers are no longer able to go on "fishing expeditions" for personal information without specifying exactly why and what data are to be used for. Companies will also have to clearly identify the individual in the organization responsible for managing privacy issues, assure access to that individual, and create an official system for handling privacy-related complaints and requests.

There are three levels of consent recognized by the new law: implied (for example, where personal information may be used to contact consumers regarding renewal of service and the like), negative-option (people are given a box to check whether or not their information may be passed on to other organizations), and express (individuals must give specific consent to use personal data — in cases where the data may be considered sensitive).[33]

Status of Marketing Research

Marketing research is a major growth area partially brought about by the new advances in technology. These advances include computer accessibility, point-of-sale data collection equipment, such as supermarket scanners, the Internet and its proliferation, and improved data-analysis software. They have enabled more efficient collection, analysis, and processing of data. The cost of computer technology has plummeted in the last decade to the point where even small businesses can collect data on their customer base. Most large companies now collect considerable amounts of data at each purchase. Frequent-buyer cards, such as those used by Zellers, A&P, and Sobeys, allow businesses to determine purchasing behaviour and patterns.

The challenge for marketers in the future will be to decide what information is needed and how it is to be integrated into decision-making. Database development and design is critical in ensuring that information is collected efficiently and meets management's need. The role of managing databases is, therefore, a crucial one, and more emphasis is being placed on proper management. One example of this is the integration of customer files throughout business departments where previously separate data was maintained in each. Hotels, for instance, now compile data on their guests that can be accessed at check-in. The individual's file will tell the front-desk clerk that the guest may require a smoke-free room, a 6:00 A.M. wake-up call, and business services, such as access to fax or e-mail, throughout the day. In addition to providing immediate information to management, the integration of this information in research design on lifestyles or travel trend patterns can identify for marketers the areas to be explored and the types of information to be collected.

As we saw earlier, the marketing environment is changing. For example, increased competition through globalization and expanded marketing borders has sometimes made it more difficult for businesses to operate. Lifestyles and value systems are changing. Since marketing research is all about obtaining information to support marketing decision-making, the changing environment is increasing its importance. The more competently marketers can zero in on what is wanted and needed, the more effective they will be in selling their products and services.

It is still true, however, that many companies are spending very large amounts on product development research, but much less on determining market opportunities for their products. Several factors account for this less-than-universal acceptance of marketing research:

◆ *Predicting behaviour is inexact.* Because of the many interrelated variables involved, marketing research often cannot predict exact future market behaviour accurately. When dealing with consumer behaviour, it is difficult to determine present attitudes or motives, let alone predict what they may be next year. As such, it is difficult to make predictions regarding sales increases for the following period. Unless it is able to convince management of the concrete value of such research, the marketing research department will often not receive enough resources to do a good job.

◆ *Conflicting objectives between researchers and managers.* Poor communication between these groups continues to be a problem. Researchers tend to be product-focused while managers will be market-focused. Managers are often forced to make quick decisions in the face of uncertainty while researchers have been trained to approach problems in a more cautious, scientific manner. It can be appreciated how this leads to disagreements regarding what research to conduct, how long it should take, the way it should be presented, and even what the goals of the research should be.

◆ *A project orientation to research.* Management is often reluctant to treat marketing research as a continuing process and further to relate it and decision-making in a more systematic fashion. Too often marketing research is viewed in a fragmented, one-project-at-a time manner and utilized only when management feels it has a "marketing problem." The expansion of MkIS and DSS into firms of various sizes will likely improve this situation.

Marketing Research, a magazine dedicated to management and applications issues within marketing, recently performed its own survey of research professionals asking what they believed to be the key influences in shaping marketing research at the beginning of the 21st century. The top responses were as follows: the Internet, globalization of business and research, one-to-one marketing, Internet/online research, privacy issues, computer technology, and e-commerce. As can be seen, the very technology issues that have come up repeatedly throughout this chapter dominate these responses. As the future and impact of these are still quite uncertain, we must also conclude the same for the future of marketing research.

Marketing research in the 21st century may become barely recognizable to a 20th century researcher. And this possibility brings the industry much optimism. The potential payoff for the pain and disruption of such a transformation as we are now experiencing is that research will evolve from an episodic contributor to a critical resource in the operation of businesses.[34]

Summary

Competitive pressure, expanding markets, the cost of making a mistake, and growing customer expectations all contribute to the need for marketing research. For a company to operate successfully today, management must develop a method for gathering and storing relevant data and converting it into usable information. Three tools used in research are the marketing information system, decision support systems, and the research project.

A marketing information system (MkIS) is an ongoing set of procedures designed to generate, analyze, disseminate, store, and retrieve information for use in making marketing decisions. An MkIS provides a manager with a regularly scheduled flow of information and reports. A decision support system (DSS) differs from an MkIS in that the manager, using a personal computer, can interact directly with data.

A marketing research project is undertaken to help resolve a specific marketing problem. The problem must first be clearly defined. Then a researcher conducts a situation analysis and an informal investigation. If a formal investigation is needed, the researcher decides which secondary and primary sources of information to use. To gather primary data, a survey, an observation, or an experiment may be used. The project is completed when the data are analyzed and the results reported. Follow-up provides information for improving future research.

Researchers have recently developed a stronger interest in finding out what competitors are currently doing and forecasting what they are likely to do in the future. Research is conducted internally by marketing research staff members and purchased externally from firms that specialize in doing research.

Marketing research has not yet achieved its potential because the value of research often cannot be directly measured, research does not always accurately predict the future, and researchers are too production-oriented. Further, researchers do not always communicate effectively with management, and research is frequently used in an ad hoc manner.

Key Terms and Concepts

Marketing research 217	Primary data 229	Personal observation 236
Marketing information system (MkIS) 220	Secondary data 229	Mechanical observation 236
	Syndicated data 229	Experiment 237
Decision support system (DSS) 222	Survey 231	Test marketing 238
Database 223	Quantitative 231	Simulated test market 238
Data warehouse 223	Personal interviews 231	Sample 240
Data mining 224	Mall intercept 231	Population 240
Retail scanner 225	Telephone survey 231	Representative sample 240
Single-source data 226	Mail surveys 232	Random sample 240
Situation analysis 228	Internet research 233	Convenience sample 241
Secondary research 228	Individual depth interview 234	Competitive intelligence (CI) 244
Hypothesis 228	Focus group interview 234	
Informal investigation 228	Observational method 236	

Questions and Problems

1. Explain how a marketing information system differs from a decision support system.

2. How involved should marketing researchers be in setting strategy for their organizations?

3. A group of wealthy business executives regularly spends some time each winter at a popular ski resort — Whistler, B.C.; Banff, Alberta; or Grey Rocks, Quebec. They were intrigued with the possibility of forming a corporation to develop and operate a large ski resort in the B.C. Rockies near the Alberta border. This would be a totally new venture and would be on federal park land. It would be a complete resort, with facilities appealing to middle- and upper-income markets. What types of information might they want to have before deciding whether to go ahead with the venture? What sources of information would be used?

4. Evaluate surveys, observation, and experimentation as methods of gathering primary data in the following projects:

    a. A sporting goods retailer wants to determine college students' brand preferences for skis, tennis racquets, and golf clubs.

    b. A supermarket chain wants to determine shoppers' preferences for the physical layout of fixtures and traffic patterns, particularly around checkout stands.

    c. A manufacturer of equipment used in the manufacture of ice cream wants to know who makes buying decisions for its product among present and prospective users.

5. Using the steps in the research process as presented in this chapter, describe how you would go about investigating the feasibility of opening a computer repair shop close to your campus.

6. What kind of sample would you use in research projects designed to answer the following questions?

    a. What brand of running shoes is most popular among the students on your campus?

    b. Should retail stores in or near your hometown be open all day on Sundays?

    c. What percentage of the business firms in the city nearest your campus have automatic sprinkler systems?

7. Would it be appropriate to interview two hundred students as they left your college hockey arena about their feelings regarding funding for athletics and then generalize the results to the student body? Why or why not?

8. If you were called in to conduct a research project for a venture capital company, what suggestions would you have for your client if they proposed that you conduct a consumer study to determine the feasibility of introducing an NBA franchise in Calgary or Montreal?

Hands-On Marketing

1. Assume that you work for a manufacturer of a liquid glass cleaner that competes with Windex and Glass Wax. Your manager wants to determine the amount of the product that can be sold throughout the country. To help her in this project, prepare a report that shows the following information for your home province and, if possible, your home city or region. Carefully identify the sources you use for this information.

    a. Number of households or families.

    b. Income or buying power per family or per household.

    c. Total retail sales in the most recent year for which you can find reliable data.

    d. Total annual sales of food stores, hardware stores, and drugstores.

    e. Total number of food stores.

2. Interview the manager of your campus bookstore about the marketing information system used in the store (keep in mind that it may be a very informal system).

    a. What are the data sources?

    b. How are the data collected?

    c. What reports are received, and on what schedule?

    d. What problems arise with the MkIS?

    e. How could the MkIS be improved?

Case 2-1

PETER TAYLOR BUYS RUNNING SHOES

April was drawing to a close, and the signs of spring were evident throughout the nation's capital. Peter Taylor was in the process of writing the final set of examinations for his master's degree in business administration at the University of Ottawa. As a marketing major and sports enthusiast, his primary job-search objective was to find a position in sports marketing, preferably in Toronto. Peter knew that Canada's largest city contained an established base of sports and fitness organizations that could be targeted as employment prospects. In addition, Toronto contained the head offices of many large corporations that are involved in sports sponsorship. He had already made tentative plans to be in Toronto by June 1.

Peter had been involved in sports and athletics for as long as he could remember. His father, also an athlete and a soccer coach, encouraged Peter's initial involvement in hockey and baseball from the time Peter was five or six years old. Up to high school, Peter's active involvement in the local minor hockey program was maintained throughout the fall and winter, and he was active in baseball during the spring and summer seasons. The high school hockey schedule demanded early morning and evening practices, which eventually led him to decrease his hockey participation to a recreational level.

At high school, Peter became an avid competitor throughout the school year — soccer in the fall, volleyball until Christmas, basketball in the new year until Easter, and then track and field in the spring.

Peter has always felt that a physically active lifestyle enhanced his academic performance and general well-being. His parents were very outdoors-oriented and concerned about health and diet. These factors contributed to Peter's performance and drive in all his athletic endeavours. After he completed high school in Peterborough and began his undergraduate program at Trent University, a heavy course schedule prevented him from participating in team sports as actively as he had previously. For recreation and to keep the old gang together, Peter and a group of his high school friends arranged for free gym time in their old school. Every couple of weeks they would round up players for an afternoon or evening of basketball or volleyball.

Peter was also an active intramural competitor. Twenty or so of Peter's friends in his business administration class were athletically inclined. They competed in a variety of intramural sports as the nucleus of the business administration teams throughout their four years at Trent.

When Peter went on after graduation to the University of Ottawa for his MBA, few of his friends were surprised. They had expected for some time that Peter would try to combine his interest in marketing with his love for sports. During the often-gruelling two-year MBA program, Peter found less and less time for organized team sports. He rarely played hockey and did not compete in intramural sports. He did find time each week to swim in the university pool, and he cycled to the university regularly from his apartment in the Glebe area of the city. He also took squash more seriously, playing at least twice a week, although he had played only a little at Trent. This was a sport he felt he could continue to play after graduation.

Now that Peter was nearing the end of his MBA program, he realized that an active involvement in team sports would become difficult. He intended to continue playing squash, however, he wished to pursue an alternative form of exercise to balance and enhance his overall fitness. He considered weight training, but preferred more active sports. Having done quite well in middle-distance track and field competitions during high school, Peter decided to take running more seriously. During his two years in Ottawa, he had done a little jogging from time to time along the Rideau Canal, which runs near the university, but the cold Ottawa winters discouraged him from maintaining a year-round schedule. He realized, however, that running was one physical activity he could do according to his own schedule. He felt he might even consider competing in some of the middle- and longer-distance runs that he knew were held on a regular basis in and around Toronto.

Although Peter considered himself quite knowledgeable about most sports, he also felt there was probably more to running than just putting on a pair of sneakers and going out for a jog. He decided he should take advantage of the fact that the head office of Athletics Canada was located in Ottawa to obtain some technical information on the sport. Intuition told him that he should expand his common-sense list of "dos" and "don'ts." By placing a telephone call to the office of Athletics Canada, he was able to obtain the address of the Ontario Track and Field Association, which he was advised could provide him with a list of track and roadrunning clubs he might wish to join in the Toronto area.

As he walked through the Rideau Centre on a Saturday afternoon, following the exam in his marketing strategy course, he stopped into a bookstore that carried a wide range of magazines. He was particularly interested in buying a running magazine that might tell him something more about the right equipment for the sport. He found two such magazines in the sports and fitness section of the magazine rack, *Runner's World* and *Running Times*. He was not familiar with either magazine, but as he thumbed through them he was surprised by the number of advertisements for running shoes, and by the "high-tech" descriptions of many of the shoes. He selected *Running Times*, primarily because of the section labelled "Annual Running Shoe Guide," which seemed to be just what he needed.

Of particular concern to Peter was the financial investment he would need to make if he was to take running seriously. Although he owned an ample supply of basic sportswear such as shorts, sweatshirts, and T-shirts, he knew that top-of-the-line running shoes and a rainsuit were two necessities that together might cost him $300 or more. Peter did not yet have a salary, but he was never one to scrimp on sports equipment. He rationalized that the time he invested in such activities deserved a comparable monetary investment. His father had always taught him the value of good equipment as insurance against accidents and injuries.

Peter decided that he would wait until he moved to Toronto to join a running club and to learn more about the technique of the sport. Right now, he determined that he needed to get back to exercising regularly again, following the past few months of the MBA program, which had left him little time to work out. The more he thought about running, and stimulated by the articles in *Running Times*, the more anxious he was to begin running regularly as soon as his exams were over. He realized that he needed to know what running shoes to purchase and how best to prevent running injuries.

He was also beginning to realize that he knew very little about the engineering and technology of running shoes. Although he had bought other athletic footwear during the past few years, he had not appreciated the diversity of styles and models available. Advertisements in *Running Times* stressed materials such as Hexalite and Dynalite, cushioning based on air, fluids, gel, and foam, and glitzy colours and styles. Peter was unaware of the benefits each system offered. He read terms such as "rearfoot control," "heel counter," and "shock distribution," but felt ignorant about what shoe he should buy.

The wide variety of running shoes displayed in retail stores and featured in running magazines and the range of prices, colours, and styles made the decision even more complex. Rapidly changing technology, eye-catching innovations, and clever marketing tended to sway Peter from brand to brand without his knowing if the shoe matched his own needs and requirements. Running shoe purchases, as Peter had learned through consumer behaviour textbooks, seemed to be determined by how the buyer wishes to be perceived, whether to be trendy or athletic. Running shoe buyers often appeared to Peter to be very fickle, depending on what appealed to them or caught their eye at the point of purchase. He knew that serious runners often buy two or three different pairs, rotating them from day to day. He concluded that, as advanced engineering has transformed running shoes into technical and fashionable articles, their purchase had become a conspicuous activity and their wearing a "fashion statement."

Peter wanted to make sure he bought the right brand of running shoe. As he mulled over his decision, he identified criteria he felt he should consider in the selection process. Despite the wide price range of the shoes advertised in the magazine, high price was not a deterrent to Peter's purchase decision. Although he expected to pay more than $100 for a pair of quality running shoes, he preferred to keep the expense close to that level if at all possible. Comfort, availability, and protection against injury were critical to Peter. Colour was not at all important, although some shoes seemed a little too flashy. He was tending toward a lighter-weight shoe, which seemed to be preferred for longer distances. Peter felt that if each of these criteria was satisfied, he could run at his optimal capability.

To ensure that he was on the right track, he arranged a meeting with Sheila Cambridge at Athletics Canada. Sheila was a consultant with the association and held the provincial record for the ten km distance. Peter had met Sheila at a campus party several weeks ago and knew that she was held in high regard in the local athletic community. She would also be well versed in the technical aspects of running shoe construction, as she had graduated from the University of Ottawa a year earlier having specialized in kinesiology. Peter felt confident that she would be able to provide the expert advice he needed to pick the right pair of running shoes. "Besides," thought Peter as he walked along the canal towards Sheila's office, "it will be nice to see Sheila again."

Peter enjoyed the meeting with Sheila, as they discussed mutual friends and Sheila's training for the summer roadracing season. Peter learned that she had been training for the past four months in preparation for her first attempt at the marathon distance, to take place in mid-May in Ottawa's National Capital Marathon. Peter began to feel a little ill at ease, as he realized that Sheila was obviously far more knowledgeable about running than he was. He wondered whether he would ever reach the same level of training that she had achieved and felt a little uncomfortable at the thought of asking very basic questions about what shoes he should buy. He wondered whether he shouldn't just end the conversation.

It was too late when Sheila said, "Enough about my running. You wanted to talk about running shoes, didn't you? How much running are you planning to do?" Peter explained that he had participated in track and field in high school, but at distances from 400 to 1500 m. He now wanted to try running some longer distances, primarily to get back in shape. He also thought he might like to run some road races and even try a little cross-country. With that, Sheila pulled from a pile of magazines and books on her desk a back issue of *Running Times*. She turned to a page that contained a diagram of the various components of a running shoe (see page 252). She explained to Peter those components to which he should pay particular attention. "In selecting a running shoe," she explained, "the factor that I consider most important is fit. If the shoe doesn't fit well, you are likely to encounter problems down the road."

Sheila further suggested that one of the main criteria Peter must satisfy in his purchase of running shoes was protection against injury and overload. Research into the causes of injury has pointed to the type of running surface as one of the possible causes. She explained that common running injuries and ailments include leg fractures, muscle pulls and tears, heel spurs, shin splints, and knee injuries.

Although Peter felt he would prefer cross-country training through wooded and grassy areas, he observed that access to scenic trails would likely be limited once he moved to Toronto. "In that case," explained Sheila, "your running shoe must provide stability and protection against the high impact of pounding on the pavement. Not only do the interior components of the shoe have to protect your feet, but the exterior components such as the outsole will be important in cushioning against impact."

Other factors Sheila mentioned as contributing to injury were the type of movement, the training distance per week, and the intensity of training. She went on to explain that protection against overloading is also important. "Load is the external force acting upon a body. It results both from dynamic factors such as the type of movement, the velocity of limbs, posture, muscular activity, and the number of repetitions, and also from boundary conditions such as the shoe surface, obstacles, anthropometric factors, and individual situation," she explained.

Peter found himself listening less intently as the information that Sheila was offering began to sound much more technical than he had expected. He really just wanted her to recommend a pair of running shoes and was not interested in all the technical jargon. When Sheila suggested that he attend a running clinic to check out what some of the local runners were wearing, Peter asked her what she would buy if she was in his position.

Glossary of Terms

Shoe Part	Term	Explanation
	Rearfoot Stability	Prevents excessive lateral wobble or sag, and is important to severe pronators (see opposite page).
	Achilles Notch	Soft, padded material above heel counter cushions Achilles tendon and is sometimes notched to prevent irritation of the tendon.
	Heel Counter	Rigid cup holds heel firmly in place to prevent lateral motion.
	Heel Counter Collar	Reinforces heel counter.
	Dual-density midsole	Higher density on medial (inner) side of shoe resists compression and makes it harder for the foot to pronate (roll or sag sideways toward the inward side).
Rear Foot	**Forefoot stability strap**	Helps to keep the upper material (usually a light nylon fabric or mesh) from sagging or bursting out; also helps to prevent excessive lateral motion of the forefoot.
	Toe Box	Should be roomy enough to let toes wiggle freely, with at least a thumb's width of space between toe and front wall of box. Foot should be snug around the heel, roomy around the toes.
	Midsole	Cushions the foot. Simplest midsoles are pieces of EVA foam. A more durable material is lightweight polyurethane (PU).
	Air Sac and Fluid Sac Midsole Components (Nike Air, Etonic StableAir, Brooks Hydroflow, Asics Gel, Reebok ERS, Hi-Tec AirBall, etc.)	Cushions impact of heel on the road, lengthens life of the shoe by preventing squashing of midsole (units are usually contained in strong PU casings) and may help stabilize ride by distributing impact.
Upper & Midsole	**Flexible Plate Midsole Components** (Nike Footbridge, Avia ARC, Etonic graphite plate, etc.)	Cushions impact by distributing impact over a wider area, and ARC combines this cushioning with a trampoline effect for greater energy return or "bounce."
	Heel Plug	Carbon/rubber resists abrasion, prevents wearing through prematurely at outside corner of the heel.
	Horseshoe Outsole (Nike Center-of-Pressure, Avia Cantilever)	Distributes weight to perimeter to maximize stability, while allowing center of rearfoot outsole to be scooped out (see Exposed Midsole, below).
	Exposed (Recessed) Midsole	Often in the center of the rearfoot bottom, and sometimes across the midfoot bottom, sections of dense outsole are scooped out in areas where foot contact with the ground isn't needed. This cuts down on the weight of the shoe, helps to keep the heel centered (by allowing it to sink down more in the center than on either side), and allows the foot to trampoline for better energy return.
	Filled-in Medial Arch	Resists pronation by preventing sag at instep. Similarly, **straight-lasted** shoe has straight shape suitable for stabilizing motion for hard heel-hitters and severe pronators. **Curved-lasted** models facilitate natural motion for forefoot-strikers and faster-paced runners.
Outsole	**Outsole Studs or Lugs**	Provide traction, especially important in the forefoot area, for both heel-strikers and forefoot-strikers. Tread patterns vary widely, but generally the smoother patterns are more effective for roads, the toothier patterns better in snow or mud or off-road.

Reprinted with permission of *Running Times* magazine.

Sheila said that she really couldn't recommend a brand or model that would be best for him, as there were many acceptable shoes available. She did say that she ran in Nike shoes and that Nike was, in her opinion, the leading running shoe in the market. She suggested that he probably wouldn't be disappointed if he bought a Nike shoe, possibly an Air Stab or an Air Span. Peter wondered if her opinion might be biased by her personal choice. He thanked her, but felt a little disappointed to have left without knowing why Nike would be a good choice.

Heading home the next day, following his final exam in marketing research, Peter decided to visit Sports Experts, a sporting goods store in the Rideau Centre, to look at the selection of running shoes and to price the various brands and styles that he had seen in a recent advertising flyer from the store. He had often found the sales clerks in sporting goods stores to be knowledgeable and hoped he might get some advice concerning running shoes. Although he was familiar with a number of sporting goods stores in the Ottawa area, Peter decided to visit only three of them, all located within the downtown area. Over the next day or two, he would check the variety and prices at Sports Experts, Elgin Sports, and Sports-4.

Sports Experts had a reputation for a wide selection and good service. Generally, Peter did not appreciate being hounded by sales clerks in stores. He had never found the sales clerks in this particular store to be pushy, but rather genuinely helpful and friendly. Many seemed to be students who were working in the store part-time. After he had been given a few minutes to scan the huge wall display of running, court, squash, tennis, aerobic, basketball, cross-training, volleyball, sprinting, cycling, and windsurfing shoes, a sales clerk approached him and offered her assistance.

Peter had been looking closely at several Nike and Brooks styles, as he had worn both brands in the court and cross-training styles in the past and had been very satisfied with them. He asked the sales clerk which of the brands was considered best and what benefits each had to offer.

The Sports Experts sales clerk, Donna Williams, proceeded to explain that neither was necessarily the best brand. She suggested that Peter's decision should be based on comfort and ensuring that the width was neither too narrow nor so wide that his feet shifted from side to side. She felt that price was generally a good measure of the quality of the shoe, but not necessarily of the brand. She recommended that Peter try one style of each of the major brands, so that he could determine the fit of each of the shoes, and whether the cushioning felt right.

Donna went on to suggest that sturdiness could be tested by bending the shoe from right to left, and by ensuring that the heel components of the shoe felt firm. The lightness of the various shoes could be compared easily. Once the most comfortable brand of shoe was identified, price could be used along with a visual test of features to determine which shoe fulfilled his need. Donna suggested that generally the higher the price, the more stability and features were associated with the running shoe. She felt that gimmicks, such as endorsements by personalities, Velcro closures, and fluorescent colours, would probably inflate the price but did not necessarily enhance the shoe's quality. So the quality-conscious consumer, as compared with the socially conscious one, would need to search beyond superficial features. Donna Williams indicated that it was often very difficult to tell, having been influenced by advertising and other marketing strategies, which features were truly beneficial for a runner such as Peter and which had merely been promoted to make a shoe stand out from the competition. She felt that the consumer did not necessarily need to be a technical expert or sports engineer to perceive the difference, but should be educated as to what was most necessary given his or her running style, training schedule, desired features, and price range.

Peter proceeded to try one Nike, one Brooks, one Saucony, and one Asics running shoe, all within the same price range. Donna Williams suggested that he walk and jog down the mall corridor outside the store for a more realistic indication of comfort and stability. This comparison would give him a better basis for comparing the features offered by each brand. Peter declined the offer to jog in the mall. Instead, he tried on each pair of shoes and walked around the store. He decided that he felt most comfortable with the Nike shoes, as the air cushioning and light weight seemed to offer more spring, and he felt this would diminish some of the impact he would experience running on hard surfaces.

Peter remembered Sheila Cambridge's recommendation. Although Peter was sold on the Nike brand, the particular style he had tried, the Air Max, felt a little wide on his narrow foot. Donna Williams explained that the only shoe manufacturer who offered shoes in a full range of widths was New Balance and asked whether he would like to try a pair. Peter explained that he really liked the feel of the Nike shoe, but he wanted to find one that felt a little less wide. Donna suggested another Nike shoe, the Air Stab, which Peter proceeded to try. Feeling satisfied with the shoe, he jogged on the spot as a test of this new style. He felt that he had finally found what he had been looking for.

Peter asked Donna to hold the shoes for him until closing that night. This would provide ample time for him to ensure that the other stores were not offering the Nike Air Stab at a lower price than $129.99. Peter thanked Donna Williams for her help and left Sports Experts to see what the other stores had to offer. As he walked toward the mall exit on Laurier Street, he passed another sporting goods store and was attracted by a large wall display of athletic shoes. Athlete's World was offering Nike Air Stab at the same price he had found at Sports Experts, so Peter left the store quickly, feeling that Sports Experts deserved the sale, considering that Donna Williams had invested considerable time helping him. Peter decided to head for Bank Street, where he could see the offerings at Elgin Sports and Sports-4. Elgin Sports was an established Ottawa sporting goods store, with its original outlet on Elgin Street. A couple of years ago, the company had opened a second store on Bank Street, which offered a wide variety of sports clothing and shoes. Sports-4 was a newer store, having opened just two or three years ago. Peter felt that the Sports-4 outlet was much more of a running specialty store, as a display near the door contained notices of forthcoming road races and triathlons.

The Elgin Sports store on Bank Street also had the Air Stabs priced at $129.99, which left Peter wondering if he was needlessly running around the city when he could have purchased the pair of shoes he had seen at Sports Experts. On entering Sports-4, Peter was pleasantly surprised, as the Nike Air Stab was on a special promotion for $99.99. Peter was thrilled with this $30 savings and asked if he could try on a size 9, feeling he really couldn't buy a pair of shoes without trying them on. The sales clerk disappeared into the storage room for a few minutes only to walk out empty-handed. He looked at Peter apologetically and informed him that unfortunately a 9-1/2 was the smallest size they had in stock.

Peter decided to try them on anyway. Perhaps the extra half-size wouldn't make much difference to the fit. After all, he would be saving $30 in the process. However, the extra space in the toe was quite noticeable, even with the thick socks the clerk had handed him to try with the shoes. Peter wondered how this difference might affect his running performance. His past experience with athletic footwear suggested that the shoe would stretch a little with wear, especially if exposed to wet conditions. Disappointed, Peter felt he would have to forfeit the $30 savings and be satisfied with the fact that he was still fairly close to his initial price range.

Geoff Wallace, the clerk at Sports-4, suggested that he measure Peter's foot to make sure that he did indeed require a size 9. Having confirmed that this was Peter's correct size, he advised strongly against buying a half-size larger, indicating it was his opinion that fit is of critical importance when selecting a pair of running shoes. He then asked Peter to walk up and down in front of the shoe display so that he might examine how his feet struck the floor as he walked.

Geoff observed that Peter tended to strike the floor first with the outer edge of his foot, a tendency referred to as supination, and suggested that Peter might like to try a pair of Brooks GFS-105 shoes, explaining that this was a shoe that offered excellent fit and the Hydroflow cushioning system. He also explained that the GFS-105 featured a curved last, which was recommended for people who tended to supinate. Peter was impressed at the time Geoff was taking to help him select the right shoe and with the fact that the Brooks GFS-105 shoe was on sale at a special price of $109. Peter declined Geoff's suggestion politely, explaining that he had decided on the Nike Air Stab.

Peter was wondering, as he left Sports-4, if he might be able to strike a deal at Sports Experts, considering he should probably think about buying a rainsuit anyway. After dinner, he walked back to the Rideau Centre, wandered into Sports Experts, and was met by Donna Williams, who had been so helpful earlier in the day. Peter requested the running shoes that he had asked her to hold for him, but expressed his dismay over the better deal offered by Sports-4. Peter asked if he might speak with the manager about the possibility of matching the Sports-4 price.

While Donna disappeared to get the manager, Peter spotted a Nike rainsuit that appealed to him and had been marked down in price. As he took the rainsuit off the display rack, he was greeted by the manager who had been directed to Peter by Donna Williams. Peter explained his dilemma and asked if Sports-4's sale price on the Nike Air Stab might be matched, provided that he purchase the rainsuit he had selected. The manager was eager for business and goodwill, especially since he considered Sports-4 to be Sports Experts' main competitor for running and triathlon equipment in the city. He nodded and offered to ring in the sale for him, all the while making conversation about running in Ottawa. Peter appreciated the concession that Sports Experts had made and thanked the manager and Donna Williams, telling them he would be sure to shop at Sports Experts stores in Toronto on a regular basis.

While running slowly along the Rideau Canal later that evening, Peter met Sheila Cambridge, who had just finished a 10 km run. The clean white of Peter's new shoes caught her eye and she commented that he had made an excellent choice. Peter continued on his run toward his apartment on the other side of the canal, feeling satisfied with his purchase. He could sense that he was going to enjoy running, and he was already thinking about entering his first road race later that summer.

Coyright ©1991, 2000. This case was written by James G. Barnes and Bernita Kiefte of Memorial University of Newfoundland and is intended to stimulate discussion of a marketing problem and not to illustrate either effective or ineffective handling of that problem. The authors wish to acknowledge the input of Ed Ayres, editor of *Running Times*, for his comments and for permission to reproduce the exhibit in this case.

Pertinent Web Sites

www.nike.com/
www.brookssports.com/

Questions

1. Identify the various factors that influenced Peter Taylor's behaviour in selecting a pair of running shoes. Why did he select the Nike brand?

2. What objectives do you feel Peter was trying to accomplish in the selection of running shoes? What motivated his final selection?

3. Why did he buy his shoes at Sports Experts? What could Geoff Wallace have done to persuade Peter to buy the Brooks shoe (or any other) at Sports-4?

Case 2-2

STARBUCKS: POURING INTO CANADA

The battle for market share in the Canadian specialty coffee market continues to heat up. The expected future potential of this market can be seen in the proliferation of coffee shops, cafés and their variations in recent years. Although only 4 percent of adult Canadians drank specialty coffees in 1994, this percentage doubled within a year, and is now believed to hover somewhere in the region of 10 percent. The popularity of these premium-priced beverages remains quite strong.

Coffee has a new cachet across North America as a culture evolves around the new café scene and as "going for a coffee" becomes part of the contemporary lifestyle. The success and creativity of Starbucks cafés in North America has set off a chain reaction of innovation in the coffee industry, producing many new brands and product variations. Many coffee outlets have become less a donut shop and more of a social meeting place.

The Bean has Landed

One of the most significant changes in the Canadian marketplace has been the entry into this country of Seattle-based Starbucks. Since arriving in Canada in 1987, Starbucks has aggressively sought to increase its market share in large urban centres. Initially, Starbucks confined its operations to Vancouver, and its success there motivated entry into other Canadian cities. In 1996, when the company planned its entry into the Toronto market, it stirred up considerable controversy when it attempted to acquire prime locations for its corporate-owned stores adjacent to existing Second Cup franchises. The casualties in this confrontation were neighbourhood shops, and this resulted in considerable negative press for Starbucks. Nevertheless, the company has continued its penetration of the Canadian market and now has locations coast to coast. Observers are questioning whether this success will continue. What is it that sets Starbucks apart from the competition? Are such differences sustainable, or are they merely part of some fad?

It was thought that the coffee sector was saturated ten years ago — yet chains have flourished in the last couple of years and the number of these shops continues to increase. As mentioned, social changes have made the café an ultimate destination for social gatherings, lunch or dinner dates. It is thought, amazingly, that there is still *much* more room for expansion (and extension). Menu extensions continue to be one area rich in potential, and there are areas such as Western Canada, greater Toronto, and Quebec that have yet to be maxed out.

Brewing Competition

How is it that Starbucks has been able to penetrate a market served by such well-known brands as Tim Hortons, Second Cup, A.L. Van Houtte, and Timothy's World's Coffees? The specialty coffee shops in Canada differentiate themselves according to various aspects of coffee drinking. Tim Hortons' president, Paul House, identifies his company as being in the "snack occasion" business and that the growth segments are lunches and bagels. The focus of Second Cup is on street-level stores — takeout coffee bars in commuter stations, hospitals, and shopping malls. The focus for Timothy's World Coffees is on the standard cup of fresh-brewed coffee. Van Houtte, primarily a wholesale distributor to supermarkets and a supplier of coffee machines in offices and institutions, also operates a number of retail outlets. Paul-Andre Guillotte, president of A.L. Van Houtte Ltee, says that his establishment caters to 18 to 25-year-olds that are increasingly using coffee shops as a meeting place. Van Houtte's customers view its coffee shops as a young, hip place serving high-quality coffee.

Van Houtte has recently partnered with Great Canadian Bagel to supply coffee bars in that company's outlets as the company follows the lead of other coffee chains in evolving their outlets into homey environments complete with comfy chairs, fireplaces, and murals. This represents another entry into this market hoping to take advantage of the current social trend. Great Canadian Bagel is also increasing its food menu as they continue to open new stores experimenting with new locales including malls and office buildings. As the new century began, such extensions have increasingly become a part of the focus for all competitors in this category.

While Starbucks offers original espresso-based products such as caffee latte, caffee mocha, cappuccino and icy-cold Frappuccino, some would argue that Starbucks' success is attributable to its ability to offer customers a total brand experience that extends beyond the mere consumption of a beverage. This process has involved a positioning of the company — its ideals and image — with various stakeholder groups: the community, its employees, and its customers. Like many other types of retailers, the company has developed a lifestyle brand — as has been joked about being served at Starbucks — would you like a coffee to go with your souvenir Starbucks' T-shirt? They have become more of a destination, or experience, than simply a service.

The Bean Lifestyle

Starbucks' ability to transform coffee into a lifestyle choice flows from its mission statement, which directs the company to a role of environmental leadership in all facets of its business. These words have been transformed into a variety of socially responsible actions, including sale of a reusable coffee tumbler designed to commemorate the one-hundredth anniversary in 1997 of the YMCA in Vancouver. In 1996, Starbucks and the Hospital for Sick Children in Toronto forged a long-term partnership that resulted in Starbucks making an annual contribution to the hospital foundation and opening a Starbucks location in the hospital's lobby. Starbucks actively supports organizations that benefit children's welfare, AIDS outreach, and environmental awareness; is involved in a variety of community cultural events; and supports programs in Guatemala, Indonesia, Kenya, and Ethiopia — all coffee-growing countries. This protection of the environment can be seen within the individual stores where "everything" that can be recycled is: from the cardboard butter patties to the used coffee grounds. Stale-dated coffee is donated to charitable organizations such as women's shelters.

To remain "hip" with particular market segments, the company has had a long association with music even to the point of releasing compilation CDs of selected artists. It has been a sponsor of the Lilith Fair tour, providing the official tour coffee and offering their brews at all tour dates from its own tour bus. The company's Web site has also served as a source of tour information as well as providing lists of charity recipients and information for purchasing concert merchandise.

The positive press that the company receives from such community involvement extends to its internal marketing efforts. Despite the recent unionization of workers at some Canadian locations, Starbucks is known for its progressive personnel policies and generous compensation packages. In a proactive move, Starbucks offered all employees, or "partners," the same wages regardless of whether or not they were unionized. Compensation packages for employees also include company stock, making them owners as well as employees. Such actions reduce the adversarial nature that often exists between employers and employees, while bolstering the firm's image in the community.

The company's claim that it is in the "people development" business as much as the coffee business is evidenced by its training programs, in which partners are encouraged to share their feelings about selling, about coffee, and about working for Starbucks. They are also encouraged to take personal responsibility for all aspects of their work, including the production of beverages to exact specifications and the encouragement of recycling and conservation wherever possible. Partners devote special attention to educating the consumer about the explanation for Starbucks' Italian drink names, the necessity to buy new beans weekly, and the requirement to never let coffee stand for more than twenty minutes. The relationship marketing efforts between Starbucks and its partners have translated into annual staff, or "barista," turnover of 60 percent, compared with 140 percent for hourly workers in the fast-food business.

Customers, 10 percent of whom visit the store twice a day, also feel this affinity toward Starbucks; the average customer visits eighteen times a month. The strength of such customer loyalty has provided the company with the luxury of using very little traditional advertising. Instead, the company has concentrated on creating an experience that customers are happy to promote. Starbucks devotees feel that the brand is defined as much by attitude as by products. It is Starbucks' treatment of its employees, the community, and the environment that has earned it respect with customers. This positive image is backed by premium products, including traditional specialty coffees and Frappuccino, a frozen coffee drink that is tremendously popular during the summer. Customers can buy Starbucks ice cream and bottled drinks in the supermarket. Some argue that the proliferation of brand extensions could serve to dilute the core concept. The company has recently decided, like its rivals, to expand its menu including breakfast-focused items, increasing sandwich offerings, and "designer" snack items.

Starbuck's also hopes to develop its Web site into a lifestyle portal by joining with gourmet food sellers and home-furnishing stores.

While far from floundering, by the end of 1999, delayed store openings and lower-than-expected sales at existing outlets depressed company earnings. The company has continued, however, to expand both in North America and internationally. In early 2000 this appeared to have paid off as earnings began to show signs of modest recovery.

Where the Competition has Bean!

What have other coffee companies been doing in the wake of Starbucks' aggressive marketing campaigns? Distribution is critical and has been extended beyond traditional retail outlets. Second Cup kiosks can be found in all Borders bookstores in Canada, while Starbucks has opened outlets in Chapters bookshops. Second Cup coffee is served on all Air Canada flights and lounges, an alliance that accounts for 10 percent of the company's coffee sales in Canada. It can also be found in Delta Hotel restaurants and on VIA Rail. Second Cup and Tim Hortons operate franchises in Canadian hospitals.

Tim Hortons coffee is available at over 1,839 company and franchise restaurants, many in rural locations, and through some Esso gas stations, and is promoted with the theme "You've always got time for Tim Hortons." Tim Hortons' coffee products are also available in supermarkets.

Tim Hortons' slogan has been supplemented by the use of emotional appeals such as in the company's "true stories" ad campaign in which the focus is on the unique role of Tim Hortons stores in the community. Lillian, age eighty-six, is shown walking through Lunenburg, Nova Scotia, on her way to enjoying her daily cup of Tim Horton's coffee. Customers have found Lillian to be warm and charming — just the image that the advertising creators were looking for. Another advertisement includes a spot on Sammi, a dog from Saint John, New Brunswick, who picks up her master's coffee from the local drive-through window. The use of such true stories is quite popular with customers in Atlantic Canada. It has portrayed Tim's as a part of everyone's day! The company believes that this campaign has really elevated the awareness of Tim Hortons and particularly coffee as a product. The company attributes much of its success to its determination to stick to its "Always Fresh" positioning.

Tim Hortons undertook an aggressive roll-out in 1999 opening 175 stores. The company continued to experience same-store sales increases during this period despite increasing competition and enjoyed a 52.6 percent national market share in the coffee and baked-goods segment. One market of particular focus has been Quebec. This has been dominated by U.S-based Dunkin' Donuts and Van Houtte. Tim Hortons is using a new Quebec-only advertising campaign created by a Montreal-based firm.

The innovation of Starbucks has led Canadian chains to introduce a variety of cold coffee products including Second Cup's "nutritional supplement" Energy Latte and Tim's Iced Cappuccino.

Regional players are also gearing up for their share of the bean. Great Canadian Bagel, as discussed, has redesigned many of its premises to more resemble the coffeehouse persona, and B.C.-based Grabbajabba is expanding fast, opening stores with a "more contemporary, upscale look." While rivals continue to increase food offerings, it has always been a sizable component of Grabbajabba's offerings. Not content to stand still, Second Cup has, after redesigning its packaging, squeezing into the juice market, and also increasing its stores, once again has decided to try its hand in the United States by merging with a coffee chain in Portland, Oregon. The company claims that it has also stood up quite well to the arrival of Starbucks as they have opened well over 150 locations since its arrival. They now feel they are ready to compete with Starbuck's in *their* "home" markets.

The expansion of regional competitors and the continued growth of each chain would appear to reflect a market that is, indeed, continuing to grow.

Fashion, Fad, or Has Bean?

There are those who question whether the specialty coffee market will continue to expand or whether it is just a fad. Supporters maintain that the proliferation of coffeehouses reflects changes in social views, particularly with young adults. Both Starbucks and Second Cup hope to capitalize on the profitability associated with catering to the time-strapped boomer by producing, selling, and playing CDs designed to attract people to the stores. Starbucks even maintains designers and architects in-house who adapt the mellow urban look to different locations and customer demographics. They even publish *JOE* magazine, available only at the 2,200 Starbucks (and Chapters with coffeehouses, of course) outlets across North America. One of the magazine's goals is to "really analyze key aspects of human behaviour" while being an extension of "the coffeehouse tradition of conversation, community and culture." The magazine has its own Web site which includes a survey filled with questions asking readers about age, income, education, and frequency of visits. While the company has no current plans to use this site as a source of research data, it has the potential to be used as a powerful relationship marketing tool.

The creation of such a comfortable environment to complement the eclectic product offerings and corporate image is proving to be quite popular with Canadians in urban centres. Will this success continue in other parts of the country? Is it even sustainable over the long-run in existing centres? What changes will be necessary over the next few years?

Pertinent Web Sites

www.starbucks.com
wwwjoemag.com
www.secondcup.com
www.timhortons.com
www.alvanhoutte.com
www.timothys.com

Questions

1. Who are the target markets for Starbucks? How do they differ from those of other coffee shops?

2. What is Starbucks' competitive advantage? Is it sustainable?

3. How is the company positioned? Illustrate this with a positioning map that reflects the major players in the coffee market.

4. Does the proliferation of Starbucks' brand extension dilute the core concept and negatively affect the company's positioning and competitive advantage?

Sources: David Chilton, "Always Room for Another Cup," *Marketing Magazine*, June 5, 2000, p.12; Jennifer Ordonez, "Starbuck's Schultz to Leave Top Post, Lead Global Effort," *Wall Street Journal*, April 7, 2000, p. B3; Shawna Cohen, "Coffee Taps Energy Trend," *Marketing Magazine*, April 3, 2000, p. 13; Astrid Van Den Broek, "Bagel Co. Nuzzles into Comfy Couch," *Marketing Magazine*, March 13, 2000; p. 4; Louise Lee, "Now, Starbucks Uses its Bean," *Business Week*, February 14, 2000, p. 92; Natalie Bahadur, "Tim Hortons Plans Aggressive Roll-Out," *Strategy*, March 29, 1999, p. 7; Vijay Vishwanath & David Harding, "The Starbucks Effect," *Harvard Business Review*, March/April 2000, pp. 17–18; David North, "King Cruller," *Canadian Business*, December 32, 1999, pp. 126–7; Ben Van-Houten, "New Brew: Starbucks Café Adding Menu Items and Units," *Restaurant Business*, December 1, 1999, p. 13; Astrid Van Den Broek, "Changes Brewing at Coffee Chains," *Marketing Magazine*, November 15, 1999, p. 3; David Eggleston, "Starbucks Grounds Direct Opportunity," *Strategy*, September 13, 1999, p. D3; Norma Ramage, "Will That be Tetley or Nabob," *Marketing Magazine*, July 5, 1999, pp. 11–13; "Brewing Up Stronger Sales for Specialty Coffee," *Canadian Grocer*, October 1996, p. 25; Simona Chiose, "A Little Jazz with Your Java?" *The Globe and Mail*, November 4, 1996, p. C1; Lesley Daw, "Tim Hortons Stars Pooch in True Story," *Marketing Magazine*, January 27, 1997, p. 4; "Dollars for Doughnuts," *Financial Post*, September 2/4, 1995, p. 7; Louise Gagnon, "Coffee Wars Perking Up in Quebec Market," *Marketing Magazine*, January 20, 1997, p. 3; Jo Marney, "Fresh-Brewed Data," *Marketing Magazine*, March 10, 1997, p. 21; Bill McDowell, "Starbucks Is Ground Zero in Today's Coffee Culture," *Advertising Age*, December 9, 1996; Jennifer Reese, "Starbucks: Inside the Coffee Culture," *Fortune*, December 9, 1996, pp.190–200; "Second Cup to Fly Air Canada with $2 Million Contract," *Financial Post Daily*, November 12, 1996, p. 11; "Starbucks and the Vancouver YMCA Announce Community Partnership," *The News Hook*, June 4, 1997; "Starbucks Coffee Company Corporate Profile," *The News Hook*, September 24, 1996; "Starbucks Invades Toronto Market," *The Globe and Mail*, January 23, 1996, p. B19; "Starbucks Makes Long-Term Commitment to The Hospital For Sick Children," *Canada NewsWire*, July 2, 1996; Karen Van Hahn, "Brewing Up a Northwest Image," The Globe and Mail, April 10, 1996, pp. E5, E7.

Case 2-3

THE RIGHT FOCUS

A focus group is like a chainsaw — a tremendous help if you know what you're doing with it. If you don't, somebody could lose a leg! This is the view of Professor Lindsey Meredith of Simon Fraser University. It would seem that he has a valid point to make about exercising concern when developing focus group research.

Focus groups can be not only expensive, but dangerous if the information collected is not accurate and relevant, or if it is misinterpreted. Information gathered may not actually affect purchase decisions, may not reflect the market at large, or can be gathered under artificial conditions that mislead researchers. Marketing decisions made from this collected information may, therefore, doom a product or service, or destroy a company's brand in the marketplace.

The Right Stuff

Perhaps the most important foundation for any marketing endeavour is to begin with thorough, sound, and comprehensive market research. This includes many facets from investigating potential market size, to how to produce and distribute the product even to what colour and shape a product should be.

Much of the initial research effort involves the accumulation of statistics and raw data and deciding alternative traits based on hard facts of availability and cost. But eventually a company must actually consider what it is that a consumer may want – or ideally what as many consumers as possible would want and would actually purchase. They are, unfortunately, not always the same things in practice.

It would seem, therefore, that the simplest thing would be to get a group of consumers together and ask them, right? Well, yes and no. What and how to ask them is just the beginning of the challenge. While often the first thought is to throw together a group of consumers, this method is inherently flawed and is like navigating through a minefield.

The depth and breadth of information gathered, as well as the format, a focus group takes varies greatly according to the needs of the market research. Participants may simply look and comment on products, share experiences, or engage in creative activities such as a diverse range of "games," challenges, and even debates. Typically, a focus group moderator will spend two or three hours talking to participants, while other researchers and perhaps the clients watch from behind two-way mirrors. Sessions may also be recorded on videotape.

The new Eatons (a subsidiary of Sears) decided in order to reposition the store for success they must first determine what existing perceptions were of the Eaton's brand. Focus groups revealed that it was seen as middle-aged, middle-class, comfortable and familiar. There remained a pent-up demand among a wide range of shoppers for the kind of retail experiences Eatons once offered and to the relief of management it was discovered that the name still carried an air of prestige and grandeur. The proposed changes for the store were also a hit in these focus groups.

To test concepts for Eatons' new fashion image, the company used the toughest group they could find — loyal Eatons shoppers between the ages of 25 and 50, each of whom had spent more than $1,000 on clothing in the past year. They were shown a variety of concept boards portraying the proposed images of the new Eatons. Feedback from groups in Toronto, Vancouver, and Calgary was very positive.

In preparing plans for expansion in Canada, Taco Bell established a long-term youth focus group to tap into youth culture and solicit advice. This panel meets regularly to discuss which music and movies are cool as well as how to market new food products in Canada. Pizza Hut has done the same thing in the United States.

The Right People

"People either lie on purpose, or lie to themselves," says Professor Meredith. "We've got to use as many methods as we can to cross reference to find out if we're getting the right stuff." Even then, it is difficult to be sure sometimes how relevant it is to actual purchase decisions.

Many factors must be given consideration. Do people who volunteer to participate in such groups actually represent the desired target segment? Do the attitudes of people who agree to take part differ from the others? Do they act as they perceive that the moderator or those behind the glass would want them to? What about people who make a habit or a hobby of volunteering for such groups? What information should be solicited from participants? Who are the people conducting these groups? How can this be done in a group environment without introducing bias? How do we ensure that these interactions are pragmatically interpreted.

Meaningful information can be difficult to uncover as consumers are bombarded by advertising, new products, and crowded store shelves each day. Many advertisements are difficult to recall and purchase decisions difficult to explain as more and more consumers spend more and more time shopping on autopilot. Consumers are often quite unconscious of how they "feel," the processes they engage in and why they do some of the things they do as consumers.

Just as "regulars" to focus groups know how to "play the game" and can skew results, so can an nonrepresentative sample — even when their responses are accurately interpreted. Enbridge Home Services, a gas company, had to pull their TV ad for gas fireplaces just for this reason. Focus groups were amused by the ad depicting an older couple grappling around on the floor in front of the fire in an amorous embrace. However many in that older age group were not amused and many complained. The focus group participants all turned out to be from younger age segments!

The Right Information

What do clients want to know? They may want to find out what colours sizes. or flavours to produce, the functions for which products are used or how much a product should cost. Retailers may want to know how to better design retail space to maximize sales and what environmental factors influence the decision to buy. Service providers who deliver largely intangible "products" may want to know what goes through the mind of prospective customers when they are selecting a service provider and how they want to be treated. Beyond design and new introductions, companies may want to obtain these types of information in order to gauge their performance or image against that of their competitors. As well, clients wishing to have such research conducted may not know exactly what they need to find out, or they may have inaccurate ideas about what it is they need to ask consumers.

New formats and derivations for focus groups have varied from using anthropologists to spend up to twelve hours following consumers during their daily routines and questioning their behaviours to inciting arguments to debate the relative merits of different brands by planting a confederate into these groups. Researchers also utilize "games" and creative exercises to express "meaning" for brands. Market research firms have each developed a tool kit of such approaches when investigating concepts such as brand perception and corporate image in the marketplace.

In a recent project for Happy Planet, a Vancouver-based organic juice company, researchers from Marktrend Research had focus group participants go shopping. Each person was to purchase juices that matched themes they were given. They also drew pictures of what they imagined Happy Planet juice buyers would look like. Bad news actually came out of the exercises, but it was news that may have prevented a serious marketing blunder. Although these are labelled as organic products, not all the ingredients of all flavours are totally organic. This is because this is not currently possible — not because the company is trying to deceive consumers as the products do meet the requirements to be labelled as such. However, if this was a central marketing theme and the competition exploited this claim as being false it could have serious repercussions for the product's image.

For Option Snowboards, Marktrend sent snowboarders, a consumer group considered difficult to understand, out with disposable cameras, asking them to document their lives. The pictures provided great insight into the attitudes of these consumers and a successful campaign was generated from the images returned by the participants.

The Right Idea

Although focus group participants can be a source of ideas and an aid to judgment, they cannot consistently be relied upon to represent the attitudes and potential behaviour of the target. In the world of brand advertising, focus groups may be a very effective way to determine what ideas resonate with consumers and which do not. What people tell you they enjoy in an advertisement, for example, may not be what make them respond to them, or make them purchase. Ask a question in a focus group and often you do not receive a factual response but an anecdote involving the respondents' relationship with the product or brand — their feelings, experience, expectations, and disappointments.

The Right Method

Given the profound power and reach of the Internet, it seems logical that it would come under scrutiny with respect to its role in marketing research. It is indeed a powerful tool and many packaged-goods companies have realized its potential as a device for understanding and anticipating consumer needs. Its application to marketing research has included adaptation of the focus group technique for cyberspace travel. It is quickly becoming a progressively popular alternative and addition to traditional market research methods. Proponents state that much of the same data can be collected — even some of the emotional factors behind a respondent's opinion — but without the cost of facility rental and transportation.

In addition, online groups promise a quicker turnaround and the respondent pool can cover a greater geographical area, instead of a single city or a couple of cities as is usually employed. There are limitations, of course such as the case when intense conversations or body language may be involved. As well, new concept testing is usually conducted quietly by researchers and use of the Internet makes it difficult to maintain privacy with regard to a firm's marketing research efforts. It would appear however, that online groups are set to play a bigger role in the future of qualitative research studies.

Although focus group research is a popular qualitative research strategy, in-depth, one-on-one interviews, conducted through various media, provide more information for less money without many of the limitations focus groups can impose. Specifically, they can provide researchers with more quality, more quantity of information, more depth, more representation, more efficiency, more statistics, and more value.

The Right Approach?

Important target segments that many marketers want to reach today are youth segments that are increasingly becoming a dominant voice in how many household dollars are spent in today's marketplace. This group has proven hard to crack as researchers try to understand how these trendsetters think and what motivates their increasingly lucrative purchase decisions. They are a secretive group that want to fit in with everybody else while at the same time think for themselves and be their own individuals. They are savvy and sophisticated, making it difficult to disguise or camouflage market research efforts. It is difficult to get their approval and it seems when something becomes too hip it suddenly ceases to be cool anymore. This has been a frustrating challenge for the marketing researchers.

Questions

1. What concerns and precautions should be addressed when preparing a focus group as a part of market research?

2. What participants' characteristics might a researcher look for when designing a focus group to design a new product introduction in the following product classes:

   a. A luxury car.

   b. A college/university.

   c. Accounting services.

   d. A children's clothing line.

   e. Cruise line holidays.

3. Discuss the strengths and weaknesses of the various research methods discussed.

4. Which method(s) would you recommend for the introduction of a new product? For the re-introduction of an updated product? A product that creates an entirely new product class? Why?

5. What method or combination of techniques discussed would you recommend for conducting marketing research among youth segments in today's environment?

Sources: Sean Silcoff, "Second Time Friendly," *Canadian Business*, May 29, 2000, pp. 34–39; Charles Newman, "Online Testing Rated," *Advertising Age*, May 8, 2000, p. 64; John Gray, "Taco Bell Establishes Youth Panel," *Strategy*, April 10, 2000, p. 11; James Heckman, "Turning The Focus Online," *Marketing News*, February 28, 2000, p. 15; CBC *Venture*, Episode #734, Focus Group segment, January 11, 2000 or see the CBC Web site at www.cbc.ca/venture; Dennis Bruce, "It Was A Dark and Stormy Night…," *Marketing Magazine*, January 24, 2000, p. 20; Mark Palmerino, "Take A Quality Approach to Qualitative Research," *Marketing News*, June 1999, pp. H35–H36; Marvin Schoenwald, "Abuse of Focus Groups Can Haunt," *Brandweek*, May 18, 1998, p. 24.

Part three

Products and Services

The planning, development, and management of the want-satisfying goods and services that are a company's products

Part Two focused on the selection and identification of target markets in accordance with the firm's marketing goals. The next step in the strategic marketing planning process is to develop a marketing mix that will achieve these goals in the selected target markets. The marketing mix is a strategic combination of four variables — the organization's products or services, pricing structure, distribution system, and promotional program. Each of these is closely interrelated with the other three variables in the mix.

Part Three, consisting of four chapters, is devoted to the product component of the marketing mix. In Chapter 9 we define the term product, consider the importance of product planning and innovation, and discuss the new-product development process. Chapter 10 deals mainly with product-mix strategies, the management of the product life cycle, and a consideration of style and fashion. Chapter 11 is concerned with branding, packaging, labelling, and other product features. Chapter 12 addresses the subject of services and how they are marketed to consumers.

Chapter Nine

Product Planning and Development

After studying this chapter, you should have an understanding of:

◆ The meaning of the word product in its fullest sense.

◆ What a "new" product is.

◆ The classification of consumer and business products.

◆ The relevance of these product classifications to marketing strategy.

◆ The importance of product innovation.

◆ The steps in the product-development process.

◆ Criteria for adding a product to a company's line.

◆ Adoption and diffusion processes for new products.

◆ Organizational structures for product planning and development.

Never Mind Your SUV, It's The Environment, Remember??!!

*T*hese days, there are new products all around us. It's easy to get tired of hearing about them. But, that's the price you pay for living in the introductory phase of a technological revolution — the information revolution. But let's not talk about that right now — let's talk about the environment. Let's talk about cars and buses and whatever else is on motorized wheels these days. Whether or not the environment is fashionable, it's still there and is still threatened and has plenty of enemies aside from you and me; for instance, cars, buses, trucks, and RVs.

Enter Ballard Power Systems of Vancouver, BC. This is high-tech stuff, but not another 24-hour dot.com story full of glory. This is about the long haul of getting a new technology to market. Dr. Geoffrey Ballard was one of the original founders of this company way back in 1979. The objective at the time was to produce an environmentally clean source of power — a fuel cell that had little or no atmospheric emissions. Today, Ballard is the world leader in develop-

ing, manufacturing and marketing zero emission PEM (proton exchange membrane, that is) fuel cells for use in transportation, electricity generation, and portable products. In 1999 *Time* magazine selected Dr. Ballard as one of the five "Heroes for the Planet." A mere twenty years after he began this work, and yet to many reading this it will probably be the first time you have ever heard of this "new" product.

The proprietary fuel cell technology, the Ballard Fuel Cell, allows manufacturers who purchase it to develop, manufacture, and market autos, electrical equipment, and portable power products which are environmentally clean. The Fuel Cell, the fundamental component of such

products, combines hydrogen (obtained from methanol, natural gas or petroleum) with oxygen (from the air) *without* combustion to generate electricity. The promise of the technology is such that today Ballard has partners like DaimlerChrysler, Ford, GPU International, ALSTROM and EBARA — all of whom are to commercialize the cell using their own products. Other customers using Ballard Fuel Cells include General Motors, Nissan, Honda, Volkswagen, Volvo, Matushita Electrical Works, and Cinergy.

The research, development, and product testing process for this kind of technology is expensive both in terms of time and dollars. The process for developing a bus for commercial use included a Phase 1 Proof of Concept (concept testing from 1993–1995); a Phase II Commercial Prototype Development (building, testing and refining, 1993–97); Phase III Demonstration Fleets (Chicago and Vancouver tests, 1997–2000) and Phase IV, Commercial Production (first bus scheduled for 2002).

Ballard, EXCELLSIS (an alliance of Ballard, Ford, and DaimlerChrysler for fuel cell engine development) and the Chicago Transit Authority has concluded the world's first fuel cell bus demonstration and testing program. This was a two-year product test of three Ballard Fuel Cell equipped buses, under real revenue-producing winter and summer conditions. During the test period, the Fuel Cells clocked more than five thousand hours in service, covered forty-five thousand kms, carried more than one hundred thousand passengers and emitted nothing more than water vapour.

The Chicago test made it possible to design and construct the next generation of fuel cell engine that is simpler in design, easier to maintain, and half the weight of those engines used in the Chicago test.

Both the Chicago and Vancouver tests had additional objectives: determining the needs of transit authorities; determining the needs of transit passengers; gathering performance data from drivers and mechanics, assessing public reaction to the fuel cell powered buses as well as the buses powered by hydrogen. Driver and passenger reaction was positive: drivers reported smooth quiet rides with an absence of fumes and smooth acceleration, passengers were pleased and there were visitors to Chicago who made a point of riding the fuel cell powered bus during their stay. In other words, these other objectives were marketing research as much as they were product development.

A bus using the new EXCELLSIS precommercial fuel cell engine went into revenue-producing service in Palm Springs,

California in mid-2000 under a partnership venture called the California Fuel Cell Partnership. Under this partnership, twenty-five buses and thirty cars will be street tested and demonstrated between 2000 and 2003. DaimlerChrysler, on the strength of the Chicago test results, is now building twenty to thirty fuel-celled buses to be available to its Mercedes-Benz division by 2003.

Finally, commercial sales are within the company's grasp; DaimlerChrysler will be the first manufacturer to offer fuel cell buses for sale — a seventy-passenger vehicle with a range of 186 miles/298 kilometres and speed up to 50 miles per hour/180 kilometres per hour. The company is also moving to develop fuel cell engines for passenger cars and expects to have the first vehicles in the market in 2004.[1]

As can be seen from this example, the process involved in developing a product to be 'market-ready' can be long and arduous. This can be magnified when the development and marketing of new technology is involved. The various stages of the product development process pursued by Ballard encompassed senior executives from a number of organizations, scientists, engineers, technicians, financial advisers and bankers, market analysts, market researchers, public and community relations people — all on the production side. And on the consumption side, more senior executives, scientists, engineers, technicians, mechanics, bus drivers, and passengers, passengers, and then more passengers.

The Meaning of Product

In a narrow sense, a product is a set of attributes assembled in an identifiable form. Each product is identified by a commonly understood descriptive (or generic) name, such as steel, insurance, tennis racquets, or entertainment. Product attributes such as brand name and post-sale service that appeal to consumer motivation or buying patterns play no part in this narrow interpretation. According to this interpretation, an Apple (www.apple.com) and a Compaq (www.compaq.com) would be the same product — a personal computer. And Canada's Wonderland (www.canadaswonderland.com), Playland, and Ontario Place (www.ontarioplace.com/) would be considered an identical service — an amusement park.

In marketing, we need a broader definition of product to indicate that consumers are not really buying a set of attributes, but rather *benefits* that satisfy their needs. Thus consumers don't want sandpaper; they really want a smooth surface. They don't want a wireless hand held personal organizer; they want quick and convenient communication almost anywhere. To develop a sufficiently broad definition, let's start with *product* as an umbrella term covering goods, services, places, persons, and ideas. Throughout this book, when we speak of products, we are most often using this broad "generic" connotation.

Thus a product that provides benefits can be something other than a tangible good. The Royal Bank's product is a host of services that provide, among other things, the benefits of convenient and secure transactions as well as asset growth and management for personal financial security. The Vancouver Visitors Bureau's product is a destination that provides recreation, romance, sun and sea, relaxation, cross-cultural experiences, and other benefits. In a political campaign, the New Democratic Party or Liberal Party's product is a person (candidate) whom the party wants you to "buy" (vote for). The Canadian Cancer Society is selling an idea and the benefits of not smoking. In Chapter 12 we discuss in more detail the marketing of intangible products such as services and ideas.

To further expand our broad definition, we treat each brand as a separate product. In this sense, this definition appears to contradict the narrow definition of a product just discussed, but this is more representative of consumers' perceptions in the marketplace regarding many purchases. For example, in our broad definition the Sony Playstation and Nintendo N64 are different products. Lantic sugar and St. Lawrence sugar are also separate products, even though the only physical difference may be the brand name on the package. But the brand name suggests a product difference to the consumer, and this brings the concept of consumer wants and satisfaction into the definition.

Any change in a feature (design, colour, size, packaging), however minor, creates another product. Each such change provides the seller with an opportunity to use a new set of appeals to reach what essentially may be a new market. Pain relievers (Tylenol, Anacin) in tablet, capsule, and gelcap forms are different products from the same brand, even though the medicinal content of each is identical. Seemingly minor product changes can be the key to success (or failure) in international markets. For example, to satisfy Japanese consumers, two modified versions of Oreo cookies were developed. One has less sugar in the cookie batter; the other omits the cream filling.[2] Now really, what would North Americans do without the cream filling? Isn't the filling the whole point? This does show, however, how individual product features impact upon a product's success with different consumer segments and in different markets.

We can broaden this interpretation still further. A Sony TV bought in a discount store on a cash-and-carry basis is a different product from the identical model purchased in a department store or from The Sony Store. In the department store, the customer may pay a higher price for the TV but can buy it on credit, has it delivered free of charge, and receives other store services. Our concept of a product now includes the *services* that *accompany* it when purchased. Hertz (www.hertz.com), for example, may offer the same model of car to rent as another company, however only Hertz vehicles come with NeverLost® — an in-car navigational system that displays maps on a small dash-mounted screen providing turn-by-turn guidance to guide customers. An invaluable component to this "product" if you consider that most rental drivers would be driving in unfamiliar locations. Hertz is

An in-car service that really makes a difference when you are in new territory.

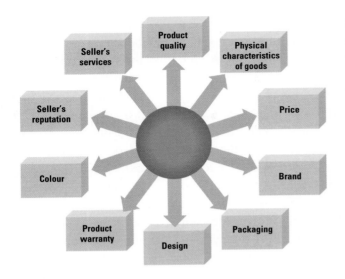

FIGURE 9-1
A Product Is Much More Than a Set of Physical Attributes

product
A set of tangible attributes, including packaging, colour, price, quality, and brand, plus the services and reputation of the seller. A product may be a good, service, place, person, or idea.

selling a little peace of mind with each car rental. The company also offers small business packages, loyalty programs, large equipment rental, and travel services.

Occasionally, a seller's support and assurances may be extraordinary. To keep with our navigation example, Mercedes Benz's TeleAid (www.mbusa.com) and the OnStar® system available on all Cadillac models (www.cadillac.gmcanada.com), most other GM products, and Saab automobiles utilize Global Positioning Systems to tell the vehicle's location at all times and link the car driver to a whole host of additional services. TeleAid provides emergency response, roadside assistance, and is guaranteed crash secure. Owners can reach OnStar® advisors at the touch of a button while still driving and receive voice and visual road directions as they progress. Communication is hands-free as there is a small microphone in the car and the advisor can be heard through the car's stereo speakers. There is also emergency roadside assistance, remote door unlock, theft detection and notification, stolen vehicle tracking, automatic notification of air bag deployment, and convenience services such as hotel reservations, the location of ATMs, and a hands-free, voice-activated cellular phone. OnStar®'s convenience and concierge service listings include over five million service providers, and the list grows each day.[3]

We're now ready for a definition that is useful to marketers: A **product** is a set of tangible and intangible attributes, including packaging, colour, price, quality, and brand, plus the seller's services and reputation. A product may be a tangible product, service, place, person, or idea (see Figure 9-1). In essence, then, consumers are buying much more than a set of physical attributes when they buy a product. They are buying want satisfaction in the form of the benefits they expect to receive from the product. The physical product is only one aspect of the marketing relationship.

Classifications of Products

To design effective marketing programs, organizations need to know what kinds of products they are offering to consumers. Thus it's helpful to separate products into homogeneous categories. First we will divide all products into two categories — consumer products and business products — that parallel our description of the market. Then we will subdivide each category still further.

consumer product
A product that is intended for purchase and use by household consumers for nonbusiness purposes.

business product
A product that is intended for purchase and use in producing other products or in rendering services in a business.

Consumer and Business Products

Consumer products are intended for use by household consumers for nonbusiness purposes. **Business products** are intended for resale, for use in producing other products, or for providing services in an organization. Thus the two types of products are distinguished on the basis of who will use them and how they will be used.

The position of a product in its distribution channel has no bearing on its classification. Kellogg's Corn Flakes are categorized as consumer products, even if they are in the manufacturer's warehouses, in a freight line's trucks, or on retailers' shelves, if ultimately household consumers will use them in their present form. However, Kellogg's Corn

Flakes sold to restaurants and other institutions are categorized as business products no matter where they are in the distribution system. Similarly, Sympatico, as an Internet service provider, can be accessed from a home computer for sending personal e-mail and surfing for information and entertainment or utilized for conducting business communications and ordering business supplies online.

Often it is not possible to place a product in only one class or the other. Seats on an Air Canada flight from Toronto to Vancouver may be considered a consumer product if purchased by students or a family going on vacation. But a seat on the same flight bought by a sales representative for business use is categorized as a business product. Air Canada, or any other company in a similar situation, recognizes that its product falls into both categories and therefore develops separate marketing programs for each market.

These distinctions may seem like "splitting hairs," but they are necessary for the strategic planning of marketing programs. Each major category of products ultimately goes to a distinctive type of market and thus requires different marketing methods.[4]

Classification of Consumer Goods

For marketing purposes, distinguishing consumer goods from business goods is helpful but only a first step. The range of consumer goods is still too broad. Consequently, as shown in Table 9-1, they are further classified as convenience, shopping, specialty, and unsought goods. This classification is not based on intrinsic differences in the products themselves. Rather, it is based on how consumers go about buying a particular product. Depending on the buying behaviour of different consumers, a single product — such as wine or software or dress pants — can fall into more than one of the four categories.

CONVENIENCE GOODS A tangible product that the consumer knows enough about before going out to buy it and then actually buys it with a minimum of effort is termed a **convenience good**. Normally the advantages resulting from shopping around to compare price and quality are not considered worth the extra time and effort required to "shop and compare." A consumer is willing to accept any of several brands and thus will buy the one that is most accessible. For most buyers, convenience goods include many food items, inexpensive candy, drug sundries such as shampoo and toothpaste, and staple hardware items such as light bulbs and batteries. Convenience services include such things as banking transactions, pay telephones, and photocopying.

Although for convenience goods the service expectation level is low, from time to time, service is a requirement and poor service can be a problem. Slow or inconsistent quality of service is, after all, not very convenient for a regular customer and will cause that consumer to seek other providers in the future. While good service will not necessarily be an advantage on a product level, it will be in terms of the consumer's relationship with the store and the store personnel. The retailer and the store personnel, if properly trained, should be developing long-term relationships with consumers.

shopping goods
A class of consumer products that are purchased after the buyer has spent some time and effort comparing the price, quality, colour, and/or other attributes of alternative products.

SHOPPING GOODS A tangible product for which consumers want to compare quality, price, and perhaps style in several stores or on several Web sites before purchasing is considered a **shopping good**. Examples of shopping goods — at least for most consumers — are clothing, furniture, major appliances, computer components, and automobiles. The process of searching and comparing continues as long as the customer believes that the potential benefits from a better purchase more than offset the additional time and effort spent shopping.

TABLE 9-1	Categories of Consumer Goods: Characteristics and Marketing Considerations		
	Type of Product*		
	Convenience	**Shopping**	**Specialty**
EXAMPLES	Canned fruit	Furniture	Expensive suits
Characteristics			
Time and effort devoted by consumer to shopping	Very little	Considerable	Cannot generalize; consumer may go to nearby store and buy with minimum effort or may have to go to distant store and spend much time and effort
Time spent planning the purchase	Very little	Considerable	Considerable
How soon want is satisfied after it arises	Immediately	Relatively long time	Relatively long time
Are price and quality compared?	No	Yes	No
Price	Usually low	High	High
Purchase frequency	Usually frequent	Infrequent	Infrequent
Marketing Considerations			
Length of channel	Long	Short	Short to very short
Retailer	Relatively unimportant	Important	Very important
Number of outlets	As many as possible	Few	Few; often only one in a market
Stock turnover	High	Lower	Lower
Gross margin	Low	High	High
Responsibility for advertising	Producer's	Retailer's	Joint responsibility
Point-of-purchase display	Very important	Less important	Less important
Brand or store name important	Brand name	Store name	Both
Packaging	Very important	Less important	Less important

*Unsought products are not included. See text explanation.

Searching for such information has become considerably easier with the development of the Internet. It remains to be seen if the availability and relative ease of cybersearches will permanently cause an overall general increase in search behaviour by consumers. A better purchase may result from saving several hundred dollars on the purchase of a new car or finally finding a software package that prepares financial statements in the exact manner desired by the buyer.

To buyers of a shopping good, the reputations of the stores or Web sites carrying the product often are more important than the "image" of the actual manufacturer of the product. For example, a consumer may be more loyal to a Future Shop store than to various brands of audio and video equipment, such as JVC or Panasonic. The quality of store personnel and the way customer interaction is handled in the shopping process contribute to the store's reputation. The vendor's return, guarantee, and post-sale service policies will also contribute to this reputation.

specialty goods
A class of consumer products with perceived unique characteristics such that consumers are willing to expend special effort to buy them.

SPECIALTY GOODS A tangible product for which consumers have a strong brand preference and are willing to expend substantial time and effort in locating the desired brand is called a **specialty good**. The consumer is willing to forgo more accessible substitutes to search for and purchase the desired brand. This can even result in a buyer searching the Internet and purchasing a preferred brand as an imported item from another country

SOME FEEL WE ELEVATE
THE WORLD OF PROFESSIONAL PHOTOGRAPHY.

ACTUALLY, WE MADE IT MORE ACCESSIBLE.

INTRODUCING THE NEW F80 FROM NIKON

The product of decades of field-proven expertise, the F80 is the SLR you've been waiting for. Drawing upon technologies, such as 10-segment 3D Matrix Metering and Five-Area Dynamic AF, developed for Nikon's pro-series F100. Additionally, the F80 features its own innovations such as Vari-Brite Focus and On-Demand Grid Lines. Explore the F80's 18 custom functions, multiple exposure capability

and depth-of-field preview. Experience its classic, friendly, ergonomic design and discover your true creative potential. Visit an Authorized Nikon Dealer or www.nikon.ca to learn more about the astounding F80 and feel like a pro.

I feel I
LIKE A PRO

Nikon

How special is the Nikon brand, will you spend time searching for it?

unsought goods
A type of consumer product that consists of new products the consumer is not yet aware of or products the consumer does not yet want.

subject to duties and taxes. Examples of products usually categorized as specialty goods include expensive men's suits, stereo sound equipment, health foods, photographic equipment, and, for many people, automobiles and certain home appliances. Various brands, such as Boss, Nikon, and BMW, have achieved specialty-good status in the minds of consumers around the globe.

Usually relatively few outlets carry such brands, and since the product's brand name is important to buyers, both manufacturer and retailer advertise the product extensively. This is both to maintain the status of the product and to make consumers aware of vendor locations. Often the manufacturer pays a portion of the retailer's advertising costs, and the name of the store carrying the specialty good frequently appears in the manufacturer's ads. Manufacturers are also prepared to provide training for store personnel because the information and service expectations of customers are high. Of course, specialized retailers have their own store reputation and image to consider, and the quality of service and manner in which the buying experience is handled can help develop trust and enable the selling of other stocked brands and repeat shopping.

UNSOUGHT GOODS There's one more, quite different category of goods. In fact, it's so unlike the other three categories that we have not included it in Table 9-1. Nevertheless, because some firms sell unsought goods, this category deserves brief discussion.

An **unsought good** is a new product that the consumer is not yet aware of or a product that the consumer is aware of but does not want right now. For that matter, some goods they may not really want to buy at all! Many new hi tech products and services may very well be unsought goods simply because while they are technologically feasible, they do not offer consumer benefits that are easily recognized as having value. These are also such things such as burial services, gravestones, or life insurance.

Newly created products and innovations begin as *unsought* goods as it is difficult to look for a product if you don't know it exists. For many people, unknown new products include computers that speak and video telephones. However, telephone companies are betting that new promotional programs will remove the latter product from the unsought category. And sometimes telephones don't come from telephone companies as was the case in mid-2000 when Cisco Systems Inc., the giant Internet equipment maker rolled out a new line of phones that could one day threaten to make the traditional phone obsolete. With it "phone" conversations can be carried over data networks using the standard Internet protocol (IP) language. As such, the phones could be plugged into any network anywhere, be able to receive calls, and never require a change of telephone number. Presently intended for business use, the company expects an uphill climb to win over their targeted customers. Cisco intends to hang in for the long run and demonstrate the increasing reliability of the technology and the "need" for this product.[5]

As the term *unsought* suggests, a firm faces a very difficult, perhaps impossible, advertising and personal-selling job when trying to market unsought goods. Having a good marketing relationship with customers allows buyers to more easily entertain unsought goods. The traditional approach would be to make consumers aware of the products so that they will buy the advertised brand when the need arises.

Classification of Business Goods

As with consumer goods, the general category of business goods is too broad to use in developing a marketing program. One factor, however, stands out, as shown in Table 9-2. For each of the five traditional categories of business goods displayed, the relationship between buyer and seller is of consequence and, in all but one case, very important. With the increasing growth in use of new Internet markets for business-goods buying, the relationships between buyer and seller are bound to weaken for some business goods, as the buying process tends to become more auction-like through this new medium. Internet markets will be discussed in more detail in Chapters 15 and 16.

We separate business goods into five categories: raw materials, manufactured parts and materials, installations, accessory equipment, and operating supplies. This classification is based on the product's broad uses. For example, a business good may be used in producing other products, in operating an organization, and in other ways we will discuss.

RAW MATERIALS Business goods that become part of another tangible product before being processed in any way (except as necessary to assist in handling the product) are

raw materials
Business goods that have not been processed in any way and that will become part of another product.

considered **raw materials**. Raw materials include:

◆ Goods found in their natural state, such as minerals, land, and products of the forests and the seas, and

◆ Agricultural products, such as cotton, fruits, livestock, and animal products, including eggs and raw milk.

Because of their distinctive attributes, these two groups of raw materials should be marketed differently. For instance, the supply of raw materials in their natural state is limited, cannot be substantially increased, and often involves only a few large producers. Further, such products generally are of a commodity nature, must be carefully graded, and, consequently, are highly standardized. Consider coal as an example; it is extracted in great quantities and then is graded by hardness and sulphur content.

The characteristics of raw materials in their natural state affect how they are marketed:

◆ Prices are normally set by supply and demand; thus producers have little or no control.

◆ Because of their bulk and low unit value, transportation costs are an important consideration; consider grain and fish as examples.

◆ Because of these same factors, natural raw materials frequently are marketed directly from producer to business user with a minimum of physical handling.

◆ There is very little branding or other product differentiation of this type of product. This puts the buyer-seller relationship in a pivotal position.

◆ It's also rare for marketers of natural raw materials to advertise or try to stimulate demand in other ways.

TABLE 9-2	Categories of Business Goods: Characteristics and Marketing Considerations				
	Type of Product				
	Raw Materials	**Fabricating Parts and Materials**	**Installations**	**Accessory Equipment**	**Operating Supplies**
EXAMPLES	Iron ore	Engine blocks	Blast furnaces	Storage racks	Paper clips
Characteristics					
Unit price	Very low	Low	Very high	Medium	Low
Length of life	Very short	Depends on final product	Very long	Long	Short
Quantities purchased	Large	Large	Very small	Small	Small
Frequency of purchase	Frequent delivery; long-term purchase contract	Infrequent purchase, but frequent delivery	Very infrequent	Medium frequency	Frequent
Standardization of competitive products	Very much; grading is important	Very much	Very little; custom-made	Little	Much
Quantity of supply	Limited; supply can be increased slowly or not at all	Usually no problem	No problem	Usually no problem	Usually no problem
Marketing Considerations					
Nature of channel	Short; no intermediaries	Short; intermediaries only for small buyers	Short; no intermediaries	Intermediaries used	Intermediaries used
Negotiation period	Hard to generalize	Medium	Long	Medium	Short
Price competition	Important	Important	Varies in important	Not main factor	Important
Presale/postsale service	Not important	Important	Very important	Important	Very little
Promotional activity	Very little	Moderate	Salespeople very important	Important	Not too important
Brand preference	None	Generally low	High	High	Low
Advance buying contract	Important; long-term contracts	Important; long-term contracts	Not usual	Not usual	Not usual

For raw materials in their natural state, competition is built around price and the assurance that a producer can deliver the product as specified. This makes these products very amenable to Internet market operations.

Many small producers located some distance from their markets supply agricultural products. Aside from imports into Canada from a variety of countries, the supply of domestic agricultural products is largely controllable by producers — frequently through marketing boards — but it cannot be increased or decreased rapidly. The product is perishable and is not produced at a uniform rate throughout the year. Most

Okanagan and Niagara soft fruits, for example, ripen in late summer and thus are readily available at that time of year and become less available in subsequent months. Standardization and grading are commonplace for agricultural products. Also, transportation costs are likely to be high relative to the product's unit value.

Close attention must be given to transportation and warehousing. Transportation costs are high relative to unit value, and standardization and grading are very important. Because producers are small and numerous, many producer co-operatives, intermediaries, and long channels of distribution are needed. For domestic production, promotional activity is usually carried out by marketing boards as well as provincial governments.

fabricating materials
Business goods that have received some processing and will undergo further processing as they become part of another product.

MANUFACTURED PARTS AND MATERIALS Business products that become part of other finished products fit into the category of **manufactured parts and materials**. Some of these undergo further processing and may be referred to as **fabricating materials**; examples include yarn that is woven into cloth and flour used in making bread. What distinguishes them from raw materials is that they have already been processed and are bought by manufacturers for assembly into their final products. Some examples are the small motors that are bought by manufacturers of furnaces and lawnmowers, and the zippers used by clothing manufacturers.

Manufactured materials and parts are usually purchased in large quantities. Buying decisions are based on the price and the service provided by the seller. In order to ensure an adequate and timely supply a buyer may place an order a year or more in advance. Because customers are concerned about price, service, and reliability of supply, most manufactured products are marketed directly from producer to user. Intermediaries are used most often when the buyers are small and/or when buyers have small fill-in orders (after the large initial order) requiring rapid delivery.

Branding manufactured materials and parts is generally unimportant. However, some firms have successfully pulled their business goods out of obscurity by branding them. Gore-Tex fabrics (www.goretex.com), YKK zippers, Intel Pentium processors (www.intel.com), Teflon coatings (www.dupont.com/teflon), and the NutraSweet brand of sweetener are examples.

installations
In the business market, long-lived, expensive, major industrial capital goods that directly affect the scale of operation of an industrial firm.

INSTALLATIONS Manufactured products that are an organization's major, expensive, and long-lived equipment are termed **installations**. Examples are large generators in a dam, a factory building, diesel engines for a railway, and servers for an Internet service provider. The characteristic of installations that differentiates them from other categories of business goods is that they directly affect the scale of operations in an organization producing goods or services. Adding twelve new Steelcase desks will not affect the scale of operations at Air Canada, but adding twelve Airbus jet aircraft certainly will. Therefore, jet aircraft are categorized as installations, but desks normally are not.

The marketing of installations presents a real challenge, because each unit sold represents a large dollar amount. Often each unit is made to the buyer's detailed specifications and much presale and post-sale servicing is essential, making buyer trust and confidence in the supplier essential. For example, a large printing press requires installation, maintenance, and — inevitably — repairs service. Sales are usually made directly from producer to business user. Because installations are technical in nature, a high-calibre, well-trained sales force is needed to provide careful, detailed explanations, and quality service and personal selling. It is not unusual for a representative of the vendor to work at a customer's location for months after installation to train employees on new technology, procedures, etc. Promotion and advertising emphasizing service and expertise might be conducted using print media in relevant trade journals or through a Web page.

accessory equipment
In the business market, capital goods used in the operation of an industrial firm.

ACCESSORY EQUIPMENT Tangible products that have substantial value and are used in an organization's operations are called **accessory equipment**. This category of business goods neither becomes an actual part of a finished product nor has a significant impact on the organization's scale of operations. The life of accessory equipment is shorter than that of installations but longer than that of operating supplies. Some examples are point-of-sale terminals (computerized register systems and scanners) in a retail store, small power tools, hand-held wireless scanners, forklift trucks, and office desks.

It is difficult to generalize about how accessory equipment should be marketed. For example, direct sale is appropriate for some products in this category when an order is for several units or when each unit is worth a lot of money. Normally, however, manufacturers of accessory equipment use intermediaries — for example, office-equipment distributors. The reasons: typically, the market is geographically dispersed, there are many different types of potential users, and individual orders may be relatively small.

operating supplies
The "convenience goods" of the business market — short-lived, low-priced items purchased with a minimum of time and effort.

OPERATING SUPPLIES Business goods that are characterized by low dollar value per unit and a short life and that aid in an organization's operations without becoming part of the finished product are called **operating supplies**. Examples are lubricating oils, ink cartridges for printers, copy paper and other stationery, and heating fuel. Purchasers want to buy operating supplies with fairly little effort. Thus operating supplies are the convenience goods of the business sector.

As with the other categories of goods, the characteristics of operating supplies influence how they should be marketed. Because they are low in unit value and are bought by many different organizations, operating supplies — like consumer convenience goods — are distributed widely. Thus the producing firm uses wholesaling intermediaries extensively. Also, because competing products are quite standardized and there is little brand insistence, price competition is normally stiff.

Importance of Product Innovation

A business exists to satisfy consumers while making a profit. Fundamentally, a company fulfils this dual purpose through its products. New-product planning and development are vital to an organization's success. A company needs new product that the market wants in order to survive over the long run.

Requirement for Growth

A guideline for management is "innovate or die." For many companies, a substantial portion of this year's sales volume and net profit will come from products that did not exist five to ten years ago and in the high technology world, from products which did not exist two years ago or less. For example, innovation is credited for ING Canada's (www.ingdirect.com) ability to move up in the financial services business. This company shot to number two among property and casualty insurers in Canada. Some of its innovations include setting up a national electronic banking service with no actual branches being opened and the introduction of a project in Quebec in which insurance brokers can sell residential mortgages, making ING one of the first insurance companies in Canada to move into this territory.[6] ING's parent company has successfully established itself around the globe to provide insurance, banking services, and asset management.

Because products, like people, go through a life cycle, new products are essential for sustaining a company's revenues and profits. This has proven especially true in high-technology industries where products often become obsolete. Sales of a product grow and then, almost inevitably, decline; eventually, most products are replaced. The concept of the product life cycle is discussed in more detail in Chapter 10, but we mention it here because it has two significant implications for product innovation:

◆ Every company's present products eventually become obsolete as their sales volume and market share are reduced by changing consumer desires and/or superior competing products.

◆ As a product ages, its profits generally decline. Introducing a new product at the right time can help maintain a company's profits.

Companies that develop innovative products can reap financial benefits. According to a research study in the United States, 39 percent of highly successful firms had introduced an innovative product during the previous five years, compared with only 23 percent of less successful firms. Consider specific examples such as microwave popcorn, fibre optic cable, and Post-It notes. Each provided benefits that were not previously available.

Innovation can mean new product development, existing product modification, or packaging and marketing innovations. Whatever helps attract new or increased attention from consumers can only help in moving the product off the shelves. Innovation isn't restricted, however, to high-technology products and industries. Often, it is the only means of growth available in mature and stagnant product categories.

The salty snack market in Canada has been predominantly characterized as having one or two leaders with some smaller players enjoying some regional success. The salty snack market is comprised of chips, cheesies, pretzels, and popcorn — of which Canadians consume about two kilograms each year (this includes U.S.-made products). Recently, several smaller players have begun to carve out their own niches with products that differ from traditional offerings. This includes pita chips, extruded snacks (corn meal formed into shapes and fried), ethnic-inspired tidbits, and vegetable chips.[7] While distribution is difficult for these smaller producers, alternative channels will provide the solution through vending machines, hotels, convenience stores, and gas stations. Product innovation such as this has been the major contributor to growth in this category for the last several years.

Kitchener, Ontario-based Dare cookies created a stir by simply redesigning the graphics on their familiar line of cookies. The standard cookie packaging didn't change, but they did lose the obligatory visual of a plate of cookies and glass of milk that is so common. Instead they went with colourful, evocative images to convey the quality of the experience obtained from each cookie flavour. French Crèmes feature images from French impressionist paintings while Lemon Cremes feature a cockatoo perched in a lemon tree. The high-impact designs have been a successful move in a market known for its conservatism.[8]

Creative innovation can provide a means of effectively entering and competing in markets with large competitive established firms. Lassonde Industries Inc. of Quebec (www.lassonde.com) has had to rely on its innovative skills to survive in an industry dominated by large multinationals.[9] This is the fruit beverage industry in which they

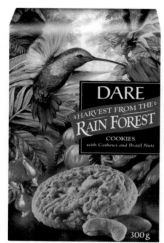

Doing the unusual, and successfully, with cookie packaging.

produce Oasis orange juice, Rougemont Apple juice, and Fruite drinks. Annual sales first topped $1 million in 1971, while sales exceeded $158 million by the year 2000. The company's marketing is one that emphasizes all facets of product innovation. To be noticed among the multinationals, Lassonde has long marched to a different drummer — through different products and packaging. Examples include the development of the first aseptic plastic bottle for their Fruite drinks — which are a cross between jelly and a fruit drink. As well, there is *Health Break* made from passion fruit, orange juice, and milk ingredients that took two years to develop and *Vegetable Delight*, the first refrigerated veggie beverage. Lassonde is the only Canadian juice maker with its own R&D team, but then again they are the only one to have won all fifteen Grand Prix product categories in the same year. They also produce 100 percent fruit juices, a cranberry cocktail, a line of sauces and marinades, and produce beverages for several private-label brands.

Innovation can also revitalize the image of a tired, sleepy product or brand. To stay with beverages for the moment, what could be a more tired product than milk? Parmalat Canada is one Canadian dairy that that has been shaking off the sleepy image with innovative packaging and marketing. It has offered Milk Mania and Shake-A-Shake single-serving flavoured milk brands as well as PurFiltre Original and PurFiltre Calcium brands.[10] These products have each been developed to recapture segments that have been steadily declining. The success of these products has caused other major dairies in the Canadian market to quickly adopt similar strategies.

Increased Consumer Selectivity

In recent years, consumers have become more selective in their choices of products. The economic environment of the early 1990s left consumers with reduced financial resources. This only began to recover by the late 1990s. Individuals, households, and organizations had to be very careful in their purchases and while consumers are currently more financially comfortable, they are still careful. Even households and individuals that were not affected by economic downturns were selective in making additional purchases because they were already reasonably well fed, clothed, housed, transported, and equipped. The nineties were a period of increasing consumer sophistication, knowledge, and selectivity. Consumers gained access to greater information and made more demands of the products and services they consumed.

Another reason for more selective buying is that consumers have to sort through an abundance (or, some would say, an excess) of similar products. Many new products are mere imitations of existing products and, as such, offer few if any added benefits. Is Procter & Gamble's introduction of HE (high energy) Tide really a new product?[11] This deluge of "new" products may lead to "product indigestion." The remedy is to develop truly new products — to innovate, not just imitate.

With the "information revolution" and the "new economy," consumers must also sort through an abundance of information. In addition to traditional sources of information about consumer purchases, there are more "channels" of information flow thanks to technology. With the Internet, there is the ability to actively and rapidly search for product and service information. This also has provided a new advertising media — the dreaded banner ad included! Also, the proliferation of satellite and specialty cable channels has caused many to focus advertising to specific target audiences, often causing new advertisers to enter the arena as harder to reach audiences are drawn together because of common interest programming.

High Failure Rates

For many years, the "rule of thumb" had been that about 80 percent of new products fail. However, because of differing definitions of *new product* and *failure*, the statistics often vary from one study to another. One company that tracks new-product introductions placed the failure rate at even higher than 80 percent. According to another firm's annual survey, 72 percent of new products do not meet their primary business objectives in terms of volume sales, market penetration consumer interest, and preference.

Why do new products fail? Most fail because they are not different from existing products. Sometimes they simply do not deliver what they imply or promise. Others simply do not have a sufficient market, a fact missed because of faulty or insufficient market research. Other factors contributing to failures include poor positioning and lack of marketing support. A good number of new dot.com services have great difficulty due to their inability to attract consumer attention among "surfers" on the Internet. Another reason a new product fails is that it is perceived as offering poor value in relation to its price.

The Bank of Montreal (www.bmo.com) felt that Canada was ready for a new banking alternative and introduced MBANX (www.mbanx.com) in 1996 as an alternative to traditional banking — banking without branches. Yet, despite all their preparations, they were wrong. Although Internet banking and branch-less providers did find success in the new economy something went terribly wrong with this "product" offering. With great confidence that customers would number a million in five years of operation, MBANX had only 160,000 clients four years later. And 80 percent of these were already Bank of Montreal customers. What the then-current chairman said would be "an acorn from which a truly mighty oak will grow" actually laid a big egg. What happened? The marketing campaign failed to communicate why people should join and exactly *what* it was they would be joining. The product was not market-ready as there were technological problems and pricing schemes were not in-line with other Internet offerings. As well, many features were not available that other providers were offering. Finally, the organization incorrectly determined what most consumers wanted. They incorrectly predicted that Canadians were ready to completely abandon the traditional banking system, many were obviously not. Some were, of course, as evidenced by the success of providers such as ING Direct and Citizens Bank of Canada. But the vast majority willing to use online services wanted a "bricks *and* clicks" bank as can be seen from the greater success of CIBC, Royal Bank, etc. It would appear that the concept was brilliant, but that they forgot one thing — the customer. MBANX continues to bleed revenues from the wound inflicted by its own cutting edge innovation.[12] The bank has since adopted a co-branding approach identifying the association between the two names and referring to the Internet option as a "direct" banking option.

Considering how vital new products are to a company's growth, the large number of new-product introductions, and the high failure rates, product innovation deserves special attention. Firms that are inattentive to their new products may face financial ruin due to the high cost of product failures. Companies that effectively manage product innovation can expect to reap a variety of benefits — differential advantage, higher sales and profits, and a solid foundation for the future.

New product development is always a risky business, and new product introductions are very expensive. Finding out what the customer really wants reduces the product development cycle and helps reduce the risk of product failures that often exceed 80 percent. The closer you take the research to the consumer's decision-making point, whether at the store shelf or in the kitchen, the more actionable the information will be.[13]

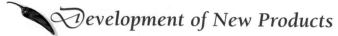 Development of New Products

It's often said that nothing happens until somebody sells something. This is not entirely true. First there must be something to sell — a product, service, person, place, or idea. And that "something" must be developed.

What Is a "New" Product?

Just what is a "new" product? Are the auto manufacturers' annual models new products? Was Ford's introduction of the 2000 Focus car models new? Or, in other product categories, is a new version of Corel's WordPerfect Office Suite software for word processing, communications, and spreadsheet work new? Or must a product be revolutionary, never before seen, before we can class it as new?

How new a product is affects how it should be marketed. There are numerous connotations of "new product," but we will focus our attention on three distinct categories of **new products**:

new product
A vague term that may refer to (1) really innovative, truly unique products; (2) replacements for existing products that are significantly different from existing ones; or (3) imitative products that are new to the given firm.

♦ Products that are really innovative — truly unique. A recent example is a security device that electronically compares the shape of a person's hand with the image of a hand encoded on an identification card. Another is a gadget developed by Hewlett-Packard that permits viewers to participate in "interactive" TV programs.[14] A new model car is not a new product, but what about if it's the first hybrid gas/electric car, it recharges itself, and gets about 110 kpg on the highway?[15] That describes the new Honda Insight coupe. Honda (www.honda.ca) was the first to make such a product commercially available. The same can be said for Sony (www.sony.ca) with AIBO, the first four-legged interactive robotic pet.

Any new product in this category satisfies a real need that is not being satisfied at the time it is introduced. Electric or hybrid vehicles are a new product as they provide new solutions to fossil fuel and pollution problems. Exactly what need is being satisfied by AIBO would have to be asked of its new owners! Still-to-be-developed products in this category would be a cancer cure and easily and inexpensively repaired automobiles.

♦ Replacements that are significantly different from existing products in form, function, and — most important — benefits provided. Johnson & Johnson's Acuvue disposable contact lenses and Panasonic's (www.panasonic.com) very thin PlasmaTV™ (42"/110 cm screen, 3.5"/9 cm thick, and only 72 lbs/32 kg) that can hang on a wall like a picture are replacing some traditional models. Similarly, thin profile computer monitors are replacing the clunky ones of the last generation. WebTV offers a different alternative to "traditional" Internet access and the Nintendo Gameboy offers video games "on-the-go." At times, new fashions in clothing are different enough to fit into this category.

♦ Imitative products that are new to a particular company but not new to the market. Usually, annual models of autos and new versions of cereals are appropriately placed in this category. In another situation, a firm may simply want to capture part of an existing market with a "me too" product. To maximize company-wide sales, makers of cold and cough remedies routinely introduce imitative products, some of which compete with a nearly identical product from the same company. Computer manufacturers and assemblers do this all the time. That's the case with Dristan Sinus and

Marketing at Work 9-1

Closing In On the Most Successful Eye Medication in History

QLT Photo Therapeutics Ltd. of Vancouver has done it. After eight years of research and $200 million in development, the company received approval to sell its new anti-blindness drug from the Food and Drug Administration in the U.S., the agency which approves new drugs for public use and whose decisions carry worldwide influence. Canadian marketing approval is expected from Health Canada at the end of 2000, Switzerland has already approved the drug, and the European regulators are expected to approve it by year end as well.

Age related macular degeneration (AMD) is the leading cause of blindness in people over age 50. In the U.S., there are 180,000 new cases diagnosed each year. In Toronto alone, one retinal specialist has over five humdred patients waiting for Visudyne. Prior to the development of the drug, only 10 percent of AMD cases were treatable; with Visudyne, doctors believe they can treat 40 percent of patients with AMD. The drug costs between US$2,000 and US$2,500 per treatment.

QLT was formed in the early 1980s and began researching AMD in 1992. By 1995, the company received approval from the FDA to begin clinical trials on humans and these were continued until 1999. Then QLT sent its results to the FDA for review and approval — all three hundred binders full.

QLT executives believe that the company will be earning $1 billion from worldwide sales of Visudyne within three years.

The marketing of the drug will be undertaken by CIBA Vision, the eye-care unit of Novartis, the giant Swiss-based drug firm. Profits will be split 50–50 between the two. For QLR, this means that by mid-2000, the company will become profitable for the first time since its inception and because of the market potential of Visudyne, QLT will be the largest biotech firm in Canada and the scond Canadian drug firm to have a "blockbuster" product. Montreal's Biochem Pharma had the first "blockbuster" with its AIDS drug 3TC.

Now that Visudyne is being launched, QLT is selling its first commercial product, Photofrin, to Axan Pharma for $60 million. QLT purchased the rights to the drug from Johnson and Johnson in 1987 and then spent $100 million developing it. In 1995, it was approved for sale in Canada, the U.S., Japan, and eight European countries. Photofrin is used to treat certain forms of cancers but it was never used as "first line" therapy and while it earned $11 million in 1999, it does not have anything like the potential of Visudyne. QLT executives want to focus on Visudyne and capitalize on it by freeing up personnel to expand the drug's research base, its applications, and to make sure financial resources are available to continue the development of more products. Product development is a risky business and requires not only time and money, but a lot of stick-to-it-iveness. And then you need a first class marketing partner.

Source: Adapted from Drew Hasselback, "QLT achieves milestone with eye drug in U.S.," *National Post*, May 2, 2000, pp. C1, C11 and Leonard Zehr, "QLT sells drug treatment to Axcan," *The Globe and Mail*, May 2, 2000, p. B7.

CoAdvil, both marketed in Canada by American Home Products. In a different field, following the early success of hotels featuring two-room suites rather than single rooms, Quality Inns added a similar accommodation to their hotels.

Ultimately, of course, whether a product is new or not depends on how the intended market perceives it. If buyers consider it to be significantly different from competitive products in some relevant characteristic (such as appearance or performance), then it is indeed a new product. As in other situations, perception is reality!

New-Product Strategy

To achieve strong sales and healthy profits, every producer of business or consumer goods should have an explicit strategy with respect to developing and evaluating new products. This strategy should guide every step in the process.

A **new-product strategy** is a statement identifying the role a new product is expected to play in achieving corporate and marketing goals. For example, a new product might be designed to protect market share or maintain the company's reputation as an innovator. The perception in the marketplace of a company as a leader or innovator in that

Company Goal		Product Strategy		Recent Examples
To defend market share.	→	Introduce an addition to an existing product line or revise an existing product.	→	Dairy desserts to complement other Healthy Choice "healthful" foods.
To strengthen a reputation as an innovator.	→	Introduce a really new product — not just an extension of an existing one.	→	Palmtop computers introduced by Hewlett-Packard.
To increase customer satisfaction.	→	Develop a mass customization system to improve service.	→	Paris Miki, world's largest eyewear retailer, developed an interactive fitting/ styling system.

product category gives that firm a great deal of power in the markets. This is easy to see when you consider companies such as Microsoft, 3M, or Sony. Or a new product's role might be to meet a specific return-on-investment goal or establish a position in a new market. With computer technology, the imperative is often to be the first to market. As the pace of technological advancement continues to increase, it is crucial to be the first on store shelves in order to maximize profit before another software package or hardware component garners the market, or the next wave of advancements renders your product an immediate fossil.

A new product's intended role also will influence the type of product to be developed, as shown in the box at the top of this page.

Only in recent years have many companies consciously identified new-product strategies. The process of developing new products has become more efficient and more effective for firms with strategies because they have a better idea of what they are trying to accomplish.

With the availability of new communication and information technology, firms are now beginning to orient their new-product strategies toward mass customization in order to provide increased product value. Individual consumer preferences can be built into new products either by requiring that a modular strategy be used for product design or by positioning the final step of individual product differentiation at the last minute in the product creation process, the delivery or consumer "try on" stage. Gateway Computers has found a happy balance between the "clicks" and the "bricks" formats of retailing PCs. The company began as with a toll-free number for ordering low priced PCs. They continue to customize systems through online and telephone orders, but now offer the opportunity to "test-drive" your options before ordering. In select regions they have opened Gateway Country stores. These black and white spotted stores (like their famous box graphics) allow you to "try on" different equipment that you can mix and match for your custom system — order at the store or after you get home and consider your options. Auto manufacturers continue to refine their Internet presence in the hope of increasing online ordering. By allowing consumers to custom order their new car, the manufacturers hope to reduce the inventories held at dealerships by producing more on demand. This ensures consumers get the exact model they want instead of simply taking what was offered at the dealership. As well, this consumer input provides rich data in determining current consumer tastes and preferences.

Stages in the Development Process

Guided by a company's new-product strategy, a new product is best developed through a series of six stages, as shown in Figure 9-2. Compared with unstructured development,

FIGURE 9-2

Major Stages in
the New-Product
Development Process

**new-product
development process**
Developmental stages
that a new product goes
through, starting with
idea generation and
continuing through idea
screening, business
analysis, limited
production, test-
marketing, and eventually
commercialization
(full-scale production
and marketing).

the formal development of new products provides benefits such as higher success rates, increased customer satisfaction, and greater achievement of time, quality, and cost objectives for new products.[16]

At each stage, management must decide whether to proceed to the next stage, abandon the product, or seek additional information.[17] Here's a brief description of what should happen at each stage of the **new-product development process**:

1. *Generating new-product ideas.* New-product development starts with an idea or a concept. A system must be designed for stimulating new ideas within an organization and then acknowledging and reviewing them promptly. Customers should also be encouraged to propose innovations. In a research study, 80 percent of companies pointed to customers as their best source for new-product ideas.[18]

2. *Screening ideas.* At this stage, new-product ideas are evaluated to determine which ones warrant further study.[19] Typically, a management team screens the pool of ideas.

3. *Business analysis.* A surviving idea is expanded into a concrete business proposal. In the **business analysis**, management (a) identifies product features, (b) estimates market demand, competition, and the product's profitability, (c) establishes a program to develop the product, and (d) assigns responsibility for further study of the product's feasibility.

4. *Prototype development.* If the results of the business analysis are favourable, then a prototype or trial model of the product is developed. In the case of tangible products, a small quantity of the trial model is manufactured to designated specifications. Laboratory tests and other technical evaluations are carried out to determine whether it is practical to produce the product. A firm may be able to construct a prototype of a new type of cellular telephone but be unable to manufacture the new product in large quantities or at a cost low enough to stimulate sales and still yield a profit. In the case of services, the facilities and procedures necessary to produce and deliver the new product are designed and tested. That certainly is a necessary step in the development of a new roller-coaster ride at an amusement park!

test marketing
A marketing research
technique in which a
firm markets its product
in a limited geographic
area, measures the
sales, and then — from
this sample — projects
(a) the company's sales
over a larger area and/or
(b) consumers' response
to a strategy before
committing to a major
marketing effort.

5. *Market tests.* Unlike the internal tests conducted during prototype development, **market tests** involve actual consumers. A new tangible product may be given to a sample of people for use in their households (in the case of a consumer good) or their organizations (a business good). Beta versions of all types of software are made available free to those who will download and make use of it. Following this trial, consumers are asked to evaluate the product. Consumer-use tests are less practical for pure services due to their intangible nature. If they can be simulated on a computer, however, some form of trial can be achieved.

This stage in new-product development often entails **test marketing**, in which the product is placed on sale in a limited geographic area. Results, including sales and repeat purchases, are monitored by the company that developed the product and perhaps by competitors as well. In this stage, the product's design and production plans may have to be adjusted as a result of test findings. Following market tests, management must make a final "go–no go" decision about introducing the product.

6. *Commercialization.* In this stage, full-scale production and marketing programs are planned and, finally, implemented. Up to this point in development, management has virtually complete control over the product. Once the product is "born" and enters its life cycle, however, the external competitive environment becomes a major determinant of its destiny.

Note that the first two stages — idea generation and screening — are tied closely to the overall new-product strategy. This strategy can provide a focus for generating new-product ideas and a basis for evaluating them.

In the six-stage process, the first three stages are particularly critical because they deal with ideas and, as such, are the least expensive. More important, many products fail because the idea or the timing is wrong — and the first three stages are intended to identify such situations. Each subsequent stage becomes more costly in terms of the budget and human resources necessary to carry out the required tasks.

Some companies, trying to bring new products to market faster than their competitors, skip stages in the development process. The most common omission is the fifth stage, market tests. Without this stage, however, the company lacks consumer reactions to the proposed product.

Historically, the marketing of goods has received more attention than the marketing of services. Thus it is not surprising that the new-product development process is not as advanced in services fields as it is in goods industries. However, on the positive side, that means services firms have more flexibility to devise a new-product development process that suits their distinctive circumstances.

Producer's Criteria for New Products

When should a company add a new product to its current assortment of products? Here are guidelines that some producers use in answering this question:

◆ *There must be adequate market demand.* Too often management begins with the wrong question, such as "Can we use our present sales force?" or "Will the new item fit into our production system?" or "Can we just put it up on our Web site — we get a lot of traffic." The necessary first question is "Do enough people really want this product?"

   Shoppers Drug Mart (www.shoppersdrugmart.com) made sure they knew what they were doing before they introduced a new private-label makeup line, *Quo*. Research indicated that the average Canadian woman visited SDM every eight days, and yet bought most cosmetics at department store "brand name" cosmetic counters. No department store, however, can boast such a customer frequency. The new private-label line was positioned between pricey high-end store brands and inexpensive mass-market offerings filling a very real gap in the marketplace. With no visible tie-in to SDM on the packaging and packaging designed in a timeless quality with clean, sleek lines and displayed in a special showcase in the cosmetics department, the product had the high-end brands in its sights. Comprehensive marketing support included TV and print media designed to be very eye-catching to make women think about the makeup they are currently using.[20]

Marketing at Work 9-2

Need Innovative Ideas??
Visit BrainStore

How does an innovative company produce a steady stream of ideas for new products, services, in-house implementation programs, and so on. Since not everyone is a 17-year-old cybergeek about to become an e-millionaire, it is just not possible to wait for the lightbulbs to flash — what if they don't? Well, these days, some firms have hired those 17-year-olds to generate ideas. But most of those firms have been in software or related e-commerce. But if you are like Wander, a subsidiary of Novartis AG (pharmaceuticals) and looking for new food-product ideas, or like the Swiss Cancer Association looking for ideas on how to promote sun protection products, you can visit the BrainStore.

The BrainStore has developed a creative approach to the hard work of creativity. The two principals and their thirty-one employees operate with the notion that you can manufacture ideas with the same discipline and rigor that you use in a production process. By examining the creative process closely, then breaking it into steps and developing tools to optimize those steps, this idea factory actually runs like an efficient assembly line without being bureaucratic about its operations. Every project that comes in must start in the Creative Lab., a large room equipped with lots of space, all kinds of supplies (crayons, glitter, glue, coloured paper, beads, model-building equipment) and a special prop — a white cast iron bathtub. Why the bathtub? To remind everyone that you have to be playful and that great ideas start with completely unrealistic thoughts.

When BrainStore has a creative challenge that is beyond the resident staff, it goes to its outside experts — kids! The kids comprise the BrainNet, a fifteen hundred strong group of youths aged 13 to 20 and a few adult professionals thrown in as window dressing. Members of the BrainNet act as trendwatchers and sources of inspiration, no matter how offbeat and crazy-seeming — just keep the bathtub in mind. The members of BrainNet — being kids — know how to talk about things in the kind of way that does not let thinking interfere. During creative workshops, young people are mixed with client team members so that one gets a blend of the professionalism of experts as well as the enthusiasm and, sometimes, the useful know nothingness of kids. The result is that you have teenagers working on products and campaigns for such firms as Nestle SA and Swiss Railways.

Credit Suisse Group wanted to phase out a passbook savings plan that Swiss families had relied upon for years but that the bank believed was obsolete. Nine kids visited the Creative Lab together with five executives from the Credit Suisse Group. Cross-generational teams developed a number of scenarios with each producing a series of ideas. The ideas go through the remaining steps in the BrainStore assembly line process: compression (a team of in-house employees and outside experts pick the best ideas — similar to concept development), testing (research and prototype development), and finishing (commercialization — marketing campaigns and positioning strategies). By keeping the creative process moving along from stage to stage, BrainStore is able to maintain the creative flow and efficiency of process.

Source: Adapted from Anna Muoio, "Brainstorming at Switzerland's BrainStore," *Financial Post*, April 12, 2000, p. C15, and the BrainStore.com Web site, April 18, 2000.

♦ *The product must satisfy key financial criteria.* At least three questions should be asked: "Is adequate financing available?" "Will the new item reduce seasonal and cyclical fluctuations in the company's sales?" And, most critical, "Can we make sufficient profits with the product?" Adequate financing means more than that required to produce the product, it must ensure sufficient market research is carried out and that sufficient marketing support is provided to bring the product to the awareness of the targeted segments.

♦ *The product must be compatible with environmental standards.* Key questions include: "Do the production processes avoid polluting the air or water?" "Will the finished product, including its packaging, be friendly to the environment?" And, "After being used, does the product have recycling potential?"

♦ *The product must fit into the company's present marketing structure.* Sherwin Williams Paint Company would probably find it quite difficult to add margarine to its line of paints. Specific questions related to whether a new product will fit the company's marketing expertise and experience include: "Can the existing sales force be used?" "Can the present channels of distribution be used?" in order to reduce risk, many organizations rely upon brand extensions. This means using an established brand name on a new product offering. Ideally, this should be a "related" product category. For example, Sunlight successfully moved out of the laundry room and into the kitchen with Sunlight dishwashing products. It seems the idea of removing stubborn dirt and stains carried over well from clothing to greasy dishes. The name was less successful, however, when it came to hand soap, and its furniture polish never made it past the test market phase.[21]

Besides these four issues, a proposed product must satisfy other criteria. For instance, it must be in keeping with the company's objectives and image. For spring 2000 Bayer (www.bayer.com) aggressively promoted its new garden bug spray showing insects choking and wheezing before their final demise. The question is — what image will parents think of the next time that they go to give that little pink Bayer aspirin to their child? Time will tell if this is a good consumer association between product lines, perhaps we'd rather not know what else they make. The product also must be compatible with the firm's production capabilities. And it must satisfy any pertinent legal requirements.

Conventional marketing wisdom says that as long as you keep making new products, consumers will keep buying them. However, according to the Marketing Intelligence Service Ltd.'s annual new-products survey the new-product's stream is drying up. One reason for this is thought to be the number of mergers and acquisitions in the consumer packaged-goods industry. Another is that the barrage of product choices available is confusing consumers, and retailers are finding it difficult to come to terms with the flood of new products. Shelf space is a big issue as thousands of *new* products compete for space each year. Some marketers have responded by decreasing the variety of products they offer, or by melding brands together into one. With too many choices it is believed that it takes too long to sort out the best value and consumers may simply reach for the tried and true. With fewer choices, it is thought, consumers will be able to see the difference between brands.[22]

Intermediary's Criteria for New Products

Intermediaries, such as retailers and wholesalers, considering whether to buy a new product for resale should apply all the preceding criteria except those related to production. In addition, an intermediary should apply the following guidelines:

◆ The intermediary must have a good working relationship with the producer. By distributing a new product, an intermediary should stand to benefit from the producer's reputation, the possibility of getting the right to be the only company to sell the product in a given territory, and the promotional and financial help given by the producer.

◆ The producer and intermediary must have compatible distribution policies and practices. Pertinent questions include: "What kind of selling effort is required for the new product?" "How does the proposed product fit with the intermediary's policies regarding repair service, alterations (for clothing), credit, and delivery?"

◆ As in the case of producers, the product must satisfy key financial criteria. At least two questions should be asked: "If adding a new product necessitates eliminating another product due to a shortage of shelf or storage space, will the result be a net gain in sales?" And "Can we make sufficient profits with the product?"

New-Product Adoption and Diffusion

The likelihood of achieving success with a new product, especially a really innovative product, is increased if management understands the adoption and diffusion processes for that product. Once again, we are stressing that organizations need to understand how consumers behave. The **adoption process** is the set of successive decisions an individual makes before accepting an innovation. **Diffusion** of a new product is the process by which an innovation spreads throughout a social system over time.[23]

By understanding these processes, an organization can gain insight into how a product is or is not accepted by consumers and which groups of consumers are likely to buy a product soon after it is introduced, later on, or never. This knowledge of consumer behaviour can be valuable in designing an effective marketing program.

Stages in Adoption Process

A prospective user goes through six **stages in the adoption process** — deciding whether to purchase something new. See the box at the bottom of this page.

Adopter Categories

Some people will adopt an innovation soon after it is introduced. Others will delay before accepting a new product, and still others may never adopt it. Research has identified five **innovation adopter categories**, based on the point in time when individuals adopt a given innovation. Non-adopters are excluded from this categorization. Characteristics of early and late adopters are summarized in Table 9-3. It is unclear what effect the Internet will have, if any, on these stages and on the process itself. It is quite possible that the instant availability of a wealth of information and opportunities ranging from new product vendors to consumer rating sites and online clearinghouses may create acceleration in the adoption process.

INNOVATORS Representing about 3 percent of the market, **innovators** are venturesome consumers who are the first to adopt an innovation. In relation to later adopters, innovators are likely to be younger, have higher social status, and be in better financial shape. Innovators also tend to have broad social relationships involving various groups of people in more than one community. They are likely to rely more on non-personal sources of information, such as advertising and the Internet, rather than on salespeople or other personal sources.

adoption process
The stages that an individual goes through in deciding whether to accept an innovation.

diffusion of innovation
A process by which an innovation is spread through a social system over time.

innovators
The first group — a venturesome group — of people to adopt something new (good, service).

Stage	Activity in That Stage
Awareness	Individual is exposed to the innovation; becomes a prospect.
Interest	Prospect is interested enough to seek information.
Evaluation	Prospect judges the advantages and disadvantages of a product.
Trial	Prospect adopts the innovation on a limited basis. A consumer buys a sample, if the product can be sampled.
Adoption	Prospect decides whether to use the innovation on a full-scale basis.
Confirmation	After adopting the innovation, prospect becomes a user who immediately seeks assurances that decision to purchase the product was correct.

TABLE 9-3   Characteristics of Early and Late Adopters of Innovations

	Early Adopters	Late Adopters
Key Characteristics		
Venturesome	Innovators (3% of total adopters)	
Respected	Early adopters (13%)	
Deliberate	Early majority (34%)	
Sceptical		Late majority (34% of total adopters)
Tradition-bound		Laggards (16%)
Other Characteristics		
Age	Younger	Older
Education	Well educated	Less educated
Income	Higher	Lower
Social relationships: within or outside community	Innovators: outside Others: within	Totally local
Social status	Higher	Lower
Information sources	Wide variety; many media	Limited media exposure; limited reliance on outside media; reliance on local peer groups

early adopters
The second group (following the innovators) to adopt something new. This group includes the opinion leaders, is respected, and has much influence on its peers.

change agent
Person responsible for introducing an innovative new product.

early majority
A more deliberate group of innovation adopters that adopts just before the "average" adopter.

EARLY ADOPTERS Making up about 13 percent of the market, **early adopters** purchase a new product after innovators but sooner than other consumers. Unlike innovators, who have broad involvement outside a local community, early adopters tend to be involved socially within a local community. Early adopters are greatly respected in their social system; in fact, other people are interested in and influenced by their opinions. Thus the early-adopter category includes more opinion leaders than any other adopter group. Salespeople are probably used more as information sources by early adopters than by any other category.

In the process of diffusion, a **change agent** is a person who seeks to accelerate the spread of a given innovation. In business, the person responsible for introducing an innovative new product must be a change agent. Consider the introduction of digital cameras. Epson's (www.epson.com) PhotoPC®650 digital camera is an example of such a product that retails at a price substantially above the market price of more conventional technology. The marketers of these products must be effective change agents, convincing consumers that it is worthwhile to pay the higher price. Also, to convince consumers they suddenly need to be able to store forty-seven images, use a 1.8"/5 cm LCD monitor to take pictures, and that they need sixteen million colour capability for pictures of their family outings. A change agent focuses the initial persuasive efforts on early adopters because other people respect their opinions and eventually will emulate their behaviour. If a firm can get early adopters to accept its innovative product, then the broader market eventually will accept the product as well.

EARLY MAJORITY The **early majority**, representing about 34 percent of the market, includes more deliberate consumers who accept an innovation just before the "average" adopter in a social system. This group is a bit above average in social and economic measures. Consumers in the early-majority group rely quite a bit on ads, salespeople, and contact with early adopters.

Marketing at Work 9-3

Targeting Early Adopting Business With a Web Timesheet

Replicon Inc., based in Calgary, makes Web TimeSheet, software that takes the hassle out of tracking employees' time and projects. Not wideband, not wireless, not streaming video, just plain work-a-day timesheet and project management. But it seems that this is an area of activity that technology had passed by — until now. Many corporations have just begun to automate their timesheets and this created an opportunity for Replicon to move quickly with smart product and smart target marketing to beat established competitors to market domination.

Replicon was founded in the mid-90s by Raj Narayanaswamy and his wife Lackshmi Raj. Both studied computer science at one of India's famous technology schools, the Indian Institute of Technology. The first software product they developed, a customer relationship program called Reach, failed. While the system design was leading edge, the program had glitches but their real problem was marketing. Potential buyers were not willing to entrust an important part of their business to an unknown startup firm. While the software was fixable, the marketing challenge was not one they thought they could overcome. They moved on to another opportunity, an aspect of doing business that, while not as vital as customer relations, was one they believed companies would be just as interested

in and not present the same unknown start-up marketing challenges of their previous product and market.

Replicon set a goal for Web TimeSheet: to grow fast enough and big enough to be a major player in the emerging market of automated timesheets. The software product was launched in March of 1998. It was priced at $30 a seat for a thirty-day five-user trial. Within a few months the firm had two or three dozen clients in ten countries. With few marketing resources, Replicon concentrated advertising and promotion on online trade publications which are followed by technology savvy people willing to "try and buy" new products — early adopters.

Currently, customers are buying "seats" or software user privileges for complete companies rather than just a department or two. Kraft Foods plans to implement Web TimeSheets for 17,000 employees in North America. Nortel Networks and Hewlett Packard are also customers. With early adopter and opinion leader clients like these, the firm is well on its way to obtaining a very large share of this market with few competitors in sight. It is now moving into the application service provider mode of operations (ASP) whereby it will allow users to rent software rather than buy it.

Source: Adapted from Wendy Stueck, "Duo clocks in with Web Timesheet," *The Globe and Mail*, April 24, 2000, p. B7.

late majority
The sceptical group of innovation adopters who adopt a new idea late in the game.

LATE MAJORITY   The **late majority**, another 34 percent of the market, is a skeptical group of consumers who usually adopt an innovation to save money or in response to social pressure from their peers. They rely on their peers — late or early majority — as sources of information. Advertising and personal selling are less effective with this group than is word-of-mouth communication.

laggards
Tradition-bound people who are the last to adopt an innovation.

LAGGARDS   **Laggards** are consumers who are bound by tradition and, hence, are last to adopt an innovation. They make up about 16 percent of the market. Laggards are suspicious of innovations and innovators; they wonder why anyone would pay a lot more for a new kind of light bulb, for example. By the time laggards adopt something new, it may already have been discarded by the innovators in favour of a newer concept. Laggards are older and usually are at the low end of the social and economic scales.

nonadopters
Consumers who never adopt an innovation.

We are discussing only adopters of an innovation. For most innovations, there are many people who are not included in our percentages. They are **nonadopters**; they never adopt the innovation.

Innovation Characteristics Affecting Adoption Rate

There are five **innovation characteristics that affect the adoption rate:**[24]

◆   *Relative advantage*: the degree to which an innovation is superior to currently available products. Relative advantage may be reflected in lower cost, greater safety, easier use, or some other relevant benefit. Safest Stripper, a paint and varnish remover introduced by 3M (www.3m.com), scores high on this characteristic. The product contains no harmful chemicals, has no odour, and allows the user to refinish furniture indoors rather than having to work outdoors.

◆ *Compatibility*: the degree to which an innovation coincides with the cultural values and experiences of prospective adopters. Since many consumers want to save time and satisfy their desires now rather than later, microwave popcorn certainly satisfies this characteristic. Supermarkets offer ethnic foods in large urban areas, and most any food is now microwave-friendly if not developed specifically for microwave use.

◆ *Complexity*: the degree of difficulty in understanding or using an innovation. The more complex an innovation is, the more slowly it will be adopted — if it is adopted at all. Combined shampoo-conditioners certainly are simple to use, so adoption of them was not impeded by complexity. However, many forms of insurance and some consumer-electronics products have problems with this characteristic. To assist in combating this problem these producers often use toll-free phone numbers for set-up and technical assistance. This reliance on toll-free numbers for customer assistance hotlines has caused the need to utilize additional number combinations beyond the familiar 1-800. This is why now 888, 877, etc, are being used.

◆ *Trialability*: the degree to which an innovation may be sampled on some limited basis. Setting aside the other characteristics, the greater the trialability, the faster will be the adoption rate. For instance, a central home air-conditioning system is likely to have a slower adoption rate than a new seed or fertilizer, which may be tried on a small plot of ground. In general, due to this characteristic, costly products will be adopted more slowly than will inexpensive products. Similarly, many services (such as insurance) are difficult to use on a trial basis, so they tend to be adopted rather slowly. Many Web-savvy consumers are still tentative regarding purchasing goods or services over the Internet. Further, paying for a good that you download is as intangible as it gets. The benefits and usage of some software "plug-ins" are difficult to appreciate unless you can use the product — very often consumers can download for a trial period that will expire in thirty days. This is sort of a high-tech equivalent to getting a sample of a product in your mailbox.

◆ *Observability*: the degree to which an innovation actually can be seen to be effective. In general, the greater the observability, the faster the adoption rate. For example, a new weed killer that works on existing weeds probably will be accepted sooner than a product that prevents weeds from sprouting. The reason? The latter product, even if highly effective, produces no dead weeds to show to prospective buyers! On the other hand it does a good service for a lawn care company to have their signs seen on a lush, green lawn and not a dry, brown garden. It also provides a sense of tangibility for consumers.

A company would like an innovative product to satisfy all five characteristics discussed above. But few do. Kodak's camcorder videotape is a good example to assess these characteristics. Kodak (www.kodak.ca) sells this product as "backcoated," which it claims enables the videotape to perform better in a VCR, especially if it is an old VCR. The backcoating reduces the likelihood of losing images. This product comes pre-packed in a cassette and is easy to use (reducing complexity), is a well-known brand name (alleviating concerns about trialability and tangibility), and offers a feature that other film does not have — the backcoating that prevents damage to the film (representing relative advantage). The customer can observe the backcoating by checking the back of the film. A flat surface as opposed to a shiny one indicates that the product is backcoated. The product is widely distributed, which enhances compatibility with consumers' desire for convenient purchase.[25]

Organizing for Product Innovation

If new-product programs are to be successful, they must be supported by a strong, long-term commitment from top management. This commitment must be maintained even when some new products fail. To implement this commitment to innovation effectively, new-product programs must be soundly organized.

Types of Organization

There is no "one best" organizational structure for product planning and development. Many companies use more than one structure to manage these activities. Some widely used organizational structures for planning and developing new products are:

- **Product-planning committee.** Members include executives from major departments — marketing, production, finance, engineering, and research — and, especially in small firms, the president and/or another top-level executive.

- **New-product department.** These units are small, consisting of five or fewer people. The department head reports to the president (which, in a large firm, may be the president of a division).

- **Venture team.** A small group, with representatives from engineering, production, finance, and marketing research, operates like a separate small business. Typically the team reports directly to top management.

- **Product manager.** This individual is responsible for planning new products as well as managing established products. Although still effective in some firms, we'll discuss in the next section why this structure is being displaced in many firms by one of the other structures discussed above.

Which organizational structure is chosen is not the key point here — each has strengths and weaknesses. What's critical is to make sure that some person or group has the specific responsibility for new-product development and is backed by top management. Product innovation is too important an activity to handle in an unorganized, nonchalant fashion, which presumes that somehow the job will get done. To maximize the chances for successful new-product development, it is vital that employees responsible for product planning have the right skills, particularly the ability to work well with other people and operate in a supportive environment.

As the new product is completed, responsibility for marketing it usually is shifted either to an existing department or a new department established just for this new product. In some cases the team that developed the product may continue as the management nucleus of the new unit.

Integrating new products into departments that are already marketing established products does carry at least two risks, however. First, executives who are involved with ongoing products may have a short-term outlook as they deal with day-to-day problems of existing products. Consequently, they may not recognize the long-term importance of new products and, as a result, neglect them. Second, managers of successful existing products often are reluctant to assume the risks inherent in marketing new products.

Product Manager

Beginning in the 1950s, many companies, such as Procter & Gamble and Kraft General Foods, assigned the responsibility for planning new products as well as coordinating the marketing efforts of existing ones to a product manager. Essentially, a product manager, sometimes called a brand manager, plans the complete marketing program for a brand or group of products. Specific tasks include setting marketing goals, preparing budgets, and developing plans for advertising and personal-selling and service activities. Developing new products along with improving established products may also be part of the job description.

Probably the biggest problem with this approach is that a company often saddles product managers with great responsibility but provides them with little authority. For instance, product managers are expected to develop the plan by which the sales force will market the product to wholesalers and retailers, but they have no real authority over the sales force. They are responsible for drafting advertising plans, but typically do not select the advertising agencies that will fully develop and execute them. Product managers have a profit responsibility for their brands, yet are often denied any control over product costs, prices, or advertising budgets. Their effectiveness depends largely on their ability to influence other executives to co-operate with their plans.

The role of product, or brand, managers is seen as becoming increasingly crucial. Today, brands are not built via a single medium and advertising is, for many, becoming a declining part of the marketing mix. In the new economy the product experience, customer service corporate culture, advertising, direct mail, promotions, the Internet, product features, public relations, and distribution channels all contribute to brand creation.[26] In this increasingly complex and competitive marketplace the role of a product manager has become no less complicated.

Many firms are relying on team efforts — such as the product-planning committees or venture teams previously discussed — to develop new products.[27] Typically, these are cross-functional teams consisting of representatives not only from marketing research and marketing but also product design, engineering, and manufacturing. Research has shown that the use of cross-functional teams at the Chrysler Design Center in Michigan have been able to reduce the time taken to design and build vehicles such as the new Durango SUV by 40 percent.

Summary

The first commandment in marketing is "Know thy customer," and the second is "Know thy product." The relative number and success of a company's new products are a prime determinant of its sales, growth rate, and profits. A firm can best serve its customers by producing and marketing want-satisfying goods or services. The scarcity of some natural resources and a growing concern for our environment make social responsibility a crucial aspect of product innovation.

To manage its products effectively, a firm's marketers must understand the full meaning of product, which stresses that consumers are buying want satisfaction. Products can be classified into two basic categories — consumer products and business products. Each category is then subdivided, because a different marketing program is required for each distinct group of products.

There are many views about what constitutes a new product. For marketing purposes, three categories of new products need to be recognized — innovative, significantly different, and imitative.

A clear statement of the firm's new-product strategy serves as a solid foundation for the six-stage development process for new products. The early stages in this process are especially important. If a firm can make an early and correct decision to stop the development of a proposed product, a lot of money and labour can be saved.

In deciding whether to add a new product, a producer or intermediary should consider whether there is adequate market demand for it. The product also should fit in with the firm's marketing, production, and financial resources. Management needs to understand the adoption and diffusion processes for a new product.

A prospective user goes through six stages in deciding whether to adopt a new product. Adopters of an innovation can be divided into five categories, depending on how quickly they accept an innovation such as a new product. These categories are innovators, early adopters, early majority, late majority, and laggards. In addition, there usually is a group of non-adopters.

Five characteristics of an innovation seem to influence the adoption rate: relative advantage, compatibility, complexity, trialability, and observability.

Successful product planning and development require long-term commitment and strong support from top management. Furthermore, new-product programs must be soundly organized. Most firms use one of four organizational structures for new-product development: product-planning committee, new-product department, venture team, or product manager. Recently, the trend has been away from product managers and toward team efforts for developing new products.

Key Terms and Concepts

Product 270
Consumer products 270
Business products 270
Convenience good 271
Shopping good 271
Specialty good 272
Unsought good 273
Raw materials 274
Manufactured parts and
    materials 276
Fabricating materials 276
Installations 276
Accessory equipment 277

Operating supplies 277
New products 281
New-product strategy 282
New-product development
    process 284
Business analysis 284
Market tests 284
Test marketing 284
Adoption process 288
Diffusion 288
Stages in the adoption process 288
Innovation adopter categories 288
Innovators 288

Early adopters 289
Change agent 289
Early majority 289
Late majority 290
Laggards 290
Nonadopters 290
Innovation characteristics that affect
    the adoption rate 290
Product-planning committee 292
New-product department 292
Venture team 292
Product manager 292

Questions and Problems

1. In what respects are the products different in each of the following cases?

   a. A Whirlpool dishwasher sold at an appliance store and a similar dishwasher sold by Sears under its Kenmore brand name. Assume that Whirlpool makes both dishwashers.

   b. A Sunbeam Mixmaster sold by a leading department store and the same model sold by a discount house.

   c. An airline ticket purchased through a travel agent and an identical ticket purchased directly from the airline.

2. a. Explain the various interpretations of the term *new product*.

   b. Give some examples, other than those cited in this chapter, of products in each of the three new-product categories.

3. "Because brand preferences are well established with regard to many items of women's clothing, these items — traditionally considered shopping goods — will move into the specialty-

goods category. At the same time, however, other items of women's clothing can be found in supermarkets and variety stores, thus indicating that some items are convenience goods."

    a.   Explain the reasoning in these statements.

    b.   Do you agree that women's clothing is shifting away from the shopping-goods classification? Explain.

4.   Compare the elements of a producer's marketing mix for a convenience good with those of the mix for a specialty good.

5.   In which of the five categories of business goods should each of the following be included? And which products may belong in more than one category?

    a.   Trucks.

    b.   Medical X-ray equipment.

    c.   Printer paper.

    d.   Copper wire.

    e.   Printers.

    f.   Nuts and bolts.

    g.   Paper clips.

    h.   Land.

6.   In developing new products, how can a firm make sure that it is being socially responsible with regard to scarce resources and the environment?

7.   Assume that the following organizations are considering additions to their product lines. In each case, does the proposed product meet the criteria for adding a new product? Explain your decisions.

    a.   McDonald's — salad bar.

    b.   Safeway — automobile tires.

    c.   Esso — personal computers.

    d.   Banks — life insurance.

    e.   General Motors Canada — outboard motors for boats.

8.   Describe the kinds of people who are most likely to be found in (a) the innovator category of adopters and (b) the late-majority category.

9.   What are some of the problems typically connected with the product-manager organizational structure?

Hands-On Marketing

1.   Arrange a meeting with the manager of a large retail outlet in your community. Discuss two topics with the manager:

    a.   What recently introduced product has been a failure or appears destined to fail?

    b.   Did this product, in retrospect, satisfy the criteria for adding a new product? (Remember to consider not just the intermediary's criteria but also applicable producer's criteria.)

2.   Design (either in words or drawings) a new product that fits into one of the first two categories of new products — a really innovative product or a significant replacement, not just an imitative product. Then evaluate how your proposed product rates with respect to the five characteristics of an innovation that influence the adoption rate.

Chapter Ten

Product-Mix Strategies

At any given time, a firm may be marketing some new products and some old ones, while others are being planned and developed. In this chapter we'll cover a number of strategic decisions pertaining to an organization's assortment of products and services. After studying this chapter, you should have an understanding of:

◆ The difference between product mix and product line.

◆ The major product-mix strategies:

◆ Positioning

◆ Expansion

◆ Alteration

◆ Contraction

◆ Trading up and trading down.

◆ Managing a product throughout a life cycle.

◆ Planned obsolescence.

◆ Style and fashion.

◆ The fashion-adoption process.

Meeting Market Demands for Change

In most industries, companies would not even consider keeping the exact same products in their product lines year after year. It is normal for marketers to be constantly changing their lines in response to changing consumer preferences and competitive pressures by introducing new products, modifying existing ones, altering packages, and repositioning brands.

Take the brewing industry. The two principal competitors in the Canadian beer industry are Molson (www.iam.ca/corp/) and Labatt (www.labatt.ca) breweries. Both companies are over two hundred years old and still retain some of their original brews. But in recent years, changes in lifestyles and drinking behaviour, cultural values, a growing interest in preservative-free products, quality concerns, and new legislation have all had an impact and have necessitated the introduction of a wide array of new products. Among these offerings are ice and dry beer products, reduced-alcohol beers, no-preservative beers, and packaged draft beer. These are meant to compete against various

market trends — increasing wine consumption among younger segments, the increasing popularity of microbrewery products and European brands, the constant stream of new distilled spirit and "cooler" products, and the presence of Mexican and American brands as trade barriers decreased.

Aside from extravagant promotions and in-box giveaways by both companies,

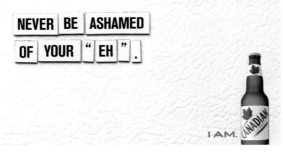

NEVER BE ASHAMED OF YOUR "EH".

Labatt released a product called "The Blue Cooler Pack," which is a container holding twelve bottles of Labatt Blue with room for ice and water. This product is meant to offer a new twist on the cold-beer image that is used in the "ice" and "glacier" beer products. Molson has attempted to guarantee "freshness" with a "brewed-on" date after which the beer will be at its peak flavour for the following 120 days.

New products have ranged from the development of "specialty" beers to that of increasing and decreasing the alcohol content, sweetness, or aftertaste. Amber, dark, as well as cream and red ales have been developed and calories have been counted and reduced for weight-conscious beer guzzlers. Labatt .5 has, of course, 0.5 percent alcohol and only eighty calories, while most other reduced brews offer between 2.5 percent and 4 percent alcohol. Labatt's Wildcat Strong, on the other hand, delivers a full 6.1 percent alcohol content and doesn't appear to be worried about calories. Molson's OV is just "slightly sweet and fruity," while Labatt offers the Twist Shandy, a beer-based cooler (available during the spring and summer) with 2.3 percent alcohol and flavoured with citrus fruit juices. The dry and ice brews also offer a higher alcohol content, with dry brews reducing sweetness and ice brews providing a "snappy taste." Each brewery has also introduced "premium" or "specialty" brews to compete with the cottage-industry feel of the microbrews. Molson's Signature series is craft-brewed in small batches, while John Labatt Classic is the number one domestic premium beer in Canada.

With such specialty products, the companies are trying to offer the virtues of a premium beer while appearing unpretentious enough to keep swimming in the mainstream. But with such a deluge of products on offer by the end of the last millennium, they have had to move past the product to develop distinctive identities in the marketplace. As well, they have had to develop profiles as responsible corporate citizens. This has meant fostering a brand personality and reflecting current social concerns.

Labatt kept young in the nineties by coming "out of the blue" with its advertising and marketing promotions, while Molson instead saw red — in the form of our national symbol the maple leaf. Molson Canadian's "I AM" campaign was so successful in the late nineties that it was continued into the new century by cranking up the volume on the patriotic appeals. Apparently market research found that there was an increasing trend in this country toward overt patriotism. The 2000 campaign, as discussed in the beginning of Chapter 5, created such frenzied patriotism that national newspapers covered its progress and the actor portraying the "average Joe" was even interviewed on American morning television.

That year, Labatt kept its finger on the national pulse by not only wrestling away sponsorship of *Hockey Night in Canada*, a venerable Canadian institution, but also by touring the country with the Stanley Cup, the most coveted trophy in sports. Aside from announced venues, it was reported that the trophy, insured for several million dollars, could show up "out of the blue" just about anywhere during the cross-country tour. This resulted in a travelling sideshow that was guaranteed to get news coverage throughout the tour. A series of TV ads also aired dramatizing the Stanley Cup cropping up unexpectedly at different locations.

Both breweries also maintained programs promoting responsible drinking. Labatt sponsored research about youth attitudes toward drinking in their efforts to help people to "know when to draw the line." They also promoted environmental issues through packaging and recycling efforts as well as employee and supplier activities. Molson also developed a politically correct persona through their toll-free network of "taxi guys" to promote the use of cabs when out on the town. They urge consumers to "take care," as drinking is a social responsibility — look after yourself but also to take care for others. Molson also supported community-based adult sports through the Local Heroes program that funded the repair and revitalization of existing sport facilities across the country.[1]

These examples illustrate how market pressures have forced these two major brewing companies to finally adapt product lines with changes that reflect customer demands, product competition, and other changes in the environment. Adaptation, as can be seen, can sometimes necessitate changes far beyond just the core product as positioning and image all impact upon the product mix.

product mix
All products offered for sale by a company.

Product Mix and Product Line

Very few firms rely on a single product or service; instead most sell many products. What each firm does about products and services is dictated by the product strategy it chooses to devise and implement (see the Product-Market Growth Matrix discussion in Chapter 3). The set of all products offered for sale by a company is called a **product mix**. The structure of a product mix has both **breadth** and **depth**. The number of product lines carried is a measure of the breadth of the product mix. The depth is measured by the variety of sizes, colours, and models offered within each product line. A product-mix strategy is illustrated in Figure 10-1.

A broad group of products, intended for essentially similar uses and having similar physical characteristics, constitutes a product line. Firms may delineate a **product line**

breadth of product mix
The number of product lines offered for sale by a firm.

depth of product line
The assortment within a product line.

FIGURE 10-1
Product Mix —
Breadth and Depth
Part of the product
mix in a lawn and
garden store.

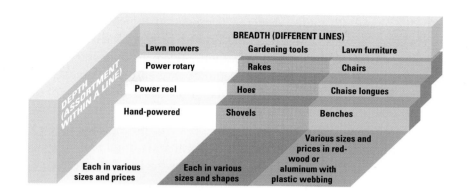

BREADTH (DIFFERENT LINES)

Lawn mowers	Gardening tools	Lawn furniture
Power rotary	Rakes	Chairs
Power reel	Hoes	Chaise longues
Hand-powered	Shovels	Benches

DEPTH (ASSORTMENT WITHIN A LINE)

Each in various sizes and prices

Each in various sizes and shapes

Various sizes and prices in redwood or aluminum with plastic webbing

product line
A broad group of
products, intended for
essentially similar uses
and possessing
reasonably similar
physical characteristics.

in different ways. Panasonic (www.panasonic.com), a company that offers a wide range of electronic products, provides a relatively uncomplicated example to demonstrate these terms. The breadth of product lines includes television, videocassette recorders, DVD players, musical keyboards, telephones, small home appliances, as well as several lines of audio components. To examine the depth of one particular product line, DVD-players for example, we would count the various models that are connected to external screens, the number of portable models offered, and then include the in-dash model for cars. For the depth of television offerings we would include Superflat™ models, HDTV-compatible digital models, and wall-mountable plasma TV models, as well as the different screen sizes available in each style.

Planned Product-Mix Strategies

Many large corporations, such as Kraft General Foods, Johnson & Johnson, Sony, and Procter & Gamble, offer a vast array of products to consumers. In service industries today, telecommunications companies such as Bell Canada and B.C. Telus and retail giants such as Sobey's and the Hudson's Bay Company offer customers many services and many ways to access them. Did these diverse assortments of products and services develop by accident? No — their existence reflects a planned strategy by the company. To be successful in marketing, producers and intermediaries need carefully planned strategies for managing their product mixes, as we'll see next.

Product Positioning

positioning
A company's strategies
and actions related to
favourably distinguishing
itself and its products
from competitors in the
minds (and hearts) of
selected groups of
consumers.

Management's ability to position a product appropriately in the market is a major determinant of company profit. As well, its ability to reposition when necessary helps to assure its long run and sustainable competitive advantage. A product's **position**, first introduced as a key part of the discussion of segmentation in Chapter 5, is the image the product projects in the minds of consumers compared with competitive products and with other products marketed by the same company.

In addition to the positioning strategies based on market segmentaion discussed in Chapter 5, marketing executives can choose from a variety of other positioning strategies in order to create the most useful meaning in the minds of consumers.[2]

POSITIONING IN RELATION TO A COMPETITOR For some products (Coca-Cola and Pepsi-Cola, for example), the best position is directly against the competition. This is a particularly effective approach if a product offering has greater features or some other differential advantage over the competition. Quebec-based Lassonde Industries Inc., makers of Oasis orange juice and Fruite beverages, have recently marketed the first available refrigerated vegetable juice. Eighty-five percent of consumers surveyed said that this product was fresher tasting, of better quality, and more practical than shelf products currently available.[3] These are important qualities to consumers of this product and are not otherwise available in the market.

One view is that underdogs should try to position themselves as the opposite, or at least much different from, established or market-dominant competitors. Canada 3000, for example, has positioned itself effectively as the low-fare alternative to full-service airlines.

POSITIONING IN RELATION TO A PRODUCT CLASS OR ATTRIBUTE Sometimes a company's positioning strategy entails associating its product with (or dissociating it from) a product class or attribute. Some firms promote their wares as being in a desirable class, such as "Made in Canada," or having an attractive attribute, such as "low energy consumption," "all natural," or "environmentally friendly."

Occasionally, a company, or a province or region can position its products based on the fact that they are manufactured in the province or country of the target market, appealing to the consumer's sense of patriotism. A survey of consumers' opinions of manufactured goods made in various countries revealed that Canadians rate their own manufactured goods more favourably than products produced in Japan, Germany, and other countries.[4] These results are good news for Canadian firms that wish to position their products on a "made in Canada" basis. It would appear that this is also effective for associative characteristics both inside and outside of Canada. Commonly referred to as the "cold north," Canada is credited with expertise in all things to do with ice from

To **optimize** crispness and **flavour, store** in refrigerator crisper **separately** from other fruits and vegetables.

For seasonal recipes, call
1-888-4BUYONT
or www.foodland.gov.on.ca

When locally grown foods are ready for market, the market should be ready for them.

APPLES

hockey to beverages — as evidenced with the success of Canadian products such as beer, ice wine, ice vodka, and bottled water made from iceberg or glacial water in various countries.[5] If a vital, or obvious benefit or feature, of the product has a favourable association with the region from which it originates this can be beneficial. Similarly oranges are marketed as being from Florida and rum from Jamaica.

The strategy of differentiating or positioning products on the basis of an attractive attribute is widely used in the food industry. Health attributes are currently very popular in differentiating products. In particular, low-fat or calcium enriched varieties of food products are being seen in increasing numbers. In some cases, the low-fat and health-food attributes are very specific and reflect current health concerns.

Warner-Lambert Co. has extended its line of Benylin cold remedies to include a naturally-sourced herbal remedy called Benylin First Defense (www.first-defense.com). It is available only in Canada, and intended to be taken at the first sign of a cold. Its ingredients include echinacea and menthol reflecting interest in the marketplace for natural, preventative alternatives. As well, Quaker Oats Co. and General Mills are introducing cereal products with soluble fibre. These products are based on the claim that soluble fibre from oatmeal, when consumed as part of a low-fat diet, can help reduce the risk of heart disease. Quaker and General Mills are positioning their cereals against breakfast products that do not provide oat bran. Low fat, as an attribute, is also showing up in traditionally high-fat areas to position these unhealthy products against more healthy ones. Häagen-Dazs Ice Cream, which established itself on the basis of its rich, high-fat products, has introduced low-fat varieties. It has recently rolled out frozen yogurt and ice-cream products that contain no more than three grams of fat per serving.[6] Low-fat products have also been showing up in fast-food chains. Their success has been minimal, however, and we are now seeing companies such as McDonald's, Taco Bell, and Kentucky Fried Chicken giving up on low-fat products. These companies are now focusing on a different attribute and are promoting products with higher levels of taste-pleasing fat![7]

Positioning is a strategy that can work for services as well as for tangible products. The Mighty Ducks of Anaheim (www.mightyducks.com) have been positioned as the "fun" team of the National Hockey League. The team's logo and colour scheme were selected with merchandising in mind and to appeal not only to hockey's traditional audience, men, but to women and children as well.[8] The Disney-owned club chose teal and purple as the team colours, and Ducks' merchandise is sold in retail stores throughout North America, including Disney stores. Such positioning with a broader range of consumers was greatly bolstered by the series of Walt Disney movies based on the hockey team.

POSITIONING IN RELATION TO A TARGET MARKET Regardless of which positioning strategy is used, the needs of the target market always must be considered. This positioning strategy doesn't suggest that the other ones ignore target markets. Rather, with this strategy, the target market — rather than another factor, such as competition — is the focal point in positioning the product.

Day-Timers Inc. (www.daytimer.com), widely known for its daily planners and organizers targeted at businesspersons, has also developed a product for the home. This was the result of a realization by the company that there was an untapped market of consumers looking for products to use for time-management in the home. The majority of this market was anticipated to be female. We all know at least one soccer mom who could use one — tooling around in their minivans most of the week full of athletic

Marketing at Work 10-1

The Power of Positioning Products and Brands For Economic Development

Continued globalization means, among other things, that in all countries there is a growing appetite for brands from somewhere else; brands that embody the country or place of origin or a locale that is exotic or admired. In developing countries, high profile brands from Western countries are often prized. The trend is also very strong in the Western world. While the marketing skills needed to successfully position a product, a brand, and a product line are generally well known in developed countries, these skills are pretty scarce in developing countries. Exporting to more economically developed countries tends to be in the form of commodities or low cost production for the owners of foreign brands. But the developing countries are sitting on a gold mine of potential products and brands that could help their growth immensely. That is the opinion of Simon Anholt, chairman of advertising agency World Writers in London, England. He feels a sense of mission to help developing countries acquire the consumer product and brand marketing skills which can raise their standards of living. "If only some of the poorer countries could emulate that process (of Western countries) to brand, finish, package and sell on to the consumer their own commodities." Then, developing countries would be emulating, say, The Netherlands or Switzerland, countries without any of their own resources but who have purchased commodities from others and added value and sold the resulting products very successfully using positioning and brand marketing.

Anholt believes that the idea of transferring marketing technology instead of money to developing countries is catching on. He debated his ideas with aid specialists and business representatives at an international advertising conference in London in mid-2000. His own agency has been sought out by a number of developing countries requesting help in creating brand images for their countries that would spur exports.

What does it take to make a product or product line successful in terms of branding and positioning? It has to be linked in a logical way to a positive image of its origins — beaches, soccer, or carnival for Brazil; the wisdom of ancient Asian philosophies and cultures for China or Asia. For example, the Indian chemicals firm Gandh Sugandh successfully exported a perfume to France, of all places. By positioning the brand at a premium price and using appropriate imagery, it worked to counter the perception that a perfume from India might be inexpensive and oddly odiferous. India also has a strong tradition of high quality technical training (as does China and Taiwan) and this could provide the foundation to position and promote high technology products. The presence of numerous citizens of China, Taiwan, and India in the Silicon Valleys of the world could also be used to position and brand products from these countries.

It wasn't too long ago that you knew nothing about Finland except, perhaps, that it had weather and climate just like Canada. Now, of course, Finland is known around the world as a hothouse of mobile and wireless communications technology and has a growing economy thanks to the Nokia brand and product line alone.

Source: Adapted, in part, from Hester Abrams, "Poorer countries need brand power: adman," *Financial Post*, April 26, 2000, p. C15.

equipment, dry-cleaning, groceries, and children on their way to some sports practice and back from music lessons! When researching the target market to design the product, the manufacturer learned that the proposed users wanted the planner to be basic, made of softer, leather-like material, with closures such as a zipper or a clasp. The product was introduced in a variety of colours, designs, and sizes, and sold at very low prices in comparison with the business products. To appeal to younger groups, the styles now offered include brighter color schemes and more generic filler sheets. To keep pace with their changing business segment, DayTimer also offers more portable models, software organizers, office accessories for the mobile office, gift products, and electronic organizers by brand name manufacturers and carrying cases. These reflect current changes in the market segment as time becomes more valuable, and as an increasingly service-based economy causes more people to work out of their cars, and spend less time in their offices.

POSITIONING BY PRICE AND QUALITY Some retail stores are known for their high-quality merchandise and high prices (Harry Rosen, Holt Renfrew). Positioned at the other end of the price and quality scale are discount stores such as Wal-Mart and Zellers. This doesn't mean such retailers position themselves as lacking quality, but rather that value and low-price is stressed.

In the hotel industry, positioning by price and quality is common, particularly when it separates products in the high-end range from those in the middle or lower-end of the market. The Four Seasons Hotel chain (www.fourseasons.com) in Canada and elsewhere is well known for its high standards in rooms and services. Luxurious furnishings and guest courtesies clearly differentiate this chain from others that target a lower-paying clientele. The Comfort chain of hotels and inns (www.comfortinns.com or www.choice-hotels.com), on the other hand, has positioned itself as offering clean, comfortable rooms and economical prices. So clean, in fact, that their Econolodge roadside lodges offer Mr. Clean® certified rooms bearing the seal of approval of the number one lemon-fresh cleaner. They have gone further to position by segment by developing senior-friendly lodgings for their roadside chains, while focusing toward the business traveller at city-centre chains.

Product-Mix Expansion

Product-mix expansion is accomplished by increasing the depth within a particular line and/or the number of lines a firm offers to consumers. Let's look at these options.

When a company adds a similar item to an existing product line with the same brand name, this is termed a **line extension**. For examples, pull the coupons out of your local newspaper or take a look at coupons that appear in your mailbox. You will probably see lots of examples of new products that are really line extensions. Dove soap, a product of the Lever Brothers Co., offers Dove Cares and Dove Skin Care products in addition to Dove bar soap. Dove added a liquid bath wash to its product mix and markets it with the Dove body puff. Procter & Gamble, which manufactures Pringles potato chips, has introduced fat-reduced and pizza-licious flavour products as extensions to its existing chip line. Crest (www.crest.com) toothpaste, a Procter & Gamble brand, has released Crest MultiCare, a toothpaste with special foaming action that is designed to deliver tartar protection in places that are hard to reach.[9] Saturn (www.saturncanada.com) recently added a new higher-end model to their value-oriented product line. What was previously one model — the SL — offered in coupe, wagon and sedan styles has been joined by the roomier, more generously appointed L-series (the L is for larger — Saturn likes to keep things simple).

The line-extension strategy is also used by organizations in services fields. For example, universities offer programs to appeal to prospective older students, as well as shorter-term diploma programs. Municipalities are running garbage programs to collect types of recyclables. Some group medical practices and some hospitals have added nutrition counselling clinics and forms of exercise counselling to their product lines, acknowledging that an important part of their role is to keep people well. Eye doctors will often offer other optical services such as glass and contact fittings through providing a retail outlet for sales. In recent years Canadian banks have continually offered greater services through telephone and Internet banking, trust services, insurance, etc. GMAC, the finance arm of General Motors took over the Better Homes & Gardens real estate network (www.gmacrealestate.com) in 2000 branding it with their own name and using a modified version of the BH&G's exist-

line extension

One form of product-mix expansion in which a company adds a similar item to an existing product line with the same brand name.

ing logo. ServiceMASTER (www.servicemaster.com), once known for commercial property maintenance also offers home cleaning and lawn maintenance services.

There are many reasons for line extensions. The main one is that the firm wants to appeal to more market segments by offering a wider range of choices for a particular product. Another reason is that companies want to take advantage of the considerable value that resides in their established brands. There is often a much lower risk involved in introducing a new product as an extension to an existing line under a recognized brand than there would be to launch a completely separate line with a new brand name. A successful brand name can possess a great deal of "equity," or value in the marketplace. Such a name on a new product gives it greater credibility and possibly quicker acceptance. Marketers have found that line extensions have a greater chance of success than a totally new brand. To increase the success rate of new-product introductions, a line-extension strategy is a very obvious part of the marketing program of many companies.

There are risks however, as can be seen with the extreme example of Gucci (www.gucci.com), which — at the time of its bankruptcy — had over twelve thousand licensed items carrying its name. Gucci allowed its name to be slapped on everything from leather goods to food. Consumers no longer understood what the brand stood for in its upscale market.[10]

Another way to expand the product mix, referred to as **mix extension**, is to add a new product line to the company's present assortment. To illustrate, when Johnson & Johnson (www.johnsonandjohnson.com) introduced a line of Acuvue disposable contact lenses, that was mix extension because it added another product to the company's product mix. This was the first contact lens offered by the company. In contrast, line extension adds more items within the same product line. When J&J, the makers of Tylenol pain relievers, produces additional versions of this line or any other brand of pain reliever, that was line extension.

Under a mix-extension strategy, the new line may be related or unrelated to current products. Furthermore, it may carry one of the company's existing brand names or may be given an entirely new name. Here are examples of these four alternatives:

◆ *Related product, same brand*: To allow their customers to enjoy their favourite cup of coffee at home, Tim Hortons added canned ground coffee and then introduced a line of Tim Hortons coffee makers that customers could buy to take home. Kimberley-Clark added Kleenex toilet tissue to its long-established line of facial tissues. Nestlé, added the Quik chocolate bar, and Crest added MultiClean toothbrushes to its toothpaste products. Sony, known for its electronic innovation, joined established video game providers with its PlayStation. Roots began with leather products — then into all sorts of other casual clothing.

◆ *Unrelated product, same brand*: Forschner Group, Inc., maker of the Original Swiss Army Knives, extended its mix by adding Swiss Army watches and sunglasses; and Swatch (www.swatch.com), the Swiss watch company, added a clothing line and then announced an even more, unlikely mix extension — small cars![11] 3M, the maker of Scotch Tape and other adhesive and abrasive products, expanded into audio and video tapes and then to computer discs, Scotch-Brite soap pads that never rust, and the famous Post-It notes. Here, in Canada Club Monaco (www.clubmonaco.com) has expanded its stores to carry a line of home goods, and Roots Inc. (www.roots.com) has gone on to put their logo on everything from watches, home furnishings, to a

B.C. getaway resort. Nike (www.nike.com), makers of, well, everything these days, has recently begun producing snowboards. While all Nike products emphasize the notion of being sports-related — there is no inherent connection between producing wicked sneakers and fast boards.

◆ *Unrelated product, different brand*: This reflects a diversification strategy, such as when a company adds a new division in a different field. This strategy was very popular in the early 1990s. Many companies today are more likely to eliminate unrelated product lines. Pepsi-Cola, for example, amassed a number of diversified companies such as Pizza Hut and KFC. Recently it has announced its intention to spin-off these fast-food outlets.[12]

◆ *Related product, different brand*: Procter & Gamble introduced Luvs as a companion to its Pampers disposable diapers. Southam Inc. has entered the information age through the development of a general purpose Internet portal named Canada.com (www.canada.com). Aside from the wide variety of services previously mentioned in Chapter 1, the *National Post's* news features originate from the newspaper which also maintains its own Internet site (www.nationalpost.com). Black & Decker produces a line of professional/industrial tools under the DeWalt brand, while Panasonic produces some of its audio equipment under the Technics brand.

Most often, the new line is related to the existing product mix because the company wants to capitalize on its expertise and experience. For example, IKEA, which has been known for offering reasonably priced, medium-quality Scandinavian home furnishings, has expanded into a line of office furniture.[13] Thomson Minwax Ltd., of Richmond Hill, Ontario, is expanding beyond its line of wood stains and producing a new line of decorative paints. The Home Decor line includes bright colours, faux finishes, and blocking patterns.[14] In both cases, the new lines benefit from consumers' familiarity with and good feeling toward the brand. We'll consider this approach in more detail when we discuss brand equity in the next chapter.

Trading Up and Trading Down

The product strategies of trading up and trading down involve a change in product positioning and an expansion of product line. **Trading up** means adding a higher-priced product to a line to attract a broader market. Also, the seller intends that the new product's prestige will help the sale of its existing lower-priced products.

Consider some examples of trading up. Facing stiff competition in the middle-price market, Holiday Inns introduced the higher-price Crowne Plaza Hotels, with nicer surroundings and more amenities. To its line of inexpensive casual watches, Swatch (www.swatch.com) added the higher-priced Chrono stopwatch and other upgraded watches as well as the SwatchTalk, the first watch with integrated cell phone. Pet-food manufacturers have traded up to "superpremium" lines, as illustrated by Kal Kan's Pedigree and Quaker Oats' King Kuts. Even home-improvement retailers, such as Home Depot, are now offering more high-end products, such as $39,500 chandeliers.[15]

A company is said to be **trading down** when it adds a lower-priced item to its line of prestige products. The company expects that people who cannot afford the original product will want to buy the new one because it carries some of the status of the higher-priced product. In line with this strategy, major manufacturers of 35 mm single-lens

trading up
A product-line strategy wherein a company adds a higher-priced, prestige product to its line in order to increase sales of the existing lower-priced products in that line and attract a higher-income market.

trading down
A product-line strategy wherein a company adds a lower-priced item to its line of prestige goods in order to reach a market that cannot afford the higher-priced items.

reflex (SLR) cameras, such as Pentax, Canon, and Minolta, have introduced smaller, simplified cameras for photography buffs who want to be seen to be using the major brands but who do not want to be bothered with the intricacies of 35 mm photography. Mont Blanc (www.montblanc.com), the West German manufacturer of the "world's most famous fountain pen," introduced a lower-priced ballpoint pen, thereby allowing its purchasers to own a Mont Blanc without having to pay more than $300 for the top-of-the-line fountain pen. Toronto-based Holt Renfrew (www.holtrenfrew.com) continues to carry the highest high-end designers in Canada but they are also greatly expanding their popular private-label clothing line. The quality line of products is not inexpensive but reflects value through its pricing. A Prada suit carried by the store may cost over $4,000 while the Holt Renfrew equivalent would retail at about $700.[16]

Sometimes the effect of trading down can be achieved through advertising, without introducing new, lower-priced products. A manufacturer might accomplish this by advertising some of the lower-priced items in its existing product lines. They are going down-market by placing increased marketing emphasis on the lower-priced products.

Trading up and trading down are risky strategies because the new products may confuse buyers, resulting in negligible net gain. It is equally undesirable if sales of the new item or line are generated at the expense of the established products. When trading down, the new offering may permanently hurt the firm's reputation and that of its established high-quality product. To reduce this possibility, new lower-priced products may be given different brand names to distinguish them from the established brands. Hewlett Packard (www.hp.com) produces a lower-priced line of computer printers under the Apollo name (www.myapollo.com), while The Gap, Inc. (www.gap.com) chose Old Navy Clothing Co. (www.oldnavy.com) for its lower-price outlets.[17]

In trading up, on the other hand, the problem depends on whether the new product or line carries the established brand name or is given a new name. If the same brand name is used, the firm must change its image enough so that new customers will accept the higher-priced product. At the same time, the seller does not want to lose its present customers. The new offering may present a cloudy image, not attracting new customers but driving away existing customers. If a different brand name is used, the company must create awareness for it and then stimulate consumers to buy the new product. This latter strategy means that the company will not be able to trade on the reputation of its existing brand.

An exception to this appears to have occurred in the automotive industry. Luxury performance cars had never come from Japan — they were supposed to be German. And they certainly couldn't be produced by Honda, Toyota, or Nissan — long famous for economy-minded products. Hence, the creation of the Acura, Lexus, and Infiniti lines of cars. Costing up to $100,000 for the Acura NSXT (www.acura.ca), lines such as Acura and Infiniti have benefited from an association with their parentage long known for high-quality products. Marketing efforts however did not emphasize the relationship between these product lines.

Alteration of Existing Products

As an alternative to developing a completely new product, management should take a fresh look at the organization's existing products. Often, improving an established product — **product alteration** — can be more profitable and less risky than developing a completely new one. The substitution of NutraSweet (www.nutrasweet.com) for saccharin in diet soft drinks increased sales of those drinks by improving flavour and reducing health-related concerns about the old additive. However, product alteration is not without risks. When Coca-Cola modified the formula for its leading product and changed its name to New Coke, sales suffered so much that the old formula had to be brought back three months later under the Coca-Cola Classic name.

For some products, redesigning is the key to their relaunching or repositioning. Many companies frequently redesign or reformulate their products to give them a fresh appeal. In recent years, disposable diapers have been redesigned to be less bulky and are now available in separate styles for girls and boys. Sometimes the redesign might simply involve the addition of a new flavour, in which case the product becomes more of a line extension, as when General Mills launched Apple Cinnamon Cheerios. Another example involves changing the shape or basic look of the product. This occurred when Hostess Frito-Lay introduced its new "flat" potato chip.

Who remembers Legos? Those bright, primary-coloured building blocks whose potential combinations were limited only by your imagination. Well, the popularity of Legos in North America has slipped as children have become increasingly seduced by the joys of the electronic age, wanting instant gratification and the latest and greatest in technology. Lego (www.lego.com) has had to adapt beyond its basic construction toy and concede to children's changing interests and shrinking attention spans. A new product line, Mindstorms, was developed to combine high-tech gadgetry with traditional Lego architecture allowing children to dream up moving and speaking creations.[18] Looking ahead to 2005, the company intends to have the powerful brand among families with children. Several specialty lines have also been evolved out of the traditional pieces and primary colours including a series of Star Wars structures and vehicles based upon the latest movie.

As a variation of this strategy, developing new uses for the existing product can be part of the relaunch and repositioning — Eagle Brand Sweetened Condensed Milk — redesigned the labelling and promoted use in mocha and other specialty coffees, five-minute fondues, no-bake bars, and as an after school beverage.[19]

Alternatively, especially for consumer products, its only the packaging that is altered. Kraft Canada Inc. relaunched its Honey-Toasted Shredded Wheat cereal with new packaging and a multimedia ad campaign. The line extension to Shredded Wheat debuted a year earlier, but sales quickly tailed off as it became lost in a sea of other cereals with yellow packaging.[20] Made to look like a bee, the packaging communicates the flavour while creating a striking image when stacked together on the store shelf.

This strategy can also be employed to gain a competitive advantage, as when Tylenol introduced its products in red-cap bottles with ridges for ease of opening or when Evian redesigned its bottle with mountain ridges to improve its ability to be crushed for recycling. Kraft, Black Diamond, and other manufacturers of cheese products are now offering their sliced and shredded cheeses in packages that reseal by using zipper-like closures. Thus, packaging can be altered to enhance appearance or to improve the product's usability. Shredded and single slice cheese products offer the benefits of convenience and time-saving, while resealable packages offer this as well as ensuring product freshness and reduced spoilage.

Product-Mix Contraction

Another product strategy, **product-mix contraction**, is carried out either by eliminating an entire line or by simplifying the assortment within a line. Thinner and/or shorter product lines or mixes can weed out low-profit and unprofitable products. The intended

Marketing at Work 10-2

Positioning by Cutting and Pasting: Unilever's Profit Pursuit

Unilever PLC, the Dutch based consumer goods giant, seems to be benchmarking Procter & Gamble with respect to profitability in global consumer goods markets. P & G's profitability has increased in each of the last five years; its operating margins are 16.4 percent; it is experiencing an 11 percent quarterly profit growth in 2000. Unilever has had fluctuating profitability; an operating margin of 11.1 percent — a new 15 percent target has been set; net income increases of around 2 percent.

To imrove its performance, Unilever announced a five year program of cutting. The workforce is to be reduced by 25,000 — 10 percent; one hundred factories will be closing; there will be a new focus on the best selling brands like Dove soap and Lipton tea. In the future, Unilever will concentrate its efforts on 400 key brands out of a line-up of 1,600 in numerous product categories. The company will invest over one billion pounds (currently about Cdn.$2.40 to the pound) to support key brands over the next five years. Those brands not meeting new performance standards will fall away in due course. This will result in a simplifying of product lines and making the supply chain more cost efficient. The Elizabeth Arden division with all its brands and lines is targeted for restructuring as is the European baking business.

While it is cutting product lines and brands that it has marketed in the past, Unilever is also adding products and brands that meet its new performance standards. The company acquired Ben & Jerry's Homemade Inc. with its rich ice cream lines and Slim Fast Foods Co., at the other end of the dietary-nutrition market. It has been attempting other acquisitions such as Bestfoods, the producer of Knorr Soups, Hellmann's mayonnaise, and Skippy Peanut Butter.

Unilever Canada expect to experience layoffs and plant closures over the next five years as product lines and brands are eliminated in the Canadian market. It currently has three thousand employees and twenty plants spread across the country.

Source: Adapted from Glen Hall, "25,000 jobs to go in Unilever's pursuit of higher profits," *Financial Post*, February 23, 2000, p. C11, and Nikhil Deogun, "Bestfoods board rebuffs $18-billion bid by Unilever," *The Globe and Mail*, May 3, 2000, p. B10.

result of product-mix contraction is higher profits from fewer products. General Mills decided to concentrate on its food business and, consequently, sold its interest in Izod (the "alligator" apparel maker) and its lines of children's toys and games. In services fields, some travel agencies have shifted from selling all modes of travel to concentrate on cruises only or specialized tours and trips to exotic places.

During the 1990s, most companies expanded — rather than contracted — their product mixes. Numerous line extensions document this trend. As firms find that they have an unmanageable number of products or that various items or lines are unprofitable, or both, product-mix pruning is occurring. As a result, many organizations now have fewer product lines, and those that remain are often thinner. This has happened with many well-known firms such as Proctor & Gamble and Unilever PLC. Unilever decided to prune more than 1,000 brands from its total of about 1,600. The company will concentrate its marketing resources on the approximately 400 remaining brands that generate almost 90 percent of annual revenues.[21]

The Product Life Cycle

As we saw in Chapter 9, a product's life cycle can have a direct bearing on a company's survival. The life cycle of a product consists of four stages: introduction, growth, maturity, and decline. The concept of product life applies to a generic category of product (microwave ovens, for example). The category can consist of a number of product lines — high powered and fully featured, medium powered with standard featues or low powered with basic features. The category thus consists of all brands of all lines being offered

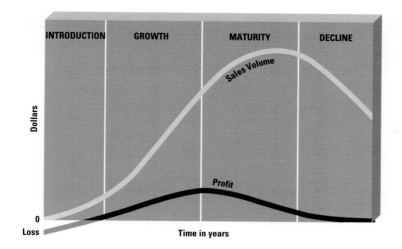

FIGURE 10-2

Typical Life Cycle of a Product Category
During the introduction stage of a life cycle, a product category — and virtually all brands within it — are unprofitable. Profits are healthy during the growth stage, but then start to decline while a product's sales volume is still increasing.

product life cycle
The stages a product goes through from its introduction, to its growth and maturity, to its eventual decline and death (withdrawal from the market or deletion from the company's offerings).

by competitors and not to specific brands (such as Sony or Braun). A **product life cycle** consists of the aggregate demand over an extended period of time for all brands making up a generic product category.

A life cycle can be graphed by plotting aggregate sales volume for a generic product category over time, usually years. It is also worthwhile to accompany the sales-volume curve with the corresponding profit curve for the product category, as shown in Figure 10-2. After all, we are interested ultimately in profitability, not just sales.

The shapes of these two curves vary from one product category to another. Still, for most categories, the basic shapes and the relationship between the sales and the profit curves are as illustrated in Figure 10-2. In this typical life cycle, the profit curve for most new products is negative (signifying a loss) through much of the introductory stage.

In the latter part of the growth stage, the profit curve starts to decline while sales volume is still rising. Profits decline because the companies in an industry usually must increase their advertising and selling efforts or cut their prices (or both) to sustain sales growth in the face of intensifying competition during the maturity stage. The length of time it takes a product to reach maturity varies considerably, depending on the nature of the product. Some products remain in the maturity stage much longer than others. Electronic equipment, such as computers, have a very short maturity stage. Continuous new developments in technology cause the life cycle of these products to be quite short.

Introducing a new product at the proper time will help maintain a company's desired level of profit. Building on its original product lines, Kraft (www.kraft.com) is constantly extending product life cycles with innovations. Macaroni and cheese is a good example of a product that has been sustained in this way. Over the past fifteen years, the company has introduced spiral pasta, pasta shaped like cartoon characters, and different flavours of cheese. These products have all sold at premium prices.[22] This has also been achieved with its Lunchables and Handi-Snacks products by introducing new varieties and flavour combinations. The Gillete Company (www.gillette.com) has had to constantly evolve to compete against the disposable variety of razors in the wet-shave market. The Sensor featured independently suspended blades and consumers were willing to pay a little more for the superior shave it provided. Trading up again, Gillette produced the triple-blade Mach3, which is considerably more expensive.[23] The product has enjoyed some success, however heavy advertising has had to be employed to convince consumers of the worth of the expensive replacement blades.

TABLE 10-1	Characteristics and Implications of Different Product Life-Cycle Stages			
Each stage of a product's life cycle has different characteristics; as a result, marketing must be modified over the course of the cycle.				
	Stage			
	Introduction	**Growth**	**Maturity**	**Decline**
Characteristics				
Customers	Innovators	Mass market	Mass market	Loyal customers
Competition	Little, if any	Increasing	Intense	Decreasing
Sales	Low levels, then rising	Rapid growth	Slow/no annual growth	Declining
Profits	None	Strong, then at a peak	Declining annually	Low/none
Marketing Implications				
Overall strategy	Market development	Market penetration	Defensive positioning	Efficiency or exit
Costs	High per unit	Declining	Stable or increasing	Low
Product strategy	Undifferentiated	Improved Items	Differentiated	Pruned line
Pricing strategy	Most likely high	Lower over time	Lowest	Increasing
Distribution strategy	Scattered	Intensive	Intensive	Selective
Promotion strategy	Category awareness	Brand preference	Brand loyalty	Reinforcement

Source: Adapted from material provided by Professor David Appel, University of Notre Dame, Notre Dame, IN.

Intel Corp. (www.intel.com) has sought a measure of control over the product life cycle of microprocessors and their prices by introducing new generations only two or three years apart. They did this even though demand was still growing for the current versions. In recent years, however, Intel has had to rely more on price cuts of existing lines than on new product introductions in order to maintain its share of the market for microprocessors used in personal computers.[24]

The product life cycle concept has been criticized as lacking empirical support and being too general to be useful in specific cases.[25] Although the concept is not perfect and must be adapted to fit different circumstances, this model is both straightforward and powerful. A company's marketing success can be affected considerably by its ability to determine and adapt to the life cycles for each of its product categories. Technology has had a sizable, and sometimes unpredictable, impact on traditional cycle predictions. The availability of information in this stage has often accelerated the adoption process while advancements in technology have quickened the cycle's pace or stopped a product in mid-cycle as it becomes prematurely outdated or obsolete.

Characteristics of Each Stage

Management must be able to recognize what part of the life cycle its product is in at any given time. The competitive environment and marketing strategies that should be used ordinarily depend on the particular life cycle stage. Table 10-1 contains a synopsis of all four stages. Each stage is highlighted below.

introduction stage
The first part of a product life cycle, during which a generic product category is launched into the market in a full-scale marketing program.

INTRODUCTION During the **introduction stage**, a product is launched into the market in a full-scale marketing program. It has gone through product development, including idea screening, prototype, and market tests. The entire product may be new, such as a substitute for fat in prepared foods. Or it may be well known but have significant new features that, in effect, create a new product category — fax machines and cordless phones are examples.

Marketing at Work 10-3

Who Will Fly High? Who Will Crash and Burn? — The Big E-commerce Question

If what we say about the introductory stage of the product life cycle has any real meaning, we should be seeing not only lots of innovation in products and services but also, lots of failures. Why?? The real test for all the innovations that reach the market is a simple one: do enough buyers — businesses or consumers — as opposed to innovators and investors, care enough? They have to so that the new venture becomes profitable and moves from the introductory stage to the growth stage.

Are the fire bells ringing? They can be heard in some places. Some lawyers who specialize in bankruptcy and receivership in New York and Toronto (although Canada is seen as eighteen months behind the U.S. in Internet business development), report an increase in business from dot.com startups. Stock markets hiccup when it comes to providing investment capital. In the marketing world, some advertising agencies and media buyers with high-tech sector clients worry about whether or not the cheque is really in the mail or will really arrive at all. Pattulo Integrated Inc., the well-known Toronto advertising agency, has some remuneration agreements with clients that include stock options as well as cash payment. Other advertising agencies are reported to have asked their advertising agencies to accept stock in lieu of cash. Fresh Advertising of Toronto, which launched the portal Yahoo! in Canada and has such clients as Holtrenfrew.com, Quicken.ca and Bid.com, believes that the riskiest clients are pure business to consumer Web site companies that rely exclusively on advertising revenues. The preferred model is an e-commerce business that relies on a revenue mix with funds coming in from product sales, advertising on their Web site and the sale of their backroom technologies.

Even some of the bestknown e-commerce names are being looked at skeptically. Amazon.com, which actually has made money selling books after years of losses, diversified from books by adding music, videotapes, toys, cookware, and other products and services. The diversification means profits continue to fade into the future and the expectation is that costly diversification will have to be reversed to gain long-run profitability. The Amazon of Canada, Chapters Online, has good book sales but very good losses. Chapters Inc. was a dominant bookseller in Canada before it added its online business. Chapter Online has also diversified from books into video games, electronics, plants, and gardening clothing and accessories. Some analysts believe that the most successful pure online marketing organizations will be those who concentrate on anything that can be digitized, anything that is low touch — does not require "hands of assessment" — or anything that can be delivered very quickly. Most others can succeed only if they are really an extension of a focused "bricks and mortar" business.

Finally, there remains the question of which e-commerce models work in which countries. Approaches pioneered in the U.S., in a very large market, may not really work in Canada where the market is one-tenth the size and widely geographically distributed. Then again, things do change! And very quickly!!

Source: Adapted, in part, from Patrick Allossery, "Check those dot.com cheques," *Financial Post*, April 10, 2000, p. C5; Robert Reguly, "Shareholders closed the book on Chapters Online long ago," *Financial Post*, April 15, 2000, p. B9; *The Economist*, Online Edition, Survey of E-commerce, "Define and Sell," February 26, 2000.

This introductory (sometimes called pioneering) stage is the most risky and expensive one, because substantial amounts of money must be spent in seeking consumer acceptance of the product. But many products are not accepted by a sufficient number of consumers and fail at this stage. For really new products, there is very little direct competition. Thus the promotional program is designed to stimulate demand for the entire product category rather than only the seller's brand.

growth stage
The second part of a product life cycle, during which the sales and profits of a generic product category rise and competitors enter the market, after which profits start to decline near the end of this part of the cycle.

GROWTH   In the **growth stage**, or market-acceptance stage, sales and profits rise, often at a rapid rate. Competitors enter the market, often in large numbers if the profit outlook is particularly attractive. Mostly as a result of competition, profits start to decline near the end of the growth stage. Appropriate marketing strategies for this stage, as well as the other three, are summarized in Table 10-1.

maturity stage
The third part of a product life cycle, during which the sales of a generic product category continue to increase (but at a decreasing rate), profits decline largely due to price competition, and some firms leave the market.

decline stage
The fourth, and final, part of a product life cycle, during which the sales of a generic product category drop and most competitors abandon the market.

MATURITY During the first part of the **maturity stage**, sales continue to increase, but at a decreasing rate. When sales level off, profits of both producers and intermediaries decline. The primary reason: intense price competition. Seeking to differentiate themselves, some firms extend their product lines with new models. During the latter part of this stage, marginal producers, those with high costs or without a differential advantage, are forced to drop out of the market. They do so because they lack sufficient customers and/or profits.

DECLINE For most products, a **decline stage**, as gauged by sales volume for the total category, is inevitable for one of the following reasons:

◆ The need for the product disappears, as when frozen orange juice generally eliminated the market for juice squeezers.

◆ A better or less expensive product is developed to fill the same need. CDs have replaced tapes and vinyl records because the sound, durability, and storage capability of the new product is far superior to that of the old product. CDs require CD players, which have, for the most part, replaced tape machines and turntables.

◆ People simply grow tired of a product (a clothing style, for instance), so it disappears from the market.

Seeing little opportunity for revitalized sales or profits, most competitors abandon the market during this stage. However, a few firms may be able to develop a small market niche and remain moderately successful in the decline stage. Some manufacturers of wood-burning stoves have been able to do this. Whether a product at this stage has to be abandoned or can be continued on a profitable basis often depends on the skills and creativity of the marketing manager responsible for the product.

Length of Product Life Cycle

The total length of the life cycle — from start of the introduction stage to the end of the decline stage — varies across product categories. It ranges from weeks or a short season (for a clothing fashion) to many decades (for autos or telephones). And it varies because of differences in the length of individual stages from one product category to the next. Furthermore, although Figure 10-2 suggests that all four life cycle stages cover nearly equal periods of time, the stages in any given product's life cycle usually last for different periods. Three variations on the typical life cycle are shown in Figure 10-3:

FIGURE 10-3
Product Life Cycle Variations

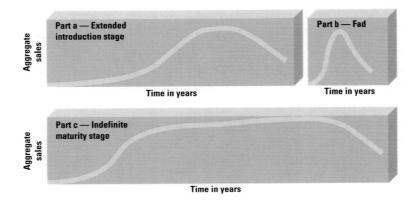

◆ In one, the product gains widespread consumer acceptance only after an extended introductory period (See Part a). The hand-held computer is an example of a current product that, for this category, has experienced a long introductory period. Companies such as Apple, Sony, and AT&T have introduced versions of this product to limited success. Recently 3Com, Compaq, Hewlett-Packard, and Philips, among others, have tried again to interest the market in paper-sized "personal digital assistants." The HP545 pocket PC is full-colour, windows-powered, enabling users to review Word and Excel documents, receive e-mail, and enjoy digital music and electronic books. It remains to be seen whether these new multi-functional versions will reach the full market potential these companies anticipate.[26]

◆ In another variation, the entire life cycle begins and ends in a relatively short period of time (Part b). This variation depicts the life cycle for a **fad**, a product or style that becomes immensely popular nearly overnight and then falls out of favour with consumers almost as quickly. Children's toys often fall into this category. Cabbage Patch dolls were immensely popular in the 1980s, in the 90s we had Elmo and Furbies, and we "evolved" into a new century with several hundred Pokemon characters. How long does it last? How can you predict it? Is it fad or trend? With childrens' toys who can tell!

Distinguishing between fad and trend, however, is crucial. Such a distinction will determine effective marketing strategies and budgeting. Marketers that can distinguish between the two in any industry have a strong competitive edge.[27]

◆ In a third variation, the product's mature stage lasts almost indefinitely (Part c). This life cycle is illustrated by canned, carbonated soft drinks and also by the automobile with a gasoline-powered, internal-combustion engine. Other forms, such as electric, hybrid, and solar-powered cars, have been proposed, but the automobile as we know it remains dominant. The Ballard engine, previously discussed, demonstrates just how much time can be involved.

Setting aside fads, which represent a special case, product life cycles are getting shorter generally. If competitors can quickly introduce a "me too" version of a popular product, it may move swiftly into the maturity stage. Or rapid changes in technology can make a product obsolete virtually overnight. Some said that would occur in the audio field, with digital audio tapes replacing compact discs (CDs), but that didn't happen. The latest forecast is that even newer formats, notably Super Audio CDs and DVD-Audio, will turn the CD into a dinosaur.[28]

Life Cycle Is Related to a Market
When we say that a product is in a specific stage of its life cycle, implicitly we are referring to a specific market. A product may be well accepted (growth or maturity stage) in some markets but still be striving for acceptance in other markets. At the time Ortho Pharmaceuticals (www.orthomcneil.com) introduced Retin-A as a treatment for acne, existing products already served this purpose. Thus the acne-treatment category probably was in the maturity stage. However, then it was discovered that Retin-A might be effective in reducing facial wrinkles. In effect, it created a new product category. Hence, Retin-A fit into both the acne-treatment category that was in the maturity stage among teenagers and into the wrinkle-remover category that was in the introductory or perhaps early-growth stage among the middle-aged.

Life Cycle Management

To a surprising extent, the shape of the sales and profit curves for a product category can be controlled. The collective actions of firms offering competing products in the same category shape the curves. But even single companies can have an impact. A giant firm may be able to shorten the introductory stage by broadening the distribution or increasing the promotional effort supporting the new product.

Most firms, however, cannot substantially affect the sales and profit curves for a product category. Thus their task is to determine how best to achieve success with their own brands within the life cycle for an entire product category. For an individual firm, successful life cycle management depends on (1) predicting the shape of the proposed product's cycle even before it is introduced and (2) successfully adapting marketing strategies at each stage of the life cycle.

ENTRY STRATEGIES   A firm entering a new market must decide whether to plunge in during the introductory stage. Or it can wait and make its entry during the early part of the growth stage, after innovating companies have proven there is a viable market.

The strategy of entering during the introductory stage is prompted by the desire to build a dominant market position right away and thus lessen the interest of potential competitors and the effectiveness of actual competitors. This strategy worked for Sony with the Walkman; Perrier (www.perrier.com) with bottled sparkling water; and Nike with running shoes. Time will tell whether or not this strategy works for Chapters Online and Amazon.com. Evidently, there is benefit to getting a head start in marketing a new type of product. The hurdles may be insurmountable when you enter with a "me too" product or service and try to play catch-up — to grow market share against an entrenched competitor.

However, delaying entry until the market is proven can sometimes pay off. Pioneering requires a large investment, and the risks are great — as demonstrated by the high failure rate among new products. Large companies with the marketing resources to overwhelm smaller innovating firms are most likely to be successful with a delayed-entry strategy. In one such case, Coca-Cola introduced Tab and Diet Coke, and Pepsi-Cola introduced Diet Pepsi — and the two giants surpassed Diet Rite Cola, an early pioneer. It is expected that the owners of strong consumer brands will be quite successful by embarking on e-commerce strategies when more is understood about how consumers respond to different styles of online marketing.

It's not clear-cut which is the better entry strategy. Each has its advantages and disadvantages, its successes and failures. As with nearly all marketing decisions, sound managerial judgment is critical.[29]

MANAGING ON THE RISE   When sales are growing strongly and profits are robust in a product category, you might think a marketing manager has little to do except tally up an anticipated bonus. Unfortunately, that's not the case. During the growth stage of the life cycle, a company has to devise the right strategies for its brand(s) and Web sites in that product category. Promotion that will cause consumers to desire the company's brand of product must be considered. Distribution must be expanded and made more efficient and rapid. And product improvements must be considered. Decisions made during the growth stage influence (a) how many competitors enter the market and (b) how well the company's brand does within a product category both in the near and distant future.

Home video games were introduced in the 1970s, but the more captivating (and perhaps addictive) Nintendo brand, in effect, created a new product category in the 1980s. As the 1990s began, this product appeared to be in the growth stage of its life cycle. However, in the mid-1990s, video games stagnated. To stimulate sales Nintendo as well as competitors Sega and Sony have been engaged in a game of "technological leap frog." The game players are in a constant struggle to gain some sort of differential advantage, even if it's only temporary, by increasing the video, audio, or graphics capabilities of their systems. At the same time they are trying to control prices.[30]

MANAGING DURING MATURITY Various strategies may be effective in maintaining or boosting sales of a product during the maturity stage of its life cycle. Of course, what works magnificently for one product may perform dismally for another. Common strategies during maturity include modifying the product, designing new promotion, and devising new uses for the product. Campbell's Soups recently celebrated its one-hundredth birthday and used this event as an opportunity to redesign its labels, thus giving a more mature look to the product.[31] Such steps may lead to added purchases by present customers and/or may attract new customers. As sales in the North American cruise industry flattened out, some cruise lines modified their services by adding fitness programs and offering special theme cruises (sometimes in conjunction with a professional sports team or celebrity entertainers).

Playskool, a division of Hasbro Canada Inc. of Longueuil, Quebec, has modified its mature product line of children's toys, equipment, and furniture. To make the products more competitive, the company has added an antibacterial agent to the plastic in the manufacturing stage.[32] Another example is CIGNA Life Insurance Company of Canada, which is marketing the Women's Health and Hope Plan. This plan provides financial aid to women diagnosed with a female-specific cancer, heart attack, stroke, or coronary artery surgery. This new twist on disability insurance is created to adapt an aging product line to a society of women with family responsibilities.[33] This recognizes the role of females as earners and heads of family units.

SURVIVING THE DECLINE STAGE Perhaps it is in the decline stage that a company finds its greatest challenges in life cycle management. For instance, the advent of video camcorders and film-less cameras may hint at the decline of photographic film as a product category. Kodak Canada is trying to prevent the decline of this product while keeping pace with competitors in examining bold new products. With one such product, which Kodak calls Photo CD, consumers take pictures as they normally have; the big difference comes at the time of film processing, when the prints can be stored on a compact disc. Then they can be shown on a TV, if you have a videodisc player! Kodak is also extending the life of the traditional film product by maintaining an aggressive research and development process to improve the overall performance of each roll. Film recently released offers improved colour accuracy, saturation, detail, and sharpness. A new product designed especially for "zoom" cameras improves light sensitivity and eliminates photographic problems with light reduction. Also the Advantix films, for use with Kodak Advantix cameras offer the ability to have pictures developed in three different sizes. The accompanying picture negatives show what would be developed with each size option should you wish a reprint. Kodak PhotoNet Online offers online processing allowing users to download their pictures once they are notified via e-mail that they are ready.[34]

Advantix cameras offer the latest in technology, come in a wide price range, and offer the greatest ease of operation. Along with the Advantix film system, this has been a very successful launch of a "traditional" product in a technologically evolving arena. Kodak does, however, also offer digital cameras.

When sales are declining, management has the following alternatives:

◆ Ensure that marketing and production programs are as efficient as possible.

◆ Prune unprofitable sizes and models. Frequently this tactic will decrease sales but increase profits.

◆ "Run out" the product; that is, cut all costs to the bare minimum to maximize profitability over the limited remaining life of the product.

◆ Best (and toughest) of all, improve the product in a functional sense, or revitalize it in some manner. Publishers of printed dictionaries may have attempted to do this. Other reference materials, including dictionaries available on personal computers and online encyclopedias, seemed to have pushed such traditional reference materials into — or at least toward — decline. However, some publishers are working hard to maintain the appeal of the dictionary. St. Martin's Press has introduced a dictionary that includes workplace slang, five thousand biographical references, geographical and cultural notes, and over four thousand illustrations. A collaboration with Microsoft, the Encarta World English Dictionary (www.worldenglishdictionary.com) is available on CD-ROM and in the traditional printed format.[35]

If one of these alternatives doesn't work, management will have to consider **product abandonment**. The expense of carrying profitless products goes beyond what shows up on financial statements. For example, there is a very real cost to the managerial time and effort that is diverted to terminally ill products. Management often is reluctant to discard a product, however, partly because it is easy to become attached to the product over the years. John Fluke Manufacturing began in 1928 as a provider of traditional testing and measurement devices for manufacturers. As manufacturing became more and more technologically advanced, these products became less useful and effective. In fact, they eventually became obsolete. As such the company is still in the same business, but the products sold for decades had to be completely discarded in favour of the development of electronic testing and measurement devices.[36]

In the final analysis, the most compelling — but often painful — alternative may be product abandonment. Knowing when and how to abandon products successfully may be as important as knowing when and how to introduce new ones. Certainly management should develop systematic procedures for phasing out weak products.

✒ Planned Obsolescence and Fashion

Consumers seem to be constantly searching for "what's new" but not "too new." They want newness — new products, new styles, new colours, new Web sites. However, they want to be moved gently out of their habitual patterns, not shocked out of them. Consequently, some manufacturers use a product strategy of planned obsolescence. The intent of this strategy is to make an existing product out of date and thus to increase the market for replacement products. Consumers often satisfy their thirst for newness through fashion. And producers of fashions rely heavily on planned obsolescence, as we'll now see.

Nature of Planned Obsolescence

Planned obsolescence may be interpreted in two ways:

◆ **Technological or functional obsolescence**. Significant technical improvements result in a more effective product. For instance, audiocassette tapes made phonograph records obsolete; and digital audiotapes threaten to make cassettes and compact discs obsolete. This type of obsolescence is generally considered to be socially and economically desirable, because the replacement product offers more benefits and/or a lower cost. As discussed, Intel Corp. has had some control over the obsolescence of their processors by releasing new upgrades while the current processor was still enjoying high sales levels. Similarly, this is occurring with video game hardware such as the Radeon graphics acceleration processor from ATI Technologies Inc. (www.atitech.com) and the video-game dimensional processor from Matrox Electrical Systems Ltd.

◆ **Style obsolescence**. Superficial characteristics of a product are altered so that the new model is easily differentiated from the previous model. Style obsolescence, sometimes called "psychological" or "fashion" obsolescence, is intended to make people feel out of date if they continue to use old models. Products subject to this type of obsolescence include clothing, furniture, and automobiles.

When people criticize planned obsolescence, they usually mean style obsolescence. In our discussion, when we refer to planned obsolescence, we will mean only style obsolescence, unless otherwise stated.

Nature of Style and Fashion

style
A distinctive presentation or construction in any art, product, or activity.

Although the words style and fashion are often used interchangeably, there is a clear distinction. A **style** is a distinctive manner of construction or presentation in any art, product, or endeavour (singing, playing, behaving). Thus we have styles in automobiles (sedans, compact, SUVs), in bathing suits (one-piece, string bikini, thong), in furniture (old Canadian pine, Mission, French Provincial), and in dance (waltz, break dancing, line dancing).

fashion
A style that is popularly accepted by groups of people over a reasonably long period of time.

A **fashion** is any style that is popularly accepted and purchased by successive groups of people over a reasonably long period of time. Not every style becomes a fashion. To be considered a fashion, or to be called "fashionable," a style must be accepted by many people. All of the styles listed in the preceding paragraph, except perhaps for break dancing, qualify as fashions. All societies, ranging from contemporary primitive groups to medieval European societies, have fashions.

Fashion is rooted in sociological and psychological factors. Basically, most of us are conformists. At the same time, we yearn to look and act a little different from others. We probably are not in revolt against custom; we simply wish to be a bit distinctive but not be accused of bad taste or disregard for norms. Fashion furnishes the opportunity for self-expression.

Values and qualities also go in and out of fashion. Values such family, conservatism, etc. as well as the concepts of "value" and "quality" themselves differ in their importance as a point of emphasis to various segments in the market at different times. These do not represent actual physical products, however, they can affect the popularity of products as well as marketing strategies directed at selling such products.

Fashion-Adoption Process

fashion-adoption process
The process by which a style becomes popular in a market; similar to diffusion of an innovation.

The **fashion-adoption process** reflects the concepts of (1) large-group and small-group influences on consumer buying behaviour and (2) the diffusion of innovation, as discussed in Chapters 6 and 9. People usually try to imitate others at the same or the next higher socioeconomic level. One way people do that is purchasing a product or using a product or service that is fashionable in the group they want to be like.

Thus the fashion-adoption process is a series of buying waves that arise as a particular style is popularly accepted in one group, then another group and another, until it finally falls out of fashion. This movement, representing the introduction, rise, popular culmination, and decline of the market's acceptance of a style, is referred to as the fashion cycle. A case can be made that synthetic fibres, such as polyester, in clothing, and the convertible model of automobile are two products that have run the full **fashion cycle**. While still consumed in limited quantities, they will most likely never gain the widespread consumption they once enjoyed.

As discussed in previous chapters, the mass communication abilities provided by the Internet has created many arenas for the exchange of product information and opinions. The existence of online reviews, newsgroups, and chat rooms has enabled the adoption process to be disseminated over larger areas in quicker times. As word, and opinions, of new products rapidly span the globe it remains to be seen if their demise will also be quickened by this technology.

There are three theories of fashion adoption (see Figure 10-4):

◆ **Trickle-down**, where a given fashion cycle flows downward through several socioeconomic levels.

◆ **Trickle-across**, where the cycle moves horizontally and simultaneously within several socioeconomic levels.

◆ **Trickle-up**, where a style first becomes popular at lower socioeconomic levels and then flows upward to become popular among higher levels.

Traditionally, the trickle-down theory has been used to explain the fashion-adoption process. As an example, designers of women's apparel first introduce a style to opinion leaders in the upper socioeconomic groups. If they accept the style, it quickly appears in

fashion cycle
Wavelike movements representing the introduction, rise, popular acceptance, and decline in popularity of a given style.

trickle-down cycle
In fashion adoption, a fashion cycle that flows downward through several socioeconomic classes.

trickle-across cycle
In fashion adoption, a fashion cycle that moves horizontally within several social classes at the same time.

trickle-up cycle
In fashion adoption, a fashion cycle by which a style becomes popular (fashionable) first with lower socioeconomic classes and then, later, with higher socioeconomic groups.

FIGURE 10-4
Fashion-Adoption Processes

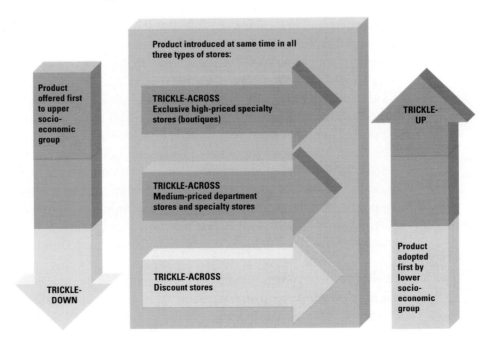

Some clothing items seem never to go out of style.

leading fashion stores. Soon the middle-income and then the lower-income markets want to emulate the leaders, and the style is mass-marketed. As its popularity wanes, the style appears in bargain-price stores and finally is no longer considered fashionable.

Today the trickle-across theory best explains the adoption process for most fashions. It's true that there is some flow downward, and obviously there is an upward flow. But, by means of modern production, communication, and transportation, we can disseminate style information and products so rapidly that all social levels can be reached at about the same time. For example, within a few weeks of the beginning of the fall season, the same style of dress (but at different quality levels) appears (1) in small, exclusive dress shops appealing to the upper social class, (2) in large department stores appealing to the middle social class, and (3) in discount houses and low-price women's ready-to-wear chain stores, where the appeal is to the portion of the lower social class that has some disposable income.

Consider the popularity of mountain-gear inspired clothing for casual wear. Functional in design, these items were available at specialty-stores for climbers and campers. Very durable and weather resistant, such items were carefully constructed from special materials. They then became available in most sports stores as people adopted them for various purposes. As they became a street fashion, clothing and department stores offered inner and outerwear based on these styles. Although these durable fabrics have become cheaper with time, many lower-priced outlets utilize common fabrics as this style becomes all about the fashion and much less about the function. Who by now doesn't have all-terrain sneakers, pants with pockets like pouches, and perhaps even zip out leg bottoms, or all-weather coats with a zillion zippers, drawstrings, and compartments. And how many members of the Mountain Equipment Co-Op do you think are actually climbing mountains on the weekends?

Well, this Mountain Co-Op member is climbing, but not on the way down!

Most apparel manufacturers produce a wide variety of essentially one style. They also produce different qualities of the same basic style so as to appeal to different income groups. When an entire cycle may last only one season, sellers cannot afford to wait for style acceptance to trickle down. They must introduce it to many social levels simultaneously.

Within each class, the dresses are purchased early in the season by the opinion leaders — the innovators. If the style is accepted, its sales curve rises as it becomes popular with the early adopters and then with the late adopters. Eventually, sales decline as the style loses popularity. This cycle is a horizontal movement, occurring virtually simultaneously within each of several socioeconomic levels.

The trickle-up process also explains some product-adoption processes. Consider how styles of music such as jazz and rap became popular. Also look at acid-wash denim, T-shirts, blacktop athletic footwear, boxer shorts peeking out over low-slung baggy pants, and even pasta in the 1990s. They all have one thing in common: They were popular first with lower socioeconomic and inner city groups. Only later did their popularity "trickle up" to higher-income markets.

Marketing Considerations in Fashion

When a firm's products are subject to the fashion cycle, management must know what stage the cycle is in at all times. Managers must decide at what point to get into the cycle and when to get out.

Accurate forecasting is critical to success in fashion merchandising. This is extremely difficult, however, because the forecaster must deal with complex sociological and psychological factors. Frequently a retailer or manufacturer operates largely on intuition and inspiration, tempered by considerable experience.

Ordinarily a retailer cannot participate successfully in all stages of the fashion cycle at the same time. Thus a specialty apparel store — whose stocks are displayed in limited numbers without price tags — should get in at the start of a fashion trend. And a department store appealing to the middle-income market should plan to enter the cycle in time to mass-market the style as it is climbing to its peak of popularity. Fundamentally, retail executives must keep in mind the product's target market in deciding at which stage(s) of the life cycle its stores should offer fashionable apparel.

Summary

Many strategic decisions must be made to manage a company's assortment of products effectively. To start, a firm must select strategies regarding its product mix. One decision is how to position the product relative to competing products and other products sold by the firm.

Another strategic decision is whether or how to expand the product mix by adding items to a line and/or introducing new lines. Alternatively, management may elect to trade up or trade down relative to existing products. Altering the design, packaging, or other features of existing products is still another option among the strategies of selecting the best mix. The product mix also can be changed by eliminating an entire line or by simplifying the assortment within a line.

Executives need to understand the concept of a product life cycle, which reflects the total sales volume for a generic product category. Each of the cycle's four stages — introduction, growth, maturity, and decline — has distinctive characteristics that have implications for marketing. Managing a product as it moves through its life cycle presents challenges and opportunities. Eventually, a product category may lack adequate acceptance from consumers; at that point, all or most companies will abandon their versions of this product.

Planned obsolescence is a controversial product strategy, built around the concepts of style, fashion, and the fashion cycle. Fashion — essentially a sociological and psychological phenomenon — follows a reasonably predictable pattern. With advances in communications and production, the fashion-adoption process has moved away from the traditional trickle-down pattern. Today the process is better described as trickle-across. There also are examples of fashions trickling up. Managing a product, such as expensive apparel, through a fashion cycle may be even more challenging than adjusting another type of product's strategies during its life cycle.

Key Terms and Concepts

Product mix 298
Breadth 298
Depth 298
Product line 298
Position 299
Product-mix expansion 303
Line extension 303
Mix extension 304
Trading up 305
Trading down 305
Product alteration 306

Product-mix contraction 307
Product life cycle 309
Introduction stage 310
Growth stage 311
Maturity stage 312
Decline stage 312
Fad 313
Product abandonment 316
Planned obsolescence 317
Technological (functional)
   obsolescence 317

Style (fashion or psychological)
   obsolescence 317
Style 317
Fashion 317
Fashion-adoption process 317
Fashion cycle 318
Trickle-down theory 318
Trickle-across theory 318
Trickle-up theory 318

Question and Problems

1. "It is inconsistent for management to follow concurrently the product-line strategies of expanding its product mix and contracting its product mix." Discuss.

2. "Trading up and trading down are product strategies closely related to the business cycle. Firms trade up during periods of prosperity and trade down during recessions." Do you agree? Why?

3. Name one category of tangible products and one category of services you believe are in the introductory stage of their life cycles. For each product, identify the market that considers your examples to be truly new.

4. What are two products that are in the decline stage of the life cycle? In each case, point out whether you think the decline is permanent. What recommendations do you have for rejuvenating the demand for either of these products?

5. How might a company's advertising strategies differ, depending on whether its brand of a product is in the introduction stage or the maturity stage of its life cycle?

6. What products, other than apparel and automobiles, stress fashion and style in marketing? Do styles exist among business products?

7. Is the trickle-across theory applicable to the fashion-adoption process in product lines other than women's apparel? Explain, using examples.

8. Planned obsolescence is criticized as a social and economic waste because we are urged to buy things we do not like and do not need. What is your opinion? If you object to planned obsolescence, what are your recommendations for correcting the situation?

Hands-On Marketing

1. Select a product category in which you are interested. Go to the library or search the Web and identify the national or provincial trade association for this product category. Then contact the association, requesting sales figures for this product over its history and other information that will allow you to plot the life cycle for this product. What stage of the life cycle is this product in? Explain.

2. Arrange a meeting with a supermarket manager or a department manager in a supermarket. Discuss how the manager handles the challenge of line extensions. In which product category are line extensions most common? When new items are added to the line, how does the manager find space for the new entries — by giving more space to this category, dropping other items carrying this same brand, pruning other brands in this category, or some other means?

Chapter Eleven

Brands, Packaging, and Other Product Features

As the Durex Canada example that opens this chapter illustrates, the success of a product or service will depend to a very great extent on the image communicated by the brand name. Otherwise, how do you account for some people paying more for Bayer Aspirin, while others prefer to buy a significantly lower priced private-label, or generic, brand of ASA tablets, when both products are commonly known to contain the same medicinal content? Consumer choice is influenced not only by the brand name, but also in the case of tangible products by the package, warranty, design, and other product features. Because these features of products and services are important elements in a marketing program, we devote this chapter to them. After studying this chapter, you should have an understanding of:

◆ The nature and importance of brands.

◆ The characteristics of a good brand name.

◆ The branding strategies of producers and intermediaries.

◆ Why and how a growing number of firms are building and using brand equity.

◆ The nature and importance of packaging and labelling.

◆ Major packaging strategies.

◆ The marketing implications of other product features — design, quality, warranty, and postsale service — that can satisfy consumers' wants.

When the Rubbers Hit the Road: Safe Sex Meets Rock n' Roll

In 1999, Saskatoon's *Wide Mouth Mason* toured Canada under the sponsorship of Durex Canada, a subsidiary of the London International Group, the world's largest prophylactic company. This was a first for both industries and was just one part of a marketing effort to develop a brand image for a product that has traditionally not been actively marketed directly to consumers.

This was part of an effort to develop a brand image that will appeal to that segment of the marketplace that represents a large part of the consumption of this product — young adults. Other components include an extensive Internet presence, distinctive packaging, and of course what every sponsored event requires — a mascot. This would be Richard, the walking Durex condom.

While most condom producers offer some variety in their product line, Durex offers a very extensive selection in the same packaging design but varied in colour to distinguish condom type. This provides a distinctive shelf presence. More distinctive, however, is the packaging for the new Durex Gold,

representing the first ever variation in packaging design. Forget the jokes about fumbling to get the package open, these condoms are uniquely packaged to be fast and easy to use. They are convenient to carry, easy to open, and oriented with the reservoir end in the upright position — heads up every time — so there's no fumbling around. Easy to remember, each condom is packaged to look like a coin.

By differentiating itself early in marketing efforts, Durex is positioning the brand to stand out from its competitors and to have greater relevance to its target market. With a brand name denoting its strength to do the job, Durex's Internet site (www.durex.com) provides any information required for getting the job done. With attention to each of the company's international markets, the site provides a large dose of entertainment while providing a forum for sensitive and private questions.

Durex Canada believes that audiences have been very receptive to the concert tour's theme, with young concert-goers accepting free samples and parents praising the effort. The tour received plenty of attention from local and national media in print, radio, and TV, plus public service announcements on MuchMusic and CBC-TV.[1]

The approach Durex is taking in differentiating itself from the competition is the equivalent of brand positioning, as was discussed in Chapter 10. If this company is to remain successful, it must be seen by prospective customers to be able to offer more than its competitors. By appearing to be an innovative company that is able to "connect" with its consumers and by distinguishing itself from the pack, Durex would emerge as a superior product in the minds of market segments of interest.

 Brands

When we think of brand names, most of us tend to think of products that we use often and that we have been using, or at least have been familiar with, for many years. Certainly, many well-established brands have been part of our consumer lives for fifty years or more. They include Tetley tea, Campbell's soup, Kodak film, Gillette shaving products, and Wrigley chewing gum. But brand names are just as important in the marketing of services. A retail store name such as Bata or Tip Top is really a brand, as are such names as Air Canada, Delta Hotels, and Canada's Wonderland, although these are not applied to tangible products. As we will see in this chapter, some retailer names have become so trusted and accepted by Canadians that they constitute widely regarded brand names in their own right.

The word *brand* is a comprehensive term, and it includes other, narrower terms. A **brand** is a name, term, symbol, or special design, or some combination of these elements, that is intended to identify the goods or services of one seller or a group of sellers. A brand differentiates one seller's products or services from those of competitors. A **brand name** consists of words, letters, and/or numbers that can be vocalized. A **brand mark** is the part of the brand that appears in the form of a symbol, design, or distinctive colouring or lettering. It is recognized by sight but may not be expressed when a person pronounces the brand name. Xerox, Bell Canada, Sony and Maple Leaf are brand names. Brand marks are illustrated by the distinctive lettering and styling of the name, for example, the Nike "swoosh," the picture of the little girl with pigtails on the Wendy's sign, and the "doughboy" character used by Pillsbury. These marks, logos, or designs are usually registered and may be used only by the company that owns the mark. In many cases the company name is the brand, and this is often the case for services companies such as Loblaw, Four Seasons, and Speedy Muffler.

A **trademark** is defined as a brand that is given legal protection because, under the law, it has been appropriated by one seller. Thus *trademark* is essentially a legal term. Trademark protection gives the legal owner of the brand the exclusive right to use that brand. All trademarks are brands and thus include the words, letters, or numbers that can be pronounced. They may also include a pictorial design (brand mark).

One major method of classifying brands is on the basis of who owns them — producers or retailers. Major brands such as Sony, Zenith, Lexus, Sunlight, Levi's, and Ivory are producers' brands, while Motomaster, President's Choice, Kenmore, Body Shop, and Life are all brands that are owned by retailers.

The term *national* has been used for many years to describe producer-brand ownership, while brands owned by retailers are generally referred to as private brands or private labels. However, more acceptable terminology for many marketers would be the terms *producer* and *retailer* brands. To say that a brand of a small manufacturer of poultry feed in British Columbia that markets in only two or three Western provinces is a

---

brand
A name, term, symbol, special design, or some combination of these elements that is intended to identify the products of one seller or a group of sellers.

brand name
The part of a brand that can be vocalized — words, letters, and/or numbers.

brand mark
The part of a brand that appears in the form of a symbol, picture, design, or distinctive colour or type of lettering.

trademark
A brand that is legally protected.

national brand, while those of Canadian Tire, Shoppers Drug Mart, Loblaw, and Sears are private brands, seems to be misusing these terms to some extent. Nevertheless, the brands of retailers generally continue to be referred to as private labels.

The issue of trademark protection arises quite often in marketing. In 1999, a dispute arose over "ownership" of, of all things, the use of a green traffic symbol on the Internet. GoTo.com, a popular search engine sued the Walt Disney Company, charging that Disney's newly-launched Go Network (www.go.com) had unlawfully adopted a logo that was confusingly similar to the unique one that GoTo.com had been using since 1997. In January 2000, the United States Court of Appeals reinstated a preliminary injunction against Walt Disney Company and other related companies. This included the ABC network (owned by Disney) that used the symbol to refer viewers to the site during credits that run after each television show. The judge ruled that the use of this symbol by Disney had caused, and was likely to continue causing, confusion among consumers. As a result GoTo.com would suffer irreparable harm.[2]

Even the names of fictional characters are brands. In Ontario, a $1 million judgment was made against Avonlea Traditions of Richmond Hill for making and selling a wide variety of Anne of Green Gables products claiming that they were authorized by the Montgomery family and bearing the signature of L.M. Montgomery. The company's licence to use the name and likeness of the turn-of-the-century P.E.I. character was terminated in 1994 for failure to pay royalties.[3] It is important to note that trademark protection under Canadian law extends not only to exact copies but to similar representations of brands as well.

What's In A Name?

A history of brand marketing will tell us that once a brand establishes a position of leadership in a product category, this position is often maintained over a very long period of time. Many of the leading brands that we buy today were purchased regularly by our parents and even our grandparents. Brands that continue to dominate their consumer product categories include Kodak, General Electric, Kellogg, Levi's, Kraft, Nabisco, Heinz, Tide, and Campbell's.

The development and protection of brand names has become a very important element of marketing management and one that demands increased attention all the time. Companies such as Colgate-Palmolive have made conscious decisions to manage their brand names in such a way as to dominate a product category. For example, this company has made a commitment to position Colgate as an all-purpose supplier of oral-health products. The importance of the Colgate name is summed up in a comment from Patrick Knight, former vice-president of marketing for Colgate-Palmolive: "We now consider the most valuable assets we have to be our trademarks."[4]

Such an attitude toward successful brands has led major companies to ensure that their brand names are assigned a value and are shown as assets on their balance sheets. Many of the leading brands have been the major targets in corporate takeovers as the purchasing companies have realized that the equity represented in successful brands is considerably more valuable than factories and distribution systems.[5]

When Canadian Pacific (CP) Hotels and Fairmont Hotels and Resorts joined to create a new hotel management company in the spring of 1999, instead of renaming and marketing these destinations under either luxury moniker, the company instead opted to leave the

In Canada, CP hotels stand for quality.

names of the hotels as they were, but to advertise the locations under both names (www.cphotels.com). Each brand has an established image and clientele — why not let each brand name benefit from the equity of the other? The brands will now each come to be associated with quality accommodations at resort destinations and city-central locations.[6] CP hotels have strong brand recognition in Canada for providing superior accommodations. Each brand will now strengthen its name in both Canada and the United States with this association. Fairmont Hotels have "Grand Hotel" locations in major U.S. cities, including such landmark properties as The Plaza in New York.

Equally important is the value of established brands in allowing their owners to apply the brand names to new products. As the cost of acquiring established brands increases, as does the cost and risk of introducing new products, many companies have been turning in recent years to the launching of brand extensions as a way of trading on the success of established brands and reducing the risk of new product failure. Hewlett-Packard, a company that had developed a strong reputation for printers, then moved into selling personal computers. The company decided to do so because the brand was so highly regarded by individuals who had purchased printers to use with personal computers. The Hewlett-Packard LaserJet printers were noted for being headache-free. The brand popularity transferred to the introduction of the extension.[7] Success with desktop computers has allowed HP to move into offering a wide range of products, including mobile computers, digital imaging, servers, information storage solutions, networking and e-services (www.hp.com).

Some companies have succeeded in keeping their brands successful and before the purchasing public for many years. Nabisco, maker of such cookies and crackers as Oreo, Ritz, Arrowroot, Chips Ahoy, and Triscuit, has been making cookies in Canada since 1861. Triscuit Crackers date from 1895, Honey Maid Graham Wafers from 1900, and Ritz from 1935. Today, the success of the Nabisco brands is obvious, and many have spawned brand extensions.

By stretching the original successful brand name to cover a number of brand extension products, the marketer is trading on the success of the original brand but is running some risk at the same time. Clearly, there may be some new products to which the original brand should not be applied. This raises the question of how far the successful brand can be "extended" before the marketer is stretching the credibility of the link between the brand and the product. Club Monaco, which successfully marketed casual wear aimed at young adults in Canada has recently moved into lifestyle marketing producing a wide range of home goods to sell in their stores. Roots, the Canadian company once famous for their revolutionary leather footwear has long sold leisure wear, but have recently tried to extend the brand to include home furnishings and a remote forest get-away resort.[8] Colgate can with confidence launch a line of toothbrushes, dental floss, and mouthwash, but would consumers buy Colgate sunglasses or suntan lotion?

Brands make it easy for consumers to identify goods or services. Brands also help assure purchasers they are getting comparable quality when they reorder. For sellers, brands can be advertised and recognized when displayed on shelves in a store. Branding

Marketing at Work 11-1

Financial Services a Staple at Loblaw

Would you shop for financial services at a supermarket? More than 300,000 Canadians have since February 1998 when *Loblaw Companies Limited* redefined banking by offering a comfortable, dressed down, and convenient banking option under an extension of its hugely successful private label brand — *President's Choice*.

The offering of *President's Choice Financial* services is a collaboration between *Loblaw Companies Limited* and *Canadian Imperial Bank of Commerce*. CIBC supplies financial products and the sales, service and electronic banking infrastructure and gains access to a new customer base. Loblaw gets a powerful brand extension under its *President's Choice* trademark and further strengthens its one-stop shopping value proposition which is already supported by in-store photofinishing, dry cleaning, and pharmacy services.

President's Choice Financial services contain the same ingredients that made other *President's Choice* products so successful — unique, high quality products that are value priced or products that are better than national brands in quality and lower than national brands in price. Using the tagline "*Fresh Financial Thinking*," the *President's Choice Financial* services offering boasts 24-hour banking, no service fees for daily banking, higher interest rates on savings accounts, low cost borrowing, and *PC* points which can be redeemed for groceries at Loblaw-owned or franchised grocery stores. Financial products such as *the unbeatable, eatable mortgage* and *The World's Best* RRSP show the same witty, contempo-

rary approach to product naming that Loblaw has become known for through its *President's Choice* products.

Loblaw's initial focus has been to leverage the real estate of its stores and the loyalty of its customers to the *President's Choice* brand to aggressively acquire customers. The challenge now is to find new and unique ways to effectively and quickly communicate its brand outside of the store so more customers can take advantage of these innovative financial offerings.

Source: Adapted from Mark de Wolf, "PC Financial winning converts," *Strategy*, June, 7, 1999, p. D3; Erica Zlomislic, "Loblaw taps CIBC for President's Choice Financial : Private-label bank offers points redeemable for Loblaw's groceries," *Strategy*, February, 16, 1998, p. 2. Numbers updated as of June 2000.

Note: *PC, President's Choice, President's Choice Financial, Fresh Financial Thinking, the unbeatable, eatable mortgage, and The World's Best* are trademarks of Loblaw Inc.

also helps sellers control their market because buyers will not confuse one branded product with another. Branding reduces price comparisons because it is hard to compare prices on two items with different brands. Finally, for sellers, branding can add a measure of prestige to otherwise ordinary commodities (Sunkist oranges, Sifto salt, Lantic sugar, Highliner fish, Chiquita bananas).[9]

Reasons for Not Branding

The two major responsibilities inherent in brand ownership are (1) to promote the brand and (2) to maintain a consistent quality of output. Many firms do not brand their products because they are unable or unwilling to assume those responsibilities.

Some items are not branded because of the difficulty of differentiating the products of one firm from those of another. Clothespins, nails, and industrial raw materials (coal, cotton, wheat) are examples of goods for which product differentiation (including branding) is generally unknown. The physical nature of some items, such as fresh fruits and vegetables, may discourage branding. However, now that these products are often packaged in typically purchased quantities, brands are being applied to the packages.

Producers frequently do not brand the part of their output that is below their usual quality. Products graded as seconds, or imperfects, are sold at discount prices and are often distributed through different channels and under different brand names than those used for usual-quality goods.

Selecting a Good Brand Name

Some brand names are so good that they contribute to the sales success of the product or service; others are so poor or inappropriate that they would appear to contribute little if anything to sales success and may even seem to be a factor in market failures. Some products seem to have been successful despite having names that may appear to add little to their appeal. Some brand names attain considerable value over time and remain consumer favourites for many years. In fact, it takes some time for the name of a product, service or company to achieve the status where it becomes a "brand." The word itself implies that customers recognize the name and attach some meaning to it.

THE CHALLENGE   Today, selecting a good name for a product or service is more challenging than ever. The reason is that we are running out of possibilities — and many of the good names have already been used. There are about ten thousand new products launched annually in North America, yet the standard desk-size dictionary contains only about fifty thousand words. When one considers that a new brand can't be labelled Panasonic, Oreo, Esso, or Timex because these brands have been used successfully for many years and that there are many other words one would not want to have associated with one's product or service, it is no surprise that companies often resort to words that aren't really words, or that they bring out the new product as an extension of an already-successful brand.

Many company and brand names have achieved a certain status over time, but at one time they probably meant very little to consumers. It is only over time that these names have truly become recognizable and respected brands. Consider for example, the names of companies like Ford, or Kraft. At one time these were family names only — the name of the person who started the company. What if Henry Ford had been born into the Murphy family? Would many families all over the world now have Murphys parked in their driveways? It will be interesting to see how long it takes for some of the new companies that are being established to do business on the Internet to achieve brand status. Names like Invensys and Getronics — both IT companies — may well become widely known brands in the future.

On the Internet restrictions apply to the selection of names. Although e-addresses often ignore rules of grammar such as removal of spaces between words, there are limits in that while two or more companies can have the same word, that word can be the basis for only one domain name in cyberspace. By the end of 1999, the organization that registers domain names had already approved over five million "dot.com" addresses.[10]

The need for names and brands that are likely to contribute to a product's success has led to the establishment of companies that specialize in coming up with attractive and appealing brand names. These firms will use database searches and will rely on unusual sources to identify likely names. Some even employ qualified linguists on staff. They often come up with names that aren't part of any language: Pentium (Intel's microprocessor chip), Zoloft (a new pharmaceutical product), Lexus, Acura, and Compaq. Branding on the Internet through Web addresses has been approached in a similar manner with sites like fundu.com or imandi.com. The creation of a new brand name will often involve research to determine whether consumers will react positively to the brand being proposed. It also is not an inexpensive process, as some firms will charge $25,000 or more for a new brand name.[11]

DESIRABLE CHARACTERISTICS Five characteristics determine the desirability of a brand name for a product or service.[12] It is difficult to think of a brand that has all five. Still, a brand should possess as many of these characteristics as possible:

◆ *Suggest something about the product's characteristics* — its benefits, use, or action. Some names that suggest desirable benefits include Beautyrest, Motomaster, and — perhaps best of all — DieHard. Product use and action are suggested by Hi-Liter, La-Z-Boy, Mr. Clean, and Easy-Off. Or site addresses such as GardenCrazy.com, or clickabid.com.

◆ *Be easy to pronounce, spell, and remember.* Simple, short, one-syllable names such as Tide, Ban, Aim, and Raid are helpful. Top-cuts, Weedman, and Speedy are additional examples of brand names that are easy to remember. However, even some short names, such as NYNEX and Aetna, aren't easily pronounced by some customers.

◆ *Be distinctive.* Brands with names like National, Star, Ideal, or Standard fail on this point. Many services firms begin their brand names with adjectives connoting strength and then add a description of the business, creating brands such as Allied Van Lines and United Parcel Service. Some brand names play on patriotism as, for example, Maple Leaf food products, Air Canada, and Molson Canadian.

◆ *Be adaptable to new products that may be added to the product line.* An innocuous name such as Kellogg or Lipton may serve the purpose better than a highly distinctive name suggestive of product benefits. Frigidaire is an excellent name for a refrigerator and other cold-image products. But when the producer expanded its line of home appliances and added Frigidaire kitchen ranges, the name lost some of its sales appeal. Amazon.com suggests huge selection and/or inventory of any product, but has come to be associated thus far with a huge choice of books and music.

◆ *Be capable of being registered and legally protected under the Trade Marks Act and other statutory or common laws.* Names that are generic and in common usage in the English language would not meet this criteria. For example, the word "water" used as a name could not by itself be registered and legally protected. Names must also not be registered or in use by other firms.

Protecting a Brand Name

generic use of brand names
General reference to a product by its brand name — cellophane, kerosene, zipper, for example — rather than its generic name. The owners of these brands no longer have exclusive use of the brand name.

Over a period of years, some brands have become so well accepted that the brand name is substituted for the **generic name** of the particular product. Examples of brand names that legally have become generic are linoleum, celluloid, cellophane, kerosene, shredded wheat, and nylon. Originally, these were trademarks limited to use by the owner.

A brand name can become generic in several ways. Sometimes the patent on a product expires. There is no simple generic name available, so the public continues to use the brand name as a generic name. This happened with shredded wheat, nylon, and cellophane. Sometimes a firm just does too good an advertising and selling job with an outstanding brand name. While not yet legally generic, names such as Xerox, Aspirin, Band-Aid, Scotch Tape, Ski-Doo®, and Kleenex are on the borderline in Canada. Some

Marketing at Work 11-2

Mike's Personality Plus

In just four years mike's hard lemonade® has become the most successful refreshment beverage in Canada with a 29.9 percent share of the Refreshment Beverage category. mike's™ has little in common, however, with its cooler counterparts. mike's™ appeals as much (maybe even more) to macho beer-drinking men as it does to the traditional cooler-drinking female between 18–24.

The reason mike's™ was able to cross the gender gap was because mike is a fun, happy-go-lucky, party guy who is infatuated with lemons, and therefore has equal appeal to both men and women.

mike's™ wasn't launched with the support of a huge advertising budget, instead it relied on a few shelf talkers, some POP materials, a strong personality, and innovative packaging. Much of its success can be attributed to the attitude that's evoked on the package. It's comfortable, laid-back, hip looking not dorky, and includes the lines "Lemons were hurt real bad in the making of this product" and "An excellent source of Vodka®."

mike's™ followed a very disciplined approach to marketing by ensuring that everything reflects the core personality of the

brand. So when advertising support began, mike's personality, along with these lines, cute stories about lemons and mike were pooled out into outdoor and TV.

mike's™ successfully took a strong personality and extended it to a wider audience without disenfranchising its loyal fans by paying careful attention to their identity as a brand.

Source: Adapted from Eve Lazarus, "Lemon-aid," *Marketing Magazine*, October 11, 1999, p. 15, with input from mike™.

of these brands have already lost their trademark protection in other countries. For example, in the United States and Great Britain, one can buy many brands of aspirin.

It is the responsibility of the trademark owner to assert the company's rights in order to prevent the loss of the distinctive character of the trademark. A number of strategies are employed to prevent the brand name from falling into generic usage. The most common strategy is to ensure that the word "trademark" or the letters "TM®" appear adjacent to the brand name wherever it appears. A second strategy is to use two names — the brand name together with either the company's name or the generic name of the product. Examples of this include Polariod Land camera and Dacron brand polyester. A third strategy for protecting a trademark involves the incorporation into the trademark of a distinctive signature or logo.

This protection is as important as ever as according to the latest estimates, imitation products cost American companies as much as $200 *billion* annually. Nintendo alone estimates the piracy of their video games cost the company over $700 million in 1998. In the U.S., a top FBI official has called product counterfeiting "the crime of the 21st century."[13]

Branding Strategies

Both producers and intermediaries face strategic decisions regarding the branding of their goods or services. Whether a firm is branding a product or a service, some fundamental things need to be kept in mind. Branding is a means of creating and maintaining a perception of customer value. There is an expectation on the part of the customer that the brand name stands for quality. Branding also provides the means of differentiating products and services from the competition. When consumers see the offerings as all being alike, there is a tendency to shop on the basis of price. Branding provides consumers with another reason to choose a product. When brands provide better quality in products and services, they tend to be remembered by the consumer.[14] This is brand differentiation.

Product-branding strategies are often viewed differently than are services-branding strategies. Services branding is generally synonymous with the name of the company. The best example of services branding is franchising in which companies such as Second Cup, Starbucks, and Tim Hortons sell the rights to their name and products. The brand or name has come to stand for a service encompassing recognizable features. For example, McDonald's represents fast service, a children's focus, and consistent products. Other examples of services branding include hotel chains like Canadian Pacific or Hilton, and professional-service companies, including consulting firms like KPMG and Ernst and Young. Sometimes, service products are licensed for sale by intermediaries. An example of this would be a training facility that delivers Microsoft training programs. The following strategies generally are used to brand tangible products. The strategic branding of services is dealt with later in the chapter.

Producers' Strategies

Producers must decide whether to brand their products and whether to sell any or all of their output under intermediaries' brands.

MARKETING ENTIRE OUTPUT UNDER PRODUCERS' OWN BRANDS Companies that market their entire output under their own brands usually are very large, well financed, and well managed. Procter & Gamble, Maytag, and IBM are examples. They have broad product lines, well-established distribution systems, and large shares of the market. They generally have sufficient demand for products branded with their own names that they have no need to make products for other companies.

Some reasons for adopting this policy have already been covered in the section on the importance of branding to the seller. In addition, intermediaries often prefer to handle producers' brands, especially when the brands have high consumer acceptance.

BRANDING OF FABRICATING PARTS AND MATERIALS Some producers of fabricating materials and parts (products used in the further manufacturing of other goods) will brand their product.[15] This strategy is used in the marketing of Fiberglas insulation, Pella windows, Dolby noise reduction, Intel processors and many automotive parts — spark plugs, batteries, oil filters, and so on. DuPont has consistently and successfully used this strategy, notably with its Lycra Spandex fibre and Stainmaster stain repellent for carpets.

Underlying this strategy is the seller's desire to develop a market preference for its branded part or material. For instance, G.D. Searle Ltd. wants to build a market situation in which customers will insist on food products sweetened with NutraSweet. In addition, the parts manufacturer wants to persuade the producer of the finished item that using the branded materials will help sell the end product. In our example, Searle hopes to convince food manufacturers that their sales will be increased if their products contain NutraSweet.

Certain product characteristics lend themselves to the effective use of this strategy. First, it helps if the product is also a consumer good that is bought for replacement purposes. This factor encourages the branding of Champion spark plugs, Atlas batteries, and Fram oil filters, for example. Second, the seller's situation is improved if the item is a major part of the finished product — a microprocessor within a personal computer, for instance. Intel Corp. developed the slogan "Intel Inside" to strengthen its product's position.[16]

MARKETING UNDER INTERMEDIARIES' BRANDS A widespread strategy is for producers to brand part or all of their output with the brands of their intermediary's customers. For example, a manufacturer of salad dressing makes products for Loblaw, and they are sold under the President's Choice label. For the manufacturer, this intermediary's brand business generates additional sales volume and profit dollars. Orders typically are large, payment is prompt, and a producer's working-capital position is improved. Also, manufacturers may use their production resources more effectively, including their plant capacities. Furthermore, refusing to sell under a retailer's or wholesaler's brand will not eliminate competition from this source. Many intermediaries want to market under their own brands, so if one manufacturer refuses their business, they will simply go to another.

Intermediaries' Strategies

The question of whether or not to brand the products they may carry must also be answered by intermediaries. There are two usual strategies, as follows:

CARRY ONLY PRODUCERS' BRANDS Most retailers and wholesalers follow this policy because they are not able to take on the dual burdens of promoting a brand and maintaining its quality. This is especially the case with smaller retailers, such as local shoe stores, whose volume of business is not sufficient to allow them to contract with a manufacturer for products labelled with the store's own brand.

CARRY INTERMEDIARIES' BRANDS ALONE OR WITH PRODUCERS' BRANDS Many large retailers and some large wholesalers have their own brands. In fact, some of the most successful brands in recent years have been retailers' own brands, including President's Choice, Sobey's Our Compliments, and Life from Shoppers Drug Mart. Intermediaries may find it advantageous to market their own brands for several reasons. First, this strategy increases their control over their market. If customers prefer a given retailer's brand, they can get it only from that retailer's store. Furthermore, intermediaries can usually sell their brands at prices below those of producers' brands and still earn higher gross margins. This is possible because intermediaries can buy at lower costs. The costs may be lower because (1) manufacturers' advertising and selling costs are not included in their prices, or (2) producers are anxious to get the extra business to keep their plants running in slack seasons.

In addition to the two strategies mentioned above, some companies are carrying brands of other producers in association with their own. For example, Air Canada has entered into an agreement to provide Second Cup coffee on all of its flights.[17] McDonald's has an agreement with Wal-Mart to set up outlets inside their stores, and Starbucks has a similar arrangement with Chapters.

Intermediaries have more freedom in pricing products sold under their own labels. Products carrying a retailer's brand become differentiated products, and this hinders price comparisons that might be unfavourable to that retailer. Also, prices on manufacturers' brands can be cut drastically by competing retail stores. This last point is what has been happening in recent years in the marketing of clothing with designer labels such as Calvin Klein, DKNY, Ralph Lauren, Fendi, and Hugo Boss. Some of the large retailers in their upper-priced clothing departments have increased their stocks of apparel carrying the store's own brand. These stores have cut back on products with designer brands such as Calvin Klein and others. The reason for this brand-switching is that some designer-labelled products are now available at much lower prices in stores such as Wal-Mart, Zellers, and other "off-price retailers."

The strategy of marketing as many products as possible under the retailer's own label has met with considerable success for such Canadian retailers as Loblaw and Canadian Tire. In fact, Loblaw is among the leading companies in the world in the private-label business, creating a situation where more than 30 percent of all Loblaw sales is accounted for by private-label products such as President's Choice Decadent chocolate chip cookies, Too Good To Be True cereals, and PC Cola. In fact, Loblaw has been so successful at developing the market for private-label products that the company has licensed the President's Choice brand to chains around the world. It has even extended the PC brand into financial services (see "Marketing at Work" File 11-1). Loblaw is an excellent example of how private-label products can replace national brands in the consumer's mind when the retailer develops products and value in which the consumer can be confident.[18]

Strategies Common to Producers and Intermediaries

Producers and intermediaries alike must adopt some strategy with respect to branding their product mix and branding for market saturation.

BRANDING A LINE OF PRODUCTS/SERVICES   At least four different strategies are widely used by firms that sell more than one product or service.

◆ The same "family" or "blanket" brand may be placed on all products. This policy is followed by Heinz, Catelli, Campbell's, McCain's, and others in the food field. Other examples include the YM-YWCA and Pizza Hut.

◆ A separate name may be used for each product. This strategy is employed by Procter & Gamble and Lever Brothers. Pampers are produced by Procter & Gamble; Dove soap is a Lever product.

◆ A separate family brand may be applied to each grade of product or to each group of similar products or services. Sears groups its major home appliances under the Kenmore name, its paints and home furnishings under Harmony House, and its insurance under Allstate.

◆ The company trade name may be combined with an individual name for the product or service. Thus there is Johnson's Pledge, Microsoft's Excel, Kellogg's Rice Krispies, Molson Export, Bank of Montreal's MasterCard, and Ford Mustang.

family-brand strategy
A branding strategy in which a group of products is given a single brand.

When used wisely, a **family-brand strategy** has considerable merit. This strategy makes it much simpler and less expensive to introduce new related products to a line.

Also, the general prestige of a brand can be spread more easily if it appears on several products rather than on only one. A family brand is best suited for a marketing situation when the products are related in quality, in use, or in some other manner. When Black & Decker, a manufacturer of power tools, purchased General Electric's line of small appliances, the Black & Decker brand was put on those appliances, but not immediately. Because of the perceived differences between kitchen products and workroom products, Black & Decker realized it was a risky proposition to switch brands. Consequently, the company mounted a year-long brand-transition campaign before making the change. Also, during those years, Black & Decker introduced several other houseware products, and this helped in the General Electric–Black & Decker brand transition.

The success of major brands and families of brands certainly makes it easier for companies, whether manufacturers or intermediaries, to introduce new products under the established family brand or as brand extensions to well-established brands. This is obvious when one considers the number of varieties of Oreo cookies and Ritz crackers now produced by Nabisco and the wide array of products marketed under the Motomaster label by Canadian Tire. But the use of family brands and established brands to launch new products places a burden on the brand owner to maintain consistently high quality across all products marketed under that brand. One bad item can reflect unfavourably on other products that carry the brand and may even lead to the creation of a negative image for the overall brand.

BRANDING FOR MARKET SATURATION Frequently, to increase its degree of market saturation, a firm will employ a **multiple-brand strategy**. Suppose, for example, that a company has built one type of sales appeal around a given brand. To reach other segments of the market, the company can use other appeals with other brands. For example, Procter & Gamble markets a line of detergents that includes Tide, Bold, Cheer, and Ivory Snow. There may be some consumers who feel that Tide, even with its many varieties (phosphate-free, with bleach, unscented, liquid, regular, and most recently, high-efficiency HE Tide), is not suitable for washing lingerie and other delicate clothing. For these people, Procter & Gamble offers Ivory Snow, a detergent whose image is gentler than that of Tide and trades on its association with the purity and gentleness of Ivory soap. With this brand line-up, Procter & Gamble is assured of having a brand or a brand variation to appeal to every segment of the detergent market.

Building and Using Brand Equity

Companies as diverse as General Motors, Microsoft, Hallmark, Kodak, and McCain recognize that the brands they own may be more valuable than their physical assets such as buildings and equipment. What we are talking about here is brand equity, one of the hottest topics in marketing for over ten years. **Brand equity** is the value a brand adds to a product. In the minds of many consumers, just having a brand name such as Sony, Kenmore, or Reebok on a product adds value to it. Beyond a product's value in its potential to do what it's supposed to do, a brand adds value to that product through its name awareness and its connotations of favourable attributes (such as quality or economy).

If you're not convinced that a brand name by itself can have much value, consider the results of two studies. In one, the proportion of subjects choosing cornflakes cereal jumped from 47 percent when the brand was not known to 59 percent when the brand was identified as Kellogg's. In another study, conducted in 1993, when a sample of computer buyers were asked how much more or less they would pay for particular brands

---

multiple-brand strategy
A strategy in which a firm has more than one brand of essentially the same product, aimed either at the same target market or at distinct target markets.

brand equity
The value a brand adds to a product.

rather than the average computer brand, there was a range of $364. Consumers said they would pay $295 and $232 more for the IBM and Compaq brands, respectively. Other brands commanding a premium include Apple, Digital, and Dell.[19] It's evident that Kellogg's, IBM, Compaq, and many other brands have substantial equity.

Today, creating brand equity is about more than positioning, packaging, and imagery. It involves developing a relationship with customers. Customers want brands that they can trust and be happy to tell others about. Developing a brand is a process of creating loyal followers who provide word-of-mouth support and ultimately add value to the product.[20] Substantial brand equity provides many benefits to the firm that owns the brand:

◆ The brand itself can become a differential advantage, influencing consumers to buy a particular product. Examples include Volvo, Tetley tea, Häagen-Dazs and BMW.

◆ Because it is expensive and time consuming to build brand equity, it creates a barrier for companies that want to enter the market with a similar product.

◆ The widespread recognition and favourable attitudes surrounding a brand with substantial brand equity can facilitate international expansion. For example, brands like Pizza Hut, McDonald's, and Baskin-Robbins are now found literally all over the world.

◆ Brand equity can help a product survive changes in the operating environment, such as a business crisis or a shift in consumer tastes.

Brand equity is most often used to expand a product line, especially to extend a brand into new varieties or even new products. In fact, it may be argued that brand extensions are not possible unless the brand has established considerable equity. Examples include Ocean Spray drinks in flavours other than the original cranberry, Tetley iced tea, and Ivory bath wash. The rationale for using an existing, strong brand name on a new item or line is that the brand's equity will convey a favourable impression of the product and increase the likelihood that consumers will at least try it.

If a brand has abundant equity that does not necessarily mean it should be applied to other products. When it was developing a spaghetti sauce, Campbell determined that its popular brand name would not convey an Italian image, so it selected Prego as the name for its new sauce. Also, strong equity does not guarantee success for new items. Examples include Harley Davidson cigarettes, Levi's tailored men's clothing, Dunkin' Donuts cereal, and Swatch clothing, to name a few.

The issue of relative brand equity was most obvious in the early 1990s in the battle that arose between established national brands on the one hand and generally newer private-label or retailers' own brands on the other. In fact, this situation developed into one of the most important issues in marketing. This battle of the brands has been most obvious in grocery and personal-care products — the items that most households buy regularly from their neighbourhood supermarkets and drugstores. As consumer confidence in the quality of such private-label products has grown, so too has their share of the packaged-goods business. It is forecasted that private-brand food business will account for $100 billion in volume in North America in 2005.[21]

Strategic Branding of Services

Throughout this chapter, we have discussed the competitive edge that a well-selected brand can give to a product. These advantages are equally applicable to tangible goods and

Marketing at Work 11-3

Keeping KD Current

"Barenaked Ladies sing about it. The cartoon characters on South Park joke about it. And millions of people eat it, some before noon."

Kraft Dinner, KD to those who know it well, faces an interesting challenge because of its enormous popularity. It is the top selling grocery item in the country, according to Kraft Canada Inc., with ninety million boxes consumed by Canadians each year. So how can they get people to eat more of it?

Kraft is facing a dilemma familiar to many packaged goods companies with mature products and increasing competition. KD has been in the marketplace since 1937 and has had to constantly innovate to keep the brand on top. Past spinoffs in the KD family include extra creamy, white cheddar, egg noodles, and spirals. Innovation is especially important now that the many private-label macaroni and cheese dinners have taken a bite out of its market share. KD holds approximately 73 percent of the national macaroni and cheese market, but this slips to as low as 40 percent within Loblaw supermarkets where it competes against Loblaw's popular President's Choice label macaroni and cheese.

Kraft feels that they can't sit back and expect the brand to continue to be popular without trying to keep it relevant to consumers. Thus KD recently underwent a face lift, the first package redesign in nearly a decade. The package now features the name Kraft Dinner in 3-D and sports a more appetizing picture of the product.

To go with its new look, Kraft has also launched a new ad campaign which focuses on special moments and memories that consumers link with KD, for example university days, or dinner with Dad when Mom was away. One of the goals of the new ad campaign is to awaken warm and fuzzy memories which will encourage consumers who haven't recently purchased the product to try KD again.

To accompany the new packaging and advertising campaign Kraft has launched another product extension under the KD brand, "Easy Mac." This new product comes in a single-serving size and can be prepared in the microwave instead of the conventional stove-top method. It is great for those who desire a portable meal, or those dining solo who want a quick fix of comfort food.

Source: Adapted from John Heinzl, "Kraft Dinner serves up a new look," *The Globe and Mail*, January 13, 1999, p. B29.

---

intangible services. Furthermore, the marketers of services have to make many of the same strategic branding decisions as do the marketers of tangible products. Perhaps the first of these decisions is to select a good brand name for the service.[22] In services marketing, more so than in the marketing of tangible goods, the company name typically serves as the brand name. For example, H&R Block has become synonymous with tax-return preparation.

The characteristics of an effective service brand are much the same as for tangible goods. Thus, a service brand should be:

◆ *Relevant to the service or its benefits.* Ticketron, the sales agency that sells tickets to sporting events, concerts, and other major attractions, conveys the nature of the service and the electronic speed with which it is delivered. Visa suggests an international activity and is relevant for a global financial service. Instant Teller is a good name for the automatic banking machines of the CIBC. Budget implies the best price for people who rent cars from that company. Four Seasons suggests a hotel chain that has something to offer year-round.

◆ *Distinctive.* This characteristic is difficult to communicate. The point is that companies should avoid branding their service with names that others could use. Thus, names like National, Canadian, and Royal should probably be avoided because, standing alone, they tell us nothing about the service or its benefits. When names such as these are used, the company will usually add words that tell us what service is being offered, such as Canada Trust or Royal Trust, and National Life Insurance.

Some service marketers differentiate themselves from the competition by using a symbol (usually referred to as a logo) or a distinctive colour. We are all familiar with the golden arches of McDonald's, the lion of the Royal Bank of Canada, and Air Canada's maple leaf. For colour, we see the green of the Toronto Dominion Bank, the red of Scotiabank, the claret of CIBC, and the blue of the Bank of Montreal. The use of a person's name such as Harvey's or Tilden, or a coined word, such as Avis, Re/Max, and Amex, also offers distinctiveness, but it tells us little about the service being offered. This is the case until the name has been firmly established and it comes to mean something to the consumer. Certainly, many such names have become very well established in the marketplace.

♦ *Easy to pronounce and remember.* Simple, short names, such as Delta and A&W usually meet this criterion. Others, such as Aetna, Clarica, and Overwaitea, pose pronunciation problems for some people. Sometimes, unusual spelling aids in having the consumer remember the name — the reverse R in Toys "Я" Us, for example.

♦ *Adaptable to additional services or regions.* Companies that change their mix of services and their geographical locations over time should be flexible enough to adapt to these extensions of their operations. Alberta Government Telephones (AGT) changed its name to Telus, and the four telecommunications companies of Atlantic Canada merged to form Aliant, as traditional telephone service became a smaller part of their business with the move into Internet services, IT, and a range of other technology-based services. The Canadian Imperial Bank of Commerce shortened its name to CIBC in anticipation of expanding its range of financial services beyond banking. When companies have names with geographic connotations, such as Canadian Pacific, they are often abbreviated when expansion takes place, as in CP Hotels.

 ## Packaging

packaging
The activities in product planning that involve designing and producing the container or wrapper for a product.

Packaging may be defined as all the activities of designing and producing the container or wrapper for a product. Services can also be packaged even though they are not wrapped in cartons or displayed in containers. Examples of services packaging include travel tours or H & R Block personal income tax service. The customer purchases a package of services that are sold as one unit and that can include many elements. With services, the container is not the tangible package we associate with products; it is, nevertheless, a package of value for the consumer, and the process of packaging involves making the appearance of the collection of goods attractive to the consumer. There are three reasons for packaging:

♦ *Packaging of products often serves several safety and utilitarian purposes.* It protects a product on its route from the producer to the final customer, and in some cases even while it is being used by the customer. Effective packaging can help prevent ill-intentioned persons from tampering with products. Some protection is provided by "child-proof" closures on containers of medicines and other products that are potentially harmful to children. Also, compared with bulk items, packaged goods generally are more convenient, cleaner, and less susceptible to losses from evaporation, spilling, and spoilage.

♦ *Packaging may be part of a company's marketing program.* Packaging helps identify a product and thus may prevent substitution of competitive products. At the point of purchase, the package can serve as a silent salesperson. Furthermore, the advertising copy on the package will last as long as the product is used in its packaged form. A package may be the only significant way in which a firm can differentiate its product. In the case of convenience goods or business operating supplies, for example, most buyers feel that one well-known brand is about as good as another. Altoids, "the curiously strong mints," are packaged in a metal tin; not because they have to be, but because it sets them apart from "ordinary" mints.

Some feature of the package may add sales appeal — a no-drip spout, a reusable jar, or a self-applicator (a bottle of shoe polish or glue with an applicator top, for example). By packaging their toothpaste in a pump dispenser — a product long used in Europe — Colgate and Close-Up brands increased their sales considerably. Crest and Aim later adopted the same type of packaging. Concentrated formulations of cleaning solutions can be marketed as adding convenience by virtue of being smaller, lighter, and more environmentally friendly. Refill pouches for several home-cleaning products served these aims when they were introduced in recent years.

◆ *A firm can package its product in a way that increases profit and sales volume.* A package that is easy to handle or minimizes damage losses will cut marketing costs, thus boosting profit. The previously discussed changes to several cleaning agents helped to reduce transportation and storage costs, as well as attracting environmentally sensitive consumers. On the sales side, packaged goods typically are more attractive and therefore better than items sold in bulk. Many companies have increased the sales volume of an article simply by redesigning its package. Coca-Cola, for instance, launched its traditionally-styled contour bottle to boost the image of the product. Smarties sold their candy in a plastic building-block shaped container for a period of time thereby encouraging multiple purchases to accumulate a set of inter-locking blocks for play. Heinz recently announced a new "trap cap" for their plastic ketchup bottles that will end the age-old problem associated with ketchup, namely the first few watery drips of ketchup before the real stuff starts to pour.[23]

Importance of Packaging in Marketing

Historically, packaging was a production-oriented activity in most companies, performed mainly to obtain the benefits of protection and convenience. Today, however, the marketing significance of packaging is fully recognized, and packaging is truly a major competitive force in the struggle for markets. The widespread use of self-service selling and automatic vending means that the package must do the selling job at the point of purchase. Shelf space is often at a premium, and it is no simple task for manufacturers even to get their products displayed in a retail outlet. Most retailers are inclined to cater to producers that have used effective packaging.

In addition, the increased use of branding and the public's rising standards in health and sanitation have contributed to a greater awareness of packaging. Safety in packaging has become a prominent marketing and social issue in recent years. Extensive consumer use of microwave ovens has had a significant impact on packaging. Many food products are now packaged so that they can go straight from the shelf or freezer into a microwave oven. Environmental concerns, as mentioned, are also influencing package design.

New developments in packaging, occurring rapidly and in a seemingly endless flow, require management's constant attention. We see new packaging materials replacing traditional ones, new shapes, new closures, and other new features (measured portions, metered flow). These all increase convenience for consumers and selling points for marketers.

To assist consumers in being able to browse through CD-ROM products, Ames Specialty Packaging has designed the CD book pack, a book-sized package with multiple configurations incorporating various tray, cover, and pocket options. This package enables customers to receive more information about the product and facilitates their ability to access that information before buying.[24]

Packaging is an important marketing tool for companies that operate in international markets. Most countries have regulations governing the packaging of products and the wording that must appear on labels. A company that wishes to export its product to another country must, therefore, be aware of the packaging laws of that country. For example, companies in other countries that export to Canada and the Canadian importers that represent them have to be aware of Canadian packaging regulations pertaining to metric package sizes, bilingual labelling, and the standard sizes of packages used in some industries. In addition to regulations, exporters must understand that packages that work in one country may not be accepted in another, because of design, illustration, or colour. Cultural differences as well as traditions and attitudes affect how consumers respond to brand colors and image as well as situations and usage portrayed in advertisements.

Packaging Strategies

CHANGING THE PACKAGE In general, management has two reasons for considering a package change — to combat a decrease in sales and to expand a market by attracting new groups of customers. More specifically, a firm may want to correct a poor feature in the existing container, or it may want to take advantage of new materials. Some companies change their containers to aid in promotional programs. A new package may be used as a major appeal in advertising copy, or because the old container may not show up well in advertisements. A package change may be an important element in a brand repositioning strategy.

family packaging
A strategy of using either highly similar packages for all products or packages with a common and clearly noticeable feature.

PACKAGING THE PRODUCT LINE A company must decide whether to develop a family resemblance in the packaging of its several products. **Family packaging** involves the use of identical packages for all products or the use of packaging with some common feature. Campbell's, for example, has uses virtually identical packaging on its condensed soup products for many years (see "Marketing at Work" File 11-4). Management's philosophy concerning family packaging generally parallels its feelings about family branding. When new products are added to a line, promotional values associated with old products extend to the new ones. On the other hand, family packaging should be used only when the products are related in use and are of similar quality.

REUSE PACKAGING Another strategy to be considered is **reuse packaging**. Should the company design and promote a package that can serve other purposes after the original contents have been consumed? Decorative biscuit tins can be used for any number of household functions, such as button boxes, containers for school supplies, or children's small-toy storage. Baby-food jars make great containers for small parts such as nuts, bolts, and screws. Reuse packaging also should stimulate repeat purchases as the consumer attempts to acquire a matching set of containers.

multiple packaging
The practice of placing several units of the same product in one container.

MULTIPLE PACKAGING For many years there has been a trend toward **multiple packaging**, or the practice of placing several units in one container. Dehydrated soups, motor oil, beer, golf balls, building hardware, candy bars, towels, and countless other products are packaged in multiple units. Test after test has proved that multiple packaging increases total sales of a product.

Criticisms of Packaging

Packaging is in the forefront today because of its relationship to environmental pollution issues. Perhaps the biggest challenges facing packagers is how to dispose of used containers, which are a major contributor to the solid-waste disposal problem. Consumers' desire for convenience (in the form of throw-away containers) conflicts with their desire for a clean environment.

In many ways, the debate over the environmental impact of packaging often appears impossible to resolve, as the issue of the disposability of packaging is weighed against that of the use of energy and other effects associated with manufacturing it. Over the last decade the use of environmentally friendly containers has become common. LMG Reliance, a Winnipeg company, manufactures the Enviro-Chem agricultural chemical container, part of a closed-loop recycling system that involves the collection of used containers from landfill sites for recycling. Dow Canada produces its Fantastik cleaner in a stand-up pouch refill, as do many other makers of cleaners and detergents. The issue is, however, not a simple one. Environmentalists argue that companies should abandon disposable products, but the alternatives are often fraught with problems, as considerable energy may be required for their production and in recycling them for reuse.

Soft-drink and beer companies have moved toward a completely refillable packaging strategy, involving the exclusive use of glass bottles. Companies that have for years been supplying the restaurant industry and providing Canadians with convenient disposable products have been greatly affected by the environmental movement and have had to adopt strategies aimed at developing products that are less harmful to the environment.

Other criticisms of packaging are:

◆ *Packaging depletes our natural resources.* This criticism is offset to some extent by the use of recycled materials in the package and the fact that packaging reduces spoilage.

◆ *Packaging is excessively expensive.* In producing beer, for example, as much as half the production cost goes for the container. On the other hand, effective packaging reduces transportation costs and losses from product spoilage.

◆ *Health hazards occur from some forms of plastic packaging and some aerosol cans.* Government regulations have banned the use of several of these suspect packaging materials.

◆ *Packaging is deceptive.* Excessive packaging may convey the impression of containing more than the actual contents. Government regulation plus improvements in business practices regarding packaging have reduced the intensity of this criticism, although it is heard on occasion.

◆ *Package disposal.* Throwaway containers contribute significantly to the volume of solid waste in landfills, as well as contributing to litter problems.

Marketing at Work 11-4

A Soup-er New Look

Campbell's Condensed Soup recently took stock of its fifty-four soup varieties and decided the time was right for an updated look which it hopes will make the brand stand out more on supermarket shelves.

Changing packaging is not an easy decision. If packaging remains the same for too long, a brand runs the risk of becoming tired and outdated. However, if the package is changed too quickly, or too dramatically, customers may believe that the product too has changed and thus the brand image suffers.

Campbell's has a lot riding on this decision. At the ripe old age of 102, it is the leader in the Canadian soup market, valued at $400 million a year, and can be found in the cupboards of 80 percent of Canadian households.

Campbell's objective was to make their packaging more uniform and make it easier for consumers to find what they are looking for. The challenge was how to update the brand's look and make it more useful for consumers, while maintaining the comfort and warmth of the original design. The result is labels with a new typeface, a picture of a bowl of soup, a recipe, and a colour banding system that categorizes the varieties. In Canada, labels will be bilingual and will also provide nutritional information as 70 percent of Canadians feel that nutritional information on packaging is important.

The colour banding system will categorize soups into subgroups such as broths, creams, half-fat, and 25 percent less sodium. It is hoped that the banding along with the photo-graph will not only make each variety more identifiable, but it may encourage consumers to try different flavours within the same subgroup.

Campbell's feels that the new cans are more contemporary, more useful and relevant, but still warm and comforting. The additional label elements should not only make it easier for consumers to shop, but encourage them to buy more.

Source: Adapted from Shawna Cohen, "Taking Stock," *Marketing Magazine*, October 11, 1999, p. 25.

 Labelling

Labelling is another product feature that requires managerial attention. The **label** is part of a product that carries information about the product or the seller. A label may be part of a package, or it may be a tag attached directly to the product. Obviously there is a close relationship among labelling, packaging, and branding.

Types of Labels

Typically, labels are classified as brand, grade, or descriptive. A **brand label** is simply the brand alone applied to the product or to the package. Thus, some oranges are brand-labelled (stamped) Sunkist or Jaffa, and some clothes carry the brand label Sanforized. A **grade label** identifies the quality with a letter, number, or word. Canadian beef is grade-labelled A, B, or C, and each grade is subdivided by number from 1 to 4, indicating an increasing fat content.

label
The part of a product that carries written information about the product or the seller.

brand label
The application of the brand name alone to a product or package.

grade label
Identification of the quality (grade) of a product by means of a letter, number, or word.

descriptive label
A label that gives information regarding the use, care, performance, or other features of a product.

eco-labelling
Seals of approval awarded by government to encourage environmentally safe products.

statutory labelling requirements
Federal and provincial laws regulating packaging and labelling.

Descriptive labels give objective information about the use, construction, care, performance, or other features of the product. On a descriptive label for a can of corn, there will be statements concerning the type of corn (golden sweet), the style (creamed or in niblet kernels), and the can size, number of servings, other ingredients, and nutritional content. There is also growing interest in **eco-labelling**, such as the Canadian government's Environmental Choice program, which encourages environmentally safe products through awarding seals of approval.[25] Many companies are now redesigning their products to qualify for environmental labels offered through such programs, which are now in operation in many countries worldwide.[26]

Statutory Labelling Requirements

The importance of packaging and labelling in its potential for influencing the consumer's purchasing decision is reflected in the large number of federal and provincial laws that contain **statutory labelling requirements** to regulate this marketing activity. At the federal level, the Competition Act[27] regulates the area of misleading advertising, and a number of companies have been convicted of misleading advertising for the false or deceptive statements that have appeared on their packages. In this case, the information that appears on a package or label has been considered to constitute an advertisement.

The Hazardous Products Act[28] gives the Government of Canada the power to regulate the sale, distribution, advertising, and labelling of certain consumer products that are considered dangerous. As such, cleaning substances, chemicals, and aerosol products, must carry on their labels a series of symbols that indicate the danger associated with the product and the precautions that should be taken with its use.

Similarly the federal Food and Drugs Act regulates the sale of food, drugs, cosmetics, and medical devices. Certain misleading and deceptive packaging and labelling practices are specifically prohibited. Without question, the strictest regulations applied to packaging in Canada pertain to the cigarette industry. Amendments to the Tobacco Products Control Act in 1993 required manufacturers to make a number of very detailed changes to their cigarette packages. Challenges to these amendments were made to the Supreme Court of Canada, and in 1995 it ruled that "the requirement to place unattributed health messages on tobacco packages infringed on the Charter."[29]

The Textile Labelling Act requires that manufacturers label their products according to the fibre content of the product, with the percentage of each fibre in excess of 5 percent listed.

The Consumer Packaging and Labelling Act regulates all aspects of the packaging and labelling of consumer products in this country. The regulations that have been passed under this Act require that most products sold in Canada bear bilingual labels. The net quantity of the product must appear on the label in both metric and imperial units. The Act also makes provision for the standardization of container sizes.

The provinces have also moved into the field of regulating packaging and labelling. A number of provinces have passed legislation regarding misleading advertising, and any information that appears on a package or label is considered an advertisement.

We can expect to see further changes in the labels required on food and grocery items in the future, as consumers demand more information about the products they are consuming and using. The most likely changes relate to the listing of nutritional information on food products, brought about by the increasing interest of consumers in their health and nutrition.

Other Image-Building Features

A well-rounded program for product planning and development will include a company policy on several additional product attributes: product design, colour, quality, warranty, and after-sale service.

Product Design and Colour

One way to satisfy customers and gain a competitive advantage is through skilful **product design**. In fact, a distinctive design may be the only feature that significantly differentiates a product. Many firms feel that there is considerable glamour and general promotional appeal in product design and the designer's name. In the field of business products, engineering design has long been recognized as extremely important. Today there is a realization of the marketing value of appearance design as well. Office machines and office furniture are examples of business products that reflect recent conscious attention to product design, often with good sales results. The marketing significance of design has been recognized for years in the field of consumer products, from big items like automobiles and refrigerators to small products like fountain pens and apparel.

Good design can improve the marketability of a product by making it easier to operate, upgrading its quality, improving its appearance, and/or reducing manufacturing costs. One example is Kohler Co.'s newly designed bathtub that has a door allowing easy, safe access for children, seniors, and the handicapped. Some designs fall in and out of favour with the buying public. The Volkswagen Beetle was re-introduced in 1998 with the unmistakable styling of the 60's version. Ford is expected to release the new Thunderbird in 2001 derived from the classic 50's version that made the nameplate legendary. Recognizing the strategic importance of design, many companies have elevated the design function in the corporate hierarchy. In fact, it has been pointed out that design changes have assisted the iMac in saving Apple and that the new Beetle has provided needed revitalization to the image of Volkswagen.[30]

Colour often is the determining factor in a customer's acceptance or rejection of a product, whether that product is a dress, a table, or an automobile. Colour by itself, however, is no selling advantage because many competing firms offer colour. The marketing advantage comes in knowing the right colour and in knowing when to change colours. Sometimes just the presence of color can be enough. In the late 90s the Apple iMac PC in vibrant colors such as grape and tangerine — expected to be popular for home use, the products sold out within months and were a hit in both home and offices. If a garment manufacturer or a retail store's fashion co-ordinator guesses wrong on what will be the fashionable colour in this season's clothing, disaster may ensue.

Product Quality

quality
How well a product or service meets the expectations of the customer.

The **quality** of a product is extremely significant, but it is probably the most difficult of all the image-building features to define. Users frequently disagree on what constitutes quality in a product, whether it is a cut of meat or a work of art or music. Personal tastes are deeply involved. One guideline in managing product quality is that the quality level should be compatible with the intended use of a product; the level need not be any higher. In fact, good and poor sometimes are misleading terms for quality. Correct and incorrect or right and wrong may be more appropriate. If a person is making a peach cobbler, grade B or C peaches are the correct quality. They are not necessarily the best quality, but they are right for the intended use. It is not necessary to pay grade A prices for large, well-formed peaches when these features are destroyed in making the cobbler. Another key to the successful management of quality is to maintain consistency of product output at the desired quality level.

In recent years, North American manufacturers have been increasingly concerned about the quality of their products.[31] For many years, consumers have complained about the poor quality of some products — both materials and workmanship. Foreign products — Japanese cars, for example — made serious inroads into the market because these products were perceived as being of better quality than their North American counterparts.

Quality of output also is a primary consideration in the production and marketing of services. The quality of its service can determine whether a firm will be successful. Yet it is virtually impossible for a firm to standardize performance quality among its units of service output. We frequently experience differences in performance quality from the same organization in appliance repairs, haircuts, medical exams, football games, or marketing courses.

To aid in determining and maintaining the desired level of quality in its goods and services, a company should establish a quality-improvement program. This should be an ongoing group effort of the design, production, marketing, and customer-service departments. A firm may then justifiably claim in its advertising that its product quality has improved. The problem is getting consumers to believe this fact.

Warranties

warranty
An assurance given to buyers that they will be compensated in case the product does not perform up to reasonable expectations.

The purpose of a **warranty** is to assure buyers they will be compensated in case the product does not perform up to reasonable expectations. In years past, courts seemed to recognize only **express warranties** — those stated in written or spoken words. Usually these were quite limited in their coverage and seemed mainly to protect the seller from buyers' claims. As a result, the following caution was appropriate: "Caveat emptor," which means "Let the buyer beware."

express warranty
A statement in written or spoken words regarding restitution from seller to customer if the seller's product does not perform up to reasonable expectations.

But times change! Consumer complaints led to a campaign to protect the consumer in many areas, including product warranties. Courts and government agencies have broadened the scope of warranty coverage by recognizing **implied warranty**. This means that a warranty was intended, although not actually stated, by the seller. Furthermore, producers are being held responsible even when the sales contract is between the retailer and the consumer. Now the caution is: "Caveat venditor," or "Let the seller beware."

implied warranty
An intended but unstated assurance regarding restitution from seller to customer if the seller's product does not perform up to reasonable expectations.

In recent years manufacturers have responded to legislation and consumer complaints by broadening and simplifying their warranties. Many sellers are using their warranties as promotional devices to stimulate purchase by reducing consumers' risks. Advertising may be designed around claims regarding the quality of the warranty. This has been popular with high-ticket items such as automobiles claiming coverage for a determined number of years or kilometres. The effective handling of consumers' complaints related to warranties can be a significant factor in strengthening a company's marketing program.

Some provinces have passed Consumer Products Warranty Acts. These Acts sometimes provide for statutory warranties and the form written warranties must take.

Postsale Service

postsale activity or service
The final stage of the selling process, including delivery, financing, installation, routine maintenance, employee training, billing, and other areas important to customer satisfaction.

Many companies have to provide **postsale service**, notably repairs, to fulfil the terms of their warranties. Other firms offer postsale services such as maintenance and repairs not only to satisfy their customers but also to augment their revenues. Companies that offer products such as automobiles and mechanical equipment such as elevators or heating and ventilation systems rely on their service contracts for a substantial portion of their sales and profits. With more complex products and increasingly demanding and vocal consumers, postsale service has become essential. A frequent consumer gripe is that manufacturers and retailers do not provide adequate repair service for the products they sell.

Many responsive companies have established toll-free 1-800 telephone numbers that connect the customer directly with a customer service representative. Many actually invite customers to complain, acting on the principle that if the customer doesn't complain, the company won't know there is a problem and can't take steps to correct it. This postsale service is also required for trouble-shooting and assembly assistance for many products and services such as audio systems or Internet installation. Many companies post their 1-800 customer service numbers on the doors of their stores and feature them in their advertising. While it may not always be pleasant to listen to customer complaints, the alternative of customers taking their business elsewhere is much worse in the long run.

Postsale service has the potential to be either a differential advantage or a disadvantage for an organization. Therefore, it is an issue that managers must monitor on a regular basis.

Summary

Effective product management involves developing and then monitoring the various features of a product — its brand, package, labelling, design, quality, warranty, and postsale service. A consumer's purchase decision may take into account not just the basic good or service but also the brand and perhaps one or more of the other want-satisfying product features.

A brand is a means of identifying and differentiating the products of an organization. Branding aids sellers in managing their promotional and pricing activities. The dual responsibilities of brand ownership are to promote the brand and to maintain a consistent level of quality. Selecting a good brand name — and there are relatively few really good ones — is difficult. Once a brand becomes well known, the owner may have to protect it from becoming a generic term.

Manufacturers must decide whether to brand their products and/or sell under an intermediary's brand. Intermediaries must decide whether to carry producers' brands alone or to establish their own brands as well. In addition, intermediaries must decide whether to carry generic products. Both producers and intermediaries must set policies regarding the branding of groups of products and branding for market saturation.

A growing number of companies are recognizing that the brands they own are — or can be — among their most valuable assets. They are building brand equity — the added value that a brand brings to a product. It's difficult to build brand equity but, if it can be done, it can be the basis for expanding a product mix. Products with abundant brand equity also lend themselves to trademark licensing, a marketing arrangement that is growing in popularity.

Packaging is becoming increasingly important as sellers recognize the problems, as well as the marketing opportunities, associated with it. Companies must choose among strategies such as family packaging, multiple packaging, and changing the package. Labelling, a related activity, provides information about the product and the seller. Many consumer criticisms of marketing target packaging and labelling. As a result, there are several laws regulating these activities.

Companies are now recognizing the marketing value of both product design and quality. Good design can improve the marketability of a product; it may be the only feature that differentiates a product. Projecting the appropriate quality image and then delivering the level of quality desired by customers are essential to marketing success. In many cases, firms need to enhance product quality to eliminate a differential disadvantage; in others, firms seek to build quality as a way of gaining a differential advantage.

Warranties and postsale service require considerable management attention these days because of consumer complaints and governmental regulations. Product liability is an issue of great consequence to companies because of the financial risk associated with consumers' claims of injuries caused by the firms' products.

Many companies provide postsale service, mainly repairs, to fulfil the terms of their warranties and/or to augment their revenues. To promote customer satisfaction, a number of firms are improving their methods of inviting and responding to consumer complaints.

Key Terms and Concepts

Brand 326
Brand name 326
Brand mark 326
Trademark 326
Generic name 331
Family-brand strategy 335
Multiple-brand strategy 336
Brand equity 336
Packaging 339

Family packaging 341
Reuse packaging 341
Multiple packaging 342
Label 343
Brand label 343
Grade label 343
Descriptive label 344
Eco-labelling 344
Statutory labelling requirements 344

Product design 345
Product colour 345
Product quality 345
Warranty 346
Express warranty 346
Implied warranty 346
Postsale service 346

Questions and Problems

1. List five brand names that you think are good ones and five you consider poor. Explain the reasoning behind your choices. Consider factors such as quality, packaging, size, image, etc.

2. Evaluate each of the following brand names in light of the characteristics of a good brand, indicating the strong and weak points of each name.

    a.   Xerox (office copiers).

    b.   Tip Top (retailer).

    c.   Holiday Inns (hotels).

    d.   Moschino (clothing)

    e.   Red Lobster (restaurant).

    f.   Ecco (footwear)

3. When does a company or product name become a brand? What distinction do you make between the concepts of "name" and "brand"? Does the term "brand" imply that the product or company has achieved a certain status?

4. Suggest some brands that are on the verge of becoming generic. What course of action should a company take to protect the separate identity of its brands?

5. What are brand extensions? Why would a company launch a new product as a brand extension rather than as a completely new brand? What are the risks associated with such a strategy?

6. In which of the following cases should the company adopt the strategy of family branding?

    a.   A manufacturer of men's underwear introduces essentially the same products for women.

    b.   A manufacturer of women's cosmetics adds a line of men's cosmetics to its product assortment.

    c.   A manufacturer of hair-care products introduces a line of portable electric hair dryers.

7. Suppose you are employed by the manufacturer of a well-known brand of skis. Your company is planning to add skates and water skis to its product line. It has no previous experience with either of these two new products. You are given the assignment of selecting a brand name for the skates and water skis. Your main problem is in deciding whether to adopt a family-brand policy. That is, should you use the snow-ski brand for either or both of the new products? Or should you develop separate names for each of the new items? You

note that Campbell's (soups) and McCain (French-fries) use family brands. You also note that Sears and Procter & Gamble generally do the opposite. They use different names for each group of products (Sears) or each separate product (P&G). What course of action would you recommend? Why?

8. A manufacturer of a well-known brand of ski boots acquired a division of a company that marketed a well-known brand of skis. What brand strategy should the new organization adopt? Should all products (skis and boots) now carry the boot brand? Should they carry the ski brand? Is there some other alternative that would be better?

9. Why do some firms sell an identical product under more than one of their own brands?

10. Assume that a large department-store chain proposed to Black & Decker that the latter company supply the chain with a line of power tools carrying the store's own label. What factors should Black & Decker management consider in making such a decision? Would the situation be any different if a supermarket chain had approached Kraft General Foods with a request to supply a private-label jelly dessert similar to Jell-O?

11. A Canadian manufacturer of camping equipment (stoves, lanterns, tents, sleeping bags) plans to introduce its line into several Eastern European countries. Should management select the same brand name for all countries or market under the name that is used in Canada? Should they consider using a different name in each country? What factors should influence this decision?

12. What changes would you recommend in the typical packaging of these products?

    a. Soft drinks.

    b. Hairspray.

    c. Adventure vacation.

    d. Toothpaste.

13. Give examples of products for which the careful use of the colour of the product has increased sales. Can you cite examples to show that poor use of colour may hurt a company's marketing program?

14. Explain the relationship between a product warranty on small electric appliances and the manufacturer's distribution system for these products.

15. How would the warranty policies set by a manufacturer of skis differ from those adopted by an automobile manufacturer?

Hands-On Marketing

1. Visit a large local supermarket and:

    a. Obtain the store manager's opinions regarding which products are excellently packaged and which are poorly packaged. Ask the manager for reasons.

    b. Walk around the store and compile your own list of excellent and poor packages. What factors did you use to judge quality of packaging?

2. Ask five students who are not taking this course to evaluate the following names for a proposed expensive perfume: Entice, Nitespark, At Risk, and Foreglow. For evaluation purposes, share with the students the characteristics of a good brand name. Also ask them to suggest a better name for the new perfume.

Chapter Twelve

Services Marketing and Customer Relationships

This chapter focuses on the marketing of services and the role of service in supporting marketing in all its forms. It discusses the changes in the field of marketing generated by the growth experienced in the services industries and through an increased emphasis on service provision across all industries. The concept of service quality and the connection between quality and profit, the linkage between human resource practices and marketing, and the development and implications of relationship marketing are key issues addressed in this chapter. After studying this chapter, you should have an understanding of:

◆ The nature of services.

◆ The importance of services in our economy.

◆ The characteristics of services, and the marketing implications of these characteristics.

◆ The issues related to the planning and marketing of services.

◆ The four Rs of services marketing.

◆ The relationship marketing approach.

◆ The impact of technology in the provision of services.

Tim Hortons: Donut Shop or National Institution?

The food services industry is a prime example of how tangible and intangible elements combine to create the majority of service industries. This also represents a traditional service industry that has benefited substantially from the considerable growth in service consumption that is expected to continue well into this new millennium.

One icon of the Canadian food service industry is Tim Hortons. In twenty-five years, the TDL Group of Oakville, Ontario has evolved into 1,624 franchised restaurants with over 42,000 employees across the country. It has its own legend, lingo, and has come to occupy a central place in Canadian life. It's where we go before, after, or instead of going to work, school, church, or club-hopping.[1] Open 24 hours a day and 364 days a year, it's always there when we want to meet friends, or just need to boost our caffeine/sugar level.

Clearly Canadian in its identity from its NHL-playing founder, its distinctive red take-out cups, friendly media

persona, to its summer camps and community sports sponsorship, each location has become for regular patrons a central part of the surrounding community. The nature and consistency of its menu permits easy, quick service — even speedier should you "drive-thru" for your order. Strict control over simple preparation processes results in consistent quality. How many places can boast of customers eager to pay for a self-advertising mug that they wash and return with each day? So familiar are many of the customers that often it isn't necessary to place your order as some counter staff already know what you will order — so much so that such customer familiarity has been spoofed in a recent series of ads. Tim Hortons has relied on the fact that Canadians can laugh and poke fun at themselves, and will when given the opportunity.

The annual R-r-roll up the Rim promotion, now in its fourteenth year, has reached a momentum that few promotions have ever seen. The expression has become part of the vernacular and has, again, spawned ads each year showing that it's a Canadian thing! It has evolved from a campaign aimed at carrying coffee sales into the summer months to a pure customer appreciation program.[2] It's quick and easy to play, with lots of chances to win. Its success has resulted from repeatedly building customer loyalty through rewarding existing customers rather than focusing on attracting new ones.

Clearly a Canadian phenomenon, Tim Hortons stores in the United States number about 110 and are reportedly not very successful — they may have failed to grasp the notion of niceness that's supposed to be served with coffee. Is it that they don't understand the experience of "going out for a coffee," or do Americans take themselves too seriously?

Nature and Importance of Services

Over the past twenty years, a major focus on the role of services in the Canadian economy has changed the thinking of marketers. In the first month of 2000, more than three-quarters of the 14.8 million working Canadians were employed in the services sector.[3] Many economists now see the services sector as holding the key to improved economic growth and job creation in the future as the services industries currently account for more than two-thirds of Canada's Gross Domestic Product.[4] Virtually all growth in employment experienced in the 1990s was due to growth in the service sector.

Some of the reasons for the rapid growth of this sector, which is undoubtedly the fastest-growing part of the Canadian economy, stem from the major environmental changes we discussed in Chapter 3. You will recall that these included such things as a more technologically oriented world and massive communication changes as well as changing work force demographics. Demands for and the ability to provide services have increased. For example, an entire industry has grown up around servicing the Internet. Other examples include increased requirements for eating out with both parents in the work force, more interest in time saving and convenience, as is acquired through home cleaning services and telephone banking, and the rapid growth in television networks and home entertainment products such as videos and direct-to-home television. All of these environmental changes have placed greater emphasis on services and increasing demands on the quality of service provision. Marketers have been required to change their focus from trying to sell tangible goods to identifying customer needs and wants in services, either to accompany those goods or on their own.

This discussion of the growth in the service sector tends to focus on the expansion of the economy in areas that have traditionally been classified as service industries. When we consider that the service sector includes transportation, entertainment, education, health care, government and public services, and financial services, it is no wonder that such a large portion of the Canadian economy is included. Advances in technology that have dramatically improved productivity in goods-producing industries have contributed to a decline in the percentage of jobs in manufacturing. While this is all very important, we should not lose sight of a very important aspect of this chapter — the need to remember that service is an integral component of the marketing of any product, whether tangible or intangible. Therefore, we will continue to refer to the provision of service and the importance of customer service in the achievement of customer satisfaction.

Traditionally, services marketing has been thought to be different from the marketing of tangible products. In concept, however, they are essentially the same. In each case, the marketer must select and analyze target markets. Then, a marketing program must be developed. There are characteristics of services that differentiate them from tangible products, and these must be considered in developing the marketing program. This section will identify these characteristics. Most tangible goods have a service element and, as consumers place more value on the services that accompany the purchase of tangible goods, the distinctions between services marketing and tangible-goods marketing become less significant.

Definition and Scope of Services

We are talking about the marketing of services, but do we have a clear understanding of what we mean by "services"? The term is difficult to define because, in addition to being the core product being sold in some instances (such as in banking or education, where the core is intangible), services are also marketed in conjunction with tangible products. Services require supporting products (you need an airplane to provide air transportation services), and products require supporting services (delivery, credit, and repair services accompany the sale of a refrigerator). Furthermore, a company may sell a combination of goods and services. Thus, along with repair service for your car, you might buy spark plugs or an oil filter. It may be helpful to think of every product as a mix of goods and services located on a continuum ranging from pure goods to pure services, as shown in Figure 12-1.

To move closer to a useful definition, we identify two classes of services. In the first group are services that are the main purpose or object of a transaction. These are what we have been referring to in this chapter as the **core services**. As an example, suppose you want to rent a car from Avis. The rental car company needs a car (tangible product) to provide the rental service. But you are buying the rental use of the car, not the car itself. The second group consists of **supplementary services** that support or facilitate the sale of a tangible good or another service. Thus, when you buy a compact disc player, you may want technical information and service from a salesperson and the opportunity to pay with a credit card. Virtually every transaction that one can think of involves both tangible and intangible elements. It is useful to distinguish between situations where the core of what is being exchanged is intangible — this is the situation that we refer to as the marketing of services — and the supplementary services and general level of customer service that accompanies the sale of everything that we buy.

Consequently, our definition of services in this chapter is as follows: **Services** are identifiable, intangible activities that are sometimes the main object of a transaction and at other times support the sale of tangible products or other services. Although we are interested primarily in the marketing of services that are the principal objective of a transaction, as in financial services, entertainment, hotel accommodations, and car rentals, we must not overlook the very important services associated with the marketing of literally every product, whether tangible or intangible. Increasingly, marketers are realizing that one of the most effective ways to compete and to differentiate one's company from the competition is to offer excellent service. Thus, even to a company selling industrial supplies, there is a challenge to deliver the product on time and in good condition and to ensure that the customer is billed correctly and called on regularly.

We are concerned here primarily with the services marketed by business or professional firms with profit-making motives — commercial services. This is in contrast to services of not-for-profit organizations, such as churches, universities and colleges, arts and cultural organizations, and the government. A useful classification of commercial services by industry is as follows:

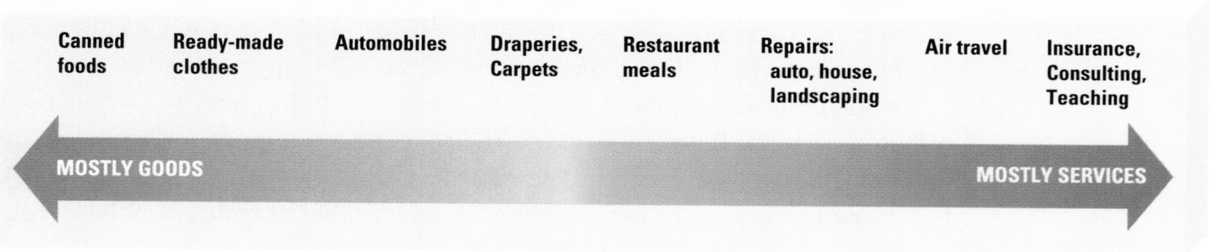

services
An activity that is separately identifiable, intangible, and the main object of a transaction designed to provide want-satisfaction for customers.

FIGURE 12-1
A Goods-Services Continuum

| Canned foods | Ready-made clothes | Automobiles | Draperies, Carpets | Restaurant meals | Repairs: auto, house, landscaping | Air travel | Insurance, Consulting, Teaching |

MOSTLY GOODS ←——————————————————————————————→ MOSTLY SERVICES

- Accommodations (includes rental of hotels, motels, apartments, houses, and cottages).

- Household operations (includes utilities, house repairs, painting and decorating, repairs of equipment in the house, landscaping, and household cleaning).

- Recreation and entertainment (includes rental and repair of equipment used to participate in recreation and entertainment activities; also admission to all entertainment, recreation, and amusement events).

- Food services (includes restaurants, fast-food outlets, and catering services).

- Personal care (includes laundry, dry cleaning, and beauty care).

- Medical and other health care (includes all medical services, dental, nursing, hospitalization, optometry, and other health care).

- Private education (courses taken at a community college, university, or private college).

- Business and other professional services (includes legal, accounting, marketing research, management consulting, and computer services).

- Insurance, banking, and other financial services (includes personal and business insurance, credit and loan services, investment counselling, and tax services).

- Transportation (includes freight and passenger services on airplanes, trains and ferries, automobile repairs and rentals).

- Communications (includes telephone, facsimile, Internet, e-mail, and specialized business communication services).

Note that no attempt was made to separate the above groups into consumer and business services, as we did with tangible products. In fact, both market groups purchase most.

Importance of Services

North America has genuinely become a service economy. More than 76 percent of all jobs in Canada are now accounted for by the service sector, and approximately 73 percent of the country's gross domestic product is accounted for by services. Also, service jobs typically hold up better during a recession than do jobs in industries that produce tangible products. Canadians have become more dependent on the service sector for their jobs. Much of that employment, particularly in retail organizations, is now on a part-time basis.

While the share of total output accounted for by manufacturing has dropped to less than 20 percent in Canada, there is some evidence that even this value is overstated, as many of the activities that add value or contribute to final output in manufacturing companies are really services. Some writers have observed that the distinction between services and manufacturing is becoming less useful. Nevertheless, governments in particular continue to classify companies as manufacturing *or* services firms, despite the fact, for example, that the largest single supplier to General Motors is not a parts manufacturer, but Blue Cross–Blue Shield, the employee health-insurance provider.

The highest-paying jobs in the services sector include a mixture of transportation, the public sector, and financial services. The absolute top dogs of the service sector work in brokerage houses and stock exchanges.[5] The rapid growth of the technology industries has created a corresponding explosion in the number of technology jobs. For example, the Internet and other advances in computer systems have created a need for systems analysts, program co-ordinators, network support specialists, systems support specialists, technical writers, and instructional technologists, among others.

The growth in the market for **personal services** is at least partially explained by the relative prosperity, and increasing standard of living, that Canadians have enjoyed during the past forty years. It could be argued that many of the tangible products that we buy tend to be necessity purchases. People buy food, housing, clothing, and automobiles to meet essential needs. On the other hand, many services tend to be purchased, by end consumers at least, from discretionary spending. The consumer usually purchases such things as travel, entertainment, restaurant meals, and home cleaning services after the essentials have been paid for. This spending has increased as the average standard of living has increased.

The Canadian population that has entered the new millennium is more sophisticated than their parents and more active in leisure and entertainment activities. Increased global transportation systems have resulted in a high-growth travel industry, and advanced communications systems have stimulated increased awareness of travel destinations. Affluence and lifestyle changes have contributed significantly to this rapid growth in personal services.

The growth of **business services** may be attributed to the fact that business has become increasingly complex, specialized, and competitive. As a consequence, management has been forced to call in experts to provide services in marketing research, taxation, advertising, labour relations, and a host of other areas. Technology has also played a major role in the expansion of demand for business services. Even amid relatively high rates of unemployment in parts of Canada, jobs in high-technology fields may still go unfilled because of a shortage of trained individuals to fill these vacancies.

Characteristics of Services

The special nature of services stems from a number of characteristics that distinguish services from tangible products. These features create special marketing challenges and opportunities. As a result, service firms often require strategic marketing programs that are substantially different from those found in the marketing of tangible goods. Also, these characteristics of services should cause us to consider certain implications for the provision of customer service in all industries.

intangibility
A characteristic of a service indicating that it has no physical attributes and, as a result, is impossible for customers to taste, feel, see, hear, or smell before buying.

INTANGIBILITY Because services are **intangible**, it is impossible for customers to sample — taste, feel, see, hear, or smell — a service before they buy it. Consequently, a company's promotional program must portray the benefits to be derived from the service, rather than emphasizing the service itself. Four promotional strategies that may be used to suggest service benefits are as follows:[6]

◆ *Visualization.* For example, virtual banks and chartered banks that offer Internet banking services depict the convenience and freedom of extensive twenty-four-hour banking services by showing clients curled up at home late at night in their comfy clothes doing their banking. Or alternatively, they are on holiday spread out on the beach with their laptops.

◆ *Association.* Connect the service with a tangible object, person, or place. The Australian airline, Qantas, uses a cuddly koala bear in its advertising to project a warm, friendly image of Australia. Prudential Insurance suggests stability and security with its logo depicting the Rock of Gibraltar. Met Life uses the familiar Snoopy character as a sales agent in television spots.

What exactly do Met Life customers associate with Snoopy?

WE CAN POINT YOU IN THE RIGHT DIRECTION.

When it comes to planning your future, we believe a little guidance goes a long way. So with the help of nationally recognized authorities, MetLife's Consumer Education Center has created the Life Advice℠ series. It's an information resource that can help you plan for more than sixty important events in your life, events that can have a major impact on your health, property and financial well-being.

Each Life Advice brochure includes practical information on the issues involved, to help you make sense of it all. Our Directory lists Life Advice pamphlets on a wide range of topics such as saving for college, getting married, becoming a parent, buying a car or home, starting a business and planning for your retirement.

They're all significant events where MetLife's Life Advice can point you in the right direction.

For your free Life Advice Directory, just visit the MetLife Web site at www.metlife.com or call 1-800-MetLife today.

INSURANCE · MUTUAL FUNDS · ANNUITIES · EMPLOYEE BENEFITS · PENSIONS · INVESTMENT MANAGEMENT

GET MET. IT PAYS.®
1-800-MetLife®

SCHULZ

PEANUTS © United Feature Syndicate, Inc.

Auto & Home Insurance offered by Metropolitan Property and Casualty Insurance Co., Warwick, R.I. Mutual Funds offered by MetLife Securities, Inc., NY, NY. Life Insurance & Annuities offered by Metropolitan Life Insurance Co., NY, NY. 96041AJ4 MLIC-LD © 1997 Metropolitan Life Insurance Co., NY, NY

◆ *Physical representation.* GM Goodwrench uses the image of their service representatives. All print and television ads show clean-cut employees in their familiar, freshly-pressed black and red uniform beaming a warm, broad smile to stress trustworthiness, dependability and cleanliness.

◆ *Documentation.* Midas muffler shops have used their warranty as print advertisements. This represents the company's commitment to the customer and supports the claim of performance, dependability and customer satisfaction. Sylvan Learning Centres use testimonials of children and parents stating the changes and improvements that have resulted from using these programs.

INSEPARABILITY Services typically cannot be separated from the creator-seller of the service. Moreover, many services are created, dispensed, and consumed simultaneously. For example, dentists and hairstylists create and dispense almost all their services at the same time, and they require the presence of the consumer for the services to be performed. Because of this **inseparability** feature, many people are involved concurrently in the production operations and the marketing effort in services firms, and the customers receive and consume the services at the production site — in the firm's service "factory," so to speak. Consequently, customers' opinions regarding a service frequently are formed through their contact in face-to-face or telephone meetings with service personnel and their impressions of the physical surroundings of the company's premises. Too often, contact personnel think of themselves as producers-creators of the service rather than as marketers.

> **inseparability**
> A characteristic of a service indicating that it cannot be separated from the creator-seller of the service.

From a marketing standpoint, inseparability frequently means that direct sale is the only possible channel of distribution, and a seller's services cannot be sold in very many markets. This characteristic limits the scale of operation in a firm. One person can repair only so many autos in a day or treat only so many medical patients.

As an exception to the inseparability feature, services may be sold by a person who is representing the creator of the service. A travel agent, insurance broker, or rental agent, for instance, may represent and help promote services that will be sold by the organizations that are producing them. Another way in which services are delivered by intermediaries is through franchising. Companies such as Swiss Chalet and National Tilden Rent-a-Car are in the service business, but their head offices deal with customers through franchise holders in various cities.

The inseparability of a service from the people providing it has important implications for companies that are operating in service-oriented businesses. This includes not only those companies in true "service" industries, such as financial services, entertainment, hotels, and restaurants, but also those who must pay particular attention to the services that support the marketing of their tangible products. For example, although Eastern Bakeries is technically a manufacturer of bakery products such as breads and cakes, it is also in the business of making sure that its products are delivered on time and in the quantity and condition the customer ordered.

For the most part, it is the employees of a company who have the greatest influence on the level of service provided to its customers. Eastern Bakeries may bake the most wholesome bread in Eastern Canada, but if employees cannot get it to the retail stores in time for consumers to buy it, then any product advantage Eastern may have had will be lost.

In fact, in many industries, particularly those where the products or services are technologically advanced or difficult for the consumer to understand, or where the customer cannot see important differences among the offerings of the various competitors, the ability to compete comes down to whether a company can deliver superior service. Most *progressive* companies have come to realize that their employees are extremely important in providing a level of service that will keep their customers happy. Sadly, many organizations have not developed the orientation necessary to produce such superior customer-contact employees.[7]

This applies to employees who come into direct contact with the customer — sales staff, repair technicians, and flight attendants — as well as to support personnel, who can damage a company's relationship with its customers even though they may never meet them directly. A clerk in the accounting department who fails to credit a customer's account correctly, or a baggage handler who sends a passenger's suitcase to Halifax when the passenger was travelling to Calgary, is just as responsible for service and customer relations as those staff members who meet and talk with customers.

HETEROGENEITY It is impossible for a service industry, or even an individual seller of services, to standardize output. Each "unit" of the service is somewhat different from other "units" of the same service. This is principally so because of the individualized approach that service providers take to the provision of a service. Because most services are delivered by people, service delivery is prone to the differences that exist across human beings. Because we are all different and our interaction with other people is affected by personality, mood, and a number of other factors, service delivery and quality are bound to vary considerably. For example, an airline does not give the same quality of service on each flight. All repair jobs an auto mechanic does are not of equal quality. An added complication is the fact that it is often difficult to judge the quality of a service. It is particularly difficult to forecast quality in advance of buying a service. A person pays to see a ball game without knowing whether it will be an exciting one (well worth the price of admission) or a dull performance. Some companies are able to address this by allowing customers to sample a service for a limited time — for example, cable television companies will give new subscribers a free trial month's service on new channels. However, it is difficult for most services companies to provide samples.

The **heterogeneity** of services is of concern to service providers, but the ability to deliver customer satisfaction is further complicated by the fact that customer expectations are not at all consistent. Although a student on a short lunch break may spend only fifteen minutes grabbing a quick meal at a restaurant near campus, the same student may take more than an hour to enjoy a pizza with a friend after a Saturday-night movie. In the first case, the customer wants to be served as quickly as possible; in the second, he or she is prepared to wait a little longer for service. Because service expectations differ across customers and even over time for the same customers, it is very difficult for service businesses to standardize their level of service.

In recent years, some service companies have turned to technology in an attempt to standardize the type and quality of service provided, but at the expense of losing personal contact and the ability to respond to customers' questions or concerns. Nevertheless, some technology-delivered services, such as those provided by automated banking machines, telephone banking, and self-service gas stations, can become standardized and are accepted by a large number of customers. Some of these services are even welcomed by customers, as in the case of the U.S. drycleaning chain, Zoots, who have employed technology to increase customer convenience. By providing customers with bar-coded garment bags, clothing is dropped off through a drive-through window, services charged to the customer's credit card, and the cleaned garments can be picked up around the clock from indoor lockers.[8] The entire process can be conducted without any customer contact.

Similarly, many companies and other organizations have installed telephone-answering and voice-mail systems that allow callers to leave messages for staff members who are out

heterogeneity of a service
A characteristic of a service indicating that each unit is somewhat different from other "units" of the same service.

of the office or unable to answer their calls when the telephone rings. Canada's telephone companies have automated directory-assistance services and have introduced a voice-response system for handling third-party collect calls. To automate service even further, the telephone industry has encouraged customers to sign up for calling cards, which eliminate the need to contact an operator to place long-distance calls billed to a third number.

While such technology-based services achieve standardization of service, in part by delegating much of the service provision or delivery to the customers themselves, there are at least some risks inherent in their use. On the other hand, some customers may resent having to do all the work, especially when they are paying for the service. Also, some customers simply prefer to deal with real people and get confused or irritated when they encounter technology. Finally, in some industries management is faced with the dilemma of not being able to keep in touch with customers or to establish relationships with them, when the customers are dealing primarily with machines or computers.[9]

Service companies should pay special attention to the product-planning stage of their marketing programs. From the beginning, management must do all it can to ensure consistency of quality and to maintain high levels of quality control. This important issue of service quality will be discussed in a later section of this chapter.

PERISHABILITY AND FLUCTUATING DEMAND Services are highly perishable, and they cannot be stored. Unused telephone time, empty seats in a stadium, and idle mechanics in a garage all represent business that is lost forever. Furthermore, the market for services fluctuates considerably by season, by day of the week, and by hour of the day. Most ski lifts lie idle all summer, whereas golf courses go unused in the winter. The use of city buses fluctuates greatly during the day.

perishability
A characteristic of a service indicating that it is highly perishable and cannot be stored.

There are notable exceptions to this generalization regarding the **perishability** and storage of services. In health and life insurance, for example, the service is purchased by a person or a company. Then it is held by the insurance company (the seller) until needed by the buyer or the beneficiary. This holding constitutes a type of storage. Similarly, many services generally considered to be "public utilities" are able to store services until they are needed. For example, telephone and electricity services are available on demand. We can access them whenever we need them. Because of this, there is a very real probability that consumers will take such services for granted, simply because they are always there. This causes potential problems for companies that are marketing such services because it makes it difficult for them to interest their customers in buying more or in adopting new services.

The combination of perishability and **fluctuating demand** offers product-planning, pricing, and promotion challenges to services marketing managers. Some organizations have developed new uses for idle plant capacity during off-seasons. Thus, during the summer, several ski resorts operate their ski lifts for hikers and sightseers who want access to higher elevations. Mont Tremblant has increased its summer traffic by more than one hundred times since 1991. This has been through increasing available facilities and other recreational activities. Also, by adding the uniqueness of the Québécois cultural experience to the marketing mix.[10]

Advertising and creative pricing are also used to stimulate demand during slack periods. Hotels offer lower prices and family packages on weekends. Telephone companies offer lower rates at nights and on weekends.

The Four Rs of Services Marketing

The recent focus on marketing in service organizations has brought about an important change in how marketers view their dealings with customers and prospective customers. In short, there has been a realization on the part of many marketing managers that the provision of the four elements of the conventional marketing mix — product, price, advertising and promotion, and distribution channels — is not sufficient to ensure customer satisfaction. While we will devote much of the next four sections of this book to coverage of these four components of the marketing mix, it is important to do so in the context of a new view of marketing, one that focuses on services and how they are delivered. We have labelled the components of this new view the four Rs of marketing.

RETENTION Most successful marketing managers today have accepted the principle that long-term customers are more profitable and that their organizations should pay at least as much attention to keeping their existing customers (or, more correctly, some of them) as they do to trying to attract new ones. Recent studies have demonstrated quite clearly that customers become more profitable the longer they continue to do business with a firm.[11] This is the case because satisfied, long-term customers spend a larger portion of their total expenditure with the firm to which they are loyal. They also cost less to serve because they are generally more satisfied and don't need to be convinced to buy. They make fewer complaints and are less likely to quibble over price, often being prepared to pay more for good service. And they tell others how satisfied they are.

With the advent of electrical utility deregulation in Canada, these service providers find themselves under a threat never before experienced — competition. B.C. Hydro quickly recognized the merits of the previous arguments and after assessing the costs associated with retaining and winning-back consumers decided to begin a customer retention program long before competitive forces began to play out in the provincial market. Print and TV spots were utilized to "humanize" B.C. Hydro and to forge an emotional connection with customers. A Web-based service was designed for business clients to provide instant access to Hydro-related information. The program has been intended to "personalize and crystallize relationships with all three customer segments."[12]

REFERRALS This last point leads to the second of our four Rs, referrals. One of the greatest benefits of satisfying customers is that they will refer their friends and associates to the firm providing them with superior service. This is one of the most important aspects of determining the benefits to be gained from satisfying customers. Through positive word-of-mouth, they can produce large volumes of new business. Conversely, a dissatisfied customer will either spread negative word-of-mouth or will disappear, never to return. Companies that provide a high level of customer service will always keep in mind the potential for existing customers to bring in new ones.

RELATIONSHIPS One of the most important developments in marketing in recent years has been the attention now being paid to the establishment of relationships between companies and their customers. This is an aspect of marketing that is gaining considerable attention and that is linked very closely to the notion that long-term customer satisfaction is a direct result of the provision of superior customer service.[13] The customer's definition of service very often extends to the establishment of a close relationship with a service provider. The idea of forming a relationship with customers makes considerable sense because it leads to the establishment of loyal customers who are likely to be very profitable. However, the establishment of a long-term customer relationship is not a simple task and is one that should be approached following much study of how the firm's customers define a relationship. Recent research has suggested that the customer must define the terms on which a relationship is to be formed with a company and that a company may feel a relationship is in place when the customer is of a quite different opinion.[14]

Many companies are now introducing relationship-marketing programs to try to get closer to their customers so that they will feel more a part of the company. The most notable of these include examples like Saturn, the automaker, which holds picnics and barbeques for Saturn owners. The company also sponsors the construction of local community playgrounds.[15] Many companies base their relationship marketing programs on the establishment of a detailed customer database that will allow them to know as much as possible about their customers so that they can direct tailored communications to each customer. For example, pharmaceutical companies have developed communications programs based upon databases that allow them to communicate with patients to ensure that they are taking their medication correctly.[16] Other higher-end service providers deliver services that exceed customer expectations, providing memorable experiences that forge relationship qualities. The Ritz-Carlton Hotel, for example, provides what they call a "technology butler," a skilled computer technologist available twenty-four hours a day to assist laptop-equipped guests with any software or hardware difficulties — a service appreciated by their high-value business travellers.[17]

RECOVERY The final element in our four Rs of services marketing relates to service recovery — what a company can do to recover customer satisfaction when something has gone wrong. Inevitably, customers will encounter problems and poor service when dealing with service providers. Even the most meticulous companies cannot completely avoid delivering poor service on occasion. The issue is, what can and should the company do when something goes wrong? Certainly, the answer is not "do nothing." Particularly in services companies in recent years, managers have been paying increasing attention to the development of procedures to deal with service problems as they arise, with a view to solving the customer's problem before he or she decides to take his or her business elsewhere. Therefore, service recovery becomes an important component in a company's program to establish and maintain customer relationships. A company taking the necessary steps to deal with customers' problems efficiently and effectively will lead to those customers being satisfied, even to the point that they will be more loyal than they would have been if the service problem had never occurred![18] In this age of high technology, the Internet, and spiraling competition, consumers are becoming increasingly sophisticated and demanding. Consumer loyalty can be achieved, but often under the consumer's conditions. It has become increasingly important that customer complaints be handled effectively, as failure to do so after a customer has invested effort and emotion in complaining will magnify the damage caused. And today's demanding consumers are complaining![19]

Some companies are so intent on dealing with customer service problems that they openly encourage their customers to complain if they have a problem.[20] If the dissatisfied customer simply leaves, vowing never to return, the company has missed a chance to deal with the problem, management may never know that the problem exists, other

Marketing at Work 12-1

Whirlpool Cleans Up on Relationship-Building

– A statement insert from CIBC Aerogold thanking you for your business. The insert states that CIBC recognizes that there are a lot of competitive offers in the marketplace and they appreciate your staying with them.
– A phone call from Bell Canada just to make sure that everything is OK with your phone service, and offering to answer any questions or clear up any confusion regarding competitive offers.
– An anniversary card and flower arrangement from your local Volvo dealership congratulating you on the one year anniversary of your new Volvo.

All are examples of relationship marketing at its best. They illustrate the same strategy — "get your customers emotionally involved with your product or service and their wallets will follow."

Whirlpool has taken this strategy one step further and develops custom catalogues for customers who call their information centre and express interest in specific appliances. Based on the caller's immediate needs a custom catalogue is developed by an outside service provider. The catalogue is personalized for the caller ("Whirlpool Washing Machine Selections for John Doe") and features complete product information and colour pictures.

Whirlpool's custom catalogue has three main objectives: it creates better one-to-one communication with prospective or repeat customers; it reduces costs of conventional printing, inventory, and waste due to frequent product changes; and it delivers a custom catalogue of comparable quality to the standard printed catalogue.

Since callers are usually only interested in one or two products at a time, the catalogue addresses their current need while saving Whirlpool substantial printing and mailing costs. Whirlpool also has better data on potential customers for follow-up as a result of their calls to the customer information centre.

Source: Adapted from David Foley, "Relationship-building an underrated enterprise," *Strategy*, January, 17, 2000, p. 18.

customers may experience the same problem, and the exiting customer has the opportunity to spread the bad news about how he or she was treated. Complaints provide an opportunity to restore customer satisfaction and even to impress the customer.

Strategic Aspects of Services Marketing

Because of the characteristics of services (notably intangibility), the development of a total marketing program in a service industry is often uniquely challenging. This is also the case because many marketers, as they have advanced through their careers, seem to have focused principally on the marketing of tangible products. In addition, it may be said that strategic approaches to marketing have only recently been accepted in services organizations, and particularly in the not-for-profit sector. Nevertheless, as we have observed before, the fundamental principles of marketing are the same, regardless of what is being marketed. Ultimately, we are interested in achieving long-term customer satisfaction. Let's consider some developments that have been emerging in services marketing in recent years.

Selecting Target Markets

Marketers of services should understand the customers who buy their services. What are their buying motives? Sellers must determine buying patterns for their services — when, where, and how do customers buy, who does the buying, and who makes the buying decisions? The psychological determinants of buying behaviour — attitudes, perceptions, and personality — become even more important when marketing services rather than tangible goods, because typically we cannot touch, smell, or taste a service offering. This has implications for how consumers buy and for the need to gain a complete understanding.

Some of the trends noted in Chapters 4 to 6 are particularly worth watching because they carry considerable influence in the marketing of services. As an example, an aging population, increases in disposable income, and discretionary buying power mean a growing market for health care services, insurance, and transportation services. Shorter working hours result in increased leisure time. More leisure time plus greater income means larger markets for recreation and entertainment services.

customer value
The categorization of customers based upon their value to the firm.

Market segmentation strategies also can be adopted by services marketers. One of the most important issues arising from our discussion of the four Rs of services marketing relates to the question of **customer value**. Many services companies have begun to develop information systems to allow them to measure or estimate the value of a customer to their firms. The question of customer value is important when companies are trying to decide upon those customers they should retain and those with whom they should establish close relationships. The principle here is one that many firms and organizations often find difficult to accept — we may not want all the customers! Typically, companies earn as much as 80 percent of their profits from as few as 20 percent of their customers. The issue is to decide which are the most valuable ones. Some larger companies collect information on customers and their purchases and utilize this database information to assess the value of each customer. By categorizing customers, for example, into A, B, C, and D categories, based upon their value to the firm, a company can ensure that its best customers receive the highest levels of service and that attempts are made to address their problems immediately.[21]

Planning of Services

New services are just as important to a service company as new products are to a goods-marketing firm. Similarly, the improvement of existing services and elimination of unwanted, unprofitable services are also key goals.

Product planning and development has its counterpart in the marketing program of a service organization. Management must select appropriate strategies based on answers to these questions:

◆ What service products will be offered?

◆ What will be the breadth and depth of the service mix?

◆ How will the services be positioned?

◆ What attributes, such as branding, packaging, and service quality, will the service have?

◆ What support services are needed?

◆ What level of customer service should be offered?

SERVICES OFFERING Many firms have become successful by identifying a previously unsatisfied consumer need and then developing a service to address that need. A good example is the number of new routes added by Canada's smaller regional airlines such as WestJet and CanJet in response to the merger of Air Canada and Canadian Airlines International. These smaller carriers identified a need for customers to have an alternative in a marketplace that many viewed as now dominated by an airline monopoly. The introduction of new services should involve a process very similar to that which may be used by manufacturers in introducing new tangible products. Attention must be paid to addressing customer needs and to knowing what will appeal to the customer. Failure to do so will lead to the same lack of success that manufacturers encounter when they do not follow these principles in launching new tangible products.[22]

The explosive growth of the Internet resulted in the creation of a new range of consumer services involving provision of street directions on the information superhighway. These new information services come in a variety of combinations, including additional services, from free e-mail, weather forecasts and daily lottery numbers, to actually providing the Internet connection service free or at a very low cost. The primary source of revenue becomes advertising driven. These are unique in that providers must attract more and more non-paying "consumers" in order to attract a different, and paying, group of consumers. They must market themselves to the first in order to demonstrate their value to the latter. The Funcow Internet Club (www.funcow.com) is one of many such Internet Service Providers that are quickly building large, captive, Internet-savvy audiences ripe for the picking by online marketers.[23]

SERVICE-MIX STRATEGIES Several of the product-mix strategies discussed in Chapter 10 can be employed effectively by services marketers. Consider the strategy of expanding or enhancing the line of services offered. This is often referred to as a process of adding value for the customer. In fact, one of the most effective ways of adding value to existing products and services is by adding new support services. Many hotel chains and even some "bed and breakfasts" have added fax machines, desks, and computer data ports to their rooms and provide photocopier and printer services on request for business guests.[24] Rental-car companies offer no-smoking cars and rent cellular telephones. Most now have computerized the process of returning rental cars at airports to speed travellers on their way. Many companies have chosen to add value for their loyal customers by establishing loyalty programs that reward them with free travel or gifts.[25]

Many firms have moved to alter their services offering in response to competition or to customer demands. To better serve customers who may have difficulty finding time to visit a conventional bank branch, the Bank of Montreal launched its MBANX service, which allows customers to access virtually all banking services through a 1-800 number, Internet, and ATMs. Some personal-care companies now offer in-home services, from foot care, to massages, to pet care for customers who are unable to get to their offices.[26]

Managing the life cycle of a service is another strategy that is being practised more and more by services marketers. Recognizing that the credit card industry is in its maturity stage, Canadian banks have explored new ways of getting their cards into the hands of new customers and of expanding use of the cards. The result in many cases is that consumers now carry several credit cards when they had only one previously. Variations on the Visa card include a deal between the Toronto Dominion Bank (www.td.com) and General Motors, which sees 5 percent of all charges on the TD Visa held as a rebate that can be saved (up to a maximum of $500 per year for five years) and applied toward the purchase of a GM vehicle. This "co-branding" of credit cards has also been used by Bank of Montreal with Wal-Mart (2 percent interest rebate) and Canada.com (exclusive discounts with participating retailers). This co-branding has also been extended to charitable organizations and personal interests. Affinity cards have been introduced by Royal Bank and Bank of Montreal that see a percentage of cardholder's purchases donated to a choice of charities, recreational sports groups, professional associations, or college or universities. Bank of Montreal (www.bmo.com) has also introduced the Star Trek MasterCard — the only credit card approved by the United Federation of Planets.™

Probably the most successful "new" credit card launch in recent years was the CIBC (www.cibc.com) Aerogold Visa card, which allows holders to accumulate Air Canada Aeroplan points by using the card. Not to be left out, American Express (www.american express.com) offers White Glove holiday packages to its cardholders. These are special Disney packages only available to cardholders that include private opportunities for children to meet Disney characters. Cardholder benefits also include preferential ticket access to live entertainment venues, travel and entertainment rewards, and airline travel points. The Royal Bank of Canada (www.royalbank.com) offers Visa card holders 30 percent off their long-distance telephone bills as well as the opportunity to accumulate travel points with the Royal Bank card. There is also the Partners Program. These are regional and national retailers that will offer discounts when using the card to pay for purchases. Also, special hotel, restaurant and car rental packages are offered to cardholders in their monthly statements. These varied programs have all served to extend the life of the credit card by developing new uses and increased usage.

SERVICE FEATURES In some respects, product planning is easier for services than for tangible goods. Packaging and labelling really are nonexistent in services marketing. However, other features — branding and quality management, for example — present greater challenges for services industries.

Branding of services is a problem because maintaining consistent quality (a responsibility of brand ownership) is difficult. Also, a brand cannot be physically attached to a label or to the service itself. A services marketer's goal should be to create an effective brand image. In most successful services companies, the company or organization name is the brand name. Thus, customers become loyal to Tim Hortons or to Air Canada or to Hilton. Although there are some exceptions, most services companies have not been successful in creating strong brands for their individual service products. Most customers probably do not remember the brand of various classes of service provided by a courier company or that placed on their particular type of chequing account. Most banks have, therefore, eliminated these distinctions between accounts and develop a client's account around his or her individual needs.

The strategy to achieve a strong services brand image is to develop a total theme that includes more than just a good brand name. To implement this strategy, the following tactics may be used:[27]

- ◆ Include a tangible good as part of the brand image — like the umbrella of Travelers Insurance, Prudential's Rock of Gibraltar, or the koala bear of Qantas Airlines.

- ◆ Tie in a slogan with the brand — for instance, "You're in good hands with Allstate" or "Membership has its privileges" (American Express).

- ◆ Use a distinctive colour scheme — such as Avis's red or the green of the Toronto Dominion Bank.

Without physical locations to reinforce an e-retailer's image or "brand," it has become a challenge for these solely Internet-based firms to develop such "personalities" in the consumer's mind's eye. With many Internet grocery portals experiencing poor returns,

Yet another variation on the classic credit card.

The Peachtree Network (www.peachtree.com) developed a national brand-building campaign for 2000/2001. The Montreal-based company prominently featured their logo in direct mail, billboard, and newspaper efforts. Traditionally, Peachtree segmented consumers in three ways: busy people, people with mobility problems, and nerds. While important to understand why these people shop online — continued growth will come from exposing the brand to (currently) offline shoppers. Sobey's-owned IGA has recently launched its own online system, called Cybermarket, and advertising is done in-store across the country serving as an online option to their 153 stores. Peachtree has recognized the need to tap the growing offline marketing by developing the brand outside of

Marketing at Work 12-2 °

Relationship Blues

The new Blue credit card from American Express combines the popularity of the Internet and the allure of a new chip technology with a 0 percent introductory interest rate and no annual fee. It is intended to appeal to the young, entertainment- and health-conscious consumer who is hip to technology.

AmEx Blue was launched in September 1999 behind a US$45 million ad campaign. Edgy and futuristic TV ads were supported by radio advertising and print ads in publications such as *Rolling Stone* and *Entertainment Weekly* and billboards in health clubs, movie theatres, transit shelters, and on buses.

Why would AmEx spend so much to support the launch of its new product? To generate interest and ultimately put AmEx Blue cards into the hands of consumers and get them spending on them. Or so one may think . . . AmEx succeeded in creating a hip image for the credit card, which many were eager to be a part of, but fell short on delivering the plastic.

Ted, a former AmEx Green cardholder and current AmEx Gold cardholder, fell for Blue's cachet hook line and sinker, and couldn't wait to get his hands on a Blue application. Then one mid-October evening Ted noted the arrival of a blue-tinted envelope bearing the AmEx logo among his daily mail. It had arrived! Without hesitation the envelope was ripped open to reveal a computer-generated brochure informing him that this was the second invitation to apply for a pre-approved Blue card. Trouble was Ted didn't recall receiving the first invitation. No matter, he completed the application and mailed it the next morning.

Ted began checking his mail daily for the new card, but that quickly grew tiresome and consistently disappointing. Mid-October turned into the end of November and finally Ted received word from American Express that his balance transfer had gone through. Now he had a couple of thousand dollars of debt sitting on an account for which he still hadn't received official approval, an account number, a bill or payment date, or even a card.

A few more days passed without receiving the much anticipated card, so Ted called AmEx's customer service department and was informed that his card would be sent in about a week, and certainly no bill would be sent nor any payment required before a card was received. That evening the same customer service rep called back to say she had made a mistake and that there was a delay. The card should be in Ted's hands by mid-January, and again reassured him that no payment would be required until the card was received. Now the beginning of December, all hopes of online Christmas shopping were dashed, one of the major draws for obtaining the new card.

In mid-December Ted received another mailing from AmEx containing a book of convenience cheques to use against his soon-to-arrive Blue account, and an online registration letter for Blue telling him among other things that he could access special offers by registering his account information exactly as it appeared on his card. Not yet having a card put a damper on this exercise.

Then two days after Christmas the fourth mailing arrived from AmEx. It was blue and definitely a bill. After placing another call to AmEx's customer service department Ted was informed that his credit card balances had been transferred as he requested, therefore, he owed money. Delivery of the card was a separate matter. His card was on back-order, no, oops, there was a manufacturing delay and the card should arrive on or before January 15, but as a courtesy finance charges on the bill would be waived until the card arrived. This meant a saving of $35 but Ted's desire for the card was waning fast.

On January 15, three months after sending in the initial application, the card arrived without fanfare and without any apology for the delay.

Source: Adapted from Lavonne Kuykendall, "AmEx Puts Marketing Might Behind 'Blue'," *Card Marketing*, vol. 3, no. 9, October 1999, p. 1; I. M. Blue, "AmEx Makes Promises, Consumer Sings Blues," *Card Marketing*, vol. 4, no. 2, February 2000, p. 1.

cyberspace. This is required to prevent click-and-brick retailers such as IGA from maintaining an in-store advantage.[28]

MANAGEMENT OF SERVICE QUALITY In our brief discussion of product quality in Chapter 11, we noted the elusiveness of this important product feature. Quality is difficult to define, measure, control, and communicate. Yet in services marketing, the quality of the service is critical to a firm's success. Two airlines each fly a Boeing 747 on the

Toronto–Paris route for approximately the same fare; two auto repair shops each use Ford or Chrysler parts and charge the same price; and two banks each offer the same investment accounts at identical interest rates. Assuming similar times and locations, quality of service is the only factor that differentiates the offerings in each of these paired situations.

However difficult it may be to define the concept of service quality, management must understand one thing: Quality is defined by the consumer and not by the producer-seller of a service. Your hairstylist may be delighted with the job she did on your hair. But if you think your hair looks terrible, then the service quality was poor. What counts is what consumers think about a service. **Service quality** that does not meet customer expectations can result in lost sales from present customers and a failure to attract new customers. Consequently, it is imperative that management strives to maintain consistent service quality at or above the level of consumer expectations. Yet it is sometimes virtually impossible to standardize service quality — that is, to maintain consistency in service output. Performance quality typically varies even within the same organization. This is true in such diverse fields as opera, legal services, landscaping, baseball, health care, and marketing courses.[29]

As part of managing service quality, an organization should design and operate an ongoing quality-improvement program that will monitor the level and consistency of service quality. A related, but also difficult, task is to evaluate service quality by measuring customer satisfaction — customers' perceptions of the quality of an organization's services.[30]

Most successful marketers of services and those responsible for the services associated with tangible products have begun to introduce programs that will allow them to measure the quality of the service they provide, as perceived by their customers. Many businesses have existed for years under the assumption that management knew what the customer wanted and how he or she wished to be treated. The most successful have now abandoned that way of thinking and have subscribed to the maxim that "good service is whatever the customer says it is." Thus, a program to measure the perceived quality of a business's service must start by defining the aspects of the contact with the company the customer considers to be most important.

Research with a number of Canadian and foreign companies in various industries has confirmed that consumers consider five components of service to be important: (1) the nature of the service itself (the core service); (2) the quality of services required to ensure that the core product performs to expectations; (3) the technical aspects of the process by which the product or service is delivered; (4) interaction with the people who deliver the service; and (5) affective dimensions of the interaction — literally, how the customer feels during his or her interaction with the company and its employees (see Figure 12-2). You will note that the components of service illustrated in Figure 12-2 correspond closely to the five "drivers of customer satisfaction" that were discussed in Chapter 1.

Let's illustrate the components of service by considering customers of Bell Canada and other telephone companies who are interested, first of all, in ensuring that their telephone systems work properly, that calls go through, and that reception is clear (the "core product" aspects of the service). In fact, as technology has improved in the telecommunications industry, customers do not expect their telephone systems ever to fail — the core service in this industry is largely taken for granted by customers; they almost never think of it.

The next component of service relates to the processes and support services that the telephone company has in place to deliver and support the core service — telephone bills, installation of new lines, telephone directories, directory assistance services, and

service quality
The value that consumers perceive they are receiving from their purchase of services; generally very difficult to measure.

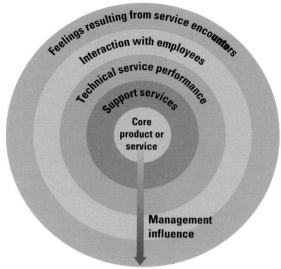

FIGURE 12-2

The Domain of Customer Service

so-called vertical services such as voice mail and call forwarding. Thirdly, we raise the issue of the technical quality of the core service and of the support services — does the telephone work? Are the telephone bills accurate? Is installation done promptly?

Finally, we must also appreciate that the quality of service as perceived by customers is related to the way in which employees of the company interact with their customers — whether operators are courteous and polite, whether salespeople know the technology, and how complaints are resolved. This not only relates to such aspects of personal service as courtesy, politeness, and general civility, but also to the final level of service, that relating to how the customer is made to feel by the service provider and by the company in general.[31]

It may be suggested that as the nature of service moves farther away from the actual product or service and more toward the "people" aspects of service, the less control management has over the delivery, and therefore the quality, of the service offered. For example, WestJet can control the actual flight from Calgary to Vancouver (the core service, getting passengers from one city to another). Barring unforeseen circumstances management can control, to a greater or lesser extent, the services that support that core product: the frequency of flights, departure and arrival times, the number of ticket agents at the counter, baggage-handling systems, and meal or beverage service.

Management loses much more control over the details of the service provided at the interface between customer and employee — how the passenger agent greets the customer at the check-in counter, whether the baggage handler puts the suitcase on the right plane, whether the flight attendants are pleasant and helpful. In fact, it is in this latter component of service that many companies feel their greatest potential lies to differentiate themselves from the competition. Among international airlines, British Airways, Singapore Airlines, and Cathay Pacific try to feature superior service and "cabin comfort" in their advertising.

It is this realization that employees have the potential to make or break a relationship with a customer that has led many companies to introduce programs of **internal marketing**. These are programs intended to ensure that employees "buy in" to the concept of customer service and appreciate that every satisfied customer means a returning customer. Again, the more progressive companies, and those that are most committed to exceptional levels of customer service, have developed elaborate training and motivation programs that emphasize excellence in treating the customer and reward those employees who treat customers well.[32]

internal marketing

The process of directing programs to staff members with the intention of encouraging them to deliver superior service to customers and generally to adopt a customer focus in all that they do.

Pricing of Services

In the marketing of services, nowhere is there a greater need for managerial creativity and skill than in the area of pricing. Earlier we noted that services are intangible, extremely perishable, and usually cannot be stored, and that demand for them often fluctuates considerably. All these features carry significant pricing implications. To further complicate the situation, customers may perform some services themselves (auto and household repairs, for example).

Because of the heterogeneity and difficulty of standardizing quality, most services are highly differentiated. Also, it is virtually impossible to have complete market information; customers often have considerable difficulty assessing the quality of the service and, therefore, the value for money that they have received. As an example, consider the issue of auto repairs. Many customers of auto dealers and repair shops do not understand how cars work, particularly with the on-board computer systems that are in most cars today. As a result, they are unable to assess whether or not they have received good value from the repair job. It's little wonder that auto repair businesses bear the brunt of large numbers of consumer complaints.

Many of the pricing strategies discussed in Chapter 13 are applicable to services marketing. Car-rental companies, for instance, use quantity discounts. Daily rates are lower if you rent the car for a week or a month at a time. Cash discounts are offered when insurance premiums are paid annually instead of quarterly. Mechanics will charge more if they must travel out of town, and engineers will usually command higher fees for work in foreign countries.

Channels of Distribution for Services

Traditionally, most services have been sold directly from producer to consumer or business user. No intermediaries are used when the service cannot be separated from the seller or when the service is created and marketed simultaneously. For example, medical care, repair services, and other personal services are typically sold without intermediaries, simply because the service could not exist without the people who are providing it. Not using intermediaries does limit the geographic markets that service providers can reach because they have to be there in person to provide the service. But it also enables sellers to personalize their services and get quick, detailed customer feedback.

The only other frequently used channel includes one agent intermediary. Some type of agent or broker is often used in the marketing of securities, travel arrangements, entertainment, and housing rentals. Sometimes dealers are trained in the production of the service and then are **franchised** to sell it. This is the case with Sanitone dry cleaning (www.fabritec.com/sanitone/), Midas Muffler shops, and similar franchises.

In recent years, some firms have realized that the characteristic of inseparability is not an insurmountable limitation to a seller's distribution system. With a little imagination, a services marketer can broaden distribution considerably. Let's look at some examples, starting with location.

The service provider or agent should be conveniently located for customers, because many services cannot be delivered. Many motels and restaurants have gone out of business when a new highway bypassed their locations, thereby drawing away customer traffic. On the other hand, banks have increased business by installing twenty-four-hour automated banking machines and by launching telephone and Internet banking, and allowing customers to access their accounts by computer from their homes or offices. Dental centres, chiropractors, and optometrists have opened offices in shopping-centre malls. They offer convenience of location, extended hours, and parking.

The use of intermediaries is another way to expand distribution of services. Some banks have arranged for companies to deposit employees' paycheques directly into their bank accounts. The employer thus becomes an intermediary in distributing the bank's service. Insurance firms have broadened distribution by setting up vending machines in airports. Canada Post now operates post offices in drugstores across Canada. Canada's

franchising
A type of contractual vertical marketing system that involves a continuing relationship in which a franchiser (the parent company) provides the right to use a trademark plus various management assistance in opening and operating a business in return for financial considerations from a franchisee (the owner of the individual business unit).

lottery corporations sell their tickets through kiosks in shopping malls and through thousands of retail agents in convenience stores and gasoline stations across the country. Courier services such as Purolator and Federal Express have made it convenient for their customers by installing drop boxes on street corners in the downtown business districts of major cities.

The characteristic of intangibility essentially eliminates physical-distribution problems for most service producers. For example, other than office and other supplies, accountants have no physical inventory to store or handle. However, not all service producers are free from physical-distribution headaches. Those who are unable to deliver their service without the support of tangible products still have to address issues relating to physical storage and logistics. Retailing, for example, is considered a service industry, but retailers certainly have to deal with inventory issues and questions relating to location. Courier companies have to maintain fleets of trucks and aircraft.

Many companies have succeeded in separating some services from the people who provide them by delegating the delivery of their services to vending machines. While we normally associate the concept of a vending machine with those that supply candy bars and soft drinks, much of the equipment and technology that now deliver services are essentially service-vending machines. When we make a telephone call from a pay phone — now virtually all converted from coin to card operated — we are using a vending machine of sorts. Similarly, ABMs supply financial services in much the same way that "Coke machines" supply soft drinks. When you use a coin-operated photocopying machine in your college library, you are buying a service.

Promotion of Services

Several forms of promotion are used extensively in services marketing, but because services are often inseparable from the people who provide them, personal selling plays the dominant role. Whether or not he or she realizes it, any employee of a service firm who comes in contact with a customer is, in effect, part of that firm's sales force. In addition to a regular sales force, customer contact personnel might include airline flight attendants, law-office receptionists, couriers, bank tellers, and ticket-takers and ushers at ballparks or theatres. We use the term **service encounter** to describe a customer's interaction with any service employee or with any tangible element such as a service's physical surroundings (bank, ballpark, law office). Customers often form opinions of a company and its service on the basis of service encounters. Consequently, it is essential that management recognize the strategic importance of service encounters and prepare contact personnel and physical surroundings accordingly. A key step in preparing to sell a service is to provide sales training and service information for contact personnel, impressing on them the importance of their role.[33]

For years, of course, advertising has been used extensively in many service fields — hotels, transportation, recreation, and insurance, for example. What is newer is the use of advertising by professional-services firms, including legal, accounting, and health services such as physiotherapists and chiropractors. Previously, professional associations in such fields prohibited advertising on the grounds that it was unethical. While some associations still control the type of advertising that may be done, the promotion of professional services is much more open and accepted than ever before.

In sales promotion, while point-of-purchase displays of services offered are often impossible, displays of the results of using a service can be effective. Many service firms,

service encounter
In services marketing, a customer's interaction with any service employee or with any tangible element, such as a service's physical surroundings.

especially in the recreation and entertainment fields, benefit considerably from free publicity. Sports coverage by newspapers, radio, and television provides publicity, as do newspaper reviews of movies, plays, and concerts. Travel sections in newspapers have helped sell transportation, accommodation, and other services related to the travel industry.

As an indirect type of promotion, engineers, accountants, lawyers, and insurance agents may participate actively in community affairs as a means of getting their names before the public. Some professional firms are even offering guarantees. Service firms (banks, public utilities, lawyers) may advertise to attract new industry to the community. They know that anything that helps the community grow will automatically mean an expanded market for their services.

Increasing Productivity

The boom in the services economy in recent years has been accompanied by a significant increase in competition in many service industries. This competition has been stimulated by several factors. One is the reduction in government regulation in many industries — airlines, telecommunications, and banking, for example. Relaxed regulations by professional organizations now permit advertising in the medical, legal, and other professions. New techniques have opened new service fields — in solar energy and information processing, for instance. Technological advances have also brought automation and other "industrial" features to service industries in which employees of organizations generally performed many manual tasks. Service chains and franchise systems are replacing the small-scale independent in many fields, including take-out food, auto repairs, beauty shops, and real estate brokerage.

With the beginning of the 21st century, companies and other organizations in virtually every industry still continued to face the challenges of becoming more efficient and productive. The pressure on businesses is to deliver greater returns to shareholders, while in public-sector organizations, governments at all levels have been looking for new ways to produce better value for taxpayers. Because service industries are very labour-intensive compared with manufacturing, the pressure to become more efficient has led in some organizations to a phenomenon that has become known as "downsizing," reducing costs by reducing the number of employees. Also, since wages in the service sector of the economy have a major impact on prices, there has been pressure on labour unions and their employers to keep wage increases to a minimum in the interest of keeping inflation down. As a result of these forces, the forecast for the next few years is for continued growth in the service sector, but also for continued pressure to keep levels of productivity up.

Service firms are employing various strategies to improve productivity. One is to invest in education and training programs, not just to teach basic skills but also to improve employees' efficiency. Another strategy is to bring in new technology and adopt methods used in manufacturing. Machines have enhanced or even replaced labour in a wide range of service industries. As technology has become more efficient, industries such as financial services are able to operate with far fewer customer-facing employees than ever before.

Elimination of many routine tasks may also occur as simple transactions are passed down to the consumer. Many banking transactions can be conducted at ATMs, or through the Internet. Consumers pump their own gas and pay for it without ever meeting an employee of the company that operates the gas station. We obtain our own information on the Internet and complete our own course registration through our university or college computerized registration system. We interact with automated telephone systems that allow us to reach individuals or to leave messages in an office without ever talking to a receptionist or operator. While this use of technology and the downloading of service tasks to the customer makes for greater efficiency and lower per-transaction costs for the company that uses these systems, they are not without their disadvantages. Firstly, there are customers out there who would prefer not to deal with machines and technology. They want to meet and talk with live people and resent being forced to interact with technology. Secondly, the increased use of technology to interact with customers is felt by many to depersonalize the interaction and lead to much weaker customer relationships than exist when customers and companies deal face to face.[34]

Moving Forward

The basic premise of the manufacturing model is that machines and technology are the primary keys to increased productivity and successful operations. The people who deliver the services are less important — so goes the premise. But this premise simply no longer works in the competitive services environment of today. Instead, we need a model that puts customer-contact employees first and then designs the business operations around these people. Four key elements in this new model are:[35]

◆ Companies value investments in people at least as much as investments in machines.

◆ Firms use technology to support the work of customer-contact people, rather than using it to monitor or replace these workers.

◆ Companies make recruiting and training as important for salespeople and other customer-contact employees as for executives.

◆ Management ties compensation to performance for employees at every level from bottom to top.

McDonald's, Taco Bell, and ServiceMASTER are examples of firms working to implement this new services model. They would agree with Ron Zemke, president of Performance Research Associates, who said, "No amount of marketing money and moxie can wash away the effect of poor frontline service."

Impact of Technology

One of the most important issues facing services marketing relates to how technology affects the way services are delivered to customers and how it influences the quality of service provided to them. Certainly, we are unable to avoid technology today. Probably no other force has had the impact on service industries that technology has had in recent years and will continue to have in the future. Everywhere we turn there is evidence of technology-delivered service, from the myriad ways we can access financial services at our banks, to the 100-channel universe being delivered by direct-to-home television services such as StarChoice, to the Internet and all that it delivers.

Many advances in technology certainly make the life of the customer easier, even though the consumer may not even realize the role that technology is playing. Such is the case when Federal Express uses its sophisticated tracking system to allow customers to know exactly where a package is at all times, when it was delivered, and who signed for it. Companies that operate call centres to receive incoming calls from customers use sophisticated number-

Marketing at Work 12-3

Roll Up the Rim to Form a Relationship

In 1987 Tim Hortons launched a promotion called "Roll up the Rim" which was intended to boost coffee sales during their slow period in the early summer and to up-sell customers to larger cup sizes. Little did they know the program would help to form relationships with their customers and foster loyalty.

One of the keys to the program's success is its simplicity. Customers are offered a chance to win with every purchase of a medium, large, or extra large coffee. As the name of the promotion suggests, customers simply roll back the rim of their coffee cups to discover whether they have won a prize. In an effort to appeal to as broad an audience as possible the program includes a wide array of prizes — from free doughnuts to big-ticket items such as vehicles.

Bill Moir, executive vice-president of marketing with Tim Hortons, says that his customers view Roll up the Rim much like a lottery — they don't really expect to win the jackpot, but they are happy to keep playing all the same. Many of Tim Hortons' customers make purchases daily and providing a program where they can win something — even a coffee, doughnut, or muffin — is a great way to recognize them and thank them for being Tim Hortons' customers.

The fundamentals of the program haven't changed much since it was first introduced. Two things that have are the timing, the program is now run for eight weeks in the late winter and early spring, and the media budget to support the promotion now includes television.

Roll up the Rim has become synonymous with Tim Hortons and is more like a brand unto itself than a promotion. To keep it fresh and interesting year after year Tim Hortons speaks to its customers regularly to determine whether they feel the promotion is maintaining its vitality. The positive feedback remains consistent — customers understand it, look forward to it, and it adds to their enjoyment of a morning coffee.

Source: Adapted from Laura Pratt, "Roll up the Rim major player for Tim Hortons," *Strategy*, May 22, 2000, p. 22.

recognition software to direct a customer's call to the person to whom the customer last spoke, thereby helping in the building of a more personal relationship between an employee and the customer. Manufacturers like Caterpillar use on-board computers to measure the wear on parts and to send a signal to a satellite in order to inform the nearest Caterpillar dealer to contact the customer to replace the part before the customer's equipment fails.

Such use of technology to deliver improved levels of customer service is impressive. But, in service industries, particularly when one considers the quality of service delivered, technology has the potential to be a two-edged sword. The reason for this is simply that all consumers are not similarly comfortable and familiar with technology. Not everyone wants to use an ATM or bank through the Internet — some people don't even know what the Internet is! To people who are not technologically literate or who simply long for the "old days," technology often gets in the way of good service. They resent efforts by their banks to encourage them to use ATMs, because they are used to dealing with their favourite bank employee. They are uncomfortable with the interactive voice-response system they encounter when they want to place a collect call. They don't enjoy dealing with voice mail. Encountering technology may cause these customers not to want to do business with a company. This is an issue that some companies have begun to address, but many also seem to want to rush headlong into the implementation of more technology without giving much thought to its impact on customers and on their view of the firm.

Performance Measurement in Services Organizations

Profit-oriented service firms can evaluate their performance by using quantitative measures such as market share or return on investment, and then compare these figures with industry averages and trends. Unfortunately, many firms, particularly smaller businesses, do not have access to such comparative data and are unable to benchmark themselves against other companies. For many, it would be inappropriate to compare themselves with much larger firms or with those that operate in quite different markets. In any event, market share and return on investment are much too broad to serve as good measures of how the service company is performing.

To measure their performance, therefore, companies that operate in service industries must address the question of how consumers perceive the quality of the service provided and how well they are doing in meeting customers' expectations of service. One of the principal issues relates to how such measurement of perceived service quality is to be carried out; another deals with what should be measured. There are many ways to measure service quality, some of which have been mentioned in this chapter. But it is not a simple process, and it is made all the more difficult by the fact that we are dealing with intangibles and that every customer's definition of acceptable quality is different. This issue of developing a sound basis for measuring the quality of service is one that will continue to command the attention of services marketers in the future.

Another issue relating to measurement deals with the question of measuring payback on investment in service and with determining where such investment should be directed. For example, should a bank or airline or hotel chain spend much to provide superb service to a customer who may bring it little business and whose account may cost the company a great deal to service? Should a retail store invest in superior service if most of the customers it serves are passing traffic and if very few can be counted on for repeat business? These questions must be addressed by services marketers in deciding where to invest in the improvement of service. Dealing with this issue will also require improved cost-accounting systems in many companies so that they can track the effectiveness of investing in service improvements.[36]

Prospects for Growth

Services will continue to take an increasing share of the consumer dollar, just as they have done over the past forty years. This forecast seems reasonable even for periods of economic decline. History shows that the demand for services is less sensitive to economic fluctuations than is the demand for goods. The demand for business services should also continue to expand as business becomes more complex and as management further recognizes its need for business-service specialists. In professional services especially, the use of marketing programs is expected to increase considerably during the coming decade. This expansion will occur as more health-care organizations, lawyers, engineers, and other professionals come to understand the economic benefits they can derive from an effective marketing program.

Unfortunately, many service firms today still do not provide a satisfactory level of service quality. Most consumers undoubtedly would agree with this assessment by Leonard L. Berry, one of the leading researchers and authors in services marketing. Any prediction of profitable growth in services firms is based on senior management's raising their aspirations, learning from past mistakes, and providing effective leadership. More specifically, future profitability depends on a company's ability to correct the following basic mistakes related to service quality:[37]

◆ *Spending money on the wrong priorities.* A major hotel planned to install colour TV sets in some guest bathrooms when 66 percent of customer calls to the housekeeping department were requests for irons and ironing boards. The hotel later reversed these priorities.

◆ *Reducing quality by flaws in service design.* Computer-generated billing statements that are impossible for customers to understand; clothing-store dressing rooms with less than two hooks — one for street clothes and one for try-on clothes.

◆ *Seeking easy solutions to quality problems.* Short-term, superficial, pep-talk solutions when the real need is an investment in managerial time, energy, and ego to change employee and management habits and attitudes regarding service quality.

◆ *Shortchanging fairness to customers.* Hotels and airlines that do not honour confirmed reservations; insurance companies that inadequately disclose important information.

◆ *Underinvesting in leadership development.* At all managerial levels, companies need leadership for employees faced with large numbers of demanding, sometimes rude, customers and other conditions that breed stress, fatigue, and discouragement.

Even manufacturers are taking an increasing interest in services as a basis for growth. Most tangible goods can be quickly and easily imitated. Consequently, manufacturers see their accompanying services as a key factor in giving a company a competitive advantage. The idea is to bundle services with goods to respond to a full range of customers' wants.

Summary

Most product offerings are a mix of tangible goods and intangible services, located on a spectrum ranging from pure goods to pure services. Services are separately identifiable, intangible activities that are the main object of a transaction designed to provide want-satisfaction for customers. Conceptually, tangible-goods marketing and services marketing are essentially the same. In reality, however, the characteristics that differentiate services from goods usually call for quite different marketing programs.

The scope of services marketing is enormous. About half of what we spend goes for services, and about two-thirds of non-governmental jobs are in service industries. Not only are services of considerable significance in our economy today, but it is predicted that the services sector will continue to grow faster than the manufacturing sector of the economy. Services generally are intangible, inseparable from the seller, heterogeneous, and highly perishable, and they have a widely fluctuating demand. Each of these distinctive characteristics has several marketing implications.

The development of a program for the marketing of services parallels that for tangible goods, but takes into account the special characteristics of services. Management first identifies its target market and then designs a marketing mix to provide want-satisfaction for that market. In the product-planning stage, the element of service quality is critical to a company's success. Similar pricing strategies are used by services and goods producers, although it is often difficult to communicate value in services. In distribution, intermediaries are used less often, and location of the service marketer in relation to the market is important, particularly when the service is delivered in person. Personal selling is the dominant promotional method used in services marketing.

As we move into the next millennium, the service environment will continue to change. One of the biggest challenges for service industries today is to develop ways to improve efficiency and productivity without impairing the quality of the service provided. Productivity becomes more important as services account for a growing share of consumer expenditures and as organizations look for ways to provide better returns to their stakeholders. Service quality is often at risk in such situations, but it should remain a priority of service companies and not-for-profit organizations as consumers pay increasing attention to the quality of service that they receive.

Key Terms and Concepts

Core services 353
Supplementary services 353
Services 353
Personal services 355
Business services 355
Intangibility 355

Inseparability 357
Heterogeneity 358
Perishability 359
Fluctuating demand 359
Customer value 363
Branding of services 365

Service quality 368
Internal marketing 369
Services franchising 370
Service encounter 371

Questions and Problems

1. How do you explain the substantial increase in expenditures for services relative to expenditures for tangible products in the past forty years?

2. What are some marketing implications of the fact that services possess the characteristic of intangibility?

3. Why are intermediaries rarely used in the marketing programs of service firms?

4. Services are highly perishable and are often subject to fluctuations in demand. In marketing its services, how can a company offset these factors?

5. Cite some examples of service marketers that you feel are customer-oriented, and describe what these firms have done to make you feel this way about them.

6. Discuss how loyalty programs such as Air Miles and Club Z add value for customers.

7. Present a brief analysis of the market for each of the following service firms. Make use of the components of a market discussed in Chapters 4 to 7.

    a. Travelocity.com.

    b. Toronto Airport Hilton hotel.

    c. Indoor tennis club.

    d. Credit union.

8. What are some of the ways in which each of the following service firms might expand its services mix?

    a. Blockbuster Video.

    b. Hairstyling salon.

    c. Internet service provider.

9. Explain the importance of demand elasticity in the pricing of services.

10. "Personal selling should be the main ingredient in the promotional mix for a marketer of services." Do you agree? Discuss.

11. Present in brief form a marketing program for each of the following services. Your presentation should start with a description of the target market you have selected for the service. Then explain how you would plan, price, promote, and distribute the service.

    a. A disc jockey for private parties in the community.

    b. Your electric company.

    c. Household cleaning.

Hands-On Marketing

1. Identify a company in your town that manufactures tangible products (a woodworking shop, a metal fabricating plant, or similar operation) and examine the services this company also must supply in supporting the sale of its tangible products.

2. Review a service encounter in which you have recently participated and in which you were not pleased with the outcome. Consider what went wrong, using the model shown in Figure 12-2. Was the problem with the "core" product or service, or in one of the outer rings? What could the service provider do to improve your experience next time?

Case 3-1

ACORN PARK HOTEL

The Acorn Park Hotel was opened in 1946 and is located in South Kensington, a quiet area of London, not far from Harrods and other fashionable shops, and very close to a number of museums and art galleries. With only eighty rooms, the Acorn Park is typical of the properties in the Redpath Group of Inns, who pride themselves as hotels that create a special atmosphere for their guests. It was Monday, July 17, and Geoffrey Thornton, guest relations manager, had just entered his office. The morning mail had arrived, and the first envelope Thornton opened contained the following letter.

Martha K. Stone, QC
Barrister and Solicitor
3265 Main Street
Fredericton, NB, Canada
E3B 4K6

Telephone: 506 624 7419
Facsimile: 506 624 8000

July 12, 2000

Mr. Geoffrey Thornton
Guest Relations Manager
Acorn Park Hotel
100 Bromley Road
London, England

Dear Mr. Thornton:

My husband and I have just returned home, having spent the past ten days in London on a combined business and pleasure trip. We decided to end our trip with a short weekend stay at the Acorn Park before returning to Canada, as your hotel had been recommended by some good friends of ours who stayed there last summer. Our friends had nothing but good things to say about the Acorn Park Hotel. But, despite the hotel's excellent reputation, the service we received during our stay was quite the opposite. I have decided to write to you to describe the treatment my husband and I received from what can only be described as your tactless and unhelpful staff.

When we arrived last Friday, we were quite tired and were looking forward to relaxing in our room for a few hours before dinner. Upon checking in we were assigned room 216 which was, if I may say, not what one would expect of a four-star hotel. The room had not been cleaned, as items of clothing had been left by the previous guest. The window looked out on scaffolding and the room was unbearably hot. The person at the front desk, when I finally was able to get through, informed me that there was nothing she could do to find us an alternate room.

The next morning, we experienced totally unacceptable treatment when we ate breakfast in the dining room. The lady on the desk as we entered the dining room pointed out to us that, as we were not members of one of the bus tours staying at the hotel, our breakfast was not included in our room rate and we would have to pay for it! This was no surprise, as we had fully expected to pay.

We were quite surprised as we were leaving the dining room to be stopped again by this lady, who insisted that we pay either in cash or by credit card. Despite our protests that we were guests in the hotel and that she should simply put the charge on our room bill, she insisted that she had instructions to accept only cash or credit card payment from us, referring to the fact that our name was on a list that had been provided to her by the front office.

While I began the process of paying by credit card, my husband went looking for the front desk manager, who was most helpful and responded immediately. He accompanied my husband to the dining room where he ascertained that an error had been made and that the name opposite room 216 on the list which had been provided to the dining room staff was not ours. He apologized and the charge was allowed to go to our room bill. The dining room staff involved were totally unaccommodating and tactless in the manner in which they handled the matter. Needless to say, we did not eat breakfast at the hotel the following morning.

We also encountered problems with your telephone system. Shortly after arriving on Friday evening, I wanted to make an outside telephone call and dialled 9 to get an outside line. I did not get a second dial tone, but rather the line rang and rang for 15 or 20 rings with no answer. I tried two or three times before I could get an answer from the switchboard, only to be told that I should dial 9. Only when I explained that I had been dialling 9 was there an effort made to find out what had happened. Evidently, our line had been switched over in some way so that dialling 9 resulted in the telephone ringing at the front desk. Once this was rectified, I was able to make outside calls.

Checking out on Sunday morning was the final frustration. It was 9 o'clock; others were checking out, bus tours were leaving, guests were trying to have travellers' cheques cashed before their buses left, and the telephones were ringing constantly. The young lady who was working alone on the front desk was trying to deal with this confusion. Guests were becoming upset, the departure of the tours was being delayed, and your employee became so frustrated with the ringing telephones that she simply lifted them and placed them back down again, without answering them!

I do not blame the employee; she was doing her best under the circumstances. I find it totally unacceptable that a hotel would have one employee serving the front desk during what is one of the busiest periods of the day, and have her try to answer the telephones at the same time.

Despite the recommendation from our friends and the Acorn Park's excellent location, I would have to say that it is very unlikely that we will be back unless we have some assurance that the problems with customer service have been overcome. I would welcome your comments.

Sincerely

M.K. Stone

Martha K. Stone, QC

Questions

1. Why did Martha Stone write her letter?

2. What factors contributed to her dissatisfaction?

3. How important were the following factors in affecting the service the Stones had received?

   Product
   Process
   Performance
   People

4. What were the Stones' expectations when they arrived at the Acorn Park Hotel?

5. What does Martha Stone expect to happen now that she has written?

6. What could or should the front desk manager have done when he was called to the dining room on Saturday morning?

7. What should Geoffrey Thornton do now? What factors will influence how he responds?

Case 3-2

MODROBES — LET THERE BE PANTS!

How often does a sore butt turn into a good business opportunity? How often does an idea rejected for an entrepreneurship competition turn into a thriving business unable to keep up with demand? This is a story that began with both a sore butt and a rejected business plan. This is the story of "Exam Pants" and a clothing company that has gone from selling pants on a folding table visiting university campuses across Ontario to a $3 million clothing marketing and design business with a mission to "Save the world one crotch at a time."

Steve "Sal" Debus, now 30, had always had something of a fascination with fashion. At age 10 he would while away the hours designing shoes for his favourite brands such as Nike and Converse. As time passed he discovered his sketchings were not too different from many of the styles that came to be popular. Sal's fashion flair didn't see much practical expression until he became tired of getting a numb behind while writing four-hour political science exams at Brock University in St. Catherines. This was when he came up with the idea of the exam pant — a lightweight, extremely comfortable utility pant for sitting in while writing lengthy exams. The secret to the pant was quilted foam padding sewn into the rear-end of the pant. They also featured widened legs, many easy access pockets as well as a secret pocket. They were so comfortable Sal wore them for a month earning the name "Fat Ass." This prompted Sal to experiment a little with the styling.

The idea went over well with other students but only earned a 75 in his entrepreneurship course at Brock and was rejected for a similar contest at Queen's University. For the contest he included a business plan detailing how he would travel to universities and colleges all over Canada and the United States directly targeting those who would best appreciate his wares. He was told that his submission did not pass the screening process for applicants. Ironically, that plan is not far from the path Modrobes has followed to success.

Modrobes Saldebus Lounge Clothing Inc.

So, here was Sal with the perfect pant and nothing to do with it! He had designed the pant for student life — "You could eat, sleep, drink, party, get up the next day and go to class in them." You could carry everything you needed. The pants were stain-resistant, needed no ironing and dried in ten minutes, hence no wasting beer money on dryers.

After university, Debus worked for a sports specialty-clothing manufacturer. He pitched the pant idea to his employers, sharing his burning desire to make pants and rule the world. Sal reports that "they didn't seem to like that." They passed on the pants, leaving Sal still sitting on his big idea.

Sal soon left the job and started Toronto-based Modrobes Saldebus Lounge Clothing Inc., better known as Modrobes (pronounced "mode robes"). Modrobes, meaning "modern, casual loose fitting garments." Sal felt that a new idea deserved a new word to describe it. In early 1996, Debus started marketing his pants the cheapest way possible — setting up tables at universities and using the pitch "If these aren't the most comfortable pair of pants you've had in your life, return them and I'll give you your money back." The pants went for $20 a pair and trade was brisk. He went wherever students congregated such as the travelling Edgefest music festival. Debus stuck to his strengths — design and marketing — contracting out manufacturing.

He has shown that if you speak loudly enough in your customers' language, both consumers and conventional partners will sit up and listen. With the realization that he was on to something, Sal expanded the Modrobes line to include skirts, jackets, bags, and shirts. Product ideas often incorporated input that came from conversations with customers. Sal has always stayed close to the customers. His designs therefore include all that his young clientele want: comfort, streetwise looks, and reasonable price tags — usually under fifty bucks.

Modrobes quickly traded up to selling out of the back of a truck — but that can only get you so far! It was time to break into retail. When traditional sales calls didn't work Sal, of course, tried the unconventional. When people asked Sal where they could get Modrobes he would tell them all the name of a particular local store, they would hound the store looking for the brand and you guessed it, the retailer would then come asking Sal to supply the Modrobes line. Independent retailers began picking up the line and by 1998 chains such as Athlete's World and Jean Machine were also carrying the brand. By the end of 1999 Modrobes fashions sold in 350 stores across Canada. This includes two company-owned retail outlets in Toronto that allow Debus to conduct informal market research by keeping in touch with the customers. After all, they are the source of his inspiration. The company's primary target is 14 to 25-year-olds. As it turns out, girls make up 75 percent of Modrobes' customers. This approach has allowed the company to develop what could be likened to a cult following – customers love their Modrobes!

Finding Your Market

Despite growing retail success, Debus remains committed to a guerilla style of marketing. The chains have requested that Modrobes do more traditional advertising, but he is resistant to go in that direction. He doesn't want to fall into the "ordinary" and certainly doesn't want to look like another big corporation. His marketing efforts have taken great pains to avoid this because he feels that his customers do not identify with this persona and do not like corporate sentiment.

He believes that his approach of speaking directly to his customers and designing cutting-edge clothes drives sales and that as long as the clothes sell, the stores should be happy. He instead believes in alternate means to spread the word — ways that speak directly to the customer. Distributing stickers, for example, that young customers can put on their skateboards or snowboards and travelling with the nine-city Edgefest Concert Tour. Throughout the tour the company offered their wares and distributed stickers with catchy slogans. Before the music starts, the booth is usually lined up six deep.

The big idea? — these stickers go many places and are seen by even more of the target market. This appears to be a very effective advertising medium with this consumer group. And as Modrobes travels the country on tour, concert-goers across the country will return home and will ask their local retailers for Modrobes.

That same idea is behind the DJ parties that Modrobes organize. The rave-style atmosphere and the entertainment appeal to typical Modrobes' customer tastes. They also provide a venue to introduce new products and get feedback. The Modrobes Web site provides a similar lifestyle atmosphere where consumers can visit and learn about different things going on, including upcoming events. Visitors can learn about staff members and are encouraged to communicate via e-mail. Products can also be viewed, but as of early 2000 purchases could not be made through the site.

Really, it's a back to basics marketing approach that means staying current with your customers and marketing where they meet.

Debus believes his age is a definite plus when trying to market to youth segments — he even advertises himself and his staff as they are a part of the market they are trying to reach. On the Web site Sal is labelled as "designer guy" while employee Heather is described as "event/sales chick." He believes this reinforces that the company isn't a major corporation. It's more than just clothing; it's a lifestyle. This is supported by peripherals such as the Web site and the events the company organizes.

Bordering on the traditional, advertising is placed in youth niche magazines such as *Tribe* and *Vice* with taglines such as "I want you in my pants." There has also been a tie-in with corporate giant Molson Inc. whereby Modrobes clothed the Molson Extreme team, the brewer's promotional teams of university students who toured Ontario bars and events in summer 1999 to promote Molson brands. Although this associated the brand with a corporate goliath, Sal felt it was still a good move as it was a natural outgrowth of

Modrobes marketing strategy to go where the target market meets. With clubs, beer and young people the Molson promotion was an obvious go for the company.

Continuing to Find New Markets

Although there have been no concrete plans as to how to invade the U.S. market, the company did travel to the 30th anniversary Woodstock '99. Although still determining effective product distribution across Canada, the company decided to rent an RV, bringing as much product as they could and join the pilgrimage to Rome, N.Y. The U.S., however, is in Sal's plans for the near future as he hopes to build a $60 million company in five years by selling on the Net and in the U.S.

Sal's big marketing idea has been hugely successful. Demand is growing, and growing, and growing. Forever the entrepreneur and marketing machine, Debus shows no sign of stopping. While a company growth crisis looms, Sal marches forward — into Woodstock as the band of merry modsters hit the road again. With an estimated 225,000 captive consumers on site for three days, how can Sal resist? And after that there's a two-month campus tour planned.

But the company's growing fast, really fast — or at least the demand for product is growing fast. The company is having trouble growing to keep up with the demand, yet Sal remains focused on fostering yet more demand. The company is overbooked and wholesale customers just keep ordering more. At the same time Sal's becoming concerned about over-saturating the market. By his own reasoning if his cool clothing brand becomes too well known, it will be therefore less cool!

The company has young management and staff. They are relatively inexperienced and the company's growth and product demand is at a point where it may take on a life of its own. While there are goals that Sal wishes the company to reach, there is no firm strategic plan as to how it will get there. Growth carries with it concerns about saturating the market and about maintaining the mutinous image of the brand. While trying to juggle growth and distribution challenges, Sal must still find the time for product design. Sal still does all the designing himself.

Sal says, "We're not the perfectly efficiently flowing company and as I am explaining the tone is do it now or I'll kill you!" Faced with such rapid growth, many challenges, and stretched thin as leader, he has begun to take "CEO lessons" from consultants. He hopes this will help him learn how to grow his company prudently. They've managed to figure out that he has a young and inexperienced management team, and that they need to grow as quickly as the company! He has also begun to consult with a mentor. The mentor, a retired recreational clothing executive discusses concerns and offers advice to Sal.

Sal wonders if the solution to becoming too well known is to drop some of the company's customers. The mentor's advice is not to cutback but to customize, so that there is a difference in what different retailers carry in their store. This seems to please Sal and the Athlete's World buyer for thirty-three stores who gets the pitch, likes it as well because it will be an exclusive for the chain. But this doesn't help with demand — if anything, the custom approach may be even more appealing to buyers for the larger retailers.

Although Sal is quiet when it comes to revealing the profitability of Modrobes, he says that it is 100 percent self-financed and has zero bank debt. He believes that his "wow factor" will continue to work in new markets and will help the company get to its goal of being a $60 million company. It helps the company stand out just as its customers wish to do. Sal Debus is just a guy who can't say no to growth.

Says Debus: "Our biggest challenge for the future is being able to maintain that level of energy doing all those events as well as being able to maintain the operation of business having the supply flow out to the stores. That's the key to whether or not we'll succeed. I'd rather not be a traditional company. I'd rather do all those things or nothing."

Pertinent Web Site

www.modrobes.com

Questions

1. Why do Modrobes' customers buy these products over other brands that are available? What social influences could be involved?

2. Modrobes' target market is primarily 14 to 25 year-old consumers. Discuss any other variables/characteristics that could describe potential consumers for these products.

3. What type of segmentation and positioning strategies is the company employing? Are these strategies effective for the company?

4. Are Sal's concerns about "oversaturating" the marketplace valid? Will increasing success of the product line contribute to decreasing its "cool factor"?

5. Has the company effectively forecasted demand for its products? Could this have been done more effectively? Discuss.

6. What types of market research projects could be undertaken at this time to assist in determining future strategic directions for the company?

7. What types of future markets may exist for the company? For example, could current consumers be targeted as they age, considering casual fashion trends for work and social environments? Perhaps this style will appeal only to this current generation of consumers and not the next generation of 14 to 25-year-olds.

Sources: The Modrobes Saldebus Lounge Clothing Inc. company Web site, www.modrobes.com, July 17, 2000; Hilary Davidson, "Out of the Mainstream: Steven Debus is Building His Fashion Business by Staying In His Customers' Faces," *Profit: The Magazine for Canadian Entrepreneurs*, November 1999, pp. 71, 73; CBC *Venture*, October 12, 1999; Astrid van den Broek, "Targeting Yourself," *Marketing Magazine*, August 2, 1999, pp. 9–10.

Case 3-3

GAMES WARS — EPISODE ONE

In 1993, Sega ruled the video gaming universe with control of almost half of the North American video game market. The industry, originally dominated by Nintendo, had been turned upside down by the arrival of the Sega Genesis system. Ironically, the word "Genesis" means beginning and it actually marked the beginning of the video game war that still rages today between three arch rivals that comprise this industry (for now).

The Genesis system by all indications marked the beginning of the end for Nintendo, however Sega fumbled in its next introduction, the Saturn, and it was blown away by the then newly introduced Nintendo 64 and Sony Playstation. The underdogs had retooled and had armed themselves to do battle with Sega

By 1999, Sega's share of the US$6 billion North American home video-game market was a paltry 1 percent, compared with 56 percent for Sony and 42 percent for Nintendo. Canada's share of this market amounts to approximately $600 million. Not willing to call it quits, Sega laboured to design a new state-of-the-art game system to arrive in stores for the 1999 holiday season. The new Dreamcast system was the centre of an extravagant product launch that fall, providing Sega with the hope of starting the new century on the comeback trail.

The Industry at a Glance

The home video-game industry began in 1976 with the introduction of what was called the Fairchild Video Entertainment System. This featured twenty-one games including Pong — basically a grainy, pixelized image resembling a ping-pong ball that players could bounce back and forth. Action-packed entertainment in its day! Interest in home games soared when Atari introduced the Video Computer System in 1977.

By the following year, hardware and software sales totalled US$200 million. Atari often used the strategy of purchasing the rights to currently successful arcade game titles such as Space Invaders. Atari became the name in home gaming and within three years became a US$2 billion international company. Of course, like any burgeoning industry, competition intensified and a lack of product focus eventually led to the company's demise. Today, however, many of the old Atari titles have been brought into the new millennium by game makers that have bought the rights to the old games, merging them with today's technology.

Today's game wars represent something of a "second coming" for the industry as the market crashed in the mid-80s largely because of the rise of the personal computer. Interest in video games continued to increase, but largely as a function of the increasing interest in PCs. Video game systems began to regain popularity once graphics were developed that were superior to those provided by computer games.

By 1990, Nintendo dominated the product category; that is until the Sega Genesis became one of the most recognized brands among North American children. It was during this period that the company enjoyed up to a 60 percent share of the market. This was to be short-lived however as its much anticipated 32-bit Saturn system was deemed a failure shortly after its launch in 1995. Largely as a result of this the company experienced losses exceeding US$300 million in 1997 and $389 million in 1998. The company has continued to lose money through the end of 1999 and with heavy debt payments looming, will need to make a big success of its latest venture in order to continue.

The failure of Saturn and its inability to capture the following of devoted game players has been attributed to a couple of key factors. First, the company itself was the primary software developer for the system. As such, third-party developers had difficulty developing additional games to be played on the system and there were not many games available to be played on the Saturn console. Secondly, the company was very often delayed producing its own software and getting it into the marketplace. This compounded the problem of limited game selection. Finally, the price of this system was high compared with the price of rival systems.

By this time Nintendo and Sony had realized the escalating competitive environment in the industry and had begun to develop competitive consoles. They were poised to benefit greatly from Sega's missteps. By the end of 1999, the Sony Playstation was in over seventy million homes. The Sony name projected an image of state of the art technology and its open design allowed easy compatibility for third party software efforts. By this time there was almost three thousand compatible titles available for the system.

When released, Sony's 32-bit technology was considered quite sophisticated and the system had appeal for older demographics than would have been expected. More than 30 percent of Playstation owners are 30 or older, and only 17 percent are grade schoolers! In contrast, most Nintendo's users are between the ages of six and thirteen. Because Nintendo maintains more control over software development, it has significantly fewer games compared to Sony.

However Nintendo 64, introduced in 1996, had 64-bit graphics and has been able to lure away customers from both competitors. In 1999, more than twenty-eight million homes were equipped with the 64 system. Having been the first to introduce an improved console, Sony still held the lion's share of the market at the end of the century, with Nintendo in second place. Sega barely registered a pulse at this point in the industry.

Sega Gets Back in the Game

It was now down to the wire — Sega needed to come up quickly with a game plan — forfeit the game or stage a comeback. A comeback would not be easy in this environment. It would require innovation and would have to capture a great deal of attention (and sales). As well, it would have to be done before either competitor could place a new console on the market.

By fall 1999, the Dreamcast was ready and Sega spent US$100 million to promote the product for its September launch. Such clamor and excitement was created that over 300,000 advance orders were received for the new console. Some retailers even opened for business at midnight on September 9, the date of release for the Dreamcast.

Teaser spots debuted prior to its release on MTV and then an epic advertisement by Irish producer John Moore debuted during the MTV Music Awards on September 9. The awards were a big affair that year for MTV in recognition of the date — 9/9/99 — prophesized as the Day of Reckoning and also feared to create computer crashes similar to the anticipated Y2K "bug." The same combination of numbers had previously been used to program mainframe computers indicating the last computer file. MTV had promoted this in their award ads. The Sega ads showed the Dreamcast console as being alive and scheming to defeat the humans playing on it.

The Dreamcast had a 128-bit system capable of generating 3-D visuals and forty CD-ROM games available in the first three months with plans for more already in the works. This time around Sega supported outside development efforts even to the point of offering substantial financial incentives for games that became highly successful. Hard-core options included a plug-in Visual Memory Unit and LCD screen allowing users to play games away from the console. As well, a microphone for voice control and a video camera for those who want to actually place themselves into the gaming action.

The company also overhauled itself — including the creation of a number of smaller wholly owned subsidiaries in an attempt to increase accountability and profitability as well as assist in transforming the company into a network services provider.

The reviews were favourable and the launch was an unqualified success. Over 372,000 systems sold in the first four days bringing in sales of US$132.7 million. Sega sold 1.5 million Dreamcast consoles and 4.5 million games in less than four months, setting new industry records. The company's market share quickly moved from 0.5 percent to 15 percent. This is especially impressive as video-game sales grew by only 11 percent in 1999.

All this despite what would seem an unforgivable gaffe for many consumers — say, like four of the seventeen launch titles not operating in the new machine — Sonic the Hedgehog (the company's new mascot), Blue Stinger, Hydro Thunder, and Ready 2 Rumble. To promote the new title and mascot, the company had even held a contest to find people that looked like its new mascot — pretty embarrassing when the game turned out not to work. It wouldn't appear to be a good omen to be let down by your own mascot on the first day of battle with your goliath rivals waiting in the wings.

More Fun and Games

Besides its impressive game capabilities, the Dreamcast includes a 56k modem, a Web browser, and a version of Microsoft's CE operating system. These are intended to allow access to the Web enabling users to play each other online. This was not initially available, but access was available to the Dreamcast Network (Sega Web) that provides product information and playing tips. Some technology buffs have complained however that the display is difficult to read and the browser is quite unwieldy. While buffs applaud the 3-D graphics and speed of the console many believe that it is not yet truly Net-worthy.

Sega, keeping an eye on the future, hopes that it will be able to gather online information and consumer profiles to help strategically market new games and the next generation console when the time comes. The company also hopes that this will help reduce defections when the competition releases their new consoles next year.

The competition is following suit and have included similar features for their next console releases. Due in late 2000, Nintendo describes its new Neptune as being built on a DVD platform with a 128-bit processor and a modem. DVD is less expensive to produce and allows greater storage. This will easily allow the machine to be used as a music and movie player. Nintendo will release its own game titles initially, followed by third-party titles.

Sony's Playstation 2, also due late 2000, will also employ DVD technology but will have the bonus of being able to play games developed for its predecessor, which is CD-based. The "backward-compatible" unit will also have a 128-bit processor. There will also be a high-speed modem that can use telephone or digital cable lines to access the Internet. Sony will be able to distribute movies, music, and games directly to its Playstation 2 owners. Positioned as an "all-around entertainment player," it will offer applications to a variety of electronic devices such as digital camcorders. Already available in Japan, Sony has had to work feverishly to meet initial demand. A similar response is expected when it is introduced in North America and Europe.

Industry insiders believe that Sega will release its next generation console by the end of 2001 and that it will also have the ability to download and play back music from the Internet.

The Price of War

At the time of its release, the Dreamcast was competing against the 64 and the original Playstation with about a year until new consoles would be introduced. At that point, the Dreamcast beat the competition in every respect. The system was introduced with a price of US$199 and games going for about US$50 each. In response to the introduction, both rivals lowered their prices to an all-time low of $99 and discounting classic titles to as low as $19.99. Nintendo also renewed its focus on the handheld Gameboy unit in order to maintain its dominance in this category. Nearly 88 million Gameboy units have been sold in the last decade.

In response, and to develop closer connections (stronger links) with its consumers Sega decided in spring 2000 that it would give consoles away at no charge in exchange for a two-year subscription to its Sega Web service at $21.95 a month. Existing owners would be entitled to receive a free keyboard and a $200 cheque.

It is estimated that Sony's new player will retail for at least US$300 while Nintendo is keeping quiet about their upcoming suggested retail price.

Who Else Wants to Play?

There are currently three main players in the industry — Nintendo, Sega, and Sony. Owing to high-product development costs and strong brand loyalty, newcomers have great difficulty entering this industry. One company, however, thinks it may be able to make it — Microsoft. The company announced in March 2000 that it had created a custom operating system with photo-realistic graphics — called the X-Box. While the company would not divulge the development costs, it is believed to be between US$5 and $7 billion. The company plans to spend over US$200 million in advertising alone for the fall 2001 launch. This move is in response to the new Sony introduction that will have functions that rival Microsoft's WebTV system. The X-Box will be much like a basic PC that connects to a TV to play games and DVD videos. As well, it would provide access to the Internet. With falling PC component prices, the X-Box may even be able to offer capabilities more advanced than the new Sony offering. The system is expected to retail at only about $299, reflecting these falling costs.

Aside from this threat, the industry itself still considers computer video games to be a stiff source of competition. In 1997, US$1.8 billion worth of PC-based games were sold, compared to US$3.3 billion of console games. However, sales of software for consoles increased by 65 percent over the previous year, compared with a meager 5 percent for PC game software. This would seem to indicate that video gamers clearly enjoy the superior graphics provided by the game machines.

Competition is also feared to come from a continual flow of new Internet companies that offer gamers the opportunity to play new games at their Web sites. The Web is changing the rules of the game for what seems like each day that goes by with new firms coming out of nowhere and scoring big, even in established markets.

What else is clear is that aside from the requirement of offering the latest technology in the game consoles, the ultimate winner will be the firm that delivers the most quality game titles to consumers. With the race to offer high technology, there still exists the possibility of losing sight of the ultimate goal — entertainment.

Although Sega is facing a variety of existing and potential competition, it does have the advantage of introducing the 128-bit console before its rivals. This strategy of being the first to market paid off big for Sony in the past. But to avoid ending up back where it was, Sega will have to remain in the forefront and continue to advance the battle line forward if they wish to be around for the next episode of the game war.

Pertinent Web Sites

www.microsoft.com/insider
www.nintendo.com
www.sega.com
www.sony.com

Questions

1. Discuss the importance of product innovation in this industry.
2. There is generally a high failure rate for new product introductions. What factors may cause a product (console, game cartridge) to fail in this category?
3. What opportunities exist in this industry for participants to position (differentiate) their products? Is branding an important component of marketing such products? Among other things, consider factors such as company image or reputation and the age profile of users.
4. Where do video game consoles fall in the product life cycle? What are the appropriate responses for manufacturers of this industry under such circumstances?
5. Should manufacturers in this industry continue to focus on product alteration to include these functions beyond gaming options? Explain your reasons.

Sources: Tobi Elkin, "Sega Ups Ante for its Online Gaming Push," *Advertising Age*, April 17, 2000, pp. 3, 69; Dean Takahashi, "Sega Will Give Away Dreamcast Players to Lure Subscribers to the Web," *Wall Street Journal*, April 4, 2000, p. B1; Joe Hutsko, "88 Million and Counting: Nintendo Remains King of the Handheld Game Players," *New York Times*, March 25, 2000, p. C1; Tobi Elkin, "Dreamcast Bolsters Sega Rebound," *Advertising Age*, March 20, 2000, p. S10; Jay Greene, "Get Ready to Rumble," *Business Week*, March 20, 2000, p. 48; Irene M. Kunii, "Sony's Indispensable Samurai," *Business Week*, March 20, 2000, p. 56; Tom Price, "Get in the Game: Prepare to be Blown Away by the New Wave of Game Consoles," *PC Computing*, February 2000, p. 190; Dean Takahashi, "'Sonic' Boom Marks Sega's Comeback in Video Games," *Wall Street Journal*, January 13, 2000, p. B6; David Ward, "Games 2000," *Video Store*, January 2/8, 2000, pp. 15–19; Janet Rae-Dupree & Irene M. Kunii, "Can Dreamcast Make Sega's Dreams Come True?" *Business Week*, December 27, 1999, p. 62; Stephanie Strom, "Sega Announces Overhaul as Losses Exceed Forecast," *New York Times*, November 27, 1999, p. C3; Dean Takahashi, "With Sony in its Sights, Microsoft Weighs Entry into Game Machines," *Wall Street Journal*, October 26, 1999, p. B1; Brian Garrity, "Video-Game Console Makers Eye New Music-Download Applications," *Billboard*, October 16, 1999, p. 3; Irene M. Kunii & Janet Rae-Dupree, "Sega's Dream Machine," *Business Week*, September 13, 1999, p. 60; David Ward, "Sega Gets 'Dream' Launch," *Video Store*, September 19/25, 1999, p. 60; Jim Carlton and David Hamilton, "Can A New Machine Called the Dreamcast End Sega's Nightmare," *Wall Street Journal*, September 7, 1999, p. A1; Peter Brown, "Send in the Freaks," *Electronic News*, September 6, 1999, p. 23; Bernadette Johnson, "Gaming Console Rivalry Heats Up," *Strategy*, July 5, 1999, p. 7; Alice Cuneo and Beth Snyder, "Sega Unleashes $100 Mil Drive for Dreamcast," *Advertising Age*, June 28, 1999, p. 3; Ben Pappas, "From Pong to Kingpin," *Forbes*, May 31, 1999, p. 54; Maryanne Murray Buechner, "The Battle Has Just Begun," *Time Digital*, April 12, 1999, pp. 28–31.

Price

The development of a pricing structure and its use as part of the marketing mix

We are in the process of developing a marketing mix to reach our target markets and achieve our marketing goals. Having completed product planning, we turn now to pricing, where we face two tasks. First, we must determine the base price for a product or service that is consistent with our pricing objectives; this endeavour is covered in Chapter 13. Second, we must decide on strategies (such as discounts and value pricing) to employ in modifying and applying the base price; these strategies are discussed in Chapter 14.

Price Determination

In this chapter we cover the role of price in the marketing mix — what price is, how it can be used, and how it is set relative to such factors as product costs, market demand, and competitors' prices. After studying this chapter, you should have an understanding of:

◆ The meaning of price.

◆ The significance of price in our economy, to an individual firm, and in a consumer's mind.

◆ The concept of value and how it relates to price.

◆ Major pricing objectives.

◆ Key factors influencing price.

◆ The types of costs incurred in producing and marketing a product.

◆ Approaches to determining prices, including cost-plus pricing.

◆ Break-even analysis.

If it's Free, is the Price Right?

*M*usic CDs are expensive, right? Music companies make a lot of money, right? And keeping up with the latest music is expensive — there is an endless supply of new groups producing an endless supply of tracks and albums. Can you sample what's out there without spending $20 for a CD? Can you get the tracks your friends have told you about at no cost? Or maybe you have already downloaded music files from an Internet site without having to spend a dime. If you haven't, will you?

Every month, more and more people are doing just that, downloading music files, storing them, compiling them, playing them, "burning" their own CDs for portable listening or trading. Is it the novelty of the new technology or is it because the price is right? Is the price right for college students only or is it right for everyone? The music industry — comprising the "big five" record companies Warner, Sony, EMI, GMG, and Universal — as well as some performers, say they are being ripped off. What do you say?

Music in digital form (MP3 is the digital data compression/ decompression standard in use) can be copied with a few computer keystrokes. MP3 as a technology has put the recording industry on its head. All you need is to travel a little through cyberspace and visit sites such as MP3.com or Napster to shop for your free music. Napster is a software program that allows you to easily copy from the Internet any MP3 digital music file you find there. And you can get Napster for nothing — it's *free*. More than ten million have registered for and downloaded the program. There are an increasing number of Internet sites as well as programs which make it easy to surf, search out your interests and download in no time at all. MP3.com alone has a database of forty-five thousand albums. It's all free — and usually illegal.

Estimates are that at any one time, there are three hundred thousand people in North America surfing the Internet with Napster software looking for music. In a one-week trial of MP3 music availability,

6,890 collections were found on the Net comprising 804,402 tracks ready for downloading. Traffic in music files is currently the largest single component on the Net. Most Napster users are college and university students although the number of older users is increasing rapidly.

If free is the right price, what is the problem? A free product has got to have some costs associated with it so the question may be: who covers the costs. One cost is that faced by North American colleges and universities. Students using college and university computers to hunt for music have overloaded the systems by using up to 20 and 30 percent of the available bandwidth thereby clogging traffic and using massive amounts of storage space. At the University of British Columbia, this has caused service slowdowns, disruptions, crashes and other computer services problems that end up being very expensive to deal with. At the University of Western Ontario, there have been times when students have utilized 50 percent of the available bandwidth for Napster causing costly system delays. The University of Guelph, in order to control costs, has banned the use of the program but relies on students to comply voluntarily. Carleton University in Ottawa has also banned Napster use. Considering the fact that most realize what they are engaging in, it is doubtful that voluntary compliance will be an effective measure.

In addition to direct system costs, in the U.S. there is the potential cost of lawsuits launched by the Recording Industry Association of America. The RIAA represents the "big five" and smaller labels who own the rights to the physical recordings of 90 percent of the music sold in North America. Artists and publishers own the words and melodies. The first ruling in music cyberspace went against this new technology in May 2000 when a New York federal judge decided for the RIAA and against MyMP3 (MP3.com) ruling that the company's database collection was a violation of copyright law. Certainly not to be the last of these cases, the RIAA has a similarly charged suit against Napster, asking up to $100,000 in damages for each copyright protected song allegedly exchanged illegally using Napster software. The RIAA has also lobbied colleges and universities, and in some cases

threatened suit, with the result that more than two hundred have banned the use of Napster on their systems.

The artists, well, they are divided. Some now use the MP3 format to make new tracks available for promotional purposes. New and up-and-coming bands like Nickelback in B.C. and performers like Damhnait Doyle of Newfoundland have used the Internet to introduce themselves and make tracks available free to gain attention and recognition. Stars like Sara McLachlin and Alanis Morissette use the MP3 format to communicate with fans in a variety of ways. Others, like Metallica and Dr. Dre have initiated lawsuits against Napster for copyright infringement since they see revenue losses just as do the record companies. Some rapsters, like Public Enemy, believe it is a great marketing tool.

With the advent of the Internet, MP3 and software like Napster, an important and sometimes income-constrained segment of the music market has questioned the established price–value equation of the music industry. While the record companies have fought the innovations with legal moves and have won some of their legal actions, the

stability of both the pricing structure and the cost structure of the industry has been undermined. While the industry reaction has been slow and defensive, many new and ambitious music entrepreneurs and performers have been innovative. With technological fixes now being developed, costs will change and consumers will be faced with access to tracks and albums at different prices based on how many "plays" they wish to purchase. There will also be fixes that will limit copying capabilities. Cape Breton Fiddler Natalie MacMaster performed two medleys that were recorded and posted on the Web site of record retailer HMV where e-buyers can download them for $2.99. Codes embedded in the music file allowed only credit card holders with Canadian addresses to download the music — and only for a limited time.

Concern with revenue and royalties is legitimate, but is the recording industry clinging to an outdated business model and pricing structure that is ignoring consumer wants and trends? The industry has been ignoring the impetus to change that technology has had on all business sectors and traditional business models.[1]

Determining Price

The issue of how much a company should charge for its products and services will depend on many factors. As the previous illustration shows, the value that consumers perceive in a product or service is always a factor influencing the price that can be charged. And costs are always present and must be paid for. As a result of technological advances as well as increased competition, lower costs generally will lead to lower prices. There are, of course, many other factors that must be taken into consideration, including the target segment for the product or service and the prices being charged by competitors. These factors must be considered when a company introduces a new product or service or considers changing the price of an existing one. Pricing is much more than how much can you get from the consumer — it should be all about delivering value for dollars — not nickel-and-diming your customers. Research indicates that by improving its pricing process, the average company can increase its profitability by a whopping 26-60 percent.[2] It, therefore, makes a great deal of sense for a company to carefully analyze its pricing strategy and options.

In this chapter we will discuss methods used to determine the price to be charged. Before being concerned with actual price determination, however, executives — and you — should understand the meaning and importance of price.

Meaning Of Price

price
The amount of money and/or products needed to acquire some combination of another product and its accompanying services.

Some pricing difficulties occur because of confusion about the meaning of price, even though the concept is easy to define in familiar terms. Simply, **price** is the amount of money and/or other resources with utility that are needed to acquire a product. Recall that **utility** is an attribute that has the potential to satisfy wants.

Generally, we tend to think of price in strictly monetary terms; a sweater costs $100, a ticket to a movie $10, a visit to a doctor, how much? Because of our health-care system, very few of us have any idea what a visit to a doctor costs, because we don't pay for it, at least not directly. It may be useful to think of price as what it costs us to acquire something, whether that something is a tangible product or service.

What it costs to acquire that sweater is more than the $100 price. It involves shopping time and effort, and it may involve other non-monetary considerations such as having to find a parking space, or arrange public transit, or having to visit several stores to find the size and other features you need. Viewing price as a monetary factor oversimplifies the buying process. When a customer decides whether he or she is satisfied with the sweater, or with the meal at the restaurant, he or she will implicitly think about the value received. As a result, we often hear customers say, "I'll never go back there. It's just not worth the _____ ." They may fill the blank with "money," but it is just as likely they will include words like "hassle" or "aggravation."

value
The quantitative measure of the worth of a product to attract other products in exchange.

Therefore, we need to consider **value** when we talk about price. A marketer who is interested in creating customer satisfaction will focus on creating value for the customer. There are many ways to create or add value, only one of which is to reduce price. But, because our economy utilizes money as the medium of exchange, we tend to state prices in monetary terms. But as you read this chapter, it may be useful to think of the effect that price has in communicating value to customers.

Price Is What You Pay for What You Get

Here are prices under various names:

• Tuition →	Education.
• Interest →	Use of money.
• Rent →	Use of living quarters or a piece of equipment for a period of time.
• Fare →	Taxi ride or airline flight.
• Fee →	Services of an accountant or lawyer.
• Retainer →	Lawyer's or consultant's services over a period of time.
• Toll →	Long-distance phone call or travel on some highways.
• Salary →	Services of an executive or other white-collar employee.
• Wage →	Services of a blue-collar employee.
• Commission →	Salesperson's services.
• Dues →	Membership in a union or a club.

And in socially undesirable situations, there are prices called blackmail, ransom, or bribery.

Source: Suggested in part by John T. Mentzer and David J. Schwartz, *Marketing Today,* 4th ed. (San Diego: Harcourt Brace Jovanovich, 1985), p. 599.

Practical problems also arise when we try to state simply the price of a product. Suppose you paid $175 for a desk, but your instructor paid $325 for one of similar style and size. At first glance, it looks as if the student has taught the instructor a lesson! Your instructor's desk — which has a beautiful finish — was delivered to his apartment, and was charged to his store credit card where it can be paid off at his convenience. But you, a do-it-yourself buff, bought a ready-to-assemble desk on cash-and-carry terms. You had to get it home, assemble it, and then stain and varnish it. The seller provided neither delivery nor credit options. Now who paid the higher price? The answer is not as easy as it first appeared. It depends on not only on the product and vendor, but also the individual consumer.

This example indicates that the definition depends on determining exactly what is being sold. A seller usually is pricing a combination of (1) the specific product or service that is the object of the transaction, (2) several supplementary services (such as a warranty), and (3) in a very real sense, the want-satisfying benefits provided by the product. Sometimes it is difficult even to define the price of the predominant good or service itself. On one model of automobile, a stated price may include radio, power steering, and power brakes. For another model of the same brand of auto, these three items may be priced separately. So, to know the real price of a product, you need to look at the identifiable components that make up that product.

Also, it is often extremely difficult to determine what the actual price of a product or service is. How much does it cost to fly from Vancouver to Winnipeg on Air Canada? It depends! The answer can depend on many factors. You may find a student who going to visit a friend in Winnipeg on a seat sale or stand-by ticket for which he or she has paid $249 seated next to a businessperson who has paid four or five times as much. Also, some examples require thought to consider what it is you are paying for — you pay $20 on average for a CD, but some of your friends pay a good deal less ordering music through CDHQ or Play music clubs. While they have to wait up to two weeks for their new music you get your hands on your new CD as soon as you decide which ones to buy.

The price paid, therefore, will depend on circumstances; how much planning has gone into the purchase, how badly the customer needs the product, and how much he or she is prepared to put into the purchase: how much it is valued. If the businessperson absolutely has to attend a meeting in Winnipeg on short notice, he or she may be prepared to pay a very high price. If you absolutely have to have your favourite group's new CD — then you will pay more for the instant gratification. It's not that much different than deciding to send your film away for processing or zipping out to the mall for one-hour processing. It all depends on how the customer defines the value associated with the purchase.

Consider once *again* the case of CDs. This product is manufactured for roughly $2.50 and sold for anywhere from $14 to $25, depending on the product and the location of the vendor. The disc version of a recording costs roughly $4 more than the tape version. The price of this product has never come close to that of the vinyl album it replaced, which was anywhere from $8 to $12. Some consumer investigators who have looked at this issue feel that it occurs because the consumer was *willing* to pay more. The music industry people say this is so because discs offer good value to the consumer.[3] Apparently, belief in the marketplace of the compact disc's superior sound quality and durability supports this higher price. As you know from the tale of Napster, the question of value is not what it used to be.

Importance Of Price

Price is significant in our economy, to an individual firm, and in the consumer's mind. Let's consider each situation.[4]

In the Economy

A product's price influences wages, rent, interest, and profits. Price is a basic regulator of the economic system because it influences the allocation of the factors of production. High wages attract labour, high interest rates attract capital, and so on. As an allocator of resources, price determines what will be produced (supply) and who will get the goods and services produced (demand).

Criticism of our system of free enterprise and, in turn, public demand for added restraints on the system are often triggered by negative reactions to prices or pricing policies. For example, concerns about rapidly rising prices (that is, inflation) may lead to a call for price controls. To reduce the risk of government intervention, businesses need to establish prices in a manner and at a level that consumers and government officials consider socially responsible.

Bell deals with the question of the meaning of price in a competitive telecommunications environment by communicating what fair value means.

In the Consumer's Mind

At the retail level, a small segment of shoppers is interested primarily in low prices. Another segment may be indifferent about price in making purchases. The majority of consumers are somewhat sensitive about price but are also concerned with other factors such as brand image, nature of shopping situation, store location, quality, and value. Consumers who utilize the Internet to comparison-shop and research prices are often much more price sensitive for some goods because they can price compare very easily — others are less so. Consumers' relative interest in price also can vary across demographic groups. Consumers with large families, single parents, and those on low incomes and/or fixed incomes are likely to be much more price sensitive. But even customers in these situations will, on occasion, be prepared to pay more to get what they consider better value. Further, even those with generous resources at their disposal may still seek out value for their money cautiously assessing benefits and features versus price before purchasing.

Another consideration is that some consumers' perceptions of product quality varies directly with price.[5] Typically, the higher the price, the better the quality is perceived to be. Have you ever questioned product quality — such as when you are looking at ads for DVD players or stereo equipment — when the price

"It seems like everybody's talking about price, when what really matters is value."

Kevin Stangeland, Ray Hueser, UFR Urban Forest Recyclers Inc.

The business.	The challenge.	The solution.	The results.
UFR Urban Forest Recyclers Inc. Recycles paper products into molded fibre egg filler flats for customers throughout North America.	"We are not the lowest-price provider out there, and we don't want to be. We could make a cheaper product, but because of breakage, it'd end up costing our customers more. And costing us our customers. Having said that, there are more competitors entering the market every day, and we have to watch costs to keep our prices competitive. I admit, it's a bit of a juggling act."	*Advantage Savings*™ program and *Advantage Toll-free*™ service.	"Over the past year, Advantage has saved us over 55% on our long distance bill. And when you consider that most of our business is done with the U.S., that translates into some serious money - about $1200 a month. But in the end, it's not really about price, it's about value. It's about getting a solid, dependable product at a fair price. That's what we deliver, that's what Advantage delivers."

New solutions for business. From the new Bell.
1-888-783-1234

provided was unexpectedly low? Or, at the other extreme, have you ever selected a restaurant for a special dinner because you heard it was fairly expensive, assuming this meant it would be very nice? Consumers' perceptions of quality are, of course, influenced by such other factors as store reputation, product colour or texture, advertising, or the nature of the service and sales encounter. Many consumers are prepared to pay more for good service.

Price is also important as a component of value. Throughout the late 1990s, more and more prospective buyers, in both consumer and business markets, have been demanding better value in the goods and services they purchase. Value is the ratio of perceived benefits to price and any other incurred costs. Time associated with shopping for the product, time spent on the Internet browsing to gather information to determine exactly what you want, gasoline used travelling in search of your purchase, and time (and perhaps aggravation) assembling the product are examples of these other incurred costs.

When we say a product has value, we don't necessarily mean it is inexpensive. Rather, good value indicates that a particular product has the kinds and amounts of potential benefits — such as product quality, image, and purchase convenience — that consumers expect from that product at a particular price level.

Many businesses are responding to consumers' calls for more value by devising new products and services. The intent is to improve value — essentially, the ratio of benefits to price. And benefits, real or otherwise, have to be perceived. This can be thought of in the following way:

$$Value = \frac{perceived\ benefits}{price}$$

Improving value can be accomplished by maintaining essential elements, adding new elements or features, dropping other elements to cut costs, lowering prices or more effectively communicating benefits that already exist. In other words, by increasing what is in the numerator of our ratio.

Other businesses are striving for better value with existing products. Fast-food firms such as Wendy's, Burger King, and McDonald's have reduced prices on basic items by taking a "combination meals" approach, which bundles several items for a lower price than they would have if purchased separately. The inclusion of small toys of popular movie and animated figures has also been seen by many consumers as adding value to these restaurants' offerings due to the popularity of these toys among children (and some adults). These restaurants believe the toys are strong premiums that provide extra value to existing customers and that they are not the primary reason customers come to their stores.[6]

Industrial goods producers such as Asea Brown Boveri, makers of transformers and heavy equipment, have worked to increase quality and pare production costs. With lower costs, the urge to increase prices to maintain profits is lessened.

Attention to value is certainly heightened when an economy heads into a recession. However, don't expect concern about real value to dissipate even after a return to better times. According to market researchers, the increased emphasis on value reflects a more fundamental shift in consumer attitudes. At least in Canada and the United States, individuals, households, and organizations alike are now more interested in the ratio of benefits to price. This has created a new approach to pricing, not surprisingly called "value pricing," which we will discuss in Chapter 14.

Marketing at Work 13-1

If They Build It, Will You Pay??

How much do you value the experience? The experience of seeing a film complete with bigger screens, bigger sound, bigger concessions, VIP boxes, retractable love seats and, perhaps, valet parking. Every major theatre chain in the country is on a building binge. Famous Players, Cineplex Odeon, and AMC are all locating new sites and building new screens. And, of course, these new cinema palaces are very expensive, so Famous Players would now like you to pay $11 for a ticket. Is it worth it? And, of course, buying a ticket is just the beginning, you can't really enjoy the experience by just sitting and watching. So you get in line; the large popcorn can cost $4, your drink goes for up to $3. Want some specialty coffee and a Nanaimo bar? Add it all up and you can be leaving behind $20. Going Dutch, that is.

Building new state-of-the-art film complexes is a very expensive proposition. It is not a surprise that ticket prices go up. Famous Players president John Bailey says that a lot of careful thought goes into increasing prices since the chain does not want to offend customers or be seen as price gougers. But price increases are a matter of business. When you pay $11 for a Famous Players ticket, 50 percent goes to the film distributor (the cost of being able to show the film); 45 percent goes to the theatre (to cover operating costs, 17 percent GST and amusement taxes, and carrying costs — paying for the facility); 5 percent for other exhibition costs. Mr. Bailey says that after you take into account carrying costs, there is no money left out of the ticket price. Where the money does come from is the concessions. From that $4 box of popcorn, 20 percent is the cost of concessions, 80 percent goes to the theatre. That's where all theatre operators make their money.

The Famous Players price increase comes a year after a similar price increase applied only to mega-plex admission prices. Industry analysts expect that competitors will soon move to increase their prices. Cineplex Odeon now charges $10 and AMC charges $9.75 for evenings. Costs are rising! What about the total experience? How does it compare to a concert, a CD, another form of entertainment? Where do you get value for your money?

Source: Adapted from Gayle MacDonald and Alexandra Gill, "If they build it, you will pay," *The Globe and Mail*, May 3, 2000, pp. R1, R2.

In the Individual Firm

A product's price is an important determinant of the market demand for it. Price affects a firm's competitive position and its market share. But more than anything, price has a considerable bearing on a company's revenues and net profits. Through prices, money comes into an organization.

Some businesses use higher prices to convey an image of superior quality, but this would make sense only to consumers who consider quality to be important. Differentiated product features, a favourite brand, high quality, convenience, or some combination of these and other factors may be more important to consumers than price. As we saw in Chapter 11, one object of branding is to decrease the effect of price on the demand for a product.

Thus we see that prices are important to a company most of the time — but not always. To put the role of pricing in a company's marketing program in its proper perspective, it is only one of the four marketing-mix elements (remember the 4 Ps? — product, price, place, and promotion) that must be skillfully combined — and then adapted over time — to achieve business success.

pricing objective
The goals that management tries to reach with its pricing structure and strategies.

Pricing Objectives

Every marketing activity — including pricing — should be directed toward a goal. Thus management should decide on its **pricing objective** before determining the price itself. Yet, as logical as this may sound, few firms consciously establish, or explicitly state, a pricing objective.[7]

To be useful, the pricing objective that management selects must be compatible with the overall goals set by the company and the goals for its marketing program. Let's assume that an established company's goal is to increase return on investment from its present level of 15 percent to 20 percent within three years. It follows that the pricing goal during this period must be to achieve some stated percentage return on investment. It would not be logical, in this case, to adopt the pricing goal of maintaining the company's market share or of stabilizing prices. We shall discuss the following pricing objectives:

◆ Profit-oriented:
    ✔ To achieve a target return.
    ✔ To maximize profit.

◆ Sales-oriented:
    ✔ To increase sales volume.
    ✔ To maintain or increase market share.

◆ Status quo-oriented:
    ✔ To stabilize prices.
    ✔ To meet competition.

Recognize that all these objectives can be sought — and, it is to be hoped, attained — not just through pricing but also through other marketing activities such as product design and distribution channels. All these objectives are ultimately aimed at satisfactory performance over the long run. For a business, that requires ample profits.

Profit-Oriented Goals

Profit goals may be set for the short or long run. A company may select one of two profit-oriented goals for its pricing policy.

target return

A pricing goal that involves setting prices so as to achieve a certain percentage return on investment or on net sales.

ACHIEVE A TARGET RETURN   A firm may price its product to **achieve a target return** — a specified percentage return on its sales or on its investment. Many established retailers and wholesalers use a target return on sales as a pricing objective for short periods such as a year or a fashion season. They add an amount to the cost of the product, called a **markup**, to cover anticipated operating expenses and provide a desired profit for the period. A chain of men's clothing stores may have a target profit of 7 percent of sales, and price its products accordingly. Safeway or Loblaw, for example, may price to earn a net profit of 1.5 percent on a store's overall sales.

markup

The dollar amount that is added to the acquisition cost of a product to determine the selling price.

Achieving a target return on investment is measured in relation to a firm's net worth (the firm's assets minus its liabilities). The leading firm in an established industry often selects this pricing goal. Target-return pricing is used by industry leaders such as DuPont (www.dupont.com), Alcan, and Esso (www.esso.ca) because they can set their pricing goals more independently of competition than can smaller firms in the industry. The leaders may price so that they earn a net profit that is 15 or 20 percent of the firm's net worth.

This approach is not necessarily useful nor even easily used in new and fast changing high technology industries. Cost and price structures, as well as competitive forces, change so rapidly these days that this method reduces effective forecasting if forecasting can even be considered accurate in some of these industries. As well, the turnover of technology can be so rapid that prices must be able to be quickly adapted to impending advancements.

Pricing databases make flexible pricing easier and may enable pricing to actually become an effective marketing tool beyond the traditional competitive pricing model. Flexible pricing allows, for example, grocery chains to offer specials to frequent shopper club members as well as allowing quantity pricing.

One such database has delivered a revolutionary approach to pricing — take whatever you're offered! Priceline.com Inc. (www.priceline.com) works to increase all their vendors' sales volumes by letting consumers pick their price — truly a new approach for one-to-one marketing. Products include airline tickets, hotel rooms, rental cars, car buying or leasing, groceries, and even gasoline in some U.S. states. A pricing system only available due to advanced technology, this auction-like approach determines price on an individual sale basis in a "private" cyber arena. Different from online auctions in that the items aren't hard to find collectibles or Beanie Babies, but "stockpiled" merchandise and services that other consumers are simultaneously consuming at list price when they enter the "brick and mortar" locations of the same providers. Also different is that the firm holds the patent on its name-your-own-price technology preventing "me-too" sites from popping up all over cyberspace. By early 2000 the service was selling about 100,000 airline tickets a week — up from five thousand a week the same time one-year earlier.[8]

profit maximization
The pricing objective of making as much money as possible.

MAXIMIZE PROFITS The pricing objective of making as much money as possible — using a "what the market will bear" approach — is probably followed more than any other goal. The trouble with this goal is that to some people, **profit maximization** has an ugly connotation, suggesting profiteering, high prices, and monopoly. Sometimes this appears too close to the mark as firms attempt to maximize their revenues as they may be the only provider. Alternatively, a firm may be trying to get what they can before other providers enter the market, or a fad or trend passes, or even the next technology arrives that lessens the "value" of the current product.

In both economic theory and business practice, and for most of us budgeting our own time, there is nothing wrong with profit maximization. Theoretically, if profits become high in an industry because supply is short in relation to demand, new capital will be attracted to increase production capacity. This will increase supply and eventually reduce profits to normal levels. In the marketplace where there is real competition, it is difficult to find many situations where profiteering has existed over an extended period of time. Substitute products are available, purchases are postponable, and competition can increase to keep prices at a reasonable level.

When prices are unduly high and entry into the field is severely limited, public outrage often is seen. In recent times this has been a highly visible issue with regard to pharmaceutical companies. For example, British Columbia hospitals have strongly objected to the price of alteplase, a blood-thinning drug used after heart attacks. The drug manufacturer Hoffman La Roche (www.rochecanada.com) sells this under the brand name Activase®, charging $2,700 per dose. This drug is generally considered the best "clot-buster" drug on the market, and hospitals want to be able to use it. Clearly, this isn't one of those products where you think — oh, I'll just go with the cheaper brand, it's probably not worth the extra money for that fancy brand. The matter is being considered by the Patent Medicine Prices Review Board, which controls the prices of many medications in Canada.[9] If market conditions and public opinion do not bring about reasonable prices for critical products such as this, agencies such as the review board are often set

Marketing at Work 13-2

Gasoline, Coffee, Cocoa: How Cartels Try To Control The Prices of Your Daily Fix

From time to time, Tim Hortons, the Second Cup, or Starbucks raises the price of a cup of coffee. Or Imperial Oil and Petro-Canada raise the price of a litre of gasoline. Or Cadbury and Lowney raise the price of a chocolate bar (or the bar gets smaller). Sometimes a natural disaster creates an expected and even a real supply shortage, so prices increase; frost in Brazil means the price of coffee beans starts to rise, a hurricane in Florida means the price of orange juice goes up. And sometimes, the prices of these and similar commodities rise because producers have banded together in an attempt to control output in order to cause price increases. It is also true that sometimes, the prices of commodities decrease. This can happen when the effect of a natural disaster has run its course or when commodity producers who are operating in concert fail to maintain their control over supply. Then, what you pay at the Esso or Petro-Canada pumps goes down. But you won't see the price of a chocolate bar or a cup of coffee decrease very often. Consumers are quite sensitive to the price of gas; they are not nearly so sensitive to the cost of coffee or chocolate.

Lately, three commodity organizations have attempted to control the production of their commodities, in various ways, in order to achieve desired price levels. The best known is OPEC (the Organization of Petroleum Exporting Countries) which controls about 60 percent of world petroleum production and, as a result, has a major influence on world prices. The member countries of OPEC used to meet once every six months to decide on what level of petroleum production they should make available in order to obtain a desired price from purchasers. Generally OPEC would attempt to restrict supply in order to increase prices as long as demand held up. From time to time, OPEC would increase supply in order to reduce prices when it felt that a price level had become so high as to threaten demand and revenue. The member countries have never agreed easily on any course of action. And whatever course was eventually agreed upon was sure to be ignored by some as they pursued their own interest in terms of generating revenues. But still, in general, the collusive action of the members provided reasonable results as far as their interests were concerned. And as long as OPEC was successful, the price of gasoline at Canadian pumps (as well as around the world outside of OPEC and a few other producing countries) was sometimes increased and sometimes decreased.

In early 2000, when world oil prices hit a peak due to increased demand and effective OPEC supply control, Canadian motorists and truckers (among others), screamed for government investigations into our oil companies and for price relief in the form of gasoline tax reductions or even subsidies. Given their success, OPEC countries met and agreed to increase production to force prices down from a very high US$34 a barrel to around US$25. OPEC did not want demand to be reduced too much in the face of the price spike. The countries agreed on an acceptable target price band of from $22 to $27 a barrel; if prices rose above $27, they would increase production to force them down, if they fell below $22, they would reduce production to force them up. Thus they attempted to establish a target price range with a mechanism to maintain it — a new price policy aimed at allowing them to meet their revenue goals. While analysts do not believe this approach can really work out well for OPEC in the long run, other commodity producers looked upon it with envy.

The most envious ones were members of the Association of Coffee Producing Countries (ACPC) and the Cocoa Producers' Alliance (CPA). Both groups are attempting to imitate OPEC so as to stabilize prices at levels which yield them target revenues; both are trying to reduce the supply of product that comes to market. Both have a much greater problem controlling supply simply because there are many more small producers and it is relatively easy to turn off the taps on oil supply but both coffee and cocoa plants take months to years to produce beans. And since the producers' supply decisions were made months and years ago and cannot be easily curtailed in the short run, their ability to control supply just doesn't compare to OPEC's. In addition, in general they need cash much more badly than do the OPEC countries

What will be the result? OPEC will continue to force prices up and down to suit dominant member country revenue needs, and you will see posted prices going up and down as a result. Canadian consumers, and others, will scream when prices go up and not make a peep when they go down. ACPC and CPA will continue to attempt to control supply and not have much success for the foreseeable future. You need not fear that on their account alone, your favourite chocolate fix or double latte will increase in price. But it could if there is a bad freeze, or a huge storm or flood in the major producing areas. Or if Tim Hortons, the Second Cup, and Starbucks decide they need to increase their margins and believe you won't mind very much.

Source: Adapted, in part, from Ross Laver, "The reality of gas prices," *MacLean's*, April 3, 2000, p. 39; Peter McKay, "Fledgling commodity cartels full of beans," *The Globe and Mail*, April 25, 2000, p. B13.

up to ensure equitable controls. For most other products and services, consumers for the most part cease to purchase when prices are perceived to reach such a point.

The goal should be to maximize profits on total output rather than on each single product. In fact, a company may maximize total profit by setting low, relatively unprofitable prices on some products in order to stimulate sales of others. In its advertising on televised athletic events, the Gillette Company (www.gillette.com) frequently promotes razors at very low prices. The firm hopes that once customers acquire products such as the Sensor Excel or Mach3 razor, they will become loyal customers for Gillette blades, which generate healthy profits for the company. In some situations accepting less profit on the initial product sale increases the potential for future revenues as it "hooks" a greater number of consumers on the refill products which actually provide a higher profit return.

Sales-Oriented Goals
In some companies, management's pricing is focused on sales volume. The pricing goal may be to increase sales volume or to maintain or increase the firm's market share.

INCREASE SALES VOLUME The pricing goal of **increasing sales volume** is typically adopted to achieve rapid growth or to discourage potential competitors from entering a market. The goal is usually stated as a percentage increase in sales volume over some period, say, one year or three years. Management may seek higher sales volume by discounting or by some other aggressive pricing strategy, perhaps even incurring a loss in the short run. Thus, clothing stores run end-of-season sales, and auto dealers offer rebates and below-market financing rates on new cars to stimulate sales. Many vacation destinations, such as golf courses and resorts, reduce prices during off-seasons to increase sales volume. Internet start-ups frequently offer free products or trials or services. The purpose of this has been twofold. These promotions are advertised on TV and on other Web sites to direct traffic to their site, but there was also a time when such promotions were required to encourage many reluctant first time e-buyers.

These promotions, for example, included a free first purchase up to a certain dollar amount (often $20 or $25) such as was done by MotherNature.com (www.mother-nature.com), a provider of herbal and preventative measure health products. This was still the infancy of e-buying for many retail consumers and significant incentives were required to get many to make their first purchase on the net. MotherNature.com decreased this incentive to $10 during 2000 as buying over the Internet became more commonplace. But, at the same time, more and more retailers were putting up their own cyberstores requiring that some incentive be available to be chosen over other vendors. Some retailers like drugstore.com (www.drugstore.com) took a more creative and personalized approach and offered a choice of free themed gift baskets — aromatherapy products, health and beauty, herbal/vitamin supplements, etc.

MAINTAIN OR INCREASE MARKET SHARE In some companies, both large and small, the pricing objective is to **maintain or increase market share**. Why is market share protected or pursued so vigorously? In growing fields such as computers, information technology, and communications, companies want large shares in order to gain leverage with vendors and to aid in driving down production and other costs that are sensitive to economies of scale.

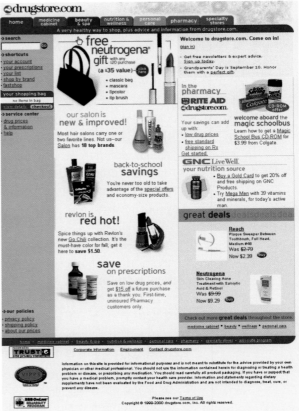

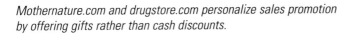

Mothernature.com and drugstore.com personalize sales promotion by offering gifts rather than cash discounts.

Most other industries today are not growing much, if at all, and, if they have not yet rationalized their operations, have excess production and operations capacity. Since the size of the "pie" isn't growing in most cases, businesses that need added volume have to grab a bigger "slice of the pie" — that is, greater market share. The North American auto and airline industries illustrate these situations. The deregulation of long-distance telephone service in Canada demonstrates what a battle can result when trying to enter a market or when trying to defend one's existing share against new players.

Other firms have had to go further back in the manufacturing process to maintain their market shares. For instance, when global organizations face currency fluctuations that result in price increases in various national markets, they must react if this affects their competitive position. When the Japanese yen rose considerably in relation to the Canadian and U.S. dollars, Japanese products — autos, for example — became more expensive in dollars and Japanese companies faced the prospect of losing market share. To maintain their shares, Toyota, Nissan, and Honda accepted smaller profit margins and reduced their costs so that they could lower their selling prices.

Honda (www.honda.ca) and Toyota (www.toyota.ca) serve as prime examples of how integral effective pricing strategies should be to the operation of an organization. The shift in the value of the yen throughout the early-90s had such an impact that sales of the Accord and Camry were significantly decreased as their prices skyrocketed. Prices rose such that buyers were opting for North American products such as the popular Ford Taurus over these models. The Accord had long battled for market share and first place sales position with the Taurus and was now at a significant price disadvantage causing it to lose its first place ranking. Unwilling to allow this model to lose the momentum it had achieved, the car

Marketing at Work 13-3

Canada's Telcos Continue The Price/Value/Market Share Wars

The long-distance price wars began in summer 1998. As new service providers entered the Canadian marketplace a struggle began for market share by these new providers while existing utilities in each province not used to competing in an open market had to struggle tooth and nail to maintain some of their previous share of the market.

Telecommunications pricing was revolutionized with Sprint Canada's offer of flat-rate pricing — unlimited calling for $20 a month. This was an all-you-could-eat-buffet with some consumers spending over one hundred hours on long distance calls in one month! What followed was a series of rate cuts and flat fee offers geared to outdo the last. Suddenly, long distance revenues dropped so low and so hard that the legs buckled out from underneath that buffet table as companies realized this was no longer profitable or healthy for the brand. Adjustments and limits were placed on these packages and firms looked for means beyond pricing. And yes, the telcos to look at value from a non-price perspective. Value creation through bundling services became what the telcos referred to as "sticky applications." Sticky because the more services you

provided to a single consumer the more attached they became to the provider — no one wants to change their home and cell numbers, e-mail address, and set up a new voice mailbox at the same time for the sake of saving a few bucks!

Now we have Burnaby, B.C.-based BCT Telus taking on Montreal-based Bell Canada on its home turf. This new company — the result of a 1998 merger between Alberta's Telus Corp. and B.C. Telecom — seems to be off to a good start with its recent takeover of QuébecTel, Quebec's second-largest phone system. BCT Telus hopes to branch out of its traditional British Columbia and Alberta markets and offer its trademark low prices to businesses in Bell-dominated Quebec and Ontario. In the meantime, Bell hardly plans to take any of this sitting down. It plans to fight back by lowering its prices to business customers from 20 percent (for small and medium-sized companies) to 37 per cent (for big corporations). Like its rival, Bell figures that an expanded market and its one-stop shopping basket of new and improved services will allow it to send prices plummeting — and still end up with a nice profit.

Source: Adapted from Zena Olijnyk, "Online Bookseller Has 'Enough Resources'," *The Financial Post*, April 20, 2000, p. C3 and Simon Tuck, "BCE, Telus battle for customers," *The Globe and Mail*, April 1, 2000, p. B4.

---

and its manufacturing costs were redesigned with an eye to reducing processes and costs which resulted in enabling the new model to sell in North America for approximately $1,200 less then the previous version. The car could now be priced back in the same category as previously. Toyota performed similar surgeries on its Camry assembly plants.

Of course growing market share and huge volumes of sales should mean streaming profits. Well, not always, or not at first! As was previously discussed, many dot-coms are generating huge sales and investing massive capital to continue expansion without yet seeing the light of profit at the end of the cyber-tunnel. Chapters Online Inc. (www.chapters.ca) as we all know by now sells books as its major business. And books are thought to be the consumer's entry point to online shopping. Considering this and that it is the number one online retailer in Canada at doing just that, you would think they were making money. But after three years, this is still not the case! However, they soon expect to be "cash generative." With a cash "burn" rate of $7.8 million per quarter the company hopes to see a profit by late 2001.[10]

Status Quo Goals

Two closely related goals — **stabilizing prices** and **meeting competition** — are the least aggressive of all pricing goals. They are intended simply to maintain the firm's current situation — the status quo. With either of these goals, a firm seeks to avoid price competition.

Price stabilization often is the goal in industries in which the product is highly standardized (such as lumber products or bulk chemicals) and in which one large firm historically has acted as a leader in setting prices. Smaller firms in these industries tend to "follow the leader" when setting their prices. What is the reason for such pricing behaviour? A price cut by any one firm is likely to be matched by all other firms in order to remain competitive; therefore, no individual firm gains, but all may suffer smaller profits. Conversely, a price boost is unlikely to be matched (except in cases of supply shortages, as we have discussed in "Marketing at Work" File 13-2), but the price-changing firm faces a differential disadvantage because other elements of a standardized product, such as gasoline, are perceived to be fairly similar.

Even in industries in which there are no price leaders, countless firms deliberately price their products to meet the prevailing market price. This pricing policy gives management an easy means of avoiding difficult pricing decisions. Many stores have adopted a price-matching policy such as Future Shop (www.futureshop.ca) and Staples (www.staples.ca). This allows the onus to be placed with the consumer to present a lower price to be matched or beaten by a fixed percentage while allowing the retailer to advertise having the lowest prices available.

Firms that adopt status quo pricing goals to avoid price competition are not necessarily passive in their marketing. Quite the contrary! Typically these companies compete aggressively using other marketing-mix elements — product, distribution, and especially promotion. This approach is called non-price competition, and its objective is to provide the customer with other reasons for buying the firm's products or services. It is never desirable to depend on differentiation based *only* upon price, as it will simply escalate price-matching and reduce profits all around. There are consumers who will pay extra for better service, greater convenience, or other attributes they believe offer incremental value.

Even among discount retailers, competing solely on price is not effective. When Zellers (www.hbc.com/zellers) tried to take on Wal-Mart when it entered Canada, they tried to do it on price. Zellers took every ounce of profitability and expended it trying to be price competitive, but to no avail.[11] Low pricing alone cannot maintain market share and profitability among such competitors. Zellers has instead moved to a new branding strategy that focuses on value, new brands including a new private label of household, nutrition, health and beauty products (Truly), and new store design.

Factors Influencing Price Determination

base price

The price of one unit of the product at its point of production or resale.

Knowing the objective of its pricing, a company then can move to the heart of price management: determining the base price of a product. **Base price**, or list price, refers to the price of one unit of the product or service at its point of production, resale, or delivery. This price does not reflect discounts or special allowances, delivery or freight charges, or any other modifications (discussed in the next chapter), such as leader pricing and value pricing.

The same procedure is followed in pricing both new and established products. Pricing an established product usually is less difficult than pricing a new product, however, because the exact price or a narrow range of prices may be dictated by the market. Other factors, besides objectives, that influence price determination are discussed next.

Estimating the Demand for a Product

In pricing, a company must estimate the total demand for the product. This is easier to do for an established product than for a new one. The steps in estimating demand are

(1) determine whether there is a price the market expects and (2) estimate what the sales volume might be at different prices.

The **expected price** of a product is the price at which customers consciously or unconsciously value it — what they think the product is worth. Expected price usually is expressed as a **range of prices** rather than as a specific amount. Thus the expected price might be "between $250 and $300" or "not over $20."

A producer must also consider an intermediary's reaction to price. Intermediaries are more likely to promote a product if they approve of its price. Sometimes they don't approve. For example, in the mid-90s, Wal-Mart (wal-mart.com) did not approve when Rubbermaid attempted to raise its prices on housewares. Rubbermaid was faced with a substantial cost increase for resin, a major ingredient in its housewares and toys. But since Wal-Mart was such an important reseller, Rubbermaid settled for a smaller increase (which hurt its profits) than it had originally planned for, thereby resulting in lower profits. Accepting this still resulted in an increase in profits than if the huge reseller decided not to carry the Rubbermaid line anymore.

It's possible to set a price too low. If the price is much lower than what the market expects, sales may be lost. For example, it probably would be a mistake for MAC Cosmetics (www.maccosmetics.com), a trendy cosmetics maker, to put a $1.49 price tag on its lipstick or for L'Oreal Paris (www.loreal.com) to price its imported perfume at $3.49 for 3 ml. In all likelihood, customers would be suspicious about product quality or their self-concept would not let them buy such low-priced products.

Although some consumers do know that a high price does not necessarily mean high quality, most realize enough to believe that a low price is an indication of quality. The prices just discussed would be significantly lower than expected from these brands and would signal inconsistency with the traditional products and images of those cosmetics companies. After all, the well-known slogan "you're worth it" doesn't say much if it's only a $1.49.

L'Oreal knows that one line says it all!

Altering product lines and prices can have a confusing and chilling effect on consumers as well as revenues. This is what initially happened to Canadian menswear retailer Tip Top Tailors when they pushed to rapidly reposition their stores in the Canadian marketplace. Overnight they tried to go from pushing acrylic sweaters to the cost conscious consumers to selling designer labels such as Sanford Bryant to the fashionable middle class. In trying to go in the reverse market direction than our cosmetic example, Tip Top moved too quickly to present its new image. Price as much as the product communicates a message to the consumer in combination with other available cues. People's impressions of brands don't change any more quickly or completely than their impressions of other things in life. In the first year sales dropped about ten percent and the retailer closed seven of its 127 outlets.[12]

After raising a product's price, some organizations have experienced a considerable increase in sales. This situation is called **inverse demand** — the higher the price, the greater the unit sales. Inverse demand usually exists only within a given price range and only at lower price levels. Suppose a cutting-edge electronics company like Sony increased the prices of their line of DVD players. Would you wonder if perhaps this was the brand everyone was buying, or that the marketplace must recognize these as superior to other players? Perhaps you would believe that it means they are in short supply and you should get one while you can. However, at some point inverse demand ends and the usual pattern — declining demand as prices rise — becomes evident.

How do sellers determine expected prices? They may submit products to experienced retailers or wholesalers for appraisal. A business-goods manufacturer might get price estimates over the Internet by showing models or blueprints to engineers working for prospective customers. Another alternative is to ask a sample of consumers what they would expect to pay for the product or which item in a list of alternatives is most similar to the test product. An Internet-based consumer experiment or "auction" could be used as well as personal surveys. Using such methods, a seller can determine a reasonable range of prices.

It is extremely helpful to estimate what the sales volume will be at several different prices. By doing this, the seller is, in effect, determining the demand curve for the product. Moreover, the seller is gauging **price elasticity of demand**, which refers to the responsiveness of quantity demanded to price changes. Estimates of sales at different prices also are useful in determining break-even points (we'll get to this topic shortly).

Sellers can choose from several methods to estimate sales at various prices. Recall some of the demand-forecasting methods discussed in Chapter 5 — survey of buyer intentions, test marketing, and sales force composite, for example. These methods can be used in this situation as well.

Competitive Reactions

Competition greatly influences base price. A new product is distinctive only until the inevitable arrival of competition. The threat of potential competition is greatest when the field is easy to enter and profit prospects are encouraging. This may provide a good opportunity for a firm to exercise its competitive intelligence skills. Competition can come from these sources:

◆ *Directly similar products:* Nike versus Adidas or Reebok running shoes.

◆ *Available substitutes:* Airfreight versus truck shipping or rail freight.

---

inverse demand
A price–volume relationship such that the higher the price, the greater the unit sales.

price elasticity of demand
The responsiveness of quantity demanded to price changes.

◆ *Unrelated products seeking the same consumer dollar:* a PalmPilot handheld PC versus a portable CD player, bicycle, or a weekend excursion.

In the case of directly similar products, a competitor may adjust its prices. In turn, other firms have to decide what price adjustments, if any, are necessary to retain their customers.

Other Marketing-Mix Elements

A product's base price is influenced considerably by the other ingredients in the marketing mix.

PRODUCT We have already observed that a product's price is affected by whether it is a new item or an established one. Over the course of the life of a product — its life cycle — price changes are necessary to keep the product competitive. The end use of the product must also be considered. For instance, there is little price competition among

Because Palm Pilot is in the early stage of the life cycle, it can protect its price not only because it is an innovation but also because it attracts dollars from unrelated products due to its features — the long list on the right-side of their ad.

manufacturers of packaging materials or producers of industrial gases, so their price structure is stable. These business products are only an incidental part of the final article, so customers will buy the least expensive product consistent with the required quality. The price of a product is also influenced by whether (1) the product may be leased as well as purchased outright, (2) the product may be returned to the seller, and (3) a trade-in is involved.

The pricing of services is somewhat more difficult in that the customer has little or no opportunity to examine the service before buying. In many service industries, the "product" being sold is the expertise and experience of the employees of the firm. Thus a law firm may charge clients $400 per hour for the time that the senior partner spends on a file, but only $100 per hour for a junior lawyer. Why does it cost so much more to get a haircut at one of those uptown hair salons than at one of those franchises like Choice Cuts or Fantasic Sam's? There must be an underlying belief among some consumers that these stylists or the products used are somehow "better."

DISTRIBUTION CHANNELS The channels and types of intermediaries selected will influence a producer's pricing. A firm selling both through wholesalers and directly to retailers often sets a different factory price for these two classes of customers. The price to wholesalers is lower because they perform services that the producer would have to perform — such as providing storage, granting credit to retailers, and selling to small retailers.

Also, in some cases, a more direct distribution channel may allow a firm to charge higher prices because customers are generally prepared to pay more for convenience and speedy delivery. Insurance companies that sell direct, as opposed to through agents, are illustrations of how cost savings can be passed to customers because of a major change in its distribution channel.

Somewhere in between this lies the Internet. As a new channel of distribution, it eliminates the middleman completely when the vendor operates only as a "click" company. While attractive pricing has lead many to begin purchasing goods on the Web, it must also be considered that shipping becomes an incremental element of the total cost for every purchase. Concern over the safety and timeliness of the products delivery to the buyer can be costs to both the vendor and the consumer.

PROMOTION The extent to which the product is promoted by the producer or intermediaries and the methods used are added considerations in pricing. If major promotional responsibility is placed on retailers, they ordinarily will be charged a lower price for a product than if the producer advertises it heavily. Even when a producer promotes heavily, it may want its retailers to use local advertising to tie in with national advertising. Such a decision must be reflected in the producer's price to these retailers.

Auto manufacturers are attempting to utilize the Internet as a means to centralize several facets of their organizations from their own parts ordering to selling the actual finished product. It is believed that by directing more consumers, distributors, and processes through their online information systems they will gain tighter inventory control and significantly reduce costs. This includes using the Web for consumer information and promotion like all other "bricks and clicks" firms. In 2000, Volkswagen (www.vw.com) gave consumers a bold push in the desired direction with its Reflex Beetle promotion. Part of the success of the new 90's version of the Beetle was its strong nostalgia twist. In 2000, VW introduced "new" colours that were in fact the colours for which people remember the old model, such as powder blue. Perhaps the best known shade was the intense yellow that made the oval-shaped car resemble a big ol' lemon. Lemon yellow was back, but only on the Web! Original advertising introduced the "new" colour now called "reflex" — only 2000 available, and obtained only on the Web.

Estimating the Cost of a Product

The pricing of a product also should consider its cost. A product's total unit cost is made up of two basic types of costs, fixed or variable.

fixed cost
A constant cost, regardless of how many items are produced or sold.

◆   A **fixed cost**, such as rent, executive or technical support salaries, or property tax, remains constant regardless of how many items are produced, how many customers walk in the door or how many "hits" there are on a Web site. Such a cost continues even if production stops completely, no one enters the shop or the Web site receives no visitors. It is called a fixed cost because it is difficult to change in the short run — it is committed. In the long run, it can be changed.

variable cost
A cost that varies or changes directly in relation to the number of units produced or sold.

total cost
The sum of total fixed costs and total variable costs, or the full cost of a specific quantity produced or sold.

◆ A **variable cost**, such as labour or materials or commissions paid to sales staff is directly related to production. Variable costs can be controlled in the short run simply by changing the level of production. When production stops, or the shop closes, all variable production or operating costs become zero.

◆ **Total costs** are the sum of the fixed and variable costs at a particular level of operation — producing five thousand units of product or selling forty printers in a week.

Total unit costs are the total costs at a particular level of operation divided by the number of units produced or sold.

We will illustrate these costs in the pricing approaches that follow.

Cost-Plus Pricing

cost-plus pricing
A major method of price determination in which the price of a unit of a product is set at a level equal to the unit's total cost plus a desired profit on the unit.

Should the builder use the cost-plus method when pricing these condominiums?

Most companies establish their prices based on *total cost plus a desired profit.*

According to a survey that examined what approaches are used to price new as opposed to existing products:

◆ 9 percent of companies "guess-timate" what the base price for a new product should be.

◆ 37 percent match what competitors charge for similar items.

◆ 50 percent of firms charge what the market will bear.

◆ 52 percent, the most common approach, choose a price to cover costs and provide a fair profit.

Since this totals 148 per cent, its clear that most firms use more than one approach — an important factor to keep in mind.[13]

Let's first discuss **cost-plus pricing**, which means setting the price of one unit of a product equal to the total cost of the unit plus the desired profit on the unit. Suppose that Regency Builders, a housing contractor, figures the labour and materials required to build and sell ten condominiums will cost $750,000, and other expenses (office rent, depreciation on equipment, management salaries, and so on) will be $150,000. The contractor wants to earn a profit of 10 percent on the total cost of $900,000. Cost plus desired profit is $990,000, so each of the ten condos is priced at $99,000.

While it is an easily applied method, cost-plus pricing has limitations. One is that it does not recognize various types of costs or the fact that these costs are affected differently by changes in level of output. In our housing example, suppose that Regency built and sold only eight condos at the cost-plus price of $99,000 each. As shown in Table 13-1, total sales would then be $792,000. Labour and materials chargeable to the eight condos would total $600,000 ($75,000 per house). Since the contractor would

TABLE 13-1 Regency Builders: An Example of Cost-Plus Pricing

Actual results often differ from planned outcomes because various types of costs react differently to changes in output.

Regency Builders costs, selling price, and profit	Number of condominiums built and sold by Regency Builders	
	Planned = 10	Actual = 8
Labour and materials costs ($75,000 per condo)	$750,000	$600,000
Overhead (fixed) costs	150,000	150,000
Total costs	$900,000	$750,000
Total sales at $99,000 per condo	990,000	792,000
Profit: Total	$ 90,000	$ 42,000
Profit: Per condo	$ 9,000	$ 5,250
Profit: As percent of cost	10%	5.6%

still incur the full $150,000 in overhead expenses, the total cost would be $750,000. This would leave a profit of only $42,000, or $5,250 per condominium instead of the anticipated $9,000. On a percentage basis, profit would be only 5.6 percent of total cost rather than the desired 10 percent.

A second limitation of this pricing approach is that market demand is ignored (which might explain why we have unsold condos). That is, cost-plus pricing assumes that all the output will be produced and sold. If fewer units are produced, each would have to sell for a higher price to cover all costs and show a profit. But if the condominium market is becoming depressed or the location of the units is not that desirable, output must be cut, as it is not wise to raise the unit price. Another limitation of this method is that doesn't recognize that total unit cost changes as output expands or contracts. However, a more sophisticated approach to cost-plus pricing can take such changes into consideration.

Prices Based on Variable Costs

Another approach to cost-plus pricing is to set prices based, at least, on variable costs only, not total costs. This is **variable-cost pricing**. Say a firm cannot obtain a price to cover its total costs because of, say, extreme short-term competitive conditions—an Air Canada seat sale on the Toronto to London route forced by a British Airways seat sale. If the firm can sell for any price in excess of its variable costs, the excess contributes to the payment of fixed costs. The firm can only persist with this kind of pricing if it has other sources of revenue to cover its total costs.

Not all orders can be priced to cover only variable costs. Contribution pricing may be feasible, however, if management wants to keep its labour force employed during a slack season. It may also be used when one product is expected to attract business for another. Thus a department store may price meals in its cafe at a level that covers only the variable costs. The reasoning is that this food service will bring shoppers to the store, where they will buy other, more profitable products.

Pricing by Middlemen

At first glance, cost-plus pricing appears to be widely used by retailing and wholesaling intermediaries. A retailer, for example, pays a given amount to buy products and have them delivered to the store. Then the retailer adds an amount, called a markup, to the acquisition cost. This markup is estimated to be sufficient to cover the store's expenses and provide a reasonable profit. Thus a building-materials outlet may buy a power drill for $30 including freight, and price the item at $50. The $50 price reflects a markup of 40 percent based on the selling price, or 66.7 percent percent based on the merchandise cost. Of course, in setting prices, intermediaries also should take into account the expectations of their customers.

Various types of retailers require different percentage markups because of the nature of the products handled and the services offered. A self-service supermarket has lower costs and thus can have a lower average markup than a full-service delicatessen. Figure 13-1 shows examples of markup pricing by intermediaries.

Is cost-plus pricing really used by intermediaries? For the following reasons, it's safe to say that cost-plus pricing is not widely used:

◆ *Most retail prices are really only offers.* If customers accept the offer, the price is fine. If they reject it, the price usually will be changed quickly, or the product may even be withdrawn from the market. Prices thus are always on trial.

◆ *Many retailers don't use the same markup on all the products they carry.* A supermarket will have a markup of 6 to 8 percent on sugar and soap products, 15 to 18 percent on canned fruit and vegetables, and 25 to 30 percent on fresh meats and produce. These different markups for distinctive products reflect competitive considerations and other aspects of market demand.

◆ The middleman usually doesn't actually set a base price but only adds a percentage to the price already set by the producer. The producer's price is set to allow each middleman to add a reasonable markup and still sell at a competitive retail price. The producer sets the key price, with an eye on the final market.

Thus what seems to be cost-plus pricing by intermediaries is usually market-influenced pricing.

Evaluation of Cost-Plus Pricing

Since a firm should be market-oriented and cater to consumers' wants, why are we considering cost-plus pricing? Simply, cost-plus pricing must be understood because it is referred to often in business. Further, it is used by numerous industrial firms.[14]

The traditional perspective has been that costs should be a determinant of prices, but not the only one. Costs are a floor under a firm's prices — particularly variable costs as

FIGURE 13-1

Examples of Markup Pricing by Retailers and Wholesalers

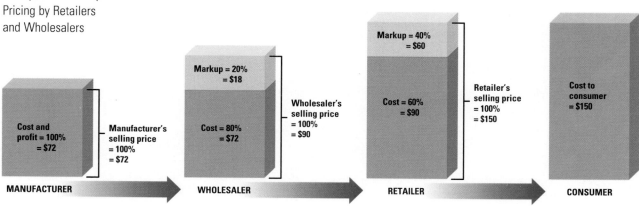

we pointed out earlier. If goods are priced under the cost floor for a long time, the firm will be forced out of business. But when it is used by itself, cost-plus pricing is a weak and unrealistic method because it ignores competition and market demand.

In recent years, with low rates of inflation in our economy as well as in the United States, a consumer-oriented concept that price should determine costs has received great emphasis. Firms using this market-based perspective must re-engineer their production and operating systems to reduce costs wherever possible. The appropriate conclusion is that used by itself, cost-plus pricing is a weak and unrealistic method because it ignores market conditions, notably demand and competition.

Break-Even Analysis

One way to consider both market demand and costs in price determination is to use **break-even analysis** to calculate break-even points. A break-even point is that quantity of output at which total revenue equals total costs, *assuming a certain selling price*. There is a different break-even point for each different selling price. Sales exceeding the **break-even point** result in a profit on each additional unit. The higher sales are above the break-even point, the higher will be the total and unit profits. Sales below the break-even point result in a loss to the seller.

break-even point
The level of output at which revenues equal costs, assuming a certain selling price.

Determining the Break-Even Point

The method of determining a break-even point is illustrated in Table 13-2 and Figure 13-2. In our example, the Futon Factory's fixed costs are $25,000 and variable costs are assumed to be constant at $30 per unit.

The total cost of producing one unit is $25,300 — the Futon Factory obviously needs more volume to absorb its fixed costs! For 400 units the total cost is $37,000 ($30 multiplied by 400, plus $25,000). In Figure 13-2 the selling price is $80 a unit, and variable costs of $30 per unit are incurred in producing each unit. Consequently, any revenue over $30 contributes to covering fixed costs (sometimes termed *overhead*). When the price is $80, that would be $50 per unit. At a price of $80, the break-even point is 500 units, because a $50 per-unit contribution will just cover overhead of $25,000.

TABLE 13-2   Futon Factory: Computation of Break-even Point

At each of several prices, we wish to find out how many units must be sold to cover all costs. At a unit price of $100, the sale of each unit contributes $70 to cover overhead expenses. The Futon Factory must sell about 357 units to cover its $25,000 in fixed costs.

(1) Unit price	(2) Unit variable costs	(3) Contribution to overhead (1) − (2)	(4) Overhead (total fixed costs)	(5) Break-even point (rounded) (4) ÷ (3)
$60	$30	$30	$25,000	833 units
80	30	50	$25,000	500 units
100	30	70	$25,000	357 units
150	30	120	$25,000	208 units

FIGURE 13-2

Break even chart for Futon Factory

Here the break-even point is reached when the company sells 500 units. Fixed costs, regardless of quantity produced and sold, are $25,000. The variable cost per unit is $30. If this company sells 500 units, total costs are $40,000 (variable cost of 500 × $30, or $15,000, plus fixed costs of $25,000). At a selling price of $80, the sale of 500 units will yield $40,000 revenue, and costs and revenue will equal each other. At the same price, the sale of each unit above 500 will yield a profit.

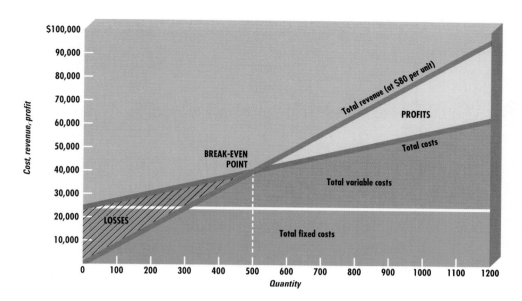

Stated another way, variable costs for 500 units are $15,000 and fixed costs are $25,000, for a total cost of $40,000. This amount equals the revenue from 500 units sold at $80 each. So, at an $80 selling price, the break-even volume is 500 units. Figure 13-2 shows a break-even point for an $80 price, but it is highly desirable to calculate break-even points for several different selling prices.

The break-even point may be found with this formula:

$$\text{Break-even point in units} = \frac{\text{total fixed costs}}{\text{unit contribution to overhead}}$$

Because unit contribution to overhead equals selling price less the average variable cost, the working formula becomes:

$$\text{Break-even point in units} = \frac{\text{total fixed costs}}{\text{selling price} - \text{average variable cost}}$$

Two basic assumptions underlie these calculations:

◆ Total fixed costs are constant. In reality they may change, although usually not in the short run.

◆ Variable costs remain constant per unit of output. Actually, average variable costs usually fluctuate.

Evaluation of Break-Even Analysis

Two basic assumptions underlie break-even analysis: total fixed costs are constant; variable costs remain constant per unit of output. Actually, fixed costs may change, although not rapidly, and average variable costs normally fluctuate. Therefore, break-even analysis cannot be used conclusively in most companies. But it does provide some guidance.

Another drawback of break-even analysis is that it cannot tell us whether we can actually sell the break-even amount. Table 13-2, for example, shows what revenue will be at the different prices if the given number of units can be sold at these prices. The number the market will buy at a given price could well be below the break-even point. If that happens, the firm will not break even — it will show a loss.

Despite these limitations, management should not dismiss break-even analysis as a pricing tool. Even in its simplest form, break-even analysis is helpful because in the short run many firms experience reasonably stable cost and demand structures.[15]

Prices Set in Relation to Market Alone

Cost-plus pricing is one extreme among pricing methods. At the other extreme are methods in which a firm's prices are set in relation only to the market price. The seller's price may be set right at the market price to meet the competition, or it may be set above or below the market price.

Pricing to Meet Competition

Pricing to meet competition is simple to carry out. A firm ascertains what the market price is and, after allowing for customary markups for intermediaries, arrives at its own selling price. To illustrate, let's take the high-end of athletic shoes and a manufacturer like Nike. Nike's market research indicates that the Air Metal Max IV cross trainer should be priced around US$130 on the store shelf. Lets suppose that usually retailers want about a 40 percent average markup of their selling price. Consequently, after allowing US$52 for the retailer's markup, Nike's price is US$78. This manufacturer then has to decide whether US$78 is enough to cover the associated costs and provide the desired level of profit. Sometimes a producer faces a real squeeze if costs are rising but the market price is holding firm. When a firm like Nike engages in so much promotion and sponsorship using so many celebrity spokespeople that command such huge fees, it's not hard for costs to escalate.

One situation in which management might price a product right at the market level is when competition is keen and the firm's product is not differentiated significantly from competing products. To some extent, this pricing method reflects the market conditions of **perfect competition**. That is, product differentiation is absent, buyers and sellers are well informed, and the seller has no discernible control over the selling price. Most producers of agricultural products and small firms marketing well-known, standardized products use this pricing method.

So far in our discussion of pricing to meet competition, we have observed market situations that involve many sellers. Oddly enough, this same pricing method is often used when the market is dominated by a few firms, with each marketing similar products. With this kind of market structure, called an **oligopoly**, which includes such industries as copper, aluminum, soft drinks, breakfast cereals, auto tires, and even among barber shops and grocery stores in a small community — oligopolists should simply set prices at a competitive level and leave them there. Typically they do. If they raise prices above the market level, their revenue quickly decreases and if they lower them below market level, their competitors quickly reduce their prices to match the cut in order to protect their revenue. The result is that no one is better off.

Pricing Below Competition

A variation of market-based pricing is to set a price below the level charged by your main competitors. **Pricing below competition** is done by discount retailers, such as Zellers and Wal-Mart, that compete against major department stores. They stress low markup, high volume, and fewer customer services (including salespeople). They price some heavily advertised, well-known brands 10 to 30 percent below the suggested list price, which is normally charged by full-service retailers. Even full-service retailers may price below the competitive level by eliminating specific services. Some gas stations offer a discount to customers who pay with cash instead of a credit card. Canadian Tire gasoline stations distribute bonus coupons for their infamous Canadian Tire money that provide consumers with four or five times the "cash" if they pay cash.

The risk in pricing below competition is that consumers begin to view the product as an undifferentiated commodity, such as coal and bulk salt, with all the focus on price differences. If that happens, and some would say it already has in fields such as personal computers, then consumers choose the brand with the lowest price. In turn, competing firms are likely to wind up in a price war that diminishes or eliminates profits.[16] One observer asked a question that applies to any industry in which firms rely on price as a way to gain an edge over competitors: "How can restaurant chains ever expect to charge top dollar again after relentlessly pushing value [low] prices?"[17]

Pricing Above Competition

Producers or retailers sometimes set their prices above the prevailing market level. Usually, **pricing above competition** works only when the product is distinctive or when the seller has acquired prestige in its field. Most communities have an elite clothing boutique and a prestigious jewellery store in which price tags are noticeably above the level set by other stores with seemingly similar products. However, a gas station that has a strong advantage based on a superior location (perhaps the only such station for many kilometres on the Trans-Canada Highway) may also be able to use above-market pricing.

Above-market pricing often is employed by manufacturers of prestige brands of high-cost products, such as automobiles (Ferrari, Mercedes), clothing (Prada, Dolce & Gabbana), leather products (Gucci, Fendi), and watches (TAG Heuer, Rolex). Some retailers feel that luxury goods in Canada are doing better than ever. The lure of high-priced goods is felt to be quality and an image of elegance. Canadian consumers were throwing money at the luxury car market in 2000. Porsche Cars North America reported that sales for April of that year were up 64 percent over the same period the previous year while BMW Canada experienced a 14 percent increase from the previous year.[18] Cartier Inc. (www.cartier.com), the famous jeweller, is one example of a retailer that is thriving at the luxury end of the scale. This establishment feels that luxury and discount price outlets often thrive at the same time that the mid-range operations show limited growth. This is because the customers who frequent these establishments are often not affected by changes in economic situations.[19] But while these luxury items continue to be popular, a changing trend has shown that more value is sought from many such items. It appears that these consumers now are focusing more on style, quality, and longer-lasting items that could become family heirlooms.[20] In other words, these consumers have become more value-oriented.

Above-market pricing is sometimes found even among relatively low-cost products — candies, for example. Godiva (www.godiva.com), a brand of imported Belgian chocolates, follows this practice in Canada and the United States. Recently, even simple daily-use products have become premium-priced niche products. The very mature, and highly competitive, oral hygiene category is one such example. For years, Colgate (www.colgate.com) and Crest (www.crest.com) have waged a grinding market share battle with almost nothing to show for it. The companies have developed extensions ranging from whitening products to specialty toothbrushes and products specifically designed for children. These offerings have all been at premium prices with pastes exceeding the $3 level and toothbrushes retailing for $6.[21] Premium-pricing, as can be seen, doesn't only apply to luxury goods.

The basic pricing methods covered in this chapter are equally applicable in the marketing of goods and services by businesses. Pricing of services was discussed in more detail in Chapter 12.

Summary

In our economy, price influences the allocation of resources. In individual companies, price is one significant factor in achieving marketing success. And in many purchase situations, price can be of great importance to consumers. However, it is difficult to define price. A rather general definition is: Price is the amount of money and/or other items with utility needed to acquire a product.

Before setting a product's base price, management should identify its pricing goal. Major pricing objectives are to (1) earn a target return on investment or on net sales, (2) maximize profits, (3) increase sales, (4) hold or gain a target market share, (5) stabilize prices, and (6) meet competition's prices.

Besides the firm's pricing objective, other key factors that influence price setting are (1) demand for the product, (2) competitive reactions, (3) strategies planned for other marketing-mix elements, and (4) cost of the product. The concept of elasticity refers to the effect that unit-price changes have on the number of units sold and on total revenue.

Two major methods used to determine the base price are cost-plus pricing, and setting the price in relation only to the market. For cost-plus pricing to be effective, a seller must consider several types of costs and their reactions to changes in the quantity produced. A producer usually sets a price to cover total cost. In some cases, however, the best policy may be to set a price that covers marginal cost only. The main weakness in cost-plus pricing is that it completely ignores market demand. To partially offset this weakness, a company may use break-even analysis as a tool in price setting.

In actual business situations, price setting is influenced by market conditions. Hence, variable costs or contribution pricing, which takes into account both demand and costs to determine a suitable price for the product, is a useful price determination method.

For many products, price setting is relatively easy because management simply sets the price at the level of competition. Because markets are constantly changing and evolving this still requires that pricing policies and strategies be assessed frequently. Pricing at prevailing market levels makes sense for firms selling well-known, standardized products and sometimes for individual firms in an oligopoly. Two variations of market-level pricing are to price below or above the levels of primary competitors.

Key Terms and Concepts

Price 395
Utility 395
Value 395
Pricing objective 399
Achieve target return 400
Markup 400
Profit maximization 401
Increase sales volume 403
Maintain or increase market
    share 403

Stabilize prices 405
Meet competition 405
Base price (list price) 406
Expected price 407
Range of prices 407
Inverse demand 408
Price elasticity of demand 408
Fixed cost 410
Variable cost 411
Total cost 411

Cost-plus pricing 411
Variable-cost pricing 412
Break-even analysis 414
Break-even point 414
Pricing to meet competition 416
Perfect competition 416
Oligopoly 416
Pricing below competition 416
Pricing above competition 417

Questions and Problems

1. Explain how a firm's pricing objective may influence the promotional program for a product. Which of the six pricing goals involves the largest, most aggressive promotional campaign?

2. What marketing conditions might logically lead a company to set "meeting competition" as a pricing objective?

3. What is your expected price for each of the following articles? How did you arrive at your estimate in each instance?

   a. A new type of cola beverage that holds its carbonation long after it has been opened; packaged in 355-ml and 2-L bottles.

   b. A nuclear-powered 23-inch table-model television set, guaranteed to run for ten years without replacement of the original power-generating component; requires no battery or electric wires.

   c. An automatic garage-door opener for residential housing.

4. Name at least three products for which you think an inverse demand exists. For each product, within which price range does this inverse demand exist?

5. Why is the status quo goal of meeting the competition considered to be the least aggressive of all the pricing goals

6. What are the merits and limitations of the cost-plus method of setting a base price?

7. In a break-even chart, is the total fixed cost line always horizontal? Is the total variable cost line always straight? Explain.

8. Referring to Table 13-2 and Figure 13-2, what would be the Futon Factory's break-even points at prices of $50 and $90, if variable costs are $40 per unit and fixed costs remain at $25,000?

9. A small manufacturer sold ballpoint pens to retailers at $8.40 per dozen. The manufacturing cost was 50 cents for each pen. Expenses, including all selling and administrative costs except advertising, were $19,200. How many dozen must the manufacturer sell to cover these expenses and pay for an advertising campaign costing $6,000?

10. If a retailer buys specialty backpacks for $30 and plans to use a 70 percent markup on selling price, what will be the retail price? What is the dollar markup?

Hands-On Marketing

1. Select ten items that college students purchase frequently at a supermarket. Be specific in describing the items (e.g., a six-pack of Diet Coke). Conduct separate interviews with five of your fellow students, asking them to indicate the price of each item at the supermarket closest to campus. Compare the students' answers with the actual prices charged by that supermarket. How many of the fifty answers were within 5 percent of the actual price? Within 10 percent? Do these results, admittedly from a small sample, suggest that consumers are knowledgeable and concerned about grocery prices?

2. Identify one store in your community that generally prices below the levels of most other firms and one that prices above prevailing market levels. Arrange an interview with the manager of each store. Ask both managers to explain the rationale and procedures associated with their pricing approaches. Also ask the manager of the store with below-market prices how profits are achieved with such low prices. Ask the manager of the store with above-market prices how customers are attracted and satisfied with such high prices.

Chapter Fourteen

Pricing Strategies and Tactics

In this chapter we discuss ways in which a firm adjusts a product's base price to coincide with its overall marketing program. After studying this chapter, you should have an understanding of:

◆ Price competition and value pricing.

◆ Pricing strategies for entering a market, notably market skimming and market penetration.

◆ Price discounts and allowances.

◆ Geographic pricing strategies.

◆ Special strategies, including one-price and flexible-price approaches, price lining, resale price maintenance, leader pricing, everyday low pricing, and odd pricing.

◆ Legal issues associated with pricing.

Buying Power to the People™

Setting the right price for a product is very important, right? A great deal of time and effort goes into calculating exactly what the right price should be, right? And once an appropriate price is found it's a done deal — that's going to be the price until conditions change to dictate re-evaluating the situation... right?

Well, there's one place where, as soon as somebody actually buys the product, the price may have to be looked at again. Actually, every time someone buys something the price is reviewed.

This is a place where setting prices is, well, not really all that important because they'll just be changed. Of course, prices are always going up, right? Uh, wrong again. Here, when prices are changed, they go down. And then, usually, down again. Of course, this is not always the case. It's just for twenty-four to ninety-six hours.

Before we begin this chapter on traditional price-setting procedures, we thought we'd look at how things *aren't* usually done and how, through the advent of Internet technology, some aspects of pricing are being revolutionized. Decide what you want to pay — the price can only go down! While many aspects of price-setting are bound in bricks and mortar tradition (as you will soon read), online commerce has provided bright alternatives based on another traditional pricing concept — volume buying.

What we have been discussing is the pricing at Mercata.Com (www.mercata.com). This is an e-retail Web site that offers brand-name products in many product categories such as appliances, electronics, baby goods, home and kitchen, lawn and garden, fitness and sports, home office, tools, watches, and jewellery. These are all offered at all times at what the company calls everyday low prices. But when an item is selected as a PowerBuy™, things start getting crazy and the price just keeps dropping — you may actually end up paying less than the amount you agreed to pay. It could be anything — an odourless diaper pail for $14.90, a reduction of more than $10.00, a drill bit kit for $29.40, a saving of $30.50, or how about a Diamond Rio MP3 player for $93.98 with a saving of $76.01. And, by the way, there's free shipping on every order!

As more and more people click-in to "bid" what they are willing to pay for an item, the lower the accepted price will actually turn out to be. PowerBuys™ operate as a reverse online auction — but you don't actually bid *against* anybody and all participants get what they want. With the

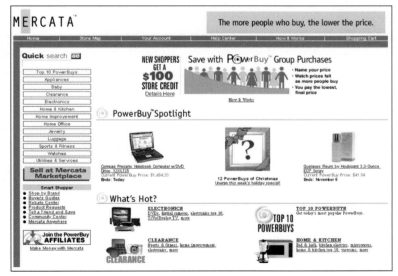

time counting down next to each item featured as a PowerBuy™, you may decide that you like the current price of an item and don't wish to miss the opportunity before it returns to its regular price and so you enter the current reduced price. It turns out, however, so many people felt the same way that once all the "bids" were processed that the lowest acceptable price got even lower — and everybody winds up paying less than expected (and never more than you want). This is the high-technology world of volume buying.[1]

It all sort of makes you wonder if prices actually mean anything, or how there can be such a thing as price competition. But price-based competition does exist as much as it ever did and has as much meaning as it ever did, as we will soon read.

 ## Price Competition

In developing a marketing program, a firm decides on the positioning of its offerings and then manages the elements of its marketing mix to achieve and maintain the position — or reposition if necessary. Some firms decide to compete primarily, but not exclusively, on price. Others use such nonprice approaches as concentrating on quality of product or service and/or distribution, advertising, and promotion, but always with a compatible pricing policy.

A firm engages in **price competition** by:

price competition
A strategy in which a firm regularly offers prices that are as low as possible, usually accompanied by a minimum of services.

1. Regularly offering products priced as low as possible and accompanied by a minimum of services. Zellers, Wal-Mart, and other discount houses and off-price retailers compete in this way.

2. Instigating changes in price that change the consumer's perception of product value without relying on other marketing factors. Supermarkets that rely on heavily discounted weekly specials to attract customers are an example of this practice. "Bay Days" that are regularly scheduled by The Bay department store is another such example.

3. Reacting to competitors' price changes with price changes of its own, for example, engaging in a price war.

nonprice competition
A strategy in which a firm tries to compete based on some factor other than price — for example, promotion, product differentiation, or variety of services.

In **nonprice competition**, vendors strive to maintain product prices and/or attempt to protect or improve their market positions by emphasizing other aspects of their marketing programs. This does not mean that price setting is not an important component of the marketing mix. If the price of your product or service appears unreasonable in the marketplace few consumers will buy it regardless of how catchy the advertising jingle, or excellent the service reputation. In nonprice competition, the seller is interested in creating value for the customer by offering something that will cause the customer not to focus on obtaining a lower price. Where marketers are successful in adding such value, either through service or attractive features, the customer is often prepared to pay more.

Price changes will occur with any product or service over time, however in nonprice competition, a manufacturer, retailer, or service provider will attempt to maintain or increase demand for their product by focusing on product differentiation, promotional activities, distribution, superior service, or some other technique. Some factor is chosen to distinguish this provider over others in the marketplace. This factor represents incremental *value* to the consumer beyond simply the cash price of the "product." This can often be a more enduring factor in consumer loyalty than price, as when consumers learn to buy a "brand" based only on price, then as prices change so may loyalties and brand preferences. Price competition generally leads to customers switching brands in search of lower prices.

This added value provides an advantage through differentiation if only on the basis of attractive design and colour offerings even though other firms offer a lower price on a comparable product. One approach to this type of competition is to increase brand equity for the firm's offerings. A strong reputation or perception in the minds of consumers will cause them to judge the brand offerings on factors other than price considerations. This can usually be achieved through high levels of quality, distinctive product features, superior service, and novel promotional programs. Price competition will often lead to overall lower levels of profits, the risk of price wars, resulting in circumstances whereby firms often find themselves no longer fully in control of their marketing programs and price levels.

Sofas à la carte is a small Vancouver business that has creatively developed a marketing mix that addresses quality, reputation, service, and price. While most furniture chains prefer discount advertising and tired advertising formats, this company wanted to get the message that its product was affordable and had fast delivery. At the same time it should build a brand name with trust behind it. The result is front-page banner ads in Saturday's *Vancouver Sun* fifty-two weeks of the year, as well as appearing on outdoor billboards. Efforts include a picture of a man in a speeding armchair with the caption "Fast. 16-day delivery" (which is speedy for custom upholstery). Another ad featured a snoozing basset hound stretched over a brown leather sofa with the words "Relax. It's Affordable."

"We don't sell our product on the basis of price," says Len Laycock, president and founder of Sofas à la carte. "And that's extremely unusual in the furniture business, where almost everything is sold by discounting."[2]

Avoiding price competition is more relaxing.

Value Pricing

In Chapter 13 and earlier, we discussed how more consumers are seeking better value in their purchases. In response, many companies in diverse industries are using what's

Relax.
It's
affordable.

VANCOUVER 909 WEST BROADWAY 731-9020   BURNABY 4361 KINGSWAY 438-3480 called **value pricing**. This form of price competition aims to improve a product's perceived value — the ratio of its benefits to its price and related costs. Using value pricing:

◆ A firm may offer products with lower prices but the same, or perhaps added, benefits. Through bundling products or services consumers may receive the benefit of reduced prices per item.

◆ At the same time, a firm may seek ways to reduce expenses so that profits do not suffer. If a company can manage to maintain costs or decrease them through increased efficiency then there is a reduced need to increase prices as often, and profit levels can be maintained.

During the 1990s, value pricing became a pivotal marketing trend in fields as diverse as air travel, groceries, personal computers, and fast food. For example, Bell Canada has attempted to recover from the ravages of the telephone price wars by shifting their focus to one where the emphasis is not on price, but rather on the value and breadth of service Bell can offer its customers. They have moved from a strategy of price slashing to one in which they bundle the most attractive service packages in order to leverage its entire range of telecommunication services. A two-pronged strategy, it is intended to raise awareness of the entire range of Bell services and to entice customers with cost savings through bundled service offerings. "Customers know we are competitive on price and now they want to know what differentiates us from others," believes Josee Goulet, Bell's vice-president, consumer market (sales and service). The move away from price to value marks a strategic shift in the ongoing Canadian telcos wars.[3]

Value pricing certainly still emphasizes the price element of the marketing mix. But that's not enough. For the value buyer, if all that is offered is price, that is not going to guarantee the sale. People who are attracted to the value that a product or service offers make their purchases by weighing attributes and analyzing trade-offs. They ultimately purchase on the basis of what provides the highest utility for the lowest price.[4] Consequently, value pricing depends on creatively combining all the elements of the marketing mix in order to maximize benefits in relation to price and other costs. With a value-pricing strategy, products often have to be redesigned to expand benefits and/or shave costs. Relationships among channel members and customers have to be strengthened to generate repeat sales. Steps toward this end include frequent-buyer programs, toll-free customer-service lines, and hassle-free warranties. And advertising has to be revamped to provide more facts and fewer emotional appeals.

Perhaps it may be helpful to think of value pricing as a compromise or blend of price and nonprice factors. Many things go into consumers' perception of value. Also, there is some variation among consumers as what represents value. As discussed, additional effort and cost must often be invested to enhance the offering and yet there is a stress on *reducing* the final cash price to the customer. But as also discussed before there are other components of total price beyond the cash that is exchanged between buyer and seller. A business can influence this by offering several value components at a number of levels — not just product features. Many times, if we can add value in some way, than this will allow us to maintain price. If a competitive price gives the consumer greater flexibility and reduces risk or commitment, then this has provided more value to the consumer while not costing the vendor a great deal.

Apple's Power Mac G4 (www.apple.ca) is an example of a product that is value priced, technologically innovative, has a high level of dealer support and is expandable to meet changing or expanding consumer needs. Considered to be technologically advanced, with high capacity and Pentium-crushing speed, the product can be modified as the user's needs change, thereby reducing the risk of its becoming outdated or of not meeting the buyer's needs. While this "package" of features has required a great deal of planning and consideration by the manufacturer it has allowed Apple to position themselves a distance away from most others and, while PC prices do normally decrease over time, Apple no longer has to rely on price slashing to boost sales.

Developing a program based on value can help firms compete with major players. By increasing the overall value provided by its outlets, a business can become more meaningful to its customers. Technology in the form of database management, loyalty programs, and even the Internet have assisted in "reaching out" to consumers to develop a range of points of contact. Toronto-based Drug Trading, Canada's leading pharmaceutical dispenser, has mounted a major marketing offensive to harmonize the operations of its more than fifteen hundred independent pharmacies to allow them to compete more effectively with major drugstore chains like Shoppers Drug Mart (www.shoppersdrugmart.ca) and Pharmasave (www.pharmasave.com). The program hinges upon PharmAssist, a new branded service offering that will link the dispensary service, technology, and consumer programs of each Drug Trading banner (such as IDA and Guardian). This will allow a loyalty program that will offer members added value on "front-shop" purchases, such as health and beauty products and convenience items. Private-label offerings will increase from six hundred to over one thousand to compete with SDM's "Life" brand offerings.[5]

Using the Internet offers other opportunities to creating a value-added pricing package. This medium allows vendors and service providers to enhance services and convenience to their customers. Edmonton-based specialty tool chain House of Tools (www.houseoftools.com) has mustered its thirty-seven years of experience and mail order expertise to create a Canadian presence on the Web — a site to be envied by the Web-nation. The site has all the bells and whistles including currency conversion, a dictionary of unique terms, an on-sale area, clearance bin, Web-exclusive pricing, VeriSign™ online security, and the ability to customize the site to preferred interests for return visits — value-adds that the company thinks will drive visitors to the site.[6] The ability to provide product information, related information (sometimes not so related), links to other services, and purchase, order, or location details by this technology that reaches into consumers' homes has great potential to add value to customer relationships.

Relationship Pricing

Some believe traditional marketing has been killed by an idea whose time has come: relationship marketing. The declining cost and increasing power of technology has given marketers an opportunity to challenge the idea that people be grouped according to the needs they have in common. Technology is allowing the same for how pricing is applied. It is allowing a focus on pricing based on customer profitability over product profitability.

Differentiated marketing is critical to attracting more loyal, longer-term customers. Those who have made advances in this area are moving toward relationship-based pricing through product packages. However, it is necessary to go beyond that and discover a way to reward the best customers for giving the company their business. Grocery stores and banks should correlate the depth of price-reduction offers to customer profitability potential and product and delivery channel preferences. Therefore, it is necessary to develop value propositions for customers that correspond to their consumption patterns and value to the firm.[7]

relationship pricing
Related to concept of value pricing where benefits are shared with customers to ensure that they receive better value and therefore remain loyal.

Related to the concept of value pricing is that of **relationship pricing**. This strategy is one of the elements of relationship marketing discussed in Chapter 12. You will recall that relationship marketing is about developing long-term, ongoing relationships with customers, the benefits of which include loyalty and reduced costs of doing business. In relationship pricing, some of these benefits are shared with customers to ensure that they receive better value and have another incentive to remain loyal. In other words, the firm gives a better price to its more valuable customers. In relationship pricing, customers are given a price incentive to encourage them to do all or most of their business with one supplier. For example, if you maintain a chequing account, savings account, mortgage account, and retirement fund with one bank, you will very likely be offered reduced interest costs on any borrowing or invited to join a plan that provides no-cost transactions. The bank is attempting to establish a relationship with you as a customer by offering you a preferred rate and is therefore encouraging you to do all of your business with them.[8] Insurance companies may offer a percentage discount based on the number of policies carried with the company.

Relationship pricing can be thought of as pricing based on bundling products or services over the longer term — sort of like a bulk purchase, but over time. It is pricing based on the long-term potential of the relationship determined on a discretionary one-to-one basis within a range of possible discount levels. Initially, it is based on the perceived potential of future business to encourage a consumer to select this provider. Future exchanges may enhance the perception of a special relationship and express to the customer his or her value to the firm, or to combat the risk of defection. Beyond special pricing considerations, this approach might involve some free services or products and extra or discretionary services.

There is potential for value to the consumer here beyond the money saved or the extra interest earned. There can be a psychological benefit that there is one familiar person looking after your needs, that your provider is knowledgeable about your details and preferences. Issues can be dealt with quickly and efficiently as your details and requirements are well known. The perception of reliability, trust, and integrity that may come from such "relationships" can be comforting and reassuring to the customer.

FIGURE 14-1
The Price-Determination Process

Market-Entry Pricing Strategies

In preparing to enter the market with a new product or service, management must decide whether to adopt a skimming or a penetration pricing **strategy**.

Market-Skimming Pricing

market-skimming pricing
A pricing strategy in which the initial price is set high in the range of expected prices.

Setting a relatively high initial price for a new product is referred to as **market-skimming pricing**. Ordinarily the price is high in relation to the target market's range of expected prices. That is, the price is set at the highest possible level that the most interested consumers will pay for the new product. Also, this assists to recover introductory costs as quickly as possible before decreasing it attracts the next price-sensitive level of customers. This allows the firm to maximize the revenue from the different segments of the market.

Intel (www.intel.com) has long utilized this strategy in the pricing of their processor chips. Possessing a very strong dominant market position, the company is able to command the highest price possible given the benefits it provides over competing products when it introduces a newest generation of their product. The price is relatively stable at this level until they have introduced the next generation or sales begin to decline as competitors begin to catch up with new product introductions. New cosmetic products are also commonly marketed this way. For example, in recent years developments in alpha hydroxy and other wrinkle-fighting cosmetic products have resulted in many new products such as L'Oreal's Niosome facial cream (www.loreal.com) which has entered the market at a very high price.[9] L'Oreal's ability to do this successfully comes from the brand equity it has established through time with the development and introduction of many cosmetic innovations. This has enabled the company to command premium prices for their various product lines.

Market-skimming pricing has several purposes. Since it should provide healthy profit margins, it is intended primarily to recover research and development costs as quickly

Many are prepared to pay more for products like this.

as possible. Further, lofty prices can be used to connote high quality, and/or cutting edge innovation and technology. Moreover, market-skimming pricing is likely to curtail demand to levels that do not outstrip the firm's production capacities. Finally, it provides the firm with flexibility, because it is much easier to lower an initial price that meets with consumer resistance than it is to raise an initial price that has proven to be too low to cover costs.

Market-skimming pricing is suitable under the following conditions:

♦ The new product has distinctive features strongly desired by consumers.

♦ Demand is fairly inelastic — most likely the case in the early stages of a product's life cycle. Under this condition, lower prices are unlikely to produce greater total revenues.

♦ The new product is protected from competition through one or more entry barriers, such as a patent.

Market skimming is often used in pricing new technological products such as cellular telephones and digital televisions (DTVs). Over time, the initial price may be lowered gradually. Consider the pricing of Panasonic DTVs. In keeping with the company's slogan of being "just slightly ahead" of the times, they offered a varied selection of DDTVs and SDTVs by 2000. Perhaps the most surprising model was the Plasma TV, a 42"/110 cm television that was only 3.5"/9 cm deep, 73 lbs/33 kg, had a 160-degree viewing angle, and could be hung on the wall. It is constructed of two glass screens 0.1 mm apart each with its own electrodes that make the plasma display. Gas is injected between these screens and becomes charged when voltage is passed through the electrodes. This generates ultraviolet rays creating the picture image. Perhaps more amazing was the price — US$13,995.95! Certainly the introduction of DTV brought with it high initial prices, but the Panasonic 51"/130 cm SDTV was only US$2995.95 — still not that cheap. It was also a projection TV weighing 200 lbs/90 kg and 24.9"/63 cm deep — not likely to be hung on *any* wall![10] It will be interesting to watch the price of digital televisions, and in particular the twin gas screen technology, to observe whether this new technology will eventually become more affordable as it is introduced to a broader consumer base.

Market-Penetration Pricing

market-penetration pricing
A pricing strategy in which a low initial price is set to reach the mass market immediately.

In **market-penetration pricing**, a relatively low initial price is established for a new product. The price is low in relation to the target market's range of expected prices. The primary aim of this strategy is to penetrate the mass market immediately and, in so doing, generate substantial sales volume and a large market share. At the same time, it is intended to discourage other firms from introducing competing products.

Market-penetration pricing makes the most sense under the following conditions:

♦ A large mass market exists for the product.

♦ Demand is highly elastic, typically in the later stages of the life cycle for a product category.

♦ Substantial reductions in unit costs can be achieved through large-scale operations. In other words, economies of scale are possible.

♦ Fierce competition already exists in the market for this product or can be expected to materialize soon after the product is introduced.

When computer firms introduced clones that imitated IBM or Apple models a number of years ago, they were relying on market-penetration pricing by undercutting the prices of the large, well-known producers. Now, a number of years later, pricing approaches have changed again. Other manufacturers have attempted to increase their penetration by joining forces with compatible or linked products/services. Lucent Technologies and Sun Microsystems had the opportunity to test their claims that their Inferno and Java operating systems could work together. Through a licensing deal allowing each to draw on each other's products and expertise, this has ensured greater market penetration for both products.[11]

As discussed in the previous chapter, Sprint Canada attempted market penetration pricing when it entered the newly deregulated telecommunications industry and introduced unlimited calling for $20 a month. This certainly aimed for deep penetration — deep into the pockets of traditional long-distance carriers across the country. Other providers followed suit and a price war ensued in order to develop or to protect market shares. These providers are currently trying to increase their market penetration in a still growing market — Internet access. Through increasing access allowances without increasing prices and through bundling access with other telecommunications products at attractive prices, each provider is hoping to increase their slice of the cyber-pie.[12]

In a departure from tradition, Canadian software manufacturer Corel Corporation (www.corel.com) has announced that its latest WordPerfect® release would be sold as a

Marketing at Work 14-1

Is that Your Best Price?

Have you ever purchased enough toothpaste to last you the whole year, driven across town to buy gas in order to receive Air Mile points, or held off on a major purchase until the item went on sale? Of course you have. Shopping incentives such as sales, bonus items, and reward programs are common practice in North America and consumers take full advantage of them. In fact, these programs are often more important in the consumer's final decision-making process than the product itself. For many, products like toothpaste and gasoline are viewed as commodities — that is, they have few discernible characteristics which differentiate one brand of the product from another. For manufacturers of such products, pricing strategies are an important way to establish a point of difference versus their competition.

Manufacturers and consumers in Europe, however, aren't as lucky. Many European countries place tough restrictions on discounts or free gifts, and others ban them outright. One of the most restrictive countries is Germany where many of its current shopping laws date from the early 1930s. German retailers cannot give products away, offer unlimited guarantees, or offer more than a 3 percent discount on cash purchases. Probably the most bizarre though are the rules that govern seasonal sales. Such sales can only be held during specified weeks and can only include an approved list of items (this list varies between summer and winter sales).

Retail lobby groups in Germany oppose liberalism and fear that competitive pricing would not only drive small shops out of business, but would also confuse the consumer. German shoppers must be offended by this view as many of these same retailers offer pricing incentives to consumers abroad.

The good news is that German shopping laws are coming under attack, due in large part to the growth of the Internet. The e-commerce directive from Brussels is that retailers must abide by the laws of their home country. This would allow companies located elsewhere in the world to dodge Germany's restrictive retail rules. The German government, fearful that its own retailers will suffer, have promised to overhaul its retailing laws. It is even rumoured that the shopping-hours law may come under attack. Currently, it forces stores to close for much of the weekend — probably to give retailers a chance to do all of their errands and shopping they couldn't do during the week because they were working.

Source: Adapted from "Handcuffs on the high street," *The Economist,* May 13, 2000, p. 62.

monthly subscription service. Rather than charging big bucks up front, there will be an ongoing monthly fee that will include automatic upgrades and enhancements, as they become available. It is believed that this new pricing scheme will reduce distribution costs, reduce barriers to online selling, and increase market penetration.[13] As can be seen, increasing penetration can sometimes be achieved through means other than price reductions.

Discounts and Allowances

Discounts and allowances result in a deduction from the base (or list) price. The deduction may be in the form of a reduced price or some other concession, such as free merchandise or advertising allowances. Discounts and allowances are commonplace in business dealings.

Quantity Discounts

quantity discount
A reduction from list price when large quantities are purchased; offered to encourage buyers to purchase in large quantities.

Quantity discounts are deductions from a seller's list price intended to encourage customers to buy in larger amounts or to buy most of what they need from the seller offering the deduction. Discounts are based on the size of the purchase, either in dollars or in units.

noncumulative discount
A quantity discount based on the size of an individual order of products.

A **noncumulative discount** is based on the size of an individual order of one or more products. A retailer may sell golf balls at $2 each or at three for $5. A manufacturer or wholesaler may set up a quantity discount schedule such as the following, used by a manufacturer of industrial adhesives:

Boxes purchased in single order	Percent discount from list price
1–5	None
6–12	2.0
13–25	3.5
Over 25	5.0

Noncumulative quantity discounts are intended to encourage large orders. Many expenses, such as billing, order filling, and salaries of salespeople, are about the same whether the seller receives an order totalling $10 or one totalling $500. Consequently, selling expense as a percentage of sales decreases as orders grow in size. With a noncumulative discount, a seller shares such savings with a purchaser of large quantities.

cumulative discount
A quantity discount based on the total volume purchased over a period of time.

A **cumulative discount** is based on the total volume purchased over a specified period. This type of discount is advantageous to a seller because it ties customers more closely to that firm. The more total business a buyer gives a seller, the greater is the discount. Air Canada frequent-flyer and hotel frequent-guest programs are a form of cumulative discount. IBM offers an assortment of volume-over-time discounts. And Bell Canada competes with Sprint Canada and other telephone companies by offering discounts to high-usage customers of long-distance telephone service.

Cumulative discounts also are common in selling perishable products. These discounts encourage customers to buy fresh supplies frequently, so that the buyer's merchandise will not become stale.

Quantity discounts can help a producer achieve real economies in production as well as in selling. On the one hand, large orders (motivated by a noncumulative discount) can result in lower production and transportation costs. On the other hand, frequent orders from a single customer (motivated by a cumulative discount) can enable the producer to make much more effective use of production capacity, even though individual orders are small and do not generate savings in marketing costs.

Trade Discounts

trade discount
A reduction from the list price, offered by a seller to buyers in payment for marketing activities that they will perform.

Trade discounts, sometimes called **functional discounts**, are reductions from the list price offered to buyers in payment for marketing functions the buyers will perform, such as storing, promoting, and selling the product. A manufacturer may quote a retail price of $400 with trade discounts of 40 percent and 10 percent. The retailer pays the wholesaler $240 ($400 less 40 percent), and the wholesaler pays the manufacturer $216 ($240 less 10 percent). The wholesaler is given the 40 and 10 percent discounts. The wholesaler is expected to keep the 10 percent to cover costs of the wholesaling functions and pass on the 40 percent discount to retailers. Sometimes, however, wholesalers keep more than the 10 percent — and it's not illegal for them to do so.

Note that the 40 and 10 percent discounts do not constitute a total discount of 50 percent off list price. They are not additive; rather, they are discounts on discounts. Each discount is computed on the amount remaining after the preceding discount has been deducted.

Cash Discounts

cash discount
A deduction from list price for paying a bill within a specified period of time.

A **cash discount** is a deduction granted to buyers for paying their bills within a specified time. The discount is computed on the net amount due after first deducting trade and quantity discounts from the base price. Every cash discount includes three elements, as indicated in Figure 14-2:

◆ The percentage discount.

◆ The period during which the discount may be taken.

◆ The time when the bill becomes overdue.

Let's say a buyer owes $360 after other discounts have been granted and is offered terms of 2/10, n/30 on an invoice dated November 8. This means the buyer may deduct a discount of 2 percent ($7.20) if the bill is paid within ten days of the invoice date —

FIGURE 14-2
Parts of a Cash Discount

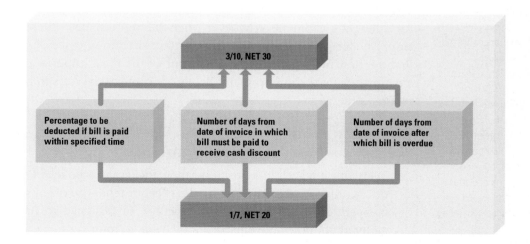

by November 18. Otherwise the entire (net) bill of $360 must be paid in thirty days — by December 8.

There are almost as many different cash discounts as there are industries. For example, in women's fashions, large discounts and short payment periods have been common; thus a cash discount of 5/5, n/15 would not be surprising. Such differences persist not so much for business reasons but because of tradition in various industries.

Most buyers are eager to pay bills in time to earn cash discounts. The discount in a 2/10, n/30 situation may not seem like very much. But this 2 percent is earned just for paying twenty days in advance of the date the entire bill is due. If buyers fail to take the cash discount in a 2/10, n/30 situation, they are, in effect, borrowing money at a 36 percent annual rate of interest. Here's how we arrived at that interest rate: In a 360-day business year, there are eighteen periods of twenty days. Paying 2 percent for one of these twenty-day periods is equivalent to paying 36 percent for an entire year.

Other Discounts and Allowances

seasonal discount
A discount for placing an order during the seller's slow season.

A manufacturer of goods such as air conditioners or toys purchased on a seasonal basis may consider granting a **seasonal discount**. This discount of, say, 5, 10, or 20 percent is given to a customer who places an order during the slack season. Off-season orders enable manufacturers to better use their production facilities and/or avoid inventory-carrying costs. Many services firms also offer seasonal discounts. For example, Club Med, other vacation resorts, and cruise lines lower their prices during the off-season.

forward dating
A combination of a seasonal discount and a cash discount under which a buyer places an order and receives shipment during the off-season but does not have to pay the bill until after the season has started and some sales revenue has been generated.

Forward dating is a variation on both seasonal and cash discounts. A manufacturer of fishing tackle might seek and fill orders from wholesalers and retailers during the winter months. But the bills would be dated April 1, with terms of 2/10, n/30 offered as of that date. Orders filled in December and January help to maintain production during the slack season for more efficient operation. The forward-dated bills allow the wholesale or retail buyers to pay their bills after the season has started and they can generate some sales revenue from the products delivered earlier.

promotional allowance
A price reduction granted by the seller as payment for promotional services rendered by the buyer.

A **promotional allowance** is a price reduction granted by a seller as payment for promotional services performed by buyers. To illustrate, a producer of builders' hardware gives a certain quantity of free goods to dealers who prominently display its line. Or a clothing manufacturer pays one-half the cost of a retailer's ad featuring its product.

The Competition Act and Price Discrimination

price discrimination
A situation in which different customers pay different prices for the same product.

The discounts and allowances discussed in this section may result in different prices for different customers. Whenever price differentials exist, there is **price discrimination**. The terms are synonymous. In certain situations, price discrimination is prohibited by the **Competition Act**. This is one of the most important federal laws affecting a company's marketing program. Below are some of the Act's implications for common pricing strategies.

Predatory Pricing

Competition Act
The major piece of federal legislation in Canada that governs the marketing and advertising activities of companies and organizations operating in Canada.

Paragraph 50(1)(c) of the Competition Act states:

> Every one engaged in a business who...engages in a policy of selling products at prices unreasonably low, having the effect or tendency of substantially lessening competition or eliminating a competitor, or designed to have such effect, is guilty of an indictable offence and is liable to imprisonment for two years.

In order for a conviction to result under paragraph 50(1)(c), it must be shown that prices are unreasonably low and that such prices have the effect, of reducing competition. The word "products" in the Competition Act includes articles and services.

Price Discrimination

Paragraph 50(1)(a) of the Act regulates price discrimination:

> 50(1) Every one engaged in a business who
> (a) is a party or privy to, or assists in, any sale that discriminates to his knowledge, directly or indirectly, against competitors of a purchaser of articles from him in that any discount, rebate, allowance, price concession or other advantage that, at the time the articles are sold to such purchaser, is available to such competitors in respect of a sale of articles of like quality and quantity, ...is guilty of an indictable offence and is liable to imprisonment for two years.

This section goes on to state in subsection 50(2):

> It is not an offence under paragraph (1)(a) to be a party or privy to, or assist in any sale mentioned therein unless the discount, rebate, allowance, price concession or other advantage was granted as part of a practice of discriminating as described in that paragraph.

The following conditions must be met in order for a conviction to be registered for price discrimination: (1) a discount, rebate, allowance, price concession, or other advantage must be granted to one customer and not to another; (2) the two customers concerned must be competitors; (3) the price discrimination must occur in respect of articles of similar quality and quantity; (4) the act of discrimination must be part of a practice of discrimination. Not all price discrimination is, per se, an offence. It is lawful to discriminate in price on the basis of quantities of goods purchased.

It should be noted that the buyer is seen as being as liable as the seller in cases of discrimination. The legislation applies to those who are party to a sale, and this includes both buyer and seller. This wording was intended to restrain large-scale buyers from demanding discriminatory prices. In addition, the buyer (as well as the seller) must know that the price involved is discriminatory.

Granting Promotional Allowances as an Offence

The Act, in section 51, requires that promotional allowances be granted proportionately to all competing customers:

> 51(1) In this section, "allowance" means any discount, rebate, price concession or other advantage that is or purports to be offered or granted for advertising or display purposes and is collateral to a sale or sales of products but is not applied directly to the selling price...
> (3) For the purposes of this section, an allowance is offered on proportionate terms only if
> (a) the allowance offered to a purchaser is in approximately the same proportion to the value of sales to him as the allowance offered to each competing purchaser is to the total value of sales to such competing purchaser.
> (b) In any case where advertising or other expenditures or services are exacted in return therefor, the cost thereof required to be incurred by a purchaser is in

approximately the same proportion to the value of sales to him as the cost of such advertising or other expenditures or services required to be incurred by each competing purchaser is the total value of sales to such competing purchaser, and

(c) in any case where services are exacted in return therefor, the requirements thereof have regard to the kinds of services that competing purchasers at the same time or different levels of distribution are ordinarily able to perform or cause to be performed.

The provisions of section 51 apply to the sale of both articles and services. Discrimination in the granting of promotional allowances is a *per se* offence, not requiring proof of the existence of either a practice of discrimination or a lessening of competition. A company that wishes to discriminate among its customers may do so through the legal practice of granting quantity discounts.

Geographic Pricing Strategies

In pricing, a seller must consider the costs of shipping goods to the buyer. These costs grow in importance as freight becomes a larger part of total variable costs. Pricing policies may be established where the buyer pays all the freight expense, the seller pays the entire cost, or the seller and buyer share this expense. The strategy chosen can influence the geographic limits of a firm's market, the locations of its production facilities, the sources of its raw materials, and its competitive strength in various geographic markets.

F.O.B. Point-of-Production Pricing

In one widely used geographic pricing strategy, the seller quotes the selling price at the factory or at some other point of production or origin. In this situation the buyer pays the entire cost of transportation. This is usually referred to as **f.o.b. factory pricing**. Of the four strategies discussed in this section, this is the only one in which the seller does not pay any of the transport costs. The seller pays only the cost of loading the shipment aboard the carrier — hence the term f.o.b., or free on board.

f.o.b. (free on board) factory price
A geographic pricing strategy whereby the buyer pays all freight charges from the f.o.b. location to the destination.

Under f.o.b. factory pricing strategy, the seller nets the same amount on each sale of similar quantities. The delivered price to the buyer varies according to the freight charge. However, this pricing strategy has serious economic and marketing implications. In effect, f.o.b. factory pricing tends to establish a geographic monopoly for a given seller, because transportation costs prevent distant competitors from entering the market. The seller, in turn, is increasingly priced out of more distant markets.

Uniform Delivered Pricing

Under the **uniform delivered pricing** strategy, the same delivered price is quoted to all buyers regardless of their locations. This strategy is sometimes referred to as "postage stamp pricing" because of its similarity to the pricing of first-class mail service. The net revenue to the seller varies, depending on the shipping cost involved in each sale.

A uniform delivered price is typically used where transportation costs are a small part of the seller's total costs. This strategy is also used by many retailers who feel that "free" delivery is an additional service that strengthens their market position.

Under a uniform delivered price system, buyers located near the seller's factory pay for some of the costs of shipping to more distant locations. Critics of f.o.b. factory pricing are usually in favour of a uniform delivered price. They feel that the transportation expense should not be charged to individual customers any more than is any other single marketing or production expense.

Zone-Delivered Pricing

zone-delivered price
A geographic pricing strategy whereby the same delivered price is charged at any location within each geographic zone.

Under a **zone-delivered pricing** strategy, a seller would divide the Canadian market into a limited number of broad geographic zones. Then a uniform delivered price is set within each zone. Zone-delivered pricing is similar to the system used in pricing parcel post services and long-distance telephone service. A firm that quotes a price and then says "Slightly higher west of the Lakehead" is using a two-zone pricing system. The transportation charge built into the delivered price is an average of the charges at all points within a zone area.

When adopting this pricing strategy, the seller must walk a neat tightrope to avoid charges of illegal price discrimination. This means that the zone lines must be drawn so that all buyers who compete for a particular market are in the same zone. Such a condition is most easily met where markets are widely distributed.

Freight-Absorption Pricing

freight absorption
A geographic pricing strategy whereby the seller pays for (absorbs) some of the freight charges in order to penetrate more distant markets.

A **freight-absorption pricing** strategy may be adopted to offset some of the competitive disadvantages of f.o.b. factory pricing. With an f.o.b. factory price, a firm is at a price disadvantage when it tries to sell to buyers located in markets nearer to competitors' plants. To penetrate more deeply into such markets, a seller may be willing to absorb some of the transportation costs. Thus, seller A will quote to the customer a delivered price equal to (1) A's factory price plus (2) the freight costs that would be charged by the competitive seller located nearest to that customer.

A seller can continue to expand the geographic limits of its market as long as its net revenue after freight absorption is larger than its marginal cost for the units sold. Freight absorption is particularly useful to a firm with excess capacity whose fixed costs per unit of product are high and whose variable costs are low. In these cases, management must constantly seek ways to cover fixed costs, and freight absorption is one answer.

one-price strategy
A strategy under which a seller charges the same price to all customers of the same type who buy the same quantity of goods.

The legality of freight absorption is reasonably clear. The strategy is legal if it is used independently and not in collusion with other firms. Also, it must be used only to meet competition. In fact, if practised properly, freight absorption can have the effect of strengthening competition because it can break down geographic monopolies.

Special Pricing Strategies

To set initial prices and evaluate existing prices, a firm needs to consider a number of distinctive strategies. It's likely that at least one, but probably not all, will apply to a particular pricing situation.

One-Price and Flexible-Price Strategies

flexible-price strategy
A pricing strategy in which a company sells similar quantities of merchandise to similar buyers at different prices.

Rather early in its pricing deliberations, management should decide whether to adopt a one-price strategy or a flexible-price strategy. Under a **one-price strategy**, a seller charges the same price to all similar customers who buy similar quantities of a product. Under a **flexible-price** (also called a **variable-price) strategy**, similar customers may each pay a different price when buying similar quantities of a product.

Marketing at Work 14-2

Virtual Yard Sale or Auction House?

The rapid growth of online ticket sales has enabled many industries to alter prices according to demand. While the benefits of a variable pricing structure are obvious from the sellers' point of view the advantage may not always be apparent from the consumers' perspective.

Airlines were one of the first industries to act on the data they gathered through online ticket sales. By offering discounted fares on light flights, airlines are able to fill empty seats and recoup a major portion of the fares that would have been foregone if the flights had left with less than a full load. Similarly, sports organizations are following this example and are offering substantial online discounts for baseball games in particular. Stadium and team owners are more than willing to fill the empty seats at a discount because so much of their revenue comes from concession sales.

For consumers, these situations are favourable. They receive the same benefits as full-fare paying customers but at much lower prices. The newest technology will even permit online buyers to print their tickets instead of having to wait for them to arrive by mail or having to pick them up at box offices. Printouts may also include directions, seating charts, and parking coupons.

So what, you may be wondering, is the downside?

The consumer will benefit when supply exceeds demand, but when seats are too few to satisfy would-be-buyers the final sale can be awarded to the highest bidder. This happened recently when Tickets.com auctioned off some prime seats for both Elton John and Backstreet Boys concerts. Consumers ended up paying on average 45 percent more than the ticket price for these seats. Although the extra proceeds went to charity, the consumer still paid considerably more than the face value of the ticket.

At this time, sports organizations are more likely to adopt variable pricing than entertainment promoters who are fearful of alienating their fans. Since supply tends to exceed demand for most sports teams, the benefits of online ticket sales, for the time being, will be in the consumers' favour.

Source: Adapted from Andrea Adelson "Filling Seats With Online Discounts," *The New York Times,* April 2, 2000, p. 10.

One price fits all.

The motel of choice for the serious traveler.

After a day of sightseeing caverns or mountains carved up into presidents, nothing makes more sense than Motel 6. You'll get just what you need for the lowest price of any national chain. Which should free up some money for the Hillbilly Wax Museum.

In Canada and the United States, a one-price strategy has been adopted more often than variable pricing. Most retailers, for example, typically follow a one-price policy — except in cases where trade-ins are involved, and then flexible pricing abounds. A one-price policy builds customer confidence in a seller, whether at the manufacturing, wholesaling, or retailing level. Weak bargainers need not feel that they are at a competitive disadvantage.

When a flexible pricing policy is followed, often the price is set as a result of buyer-seller bargaining. In automobile retailing — with or without a trade-in — price negotiating (bargaining) is quite common, even though window-sticker prices may suggest a one-price policy. Variable pricing may be used to meet a competitor's price. Canada's major airlines used aggressive flexible-price strategies to enter new markets in the United States after deregulation and to increase their market share on existing routes. Their new business comes from two sources — passengers now flying on other airlines and passengers who would not fly at higher prices. In the second group, especially, the demand for air travel is highly elastic. The trick is to keep the market segment of price-sensitive passengers separate from the business-traveller segment, whose demand is inelastic. The airlines keep these segments apart by placing restrictions on the lower-priced tickets — requiring advance purchases, over-the-weekend stays in destination cities, and so on.

A **single-price strategy** is an extreme variation of the one-price strategy. Not only are all customers charged the same price, but all items sold by the firm carry a single price! The origins of this approach may be traced to budget motels of thirty years ago. For instance, Motel 6 (www.motel6.com) in the United States (where they "leave the light on" for you) originally priced all rooms at $6 a night for single occupancy.

Single-price stores, selling all goods at $1 or $2, were popular for a time but have now become more scarce. These stores typically purchase close-out and discontinued products as well as production overruns from a variety of sources at a small fraction of their original costs. Some analysts question whether single-price stores can be successful not just during a recession but during prosperous times as well.

🌶 *Price Sensitivity*

There have always been those segments in the marketplace that have been price sensitive — through both necessity and through personal values. This will always be the case. As well, there are those that are not very sensitive to changes in prices. Some because they don't have the necessity, they aren't that observant, and those that don't believe it really worth the effort to notice and shop around for the difference. However, there are segments that will vary in the marketplace as a result of external forces such as economic conditions, contemporary social values, and changing lifestyles. And, of course, there is a limit to anything — even price sensitivity. Studies reveal that price rises of 5 percent go virtually unnoticed, price rises of 10 percent will be noticed, and price rises of 15 percent will result in massive switching.[14]

Technology, in the form of the Internet, has unquestionably made easy the search process for the lowest prices and other related information enabling the price-conscious consumer to more ably arm themselves in record-breaking time with a large reduction of effort. What will be the overall effect of this technology on the price sensitivity of the marketplace? Only time will tell.

Economic conditions may dictate that the lowest price wins, but in today's increasingly hectic environment other costs, as previously discussed, beyond the cash price are figuring into the calculation of these costs — maybe think of it as *cost* sensitivity. And as already stated there will always be those that are not looking primarily for the lowest price. For many daily and routine products and services access to the Internet will not influence some of these decisions as the greatest price to some consumers is time — seeking, searching, and just the mental effort involved in an already hectic schedule (and life!). Time and psychological effort may be more expensive than money, and as such these consumers will pay extra for convenience, expediency, or just to get exactly what they want.

There are consumers who will knowingly pay more for these reasons and for reasons such as higher quality or even prestige value. There are consumers that prefer to develop a relationship with a vendor or service provider enabling better service, efficient transactions, and the ability to build trust and a sense of reliability. In other words, not everyone is looking for the lowest price.

Psychology of Pricing

Considerations for final pricing decisions may often involve more than just calculations about covering costs and how much you can get the customer to pay — thought is also given to how the price of an item or service can be used to communicate information to the consumer — to let it tell the consumer, or let consumers think, something about the product. Price is used to communicate price level, of course, but the use of certain numbers influence the consumer's perception of that level and therefore the value received. Price also is used to connote quality, value, up-to-date and cutting-edge innovation. While a high price does not mean high quality, it can be taken as an indication in many consumers' minds.

Psychological pricing means setting a price to have a special appeal to a particular segment of consumers. **Leader pricing** is intended to attract customers by selling some products at a very low price, perhaps at a loss, to get people into the store. This is often used for weekly supermarket sales. Or there is **bait pricing**, or baiting consumers with a low-priced feature item but then pointing out its weaker details in order to sell-up to a more expensive model. This is common with electronics outlets. This approach also can work in the other direction — with *raising* prices above competitive levels, sometimes to such a degree that it is referred to as **prestige pricing**. Swiss watchmaker TAG Heuer is one such example — the company's average watch price went from $250 to almost $1000. The company's sales also increased — by sevenfold![15] Two other psychological pricing approaches, price lining and odd pricing are discussed in the following sections.

Price Lining

Price lining involves selecting a limited number of prices at which a business will sell related products. It is used extensively by retailers of apparel. A sporting goods store, for instance, may sell several styles of running shoes at $69.95 a pair, another group at $89.95, and a third assortment at $119.95.

For the consumer, the main benefit of price lining is that it simplifies buying decisions. For the retailer, price lining helps in planning purchases. The buyer for the sporting goods store can go to market looking for shoes that can be retailed at one of its three prices.

Rising costs can put a real squeeze on price lines. That's because a company hesitates to change its price line every time its costs go up. But if costs rise and prices are not increased accordingly, profit margins shrink and the retailer may be forced to seek products with lower costs.

Odd Pricing

Odd pricing, another psychological strategy, is commonly used in retailing. Odd pricing sets prices at uneven (or odd) amounts, such as 49 cents or $19.95, rather than at even amounts. Autos are priced at $19,995 rather than $20,000, and houses sell for $189,500 instead of $190,000. Odd pricing is often avoided in prestige stores or on higher-priced luxury items. A man's suit at Holt Renfrew, for example, may be priced at $1000, but not $999.95. The Hyundai Tiburon is advertised at $13,999 while the Infiniti I30 is advertised for $41,000.

The rationale for odd pricing is that it suggests lower prices and, as a result, yields greater sales than even pricing. According to this reasoning, a price of 98 cents will bring in greater revenue than a $1 price for the same product. Research indicates that odd pricing can be an effective strategy for a firm that emphasizes low prices.[16]

---

psychological pricing
Setting a price to have a special appeal to a particular customer.

leader pricing
Temporary price cuts on well-known items. The price cut is made with the idea that these "specials" (loss leaders) will attract customers to the store.

bait pricing
Attracting consumers with a low-priced feature item and then pointing out weaknesses in order to sell up to a more expensive item.

prestige pricing
Raising pricing above competitive levels.

price lining
A retail pricing strategy whereby a store selects a limited number of prices and sells each item only at one of these selected prices.

odd pricing
A form of psychological pricing that consists of setting prices at odd amounts ($4.99 rather than $5.00, for example) in the belief that these seemingly low prices will result in larger sales volume.

Resale Price Maintenance

Some manufacturers want control over the prices at which retailers resell the manufacturers' products. This is most often done in Canada by following a policy of providing manufacturers' suggested list prices, where the price is just a guide for retailers. It is a list price on which discounts may be computed. For others, the suggested price is "informally" enforced. Normally, enforcement of a suggested price, termed resale price maintenance, has been illegal in Canada since 1951. In this country, attempts on the part of the manufacturers to control or to influence upward the prices at which their products are sold by retailers have been considered akin to price fixing.

Section 50 of the Competition Act prohibits a manufacturer or supplier from requiring or inducing a retailer to sell a product at a particular price or not below a particular price. On occasion, a supplier may attempt to control retail prices through the use of a "suggested retail price." Under section 50, the use of "suggested retail prices" is permitted only if the supplier makes it clear to the retailer that the product may be sold at a price below the suggested price and that the retailer will not in any way be discriminated against if the product is sold at a lower price. Also, where a manufacturer advertises a product, and in the advertisement mentions a certain price, the manufacturer must make it clear in the advertisement that the product may be sold at a lower price. While retailers are free to sell a product at whatever price they deem appropriate, from time to time manufacturers attempt to exert pressure on retailers to sell at a particular price.

Leader Pricing and Unfair-Practices Acts

Many firms, primarily retailers, temporarily cut prices on a few items to attract customers. This price and promotional strategy is called leader pricing, and the items whose prices may be reduced below the retailer's cost are called **loss leaders**.

loss leaders
Products whose prices are cut with the idea that they will attract customers to the store.

Leaders should be well-known heavily advertised articles that are purchased frequently. The idea is that customers will come to the store to buy the advertised leader items and then stay to buy other regularly priced merchandise. The net result, the firm hopes, will be increased total sales volume and net profit.

Three provinces — British Columbia, Alberta, and Manitoba — have had legislation dealing with loss-leader selling. The approach has been to prohibit a reseller from selling an item below invoice cost, including freight, plus a stated markup, which is usually 5 percent at retail. The general intent of these laws is commendable. They eliminate much of the predatory type of price-cutting; however, they permit firms to use loss leaders as a price and promotional strategy. That is, a retailer can offer an article below full cost but still sell above cost plus 5 percent markup. Under such Acts, low-cost, efficient businesses are not penalized, nor are high-cost operators protected. Differentials in retailers' purchase prices can be reflected in their selling prices, and savings resulting from the absence of services can be passed on to the customers.

On the other hand, the laws have some glaring weaknesses. In the first place, the provinces do not establish provisions or agencies for enforcement. It is the responsibility and burden of the injured party to seek satisfaction from the offender in a civil suit. Another limitation is that it is difficult or even impossible to determine the cost of doing business for each individual product. The third weakness is that the laws seem to disregard the fundamental idea that the purpose of a business is to make a profit on the total operation, and not necessarily on each sale of each product.

Everyday Low Pricing and High-Low Pricing

everyday low pricing (EDLP)
A pricing strategy that involves consistently low prices and few, if any, temporary price reductions.

Everyday low pricing (EDLP) is "the hottest retailing price trend," according to one analyst.[17] While it may be trendy, it certainly is not new. Basically, it involves consistently low prices and few if any temporary price reductions. Both Wal-Mart and Zellers have been extremely successful with this type of pricing, as have the various warehouse stores such as Price Club/Costco and Staples Business Depot. Some of these stores support this pricing policy with a guaranteed price-matching or price-beating policy. This feels like "insurance" to the consumer and may reassure them that this particular store must offer the lowest prices in order make this claim.

high-low pricing
A pricing strategy that involves using relatively low prices on some products and higher prices on others.

Many firms do not engage in EDLP but rather in **high-low pricing**. High-low pricing involves using relatively low prices on some products and higher prices on others. This strategy combines frequent price reductions and aggressive promotion to convey an image of very low prices. Many supermarkets, some department stores, and chain drugstores rely on this approach.

The grocery business in Quebec is an example both approaches to pricing. At least, grocery stores and chains in that province have switched formats in recent times as buyouts and mergers have altered the playing field, leaving only three big players. The Super C stores of the Metro Inc. group operate on an EDLP strategy. Loblaw, now the owners of Provigo and Maxi stores, is focusing on delivering value through their private-label lines which comprise 32 percent of sales. The Loblaw-owned Provigo stores (www.provigo.com) have been positioned in the high-low format, as has the franchised stores of Metro Inc. of Montreal, offering high regular prices and low sale prices. Sobey's, through their newly-acquired IGA stores (www.iga.net/qc/), go head-to-head with the Metro stores, as both tend to reference themselves as "neighbourhood stores."[18]

Which is better — EDLP or high-low pricing? A controlled experiment that compared the effects of the two pricing strategies on twenty-six product categories in a chain of eighty-six grocery stores provides an answer. EDLP increased sales somewhat, whereas high-low pricing resulted in slightly lower volume. More important, profits fell 18 percent with EDLP but jumped almost as much with high-low pricing.[19]

The use of EDLP has continued to expand because some manufacturers, notably Procter & Gamble (www.pg.com), have replaced the special discounts, allowances, and other price deals they offered retailers with consistently lower prices. P&G did this to even out supermarket orders, which would allow them to control production more easily and reduce costs. As one of North America's largest advertisers, P&G has been very effective in this strategy.[20]

Proactive and Reactive Changes

After an initial price is set, a number of situations may prompt a firm to change its price. As costs increase, for instance, management may decide to raise its price rather than to maintain price, and either cut quality or promote the product aggressively. Larger firms tend to be less reluctant to raise prices than are smaller ones.

Temporary price cuts may be used to sell excess inventory or to introduce a new product. Also, if a company's market share is declining because of strong competition, its executives may react initially by reducing price. Cereal makers, faced with strong growth from private-label products, began aggressive pricing competition for a share of the market in the late 1990s and dropped the supermarket price of some cereals by as much as 20 per cent. Kellogg Co. (www.kellogg.com) was one of these cereal makers who did this in their American markets. For many products, however, a better long-term alternative to a price

Marketing at Work 14-3

Coke Charges More for Same Fizz

Coca-Cola is the world's best selling cola and most recognized brand. So why is the company introducing a new advertising campaign designed to stimulate demand?

Coca-Cola, and its rival Pepsi-Cola, have begun to increase prices for the concentrate they sell to bottlers in an effort to make their retail business more profitable. This price increase comes at a time when consumers have more beverage options than ever — teas, fruit drinks, sports beverages, and a vast array of bottled waters.

Coca-Cola is, therefore, launching a new advertising campaign intended to persuade U.S. consumers to pay more for their favourite beverage.

The new ads focus on the product qualities and benefits of Coke — the flavour, the composition, the spice and aromatics, the good memories, the feel of the bottle, and of course how it adds a little bit of magic to everyday life. According to Charles Frenette, chief marketing officer of Coca-Cola, the campaign is intended to make Coke more useful, by talking about what Coke does for the user.

The slogan too has changed from "Always Coca-Cola" which has been around since 1993, to "Coca-Cola. Enjoy." The new slogan is a softer sell, an invitation, says Ian Rowden, VP and advertising director of Coca-Cola, to enjoy life through the optimistic lens provided by Coke.

Coke is promising a lot more than quenching a parched throat. The new campaign suggests fun and good times, and refreshment through renewal. That's a lot for a little can of carbonated sugar and water to deliver. But then again **It's the real thing,** and you just **Can't beat the real thing**. **Coke is it**. It's **The pause that refreshes**, and **Things go better with Coke**. In fact, **I'd like to buy the world a Coke** because **It's the refreshing thing to do**. It's the **Global high sign**. **Coke adds life**. It's **Red white and you**. So go ahead **Be really refreshed**, you just **Can't beat the feeling**, it's **Always Coca Cola**. So what if it costs a little more… **Coca-Cola. Enjoy!**

Source: Adapted from Stuart Elliott and Constance L. Hays, "Coca-Cola refreshes ad campaign," *The Globe and Mail*, January 14, 2000, p. M1.

---

reduction is improving the overall marketing program. Once again, Kellogg is one such company. By the end of 1998 the market had really gone soggy — it had shrivelled to US$7.1 billion from US$8 billion five years earlier. Private-label brands are continuing to chip away at the market as well as consumers are opting for more portable alternatives like bagels and cereal bars. Kellogg Co. has realized however that this decline was not happening in Canada where there was a slightly increasing sales trend. In Canada, the company had maintained price levels and had continued to try fresh marketing approaches. In the U.S. markets price cuts meant that less was available to invest in new product development and advertising — two stiff requirements in this category to guard market share. Kellogg will now streamline its operations to reduce costs, price hikes on certain brands will occur, and they will increase promotion of the brands that are familiar to most consumers, such as placing their three different bran varieties all under the well-known All-Bran banner. New campaigns will develop a more unified health-promotion message to Canadian and American consumers. The company may also begin to highlight the nutritional benefits of cereal in its marketing as recommended by health professionals.[21]

Any firm can safely assume that its competitors will change their prices — sooner or later. Consequently, every firm should have guidelines on how it will react. If a competitor raises its price, a short delay in reacting probably will not be perilous. However, if a competing firm reduces price, a prompt response normally is required to avoid losing customers.

Occasional price reductions occur even in an oligopoly, because all sellers of the product cannot be controlled. In the absence of collusion, every so often some firm will cut its price. Then all others usually follow to maintain their respective market shares. However, vigorous short-term discount plans indicate that the major competitors are engaging in vigorous price competition at the initial stage of market and brand development.

From a seller's standpoint, the big disadvantage in price-cutting is that competitors will retaliate — and not let up. A **price war** may begin when one firm decreases its price in an effort to increase its sales volume and/or market share. The battle is on if other firms retaliate, reducing price on their competing products. Additional price decreases by the original price cutter and/or its competitors are likely to follow until one of the firms decides it can endure no further damage to its profits. Most businesses would like to avoid price wars, but they always break out.

Always part of business, price wars were almost epidemic in the 1990s, breaking out in numerous fields: airlines, vacation packages, many grocery items, computers and computer software, gasoline on a local basis, long-distance telephone services, even bank service charges. Price wars can be extremely harmful to firms, particularly financially weak ones. Unless trying to drive small competitors out of the market completely, there is likely to be no long-term advantage to this approach. Market gains will be temporary as consumer loyalty is weakened while destroying profits and encouraging unstable market conditions creating havoc on any planning that was developed. If this is the goal, the company should have deep pockets and be prepared to shell a great deal out of them to achieve its goal.

In the short term, consumers benefit from price wars through sharply lower prices. But over the longer term, the net effects on consumers are not clear-cut. What is evident is that price wars can be harmful to many firms, especially the weaker ones, in an industry. Lower profits typically decrease the number of competitors and, over a longer period, possibly the vigour of competition. After extended price wars, some companies in industries as different as groceries and personal computers have gone out of business. Ultimately, a smaller number of competing firms might translate to fewer product choices and/or higher prices for consumers. Gaining sales and market share with price competition is only valid when it is managed as part of a longer-term marketing strategy for achieving, exploiting, or sustaining a longer-term competitive advantage.[22]

Summary

After deciding on pricing goals and setting the base (or list) price, marketers must establish pricing strategies that are compatible with the rest of the marketing mix. Another basic decision facing management is whether to engage primarily in price or nonprice competition. Although price competition was widespread in the 1990s, most firms prefer nonprice competition. Price competition establishes price as the primary, perhaps the sole, basis for attracting and retaining customers. A growing number of businesses are adopting value pricing to improve the ratio of benefits to price and, in turn, win customers from competitors.

When a firm is launching a new product, it must choose a market skimming or a market-penetration pricing strategy. Market skimming uses a relatively high initial price, market penetration a low one.

Many things must be considered when setting prices for products and services. The price, at times, may be used to communicate information to consumers regarding quality and innovation. It is also important to consider that the lowest price is not always the most important variable to a consumer at all times, or for all products.

Strategies also must be devised for discounts and allowances — deductions from the list price. Management has the option of offering quantity discounts, trade discounts, cash discounts, and/or other types of deductions.

Transportation costs must be considered in pricing. A producer can require the buyer to pay all freight costs (f.o.b. factory pricing), or a producer can absorb all freight costs (uniform delivered pricing). Or the two parties can share the freight costs (freight absorption). Decisions on discounts and allowances must conform to the Competition Act, a federal law regulating price discrimination.

Management also should decide whether to charge the same price to all similar buyers of identical quantities of a product (a one-price strategy) or to set different prices (a flexible-price strategy). Many organizations, especially retailers, use at least some of the following special strategies:

price lining — selecting a limited number of prices at which to sell related products; odd pricing — setting prices at uneven (or odd) amounts; and leader pricing — temporarily cutting prices on a few items to attract customers.

Many manufacturers are concerned about resale price maintenance, which means controlling the prices at which intermediaries resell products. Some approaches to resale price maintenance are stronger than others; moreover, some methods may be illegal.

Market opportunities and/or competitive forces may motivate companies to initiate price changes or, in other situations, to react to other firms' price changes. A series of successive price cuts by competing firms creates a price war, which can harm the profits of all participating companies.

Key Terms and Concepts

Price competition 422	Seasonal discount 432	Single-price strategy 437
Nonprice competition 422	Forward dating 432	Psychological pricing 438
Value pricing 424	Promotional allowance 432	Leader pricing 438
Relationship pricing 426	Price discrimination 432	Bait pricing 438
Strategy 427	Competition Act 432	Prestige pricing 438
Market-skimming pricing 427	F.o.b. factory pricing 434	Price lining 438
Market-penetration pricing 428	Uniform delivered pricing 434	Odd pricing 438
Quantity discount 430	Zone-delivered pricing 435	Loss leaders 439
Noncumulative discount 430	Freight-absorption pricing 435	Everyday low pricing (EDLP) 440
Cumulative discount 430	One-price strategy 435	High-low pricing 440
Trade (functional) discount 431	Flexible-price (variable-price)	Price war 442
Cash discount 431	strategy 435	

Questions and Problems

1. For each of the following products, should the seller adopt a market-skimming or a market-penetration pricing strategy? Support your decision in each instance.

   a. High-fashion dresses styled and manufactured by Yves St. Laurent.

   b. An exterior house paint that wears twice as long as any competitive brand.

   c. A cigarette that is totally free of tar and nicotine.

   d. A tablet that converts a litre of water into a litre of automotive fuel.

2. Carefully distinguish between cumulative and noncumulative quantity discounts. Which type of quantity discount has the greater economic and social justification? Why?

3. A manufacturer of appliances quotes a list price of $800 per unit for a certain model of refrigerator and grants trade discounts of 35, 20, and 5 percent. What is the manufacturer's selling price? Who might get these various discounts?

4. The Craig Charles Company (CCC) sells to all its customers at the same published price. One of its sales managers discerns that Jamaican Enterprises is offering to sell to one of CCC's customers, Mountain Sports, at a lower price. CCC then cuts its price to Mountain Sports but maintains the original price for all other customers. Is CCC's price cut a violation of the Competition Act?

5. "An f.o.b. point-of-production price system is the only geographic price system that is fair to buyers." Discuss.

6. An eastern firm wants to compete in western markets, where it is at a significant disadvantage with respect to freight costs. What pricing alternatives can it adopt to overcome the freight differential?

7. Under what conditions is a company likely to use a variable-price strategy? Can you name firms that employ this strategy other than when a trade-in is involved?

8. On the basis of the topics covered in this chapter, establish a set of price strategies for the manufacturer of a new glass cleaner that is sold through an intermediary to supermarkets. The manufacturer sells the cleaner at $15 for a case of a dozen 482-ml bottles.

Hands-On Marketing

1. Talk to the owner or a top executive of a firm in your community regarding whether this company emphasizes price or nonprice competition and the reasons for following this course. Also ask whether its approach is similar to or dissimilar from the normal approach used by competitors to market the primary product sold by this firm.

2. Visit a local discount store such as Wal-Mart or Zellers. Note the prices of three products including a child's toy, a piece of electronic equipment such as a CD player, and a small appliance. Check these prices with other outlets that sell on the basis of high-low pricing, such as Sears or The Bay. Determine whether there is a difference in price. Are the products selling at high or low prices in the nondiscount outlets?

3. Karina's Pizza produces two products, 12-inch pizzas and 16-inch pizzas, with the following characteristics:

	12-Inch Pizza	16-Inch Pizza
Selling Price	$500,000 ($5/unit)	$900,000 ($6/unit)
Variable Cost	$300,000	$300,000
Expected Sales (Units)	100,000	150,000

The total fixed costs for the company are $700,000.

a. What is the anticipated level of profits for the expected sales volumes?

b. Assuming that the product mix in units would be the same as above at the break-even point, compute the break-even point in terms of number of units of each of the products.

c. If the product sales mix were to change to four 12-inch pizzas for each 16-inch pizza, what would be the new break-even volume for each of the products? Comment on number of units required to break even for this sales mix, compared with the original sales mix.

4. The following income statement represents Matthew's Mining Company's operating results for the fiscal year just ended. The company had sales of 1,600 tonnes during the current year. The manufacturing capacity of Matthew's facilities is 2,800 tonnes per year. (Ignore income taxes.)

Matthew's Mining Company
Income Statement
For the Year Ended December 31, Year One

Sales		$800,000
Variable costs:		
Manufacturing	$280,000	
Selling costs	160,000	
Total variable costs	$440,000	440,000
Contribution margin		360,000
Fixed costs:		
Manufacturing	$ 90,000	
Selling	112,500	
Administrative	45,000	
Total fixed costs	$247,500	247,500
Net income		$112,500

a. Calculate the company's break-even volume in tonnes for Year One.

b. If the sales volume is estimated to be 1,900 tonnes in the next year, and if the prices and costs stay at the same levels and amounts, what is the net income that management can expect for Year Two?

c. The company has a potential foreign customer that has offered to buy 1,700 tonnes at $450 per tonne. Assume that all of Matthew's costs would be at the same levels and rates as in Year One. What net income would the firm earn if it took this order and rejected some business from regular customers so as not to exceed capacity? Why might Matthew's consider accepting this order at a reduced selling price?

d. Matthew's plans to market its product in a new territory. Management estimates that an advertising and promotion program costing $42,000 annually would be needed for each of the next two or three years. In addition, a $15 per tonne sales commission to the sales force in the new territory, over and above the current commission, would be required. Assume that all of Matthew's costs would be at the same levels and rates as in Year One, with the only incremental costs being those related to advertising and promotion and the additional sales commission. How many extra tonnes would have to be sold in the new territory to maintain Matthew's current net income? (Ignore the information in question 3.)

e. Refer to the original data. Matthew's is considering replacing its labour-intensive process with an automated production system. This would result in an increase of $56,000 annually in fixed manufacturing costs. The variable manufacturing costs would decrease by $25 per tonne. Compute the new break-even volume in tonnes and in sales dollars.

Questions 3 and 4 were prepared by Judith A. Cumby, assistant professor, Faculty of Business Administration, Memorial University of Newfoundland, as a basis for class discussion and is not intended to reflect either an effective or an ineffective handling of a management problem.

Case 4-1

BUY.COM
The Lowest Prices on Earth — But at What Cost?

Apparently, finding low prices is a snap! Well, actually it's more of a click. A little typing and a click of the mouse to be precise and, voila, you arrive at Buy.com where you will find "the lowest prices on Earth." At this shopping utopia visitors can find pretty much anything at prices that won't be beaten, even if it means that the company has to sell items at less than it actually paid for them. It doesn't sound like a profitable business plan, but Buy.com has become one of the fastest growing companies in North American history. But, you say, that may not be a good thing unless there are profits to back up this business strategy. Only time will tell when and if that will happen. The company hopes to generate US$10 billion in revenue by 2003. The company's chances at turning a profit arise from its ability to cut costs. It never touches any inventory because of the fact that order fulfillment is completely outsourced.

Buy.com believes advertising revenue will provide profit in the future as it builds a "loyal" customer base and an increasingly high flow of traffic to the Buy.com site. Nonetheless, protest Web sites have arisen admonishing Buy.com's poor customer service and business practices, while customers who buy in large quantities have criticized its distributors.

How it All Began

Like other growing Internet companies, this one began with a much narrower focus. The company started in 1996 as BuyComp.com selling computer products at discount prices. The founder, Scott Blum, began looking for ways to expand the business and eventually found an opportunity — he bought another Internet company that sold books and videos. This became BuyBooks.com and BuyVideos.com. Blum then decided he would establish an e-commerce portal that would allow continued expansion when opportunities arose — Buy.com was the result. In fact, Blum has purchased thousands of Internet domain names with the word "buy." With unswerving intentions to revolutionize all of retailing, Blum came up with a bold, some say reckless, business plan to build up a loyal customer base that would return again and again when looking for products.

The company broke records for first year sales with sales of US$125 million for 1998, but the company was losing several million each month (and still is!). As with most Internet start-ups, this was anticipated and the strategy has been to develop as large a customer base as possible. It was thought this would be achieved by offering some products below cost and the others would sell just above cost, allowing the company to keep its head above water.

If all went as anticipated this large customer base would begin to click into Buy.com whenever they needed to make purchases, creating considerable traffic flow on a regular basis. With the goods as the bait, advertising and ancillary services would come to provide revenue opportunities leading to profit.

Over time, this high traffic flow would make the site a very desirable advertising space. As the goal of a general e-commerce portal came to be realized, the company would generate considerable revenues from advertising and through offering leasing arrangements and product warranties. Losing money initially would be the cost of developing the "brand." Many well-known companies that manufacture a wide range of products have purchased space on the site, including Lexus, Pepsi-Cola, and The Gap.

The goal of Buy.com has been to keep expanding and to offer whatever can be sold over the Internet. By 1999, Buy.com was selling books, gifts, electronics, software, computer equipment, games, videos, travel, and golfing equipment. Blum has purchased the rights to more than four thousand Web addresses in anticipation of future exploits. The range of anticipated future product offerings could be assumed from names such as BuyInsurance.com and BuyCars.com, but the imagination wonders at domains such as

BuyStuff.com. How earnestly Blum takes his goal to be the largest commerce portal on the Internet can be seen from his buying the rights to "10percentoffamazon.com." Becoming number one means first getting past Amazon, which has also been expanding its product categories. For example, Amazon became the number one online toy retailer in only a few weeks in 1999, shooting past specialty sites such as eToys and toys-rus.com. It will take a great deal to move past the momentum achieved by Amazon.

With having to offer the lowest prices and the ultimate goal of eventually achieving only a 1 percent gross margin on product sales, this requires having to maintain tight control over prices. At Buy.com, almost every expense is cut to the bone. There isn't any inventory and most functions, including customer service, is outsourced.

The only function that seems to have unlimited resources, like many Internet start-ups, is marketing and advertising. Again, this is how the company builds its brand and attracts traffic. At this stage of e-commerce development, it is still critical to keep the brand name in front of potential consumers. The strength of the new economy may be largely confined by people's ability to remember Web addresses. Unforgettable URLs are either uniquely relevant or extremely curt. Luckily, Buy.com is making the name (and address) impossible to forget. The company spent millions of dollars in early 2000 alone on TV ads and billboards that featured only the Buy.com name printed in white on a black background.

However, many Internet companies have had to become more accountable for advertising expenditures and many are pulling back on marketing spending as businesses mature. Investors and venture capitalists are demanding more accountability and value for these marketing expenditures and it is unclear how much longer new capital will keep flowing to pay for all the consumer advertising and promotion. Many wonder when the Internet gold rush will end.

Anything You Can Sell, I Can Sell Cheaper

Blum isn't the only Web retailer using this model on the Internet. For example, OnSale Inc. sells computer equipment as well without any markup. Instead, they apply a small ordering fee and the firm offers leasing and equipment service contracts. And, of course, it also sells advertising space on its Web site. In an attempt to develop early market share in the cyber marketplace, many e-tailers have become fiercely price-oriented. These e-tailers exist in almost every product category that can be thought of on the Internet. While it can be argued that lower prices are a logical benefit from this form of retailing as it can be performed in a more efficient manner than most physical retailing and personal selling, where will it end? The battle for business in categories such as music and books has already seen what can only be described as price wars as sites promise to outdo other prices.

This one-upmanship — or down-manship in this instance — cannot logically continue. How can varied-line retailers continue to outdo the "category-killer" sites that also often price competitively? These vendors customarily have greater leverage with their manufacturers.

Buy.com has committed itself to being the lowest-priced vendor in each category that it enters. This goes beyond those guarantees that we see in traditional stores whereby the consumer demonstrates a lower price at another store by providing a flyer, availability is checked, and then the price is matched. Buy.com uses stealth software technology that continually searches the Internet to monitor prices and maintain its own prices as the lowest available. This can entail the repricing of up to thirty thousand items a day. Buy.com doesn't just try to match prices, it aims for lower prices than it finds at other Web sites.

Professional marketers tell retailers to avoid competing solely on price as all retailers lose out in the long term as profit margins become smaller and smaller. Price alone cannot provide a sustainable competitive advantage. Many observers wonder how this principle will work in the cyber marketplace, and if in the long run such a strategy will enable companies such as Buy.com to persevere.

The Internet is shrinking margins, and only the creative or those with the deepest pockets can survive. While comparison shopping in the physical world involves time and effort, in the cyber world it takes a few keystrokes to arrive at each new retailer. It is worth the consumers' effort to exert that much more time and effort to get the best price, even if it is only a minimal improvement.

As has been asked before, experts wonder — what proportion of the market will make buying decisions on the basis of price alone? For those that don't, what else will they use to make such decisions? In other words, is this a viable strategy in the long term? Is it sustainable? The problem is that in setting themselves up to be price leaders, a Web retailer's customer base becomes rooted upon this and will leave when the next lower price comes along. There is actually no customer "base" established, as there is no customer loyalty — the relationship is based solely upon price.

The focus on price may not currently exist to the same degree in the cyber marketplace, as the average Internet shopper may not be the average shopper in general. According to a study conducted in the United States in May 1999, price is often not the most important factor for many Internet shoppers. Instead, these consumers on average are more concerned with factors such as branding and trust. This is one reason why e-tailers are justified in spending such a disproportionate amount of funds on promotion and branding, turning their names and slogans into familiar phrases.

Ploy or Honest Mistake?

The primary activity in e-tailing remains getting visitors onto your Web site. And then like with any other vendor, ensure that the visitor has a positive shopping experience. It is here that Buy.com has had a few problems. In early 1999 a computer monitor that retails for about $560 was advertised on the site for $165, leading to a rapid flow of hundreds of orders for the item. Unfortunately, the price was a mistake, and claiming that the distributor (Ingram Micro/Ingram Entertainment, Inc.) did not have stock to cover these orders, the company refused to fill the orders. Very soon there were dozens of lawsuits to force the company to honour the price posted on the site.

This caused the company to alter its policies, thereby protecting itself against typographical errors that might create similar circumstance in the future. Again in 1999, a number of customers began to complain that Buy.com had charged their credit cards for items that were not in stock. The company provided little explanation even though their distributors employ real-time inventory reporting systems that indicate the current status of products. Also in that year, e-mails were sent out to customers advertising that all DVDs were $14.99 or less. When customers visited the site they found that popular titles were more expensive than the advertised price. Many complained, but their complaints either went unanswered or they were told that the offer had expired.

At this point the anti Buy.com sentiment had reached a dull roar and some customers even started Web sites protesting the actions of the company. Buy.com had to go so far as to invite a group of customers to the company's headquarters in California to discuss their grievances and explain what the company would do. One invited guest declined the invitation, believing that there was no real indication that the company would change their business practices. This could be interpreted to reflect the sentiment that these "problems" had not been mistakes or poor judgment but rather deliberate sales ploys intended to dupe consumers.

New Leader

During the same year the company was preparing to go "public." Blum, the entrepreneur that he is, also had other ideas he wanted to start pursuing. He had developed the idea of starting a company that would provide services to assist new Internet companies to get set up on the Web. It would be called ThinkTank.com. His resignation was announced a couple of months before the company's IPO. Greg Hawkins was announced as CEO in spring of 1999.

This was most likely scheduled as a part of a larger strategic scheme as Blum had been previously involved with a company that had been the subject of an SEC investigation. As well, new day-to-day leadership could also help in positioning the previous bad publicity as an irrelevant issue and position the new leadership as a sign of change to investors and consumers. By ending his direct involvement with the company, this would help to appease prospective stakeholders. He remains the company's largest shareholder with about 60 percent of its stock.

Hacking into the Market

In February 2000, Buy.com entered the financial markets offering 14 million shares of common stock. Within hours, the price of the stock rose from its original offer price of $13 to $35; a great show of faith from investors for a company which had been reported to have lost somewhere between $145 million and $600 million in 1999. The company posted sales of $597 million for the year making it the number two online retailer after Amazon. The euphoria was short lived however as that same day several of the largest vendors on the Internet were hit by hackers and brought crashing.

Because of the activity surrounding the IPO the Buy.com site was already receiving a great deal more traffic than usual. The hackers bombarded the sites over February 7 and 8 with volumes of data that far exceeded the capacity of each site causing them to crash. Sites were down for up to five hours. Other victims of the attack included CNN.com, E*Trade, Yahoo!, and Amazon. A great deal of publicity and public concern was generated as a result of these successful attacks on such well known and "established" Web sites. The price of Buy.com stock began to decline that same day, but it was not until two weeks later that the price declined to its original price level.

While some claim the fallout from the hacker attack and its implications are responsible for the outcome of the IPO, there are others that believe it reflects a more fundamental concern — a lack of faith in the business model. Many analysts are critical of the policy of selling merchandise at a loss to generate sales and attract customers. Although profit is hoped to come through advertising, the company has yet to prove that its approach can ever make money.

The attacks sent a wake-up call to the cyber business community. For all the talk of firewalls, encryption, and intrusion-detection systems, these systems were disabled by a strategy no more complicated than dialing a telephone number continually so that everyone else gets a busy signal. The equipment to perform this can be easily obtained from hacker sites all over the Internet. Therefore, the $100 million headache was not so much an inherent flaw in the e-commerce model as it was a case of not really anticipating that anyone would actually attempt to shut such sites down.

Advertisers united to support the affected sites and supported assertions by Internet companies that such a disruption is a problem typical of any evolving technology.

David Ingram, chairman of Ingram and board member of Buy.com (remember the computer monitor fiasco?) purchased 5.1 million shares, but quickly announced that he would sell them as soon as was legally possible. Stocks must be retained for 180 days after an IPO. It is believed this announcement was in response to customer complaints about the prospect of the world's largest distributor of videos, DVDs, and video games becoming an e-commerce competitor. In the fall of 1999 Ingram had planned to sell his $1.5 billion distributorship to Barnes and Noble until the Federal Trade Commission put a stop to the deal that would have seen the world's largest book wholesaler combine with the world's largest bookstore chain. Since this, the company's two largest customers, B&N and Amazon have begun to assume more of their own distribution tasks. The Ingram book group remains the sole shipper of Web orders for Buy.com.

A Happy Ending?

Buy.com's business strategy is a model not unlike that used by many of the largest-volume vendors on the Internet. It can be seen to benefit consumers who surf the Web to navigate the deepest discount that they can find, but will it benefit the vendors. When and how will they stop this battle for cyber-sales? How will consumers respond? For now, it would appear that price is the key to generating revenues and creating a "loyal" customer base. In the long run, however, more is needed. But what is it? Only time and the customer will determine what is the best strategy in the long run.

Pertinent Web Site
www.buy.com

Questions

1. What type of pricing does this company utilize? What may be the impact of this practice in the longer term? Will this prove successful for the company?

2. Which pricing objective is the company pursuing? What potential impact might this have on the e-commerce of the future?

3. What do you think may happen when e-tailers stop following these types of pricing policies as their key means to acquire market share?

4. We have read in the text about the importance of price and how it is a component of value. Has the Internet increased the value received by consumers?

Sources: Alice Cuneo, "E-volution: Dot-Coms Face the Bottom Line," *Advertising Age,* March 27, 2000, pp. 46, 47; Ryann Bigge, "Finding A Name That Sticks," *Marketing Magazine,* March 20, 2000, p. 10; Kevin Brass, "Soaring E-Commerce Stocks Obliterate Economic Reality," *Video Store,* March 19/25, 2000, p. 15; Ann Mack, "Web Advertisers Support Sites After Hack Attacks," *Adweek,* February 21, 2000, p. 46; Zena Olijnyk, "RCMP to Swap notes With FBI on Hackers," *Financial Post,* February 14, 2000, pp. C1, C5; Brett Sporich, "Ingram Vows to Sell Off 'Buy' Shares," *Video Store,* February 13/19, 2000, pp. 1, 56; Brett Sporich, "Buy.com Soars," *Video Store,* February 13/19, 2000, pp. 1, 56; Jill Vardy, "E-commerce Gets a Wake-up Call: Hacker Attacks Should Spark Security Overhaul," *Financial Post,* February 10, 2000, pp. C1, C4; "Playing i-Ball," *The Economist,* November 6, 1999, p. 65; George Anders, "Buy.com's Blum Leaves to Launch ThinkTank.com," *The Wall Street Journal,* October 22, 1999, p. B9; Zina Moukheiber, "Beleaguered Brother," *Forbes,* September 6, 1999, pp. 196–7; Wendy Taylor & Marty Jerome, "First One's Free," *PC Computing,* August 1999, p. 91; David Bank, "A Site-Eat-Site World," *The Wall Street Journal,* July 12, 1999, pp. R8, R10; Scott Campbell, "Buy.com Loses One in Court, But Precedent is Unclear," *Computer Reseller News,* July 12, 1999, p. 6; Brett Sporich, "The Cyber-Power Players," *Video Store,* July 11/17, 1999, p. 22; Ed Foster, "Dubious Marketing Ploys at Buy.com Expose the Seamy Side of E-Commerce," *Infoworld,* May 3, 1999, p. 99; Eric Nee, "Meet Mister Buy (Everything).com," *Fortune,* March 29, 1999, pp. 119–124; William Gurley, "Buy.com May Fail, But If It Succeeds Retailing May Never Be The Same," *Fortune,* January 11, 1999, pp. 150–151; Larry Armstrong, "Anything You Can Sell, I Can Sell Cheaper," *Business Week,* December 14, 1998, p. 130.

Case 4-2

PRICING

A Great Deal on Heating Oil

The Maxwell Oil Company had been marketing home heating oil to homeowners in the Westville area for more than fifty years. This company operated an annual payment/purchase plan that offered customers a package that, for $99 per year, gave them regular maintenance, service and insurance on their furnaces, and the fuel at 34 cents per litre.

During the past year or so, the company had noticed it was receiving a number of telephone calls from customers who were calling to cancel their annual plan because a local competitor was offering them home heating oil at 30 cents per litre. Maxwell management agreed to match the deal for any customer who called in the future, thereby giving any customer who contacted the company a reduction of 4 cents per litre from the current contract price.

The net result was that many customers started to call, once it became generally known in certain Westville neighbourhoods that Maxwell was prepared to match the competitor's price. Then the company began to receive a number of calls from very angry customers who were upset at the fact that some of their neighbours, who apparently had signed up for the same contract, had been receiving their fuel at 4 cents per litre less — merely because they had called up and asked for it. Those who were still paying the higher price were not happy and threatened to leave. Some had been Maxwell customers for thirty years or more and felt "hurt" at being treated this way.

Questions

1. What obligation, if any, did the Maxwell company have to offer the same price reduction to all customers who were currently under contract with the annual plan?

2. What options did the company have when it first encountered the fact that the competition was offering fuel at 4 cents per litre less? Should it have let some of its customers go or tried to keep as many as possible?

3. Is there an ethical issue involved when prices are lowered for some customers and not for others?

Sale Day at The Bay

Bob Jones was walking through the men's wear department of The Bay department store in downtown Westville, taking a shortcut to the restaurant where he was meeting Gail for lunch. As he neared the door, Bob noticed a rack of men's cotton slacks, above which was displayed a large sign announcing "Special! 50% off." Although Bob had not intended to buy slacks that day, he was attracted by the sign and stopped to look at the goods.

As Bob examined the slacks on the rack, he noticed that the brand was Ruff Hewn and that the original price was $80. He thought, "I could use a pair of slacks and this is a really good price." He had a couple of Ruff Hewn cotton shirts hanging in his closet, and he thought the sweater Gail had given him for his birthday was Ruff Hewn as well. He picked out a dark green pair, size 32 waist, and tried them on. They fitted perfectly, so he decided to buy them.

"Is that on your Bay account, sir?" asked the sales clerk. Bob replied that he would be paying cash and took a $50 bill from his wallet. The clerk then asked, "Do you have your Bay Day card?" Bob indicated that he wasn't familiar with a Bay Day card. The clerk explained that he should have been handed a Bay Day card as he entered the store and that, since this was Bay Day, he was entitled to scratch a certain part of the card to reveal the discount that he would receive on his purchase. As Bob didn't have a card, she reached under the counter and gave him one. Bob scratched the latex portion of the card and saw the words "30% off."

"Too bad I can't use this," Bob commented. "The pants are already 50 percent off." "Oh no," replied the sales clerk. "You get an additional 30 percent off the sale price. Let's see, that's another $12, so the price of the slacks will be $28." Bob was delighted. He really hadn't expected to get the pants for such a low price. He had thought he was getting a good deal at $40. He paid the $28, plus tax, thanked the sales clerk, and rushed off to apologize to Gail for being late.

Questions

1. What was the price of the pants that Bob bought?

2. What factors influenced his decision to buy?

3. What would Bob have done if he had seen a rack of pants at The Bay with a sign reading "cotton slacks $28" or a sign that said "cotton slacks $80"?

Sandstrom Stereotactic System

Pia Sandstrom of Welland, Ontario, was studying medical technology at the University of Umea, Sweden, when her mother, Monica, came to see her and to visit her homeland. Monica, trained as a chemical engineer, was looking for a new career, having retired from her research job at a Hamilton chemical company. She decided to check out the possibility of importing Swedish medical devices to Canada. She and Pia came upon a revolutionary device that helps locate brain tumours. They decided to begin importing the product into North America, only to find that the product could not meet U.S. health department standards.

They decided to begin manufacturing the device themselves and, three years later, having dipped into savings, sold off investments, and mortgaged the family home, the Sandstroms expected to sell forty of their Stereotactic Systems a year at $25,000 each. They rely on a chain of suppliers in the Hamilton area to make the components of the system and to assemble the final product.

Most North American hospitals have been using a device that is screwed into the patient's forehead with sheet-metal screws. These machines are heavy, painful, and expensive — at $60,000 to $100,000 each. The Sandstrom system attaches painlessly to the patient's ears and nose and can be worn all day without discomfort. And it sells for only $25,000.

Stereotactic systems work much like a sailor's sextant. A technician, working from X-rays or ultrasound, reads off the co-ordinates of the tumour and gives the information to the neurosurgeon. By pinpointing the location of the tumour, 85 percent of the cost of the surgery is saved. A professor of neurosurgery at the University of Saskatchewan observed, "The patient can go home the next day, instead of being hospitalized for three weeks. That makes the patient less costly to look after."

The Sandstroms are a two-person company. They spend their time networking at medical trade shows where they meet doctors and academics and develop leads, which they then follow up. They have come to realize that it takes a considerable amount of time and effort to generate sales. It also took them some time to accept that a machine that costs only $1,700 to manufacture can be sold for 15 times that amount when it reaches the market.

Questions

1. What is the relationship between cost and price in the marketing of the Sandstrom Stereotactic System?

2. How would you explain to a professor of neurosurgery why the price of the device is $25,000?

3. How important is price to a senior hospital administrator who must justify the purchase of this device in an economic climate where hospital budgets are being severely cut by governments?

Case 4-3

SALVATION ARMY THRIFT STORES
Cool Threads! Cheap!

They seem like they have always been around — the Salvation Army Thrift Stores, that is. But never have they been so popular, and with so many different types of people. These and other used clothing outlets were usually drab or functionally decorated stores that didn't really try to compete with other retailers. Donations of clothing and other items were revitalized and presented as attractively as possible, with the hope that these items would meet the needs of the less advantaged who would come to these stores and purchase clothing and other items for a few dollars. These Salvation Army stores were actually charities with the goal of raising money so the Army could continue to do their work in countries around the world. As a registered charity, these "businesses" were tax-exempt. But, those days are over, as the Thrift Stores lost this status a few years ago.

Of course, the mission of the organization hasn't changed, nor has the presence of these stores across the country. But these outlets are a real going concern today as people flock to the stores in record numbers. But no, this isn't the result of record poverty levels in the country, but because it has become chic to be cheap! Many privately run stores have sprung up in the past few years. In fact, in the next five years there are plans to open one hundred new and newly renovated Thrift Stores across Canada. Actually, The Salvation Army is now one of the fastest growing retailers in Canada.

Instead of simply advertising the locations of their stores and maintaining awareness among the lower economic segments, the Thrift Stores now focus on great selection and great prices, in other words — cool threads, cheap! Marketing efforts now attempt to reach a much wider audience as interest in such goods now appeal to segments in many socioeconomic levels.

Cheapening Trends

In recent years, there has been a proliferation of retailers catering to the lower end of the marketplace. U.S. retailers Wal-Mart and Value Village have entered Canada with thundering success. As well, there have been trends toward retro styles and vintage clothing that has brought a new cachet to bargain hunting and used clothing. Or as it is often referred to today — pre-owned, previously-loved, gently-used, or second-time-round clothing and goods. Stores that specialize in used children's apparel and accessories have also become popular.

Although Wal-Mart sells new merchandise ranging from clothing to groceries to tools, its "Everyday Low Price" focus on "falling prices" has created such a demand for the retailer that its Canadian head office has even received requests and petitions from consumers pleading for stores to be opened in their areas. There is also an increasing popularity of discount and so-called "dollar store" retailers. As well, Zellers has done well in recent years, even introducing its own successful line of private-label products.

There are a variety of influences that can be seen to be driving this interest in lower priced and even used items. The economies of North America have been doing well in recent years, but Canadians have less money in their pockets than they did in the past. In the last decade, disposable income in Canada has dropped by 2 percent while in the United States it has risen 18 percent in the same period. Canadians have record levels of debt and a significant portion of earnings is lopped off for the taxman. This all translates into limited buying power. It is easy to see how Eaton's last ditch effort to reposition itself as a high-end retailer was a fateful decision. Canada's population base consists of a relatively small segment of well-off and wealthy consumers making the high-end portion of the marketplace out of reach for most Canadian shoppers.

Another trend, this one more socially-oriented, that may be having an influence is the increasing trendiness of the "value" concept. Consumers are becoming more value-conscious. Cheap isn't always enough. Poor quality has become less tolerable to consumers and consumers want to see a consistent relationship between the price paid and the value received. This attitude carries across to the higher end as well — paying a high price for a brand name that doesn't provide value is not tolerated for very long. Some consumers are happy to pay higher prices when higher quality results. Consumers are also increasingly suspicious of retailers and corporations and are not forgiving of those they feel are trying to deceive consumers with respect to value and pricing.

The rise of these "low end" stores may be having a more pervasive impact than may have been thought. An independent study by Ryerson Polytechnic University has indicated that, in markets where there are Wal-Mart stores, the cost of living has actually decreased by as much as 5 to 10 percent. The impact of Wal-Mart's arrival in Canada has been widespread.

The success of this retailer in Canada has caused other retailers to pay attention and to respond to remain competitive. Wal-Mart, once feared and the target of smear campaigns when it expanded into Canada in the mid-nineties is now heralded as having caused a rejuvenation in the stale Canadian retail community. Lax retailers must now remain alert to consumer wants and demands for value pricing and selection. Wal-Mart has been credited with delivering value through forcing other retailers to respond to consumer wants.

Second Time Around

There is a fortune in used goods. This has been both good and bad for charitable organizations such as The Salvation Army and St. Vincent de Paul both of whom aim to help the poor and the destitute. The lure of big money, however, has led many retailers into the used goods business including U.S.-based Value Village. The company now has almost seventy stores across Canada (180 in North America) that are cutting into the donations and revenues of the operations run by these charitable organizations.

Technically, The Salvation Army stores might not be considered a charity as Revenue Canada revoked its tax-exempt status, but its goal is still to help the needy. Value Village contracts with other charity focused organizations to collect merchandise through the use of aggressive telemarketing campaigns using the names of these organizations. These charities include Canadian Diabetes Association and the Ontario Federation for Cerebral Palsy.

Those who are solicited are not aware that it is actually the retailer that is soliciting and collecting these items to resell in Value Village stores across the country. Although these are registered charities they have not in the past used this form of fundraising campaign.

There is a rag war threatening to break out across the country with a large U.S. empire on one side and a tiny consortium of charities struggling to help the poor on the other side. A representative of Value Village says that this is a growing industry and that they are experiencing a real renaissance in thrift shopping. As the battle for the thrifty dollar heats up, charitable organizations will have to develop more aggressive and systematic ways of marketing themselves to remain in the game and to go up against the marketing savvy and shrewd opportunism of Value Village.

Ironically, Value Village's founders, brothers Bill and Orlo Ellison, began their professional careers with The Salvation Army more than fifty years ago, gathering and sorting clothes for the needy. They broke ranks with the church when they realized there was gold in the unbecoming mass of rags and cast-offs that poured in from donation boxes.

Thrift is not necessarily an archaic word and many are quite proud to call themselves cheapskates. Further, the consumerism, greed, and excess that was so stylish in the eighties appears to be no longer politically correct in this age of the environment, recycling, and value consciousness.

Marketing to the Mainstream

Once the territory of the trendy and the cash-strapped, Canada's thrift-shop retailers are seeing a resurgence as shopping for second-hand goods loses its stigma with the mainstream. As a result of this new popularity of resale retail the competition for young urban shoppers is increasing. This is especially the result of the aggressive expansion of Value Village across Canada.

Instead of marketing itself as a charity, The Salvation Army shops must now market like retailers. They must *think* like a retailer. The clamor for young shoppers is evident from recent campaigns by Value Village featuring younger talent and being much more playful than in the past. They still also focus on good deals and bargains. The Salvation Army and Goodwill Industries have also begun to adopt such approaches in recent campaigns.

The lure of resale retail is still attracting new entrants into the marketplace. Urban Outfitters features used clothing items alongside new merchandise and new "independent" stores continue to open such as Double Take in Toronto hoping to appeal to students by locating near universities and colleges. The company has even been working on plans to have fashion students display their designs in Double Take stores. These types of marketing efforts have increased the need for charity shops to reintroduce their "brands" to a new generation of 18 to 34-year-olds. Goodwill with its "Goodwear — it's not a label. It's a headspace" campaign focusing on fashion, creating your own image, and savings. The intention is to make the brand "fresh, hip, and yours." Salvation Army Thrift Shops has a similar youthful approach with its "Cool Threads. Cheap!" advertisements.

The tide has turned for second hand stores — they are no longer dark, dank, musty-smelling places where you have to sift through piles of merchandise to find hidden treasures. Environments are being created that are more suited to mainstream shoppers — moves also reflected in these retailer's marketing campaigns.

Pertinent Web Sites

www.salvationarmy.ca
www.valuevillage.com
www.goodwill.org/canada/toronld.htm

Questions

1. What factors (social, psychological, etc.) other than price influence a consumer's decision to buy at these types of stores?

2. Should The Salvation Army Thrift Shops rely only upon pricing to compete with retailers such as Value Village? How should they handle this competition?

3. What impact will the success of Wal-Mart and the proliferation of discount retailers have on the mainstream popularity of shopping at resale retailers such as the Salvation Army stores?

Sources: "Making Cheap Look Like A Million Dollars," *National Post,* December 1, 1999, p. B2, *CBC Venture,* "Downscale Retail," Episode #731, November 30, 1999; Shawna Cohen, "Resale Retail Takes On Mainstream," *Marketing Magazine,* July 19/26, 1999, p. 4; Michael Geisterfer, "Rag War Between U.S. Empire and Tiny Charity," *Financial Post,* April 3, 1999, p. D6; Jonathon Chevreau, "More to Being A Cheapskate Than Being Cheap," *Financial Post,* May 14, 1998, p. 32.

Part five

Distribution

Channels of distribution from producer to user, wholesaling, and retailing institutions

We are in the process of developing a marketing program to reach the firm's target markets and achieve the goals established in strategic marketing planning. So far, we have considered the product and pricing structure in that marketing mix. Now we turn our attention to the distribution system — the means for getting products and services to the market.

The distribution ingredient in the marketing mix encompasses two broad topics: (1) strategies for selecting and operating channels of distribution — Chapter 15, and (2) the wholesaling and retailing institutions used in distribution — Chapters 16 and 17.

Chapter Fifteen

Channels of Distribution: Conflict, Co-operation, and Management

We will discuss distribution channels in this chapter from the point of view of the producer or the developer of the product or service. As you will see, however, the problems and opportunities that intermediaries face in managing their channels are similar to those faced by distributors. After studying this chapter, you should have an understanding of:

◆ The nature and importance of intermediaries.

◆ What a distribution channel is.

◆ The sequence of decisions involved in designing a channel.

◆ The major channels for consumer goods, business goods, and services.

◆ Vertical marketing systems.

◆ Intensity of distribution.

◆ How to choose individual intermediaries.

◆ The nature of conflicts and control within distribution channels.

◆ Legal considerations in channels management.

◆ Channel arrangements to distribute to international markets.

An Apple of a Different Colour

Apple Computer has come back from the near dead in Canada, in the U.S. and around the world. More than one million "Macs" were sold in the first three months of 2000 — with half of these sales outside the U.S. Everyone thinks Apple's success is because of the loyalty of Mac fans — and this is true. Everyone thinks it's because of the technology of the new PowerMac G4 desktop and the PowerBook portables' capabilities — also true. And, of course, everyone thinks its because of the popular new designs for the box and the portable, the see-through case, the colours, the new curves and lines, the sheer attention-getting value of these designs in a sea of beige boxes. Well, that is also true. But so is something else — something not so easily recognized — Apple has focused hard on something it has not done before, it has focused hard on distribution and reselling. And it has been this new attention that has played a major role in the revitalization of the company. After all, no matter how great a product may be, you can't sell 'em if you don't get 'em out there!

During the 80s and early 90s, when Apple received praise for its products and could not manufacture enough and keep them in stock, it was said to have become arrogant with its distributors, wholesalers, resellers, and retailers — the very people it relied upon to sell their products. Now, Apple is paying much closer attention to its channel structure and its channel members and their needs. Steve Jobs, in his second term as head of Apple, has promised distributors and

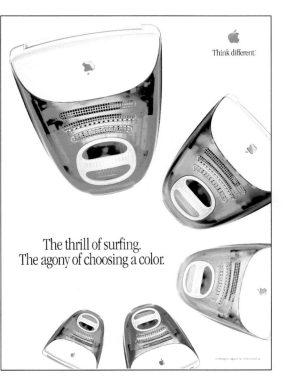

The thrill of surfing.
The agony of choosing a color.

Think different.

retailers that the company would do more to support them, and in return, it wanted them to provide more support to Apple products. Intermediaries who did not wish to provide more display and shelf space for Apple products or train staff to sell Macs were to be cut out of the channel system. The result of the new approach was to change Apple's channel systems in many markets.

The implementation of the new focus has differed somewhat from national market to national market. The Apple Canada version of the company's new direct-to-consumer-Internet-based sales channel, termed the Apple Store, began operating in the U.S. in 1998, and was not launched to serve Canadian markets until 2000. Another channel, the Apple catalogue, is used by a greater proportion of Apple buyers in the U.S. than in Canada. Apple Canada believes that the difference in the importance of the catalogue channel reflects the difference in the Canadian consumer's need and desire for more face-to-face service and aid in the buying process compared with American consumers. This difference in the

Canadian consumer's purchasing approach is also reflected in the other retail channels Apple uses. Apple Canada relies much less on distribution in mass merchandising outlets than is the case in the U.S. Canadian consumers, on the average, are not as comfortable shopping for and buying computers in a mass merchandis-ing setting as are Americans. As a result, Apple Canada provides independent Canadian resellers with a higher level of training and support than does the U.S. company in the American market.

Apple Canada's channels have been consolidated and revamped; one major addition, the Apple Store, is operating suc-cessfully; the second major change has been the creation of a completely direct in-house channel with more expert personnel to serve the education market, which has always been an important segment for Apple products.[1]

Intermediaries and Distribution Channels

As the Apple Canada story highlights, the ownership of a product, such as a computer, has to be transferred somehow from the individual or organization that makes it to the consumer who needs and buys it. Goods also must be physically transported from where they are produced to where they are needed. The distribution channels for services can be viewed somewhat differently from those of goods. As we saw in Chapter 12, services are produced and consumed in the same place. To market services, those concerned with distribution must consider producing them in locations where they are wanted and accessible by the customer.[2]

intermediary
A firm that renders services directly related to the purchase and/or sale of a product as it flows from producer to consumer.

Distribution's role within a firm's marketing program is getting the product or service efficiently and conveniently to its target market wherever it is located and whenever it is needed. The most important activity in getting a product to market is arranging for its sale (and the transfer of title) from producer to final customer. Other common activities (or functions) are promoting the goods or services, storing goods, ensuring that production capacity exists for services, and assuming some of the financial risk during the distribution process.

A producer can carry out these functions in exchange for an order (and, it is hoped, payment) from a customer. Or producer and consumer can share these activities. Typically, however, firms called intermediaries perform some of these activities on behalf of the producer or the consumer.

Travelocity.ca makes it all available with just a few clicks.

An **intermediary** is a business firm that renders services related directly to the sale and/or purchase of a product as it flows from producer to consumer. An intermediary either owns the product at some point or actively aids in the transfer of ownership. Often, but not always, an intermediary takes physical possession of the product. Most services don't involve the use of intermediaries because they are generally inseparable from the service provider. There are exceptions to that situation: The travel industry is an example of a situation in which services are transferred via intermediaries. Traditional travel agents arrange flights, book hotels, purchase theatre tickets, and assist the traveller in many ways to plan a vacation or business trip. Internet-based travel services, such as Travelocity (www.travelocity.ca) are intermediaries that provide the information, options and mechanisms enabling consumers to make decisions and conclude necessary transactions themselves.

Intermediaries are commonly classified on the basis of whether they take title to the products being distributed. **Merchant intermediaries** actually take title to the products they help to market. The two groups of merchant intermediaries are wholesalers and retailers. A distributor for Neilson chocolate bars is an example of a wholesale intermediary. Franchisee operators can be viewed as retail intermediaries in the service industry. **Agents** never actually own the products, but they do arrange the transfer of title. Real estate brokers, manufacturers' agents, and travel agents are examples of agents.

agent

A firm that never actually owns products that are being distributed but actively assists in the transfer of title.

How Important are Intermediaries?

Some critics say prices are high because there are too many intermediaries performing unnecessary or redundant functions. In recent years, some manufacturers also reached this conclusion and sought to cut costs by eliminating wholesaling intermediaries, that is, engaging in *disintermediation*. Some manufacturers feel as though they are losing control over their ability to market their products. With many intermediaries in wide distribution channels, some manufacturers find it difficult to maintain a consistent price and brand image.[3] While intermediaries can be eliminated from channels, lower costs are not necessarily achieved. The outcome is not predictable because of a basic axiom of marketing: You can eliminate intermediaries, but you cannot eliminate the essential distribution activities that they perform. These activities — such as creating assortments and storing products — can be shifted from one party to another in an effort to improve efficiency. However, someone has to perform the various activities — if not an intermediary, then the producer or the final customers.[4]

Intermediaries, whether they are physical "brick" outlets or cyberspace "click" outlets, may be able to carry out distribution activities better or more cheaply than either producers or consumers. Moreover, for some products and services — those called "high touch" (needing consumer interaction or close inspection), it is usually not practical for a producer to deal directly with ultimate consumers. Think for a moment how inconvenient your life would be if there were no local retail intermediaries such as Harvey's, Sobey's supermarket, or auto dealers. Without these middlemen we would have to go to the butcher, the bakery, who knows where for our canned goods. As well, there would be no such thing as being able to choose from an offered selection. Buying a new car would mean going to the assembly plant which may be somewhere in Canada, but it could also be in Detroit, Germany, or Japan. Unless you travel to the plant to get the vehicle, than you must make arrangements and pay to have it shipped to where you live all the while hoping it arrives in one piece. And then you have to worry about service and maintenance.

Intermediaries create value through making it easier and more efficient to sell goods and services by minimizing the number of sales contacts necessary to complete the transaction. They facilitate the flow of products to consumers through the performance of three functions. They perform a transactional function through buying, selling, and risk-taking in the pursuit of making future sales. It is also a logistical function in that they select, store, transport, and disperse products. Further, it is a facilitative function in that they gather market information and research, test or inspect products, and possibly arrange financing. These activities make the goods and services of producers more attractive to consumers.[5]

As illustrated in Figure 15-1, intermediaries serve as purchasing agents for their customers and as sales specialists for their suppliers. They provide financial services for both suppliers and customers. And their storage services, their capability to divide large shipments into smaller ones for resale, and their market knowledge benefit suppliers and customers alike.

FIGURE 15-1
Typical Activities of
an Intermediary

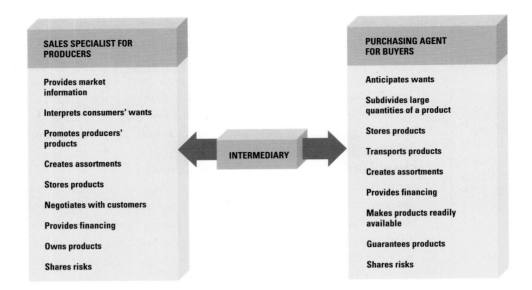

What Is a Distribution Channel?

distribution channel
The set of people and
firms involved in the
flow of the title to a
product as it moves
from producer to
ultimate consumer
or business user.

A **distribution channel** consists of the set of people and firms involved in the transfer of title to a product as the product moves from producer to ultimate consumer or business user. A channel of distribution always includes both the producer and the final customer for the product in its present form, as well as any intermediaries such as retailers and wholesalers. In the case of services, the producer and the retailer are often one and the same.

The channel for a product extends only to the last person or organization that buys it without making any significant change in its form. When its form is altered and another product emerges, a new channel is started. When lumber is milled and then made into furniture, two separate channels are involved. The channel for the lumber might be lumber mill → broker → furniture manufacturer. The channel for the finished furniture might be furniture manufacturer → retail furniture store → consumer.

Besides the producer, intermediaries, and the final customer, other institutions aid the distribution process. Among these intermediaries are banks, insurance companies, storage firms, voice and data transmission service providers, and transportation companies. However, because they do not take title to the products and are not actively involved in purchase or sales activities, these intermediaries are not formally included in the distribution channel.

This chapter focuses on the flow (or transfer) of ownership for a product, while part of Chapter 16 examines the physical flow of goods. These flows are distinct; consequently, different institutions may carry them out. For example, a contractor might order roofing shingles from a local building-materials distributor. To minimize freight and handling costs, the product might be shipped directly — for example, shingles manufacturer → contractor. But the channel for title (and ownership) would be manufacturer → distributor → contractor.

Designing Distribution Channels

Companies that appear to be similar often have very dissimilar channels of distribution. For example, Tupperware (www.tupperware.ca) sells its housewares primarily through a party-plan arrangement, in which customers buy products at Tupperware "parties" held in the homes of friends and neighbours. Rubbermaid (www.rubbermaid.com), on the other hand, sells its similar line of housewares through conventional department and variety stores. Some companies use multiple channels of distribution. Hotels, such as the Westin (www.westin.com), sell their products and services directly to walk-in customers, through travel agents who make reservations and guarantee bookings with the customer, by mail, fax, or telephone, through their Web site, or even through an Internet-based hotel room broker.

Why do seemingly similar firms or the same firm wind up with such different channels? One reason is that there are numerous types of channels and intermediaries from which to choose. Also, a variety of factors related to the market, product, intermediaries, and company itself will influence the choice of channels actually used by a firm.

A company wants a distribution channel that not only meets customers' needs but also provides an edge on the competition. Some firms gain a differential advantage with their distribution channels. Major corporations such as Caterpillar (www.caterpillar.com) in construction equipment and John Deere (www.deere.com) in farm equipment use dealers to provide many important services, ranging from advice about financing programs to rapid filling of orders for repair parts. While Apple Computers (www.apple.com) has worked to revitalize and redevelop its retail network, Dell Computers (www.dell.ca) pioneered direct sales by phone and Internet and Gateway Computers (www.gateway.com) has eliminated intermediaries in selling its products and deals directly with customers via the Internet. Using this formula, Gateway is able to reap higher margins while selling computers at competitive prices making them the world's second-largest direct marketer of personal computers. In a unique twist on this distribution method Gateway has opened fifty-eight Gateway Country showrooms. But not to sell computers! These support the strategy of custom-ordered direct delivery by allowing consumers to try various components to determine what they would best like in a system. Computers are not sold on the premises, they must still be ordered by phone or online. But nobody will stop you from ordering at the store while you are online! It's estimated that 80 percent of Gateway's sales growth can be linked to these non-retail outlets.[6]

Gateway goes direct but uses the Gateway Country showroom to take care of those buyers who want "high touch."

To design channels that satisfy customers and outdo competition, an organized approach is required.[7] As shown in Figure 15-2, we suggest a sequence of four decisions:

1. *Specifying the role of distribution.* A channel strategy should be designed within the context of the entire marketing mix. First the firm's marketing objectives are reviewed. Next the roles assigned to product, price, and promotion are specified. Each element may have a distinct role, or two elements may share an assignment. For example, a manufacturer of pressure gauges may use both traditional intermediaries and direct marketing via mail and Internet advertising to convince prospective customers that it is committed to servicing the product following the sale.

In services marketing, the role of distribution is generally related to accessibility. Because the consumer is often involved during the process of service provision, as, for example, in legal services, the ability to access the service product directly is crucial to its saleability.

FIGURE 15-2
Sequence of Decisions to Design a Distribution Channel

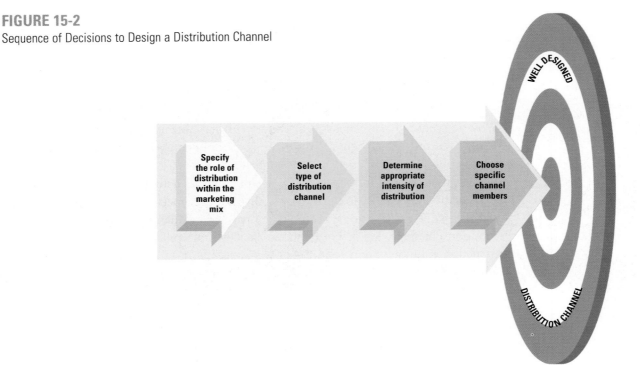

Determining the role of distribution in the marketing plan includes consideration of the human resources that will be applied to the delivery of the service. While more and more services are being delivered over the Internet — financial, travel, information and entertainment — most cannot be delivered by e-mail or the post office, stored on a shelf and passed over a counter by an intermediary, or delivered through indirect systems. The producer must be able to meet face-to-face with the buyer.

A company must decide whether distribution will be used defensively or offensively. Under a defensive approach, a firm will strive for distribution that is as good as, but not necessarily better than, other firms' distribution. With an offensive strategy, a firm uses distribution to gain an advantage over competitors. Banks provide a good example of the use of offensive strategies. Canadian banks are world leaders in moving rapidly to get the jump on their competitors with the use of telephone service options and secure online services. Bank of Montreal has gone so far as to develop a separate identity for their online services, Mbanx (www.mbanx.com). These institutions continue to battle with each other by trying to offer an increasing number of services online such as investment, trust, and insurance services. At the same time, these service providers are restructuring traditional branches so that specially trained employees can go out to clients with specialized requirements in areas of investment, retirement planning and trust services. They are covering all direct marketing bases — with both high and low technology.

2. *Selecting the type of channel.* Once distribution's role in the overall marketing program has been agreed on, the most suitable type of channel for the company's tangible product or service must be determined. At this point in the sequence, a firm needs to decide whether intermediaries will be used in its channel and, if so, which types of intermediaries will be used.[8]

To illustrate the wide array of institutions available, as well as the difficulty of channel selection, consider a manufacturer of compact disc players. If the firm decides to use intermediaries, it must choose among many different types. At the retail level, the range of institutions includes specialty audio-video outlets, department stores, discount houses, mail-order firms, and Internet retail services. Sony, for example, utilizes all of these intermediaries for their various lines of CD players. Further, they also operate a limited number of "Sony Stores" to enhance the brand image for all of their product lines.[9] As well, they have chosen to sell direct to consumers through their American (www.sony.com) and Canadian (www.sony.ca) Web sites.

Which single type or combination of types would permit the manufacturer to achieve its distribution objectives? Another choice must be made if the firm decides to also use wholesaling intermediaries. In a subsequent section, this decision as well as the major types of channels for goods and services will be discussed in detail.

3. *Determining intensity of distribution.* The next decision relates to intensity of distribution, or the number of intermediaries used at the wholesale and retail levels in a particular territory. The target market's buying behaviour and the product's nature have a direct bearing on this decision, as we will see later.

4. *Choosing specific channel members.* The last decision is selecting specific firms to distribute the product. For each type of institution, there are usually numerous specific companies from which to choose.

Recalling our CD player example, assume that the manufacturer prefers two types of intermediaries: department stores and specialty outlets. If the CD players will be sold in Toronto, the producer must decide which department stores and audio retail outlets — Sears, The Bay, Bay Bloor Radio, Toronto Music Super Store — will be asked to distribute its product line. Also one or more audio Internet distributors — including, among others, GetPlugged.com (www.getplugged.com) and The Microsoft network (MSN) (www.eshop.msn.com) — may need to be considered. Similar decisions may be required for each territory in the firm's market.

When selecting specific firms to be part of a channel, a producer should assess factors related to the market, the product, its own company, and intermediaries. Two additional factors are whether the intermediary sells to the market that the manufacturer wants to reach and whether the intermediary's product mix, pricing structure, promotion, and customer service are all compatible with the manufacturer's needs.

Selecting the Type of Channel

Firms may rely on existing channels, or they may use new channels to better serve current customers and reach prospective customers. In selecting its channels, a firm should seek to gain a differential advantage. For instance, besides selling through various types of retailers, Levi Strauss & Co. has opened its own stores featuring, of course, Levi's apparel.[10] Alberto-Culver Canada Inc. of Toronto (www.alberto.com), which has been distributing its products — Alberto VO5 hair care, Alberto European toiletries — through drug store chains, has moved into mass-market distribution and is selling its products through supermarkets and mass-merchandise outlets.[11] L.L. Bean (www.llbean.com), the outdoor clothing distributor, who has distributed merchandise through a mail-order system since its creation, is now focusing on distributing via the Internet. This company is finding that this is the company's best source for new customers. Marketing through this channel also reduces costs for L.L. Bean by eliminating the need for paper usage in catalogue production.[12]

Lands' End (www.landsend.com) and J. Crew (www.jcrew.com) have adopted similar strategies to convert mail-order customers as well as attract new business. To allow customers to have the same interactive experience as with telephone shopping, Lands' End has made it possible to indicate on their site if a visitor wishes to be contacted. Shoppers can chose to be contacted by telephone or through live text chat. The shopper can then communicate with a service representative who can guide them through the site even making a different catalogue page pop-up on the customer's computer screen according to the shopper's input. In a sense, this allows a retail service experience without leaving home.

Most goods distribution channels include intermediaries, but some do not. A channel consisting only of producer and final customer, with no intermediaries providing assistance is called **direct distribution**. ServiceMASTER (www.servicemaster.com) uses a direct approach to sell its cleaning and property maintenance services to both residential and commercial customers. Schwan's Sales Enterprises sells a wide range of frozen food products from refrigerated trucks by door to door salespeople. Services are generally distributed directly because production and consumption usually occur simultaneously. Swiss Chalet restaurants, for example, produce the food they sell and distribute it directly to the consumer.

Universities have developed new ways to distribute their service offerings. Correspondence was once the only alternative to the traditional classroom, but technology has allowed video and teleconference teaching while the Web has ushered in the introduction of Internet-based courses. Service distribution can also be a matter of altering the delivery schedule for particular groups. Executive MBA programs, for example, "bundle" classes on Fridays or weekends, or cluster them into one full day a month to enable business executives to participate.

In contrast, a channel of producer, final customer, and at least one level of intermediaries represents **indirect distribution**. Air Canada and other airlines, while selling direct to consumers through offices and over the Internet, still rely largely on an indirect approach, through both travel agents and Internet-based travel services.

One level of intermediaries — retailers but no wholesaling intermediaries, for example — or multiple levels may participate in an indirect channel. (For consumer goods, sometimes a channel in which wholesalers are bypassed but retailers are used is termed *direct*, rather than indirect, distribution.) With indirect distribution, a producer must determine the type(s) of intermediaries that will best serve its needs. The range of options at the wholesale and retail levels will be described in the next two chapters.

Now we'll look at the major channels traditionally used by producers of tangible products and at two special channels. Then we can consider the factors that most influence a company's choice of channels.

direct distribution
A channel consisting only of producer and final customer with no intermediaries providing assistance.

indirect distribution
A channel consisting of producer, final customer, and at least one level of intermediary.

Major Channels of Distribution

Diverse distribution channels exist today. The most common channels for consumer goods, business goods, and services are described next and are summarized in Figure 15-3. In viewing this figure, keep in mind that the producer, and/or any one or more intermediaries can be located in Canada or any other national market.

DISTRIBUTION OF CONSUMER GOODS Five channels are widely used in marketing tangible products to ultimate consumers:

FIGURE 15-3
Major Marketing
Channels for
Different Categories
of Products

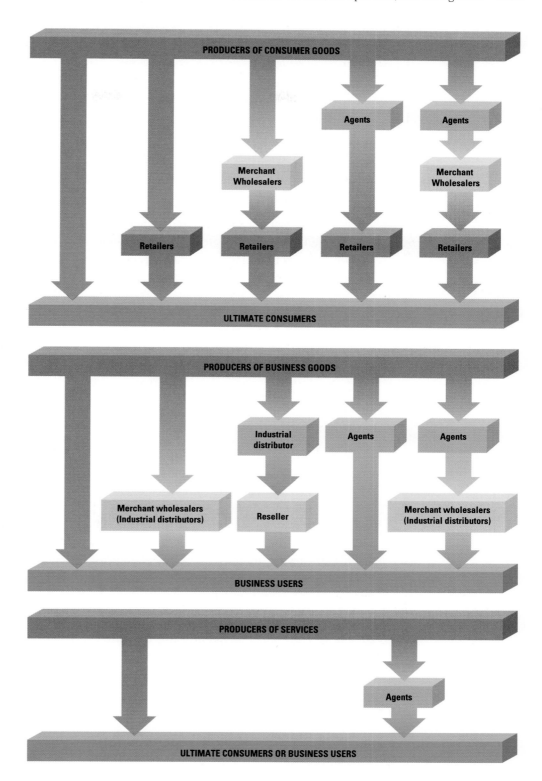

◆   *Producer → consumer.* The shortest, simplest distribution channel for consumer goods
involves no intermediaries. The producer may sell from door to door, by mail, or on
the Internet from Canada or another country, frequently the U.S. For example, Arcuri
Jewellers (www.arcuri-jewellers.com) offers complete catalogue jewellrey sales direct

to the consumer through its Canadian Web page, and J. Crew (www.jcrew.com) sells in Canada from its U.S. Web site.

◆ *Producer → retailer → consumer.* Many large retailers buy directly from manufacturers and agricultural producers. Companies such as Loblaw and Wal-Mart maintain direct dealings with producers in a number of countries.

◆ *Producer → wholesaler → retailer → consumer.* If there is a traditional channel for consumer goods, this is it. Small retailers and manufacturers by the thousands find this channel the only economically feasible choice. For imported goods, a foreign-based producer may use this channel as well.

◆ *Producer → agent → retailer → consumer.* Instead of using wholesalers, many producers prefer to use agents to reach the retail market, especially large-scale retailers. For example, a manufacturer of a glass cleaner selected a food broker to reach the grocery store market, including large chains.

◆ *Producer → agent → wholesaler → retailer → consumer.* To reach small retailers, producers often use agents, who in turn call on wholesalers that sell to large retail chains and/or small retail stores.

DISTRIBUTION OF BUSINESS PRODUCTS A variety of channels are available to reach organizations that incorporate the products into their manufacturing process or use them in their operations.[13] In the distribution of business products, the terms industrial distributor and merchant wholesaler are synonymous. The four common channels for business goods are:

◆ *Producer → user.* This direct channel accounts for a greater dollar volume of business products than does any other distribution structure. Manufacturers of large installations, such as airplanes, generators, and heating plants, usually sell directly to users. Companies also allow direct consumer purchases — computers and electronics although they do offer retail networks through other channels. Auto manufacturers have been trying to move consumers in this direction as well as evidenced by Volkswagen (www.vw.com) in 2000 when they introduced limited-edition colours for the Beetle that could only be purchased directly through the Volkswagen Web site.

◆ *Producer → industrial distributor → user.* Producers of operating supplies and small accessory equipment frequently use industrial distributors to reach their markets. Manufacturers of building materials and air-conditioning equipment are two examples of firms that make heavy use of industrial distributors.

◆ *Producer → industrial distributor → industrial distributor → user.* This channel has been common for computer products and related high technology items. The initial industrial distributor, usually a large firm, buys products from various manufacturers and then bundles them with related products for resale. These are often called value-added resellers. These firms then sell directly to the user as above or sell to smaller local firms working closely with end users to meet their needs for computer or communication system equipment and system design.

◆ *Producer → agent → user.* Firms without their own sales departments find this a desirable channel. Also, a company that wants to introduce a new product or enter a new market may prefer to use agents rather than its own sales force. Producers in

Marketing at Work 15-1

Nygard International Designs a Channel for the Fashion Market

The 60-year-old, 6-foot-2, cowboy-booted Finn with the Farrah Fawcett mane still remembers coming to Canada from Helsinki back in 1952. When Peter Nygard and his family first arrived they lived in a coal bin in Deloraine, Manitoba before moving to Winnipeg. Little did young, but towering, Nygard know when he began his professional career — as a management trainee at Eaton's department store — that a few decades later he would be the largest manufacturer of women's sportswear in Canada (and the fifth largest in North America).

Nygard is chairman of the board and owner of Nygard International, a $300 million company that manufactures and distributes women's fashions. The firm has 2,600 employees most of whom work at the two manufacturing plants in Winnipeg. Other staff are located in research and design studios in New York, Hong Kong, Montreal, and Europe. Still others work in joint-venture manufacturing operations in Mexico and Asia and in over 200 retail stores in both Canada and the United States. Clothing sales are over $200 million in Canada and $100 million in the U.S.

Although Nygard pays attention to quality manufacture and clothing design, he is pretty confident that his product is already about as good as it is going to get. Satisfied that he can spin cartwheels around American competitors who try to break in from down south, Nygard is looking in new directions to keep business booming. With product design and manufacturing under control, Nygard believes the secret to his success has and will continue to be streamlining the company's channels of distribution.

Over the last ten years, the firm has spent $30 million to automate the entire organization with an IT system. Using a program called Automatic Reorder to Sale (ARTS2), customers type in their orders and trigger a chain reaction of supply that begins with the fabric and component suppliers and ends with the billing department. Along the way, customers are guaran-

teed delivery of what is needed in the amount of time requested. More than half of his retailers are connected to the system with more to come. To encourage the other half to jump on the bandwagon, Nygard covers the cost of the system's required equipment and training for them.

Even so, he isn't content to rest on his $300-million laurels. Ever ambitious to increase the service aspect of his company, he is determined to make shopping at Nygard more convenient than ever. And how does one gain the edge in both service and convenience? Simple — the Internet. In fact, Nygard is banking on the fact that his Web site will actually double company sales. The Web site in question will be mainly a business-to-business site. With the help of a program called Locator, a customer can just walk into any store and get a retailer to log on and track down the exact model, colour, or size of an article of clothing in any Nygard store or any store selling Nygard products. No matter where in the world the garment is, it will be shipped to the customer in under 24 hours.

Although Nygard sees his Web site as a whole new way of doing business, it's a way he doesn't see working too well with his mainly thirtysomething female clientele. At least not right now. This is because his target buyer has been slow to start shopping out in cyberspace. The Nygard woman has been the last to log onto the Net overall, far behind men, young people in general, and twentysomething women in particular. And the fact that Nygard sells fashion, the hardest product to sell on the Net due to buyers' desire to touch, squeeze, and try on the products, has only increased difficulties.

None of these obstacles seem to phase Nygard, however. Confident that no other clothing brand name in Canada enjoys the same trust and loyalty that Nygard does, he is certain that his cyber-time will come.

Source: Adapted from Serena French, "In the company of women," *National Post*, May 4, 2000, p. B1.

a growing number of industrial sectors are using Internet-based agents who create a virtual marketplace for them and buyers.

◆ *Producer → agent → industrial distributor → user.* This channel is similar to the preceding one. It is used when, for some reason, it is not feasible to sell through agents directly to the business user. The unit sale may be too small for direct selling. Or decentralized inventory may be needed to supply users rapidly, in which case the storage services of an industrial distributor are required.

DISTRIBUTION OF SERVICES The intangible nature of services creates special distribution requirements. There are only two common channels for services:[14]

◆ *Producer → consumer.* Because a service is intangible, the production process and/or sales activity often require personal contact between producer and consumer. Thus a direct channel is used. Direct distribution is typical for many professional services, such as health care and legal advice, and personal services, such as haircutting and weight-loss counselling. However, other services, including travel, insurance, and entertainment, may also rely on direct distribution.

◆ *Producer → agent → consumer.* While direct distribution often is necessary for a service to be performed, producer-consumer contact may not be required for distribution activities. Agents frequently assist a services producer with transfer of ownership (the sales task) or related tasks. Many services, notably travel, lodging, advertising media, entertainment, and insurance, are sold through agents. For example, how often have you purchased tickets to a concert, sports event, or theatre production that were labelled TicketMaster (www.ticketmaster.com). This firm is an agent that handles the logistics of selling admission to different venues. They don't know anything about organizing concert tours, directing plays, or running a circus or sports arena — their expertise is for ticket sales and distribution.

Multiple Distribution Channels

Many, perhaps most, producers are not content with only a single distribution channel. Instead, for reasons such as achieving broad market coverage or avoiding total dependence on a single arrangement or entering a foreign market, they employ **multiple distribution channels**. (Similarly, many companies establish multiple supply channels to ensure that they have products when needed.)

dual distribution
The use by a producer of multiple and competing channels of distribution.

Use of multiple channels, sometimes called **dual distribution**, occurs in several distinct situations.[15] A manufacturer or producer is likely to use multiple channels to reach different types of markets when the following pertain:

◆ The same product or service (for example, sporting goods or adventure tour packages) is being marketed to both consumer and business markets.[16]

◆ When unrelated products are being sold (margarine and paint; rubber products and plastics).

Multiple channels are also used to reach different segments within a single national market when:

◆ Size of the buyers varies greatly. An airline may sell directly to travel departments in large corporations but use travel agents with physical outlets and Web-based solutions to reach small businesses and individual consumers.

◆ Geographic concentration differs across parts of the market. A manufacturer of industrial machinery may use its own sales force to sell directly to customers that are located close together, but may employ agents in sparsely populated markets.

A significant trend involves selling the same brand to a single market through channels that compete with each other. Nike shoes (www.nike.com), Guess jeans, Levi's jeans, Maytag appliances, Sony Electronics, Sherwin-Williams paints, and Goodyear tires (www.goodyear.com) are distributed through the manufacturers' own retail stores as well as through wholesalers, independent retailers, and large retail chains. Producers may open their own stores, thereby creating dual distribution, when they are not satisfied with the market coverage provided by existing retail outlets. Or they may establish their own stores primarily as testing grounds for new products and marketing techniques.

Although multiple distribution channels provide benefits to the producer, they can annoy intermediaries. One approach, which is difficult to achieve, is to develop separate pricing and promotion strategies for each different channel.[17]

Home Depot became so concerned with this increasing trend toward using the Internet as a "cyber-intermediary" that it wrote to many of its key suppliers in 1999 advising them that it would view any attempt to sell direct-to-consumer in a very negative way. It implicitly threatened suppliers — such as toolmaker Black & Decker — that it might drop their products from stores if they chose to sell directly through the Web. Levi-Strauss, on the other hand, a pioneer in e-commerce forbade several of its sales-channel partners like J.C. Penney from selling Levi's on their own Web site. Incidentally, Levi-Strauss has since stopped selling directly through the Internet.[18]

Vertical Marketing Systems

Historically, distribution channels stressed the independence of individual channel members. That is, a producer used various intermediaries to achieve its distribution objectives; however, the producer typically was not concerned with intermediaries' needs. Conversely, wholesalers and retailers were more interested in maintaining their freedom than in co-ordinating their activities with those of a producer. These priorities of conventional distribution channels provided an opportunity for a new type of channel.

During the past three decades, the vertical marketing system has become perhaps the dominant form of distribution channel. A **vertical marketing system (VMS)** is a tightly co-ordinated distribution channel designed specifically to improve operating efficiency and marketing effectiveness. A VMS illustrates the concept of function shifting discussed earlier. In a VMS no marketing function is sacred to a particular level or firm in the channel. Instead, each function is performed at the most advantageous position in the channel.

The high degree of co-ordination or control characterizing a VMS is achieved through one of three means: common ownership of successive levels of a channel, contracts between channel members, or the market power of one or more members. Loblaw (www.loblaw.com), for example, is owned by George Weston Inc., which also owns a full range of bakery facilities, an ice cream production facility and a soft drink bottling plant. Future plans involve the creation of a separate online grocery division.[19] As shown in Table 15-1, there are three distinct forms of vertical marketing systems.

vertical marketing system (VMS)
A tightly co-ordinated distribution channel designed to achieve operating efficiencies and marketing effectiveness.

TABLE 15-1	Types of Vertical Marketing Systems	
Type of System	**Control Maintained By**	**Examples**
Corporate	Ownership	Singer (sewing machines), Goodyear (tires), Radio Shack (electronics), Bata (shoes)
Contractual:		
Wholesaler-sponsored voluntary chain	Contract	IDA and Guardian Drugs, IGA stores
Retailer-owned co-operative	Stock ownership by retailers	Canadian Tire stores
Franchise systems:	Contract	
Manufacturer-sponsored retailers		Ford, Chrysler, and other auto dealers
Manufacturer-sponsored wholesalers		Coca-Cola and other soft-drink bottlers
Marketers of services		Wendy's, Speedy Muffler, Harvey's, Holiday Inn, Tilden car rentals
Administered	Economic power	Samsonite luggage, General Electric, Labatt

**corporate vertical
marketing system**
An arrangement under
which a firm at one level
of a distribution channel
owns the firms at the
next level or owns the
entire channel.

In a **corporate vertical marketing system**, a firm at one level of a channel owns the firms at the next level or owns the entire channel. Sherwin-Williams and Goodyear, for example, own retail outlets. Also, a growing number of apparel makers, such as Roots and Ralph Lauren, have opened retail stores to feature their brands of clothing.

Intermediaries may also engage in this type of vertical integration. For example, some grocery chains own food-processing facilities, such as dairies, which supply their stores. And some large retailers, including Sears, own all or part of manufacturing facilities that supply their stores with many products.

**contractual vertical
market system**
An arrangement under
which independent
firms — producers,
wholesalers, and
retailers — operate
under a contract
specifying how they
will try to improve their
distribution efficiency
and effectiveness.

In a **contractual vertical marketing system**, independent producers, wholesalers, and retailers operate under contracts specifying how they will try to improve the effectiveness and efficiency of their distribution. Three kinds of contractual systems have developed: wholesaler-sponsored voluntary chains (for example, IGA grocery stores), retailer-owned co-operatives (Canadian Tire), and franchise systems (Pizza Delight and Midas automotive maintenance and repairs). All will be discussed in Chapter 16.

**administered vertical
marketing system**
A distribution system in
which channel control is
maintained through the
economic power of one
firm in the channel.

An **administered vertical marketing system** co-ordinates distribution activities through the market and/or economic power of one channel member or the shared power of two channel members. This is illustrated by Corning in ovenware, Rolex in watches, and Kraft General Foods in food products. Sometimes a producer's brand equity and market position are strong enough to gain the voluntary co-operation of retailers in matters such as inventory levels, advertising, and store display. However, retailers — especially giant ones such as Loblaw and The Bay — are more likely to dominate channel relationships now than in prior years.

In the distant past, competition in distribution usually involved two different conventional channels. For instance, two Producer → Retailer → Consumer channels tended to compete with each other. More recently, competition pitted a conventional channel against some form of VMS. Thus a traditional Producer → Retailer → Consumer channel battled a contractual VMS for business. Increasingly, the most common competitive battles are between different forms of vertical marketing systems. For example, a corporate system (such as the stores owned by Goodyear) competes with a contractual

*Well-run vertical
marketing systems
have benefited
consumers, operators,
and suppliers.*

system (such as General Tire's franchised dealers). Considering the potential benefits of vertical marketing systems with respect to both marketing effectiveness and operating efficiencies, they should continue to grow in number and importance.

Factors Affecting Choice of Channels

If a firm is customer-oriented, its channels are determined by consumer buying patterns. The nature of the market should be the key factor in management's choice of channels. Other considerations are the product or service being marketed, the intermediaries, and the company itself.

MARKET CONSIDERATIONS A logical starting point is to consider the target market — its needs, structure, and buying behaviour:

◆ *Type of market.* Because ultimate consumers behave differently from business users, they are reached through different distribution channels. Retailers, by definition, serve ultimate consumers, so they are not in channels for business goods.

◆ *Number of potential customers.* A manufacturer with few potential customers (firms or industries) may use its own sales force to sell directly to ultimate consumers or business users. Canadair uses this approach in selling its jet aircraft. For a large number of customers, the manufacturer would likely use intermediaries. Tim Hortons relies on numerous franchisee outlets to reach the large number of consumers buying coffee. A firm using intermediaries does not need as large a sales force as a company selling directly to final consumers.

◆ *Geographic concentration of the market.* When most of a firm's prospective customers are concentrated in a few geographic areas, direct sale is practical. This is the situation in the textile and garment manufacturing industries. When customers are geographically dispersed, direct sale is likely to be impractical due to high travel costs. Sellers may establish sales branches in densely populated markets and use intermediaries in less concentrated markets.

◆ *Order size.* When either order size or total volume of business is large, direct distribution is economical. Thus a food-products manufacturer would sell directly to large grocery chains. The same manufacturer, however, would use wholesalers to reach small grocery stores, whose orders are usually too small to justify direct sale.[20]

PRODUCT CONSIDERATIONS While there are numerous product-related factors to consider, we will highlight three:

◆ *Unit value.* The price attached to each unit of a product affects the amount of funds available for distribution. For example, a company can afford to use its own employee to sell a large aircraft engine part that costs more than $10,000. But it would not make sense for a company salesperson to call on a household or a business firm to sell a $2 ballpoint pen. Consequently, products with low unit value usually are distributed through indirect channels (that is, through one or more levels of intermediaries). There are exceptions, however. For instance, if order size is large because the customer buys many products at the same time from the company, then a direct channel may be economically feasible.

◆ *Perishability.* Some goods, including many agricultural products, physically deteriorate fairly quickly. Other products, such as services, can only be consumed in the presence of the producer. Legal advice, for example, is only available directly from a law firm. As was discussed in Chapter 12, services are perishable due to their intangible nature. Perishable products require direct or very short channels.

◆ *Technical nature.* A business product that is highly technical is often distributed directly to business users. The producer's sales force must provide considerable pre-sale and post-sale service; wholesalers normally cannot do this. Consumer products of a technical nature provide a real distribution challenge for manufacturers. Ordinarily, manufacturers cannot sell the goods directly to the consumer. However, with the development of the Internet, it is easier for products to be distributed directly from the manufacturer with substantial amounts of technical support being provided on the Internet.

INTERMEDIARIES CONSIDERATIONS Here we begin to see that a company may not be able to arrange exactly the channels it desires:

◆ *Services provided by intermediaries.* Each producer should select intermediaries that will provide those marketing services that the producer either is unable to provide or cannot economically perform. Foreign producers seeking to gain market share in Canada will utilize industrial distributors or importers.

◆ *Availability of desired intermediaries.* The intermediaries preferred by a producer may not be available. They may be carrying competitive products and may not want to add another line.

◆ *Producer's and intermediaries policies.* Sometimes manufacturers' choices of channels are limited because their marketing policies are not acceptable to certain types of intermediaries. Some retailers or wholesalers, for example, are interested in carrying a line only if they receive assurance that no competing firms will carry the line in the same territory.

◆ *Channel or intermediary position.* In some cases, an intermediary has achieved such a strong or even dominant position in the market that a manufacturer cannot afford not to distribute through them. For example, Business Depot and Chapters occupy these types of positions.

COMPANY CONSIDERATIONS Before choosing a distribution channel for a product, a company should consider its own situation:

◆ *Desire for channel control.* Some producers establish direct channels because they want to control their product's distribution, even though a direct channel may be more costly than an indirect channel. By controlling the channel, producers can achieve more aggressive promotion and can better control both the freshness of merchandise stocks and their products' and services' retail prices. In mid-1992, IBM (www.ibm.ca) started experimenting with mail-order sales of its personal computers. It has experienced limited success with this move. Dell Computers, however, are extremely successful with direct distribution systems via the Internet and mail order.

◆ *Services provided by seller.* Some producers make decisions about their channels based on the distribution functions desired (and occasionally demanded) by intermediaries. For instance, numerous retail chains will not stock a product unless it is presold through heavy advertising by the producer.

◆ *Ability of management.* The marketing experience and managerial capabilities of a producer influence decisions about which channel to use. Many companies lacking marketing know-how turn the distribution job over to intermediaries.

◆ *Financial resources.* A business with adequate finances can establish its own sales force, grant credit to its customers, and/or warehouse its own products. A financially weak firm uses intermediaries to provide these services.

In a few cases, virtually all factors point to a particular length and type of channel. In most cases, however, the factors send mixed signals. Several factors may point to the desirability of direct channels, others to the use of wholesalers and/or retailers. Or the company may find the channel it wants is unavailable. If a company with an unproven product having low profit potential cannot place its product with intermediaries, it may have no other option but to try to distribute the product directly to its target market.

Determining Intensity of Distribution

intensity of distribution
The number of intermediaries used by a producer at the retailing and wholesaling levels of distribution.

At this point in designing a channel, a firm knows: what role has been assigned to distribution within the marketing mix; whether direct or indirect distribution is better; and which types of intermediaries will be used (assuming indirect distribution is appropriate). Next the company must decide on the **intensity of distribution** — that is, how many intermediaries will be used at the wholesale and retail levels in a particular territory.

There are many possible degrees of intensity. As shown in Figure 15-4, we will consider the three major categories, ranging from intensive to selective to exclusive. Distribution intensity ordinarily is thought to be a single decision. However, if the channel has more than one level of intermediaries (wholesaler and retailer, for example), the appropriate intensity must be selected for each level.

Different degrees of intensity may be appropriate at successive levels of distribution. A manufacturer can often achieve intensive retail coverage with selective, rather than intensive, wholesale distribution. Or selective intensity at the retail level may be gained through exclusive intensity at the wholesale level. Of course, the wholesaling firm(s) will determine which retail outlets actually receive the product. Despite this lack of control, a producer should plan the levels of intensity needed at both the wholesale and retail levels. Making only one decision about distribution intensity is simplistic and can create serious problems.

FIGURE 15-4
The Intensity-of-Distribution Continuum

INTENSIVE   SELECTIVE   EXCLUSIVE

Distribution through multiple, but not all, reasonable outlets in a market

Intensive Distribution

Under **intensive distribution**, a producer sells its product through every available outlet in a market where a consumer might reasonably look for it. Ultimate consumers demand immediate satisfaction from convenience goods and will not defer purchases to find a particular brand. Thus manufacturers of this category of product often use intensive distribution. Retailers often control whether a strategy of intensive distribution actually can be implemented. For example, a new manufacturer of toothpaste or a small producer of potato chips may want distribution in all supermarkets, but these retailers may limit their assortments to four fast-selling brands.

Retailers typically will not pay to advertise a product that is sold by competitors. Therefore, intensive distribution places most of the advertising and promotion burden on the producer.

Selective Distribution

selective distribution
A strategy in which a producer sells its product through multiple, but not all, wholesalers and/or retailers in a market where a consumer might reasonably look for it.

In **selective distribution**, a producer sells its product through multiple, but not all possible, wholesalers and retailers in a market where a consumer might reasonably look for it. Selective distribution is appropriate for consumer shopping goods, such as various types of clothing and appliances, and for business accessory equipment, such as office equipment and handheld tools.

A company may shift to a selective distribution strategy after some experience with intensive distribution. The decision to change usually hinges on the high cost of intensive distribution or the unsatisfactory performance of intermediaries. Certain intermediaries perennially order in small, unprofitable amounts; others may be poor credit risks. Eliminating such marginal intermediaries may reduce the number of outlets but increase a company's sales volume. Many companies have found this to be the case simply because they were able to do a more thorough selling job with a smaller number of accounts.

A firm may move toward more selective distribution to enhance the image of its products, strengthen customer service, and/or improve quality control. For instance, the Italian firm of Guccio Gucci concluded that its brand was on too many leather goods and fashion accessories and that it was carried by too many retailers. Hence, as part of a new marketing strategy, Gucci slashed both its product line and the number of outlets carrying its goods.[21] Such distribution is not desirable for an upscale, "exclusive" brand such as Gucci. Such a line available in so many places diminished the equity of the brand confusing consumers as to what the brand meant. This also causes decreased sales. Distribution can, therefore, be seen to have far-reaching marketing effects beyond simply availability.

Exclusive Distribution

exclusive distribution
A strategy in which a producer agrees to sell its product to only a single wholesaling intermediary and/or retailer in a given market.

Under **exclusive distribution**, the supplier agrees to sell its product only to a single wholesaling intermediary and/or retailer in a given market. At the wholesale level, such an arrangement is normally termed an exclusive distributorship; at the retail level, an exclusive dealership. A manufacturer may prohibit an intermediary that holds an exclusive distributorship or dealership from handling a directly competing product line.

Producers often adopt an exclusive distribution strategy when it is essential that the retailer carry a large inventory. Thus exclusive dealerships are frequently used in marketing consumer specialty products such as expensive suits. This strategy is also desirable when the dealer or distributor must furnish installation and repair service. For this reason, manufacturers of farm machinery and large construction equipment grant exclusive distributorships.

Exclusive distribution helps a manufacturer control the last level of intermediary before the final customer. An intermediary with exclusive rights is usually willing to promote the product aggressively. Why? Interested customers will have to purchase the product from this intermediary because no other outlets in the area carry the same brand. However, a producer suffers if its exclusive intermediaries in various markets do not serve customers well. Essentially a manufacturer has "all its eggs in one basket."

An exclusive dealer or distributor has the opportunity to reap all the benefits of the producer's marketing activities in a particular area. However, under exclusive distribution, an intermediary may become too dependent on the manufacturer. If the manufacturer fails, the intermediary also fails (at least for that product). Another risk is that once sales volume has been built up in a market, the producer may add other dealers or, worse yet, drop all dealers and establish its own sales force.

 ## Conflict and Control in Channels

Distribution occasionally is characterized by goals shared by suppliers and customers and by co-operative actions. But conflicts as well as struggles for control are more typical. To manage distribution channels effectively requires an understanding of both conflict and control, including techniques to (1) decrease conflict, or at least its negative effects, and (2) increase a firm's control within a channel.

Channel conflict exists when one channel member perceives another channel member to be acting in a way that prevents the first member from achieving its distribution objectives. Firms in one channel often compete vigorously with firms in other channels; this represents horizontal conflict. Even within the same channel, firms argue about operating practices and try to gain control over other members' actions; this illustrates vertical conflict.

Horizontal Conflict

Horizontal conflict occurs among firms on the same level of distribution. The cellular telephone field provides an excellent example. Cell phones and services can be purchased at a multitude of outlets — office-supply outlets, department stores, warehouse clubs, consumer-electronics retailers, and telecommunications providers such as B.C. Telus and Bell Canada with their own stores, toll-free lines and Web sites.

Horizontal conflict may occur between:

◆ *Intermediaries of the same type:* Maryvale Home Hardware versus Fred's Friendly Hardware, for example.

◆ *Different types of intermediaries on the same level:* Maryvale Home Hardware versus St. Clair Paint and Wallpaper versus Wal-Mart.

The main source of horizontal conflict is **scrambled merchandising**, in which intermediaries diversify by adding product lines not traditionally carried by their type of business. Supermarkets, for instance, expanded beyond groceries by adding health and beauty aids, small appliances, records, snack bars, and various services. Retailers that originally sold these product lines became irritated both at supermarkets for diversifying and at producers for using multiple distribution channels.

channel conflict
A situation in which one channel member perceives another channel member to be acting in a way that prevents the first member from achieving its distribution objectives.

horizontal conflict
A form of channel conflict occurring between firms on the same level of distribution — between intermediaries of the same type or between different types of intermediaries.

scrambled merchandising
A strategy under which an intermediary diversifies its assortment by adding product lines not traditionally carried by its type of business.

Scrambled merchandising and the resulting horizontal competition may stem from consumers, intermediaries, or producers. Many consumers prefer convenient, one-stop shopping, so stores broaden their assortments to satisfy this desire. As Shoppers Drugstores expands its offerings, it runs into Loblaw's inventory expansion as each begins to carry some of the same product categories and products. Intermediaries constantly strive for higher gross margins and more customer traffic, so they increase the number of lines they carry. Producers seek to expand their market coverage and reduce unit production costs, so they add new outlets. Such diversification intensifies horizontal conflict.

Vertical Conflict

vertical conflict
A form of channel conflict occurring between firms at different levels of the same channel, typically producer versus wholesaler or producer versus retailer.

Perhaps the most severe conflicts in distribution involve firms at different levels of the same channel. **Vertical conflict** typically occurs between producer and wholesaler or producer and retailer.

PRODUCER VERSUS WHOLESALER Tensions occasionally arise between producers and wholesalers. A producer and wholesaler may disagree about aspects of their business relationship. For instance, John Deere has argued with distributors about whether they should sell farm equipment made by other companies or should restrict their efforts to the Deere brand.

Why do conflicts arise? Manufacturers and wholesalers have differing points of view. On the one hand, manufacturers think that wholesalers neither promote products aggressively nor provide sufficient storage services. And wholesalers' services cost too much. On the other hand, wholesalers believe producers either expect too much or do not understand the wholesaler's primary obligation to customers.

Channel conflict typically stems from a manufacturer's attempts to bypass wholesalers and deal directly with retailers or consumers. The presence of the Internet makes this much easier to do. Direct sale occurs because (1) producers are dissatisfied with wholesalers' services or (2) market conditions call for direct sale. Ordinarily battles about direct sale are fought in consumer goods channels. Such conflicts rarely arise in channels for business goods because there already exists a tradition of direct sale to ultimate customers in business markets.

To bypass wholesalers, a producer has two alternatives:

◆ *Sell directly to consumers.* Producers may employ Internet, house-to-house or mail-order catalogue selling. Producers may also establish their own distribution centres in different areas or even their own retail stores in major markets.

◆ *Sell directly to retailers.* Under certain market and product conditions, selling directly to retailers is feasible and advisable. An ideal retail market for this option consists of retailers that buy large quantities of a limited line of products.

Direct distribution — a short channel — is advantageous when the product (1) is subject to physical or fashion perishability, (2) carries a high unit price, (3) is custom-made, or (4) requires installation and technical service. Direct distribution, however, places a financial and managerial burden on the producer. Not only must the manufacturer operate its own sales force and handle physical distribution of its products, but a direct-selling manufacturer also faces competition from its former wholesalers, who no doubt now sell competitive products.

Wholesalers too can improve their competitive position and thereby reduce channel conflict. Their options include:

◆ *Improve internal management.* Many wholesalers have modernized their operations and upgraded the calibre of their management. Functional, single-store warehouses have been built outside congested downtown areas, and mechanized materials-handling equipment has been installed. Computers and specialized software have improved order processing, inventory control, and billing immensely.

◆ *Provide management assistance to retailers.* Wholesalers have realized that improving retailers' operations benefits all parties. Wholesalers help meet certain retailers' needs, such as store layout, merchandise selection, promotion, and inventory control.

◆ *Form voluntary chains.* In a voluntary chain (discussed in Chapter 16), a wholesaler enters into a contract with a group of retailers, agreeing to furnish them with management services and volume buying power. In turn, retailers promise to buy all, or almost all, of their merchandise from the wholesaler. IDA and Guardian Drugstores and IGA Supermarkets are examples of this approach.

◆ *Develop private brands.* Some large wholesalers have successfully established their own brands. A voluntary chain of retailers provides a built-in market for the wholesaler's brand.

slotting allowance
The fee that retailers demand from manufacturers to place manufacturers' products on store shelves.

Well-known brands present their own face as well as being represented in other outlets.

PRODUCER VERSUS RETAILER Another struggle for channel control takes place between manufacturers and retailers. Conflict can arise over terms or conditions of the relationship between any two parties. Or producers may compete with retailers by selling direct via the Internet or catalogue or through producer-owned stores. A number of apparel makers — including Ralph Lauren, Levi-Strauss, and Liz Clairborne — have opened retail outlets. In doing so, they have annoyed department stores and specialty retailers that also carry their brands.

Producer and retailer may also disagree about terms of sale or conditions of the relationship between themselves. Large retail outlets continually demand lower prices as well as more service from suppliers. Some retailers demand a so-called **slotting allowance** to place a manufacturer's product on store shelves. This is most evident in the grocery-products field. In some cases, companies with new products are required to pay a fee of $100

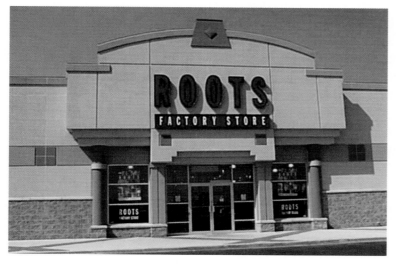

to over $1,000 per store for each version of the product. Or payment may be in the form of free products. Of course, not all manufacturers are paying all of these fees. And some small producers cannot afford them. Manufacturers criticize slotting allowances, claiming they stifle the introduction of new products, particularly those developed by small companies. On the other hand, retailers vigorously defend slotting allowances. Supermarkets contend they must find a way to recoup the costs of reviewing the flood of new products, stocking some of them, and removing failures.

Producers and retailers both have methods to gain more control. Manufacturers can:

◆ *Build strong consumer brand loyalty.* Creative and aggressive promotion is a key in creating such loyalty.

◆ *Establish one or more forms of a vertical marketing system.*

◆ *Refuse to sell to uncooperative retailers.* This tactic has to be defensible from a legal standpoint.

Effective marketing weapons are also available to retailers. They can:

◆ *Develop store loyalty among consumers.* Skilful advertising and strong store brands are means of creating loyal customers.

◆ *Improve computerized information systems.* Information is power. Knowing what sells and how fast it sells is useful in negotiating with suppliers.

◆ *Form a retailer co-operative.* In this form of vertical marketing system, a group of retailers (usually fairly small ones) band together to establish and operate a wholesale warehouse. Their primary intent is to gain lower merchandise costs through volume buying power.[22]

Who Controls Channels?

channel control
The ability to influence the behaviour of other channel members.

channel power
The ability to influence or determine the behaviour of another channel member.

Every firm would like to regulate the behaviour of the other companies in its distribution channel. When a channel member is able to do this, it has **channel control**. In many situations, including distribution channels, power is a prerequisite for control. **Channel power** is the ability to influence or determine the behaviour of another channel member. There are various sources of power in the context of channels. They include: *expertise* (for example, possessing vital technical knowledge about the product), *rewards* (providing financial benefits to co-operative channel members), and *sanctions* (removing uncooperative members from the channel).

Traditionally, manufacturers have been viewed as controlling channels — that is, making the decisions regarding types and number of outlets, participation of individual intermediaries, and business practices to be followed by a channel. But this is a one-sided, outdated point of view. In many lines of trade, power has shifted to the big-box store brands and the category killer retailers because of the volume of sales they control. Other strong retailers have gained much control because of the loyalty of their patrons.

Intermediaries often have considerable freedom to establish their own channels. Certainly the names Safeway, Loblaw, and Sears Canada mean more to consumers than the names of most brands sold in these stores. Large retailers are challenging producers for channel control, just as many manufacturers seized control from wholesalers years ago. Even small retailers can be influential in local markets, because their prestige may be greater than their suppliers' prestige.

Manufacturers contend they should assume the leader's role in a channel because they create the new products and need greater sales volume to benefit from economics of scale. Conversely, retailers also stake a claim for leadership, because they are closest to final customers and, as a result, are best able to know customers' wants and to design and oversee channels to satisfy them. Various factors have contributed to retailers' growing ability to control channels. For instance, many retailers have implemented electronic scanning devices, which gives them access to more accurate, timely information about sales trends of individual products than producers have.[23]

Marketing at Work 15-2

The Sometimes Pain of Working With Chapters

First it was the mom & pop grocery stores that closed down because of the mega Loblaw. Then it was the little corner hardware stores that couldn't keep up with the super-sized Canadian Tires. It was perhaps only a matter of time before the little independent bookstores — you know the ones where goateed poets sat on piles of books reading obscure limited edition tomes penned by brilliant but undiscovered authors — started going belly-up in the wake of the new whale on the block.

Chapters is to bookstores what Loblaw is to supermarkets. With a few comfortable sofas, plush chairs, and a cappuccino bar to boot. And its control of all aspects of Canada's book industry is getting bigger and bigger by the minute. Currently, Toronto-based Chapters sells about one-quarter of all books bought by Canadian consumers. This makes it the biggest client for most of Canada's publishers and distributors. The retail book giant recently extended its control even further over the market when it paid out a lot of money to launch its Chapters Online Inc. Internet book selling service. Then it spent over $50 million and bought 82 percent of Pegasus Wholesale Inc., the largest book distributor in Canada.

These vertical and horizontal moves by such a major competitor has created strong reverberations up and down the book chain. And it seems that everybody involved in books, from the authors who pen them to the readers who peruse them, is being affected, for better or for worse.

If you're a big name along the lines of Atwood or Ondaatje, it's good to have your bestsellers prominently featured and promoted in large numbers at a Chapters megastore where they are sure to sell. However, if you're an unknown budding Balzac whose first post-Post modern novel was published in a small edition by a tiny press, this may not happen to you. Smaller names and new authors worry about getting attention and access to the reading public.

In the same way, if you're a big publisher with big names, a big list and a big budget, you'll do just fine. But you do have

to watch out: there is always the problem of what to do with all those unsold returns sent back from your biggest book seller. However, if you're a medium sized or small publisher and engage in publishing new names and topics; those that are risky, avant-garde, alternative, or underground, then it can be a very difficult world. Some small publishers find that 40 percent of their sales go to Chapters and this makes them feel very vulnerable to fast returns. There have been complaints about slow payment as well. With an industry standard of payment for orders of within 30 to 60 days, some publishers have complained that Chapters can take from 90 to 120 days to pay for orders. Some feel that large orders, fast returns, and slow payment make them very vulnerable to having difficult terms and conditions imposed on them. The new balance of power is being questioned.

Then there are the distributors who feel that Chapters' takeover of Pegasus is nothing short of monopolistic in terms of creating unfair competition. There are also the small, and not so small, independent bookstores forced to file for bankruptcy because they just can't compete with the megastore and its large array of titles, promotional prices, free parking, and convenient hours and locations. Gone are such names as Duthie's and Bollum's of Vancouver, Lichtman's and Classic Books of Toronto.

What all of these book industry players fear is the rising power of one retail giant who may increasingly control what gets written, commissioned, published, ordered, distributed, and sold. It is clear the competitive rules of the game have changed and all those involved in the trade are learning new ways of operating. But then there are the people who actually buy the books. And these consumers seem to like things just the way they are. After all, they are the ones snapping up record numbers of books at Chapters and other similar "big-box" stores. And drinking a whole lot more cappuccino in the bargain.

Source: Adapted, in part, from Ann Gibbon, "The Catch-22 of Working with Chapters," *The Globe and Mail*, April 24, 2000 and Charles Gordon, "The big-box conundrum," *MacLean's*, March 13, 2000.

A Channel Viewed as a Partnership

Sometimes, members see a channel as a fragmented collection of independent, competing firms. Suppliers and intermediaries should not think of channels as something they "command and control," but rather as partnerships aimed at satisfying end users' needs.[24] Thus co-ordination is needed throughout a distribution channel.

One possible reason for channel problems is that not enough producers have a person in the organization that is responsible for co-ordinating the firm's channel activities.

While most producers have an advertising manager and a sales manager, not enough have a channel manager.

Legal Considerations in Channel Management

In various ways, organizations may try to exercise control over the distribution of their product as it moves through the channel. Generally speaking, any attempts to control distribution may be subject to legal constraints. In this section, we shall discuss briefly four control methods that are frequently considered by suppliers (usually manufacturers):

◆ **Dealer selection.** The manufacturer wants to select its customers and refuses to sell to some intermediaries.

◆ **Exclusive dealing.** The manufacturer prohibits its dealers from carrying products of the manufacturer's competitors.

◆ **Tying contracts.** The manufacturer sells a product to an intermediary only under the condition that this intermediary also buys another (possibly unwanted) product from the manufacturer. Or, at least, the intermediary agrees not to buy the other product from any other supplier.

◆ **Exclusive (closed) territories.** The manufacturer requires each intermediary to sell only to customers who are located within the intermediary's assigned territory.

None of these arrangements is automatically illegal. The Competition Act deals with such practices in Part VII, in which certain dealings between manufacturers and intermediaries are deemed illegal if they restrict competition.

Dealer Selection

Under section 75 of the Competition Act, it is illegal for a manufacturer or supplier to refuse to supply an intermediary with the supplier's products. Under certain circumstances, however, a supplier may refuse to deal with retailers or other intermediaries if they are unwilling or unable to meet the usual trade terms of the supplier. In other words, for example, if the intermediary engaged in selling the supplier's product as a loss leader, or failed to provide adequate post purchase service, or in some other way failed to support the product, the supplier could refuse to deal with that company. Generally, it would be illegal to refuse to supply an intermediary if the company carried a competitor's product or resisted a tying contract.

Exclusive Dealing

Exclusive dealing contracts have been declared unlawful if the manufacturer's sales volume is a substantial part of the total volume in a market or if the volume done by the exclusive dealers is a significant percentage of the total business in an area. That is, the law is violated when the competitors of a manufacturer are essentially shut out from a substantial part of the market because of this manufacturer's exclusive dealing contract.

By inference, it is clear that exclusive dealing is not illegal in all situations. In fact, in cases where the seller is just getting started in a market or where its share of the total market is so small as to be negligible, its negotiation of exclusive dealing agreements may not only improve its competitive position but also strengthen competition in general.

Ordinarily there is no question of legality when a manufacturer agrees to sell to only one retailer or wholesaler in a given territory, provided there are no limitations on competitive products. Also, a manufacturer can sell to dealers who do not carry competitors' products, as long as this is a voluntary decision on the part of the franchise holder.

Tying Contracts

A supplier is likely to push for a tying agreement when:

◆ There are shortages of a desired product, and the supplier also wants to push products that are less in demand.

◆ The supplier grants a franchise (as in fast-food services) and wants the franchisee to purchase all necessary supplies and equipment from this supplier.

◆ The supplier has exclusive dealers or distributors (in appliances, for example) and wants them to carry a full line of the supplier's products.

With regard to tying contracts, apparently a dealer can be required to carry a manufacturer's full line as long as this does not impede competition in the market. The arrangement may be questionable, however, if a supplier forces a dealer or a distributor to take slow-moving, less attractive items in order to acquire the really desirable products.

Exclusive Territories

Traditionally, the strategy of exclusive (or closed) sales territories has been used by manufacturers in assigning market areas to retailing or wholesaling intermediaries. However, closed sales territories can create area monopolies, lessen competition, and restrict trade among intermediaries who carry the same brand. Exceptions are generally provided when a company is small or is a new entrant to the market, in order to facilitate market entry.

These limitations on closed sales territories are likely to foster vertical marketing systems, where the manufacturer retains ownership of the product until it reaches the final buyer. That is, the manufacturer could either (1) own the retail or wholesale outlet or (2) consign products on an agency basis to the intermediaries but retain ownership. In either of these situations, exclusive territories are quite legal.

Distribution to Foreign Markets

In deciding to market in a foreign country, management must select an appropriate channel and organizational relationship. There is a range of channels and organizational forms for operating in foreign markets (see Table 15-2), representing successively greater levels of market involvement and intensity of distribution. All of the considerations discussed concerning channels in the Canadian market apply when a firm wishes to distribute to foreign markets or within foreign markets if they undertake production in those countries. While the basic considerations for distribution to foreign markets are the same as those for the Canadian market, the details of these markets are different. They exist in a different context, and these differences range from those that are market structure related such as economic, governmental, legal, and social systems to such specifics as the trade practices of the intermediaries and the channels that are available. Because of these differences, we will include in our discussion of distribution for and in foreign markets matters of producer investments in foreign production or sales facilities as a means of gaining effective distribution.

TABLE 15-2	The Range of Channels and Structures for Distributing in International Markets					
Exporting directly or through import-export intermediaries	Company sales branches	Licensing foreign producers	Contract manufacturing by foreign producers	Joint ventures and strategic alliances	Wholly owned subsidiaries	Multinational corporation

Low involvement abroad ◄─────────────────────────────────────► High involvement abroad

Exporting

export merchant
A middleman operating in a manufacturer's country that buys goods and exports them.

The simplest way of distributing goods to foreign markets is by **exporting**, either directly to foreign importers or through import-export intermediaries. In international markets, just as in domestic markets, there are both merchant and agent wholesalers.

An **export merchant** is an intermediary operating in the manufacturer's country that buys goods and exports them. Very little risk or investment is involved. Also, minimal time and effort are required on the part of the exporting producer. However, the exporter has little or no control over merchant wholesalers.

export agent
A middleman that operates either in a manufacturer's country or in the destination country and that negotiates the sale of the product in another country and may provide additional services such as arranging for international financing, shipping, and insurance on behalf of the manufacturer.

An **export agent** may be located in either the manufacturer's country or in the destination country. The agent negotiates the sale of the product and may provide additional services, such as arranging for international financing, shipping, and insurance on behalf of the manufacturer. Greater risk is involved, because the manufacturer retains title to the goods. Because they typically deal with a number of manufacturers, both these types of middlemen generally are not aggressive marketers, nor do they generate a large sales volume.

To counteract some of these deficiencies, management can export through its own **company sales branches** in foreign markets. Operating a sales branch enables a company to (1) promote its products more aggressively, (2) develop its foreign markets more effectively, and (3) control its sales effort more completely.

company sales branch
A sales facility that carries a stock of the product being sold.

Because it is the easiest way to distribute to international markets, exporting is popular with small firms.

Contracting

contracting
A legal relationship that allows a firm to enter a foreign market indirectly, quickly establish a market presence, and experience a limited amount of risk.

Contracting involves a legal relationship that allows a firm to enter a foreign market indirectly, quickly establish a market presence, and experience a limited amount of risk. One form of contracting is a licensing arrangement. **Licensing** means granting to another producer — for a fee or royalty payment — the right to use one's production process, patents, trademarks, or other assets. For example, in Japan, the Suntory brewery is licensed by Anheuser-Busch to produce Budweiser beer, while in England, Budweiser is brewed under licence by the Watney Brewing Company. La Senza of Montreal has licensed its successful lingerie brand for use in Saudia Arabia (see "Marketing at Work" File 15-3).

licensing
A business arrangement whereby one firm sells to another firm (for a fee or royalty) the right to use the first company's brand, patents, or manufacturing processes.

Franchising has allowed Canadian service retailers, such as Pizza Pizza, Swiss Chalet, and Uniglobe Travel, to expand overseas. **Franchising** combines a proven operating formula with local knowledge and entrepreneurial initiative.

In **contract manufacturing**, a marketer, such as The Bay, contracts with a foreign producer to supply products that are then marketed in the producer's country. For example, rather than importing certain tools and hardware for its planned stores in China, The Bay contracts with local manufacturers to supply certain items.

Contracting offers companies flexibility with minimal investment. It allows a producer to enter a market that might otherwise be closed to it because of exchange restrictions,

Marketing at Work 15-3

Canadian Lingerie Heads East

You would think that when a retailer that specializes in racy ladies' lingerie is looking to market its sultry wares internationally, it would look somewhere in the direction of Brazil, where "dental floss" bikinis are as common as a tan. Not so for Montreal-based Suzy Shier Ltd. When the Canadian retailer decided to license its successful La Senza intimate apparel brand, it looked in quite another direction altogether. And what it saw was the conservative Muslim nations of the Middle East.

The first country to (very discretely) reap the lacy benefits of La Senza's presence was the ultra-conservative kingdom of Saudi Arabia. Although in public, Saudi women are required to always wear a hijab, which covers up most of their faces and all of their bodies, what goes on beneath the veil is up to the lady in question and her husband. As such, fine and fashionable lingerie has become a highly liberating, not to mention titillating, form of expression. And clearly many Saudi women want to express themselves in such a manner. As a result, there are now eighteen La Senza stores successfully operating in Saudi Arabia.

Although the stores, run under an agreement with Saudi-based F.A. Al-Hokair Ltd., are modelled after the 211 La Senza stores in Canada, there are a few regional differences. One is that there are no fitting rooms. Another — which partially explains the first — is that all the sales clerks are male. So while a woman might be able to consult a clerk about fabric, colour, and price, she is on her own when it comes down to determining how the lingerie actually fits.

Suzy's Saudi success story has led the retailer to branch out even further in the Gulf States. A licensing agreement with United Arab Emirates-based Liwa Trading Co. will see the opening of fifteen new La Senza boutiques in the United Arab Emirates, Bahrain, Kuwait, Oman and Quatar over the next three years.

Interestingly, the radically different Arab culture is probably one of the biggest reasons for La Senza's success. The differences were of such a magnitude that they forced the company to really study the market and link up with local experts who provided invaluable guidance in terms of the market, its structure, and the consumer behaviour for the lingerie. It was also important to know about the legal, political, social and religious aspects of the country and about the nature of local business practices. An earlier foray into seemingly similar Britain lost so much money that La Senza was forced out of business in the U.K. — an interesting lesson in what happens when a firm enters a foreign market which it believes is not very foreign. And just to underscore the point, Marks and Spencer, who up until recently was Britain's foremost retailer, finally closed all its Canadian retail stores after trying, for more than ten years, and failing, to make a go of it in Canada. It seems they didn't understand the nature of competition here. It was also clear that Canadians just did not appreciate the British M&S format and product lines in large enough numbers.

Source: Adapted, in part, from Zena Olijnyk, "La Senza Lingerie heads east," *National Post*, April 25, 2000, pp. C1, C8.

---

import quotas, or prohibitive tariffs. At the same time, by licensing, producers may be creating future channel conflicts by building future competitors. A licensee may learn all it can from the producer and then proceed independently when the licensing agreement expires.

Direct Investment

direct investment
The actions of a company to build or acquire its own production facilities in a foreign country.

Another alternative is **direct investment**, in which a company can build or acquire its own production facilities in a foreign country as well as establish a distribution system. The organizational structure can be a joint venture or a wholly owned foreign subsidiary.

A **joint venture** is a partnership arrangement in which the foreign operation is owned in part by the Canadian company and in part by a foreign company. A Canadian manufacturer of children's clothing with a well-accepted brand name operates a joint venture with a foreign producer of children's apparel. This arrangement provides a network of manufacturing, sales, and distribution operations in the market.

joint venture
A partnership arrangement in which a foreign operation is owned in part by a Canadian company and in part by a foreign company.

When the controlling interest (more than 50 percent) is owned by foreign nationals, the Canadian firm has no real control over production, marketing and distribution activities. However, a joint venture may be the only structure, other than licensing, through which a firm is legally permitted to enter some foreign markets.

Joint ventures are frequently undertaken on a country-by-country basis. For example, Canadian generic drug giant Apotex formed a joint venture with a large French pharmaceutical company, Expanscience Group, to market a variety of generic drugs manufactured in Canada. The Beck Electric Division of Noma Industries Ltd. has agreements with different joint-venture partners to sell wire harnesses for automobile assembly by auto makers in India, China, and Eastern Europe.[25]

Some major firms have taken the notion of a joint venture to a higher level and formed strategic alliances. A **strategic alliance** is a formal, long-term agreement between firms to combine their capabilities and resources to accomplish global objectives. For example, Air Canada and a growing number of airlines (United Airlines, Thai Airways, Varig of Brazil, Scandinavian Airways, and Lufthansa) have formed the Star Alliance. Through it, members have integrated their flight schedules, ticketing, and catering. The arrangement gives Air Canada access to cities around the world that it does not directly service and allows its partners to offer their customers convenient routes to Canada as well as some South American and Asian destinations that the partners share or which Air Canada does not serve.

Wholly owned subsidiaries in foreign markets are commonly used by Canadian companies operating in the United States and by firms that have evolved to an advanced stage of international business. With a wholly owned foreign subsidiary, a company has maximum control over its production, marketing, and distribution operations. Quebecor Printing Inc. of Montreal purchased Arcata Corp. in the United States to move from being North America's seventh-largest book manufacturer to being the second largest. Bata Shoes operates in sixty-one countries and runs five thousand stores through reasonably autonomous local subsidiaries.[26] A wholly owned subsidiary, however, requires a substantial investment of money, labour, and managerial attention. John Labatt Ltd. spent $210 million to acquire 168 pubs in the United Kingdom so that Labatt U.K. could expand its market share.

The Changing Face of Distribution

Largely as a result of advancing technology and the changing balance of power within distribution channels, we are witnessing a change in the nature of distribution and in the means by which products and services reach the end consumer. It should be obvious from the examples in this chapter that many of the traditional channels by which products and services moved from their producers to consumers are under threat and may be expected to undergo considerable modification and change in the years to come.

As we have seen earlier in this chapter, shopping from home is expected to be a major growth area in retailing in the future as systems become more sophisticated and as catalogue companies and other direct retailers become even better at serving their customers. We will see much more use of the Internet and a host of personal wireless appliances that can be used to connect with retailers, as well as others, from anywhere. As many consumers tire of the retail shopping-mall experience and have less time to indulge in it, more will turn to electronic shopping.

Distribution involves the movement of more than just the physical product. There are many "costs" involved in the administrative function of distribution. Further, as already mentioned when discussing the value created by intermediaries and previously when discussing the marketing function in general, there is also the need for information transfer and communication between buyers and sellers for transactions to ever occur. While the Internet seems to come up in every topic discussed in this text, this only

strategic alliance
A formal, long-term agreement between firms to combine their capabilities and resources to accomplish global objectives.

wholly owned subsidiary
A business arrangement in foreign markets in which a company owns the foreign operation in order to gain maximum control over its marketing program and production operations.

contract manufacturing
An arrangement in which a firm in one country arranges for a firm in another country to produce the product in the foreign country.

franchising
A type of contractual vertical marketing system that involves a continuing relationship in which a franchiser (the parent company) provides the right to use a trademark plus various management assistance in opening and operating a business in return for financial considerations from a franchisee (the owner of the individual business unit).

underscores the impact that it has had on the fundamental functioning of various marketing functions. As such, while very few products can actually, physically be distributed through this medium (some entertainment exceptions excluded of course) most firms have found ways to aid distribution through the Internet if only for its "promotional" value. There are real costs, however, to be saved through this medium. Transaction costs have three parts, which individually or together can be quite prohibitive. These are:

◆ *Search costs.* Finding what you need takes time, resources, and out of pocket costs. Determining whether to trust a supplier adds more costs.

◆ *Contracting costs.* Every exchange requires a separate price negotiation and contract. Such processes can be expensive arrange and formalize.

◆ *Co-ordination costs.* These are the costs of co-ordinating resources and processes.

More and more of these searching and acquisition activities are taking place in cyber-space markets with examples of dramatic saving in the online market appearing daily as manufacturers in all industries post their requirements on the Web and watch prices plummet. Ford and General Motors have developed parts-supply marketplaces for their requirements while three of the top five computer manufacturers have announced plans to join with nine suppliers to create a similar marketplace for that industry.[27]

As mentioned some services and products can be delivered to the consumer through this medium making it a true cyber-intermediary of sorts. Financial services have found their way onto the Web allowing many transactions, including trading, to be conducted directly by the consumer — not otherwise possible. In the first quarter of 2000, online investing activity increased by nearly 70 percent to top US$1 trillion.[28] Online gambling is even available.

Magazines and periodicals can be received via the Internet, as well as the ever-popular pornography. Books can be downloaded to portable reading devices. Even Hollywood has taken a bow to the Internet with the introduction of the first online feature in May 2000. From SightSound.com Inc. (www.sightsound.com), the feature, Quantum Project, took four hours to download and 37 minutes to watch. Starring John Cleese and Stephen Dorff, the feature cost $3.95 to download and could be played on Microsoft's Media Player.[29]

Summary

The role of distribution is getting a product to its target market. A distribution channel carries out this assignment with intermediaries performing some tasks. An intermediary is a business firm that renders services directly related to the purchase and/or sale of a product as it flows from producer to consumer. Intermediaries can be eliminated from a channel, but someone still has to carry out their essential functions.

A distribution channel is the set of people and firms involved in the flow of title to a product as it moves from producer to ultimate consumer or business user. A channel includes producer, final customer, and any intermediaries that participate in the process.

Designing a channel of distribution for a product occurs through a sequence of four decisions: (1) delineating the role of distribution within the marketing mix; (2) selecting the proper type of distribution channel; (3) determining the appropriate intensity of distribution; and (4) choosing specific channel members. A variety of channels are used to distribute consumer goods, business goods, and services. Firms often employ multiple channels to achieve broad market coverage, although this strategy can alienate some intermediaries. Because of deficiencies in conventional channels, vertical marketing systems have become a major force in distribution. There are three forms of vertical marketing systems: corporate, contractual, and administered.

Numerous factors need to be considered prior to selecting a distribution channel for a product. The primary consideration is the nature of the target market; other considerations relate to the product, the intermediaries, and the company itself.

Distribution intensity refers to the number of intermediaries used at the wholesale and retail levels in a particular territory. It ranges from intensive to selective to exclusive.

Firms distributing goods and services sometimes clash. There are two types of conflict: horizontal (between firms at the same level of distribution) and vertical (between firms at different levels of the same channel). Scrambled merchandising is a prime cause of horizontal conflict. Vertical conflict typically pits producer against wholesaler or retailer. Manufacturers' attempts to bypass intermediaries are a prime cause of vertical conflict. Channel members frequently strive for some control over one another. Depending on the circumstances, either producers or intermediaries can achieve the dominant position in a channel. All parties may be served best by viewing channels as a system requiring co-ordination or distribution activities. Moreover, attempts to control distribution may be subject to legal constraints.

Devising distribution channels for international markets requires an examination of the same considerations as are necessary for distribution in Canadian markets. Gaining access to some international markets requires that companies establish arrangements with local businesses that would not be needed in the Canadian market.

Key Terms and Concepts

Intermediary 460	Corporate vertical marketing system 472	Scrambled merchandising 477	Export agent 484
Merchant intermediary 461	Contractual vertical marketing system 472	Vertical conflict 478	Company sales branches 484
Agent 461		Slotting allowance 479	Contracting 484
Distribution channel 462	Administered vertical marketing system 472	Channel control 480	Licensing 484
Direct distribution 466	Intensive distribution 476	Channel power 480	Franchising 484
Indirect distribution 466	Selective distribution 476	Dealer selection 482	Contract manufacturing 484
Multiple distribution channels 470	Exclusive distribution 476	Exclusive dealing 482	Direct investment 485
Dual distribution 470	Channel conflict 477	Tying contracts 482	Joint venture 485
Vertical marketing system (VMS) 471	Horizontal conflict 477	Exclusive territory 482	Strategic alliance 486
		Exporting 484	Wholly owned subsidiaries 486
		Export merchant 484	

Questions and Problems

1. "You can eliminate intermediaries, but you cannot eliminate their functions." Discuss this statement.

2. Which of the following institutions are intermediaries? Explain.

   a. Avon salesperson.

   b. Electrical wholesaler.

   c. Real estate broker.

   d. Railway.

   e. Auctioneer.

   f. Advertising agency.

   g. Grocery store.

   h. Stockbroker.

   i. Bank.

   j. Radio station.

3. Which of the channels illustrated in Figure 15-3 is most apt to be used for each of the following products? Defend your choice in each case.

   a. Fire insurance.

   b. Single-family residences.

    c.   Farm hay balers.

    d.   Washing machines.

    e.   Hair spray.

    f.   An ocean cruise.

4. "The great majority of business sales are made directly from producer to business user." Explain the reason for this first in relation to the nature of the market, and then in relation to the product.

5. Explain, using examples, the differences among the three major types of vertical systems — corporate, administered, contractual. Which is the best kind?

6. A small manufacturer of fishing lures is faced with the problem of selecting its channel of distribution. What reasonable alternatives does it have? Consider particularly the nature of its product and the nature of its market.

7. Is a policy of intensive distribution consistent with consumer buying habits for convenience goods? For shopping goods? Is intensive distribution normally used in the marketing of any type of business goods?

8. From a producer's viewpoint, what are the competitive advantages of exclusive distribution?

9. What are the drawbacks to exclusive distribution, from a retailer's point of view? To what extent are these alleviated if the retailer controls the channel for the particular brand?

10. A manufacturer of a well-known brand of men's clothing has been selling directly to one dealer in a small Canadian city for many years. For some time the market has been large enough to support two retailers very profitably. Yet the present dealer objects strongly when the manufacturer suggests adding another outlet. What alternatives does the manufacturer have in this situation? What course of action would you recommend?

11. "Manufacturers should always strive to select the lowest-cost channel of distribution." Do you agree? Should they always try to use the intermediaries with the lowest operating costs? Why or why not?

12. What role is the Internet playing in changing distribution networks? Provide examples to illustrate the changes that are occurring.

13. Why are full-service wholesalers relatively unimportant in the marketing of women's high-fashion wearing apparel, furniture, and large electrical equipment?

14. If a company uses foreign intermediaries, it must usually be prepared to supply them with financial, technical, and promotional help. Considering this, why isn't it the practice to simply bypass them and deal directly with the ultimate foreign buyers?

15. Of the alternatives discussed for foreign distribution, which option poses the greatest risks for the expanding company? The least risk? The greatest potential for profit and growth?

Hands-On Marketing

1. Arrange an interview with either the owner or a top-level manager of a small manufacturing firm. Inquire about (a) what distribution channel(s) the company uses for its primary product, (b) what factors were the greatest influences in arriving at the channel(s), and (c) whether the company would prefer some other channel(s).

2. Visit with either a supermarket manager or a buyer for a supermarket chain to learn more about slotting allowances and any other charges they levy on manufacturers. Inquire whether such charges have led to channel conflict and how the supermarket chain is handling this type of situation. Also ask whether any grocery-products manufacturers refuse to pay slotting allowances and whether the chain ever waives the fees.

Chapter Sixteen

Wholesaling and Distribution: Markets and Institutions

This chapter will provide you with insight into how wholesale markets, wholesaling institutions, and physical-distribution activities relate to marketing. After studying this chapter, you should have an understanding of:

◆ The nature and economic justification of wholesaling and the role of wholesaling intermediaries.

◆ Differences across three categories of wholesaling intermediaries.

◆ Major types of merchant wholesalers, agent wholesalers, and manufacturers' sales facilities, and the services they render.

◆ What physical distribution is.

◆ The systems approach to physical distribution.

◆ How physical distribution is used to strengthen a marketing program and reduce marketing costs.

◆ The five subsystems within a physical distribution system: inventory location and warehousing; materials handling; inventory control; order processing; and transportation.

◆ Trends in wholesaling and physical distribution.

New Tricks for an Old Firm

Every time there is a new piece of information technology, someone somewhere says, "This will finally eliminate the middleman." It was believed that the Internet would put wholesalers out of business. Some have already gone and more will yet leave this line of trade. But David Weber, president of 140-year-old Weber Supply Inc., which his family has owned since 1923, says, "We have that threat all the time; there is still a cost to bring that product to market."

Weber Supply (www.webersupply.com) of Kitchener, Ontario, operates two divisions: 1) Building Supply which is a wholesaler and distributor of hardware for eight hundred home building centres, and 2) Industrial Supply which stocks over thirty thousand items for industrial maintenance, repair, and operations for manufacturing, mining, and extraction businesses. The firm has ten branches in Ontario and one in each of Manitoba and Saskatchewan, staffed with 175 employees and generating annual sales of over $100 million. From the Kitchener head office, the company is completely integrated by computer so that customer-service representatives can instantly access, from any warehouse location, a complete range of customer and supplier information. A new and unique radio frequency based warehouse management system provides a speedy highly efficient digitally based system for receiving orders, scheduling and picking them, maintaining perpetual inventory and providing instructions for either holding or shipping purchases.

David Ticoll, president of the Alliance for Converging Technologies in Toronto (www.actnet.com), believes that the Internet will cut the cost of distribution to the point where many retailers will simply deal directly with manufacturers — bypassing intermediaries. Weber, however, set up its own Web site in what can be called a pre-emptive strike. In building the site, David Weber aimed to protect his core business. He believes that he has a head start in the sense that he has a large number of small-business customers who are the least likely to bypass the intermediary.

With the launching of the Internet service, Weber now has a much wider variety of ordering systems to offer customers than in the past. These range from his direct-sales force to telephone, fax, custom EDI (electronic data interchange) for large accounts, as well as a system that uses specialized software and modems connected to buyers' computers. All the electronic systems

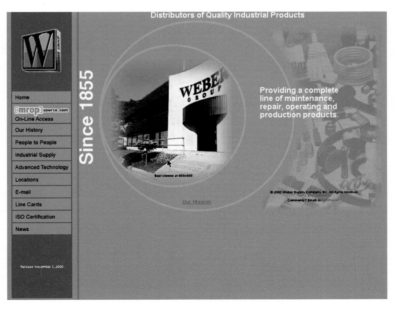

are designed to increase the productivity of Weber Supply's customers, the field sales force, as well as the warehouse order-picking, processing and shipping, and delivery systems.

The EDI systems, with private lines and specialized hardware and software, are expensive to operate, while the modem-PC systems are less expensive but sometimes are also less reliable. With the Web site, buyers tap into the Weber computerized inventory system and place orders from the 30,000-item catalogue. Customers with EDI systems are informed immediately about out-of-stock items; PC-based systems get the information when they access the system. Weber has now intro-

duced a portable order entry system using sophisticated hand held scanning devices that read UPC codes from customers' products or shelves and electronically places orders on the buyer's computer.

The Web-based and other systems are user friendly, have good technical support detail, and the electronic catalogue contains product photos. One convert from fax orders says that he can do his ordering in seconds. While never having used the Internet before, he was able to log on and navigate easily. He believes he will save many hours of ordering time. Mr. Weber is pleased with how things are working; he is pleased to be one of the first wholesalers to make this technological leap and

he will continue to try to keep ahead of his competition. He believes that his group of companies is a technological leader in Canada and is fast becoming one of the lowest cost distributors in North America. And at the same time, Weber continues with the "old stuff" that comprises personal service and makes customer relationships. This means a one-on-one attitude towards customers, assistance with merchandising concepts and techniques, providing store planners for home depots, arranging co-op advertising and giving technology training seminars for buyers who want and need them.[1]

Although consumers shop regularly at the stores of retailing intermediaries, they rarely see, or hear of, wholesalers such as Weber Supply. Also, beyond noticing company names on transportation carriers such as trucks and trains, consumers have little exposure to the way in which products actually are moved from the point of production to the point of final sale and consumption. As a result, wholesaling and physical distribution are often misunderstood — and sometimes criticized — by consumers. Nevertheless, wholesalers can be essential members of a distribution channel, and physical distribution is an integral aspect of marketing most goods. Therefore, it's critical that you understand the nature and managerial issues of both wholesaling and physical distribution.

Nature and Importance of Wholesaling

Wholesaling and retailing enable goods that are produced to be purchased for consumption. We already know that retailing involves sales to ultimate consumers for their personal use. Now we'll see that wholesaling has a different role in the marketing system.

Wholesaling and Wholesaling Intermediaries

wholesaling
All activities directly related to the sale of goods and services to parties for resale, use in producing other goods and services, or operating an organization.

Wholesaling (or *wholesale trade*) is the sale, and all activities directly related to the sale, of goods and services to businesses and other organizations for (1) resale, (2) use in producing other goods or services, or (3) operating an organization. When a business firm sells shirts and blouses to a clothing store that intends to resell them to final consumers, this is wholesaling. When a mill sells flour to a large bakery for making bread and pastries, this is also a wholesale transaction. And when a firm sells uniforms to a business or another organization for its employees to wear in carrying out their duties, this is wholesaling as well.

Sales made by one producer to another are wholesale transactions, and the selling producer is engaged in wholesaling. Similarly, a discount house is involved in wholesaling when it sells software, laser printers, calculators, and office supplies to a business firm. Thus wholesaling includes sales by any firm to any customer except an ultimate consumer who is buying for personal, non-business use. From this perspective, all sales are either wholesale or retail transactions — distinguished only by the purchaser's intended use of the good or service.

Most every retailer, at some point or to some degree, is involved in wholesale transactions — even the local bagel man. Markham, Ontario-based, The Great Canadian Bagel Company (www.greatcanadianbagel.com) has in recent years looked for ways to expand operations beyond additional franchising and the development of new international markets such as England and Russia (where its known as Canadski Bagel). They have also developed wholesaling operations to supply local supermarkets with fresh product including discount retailer Price Club/Costco. So is the bagel man a retailer or a wholesaler by trade?[2]

In this chapter we will focus on firms engaged *primarily* in wholesaling. This type of company is called a **wholesaling middleman** or **intermediary**. We will not be concerned with retailers involved in occasional wholesale transactions. And we will not focus on manufacturers and farmers because they are engaged primarily in production rather than wholesaling. Keep in mind, then, that wholesaling is a business activity that can be carried out by various types of firms, whereas a wholesaling intermediary is a business institution that concentrates on wholesaling.

Economic Justification for Wholesaling

Most manufacturing firms are small and specialized. They don't have the capital to maintain a sales force to contact the many retailers or final users that are (or could be) their customers. Even for manufacturers with sufficient capital, some of their products or lines generate such a small volume of sales that it would not be cost-effective to establish a sales force to sell them.

At the other end of the distribution channel, most retailers and final users buy in small quantities and have only a limited knowledge of the market and sources of supply. Thus there is often a gap between the seller (producer) and the buyer (retailer or final user).

A wholesaling intermediary can fill this gap by providing services of value to manufacturers and/or retailers. For example, a wholesaler can pool the orders of many retailers and/or final users, thereby creating a market for the small producer. At the same time, a wholesaling intermediary selects various items from among many alternatives to form its product mix, thereby acting as a buying service for small retailers and final users. Essentially, as we will see at various points in this chapter, the activities of a wholesaling intermediary create time, place, and/or possession or ownership value.

Let's look at two situations, one very specific and the other very broad and significant. A manufacturer of modular office dividers, the Pleion Company (www.pleion.com), decided to replace most of its own outside salesforce with independent dealers — a traditional type of channel change. The switch allowed Pleion to expand into new regions more quickly and halved the company's marketing expenses. While the company does maintain a comprehensive Internet site to showcase products and features, they are not e-retailers. The Pleion Company does not sell its products over the Web, but will respond to sales queries and the site provides the location of the nearest Pleion dealer.

From a broader perspective, there were numerous predictions that the rise of electronic commerce would harm distributors and even eliminate a large number of them. Currently, many wholesaling firms are thriving by moving quickly to adopt new technology as did Weber Supplies in the chapter opening illustration. Others are thriving by providing needed inventory and services to many new online retailers who have a retailing concept and a Web site where they can make a sale. They, however, need wholesalers to actually fill and ship ordered goods since many e-retailers have neither the product, the storage capabilities, or the order fulfillment capacity.[3]

From a broad point of view, wholesaling brings to the total distribution system the economies of skill, scale, and transactions:

◆ Wholesaling *skills* are efficiently concentrated in a relatively few hands. This saves the duplication of effort that would occur if many producers had to perform wholesaling functions themselves. For example, one large warehouse belonging to a wholesaler in Winnipeg or Moncton saves many manufacturers from each having to build and manage their own warehouses at each location to provide speedy service to customers in these and other areas.

◆ Economies of *scale* result from the specialization of wholesaling intermediaries performing functions that might otherwise require several small departments run by producing firms. Wholesalers typically can perform wholesaling functions more efficiently than can most manufacturers.

◆ *Transaction* economies come into play when wholesaling or retailing intermediaries are introduced between producers and their customers. Let's assume that four manufacturers want to sell to six retailers. As shown in Figure 16-1, *without* an intermediary, there are 24 transactions; *with* one wholesaling intermediary, the number of transactions is cut to ten. Four transactions occur when all the producers sell to the intermediary, and another six occur when the intermediary sells to all the retailers.

FIGURE 16-1
The Economy of
Transactions in
Wholesaling

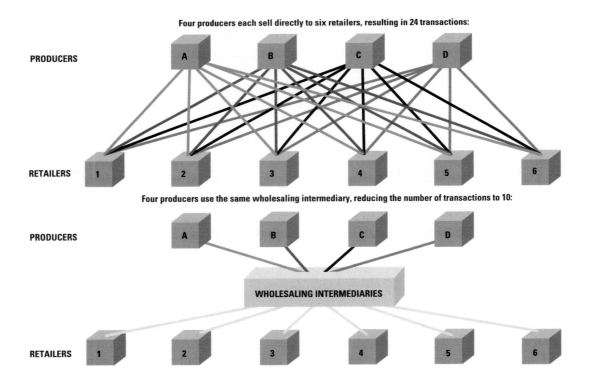

Four producers each sell directly to six retailers, resulting in 24 transactions:

PRODUCERS   A   B   C   D

RETAILERS   1   2   3   4   5   6

Four producers use the same wholesaling intermediary, reducing the number of transactions to 10:

PRODUCERS   A   B   C   D

WHOLESALING INTERMEDIARIES

RETAILERS   1   2   3   4   5   6

Size of the Wholesale Market

In 1996, the latest year for which data are available, there were more than fifty-four thousand wholesaling locations in Canada, with total annual operating revenue of over $307 billion. As is the case in retailing, the sales generated by wholesaling establishments have increased dramatically in recent years. This has been especially the case for wholesalers of computers, packaged software, and other electronic machinery suggesting that businesses are seeking further productivity gains by increasing their investment in new technologies. Part of this increase is accounted for by increases in prices that have occurred during the past ten years or so, but even if sales were expressed in constant dollars, we would still see a substantial increase.

 Profile of Wholesaling Intermediaries

A producer or retailer considering indirect distribution and the use of wholesaling intermediaries must know what alternatives are available, whom these intermediaries serve, and how they operate. Having this information increases the likelihood of establishing effective distribution arrangements.[4]

Four Major Categories

Classifying wholesaling intermediaries is difficult because they vary greatly in (1) products they carry, (2) markets to which they sell, and (3) methods of operation. To minimize the confusion, we will use the classification scheme shown in Figure 16-2. There, all wholesaling intermediaries are grouped into only four broad categories: wholesale merchants, manufacturers' sales branches and offices, agents and brokers, and primary-product dealers. These four groups are the classifications used by Statistics Canada, which is the major source of quantitative data covering wholesaling institutions and markets. Later in this chapter we shall discuss merchant wholesalers, agents and brokers, and primary-products dealers in more detail.

- **Merchant wholesalers** are firms we usually refer to as wholesalers, jobbers, or industrial distributors. They typically are independently owned, and they take title to the merchandise they handle. They form the largest single segment of wholesaling firms when measured either by sales or by number of establishments. Statistics Canada reports that merchant wholesalers, along with manufacturers' sales branches and primary-product dealers discussed below, account for almost 85 percent of total wholesale trade.[5]

- **Manufacturers' sales facilities and offices** are owned and operated by manufacturers, but they are physically separated from the manufacturing plants. The distinction between a sales branch and sales office is that a branch carries merchandise stock and an office does not.

- **Agents and brokers** do *not* take title to the merchandise they handle, but they do actively negotiate the purchase or sale of products for their principals. The main types of agents are manufacturers' agents, commission merchants (in the marketing of agricultural products), and brokers. As a group, agents and brokers represent less than 20 percent of total wholesale trade.

- **Primary product dealers** are principally engaged in buying for resale primary products such as grain, livestock, furs, fish, fruit, and vegetables from the primary pro-

---

merchant wholesaler
An independently owned firm that primarily engages in wholesaling and ordinarily takes title to the products being distributed. Same as *wholesaler*.

manufacturer's sales facility
An establishment that primarily engages in wholesaling and is owned and operated by a manufacturer but is physically separated from manufacturing plants.

manufacturer's sales office
A manufacturer's sales facility that does not carry a stock of the product being sold.

manufacturers' agent
An independent agent wholesaler that sells part or all of a manufacturer's product mix in an assigned geographic territory.

broker
An independent agent wholesaler that brings buyers and sellers together and provides market information to either party.

FIGURE 16-2
Types of
Wholesaling
Institutions

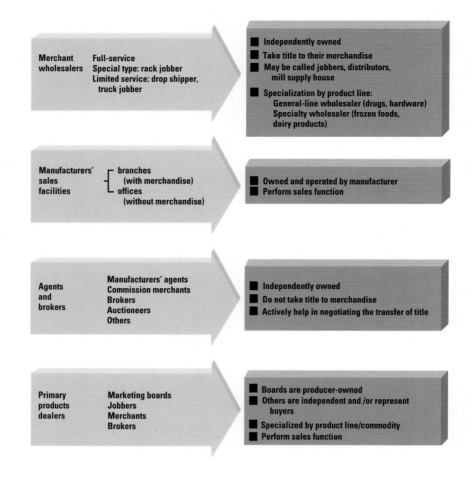

ducers of these products. On occasion, they will act as agents of the producer. Co-operatives that market the primary products of their members are also included in this category.

Some other subcategories used in classifying the wholesaling business are reflected in Figure 16-2. For example, wholesaling intermediaries may be grouped by:

Ownership of products — merchant wholesalers versus agents.

Ownership of establishments — manufacturers' sales branches versus independent merchants and agents.

Range of services offered — full-service wholesalers versus limited-service firms.

Depth and breadth of the line carried — general-line wholesalers (drugs, hardware) versus specialty firms (frozen foods, dairy products).

Wholesalers' Customers

One might expect that total retail sales would be considerably higher than total whole-sale trade, because the retail price of a given product is higher than the wholesale price. Also, many products sold at retail never pass through a wholesaler's establishment and so are excluded from total wholesale sales.

Total sales figures belie this particular line of reasoning (see Table 16-1). In each year, the volume of wholesale trade is considerably higher than total retail sales.

FIGURE 16-3
Wholesale Trade
Customers

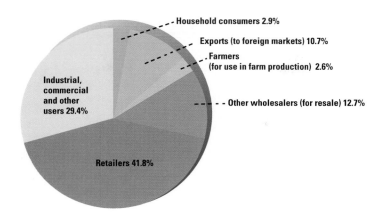

Most merchant wholesalers' sales are made to customers other than retailers. That is, large quantities of business and industrial products are now sold through merchant wholesalers. Moreover, sales by the other types of wholesalers show this same pattern. Thus, overall, sales to retailers account for much less than total sales by merchant wholesalers.

Another trend that has become obvious in recent years is the increase in the percentage of consumer goods sold directly to retailers by manufacturers. Yet, in spite of this increased bypassing of the wholesaler, wholesaling is on the increase — an indication of the value of wholesaling to the business world.

Operating Expenses and Profits of Wholesaling Intermediaries

The average total operating expenses for wholesaling combined has been estimated at about 16.7 percent of *wholesale* sales. It has also been estimated that operating expenses of retailers average about 34 percent of *retail* sales (omitting bars and restaurants, which do some processing of products).

Profit margins for the wholesaling industry are approximately equivalent to profit margins for retailing. In 1996, gross profit margins (before taxes) for the wholesale trade equalled approximately 5.4 percent; corresponding profit margins for the retail trade equalled 5.05 percent.[6]

 *Merchant Wholesalers*

Merchant wholesalers take title to the products they handle, and they account for the largest segment of wholesale trade.

TABLE 16-1	Total Wholesale and Retail Trade, Selected Years	
Year	Wholesale Trade ($millions)	Retail Trade ($millions)
1986	188,236	152,880
1988	227,173	180,545
1990	255,081	192,555
1992	237,468	185,049
1994	282,438	208,856
1996	307,043	217,353

Source: Statistics Canada, "Wholesale Trade — Historical Series, 1986–1996" and "Retail Trade — Historical Series, Canada, 1986-1996," *Wholesaling and Retailing in Canada*, 1996. The explanation for this situation may be found in an analysis of the customers of wholesalers (see Figure 16–3).

TABLE 16-2	**Full-Service Wholesalers' Typical Services to Customers and Producers**
Service	**Description**
Buying	Act as purchasing agent for customers.
Creating assortments	Buy from many suppliers to develop an inventory matching needs of customers.
Subdividing	Buy in large quantities (such as a truckload) and then resell in smaller quantities (such as a dozen).
Selling	Provide a sales force for producers to reach small retailers and other businesses, at a lower cost than producers would incur by having their own sales forces.
Transportation	Make quick, frequent deliveries to customers, reducing customers' risks and investment in inventory.
Warehousing	Store products in facilities that are nearer customers' locations than are manufacturing plants.
Financing	Grant credit to customers, reducing their capital requirements. Aid producers by ordering and paying for products before purchase by customers.
Risk taking	Reduce a producer's risk by taking title to products.
Market information	Supply information to customers about new products and producers' special offers and to producer-suppliers about customers' needs and competitors' activities.
Management	Assist customers, especially small retailers, in areas such as inventory control, allocation assistance of shelf space, and financial management.

Full-Service Wholesalers

full-service wholesaler
An independent merchant wholesaler that normally performs a full range of wholesaling functions.

An independent merchant wholesaler that performs a full range of wholesaling functions (from creating assortments to warehousing) is a **full-service wholesaler**. This type of intermediary may handle consumer and/or business products that may be manufactured or otherwise (such as grown or extracted), and imported, exported, or made and sold domestically.

Full-service suppliers comprise the majority of merchant wholesalers. They have held their own in competitive struggles with other forms of indirect distribution, including manufacturers' sales facilities and agent wholesalers. Actually, there has been an increase in full-service wholesalers' share of wholesale trade. But this trend may be a bit misleading. While full-service wholesalers have made gains in some industries, they have lost ground in others.

Individual manufacturers in some industries have begun to distribute their products directly, eliminating some or all of the wholesalers in their channels. For example, Concord, Ontario-based Janes Family Foods (www.janesfamilyfoods.com), a major frozen-foods manufacturer that produces over twenty-five fish, chicken, cheese, and vegetable products, is now marketing directly to big restaurant chains, which follows its trend of selling directly to most major food retailers in Canada.[7]

Full-service wholesalers survive and prosper by providing services needed by both their customers and producers. These services are summarized in Table 16-2. Large wholesalers use their clout to obtain good prices from producers. They also apply the latest technology to develop computerized inventory systems for their customers — recall Weber Supplies. By helping customers keep their inventories lean, a full-service intermediary can garner added loyalty.

Other Merchant Wholesalers

truck jobber
A limited-function merchant wholesaler that carries a selected line of perishable products and delivers them by truck to retail stores.

We should also consider two types of merchant wholesalers with distinctive operations:

◆ **Truck jobbers**, also called *truck distributors*, carry a selected line of perishable products and deliver them by truck to retail stores. Truck jobbers are common in the food-products field. Each jobber carries a nationally advertised brand of fast-moving, perishable or semi-perishable goods, such as candies, dairy products, potato chips, and tobacco products. Truck jobbers furnish fresh products so frequently that retailers can buy perishable goods in small amounts to minimize the risk of loss. But truck jobbers are saddled with high operating costs, caused primarily by the small order size and inefficient use of their trucks (for example, only during parts of the day). Fresh food producers such as bakeries must ensure fresh, daily delivery of their products often over a wide geographic area. Calise & Sons Bakery supply Italian rolls and bread products daily across three New England states from their Providence, R.I. headquarters. This requires over forty trucks that must make deliveries between 10 P.M. and 5 A.M. to bakery outlets, restaurants, and food stores throughout the region.

drop shipper
A limited-function merchant wholesaler that does not physically handle the product.

◆ **Drop shippers**, also known as *desk jobbers*, sell merchandise for delivery directly *from the producer to the customer*. Drop shippers do not physically handle the product. They are common in only several product categories, including coal, lumber, and building materials, that are typically sold in very large quantities and that have high freight costs in relation to their unit value. An interesting number of new dot.com retailers and have all the appearances of drop shippers except they are in consumer products and do not have the volume of traditional drop shippers.

 Agent Wholesalers

As distinguished from merchant wholesalers, agent wholesalers (1) do *not* take title to products and (2) typically perform fewer services. Agent wholesalers receive a commission intended to cover their expenses and to provide a profit. Commission rates vary greatly, ranging from about 3 to 10 percent, depending mainly on the nature of the product and the services performed.

Agent wholesalers have lost one-third of their wholesale trade since the late 1960s. In the case of agricultural products, agents are being replaced by merchant wholesalers or by direct sales to food-processing companies and grocery stores. Similarly, for manufactured goods, agents are being replaced by merchant wholesalers or direct distribution. As shown in Table 16-3, product characteristics and market conditions determine whether a distribution channel should include agent or merchant wholesalers.

TABLE 16-3	Factors Suggesting Which Type of Wholesaling Middleman Should Be Used in a Channel	
	Favouring Agent	**Favouring Merchant**
Nature of product	Nonstandard, perhaps made to order	Standard
Technicality of product	Simple	Complex
Product's gross margin	Small	Relatively large
Number of customers	Few	Many
Concentration of customers	Concentrated geographically and in a few industries	Dispersed geographically and in many industries
Frequency of ordering	Relatively infrequently	Frequently
Time between order and receipt of shipment	Customer satisfied with relatively long lead time	Customer requires/desires shorter lead time

Source: Adapted from Donald M. Jackson and Michael F. d'Amico, "Products and Markets Served by Distributors and Agents," *Industrial Marketing Management*, February 1989, pp. 27–33.

On the basis of sales volume, the most significant types of agent wholesalers are manufacturers' agents, brokers, and commission merchants. These three types as well as several special types of agent wholesalers are described next.

Manufacturers' Agents

An independent agent wholesaler that sells part or all of a manufacturer's product mix in an assigned geographic territory is a **manufacturers' agent**, or *manufacturers' representative*. Agents are not employees of the manufacturers; they are independent business firms. Still, they have little or no control over prices and terms of sale, which are established by the manufacturers they represent.

Because a manufacturers' agent sells in a limited territory, each producer uses multiple agents for full coverage of its markets. Manufacturers' reps have continuing, year-round relationships with the companies (often called principals) they represent. Each agent usually serves several non-competing manufacturers of related products. For example, a manufacturers' agent may specialize in toys and carry an assortment of non-competing lines in board games, dolls, learning materials, and outdoor play equipment.

When a manufacturer finds it is not feasible to have its own sales force, a manufacturers' agent is often practical. An agent can be cost-effective because its major expenses (travel and lodging) are spread over a number of product lines. Also, producers pay agents a commission, which is a percentage of sales volume, so agents are paid only for what they actually sell.

Manufacturers' agents are used extensively in distributing many types of consumer and business goods, ranging from sporting goods to heating and air-conditioning vents and ductwork. Their main service to manufacturers is selling. Because a manufacturers' agent does not carry nearly as many lines as a full-service wholesaler, an agent can be expected to provide knowledgeable, aggressive selling — an important advantage.

Manufacturers' agents are most helpful to:

◆ A small firm that has a limited number of products and no sales force.

◆ A business that wants to add a new and possibly unrelated line to its existing product mix, but whose present sales force either is not experienced in the new line or cannot reach the new market. In this situation, a company's own sales force and its agents may cover the same geographic market, but for different product lines.

◆ A firm that wants to enter a new market that is not yet sufficiently developed to warrant the use of its own sales force.

There are limitations to what manufacturers' agents do. Agents do not carry an inventory of merchandise, usually do not install machinery and equipment, and typically are not equipped to furnish customers with extensive technical advice or repair service.

Depending on how difficult the product is to sell and whether it is stocked by the agent, operating expenses of manufacturers' agents can vary greatly. However, they average about 7 percent of sales. Some reps operate on a commission as low as 2 percent of net sales; others earn as much as 20 percent; the average is about 5.5 percent.

Brokers

Brokers ordinarily neither physically handle products being distributed nor work on a continuing basis with sellers or buyers. Instead, a **broker** is an independent agent wholesaler that brings buyers and sellers together and provides market information to either

commission merchant
An independent agent wholesaler, used primarily in the marketing of agricultural products, that may physically handle the seller's products in central markets and has authority regarding prices and terms of sale.

auction company
An agent wholesaler that provides (1) auctioneers who do the selling and (2) physical facilities for displaying the sellers' products.

The number of auction sites continues to grow with eBay and FreeMarkets being pioneers in their early development. One is popular with the young and the other is a B2B site.

party. The broker furnishes information about many topics, including prices, products, and general market conditions. In recent years, manufacturers' agents and brokers have become more similar with respect to attributes and services.

Most brokers work for sellers, although some represent buyers. Brokers have no authority to set prices. They simply negotiate a sale and leave it up to the seller to accept or reject the buyer's offer.

Brokers are used in selling real estate and securities, but they are most prevalent in the food field. For example, a seafood broker handles the output from a salmon cannery, which operates only about three months each year. The canner employs a broker to find buyers among retail stores, wholesalers, and other outlets. When the entire output has been sold, the canner-broker relationship is discontinued — although it may be renewed the next year.

Brokers provide limited services and, as a result, incur fairly low expenses, about 3 percent of sales. Likewise, they receive relatively small commissions — normally less than 5 percent.

Other Agent Wholesalers

Four additional types of agent wholesalers account for smaller shares of wholesale trade than manufacturers' reps and brokers. Nevertheless, they provide valuable services for certain products and in specific markets. These intermediaries are:

◆ **Commission merchants**, common in the marketing of many agricultural products, set prices and terms of sale, sell the product, and perhaps physically handle it. (Despite the word *merchant*, a commission merchant is an *agent* wholesaler that normally does not take title to the products being handled and sold.)

◆ **Auction companies** help assembled buyers and sellers complete their transactions. They provide (1) auctioneers who do the selling and (2) physical facilities for displaying the sellers' products. Although they made up only about 1 percent of total wholesale trade, auction companies are extremely important in the wholesaling of used cars and certain agricultural products (such as tobacco, livestock, and fruit). Auction companies in wholesale trade are now appearing on the Internet (see "Marketing at Work" File 16-1). Internet-based auction companies offer

Marketing at Work 16-1

The New Auctions: Reach and Speed in Space

Here's a roundabout way of doing business: Down in Brazil, an orchid cultivator harvests his highly delicate and perishable blossoms. They get transported to an airport, onto a plane, off a plane, and to an auction house — halfway across the world in Holland. At the Dutch auction house (where the majority of the world's flowers assemble to get auctioned off), the orchids are bid on and bought by a Chilean wholesaler. A little older and worse for wear, the same orchids now go back to the airport, onto a plane, off a plane, and to a wholesaler — halfway across the world to Chile (which, coincidentally, happens to be pretty close to Brazil).

Does this method of selling flowers seem costly, inefficient, time-consuming, and not so great for the petally products' well-being? Of course. But you might be surprised to discover that 80 percent of the world's flower business is conducted this way. Even if it means that up to 30 percent of what is being sold rots, wilts, or ups and dies on the long and winding road that leads from supplier to consumer.

Then there is the way the other 20 percent of the world's flowers are sold: over the Net. In cyber auction houses such as that developed by Toronto-based software firm e-Auction Global Trading Inc., perishable products such as flowers, fruit, and fish are getting a new lease on life. This is because electronic auction systems allow the supply chain to become more efficient. By streamlining industry processes in which time-to-market is key, losses are fewer, profits are higher, fish and flowers are fresher.

It is thus unsurprising that business-to-businesses (B2B) electronic auction sites have been mushrooming. e-Auction, for example, began life several years ago with electronic livestock auctions. However, when the mad-cow scare in Europe sent meat eaters scurrying, the fledgling firm looked to other perishable goods. In 1999, it bought Belgium-based Schelfhout Computer Systemen N.V., a provider of electronic auction hardware and software that boasted a customer base of over 150 auction houses. This acquisition allowed e-Auction to create three Internet auction portals: one for fish, one for flowers, and a third for fruits and vegetables. The fruits and vegetables portal alone runs around thirty regular online auctions. Although most are still run out of Europe, participation is global.

The advantages are endless. A canning firm, for example, can reap the benefits of a Web site that auctions off raw tin as well as the equipment that processes it. And it doesn't matter if the canning firm in question is in Moncton or Mozambique. Internet auctions allow buyers or sellers from all over the world to join in the bidding. Geography is no object. For once, your presence is not required. Other advantages include less market fragmentation, fewer middlemen in the supply chain, and less surplus inventory and spoilage. This in turn means sellers can sell more stuff, more quickly, while buyers get better selection and lower prices. And to think that "e-auctions" are just one feature of "eMarketplaces" — areas on the Internet in which businesses can share information, exchange goods and services, and procure contracts.

So if e-auctions are such a wonderful way of doing business, why aren't more industries logging on? The truth is that in their pre-adolescent form, e-auctions are somewhat gangly and awkward. Major limitations are the absence of related services ranging from insurance and foreign exchange to transportation and lines of credit. The fact that none of these essential services are offered in an all-in-one convenient package makes e-auctions a sometimes time-consuming and expensive alternative to traditional wholesaling.

Growing pains aside, however, electronic auctions have made a difference for both the Brazilian orchid cultivator and the Chilean wholesaler. These days, two weeks before snipping his orchids, the cultivator lets the auction-house know how many flowers bidders can expect. By the time they have actually been harvested, the wholesaler will have already made a successful online bid and business will have been done. The minute the orchids are cut, they will be shipped directly from the supplier in Brazil to the seller in Chile. Nobody will have to go anywhere near the Netherlands. And chances are the flowers will smell sweeter too.

Source: Adapted from Tyler Hamilton. "Net auctions catch on," *The Globe and Mail*, April 27, 2000, p. T1.

cybermarkets in which sellers offer products for sale and a Web site at which all types of consumers and organizations search for bargains, rare products, or the best prices on industrial goods and services. According to one estimate there are now over fifteen hundred of these auction sites including eBay (www.ebay.com), Onsale (www.onsale.com), and FreeMarkets (www.freemarkets.com).[8]

◆ **Selling agents** essentially substitute for a marketing department by marketing a manufacturer's entire output. Although selling agents transact only about 1 percent of wholesale trade, they play a key role in the distribution of textile products and coal and, to a lesser extent, apparel, food, lumber, and metal products.

◆ **Import-export agents** bring together sellers and buyers in different countries. Export agents work in the country in which the product is made; import agents are based in the country where the product will be sold.

Nature and Importance of Physical Distribution

selling agent
A type of independent intermediary that essentially takes the place of a manufacturer's marketing department, marketing the manufacturer's entire output and often influencing the design and/or pricing of the products.

import–export agent
An agent wholesaler that arranges for distribution of goods in a foreign country.

physical distribution
Activities involved in the flow of products as they move physically from producer to consumer or industrial user.

After a company establishes its channels of distribution, it must arrange for the physical distribution of its products through these channels. **Physical distribution**, which we use synonymously with *logistics*, consists of all the activities concerned with moving the right amount of the right products to the right place at the right time. In its full scope, physical distribution for manufacturers includes the flow of *raw materials* from their sources of supply to the production line and the movement of *finished goods* from the end of the production line to the final users' locations. Intermediaries manage the flows of goods *onto* their shelves as well as *from* their shelves to customers' homes, stores, or other places of business.

The activities making up physical distribution are:

◆ Inventory location and warehousing.

◆ Materials handling.

◆ Inventory control.

◆ Order processing.

◆ Transportation.

A decision regarding any one of these activities affects all the others. Location of a warehouse influences the selection of transportation methods and carriers; the choice of a carrier influences the optimum size of shipments.

Increasing Attention to Physical Distribution

Through the years, management has made substantial progress in reducing production costs. Reductions have also been achieved in other costs of marketing. Physical distribution may be the last marketing area with substantial opportunities for cost cutting. And the potential savings are great. For certain products, such as furniture and building materials, the largest operating expenses are related to physical distribution. For other products, as much as one-half the wholesale cost is incurred in transportation and warehousing. For some businesses engaged in distribution, profits are small, so any savings are appreciated. A supermarket, for instance, may earn a net profit of 1 percent on sales. Thus every $1 a supermarket saves in physical distribution costs has the same effect on profit as a $100 increase in sales!

Effective physical distribution also can be the basis by which a firm gains and sustains a strong differential advantage. On-time delivery, which requires effective physical distribution, can provide a competitive edge. To accomplish this efficiency for their customers, many companies involved in distributing goods have streamlined their operations in recent years. PBB

PBB provides all the services that are needed along the supply chain.

(www.pbb.com) has three major distribution centres in Vancouver, Toronto, and Montreal. They offer specific services at every point along the supply chain. Customers receive software that permits them to dial into PBB's system and view orders being shipped, see which jobs have been completed and which are still open, and check a part number to see how much is in the warehouse. The company provides EDI and global logistics systems through their e-global logistics™ network (www.e-globallogistics.com) as well as corporate audit and travel services.[9]

A business faces a problem (or perhaps it's an opportunity) when it has a warehouse full of goods in Edmonton but unsatisfied customers in Calgary. Marks Work Warehouse (www.marks.ca) has a problem if, in the middle of January, there is too much thermal underwear in balmy British Columbia while their stores have run out in icy Saskatchewan. Snug (www.snugind.com) has a problem when shelves in Toronto have none of their baggy pants, sparkly vinyl shoulder bags, and horizontal corduroy pants while in Halifax this inventory sits in a warehouse. These examples point up the importance of location in marketing, especially with respect to merchandise. That is, the appropriate assortment of products must be in the right place at the right time to maximize the opportunity for profitable sales. That's what physical distribution can help achieve.[10]

Since deregulation, transportation firms have been able to decide which rates (prices) and levels of service would best satisfy their target markets. For example, Challenger Motor Freight (www.challengerfreight.com) of Cambridge, Ontario, with 450 trucks operating in Canada and the United States, promises on-time deliveries and works hard to keep its promise — as the company's motto attests, "On time, every time, no excuses." Toward this end, Challenger has equipped its trucks with satellite-tracking devices that allow the company to monitor their progress and to communicate with its drivers. Customers can go to the company's Web site and can track the progress of their goods. From another perspective, companies that ship goods shop around for rates and service levels that best meet their needs. Some transportation firms, Challenger Motor freight included, provide potential customers with the convenience of obtaining estimates or quotes through the company Web site.

Systems Approach to Physical Distribution

We have occasionally alluded to marketing as a *total system* of business action rather than a fragmented series of operations. Nowhere is this clearer than in physical distribution. But it has not always been this way. Traditionally, physical distribution activities were fragmented.

In many firms, physical distribution is still uncoordinated. Managerial responsibility for it is delegated to various units that often have conflicting, perhaps opposite, goals. The production department, for instance, is interested primarily in long production runs to minimize unit-manufacturing costs, even though the result may be high inventory costs. In contrast, the finance department wants a minimum of funds to be tied up in inventories. At the same time, the sales department wants to have a wide assortment of products available at locations near customers. Of course, there's always the temptation to select carriers with low shipping rates, even though this may mean longer time in transit.

Uncoordinated conditions like these make it impossible to achieve a flow of products that satisfies the firm's goals. To alleviate this problem, firms are establishing separate

Marketing at Work 16-2

Better Links for Supply Chain Management

It was B2B as usual when six of the world's largest airlines recently locked wings to create an e-commerce company that would connect them to their suppliers through a unique Internet portal. Instead of using phones and faxes, Air France, American Airlines Inc., British Airways PLC, Continental Airlines Inc., Delta Air Lines Inc., and United Airlines Inc. will be logging-on to make their combined US$32 billion purchases of everything from fuel and parts to maintenance.

If everything goes according to plan, this business-to-business decision will make doing business a much more efficient and collaborative process. It will also significantly reduce the airlines' transaction, processing, and inventory costs. It is estimated that companies that succeed in implementing online supply chains can save between 5 and 25 percent of their supply chain costs. Supply chain costs typically amount to 10 percent of total costs. For a company that spends $100 million a year, this could mean cutting out unnecessary transportation and warehousing expenditures and saving between US$500,000 to $2.5 million.

B2B e-commerce isn't just about money though. It's also about efficiency. Taking care of cyber business means getting quotes on products and services, placing and receiving orders, scheduling deliveries, doing inventory, billing, even payroll over the Net. It is estimated that companies that move their operations online can increase the percentage of orders fulfilled as promised from 80–90 percent up to 99 percent. Bringing every link in the supply chain together into one clickable reality represents nothing less than a revolution.

With benefits like these, everybody is hopping on the cutting-edge B2B bandwagon. Aside from the obvious high-tech Silicon Valley-type candidates, big industrial dinosaurs — ranging from car czars General Motors Corp., Ford Motor Co., and DaimlerChrysler AG (all of whom recently got together to form an e-commerce site that should significantly cut their US$240 billion annual supply purchasing costs) to defense and aerospace giants Boeing Co., Raytheon Co., Lockheed Martin Corp., and BAE Systems PLC (whose Web-based bazaar for aerospace goods and services will link them to 37,000 business suppliers) — have been lumbering onto the Web at surprising speed for such supposedly large, unwieldy corporate creatures.

With the numbers at stake, it is little wonder B2B e-commerce is set to leave B2C (business-to-consumer) commerce in the dust. After all, we're not just talking a few CDs from HMV Canada's online store or a few books from Chapters.com. According to Toronto-based marketing research and consulting firm International Data Corp. (Canada) Ltd., in Canada alone, B2B transactions are set to leap from $9.6 billion in 1999 to $129 billion by 2004. Nothing in the offline world quite compares. Toronto-based Celestica, maker of computers and telecommunications equipment with expected revenues of $10 billion in 2001, has moved nearly all of its communications with customers and suppliers onto the Net. Some other Canadian-based operations that have done the same include Nortel Networks, IBM, Sisco Systems, Dell, and HMV.

Source: Adapted from Simon Tuck, "Size counts in the B2B stampede to the Internet," *The Globe and Mail.* p. T8, April 27, 2000; Simon Tuck, "The supply chain gang," *The Globe and Mail*, p. T6, April 27, 2000; and Dawn Walton, "Net B2B soaring to lofty heights," *The Globe and Mail.* p. B10, April 28, 2000.

departments responsible for all logistics activities. Even when this occurs in large firms, physical distribution is usually separated from the marketing department. This separation causes problems when a company is trying to formulate and implement coordinated marketing strategies, including logistics. With supply chain management, individual logistics activities are brought together in a unified way.

total cost concept
In physical distribution, the optimization of the cost-profit relationship for the entire physical distribution system, rather than for individual activities.

The **total cost concept** is integral to effective chain management. A company should determine the set of activities that produces the best relationship between costs and profit for the entire physical distribution system. This approach is superior to focusing strictly on the separate costs of individual distribution activities.

Sometimes, a company attempts to minimize the cost of only one aspect of physical distribution — transportation, for example. Management might be upset by the high cost of airfreight. But the higher costs of airfreight may be more than offset by savings from (1) lower inventory costs, (2) less insurance and interest expense, (3) lower crating costs, and (4) fewer lost sales due to out-of-stock conditions. The point is not that airfreight is the best method of transportation. Rather, the key point is that physical distribution should be viewed as a total *process*, with all the related costs being analyzed — maybe why a company should outsource to a professional in transportation systems management.

Effective supply chain management can improve several aspects of performance. A consultant estimated that superior supply chain management can (1) improve on-time delivery by about 20 percent, (2) reduce necessary inventory levels by about 50 percent, and (3) and boost the firm's profits by from 3 to 6 percent of sales.

As part of supply chain management, some companies are contracting out, or *outsourcing*, their physical distribution function. It is more and more common for logistics companies to manage firms' distribution processes under a multiyear contract. The growth of **contract logistics**, also called *third party logistics* or simply *3PL*, reflects a broader trend in North America where firms are more and more outsourcing various business activities ranging from payroll to public relations and market research. With 3PL the outside firm may be come responsible for every function involved with getting customer's product to market. This can include many administrative duties such as record maintenance for income tax purposes, monitoring environmental and safety regulations, and customs reports. The growth in contract logistics is being simultaneously driven by the desire to reduce operational costs and to reduce operations so that companies can focus on their core competencies.

The scope of contract logistics is evident in the following examples. Caliber Logistics (www.fedexgloballogistics.com) operates a warehouse for a unit of Hewlett-Packard that produces laser and ink-jet printer lines. In addition to handling the storage function, Caliber employees deliver needed parts and materials to nearly all HP plants. Ryder Systems (www.ryder.com) takes on a larger task with the Saturn Division of General Motors by overseeing all physical distribution from suppliers' shipments to deliveries of new vehicles to dealer showrooms. Aside from being able to completely manage the logistics of distribution for clients, the company has also created do-it-yourself solutions for clients that allow vehicle leasing and maintenance that is supported by a wide range of online management and maintenance tools.

Companies are turning to contract logistics essentially for the same reasons they are outsourcing other business tasks. By doing so, they can concentrate on their core business of producing lingerie or power hand tools. In addition, firms expect to become more effective (as indicated by greater customer satisfaction) and/or more efficient (as indicated by lower costs and greater return on investment) in the area of logistics. Currently, about two thirds of large North American manufacturers are outsourcing part of their physical distribution activities.

In Canada, Nabisco Biscuits has contracted the Hub Group as its single-source intermodal shipment company. John Deere's (www.deere.com) Ontario plant has outsourced its logistics to Caliber Logistics to ease the space and labour crunch that it experiences as a result of continuous annual production increases. The company has achieved space savings, labour redeployment, improved inventory accuracy, and lowered transportation and materials costs.[11]

Strategic Use of Physical Distribution

The strategic use of physical distribution may enable a company to strengthen its competitive position by providing more customer satisfaction and/or by reducing operating costs. The management of physical distribution can also affect a firm's marketing mix, particularly distribution channels. The opportunities that can result from the strategic use of physical distribution are described below.

IMPROVE CUSTOMER SERVICE A well-run logistics system can improve the service a firm provides its customers, whether they are intermediaries or ultimate users. Furthermore, the level of customer service directly affects demand. This is true especially in marketing undifferentiated products (such as chemicals and most building materials), where effective service may be a company's only differential advantage.

To ensure reliable customer service, management should set standards of performance for each subsystem of physical distribution. These standards should be quantitatively measurable. Some examples:

◆ *Electronics manufacturer*: Make delivery within seven days after receiving an order, with no more than 20 percent of the shipment by air.

◆ *Sporting goods wholesaler*: Fill 98 percent of orders accurately without increasing the size of the order-fulfillment staff.

◆ *Industrial distributor*: Maintain inventory levels that enable fulfillment of at least 85 percent of orders received from inventory on hand, but maintain a stock turn of thirty days.

REDUCE DISTRIBUTION COSTS Many avenues to cost reductions may be opened by effective physical distribution management. For example, eliminating unneeded warehouses will lower costs. Inventories — and their attendant carrying costs and capital investment — may be reduced by consolidating stocks at fewer locations.

CREATE TIME AND LOCATION VALUE Storage, which is part of warehousing, creates *time value*. Storage is essential to correct imbalances in the timing of production and consumption. An imbalance can occur when there is *year-round consumption* but only *seasonal production*, as in the case of agricultural products. For instance, time value is added when bananas are picked green and allowed to ripen in storage. And skilful use of warehousing allows a producer to store a seasonal surplus so that it can be marketed long after the harvest has ended. In other instances warehousing helps adjust year-round production to seasonal consumption. A manufacturer may produce lawn mowers on a year-round basis; during the fall and winter, the mowers are stored for sale in the spring and summer.

Transportation adds value to products by creating *location value*. A fine suit hanging on a manufacturer's rack in Montreal has less value than an identical suit displayed in a retailer's store in Vancouver. Transporting the suit adds value to it.

STABILIZE PRICES Careful management of warehousing and transportation can help stabilize prices for an individual firm or for an entire industry. If a market is temporarily glutted with a product, sellers can store it until supply and demand conditions are better balanced. Such use of warehousing facilities is common in the marketing of agricultural products and other seasonally produced goods. The judicious movement of products from one market to another may enable a seller to (1) avoid a market with depressed prices or (2) take advantage of a market that has a shorter supply and higher prices. If

Ryder offers a system-wide management view to handling logistics rather than providing a piecemeal approach.

demand for heating oil is stronger in Kamloops than in Kelowna, a producer should be able to achieve greater revenues by shifting some shipments from Kelowna to Kamloops.

INFLUENCE CHANNEL DECISIONS Decisions regarding inventory management have a direct bearing on a producer's selection of channels and the location of intermediaries. Logistical considerations may become paramount, for example, when a company decides to decentralize its inventory. In this case management must determine (1) how many sites to establish and (2) whether to use wholesalers, the company's own warehouses, or public warehouses. One producer may select merchant wholesalers that perform storage and other warehousing services. Another may prefer to use a combination of (1) manufacturers' agents to provide aggressive selling and (2) public warehouses to distribute the products ordered.

CONTROL SHIPPING COSTS Managers with shipping responsibilities need to ensure that their companies enjoy the fastest routes and the lowest rates for whatever mode of transportation they use. The pricing of transportation services is one of the most complicated parts of North American business. The rate, or tariff, schedule is the carrier's price list. Typically it is complex; to cite one example, shipping rates vary for many different types of goods, depending on many factors including not only distance to the destination but also the bulk and weight of the products. Therefore, being able to interpret a tariff schedule properly is a money-saving skill for a manager with shipping responsibilities.

Tasks In Physical Distribution Management

physical distribution management
The development and operation of efficient flow systems for products.

Physical distribution refers to the actual physical flow of products. In contrast, **physical distribution management** is the development and operation of processes resulting in the effective and efficient physical flow of products.

Regardless of whether a firm is part of a logistics alliance or handles this function by itself, an effective physical distribution system is built around five interrelated activities:

◆ Order processing

◆ Inventory control

◆ Inventory location and warehousing

◆ Materials handling

◆ Transportation

Each of these must be carefully coordinated with the others.

Order Processing

order processing
The subsystem of physical distribution management that consists of the set of procedures for receiving, handling, and filling orders.

electronic data interchange (EDI)
Computer-to-computer transmission of orders, invoices, or other business information.

The starting point in a physical distribution system is **order processing** — a set of procedures for receiving, handling and filling orders promptly and accurately. This activity should include provisions for billing, granting credit, preparing invoices, and collecting past due accounts. Errors in order processing are costly in terms of loss of buyer goodwill and increased handling costs.

There have been various computer-based advances in order processing, notably **electronic data interchange** (EDI). Under EDI, orders, invoices, and other business information are transmitted by computer network. EDI speeds up the process and reduces paperwork. It allows invoices, payments, and order information to pass instantaneously between manufacturers, suppliers, and retailers. Since the Internet can carry the necessary information, EDI costs are lower than when dedicated transmission lines and highly specialized computer equipment and software were the only mode available and more firms can become involved in the process. While traditional EDI network use is expected to continue to grow by about 10 percent in the next few years, it is believed that Internet-based transactions will grow by 80–90 percent during the same period.[12] The number of small retailers using electronic information exchange is increasing rapidly as Internet technology becomes more financially accessible. Large firms, individually and in alliances, moved quickly to take advantage of Internet-based virtual markets and supply chains.

IBM expects that all order processing from suppliers to be done electronically by the end of 2000. General Motors and Ford Motor Company are *demanding* the same of all their suppliers by the end of 2001. Even the field of medicine has entered the stage of being able to distribute medical services to far-flung areas where specialists may be in short supply. The use of EDI systems in medicine has yielded what has been termed *telemedicine*, whereby consultations no longer require that doctor and patient be available at the same time. Technology has allowed CT scans, MRIs, and X-rays to be viewed by specialists across the globe at the same time. On the low-tech side, Kiwi Brands (www.kiwicare.com), who make shoe polishes and household cleaning products, receive approximately three-quarters of its product orders through electronic channels.

Inventory Control

inventory control
The subsystem of physical distribution management that involves maintaining control over the size and composition of inventories in order to fill customers' orders promptly, completely, and accurately while minimizing both the investment and fluctuations in inventories.

Maintaining control over the size and composition of inventories, which represent a sizable investment for most companies, is essential to any physical distribution system. The goal of **inventory control** is to fill customers' orders promptly, completely, and accurately while minimizing both the investment and fluctuations in inventories.

CUSTOMER-SERVICE REQUIREMENTS Inventory size is determined by balancing costs and desired levels of customer service. That is, what percentage of orders does the company expect to fill promptly from inventory on hand? Out-of-stock conditions result in lost sales, loss of goodwill, even loss of customers. Yet to be able to fill 100 percent of orders promptly may require an excessively large and costly inventory. Generally speaking, about 80 percent more inventory is required to fill 95 percent of the orders than to fill only 80 percent. For example, if a firm now satisfies 80 percent of its requests by stocking 20,000 units, it would have to increase its inventory to 36,000 units to improve its rate of order fulfillment to 95 percent.

Perhaps the greatest boon to inventory control in recent years has been improvements in computer technology. These advancements have enabled management to shorten the order delivery time and substantially reduce the size of inventories. Canadian Tire is one of countless firms that has benefited from computer-based inventory control. Through its inventory-control system, goods reach the selling floor much more quickly when they are reordered electronically than they would under conventional inventory ordering systems.

economic order quantity (EOQ)
The optimal quantity for reorder when replenishing inventory stocks, as indicated by the volume at which the inventory-carrying cost plus the order-processing cost are at a minimum.

ECONOMIC ORDER QUANTITY Management must establish the optimal quantity for reorder when it is time to replenish inventory stocks. The **economic order quantity (EOQ)** is the volume at which the sum of inventory-carrying costs and order-processing costs are at a minimum. Typically, as order size increases, (1) inventory-carrying cost goes up (because the average inventory is larger) and (2) order-processing cost declines (because there are fewer orders).

In Figure 16-4, point EOQ represents the order quantity having the lowest total cost. Actually, the order quantity that a firm considers best (or optimal) often is larger than the EOQ. That's because management must try to balance the sometimes conflicting goals of low inventory costs and responsive customer service. For various reasons, such as gaining a differential advantage, a firm may place a higher priority on customer service than inventory costs. To completely fill orders in a timely manner may well call for a larger order quantity than the EOQ — for example, quantity X in Figure 16-4.

FIGURE 16-4
Economic Order Quantity

Marketing at Work 16-3

Logistics Lessons from Wal-Mart

Wal-Mart, whatever else it might be, was an early benchmark for logistics — other firms have watched it, have tried to do as well, and some have done even better. But Wal-Mart was the first major operator to do things very very right. It all started with a vision of a complete dedication to fulfilling the needs of its customers that was to shape its goals: to provide customers with quality goods, to make these goods available where and when customers wanted them, to create a cost structure that would allow competitive pricing, and to develop a reputation for absolute trustworthiness. Of course, it is one thing to state such goals, and quite another to achieve them. Wal-Mart, however, hit on a valuable competitive strategy — "cross-docking." It was based on the way the company replenished its inventory, and it provided the nucleus for all its subsequent strategies and subsequent successes.

"Cross-docking" refers to a system whereby goods are constantly delivered to Wal-Mart's warehouses, where they are selected, repacked, and then transported to stores, often without having to sit in inventory. The expensive warehouse costs saved by simply rapidly moving products from one loading dock to another proved significant. This means that while bypassing the usual inventory and handling costs, Wal-Mart is able to reap the full savings that result from buying trucks carrying large volumes of goods. While early competitor Kmart was able to run only 50 percent of its goods through its warehouse system, Wal-Mart could boast that almost 90 percent of its products avoided these costs. Such savings reduced Wal-Mart's costs of sales by 2 to 3 percent, a significant difference that made possible its strategy of everyday low prices.

These low prices in turn lead to further savings by eliminating the cost of frequent promotions, as well as stabilizing prices so that sales are more predictable, thus reducing stockouts and excess inventory. And, of course, low prices attracted more customers, which meant more sales per retail square foot.

If "cross-docking" was so successful, why don't all retailers use it? The reason is that it's very difficult to manage. In order to make cross-docking work, Wal-Mart had to make strategic investments in a variety of interlocking support systems far beyond what could be justified by usual return-on-investment criteria. For example, cross-docking demands constant contact between Wal-Mart's distribution centres, suppliers, and every checkout in every store so that orders can flow in, be consolidated, and executed within a matter of mere hours. This could be done only by investing in a private satellite communication system that daily sends point-of-sale data directly to Wal-Mart's four thousand vendors.

Wal-Mart maintains an information technology system that is totally integrated with its suppliers. Its system, developed in-house, openly shares information with its suppliers. The system is dubbed RetailLink and it puts each supplier roughly on an equal footing, in terms of the information available, with Wal-Mart's own internal buyers and financial analysts.

Another key investment was in the development of a rapid and responsive transportation system. Distribution centres are serviced by a fleet of company-owned trucks, allowing Wal-Mart to ship goods from warehouses to stores in less than forty-eight hours and to replenish store shelves twice a week, compared with the industry average of twice a month.

Finally, however, all the logistical facets of the cross-docking strategy could never have functioned if it weren't for the fundamental changes made on the management level. Traditionally in retail, decisions about merchandising, pricing, and promotions have remained in the highly centralized hands of a few corporate executives, but the very nature of cross-docking turned this command-and-control logic upside-down. For, instead of the retailer pushing products into the system, cross-docking has customers "pulling" products when and where they need them. The upshot was a managerial style emphasizing frequent, informal co-operation between stores, distribution centres, and suppliers — with much less centralized control. Thus, instead of giving directives to individual store managers, senior managers at Wal-Mart were helping to create an environment where they could learn from the market — and from each other.

Source: Adapted from George Stalk, Philip Evans, and Lawrence Shulman, "Competing on Capabilities," *Harvard Business Review*, 1992; and Charles B. Darling and J. William Semich, "Wal-Mart's IT Secret: Extreme Integration," *Datamation*, November 1996; www.datamation.com/Plugin/issues/1996/nov/11cover.html. (August 11, 1997).

JUST-IN-TIME A popular form of inventory control, purchasing, and production scheduling is the **just-in-time (JIT)** concept. The idea of JIT is that you buy in small quantities that arrive *just in time* for production and then produce in quantities *just in time* for sale. JIT has commanded the attention of top management — not just marketing or physical distribution management — in many North American companies.

just-in-time (JIT)
An inventory control system that involves buying parts and supplies in small quantities just in time for use in production and then producing in quantities just in time for sale.

When effectively implemented, the just-in-time concept has many benefits. By purchasing in small quantities and maintaining low inventory levels of parts and finished goods, a company can achieve dramatic cost savings because fewer items are damaged or stolen, or otherwise become unusable. Production and delivery schedules can be shortened and made more flexible and reliable. The Japanese have found that quality improves with JIT purchasing. When order quantities are small and deliveries frequent, a company can more quickly spot and then correct a quality problem in the products received.[13]

In Canada and the United States, the JIT philosophy was first adopted in the auto industry. But the concept has been adopted by leading firms in other industries, such as IBM, Xerox, Apple, Black and Decker, and General Electric. For some firms the results have been quite positive. Xerox eliminated forty-seven hundred suppliers in one year, and Black and Decker cut more than 50 percent of its suppliers in two years.[14] A producer that relies on JIT tends to use fewer suppliers because they must be close to the producer's facilities and also because there must be strong partnerships with suppliers, which is not feasible with large numbers of suppliers. Channel members — even entire channels — that employ JIT effectively can gain a differential advantage. As JIT becomes widespread, firms or channels that ignore it risk a differential disadvantage.[15] Ford of Canada's JIT strategy allows it to bring to St. Thomas, Ontario, twenty-six hundred different types of auto parts from every continent except Africa to allow it to assemble the Crown Victoria and the Mercury Grand Marquis. Perhaps the most highly developed JIT system is that used by Saturn and Ryder Integrated Systems as was already mentioned. This system operates six days a week for twenty-one hours each day directing drivers how and where to deliver various parts to the plant's fifty-six receiving docks. A key-shaped disk is inserted into the on-board computer by the driver — the computer screen instructs the driver where to pick up parts, where to deliver them, how to get there, and how much time there is to do each. By the time parts arrive they go directly to the assembly area for use. The production line has had to shut down only once when a part was eighteen minutes late being delivered to the plant.[16]

An updated version of JIT, labelled JIT II, stresses closer working relationships between manufacturers and suppliers. Under JIT II, a company provides a supplier with sales forecasts and other useful information, some of which may be confidential. In turn, a supplier may place one of its employees at the customer's plant to handle all or part of the purchasing function.[17] This, obviously, can't be done unless there is a substantial relationship between the two firms with high levels of trust. Such an arrangement has developed between The Foxboro Company, Dell Computers, and Software House International. Foxboro's purchasing unit has established a strategy for buying personal computers and peripherals that allows the company to cut buying costs, improve process efficiencies, and satisfy internal and external customer requirements. Global agreements between these firms as well as with an in-plant supplier that uses JIT II practices has resulted in a 20 percent reduction in the costs of buying PCs.[18]

Electronic data interchange (EDI) and company alliances in a channel allow for substantial cost savings and differential advantages to those involved.[19]

MARKET RESPONSE SYSTEMS JIT's focus tends to be on production and the relationship between the producer and its suppliers. A parallel trend involves producers or intermediaries of finished goods and their customers. We refer to this counterpart to JIT

market response system
A form of inventory control in which a purchase by a final customer activates a process to produce and deliver a replacement item.

as **market response systems**; they are sometimes called *quick response systems*. The central idea is that a purchase by a final customer, one who intends to consume the product, should activate a process to produce and deliver a replacement item. In this way, a product is pulled through a channel on the basis of demand rather than being pushed through on the basis of short-term price reductions or other inducements that often result in excessive inventory costs.

The intent of a market response system is similar to that of JIT — to have the right volume of goods to satisfy consumers and to replenish exhausted stocks rapidly. By resulting in better inventory control, a market response system can both reduce stock carrying and operating costs. In the grocery industry, market response has been labelled *efficient consumer response* (ECR). Such systems are in the early stages of implementation. One method currently being tested is for a wholesaler and a customer, usually a retail chain, to jointly and interactively develop sales forecasts through a shared Web site. Again, this method relies upon trust, as confidential information must be shared between participants. A test pilot of this program between Wal-Mart and Warner-Lambert, Inc., makers of Listerine mouthwash has shown promising results. Of particular interest was a 25 percent reduction in Listerine inventories.[20]

Inventory Location and Warehousing

Management must make critical decisions about the size, location, and transporting of inventories. These areas are interrelated often quite complex ways. The number and location of inventory sites, for example, influence inventory size and transportation method. One important consideration in managing inventories is **warehousing**, which embraces a range of functions such as assembling, bulk breaking, and storing products and preparing them for reshipping.

warehousing
A broad range of physical distribution activities that include storage, assembling, bulk breaking, and preparing products for shipping.

While many components of wholesaling and distribution have been altered by EDI and Internet technology, there still remains a role for some traditional intermediaries. The logistical function of storing a physical good will always require a physical location in which to store and process orders. A virtual bookstore like Indigo (www.indigo.ca) will require warehousing until the day comes that all books can be downloaded directly or publishers print them individually upon receipt of order and ship them individually to customers. The first alternative is a long way off, and, ironically the second alternative makes the virtual bookseller just another dispensable intermediary. Many leading e-commerce firms such as Amazon, eToys, and Webvan are building distribution centres at carefully selected locations around the U.S. Amazon, for example, has constructed centres in Kansas, Kentucky, and Nevada to serve as the hubs of its physical distribution system.[21]

private warehouse
A warehouse that is owned and operated by the firm whose products are being stored and handled at the facility.

TYPES OF WAREHOUSES Any producer, wholesaler, or retailer has the option of operating its own private warehouse or using the services of a public warehouse. A **private warehouse** is more likely to be an advantage if (1) a company moves a large volume of products through a warehouse and (2) there is very little, if any, seasonal fluctuation in this flow, and (3) the goods have special handling or storage requirements.

public warehouse
An independent firm that provides storage and handling facilities.

A **public warehouse** offers storage and handling facilities to individuals or companies. Public warehousing costs are a variable expense. Customers pay only for the space they use, and only when they use it. Public warehouses can also provide office and product display spaces, and accept and fill orders for sellers. Furthermore, warehouse receipts covering products stored in public warehouses may be used as collateral for bank loans.

distribution centre
A concept in warehousing that develops under one roof an efficient, fully integrated system for the flow of products — taking orders, filling them, and delivering them to customers.

DISTRIBUTION CENTRES An effective inventory-location strategy may involve the establishment of one or more **distribution centres**. Such facilities are planned around markets rather than transportation requirements. The idea is to develop under one roof an efficient, fully integrated system for the flow of products — taking orders, filling them, and preparing them for delivery to customers.

Distribution centres have been established by many well-known firms. They can cut distribution costs by reducing the number of warehouses, pruning excessive inventories, and eliminating out-of-stock conditions. Storage and delivery time have been cut to a minimum, recognizing the adage that companies are in business to sell goods, not to store them.

IKEA, the Scandinavian furniture retailer, expanded very slowly in Canada and the United States because the company wanted to find locations and facilities that effectively met the needs of its distribution centres. Nintendo of America has a 380,000 square-foot distribution centre in North Bend, Washington. It ships video games and related accessories to over ten thousand locations. The products are received in large sealed containers shipped from Japan. Orders are filled with a 99.996 percent accuracy rate. Given the intense competition in the video-game market, efficiency and accuracy are key goals at the Nintendo distribution centre.[22]

Materials Handling

materials handling
The subsystem of physical distribution management that involves selecting and operating the equipment and warehouse building that is used in physically handling products.

Selecting the proper equipment to physically handle products, including the warehouse building itself, is the **materials handling** subsystem of physical distribution management. Equipment that is well matched to the task can minimize losses from breakage, spoilage, and theft. Efficient equipment can reduce handling costs as well as time required for handling.

Modern warehouses are often huge, one-storey structures located in outlying areas, where land is less expensive and loading platforms are easily accessed by trucks and trains. Conveyor belts, forklift trucks, and other mechanized equipment are used to move merchandise. In some warehouses the order fillers are even outfitted with in-line skates!

Online grocers use different methods by which to deliver the goods — Montreal-based The PeachTree Network (www.peachtree.com) has a network of "traditional" grocers that receive the customer orders from PeachTree which they then fill and deliver. San Francisco-based Webvan Group (www.webvan.com), on the other hand, has invested $35 million to set up a distribution network in the San Francisco bay area including 120 delivery vans and 170 drivers. Processing some two thousand orders a day, the company has set up a "hub and spokes" delivery system of delivery routes.[23]

containerization
A cargo-handling system in which shipments of products are enclosed in large metal or wood receptacles that are then transported unopened from the time they leave the customer's facilities until they reach their destination.

Containerization is a cargo-handling system that has become standard practice in physical distribution. Shipments of products are enclosed in large metal or wood containers. The containers are then transported unopened from the time they leave the customer's facilities (such as a manufacturer's plant) until they reach their destination (such as a wholesaler's warehouse). Containerization minimizes physical handling, thereby reducing damage, lessening the risk of theft, and allowing for more efficient transportation.

Transportation

A major function of the physical distribution system in many companies is **transportation** — shipping products to customers. Management must decide on both the **mode of transportation** and the particular carriers. In this discussion we will focus on inter-city shipments. In arranging transportation, firms are trying to satisfy customers while controlling expenses. Assistance for this can be found at Web sites such as iShip.com (www.iship.com) that feature current rates charged by various transportation firms for different types of service. Such a service is particularly valuable for small Internet merchants and also for customers of online auctions.[24]

MAJOR MODES Railways, trucks, ships, and airplanes are the leading modes of transportation. In Table 16-4 these four methods are compared on the basis of criteria likely to be used by physical distribution managers in selecting a mode of transportation. Of course, the comparisons in the table are generalizations, and the ratings of alternative modes of transportation can vary from one manager to the next, even within the same buying centre in an organization.[25] Virtually all intra-city freight movements are made by truck. The use of trucks has expanded greatly and accounts for roughly half the expenditures for transportation services, with rail accounting for between 25 and 30 percent.

INTERMODAL TRANSPORTATION When two or more modes of transportation are used to move freight, this is termed **intermodal transportation**. The intent of intermodal transportation is to seize the advantages of multiple forms of transportation.

piggyback freight service
The service of transporting loaded truck trailers on railroad flatcars.

One type of intermodal transportation involves trucks and railways. So-called **piggyback service** involves carrying truck trailers on railway flatcars. This type of intermodal transportation provides (1) more flexibility than railways alone can offer, (2) lower freight costs than trucks alone, and (3) less handling of goods.

fishyback service
The service of transporting loaded trailers on barges or ships.

A similar type of intermodal transportation combines ships or barges with either railways or trucks, or both. One version of **fishyback service** transports loaded trailers on barges or ships. The trailers may be carried piggyback fashion by railway to the dock, where they are transferred to the ship. Then, at the other end of the water trip, the trailers are loaded back onto trains for completion of the haul. In an alternative use of the fishyback service, merchandise is trucked directly to ports, where the trailer vans are loaded on barges. At the end of the water journey, the vans are trucked to the receiving station.

TABLE 16-4 Comparison of Transportation Methods

Selection Criteria	Transportation Method			
	Rail	Water	Highway	Air
Speed (door-to-door time)	Medium	Slowest	Fast	Fastest
Cost of transportation	Medium	Lowest	High	Highest
Reliability in meeting delivery schedules	Medium	Poor	Good	Good
Variety of products carried	Widest	Widest	Medium	Somewhat limited
Number of geographic locations served	Very many	Limited	Unlimited	Many
Most suitable products	Long hauls of carload quantities of bulky products, when freight costs are high in relation to product's value	Bulky, low-value nonperishables	Short hauls of high-value goods	High-value perishables, where speed of delivery is all-important

245 years old and still at the leading edge.

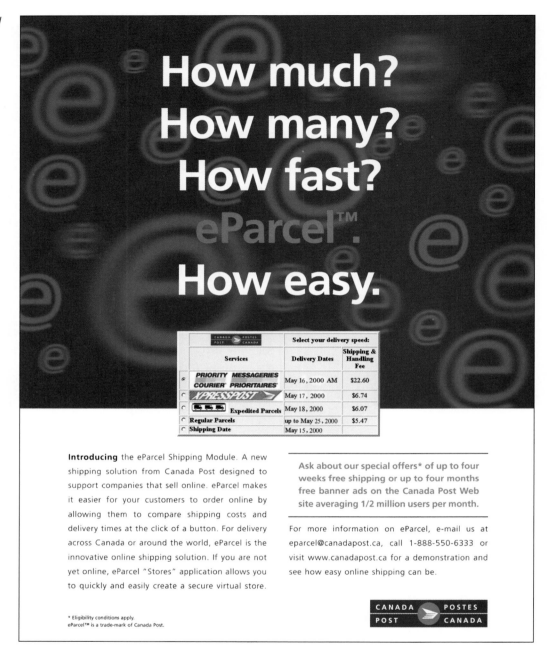
freight forwarder
A specialized transportation agency that consolidates less-than-carload or less-than-truckload shipments into carload or truckload quantities and provides door-to-door shipping service.

FREIGHT FORWARDERS A specialized marketing institution serving firms that ship in less-than-carload quantities is called a **freight forwarder**. Its main function is to consolidate less-than-carload or less-than-truckload shipments from several shippers into carload and truckload quantities. The freight forwarder picks up the merchandise at the shipper's place of business and arranges for delivery at the buyer's door. A small shipper benefits from the speed and minimum handling associated with large shipments. A freight forwarder also provides the small shipper with traffic management services, such as selecting the best transportation methods and routes.

PACKAGE-DELIVERY FIRMS A major development of the past thirty years has been the formation of companies that deliver small shipments of packages and high-priority mail. You certainly are familiar with United Parcel Service (UPS), Federal Express (FedEx), and Loomis. All these firms compete directly with Canada Post for package delivery services. These commercial package delivery giants attempt to position themselves more favourably than their competition by trying to surpass each other with respect to delivery times, technology that allows customers to prepare and track their shipments, and — of course — low prices.[26]

Canada Post is embracing the new economy with a series of new initiatives including partnerships with e-commerce sites to deliver goods purchased on the Internet. It looks after such accounts as Chapters Online, La Senza, and Sears Canada Inc.

In many respects, these companies offer the same services as freight forwarders. However, whereas the typical freight forwarder does not have its own transportation equipment, package-delivery firms do. Companies such as UPS and FedEx essentially are integrated as cargo airlines and trucking companies. Furthermore, package-delivery firms, in effect, use intermodal transportation. Consider FedEx, for example. A package is picked up by truck, shipped intercity or overseas by plane, and delivered locally by truck.

Summary

Wholesaling consists of the sale, and all activities directly related to the sale, of goods and services for resale, use in producing other goods or services, or operating an organization. Firms engaged primarily in wholesaling, called wholesaling intermediaries, provide economies of skill, scale, and transactions to other firms involved in distribution.

Three categories of wholesaling intermediaries are merchant wholesalers, agent wholesaling intermediaries, and manufacturers' sales facilities. The first two are independent firms; the third is owned by a manufacturer. Merchant wholesalers take title to products being distributed; agent wholesaling intermediaries do not.

Merchant wholesalers, who account for the majority of wholesale trade, include both full- and limited-service firms. Of the three major categories of wholesaling intermediaries, merchant wholesalers offer the widest range of services and thus incur the highest operating expenses. The main types of agent wholesalers are manufacturers' agents and brokers. Because they perform more limited services, agent wholesalers' expenses tend to be lower than those of merchant wholesalers.

Physical distribution is the flow of products from supply sources to the firm and then from the firm to its customers. The goal of physical distribution is to move the right amount of the right products to the right place at the right time. Physical distribution costs are a substantial part of total operating costs in many firms. Moreover, physical distribution is probably the only remaining source of possible cost reductions in many companies.

Although physical distribution activities are still fragmented operationally and organizationally in many firms, they should be treated as a system. The total cost concept should be applied to physical distribution — that is, the focus should be on the cost of physical distribution in its entirety, rather than on the costs of individual elements. However, management should strive *not* for the lowest total cost of physical distribution, but for the best balance between customer service and total cost. Effective management of physical distribution can help a company gain an advantage over competitors through better customer service and/or lower operating costs. To improve their physical distribution, some firms are turning to contract logistics.

The operation of a physical distribution system requires management's attention and decision-making in five areas: (1) inventory location and warehousing, (2) materials handling, (3) inventory control, (4) order processing, and (5) transportation. They should not be treated as individual activities but as interrelated components within a physical distribution system. Effective management of these five activities requires an understanding of distribution centres, economic order quantity, just-in-time processes, and intermodal transportation.

Key Terms and Concepts

Wholesaling 492
Wholesaling middleman or
    intermediary 493
Merchant wholesaler 495
Manufacturers' sales facilities
    and offices 495
Agents and brokers 435
Primary product dealers 495
Full-service wholesaler 498
Truck jobber 498
Drop shipper 499
Manufacturers' agent
    (manufacturers'
    representative) 500

Broker 500
Commission merchant 501
Auction company 501
Selling agent 503
Import-export agents 503
Physical distribution (logistics) 503
Total cost concept 505
Contract logistics 506
Physical distribution
    management 509
Order processing 509
Electronic data interchange (EDI) 509
Inventory control 510
Economic order quantity (EOQ) 510

Just-in-time (JIT) 511
Market response system 513
Warehousing 513
Private warehouse 513
Public warehouse 513
Distribution centre 514
Materials handling 514
Containerization 514
Transportation 514
Mode of transportation 514
Intermodal transportation 515
Piggyback service 515
Fishyback service 515
Freight forwarder 516

Questions and Problems

1. Which of the following are wholesaling transactions?

    a. Colour Tile sells wallpaper to an apartment building contractor and also to the contractor's family for their home.

    b. General Electric sells motors to Whirlpool for its washing machines.

    c. A fish "farmer" sells fish to a local restaurant.

    d. A family orders carpet from a friend, who is a home decorating consultant, at 50 percent off the suggested retail price. The carpet is delivered directly to the home.

    e. Weber Supply sells nails to Home Hardware.

    f. A local bakery delivers goods to Sobey's.

2. Why is it that manufacturers' agents often can penetrate a market faster and at a lower cost than a manufacturer's sales force can?

3. Which type of wholesaling intermediary, if any, is most likely to be used by each of the following firms? Explain your choice in each instance.

    a. A small manufacturer of a liquid glass cleaner to be sold through supermarkets.

    b. A small canner in Nova Scotia packs a high-quality, unbranded fruit product.

    c. A small-tools manufacturing firm that has its own sales force selling to the business market and now wants to add backyard barbecue equipment to its product mix.

    d. A Quebec textile mill producing unbranded towels, sheets, pillowcases, and blankets.

    e. A virtual bookstore that has no existing physical infrastructure other than its call-centre for receiving orders.

    f. A software e-retailer that features only downloadable products.

4. Looking to the future, which types of intermediaries do you think will increase in importance and which ones will decline? What continuing role, if any, will Internet technology have on the role of intermediaries in distribution? Explain.

5. "The goal of a modern physical distribution system in a firm should be to operate at the lowest possible *total* costs." Do you agree?

6. Name some products for which you think the cost of physical distribution constitutes at least one-half the total price of the goods at the wholesale level. Can you suggest ways of decreasing the physical distribution cost of these products?

7. "A manufacturer follows an inventory-location strategy of concentration rather than dispersion. This company's inventory size will be smaller, but its transportation and warehousing expenses will be larger than if its inventory were dispersed." Do you agree? Explain.

8. "The use of public warehouse facilities makes it possible for manufacturers to bypass wholesalers in their channels of distribution." Explain.

9. For each of the following products, determine the best transportation method for shipping them to a distribution centre in the community where your school is located. In each case the buyer (not the seller) will pay all freight charges, and, unless specifically noted, time is not important. The distribution centre has a rail siding and loading/unloading dock for trucks.

    a. Disposable diapers from Ontario. Total shipment weight is 60,000 kg.

    b. A replacement memory card for your computer, which is now inoperative. The weight of the shipment is 1 kg, and you need this card in a hurry.

    c. Blank payroll cheques for your company. (There is a sufficient number of cheques on hand for the next two weekly paydays.) Shipment weight is 50 kg.

    d. Ice cream from London, Ontario. Total shipment weight is 21,000 kg.

    e. A standing order for five dozen cut roses — to be delivered each morning to a flower shop.

Hands-On Marketing

1. Interview the owner or a manager at a firm that is a type of merchant wholesaler (such as a full-service wholesaler). Ask the owner or manager to describe the firm's activities, its differential advantage or disadvantage at the present time, and the company's prospects for the future. Conduct a similar interview with the owner or a manager at a firm that is a type of agent wholesaler (such as a broker). How do you explain any discrepancies between the interview results and the content of this chapter (other than saying that the chapter must be wrong)?

2. A manufacturer of precision lenses used in medical and hospital equipment wants to ship a 5 kg box of these lenses from your town to a laboratory in Stockholm, Sweden. The lab wants delivery in five days or less. The manufacturer wants to use a package-delivery service but is undecided as to which shipper to choose. Compile and compare the types of services provided and prices charged by Federal Express, United Parcel Service, and one other package-delivery firm.

Chapter Seventeen

Retailing: Markets and Institutions

You have abundant experience with retailing — as a consumer. And perhaps you also have worked in retailing. This chapter builds on that experience and provides insights about retail markets, different types of retailers, and key strategies and trends in retailing. After studying this chapter, you should have an understanding of:

◆ The nature of retailing.

◆ What a retailer is.

◆ Types of retailers, classified by form of ownership.

◆ Types of retailers, classified by marketing strategies.

◆ Forms of nonstore retailing.

◆ Trends in retailing.

Would You Like Anything From the Bar? — Perhaps Butter for Your Popcorn?

Famous Players, Inc. (www.famous players.com) has been entertaining Canadians in its shadowy movie theatres for almost eighty years. Going to the movies is one of the few forms of entertainment that has remained popular over time and that is enjoyed across a wide variety of cultures and all age ranges. While still popular, it has become a rather routine event that has become a little lost among a myriad of entertainment options all vying for our entertainment dollars. Home movie rentals have, for several years now, nibbled away at theatre revenues. The siphoning of movie revenues has become an escalating problem in recent years with the onslaught of hi-tech entertainment choices such as DVD, virtual reality, satellite, and Internet options that are available today. Even the resurgence of home video-game systems and rentals are competing for discretionary entertainment dollars. While increases in the standard of living have resulted in an increase in the level of discretionary spending in Canada, the growth in entertainment options from developments in technology and the service sector has, perhaps, been even greater.

What can a tired old movie theatre do in the face of such evolution and changing competition in entertainment? With 114 theatres and over seven thousand employees across Canada, Famous Players has struggled with this issue for too long to give up… yet it is unable to control what movies the studios are making. Famous Players now believes that they have created an experience that will be better able to com-

pete and deliver entertainment value to the consumer in the new marketplace.

The company is in the middle of a $500 million expansion program with the end-goal to deliver the "finest out-of-the-home film entertainment in the ultimate theatrical environment." It seems that today's buzzwords in entertainment and marketing are "extreme" and "ultimate" as competition increases to provide extreme experiences for consumers. Famous Players theatres are becoming movie palaces of the future, totally immersing the audience in the cinematic experience, and restoring for patrons the glamour, excitement, and fun evoked by the movie theatres of the past. They are becoming more than a corridor of dark concrete theatres — the company is developing "entertainment destinations" — locations with theme lobbies, interactive game centres, and party rooms. This in addition to being able to go see a selection of movies and dine at a choice of well-known concessions within the complex, including offering Canada's first fully licensed bar in a movie theatre. The entire family can come and spend an afternoon or evening and enjoy the "ultimate" in movie-going entertainment.

Taking the industry in new directions, beginning in 2000, Famous Players, Inc. will join with World Wrestling Federation Canada Inc. and Bell ExpressVu to deliver monthly WWF pay-per-view events. As satellite technology transforms entertainment across the country, Famous Players is ensuring they will remain a competitive part of the changing landscape. Other featured entertainment includes showcasing private concerts in its movie theatres such as Chantal Kreviazuk and the Matthew Good Band. These events go for the "unplugged" performance atmosphere as the venues can only accommodate up to five hundred guests.

With thirty-one of these "environments" already open, Famous Players will have another thirteen open across the country by 2001. These changes go to show that if you can't beat 'em, have them join you instead!

As the marketplace changes, so must Famous Players in order to remain a viable business concern. As consumers want more, or different, "products" from a retailer — a retailer must adapt and meet these new needs. This may be a change in the product itself, or it may be a change in how the product or service is delivered. The experience of Famous Players describes both — how a retailer has evolved with changing consumer markets and tastes to provide a modernized selection of products and services.

"We're trying to get people to, when they think of Famous Players, think that we're an entertainment location and not just a movie theatre," says Stuart Pollack, vice-president marketing for Famous Players in Toronto.[1]

Retailing is one of the distribution links between the producer and the ultimate consumer. As Famous Players illustrates, even the most traditional sectors of this industry has had to undergo changes in the face of advancing technologies and new forms of electronic entertainment. The many types of retailing institutions and their marketing activities are the subjects of this chapter.

Nature and Importance of Retailing

For every far-reaching retail superstar like Wal-Mart, Chapters, or Loblaw, there are thousands of small retailers serving consumers only in very limited areas. Despite their differences, all these firms do have two common features: They link producers and ultimate consumers, and they perform valuable services for both parties. In all likelihood these firms are retailers, but all their activities may not qualify as retailing. How can that be? Explanations follow.

Retailing and Retailers

If Safeway (www.safeway.com) or Sobey's sells some floor wax to a gift-shop operator to polish the shop floor, is this a retail sale? When a Shell (www.shell.com) or Petro-Canada (www.petro-canada.ca) service station advertises that tires are being sold at the wholesale price, is this retailing? Can a wholesaler or manufacturer engage in retailing? When a service such as hair styling or auto repair is sold to an ultimate consumer, is this retailing? Obviously we need to define some terms, particularly retailing and retailer, to avoid misunderstandings later.

retailing
The sale, and all activities directly related to the sale, of goods and services to ultimate consumers for personal, nonbusiness use.

Retailing (or **retail trade**) consists of the sale, and all activities directly related to the sale, of goods and services to ultimate consumers for personal, non-business use. While most retailing occurs through retail stores, it may be done by any institution. A manufacturer selling brushes or cosmetics door to door is engaged in retailing, so is a bookseller on the Internet or a farmer selling vegetables at a roadside stand.

Any firm — manufacturer, wholesaler, or retailer — that sells something to ultimate consumers for their own non-business use is making a retail sale. This is true regardless of how the product is sold (in person or by telephone, mail, or vending machine) or

retailer
A firm engaged primarily in retailing.

where it is sold (in a store or at the consumer's home). However, a firm engaged primarily in retailing is called a **retailer**. In this chapter, we will concentrate on retailers rather than on other types of businesses that makes only occasional retail sales.

While this chapter focuses primarily on retailers of goods, much of what is said — particularly regarding marketing strategies — applies equally well to retailers of services. As we saw in Chapter 12, and in our discussion about the Famous Players' "makeover," one of the characteristics of services relates to the inseparability of the service from the individual or company that provides it. Although this is certainly the case, the marketing of services is often delegated to retailers. For example, travel agents are really retailers who sell to end consumers the services offered by airlines, hotels, railways, and car rental companies. Banks and other financial services companies retail Canada Savings Bonds on behalf of the Government of Canada. Ticketmaster (www.ticketmaster.com) retails theatre and concert tickets.

Economic Justification for Retailing

All intermediaries basically serve as purchasing agents for their customers and as sales specialists for their suppliers. To carry out these roles, retailers perform many activities, including anticipating customers' wants, developing assortments of products, acquiring market information, and financing.

It is relatively easy to become a retailer. No large investment in production equipment is required, merchandise can often be purchased on credit, and store space can be leased with no "down payment." Some retailers don't actually need to do this much. Those retailers that sell over the Internet need only a virtual storefront — many Internet service providers will even assist their subscribers "set up shop." If not retailing a downloadable product such as software or information, there is still a requirement (as discussed in the last chapter) to have some sort of warehousing — but even this can be all outsourced, eliminating the need for capital investment or expertise. This ease of entry results in fierce competition and better value for consumers.

To get into retailing is easy but to be forced out is just as easy. To survive in retailing, a company must do a satisfactory job (at least) in its primary role — catering to consumers — as well as in its secondary role — serving producers and wholesalers. This dual responsibility is both the justification for retailing and the key to success in retailing.

SIZE OF THE RETAIL MARKET Statistics Canada reported in 1999 that there were about 177,237 retail stores in Canada in 1996, and the total sales volume of retail trade for 1999 was more than $260 billion (see Figure 17-1). In spite of growth in total population and consumer incomes over the past thirty years, the total number of retail stores has not increased consistently. In fact, the volatility of the retail business is reflected in the fact that the total number of retail stores in Canada actually dropped from 227,200 to 174,121 between 1988 and 1994, but this number has risen again. Incorporated into this trend is the recent trend of retail mergers in North America impacting retail outlets in both Canada and the United States.

Total retail sales actually dropped from $185.19 billion in 1991 to $184.90 billion in 1992, a level virtually unchanged from total retail sales in 1988. Subsequent to that recession period, sales have continued to increase to $208.8 billion in 1994 and to $260.3 billion in 1999. Much of the gain in the last two years was mainly the result of solid growth in the automotive sector in Alberta, Saskatchewan, and Ontario. Higher revenues, in these years, in the retail sector have been noted in all regions of the country.[2]

Marketing at Work 17-1

LCBO's New Stores Going Down Well

Gone are the original nondescript Ontario liquor stores — made of brown brick complete with barred windows and located on back streets, well out of sight of passers-by. These first liquor stores were more about control than providing a pleasant shopping experience. Consumers had to complete a detailed order form at the front counter and wait anxiously while a clerk hunted for the requested products among the crowded shelves in the back room. Despite the environment the stores were successful at selling booze.

In the mid-1980s, however, sales sharply declined for the first time and the Ontario government decided it was time for a change. A brand new image was developed for the LCBO that would move it away from being merely a distributor of alcohol to a leading-edge, customer-focused retailer.

Today, almost one-third of the province's six hundred liquor stores have been given a new look. The colour scheme has moved away from dark forest green to soft yellows to give the appearance of sun-drenched fields. The cash registers have been moved further back to make the store entrance more open and welcoming, and other cosmetic changes include wider aisles, colourful signage, softer lighting, and maple cabinetry.

The changes that have taken place at the LCBO, however, are not just skin deep and some of the most important additions have little to do with selling alcoholic beverages. About twenty-five LCBO locations also offer elements of a larger entertainment centre such as cooking demonstrations, and lectures on wine or how to throw a perfect dinner party.

The LCBO has even revamped its free quarterly magazine which premiered in 1988 as a two-colour tabloid called *LCBO Today*. The new and improved magazine, now called *Food & Drink*, features colourful product displays as well as recipes, gift ideas, and articles on how to be the perfect host. *Food & Drink* will soon play a larger role in the stores' marketing

strategy with the main theme of a recent issue being featured on exterior signs and interior banners on walls and shelves. The publication's monthly food features will be prepared in the LCBO's demo kitchens, the drink of the month will be available for sampling, and end-of-aisle displays will include take-away recipe cards that feature products that relate to the overall theme.

According to Nancy Cardinal, director of marketing and communications at the LCBO, the in-store thematic themes, cooking demos, and gift boutiques will help bring the LCBO's vision statement "The Source for Entertaining Ideas" to life and will hopefully translate into higher sales.

At the end of its 1999 fiscal year, LCBO revenues increased to $2.34 billion — up 9 percent over the previous year. This seems to indicate that its new marketing strategy is going down well with LCBO patrons. This revenue growth, however, also benefits Ontario residents who do not frequent the LCBO as $780 million of last year's revenues were transferred as dividends to the province's consolidated revenues funds to be used by the Ontario government for general programs and services, while an additional $220 million was collected in provincial sales tax.

Source: Adapted from Shawna Cohen, "Style & Drinks," *Marketing Magazine*, September 13, 1999, p. 30.

Costs and Profits of Retailers

Information regarding the costs of retailing is very meager. By gleaning data from several sources, however, we can make some rough generalizations.

TOTAL COSTS AND PROFITS As nearly as can be estimated, the total average operating expense for all retailers combined is about 25 to 27 percent of retail sales. Wholesaling expenses are estimated at about 8 percent of the retail dollar, or about 10 to 11 percent of wholesaling sales. Thus, retailing costs are about two and a half times

FIGURE 17-1 Total Retail Trade in Canada, Selected Years
Sales volume has increased tremendously. However, note the reduction in number of stores since 1988.
Source: Statistics Canada

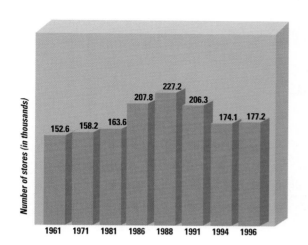

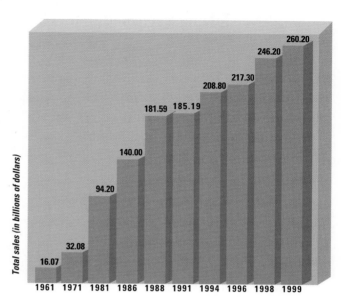

the costs of wholesaling, when both are stated as a percentage of sales of the intermediaries in question (see Figure 17-2).

The proportionately higher retailing costs are generally related to the expense of dealing directly with the consumer. In comparison with wholesalers' customers, end consumers demand more services. The average retail sale is smaller, the rate of merchandise turnover is lower, merchandise is bought in smaller lots, rent is higher, and expenses for furniture and fixtures are greater. And retail salespeople cannot be used efficiently because customers do not come into retail stores at a steady rate.

COSTS AND PROFITS BY KIND OF BUSINESS The expense ratios of retailers vary from one type of store to another. Table 17-1 shows average gross margins as a percentage of operating revenue for different kinds of stores. These margins range from 17.1 percent for motor vehicle dealers to about 44 percent for shoe and clothing stores and for automotive parts and accessories. For 1996 the overall gross margin was 26.9 percent of total operating revenue, a slight drop of 0.4 percent from the previous measurement. Table 17-1 also shows average profit (before depreciation and income taxes) for each type of store. These figures range from 0.83 percent for supermarket and grocery stores to 9.42 for shoe stores and 17.32 for other retail stores.

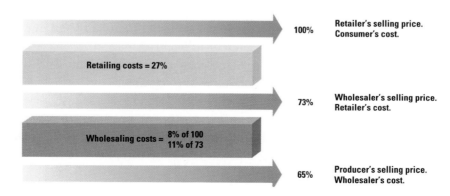

FIGURE 17-2
Average Costs of Retailing and Wholesaling

TABLE 17-1	Gross Margin and Net Profit as Percentage of Total Operating Revenue for Selected Types of Retailers	

Gross margin (net sales minus cost of goods sold) is the amount needed to cover a company's operating expenses and still leave a profit. How do you account for the differences in operating expenses among various types of retailers?

Line of Business	Gross Margin (%)	Operating Profit (%) (taxes and depreciation not included)
Supermarkets and other grocery stores	20.75	0.83
All other food stores	36.74	6.17
Drug and patent medicine stores	28.57	4.29
Shoe stores	44.39	9.42
Men's clothing stores	43.74	5.98
Women's clothing stores	44.60	5.81
Other clothing stores	43.47	5.86
Household furniture and appliances	35.30	2.15
Household furnishings	39.75	4.89
Motor vehicle and RV	17.11	5.05
Gasoline service stations	20.33	6.71
Automotive parts and accessories	43.95	6.39
General merchandise	25.77	1.38
Semi-durable goods stores	38.46	5.24
Other durable goods stores	39.07	6.05
Other retail stores	41.17	17.32
TOTAL RETAIL TRADE	26.86	4.52

Source: Statistics Canada, "Wholesaling and Retailing in Canada, 1996," cat. no. 63-236-XPB, p. 60.

Store Size

Most retail establishments are very small; with 15–20 percent of all retailers having annual sales of $100,000 or less. However, despite their numbers, such stores account for a very small percentage of total retail sales.

At the same time, there is a high degree of concentration in retailing. This becomes increasingly the case as large retailers merge and departments stores decline in number. A small number of companies account for a substantial share of total retail trade. These companies, such as Loblaw (part of the George Weston group of companies) (www.loblaw.com) and the Hudson's Bay Company (The Bay and its sister store Zellers can both be found at www.hbc.com), own many individual stores and account for the considerable degree of concentration in the industry. For example, the companies highlighted in Table 17-2 and a small number in other selected categories, while numbering fewer than forty, probably account for *close to half* of all retail sales in Canada.

Stores of different sizes present different management challenges and opportunities. Buying, promotion, personnel relations, and expense control are influenced significantly by whether a store's sales volume is large or small.

Size, or the lack thereof, brings with it certain advantages, several of which are evaluated in Table 17-3. This assessment suggests that relatively large stores have a competitive advantage over small stores. Small retailers do face many difficulties. The ones that cannot meet the challenges fail. If that's the case, how do so many small retailers succeed? The answer is twofold:

TABLE 17-2 Canada's Largest Retailers (1998–99 Sales and Profits)

Company	Revenue ($000)	Profit ($000)
Department Stores		
Hudson's Bay Co.	7,074,978	39,677
Sears Canada	4,966,600	146,400
Zellers Inc.	4,498,000	n/a
Costco Canada	2,888,558	n/a
Jean Coutu Group	1,940,074	63,236
T. Eaton Co.	1,688,200	−155,860
Clothing Stores		
Dylex Ltd.	1,077,381	19,911
Reitmans (Canada)	423,563	12,391
Mark's Work Warehouse	417,468	5,752
Suzy Shier	327,942	−12,192
Boutiques San Francisco	203,194	6,510
Château Stores of Canada	160,921	5,870
Specialty Stores		
Canadian Tire Corp.	4,347,283	166,980
Future Shop	1,760,160	3,961
RONA Inc.	818,051	13,511
Katz Group	800,000	n/a
Hartco Enterprises	717,495	12,437
SMK Speedy International	630,601	−2,559
Grand & Toy Ltd.	495,577	n/a
Chapters, Inc.	456,611	8,420
Food Distribution		
George Weston Ltd.	15,161,000	773,000
Loblaw Cos.	12,530,000	261,000
Southland Canada	7,349,811	50,724
Provigo Inc.	5,974,400	84,900
Canada Safeway	4,719,500	n/a
Westfair Foods	4,310,912	135,318
Metro-Richelieu Inc.	3,659,100	65,400
Empire Co.	3,403,645	87,782
Hospitality Serices		
McDonald's Restaurants of Canada	1,818,912	n/a
Cara Operations	801,935	35,027
C.P. Hotels & Resorts	526,871	82,833
Scott's Restaurants	349,210	14,800
A&W Food Services of Canada	341,000	n/a
Second Cup	73,442	9,100

Note: This list of retail chains is incomplete. Also, the reader may be unfamiliar with certain corporate names listed here, for example, Cara Operations operates Harvey's and Swiss Chalet restaurants; Dylex Limited operates a number of clothing stores including Tip Top Tailors, Fairweather, and Braemar.

Source: "The Top 1000," *Report on Business Magazine*, July 1999. Reprinted with permission from *The Globe and Mail*.

TABLE 17-3 Competitive Positions of Large and Small Retail Stores

Selected Bases for Evaluation	Who Has the Advantage?
Division of labour and specialization of management	Large-scale retailers — their biggest advantage.
Flexibility of operations — merchandise selection, services offered, store design, reflection of owner's personality	Small retailers — their biggest advantage.
Buying power	Large retailers buy in bigger quantities and thus get lower costs.
Access to desirable merchandise	Large retailers promise suppliers access to large numbers of customers, whereas a single small retailer may be viewed as insignificant.
Development and promotion of retailer's own brand	Large retailers.
Efficient use of advertising, especially in citywide media	Large retailers' markets match better with media circulation.
Ability to provide top-quality personal service	Small retailers, if owners pay personal attention to customers and also to selecting and supervising sales staff.
Opportunity to experiment with new products and selling methods	Large retailers can better afford the risks.
Financial strength	Large retailers have resources to gain some of the advantages noted above (such as private brands and experimentation).
Public image	Small retailers enjoy public support and sympathy. However, this same public often votes with its wallet by shopping at big stores.

◆ Some small retailers have formed or joined contractual vertical marketing systems. These entities — called retailer co-operatives, voluntary chains, or franchise systems — give individual members certain advantages of large stores, such as specialized management, buying power, and a well-known store name.

◆ Many consumers seek benefits that small stores can often provide better than large stores can. For instance, some people seek high levels of shopping convenience. Small outlets located near residential areas offer such convenience. Other consumers desire high levels of personal service. A small store's highly motivated owner-manager and well-supervised sales staff may surpass a large store on this important shopping dimension.

Many small stores take advantage of their comparative strengths and compete successfully against other retailers of varying sizes and types.

Physical Facilities

Later in this chapter we will classify retailers according to their product assortments, price strategies, and promotional methods. Here, we'll look at **physical facilities**, which represent the distribution element of a retailer's marketing mix.

Some firms engage in nonstore retailing — by selling through catalogues, the Internet, or door to door, for example — but many more firms rely on retail stores. The proliferation of Internet technology and adaptation of Internet commerce by many consumers continues to lead many traditional retailers to also enter nonstore retailing by opening cyberstores on the information superhighway.

Firms that operate retail stores must consider three aspects of physical facilities:

◆ *Location*. It is frequently stated that there are three keys to success in retailing: location, location, and location! Although overstated, this axiom does suggest the importance that retailers attach to location. Thus a store's site should be the first decision made about facilities. Considerations such as surrounding population, traffic, and cost determine where a store should be located. For Internet retailers as well as other nonstore retailers, location does matter as well, as they require warehousing and call-centres. But instead of wanting to be located in highly populated areas these retailers focus more on outlying areas where property and labour costs are usually lower. This must, of course, also be balanced with an optimal location that provides for timely and low-cost shipping provisions.

◆ *Design.* This factor refers to a store's appearance, both exterior and interior. This is important for attracting and retaining customers, as well as setting the image or tone for the location. For the nonstore retailer, this is of little importance except to ensure that the working environment is not a source of dissatisfaction for employees. It is important to provide a pleasant working environment for employees, but not to the degree it is important for traditional retailers to design environments with customer appeal.

◆ *Layout.* The amount of space allocated to various product lines, specific locations of products, and a floor plan of display tables and racks make up the store's layout. The layout should be convenient for customers while showcasing merchandise in the most prudent manner. For nonstore retailers the location's layout, like its design, is not to enhance the consumer's shopping experience but to facilitate the efficient, safe processing of customer orders.

As might be expected, retail store locations tend to follow the population. Consequently, the bulk of retail sales takes place in urban, rather than rural, areas. And suburban shopping areas have become more popular, while many downtown areas have declined.

Shopping centres have become the predominant type of retail location in most suburban areas. A **shopping centre** consists of a planned grouping of retail stores that lease space in a structure that is typically owned by a single organization and that can accommodate multiple tenants. Shopping centres can be classified by size and market served:

◆ **Convenience centre.** Usually consists of five to ten outlets, such as a dry cleaner, branch bank, convenience grocery store, and video rental store.

◆ **Neighbourhood centre.** Has ten to twenty-five tenants, including a large supermarket and perhaps a drugstore.

◆ **Community centre.** Includes twenty-five to fifty stores and features a discount house or junior department store. It may also include a supermarket. Given its composition of stores, a community centre draws shoppers from a larger area than does a neighbourhood centre.

◆ **Regional centre.** Anchored by one or more department stores and supermarkets and complemented by as many as two hundred smaller retail outlets and is typically enclosed in a climate-controlled mall.

Many regional shopping centres are very large. They have become the hubs of shopping and social activities in many communities; in fact they are "the meeting place" for many seniors and high school students. In the past twenty years, construction of new regional centres slowed considerably as the market became saturated. It is expected that relatively few shopping malls will be built in the future but that many existing ones will be renovated and modernized.

The growth of suburban shopping, especially in regional malls, led to decreased retail sales in many urban downtown areas. In recent years, therefore, some cities have worked to revitalize their downtown shopping districts. Often historical buildings or neighbourhoods are converted to shopping areas (for example, St. Lawrence Market in Toronto (www.stlawrencemarket.com) and the Cours de Mont Royal in Montreal). Enclosed shopping malls featuring distinctive designs have also been built in all major cities. Possibly the best known of these shopping centres is the West Edmonton Mall (www.westedmall.com), which has become something of a tourist attraction in western Canada.

Classification of Retailers

To understand how retailers serve both suppliers and customers, we will classify retailers on two bases:

1. Form of ownership.

2. Marketing strategies.

Any retail store can be classified according to both bases, as illustrated by the comparison below of The Bay and a neighbourhood paint store.

	Classification Bases	
Sample Store	**Form of Ownership**	**Marketing Strategies**
The Bay	Corporate chain	Department store with broad, relatively deep assortments, moderate prices, and levels of personal service that vary across departments.
Neighbourhood paint store	Independent	Limited-line store that has narrow, relatively deep assortments, avoids price competition, and provides extensive personal service.

Retailers Classified by Form of Ownership

The major forms of ownership in retailing are corporate chain, independent, and vertical marketing system (VMS). Within the VMS category are several types of organizations: wholesaler-sponsored voluntary chains, retailer-owned co-operatives, and franchise systems.

Corporate Chains

corporate chain
An organization of two or more centrally owned and managed stores that generally handle the same lines of products.

A **corporate chain**, sometimes called a *chain-store system*, is an organization of two or more centrally owned and managed stores that generally handle the same lines of products. Three factors differentiate a chain from an independent store and contractual vertical marketing system:

◆ Technically, two or more units constitute a chain. Today, however, many small-scale merchants have opened two or three units in shopping centres and in newly populated areas. These retailers ordinarily do not think of themselves as chains. Having four or more units is a good definitional basis for discussing chain stores.

◆ Central ownership distinguishes corporate chains from contractual vertical marketing systems.

◆ Because of their centralized management, individual units in a chain typically have little autonomy. Strategic decisions are made at headquarters, and there is considerable standardization of operating policies for all the units in a chain.

Corporate chains continue to play a major role in retail trade in Canada, as shown in Table 17-4. The predominance of chains varies considerably, however, depending on the kind of business. Organizations with four or more stores did about 38 percent of all retail business in Canada in 1997. The importance of chains varies considerably from one type of business to another. Chains account for 70 percent or more of total sales in the general merchandise and variety stores categories and in family clothing and shoes. Among grocery stores, hardware stores, and pharmacies, however, chains account for 30 percent of sales or less. In the retail food business, there are several giant food chains (Loblaw, A&P, Provigo, Sobey's, Safeway, etc.). In 1994, chains made up 47.06 percent of supermarket and grocery stores and 11.74 percent of other food stores. There are still a large number of independent food retailers in small towns and neighbourhoods throughout Canada.

COMPETITIVE STRENGTHS AND WEAKNESSES Chain-store organizations are large-scale retailing institutions. As such, they are subject to the general advantages and limitations of all large retailers that we discussed earlier in this chapter. Let's look at a few of these points, especially as they relate to chain stores.

LOWER SELLING PRICES Chain stores have traditionally been credited with selling at lower prices than independents. But the claim of lower prices needs careful scrutiny, because it can be misleading. It was probably more justified in the past than it is today. Many independents have pooled their buying power so that, in many instances, they can buy products at the same price as the chains can. However, it is almost certainly true that chains will have a cost advantage over independents.

It is very difficult to compare the prices of chains with those of independents. The merchandise is often not exactly comparable, because many chains sell items under their own brands. It is difficult to compare the prices of Del Monte peaches with Loblaw's or Safeway's brand of peaches. It is even more difficult to compare an item of apparel from Zellers with one from a "designer" store. The quality and durability of the fabric, the garment's construction, etc. are almost impossible for the average person to knowledgeably compare — at least with peaches, the proof is in the eating! Also, it is not accurate to compare the price of the product sold in a cash-and-carry, no-customer-service store with the price of an identically branded product in a full-service store. The value of services should be included in the comparison.

MULTISTORE FEATURE OF CHAINS Chain stores do not have all their eggs in one basket (or in one store). Even large-scale independent department stores or supermarkets cannot match this advantage of the chains. A multiunit operation has automatically spread its risks among many units. Losses in one store can be offset by profits in other

TABLE 17-4 Chain-Store Share of Total Retail Sales Volume (1974–1997)							
	1974	**1979**	**1986**	**1989**	**1994**	**1996**	**1997**
Percentage of total annual retail sales	41.1	41.5	41.5	39.3	37.3	37.5	38.4

Source: Statistics Canada, "*Marketing Research Handbook*," cat. no. 63-224-XPB, various years.

units. Multistore organizations can experiment quite easily. They can try a new store layout or a new type of merchandise in one store without committing the entire firm.

A chain can make more effective use of advertising than even a giant single-unit independent store can. To illustrate, a grocery chain may have fifteen medium-sized stores blanketing a city. An independent competitor may have one huge supermarket doing three to four times the business of any single unit of the chain. Yet the chain can use the metropolitan daily newspaper as an advertising medium, with much less waste in circulation than the independent can. Many chains can also make effective use of national advertising media.

ON THE NEGATIVE SIDE Standardization, the hallmark of a chain-store system and a major factor in its success, is a mixed blessing. Standardization also means inflexibility. Often a chain cannot adjust rapidly to a local market situation. Chains are well aware of this weakness, however, and have consequently given local store managers somewhat greater freedom to act in various situations. Also, with improved information systems, chains can better tailor their merchandising efforts to local markets.

Independent Stores

independent retailer
A company with a single retail store that is not affiliated with any type of contractual vertical marketing system.

An **independent retailer** is a company with a single retail store that is not affiliated with any type of contractual vertical marketing system. Most retailers are independents, and most independents are quite small. Of course, an independent department store or supermarket can have $10 million or more in annual sales, so it may have more economic power than small chains consisting of only a few stores. Still, independents usually have the characteristics of small retailers that were presented in Table 17-3.

Independents typically are viewed as having higher prices than chain stores. However, because of differences in merchandise and services, it is difficult to compare directly the prices of chains and independents. For instance, chains often have their own private brands that are not sold by independents. Also, the two types of retailers frequently provide customers with different levels — and perhaps quality — of services. Many customers are willing to pay extra for services that are valuable to them, such as credit, delivery, alterations, installation, a liberal returns policy, and friendly, knowledgeable personal service.[3]

contractual vertical market system
An arrangement under which independent firms — producers, wholesalers, and retailers — operate under a contract specifying how they will try to improve their distribution efficiency and effectiveness.

Contractual Vertical Marketing Systems

In a **contractual vertical marketing system**, independently owned firms join together under a contract specifying how they will operate. The three types of contractual VMS are discussed below.

retailer co-operative
A type of contractual vertical marketing system that is formed by a group of small retailers who agree to establish and operate a wholesale warehouse.

RETAILER COOPERATIVES AND VOLUNTARY CHAINS These both exist to increase the competitiveness of members and to provide members with management and administrative systems/assistance. The difference lies in how they are organized. A **retailer cooperative** is formed by a group of small retailers that agree to establish and operate a wholesale warehouse. In contrast, a **voluntary chain** is sponsored by a wholesaler who enters into individual supply contracts with interested retailers.

voluntary chain
A type of contractual vertical marketing system that is sponsored by a wholesaler who enters into a contract with interested retailers.

Historically, these two forms of contractual VMS have been organized for defensive reasons — to enable independent retailers to compete effectively with larger chains. These forms of VMS are able to do this by creating volume-buying power for members. Assistance is also provided with regard to store layout, training programs, promotion, accounting, and inventory control systems.

Voluntary Chain	Retailer Cooperative Chain
1. Sponsored by wholesalers, with a contract between wholesalers and independent retailer members.	1. Sponsored by retailers. They combine to form and operate a wholesale warehouse corporation.
2. Wholesaler provides a wide variety of management services — buying, advertising, store layout, accounting, and inventory control. Retailers agree to buy all (or almost all) their merchandise from wholesaler. Members agree to use common store name and design and to follow common managerial procedures.	2. Services to retailer members are primarily large-scale buying and warehousing operations. Members maintain their separate identities.
3. Most prevalent in grocery field (IGA). These chains also exist in hardware and building supplies (Castle), auto supplies (Western Auto), and variety stores.	3. Quite significant in grocery field in local areas, but not in other lines.

Retailer cooperatives are declining, but still have strong representation in groceries and hardware, such as True Value Hardware. Voluntary chains have been common in the grocery field, but are also found in hardware and auto supply stores.

franchising

A type of contractual vertical marketing system that involves a continuing relationship in which a franchiser (the parent company) provides the right to use a trademark plus various management assistance in opening and operating a business in return for financial considerations from a franchisee (the owner of the individual business unit).

franchise system

The combination of franchiser, franchisees, and franchiser-owned business units.

FRANCHISE SYSTEMS **Franchising** involves a continuing relationship in which a parent company provides the right to use a trademark and management assistance in return for payments from the owner of the individual business unit. The parent company is called a **franchiser**, and the owners of the individual business units are called **franchisees**. The combination of these individuals is called the **franchise system**. This type of contractual VMS is growing rapidly. According to the International Franchise Association (www.franchise.org), roughly six hundred thousand units are affiliated with about twenty-five hundred different franchise systems.[4]

There are two kinds of franchising:

◆ **Product and trade name franchising.** Historically the dominant kind, product and trade name franchising is most prevalent in the automobile (Ford, Honda) and petroleum (Esso, Ultramar, Petro-Canada) industries. It is a distribution agreement wherein a franchiser authorizes a franchisee-dealer to sell a product line, using the parent company's trade name for promotional purposes. The franchisee agrees to buy from the franchiser-supplier and also to abide by specified policies. The focus in product and trade name franchising is on what is sold.

◆ **Business-format franchising.** Much of franchising's growth and publicity over the past two decades has been associated with business-format franchising (including names such as Kentucky Fried Chicken, Tim Hortons, Midas, and H&R Block). (See Table 17-5.) This kind of franchising covers an entire format for operating a business. A firm with a successful retail business sells the right to operate the same business in different geographic areas. Quite simply, the franchisee expects to receive from the parent company a proven business format; in return, the franchiser receives from the individual business owner payments and conformance to policies and standards. The focus here is on *how the business is run*. And the business *must* be run according to the format provided.

In business-format franchising, the franchiser may be a manufacturer that provides franchisees with merchandise. More often, though, this is not the case. For example, some such franchisers do not sell products to their franchised stores; rather the stores

TABLE 17-5   Numerous Products Reach Consumer Markets through Business-Format Franchises

Product/Service Category	Sample Franchises
Fast food	McDonald's, Tim Hortons, Harvey's, Druxy's, Pizza Hut, Treats, A.L. Van Houtte
Auto rental	National, Avis, Thrifty, Budget, Hertz
Auto repair	Ziebart, Midas, Speedy, Thruway Muffler, Jiffy Lube, Mister Transmission
Personal care/services	Regis, H&R Block, Money Concepts, Nautilus Fitness, Body Shop
Home decor/services	Color Your World, Bathtub Doctor, Molly Maid, Weed Man, ServiceMASTER, College Pro Painters
Printing/photography	Kwik-Kopy, Japan Camera, U Frame It, Kinko's
Clothing	Sportchek, Benetton, Cotton Ginny, Mark's Work Warehouse, Rodier
Computers and video	Compucentres, Computerland, Jumbo Video, Radio Shack
Health and personal care	Nutri/system, Shoppers Drug Mart, Optical Factory, Tridont Health Centre
Convenience stores	7-Eleven, Mike's, Mac's, Becker's, Green Gables, Red & White

buy their inventory from wholesalers. The franchiser may also operate a wholesaling operation that supplies raw materials for the outlet's products or services — franchisees may be required to purchase here or from certain approved firms. This ensures consistency or quality of product across locations.

What the franchiser provides to franchisees in this format is management assistance, especially marketing expertise. There is also a great deal of proven brand equity in the "brand name" of the organization.

For a successful retail business that wants to expand, franchising provides critical advantages:

◆ Rapid expansion is facilitated, because franchisees provide capital when they purchase franchises.

◆ Because they have an investment at risk, franchisees typically are highly motivated to work hard and adhere to the parent company's proven format.

For an independent store facing stiff competition from chains and for a prospective new retail store, franchising offers advantages:

◆ Franchisees can use the parent company's well-known name, which should help attract customers.

◆ Various forms of management assistance are provided to franchisees prior to, as well as after, opening the store, including site selection and store-layout guidance, technical and management training, promotional programs, and inventory control systems.

Franchising is not without problems. Some franchises are based on poor products or unsound business practices and consequently fail. Further, a number of franchisees criticize franchisers for practices such as the following: enticing prospective franchisees by projecting unrealistically high revenues or unrealistically low operating costs; not providing franchisees with the promised and necessary levels of business support; locating too many of the company's outlets in the same market; or unjustifiably terminating or not renewing the franchise agreement. Conversely, franchisers have their own complaints, notably that some franchisees deviate from the system's policies and practices. As in most business fields, if self-regulation is ineffective, added regulation at the federal and provincial levels is likely.

Despite some challenges, continued growth in franchising is expected. Ambitious, successful retailers will exploit it as an offensive tool — for rapid expansion. Many small retailers will use it defensively — to achieve a viable competitive position against corporate chains. And prospective business owners will continue to buy franchises because of the two key attributes — a degree of independence and a variety of management assistance. In fact, many people with little or no business experience have purchased franchises for this reason.

Despite some challenges, continued growth in franchising is expected. It has been reported that a full 92 percent of existing franchisees consider themselves successful, a statistic widely publicized by franchisers. This however does not include those franchisees that have failed and terminated their contractual arrangements. It also leaves one to wonder how the term successful is defined in this case. But, there is evidence that some franchisers are trying to work more closely with their franchisees. For example, Burger King, allows its franchisees to request an impact study be conducted before new units are opened in the surrounding vicinity.[5]

Retailers Classified by Marketing Strategies

Whatever its form of ownership, a retailer must develop marketing-mix strategies to succeed in its chosen target markets. In retailing, the marketing mix emphasizes product assortment, price, location, promotion, and customer services. This last element consists of services designed to aid in the sale of a product. They include credit, delivery, gift-wrapping, product installation, merchandise returns, store hours, parking, and — very importantly — personal service. (When personal service is intended to create a sale, then it is personal selling — a type of promotion.)

We will now describe the major types of retail stores, paying particular attention to three elements of their marketing mixes:

◆ Breadth and depth of product assortment.

◆ Price level.

◆ Number of customer services.

Table 17-6 classifies retail stores on the basis of these three elements.

Some types of retail stores, such as category-killer stores, are new and growing rapidly. Others, notably variety stores, are diminishing in importance. And still others, particularly department stores, are under competitive pressure to modify some strategies. We will see that certain retailers are similar to others because new or modified institutions have filled the "strategic gaps" that once separated different types of retail institutions.

department store
A large-scale retailing institution that has a very broad and deep product assortment, prefers not to compete on the basis of price, and offers a wide array of customer services.

Department Stores

A mainstay of retailing in Canada is the **department store**, a large-scale retailing institution that has a very broad and deep product assortment, tries not to compete on the basis of price, and provides a wide array of customer services. Familiar department store names that can be found across the country include Sears and The Bay.

TABLE 17-6 Retail Stores Classified by Key Marketing Strategies

Type of Store	Breadth and Depth of Assortment	Price Level	Number of Customer Services
Department store	Very broad, deep	Avoids price competition	Wide array
Discount house	Broad, shallow	Emphasizes low prices	Relatively few
Limited-line store	Narrow, deep	Traditional types avoid price competition; newer kinds emphasize low prices	Vary by type
Specialty store	Very narrow, deep	Avoids price competition	At least standard and extensive in some
Off-price retailer	Narrow, deep	Emphasizes low prices	Few
Category killer store	Narrow, very deep	Emphasizes low prices	Few to moderate
Supermarket	Broad, deep	Some emphasize low prices; others avoid price disadvantages	Few
Convenience store	Narrow, shallow	High prices	Few
Warehouse club	Very broad, very shallow	Emphasizes very low prices	Few (open only to members)
Hypermarket	Very broad, deep	Emphasizes low prices	Some

Traditional department stores offer a greater variety of merchandise and services than any other type of retail stores. They feature both "soft goods" — such as apparel, sheets, towels, and bedding — and "hard goods" — including furniture, appliances, and consumer electronics. Department stores also attract — and satisfy — consumers by offering many customer services. The combination of distinctive, appealing merchandise and numerous customer services is designed to allow the stores to maintain the manufacturers' suggested retail prices. That is, department stores strive to charge "full" or "nondiscounted" prices.

Department stores face mounting problems, however. Largely due to their prime locations and customer services, their operating expenses are considerably higher than those of most other kinds of retail business. Many manufacturers' brands that used to be available exclusively through department stores are now widely distributed and often carry discounted prices in other outlets. And the quality of personal service, especially knowledgeable sales help, has deteriorated in some department stores.

Intense horizontal competition is also hurting department stores. Other types of retailers are aiming at consumers who have long supported department stores. Specialty stores, off-price retailers, and even some discount houses have been particularly aggressive in trying to lure shoppers away from department stores. To varying degrees, retail chains such as Wal-Mart and Zellers compete directly against the conventional department stores.

As a result of competitive pressures, primarily from large discount chains, some department stores have disappeared from the Canadian market in recent years. Simpson's, one of Canada's oldest retailing institutions, was closed by its parent company, Hudson's Bay Company, and some of its stores were converted to The Bay. Woodwards, a fixture in retailing in western Canada for generations, ran into difficulties in the early 1990s and closed many stores. The Bay acquired the remainder in early 1993. K-Mart no longer operates in Canada, having sold its Canadian operation in a merger to the Zellers component of The Hudson's Bay Company. In 1999, after several difficult years, Eaton's was finally forced to close its doors. Sears Canada purchased several Eaton's stores and ownership of Eaton private label brands.

Seeking to gain a competitive advantage in a market increasingly dominated by the large discounters and category killers, the more conventional department stores have had to adopt new ways of doing business. For example, Sears (www.sears.ca), Canada's leading department store chain, is working on a strategy that involves creating a brand(s). Sears is striving to establish its trademark as a statement of quality and value. Following a major restructuring in the mid-1990s, this department store has been showing remarkable strength, with 7 to 8 percent annual growth figures. Other strategies being used include redesigning stores, dropping or moving entire product lines, launching new ad campaigns, and stepping-up sales and promotions. Sears is trying to increase strength in products like apparel and home furnishings. The store has focused on building the brands of their own label apparel and has developed the *Whole Home* brand of furnishings and accessories for the entire home. Sears has also opened specialty format stores under this brand. To combat increasing competition from discount retailers, they have focused marketing efforts on positioning the store "brand" as representing good value at a moderate price. Despite the problems experienced by the department stores, many feel they still have a major role to play in retail sales.[6]

Discount Houses

Discount retailing uses price as a major selling point by combining comparatively low prices and reduced costs of doing business. Several institutions, including off-price retailers and warehouse clubs, rely on discount retailing as their main marketing strategy.

discount house
A large-scale retailing institution that has a broad and shallow product assortment, emphasizes low prices, and offers relatively few customer services.

Not surprisingly, the prime example of discount retailing is the **discount house**, a large-scale retailing institution that has a broad, shallow product assortment, emphasizes low prices, and offers relatively few customer services. A discount house normally carries a broad assortment of soft goods (particularly apparel), grocery items and may carry well-known brands of hard goods (including appliances and home furnishings). It also advertises extensively. Zellers and Wal-Mart are leading discount-house chains in Canada.

The success of discount houses can be attributed to two factors. First, other types of retailers normally had large markups on appliances and other merchandise, thereby providing discount houses with the opportunity to set smaller margins and charge lower prices. Second, consumers were receptive to a low-price, limited-service format. Discount houses have had a major impact on retailing, prompting many retailers to lower their prices.

Wal-Mart (www.wal-mart.ca) has experienced tremendous success in Canada since it acquired the Woolco chain in 1994. Before the store's arrival, it was widely anticipated as retail's version of the devil — nervous merchants warned of Wal-Mart's "greed" and went to seminars hoping to learn how to survive the "Wal-Mart threat." Seven years later the store is credited with waking up the complacent Canadian retail community that was once plagued by inefficiency. The discount giant has raised the bar on value, selection, and service for *all* marketers in Canada. To the retail community, Wal-Mart's success in Canada has meant — get smart, or pack up your bags! That success has been built on the image of lowest prices, a position that has been promoted extensively by the chain. It also maintains a state-of-the-art distribution technology, which builds on strong supplier relationships, behind-the-scenes ordering, and inventory management systems. Wal-Mart also prides itself on an up-front emphasis on customer service.[7]

Zellers has felt the impact of the competition from Wal-Mart. In preparation for battle, Zellers has developed "Best Value" format locations, opened in many former K-Mart locations, it has amended its low-price strategy and complemented it with broader assortments. This has included the addition of the private label, "Truly," and a selection of Martha Stewart products. The Truly line, consistent with the company's positioning as being truly Canadian was selected by the U.S. trade magazine *Private Label* as being one of the top five brands of its type. Zellers expanded its loyalty program to include a children's component called Generation Z with a redesigned catalogue to appeal to tween-aged consumers (www.gen-z.com), free giveaways with the Club Z loyalty card, and the merchant's own More credit card. It is also bringing in higher-priced merchandise.[8]

Limited-Line Stores

Much of the "action" in retailing in recent years has been in **limited-line stores**. This type of institution has a narrow but deep product assortment and customer services that vary from store to store. Traditionally, limited-line stores strived for full or non-discounted prices. Currently, however, new types of limited-line retailers have gained a foothold by emphasizing low prices.

Breadth of assortment varies somewhat across limited-line stores. A store may choose to concentrate on:

◆ Several related product lines (shoes, sportswear, and accessories),

◆ A single product line (shoes), or

◆ Part of one product line (athletic footwear).

We identify limited-line stores by the name of the primary product line — furniture store, hardware store, clothing store, for example. Some retailers such as grocery stores and drugstores, which used to be limited-line stores, now carry much broader assortments because of scrambled merchandising.

specialty store
A type of retail institution concentrating on a specialized product line, or even part of a specialized product line.

SPECIALTY STORES A very narrow and deep product assortment, often concentrating on a specialized product line (baked goods) or even part of a specialized product line (cookies), is offered to consumers by a **specialty store**. Examples of specialty stores are bakeshops, furriers, athletic footwear stores, meat markets, and dress shops. (Specialty stores should not be confused with specialty goods. In a sense, specialty stores are misnamed because they may carry any category of consumer goods, not just specialty goods.)

Most specialty stores strive to maintain manufacturers' suggested prices and provide at least standard customer services. Some specialty stores, however, emphasize extensive customer services and particularly knowledgeable and friendly sales help. The success of specialty stores depends on their ability to attract and then serve well customers whose two primary concerns are deep assortments and extensive, top-quality services. In general, specialty stores in Canada are doing quite well. Some of their success can be attributed to clear strategies with a narrow focus, rather than the broad approach of department stores.[9]

Some such retailers, however, are broadening their reach with what has been termed *lifestyle retailing*. These retailers have realized that their store "is the brand' and are leveraging their brands by selling a lifestyle concept that goes far beyond just clothing. The cachet of their labels have allowed once very limited line retailers such as Club Monaco, Roots, Le Senza, La Vie en Rose, Le Chateau (Chateauworks), and Northern Getaway to label products as varied as fragrance, household goods, furniture, massage oil, and feather-applied edible powder![10]

Some retailers like Winners specialize in offering the lowest price.

IKEA has become synonymous with assemble-it-yourself.

OFF-PRICE RETAILERS **Off-price retailers** position below discount houses with lower prices on selected product lines. These new discount retailers are most in evidence in the areas of clothing and consumer electronics; they offer a narrow, deep product assortment, emphasize low prices, and offer few customer services. Store names such as Labels, Winners, BiWay (www.biway.com) and Future Shop (www.futureshop.ca) are now well known to consumers in many cities in Canada. A number of chains of off-price retailers now operate in various regions of the country.

Some off-price retailers buy manufacturers' excess output, inventory remaining at the end of a fashion season, or irregular merchandise at lower-than-normal wholesale costs. In turn, their retail prices are much lower than those for regular, in-season merchandise sold in other stores. Customers are attracted by the low prices and fairly current fashions.

Factory outlets are a special type of off-price retailer. They are owned by manufacturers and usually sell a single manufacturer's clearance items, regular merchandise, and perhaps even otherwise unavailable items. Many well-known and popular brands such as L.L. Bean, Esprit, Calvin Klein, Royal Doulton, and Wabasso can be found in factory outlets in the United States and occasionally in Canada. This is a retailing form that is well established south of the border and became increasingly popular in Canada throughout the nineties as many outlet malls set up outside densely populated areas. As Canadian consumers become more familiar with shopping at factory outlets in the United States and as cross-border shopping continues to be part of the retailing scene in this country, we can expect the factory outlet to have a continued, and perhaps growing, presence here as well.

CATEGORY-KILLER STORES These outlets have a narrow but very deep assortment, emphasize low prices, and have few to moderate customer services. They are so named because they are designed to destroy all competition in a specific product category. Highly successful **category killers** include IKEA (www.ikea.com) with a broad assortment of assemble-it-yourself furniture, Future Shop in consumer electronics, and Toys "R" Us (www.toysrus.com). Other product areas where category killers tend to operate include office supplies, sporting goods, housewares, and records, tapes, and compact discs.

This relatively new form of retail institution concentrates on a single product line or several closely related lines. The distinguishing feature of a category killer is a combination of many different sizes, models, styles, and colours of the product, coupled with low prices. For example, IKEA stocks literally thousands of furniture and home furnishing items. Record retailers such as the major stores of Sam's (www.samtherecord-man.com) and HMV (www.hmv.ca) carry such an assortment that the consumer needs to make only one stop to ensure that he or she can find a particular compact disc.

That is the objective of the category killer in retailing: to dominate a category in such a way that the consumer believes this is the first store to visit and that the value will be better there. Although the major category killers tend to be found in large metropolitan markets, it is in fact easier for a major retailer to dominate a category in a smaller market, where the competition is not likely to be as fierce and where competitors tend to be smaller, local independents.

Sustained growth is forecast for category killers. However, most kinds of merchandise as well as many geographic areas will not generate the large sales levels that permit low prices through high-volume buying power. Furthermore, existing category killers are not without problems. In particular, they face a major challenge in maintaining inventories that are large enough to satisfy customer demand but not so large as to result in excess inventories, requiring significant markdowns.

Supermarkets

supermarket retailing
A retailing method that features several related product lines, a high degree of self-service, largely centralized checkout, and competitive prices.

As was the case with discount, the word supermarket can be used to describe a method of retailing and a type of institution. As a method, **supermarket retailing** features several related product lines, a high degree of self-service, largely centralized checkouts, and competitive prices. The supermarket approach to retailing is used to sell various kinds of merchandise, including building materials, office products, and — of course — groceries.

supermarket
A type of retailing institution that has a moderately broad and moderately deep product assortment spanning groceries and some nonfood lines, that offers relatively few customer services, and that ordinarily emphasizes price in either an offensive or defensive way.

The term *supermarket* usually refers to an institution in the grocery-retailing field. In this context a **supermarket** is a retailing institution that has a moderately broad, moderately deep product assortment spanning groceries and some nonfood lines and offers relatively few customer services. Most supermarkets emphasize price. Some use price *offensively* by featuring low prices in order to attract customers. Other supermarkets use price more *defensively* by relying on leader pricing to avoid a price disadvantage. Since supermarkets typically have very thin gross margins, they need high levels of inventory turnover to achieve satisfactory returns on invested capital. In recent decades, supermarkets have added various nonfood lines to provide customers with one-stop shopping convenience and to improve overall gross margins.

Today, stores using the supermarket method of retailing are dominant in grocery retailing. However, different names are used to distinguish these institutions by size and assortment:

◆ A *superstore* is a larger version of the supermarket. It offers more grocery and nonfood items than a conventional supermarket does. Many supermarket chains are emphasizing superstores in their new construction.

◆ *Combination stores* are usually even larger than superstores. They, too, offer more groceries and nonfoods than a supermarket but also most product lines found in a large drugstore.

For many years the supermarket has been under attack from numerous competitors. For example, a grocery shopper can choose among not only many brands of supermarkets (Loblaw, Safeway, A&P, and Sobey's) but also various types of institutions (warehouse clubs, gourmet shops, meat and fish markets, and convenience stores). Supermarkets have reacted to competitive pressures primarily in one of two ways: Some cut costs and stressed low prices by offering more private brands and generic products and few customer services. Others expanded their store size and assortments by adding more nonfood lines (especially products found in drugstores), groceries attuned to a particular market area (foods that appeal to a specific ethnic group, for example), and various service departments (including video rentals, restaurants, delicatessens, financial institutions, and pharmacies).

The trend to eating out has also cut into the profits of supermarkets. As well, the days of "made-from-scratch" are a thing of the past — consumers today are looking for a 20/20 solution — that is, twenty minutes to get the shopping done and just as quickly to prepare most meals. Supermarkets have responded by expanding home meal replacement (HMR) offerings. An HMR is any frozen or fresh meal prepared in-store for immediate consumption at home — many supermarkets provide café areas where many of the products can be consumed on-site. From bagged salads to frozen lasagna, the trend has reshaped supermarkets across the country. It has become a battle to recapture food dollars that time-strapped Canadians have been shelling out to restaurants and fast-food outlets. In Southern Ontario, Fortino's has added a sushi bar along with a wine shop, and a cigar counter. Brampton's Longo's has created a mammoth snack zone and over thirteen metres of salad bar. And Pete (otherwise known as the Fresh Prince of Papaya) of Pete's Frootiques in Bedford, Nova Scotia, has a power-juice bar and a professional piano player positioned over the grapes.[11]

Convenience Stores

To satisfy the increasing consumer demand for convenience, particularly in suburban areas, the **convenience store** emerged several decades ago. This retailing institution concentrates on convenience groceries and nonfoods, has higher prices than most other grocery stores, and offers few customer services. Gasoline, fast foods, and selected services (such as car washes and automated teller machines) can also be found in many convenience stores.

The name *convenience store* reflects its main appeal and explains how the somewhat higher prices are justified. Convenience stores are typically located near residential areas and are open extended hours; some never close. Hence, the reputation for being convenient! Examples of convenience-store chains are 7-Eleven (originally open from 7 A.M. to 11 P.M. but now always open in most locations), Mac's, Mike's, and Beckers. Toronto-based Silcorp Ltd. who operates these last three convenience chains, and who is the largest convenience store operator in Canada, has recognized the same trends as the supermarkets. They have adapted to target the meal replacement market thereby hoping to allow the stores to expand their customer base and lessen their reliance on tobacco product sales. Aside from increasing fresh and frozen meal offerings, these stores have also added branded products such as Subway, Taco Bell, and Timothy's Coffee. Through these increased offerings and store renovations the chains have increased their appeal beyond the typical 18 to 34 age market and are attracting more women and 35-plus customers.[12]

Convenience stores compete to some extent with both supermarkets and fast-food restaurants. Furthermore, since the 1980s, gasoline companies have modified many service stations by phasing out auto repairs and supplies and adding a convenience store section. This has evolved as the convenience store has — Chevron advertises the fresh-baked *Bread Garden* products they carry in their convenience stores while Laval, Quebec-

---

convenience store
A type of retailing institution that concentrates on convenience-oriented groceries and nonfoods, has higher prices than found at most other grocery stores, and offers few customer services.

based Couche-Tard plans to steal market share away from Tim Hortons and Dunkin' Donuts with their freshly brewed coffee and its fresh sandwiches, donuts and muffins.[13]

Warehouse Clubs

Another institution that mushroomed during the 1980s is the **warehouse club**, sometimes called a **wholesale club**. A combined retailing and wholesaling institution, it has very broad but very shallow product assortments, extremely low prices, and few customer services, and is open only to members. This format originated in Europe many years ago and was first applied successfully in the United States in the mid-1970s by the Price Club. In this country, Price Club/Costco (www.costco.com) is the major warehouse club chain. Costco is the result of a merger of two U.S. warehouse giants, Price Co. and Costco Wholesale Corp. Another warehouse club operating in Canada is Club Biz. Unlike Costco, anyone can join Club Biz, which carries a wider selection and provides service staff.

A warehouse club, or big-box store, carries about the same breadth of assortment as a large discount house but in much less depth. For each item, the club stocks only one or two brands and a limited number of sizes and models. Many products are sold in larger, bulk sizes. It is housed in a warehouse-type building with tall metal racks that display merchandise at ground level and store it at higher levels. Customers pay cash (credit cards are generally not accepted) and handle their own merchandise — even bulky, heavy items.

Market research suggests that the big-box trend will continue in Canada for at least another while as more new theme retailers from the U.S., such as Home Depot, continue to expand across the country. This will last as long as, among other things, the demand for commercial real estate remains high — office leasing, industrial, investment and retail — at which time growth will taper off. As with other retailing institutions, modifications and refinements can be anticipated as new demand slows and competition intensifies. Some warehouse clubs, for instance, are already experimenting with more service departments.[14]

Nonstore Retailing

A large majority — perhaps 80 percent — of retail transactions are made in stores. However, a growing volume of sales is taking place away from stores. Retailing activities resulting in transactions that occur away from a retail store are termed nonstore retailing.

We will consider four types of "traditional" **nonstore retailing**: direct selling, telemarketing, direct marketing, and automatic vending. (These names may be confusing, so don't worry about the names. Focus instead on the distinctive features and competitive standings of the four types.) Each type may be used by producers and/or retailers.

In the section following this we will then discuss the most turbulent form of nonstore retailing today — electronic transactions, or Internet retailing...or e-commerce, or e-retailing, or cybercommerce...or...whatever term you would prefer to use. It is turbulent in that growth continues to be exponential and there have been many obstacles to its success. But do not doubt that it is a success. So successful that it has almost developed a world unto itself — with the development of special payment systems and forms of cyber-currency. Despite the fact that many e-retailers are continuing forward without any profits — and these are the "stars" of e-commerce — growth is anticipated to continue for the foreseeable future.

Marketing at Work 17-2

Cozying Up with a Compatible Retail Partner

The concept of multi-branding isn't brand new. We've seen it for a number of years at highway service centres where Swiss Chalet and Harvey's, both owned by Cara Operations Ltd., live amicably under the same roof. What is new is the pairing up, even tripling up, of franchises that aren't owned by the same parent company. Even more radical, and growing in popularity, is the existence of franchises within another retail establishment — Tim Hortons located in Esso gas stations, McDonald's within Wal-Mart stores, and Starbucks inside Chapters.

Multi-branding makes good business sense for many franchisers who are reluctant to expand beyond their existing market because of the high cost of real estate and labour, and the time it takes to build a brand. Partnering with an already well-established brand drastically reduces real estate and labour costs and provides a ready group of potential customers.

This practice has gone one step further in Burnaby, B.C. where the first "trombo" location opened last year. Dunkin' Donuts and Togo's Great Sandwiches, two new brands to the B.C. market, were added to an existing Baskin-Robbins ice cream franchise. The trombo allows Dunkin' Donuts and Togo's to benefit from the recognition of Baskin-Robbins while providing consumers with a food option for each segment of the day.

In other situations one brand resides inside the retail establishment of another brand. The larger, dominant retailer acts almost as a carrier for the smaller retailer. A great example is the pairing of Chapters and Starbucks where Chapters uses Starbucks to reinforce its quality image, while Starbucks gets an instant customer base, another location, and locks out the competition.

Many retailers, however, fear losing control of their brand by partnering with another. Starbucks is committed to producing a high quality cup of coffee every time. It receives great exposure through Chapters' stores, but risks losing control of the quality delivered to its customers which could negatively impact its brand image.

Despite the potential downside, multi-branding is likely to grow according to Richard Cunningham, president of the Canadian Franchise Association, as the issue of expensive and ever-more-elusive locations is driving franchisers to look for non-traditional locations.

Source: Adapted from Eve Lazarus, "Branding Together," *Marketing Magazine*, November 1, 1999, p. 13.

Aside from confusion over the names, students will also notice the overlap that exists in the practice of these various retailing approaches. In reality, firms will practice a combination of these and retail stores often include one or more of these in their marketing efforts. The prevalence of the Internet in today's retail environment has led most types of store and nonstore retailers to experiment with Web selling alongside their original formats.

Direct Selling

direct selling
A form of nonstore retailing in which personal contact between a salesperson and a consumer occurs away from a retail store.

Statistics Canada defines **direct selling** as the retail marketing of consumer goods to household consumers by other than the regular retail store outlet. This represents a major growth area in Canadian retailing, as consumers increasingly turn to nonstore retailers for the purchase of many products. In Canada, sales by direct selling total about $3.5 billion, a figure that does not include sales by foreign mail-order retailers, direct sales made to Canadians by the mail-order divisions of department stores (such as the Sears catalogue), or direct sales through vending machines or by wholesalers. We can expect the impact of nonstore retailers to increase in the future, as consumers demand the convenience of shopping from locations that are convenient to them and at times at which they are available.

The annual volume of direct selling in Canada has increased from approximately $772 million in 1969 to more than $3.5 billion in 1998. An increasing number of companies are turning to the direct-selling route to reach consumers in their own homes. There are many well-known direct-selling companies, including Avon, Tupperware, Mary Kay (www.marykay.com), Amway (www.amway.com), Electrolux (www.electrolux.com), and The Pampered Chef. Many diverse products are sold through the direct-selling route, most of which require some form of testing or demonstration (cosmetics, water purifiers, vacuum cleaners). Essentially, the direct-selling approach involves a salesperson contacting potential customers outside of a conventional retail store environment.

The two major kinds of direct selling are door-to-door and party plan. Sometimes **door-to-door selling** simply involves "cold canvassing" without any advance selection of prospects. The use of door-to-door techniques has declined considerably as both adult partners increasingly work outside the home. More often there is an initial contact in a store, by telephone, or by a mailed-in coupon. A relatively new form of direct selling has emerged in recent years, known as network marketing. This approach to nonstore retailing involves a series of levels of sales personnel, each of which reports to an area or territory manager or captain. Sales are generated by salespeople contacting prospects directly, usually in their homes. Commissions on sales are paid to each level in the sales hierarchy. Products currently sold by this method include cosmetics like NuSkin (www.nuskin.com) and water purification systems (such as NSA).

With the **party-plan** approach, a host or hostess invites some friends to a party. These guests understand that a salesperson — say, for a cosmetic or a housewares company — will make a sales presentation. The sales rep has a larger prospective market and more favourable selling conditions than if these people were approached individually, door to door. And the guests get to shop in a friendly, social atmosphere. Pampered Chef (www.pamperedchef.com) "parties" involve food preparation involving the company's products with gifts of the firm's merchandise for the person who hosts the gathering and the food preparation in his or her home.

With such a large percentage of people now working outside the home, direct-selling firms have had to find new ways of making contact with prospective customers. For instance, Avon (www.avon.com) has moved in recent years to reach its target customers at their place of work by distributing catalogues at offices. They will call on customers at their work and even have parties at lunch time in offices. The Internet has also become one of the tools used by Avon to adapt to the changing environment. Tupperware (www.tupperware.ca), possibly the best known of the party-plan retailers, continues to market its extensive range of plastic houseware products primarily through in-home parties, involving its 374,000 dealers in more than forty countries. However, because of the changing nature of the North American market, Tupperware is now also marketed through catalogues, office parties, shopping mall kiosks, television infomercials, and the Internet.[15]

There are other drawbacks to direct selling. It is the most expensive form of retailing, with sales commissions as high as 40 to 50 percent of the retail price. Also, good salespeople are extremely hard to recruit and retain. Some salespeople have been too persistent or even fraudulent. As a result, a number of provinces have "cooling off" laws that permit consumers to nullify a door-to-door or party-plan sale during a period up to several days after the transaction.

Direct selling does give consumers the opportunity to buy at home or another convenient nonstore location. For the seller, direct selling provides the most aggressive form of retail promotion as well as the chance to demonstrate a product in the shopper's (rather than the seller's) environment.

---

door-to-door selling
A kind of direct selling in which the personal contact between a salesperson and an individual prospect occurs at the prospective customer's residence or business.

party-plan selling
A kind of direct selling in which a host or hostess invites some friends to a party at which a salesperson makes a sales presentation.

Telemarketing

telemarketing
A form of nonstore retailing in which a salesperson initiates contact with a shopper and closes the sale over the telephone.

Sometimes called *telephone selling*, **telemarketing** refers to a salesperson initiating contact with a shopper and also closing a sale over the telephone. As with door-to-door selling, telemarketing may mean cold canvassing from the phone directory. Or it may rely on prospects who have requested information from the company or whose demographics match those of the firm's target market.

The telemarketing business has really developed only within the past ten years, as marketers found it increasingly difficult to reach consumers through conventional means. Also, the development of computerized mailing or calling lists and auto-dialling technology have meant that literally hundreds of calls can be made during a day by a single telemarketer. Many products that can be bought without being seen are sold over the telephone. Examples include home cleaning and pest-control services, magazine subscriptions, credit card and other financial services, and athletic club memberships.

This form of selling is not without concerns. Few sales representative last very long in this job — encountering hostile responses on the other end of the phone, receiving more rejections than closed sales, and often working under high pressure conditions – it's not uncommon for these centres to be referred to as "boiler rooms." Annual turnover rates often average 100 percent. Telemarketing's reputation has been damaged by the unethical sales practices of some firms. These firms tell consumers that they are conducting marketing research and "are not selling anything." Such unethical procedures hurt other telemarketing companies as well as legitimate research firms that conduct telephone surveys. Such practices are known as "sugging" — selling under the guise of research. The approaches used by some telemarketing companies, coupled with a desire on the part of many consumers not to be bothered at home, has led to a consumer backlash against telemarketing in some areas. Aside from high pressure tactics used by some of these firms, it has also become a popular vehicle for outright fraud, particularly targeting seniors. The illegal use of credit card numbers obtained through fraudulent telemarketing practices has been estimated at $40 billion annually.[16]

Despite this problem, telemarketing sales have been increasing for several reasons. Certain consumers appreciate the convenience of making a purchase by phone. Also, the introduction of outgoing WATS lines has made telemarketing to consumers in distant locations more cost effective. Finally, computer systems today can automatically dial a telephone number or, going a step further, play a taped message and then record information that the consumer gives to complete the sale. Such systems reduce the normally high labour costs associated with telemarketing. These advances in technology, despite their obvious contribution to the efficiency of the process, contribute further to the negative feeling that many consumers have toward being sold products and services in such an intrusive manner. The truly effective telemarketing programs are being run by companies that have adopted an approach to telemarketing that involves doing a better job of targeting those customers who are likely to be actually interested in the products or service being offered and conveying their sales message to the consumer in a polite, caring manner without pressuring the listener.

Direct Marketing

direct marketing
A form of nonstore retailing that uses nonpersonal media to contact consumers, who, in turn, purchase products without visiting a retail store.

There is no consensus on the exact nature of direct marketing; in a sense, it comprises all types of nonstore retailing other than the three already discussed. We define **direct marketing** as the use of nonpersonal media to contact consumers who, in turn, purchase products without visiting a retail store. (Be sure to distinguish among the terms direct *marketing*, direct *selling*, and direct *distribution*.)

To contact consumers, direct marketers use one or more of the following media: radio, TV, newspapers, magazines, catalogues, and mailings (direct mail). Consumers typically place orders by telephone or mail. Direct marketing is big business. Everywhere we go today, we are exposed to direct-marketing efforts. We see advertisements on television from direct-marketing retailers of records and exercise aids, and we are encouraged to telephone a 1-800 number with our VISA or MasterCard number. We receive "bill stuffers" with our monthly gasoline bills, retail store bills, and credit card statements. We order clothing and other items from mail-order catalogues, by either mailing back an order form or more likely calling a toll-free long-distance telephone number. A large volume of direct-marketing effort is rarely seen by end consumers because it is directed at the business-to-business market, where direct marketers have relied on catalogues and mailing pieces for many years.

Given its broad definition, there are many forms of direct marketing. The major types are as follows:

◆ **Direct mail.** Companies mail consumers letters, brochures, and even product samples, and ask that orders be placed by mail or telephone, or through the Internet. Music and book clubs, magazine clearing houses, and credit card companies make wide use of this practice. Store retailers, such as Holt Renfrew, also use this approach — mailing out postcards to remind customers of their semi-annual sale or new product arrivals.

◆ **Catalogue retailing.** Companies mail catalogues to consumers and to businesses or make them available at retail stores. Examples of the latter include Tilley Endurables (www.tilley.com) and Canadian Tire (www.canadiantire.ca). Although catalogues can be picked up at their retail stores, Sears Canada operates its catalogue retailing operation as a separate unit. Merchandise in the catalogue may not be available in the store, prices may vary on the same product, and may even be on sale at different times. Catalogue retailers appear well suited to operating on the Internet as they have systems and distribution experience required for such an undertaking. In fact, according to one research firm, two catalogue retailers (Lands' End and L.L. Bean) quickly earned the top ratings in online apparel retailing.[17]

◆ **Television shopping.** There are basically two approaches to retailing through television. One we have mentioned above, in which individual products are advertised and the consumer places an order by telephoning a toll-free number and giving his or her credit card number. These can be regular length TV commercials, or feature length commercials called infomercials. The second involves the use of a dedicated television channel such as The Shopping Channel (www.tsc.ca), which represents a continuous advertisement for a variety of products such as housewares, jewellery, and other items that can be sold without the need for demonstration or trial.

◆ **Internet shopping.** Stated simply, this is the use of the Internet to offer products for sale. While this may be considered the newest form of direct marketing, its impact and nature is so broad, and still unknown, that it is considered separately in our discussion. It is a form of marketing that almost every type of retailer has exploited – whether simply to advertise and provide information regarding products and services, or to actually provide an alternative way to purchase products.

Some companies operate mail-order divisions as components of their department store operations — Sears is the best example. Others have launched catalogues as an additional vehicle for the distribution of their products. Others, such as The Added Touch (www.theaddedtouch.ca), distribute only through their catalogues. Direct marketers can be classified as either general-merchandise firms, which offer a wide variety of product lines, or specialty firms, which carry merchandise in only one or two product categories.

Direct marketing represents a major growth area in retailing. Its advantages relate particularly to its ability to direct the marketing effort to those consumers who are most likely to respond positively. Also, it offers products and services in a way that is most convenient for the consumer. Companies that are using catalogues and direct mail to reach their target customers maximize the effectiveness of their marketing programs by having the most accurate and complete mailing list possible. In fact, the success of most direct-marketing programs lies to a very great extent in the preparation and maintenance of an accurate mailing list.

Technology has kept pace with (or even led) developments in the direct-marketing field as companies are now developing sophisticated computer databases of customers and prospective customers. These databases contain not only mailing addresses, but other data on the characteristics of the consumer and his or her household, and a history of purchases that the consumer has made. Companies such as VISA and American Express make very effective use of such databases to direct mailings to cardholders in their monthly statements. The types of advertisements that are sent to certain customers are determined to an extent by an analysis of their purchasing history using the credit card.[18]

Like other types of nonstore retailing, direct marketing provides consumers with shopping convenience. Direct marketers often benefit from relatively low operating expenses because they do not have the overhead of retail stores. There are drawbacks to direct marketing, however. Consumers must place orders without seeing or trying on the actual merchandise (although they may see a picture of it). To offset this limitation, direct marketers must offer liberal return policies. Furthermore, catalogues and, to some extent, direct-mail pieces are costly and must be prepared long before they are issued. Price changes and new products can be announced only through supplementary catalogues or brochures.

In addition, some consumers have reacted negatively to receiving unsolicited mailing pieces at their homes, in much the same way that they are not exactly delighted to receive telemarketing solicitations. This negative reaction to direct-mail advertising in particular is exacerbated by the opinion shared by many that direct mail is "junk mail," in that much of it is wasted and represents a waste of paper at a time when more and more people are interested in conserving forest products. Some equate the receiving of "junk mail" to killing a tree and request that their names be taken off mailing lists to reduce the amount of unsolicited printed materials sent through the mail. The Canadian Direct Marketing Association (www.cdma.org) has encouraged its 750 members to comply with these requests.

automatic vending
A form of nonstore retailing where the products are sold through a machine with no personal contact between the buyer and seller.

Automatic Vending

The sale of products through a machine with no personal contact between buyer and seller is called automatic vending (or *automated merchandising*). Most products sold by **automatic vending** are convenience-oriented or are purchased on impulse. They are usually well-known brands with a high rate of turnover. For many years, the bulk of

You can get just about anything from a vending machine.

automatic vending sales has come from four main product categories: coffee, soft drinks, confectionery items, and cigarettes. In Canada, most recent available data show that sales made through 203,758 vending machines in 1995 totalled $391 million, of which 34.4 percent was from coffee and 28 percent from soft drinks. Confectionery items, including ice cream, accounted for 17 percent of vending machine sales, while sales of cigarettes accounted for only 5.9 percent, down from 20.5 percent in 1989. Vending machines can expand a firm's market by reaching customers where and when it is not feasible for stores to do so. Thus they are found virtually everywhere, particularly in schools, work-places, and public facilities. Automatic vending has to overcome major challenges, however. Operating costs are high because of the need to con-tinually replenish inventories. The machines also require occasional maintenance and repairs.

Technology can allow these machines to be monitored from a distance, thereby reduc-ing the number and revenue from out-of-stock and out-of-order machines. Coca-Cola is testing a machine with two-way communications ability that would allow long-distance price changes based on supply and demand considerations. These technological advances, however, are costly.[19]

While sales through vending machines have been somewhat volatile in recent years, there is reason to believe that we can expect to see more products sold through this form of nonstore retailing in the future. The reason for this optimism relates to changes in vending machine technology and the continual flow of new products for these machines. As well, they can be set up to accept credit and debit cards. New product offerings include movie soundtracks (sold in theatre lobbies), freshly squeezed orange juice, prepaid call-ing cards, reheatable dinners, office supplies, and even live bait for fishing. In Japan, they dispense everything from life insurance, to adult movies, to custom-made business cards.

Calgary native, and founder of Joe Boxer Corp., Nicholas Graham now has some-thing else in mind for vending machines. You know Joe Boxer, it's the company that brought you 3D boxers and the Double Dipper two-fly boxer (for lefties and righties). Now they're set to bring us "Underwear to go" — vending machines that dispense men's underwear for between $14–$18, the same prices as at the four thousand out-lets where the products can be otherwise found. Just insert your credit card and out pops the aluminum can with your selection. But there's more to these machines than meets the eye, or the derriere! These machines talk — a purchase brings with it a host of praise from a host of outrageous characters whose commentary is guaranteed to bring a hot blush to even the coldest cheek.[20]

 *O*nline Retailing

electronic transactions
Purchases made directly from a firm's Web site.

When a firm uses a Web site to offer products and services for sale, leading individuals or organizations to use their computers to make purchases from this company, these par-ties are engaging in **electronic transactions**. It is these transactions that are the basis of online, or Internet, selling which has been discussed throughout this book. The majority of these transactions take place between businesses, while this chapter is interested in sales by firms to ultimate, or end, consumers. Therefore, we are currently interested in **online retailing**, which consists of these electronic transactions where the purchasers are end consumers.

online retailing
Electronic transactions made over the Internet in which the purchaser is the ultimate consumer.

Online retailing is being carried out by almost a countless number of firms — many of them new companies, but also many existing retailers have been attracted to the Internet. New retailers that have chosen the Web include Indigo.ca and Buy.com while familiar retailers such as Sears and Lands' End have also found their way onto the Internet. Traditional retailers either operate on their own or in alliance with an Internet firm.[21] Some sites feature broad assortments, such as those of general-merchandisers such as Wal-Mart. However, most e-tailers concentrate on limited product lines or categories that are obvious from their names — which usually are also the addresses where they can be found — garden.com, 1-800-flowers.com, or furniture.com to name a few of the more obvious.

Whatever their differences, firms engaged in online retailing are likely to share a common attribute: they are unprofitable or, at best, barely profitable. For those that are both "brick and click" in their structure, this doesn't mean that the company is unprofitable — but that the cyber component probably isn't. There are substantial expenses in establishing an online operation; many of which do not diminish once set up — marketing costs continue to be high as these still early stages of Internet commerce require that firms continually remind consumers that they are actually there to serve their needs. Without a physical presence of some sort it is difficult to remain in consumers' minds. A study by the Boston Consulting group (BCG) in conjunction with Shop.Org (www.shop.org), an association for online retailers, has shown that by 2000, only 38 percent of Web retailers were actually making any money — and just how much they were making was not for certain! Also of interest was that 72 percent of catalogue firms with online operations *were* profitable.[22] Again, there is a reminder for the consumer — the catalogue!

Aggressive efforts to attract shoppers and retain customers, through extensive advertising, low prices and giveaways, are also clearly hampering profitability — at least in the short run. To this point the substantial losses racked up by online enterprises have been accepted — even encouraged, by investors and industry analysts. The rationale was that all available funds should be used to gain a foothold in this growing market subscribing to the principle of the first mover advantage — the pioneers in this new marketplace should do whatever they could to stake the biggest claim possible. Seemingly limitless financing was available to anyone with an idea for an Internet start-up. The values of Internet stocks were through the roof! But, what goes e-round eventually comes e-round. Attitudes changed as the new century began — as cash burn-rates for Web enterprises remained high and more "successful" sites were swallowed by black holes in cyberspace, the value of hi-tech stocks dropped quickly and many predicted a shakeout in the e-retail arena. It was predicted that "click and brick" firms stood the best chance of surviving, but that in the long run as many as half of the e-tailers would disappear.

Survival of the fittest is predicted as it is thought that those firms with unique products or services, strong brand names and, of course, cash reserves will go on to survive. They will probably prosper as they will be able to purchase flailing competitors for pennies on the dollar.[23]

Besides figuring out how to maintain investment and to turn a profit (eventually), online merchants have also had to address the dual challenges of order fulfillment and customer service. A study of the top fifty retail Web sites in 2000 underscored these challenges. The conclusion: "shoppers were unable even to place an order 25 percent of the time; 20 percent of packages arrived late or never; and 36 percent of sites had busy or unhelpful customer-service numbers."[24] Consumers are very unforgiving when e-tailers disappoint them — a bad experience and many decide they won't return to the site. A bad Web experience can also cause some consumers to sour on the "bricks" outlet of a firm that has displeased them. It appears that people have higher expectations, and lower tolerances, when using technology to shop — items should not be out of stock and even a slow-loading Web page or a difficult to navigate site may be enough to turn off some consumers to the point that they will not return.[25]

Despite these inherent challenges, online retailing has continued to grow — rapidly and significantly. Online sales represented about 1 percent of retail spending in 1999, however Forrester Research projects that Internet sales will reach almost $185 billion by the year 2004.[26] It is estimated that approximately 6 percent of this would come from online retailing (the rest being B2B transactions). While it is difficult to estimate practical values spent by Canadian consumers, it is believed that this would represent about 5 percent of retail trade in 2004.

Retail on the Internet is difficult to classify by country, as by its very nature, marketers are not bounded by geographical marketplaces. Firms may be based anywhere and may have orders from anywhere, creating one truly global marketplace. Like most other trends in Canada, we usually adapt those behaviours that "catch on" in the United States. This makes sense because of proximity and many cultural similarities. There is a lag effect, however, with regard to retail shopping on the Internet. Canadians do seem to welcome this opportunity, but there is a delayed acceptance. While it is not clear that this is because we are a more conservative culture, simply leery of Internet commerce — or if it's just that the same momentum has not yet been established as in the United States that has a population ten times that of Canada. Either way, it would seem that we lag in these shopping patterns by about eighteen months to two years. But, as e-commerce evolves this lag probably will as well.

Which product categories are consumers most likely to buy on the Internet? Well *this* doesn't seem to vary much by geography. At the top of the list: books, music and videos, computer hardware and software, travel, and apparel. What will they be most likely to buy on the Internet in the future? — given the speed of change in cyberspace, these categories soon may be surpassed by others — perhaps groceries, toys, health and beauty aids, auto supplies, or pet supplies.[27]

ℛetailing Management

Fundamental to managing a retailing firm is the planning of sound strategies. Central to strategic planning are the selection of target markets and the development of customer relationships. Also, in the future, a factor called retail positioning will probably be even more critical. Let's briefly discuss these topics.

positioning
A company's strategies and actions related to favourably distinguishing itself and its products from competitors in the minds (and hearts) of selected groups of consumers.

Positioning

Retailers are increasingly thinking about positioning as they develop marketing plans. **Positioning** refers to a retailer's strategies and actions designed to favourably distinguish itself from competitors in the minds (and hearts) of targeted groups of consumers.

Marketing at Work 17-3

The Many Sides of Sears

Last year was not a good year for retailers in Canada — Eaton's closed its doors after a failed attempt at repositioning its department stores, and international retailer Marks & Spencer pulled out of the Canadian marketplace declaring this country the worst possible retail market to make a buck. Other retailers have been affected by the same difficulties plaguing the Canadian retail industry, but have been much more successful at turning things around. Their secret — understanding their target market and delivering what they want better than anyone else.

Six years ago Sears Canada posted a loss of more than $91 million, and last year reported earnings of more than $146 million. The company invested more than $500 million in refurbishing its stores and increasing its brand selection, but one of the main reasons for Sears' success was its focus on its key customer group — women.

Women are now at the core of all of Sears' marketing initiatives. Sears has not ignored its male customers, but has made a conscious decision to focus on its key customer group.

As a result almost all of Sears' advertising and promotional campaigns are directed at women.

The first example of its repositioning came with the launch of the "Softer Side of Sears" campaign which used fashion to entice women back to the stores. Sears had learned through extensive customer research that women were going to its stores to buy home furnishings but elsewhere to buy clothes and other items. They wanted more selection, more brand names, more sizes, more colours, more choice, and more convenience. As a result, brands such as Jones Studio, Calvin Klein, and Dockers were added as well as an increased selection within these brands.

Instead of trying to redefine the department store by paring down product offerings and eliminating departments, Sears listened to its customers and now offers the brands and selection they are looking for. Shoppers can still find everything from lingerie to appliances but now they can consider Maytag and Bosch in addition to Kenmore.

Source: Adapted from John Gray, "Top Client, Retail: Sears right on target," *Strategy*, August 2, 1999, p. B5.

Positioning centres on the three variables we have stressed in this chapter: product assortment, price, and customer services.

Let's briefly examine several positioning strategies.[28] When only price and service levels are considered, two strategies that have potential value are *high price–high service* and *low price–low service*. The former is difficult to implement because it requires skilled, motivated employees (especially salespeople); the latter necessitates careful management of operating expenses because gross margins are small.

When all three variables — product assortment, price, and customer services — are considered, two new options emerge. One is product differentiation, in which a retailer offers brands or styles different from those sold in competing stores. A second is service and personality augmentation, in which a retailer offers similar products but sets itself apart by providing special services and creating a distinctive personality or atmosphere for its stores.

A retailer's positioning strategy may include one or a combination of these options. Retail executives need to exhibit creativity and skill in selecting positioning strategies and implementing them.

Customer Retention

In recent years, marketers in many businesses, especially in retailing, have begun to subscribe in increasing numbers to the philosophy that it makes considerably greater sense to retain the customers they have than to compete vigorously in order to attract new ones. This viewpoint acknowledges what should have been obvious to all marketers — namely that a company's most valuable assets are loyal customers. While not denying the importance of going out to attract new customers, this approach to doing business places at least equal emphasis on keeping existing customers happy.

Two elements of a customer-retention strategy involve getting to know customers in as much detail as possible and rewarding those who are loyal and continue to give us their business. The former implies the development and maintenance of a customer database, and the latter often involves the establishment of a bonus program for frequent shoppers. Some of the most effective customer-retention programs combine these elements.

The best example of a customer-retention program (often called a *loyalty program*) in Canadian retailing is Club Z, operated by Zellers, the successful discount arm of the Hudson's Bay Company. Established in 1986 as a frequent-buyer program and modelled along the lines of the airlines' frequent-flyer programs, Club Z and Generation Z awards "points" to Zellers' shoppers based on the amount of their purchases. These points may be redeemed for "gifts" from a Club Z gift catalogue. The program has been wildly successful in differentiating Zellers from the competition and in creating a very loyal customer base — close to half of all Canadian households are Club Z members and points have been redeemed for over ten million gifts.[29]

Other retailers have had or have recently established similar programs to encourage shopper loyalty. High-end retailer Holt Renfrew has its Club-Select and Canadian Tire has issued its well-known "Canadian Tire money" for many years, essentially giving customers discounts of up to 5 percent on purchases made in the store. Sears Canada relaunched its Sears Club, a frequent-shopper program that rewards users of the Sears credit card with savings of up to 4 percent on purchases. Even Tim Hortons has found a way to reward faithful customers through its annual "R-R-Roll Up The Rim to Win" promotion.

Retailing in the Future

As consumers change, so do forms of retailing. And one thing is for sure — consumers will change! Retailers would, of course, like to anticipate changes *before* they occur. But, when change can be as revolutionary as the sudden and dramatic emergence of online retailing, that can be difficult to do. Many trends represent threats to retailers. But, as we know, a threat perceived and handled properly is really an opportunity. We will illustrate the dynamics of retailing by focusing on eight diverse, significant trends.

◆ *Changing demographics and industry structure.* The Canadian population is growing older, with proportional decreases in the 16 to 34 age group and increases in the 45 and over age group. Real growth in retail sales is expected to be substantially less than in the 1970s and 1980s. Thus there may be too many shopping centres and retail stores, particularly as so many major chains entered the market in the mid-1990s.

◆ *Expanding computer technology.* Advancing technology dramatically affects both consumer behaviour and retail management. In particular, sophisticated computer systems that capture sales and inventory data influence the items retailers stock as well as what and when they reorder. Newer systems permit retailers to automatically place orders and reorders with suppliers that are linked to them via computer.

◆ *Emphasis on lower prices and lower costs.* An expanding number of retailers are expected to stress value. For most of them, that strategy will dictate reducing prices and — if they intend to remain profitable — cutting costs. To pare their expenses over a period of years, more and more chains will need to take steps such as eliminating one or more layers of management, cutting advertising, and investing in labour-saving equipment such as computers that monitor inventory levels and automatically reorder merchandise as needed.

◆ *Accent on convenience and service.* Compared with the situation in past decades, consumers are busier, are older, and have more money to spend. They want products and ways to buy them that provide maximum convenience and service. Convenience means nearby locations, extended hours, short waiting times, and other factors that make shopping easier. Service also includes friendly, knowledgeable sales staff, easy credit, liberal return policies, and ample post-sale service.

◆ *Experimentation.* Largely because of competitive pressures, many retailers are experimenting with new or modified formats and with nontraditional locations. For example, department stores are scaling back product assortments by eliminating "commodity" lines (such as fabrics and mattresses) and stressing fashion and quality. Discount houses are either trading up to become so-called promotional department stores or are digging in for price battles. Some retailers are expanding their markets through new types of locations, or by moving toward more nonstore retailing. Others are welcoming smaller, specialized retailers into their stores to operate specific departments as tenants or partners.

◆ *Internet.* Developments in this technology are enabling retailers to reach consumers through a new distribution network. The frequency of online shopping is increasing. One survey reveals that computer software, books, clothing, and airline tickets are the most common buys on the Internet. It is projected that the biggest growth in Internet buying will be in airline tickets and hotel reservations.[30] Retailing is seeing the development of online shopping malls. One Canadian project combines banking and shopping. Once an Internet access kit is purchased, consumers can make purchases from any number of cyber-stores using Paypro — Internet Payment Processing Inc. (www.paypprocorp.com). Also, Internet currency, such as is available from Flooz.com (www.flooz.com), and sites like it demonstrate that we have just seen the beginning of a system of commerce based upon electronic transactions.[31]

Now the Internet has its own currency.

◆ *Emphasis on productivity.* Extremely small profits are forcing retailers to squeeze more revenues out of their resources (floor space, people, and inventories). Hence, virtually all products are being sold, at least to some extent, on a self-service basis. To boost motivation, some retailers have put salespeople completely on commissions rather than on salaries plus commissions. Computer systems, as discussed above, can also help achieve greater productivity.

◆ *Continuing growth of nonstore retailing.* Retail stores will continue to be dominant. But more and more retailers are complementing their stores with one or more types of nonstore retailing. Many consumers prefer the novelty or convenience of nonstore retailing. As the chapter discusses, growth is expected within most areas of nonstore retailing.

wheel of retailing
The cyclical pattern of changes in retailing, whereby a new type of store enters the market as a low-cost, low-price store and over time takes business away from unchanging competitors; eventually, the successful new retailer trades up, incurring higher costs and higher prices and making the institution vulnerable to a new type of retailer.

As consumers change, so do forms of retailing. Retail executives would like to anticipate changes in retailing before they occur. To some extent this is possible, as many of the evolutionary changes in retailing have followed a cyclical pattern called the **wheel of retailing**.[32] This theory states that a new type of retailer often enters the market as a low-cost, low-price store. Other retailers, as well as financial firms, often do not take the new type retailer seriously. However, consumers respond favourably to the low prices and shop at the new institution. Over time, this store takes business away from other retailers that initially ignored it and retained their old strategies.

Eventually, according to the wheel of retailing, the successful new institution trades up in order to attract a broader market, achieve higher margins, and/or gain more status. Trading up entails improving the quality of products sold and adding customer services. Sooner or later, high costs and, ultimately, high prices (at least as perceived by its target markets) make the institution vulnerable to new retail types as the wheel revolves. The next innovator enters as a low-cost, low-price form of retailing, and the evolutionary process continues.

There are many examples of the wheel of retailing. To mention a few, chain stores grew at the expense of independents during the 1920s, particularly in the grocery field. In the 1950s, discount houses placed tremendous pressure on department stores, which had become staid, stagnant institutions. The 1980s saw the expansion of warehouse clubs and off-price retailers, which have forced many institutions — supermarkets, specialty stores, and department stores — to modify their marketing strategies.

What will be the retailing innovations of the future? The 1990s brought growth in nonstore retailing, direct marketing, and the use of the Internet. These trends will likely continue well into the future. The wheel of retailing can help retailers identify changes in retail institutions. Retail firms must identify and respond to significant trends that affect retailing, including institutional changes, by developing customer want-satisfying marketing strategies.

It would appear that the retail world does now take the "threat" of a retail Internet seriously, but at the same time many believe that it will never take the place of "real" shopping experiences. It need not replace the experience to still pose a very real threat to the revenues of traditional retail outlets. As well, retailers may need to continue experimenting with ways to get consumers away from their computers and into their stores.

What innovations are next — given the surge in Internet usage, perhaps various new kinds of e-tailing? Perhaps some other form of retailing that has yet to be considered? Perhaps even bigger supercentres or giant specialty retailers that dwarf existing category killers?

Whatever happens, retail experts predict that those merchants that will prosper in the future will (1) provide consumers with a distinctive bundle of benefits, (2) stress value, not just low prices, (3) save their customers time and energy, and (4) make shopping fun. Many retailers and even large malls, in fact, are stressing entertainment-based selling.[33]

Summary

Retailing is the sale of goods and services to ultimate consumers for personal, non-business use. Any institution (such as a manufacturer) may engage in retailing, but a firm engaged primarily in retailing is called a retailer.

Retailers serve as purchasing agents for consumers and as sales specialists for wholesaling intermediaries and producers. They perform many specific activities, such as anticipating customers' wants, developing product assortments, and financing.

Almost two hundred thousand retail stores in Canada collectively generate over $260 billion in annual sales. Retailers' operating expenses run about 27 percent of the retail selling price; profits are usually a very small percentage of sales.

Most retail firms are very small. However, small retailers can survive — and even prosper — if they remain flexible and pay careful attention to personally serving customers' needs.

Retailers can be classified in two ways: (1) by form of ownership, including corporate chain, independent store, and various kinds of contractual vertical marketing systems such as franchising; and (2) by key marketing strategies. Retailer types are distinguished according to product assortment, price levels, and customer service levels: department store, discount house, catalogue showroom, limited-line store (including specialty store, off-price retailer, and category-killer store), supermarket, convenience store, and warehouse club. Mature institutions such as department stores, discount houses, and supermarkets face strong challenges from new competitors, particularly different kinds of limited-line stores.

Although the large majority of retail sales are made in stores, an increasing percentage now occur away from stores. And this proportion is growing steadily. Four major forms of nonstore retailing are direct selling, telemarketing, automatic vending, and direct marketing. Each type has advantages as well as drawbacks. Perhaps the greatest change in nonstore retailing will be from the Internet as Web-shopping continues to increasingly come "online" as more and more retailers open stores on the Internet and as marketers refine their skills to attract shoppers to this new retail medium.

Retailers need to carefully select markets and plan marketing mixes. Besides product, price, promotion, and customer services, executives also must make strategic decisions regarding physical facilities. Specific decisions concern location, design, and layout of the store. Downtown shopping areas have suffered, while suburban shopping centres have grown in number and importance. Retailers also should consider positioning — how to favourably distinguish their stores from competitors' stores in the minds of consumers.

Various trends present opportunities or pose threats for retailers. Institutional changes in retailing can frequently be explained by a theory called the wheel of retailing. To succeed, retailers need to identify significant trends and ensure that they develop marketing strategies to satisfy consumers.

Key Terms and Concepts

Retailing (retail trade) 522	Franchisee 533	Warehouse club (wholesale club) 542
Retailer 523	Franchise system 533	Nonstore retailing 542
Physical facilities 528	Product and trade name	Direct selling 543
Shopping centre 529	franchising 533	Door-to-door selling 544
Convenience centre 529	Business-format franchising 533	Party-plan selling 544
Neighbourhood centre 529	Department store 535	Telemarketing 545
Community centre 529	Discount retailing 537	Direct marketing 545
Regional centre 529	Discount house 537	Direct mail 546
Corporate chain 530	Limited-line store 538	Catalogue retailing 546
Independent retailer 532	Specialty store 538	Television shopping 546
Contractual vertical marketing	Off-price retailer 539	Internet shopping 546
system 532	Factory outlet 539	Automatic vending 547
Retailer cooperative 532	Category-killer store 539	Electronic transactions 548
Voluntary chain 532	Supermarket retailing 540	Online retailing 549
Franchising 533	Supermarket 540	Positioning 550
Franchiser 533	Convenience store 541	Wheel of retailing 554

Questions and Problems

1. Explain the terms *retailing*, *retail sale*, and *retailer* in light of the following situations:

   a. Avon cosmetics salesperson selling in offices.

   b. Farmer selling produce door to door.

   c. Farmer selling produce at a roadside stand.

   d. Sporting-goods store selling uniforms to a semiprofessional baseball team.

   e. Indigo.ca selling books and music through its Web site.

2. How do you explain the wide differences in operating expenses among the various types of retailers shown in Table 17-1?

3. What recommendations do you have for reducing retailing costs?

4. Reconcile the following statements, using facts and statistics where appropriate:

   a. "Retailing is typically small-scale business."

   b. "There is a high degree of concentration in retailing today; the giants control the field."

5. Of the criteria given in this chapter for evaluating the competitive positions of large-scale and small-scale retailers, which ones show small stores to be in a stronger position than large-scale retailers? Do your findings conflict with the fact that most retail firms are quite small?

6. The ease of entry into retailing undoubtedly contributes to the high failure rate among retailers, which — in the view of some — creates economic waste. Should entry into retailing be restricted? If so, how could this be done?

7. What course of action might small retailers take to improve their competitive position?

8. In what ways does a corporate chain (Loblaw, Zellers, or Sears) differ from a voluntary chain such as IGA?

9. What can department stores do to strengthen their competitive positions?

10. "The supermarket, with its operating expense ratio of 20 percent, is the most efficient institution in retailing today." Do you agree with this statement? In what ways might supermarkets further reduce their expenses?

11. "Door-to-door selling is the most efficient form of retailing because it eliminates wholesalers and retail stores." Discuss.

12. What is the relationship between the growth and successful development of regional shopping centres in suburban areas and the material you studied in Chapters 4, 5, and 6 regarding consumers?

13. Which of the retailing trends discussed in the last section of the chapter do you think represents the greatest opportunity for retailers? The greatest threat?

14. Do you agree with the axiom that there are three keys to success in retailing — location, location, and location? How do you reconcile this axiom with the fact that there is so much price competition in retailing at present?

15. With the widespread acceptance of the Internet as a means of shopping, how do you think this will affect the axiom discussed in the previous question?

16. Of the types of retail stores discussed in this chapter, which one(s) do you think have been or would be most successful in foreign countries? Which one(s) have been or would be unsuccessful in other countries? Explain your answers.

Hands-On Marketing

1. Arrange an interview with a small retailer. Discuss with this merchant the general positions of small and large retailers, as covered in this chapter. Which if any of these points does the small retailer disagree with, and why? Also ask what courses of action this merchant takes to achieve or maintain a viable competitive position. Interview a second small retailer, ask the same questions, and compare your answers.

2. Contact the headquarters of two retail franchise systems with which you are familiar and request information provided to prospective purchasers of a franchise. (Local units of the franchise systems should be able to supply you with the headquarters' mailing or e-mail addresses.) Once you have received the information, evaluate whether you would like to own either of these franchises. What criteria did you use in making this evaluation?

Case 5-1

AMAZON, CHAPTERS, INDIGO
A New Chapter in Bookselling

Amazon.com Inc.'s success in Internet retailing has become legendary. Founded in July 1995 by Jeff Bezos, Amazon.com generated $1.6 billion in revenue during 1999. This represents a 169 percent growth from the previous year, leaving the company with an $18 billion market valuation before ever turning a profit. Driving those sales, the company says, is a continuing increase in customer traffic, which is now about 20 million.

The company lists over three million titles in its online catalogue, yet it originally kept only a couple of hundred titles in stock at its headquarters in Seattle. Customer orders were filled from the nearby warehouse of one of America's largest book distributors, Ingram Book. This kept employees and overhead costs to a minimum. As growth continued and increasing competitive forces necessitated quicker distribution, the last year has seen hundreds of millions of dollars go toward capital expenditures. This has included the construction of massive distribution centres. Virtual retailing on this scale requires actual premises and many employees to run dependably. More obscure books are still obtained directly from the publishers. However, it is not just the availability of products that is contributing to the company's growth. Amazon's success seems to be attributable to its investment in customers.

Shopping in Cyberspace

Amazon offers a variety of online features that make it easier for customers to find books that match their tastes and suit their needs. Although an Internet retailer cannot offer its customers the physical comforts of cozy furniture and specialty coffees, Amazon.com creates a special ambiance in other ways. Authors drop by electronically to post comments about their books. Customers are encouraged to do the same, regardless of their opinions on what they have read. Browsers find this type of openness refreshing. Value to the customer is enhanced by discount pricing, up to 50 percent off bestsellers, and availability of shipping alternatives designed to meet customers' needs of timeliness and economy. Customers have the convenience of setting their own shopping hours.

Recognizing the value associated with loyal customers, Amazon has devoted considerable resources to the development of a customer database, detailing customers' preferences and buying patterns. This information is linked to customers' postal and e-mail addresses, which are used to solicit customer feedback on changes to the Web site. The completion of these forms provides the company with valuable information for the building of good customer relationships.

Personalized e-mails can be sent about new releases that would be of interest, make recommendations, and advise regular customers about sale items. At the same time, it keeps customers aware of, and involved in, Amazon's retail site. This leaves an obvious question to be asked — why would customers ever need to go to a bookstore again?

Seeking Profits

Not satisfied with being the largest Internet bookseller, Amazon has diversified its offerings to include music, videos, electronics, toys, online auctions, and more. Within weeks of its entry into the toy business, Amazon became the #1 online retailer of toys. It is the only major online "bookseller" to offer such a diversified range of products. Amazon has also become the #1 online retailer in the United Kingdom.

Each year, sales have skyrocketed beyond expectations. But so have the losses, now estimated at over $900 million and counting. This has caused many to speculate if Amazon.com would ever make a profit and whether success would ever be achieved utilizing such business models. The turnaround began in January 2000 when the company announced that a series of deals to rent Web space to other e-tailers yielded Amazon a stunning $607 million. Not only is the company selling more and more products to its customers, but selling the attention of those customers to other e-tailers. This is the beginning of Bezos' intention to develop the Amazon site into a more general-purpose portal that will continue to attract more and more traffic.

Soon after, in February 2000, it was announced that the company's original books business was profitable — a sign that its core e-tailing model just might have legs after all. This has all led analysts to now think that Amazon will be profitable by 2002. But, as Amazon's leader continues to expand its breadth, it is difficult to foresee how this may affect these forecasts.

Maintaining Profits

With so many visitors, features, and products it is not surprising, then, to learn that 76 percent of Amazon's sales in the first quarter of 2000 came from repeat customers. Despite the high percentage of repeat customers and a registered customer base of eight million people in more than one hundred countries, the company is not profitable. This is despite the fact that the company sells 75 percent of all books that are ordered online. Because Amazon has built up a vast infrastructure of warehouse and distribution centres to house burgeoning inventories of product lines, relies on brand-name identification, and needs to spend relentlessly to attract each dollar of sales, it faces many of the same difficulties managing its business as old-line retailers do.

Financial stresses are attributable to too little Web traffic, which continues to force Web companies to spend a great deal of money on marketing and sales. Links to the Amazon site are available at a variety of other Internet locations, and the company has developed an "associates program" to encourage the promotion of these referrals. Associates at other Web sites, such as Yahoo!, are offered a share of each sale they direct to the online bookshop, further reducing profit potential.

These results have not gone unnoticed by two of North America's largest booksellers: Borders Books and Barnes & Noble. In early 1997, these well-established retailers each decided to develop their own Internet destinations to accompany their traditional stores. When Barnes & Noble first entered the cyber market, management of Amazon.com indicated that they had been expecting competition for a long time and did not intend to budge. However, by June 1997, Amazon.com indicated that it would slash prices at its site by up to 40 percent. This eventually reached 50 percent. Such actions are characteristic of an industry entering the growth stage of the product life cycle — new competitors entering the market are creating a downward pressure on prices. Despite these growing pains and the fragmentation of the book industry, many book retailers of all sizes are rushing to establish Internet storefronts.

Although Borders has committed itself to developing an Internet presence, it still believes that its future growth will come from "bricks and mortar" locations. It has been criticized for poor Internet sales performance as it has captured only 1 percent of the online book market. The Barnes and Noble chain has been more aggressive and creative in establishing its online persona. It has developed bnradio.com where visitors can listen to full-length music clips and sample five-minute portions of books. As well, they have developed a section of its site to offer thousands of free distance-learning courses based on works from yoga to Shakespeare. They have also obtained a stake in notHarvard.com that provides distance-learning software packages. The expected growth in video game sales has led the company to once again offer an expanded selection of game titles online and in its superstores.

Booksellers in Canada and the United States have all experienced growth in revenues over the past six years, however the lion's share of this has been enjoyed by the large national chains in each country. What is not known is how many players the industry can sustain and whether it is possible to generate a profit by operating solely in cyberspace. As 2000 began, some analysts still wondered if buying books over the Internet might simply be a temporary fashion, with limited growth and nonexistent profit.

North of Borders

How are these Internet booksellers affecting retailers in Canada? Canada's largest bookseller, Chapters Inc., which was created in March 1995 by the merger of Coles Book Stores and SmithBooks, also operates Classic Bookstores, The Book Company, and World's Biggest Bookstore. It also has a majority stake in Pegasus Wholesale Inc., a nationwide book distribution company. The company has also spun off a separate Internet company, Chapters Online, which the company has been aggressively marketing since early 1999 when Chapters began preparations to take the Internet company public. Chapters earned $234.7 million in revenue in the final quarter of 1999, representing a significant increase over previous quarters. Actual profits have been decreasing, however, as a result of the online division. The last quarter of 1999 saw an $8.5 million loss from Chapters Online.

Aside from the new cross border competition via the Internet, there is also renewed competition in the traditional medium as Indigo Books Music and Cafe, the second largest bookseller in Canada steps up its presence and competitive pressures. Although the company currently has fewer than twenty superstores, compared with the seventy operated by Chapters, it has plans to open twenty-five to thirty more but believes that the Canadian market will ultimately only support about seventy. Indigo can also be found on the Internet, and like its stores has a heavy emphasis on music products.

Both Canadian retailers continue to modify their superstore concepts, trying to find the right blend of decor, comfort, and amenities. Chapters Inc. has been recently attempting to reconfigure their outlets to differentiate itself from the newer Indigo locations. As well, they continue to work on their Web personas with the potential advantage of offering Canadian flavour by featuring Canadian titles and currency.

In 1995, U.S. retail giant Borders was prevented from entering the Canadian market by a government ruling that indicated that a controlling interest of a Canadian bookstore by a U.S. retailer would be a threat to the Canadian publishing industry. However, in June 1996 the U.S. book retail giant, Barnes & Noble, was able to create a Canadian presence through acquisition of a 20 percent interest in Chapters Inc. However, with the large-scale popularity of online bookstores location is no longer relevant as sophisticated distribution systems enable overnight shipment to most locations.

Seeking Growth

How is it that Chapters has identified a growth opportunity in the retail book market when Canadians have access to limitless choices of books from Internet retail locations? Traditionally, retailers have argued that location is the key to success. So why is it that Chapters' management thinks that it can be successful operating stand-alone stores? The answer lies in how the company positions itself. It is not just selling books; it is catering to the demands and lifestyles of its marketplace. The company locates its superstores in a market with between 15,000 and 18,000 university graduates and then attempts to create an atmosphere conducive to a sense of community among customers.

While Chapters stores have common design elements, with soft green and yellow colours with lots of wood accents, they also have features unique to their location. The superstore in Guelph, Ontario, has beautiful cathedral ceilings. The three-storey outlet in Victoria is located in a fully restored marble-faced heritage building. The MacLeod Trail Chapters superstore in Calgary features one-of-a-kind western-theme decor, including rotating western art exhibits, a kids-own corral, and a giant teepee in the children's department. The West Hills superstore in Calgary has hardwood floors and cherrywood fixtures, providing a rich, warm atmosphere.

All stores are equipped with cozy furniture and various seating areas in which customers can relax and browse through a book or select from the large and eclectic assortment of magazines. Most locations have a Starbucks cafe. Within each superstore is a "My Books" children's section featuring CD-ROM terminals, colourful kid-sized seating, an assortment of books, and hopscotch. This combination of comforts is designed to encourage the customers to stay in the store as long as they wish.

The managers of many of the superstore locations have expressed their hopes of turning the store into a gathering place for the community. Many locations have a meeting room that is made available to community groups. There are a variety of events scheduled at the stores most weekends: live music, multimedia demonstrations, cooking demonstrations, and readings by Canadian authors. The stores prominently feature local content and participate in local charity events. For example, Chapters Inc. is a partner with Frontier College, an organization that has been teaching people to read since 1899. For one event Chapters Inc. teamed up with author Mordecai Richler and TV personality Peter Gzowski to present a benefit evening for Frontier College.

Chapters Inc. has created a college book division that operates the bookstore at McGill University in Montreal. Company officials anticipate that the college division will have revenues of up to $100 million, but if history is to repeat itself, this will not happen without controversy. When Follett Corporation took over the management of the campus bookstore at Sheridan College in Oakville, Ontario, in 1996, it attracted the attention of many critics. Concerns included queries as to the propriety of diverting profits from operations at a tax-funded institution to corporate headquarters in the United States.

Where does all this competition from Internet retailers, superstores, and foreign operators leave the small, independent Canadian book retailer? Canadian booksellers, in fact, have recently begun asking Ottawa to protect them against the Chapters superstore chain.

Small booksellers have recognized the need to distinguish themselves from the large retailers. One small American chain, Chapter 11, has decided to stay with smaller-sized locations allowing the store to locate in neighbourhood strip malls and other suburban locations. It also relies more on in-store events than on advertising expenditures. Other options include specializing in local-interest products, supplying personal service, and forging ties with individuals and groups in the community.

Some have recognized the need to establish a Web site to complement their physical location. However, there is the very real concern of how enough buyers can be attracted to their Internet location. If Amazon.com is having trouble generating sufficient traffic with its "associates programs," which encourages referrals, how then can a small entrepreneur hope to succeed in such a market? There are those who maintain that it is possible to carve out a niche through specialization. Such a strategy would require a total rethinking of the manner in which business is conducted: from the physical design of the store to the building and nurturing of customer relationships. Is it realistic to think that success can be achieved by independent operators who alter their way of business? Or should Canadians come to accept that their literary choices will be controlled by large corporations operating in exclusive locations or through the Internet?

Pertinent Web Sites

www.amazon.com
www.barnesandnoble.com
www.bnradio.com
www.borders.com
www.chapters.ca
www.indigo.ca

Questions

1. How do bookstores operating on the Internet position themselves relative to competition operating from "traditional" stores? Illustrate this through use of a positioning map.

2. How do the superstore book retailers position themselves relative to stores operated by independent owners, those operated in shopping malls, and those operating solely through the Internet?

3. What role has store design played in the positioning of Chapters superstores?

4. What role should national and international bookstores play in the operation of bookstores on college and university campuses?

5. As book retailing via the Internet proceeds through the various stages of the product life cycle, what changes do you predict for the industry as a whole and for individual players?

6. What responses are available for small chains and independent booksellers to take to the changing conditions in this industry?

Sources: Robert Hof, Ellen Neuborne, and Wendy Zellner, "Can Amazon Make It?" *Business Week*, pp. 38–43; Rebecca Quick, "Web Bookseller Plans to Offer Array of Courses," *The Wall Street Journal*, May 30, 2000, p. B1; Rebecca Quick, "Barnes and Noble Makes Another Play in Video Games," *The Wall Street Journal*, May 8, 2000, p. B6; Carol Loomis, "Amazon" *Fortune*, May 1, 2000, pp.129–132; Jim Carlton, "Amazon.com Beats Analysts Estimates," *The Wall Street Journal*, April 27, 2000, p. A3; Joann Muller, "Can Borders Turn the Page?" *Business Week*, April 3, 2000, pp. 75–78; George Bragues, "Bookstore Protectionism," *Financial Post*, March 31, 2000, p. C7; Leah Eichler " Indigo Owner Optimistic on Stores," *Publishers Weekly*, March 20, 2000, p. 17; Zena Olijnyk, "Indie Bookseller Takes on Book Chains," *Financial Post*, March 13, 2000, pp. C1, C6; "Mixed Results in Third Quarter for Chapters," *Publishers Weekly*, February 21, 2000, p. 16; Robert Hof, Heather Green, and Diane Brady, "Suddenly, Amazon's Books Look Better," *Business Week*, February 21, 2000, pp. 78–84; Mikala Folb, "Above the Crowd," *Marketing Magazine*, January 25, 1999, pp. 15–16; Larry LeBlanc, "Indigo Seen as Major Retail Player," Billboard, January 10, 1998, p. 36; "Media Alert — Chapters Presents an Evening with Mordecai Richler and Peter Gzowski," *Canada News Wire*, October 2, 1997; Randell E. Stross, "Why Barnes & Noble May Crush Amazon," *Fortune*, September 29, 1997, pp. 248, 250; "Hot on the Trail — New Chapters for Calgary," *Canada News Wire*, September 24, 1997; "Guelph Previews Chapters Book Superstore," *Canada News Wire*, July 29, 1997; "Chapters Book Superstore Opens in Victoria," *Canada News Wire*, July 28, 1997; Amanda Lang, "Still Searching for the Holy Grail," *Financial Post*, June 19, 1997, p. 17; "A River Runs Through It," *The Economist* (Electronic Commerce Survey), May 10, 1997, pp. 9–10; Kurt Opprecht, "Barnes & Noble Undercuts Amazon.com Discount," *Wired News*, February 25, 1997; John Lorinc, "Chapters Unveils New Mall Design in Yorkdale Mall, Toronto," *Quill & Quire*, November 1996, p. 8; "Large Format Independents Challenge Chapters at Its Own Game," *Quill & Quire*, October 1996, pp. 8–9.

Case 5-2

TOYS "R" US
Playing Around With Distribution

Several years ago there were a handful of companies that quickly recognized the commercial (i.e., retail) potential of the then new and emerging Information Superhighway. Recognizing its vast potential, these pioneering companies were the first to establish their virtual storefronts on the Internet. As is found in most business strategies, this first mover advantage has afforded these companies a significant head start. In 1997 eToys, Inc. was one of these companies that established themselves as an online e-tailer banking on this new method of distribution as a strategy for success. And successful it has been, allowing the company to develop a considerable consumer base of loyal shoppers and becoming an e-tailer with enviable brand recognition in the American marketplace. Needless to say, these events have become a concern for the largest specialty toys retailer in North America, Toys "R" Us.

Toys "R" Us is also on the Internet — since 1998 — *presumably* affording the company the advantages of multiple distribution channels, considerable industry experience, substantial buying power, and existing brand recognition and equity. However, the company has encountered operational problems in trying to devote itself to both the "click" and "brick" marketing environments. Most noticeable have been conflicts between its traditional retail locations and its Web site.

Snakes and Ladders

During the 1980s and before, there were retailers who developed a specialized focus and became known as category killers. Toys "R" Us is one such retailer. In fact, the store's founder, Charles Lazarus, is credited with having created the concept. As the Internet has evolved it can be seen that many of the most successful e-tailers may also be categorized as such. The Internet provides a means of reaching a potentially massive audience while focusing on the most specialized products and categories. Category killers have arisen in many categories in the brick environment and we are now seeing the same happen in the cyber marketplace.

Toys "R" Us was so successful throughout the 1980s that it forced some large competitors out of business and expanded at an average of about 30 percent a year. But like many retailers that experience such success, the company then seemed to lose touch with the marketplace. Complacency or overconfidence set in and the company did not notice that, as the 1990s began, its stores needed renovation and customer service had slipped. Customers, however, did notice these things. As well, the company began to miss trends in toys — such as the substantial interest in educational toys.

As would be expected, market share dropped and the company's stock price fell considerably by the late 1990s. If that wasn't bad enough, eToys gained considerable momentum on the Internet and giant retailer Wal-Mart had overtaken the company, becoming the largest volume seller of toys in the United States.

E-Toys Gets in the Game

Becoming a success on the Internet involves more than simply getting a Web site up and operating, in fact many of the initial problems eToys experienced were of a more traditional variety. Ironically, eToys' first order was placed secretly by Toys "R" Us. It was an order for five items. The inventory tracking system was not yet in place and four of the items were mysteriously unavailable. It must have appeared to Toys "R" Us management that no real threat existed from the Internet start-up.

Once these kinks were ironed out, eToys focused on developing product selection. After all, what distinguishes these cyber merchants? One advantage is that e-stores are not restricted by limited shelf space — the company decided therefore to offer whatever they could — let the customer choose. The company quickly expanded to include children's music, videos, software, and books. eToys also acquired an Internet firm that sells baby-related products and provides information services about raising babies. The cyberstore had developed a product assortment of more than one hundred thousand available items by 1999. The goal was to become the top retailer of merchandise for children up to 12 years of age.

The eToys Web site has received very positive reviews since its inception for its attractiveness and its simplicity. It offers an advanced search engine that greatly assists in selecting items based on the interests of the child. Gift shopping is aided by wrapping services and the ability to specify multiple addresses. Outside packaging is unmarked so as not to arouse the suspicions of observant children upon delivery — important features when holiday shopping can account for up to 50 percent of online toy sales.

Half a million dollars in sales in 1997 quickly soared to $32 million for 1998. Not in the same ball park as Toys "R" Us but clearly a threat to the conventional "bricks and mortar" retailer as it was now venturing onto the Internet. Further, there was great confidence in the eToys enterprise, as on the day of its IPO stock price almost quadrupled, making the company's market capitalization considerably more than that of Toys "R" Us.

Channel Surfing

Changes in the company's fortune now required Toys "R" Us to rethink what it was doing. Serious threats now existed from retailers outside of their "category." The "category killer" strategy was no longer enough, Geoffrey the Giraffe was being shown up by a toy store that existed only in cyberspace, and a discount department store of which toys was but only one of many product assortments it carried. Further, Wal-Mart is expected to soon extend its retailing efforts onto the Internet.

A new business strategy was needed. During 1999, the company committed millions of dollars to store renovations, it significantly increased the number of products carried in its stores, and redesigned its supply chain, including adding distribution centres to reduce or eliminate stock-outs.

The fledgling Internet component of Toys "R" Us was made a separate unit in order to provide the focus and attention that would be required to compete with eToys. Pricing became a contentious issue for the online component as many retailers during the early development of e-commerce relied or competed on price in order to lure consumers to the Internet and to capture sales from other e-tailers. The toy category was no different. The issue was difficult for vendors such as Toys "R" Us because of the inherent problems of offering one set of prices online and another in its physical stores.

The site itself did not earn favourable reviews, as it was difficult to use and provided a low level of service. The 1998 holiday season quickly became a nightmare, as during November and December there were several site crashes and order-fulfilment problems.

A new site was unveiled in April 1999 as the company sought to find advantages they held over online-only toy vendors. One answer was to allow purchases from toysrus.com to be returned to the company's physical locations. The company also focused attention on determining key products with great demand and using the company's buying clout to ensure supply — items such as Pokemon products and Furbys. The new site featured Pokemon Central, an area devoted to all that is Pokemon. A variety of search methods are available as well as a guide to selecting toys, including product reviews. Visitors can link to a site devoted to the youngest of consumers — Babies "R" Us. Also a Web address has been developed for the U.K. market.

Another glitch in Toys "R" Us comeback plans occurred when Amazon.com began to sell toys online the summer of 1999 and within weeks was purported to have become the number one online seller of children's products.

By Christmas 1999 the new Toys "R" Us site had closed much of the gap between themselves and eToys.com, receiving nearly as much traffic as its cyber rival. It was the fourth most visited e-retail site during the season. They both were in the wake of Internet phenomenon Amazon.com.

A Hit! Again and Again and, uh, Again!

It would seem that Toys "R" Us had mastered distribution via the Internet at this point. But, guess again, although the company had successfully employed its familiar name to attract visitors, even orders — it was more than they were prepared for! Much, much more! Perhaps, as a result, they were in fact creating more trouble for the brand than benefits.

Overall, the 1999 holiday season heralded indications that mainstream online buying was soon to be a reality after its anticipation for the past few years. Growth during this holiday season over the last was so great in fact that it strained the abilities of both toysrus.com and eToys.

Although eToys successfully expedited 96 percent of its orders on time during November and December, it claims that its resources were sorely tested and that customer service declined as a result. The company felt that they had not performed adequately and that they would continue to work towards improving its record. During this same period the company had been also concentrating on expansion, focusing on developing the first service of its kind in the U.K. This required the development of a distribution system in England to service that area.

Toys "R" Us' woes were much greater and, of course, the focus of much more publicity. A typical e-commerce strategy, the company launched a huge campaign to begin the season complete with $10 off first time orders. Traffic to the site was overwhelming for the company and its server — the site crashed. Despite its guaranteed Christmas delivery policy, the company announced shortly before Christmas that it would not be able to meet the demand that had been experienced. There was a backlog of orders and inventory shortages despite recent investments in a new distribution system, and customers were informed that they would have to pay extra for priority shipping.

Customers were shocked and enraged that they had been let down by the established retailer and a furor of publicity ensued. Many were so disgusted that the offer of $100 coupons did little to pacify their anger at having been let down so close to Christmas. It would be the children that would be the most disappointed come Christmas morning if parents couldn't fill wish lists at the last moment. On December 22, the company announced that the free gift certificates would be delivered by overnight courier, giving the parents two days to try to buy the gifts they had thought were taken care of up to a month before. The company would not disclose the cost of this gaffe, but claimed that less than 5 percent of orders were affected.

Tremors were also felt at the management level as the company worked tirelessly to close a beneficial deal for venture capital for the battered Web site. As well, board pressure forced the CEO to resign. During the year a number of executives left the company. The replacement was John Eyler, former CEO and chairman of FAO Schwarz. FAO quickly filed suit against their former chairman for contract violations stating that his contract required a one-year notice period and barred him for working for a competitor for at least two years.

Now, with almost twenty online specialty toy retailers, the pie was breaking into smaller pieces — and both toysrus.com and eToys had some of their customers lured away. The biggest single nemesis was perhaps Amazon, who managed to get 99 percent of its orders on their way (on time) during the 1999 holiday season. And to prevent any future problems, that company then invested another $300 million to increase the capacity of its system.

Notwithstanding the problems of the holiday season, some analysts believed that reports compiled on the Christmas season indicate that, despite huge sums thrown at advertising by Web start-ups, traditional bricks-and-mortar brands, such as Best Buy and Toys "R" Us, Inc. won on the net. Despite this, these retailers have to realize that it is not enough to rely upon previously won reputations when setting up on the Web.

eToys also prepared for increasing Internet shopping by fine-tuning its order fulfilment strategy. Where it once used an outside catalogue company, Fingerhut, it has begun handling the process in-house through drastic expansion of its own distribution centres. It believes this will streamline the process while also reducing costs. These e-tailers believe online-only distribution will be the key to their future success, while Toys "R" Us believes that its combination of online and offline operations will prove itself more beneficial for success in the long run.

With concerns about continued investment in Internet enterprises, eToys announced in spring 2000, in a bid to convince investors that it can became profitable, a new US$8 million summer marketing campaign featuring a wide variety of summer-themed children's products. This included items not usually exploited by toy retailers such as car games and travel music. The company hopes to distribute sales more evenly through the year to make better use of its customer service and distribution network.

The 1999 season may be remembered as the year that e-commerce flourished to a $10 billion business, but it will also go down as the year that many became very annoyed at e-commerce sites. Andersen Consulting, in December of that year, attempted 480 e-purchases, only to find that 130 failed. These failures occurred because the sites were unable to process the transactions without crashing.

Are the glitches experienced by these retailers actually errors on the part of the retailers or growing pains related to the new technology? With new technology and distribution methods aren't there likely to be learning curves? One thing is for sure, however, the 1999 holiday season represented a coming of age for Internet retailers.

Toys Were Us?

The Toys "R" Us stock price has declined in value for the past five years, while management has continued to argue over who and what is responsible for its ailing fortunes. The company faces rising competition in both the brick and click marketplaces while continuing to cling to the strategies introduced by the company's founder in the 1980s. Although retired, Lazarus remains an influential figure in the company, and has been a hard sell for even the smallest of changes.

Pertinent Web Sites

www.toysrus.com
www.babiesrus.com
www.toysrus.co.uk
www.etoys.com
www.amazon.com

Questions

1. What are the strengths and weaknesses of each of these three e-tailers regarding the selling of children's merchandise online?

2. In the longer-term, which of these e-tailers will continue to be successful? Why?

3. With price-cutting a popular means to promote Internet traffic and sales, how can Toysrus.com position itself as a strong competitor without creating conflict with its physical stores?

4. Should the company continue to employ both distribution channels in the future or focus on only one channel? Explain your reasoning.

Sources: Lisa Bannon, "E-Toys Strategy To Stay in The Game," *The Wall Street Journal*, April 25, 2000, p. B1; William Bulkeley & Kara Swisher, "Toys 'R' Us to Announce Softbank Deal," *The Wall Street Journal*, February 23, 2000, p. B10; Dana Canedy, "Scharz Sues Chief For Move to Toys 'R' Us," *New York Times*, February 18, 2000, p. C1; Stephanie Neil, "Santa's IT Helpers: E-Com Sites That Weathered the Holidays Just Fine Now Face the Next Step," *PC Week*, January 31, 2000, p. 65; Lisa Bannon, "Etoys Meets Expectation but Stock Falls," *The Wall Street Journal*, January 28, 2000, p. B2; Katrina Brooker, "The Nightmare Before Christmas," *Fortune*, January 24, 2000, pp. 24–25; Heather Green, Catherine Yang & Paul Judge, "The Dot.coms Falling to Earth," *Business Week*, January 17, 2000, pp. 38-9; Kevin Brass, "E-Commerce Sites Need to Iron Out the Kinks," *Video Store*, January 9/15, 2000, p. 16; David Orenstein, "E-Retailers Learn Delivery Lesson," *Computerworld*, January 3, 2000, p. 1; Rebecca Smith, "Etoys Lured Holiday-Season Shoppers But Concern About Service Hurts Stock," *The Wall Street Journal*, December 28, 1999, p. A3; Maryanne Murray Buechner & Marc Hequet, "Clicks and Bricks: E-tailers Don't Own the World Yet," *Time*, December 27, 1999, p. 88; Saul Hansell, "Toys 'R' Us Falls Behind on Shipping," *New York Times*, December 23, 1999, p. C5; "Some Web Customers Cry: 'All I Want For Christmas is my Order!'" *The Wall Street Journal*, December 13, 1999, p. B1; Matt Krantz, "Stocking a Giant Toybox," *USA Today*, November 24, 1999, pp. 1B, 2B; George Anders, "Amazon, Etoys make Big, Opposing Bets; Which One is Right?" *The Wall Street Journal*, November 2, 1999, pp. A1, A10; Katrina Brooker, "Toys Were Us," *Fortune*, September 27, 1999, pp. 145–6.

Case 5-3

FALLING INTO THE GAP
Changing Consumer Preferences

By all accounts, The Gap is a marketing success story. The retail chain began by offering basic T-shirts and jeans that looked like designer clothes without the designer image or price. The Gap quickly grew into the most profitable specialty-clothing store chain in North America by positioning itself as offering "good style, good quality, good value." Its eight hundred stores do more than $8.3 billion in sales, and its divisions include GapKids, BabyGap, Banana Republic, and Old Navy stores. *Advertising Age* magazine named the company Marketer of the Year in 1997.

The Gap's road to becoming a leader in specialty retailing was not without bumps. Donald Fisher started The Gap in 1969 out of frustration when a store refused to allow him to return a pair of Levi jeans that were too short. The first Gap store was located in San Francisco and it stocked jeans in a wide range of sizes. The Gap soon expanded across the United States, supported by a fixed 50 percent markup that Levi Strauss required of all retailers selling its jeans. However, as a result of government regulatory changes and other factors in the mid-1970s, the price of jeans could no longer be set by manufacturers. This forced The Gap, which was totally dependent on jeans, to find a new position.

After a futile attempt to position itself as a retailer of higher-margin clothing carrying its own brand, a back-to-basics merchandise strategy was found to have the greatest appeal among The Gap's customers. Gap stores stocked all-cotton apparel items in a deep assortment of colours. The Gap's strong ties to manufacturers, developed during its earlier efforts to sell its own store label, allowed the company to manage the quality of its products. Furthermore, the company was able to control costs by designing its clothes in-house.

Expansion into children's clothing followed the success of Gap stores in the 1980s. BabyGap and GapKids stores feature simple, basic apparel items (for example, dresses and overalls) for newborns to young children. The Gap acquired Banana Republic in 1983. Banana Republic grew rapidly as safari fashion became very popular with the release of movies such as the *Indiana Jones* series, *Out of Africa*, and *Romancing the Stone*. However, the safari image waned by the late eighties, necessitating a change in position for the 150-store chain. The position that produced the best financial results was as an upscale Gap with more adventurous fashions. As all-occasion casual dressing and khaki apparel regained popularity at the end of the nineties so did the popularity of Banana Republic.

The Gap's merchandise assortment allowed it to become the "uniform of the middle class and middle aged." However, two core customer groups, teens and Generation Xers, began to turn away from The Gap's staple clothing items. Leo Burnett Co.'s semiannual "What is hot among kids" market research survey indicated that a negative image of The Gap began developing among teens as early as 1992. In that year, over 90 percent of teens surveyed labelled Gap clothes as "cool." This rating slipped to 83 percent by the summer of 1993, 75 percent by the winter of 1993, and 66 percent by the end of 1994. The loss of interest by these important market segments forced The Gap to appeal to new customers by becoming more fashion-oriented and launching new products and retail store concepts.

The Gap shifted its emphasis in merchandise away from unisex items to clothing that is gender-specific and fashion-oriented. The effort worked, as the company's earnings increased by 23 percent from 1992 to 1993 despite a less favourable image among younger consumers. In addition, an effort was made to present a uniform picture of a Gap store by stocking all styles available in all Gap stores, whereas smaller stores previously received only a narrow selection of inventory.

Another attempt to expand The Gap's customer base resulted in its entry into discount retailing in the United States in 1993. Forty-eight low-performing Gap stores were converted into Gap Warehouse discount stores. This decision represented a radical departure from The Gap's success formula, which focused the company on being the leader in specialty clothing retailing. To prevent the cannibalization of sales at Gap stores, Gap Warehouses sold separate lines of clothes that were similar to the Gap's basic products — jeans, khaki pants, and T-shirts — but carried everyday low prices. In addition, the material used in Gap Warehouse clothes was different from those stocked at Gap stores. Jeans received fewer stone-washed treatments, and stitching was less detailed. And lighter-weight fabrics containing more polyester were used to control costs and keep retail prices low. Unlike The Gap, which targets only adults, Gap Warehouses targeted adults and children.

The following year, The Gap launched in the United States a second entry into discount retailing to compete with mass merchants. Its Old Navy Clothing Co. stores carry specially designed apparel and accessories for consumers with incomes of $20,000 to $50,000. The Old Navy stores offer a wide selection of casual apparel items priced 20 to 25 percent below The Gap's clothing lines. Old Navy stores are positioned as one-stop clothing outlets with department store-style assortments of clothing for men, women, boys, girls, and babies. In addition, the stores stock The Gap's non-clothing products (for example, picture frames, address books, and decorative shopping bags).

The Gap introduced increasingly more lifestyle products such as a line of bath and body products in a further attempt to serve new market segments. Gap Scents includes a line of soaps, lotions, shampoos, conditioners, shower gels, bath salts, and scented candles. The bath and body products are designed to target a market estimated to be worth more than $1 billion annually and growing at 5 percent per year. In part, the development of Gap Scents was in response to the introduction of the Bath & Body Works chain by The Limited, The Gap's major competitor. The bath and body products are viewed by Gap management as the first step in making The Gap a lifestyle brand. If consumers begin to view The Gap as more than just a place for clothes, other product categories can be added. The company has also made inroads in developing Old Navy as a lifestyle brand with the introduction of its own cosmetics offerings.

Where Next?

Although The Gap has been presented as a fairy re-tale story, the company is not today without its challenges. These include imitation by competitors of both its clothing and its marketing style, a significant public relations problem arising from protests against its labour policies, having been targeted by anti-sweatshop activists, as well as opposition from environmentalists to the logging of old growth redwood trees by the founder's family. Finally, a drop in sales at stores open more than a year; down from double digit increases. While the company itself has seen growing sales this has been the cumulative effect of increasing sales at Banana Republic (20 percent) and Old Navy stores (10 percent).

It would seem that Old Navy sales increases are cannibalizing Gap sales. Also, the increasing extension of high-equity brands such as Roots and Nike into the casual wear market increases competition for these spending dollars. Even makers like Russell Athletics have increased marketing efforts to fend off the casual retail chains like The Gap and Abercrombie & Fitch.

During the first quarter of fiscal 2000, same-store sales at The Gap sank 5 percent; Old Navy and Banana Republic same-store sales fell 2 percent. In a healthy economy, is this a brief aberration or a sign of something bigger? One of The Gap's responses to falling sales will give new meaning to the phrase "expanding markets." The company has enlarged the range of sizes available in all three chains. The selection will now top out at a full-figured size 20. In the past cellulite has been a feminist issue and even a medical issue — The Gap now sees it as a business opportunity. While 40 percent of the female population wear a size 12 or bigger, only 26 percent of women's clothing sales are in the plus size category. This is an apparel market estimated at US$23 billion.

Retailing also is undergoing radical changes. Data on North American shopping habits indicate that both the number of mall visits and the number of stores visited per shopping trip have dropped dramatically over the last twenty years. In addition, new technology is allowing retailers to control their costs as never before and devise new ways to offer products to meet the needs of their customers (for example, the Internet). The face of specialty retailing will continue to be shaped in the 2000s as the echo boomer generation continues to move through its teens.

These consumers switch brands easily and are comfortable with technology. One in three North American echo boomers belongs to a minority group, compared with one in four in the general population. These teens have more purchasing power than previous generations and make many of their own purchase decisions, including those about clothes. Research indicates that this age group has great influence over a range of family purchase decisions. The key to success for The Gap will be its ability to refine the position of its stores to meet the needs of its target markets while operating in an increasingly dynamic environment.

Online Strategy

It is thought by many retailing experts that perhaps the best survival strategy in the retailing world of the future is to find that optimal mixture between online and offline components. But when will a retailer ever strike that perfect balance — and will it be the same balance for all? The Gap has attempted to develop a Web presence that is friendly across a wide range of targets while trying to stimulate enough to keep the attention and interest of the digital generation. Aside from the sale pages, the store offers maternity wear exclusively online and any purchase made through the Web site can be returned to any store in the U.S. There is also a guide for recommending items suitable for casual work attire. Web sales are only available in the United States.

Another trend that has greatly influenced retailers such as The Gap is the move toward casual attire in the workplace. While this may mean that consumers, overall, may require a less varied wardrobe and there-fore buy less clothing, more demand will exist for good quality casual clothing. But, the population is also aging — into an age bracket that has traditionally considered "fashion" as a discretionary category and therefore not very crucial. It is believed that "lifestyle leaders" such as Club Monaco, Eddie Bauer, and The Gap will weather this change well as they appear to have an intimate understanding of their customers and are usually successful at editing their merchandise down to what their customers need. Perhaps, however, it is that they have the ability to convince consumers what they need!

Gap Ads appeal a little to the nostalgia of some segments, the current appeal for retro, and that elusive "invisible cool" so important with tweens and portions of the Nexus generation (Canadians aged 18 to 34). Campaigns have been developed around recurrent themes with a little modification for different targets — Christmas 1998 ads featured popular musicians performing seasonal faves in their own key — from Lena Horne to Aerosmith to all-girl group Luscious Jackson — similar and yet different — all ending with the "Fall into the Gap" slogan.

More recent ads featuring similarly attired dancers moving to different musical genres were very popu-lar with viewers. A second wave of these ads, again featuring similarly dressed models, appeared drone (everybody in vests; corduroys; leather) and felt to some viewers that they made "Shopping at The Gap like being in a cult." Invisible cool incites the desire to follow a trend, yet appear to be non-conformist. It all combines to create an image — reflect a lifestyle — trendy, chic, but somehow individualistic. The com-pany did actually fall into a gap with this second group of ads.

The increasing popularity of khaki fashions prompted Gap to vary slightly with "Are you a jean or a khaki?" The reviews have been mixed and the jury is still out on this campaign.

Pertinent Web Sites

www.gap.com
www.gapkids.com
www.babygap.com
www.bananarepublic.com
www.oldnavy.com

Questions

1. What social influences will have an effect on The Gap's future marketing strategy?

2. Evaluate Gap's entry into discount retailing in the United States with Gap Warehouse and Old Navy stores. Given the changes that have taken place over the last few years in discount retailing in Canada, where is The Gap positioned relative to the competition? Illustrate with use of a positioning map.

3. Given the changes taking place in retailing, what new products might The Gap offer? What changes to their marketing strategy can you suggest?

4. How significant a role does TV advertising play in the positioning and image of a retailer such as this one? Where should this retailer advertise? Explain.

5. Visit The Gap's Web site and those of various competitors. How does The Gap's Web site compare with those of some of its competitors? How does the function(s) each site serves differ for each firm? How are they similar?

www.dockers.com
www.ebauer.com
www.jcrew.com

Sources: Emily Eakin, "Everybody in Size 20," Salon.Com, June 16, 2000, www.salon.com; Barbara Lippert, "Be Cool Boy: The Gap is Gonna Rumble Tonight," *Adweek*, April 3, 2000, p. 22; Linsey Bisset & Bani Dheer, "The Nexus Generation Talks Back," *Marketing Magazine*, January 31, 2000, p. 36; Alice Cuneo, "Bridging the Gap," *Advertising Age*, December 13, 1999, p. 22; Louise Lee, "Why Gap isn't Galloping Anymore," *Business Week*, November 8, 1999, p. 136; Louise Lee, "'Clicks and Mortar' at Gap.com," *Business Week*, October 18, 1999, p. 150; Leslie Kaufman, "Gap Inc. Looks Vulnerable as Sales Decline at Flagship Stores," *New York Times*, October 9, 1999, pp. C1, C2; Kelly Barron, "Gaplash," *Forbes*, June 14, 1999, p. 110; Mikala Folb, "All Dressed Down," *Marketing Magazine*, April 5, 1999, p. 12; Becky Ebencamp, "Old Navy Continues to Push Brand Scope With Cosmetics," *Brandweek*, April 20, 1998, p. 1; Barry Base, "Gap Spots Executed With Grace and Flair," *Strategy*, January 5, 1998, p. 12; Mary Kuntz, "Reinventing the Store: How Smart Retailers are Changing the Way We Shop," *Business Week*, November 27, 1995, p. 84; Christina Duff, "Bobby Short Wore Khakis — Who's He and Who Cares?" *The Wall Street Journal*, February 16, 1995, p. A1; Elaine Underwood, "Gap Sets Scent for November," *Brandweek*, August 22, 1994, p. 4; Alice Cuneo, "Gap Floats Lower-Price Old Navy Stores," *Advertising Age*, July 25, 1994, p. 36; Laura Zinn, "Teens Here Comes the Biggest Wave Yet," *Business Week*, April 11, 1994, p. 76; Russell Mitchell, "The Gap Dolls Itself Up," *Business Week*, March 21, 1994, p. 46; Russell Mitchell, "A Humbler Neighborhood for The Gap," *Business Week*, August 16, 1993, p. 29; Russell Mitchell, "A Bit of a Rut at The Gap," *Business Week*, November 30, 1992, p. 100; Russell Mitchell, "The Gap: Can the Nation's Hottest Retailer Stay on Top?" *Business Week*, March 9, 1992, p. 58.

Part six

Marketing Communications

Informing, persuading, and reminding current and potential customers

We have now examined product, price, and distribution — three of the four marketing-mix elements that are necessary but not by themselves sufficient to achieving our marketing goals. To complete the marketing mix, we now turn our attention to marketing communications.

Chapter 18 presents an overview of integrated marketing communications, including the various types of marketing communications, how marketing communications work and the management issues involved in developing marketing communications programs. Chapter 19 looks at the personal selling process and sales-force management. Advertising, sales promotion, public relations and publicity are the subjects of Chapter 20.

Chapter Eighteen

The Marketing Communications Program

This chapter will help you understand how marketing communications decisions are made by describing what marketing communications is and how it fits into a firm's total marketing program. After studying this chapter, you should have an understanding of:

◆ The role of marketing communications.

◆ The different methods of marketing communications.

◆ The concept of integrated marketing communications.

◆ How the process of communicating relates to effective marketing communications.

◆ The concept and design of the marketing communications mix.

◆ The considerations in developing a marketing communications program.

◆ Alternative marketing communications budgeting methods.

◆ The regulation of marketing communications.

Top of the Pops

Take one finely tuned marketing communications program, add a good dose of verve and nerve, and you too can create another hit pop group. Hit groups are created all the time, it is a pretty established practice in the popular music business. The list of prefabricated pop bands includes The Monkees, Spice Girls, New Kids on the Block, Milli Vanilli…want more? Okay, The Archies, Backstreet Boys, Menudo (where it all began for Ricky Martin), N'Sync, and probably a few others that you have heard about.

Take a band called Bardot. In the beginning it had no name recognition, hadn't been heard to sing — in fact, had no members. Then, in a matter of a few months, five unknown girls *became* Bardot and the biggest pop sensation in Australia. How? Well, it all started with a small group of entrepreneurs who had a marketing goal: to create the next all girl super group targetted for a market similar to that of the Spice

Girls. This is a risky business so it is essential that you have a pretty good strategy and the plan to implement it. The first step was to do the usual, get a manager and get a record deal. The manager (a.k.a. the brand manager) was the same firm that took care of the group Crowded House. A major record label provided the initial three-recording agreement (the distribution). With these basics in hand, what was necessary was a marketing communications program whose objective was: (1) provide the band members, (2) create instant awareness, (3) obtain fast conviction and (3) motivate a high level of pur-

chase of CDs, tour tickets, and associated merchandise from the target market.

The first step in the marketing communications program was pretty creative and strategic. To implement the first three objectives, the introduction of Bardot would be caught on camera for Australia's Seven Network as part of its newly popular fly-on-the-wall television series. The vehicle, a TV show called Popstars, was broadcast every Sunday night and featured applicants going through a selection process to become members of the band. Each broadcast was full of tension, tears and excitement as twenty-five hundred applicants, some talented and lots not, vied for the five available spots. Australians were completely captured by the process. Commentators called it "cringe TV," compelling viewing because even though a lot of it was awful…you had to watch. By the fifth episode, the five lucky ones had been selected and Popstars had become #1 in the TV rat-

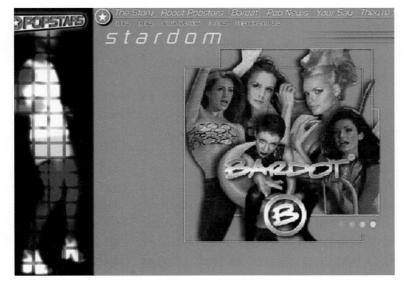

ings. Within weeks, the group's first single, Poison, was released and it went to #1 on the Australian charts and stayed there for a number of weeks. At the same time, and for six months, TV cameras followed all the group's movements.

As for the group itself, the five winners came from Australia's main cities thus assuring national appeal to the target market. The girls received daily gym workouts, dancing and singing lessons by top trainers and choreographers, makeovers by top stylist, and choice material provided by songwriters and producers from around the world. Bardot had the backing of Warner Music, the Seven-TV Network, a national radio syndicate — Austereo, and a best selling magazine called *New Idea*.

Wherever the group appeared, there was a TV camera and thousands of screaming kids, the fans. After the release of its first album, Bardot toured New Zealand to more hordes of screaming fans and plans are in place for more and more tours as the market becomes more interested in seeing the girls perform live rather than in just listening to their CD.

The TV production firm that made Popstars is negotiating with TV stations in a number of countries in hopes of selling the series or the series format rights so that another TV station can reproduce the process and create a star group in its own market. Lone Eagle Entertainment, made the largest Canadian casting call ever. In August of 2000, girls between the ages of 18 and 25 were auditioned in Calgary,

Montreal, Toronto, and Vancouver. The same approach pioneered in Australia will be used here and it is expected that Global TV will broadcast the first show in 2001.

In the United States, ABC has already introduced this format to TV viewers to a very enthusiastic response. Whether or not the new boy-band that results will be a musical success is still unknown, but the network has found a winner for its own marketing goals — increased advertising revenues. An American Popstars is expected to be launched at the same time as the Canadian version.

Some commentators say that this kind of marketing is pretty cynical, others say that's just the music business. What do you say? Is it too cynical?[1]

The Role of Marketing Communications in Marketing

One of the attributes of a market system is the right to use communication as a tool of influence. The Bardot example makes the "creating of fad" point in no uncertain terms. In our society, that freedom is reflected in the efforts by business to influence the feelings, beliefs, and behaviour of prospective customers. Let's examine how communication works from an economic perspective and then from a marketing perspective.

Marketing Communications and Imperfect Competition

The North American marketplace operates under conditions of imperfect competition characterized by product differentiation, emotional buying behaviour, and incomplete market information. A company uses marketing communications to provide more information for the decision-maker's buying-decision process, to assist in differentiating its product, and to persuade potential buyers.

Through marketing communications, a company strives to increase its sales volume at a given price. Simply stated, marketing communications is intended to make a product, service, or organization more attractive to prospective buyers or clients.

A firm also hopes that marketing communications will affect consumer responses to price increases and decreases (demand elasticity) so that when prices go up, demand will decrease very little and when prices go down demand will increase quite a bit. Also, management wants marketing communications to create an image and to send certain messages that will give the consumer a number of non-price reasons to buy. One of the main functions of marketing communications is to differentiate the offerings of a company from those of its competitors. In the absence of such differentiation, consumers are likely to conclude that there are no differences and will make their purchase decisions based

Microcell cuts through the competitive clutter with a clear, sharp, and appealing image to carry its message.

largely on price. Therefore, differences are emphasized such as President's Choice bottled water and Banff Ice vodka being made from iceberg and glacial water, or Becel margarine (www.becelcanada.com) being the "best margarine for heart health." And how can we forget Buckley's "It tastes awful, and it works!" cold medicine (www.buckleys.com). Attempts are made to focus attention on those traits that distinguish the product from others competing in the market.

Then there are products and services that would appear to actually be the same across providers — here you provide a little "personality" to the product or company through your communication efforts. In Quebec, people may say, "call me on my Fido" — referring to their cell phone from Fido Microcell Solutions of Montreal (www.fido.ca), a personal communications services provider. The bilingual canine term has come to be used generically much like people use terms like Kleenex or Band-Aid. The marketing communication program has successfully branded a product and a service that has been fraught with price competition and has come to be perceived as a commodity product.

The user-friendly approach using friendly canine imagery in all the advertisements has been immensely successful in developing brand recognition, product differentiation, and immediate visualization of what the service stood for.[2] The marketing communications program of a company has the responsibility to convey the right messages that will lead the consumer to conclude that there are many non-price reasons to buy from the firm.

Communications in the Context of Marketing

marketing
communications
All of the elements of an
organization's marketing
mix — usually
advertising, publicity,
public relations,
personal sales, and
sales promotion — that
serve to inform actual
and potential customers.

Marketing communications serves three essential roles: It **informs**, **persuades**, and **reminds** prospective customers about a company and its products. It is an attempt to influence. The relative importance of these roles varies according to the circumstances faced by a firm.

COMMUNICATING TO INFORM The most attractive product or brand will be a failure if no one knows it is available! Because distribution channels are often long, a product may pass through many hands between its producer and consumers. Therefore, a producer must *inform* intermediaries as well as ultimate consumers or business users. Wholesalers, in turn, must inform retailers, and retailers must inform consumers. As the number of prospective customers grows and the geographic dimensions of a market expand, the problems and cost of informing target consumers increase. As can be seen from this, simply making available a good or useful product is not enough. A program of communication must be designed to reach different groups, and to reach them effectively persuading them through word and imagery. The use of imagery and visuals transfers a great deal of information rapidly and often remains after the words have been forgotten.

You can't rely on the idea that once it gets packaged and to the store shelf all has been done. It's not over yet. A communication plan must be designed and implemented that will cause consumers to seek the product, recognize the product, and keep coming back for it. Keep in mind that people can see hundreds of "marketing communications" each day and that the average shopper spends slightly more than twenty minutes buying groceries, covering less than a quarter of the supermarket in the process. Add to this the fact that the eye lingers just 2.5 seconds on each product.

Canadian digital culture magazine, *Shift*, after recently extending into the U.S. market, is planning yet another extension of its identity. Moving beyond its existing magazine, Web site (www.shift.com), Internet radio station, and upcoming television show, Shift is now planning to launch a retail and e-commerce venture. So, you say, with these resources at their disposal they don't really need to worry about developing a communication strategy — well, wrong! The new stores will carry Shift-branded merchandise and a variety of computer electronics, technology, entertainment and fashion suitable to the magazine's audience — urban, well-educated, computer-literate 25 to 35-year-olds. In keeping with Shift's identity as "a multimedia brand," communications will blur the lines between technology, pop culture, fashion, and art. Aside from their own media resources, the program will include subway ads, outdoor, as well as online advertising. Initial ads seem to have worked well, and after testing price points, creative and lists, Shift will push its magazine to one million Americans in a direct mail campaign. Online advertising has included five "outside" sites including Salon (www.salon.com) and The Onion (www.theonion.com). Sites are currently under review for the best fits with Shift's target audience. Once found, "partnerships will be set up to swap online advertising, content, and other assets in order to get its name out."[3]

When Panasonic (www.panasonic.ca) wanted to launch the new line of Power Activator (PA) batteries aimed at the battery-eating electronics of today's youth markets, it knew it had to be "cool" about it, but without looking as if trying. The solution was to employ "guerilla" tactics aimed at building grassroots awareness within the target's own environment and culture.

First the product's logo was circulated without product identification through underground channels — posters were used in and surrounding dance clubs showing blown out electronics and just the PA logo. The logo was also emblazoned on T-shirts, hats, stickers

Shift communicates its multimedia brand image with a sophisticated program as well as through its pages.

that were distributed at more than thirty events in major Canadian cities. Club DJs were also enlisted to assist by wearing the PA T-shirts at their clubs — sister brand Technics' turntables are very popular with this group so they were quite willing to participate. Eventually this merchandising was replaced with similar gear, but this time revealing the product. At this stage, the campaign tied in with MuchMusic and the Much Dance 2000 CD release began. Also, a contest mini-site was connected to the MuchMusic Web site (www.muchmusic.com) with prizes consisting of Panasonic electronics and, of course, batteries.[4]

COMMUNICATING TO PERSUADE Another purpose of marketing communications is persuasion. The intense competition among different industries, as well as among different firms in the same industry, puts tremendous pressure on the communications programs of marketers. In our economy, even a product designed to satisfy a basic physiological need requires strong persuasive marketing communications, since consumers have many alternatives from which to choose. Campbell Soup Company (www.campbellsoup.com) has been selling soup for over 120 years and has annual soup sales of close to $2 billion. Studies show that 96 percent of Canadian households have some canned soup in the kitchen cupboard. Yet the firm spends over $60 million a year advertising soup because there is still room to "win more stomachs for Campbell's." To remain competitive and to increase its share of the fast growing home-prepared soup market, Campbell's continues to innovate by launching new varieties of canned soup, freeze-dried and fresh-frozen soups. All these new products have to be advertised to make consumers aware of their existence.[5]

In a luxury product category such as automobiles, demand depends upon the firm's ability to convince consumers that the product's benefits exceed those of other luxuries. Therefore, persuasion is even more important. Lincoln (www.ford.ca) says they are "what a luxury car should be," but with Infiniti (www.infiniti.com) "own one and you'll understand" the superiority of its products. Lincoln has communicated its new SUV entry, the Navigator, as, well, not really being an SUV, but something completely unique and therefore without comparison. The tagline goes "What a luxury _____ should be" letting the consumer fill in the blank. Perhaps, over time BMW (www.bmw.ca) has had the most success by developing, in many consumers' perception, into what their slogan calls "the ultimate driving machine," thus taking the product and the experience one level beyond that of the physical luxury amenities and prestigious badge to something of a more spiritual or personal experience.

Persuading consumers to buy a company's offering also includes the packaging appearance and style — whether it's sitting on the shelf or making an impression in advertising — packaging says something. All communication uses "visual vocabulary" — more than 40 percent of communication is visual. And what is more visual than packaging. Further, 80 percent of this visual communication is driven by colour and shape — words tell and pictures sell! Text will most often be forgotten, so one must rely on images, colours, and shapes to elicit a positive emotional response while remaining true to brand character.

Corby Distilleries recently launched a line of ready-to-drink and ready-to-mix fruit-blended cocktails called Shocktales to meet changing tastes and preferences in the distilled beverage market. To reach their young target demographic of "entry-level" drinkers the flavours have been boldly titled and the product has been communicated through clean, simple, and bold packaging that reaches out from the shelf and captures the consumer's attention. Simple graphics, stylized fonts on transparent labels, leveraging the jewel-toned colours of the product, have resulted in a vibrant new entry to this category.[6]

Music not only soothes but also keeps consumers from tuning out an advertiser's message and sometimes a little help is needed persuading consumers to listen to or watch a message. According to a recent woman's magazine survey, nearly 47 percent of women 45–54 cited music as a key element in holding their attention during television commercials. Also, 43 percent of women 18–34 cited music as a top reason why they watch commercials.[7] This doesn't mean spending a fortune for the rights to a rock and roll classic, just simply matching the music to the product or market. But, sometimes a classic might be just what is needed.

COMMUNICATING TO REMIND Consumers must also be *reminded* about the availability of a product or brand and its potential to satisfy. In addition, they need to be reminded on occasion of broader messages that are related to the image of corporations and not-for-profit organizations. Advertisers bombard the marketplace with thousands of messages every day in the hope of attracting new consumers, leaving positive reinforcing messages with existing customers and establishing markets for new products and services. Given the intense competition for the attention of consumers, even an established firm must constantly remind people about its brand to retain a place in their minds. It is unlikely that a day goes by, for example, in which you don't see some form of communications (an ad, in-store display, counter sign, billboard, or imprinted T-shirt) for Coca-Cola. Similarly, we all grew up with Wrigley gums — Juicy Fruit, Doublemint, etc. — but the company still spends tens of millions each year on advertising.[8] Thus, much of a firm's marketing communications activity may be intended simply to offset competitors' marketing efforts by reinforcing its familiar brand in the market.

Marketing Communications Methods

Marketing communication, whatever form it takes, is an attempt to influence. There are five basic forms: personal selling, advertising, sales promotion, public relations, and publicity. Each has distinct features that determine what role it can play in a communications program.

- **Personal selling** is the direct presentation of a product or service to a prospective customer by a representative of the organization selling it. Personal selling takes place face-to-face, over the phone, or by means of an Internet "chat," and it may be directed to an intermediary or a final consumer. We list it first because, across all businesses, more money is spent on personal selling than on any other form of marketing communications.

- **Advertising** is non-personal mass communication that the sponsor has paid for and in which the sponsor is clearly identified. The most familiar forms of ads are found in the broadcast (TV and radio) and print (newspapers and magazines) media. However, there are many other advertising alternatives, from spots on heavily visited World Wide Web pages, to direct mail, billboards, and the Yellow Pages.

- **Sales promotion** is demand-stimulating activity designed to supplement advertising and facilitate personal selling. It is paid for by the sponsor and frequently involves a temporary incentive to encourage a purchase. Many sales promotions are directed at consumers, including the coupons that arrive in the mail and the contest that allows you to win tickets to a Blue Rodeo concert. Many sales promotions, however, are designed to encourage a company's sales force or other members of its distribution channel to sell its products more aggressively. This latter category is called *trade promotion*. Included in sales promotion is a wide spectrum of activities, such as contests, trade shows, in-store displays, rebates, samples, premiums, discounts, and coupons.

- **Public relations** encompass a wide variety of communication efforts to contribute to generally favourable attitudes and opinions toward an organization and its products. Unlike most advertising and personal selling, it does not include a specific sales message. The targets may be customers, shareholders, a government agency, or a special-interest group. Public relations can take many forms, including newsletters, annual reports, lobbying, and sponsorship of charitable or civic events. The Labatt hot-air balloon is a familiar example of a public-relations device. Many large companies, such as the Royal Bank of Canada and Air Canada, gain national attention through their sponsorship of organizations and events such as symphony orchestras and the Special Olympics.

- **Publicity** is a special form of public relations that involves creating and placing a news story, editorial, or announcement about an organization or its products or services. Like advertising, it involves a non-personal message that reaches a mass audience through the media. But several things distinguish publicity from advertising: It is not paid for, the organization that is the subject of the publicity has little control over it, and it appears as news and therefore may have greater credibility or "legitimacy" than advertising. Organizations seek good publicity and frequently provide the material for it in the form of news releases, press conferences, and photographs. There is, of course, also bad publicity, which organizations try to avoid or deflect.

When becoming involved with "events" not totally under one's "creative" control, there are risks involved. Sometimes additional publicity occurs that wasn't expected — this can be good or bad. Olympic sponsorship in any shape or form was long thought a good investment — sponsors traditionally pasted the official Olympic rings on anything and everything to bask in Olympic glory. But the logo became notably absent recently attributable to the negative publicity from the Salt Lake City 2002 Games bribery story and the allegations that this may not be an isolated event in the Olympic council's history or its method of operation. At one point, the Sydney 2000 games suffered from a similar problem, and from controversies over ticket distribution resulting in companies such as Coca-Cola and McDonald's cooling their heels after gaining much momentum in the marketplace with their marketing efforts. One company did however manage to generate positive publicity in the Australian marketplace — perhaps Nike was the only firm to benefit from this Olympic sponsorship as they belatedly came to the rescue in a blaze of publicity as rival Reebok withdrew their sponsorship.[9]

In 2000, in Canada and the U.K. public concern regarding genetically modified organisms/foods (GMOs) reached the point that public protests were held — resulting in a series of supermarket protests in Quebec that made national news stories. The fearmongering over "frankenfoods" and "frankenfruits" had reached a stage where key stakeholders such as retailers, environmentalists, and food processors all began to compete to shape public opinion and direct the brunt of public condemnation.[10] To avoid the damning publicity, some chains in U.K. stopped carrying products that could not prove they did not contain modified ingredients. This policy was heavily advertised to the public.

When MuchMusic decided to look for a new VJ, they truly made it an integrated marketing effort. They "went public" in their search, holding auditions across the country at HMV stores. A great deal of media coverage was received at the local level as they moved across the country. As well, national papers covered the story. Through this, the use of their own media resources and allowing the input of their viewing audience, the station secured a great deal of positive publicity and viewer buy-in for the new on-air personality. This resulted in over 1.5 million viewers tuning in to the final selection that was televised at the same time as the Super Bowl. The Super Bowl had 3.5 million Canadian viewers. That's not bad considering the 20th annual Genie Awards were also on, and instead of watching to see Canada's home-grown celebrities that many people instead chose to watch the crowning of Bradford How as the newest Much VJ — a 22-year-old first-year Red River Community College student who describes himself as, "Very quick to speak; slow to communicate."[11]

Integrated Marketing Communications

While marketers have a variety of communication tools at their disposal, making effective use of them means that a company's personal selling, advertising, and other communications activities should form a coordinated program within its total marketing plan. However, in many firms, these activities are not well coordinated with potentially damaging consequences. For example, advertising directors and sales force managers sometimes come into conflict over resources, or the sales force may not be adequately informed about the details of a sales promotion effort. This wouldn't happen if the elements comprising the marketing communications program were part of an **integrated marketing communications (IMC)** effort. The IMC is a strategic business process used to plan, develop, execute and evaluate coordinated communication with an organization's customers and other publics.[12]

integrated marketing communications (IMC)
A strategic business process used to plan, develop, execute and evaluate coordinated communication with an organization's customers and other publics.

IMC begins with a strategic planning effort designed to coordinate marketing communications with product planning, pricing, and distribution, the other marketing mix elements. The communication program is influenced, for example, by how distinctive a product is and whether its planned price is above or below the competition. A manufacturer or intermediary must also consider its promotional links with other firms in the distribution channel. For example, Daimler Chrysler recognizes that its success is closely tied to the performance of its dealers. Therefore, in addition to advertising its automobiles directly to consumers, the firm trains dealers' salespeople in how to show a car and conduct a test drive. It also offers cash incentives to dealers with high customer satisfaction scores.

An Audience Perspective

An IMC approach adopts the position that a customer or prospect is exposed to many bit and pieces of information about a company or brand. Certainly some of these bits are designed and presented by marketers but others, possibly the majority, come from other sources. These sources can include personal experience, the opinion of others, and comparisons made by competitors in their advertising. Based on all of this information, an individual makes an evaluation and forms a judgment. With so little control over what information the audience uses, or how the information is used, a marketer's efforts must be highly coordinated and complementary to have impact. That means anticipating the opportunities when the target audience will be exposed to information about the company or brand, and effectively communicating the appropriate message in those "windows of opportunity." Usually, this involves using several different communication methods and requires a high degree of coordination.

IMC Elements

The use of the IMC approach to marketing communications is reflected in how managers think about the information needs of the message recipients. Organizations that have adopted an IMC philosophy tend to share several characteristics:

◆ An awareness of the target audience's information sources, as well as their media habits and preferences.

◆ An understanding of what the audience knows and believes that relates to the desired response.

◆ The use of a mix of communications tools each with specific objectives but all linked to a common overall goal.

◆ A concerted effort in which personal selling, advertising, sales promotion and public relations are coordinated in order to communicate a consistent and continuous flow of information adapted to the audience's needs.

Implementing IMC

IBM practices the maxim of international marketers, "think globally, act locally."

It is clear that IMC encompasses the entire marketing communications program. In developing integrated communications, a company coordinates its advertising, personal selling, sales promotion, public relations, and direct marketing to accomplish specific objectives. For example, in the early 1990s, IBM's communication efforts had become highly fragmented. The company was using over eighty advertising agencies around the world and its ads were sending mixed messages. To take care of the problem and coordinate efforts:

◆ The eighty agencies were replaced by one;

◆ All packaging, brochures, and trade show booths were standardized to present a unified image;

◆ Sports sponsorships were consolidated into a few big events such as the Olympics in order to better showcase IBM technology; and

◆ Internet home pages with a consistent look and content were developed for seventy-seven countries in their native languages. Some differences must of course be accommodated due to differences in technology and infrastructure, but they are otherwise a consistent offering. Good comparisons can be seen by looking at the U.S. (www.ibm.com), Canadian (www.ibm.ca), and German (www.de.ibm.com/) IBM pages. Many international companies will host a common "cover" page and have visitors choose a language and country/region option which will direct the visitor to relevant information for that region.

Communication at IBM is now built around the theme and content of being a technology innovator that is accessible and responsive.[13]

An IMC program may incorporate several different communications campaigns, with some even running concurrently. Depending on objectives and available funds, a firm may undertake simultaneous local, regional, national, and international programs. Moreover, a firm may have one

Coca Cola provides the most striking example of a simple global image and message.

campaign aimed at consumers and another at wholesalers and retailers. We have discussed how, with so many products available, that you must go beyond designing an attractive product to actually communicating and attracting attention of the marketplace. This includes those in the supply chains that make decisions regarding carrying a product and reordering.

Coca-Cola (www.cocacola.com) is probably the best example of a truly global product — around the world "it's the real thing." The company uses this phrase, which it owns, as a part of its global message — at least as close to it as can be literally and culturally communicated and translated. Another global campaign is the "enjoy" branding campaign. Such efforts usually have a minimum of text communication, emphasizing visual and brand images. These global programs are designed to be easily tailored to specific markets. Coca-Cola also acts nationally, regionally, and locally to bolster individual markets. Coke has always initiated a variety of programs unique to Canada such as the Coke Card promotion, but also programs with regional "flavouring" such as the Hockey-themed campaign featuring a young girl singing the Canadian anthem. And to show that it's still "the real thing" in Atlantic Canada, the company produced an advertisement that showcased a series of well-known and familiar sites throughout the Atlantic provinces in which Atlantic Canadians were shown enjoying the product.[14]

Evaluating IMC

The final step in an IMC is evaluation. A program can be evaluated in a number of ways. One approach is to examine how it is implemented. For example, if the communications program of a large manufacturer of consumer goods is being carried out in a manner consistent with the notion of IMC, we would expect to find:

◆ An advertising program consisting of a series of related, well-timed, carefully placed ads that reinforce personal selling and sales promotional efforts.

◆ A personal selling effort that is coordinated with the advertising program. The firm's sales force would be fully informed about the advertising portion of the campaign — the theme, media used, and the schedule for appearance of the ads. The salespeople would be able to explain and demonstrate the product benefits emphasized in the ads, and be prepared to transmit the promotional message and supporting material to intermediaries so they could take part in the campaign.

◆   Sales promotional devices such as point-of-purchase display materials, that are coordinated with other aspects of the program. Incentives for middlemen would be clearly communicated and understood. Retailers would be briefed about consumer promotions and adequate inventories would be in place.

◆   Public relations efforts scheduled to coincide with the other mix components and emphasizing the same theme.

More rigorous evaluation examines the results of the program. The outcome of each component is compared with the objectives set for it to determine if the effort was successful. Below are some typical objectives and some common measures associated with each of them:[15]

◆   Awareness of a company or brand: competitive brand position studies; focus groups with distributors at trade show; Web site "hits."

◆   Interest in a product or brand: number of brochures or other company publications distributed; attendance at company-sponsored seminars; Web site traffic — number of pages viewed/time spent at site.

◆   Action: usage results support tools by distributors and retailers; responses to direct mail; customer inquiries or store visits; and sales.

To be meaningful, most of these measures need to be taken before and after the communications effort, with the difference between the two measures indicating its effect. For example, The Gap did not experience a meaningful increase in store traffic and sales during and after some recent TV campaigns. One in particular, featuring young people in Khakis dancing the swing, was disappointing because it was lauded by industry observers as an outstanding commercial. As a result, the retailer de-emphasized the TV component of its communications strategy, shifting more funds to in-store promotion, print advertising, and online advertising.[16] After an appropriate period of time, these new tools will also be evaluated. Sometimes a campaign can be spectacularly successful in that it generates a great deal of publicity and press beyond the placements paid for by the company.

In Britain, super model Claudia Schiffer's striptease for Citroen motor cars got a reaction from everyone *but* car buyers. The launch of the Citroen Xsara Coupe in June 1999 wouldn't have been all that newsworthy if it wasn't for the so-called "Schiffer Stripper" routine. Ms Schiffer, dressed up to the nines in Chanel, Versace, and Agent Provacateur, shed every last item before smiling naughtily and driving away. It was Britain's most ever talked about commercial — although some of the talk was a little hostile. Ms. Schiffer received $2.9 million for her appearance! The ad was seen as "overly provocative" and banned from being broadcast before 9 P.M. Regardless, the campaign has the highest recall in automotive advertising a year later, yet sales of the Xsara Coupe have been disappointing.[17]

Barriers to IMC

Despite its attractiveness, an IMC approach is not universally supported. In some organizations, the communications functions are in different departments. The sales force may be in a unit separate from where advertising decisions are made. As a result, there is a lack of internal communication and coordination. In other firms, there is a belief that communications are such an imprecise activity that effort to carefully design objectives and coordinate efforts would be unproductive. In still other firms there is a history of relying on particular forms of communication and a resistance to consider alternatives.

Fully utilizing an IMC approach would likely require a firm to make several changes. One involves restructuring internal communication to ensure that all relevant parties involved in communication work together. Some firms have approached this by creating a marketing communications (or marcom) manager who oversees the planning and coordination of all promotional and communications efforts. A second change involves conducting research to gather the necessary information about the target audience. Firms utilize extensive databases for this purpose but they are costly to create and expensive to maintain. Finally, and most important, senior management must support the effort to integrate marketing communications efforts. Strong leadership is essential to break down barriers and help create cooperative situations.

Next we will examine how basic communication, the core of all marketing communication, actually works. We will then move on to key managerial issues in the marketing communications program.

The Communication Process

Communication is the verbal or nonverbal transmission of information between someone wanting to express an idea and someone else expected or expecting to get that idea. Because the components of marketing communications are examples of communication between two or more parties, much can be learned about structuring effective marketing messages by examining the communication process.

Fundamentally, communication requires only four elements: a message, a source of the message, a communication channel, and a receiver. In practice, however, important additional components come into play:

♦ The information that the sending source wants to share must first be **encoded** into a transmittable form. In marketing, this means changing an idea into words, pictures, or some other form such as a product display in a supermarket, a coupon, or a "hot button" on a Web site.

♦ Once the message has been transmitted through some communication channel, the symbols must be **decoded**, or given meaning, by the receiver. The received message may be what the sender intended or something else, depending on the recipient's knowledge and experience.

♦ If the message has been transmitted successfully, there is some change in the receiver's knowledge, beliefs, or feelings. As a result of this change the receiver formulates a **response**. The response could be nonverbal (a positive reaction as indicated by a smile while watching an ad), verbal (suggesting to a friend that she try an advertised product), or behavioural (purchasing the advertised product).

♦ The response serves as **feedback**, telling the sender whether the message was received and how it was perceived by the recipient. Through feedback, the sender can learn why a communication failed and how to improve future communication.

♦ All stages of the process can be affected by **noise** — any external event or factor that interferes with successful communication, such as a competitive ad. Noise is occurring when a television viewer sees ads for both Speedy and Midas within a short time period or when your system crashes while filling your shopping cart at a retail Web site.

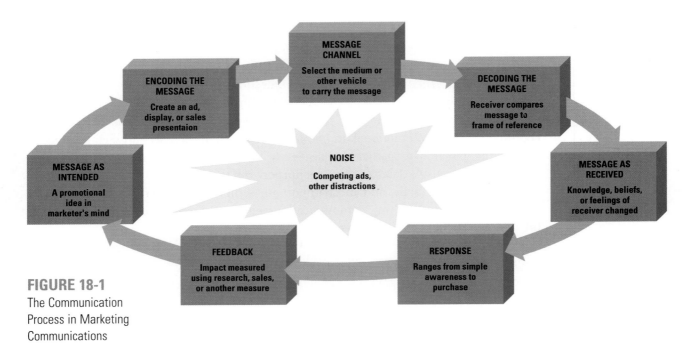

FIGURE 18-1

The Communication
Process in Marketing
Communications

Figure 18-1 illustrates these components of a communication process and relates them to marketing communications activities.

What does the communication process tell us about producing effective marketing communications programs? First, the act of encoding reminds us that messages can take many forms. Messages can be physical (a sample, a premium) or symbolic (verbal, visual), and there are a myriad of options within each of these categories. For example, a verbal message can be factual, humourous, or even threatening.

Second, the number of channels or methods of transmitting a message is limited only by the imagination and creativity of the sender. Most marketing communications messages are transmitted by familiar channels, such as the voice of a salesperson, the airwaves of radio, the mail, the side of a bus, or the lead-in to a feature film in a movie theatre. Each channel has its own characteristics in terms of audience reach, flexibility, permanence, credibility, and cost. In selecting a channel, a marketer must have clearly defined objectives and a familiarity with the features of the many alternatives.

Third, how the message is decoded or interpreted depends on its form (encoding and transmission) and the capability and interest of the recipient. In designing and sending messages, marketers must be sensitive to the audience. What is their vocabulary and level of verbal sophistication? What other messages have they received? What experiences have they had? What will get and hold their attention?

Finally, every component of the marketing communications program should have a measurable objective that can be determined from the response and feedback provided by the recipients. Feedback may be collected in many forms — changes in sales, recall of advertising messages, more favourable attitudes, increased awareness of a brand or an organization — depending on the objective of the marketing communications message. For some promotional activities the objective may be modest, for example, an increase in the audience's awareness of a brand or stimulating trial of a new product. For others, such as a direct mail solicitation, the objective would be a particular level of sales. Without objectives, there is no way of evaluating the effectiveness of a message.

Determining the Marketing Communications Mix

marketing communications mix
The combination of personal selling, advertising, sales promotion, publicity, and public relations that is intended to help an organization achieve its marketing objectives.

A **marketing communications mix** is an organization's combination of personal selling, advertising, sales promotion, public relations, and publicity. An effective mix is a critical part of virtually all marketing communications strategies. Product differentiation, market segmentation, trading up and trading down, and branding all require effective communications with target audiences. Designing an effective marketing communications mix requires a number of strategic decisions, as we shall now see.

Factors Influencing the Marketing Communications Mix

These five factors should be taken into account when determining the marketing communications mix: (1) the target market; (2) objective of the communications effort; (3) the nature of the product or service being promoted; (4) the stage in the life cycle of the product or service; and (5) the amount of money available for marketing communications.

TARGET MARKET As in most areas of marketing, decisions on the marketing communications mix will be greatly influenced by the audience or target market. At least four variables affect the choice of an approach to communicating with a particular market segment:

◆ *Readiness to Buy.* A target segment may be in any one of six stages of buying readiness. These stages — awareness, knowledge, liking, preference, conviction, and purchase — are called the hierarchy of effects because they represent stages a buyer goes through in moving toward a purchase and each defines a possible goal or effect of marketing communications.

At the awareness stage, the marketer's task is to let buyers know that the product or brand exists. Here the objective is to build familiarity with the product and the brand name. Recall the unconventional "shock" ads that Benetton (www.benetton.com) used to attract attention. A controversial series of print ads depicted various forms of human suffering, including a dying AIDS victim, refugees jumping overboard from a ship, and a pool of blood from a war casualty. These ads attracted attention but were heavily criticized in some quarters, and some were banned in Germany. And Claudia Schiffer certainly created awareness of the new Citroen coupe.

Knowledge goes beyond awareness to learning about a product's features. Goodyear (www.goodyear.com) and BF Goodrich (www.bfgoodrich.com) are tire brands that are often confused simply because the founders had similar names. And the effectiveness of the Goodyear blimp as a corporate symbol led many consumers to confuse the two companies. For example, Goodrich introduced steel-belted radial tires to the North American market, but most consumers attribute the innovation to Goodyear. To establish itself as an industry leader in consumers' minds, Goodrich developed an information campaign to increase the knowledge of consumers about the company's innovations.

Liking refers to how the market feels about the product or brand. Marketing communications can be used to move a knowledgeable audience from being indifferent to liking a brand. A common technique is to associate the item with an attractive symbol or person, which explains why Adidas Canada (www.adidas.com) selected Olympic Gold Medal winner Donovan Bailey, "the world's fastest human," as a spokesman. But when Bailey made critical comments in public about his opponent in a key race and then apologized, the risk to Adidas had to be assessed by management. At the time, Adidas Canada stood by its spokesman, but critics felt he may have lost his credibility.[18] Roots Canada looked to gain leverage with the edgy boarding crowd by selecting Ross Rebagliati as a celebrity endorsement after the 1998 Nagano games. The first year this sport was featured in the Olympic games, the medal-winning B.C. native tested positive for marijuana use. The ruling was appealed and Rebagliati got to keep his medal. Was this scandal a good thing or a bad thing in the minds of the Roots' marketing people? While this stripped him of credibility with some groups, it may have added to his sales power with more relevant groups of consumers.

Creating preference involves distinguishing among brands such that the market prefers yours. It is not uncommon for consumers to like several brands of the same product, but the customer can't make a decision until one brand is preferred over the alternatives. Ads that make direct comparisons with the competition are intended to create a preference. In the vigorous competition for long-distance customers, Sprint Canada (www.sprint.ca), frequently using spokesperson Candice Bergen, compares the simplicity of its rate structure with that of Canada's established telephone companies.

Conviction entails the actual decision or commitment to purchase. The marketing communications objective here is to increase the strength of the buyer's need. Trying a product and experiencing the benefits that come from using it are very effective in strengthening the conviction to own it. Consider how video game and WebTV systems are set up to use in stores. Or, if we go back to tire products, consider how these manufacturers convince consumers of their "fixes" to the problem of a flat tire in their television ads. Goodyear (www.goodyear.ca) Run-Flat technology was demonstrated through dramatization of how the tire allows the driver to maintain control and continue driving at normal speeds without damaging the tire or the vehicle. It was dramatic because it portrayed a family driving at night in stormy conditions on an isolated road — instead of losing control, being stranded, etc. The family arrives home again right into their garage never even getting wet. Uniroyal® (www.uniroyal.ca) chose to use a demonstration of the process to convince viewers of the merits of its NailGard™ self-sealing technology. They showed a woman parallel parking an SUV and having to maneuver back and forth several times to get it just right — unfortunately there was a board with nails in the parking spot which couldn't be seen from inside the SUV. Back and forth but no damage — she never knew it happened! Then diagrams and an explanation of how it works to seal itself. Such "role-plays" as these explain the product and provide many cues to convince consumers of the potential benefits they can experience.

◆ *Purchase* can be delayed or postponed indefinitely, even for customers who are convinced that they should buy a product. The inhibitor might be a situational factor, such as not having enough money at the moment, or a natural resistance to change. Action may be triggered through a marketing communications price discount or offering additional incentives. The vast marketing communications behind Microsoft's Windows 95 was used by computer manufacturers as well as retailers such as Future Shop to speed purchases by providing the software free or at a special discount. Many retailers will supply financing arrangements in order to get merchandise out the doors — such as Leon's furniture stores' "HO! HO! Hold the Payments" events that promise no payments for at least one full year. Postponement or cancellation can also be a challenge for Internet retailers, as e-shoppers will often abandon their cyber shopping carts containing merchandise at the last minute before submitting their orders. E-retailers try to encourage follow-up of this purchase intent by holding these items in the customer's cart until the customer removes the products themselves. Customers are also reminded upon each return to the site that there are items in their shopping cart.

◆ *Geographic scope of the market.* Personal selling may be adequate in a small local market, but as the market broadens geographically, greater emphasis must be placed on advertising using a variety of media. The exception would be a firm that sells to concentrated pockets of customers scattered around the country. For example, the market for certain plastics is heaviest in Ontario and Quebec, because these plastics are used by component suppliers to the auto industry. In this case, emphasis on personal selling may be appropriate because spending on advertising that is widely distributed would be wasteful.

◆ *Type of customer.* Marketing communications strategy depends in part on what level of the distribution channel the organization hopes to influence. Final consumers and resellers sometimes buy the same product, but they require different marketing communications. This is common among computer products that are targeted toward business and personal applications. To illustrate, Staples/Business Depot (www.staples.ca) serves both consumer and business markets. Aside from other differences utilized the company designs TV advertisements that communicate to both audiences. Back-to-school time shows a delighted father practically dancing through the aisles as his less than delighted children trudge behind to pick out supplies from the wide selection offered, Christmas brings us ads showing a husband following his wife to Staples to ensure she selects the items he wants. Among those geared toward business buyers, one television spot shows a group of office workers gathered around a computer cheering on a co-worker who is using the computer — it sounds like they're cheering her on to victory in some sort of video game. But, in reality they are cheering as she navigates through the retailer's Web site ordering office supplies. The focus is still on selection, but also online ordering, delivery, and more business-oriented supplies.

Another consideration is the variety among the target markets for a product. A market with only one type of customer will call for a different marketing communications mix than a market with many target markets. A firm selling large power saws used exclusively by lumber manufacturers may rely only on personal selling. In contrast, a company selling portable handsaws to consumers and to construction firms will probably include an ample portion of advertising in its mix. In this latter example, personal selling would be prohibitively expensive in reaching the firm's many customers.

◆ *Concentration of the market.* The total number of prospective buyers is another consideration. The fewer potential buyers there are, the more effective personal selling is, compared with advertising. For example, in Canada there are only a handful of manufacturers of household vacuum cleaners. Clearly, for a firm selling a component part for vacuum cleaners, personal selling would be the best way to reach this market.

Marketing at Work 18-1

Speaking of Type of Customer, Getting the Cat's Attention Works

Move over Morris! Canadian cats never gave a meow about you anyway even if their masters did. However, our cats do seem to be purr-fectly excited about a TV commercial for a new Whiskas cat food brand extension called Homestyle Favorites.

Created by London's M&C Saatchi ad agency and adapted for the Canadian market by Toronto-based Bensimon Bryne D'Arcy, the spot consists of a thirty-second string of images, among them bright lights, furry toys, glittery objects, and (of course) a bundle of string. The soundtrack is just as abstract and alienating, at least by human standards. Instead of a catchy jingle, there are some high-pitched squeals. If non-furry viewers are at a loss at what to make of these commercials, felines on both sides of the Atlantic are no doubt pleased that someone's finally talking their language.

The someone in question is Whiskas' manufacturer, the London-based Mars Inc., who first aired the spot in Great Britain back in 1998. The commercial was revolutionary because it was the first to actually gear its message to feline viewers. In doing so, it set itself apart from its cat food competitors who have all been too happy to rely on tired clichés and tried-and-true approaches ranging from yummy taste and multi-vitamins to cuter-than-thou balls of fuzz. Instead, willing to innovate and strike out on new advertising terrain, Mars turned to a strategy of pure kitty science. Because cats are nocturnal beasts, their vision — and thus the commercial — relies much more on strong contrasts than on colors. And their sensitivity to high-pitched sounds explains the attention-getting mouse-like squeals.

In general, cats don't care a flea about what's on the boob tube. However, researchers at England's Waltham Centre for Pet Nutrition, noted that 60 percent of feline viewers actually stop what they're doing or wake up from their cat naps when the commercial shows up on their owners' TV screen. While some adopt a listening pose, others snoop around the TV set itself, or sniff suspiciously at the screen.

Of course, cats don't actually buy cat food. Their owners do. But just imagine the reaction of any self-respecting cat owner when Fluffy or Muffy suddenly runs up to the TV and starts pawing the picture. Every time the commercial comes on, they'll be beside themselves — and their cats — with excitement. Will they register the Whiskas brand name? Undoubtedly. Will Whiskas sell a lot of cat food? Most probably.

Source: Adapted from Patrick Allossery, "Boring TV pet food ad still the cat's meow for sales," *National Post*, April 24, 2000, p. C5.

NATURE OF THE PRODUCT Several product attributes influence marketing communications strategy. The most important are:

◆ *Unit value.* A product with low unit value is usually relatively uncomplicated, involves little risk for the buyer, and must appeal to a mass market to survive. As a result, advertising would be the primary marketing communications tool. In contrast, high-unit-value products often are complex and expensive. These features suggest the need for personal selling. BMW dealers are being encouraged to have salespeople get out of the showroom and call on prospects. By increasing the personal selling effort through techniques such as delivering cars to potential customers for test-drives, BMW hopes to stimulate North American sales. Such a component to the program would be consistent with the service ideology of such a high-end product offering.

◆ *Degree of customization.* If a product must be adapted to the individual customer's needs, personal selling and service, or sometimes a technology-based equivalent, is necessary. Thus, you would expect to find an emphasis on personal selling for something like home remodelling or an expensive suit. However, the benefits of most standardized products can be effectively communicated in advertising. The increasing number of firms making use of advanced production techniques and information management have made it possible to customize some products for large markets without a great deal of personal service by relying on data warehousing and electronic communication.

◆ *Presale and post-sale service.* Products that must be demonstrated, for which there are trade-ins, or that require frequent servicing to keep them in good working order lend themselves to personal selling, sometimes combined with Internet-based demonstrations and displays of product performance. Typical examples are riding lawn mowers, powerboats, and personal computers. For example, Bombardier would want to show its Ski-Doo® (www.ski-doo.com) and Sea-Doo® (www.sea-doo.com) machines in action.

STAGE OF THE PRODUCT LIFE CYCLE Marketing communications strategies are influenced by a product's life-cycle stage. When a new product is introduced, prospective buyers must be informed about its existence and its benefits, and intermediaries must be convinced to carry it. Thus both advertising (to consumers) and personal selling (to intermediaries) are critical in a product's introductory stage. At introduction, a new product also may be something of a novelty, offering excellent opportunities for publicity. Later, if a product becomes successful, competition intensifies and more emphasis is placed on persuasive advertising. Table 18-1 shows how marketing communications strategies change as a product moves through its life cycle.

TABLE 18-1	Communication Strategies for Different Product Life-Cycle Stages
Market Situation	**Promotional Strategy**
	Introduction Stage
Customers are not aware of the product's features, nor do they understand how it will benefit them.	Inform and educate potential customers that the product exists, how it might be used, and what want-satisfying benefits it provides. In this stage, a seller must stimulate *primary demand* — the demand for a type of product — as contrasted with *selective demand* — the demand for a particular brand. For example, producers had to sell consumers on the value of compact discs in general before it was feasible to promote a particular brand. Normally, heavy emphasis must be placed on personal selling. Exhibits at trade shows are also used extensively in the communications mix. A trade show gives a new product broad exposure to many intermediaries. Manufacturers also rely heavily on personal selling to attract intermediaries to handle a new product.
	Growth Stage
Customers are aware of product's benefits. The product is selling well, and intermediaries want to handle it.	Stimulate selective (brand) demand as competition grows. Increase emphasis on persuasive advertising. Intermediaries share more of the total communications effort.
	Maturity Stage
Competition intensifies and sales level off.	Advertising is used more to remind and persuade rather than only to provide information. Intense competition forces sellers to devote larger sums to advertising and thus contributes to the declining profits experienced in this stage.
	Decline Stage
Sales and profits are declining. New and better products are coming into the market.	All communications efforts are cut back substantially. The focus becomes reminding remaining customers.

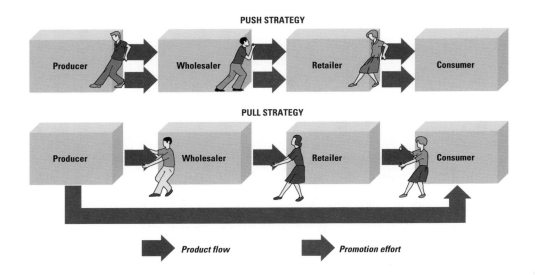

FIGURE 18-2
Push and Pull
Strategies of
Marketing
Communications

FUNDS AVAILABLE Regardless of what may be the most desirable marketing communications mix, the amount of money available for marketing communications is the ultimate determinant of the mix. A business with ample funds can make more effective use of advertising than can a firm with limited financial resources. Small or regionally based companies are likely to rely on personal selling, dealer displays, or joint manufacturer-retailer promotions. For example, the Vancouver Grizzlies partner with corporate sponsors like Air Canada, B.C. Tel Mobility, and IBM Canada to produce premiums like magnet game schedules, megaphones, and mouse pads, which add value for basketball fans and keep them coming back to the Grizzlies games.[19]

Lack of money may limit the options a firm has for its marketing communications effort. For example, television advertising can carry a particular message to far more people and at a lower cost per person than can most other media. Yet a firm may have to rely on less expensive media, such as Yellow Pages advertising, because it lacks the funds to take advantage of television's broad coverage.

Choosing a Push or a Pull Strategy

As we have seen, producers aim their marketing communications mix at both middlemen and end users. A communications program aimed primarily at intermediaries is called a **push strategy**, and a program directed primarily at end users is called a **pull strategy**. It is not unusual for firms to use both types of strategies for the same brand. Figure 18-2 contrasts these two strategies.

When using a push strategy, a channel member directs its message primarily at the intermediaries who are the next link forward in the distribution channel. The product is "pushed" through the channel. Take the case of a hardware manufacturer like Stanley tools that sells its products to household consumers through wholesalers and retailers such as True Value (www.truevalue.com) and Home Hardware (www.homehardwaredealers.com). The producer will promote heavily to wholesalers, which then also use a push strategy to retailers. In turn, the retailers promote to consumers. A push strategy usually involves a lot of personal selling and sales promotion, including contests for salespeople and displays at trade shows. Also, awards/prizes are promoted based on the volume of product sold through individual outlets. Attractive display cases to showcase products may also serve as incentive if space isn't a restriction such as in large hardware and other warehouse-sized

push strategy
A communications program aimed primarily at intermediaries.

"pull" promotional strategy
Promotional effort directed primarily at intermediaries that are the next link forward in distribution channels.

outlets. Discounting may also be used to encourage carrying a new product or buying larger quantities. This marketing communications strategy is appropriate for many manufacturers of business products, as well as for various consumer goods.

With a pull strategy, marketing communications messages are directed at end users — usually ultimate consumers. The intention is to motivate them to ask retailers for the product. The retailers, in turn, will request the product from wholesalers, and wholesalers will order it from the producer. In effect, marketing communications to consumers is designed to "pull" the product through the channel. This strategy relies on heavy advertising and various forms of consumer-directed sales promotion such as coupons or samples in consumer's mailboxes or in-store demonstrations. To promote its new Oil of Olay collection of cosmetics, Proctor & Gamble (www.pg.com) sent out over 1.5 million tiny lipstick samples in a first ever mail-out campaign of this sort. The cosmetics, aimed at women 25 and older, were sent to let consumers actually try the product and see the benefits.[20] Sunny Delight fruit juice (www.sunnydelight.com) sent out small bottles of juice to consumers — same unique bottle shape as the large bottles packaged in cardboard refrigerators with doors that open to reveal the product and coupons toward purchase. These are obviously expensive to produce and distribute, but they get the product into the consumer's hands — or, well, consumer's mouths in these examples.

There is little incentive for retailers to provide shelf space for minor variations of existing brands unless they are confident that they will sell. So manufacturers of consumer packaged goods often use a pull strategy to get new products stocked on supermarket shelves. For example, Johnson & Johnson (www.johnsonandjohnson.com) spent over $40 million on North American advertising and sales promotion to introduce Tylenol Extra Strength Headache Plus, a line extension. At this spending level, retailers had some assurance that the brand would sell.

Toronto-based Aqua Terra has reached out to major grocery- and convenience-chain buyers with a new direct mail piece for Crystal Springs bottled water (www.crystal-springs.ca), one that relies on a crumpled ball of paper to make its point. The effort features a miniature recycling "blue box" with a crumpled-up poster inside. Open it up and the poster shows the company's new collapsible bottle, which can be compacted to take up less space in recycling bins. One of the main benefits of the mailing is a 20 percent increase in purchase intent over normal bottles — the mailing lets buyers know about the change and what to look for. The new bottle incorporates a new tactile element — embossed waves that make the bottle more visually compelling in a "sea" of waters and helps in collapsing the bottle. Also included in the effort are busboards picturing children engaged in summer activities. The captions play on water's elemental cachet: "The Earth isn't 2/3 root beer," "In the beginning, God did not create cream soda." Point-of-sale displays use tag lines "Honey, I shrunk the bottle" and "Drink before you collapse."[21]

The Marketing Communications Budget

Establishing marketing communications budgets is extremely challenging because management generally lacks reliable standards for determining how much to spend altogether on advertising or personal selling and determining how much of the total budget to allocate to each element of the marketing communications mix. A firm may have the alternative of adding seven salespeople or increasing its trade show budget by $400,000 a year, but it cannot determine precisely what increase in sales or profits to expect from

Marketing at Work 18-2

Cross Border Pull Strategy for Captain Crunch

In days of yore, any self-respecting Canadian kid would come home from school, grab a couple of cookies, and plunk him or herself in front of the TV. These days, however, more and more young people are deserting the television screen for the computer screen. According to a recent survey conducted by Toronto marketing research firm Young Culture Inc., 85 percent of the country's 2.4 million teens are spending an average of 9.3 hours online every week. This is roughly the same amount of time, or even more, than they spend channel surfing. Although parents might be pleased at the new shift, advertisers — who spend close to $5 billion a year trying to target impressionable teens — are less than impressed with a lifestyle change that threatens to be more than just a phase.

One advertiser that has been quick to jump off the televisual sinking ship is Quaker Oats of Canada who, together with its U.S. parent company, recently launched a major Internet-based promotion of its Cap'n Crunch cereal. Because the sugary cereal is more popular in the United States than in Canada (where it represents a small 1.1 share of the ready-to-eat cereal market), joint promotions were pretty rare up until now. What hooked American markets seldom worked north of the border. However, true to hype, the Internet has proved to be a great equalizer. When it comes to advertising and promotional campaigns, borders don't exist when you're surfing. The result has been the biggest-ever Web promotion of any Quaker Oats cereal, organized over three stages.

Stage one begins with getting 6 to 12 year-old breakfasters riled up by the fact that the friendly Cap'n is suddenly missing from the boxes of his self-named cereal. To solve the mystery of his disappearance, kids must buy boxes of the cereal, each of which offers various clues as well as a "crunchiscope" clue decoder. Armed with the latter piece of equipment, kids can log onto www.capncrunch.com and decipher on-line clues.

They can also find clues at www.ytv.com, homepage of the YTV network. This tie-in stems from the fact that the Peterborough, Ontario-based Quaker Oats spends most of its Cap'n Crunch advertising budget on Canada's public television network for kids. Such a media-buying strategy results in relatively narrow audience reach, but frequent air-play means the target market really gets the message. In fact, in the case of this Cap'n Crunch promotion, the entire campaign will be presented only on the youth network.

Stage two of the promotion will have kids who are hungry enough (and parents who are indulgent enough) to buy a double pack of cereal, receiving a free Cap'n Crunch Crunchling Adventure CD-ROM, with a retail value of $30. And stage three will see the happy return of the Cap'n to the rightful helm of his cereal box, accompanied by a limited edition breakfast goodie tentatively named "Mystery Crunch."

Although the disappearance of the charismatic cartoon Cap'n is sure to trouble his young fans — perhaps enough to motivate them to purchase more cereal for clues as to his whereabouts — Quaker Oats is taking no chances. In the cash crazy age of "Who Wants to Be a Millionaire?," the company is sweetening the pot and egging on young cyber-sleuths with the promise of a $100 draw-prize for ten thousand junior detectives who track the Cap'n down. It is also banking on kids taking to the Net to trade cyber-clues in chat groups and e-mails. In doing so, they will be bringing the Cap'n into the Internet age.

Source: Adapted from Patrick Allossery, "Canada joins U.S. in cross border promotion," *The National Post*, May 22, 2000, p. C4.

---

marketing communications budgeting methods
The means used to determine the amount of dollars to be allocated to the marketing communications elements.

either expenditure. As a result, rather than one generally accepted approach to setting budgets, there are four common **marketing communications budgeting methods**: percentage of sales, all available funds, following the competition, and budgeting by task or objective. These methods are frequently discussed in connection with the advertising budget, but they may be applied to any communications activity as well as to determine the total marketing communications budget.

Percentage of Sales

The marketing communications budget may be related in some way to company income, as a percentage of either past or anticipated sales. A common approach for determining the sales base is to compute an average of the previous year's actual sales and expected sales for the coming year. Some businesses prefer to budget a fixed amount of money per unit of past or expected future sales. Manufacturers of products with a high unit value and a low rate of turnover (automobiles or appliances, for example) frequently use the per unit approach to setting budgets.

Because the percentage-of-sales method is simple to calculate, it is probably the most widely used budgeting method. Moreover, it sets the cost of marketing communications in relation to sales income, making it a variable rather than a fixed expense.

There are two things you need to realize about basing marketing communications expenditures on past sales. First, management is effectively making marketing communications a result of sales when, in fact, it is a cause of sales. Second, a percentage of past sales method reduces marketing communications expenditures when sales are declining — just when advertising and other forms of communications usually are most needed.

All Available Funds

A new company or a firm introducing a new product or service frequently ploughs all available funds into its marketing communications program. The objective is to build sales and market share as rapidly as possible during those early, critical months and years. We have seen many Internet start-ups spending all their funds in trying to get awareness and Web site traffic, a few successful, many not so. After a time, management generally finds it necessary to invest in other things, such as new equipment or expanded production or distribution capacity, so the method of setting the marketing communications budget is changed.

Many Internet shops trying to establish online markets for product classes have pulled out all the stops and continue to promote despite yet making any actual profit. Much of the "communication" budget is often tied up in free purchases and cash and prizes in order to entice traffic through the site and encourage purchase through this medium. Print and TV is distributed throughout the many available specialty channels and publications consumed by computer-savvy consumers. Also, for access to wider audiences less specialized channels and print is used. Because of this fragmentation, a balance between the two may be advisable to "harvest" both groups. A considerable e-retail shakeout is expected by the end of 2000 as second-tier sites become overtaken by larger interests. Money quickly evaporates on communication budgets in cyberspace and there never seems to be enough. Gloss.com had been fighting for attention in the crowded online beauty products category — only to be taken over by Estee Lauder Cos. as a part of that cosmetic giant's efforts to step-up its online presence. It seems success goes largely to those brands that are well communicated in the "bricks" world. There are of course some exceptions.[22]

Advertising costs for an Internet-only retailer are huge. The e-retailer must become established in a cyber-arena that is not unlike the impulses that carry information along the information superhighway itself — moving, fleeting, here and then gone. Consumers need to be constantly reminded, as there is no physical representation of the retailer. Physical outlets act almost like billboard advertisements. Business models are difficult to apply to these untried formats and success may be fleeting. In mid-2000, two high-profile sites crashed and burned within days of each other leaving experts to ponder the future of this retail venue. Boo.com, seller of high-end sportswear and accessories such as DKNY and Jil Sander, burned through US$120 million in the six months it operated. It appeared to be a success story, with sales increasing and expectations to continue increasing. In retrospect, the company wished it had kept a stronger control on costs! — perhaps one of their more obvious mistakes!

DEN, the high profile, Hollywood-based purveyor of Net-based entertainment, was the other burn victim that week. The company assumed that because they understood how the entertainment industry worked, that they also knew how to entertain people on the Web. They failed to recognize that communication differed on this new medium. Similarly, Boo.com constructed a site that did not "communicate" well with visitors. The site was slow, pop-up windows came out of everywhere, and plug-ins were often required to continue to the following page.[23]

With the proliferation of clicks only shops, it is important to quickly and to soundly stamp a branding impact on your marketing – or they drive past on the superhighway. Money is spent so rapidly here that rate of cost of operations is often referred to as the "burn rate" of money, not that this is a dilemma isolated to the Internet — that is, running out of money before seeing a profit, or growing too fast.

Follow Competition

A weak method of determining the marketing communications budget, but one that is used occasionally, is to match the marketing communications expenditures of competitors or to spend in proportion to market share. Sometimes only one competitor is followed. In other cases, if management has access to industry average expenditures on marketing communications through a trade association, these become company benchmarks.

There are at least two problems with this approach. First, the firm's competitors may be just as much in the dark regarding how to set a marketing communications budget. Second, a company's goals may be quite different from those of its competitors because of differences in the marketing strategies being followed.

Again, in the new e-retail markets where no real long-term patterns or guidelines exist, competitors try many different approaches. One highly visible one is giving money away each day to get attention. For example, IWon.com (www.iwon.com) which is a comprehensive general purpose Internet portal gives away money everyday — lots of it. For using this service, visitors can enter to win a $10,000 daily prize, weekly prizes, $1 million monthly prizes, and $10 million annual prizes. Competitive parity is pretty difficult in this case.

Task or Objective

The best approach for establishing the marketing communications budget is to determine the tasks or objectives the communications program must accomplish and then decide what they will cost. The task method forces management to define realistically the goals of its marketing communications program. Sometimes, it may be defined as straightforwardly as wanting to increase revenue by 10 percent or unit sales by 5 percent, or increasing the price while maintaining a particular level of sales.

Sometimes this is called the buildup method because of the way it is constructed. For example, a company may decide to enter a new geographic market. Management determines this venture will require ten additional salespeople. The compensation and expenses of these people will cost a total of $520,000 per year. Salary for an additional sales supervisor and expenses for an extra office and administrative needs will cost $70,000. Thus in the personal selling component of the marketing communications mix, an extra $590,000 must be budgeted. Similar estimates can be made for the anticipated costs of advertising, sales promotion, and other communications tools. The budget is built up by adding up the costs of the individual marketing communications tasks needed to reach the goal of entering a new territory.

Regulation of Marketing Communications Activities

Because the primary objective of marketing communications is to sell something by communicating with a market, marketing communications activities attract attention. Consequently, abuses by individual firms are easily and quickly noted by the public. This situation in turn soon leads to (1) public demand for correction of the abuses, (2) assurances that they will not be repeated, and (3) general restraints on marketing communications activities. To answer public demand, laws and regulations have been enacted by the federal government and by most provincial governments. In addition, many private business organizations have established voluntary codes of advertising standards to guide their own marketing communications activities. In addition, the advertising industry itself, through the Advertising Advisory Board and its Advertising Standards Councils, does a considerable amount of self-regulation.

The Federal Role

Broadcasting Act
Established the CRTC and provided for sweeping powers of advertising regulation.

A number of departments of the federal government administer legislation aimed at controlling various aspects of marketing communications, particularly advertising. The **Broadcasting Act** established the Canadian Radio-television and Telecommunications Commission (CRTC) (www.crtc.gc.ca) in 1968 and provided for sweeping powers of advertising regulation. Under section 16 of the Act, the CRTC may make regulations concerning the character of broadcast advertising and the amount of time that may be devoted to it. While the potential for substantial control exists, the CRTC does not in reality approve each radio and television commercial. What it has done is delegate authority in certain fields to other agencies such as the Health Protection Branch of Health Canada and the Combines Investigation Branch of Industry Canada.

Investigation Branch of Industry Canada.

The Health Protection Branch deals with advertising in the fields of drugs, cosmetics, and devices (officialese for birth-control products), and it has sweeping powers to limit, control, rewrite, or ban certain communications for the products under its authority. The authority itself is embodied in such Acts, and regulations associated with them, as the Health and Welfare Department Act, the Proprietary or Patent Medicine Act, the Food and Drug Act, the Criminal Code of Canada, and the Broadcasting Act. The various Acts and regulations result in general types of prohibition aimed at preventing the treatment, processing, packaging, labelling, advertising, and selling of foods, drugs, and devices in such a manner as to mislead or deceive, or even to be likely to create an erroneous impression concerning the nature of the products.

The Health Protection Branch also prohibits the advertising of whole classes of drugs. It has developed a list of diseases or conditions for which a cure may not be advertised under any circumstances. This prohibition stands even if a professionally accepted cure exists. The logic for the prohibition of advertising, in spite of the existence of a cure, is that the Health Protection Branch does not wish members of the general public to engage in self-diagnosis of the condition that can be treated.

By virtue of the powers delegated to it by the CRTC, the Health Protection Branch has absolute control over radio and television advertisements for the products under its jurisdiction. All such advertisements must be submitted to it at least fifteen days prior to airing, and no radio or television station can air an ad without its having been approved by the branch and, thereby, the CRTC. In practical terms, the Health Protection Branch, even though an appeal route to the CRTC is available, has complete authority and advertisers have no recourse of any consequence.

In contrast to the delegated review powers the Health Protection Branch has over advertisements using the broadcast media, its position with reference to the print media is weak. Its formal control is over alleged Food and Drug violations, which must be prosecuted in court. Given the lack of jurisprudence in this area, the branch is loath to go to court in case it loses and thus sets a precedent or in case its regulations (many of which have not been tested in court) are found to be illegal. What the branch does is advise advertisers of its opinion of advertisements that are prepared for the print media. This opinion is not a ruling, and ads submitted, as well as those that are not, are still subject to the regulations for which the branch has responsibility. This does not mean that the branch does not monitor the print media. Newspapers and magazines are sampled and advertisements examined.

What is actually on the product package is also a part of the marketing communication package — and is subject to regulation. Aside from legalities about labelling of contents, size, etc., there are also regulations about what else you can say about your product. In recent years the health dimension of a product has become a very popular marketing focus for many foods from Becel margarine to Quaker rice cakes to Kellogg's Nutri-Grain bars.

One sector that has tried to capitalize on medical study results claiming the benefits of fibre is the very mature cereal industry. The industry has lobbied Ottawa for the right to link health claims to its products as is allowed in the United States. Competitors at the breakfast table, the Quaker Oats Company (www.quakeroats.ca) and Kellogg (www.kellogg.ca) have teamed up to revolutionize food marketing in Canada by removing these prohibitions under the federal Food and Drugs Act. The stakes are high as the boom in these healthy edibles, called nutraceuticals or functional foods, is estimated at $500-billion worldwide. The change would allow, for example, the claim that oat bran products can lower cholesterol and reduce the risk of heart disease.[24] While still working toward change, the Quaker Oats Company has found a way to begin promoting such statements other than through publicity over this Food and Drug Act debate. On their Canadian Web site under "frequently asked questions," or FAQs, there are a series of questions asking about such studies and associated claims by the medical profession. The answers discuss the studies and the American legislation and make statements inferring that differences in regulations prevent them from telling more. The site does, however, manage to report most of the available information. Visitors are also encouraged to visit their American site (www.quakeroatmeal.com) if they want more information and a hypertext link is provided to bring those interested to the site.

Industry Canada has substantial and major responsibility in the area of regulating marketing communications. The Bureau of Competition Policy of Industry Canada carries the major burden of marketing communications regulation. The Acts administered include: (1) the Hazardous Products Act (concerning poisonous compounds for household use), (2) the Precious Metals Marketing Act (i.e., definitions of sterling and carat weight), (3) the Trade Marks Act, (4) the Consumer Packaging and Labelling Act, and of greatest significance, (5) the **Competition Act**. Within the Competition Act, a number of sections pertain directly to the regulation of advertising and marketing communications activities. Section 35, for example, requires that manufacturers or wholesalers who offer marketing communications allowances to retailers must offer such allowances on proportionate

Competition Act
The major piece of federal legislation in Canada that governs the marketing and advertising activities of companies and organizations operating in Canada.

Marketing at Work 18-3

Wyeth-Ayerst Looks for The Better Way

Although they have been on the Canadian market since 1961, as consumer products, birth control pills, and those who manufacture them, have always been content to remain shy, discrete, and demure. Now, however, they are set to take centre stage — in more ways than one. For the first time in Canadian history, Wyeth-Ayerst Canada Inc., the pharmaceutical company that makes the Alesse® birth control pill, is promoting its sometimes controversial product on national television with ads geared specifically to young people. Pharmaceutical companies may advertise their drugs as long as they stay within the guidelines of name, price, and quantity.

But, they *can* provide viewers with the name, quantity and price of their product — and that's as far as it goes. The rationale behind this exception is that this is the bare minimum required for manufacturers to promote their product in a pharmacy. Manufacturers are also free to produce informational TV shots that make *no* mention of any specific product, but discuss the disease or condition a product treats. And that's as far as that goes as well. The strategy is to motivate consumers to seek more information from their doctors who will be able to list all available treatments, including (hopefully) the advertiser's.

Wyeth-Ayerst Canada Inc. has *not* developed commercials that name the drug and talk about what it does. They developed two commercials, one talking about birth control options, the other provides a lesson learned and abides with Health Canada's guidelines of name, price, and quantity.

Instead, the agency has come up with two 15-second TV spots advertising the Alesse® brand (there is also a 60-second cinema ad) and one 30-second informational TV spot that discusses the importance of birth control in general. With a ten-week run on Canada's MuchMusic network, the commercials are destined to hit their target market of "with it" young women. In fact, all of the commercials feature such women engaging in talk about men and relationships. Each woman discusses "a lesson," such as "a lesson in breakups. Don't lend him anything you ever expect to get back," and "a lesson in guys. Never play hard to get. Be hard to get."

Yet while the 15-second commercials identify the brand name and show a package of Alesse® pills, the 30-second "info-mercial" reveals neither. It does however wind up with a woman saying: "Talk to your doctor about your birth control options," to which another woman adds: "Less could make sense for you." Although the line refers to the pill's low-dose formula, it also sounds coincidentally like: "Alesse® could make sense for you." Come to think of it, all those "a lessons" sound coincidentally like "Alesse®" too.

Wyeth-Ayerst's integrated advertising strategy — along with the TV and cinema commercials, posters will appear throughout the city transit system — is a classic device. Sending similar messages about a product through multiple media channels so that the consumer associates one with another and then combines them all into a unique, more complex message is nothing new. What is new is Wyeth-Ayerst's take on the integrated advertising approach. The information commercial and the branded commercial are not run at the same time. Wyeth-Ayerst Canada Inc. has spaced these commercials according to ASC guidelines. After all, similarity in the casting, copy, and overall look and feel of the ads ensures there will be overlap between the various "Alesse®" "lessons." The fact that the ads are set to run during the same time period makes the overlap even more pronounced. The deciding factor will be how much an overlap will be too much?

If, for example, Wyeth-Ayerst placed the two kinds of ads in the same media time and space, where a consumer who saw one and then the other was likely to make a connection between birth control and Alesse®, Health Canada would be forced to make a fuss. Or would they? Health Canada doesn't prescreen prescription drug ads. That role is performed by Advertising Standards Canada (ASC), the ad industry's self-regulating organization. And the ASC has given the Alesse® campaign the thumbs-up signal.

For years now prescription drug makers have been pushing to loosen tight advertising regulations. They argue that consumers are being bombarded by brand-name drug ads from U.S. media and the Internet anyway. If they can't compete on the same tough turf, how will Canadian manufacturers survive? Maybe Wyeth-Ayerst is giving more "Alessons" than it originally planned on.

Source: Adapted, in part, from Patrick Allossery "Health Canada challenge," *Financial Post*, May 15, 2000, p. C5. And John Heinzl, "A lesson in drug advertising," *The Globe and Mail*, May 5, 2000, p. M1 and Shawna Cohen, "The Pill is Controversial Once Again," *Marketing Magazine Online*, May 15, 2000.

terms to all competing purchasers. Section 36 of the Act regulates misleading advertising in general, while section 37 pertains specifically to "bait and switch" advertising.[25]

Section 36 of the Competition Act makes it illegal for an advertiser to make any false or misleading statement to the public in advertising or marketing communications materials or with respect to warranties. This section also regulates the use of false statements regarding the expected performance or length of life of a product and the use of testimonials in advertising. Section 36.2 of the Act regulates the use of "double ticketing" in retail selling and requires that, where a retailer promotes a product at two different prices or where two prices appear on a product or at the point of sale, the retailer must sell the product at the lower of the prices. Businesses or individuals who are convicted of violating section 36 are subject to fines as large as $25,000 or to imprisonment for up to one year.

Paragraph 36(1)(d) of the Competition Act regulates "sale" advertising and would apply particularly to retail advertisers. Section 37 requires that an advertiser who promotes a product at a "sale" price have sufficient quantities of the product on hand to satisfy reasonable market demand. Section 37.1 prohibits an advertiser from selling a "sale" item at a price higher than the advertised "sale" price. Finally, section 37.2 regulates the conduct of contests, lotteries, and games of chance. This section requires that advertisers who promote such contests disclose the number and value of prizes and the areas in which prizes are to be distributed, and further requires that prizes be distributed on a basis of skill or on a basis of random selection.

The provisions of the Competition Act relating to misleading advertising do not apply to publishers and broadcasters who actually distribute the advertising in question to the general public, provided that these publishers have accepted the contents of the advertising in good faith. In essence, this means that a newspaper cannot be prosecuted for misleading advertising if it accepted the advertising on the assumption that its contents were not misleading. Although no newspaper can be prosecuted for misleading advertising if it accepted the advertising in good faith, there is still some question concerning whether media production departments and advertising agencies, which actually participate with the advertiser in the production of misleading advertising, might not in the future be considered jointly responsible with the advertiser for the contents of the offending advertisement. This is a question with which Canadian courts may deal in the future.

The Provincial Role

In each of the provinces, a considerable variety of legislation exists that is aimed at controlling various marketing communications practices. For instance, in Ontario, various degrees of control are exercised by the Liquor Control Board of Ontario, the Ontario Board of Film Censors, the Ontario Superintendent of Insurance, the Ontario Human Rights Commission, the Ontario Securities Commission, the Ontario Police Commission, the Ontario Racing Commission, various ministries of the Ontario government responsible for financial, commercial, consumer, and transportation functions and services, and more. Most of the provinces have similar sets of legislation, regulatory bodies, and provincial departments. Each of the provinces, for example, regulates various aspects of the promotion of alcoholic beverages.[26] While much of the federal regulation must in the end result in argument and prosecution in a courtroom, the provincial machinery would appear to be much more flexible and potentially regulatory in nature, and if pursued, may have a more substantial effect on undesirable practices.

The powers of provincial governments in relation to the regulation of misleading advertising have been increased considerably in recent years. A number of provinces have legislation in place dealing with unfair and unconscionable trade practices. The "trade practices" Acts of British Columbia, Alberta, and Ontario, for example, contain "shopping lists" of practices that are made illegal by these Acts. In reality, these pieces of legislation write into law practices that have been considered illegal by federal prosecutors for a number of years.

Relating to advertising, these Acts prohibit such practices as advertising a product as new when it is in fact used; advertising that fails to state a material fact, thereby deceiving the consumer; and advertising that gives greater prominence to low down payments or monthly payments rather than to the actual price of the product. The Alberta Unfair Trade Practices Act also contains a provision for corrective advertising. This provision means that a court, upon convicting an advertiser for misleading advertising, can order that advertiser to devote some or all of its advertising for a certain period to informing customers that the advertiser had been advertising falsely in the past and to correcting the misleading information that had been communicated in the offending advertisements.

The Province of Quebec has within its Consumer Protection Act a section that regulates advertising directed at children. This section forbids the use of exaggeration, endorsements, cartoon characters, and statements that urge children to buy. Quebec's Official Language Act also contains a number of sections that govern the use of French and English in advertising in that province.

Regulation by Private Organizations

Several kinds of private organizations also exert considerable control over the marketing communications practices of businesses. Magazines, newspapers, and radio and television stations regularly refuse to accept advertisements that they feel are false, misleading, or generally in bad taste, and in so doing they are being "reasonable" in the ordinary course of doing business. Some trade associations have established a "code of ethics" that includes points pertaining to sales force and advertising activities. Some trade associations regularly censor advertising appearing in their trade or professional journals. Better Business Bureaus located in major cities across the country are working to control some very difficult situations. The Advertising Advisory Board administers the Canadian Code of Advertising Standards, a number of other advertising codes, including the Broadcast Code for Advertising to Children (on behalf of the Canadian Association of Broadcasters), and a code regulating the advertising of over-the-counter drugs, which was developed in co-operation with the Proprietary Association and Health Canada.

Summary

Marketing communications, the fourth component of a company's total marketing mix, is essential in modern marketing. The three primary methods of marketing communications are personal selling, advertising, and sales promotion. Other forms include public relations and publicity.

Fundamentally, the marketing communication process consists of a source sending a message through a channel to a receiver. The success of communication depends on how well the message is encoded, how easily and clearly it can be decoded, and whether any noise interferes with its transmission. Feedback, the response created by a message, is a measure of how effective communication has been.

The purposes of marketing communications are to inform, persuade, and remind customers. That means being able to make a product, service, or organization attractive to potential customers at any given price. It also means that marketing communications aims to increase the attractiveness of a product or service by providing the customer with evidence that it is different from the competition, thereby offering a number of nonprice reasons for buying.

Marketing communications must be integrated into a firm's strategic planning because effective execution requires that all elements of the marketing mix — product, price, distribution, and marketing communications — be co-ordinated. An IMC approach helps to assure necessary coordination.

When deciding on the communications mix (the combination of advertising, personal selling, and other marketing communications tools), management should consider: (1) the nature of the market, including the type of customer, the prospect's readiness to buy, and the geographic scope of the market; (2) the nature of the product or service, including unit value, the degree of customization required, and the amount of presale and postsale service; (3) the stage of the life cycle of the product or service; and (4) the funds available for all forms of marketing communications.

A basic decision is how much marketing communications effort should be focused on intermediaries and how much should be directed to end users. The options are a push strategy, which involves concentrating marketing communications efforts on the next link forward in the distribution channel, and a pull strategy, in which marketing communications is focused primarily on the final buyer.

Because the effects of communications are unpredictable, it is difficult to set a dollar figure for the total marketing communications budget. The most common method is to set the budget as a percentage of past or anticipated sales. A better approach is to establish the communications objectives and then estimate how much it will cost to achieve them.

As a result of criticism and concern regarding the use of advertising and marketing communications techniques, the federal government has enacted legislation that regulates marketing communications. The main federal laws are the Competition Act and the Broadcasting Act. Industry Canada and the Canadian Radio-television and Telecommunications Commission are charged with administering the legislation in this area. Marketing communications practices are also regulated at the provincial level through trade practices legislation, through voluntary codes of businesses and trade associations, and by the advertising industry itself.

Key Terms and Concepts

Marketing communications 578	Publicity 581	Noise 587
Inform 578	Integrated marketing	Marketing communications mix 589
Persuade 578	communications (IMC) 583	Push strategy 594
Remind 578	Communication 587	Pull strategy 594
Personal selling 581	Encoding 587	Marketing communications
Advertising 581	Decoding 587	budgeting methods 596
Sales promotion 581	Response 587	Broadcasting Act 599
Public relations 581	Feedback 587	Competition Act 600

Questions and Problems

1. Describe and explain the components of the marketing communications process in the following situations:

    a.   A college student trying to convince her parents to buy her a used car.

    b.   A salesperson trying to sell a car to a college student.

2. Explain how the nature of the market affects the marketing communications mix for the following products:

    a. Auto insurance.

    b. Golf balls.

    c. Plywood.

    d. Aircraft maintenance.

    e. Compact discs.

    f. Computers used as servers.

3. Describe how classifying consumer goods as convenience, shopping, or specialty goods helps determine the best marketing communications mix.

4. Explain whether personal selling is likely to be the main ingredient in the marketing communications mix for each of the following products:

    a. Chequing accounts.

    b. Home swimming pools.

    c. Liquid laundry detergent.

    d. Large order of fries at McDonald's.

5. Explain whether retailer trade promotion efforts should be stressed in the marketing communications mix for the following:

    a. Levi's jeans.

    b. Sunkist oranges.

    c. Canada Saving Bonds.

    d. VISA card.

6. Identify the central idea — the core or basic theme — in three current marketing communications campaigns.

7. Assume you are marketing a liquid that removes creosote (and the danger of fire) from chimneys used for wood-burning stoves. Briefly describe the roles you would assign to advertising, personal selling, sales promotion, and publicity in your marketing communications campaign.

8. Do you think we need additional legislation to regulate advertising? To regulate personal selling? If so, explain what you would recommend.

Hands-On Marketing

1. An advertisement should have a particular objective that should be apparent to a careful observer. For each of the following marketing communications objectives, find an example of a print ad:

    a. Primarily designed to inform.

    b. Primarily designed to persuade.

    c. Primarily designed to remind.

2. An IMC program or campaign is a co-ordinated series of marketing communications efforts built around a single theme and designed to reach a predetermined goal. It often includes advertising, sales promotion, personal selling, public relations, and publicity. For an important event at your school (such as homecoming, recruiting new students, fund raising), describe the marketing communications tools used in the campaign and evaluate their appropriateness based on the criteria in the chapter for designing a marketing communications mix.

Chapter Nineteen

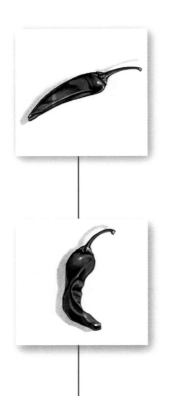

Management of Personal Selling

This chapter examines personal selling, directing a sales force, and evaluating a salesperson's performance. After studying this chapter, you should have an understanding of:

◆ The role that personal selling plays in our economy and in an organization's marketing program.

◆ The nature and variety of the sales job.

◆ The personal selling process and its changing patterns.

◆ The major tasks in staffing and operating a sales force.

◆ Key issues in evaluating a salesperson's performance.

Creating an International Sales Success

oston Scientific Corporation (BSC) (www.bsci.com) is the leading developer, manufacturer, and marketer of medical products for lesser invasive medical procedures. While it has a sales office in Southern Ontario and a direct sales force that covers Canada, it is Boston-based and is a global provider of vascular and non-vascular applications and catheter-based devices for diagnosis and treatment. It is a vigorous firm and in less than two years has acquired ten new businesses and increased its product line from 3,000 to 8,500 offerings. It has also put in place a state-of-the-art management information system which includes sales and administrative reporting, order entry, customer order fulfilment information, automated data collection, worldwide documentation control, product-lot tracking, and inventory management.

BSC sells it products to over ten thousand hospitals, clinics, outpatient facilities, and medical offices. It now has eleven hundred direct sales representatives in forty countries, eight hundred of these are in the North American market. Canada is a new market for BSC. The direct sales reps account for over 90 percent of the dollar volume of the firm and a network of distributors and dealers in thirty small-market countries account for the remainder. International sales represent 40 percent of total volume and are growing rapidly.

With 85 percent of the world's population in emerging market countries, BSC's emerging markets division launched a four year plan to increase its market position in these countries. This meant shifting from the use of local distributors to developing a direct sales presence in twenty national markets in Asia, Latin America, the Middle East, and Africa. Within two years, BSC hired nearly two hundred sales and marketing employees in order to make the change from distributors to direct sales. The director of strategy and market development, Sandy Zinke, wanted to establish common sales processes that could be translated and adapted to a variety of cultures and languages. Zinke felt that an integrated sales and marketing approach, one that would better serve customers and foster long-term partnerships, was needed. He wanted a selling strategy that was not focused on product-feature dumping but rather a process that would engage customers and meet their needs and preferences. This meant that he needed to put in place a lot of sophisticated training to develop the two hundred new sales and marketing people. But BSC didn't have the internal resources or experience to do this for itself.

As a result, BSC selected AchieveGlobal (www.achieveglobal.com), a well-recognized global training organization, to carry out the necessary training. BSC and AchieveGlobal agreed that the new staff was to be trained in the language of their specific country and that the program would be adapted to meet each local culture. AchieveGlobal account executives made the point that while many firms are international, they are not necessarily global unless their products, services, and approaches are truly culturally adapted. The sales training for all employees consisted of a three-day program containing product knowledge orientation, customer needs satisfaction selling, extensive role playing, and case studies. An important focus of this training was to equip these employees with the skills they would need to train and educate themselves in the future as new technologies and products evolve.

A two-day coaching seminar for sales managers was also presented with a focus on effective coaching and reinforcement of appropriate skills and attitudes. For sales managers, a key aspect of the training was to develop the ability to coach their staff without being over-controlling thereby allowing employee initiative and independence to be fostered.

A team of twelve international trainers and the entire sales and marketing staff in emerging markets, from such countries as Brazil, China, Korea, and Mexico, spent their training time in Newport Beach, California. An IMC approach was used with marketing staff in the sales training to assure that sales and marketing teams could carry on business with the same orientation thus minimizing conflict. AchieveGlobal facilitators trained each employee in his country's language rather than use English. The latter is a common practice with many international firms.

As a follow-up to the five-day conference, AchieveGlobal conducted thirteen sessions around the world, with the same facilitators and trainees, focusing on skill mastery, product knowledge, and using real BSC sales situations as a basis for role-playing exercises.

Since the training, BSC has had substantial sales growth, its salespeople are becoming solutions providers and customer partners, sales managers have developed a consistent coaching environment and continue to train people who conduct business autonomously. David McFaul, general manager for Canada, believes that the training has integrated the concepts of BSC's common language so well that salespeople have now have an unconscious competence when it comes to getting to customers' needs.[1]

Nature of Personal Selling

The goal of all marketing efforts is to increase profitable sales by offering want-satisfaction to consumers over the long run. Personal selling is by far the major communications method used to reach this goal. The number of people employed in advertising is a small fraction of the number employed in personal selling. In many companies, personal selling is the largest single operating expense, often 8 to 15 percent of sales. In contrast, advertising costs average 1 to 3 percent of sales.

In Chapter 18 we discussed five factors that influence an organization's marketing communications mix — the target market, the objective, the product, the product's life-cycle stage, and the budget available for promotion. Of the five factors, personal selling is likely to be responsible for a large portion of the marketing communications load when:

◆ The market is concentrated either geographically or in a few industries, or in a few large customers.

◆ The value of the product is not readily apparent to potential customers.

◆ The product has a high unit value, is quite technical in nature, or requires demonstration.

◆ The product must be fitted to an individual customer's need, as in the case of securities or insurance.

◆ The sale involves a trade-in.

Direct contact enables tailoring the message to the needs of the buyer.

◆ The product is in the introductory stage of its life cycle.

◆ The organization does not have enough money for an adequate advertising campaign.

Merits of Personal Selling

personal selling
The personal communication of information to persuade a prospective customer to buy a good, service, idea, or other product.

Personal selling is the *direct* personal communication of information, in contrast to the *impersonal* communication of advertising, sales promotion, and other marketing communications tools. This means that personal selling can be more flexible than these other tools. Salespeople can tailor their presentations to fit the needs and behaviour of individual customers. They can see their customers' reaction to a particular sales approach and make adjustments on the spot.

Also, personal selling usually can be focused or pinpointed on prospective customers, thus minimizing wasted effort. In contrast, advertising messages are directed at much larger audiences, many of who are not realistic prospects.

Another advantage of personal selling is that its goal is to actually secure a sale. Other forms of promotion are designed to move a prospect closer to a sale. Advertising, for example, often has the less ambitious goal of attracting attention, providing information, and arousing desire. Aside from retail and direct response advertising, it is rarely the sole factor responsible for stimulating buying action or completing the transfer of ownership from seller to buyer.

On the other hand, full-fledged personal selling is costly. Even though personal selling can minimize wasted effort, the cost of developing and operating a sales force is high. Another disadvantage is that a company may often find it difficult to attract and retain the quality of salespeople needed to do the job. A successful career in sales requires a certain personality disposition, otherwise the person most often does not enjoy their job — and customers often don't enjoy them either! At the retail level, many firms have abandoned their sales staff and shifted to self-service for this very reason.

Scope of Personal Selling

Elements of personal selling are to be found in almost every human interaction: when a marketing major tries to convince a Holt Renfrew human resource specialist to recruit her; when a boy tries to convince his mother why she should get him that shirt from The Gap; when your friends try and convince you to attend a dance club with them.

There are two kinds of personal selling, as shown in Figure 19-1. One is where customers come to the salespeople. Called **inside selling**, it primarily involves retail-store selling. In this kind of selling, we also include the thousands of employees who work in call-centres across the country and who take orders over the telephone. This, too, is retail selling because it involves sales to the end consumer. By far, most salespeople in Canada fall into this first category.

With advancements in telecommunication systems as integrated components of overall management information systems, the use of call-centres and telemarketing representatives grew exponentially during the nineties. This practice became particularly popular with financial service providers. This sales approach works particularly well in combination with a significant Internet presence. Dell (www.dell.ca) and Gateway (www.gateway.com) computers have both become specialists in selling computer equipment and accessories through these mediums.

Companies such as Kodak Canada (www.kodak.ca) and Molson Breweries (www.iam.ca) have also begun using telesales people. To facilitate business clients, Kodak Canada sends clients flow charts explaining how client requests for service move through the company's system. They also send clients a photo of their teleservice representative to maintain that "personal" touch. Molson has substantially reduced their personal sales force by hiring telephone reps to manage inventories and merchandising for smaller clients. Such telemarketing applications can cost as little as one tenth that of a personal sales call and an efficient, experienced rep can often reach as many companies in a day as an employee in the field can in a week.[2]

In the other kind of personal selling, known as **outside selling**, salespeople go to the customer. Telemarketing actually falls under the rubric of outside selling as it generally refers to outgoing calls directed at the solicitation of new business and sales in contrast to the previous discussion which was more customer service and maintenance focused.

outside selling
The kind of personal selling in which salespeople go to the customers, making contact by mail, telephone, or face-to-face.

FIGURE 19-1
Scope of
Personal Selling

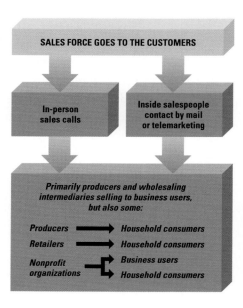

outside sales force
A group of sales reps engaged in field selling, that is, selling in person at a customer's place of business or home.

Most **outside sales forces** usually represent producers or wholesaling intermediaries, selling to business users and not to household consumers. However, in our definition of an outside sales force we also include: (1) producers whose representatives sell directly to household consumers — for example, insurance companies such as Great-West Life, and in-home sellers such as those for Avon Products (www.avon.ca) or Mary Kay Cosmetics (www.marykay.com); (2) representatives of retail organizations such as those from home heating, furniture and decorating, and insulation retailers; and (3) representatives of non-profit organizations — for example, charity fund-raisers and workers for political candidates.

Nature of Sales Jobs

The sales job of today is quite different from the stereotype of the past. The images of high pressure, false friendship, and glibness are largely outdated. Even the stereotype of the salesman is outdated, as today more and more women are entering the profession selling products as varied as financial products to automobiles.

Tenacity, optimism, and training make a professional salesperson.

THE PROFESSIONAL SALESPERSON A new type of sales rep is emerging: the **professional salesperson**. Today these salespeople are managers of a market area — their territories or a category of customers. They engage in a total selling job — servicing their customers, building goodwill, selling their products, and training their customers' salespeople. Today's sales representatives act as a mirror of the market by relaying market information back to the firm. They organize much of their own time and effort. They often take part in recruiting new salespeople, sales planning in their territories, and other managerial activities.

Sales and Marketing Management Magazine, in its surveys among sales executives and customers concerning the factors that are considered in selecting good sales employees, point to the following criteria:[3]

◆ *Accuracy:* Do the salespeople take care of details?

◆ *Availability:* Are the salespeople responsive to customers' requests?

◆ *Credibility:* Do customers view the salespeople as important resources?

◆ *Partnership:* Are the salespeople sought out for advice?

What does it take to be a great sales professional?

Tenacity, optimism and membership in the Canadian Professional Sales Association.

Professional Development Services
➤ affordable national seminar program
➤ regional networking events
➤ a comprehensive collection of audio, video and print material at 10 - 30% off
➤ access to the Sales Resource Centre, a library specifically designed to meet the needs of sales and marketing professionals

CPSA Benefits and Savings
➤ hotel/motel discounts of up to 50%
➤ car rentals at 35% off daily rate
➤ vehicle leasing at prime rate financing
➤ gasoline and car maintenance discounts
➤ cellular airtime/hardware savings
➤ long distance savings of up to 50%
➤ group insurance programs

Plug into the CPSA benefit network for only $65* annually and find out what 30,000 CPSA members see in North America's largest sales association.

Canadian Professional Sales Association

1-800-268-3794
In Toronto (416) 408-2685 *Plus a one time $20 enrolment fee

◆   *Trust:* Are customers confident that the salespeople will keep their word?

◆   *Discovery:* Do the salespeople offer ideas that improve customers' businesses?

WIDE VARIETY OF SALES JOBS The types of selling jobs and the activities involved in them cover a wide range. Consider the job of a Humpty Dumpty potato chip driver-salesperson (www.humptydumpty.com) who calls routinely on a group of retail stores. That job is completely different from that of the IBM (www.ibm.ca) systems consultant who sells a computer system for managing hotel reservations to a major hotel chain like CP Hotels (www.cp.ca). Similarly, a sales rep for Avon selling door-to-door in Japan or China has a job only remotely related to that of a Challenger 604 Aircraft (www.businessaircraft.bombardier.com) sales engineer who leads the team that sells executive-type aircraft to large corporations around the world.

One way to classify sales jobs are on the basis of the creative selling skills required, from the simple to the complex. The classification that follows are updated and adapted from several classification schemes developed over time.[4]

driver salesperson
A selling job in which the job is primarily to deliver the product. Selling responsibilities, if any, are secondary to seeing that orders are filled correctly and on time.

1. **Driver-salesperson.** In this job the salesperson primarily delivers the product — for example, soft drinks or fuel oil. The selling responsibilities are secondary though most of these salespeople are authorized to and rewarded for finding opportunities to increase sales to existing accounts.

inside order taker
A selling job in which the primary function of the salesperson is to take orders in person or by phone inside a store or other type of business.

2. **Inside order taker.** This is a position in which the salesperson takes orders at the seller's place of business — for example, a retail clerk standing behind the counter at a Bay store or a telephone representative of the Eddie Bauer catalogue retail operation. Most customers have already decided to buy. The salesperson's job is to serve them efficiently.

outside order taker
A selling job in which salespeople are primarily going to customers in the field.

3. **Outside order taker.** In this position, the salesperson goes to the customer in the field and accepts an order. An example is a sales representative for Para Paints (www.para.com) who calls on a building supplies store. The majority of sales made by outside order takers are repeat orders to established customers, and much of the salesperson's time is devoted to support activities such as assisting with promotion and helping train the account's salespeople. Outside salespeople are assigned targets, or goals, that require them to seek new customers and to introduce new products to existing customers.

missionary seller
A selling job in which the salespeople are not expected to solicit orders but are expected to influence decision-makers by building goodwill, performing promotional activities, and providing service to customers. In pharmaceuticals marketing, called "detail salesperson."

4. **Missionary salesperson.** This types of sales job is intended to build goodwill, perform promotional activities, and provide information and other services for the customers. This salesperson does not solicit orders. These people may also be called merchandisers or detailers. An example of this job is a missionary sales rep for Procter & Gamble (www.pg.com) who visits retailers regularly and may offer presentation suggestions, as well as assist in setting it up. They would also help with special promotions. Also, there are "drug reps" from companies such as Merck (www.merck.com) or Eli Lilly (www.lilly.com), who call on doctors to introduce new products, educate, and leave professional samples to be distributed to patients. This can be for both prescription and non-prescription products. Clearly, doctors don't buy these products to resell — they can potentially recommend or write prescriptions for these products.

5. **Sales engineer.** In this position the major emphasis is on the salesperson's ability to explain the product to a prospective customer, and also to adapt the product to the customer's particular needs. The products involved here typically are complex, technically sophisticated items. A sales engineer usually provides technical support and works with another sales rep who regularly calls on a given account. Examples include producers of industrial equipment that would develop manufacturing systems according to a client's requirements. Sales would be to new clients, replacement systems and replacement parts. As new developments arise reps would continue to sell to existing clients as they "sell" them on the increased benefits of the new technology. New clients and newly developed systems often require ongoing support while "bugs" are worked out, systems are fine-tuned to the particular processing requirements, and staff learn to run and maintain equipment. Also applicable here is the development and implementation of computer systems within organizations, or helping a company learn to operate on the Internet.

6. **Consultative salesperson.** The person engages in the creative selling of goods and services. This category contains the most complex, difficult selling jobs — especially the creative selling of services, because you can't see, touch, taste, or smell them. Customers often are not aware of their need for a seller's product. Or they may not realize how that product can satisfy their wants better than the product they are now using. Consultative selling requires that a relationship of trust be established with the customer. It often involves designing a system to fit the needs of a particular customer. For example, to make a sale, Nortel (www.nortel.ca) may design a customer relationship system for a business, or Otis Elevator (www.otis.com) may develop a vertical lift system especially for a new office building. Such positions also involve technologically advanced products and computer systems.

An effective insider order taker can adjust to a customer's reactions and can build good customer relations.

In summary, the above six types of sales jobs fall into three groups: **order taker** (categories 1, 2, and 3), **sales-support personnel** (categories 4 and 5), and **order-getter** (category 6). Order takers, unless they can find ways to provide added value to their customers, are the sales positions most threatened by Internet commerce.

THE COST OF PERSONAL SELLING The cost of a sales call depends on the sales approach used. For firms selling commodities and emphasizing price, the cost can be from $80 to $100 per call. When the sales approach is to identify and design solutions for customers' problems, costs can range from $160 to $200 per call. Add to this the fact that it can take from three to six calls to conclude a sale with a new customer, and it is clear that personal selling is costly. Turnover can also be high as certain personality traits are required for success and to enjoy this profession. New salespeople require training and initially they are less productive, and perhaps less successful. High turnover appears unprofessional to clients, and sales may be lost.

THE UNIQUENESS OF SALES JOBS The features that differentiate sales jobs from other jobs are:

◆ *The sales force is largely responsible for implementing a firm's marketing strategies.* Moreover, it's the sales reps that generate the revenues that are managed by the financial people and used by the production people.

◆ *Salespeople represent their company to customers and to society in general.* Many sales jobs require the salesperson to socialize with customers who frequently are upper-level managers in their companies. Opinions of the firm and its products are formed on the basis of impressions made by salespeople in their work and outside activities. The public ordinarily does not judge a company by its factory or office workers.

◆ *Salespeople often operate with limited direct supervision.* For success in selling, a sales rep must work hard physically and mentally, be creative and persistent, and show considerable initiative. This all requires a high degree of motivation.

◆ *Sales jobs often involve considerable travelling and time away from home.* Many companies have reduced sales travel time by redesigning sales territories, routing sales trips better, and relying more on telemarketing. Nevertheless, being in the field, salespeople must deal with an endless stream of customers who may seem determined not to buy their products. These stresses, coupled with long hours and travelling, require a mental toughness and physical stamina rarely demanded in other jobs. Personal selling is hard work!

Changing Patterns in Personal Selling

Traditionally, personal selling was a face-to-face, one-on-one situation between a sales person and a buyer. This situation existed both in retail sales involving ultimate consumers and in business-to-business transactions. In recent years, however, some very different selling patterns have emerged. These new patterns reflect a growing purchasing expertise among consumers and business buyers, which, in turn, has fostered a growing professionalism in personal selling. Three of these patterns are discussed below.

Marketing at Work 19-1

Whatever It Takes

What happens when somebody is selling? Let's say you're an advertising sales representative. You're not in downtown Edmonton, Toronto, or Winnipeg; you're not representing the *Edmonton Sun*, the *Toronto Star* or the *Winnipeg Free Press*; and your clients are not major department stores or corporate headquarters or provincial trade associations. No, you are Sharon Riley, and you're a sales rep for the Montague Eastern Graphic, in Montague, Prince Edward Island. Or you're Bernadette Jordan, a sales rep for three community weeklies owned by Lighthouse Publishing of Bridgewater, Nova Scotia.

When Sharon Riley dresses for work she puts on a skirt, a blazer, and her three-inch heels — pretty straightforward. Except that her clients could not only be in a shop or office building in Montague but also in a pig barn in the surrounding countryside or on a wharf at the equally near seaside. Sharon jokes about the range of accounts and the question of how to present "self" so as to use the "perceived similarity principle" to help clients feel comfortable with her. "I've thought of dressing down…but whenever I do, they ask me why I'm not working today." Riley's actions and comments reflect the nature of sales work at Canada's weekly newspapers from Port Hardy, British Columbia to Carbonear, Newfoundland. She is likely to be referred to by customers as the "ad girl," but "client sales and marketing consultant" would be more accurate. And she is as much educator, confidante, and friend, as she is a salesperson.

Being able to do a good job for clients also means understanding their business and even getting involved in it. For Riley, more than once it meant helping out when help was needed. "They told me, 'You want to sell something to us today, you'll have to help us find the time.' So I slapped on an apron and washed up the backlog of dishes in the diner's sink." She got the ad, and the small cafe is now a regular client. When competing with larger regional papers and dealing with small local firms that sit on the fence regarding whether or not to advertise you have to be creative and innovative. And it has to be done on a shoestring budget.

Bernadette Jordan, who represents three weeklies and works in southern Nova Scotia, cites trust as the most important factor in the client-salesperson relationship. "If they can't confide in me about how their children are doing in school, how can they trust me with the important financial details of their business?" And, of course, if you don't know the important details of their business, how can you really help them? "Most of my clients have never heard of Geographic Information Systems, but they sure want to know how I can bring more shoppers in their front door." That has a lot more to do with knowing how many boats are still fishing from the Lunenberg waterfront than any national buying trend. If Jordan doesn't meet her clients' expectations just once, they won't be interested in seeing her again.

Ad reps such as Riley and Jordan are constantly participating in training programs; they attend seminars and conventions such as those sponsored by the Atlantic Community Newspapers Association or the Canadian Community Newspapers Association (www.ccna.ca). It's the information picked up from colleagues at "Ideas Exchanges" held at conferences that excites Jordan. It's there that the innovation and creativity of these sales professionals combine to brainstorm new ideas. Jordan says, "I sit there thinking, 'That's the perfect campaign for so and so.' I come home bursting with ideas, and that's good for my clients."

Remember, these salespeople are involved, interested, trustworthy, persevering, helpful, and more. And they are paid on commission — they make money only when they are out there doing their jobs and clients can tell that they have been helped.

Source: Adapted, in part, from, Sheilah Allan, "Small Town Selling," *Marketing Magazine*, February 3, 1997, pp. 15–16 and Gordon Brewerton, "Old Idea, New Twist," *Marketing Magazine*, February 7, 2000, p. 26.

Selling Centres — Team Selling

To match the expertise on the buying centre in business markets, a growing number of firms on the selling side have adopted the organizational concept of a **selling centre**. A selling centre is simply a group of people representing a sales department as well as other functional areas in a firm such as finance, production, and research and development (R&D). This is sometimes called *sales team* or *team selling*.

Team selling is expensive and is used only when there is a potential for high sales volume and profit. Procter & Gamble (www.pg.com), for example, has selling teams comprising salespeople and representatives from finance, distribution, and manufacturing assigned to cover a large retailer such as Wal-Mart. As an international retailer for most all of P&G's products, the two firms work so closely that Wal-Mart's scanner and inventory system is directly linked to P&G allowing the company to perform many inventory control functions. The P&G sales team works closely with the retailer to develop, promote, and deliver products. The company also has similar, but less sophisticated, relationships with other retailers such as Zellers, Loblaw, and Shoppers Drug Mart.

Most sales teams are ad hoc groups, assembled only to deal with a particular client or opportunity. Except for the salesperson, the team members have other duties within the firm. This raises certain managerial issues. For example, who shall direct the team, the person most senior, the person with the most experience with the situation at hand or the salesperson who organized the team? What happens if the buying centre decides it prefers working with a senior manager on the team or a technical expert who "speaks their language" rather than the salesperson? How should the team members be evaluated and compensated? Despite having to deal with these types of issues, the increasingly complexity of sales has made team selling increasingly popular.

Systems Selling

The concept of **systems selling** means selling a total package of related goods and services — a system — to solve a customer's problem. The idea is that the system — the total package of goods and services — will satisfy the buyer's needs more effectively than selling individual products separately. Xerox (www.xerox.ca), for example, originally sold individual products, using a separate sales force for each major product line. Today, using a systems-selling approach, Xerox studies a customer's office information and operating problems, then provides a total automated system of machines and accompanying services to solve that customer's office problems.

Systems selling has several benefits. The most obvious is that it produces a larger initial sale since a system rather than a product is being purchased. Second, it reduces compatibility problems since either all parts of the system come from the same supplier or they have been selected for their compatibility. Third, the supplier is usually retained to service the system because of its familiarity with it and its components. Finally, if the system performs effectively, the provider is in an excellent position for upgrades as they are required. In some very technical situations, systems selling may involve a number of firms on the suppliers' side. This evolution into a "solutions" provider for the client fosters a reliance on the provider as well as a stronger "relationship" between the two firms.

Global Sales Teams

As companies expand their operations to various corners of the world, they expect their suppliers to do the same. Having products readily available and providing quick service became essential to maintaining global customers. Thus, many larger firms have established sales offices or distribution centres in some foreign locations to serve these customers. Now, to service their largest and most profitable customers, companies such as Nortel, Bombardier (www.bombardier.ca), Magna International (www.magna.ca), and IBM Canada are forming global sales teams. A global sales team is responsible for all of a client's requirements, for any of their locations, around the world.

Relationship Selling

Relationship selling means developing a mutually beneficial relationship with selected customers over time. Relationship selling can be a natural development to come from team selling or it can be developed by individual sales representatives in their continued dealings with customers. Relationship selling is based on the notion that instead of maximizing the number and size of individual transactions, the seller works to develop a deeper, longer-lasting relationship built on trust and mutual benefit. The salesperson must work with the client to determine what is in the best interest of the client and not the sales firm or the individual salesperson. This may mean taking the time and effort to understand the true needs and goals of the client's firm. The salesperson must place as much emphasis on the buyer-seller relationship as the immediate sale during transactions and sales efforts. Sales representatives must receive the full support of the firm in these efforts in that their performance must be evaluated on relationship measures as well as sales performance.

Unfortunately, frequently there is a lack of trust found in the buyer–seller relationship both in retailer–consumer selling and business to business selling. Too often selling can become adversarial with one side winning and the other side losing. Often the perception is that the sales representative's sole purpose is to increase the value of current sales without regard for future consumer interactions. The potential consumer, therefore, is suspicious of the actions and motive of the sales rep. When this does occur, it can be said that a relationship has either failed or did not really exist.

When dealing with a customer, a successful sales rep will always consider the potential for future transactions. He/she will consider the long-term potential of that client as well as the effect that his/her behaviour will have on their reputation. Being less than forthcoming, selling unneeded products and services will damage future potential of a client as well as possibly influencing whether other potential clients will wish to do business with that person. Being straightforward, putting the concerns and interests of the client first will cause trust to be developed and provide a reputation of the same. Existing clients will remain loyal and will refer new business and clients when the opportunity arises.

Many large companies such as Kraft General Foods (www.kraftfoods.com), Procter & Gamble, and Hyatt Hotels (www.hyatt.com) have realigned their sales forces to engage in relationship selling within a framework of relationship marketing. Proctor & Gamble has developed an "everyday low price" program to simplify client relations and to remove an element of the adversarial bartering that often accompanies such transaction negotiations. Hyatt Hotels has empowered employees to do whatever is required to provide for the needs of clients. This practice stresses to members of the organization that client satisfaction is paramount over minor company rules and regulations. Clients receive the same impression from the service that they experience.

Telemarketing

telemarketing
A form of nonstore retailing in which a salesperson initiates contact with a shopper and closes the sale over the telephone.

Telemarketing is the innovative use of telecommunications equipment and systems as part of the "going to the customer" category of personal selling. Under certain conditions, telemarketing is attractive to both buyers and sellers. Buyers placing routine reorders or new orders for standardized products by telephone use less of their time than with personal sales calls.

Many sellers find that telemarketing increases selling efficiency. With the high costs of keeping salespeople on the road, telemarketing reduces the time they spend on routine order-taking. Redirecting routine reorders to telemarketing allows the field sales force to devote more time to creative selling, major account selling, and other more profitable selling activities. Here are examples of selling activities that lend themselves nicely to a telemarketing program:

◆ Seeking leads to new accounts and identifying potentially good customers that sales reps can follow up with in-person calls.

◆ Processing orders for standardized products. In the case of Baxter International (www.baxter.com) and some of the customers for its hospital supplies, for example, the buyer's computer talks with Baxter's computer to determine shipping dates and to place orders.

◆ Dealing with small-order customers, especially those with whom the seller would lose money if field sales calls were used.

◆ Improving relations with intermediaries. John Deere (farm equipment) (www. deere.com) "talks" via computers with its dealers about inventories, service, and financial management.

◆ Improving communications with intermediaries in foreign countries and competing better against manufacturers in those countries. In Europe, for example, the auto, chemical, steel, and shipbuilding industries have developed electronic communication systems involving manufacturers, suppliers, and even customs and shipping agents.

Internet Selling: The Business-to-Business Auction

Internet selling
The offering of goods or services to customers over the Internet.

Most sales efforts over the Internet would not be considered personal, and therefore would not be part of a discussion of *personal* selling. For example, when a large wholesaler posted its 4,000-page catalogue of repair and maintenance parts on its Web site so customers could order items electronically, the resulting transactions are impersonal. In fact, the impersonal nature of the process is one of its strengths because it speeds up purchasing and reduces the frequency of errors. However, one category of **Internet selling**, the business-to-business auction, qualifies as personal selling because of its interactive nature.[5]

Using the *traditional auction* format, a seller (working through an intermediary such as PurchasePro.com (www.purchasepro.com) that provides the linking technology) notifies potential bidders of a product available for sale. Typically the item for sale is a discontinued model of a product or excess inventory of some raw material. According to a predetermined schedule, bids are submitted electronically in round-robin fashion in real time. Both the seller *and* all the bidders see each bid and have the opportunity to respond.

Another version is called a *reverse auction*. The prospective buyer notifies potential sellers of its willingness to purchase a specified product and an electronic auction is held to select a seller. As the auction progresses, "bids" decrease until the "bid" reaches a level that the prospective buyer is willing to pay. In both auction formats, there is an interchange of information between buyers and sellers, negotiation of terms, and intense price competition.

Thus far, the largest volume of Internet auctions have been limited to commodities or standardized goods. For example a local government bought salt for use on icy roads, and a computer memory-chip maker sold microprocessors. However, there is little doubt that as communications technology improves in terms of speed and ease of use, the Internet will become more and more significant as a sales tool.

The traditional auction format, with increasing bidding, has become popular with many collectible and hard-to-find items. Retail markets, however, have also found creative way to "auction" merchandise. Already discussed has been PriceLine.com and Mercata.com that have used Internet technology to develop "new" ways to buy and sell. The Internet also provides a medium to find markets for specialty products and services that may not otherwise find a large marketplace due to their specialized appeal. These, however, are no real threat to replacing personal selling.

Retailers, such as L.L. Bean and J. Crew, that have developed reputations for their quality of personal selling through telephone order centres, have remained in the forefront with their Internet presence. J Crew (www.jcrew.com) has combined Internet and telephone selling with interactive software that allows sales reps to communicate through voice or text while customers peruse their sites. Reps can even direct catalogue pages to appear on the customer's computer screen when making recommendations and providing advice. This has enabled the retailer to enhance the quality of personal selling offered through this established format.

Sales Force Automation

sales force automation (SFA)
Strategy of equipping salespeople with laptop computers, cellular phones, fax machines, and pagers to give them access to databases, the Internet, and e-mail to help them manage accounts more effectively.

Equipping salespeople with laptop computers, wireless mobile phones, fax machines, and pagers in order to give them access to data bases, the Internet, e-mail, and other information and communication tools is called **sales force automation (SFA)**. The concept is quite simple. A great deal of software has been developed to help salespeople manage information about their accounts and prospects, generate proposals, submit reports, and manage their time and territories more efficiently. For example, JVC, a video equipment manufacturer, found its sales force was spending time every morning tracking down information about customers' purchase orders. To reduce the search time, the company designed a system that allows the sales force to download the information from the company's main database to their laptops every day. Now the salespeople have the information they need available immediately.[6] By arming sales representatives with the appropriate technology, a firm can increase a salesperson's productivity and efficiency. By reducing time spent on routine administrative tasks, more time is free for pursuing new clients, following up on existing clients, and strengthening relationships. Sales reps can, therefore, provide a higher level of service.

Automating a sales force can be expensive, depending on the level and the degree of customization. For example, providing salespeople with pagers so they can keep in touch with customers would be a modest investment compared to a system that permitted access to corporate databases. Implementing SFA involves several challenges:

◆ Identifying the parts of the sales process that can benefit the most from automation.

◆ Designing a system that accomplishes the objectives and is user friendly.

◆ Gaining the cooperation of the sales force in changing the way they do their jobs to incorporate the technology.[7]

Experiences with automation have been mixed. According to a firm that implements these programs, 55 percent fail to meet expectations.[8] However, many of the problems that crop up seem to result from inadequate planning or implementation. Despite these difficulties, increasingly sales forces are being automated. The growth in revenue from the sale of SFA equipment is increasing at a high rate and recent surveys indicate that from 70 to 85 percent of firms now using different SFA approaches indicated plans to upgrade their systems. Many firms rush to automate without serious consideration for correct or meaningful implementation. Unless employees really appreciate how to use the technology, and how to use it to benefit their role and their clients, then time and money may be wasted.

The Personal Selling Process

The personal selling process (see Figure 19-2) is a logical sequence of four steps that a salesperson takes in dealing with a prospective buyer. This process is designed to lead to some desired customer action and ends with a follow-up to ensure customer satisfaction. The desired action usually is to get the customer to buy a product or a service. However, the same four-step process may be used equally well in other selling situations. For example, Nabisco (www.nabisco.ca) persuades Safeway and Sobey's to give Oreo cookies a prominent shelf location in a special promotion program; or Carleton University persuades alumni to contribute to a special fund-raising effort; or BMW wants its dealers to do local advertising for these automobiles.

Prospecting

prospecting
The stage in the personal selling process that involves developing a list of potential customers.

The first step in the personal selling process is called **prospecting**. It consists of two activities, identifying prospective customers and then qualifying them — that is, determining whether they have the necessary needs, purchasing power, authority, and willingness to buy.

IDENTIFYING PROSPECTIVE CUSTOMERS. The identification process is an application of market segmentation. By analyzing the firm's database of past and current customers, a sales representative determines the characteristics of the ideal prospect. Comparing this profile to a list of potential customers will produce a set of prospects.

Many other sources can be used to build the list of prospects. The representative's sales manager may prepare a list; current customers may suggest new leads; trade association and industry directories can be a good source; and leads can come from people responding to the firm's marketing communications. This includes mailing in a coupon, phoning a 1-800 number stated in an advertisement, or responding to a Web site.

A little thought often will suggest logical prospects. For example, The Brick furniture store (www.brick.com) can find prospects in lists of building permits issued. Toyota and Nissan auto dealers in Japan go door to door to seek prospects for new car sales. Insurance companies, real estate firms, and even local diaper services use such sources as marriage and birth announcements in newspapers. Home and auto insurance companies, when making outbound telemarketing calls, will try to obtain the customer's policy renewal date.

QUALIFYING THE PROSPECTS After identifying prospective customers, a marketer should **qualify** them — that is, determine whether they have the necessary willingness,

FIGURE 19-2
The Personal
Selling Process

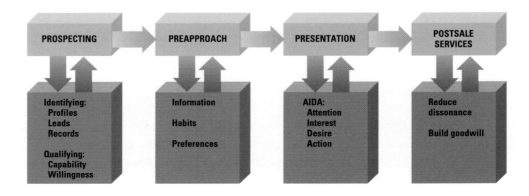

purchasing power, and authority to buy. To determine willingness to buy, a company can seek information about a prospect's relationship with its present suppliers. For example, a business firm or a household consumer may have had a long, satisfying relationship with Co-operators Insurance for auto insurance. In this case, there would seem to be little chance that an Allstate (www.allstate.ca) salesperson could get that prospect's business, so he or she may be better advised to target other customers.

To determine a prospect's ability to pay, a marketer may refer to credit-rating services such as Dun & Bradstreet (www.dnbcorp.com). For household consumers or small businesses in an area, a seller may obtain credit information from a local credit bureau. Identifying the person who has the authority to buy in a business or a household can be difficult, as we saw in Chapters 6 and 7. In a business, the buying authority may rest with a committee or a senior manager in a distant location. Besides determining the buying authority, a seller also should identify the one or more persons who influence the buying decision. A purchasing agent may have buying authority, but what he or she buys may depend on the recommendation of office staff, factory engineers, or senior managers.

Preapproach to Individual Prospects

Before calling on prospects, salespeople should learn all they can about them. This could mean finding out what products and services the prospects are now using and their reactions to these products. In business-to-business selling, a salesperson or selling team should find out how buying decisions are made in the customer's organization. (Remember, in Chapter 7 we discussed the various roles played in the buying-decision process in business firms.) A sales rep can target the right people if he or she knows whom the information gatekeeper is, who influences and/or makes the buying decision, and who actually makes the purchase.

Finding out something about the prospect's personal interests and preferences can be helpful. Salespeople should try to get all the information they can, so that they will be able to tailor their presentations to individual buyers.

Presenting the Sales Message

With the appropriate **preapproach information**, a salesperson can design a **sales presentation** that will attract the prospect's attention. The salesperson will then try to hold the prospect's interest while building a desire for the product; and, when the time is right, attempt to stimulate action by closing the sale. This approach, called AIDA (an acronym formed by the first letters of Attention, Interest, Desire, and Action), is used by many organizations.

ATTRACT ATTENTION — THE APPROACH The first task in a sales presentation is to attract the prospect's attention and to generate curiosity. In cases where the prospect is aware of a need and is seeking a solution, simply stating the seller's company and product will be enough. However, more creativity often is required.

For instance, if a customer referred the salesperson to the prospect, the right approach might be to start out by mentioning this common acquaintance. Or a salesperson might suggest the product benefits by making some startling statement. One sales training consultant often greets a prospect with the question, "If I can cut your selling costs in half, and at the same time double your sales volume, are you interested?"

HOLD INTEREST AND AROUSE DESIRE After attracting the prospect's attention, the sales representative can hold it and stimulate a desire for the product with a sales talk. There is no common pattern here. Usually, however, a product demonstration is invaluable. Whatever pattern is followed in the talk, the salesperson must always show how the product will benefit the prospect.

Some companies train their salespeople to use a "canned" sales talk — a memorized sales presentation designed to cover all points set by management. Many companies engaging in telephone selling or door-to-door selling often use canned sales talks or scripts. Although many people feel that this is a poor practice, canned talks have time and again proved to be effective. Nevertheless, they are used less and less today in face-to-face sales situations, because companies believe that flexible presentations can be more personal and tailored for individual customers' needs. Telemarketing companies, on the other hand, seem to continue to rely on scripted sales calls.

MEET OBJECTIONS AND CLOSE THE SALE After explaining the product and its benefits, a salesperson should try **closing the sale** — obtaining the customer's agreement to buy. (This is the final A in AIDA — achieving the desired action.)

As part of the presentation, the salesperson may periodically venture a **trial close** to test the prospect's willingness to buy. By posing some "either–or" questions, a salesperson can bring the presentation to a head. For example, "Would you like the installation to begin next Monday or shall we book another time later in the week?"

The trial close is important because it gives the salesperson an indication of how near the prospect is to a decision or what objections the prospect has. If objections are stated, the salesperson then has an opportunity to meet them and clarify additional product or service benefits and to reinforce those that have already been presented.

Postsale Services

An effective selling job does not end when the order is written up. The final stage of a selling process is a series of **postsale activities** that can build customer goodwill and lay the groundwork for future business. An alert salesperson will follow up sales to ensure that no problems occur in delivery, financing, installation, employee training, and other areas that are important to customer satisfaction.

postsale activity or service
The final stage of the selling process, including delivery, financing, installation, routine maintenance, employee training, billing, and other areas important to customer satisfaction.

Postsale service reduces the customer's postpurchase anxiety (cognitive dissonance, as discussed in Chapter 6) — the anxiety that usually occurs after a person makes a buying decision. In this final stage of the selling process, a salesperson can minimize the customer's dissonance by (1) summarizing the product's benefits after the purchase, (2) repeating why the product is better than alternatives not chosen, and (3) emphasizing how satisfied the customer will be with the product.[9]

Staffing and Operating a Sales Force

Most sales executives spend the bulk of their time in staffing and operating their sales forces. Hence, we now discuss what they do in these activities, as shown in Figure 19-3.

Recruitment and Selection

Staffing (personnel selection) is the most important management activity in any organization. This is true whether the organization is a business, an athletic team, or a univer-

FIGURE 19-3 Staffing and Operating a Sales Force

sity or college faculty. Consequently, the key to success in managing a sales force is selecting the right people. No matter what the calibre of sales management, if a sales force is distinctly inferior to that of a competitor, the competitor will win.

Sales force selection includes three tasks:

sale force selection
The three steps in assembling a sales force, consisting of (1) determining the number and type of people wanted by preparing a written job description, (2) recruiting an adequate number of applicants, and (3) selecting the most qualified persons from among the applicants.

1. Determining the type of people wanted, by preparing a written job description.

2. Recruiting an adequate number of applicants.

3. Selecting the most qualified persons from among the applicants.

DETERMINING HIRING SPECIFICATIONS The first step is to establish the proper hiring specifications, just as if the company were purchasing equipment or supplies rather than labour. To establish these specifications, management must first know what the particular sales job entails. This calls for a detailed review of the marketing strategy to determine the salesperson's role. Then a detailed job analysis and a written job description can be developed. This description will later be invaluable in training, compensation, and supervision.

Determining the qualifications needed to fill the job is the most difficult part of the selection function. We still really do not know all the characteristics that make a good salesperson. We cannot measure to what degree each quality should be present. Nor do we know to what extent an abundance of one can offset the lack of another.

The search for the qualities that make a good salesperson continues. As one approach, some companies have analyzed the personal histories of its past sales representatives in an effort to determine the traits common to successful (and unsuccessful) performers.

RECRUITING APPLICANTS A planned system for recruiting a sufficient number of applicants is the next step in selection. A good recruiting system:

◆ Operates continuously, not only when sales force vacancies occur.

◆ Is systematic in reaching all appropriate sources of applicants.

◆ Provides a flow of more qualified applicants than is needed.

To identify recruits, large organizations often use placement services on university and college campuses or professional employment agencies or "head-hunters," some of which specialize in locating applicants for marketing and sales positions. Smaller firms that need fewer new salespeople may place classified ads in trade publications and daily newspapers. Many firms solicit recommendations from company employees, customers, or suppliers.

MATCHING APPLICANTS WITH HIRING SPECIFICATIONS. Sales managers use a variety of techniques to determine which applicants possess the desired qualifications, including application forms, interviews, references, credit reports, psychological tests, aptitude tests, and physical examinations. Virtually all companies ask candidates to fill out application forms. In addition to providing basic screening information, the application indicates areas that should be explored in an interview.

No salesperson should be hired without at least one personal interview. It is usually desirable to have several interviews conducted by different people in different physical settings. Pooling the opinions of a number of people increases the likelihood of discovering any undesirable characteristics and reduces the effects of one interviewer's possible bias. An interview helps an employer to determine (1) the applicant's degree of interest in the job, (2) the match between the requirements of the job and the applicant's skills, and (3) the applicant's motivation to work hard.

The individuals involved in the selection process should be aware of the various provincial laws against discrimination to avoid inadvertent violations. Testing for intelligence, attributes, or personality, while legal, is somewhat controversial. Some companies avoid testing for fear that they will be accused of discrimination. However, employment tests are legitimate selection tools as long as they can be shown to predict job performance accurately.

Assimilating New Salespeople

After salespeople are hired, management should ensure that they are integrated into the company family. Often this step is overlooked entirely. Prospective salespeople are carefully screened and are often wined and dined to recruit them into the firm. Then, as soon as they are hired, the honeymoon is over and they are left to fend for themselves. In such cases, the new people often become discouraged and may even quit. A wise sales manager will recognize that the new salespeople know very little about the details of the job, their fellow workers, or their status in the firm and must be informed and made comfortable if they are to become successful.[10]

Training a Sales Force

Both new and experienced salespeople need an effective **sales training program** to improve their selling skills, learn about new products, and improve their time and territory management practices. Recognizing that the recent college graduates it hires into its sales force are unlikely to have much experience with its appliances, Whirlpool devised an unusual training experiment.[11] Eight new hires spent two months living in a house together, using the products the company sells. Under the supervision of trainers, they cooked, cleaned, baked and washed using their company's products. At the end of the program the trainees had the experience and confidence to go into the field and teach retail sales clerks how to demonstrate and sell whirlpool appliances.

Even experienced salespeople need continual training to improve their selling skills, learn about new products, and improve their time and territory management practices. One of the important training areas for experienced salespeople is in the use of sales automation tools.

Motivating a Sales Force

Salespeople, especially outside sales forces, require a high degree of motivation. Consider how a sales job is different from most other jobs. Salespeople often work independently, without supervision and guidance from management. Outside salespeople work most of the time away from the support and comfort of home-office surroundings.

Consequently, management faces a challenge in **motivating salespeople**. One key is to determine what motivates the sales representatives — is it a need for status, control, accomplishment, or something else? People differ in what motivates them, and motivations change over time. A young person may be more motivated by monetary rewards alone, while older salespeople may be more interested in receiving recognition for building long-term relationships with important buyers. This means, of course, that a motivational program, as much as possible, should reach the reps individually.

Sales executives can draw from a wide assortment of specific motivational tools.[12] Financial incentives — compensation plans, expense accounts, fringe benefits — usually are frequently effective. Non-financial awards — job enrichment, good consistent feedback from management, recognition and honour awards (pins, trophies, or certificates) — may be appropriate. Sales meetings and sales contests are often-used and enjoyable alternatives. Many firms provide cruises, resort trips, and other travel incentives as rewards to sales reps who meet or exceed various qualitative and quantitative sales goals.[13]

Compensating a Sales Force

Financial rewards are still by far the most widely used tool for motivating salespeople. Consequently, designing and administering an effective **sales compensation plan** is a big part of a sales manager's job. Financial rewards may be direct monetary payments (salary, commission) or indirect monetary compensation (paid vacations, pensions, insurance plans).

Establishing a compensation system calls for decisions concerning the level of compensation as well as the method of compensation. The level refers to the total dollar income that a salesperson earns over a period of time. The type of person required and the competitive rate of pay for similar positions influence the compensation level. The method is the system or plan by which the salesperson will reach the intended level.

salary
A fixed payment for a period of time during which the person is working.

Three widely used methods of compensating a sales force are straight salary, straight commission, and a combination plan. A **salary** is a fixed payment for a period of time during which the salesperson is working. A *salary only* plan (called a straight salary) provides security and stability of earnings for a salesperson. This plan gives management control over the selling efforts of the salesperson, and the sales representatives themselves are likely to cater to the customer's best interests. The main drawback of a straight salary is that it does not offer adequate incentive for salespeople to increase their sales volume. Also, a straight salary is a fixed cost, unrelated to sales volume or gross margin.

Straight-salary plans typically are used when:

◆ Compensating new salespeople or missionary salespeople.

◆ Opening new territories.

◆ Selling a technical product with a lengthy period of negotiation.

commission
Compensation tied to a specific unit of accomplishment.

A **commission** is a payment tied to a specific unit of accomplishment. Thus a sales representative may be paid 5 percent of sales or 8 percent of gross margin. A *straight-commission plan* (commission only) tends to have just the opposite merits and limitations of a straight salary. A straight commission provides considerable incentive for salespeople, and it is a variable cost related directly to a representative's sales volume or gross margin. On the other hand, it is difficult to control straight-commission people. And it is especially difficult to get them to perform tasks for which no commission is paid.

Straight-commission plans may work well when:

◆ A strong incentive is needed to get the sales.

◆ Very little non-selling work is required, such as setting up displays in retail stores.

◆ The company is financially weak and must relate its compensation expenses directly to sales or gross margins.

The ideal method of compensation has the best features of both the straight-salary and the straight-commission plans, with as few of their drawbacks as possible. To reach this ideal, a combination plan must be tailored to a particular firm, product, market, and type of selling. Today about three-quarters North American firms utilize some form of **combination compensation plan**.

Supervising a Sales Force

Sales force supervision is difficult because salespeople often work independently and where they cannot be observed. Yet supervision serves both as a means of continuing training and as a device to ensure that company policies are being carried out.

An issue that management must resolve is how closely to supervise. If too close, it can create a role conflict for the salesperson. One of the attractions of selling is the freedom it affords salespeople to develop creative solutions to customers' problems. Close super-vision can stifle that sense of independence. Conversely, too little supervision can also cause problems. Salespeople who are not closely supervised may lack an understanding of the expectations of their supervisors and companies. They may not know, for example, how much time should be spent in servicing existing accounts and how much in developing new business.

The most effective supervisory method is personal observation in the field. Typically, at least half of a sales manager's time is spent travelling with or spending time on the sales floor with salespeople. Other supervisory tools are reports, e-mail and sales meetings.

quantitative research
A form of marketing research that is intended to obtain statistical information about a sample of consumers or members of the public. Usually relies on surveys to collect the data.

Evaluating a Salesperson's Performance

Managing a sales force includes **evaluating the sales performance** of salespeople. Sales executives must know what the sales force is doing in order to reward them or to make constructive proposals for improvement. By establishing performance standards and studying salespeople's activities, management can develop new training programs for upgrading the sales force's efforts. And, of course, performance evaluation should be the basis for compensation decisions and other rewards.

Performance evaluation can also help salespeople identify opportunities for improv-ing their efforts. Employees with poor sales records know they are doing something wrong. However, they may not know what the problem is if they lack objective standards by which to measure their performance.

Both quantitative and qualitative factors should be used as bases for performance evaluation. **Quantitative evaluation bases** generally have the advantage of being spe-cific and objective. **Qualitative evaluation bases**, although often reflecting broader dimensions of behaviour, are limited by the subjective judgment of the evaluators. For either type of appraisal, however, management faces the difficult task of setting standards against which a salesperson's performance may be measured.

qualitative research
A form of marketing research that is usually employed for exploratory purposes that examines consumers' deeply held views, opinions, and feelings. Includes focus group interviews and one-on-one depth interviews.

Marketing at Work 19-2

Yes! Female-Led Sales Teams Are Really Superior

A recent study of men and women in first-line sales management positions found that women consistently showed superior results to men on a wide range of performance measures.

The research was conducted in a B2B company setting and results were based on a survey of 214 male and female salespeople. The survey compared the responses of salespeople reporting to a male sales manager with those of salespeople reporting to a female one. The sales managers, of whom 20 percent are female, were also questioned.

Women-led teams provided the following food for thought results:

- higher levels of effectiveness
- higher levels of job satisfaction
- lower levels of burnout
- lower levels of on-the-job-conflict
- less likely to express a desire to leave the firm
- less anxious about their work
- less anxious about their performance

The researchers were a bit surprised. David Cravens, who had conducted previous research among male and female sales staff, had found no difference in performance and attitude. Thus it was a surprise to him to find such dramatic differences at the sales manager level. Professor Cravens, who has done a good deal of work in the sales and sales management area, offered the following reasons for the differences:

- The changing role of sales staff and their managers — in the past, most sales teams focused on closing the deal; this was reflected in the wide use of incentive pay; the sales manager played the role of commander and score keeper. Currently, companies work to establish long-term relationships, sometimes partnerships, with customers; this makes the sales manager a coach and facilitator rather than a scorekeeper. Could it be that women are more effective in the coaching and collaborative role than are men? Could it be that after being number two for so long in the business world, they simply try harder?
- The glass ceiling — since women face greater barriers to promotion beyond the sales management level, women who are higher performers may be held at this level while men of similar caliber may have been promoted. No evidence of a glass ceiling or that this had occurred in the firm under study was apparent.

Other reasons for the findings could be advanced, perhaps cultural differences play a role. Regardless, the results should give companies pause for thought. What stereotypes are they working with? Should they be looking for more female salespeople and sales managers. Should they be thinking about different approaches to training? While we know that more research is needed, it can only be done with more females in the jobs at issue. After all, what if a finding that women are simply better than men is valid and reliable?

Source: Adapted from Elizabeth Church, "Female-led sales teams have superior morale, performance, study finds," *The Globe and Mail*, February 17, 2000, p. B14.

Quantitative Bases

Sales performance should be evaluated in terms of inputs (efforts) and outputs (results). Together, inputs such as number of sales calls per day or customer service activity, and outputs such as sales volume or gross margin over six months or even two years, with certain relationship marketing accounts, provide a measure of selling effectiveness.

Useful quantitative input measures include:

- Call rate — number of calls per day or week.

- Number of formal proposals presented.

- Non-selling activities — promotion displays set up, training sessions held with distributors or dealers, client problem-solving sessions.

Some quantitative output measures useful as evaluation criteria are:

- Sales volume by product, customer group, and territory.

◆ Sales volume as a percentage of quota or territory potential.

◆ Gross margin by product line, customer group, and territory.

◆ Orders — number and average dollar amount.

◆ Closing rate — number of orders divided by number of calls.

◆ Accounts — percentage of existing accounts sold, and number of new accounts opened.

An increasing number of firms, among them IBM and Hallmark, are using measures of customer satisfaction or of service quality as a performance indicator. Satisfaction is measured a number of different ways from detailed questionnaires that customers complete to counting the number of complaints received per customer. Assessing satisfaction reflects a recognition by companies that there is more to selling than making a sale and it also allows salespeople more scope in working with new and established customers.

Qualitative Bases

Performance evaluation would be much easier if it could be based only on quantitative criteria. It would minimize the subjectivity and personal bias of the evaluators. However, many qualitative factors must be considered because they influence a salesperson's performance. Some of these factors are:

◆ Knowledge of products, company policies, and competitors.

◆ Time management and preparation for sales calls.

◆ Customer relations.

◆ Personal appearance.

A successful evaluation program will appraise a salesperson's performance on as many different bases as possible. Otherwise management may be misled. A high daily call rate may look good, but it tells us nothing about how many orders are being written up. A high closing rate (orders divided by calls) may be camouflaging a low average order size or a high sales volume on low-profit items.

Summary

Personal selling is the main marketing communications tool used in North American business — whether measured by number of people employed, by total expenditures, or by expenses as a percentage of sales. The total field of personal selling comprises two broad categories. One covers selling activities where the customers come to the salespeople — primarily retail-store or inbound telephone-based selling. The other includes all selling situations where the salespeople go to the customer — primarily outside sales forces.

The sales job has evolved. A new type of sales representative — a professional salesperson — has been developing over the past few decades. Sales jobs today range from order takers through support salespeople (missionary sellers, sales engineers) to order-getters (creative sellers). Sales jobs differ from other jobs in several respects. Some changing patterns in personal selling have emerged in recent years — patterns such as selling centres (team selling), systems selling, relationship selling, global team selling, Internet selling, and telemarketing.

The personal selling process consists of four steps, starting with prospecting for prospective buyers and then preapproaching each prospect. The third step is the sales presentation, which includes attracting attention, arousing buyer interest and desire, meeting objections, and then hopefully closing the sale.

Finally, postsale activities involve follow-up services to ensure customer satisfaction and reduce dissonance regarding the purchase.

The role of the salesperson in relationship marketing can be viewed from the five-stage trust-building process. For each stage of the process, there is a combination of company and salesperson characteristics that affect the particular stage of trust building. In the final analysis, a buyer's decision to buy is affected not only by the specific details of a transaction but also by his or her view of the amount of trust that can be placed on the supplying firm as well as in the salesperson.

The sales management process involves planning, implementing, and evaluating sales force activities within the guidelines set by the company's strategic marketing planning. The tasks of staffing and operating a sales force present managerial challenges in several areas. The key to successful sales force management is to do a good job in selecting salespeople. Then plans must be made to assimilate these new people into the company and to train them. Management must set up programs to motivate, compensate, and supervise a sales force. The final stage in sales force management is to evaluate the performance of the individual salespeople.

Key Terms and Concepts

Personal selling 609	Order-getter 614	Trial close 622
Inside selling 610	Selling centre 615	Postsale activities 622
Outside selling 610	Systems selling 616	Sales force selection 623
Outside sales forces 611	Relationship selling 616	Sales training program 624
Professional salesperson 611	Telemarketing 617	Motivating salespeople 625
Driver-salesperson 612	Internet selling 618	Sales compensation plan 625
Inside order taker 612	Sales force automation (SFA) 619	Salary 625
Outside order taker 612	Prospecting 620	Commission 625
Missionary salesperson 612	Qualify 620	Combination compensation plan 626
Sales engineer 613	Preapproach information 621	Evaluating sales performance 626
Consultative salesperson 613	Sales presentation 621	Quantitative evaluation bases 626
Order taker 614	AIDA 621	Qualitative evaluation bases 626
Sales-support personnel 614	Closing a sale 622	

Questions and Problems

1. The cost of a full-page, four-colour advertisement in one issue of a national magazine is higher than the cost of employing two salespeople for a full year. A sales manager is urging her company to eliminate a few of these ads and, instead, to hire a few more salespeople. This executive believes that one good salesperson working for an entire year can sell more than one ad in one issue of a magazine. How would you respond?

2. Refer to the classification of sales jobs from driver-salesperson to creative seller, and answer the following questions:

   a. In which types of jobs are salespeople most likely to be free from close supervision?

   b. Which types are likely to be the highest paid?

   c. For which types of jobs is the highest degree of motivation necessary?

3. What are some sources you might use to acquire a list of prospects for the following products and services?

   a. Bank accounts for new area residents.

   b. Dental X-ray equipment.

   c. Laptop computers.

   d. Contributors to the United Way.

   e. Baby furniture and clothes.

   f. Web page design services.

   g. House painting.

4. If you were preparing a sales presentation for the following products and services, what information about a prospect would you seek as part of your preparation?

   a. Two-bedroom condominium.

   b. New automobile.

   c. Carpeting for a home redecorating project.

   d. Marketing research project for a local department store.

   e. Building cleaning service.

5. What sources should be used for recruiting sales applicants in each of the following firms? Explain your choice in each case.

   a. The Delta Chelsea hotel.

   b. IBM, for sales of mainframe (large) computers.

   c. Mount Pleasant Cemetery.

6. Compare the merits of straight-salary and straight-commission plans of sales compensation. What are two types of sales jobs in which each plan might be desirable?

7. How might a firm determine whether a salesperson is using high-pressure selling tactics that might injure customer relations?

8. How can a sales manager evaluate the performance of salespeople in getting new business?

Hands-On Marketing

1. Review your activities of the past few days and identify those in which:

    a. You did some personal selling.

    b. People tried to sell something to you.

    Select one situation in each category where you thought the selling was particularly effective, and tell why it was so.

2. Interview three students from your school who recently have gone through the job-interviewing process conducted by companies using your school's placement office. Ask the students to compare, contrast, and generally evaluate the recruiting practices of the companies they interviewed. Prepare a report covering your findings.

Chapter Twenty

Management of Advertising, Sales Promotion, and Public Relations

This chapter examines nonpersonal, mass communication promotional tools — advertising, sales promotion, and public relations. After studying this chapter, you should have an understanding of:

◆ The nature of advertising, what it means to the individual firm, and its importance in our economy.

◆ Characteristics of the major types of advertising.

◆ How advertising campaigns are developed and advertising media are selected.

◆ What sales promotion is, and how to manage it.

◆ The role of public relations and publicity in the marketing communications mix.

Suds and Surfing

"It was the best of times, it was the worst of times." Charles Dickens didn't know it, but he could have been writing about marketing at the beginning of the 21st century.

Never have marketers paid so much to reach so few consumers — media fragmentation characterizes whatever medium advertisers choose to consider. Twenty years ago, television networks dominated and accounted for over 90 percent of viewers; cable was as popular as CB radio (if you even know what that is — but that also makes the point!). The only outdoor advertising was the vacancy signs outside of motels and Bill Gates was a nerd with a dream and a bad haircut.

But, now that has all changed (well, you can judge for yourself about Mr. Gates). Cable practically dominates television offerings. Out-of-doors advertising is everywhere, from transit shelters to restaurant tables. The number of special-interest magazines has exploded; and then there's the Internet. The Internet, delivered through computers and other personal-communication devices, has turned marketing communications on its head.

No industry is perhaps more aware of the fragmentation of media than the beer industry, in fact this industry is one of the largest contributors to television revenues globally. This is probably *not* a surprise to any reader. Carpet-bombing-style marketing that was so efficient for beer advertisers in the past is getting more difficult to justify as the cost per bomb increases and the suds gets soaked up into smaller and smaller carpets — more like little rugs actually! Fewer people can now be reached with each advertising "bomb."

The beer industry is not going to abandon television soon, but it will have to respond to issues of efficiency and impact as this information revolution continues to unfold. The Internet will be a part of their response. And buying banner ads is not the answer — they are expensive and click-through rates are collapsing while software becomes fine-tuned for extracting banners so that surfers don't have to see them. Besides, this fails to take advantage of the best features of advertising on the Internet — interactivity and segment-of-one marketing!

However, taking the brand. com approach also poses challenges of its own. With millions of Web sites in existence and forty thousand new addresses registered globally each week,

trying to build meaningful scale with multiple brands is expensive and frustrating. This is particularly the case in brewing where the top five brewers control less than 25 percent of global consumption.

Enter Beer.com (www.beer.com) — a beer-lifestyle Web destination where folks can live *la vida cerveza* 24/7! It's kind of like, well, building a shrine to beer — or like having a beer channel! But really, it's a beer-marketing machine — developing membership profiles and initiating one-on-one marketing for brewers and beer-related companies is a key driver of the business model. The ability to advertise and promote brands and products while doing instant surveys and online focus groups with the world's largest beer community is probably what attracted Interbrew (www.interbrew.com), the world's second-largest brewer to become the site's initial investor and sponsor. The company promotes itself as the world's local brewer operating in twenty-three countries and three continents. The company buys brands and distribution, thereby maintaining a local platform and power base.

To become a "destination" that attracts a large audience, other brewers and other beer-related products will be needed to build upon the present content of Beer.com. To become a global destination, other languages and geographies will have to participate. That authenticity will be important to the consumer, and ultimately to the success of any "publishing" venture.

The Beer.com name has been a great asset, allowing the company to immediately develop a membership of almost one hundred thousand with almost no content or advertising support. It's simple and it's fun and says all that it needs to say in order to get the massage across, as proven by early interest generated by the name alone. Success will also depend upon leveraging offline resources to keep driving online traffic. The core competency and biggest cost for dot-com success is the ability to get users.

Offline leverage for Beer.com was achieved through the altering of packaging on Interbrew's major brands. In the first year, over one billion impressions were generated through Beer.com neck labels, bottle caps, and flashes on cans and cartons of brands such as Rolling Rock, Labatt Blue, and Stella Artois. All brewers wishing to participate will be required to provide the same advertising support. The site now has companies participating in over fifty countries, with links to more than fifty Canadian companies alone. The site features sports, entertainment, contests — even personals.

Getting back to Dickens, the advertising and promotion challenges as well as the pace of change *are* daunting in the early years of this new millennium, but never has there been greater opportunity to innovate, create, pioneer, and have a little fun. Welcome to the new beerlennium![1]

Advertising, sales promotion, and public relations are the mass communication tools available to marketers. As the terminology suggests, *mass communication* uses the same message for everyone in an audience. The mass communicator trades off the advantage of personal selling, the opportunity to tailor a message to each prospective customer, for the advantage of reaching many people at a lower cost per person. However, as the emergence of interactive television advertising and the use of the World Wide Web illustrate, mass communication is not indiscriminate. Advertisers are constantly seeking ways to present their messages to more clearly defined target audiences, and the use of new technology is making it increasingly possible to get a specific message into the hands of specific target customers.

Nature and Scope of Advertising

All advertisements have four features:

◆   A verbal and/or visual message.

◆   A sponsor who is identified.

◆   Delivery through at least one medium.

◆   Payment by the sponsor to the media carrying the message.

advertising
All activities involved in presenting to a group a nonpersonal, sponsor-identified message regarding a product or organization.

Advertising, then, consists of all the activities involved in presenting to an audience a nonpersonal, sponsor-identified, paid-for message about a product or organization. Advertising in one form or another is used by most organizations. One of the most interesting changes taking place in advertising is the increasing ability of marketers to reach specific audiences with tailor-made messages. Thus, in the future, we will see advertising becoming less non-personal in nature as specialty channels and publications continue to flourish, viewers become able to program their viewing, database marketing continues to be refined, and as people utilize the Web more and more for entertainment and recreation.

Types of Advertising

Advertising can be classified according to (1) the target audience, either consumers or businesses; (2) what is being advertised, a product or service versus an organization or company; and (3) the objective sought, the stimulation of primary or selective demand. To fully appreciate the scope of advertising, it is essential to understand these three classifications.

CONSUMER AND BUSINESS-TO-BUSINESS ADVERTISING An ad is generally directed at either consumers or businesses — thus it is either **consumer advertising** or **business-to-business advertising**. Most retailers by definition sell only to end consumers, so they are generally organizations that are not faced with the choice of whether to target a consumer or a business audience. There are exceptions, such as Staples, which will target both. The publishers of the *National Post* and similar newspapers and magazines must decide what portion of their advertising budget will be used to attract advertisers (called trade advertising), and what portion will go toward gaining subscribers and selling magazines and newspapers.

PRODUCT AND INSTITUTIONAL ADVERTISING All advertising may be classified as product (or service) or institutional (or corporate). Remember here that we are using the term "product" to include both tangible products and services. **Product advertising** focuses on a particular product or brand.

product advertising
Advertising intended to inform or stimulate the market about an organization's products.

Product advertising is subdivided into direct-action and indirect-action advertising:

◆ **Direct-action advertising** seeks a quick response — for instance, a magazine ad containing a coupon or a 1-800 number may urge the reader to send or call immediately for a free sample, or a supermarket ad in a local newspaper may stress this week's specials. Many advertisements today include the advertiser's Web site address, inviting the consumer to "check us out on the Web." Successfully directing consumers to take advantage of these "contact" points provides an entirely new opportunity to communicate with a potential customer that has indicated an express interest in your product or service. The direction of the "advertising" can then be tailored to the questions and concerns of that potential customer.

◆ **Indirect-action advertising** is designed to stimulate demand for a company's products or services over a longer period of time. It is intended to inform or remind consumers that the product exists and to point out its benefits. Most television advertising is of this type. Often the purpose of this form of advertising is to build awareness and recognition of a brand.

institutional advertising
Advertising designed either to present information about the advertiser's business or to create a good attitude — build goodwill — toward the organization.

Institutional or corporate advertising presents information about the advertiser's business or tries to create a good impression. It is intended to build goodwill toward the organization. This type of advertising is not intended to sell a specific product; at least not in the short term. It is intended to create a positive image of the company and its brands in the eyes of customers, prospective customers, and the general public. Two forms of corporate advertising are:

◆ **Customer service advertising**, which presents information about the advertiser's operations. Advertisements describing the level of personal service available at Esso service stations are an example. Avis (www.avis.com) has long been known for its "We try harder" slogan, demonstrating in their ads how their staff go the "extra mile" to provide superior service.

◆ **Public service advertising (PSA)**, which is designed to improve the quality of life and show that the advertiser is a responsible member of the community. Such ads may urge the audience to avoid drugs or to support a local anti-pollution campaign, or may show how the advertiser is making a contribution by supporting worthwhile projects and community activities. For the past couple of years NBC television has produced a series of PSAs called TMYK (www.nbc.com/tmyk) — the more you know — featuring actors from their most popular dramas and sit-coms communicating messages about current topics important to raising families. These have included topics such as tolerance, diversity, the importance of education, drugs, being available, and discussing important issues with your children, and even the value of reading to your children, etc. Cast members from *Friends*, *Will & Grace*, and *ER* are among those that have been featured. These have often been aired during prime time commercial slots.

PSAs have usually been generic and tame in nature and content, but in order to compete for attention with the increasingly extreme ads used today, some not-for-profit organizations have also moved in that direction. The Breast Cancer Fund, a non-profit organization in San Francisco, decided to take the approach used by the likes of Victoria's Secret and Calvin Klein in advertising their undergarments. In posters that resemble the cover of women's magazines, for example, a Victoria's Secret catalogue, attractive and shapely models are featured in scanty outfits revealing mastectomy scars. These outdoor advertisements created such a stir that they were discontinued as ad companies retreated from the scandal that was created.[2]

primary-demand advertising
Advertising designed to stimulate demand for a generic product.

selective-demand advertising
Advertising that is intended to stimulate demand for individual brands.

pioneering advertising
Primary-demand advertising in the introductory stage of the product life cycle.

PRIMARY- AND SELECTIVE-DEMAND ADVERTISING **Primary-demand advertising** is designed to stimulate demand for a generic category of a product such as Colombian coffee or garments made from cotton. This is in contrast to **selective-demand advertising**, intended to stimulate demand for individual brands such as Nabob coffee, B.C. produce, Sunkist oranges, and clothing from The Gap.

Primary-demand advertising is used in either of two situations. The first is when the product is in the introductory stage of its life cycle. This is called **pioneering advertising**. A firm may run an ad about its new product, explaining the product's benefits, but not emphasizing the brand name. The objective of pioneering primary-demand advertising is to inform, not to persuade, the target market. The buying-decision-process model explains why such ads are limited to information. Recall from our discussion in Chapter 6 that a consumer must first be made aware of a product before becoming interested in or desiring it. Combine this with the fact that only so much information can be communicated in a single ad, and it becomes clear that only one objective can be accomplished at a time. In recent years, pioneering ads have been run for personal

Like buying milk with the cow still attached.

www.bchothouse.com

BC growers just want you to eat their produce.

differential advantage
Any feature of an organization or brand perceived by customers to be desirable and different from the competition.

comparative advertising
Selective demand advertising in which the advertiser either directly (by naming a rival brand) or indirectly (through inference) points out how the advertised brand is better.

data assistant products like the Palm Pilot, MP3 players telling people what they could do with music they had downloaded, or the Sony Glasstron® — a 97-gram eyeglass-design virtual 130-cm TV screen as viewed from two metres away.

The second use of primary-demand advertising occurs throughout the product life cycle. It is usually done by trade associations trying to stimulate demand for their industry's product. Thus the Dairy Farmers of Canada's ads (www.dairybureau.org) urge us to drink more milk. They don't really care what brand of milk and dairy products we buy, just that we use more of them.

Selective-demand advertising essentially is competitive advertising — it pits one brand against another. This type of advertising typically is employed when a product has gone beyond the introductory life-cycle stage. The product is reasonably well known and in competition for market share with several brands. The objective of selective-demand advertising is to increase the demand for a brand. To accomplish this goal, it emphasizes the particular benefits — the **differential competitive advantages** — of the brand being advertised.

Comparative advertising is an important kind of selective-demand advertising that is used for a wide variety of products. In comparative advertising, the advertiser either directly, by naming a rival brand, or indirectly, through inference, points out differences between the brands. We have all seen the comparative advertising for Coke and Pepsi, both of which show the competitor's brand. In some comparative advertising, the competitor's name is not mentioned, but it is obvious to the reader or viewer. In other cases, the competitor's product is named or even shown. Kibble'n Bits dog food even mimicked a well-known series of Pedigree dog food ads by using the same "story" of a professional breeder with a group of her dogs at feeding time — it even used a bag of Pedigree food. The breeder's dogs run off chanting — "I'm gonna get me some Kibble'n Bits, and bits, and bits…." This is followed with the statement that dogs preferred the taste of Kibble'n Bits over Pedigree 3 to 1 — the trainer, of course, had to concede and give her champions the food they preferred. Similar direct comparisons have been frequently used by Burger King, Subaru, and Kia cars.

There has been considerable debate in Canada over the years concerning the use of comparative advertising techniques. Duracell (www.duracell.com) was prohibited from using Eveready's (www.eveready.com) Energizer bunny in its ads. The Duracell commercial had the pink bunny expiring on the dance floor, unable to keep up with a dancing doll powered by Duracell batteries. The judge in the case said that the commercial amounted to a "visual humiliation of a trademark at the hands of the other party."[3]

Advertisers do not have to name a competitor explicitly to run afoul of the law. In another case involving Procter & Gamble (www.pg.com), a judge of the Ontario Court rejected claims from Unilever Canada (www.unilever.ca) and allowed P&G to continue to promote its new Oil of Olay beauty bar as superior to "a leading beauty bar" — a direct reference to Unilever's Dove. Judge Dunnet acknowledged that Dove was indeed the leading beauty bar "by both dollar and tonnage market share," but said she was satisfied that P&G had a reasonable basis for the claim of superiority.[4]

The Bureau of Competition Policy of Industry Canada (www.strategis.gc.ca/ssg) has taken the position that truthful comparative advertising can be a pro-competitive force in the marketplace. In fact, the bureau has periodically published guidelines for the consideration of advertisers. The main point to be learned from the discussion of comparative advertising and its regulation is that a company planning to use the technique had better be very sure that what is being said in its advertising about the competition is completely accurate.

co-operative advertising

Advertising in which two or more firms share the cost.

vertical co-operative advertising

Advertising in which firms at different levels of the distribution channel share the cost.

advertising allowance

A payment or cash discount offered by a manufacturer to a retailer to encourage the retailer to advertise or prominently display the manufacturer's product.

horizontal co-operative advertising

Advertising that involves firms on the same level of distribution sharing the cost.

CO-OPERATIVE ADVERTISING **Co-operative advertising** promotes products of two or more firms that share the cost of the advertising. There are two types — vertical and horizontal. **Vertical co-operative advertising** involves firms on different levels of distribution. For example, a manufacturer and a retailer share the cost of the retailer's advertising of that manufacturer's product. Bombardier will share with its dealers across the country the cost of advertising Ski-doo® and Sea-doo® machines in local newspapers and sometimes on television. Frequently, the manufacturer pays for the preparation of the actual ad, leaving space for the retailer's name and location. Then the manufacturer and retailer share the media cost of placing the ad. Many retail ads in newspapers are co-operative ads.

Another type of vertical co-operative advertising uses an **advertising allowance**, or cash discount offered by a manufacturer to a retailer, to encourage the retailer to advertise or prominently display a product. This approach is often used in retail advertising of grocery products and other household items. Major retailers such as Loblaw, Canadian Tire, and Wal-Mart Canada will have much of the cost of preparing their flyers covered by the advertising allowances provided by the manufacturers whose products are featured in the flyers. The difference between co-operative advertising and allowances is the amount of control exerted by the manufacturer over how the money is actually spent. There is some question as to whether co-operative advertising allowances represent a form of advertising or a sales promotion activity. This illustrates the difficulty of classifying some forms of marketing communications as either advertising or sales promotions.

These co-op arrangements benefit retailers by providing them with extra funds for promotion. Manufacturers benefit from advertising at the local level. In addition, ad dollars go farther because rates for local media are typically lower for ads placed by local firms than for ads placed by national advertisers.

Horizontal co-operative advertising is undertaken by firms on the same level of distribution — such as a group of retailers — that share the costs of advertising. For example, all stores in a suburban shopping centre may run a joint newspaper ad. The principal benefit is that by pooling their funds, the firms can achieve much greater exposure than if they advertised individually.

Companies that normally would not have a close association often co-operate in joint promotions. More and more companies are realizing that they can stretch their promotion dollars, benefit from the reputation of non-competing successful brands, and open new markets with joint promotional programs. In Canada, Pillsbury entered into a special promotion with Panasonic (www.panasonic.ca) and sister company Technics to offer over $75,000 in electronics, with the hope that it would promote the Pizza Pops brand and draw teens to their nearest grocery store in search of the product. Although not all teens would win, the company also teamed up with CDPlus.com (www.cdplus.com) to provide in-package three-dollar coupons that could be used in-store, online, or through the catalogue for, of course, CDs. Other prizes offered included a trip to see the band Filter on their U.S. tour.

It was a well-coordinated promotion, offering opportunities for TV advertisements, POS displays in supermarkets, CDPlus stores, and each participant's Web site. It was a natural promotion, because all products appealed to a largely pizza-eating, music-oriented youth audience. Other companies often decide to partner with appropriate firms or brands in other industries.

Another interesting combination was Blockbuster Video (www.blockbuster.com) and La-Z-Boy recliners — Win A Seat with the Stars – it's the power of sitting! Advertisements welcomed viewers to visit their local Blockbuster to sit in a La-Z-Boy recliner for a chance to win a trip to the 2001 Blockbuster awards where they would sit and schmooze with the stars. Another natural combination — a recliner and a movie! Even in the auto industry this works — prestige automaker Lexus produced a special edition using Coach leathers (www.coach.com) — from the maker of prestige leather products. SUV maker Jeep produced a specially outfitted Grand Wagoneer Orvis Edition in conjunction with the Orvis Outfitting Company (www.orvis.com) that even included a pair of Orvis fishing rods.

Cost of Advertising

Advertising in one form or another is used by most marketers. The significance of advertising is indicated by the amount of money spent on it. In 1997, the gross expenditures on advertising in Canada totalled over $8 billion. Table 20-1 shows the estimated total expenditure by medium.[5] For many years, daily newspapers have been the most widely used medium, but the percentage of total expenditures accounted for by newspapers has been declining steadily from approximately 30 percent in the mid-1970s to 19 percent in 1997. In fact, the percentage of total advertising expenditures going to the traditional mass media — radio, television, newspapers, and magazines — has been declining steadily, as many advertisers have been switching at least part of their advertising budgets to established media such as direct mail, directories, and weekly papers, and to so-called new media such as the Internet and CD-ROMs, that can often do a better job of reaching targeted segments.

Another change in advertising expenditures includes that now expended on Internet advertising. A study by Ernst & Young and the Internet Advertising Bureau of Canada (www.iabcanada.com) shows that in 1997 this was $9.5 million. While not officially verified at the time of preparation, the estimates for Internet revenues in Canada have been estimated at $20.7 million for 1998 and $37.7 million in 1999. This can be contrasted with 1998 estimates for the United States of US$1.9 *billion*.[6]

ADVERTISING EXPENDITURES BY INDUSTRY Some industries in Canada spend a lot more money than others on advertising. The information presented in Table 20-2 indicates that the retail industry spent over $950 million on advertising in 1998 —

TABLE 20-1 Net Canadian Advertising Revenues by Medium, 1996–97

Medium	Revenues ($millions) 1997	1996	% Change 1996–97
Television[1]	2,100	1,975	+6.3
Daily newspapers	1,545	1,315	+17.5
Catalogues, direct mail	1,168	1,110	+5.2
Yellow Pages	894	892	+0.2
Radio	849	792	+7.2
Weeklies/community papers	634	597	+6.2
General magazines	347	318	+9.1
Business publications	252	233	+8.2
Outdoor and transit	220	200	+10.0
Other print[2]	48	48	0.0
TOTAL ADVERTISING	**$8,057**	**$7,480**	**+7.7**

1 Includes network, selective, specialty, and informercial.

2 Includes religious, school, farm, weekend supplements.

Source: As compiled by IVB from Statistics Canada, CRIC, CAN, CARD, Magazines Canada, Mediacom/CAN, Tele-Direct, Canada Post, and industry estimates. As published in *Marketing Magazine*, September 13, 1999.

Note: Revisions made to previous years' estimates for radio, general and business magazines, and other print. Internet advertising revenues are not included in this study.

much more than the $750 million spent by automobile manufacturers. The A.C. Nielsen Annual Summary of Expenditures indicates that there have been many changes in the ranking of industries in the past couple of years with regard to spending. Prior to this period, these rankings had been relatively stable. This recent flux in rankings is in part the result of advertisers' increased awareness of consumers' changing media patterns and attempts to experiment with more effective applications.

Retailers represent a very large proportion of this spending because there are so many of them, and some are very large.

It is important also to note that some of the advertisers who spend a large amount of money on advertising each year actually devote a very small percentage of their total sales to advertising. Data collected by Statistics Canada indicate that the largest percentage of sales spent on advertising is by companies that manufacture health and beauty aids, soaps, and cleaning products. In general, companies in the consumer products field spend a higher percentage of sales on advertising than do manufacturers of industrial products. Major companies spend an average of about 2 percent of total sales on advertising, while companies that manufacture consumer products spend approximately 3 percent on average.

ADVERTISING COST VERSUS PERSONAL SELLING COST While we do not have accurate totals for the costs of personal selling, we do know they far surpass advertising expenditures. In manufacturing, only a few industries, such as drugs, toiletries, cleaning products, tobacco, and beverages, spend more on advertising than on personal selling. Advertising runs from 1 to 3 percent of net sales in many firms, whereas the expenses of recruiting and operating a sales force are typically 8 to 15 percent of sales.

At the wholesale level, advertising costs are very low. Personal selling expenses, however, may run ten to fifteen times as high. Even among retailers in total — and this

TABLE 20-2 Top Twenty-five Advertising Categories, Canada, 1998

1998 Rank	Category	Number of Classes	Category Spending ($) 1998	1997 Rank	1996 Rank
1	Retail	72	953.5	1	1
2	Automotive: cars, minivans; trucks; vans; dealer associations	19	753.8	2	2
3	Business equipment & services	70	521.6	3	3
4	Food	160	395.6	4	4
5	Financial & insurance services	48	388.0	5	6
6	Entertainment	32	314.8	6	5
7	Local automotive dealers	5	266.6	8	9
8	Travel & transportation	24	249.3	7	7
9	Restaurants; catering; nightclubs	10	199.3	9	8
10	Media: TV; radio; out of home; station promo	7	165.5	12	14
11	Cosmetics & toiletries	36	154.5	10	10
12	Brewers & related products	8	125.5	11	13
13	Drug products	40	112.4	13	11
14	Petroleum products & related services	34	110.8	14	12
15	Government	17	93.2	15	19
16	Publishing	5	89.5	18	17
17	Lotteries	1	63.2	19	18
18	Entertainment equipment	16	62.9	17	15
19	Hair products	12	54.4	16	16
20	Schools; correspondence courses, seminars	6	49.7	21	22
21	Sporting goods & recreational products	45	42.8	22	21
22	Household supplies	31	40.0	20	20
23	Apparel	23	35.6	23	24
24	Real estate	5	34.8	25	25
25	Toys; games; dolls	6	33.9	24	23
TOTAL ALL CLASSES		**995**	**5,714.5**		

Source: A.C. Nielsen, Markham, Ontario.

Note: Total for Canada, January to December. Based on estimated media spending on television, daily newspapers, magazines, out-of-home advertising, and radio. The estimates for daily newspaper exclude career, professional, and classified ads, and the radio estimates cover national, Toronto, and Vancouver advertising only. A.C. Nielsen improved its coverage over the period, which may affect some numbers. The figures for classes represent the number of classes that make up each category.

includes those with self-service operations — the cost of personal selling is substantially higher than that of advertising.

Developing an Advertising Campaign

advertising campaign
The total advertising program for a product or brand that involves co-ordination, central theme, and specific goals.

An **advertising campaign** consists of all the tasks involved in transforming a theme into a co-ordinated advertising program to accomplish a specific goal for a product or brand. For example, you have probably noticed the transit and television advertising campaign for Buckley's Mixture, the famous cough remedy from W.K. Buckley Limited (www.buckleys.com), which uses the line, "It tastes awful. And it works." This campaign has been running successfully for many years and has now been extended to include recent additions to the Buckley's line. It relies on a blend of humour and trust in the grandfatherly figure of the company's president, Frank Buckley. The campaign theme has been very effective and has transferred successfully to international markets as the company has extended distribution. Most products are not this fortunate — but a taste this bad is truly a global thing. A selection of ads can be seen (and heard) on the company Web site, as well as some that didn't make the final cut.

An advertising campaign such as this is planned within the framework of the overall strategic marketing program and the promotional campaign. Before designing an advertising campaign, management must:

◆ Know who the target audience is.

◆ Establish the overall promotional goals.

◆ Set the total promotional budget.

◆ Determine the overall promotional theme.

With these tasks completed, the firm can begin formulating an advertising campaign. The steps in developing a campaign are: defining objectives, establishing a budget, creating a message, selecting media, and evaluating effectiveness.

Defining Objectives

The purpose of advertising is to sell something — product, service, idea, person, or place — either now or later. This goal is reached by setting specific objectives that can be expressed in individual ads that are incorporated into an advertising campaign. Recall again from the buying-decision process that buyers go through a series of stages from unawareness to purchase. Thus the immediate objective of an ad may be to move target customers to the next stage in the hierarchy — say, from awareness to interest. Note also that advertising seldom is the only promotional tool used by a firm. Rather, it is typically one part of a strategy that may also include personal selling, sales promotion, a company Web site, and other tools. Therefore, the objective of advertising may be to "open doors" for the sales force.

Specific advertising objectives will be dictated by the firm's overall marketing strategy. Typical objectives are:

◆ *Support personal selling.* Advertising may be used to acquaint prospects with the seller's company and products, easing the way for the sales force.

◆ *Improve dealer relations.* Wholesalers and retailers like to see a manufacturer support its products.

◆ *Introduce a new product.* Consumers need to be informed even about line extensions that make use of familiar brand names.

◆ *Expand the use of a product category.* Advertising may be used to lengthen the season for a product (as Lipton did for iced tea); increase the frequency of replacement (as Fram and Purolator did for oil filters); or increase the variety of product uses (as Arm & Hammer and Cow Brand did for baking soda).

◆ *Counteract substitution.* Advertising reinforces the decisions of existing customers and reduces the likelihood that they will switch to alternative brands.

Marketing at Work 20-1

Sunlight Benefits from Dirty Advertising Message

How do you challenge a brand that is synonymous with the category, outspends you year after year, and has three times your market share? One approach is to analyze what the market leader is doing and do the same thing, only better. This may seem logical, but it isn't the approach that Sunlight's ad agency chose to pursue. In fact, they decided to do the opposite. They determined that if Tide owned "clean," Sunlight should own "dirt."

Historically Sunlight's advertising campaigns tried to develop an appealing personality for the brand by focusing on the after-wash sensory benefits of doing laundry — scent and freshness. This resulted in Sunlight being well liked, but not necessarily trusted to get clothes clean. Meanwhile, Tide was being heavily supported with an aggressive and consistent approach of showing problem/solution advertising.

Sunlight needed a message which reinforced its cleaning power and instilled confidence in its users. The result was Sunlight's *"Go Ahead. Get Dirty"* campaign which offered a sense of freedom and promised that no matter how dirty you get, Sunlight will get your clothes clean.

The campaign was a huge success and had a direct impact on Sunlight's bottom line. Shipments of Sunlight surpassed market growth by more than 400 percent, and the company gained 2.5 share points directly at the expense of Tide.

Two years later, Tide is still pursuing its problem/solution approach to advertising but with a new focus — dirt. Tide recently launched an outdoor campaign bringing its cleaning power message to people in transit shelters, subways, and buses. Interestingly, the message has changed from *"Trust Tide to get your clothes clean."* to *"Dirt happens. But don't worry, because Tide is there."* What is that saying...? Imitation is the sincerest form of flattery.

Source: Adapted from "Advertising Success Stories," *Marketing Magazine*, November 22, 1999, p. 48; and David Todd "Tide takes dirty message to the streets," *Strategy*, June 5, 2000, p. B9.

Establishing a Budget

Once a marketing communications budget has been established (discussed in Chapter 18), it must be allocated among the various activities making up the overall marketing communications program. In the case of a particular brand, a firm may wish to have several ads, as well as sales promotion and public relations activities, directed at different target audiences all under way at the same time.

When Vancouver-based SUMmedia (www.summedia.com) launched its Savingumoney.com (www.savingumoney.com) enterprise there were several goals to be considered — first, this was an entirely new concept and method of distribution for coupons. Instead of sending out coupons, consumers surf onto the Internet to select and print coupons. But it was thought that the name was, at least, a good start to introducing the concept.

Next, enough awareness and interest had to be generated to create revenue (which we can assume is the ultimate goal of the enterprise). Enough interest had to be generated to attract companies to supply coupons and consumers to use coupons. The conundrum is that attracting each required the presence of the other. The company had to promote and to position themselves — and like the Beer.com story at the beginning of this chapter, this would require a little more consideration than a couple of banner ads on a couple of Web sites. The target for this "product" wasn't a perfect match with the typical web-savvy shopper — these were largely store coupons for traditional everyday products. Coupon clippers are largely female and skewed to a mature age category (45 to 54).

The theme of the $6 million campaign was to convey the essence of Savingumoney.com's positioning — "coupons online for just about anything." It was also to cultivate an engaging brand image: friendly, helpful and just a little on the clever side. This budget was about one hundred times the original budget used when the site was quietly

Coupons go online to save you even more.

launched the previous year. Aside from some online advertising, the linchpin to the campaign was newspapers — this allowed a broad reach (very critical), flexibility, and fast turnaround times. A consistent newspaper presence was maintained through early 2000 while also utilizing outdoor and radio ads. Television was used in some U.S. markets where there were significant coupon offerings available.

Ads were outlined like a coupon — with the depiction of a dotted line and scissors. Examples include an image of a completely bare room with an offer for "free burglar alarm installation." Another shows a seagull, and the line "20% off dry cleaning."[7]

More often than not the goal of advertising is not category awareness, but simply trying to get a larger piece of the market action. This was the case when Lexus Canada decided they were going to get a larger share of the burgeoning SUV market. In 1997, Lexus managed to sell 195 of the 649,393 light trucks sold in Canada. At over $80,000 each for the LX 470, this is not a really big surprise. To introduce its new $46,000 RX 300, as well as the redesign of their entire vehicle line, the company is reported to have increased their spending from $2.9 million to $15 million. Such a steep increase was the result of deciding: (1) not to use U.S advertising and (2) to use television for only the second time in Canada. The company felt the Canadian market was unique and it was necessary to create appeal for the French-speaking and Chinese markets. These represent important segments in Canada for prestige automobiles. Direct mail was also employed using personalized letters customized for twenty different segments.[8]

One method that firms use to extend their advertising budgets is co-operative advertising, discussed earlier in this chapter. But not all firms are in a position to participate in co-operative advertising programs. Generally, such programs are available only to retailers and wholesalers who distribute the products of large manufacturers and who can take advantage of the co-operative budgets made available by those companies. This leaves many companies and other organizations that must plan and execute their own advertising programs and must pay the entire cost.

Many firms, particularly smaller ones, find the establishment of an advertising budget to be a very difficult exercise. This is related to the fact that most business people find it equally difficult to measure the payback from advertising and, therefore, do not feel that they are in a position to decide where to place their advertising dollars to get the greatest return. The result is that a lot of advertising money is wasted, and many companies probably pay much more than they should for effective advertising.

Creating a Message

Whatever the objective of an advertising campaign, the individual ads must accomplish two things: get and hold the **attention** of the intended audience, and **influence** that audience in the desired way. Remember that the ultimate purpose of advertising is to sell something (that something may be a product or service; or it may be an idea), and that the ad itself is a sales message. The ad may be a fast-paced sales talk, as in a direct-action

TV ad by a car dealership. Or it may be a very long-range, low-key message, as are many institutional ads. Whatever the method, the goal is to sell something sooner or later.

Attention can be achieved in many ways (recall our discussion of perception in Chapter 6). The most common approach is to present the material in an unexpected manner or to use an unconventional technique to capture the attention of the audience. Thus a print ad may be mostly white space or a television commercial might show the product in an unusual setting or address a topic from a new perspective. American Express gets attention when it features well-known personalities in the advertising for its credit cards. Nike (www.nike.com) uses dramatic special effects (and personalities) in its television commercials. Nike has intensive, adrenaline pumping high-impact ads that stop in a sudden freeze-frame — if you want to see how these cliffhangers could end the viewer had to go to a special Nike Web site. Here alternative endings could be viewed and voted for to determine what endings would eventually be selected. Ford used a similar approach, allowing consumers to select cast and plot lines for new Ford Focus ads (www.focus247.com).[9] Some advertising for social programs, such as anti-smoking campaigns and appeals against drinking and driving, will use dramatic emotional content to shock viewers and to get their attention.

If the ad succeeds in getting the audience's attention, the advertiser has a few seconds to communicate a message intended to influence beliefs and/or behaviour. The message has two elements: the appeal and the execution. The **appeal** in an ad is the reason or justification for believing or behaving. It is the benefit that the individual will receive as a result of accepting the message.

Some advertisers mistakenly focus their appeal on product features or attributes. They either confuse attributes with benefits or assume that if they present the product's attributes, the audience will infer the correct benefits. Telling customers that a cereal contains fibre (an attribute) is much less meaningful than telling them that, because it contains fibre, consuming it reduces the likelihood of colon cancer (the benefit). Common appeals or benefits and examples of product categories in which they are frequently used include:

◆ Health (food, nonprescription drugs).

◆ Social acceptance (cosmetics, health and beauty aids).

◆ Material success (automobiles, investments).

◆ Recognition (clothing, jewellery).

◆ Sensory pleasure (movies, candy).

◆ Time savings (prepared foods, convenience stores).

◆ Peace of mind (insurance, tires).

Execution is combining in a convincing, compatible way the feature or device that gets attention with the appeal. An appeal can be executed in different ways. Consider the ways you could communicate the benefit of reliable performance in a home appliance — presenting operating statistics, obtaining the endorsement of a respected person or organization, collecting testimonials from satisfied owners, or describing the meticulous manufacturing process. Rather than doing any of these, Maytag opted for "the lonely repairman," an amusing and memorable execution that gets attention and conveys the benefit of reliability.

www.keepyourhead3dayslonger.com

Keep lettuce fresh up to 3 days longer* with the new Maytag refrigerator. Its breakthrough ClimateZone™ technology keeps food at its ideal temperature so it stays fresh longer. Visit our Web site or call 800-234-4320, and bring innovation home.

MAYTAG.COM

*When stored at 34°F compared to 37°F. © 2000 Maytag Co.

Maytag has long used this device to communicate the reliability of its major appliances.

Creating an advertisement involves writing the **copy**, selecting the illustration (for visual media), preparing the visual or verbal layout, and reproducing the ad for the selected media. The copy in an ad is all the written or spoken material in it; it's the words. Copy in a print ad includes the headline, coupons, advertiser's identification, and the main body of the message. In a broadcast ad the copy is the script.

For visual ads, the **illustration** is a powerful feature. The main points to consider about illustrations are (1) whether they are totally appropriate to the product advertised and (2) despite the adage "a picture is worth a thousand words," whether they represent the best use of the space. The **layout** is the physical arrangement of all the elements in an advertisement. In print ads, it is the appearance of the page. For television, layout is the set as well as the positioning of actors and props. The layout of a radio ad is the sequence in which information is presented. A good layout can hold interest as well as attract attention. It should lead the audience through the entire ad in an orderly fashion.

The cost of creating an ad can vary from almost nothing for a local radio spot written by the staff at a radio station to as much as $500,000 or even more for a complex television commercial. In recent years, production costs for network TV ads have escalated dramatically. As a result, fewer commercials are being made, and they are kept on the air longer or are modified to create a number of variations.

Selecting Media

advertising media
The communications vehicles (such as newspapers, radio, and television) that carry advertising.

In describing the steps in developing an advertising campaign, we have discussed creating an advertising message before describing the selection of **advertising media** in which to place the ad. In reality these decisions are made simultaneously. The appeal and the target audience determine both the message and the choice of media. The following discussion focuses on selecting appropriate mass media in which to place advertising. As was suggested earlier in this chapter, advertisers are increasingly facing the decision of whether to use the mass media or to try to reach targeted audiences with more direct messages. This refers to using any of a number of alternatives to the traditional mass media that advertisers have been using for the past fifty years or more. Remember that "media" doesn't have to mean mass media.

Advertisers need to make decisions at each of three successive levels to determine which specific advertising medium to use:

1. Which type of medium will be used — newspaper, television, radio, magazine, or direct contact through mail or the Internet? What about the less prominent media of billboards, specialty items, and Yellow Pages?

2. Which category of the selected medium will be used? Television has network and cable, and a host of different channels; magazines include general-interest (*Maclean's, Time*) and special interest (*Chatelaine, Ski Canada, Teen People*) categories; and there are national as well as local newspapers. On the Internet, there are e-magazines, news sites, along with a variety of retail and general-purpose portals to choose from.

3. Which specific media vehicles will be used? An advertiser who decides first on radio and then on local stations must determine which stations to use in each city.

Here are some general factors that will influence media choice:

◆ *Objectives of the ad.* The purpose of a particular ad and the goals of the entire campaign influence the choice of which media to use. For example, if the campaign goal is to generate appointments for salespeople, the company may rely on direct mail or telephone contact. If an advertiser wants to produce quick action, newspaper or radio may be the medium to use.

◆ *Audience coverage.* The audience reached by the medium should match the geographic area in which the product is distributed. Furthermore, the selected medium should reach the desired types of prospects with a minimum of wasted coverage. Wasted coverage occurs when an ad reaches people who are not prospects for the product. Many media — even national and other large-market media — can be targeted at small, specialized market segments. For example, *Maclean's* magazine publishes regional editions with different ads in the Atlantic, Ontario, and Western editions, and a French-language edition for Quebec.

◆ *Requirements of the message.* The medium should fit the message. For example, food products, floor coverings, and apparel are best presented visually. If the advertiser can use a very brief message (the rule of thumb is six words or less), as is common with reminder advertising, billboards may be a suitable medium — provided, of course, that the audience includes people who are likely to drive or walk by the billboards.

◆ *Time and location of the buying decision.* The medium should reach prospective customers when and where they are about to make their buying decisions. Research shows that radio scores the highest in immediacy of exposure; over 50 percent of adults were last exposed to radio within one hour of making their largest purchase of the day. This factor highlights one of the strengths of place-based advertising. Likewise, in-store ads — for example, on shopping carts and in the aisles of supermarkets — reach consumers at the actual time of purchase.

◆ *Media cost.* The cost of each medium should be considered in relation to the budget available to pay for it and its reach or circulation. For example, the cost of network television exceeds the available funds of many advertisers.

cost per thousand (CPM)
The media cost of gaining exposure to one thousand persons with an ad.

Cost per thousand (CPM) persons reached (M is the Roman numeral for a thousand) is a standard measure routinely provided to prospective advertisers by all media. It allows an advertiser to compare costs across media. CPM is computed as follows:

$$CPM = \frac{ad\ cost \times 1,000}{circulation}$$

For example, let's assume that the advertising rate for a full-colour, one-page ad in *Holiday Getaways*, a magazine with an international circulation, is $42,000 and the circulation is 1,200,000. Therefore, CPM for the magazine is:

$$CPM = \frac{(\$42,000 \times 1,000)}{1,200,000} = \$35$$

Of course, it is essential to estimate what proportion of all persons reached are truly prospects for the advertiser's product. If an advertiser is interested only in females over fifty years of age, we might find that there are 650,000 *Holiday Getaways* readers in this category. Therefore, we would have to calculate a weighted CPM:

$$Weighted\ CPM = \frac{(\$42,000 \times 1,000)}{650,000} = \$64.62$$

Beyond these general factors, management must evaluate the advertising characteristics of each medium it is considering. We have carefully chosen the term characteristics instead of advantages and disadvantages because a medium that works well for one product is not necessarily the best choice for another product. To illustrate, a characteristic of radio is that it makes its impressions through sound and imagination. The roar of a crowd, running water, the rumbling of thunder, or screeching tires can be used to create mental images quickly and easily. But radio will not do the job for products that benefit from colour photography. Let's examine the characteristics of the major media.

NEWSPAPERS As an advertising medium, newspapers are flexible and timely. They account for the largest portion of total advertising dollars spent in Canada. They can be used to cover a single city or a number of urban centres. With the development of computer technology and regional printing in the publishing industry, once-local newspapers may now be printed in regional centres for distribution across the country. The daily *National Post* and *The Globe and Mail*, for example, are headquartered in Toronto but printed regionally and are true national daily papers.

While newspapers are becoming more attractive to the national advertiser, they remain the principal advertising vehicle for the local advertiser, particularly when they are used as the distribution vehicle for advertising flyers. Ads can be cancelled on a few days' notice or inserted generally on one day's notice. Newspapers can give an advertiser an intense coverage of a local market because a very large percentage of consumers read newspapers. The local feature also helps in that the ads can be adapted to local audiences and to social and economic conditions. Circulation costs per prospect are low. On the other hand, the life of a newspaper advertisement is very short.

It can be a cost-effective way to provide continuity in a campaign allowing the advertiser to stretch the advertising budget and remain visible to consumers through repetitive exposure. Recent improvements in colour printing have also improved the visual impact of this alternative, allowing for more appealing graphic representations.

TELEVISION Television is probably the most versatile and the most rapidly changing of all media. It makes its appeal through both the eye and the ear; products can be demonstrated as well as explained. It offers considerable flexibility in the geographic market covered and the time of message presentation. By making part of its impression through the ear, television can take advantage of the personal, dramatic impact of the spoken word.

On the other hand, television can be an extremely expensive medium. The message is not permanently recorded for the message receiver. Thus the prospect who is not reached the first time is lost forever, as far as a particular message is concerned. Television does not lend itself to long advertising copy, nor does it present pictures as clearly as magazines do. As with direct mail and radio, television advertisers must create their own audiences.

Cable has also changed television as an advertising medium. Canada is among the most heavily "cabled" nations in the world, with more than 90 percent of homes in many urban areas wired for cable. In this country, having cable television often allows Canadians access to upwards of one hundred channels, many of which originate in the United States, while some French-language programming comes from as far away as France. Some "local" channels also carry ethnic language programming appealing to very specific markets. Many channels carry specialized programming, including sports, weather, movies, youth programs, country music, arts and entertainment, and popular music formats. This increased access to television channels has resulted in a dramatic change in the nature and effect of television as an advertising medium.

In households with cable, television is now a much more focused medium, offering specialized television channels to people with particular interests. The sheer variety of channels has led to a situation described as **fragmentation**, where viewers regularly "zap" their way through the range of channels available, often when a commercial appears. This proliferation of channels through cable, coupled with the use of VCRs and DVD players, remote control devices, commercial-skip devices, video games, and the Internet, has meant that the audience likely to be exposed to a television commercial is reduced, thereby limiting the effectiveness of television in reaching a mass market. As a result, some advertisers have begun to use shorter, more attention-getting commercials, or have moved some of their advertising budgets away from television to other media.

In the cluttered world of television, advertisers are constantly looking for ways to reach targeted audiences and to make their advertising messages stand out. Some large advertisers are experimenting with interactive television, which many feel will become a major element in media advertising in the near future. Others are developing infomercials, which are intended to stand out from other forms of advertising on television. Finally, some companies have moved their advertising from the mainstream television networks to specialty channels in order to increase the likelihood of reaching their targeted audiences. Advertising on such specialty cable channels as CBC Newsworld, The Weather Network, MeteoMedia, TSN, Outdoor Life Network, CMT, MuchMusic, MusiquePlus, YTV, Bravo, Showcase, and Vision TV reach millions of viewers every day in Canada. The result is that television is fast becoming much more of a targeted medium and less of a mass medium to reach mass audiences.[10]

We can expect to see television become even more fragmented and more competitive in the future. With the introduction of two national direct-to-home satellite TV services, Star Choice and ExpressVu, Canadians who subscribe to these services can now have access to up to three hundred channels from all over the world and satisfying a multitude of interests.[11] Cable companies have responded by launching a host of cable channels, including the Comedy Channel, Teletoon, The History Channel, Home and Gardening, CTV all-news, and a science fiction channel. The result may be a confusing array of television-based options that lead some advertisers to rethink their use of the medium.[12]

While specialty channels may offer some advertisers a prime group of viewers, they often deliver in total about 1 percent share point in key demographics. This can be compared to "generic" broadcasters, such as CTV, which has about 12 percent share of the audience in Canada. These channels are, however, beginning to understand the challenges of attracting advertisers and have begun to develop a better understanding of programming that appreciates audience flow and narrower targeting. Strategies include "theme" events or "appointment television," personality programming such as Debbie Travis' Painted House on WTN, and when all else fails — if it succeeds on A&E — borrow the concept![13]

Many information-based specialty channels such as CTV Newsnet, Headline Sports, CP24, or The Weather Channel are more challenging to analyze for buyers — without scheduled programming — information is the programming — regular updates on given topics. These are typically watched by "light" viewers who can tell if the ads are seen or acknowledged.[14]

Concern about television viewing also arises from increasing Internet usage. While many are using the Internet for more reasons, this concern arises over increasing usage by 12 to 17-year-olds. This age group spends considerable amounts of time on the Web for entertainment purposes. As discussed in other parts of this text, this is an important consumer group in Canada, and if they are spending more time *somewhere* on the Internet then they are not watching TV advertisers' carefully-designed ads placed just for them! While Nielsen Media Research says that levels have remained the same since 1996 — at about sixteen hours a week, other youth-oriented research groups (Youth Culture and Corus Enterainment) believe there is cause for concern. Some suggest multi-tasking is the answer — but, if the teen target is using the computer while watching TV, is the advertising message getting through?[15]

DIRECT MAIL Direct mail has probably become the most personal and selective of all the media. Because it reaches only the market that the advertiser wishes to contact, there is a minimum of waste circulation. Articles or other editorial matter does not accompany direct mail unless the advertiser provides it. That is, most direct mail is pure advertising. As a result, a direct-mail ad creates its own circulation and attracts its own readers. The cost of direct mail per prospect reached is quite high compared with that of other media. But other media reach many people who are not real prospects and thus have higher waste-circulation costs. A severe limitation of direct mail is the difficulty of getting and maintaining good mailing lists. Direct-mail advertising also suffers from the stigma of being classed as "junk mail."

The effectiveness of direct mail has been increased in recent years through the application of technology to the process of identifying prospects to which advertising materials are to be mailed. Highly specialized mailing lists can be purchased from mailing-list brokers, but many firms are now able to produce their own highly targeted mailing and contact lists from their own databases. Buying lists can be expensive, but they do offer the advertisers the ability to target precisely the group in which they are interested. Many companies have developed their own mailing lists through an effective design of their internal information systems. By capturing sales data in an appropriate way, for example, a travel agency can produce a list of all the clients who made a business trip to Europe in the past year, or took a vacation in the southern United States, or made more than fifteen business trips. These individuals then represent target segments for special-interest mailings. Wastage is dramatically reduced because the advertising reaches precisely those people who are most likely interested.

Technology, and the development of databases, has taken many forms and made many contributions to furthering direct mail effectiveness. And we have yet to fully realize the impact or advancements that will finally result from the adoption of the Internet as a component of direct marketing. The refinement of database software along with a better understanding of how to meaningfully combine demographic or customer data has led many firms, both store and nonstore retailers, to tailor it into a mix that works for their organization. Loyalty programs, as we have already discussed, allow retailers to maintain much information on regular customers. It also allows the company to maintain a link or "personalized" connection to the consumer. Not unlike cookie programs used by Internet retailers. Maintaining information on past consumers, those that have responded by mailing in cards, calling toll-free numbers, or visiting the company's Web site provides a valuable target list for information regarding new products, services, or other information changes. These data banks can also be generated from delivery information, or simply asking for name and postal code information at the cash register to be keyed into the terminal at the time of sale. This can be used to generate a mailing list for flyers or promotional information.

Bank of Montreal's First Canadian Funds (www.bankofmontreal.com) developed an interactive DM program to position its In-tuition fund as the most appropriate education savings plan through the use of a floppy disk. In a few minutes, recipients could quickly calculate the funds required for their children's education and how they could get these funds. The target for this campaign was selected by vetting customer lists in the bank's database and selecting those that had indicated that they were parents. The program was a success, generating a response three-and-a-half times what was expected. Some retailers offer discount cards for purchases that enable them to maintain customer information. LaSenza Girl's VIP card (www.lasenzagirl.com) — aimed at girls 8 to 14 — costs $20 and offers 10 percent off all purchases and $15 dollars in coupons. To purchase the card they must supply their name, address, and e-mail address. Other retailers such as Coles/Smithbooks offer similar programs.[16]

Richmond Hill, Ontario-based Westminster International (www.westminster.ca) has extended its mailing services company to combine the Internet with traditional direct marketing as a response mechanism thereby bringing direct mail into the information age. The database-driven electronic business reply service allows recipients of direct mail to interact with the sender via a personalized Web page. Every outbound response card has a unique URL printed on it — this allows a recipient that responds to enter his or her own page — being greeted by name and responding with any information that may have been entered with previous responses.[17]

As of the middle of 1999, an extra pair of eyes has been watching over the activities of Canada's direct mailers. It was at this time that Advertising Standards Canada (ASC) (www.adstandards.com) revised its guidelines to include direct mail in the media it scrutinizes for violations of the ASC codes. This newly extended reach includes advertising on the Internet and point-of-sale messages.[18]

While direct mail is widely regarded as one of the most cost-effective of advertising media, it is also one that must be managed very carefully. In the first place, the effectiveness of a direct-mail advertising program is very heavily dependent on the accuracy of the mailing list being used. Some users of direct mail spend too little time on ensuring the accuracy of the mailing list, with the result that many people on the list may not be at all interested in the product or service, while some will receive two or three mailing pieces because their names appear on the list in a number of different forms. You have probably been mailed advertising material that you are not the least bit interested in. This contributes to the fact that many people have a low opinion of direct mail. In a study conducted for National Public Relations, seven out of ten respondents considered direct mail to be the least credible way for them to learn about a company's new product or service.

RADIO Radio is enjoying a renaissance as an advertising and cultural medium and as a financial investment. When interest in television soared in the 1950s, radio audiences (especially for national network radio) declined so much that people were predicting radio's demise. But during the last decades of the twentieth century, this medium made a real comeback. Local radio (as contrasted with national networks) is especially strong. Radio accounts for just over 10 percent of all advertising revenues in Canada, attracting almost $840 million in sales annually.

As an advertising medium, radio's big advantage is its relatively low cost. You can reach almost everybody with radio. At the same time, with special interest, targeted programming, certain radio stations can do a very effective job of reaching specific target market segments. In recent years, for example, a number of Canadian radio stations began to pay more attention to the growing segment of the market in the 30 to 50 age group. As a result, the top three formats in Canadian radio stations are country and western, adult contemporary, and news/talk, all of which are likely to appeal to a more mature audience than are the rock music stations that were more popular in the 1970s and 1980s. Other specialty stations have emerged in many of the larger radio markets in Canada, ranging from Toronto's 680News news/talk station, to Saskatoon's CFMC-FM adult contemporary station, to Alberta's aboriginal station (CFWE), to Vancouver's "The Bridge" (CKBD), which billed itself as Canada's first contemporary Christian music station.

Although radio is one of the more targeted of the mass media and can deliver an audience at a fairly low CPM (cost per thousand), it does have its limitations. On the one hand, it makes only an audio impression, so it is of limited value where a visual impact is needed. On the other hand, some advertisers who believe in the value of radio consider this to be one of radio's strong points — it is able to stimulate the imagination of the listener. Radio also does not have a captive audience, in that many people listen to the radio for "background" entertainment while they are working around the house, driving in their cars, or doing homework! The exposure life of a radio commercial is quite short, resulting in a need to deliver multiple exposures to gain impact.

MAGAZINES Magazines are an excellent medium when high-quality printing and colour are desired in an ad. Magazines can reach a national market at a relatively low cost per reader. Through special-interest or regional editions of general-interest magazines, an advertiser can reach a selected audience with a minimum of waste circulation. Magazines are usually read in a leisurely fashion, in contrast to the haste in which other print media are read. This feature is especially valuable to the advertiser with a lengthy or complicated message. Magazines have a relatively long life, anywhere from a week to a month, and a high pass-along readership.

With less flexible production schedules than newspapers, magazines require ads to be submitted several weeks before publication. In addition, because they are published weekly or monthly, it is more difficult to use topical messages. Magazines are often read at times or in places — on planes or in doctors' offices, for instance — far removed from the place where a buying impulse can be acted on.

OUT-OF-HOME ADVERTISING Out-of-home advertising, which includes billboards, posters, bus shelter ads, and electronic digital billboards, has a low cost per exposure. Because of the mobile nature of our society, outdoor ads reach a large percentage of the population. But, because it is typically seen by people "on the go," billboard advertising is appropriate only for brief messages. It is excellent for reminder advertising, and it carries the impact of large size and colour. Motion and three-dimensional figures can be incorporated in a billboard's design for increased attention-getting ability. Billboards provide flexibility in geographic coverage and intensity of market coverage within an area. However, unless the advertised product or service is widely used, considerable waste circulation will occur. Although the cost of reaching an individual person is low, the total cost of a national billboard campaign can be quite high. Finally, the landscape-defacing aspect of outdoor advertising has aroused considerable public criticism. Another issue is that posters and billboards have to be maintained by the companies that erected them if they are going to have an appeal to passing consumers.[19]

SPECIALTY ADVERTISING An item of merchandise imprinted with the advertiser's name, message, or logo and given free is specialty advertising. According to the Specialty Advertising Association International, more than fifteen thousand different items, from pens and baseball caps to coffee cups and calendars are used in specialty advertising, and annual expenditures are more than $5 billion in North America.

Specialty advertising is usually used in conjunction with other promotional activities, though it is sometimes used alone by firms with very small advertising budgets. Its greatest strength is its long life. Every time the specialty item is used, the advertising message is repeated.

EMERGING MEDIA Many advertisers consider several lesser-known media to be valuable, especially when used in conjunction with the better-known media:

◆ *World Wide Web.* Much has been written in recent years about the advertising potential of the World Wide Web and revenues from advertising on the Internet are growing exponentially. We have reached a turning point for the acceptance of e-advertising where there is a critical mass of advertisers on the Net. For the first time, it is attracting mainstream advertisers, particularly Canadian retailers. Financial services, retailing, computer products, consumer services, and communications make up the top five spenders of 1999.[20] Many companies have had Web pages created and have begun to reach their target market utilizing this new medium. While trends are increasing, Canadian e-tailers are not keeping pace with southern counterparts. The high cost of shipping across Canada and the lower population density of the Canadian marketplace make it more difficult for Canadian electronic retailers. Traditional retailers such as Canadian Tire and Sears have an advantage over pure Internet firms in maximizing their e-commerce potential since they have established distribution networks. These companies send e-flyers that allows consumers to receive selective promotional information at their individual e-mail addresses.[21]

◆ *Infomercials.* These are the lengthy television advertisements that generally run for up to sixty minutes and combine information with entertainment and product promotions. They have been popular in the United States for many years, and many have been beamed into Canada on American channels. They often feature well-known presenters like Cher, George Foreman, Suzanne Somers, and motivational speaker Tony Robbins, promoting everything from diet plans and personal-improvement programs to baldness remedies and the "Lean, Mean, Fat-Reducing Grilling Machine." While infomercials are not as widely used in Canada as they are in the United States, a number of companies, including the Royal Bank of Canada, have utilized this format.

Growth of this format has been hampered in Canada by a couple of factors. Originally, these "programs" were only seen by insomniacs as CRTC (www.crtc.gc.ca) rules allowed their broadcast only between midnight to 6 A.M., as during other times any given broadcast hour was only permitted twelve minutes of advertising — an exception has now been made for infomercials. However, problems still exist in that infomercials are not permitted on any channel receiving public money — such as CBC or TVOntario. And specialty channels must make special applications to show them on their airwaves. Perhaps the biggest problem is the issue of Canadian content. Even if an infomercial is made in Canada with Canadian actors it is still ruled as "neutral" broadcasting content. CRTC requires 60 percent Canadian content meaning that this "programming" must cut into the 40 percent left for American network shows — these American network shows are responsible for generating a great portion of advertising revenue.[22]

◆ *Place-based media.* As we discussed earlier in this chapter, certain attractive target segments, such as young professionals, teenagers, and dual-career families, have become increasingly difficult to reach through traditional advertising media. The solution is to place the advertising where the people are. Consequently, we have seen an increase in advertising in airports, shopping malls, waiting rooms, supermarkets, phone booths, and even public washrooms. Advertisements can also been seen in movie theatres preceding the feature attraction. One new approach to entertaining a captive audience has been the use of video screens in office elevator buildings. This can allow some segmentation according to where the elevator is located. The Elevator News Network (www.enn.net) claims to have video screens located in the elevators of the

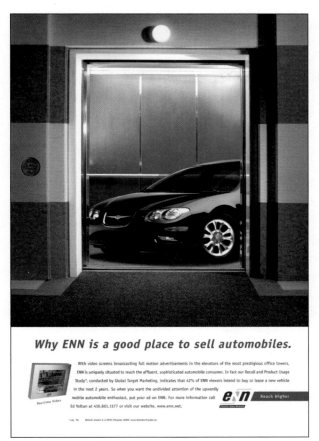

Why ENN is a good place to sell automobiles.

With video screens broadcasting full motion advertisements in the elevators of the most prestigious office towers, ENN is uniquely situated to reach the affluent, sophisticated automobile consumer. In fact our Recall and Product Usage Study*, conducted by Global Target Marketing, indicates that 42% of ENN viewers intend to buy or lease a new vehicle in the next 2 years. So when you want the undivided attention of the upwardly mobile automobile enthusiast, put your ad on ENN. For more information call Ed Voltan at 416.861.1177 or visit our website, www.enn.net.

Ads in elevators appeal to captive audiences.

most prestigious office towers in the country affording them access to affluent, sophisticated consumers. This would give advertisers the undivided attention of the upwardly (pun intended!) mobile consumer. Brewers Retail in Ontario installed its own television network that beams programming to customers through its Beer Stores throughout the province. Athletic stores such as Sportchek also broadcast a variety of extended length merchandise ads between popular music videos.

◆ *Videos and CD-ROMs.* Bothered by the erosion of their network television audience by videos, some national advertisers have moved their advertising to reach the video watchers by placing ads on rental video movies or by co-sponsoring or co-producing them. Other companies are able to get their messages, especially complex messages, directly into the hands of prospective customers by having their own videos or CD-ROMs produced and then mailed directly to targeted customers.

◆ *Yellow Pages.* The traditional Yellow Pages is a directory of local businesses and their telephone numbers, organized by type of product or service. Although such advertising media have been around for many years, there are some new twists as similar directories are being printed by companies in competition with the telephone companies, and directories of fax numbers are being issued. Tele-Direct, the national publisher of the Yellow Pages, now produces a CD-ROM version. The availability of these listings online offers the ability to generate ads relevant to the desired product or service being requested.

Many believe that advertising on the Web will become so commonplace in a few years and that it will take the place of more conventional mass media. One of its obvious advantages is that it allows the customer to seek out the advertiser; in this regard it is like the Yellow Pages, in that whomever approaches a company's Web site is very likely interested in buying. A second feature of advertising on the Web is that it is easy. Many smaller companies in particular have turned to in-house personnel or to programmers who are not trained in advertising or marketing to develop their Web pages at very low cost. The result is often embarrassingly poor. Advertisers must realize that the Web will become an extremely important advertising medium in the future and that it has to be approached in the same way as other advertising media — with appropriate strategic planning and investment — if high-quality, effective communication is to be the result.

Evaluating the Advertising Effort

In managing its advertising program, a company should carefully evaluate the effectiveness of previous ads and use the results to improve the quality of future ads. Shrinking profit margins and increasing competition — both foreign and domestic — force management to appraise all expenditures. Top executives want proof that advertising is worthwhile. They want to know whether dollars spent on advertising are producing as

Bringing the ads to where the customers are.

direct tests (in advertising)
Measures of the sales volume produced by an ad or an entire advertising campaign.

indirect tests (in advertising)
Measures of advertising effects that use something other than sales volume.

advertising recall
A measure of advertising effectiveness based on the premise that an ad can have an effect only if it is perceived and remembered.

many sales as could be reaped from the same dollars spent on other marketing activities.

DIFFICULTY OF EVALUATION It is hard to measure the sales effectiveness of advertising. By the very nature of the marketing mix, all elements — including advertising — are so intertwined that it is nearly impossible to measure the effect of any one by itself. Factors that contribute to the difficulty of measuring the sales impact of advertising are:

◆ *Ads have different objectives.* Though all advertising is ultimately intended to increase sales, individual ads may not be aimed at producing immediate results. Some ads simply announce new store hours or service policies. Other ads build goodwill or contribute to a company's image.

◆ *Ads can have an effect over time.* Even an ad designed to have immediate sales impact may produce results weeks or months after it appears. A consumer may be influenced by an ad but not be able to act on it immediately. Or an ad may plant in the consumer's mind a seed that doesn't blossom into a sale for several weeks. It is impossible to determine, with the exception of mail-order advertising, when a particular ad or campaign produced results.

◆ *Measurement problems.* Consumers cannot usually say when or if a specific ad influenced their behaviour, let alone if it caused them to buy. Human motivation is too complicated to be explained by a single factor.

In spite of these problems, advertisers try to measure advertising effectiveness because they must — and some knowledge is better than none at all. An ad's effectiveness may be tested before it is presented to the target audience, while it is being presented, or after it has completed its run.

METHODS USED TO MEASURE EFFECTIVENESS Ad effectiveness can be measured directly and indirectly. **Direct tests**, which measure or predict the sales volume attributable to an ad or a campaign, can be used only with a few types of ads. Tabulating the number of redemptions of a reduced-price coupon incorporated in an ad will indicate its effectiveness. Coupons frequently are coded so they can also be traced to the publications from which they came. Another direct test used to predict sales measures the number of inquiries received from an ad that offers additional information to prospects that call or write in.

Most other types of measures are **indirect tests** of effectiveness, or measures of something other than actual behaviour. One of the most frequently used measures is **advertising recall**. Recall tests are based on the premise that an ad can have an effect only if it is perceived and remembered. Three common recall tests are:

◆ *Recognition* — showing people an ad and asking if they have seen it before.

◆ *Aided recall* — asking people if they can recall seeing any ads for a particular brand.

◆ *Unaided recall* — asking people if they can remember seeing any ads within an identified product category.

For broadcast media this kind of testing can be conducted using a telephone survey, calling people at home within a few hours after an ad is aired, or after a campaign has been running for several weeks.

Television ads are often tested before they are presented to the general public in what are called **pretests**. Commercials in finished or nearly finished form (to save production costs) are presented to panels of consumers for their reactions. This is often done in theatre settings, with the test ad shown along with other ads in the context of a regular TV program. After viewing the program and the ads, the consumers are quizzed about the commercial being tested.

A criticism of pretests is that the situation is unrealistic. The ads often are not in the final forms that the actual target audience would see; the research respondents have been invited to a theatre to participate; and the respondents are usually given an incentive for their involvement. The testers argue that since these factors exist across all commercials tested, they in effect "wash out" and the scores provide useful comparative information.

Refinements are constantly being made in advertising testing. Developments in areas such as laboratory test markets and computer simulations hold promise for the future. However, the complexity of decision-making, combined with the multitude of influences on the buyer, will continue to make measuring the effectiveness of advertising a difficult task.

pretest
An activity in which commercials in finished or nearly finished form are presented to panels of consumers in order to gauge their reactions.

Organizing for Advertising

A firm can manage its advertising in three ways:

◆ Develop an internal advertising department.

◆ Use an outside advertising agency.

◆ Use a combination of an internal department and an outside advertising agency.

Regardless of which alternative is selected, generally the same specialized skills are necessary to do the advertising job. Creative people are needed to prepare the copy, generate illustrative material, and design the layouts. Media experts are required to select the appropriate media, buy the time or space, and arrange for the scheduled appearance of the ads. And managerial skills are essential to plan and administer the entire advertising program.

Internal Departments
All these advertising tasks, some of them, or just the overall direction can be performed by an internal department. A company whose advertising is a substantial part of its marketing mix will usually have its own advertising department. Large retailers, for example, have their own advertising departments, and many do not use advertising agencies at all.

advertising agency
An independent company rendering specialized services in advertising in particular and in marketing in general.

Advertising Agencies
Many companies, especially manufacturers of consumer products, use advertising agencies to carry out some or all of their advertising activities. An **advertising agency** is an

independent company that provides specialized advertising services and may also offer more general marketing assistance, including public relations and media relations.

Advertising agencies plan and execute entire advertising and communications campaigns. They employ more advertising specialists than their clients do, because they spread the cost over many accounts. A client company can benefit from an agency's experience gained from other products and clients. Many large agencies have expanded the services they offer to include sales promotion and public relations, and they are frequently called upon to assist in new-product development, package design, and selecting product names. In fact, many of these firms have become integrated agencies, offering a full range of services from strategic planning to market research and Web page design that heretofore were performed by other outside specialists or by the advertisers themselves.

Inside Department and Outside Agency

Many firms have their own advertising department and also use an advertising agency. The internal advertising department acts as a liaison with the agency, giving the company greater control over this major expenditure. The advertising department approves the agency's plans and ads, is responsible for preparing and administering the advertising budget, and co-ordinates advertising with personal selling. It may also handle direct marketing, dealer displays, and other promotional activities if they are not handled by the agency.

Sales Promotion

Sales promotion is one of the most loosely used terms in the marketing vocabulary. We define **sales promotion** as demand-stimulating devices designed to supplement advertising and facilitate personal selling. Examples of sales promotion devices are coupons, premiums, in-store displays and demonstrations, trade shows, samples, and contests.

Producers and intermediaries can each conduct sales promotions. The target for producers' sales promotions may be intermediaries, end users — households or business users — or the producer's own sales force. Intermediaries direct sales promotion at their salespeople or prospects further down the channel of distribution.

Nature and Scope of Sales Promotion

Sales promotion is distinct from advertising or personal selling, but these three forms of promotion are often used together in a coordinated fashion. For example, an in-store display (sales promotion) furnished by Michelin to dealers selling its tires may feature a slogan and illustrations (including, of course, the Michelin Man) from Michelin's current advertising campaign. This display, which helps retailers sell tires, also makes them more receptive to talking with Michelin salespeople. Or, as another example, prospective customers may be generated from people who enter a contest at the Canon copier exhibit at an office equipment trade show. These prospects might be sent some direct-mail advertising and then be contacted by a salesperson.

There are two categories of sales promotion: **trade promotions**, directed to the members of the distribution channel; and **consumer promotions**, aimed at consumers. Manufacturers as a group spend about twice as much on trade promotion as they do on advertising, and an amount about equal to their advertising on consumer promotions.

The numbers attached to some sales promotion activities are mind-boggling. Packaged-goods manufacturers alone distributed almost 3.3 billion coupons directly to

trade promotion
The type of sales promotion that is directed at members of a distribution channel.

consumer promotion
The type of sales promotion that is aimed at consumers.

Marketing at Work 20-2

Promos with Staying Power

Promotions have long been an important element in the marketing mix because they have the ability to generate increased sales and market share within a specific time frame. They should not be viewed, however, as one-off initiatives, rather as an ongoing element of an integrated marketing plan with the ability not only to contribute to short-term sales, but to enhance the overall strength of a brand.

Two companies who have achieved great success as a result of the longevity of their promotions are Pepsi and Robin Hood. Pepsi first introduced the "Pepsi Taste Challenge" to Canadians in 1978 by offering a chance to win prizes in exchange for taking a blind taste test. This promotion continued until 1995 when it was replaced for a short time by "Pepsi Stuff" — a retail-focused promotion in which consumers could collect points redeemable for Pepsi merchandise.

In the summer of 1999 Pepsi brought back the Taste Challenge in Ontario, Alberta, and British Columbia. The consumer response was so strong that the company decided to expand the program by adding the "Diet Pepsi Taste Challenge" in 2000, running in Ontario and Atlantic Canada. The program is so powerful in its appeal because it reinforces what is key to the brand — choice. The Pepsi brand is all about choice, which is exactly what the promotion is all about.

The challenge associated with a long-term promotion is finding a way to keep it fresh. Pepsi accomplishes this by offering prizes that capture the interest and imagination of consumers. In 2000, for example, participants in the challenge could instantly win prizes ranging from lollipops to portable CD players, and all received a Pepsi Taste Challenge card good for

discounts at Famous Players, Playdium, KFC, New York Fries, and Music World.

Another promotion that has stood the test of time is the annual "Robin Hood Baking Festival" which is now in its eighteenth year. To promote its Robin Hood flour, every fall Robin Hood Multifoods distributes five hundred thousand recipe books through grocery stores, and another two million copies in consumer magazines such as *Canadian Living, Chatelaine,* and *Elm Street.* The goal is to attract the attention of the brand's target audience — women with families.

The promotion has a second component, aimed at retailers, which results in Robin Hood displays appearing in fifteen hundred grocery stores across the country during the Baking Festival promotional time period — September through December. Retailers quickly recognize the value in featuring a Robin Hood display as consumers who pick up a bag of flour then go on to purchase nuts, raisins, and the other additional ingredients necessary to complete their baking. As with the Pepsi Taste Challenge, the Robin Hood Baking Festival must not become stale. To prevent this, the recipe book is constantly updated to include new recipes that reflect consumers' ever-changing tastes.

One key element in determining a promotion's long-term potential is to ensure that the chosen concept is right for the brand, and that it will build equity over the long term. Promotions of this magnitude, no matter how conceptually sound, do not survive without a strong commitment to the tactics and to the budget needed to execute them. A promotion with staying power, however, can pay for itself over time and eventually become cheaper to run each year as the organization becomes more proficient in its execution.

Source: Adapted from Liz Adams, "Promotions with legs," *Strategy*, May 22, 2000, p. 17.

consumers in Canada in 1996. This declined to 2.7 billion by 1998. Coupon redemptions, however, have remained relatively static at about 130 million. This is thought to be due to two forces. The average value of coupons has increased by roughly 8 percent and coupon distributors have improved their aim through advances in database management.[23] These numbers do not include coupons issued by restaurants, retailers, and other major users. The percentage of coupons delivered to consumers by direct mail has grown to 9 percent as has the percentage delivered by freestanding inserts (FSIs) inside newspapers, which can be effectively targeted geographically by forward sortation area (that part of your postal code that indicates the neighbourhood in which you live).

In recent years more and more coupons distributed have been for non-food items. Fastest growing has been the use of coupons for health and beauty aids. Food, however, still remains the biggest single couponing sector.

This growth in the distribution of paper coupons to Canadian households continues despite an increasing acceptance of technology in the distribution of coupons, as some retailers use a system to distribute coupons selectively — for example, targeting them only to customers who purchase a competitor's product. Some supermarket chains, such as Sobey's, have used electronic couponing, which involves issuing discounts automatically to all purchasers who have a special card that scans for discounts as their purchases are checked in. They have also used the reverse side of their receipts to print coupons based on purchases made on the current visit.

Many retailers, such as Sobey's, Chapters, and many fast food chains have used their Web sites to issue coupons — "click and save" becomes "print and redeem" as sites begin to exist for the sole purpose of coupon distribution. Aside from Savingyoumoney.com, which we have already discussed, existing distribution firms have also taken to the Web. Toronto-based Val-Pak of Canada (www.valpak.com) has over forty thousand coupons online while Montreal-based GTC Transcontinental Group has brought its twenty year-old Ad-Bag (Publi-Sac in French) to cyberspace in both English and French (www.adbag.ca and www.publisac.ca).[24] Another well-known entrant in the e-coupon business is CoolSavings (www.coolsavings.com). Well-known for its spokesperson (a spokespig, actually), a healthy pink cherubic-looking piggy bank, in the role of company CEO, sporting wayfarer sunglasses and shown coaching his employees to develop better savings opportunities for consumers.

Several factors in the marketing environment contribute to the surging popularity of sales promotion:

◆ *Short-term results.* Sales promotions such as couponing and trade allowances produce quicker, more measurable sales results. However, critics of this strategy argue that these immediate benefits come at the expense of building brand equity. They feel that an overemphasis on sales promotion may undermine a brand's future. While the intent (for the longer term) is to stimulate new trial, it is thought that as much as half of coupon redemptions are from existing users.[25]

◆ *Competitive pressure.* If competitors are offering buyers price reductions, contests, or other incentives, a firm may feel forced to retaliate with its own sales promotions.

◆ *Buyers' expectations.* Once they are offered purchase incentives, consumers and channel members get used to them and soon begin expecting them.

◆ *Low quality of retail selling.* Many retailers use inadequately trained sales clerks or have switched to self-service. For these outlets, sales promotion devices such as product displays and samples often are the only effective promotional tools available at the point of purchase.

Management of Sales Promotion

Sales promotion should be included in a company's marketing communications plans, along with advertising and personal selling. This means setting sales promotion objectives and strategies, determining a budget, selecting appropriate techniques, and evaluating the performance of sales promotion activities.

One problem management faces is that many sales promotion techniques are short-run, tactical actions. Coupons, premiums, and contests, for example, are designed to produce immediate (but short-lived) responses. As a result, they tend to be used as stop-gap measures to reverse unexpected sales declines rather than as integrated parts of a marketing program.

DETERMINING OBJECTIVES AND STRATEGIES We identified three broad objectives of sales promotion when we defined the term:

◆ Stimulating business-user or household demand for a product.

◆ Improving the marketing performance of intermediaries and salespeople.

◆ Supplementing advertising and facilitating personal selling.

One sales promotion technique may accomplish one or two — but probably not all — of these objectives.

More specific objectives of sales promotion are much like those for advertising and personal selling. Examples are:

◆ *To gain trial for a new or improved product.* Tetley Tea or Neutrogena shampoo might send a free sample through the mail.

◆ *To disrupt existing buying habits.* A coupon offering a large discount might cause a consumer to switch brands of a product that is viewed as generic, such as orange juice or motor oil.

◆ *To attract new customers.* Financial institutions have offered small appliances and other premiums to encourage consumers to open accounts.

◆ *To encourage greater use by existing customers.* Air Canada and most other airlines have "frequent flyer" programs to encourage travellers to use their airlines more often. Other businesses have established similar "loyalty" programs, including the popular Air Miles program, to which a number of major retailers belong.

◆ *To combat a competitor's promotional activity.* One supermarket chain runs a lottery or game to attract shoppers, and a competitor retaliates by offering triple-value coupons.

◆ *To increase impulse buying.* End-of-aisle and island displays in supermarkets can increase sales of a product by as much as 50 percent.

◆ *To get greater retailer co-operation.* A sporting-goods manufacturer gets additional shelf space by setting up excellent point-of-purchase displays, training retailers' salespeople, and providing tote bags to be given away with purchases.

The choice of sales promotion tools derives directly from the objectives of the total marketing program. Consider the following situations and the different strategies available:

◆ A firm's objective is to increase sales, which calls for entering new geographic markets using a pull strategy. To encourage product trial and attract consumers away from familiar brands, possible sales promotion tactics are coupons, cash rebates, free samples, and premiums.

◆ A firm's objective is to protect market share in the face of intense competition. This goal suggests a push strategy to improve retailer performance and goodwill. Training retailers' sales forces, supplying effective point-of-purchase displays, and granting advertising allowances would be appropriate sales promotion options.

DETERMINING BUDGETS The sales promotion budget should be established as a specific part of the budget for the total marketing communications mix. Including sales promotion in an advertising or public relations budget is not likely to foster the development of a separate sales promotion strategy. And as a result, sales promotion may be overlooked or poorly integrated with the other components of marketing communications. Setting a separate budget for sales promotion forces a company to recognize and manage it.

Within the concept of developing an integrated marketing communications strategy, the amount budgeted for sales promotion should be determined by the task method. This forces management to consider specific objectives and the sales promotion techniques that will be used to accomplish them.

SELECTING THE APPROPRIATE TECHNIQUES Common sales promotion techniques are shown in Table 20-3, where they are divided into three categories based on the target audience:

◆ *Sales promotion directed at final consumers.* Many of the tools in Table 20-3 probably are quite familiar to you, but a brief discussion of some of them will give you a better sense of their significance.

"Advertising specialties" is a miscellaneous category of small, usually inexpensive items imprinted with a company's name or logo that are given or sold by producers or intermediaries to customers and prospects. Examples are pens, calendars, key rings, paperweights, coffee cups, hats, and jackets.

◆ *Sales promotion directed at intermediaries.* Some of the tools just discussed may also be directed at intermediaries and their sales forces. In addition, trade associations in industries as diverse as shoes, travel, and furniture sponsor trade shows that are open only to wholesalers and retailers. Many producers also spend considerable time and money to train the sales forces of their wholesalers and retailers.

◆ *Sales promotion directed at a producer's own sales force.* Again, there is overlap between the tools directed at intermediaries and those designed for the producer's own sales force. Sales contests are probably the most significant of these tools, with many firms offering one kind or another. The most common incentive is cash, used in over half of all contests. Other incentives include merchandise, plaques, jewellery, and travel. Visual sales aids (flipcharts, slides) are prepared for salespeople, and brochures are developed to reinforce sales presentations.

TABLE 20-3 Major Sales Promotional Tools, Grouped by Target Audience

End Users (Consumer or Business)	Intermediaries and Their Sales Forces	Producers' Own Sales Force
Coupons	Trade shows and exhibitions	Sales contests
Cash rebates	Point-of-purchase displays	Sales training manuals
Premiums (gifts)	Free goods	Sales meetings
Free samples	Advertising allowances	Packets with promotional materials
Contests and sweepstakes	Contests for salespeople	Demonstration model of product
Point-of-purchase displays	Training intermediaries' sales force	
Product demonstrations	Product demonstrations	
Trade shows and exhibitions	Advertising specialties	
Advertising specialties		

A key step in sales promotion management is deciding which devices will help the organization reach its promotional goals. Factors that influence the choice of promotional devices include:

◆ *Nature of the target audience.* Is the target group loyal to a competing brand? If so, a high-value coupon may be necessary to disrupt customers' purchase patterns. Is the product bought on impulse? If so, an eye-catching point-of-purchase display may be enough to generate sales.

◆ *The organization's marketing communications objectives.* Does a pull or a push strategy best complement the rest of the marketing communications program?

◆ *Nature of the product.* Does the product lend itself to sampling, demonstration, or multiple-item purchases?

◆ *Cost of the device.* Sampling to a large market may be prohibitively expensive.

◆ *Current economic conditions.* Coupons, premiums, and rebates are good options during periods of recession or inflation, when consumers are particularly price conscious.

EVALUATING SALES PROMOTION Evaluating the effectiveness of sales promotions is much easier and the results are more accurate than is evaluating the effectiveness of advertising. For example, responses to a premium offer or a coupon with a specified closing date can be counted and compared with a similar period when no premiums or coupons were offered. It is easier to measure sales promotion because:

◆ *Most sales promotions have definite starting and ending points.* Coupons must be redeemed by a certain date. Contest entries must be submitted before a particular deadline. Contests for the sales force include only the sales made during a specified period. This is quite different from advertising, where there can be significant residual effects, and the results of one campaign may overlap with those of another.

◆ *Most sales promotions are designed to affect sales directly.* It is more difficult to measure a change in attitude or an increase in information about a product or brand than it is to count sales.

However, there are some pitfalls in measuring sales promotion effects. First, not all sales promotions meet the conditions just mentioned. For instance, training given to a distributor's sales force may be valuable but may not produce immediate results. Second, current sales promotion results may be inflated by sales "stolen" from the future. That is, a sales promotion may get buyers to act now but they may have bought the product in the future anyway. An indication of this "cannibalizing" effect is a lower level of sales after the promotion ends, compared with the level before the sales promotion began. Third, any attempt at measurement must take into consideration external conditions, such as the behaviour of competitors and the state of the economy. A firm's market share may not increase following an expensive sales promotion, for example, but the promotion may have offset the potentially damaging impact of a competitor's promotional activity.

Public Relations

public relations
A broad communications effort designed to build or maintain a favourable image for an organization with its various publics.

Public relations[26] is a management tool designed to favourably influence attitudes toward an organization, its products, and its policies. It is an often overlooked form of promotion. In most organizations this promotional tool is typically a stepchild, relegated far behind personal selling, advertising, and sales promotion. It is also often ignored until the company is facing a crisis or a problem that brings it into the public eye. In this sense, it is often viewed as a defensive tool. There are several reasons for management's lack of attention to public relations:

◆ *Organizational structure.* In most companies, public relations is not the responsibility of the marketing department. If there is an organized effort, it is usually handled by a small public relations department that reports directly to top management.

◆ *Inadequate definitions.* The term public relations is used loosely by both businesses and the public. There are no generally accepted definitions of the term. As a result, what actually constitutes an organized public relations effort often is not clearly defined.

◆ *Unrecognized benefits.* Only recently have many organizations come to appreciate the value of good public relations. As the cost of marketing communications has gone up, firms are realizing that positive exposure through the media or as a result of community involvement can produce a high return on the investment of time and effort.

Marketing at Work 20-3

P&G Makes a Clean Sweep of the Press

The Swiffer needs no introduction. Almost every household in Canada has been exposed to the wonders of this revolutionary broom through the mass media advertising campaign Procter & Gamble used to launch the product.

For those who have somehow missed the TV ads, the Swiffer is a flat-bottomed broom to which dry disposable cloths are attached. It is these cloths which are the key to the Swiffer's magic. Using electrostatic action, the cloths promise to attract and trap household dirt instead of merely stirring it up as a conventional broom might.

Procter & Gamble recently introduced a line-extension of their hugely successful product, called the Swiffer WetJet. The newer Swiffer is more like a mop than a broom and is battery-operated. The biggest difference, however, doesn't lie in the product's design or function but the way in which it was launched.

Instead of relying on a mass media advertising campaign, the Swiffer WetJet was launched behind a simple but extremely effective public relations campaign. Activities surrounding the product launch included sending the media a series of gimmicks prior to the press conference and using a celebrity spokesperson — Mary Walsh of *This Hour Has 22 Minutes.*

Using teasers and celebrities is nothing new in public relations strategies. Yet holding a press conference to launch a new product just hours before the product's spokesperson receives the Order of Canada is rather unique.

We may never know if the perfect timing was a result of good planning or good fortune, nevertheless the product launch was a huge success for P&G. Mary Walsh and the Swiffer WetJet made front-page news in the *National Post* the day after the press conference, while more stories followed in *The Globe and Mail* and *Toronto Sun.* Television and radio stations were also in attendance and the Swiffer WetJet debuted on Global TV, CTV, CFTO-TV and CFRB-AM radio.

Source: Adapted from Lesley Young, "P&G swiffers up media coverage," *Marketing Magazine,* July 24, 2000.

Nature and Scope of Public Relations

Public relations activities typically are designed to build or maintain a favourable image for an organization and a favourable relationship with its various publics — customers, prospects, stockholders, employees, labour unions, the local community, and the government. Senior managers in a variety of industries are increasingly recognizing the importance of maintaining a positive reputation among the public.[27]

Unlike advertising, public relations need not use the media to communicate its message. Good public relations can be achieved by supporting charitable projects (by supplying volunteer labour or other resources), participating in community service events, sponsoring athletic teams, funding the arts, producing an employee or customer newsletter, and disseminating information through exhibits, displays, and tours. Major companies often sponsor public events or special programs on television as part of their public relations efforts. Cultural organizations such as ballet companies and symphony orchestras would not survive without the support they receive from major corporations.

Publicity as a Form of Public Relations

publicity

A news presentation for a product or organization presented in any medium that is not paid for and has the credibility of editorial material.

Publicity is any communication about an organization, its products, or policies through the media that is not paid for by the organization. Publicity usually takes the form of a news story appearing in a mass medium or an endorsement provided by an individual, either informally or in a speech or interview. This is good publicity.

There is also, of course, bad publicity — a negative story about a firm or its product appearing in the media. In a society that is increasingly sensitive about the environment and in which news media are quick to report mistakes, organizations tend to focus on this negative dimension of publicity. As a result, managers are so concerned with avoiding bad publicity that they overlook the potential of good publicity.

There are three means for gaining good publicity:

◆ *Prepare a story (called a news release) and circulate it to the media.* The intention is for the selected newspapers, television stations, or other media to report the information as news.

◆ *Communicate personally with a group.* A press conference will draw media representatives if they feel the subject or speaker has news value. Company tours and speeches to civic or professional groups are other forms of individual-to-group communications.

◆ *Engage in one-on-one personal communication, or lobbying.* Companies lobby legislators or other powerful people in an attempt to influence their opinions and, subsequently, their decisions.

Publicity can help to accomplish any communication objective. It can be used to announce new products, publicize new policies, recognize employees, describe research breakthroughs, or report financial performance — if the message, person, group, or event is viewed by the media as newsworthy. This is what distinguishes publicity from advertising — publicity is not "forced" on the audience. This is also the source of its primary benefit. The credibility of publicity typically is much higher than that of advertising. If we tell you our product is great, you may well be skeptical. But if an independent, objective third party says on the evening news that our product is great, you are more likely to believe it.

Other benefits of publicity are:

◆ *Lower cost than advertising or personal selling.* Publicity usually costs less because there are no media space or time costs for conveying the message and no salespeople to support.

◆ *Increased readership.* Many consumers are conditioned to ignore advertising or at least pay it scant attention. Publicity is presented as editorial material or news, so it gets greater readership.

◆ *More information.* Because it is presented as editorial material, publicity can contain greater detail than the usual ad. More information and persuasive content can be included in the message.

◆ *Timeliness.* A company can put out a news release very quickly when some unexpected event occurs.

Of course, publicity also has limitations:

◆ *Loss of control over the message.* An organization has no guarantee that a news release will appear in the media. In fact, only a small proportion of all the news releases a firm prepares are ever used. In addition, there is no way to control how much or what portion of a publicity release the media will print or broadcast.

◆ *Limited exposure.* The media will typically use publicity material to fill space when there is a lack of other news and only use it once. If the target audience misses the message when it is presented, there is no second or third chance. There is no opportunity for repetition, as is the case in advertising.

◆ *Publicity is not free.* Even though there are no media time and space costs, there are expenses in staffing a public relations department and in preparing and disseminating news releases.

Recognizing the value of publicity, some organizations have special units or programs to generate information. For example, Campbell Soup Company sponsors a major national survey of the attitudes of Canadians toward health and nutrition; Christie's, the cookie company, sponsors the Christie Children's Book Awards; and The Body Shop actively supports the World Wildlife Fund and other environmental groups. All these activities are designed to link the companies involved with causes and activities that consumers believe to be important. Through their association, the companies intend to improve their corporate image. To fulfil its potential, however, publicity must be treated as part of the promotional strategy of the firm and be co-ordinated with the other promotional tools.

Evaluating Public Relations

Although few executives would argue that having a good image and staying in touch with an organization's publics are unimportant, evaluating public relations and publicity is difficult. In the past, evaluation usually involved a report of activities rather than results. Public relations departments maintained "scrapbooks" to show management how many stories were written and published, the number of employees who volunteered for civic projects, and the like. These days, to justify expenditures, more organizations are requiring publicity departments to provide specific public relations objectives and show measurable results. Because it is impossible to relate public relations and publicity directly to sales, other measures must be used. One is behavioural research to show, for example, increased awareness of a product or brand name, or changes in attitudes and beliefs about a firm.

Summary

Advertising is the nonpersonal, mass-communications component in a company's marketing communications mix. Advertising can be directed to consumers or businesses and can focus on products or institutions. Direct-action product ads call for immediate action, whereas indirect-action product ads are intended to stimulate demand over a longer time period. Product ads are also classified as primary-demand and selective-demand stimulating. Primary-demand ads are designed to introduce a new product, to stimulate demand for a generic product, or to sustain demand for an industry's products. Selective-demand ads, which include competitive and comparative advertising, are intended to increase the demand for a particular brand.

In vertical co-operative advertising, manufacturers and their retail dealers share the cost of advertising the manufacturers' product at the local level. Horizontal co-operative advertising involves joint sponsorship of ads by firms at the same level of distribution.

Advertising expenditures are large, but the average cost of advertising in a firm is typically 1 to 3 percent of sales. This is considerably less than the average cost of personal selling. Other frequently used advertising media are radio, magazines, Yellow Pages, and outdoor displays.

An advertising campaign should be part of a total marketing communications program. The steps in designing a campaign include defining specific objectives, establishing a budget, creating a message, selecting media, and evaluating the advertising effort. Objectives can range from creating awareness of a brand to generating sales. Vertical and horizontal co-operative arrangements can have a significant impact on advertising budgets. The advertising message — consisting of the appeal and the execution of the ad — is influenced by the target audience and the media used to deliver the message.

A major task in developing a campaign is to select the advertising media — the general type, the particular category, and the specific vehicle. The choice should be based on the characteristics of the medium, which determine how effectively it conveys the message, and its ability to reach the target audience.

With increasing fragmentation of viewing audiences for various media, it is becoming increasingly challenging to develop cost-effective strategies to maximize advertisement viewership. More and more advertisers will turn to newly emerging forms of advertising such as the Internet and newly developed forms of direct marketing. While many of the evolutions in advertising media are each reaching smaller audiences, these are more similar groups of consumers allowing advertisers to better target individual efforts.

A difficult task in advertising management is evaluating the effectiveness of the advertising effort — both the entire campaign and individual ads. Except for sales results tests, commonly used techniques measure only recall of an ad. To operate an advertising program, a firm may rely on its own advertising department, an advertising agency, or a combination of the two.

Sales promotion consists of demand-stimulating devices designed to supplement advertising and facilitate personal selling. The amount of sales promotion has increased considerably in recent years, as management has sought measurable, short-term sales results.

Sales promotion should receive the same strategic attention that a company gives to advertising and personal selling, including setting objectives and establishing a budget. Sales promotion can be directed toward final consumers, intermediaries, or a company's own employees. To implement its strategic plans, management can choose from a variety of sales promotion devices. Sales promotion performance also should be evaluated.

Public relations is a management tool designed to favourably influence attitudes toward an organization, its products, and its policies. It is a frequently overlooked form of promotion. Publicity, a part of public relations, is any communication about an organization, its products, or policies through the media that is not paid for by the organization. Typically these two activities are handled in a department separate from the marketing department in a firm. Nevertheless, the management process of planning, implementing, and evaluating should be applied to their performance in the same way it is applied to advertising, sales promotion, and personal selling.

Key Terms and Concepts

Advertising 634
Consumer advertising 635
Business-to-business advertising 635
Product advertising 635
Direct-action advertising 635
Indirect-action advertising 635
Institutional (corporate)
    advertising 635
Customer service advertising 636
Public service advertising (PSA) 636
Primary-demand advertising 636
Selective-demand advertising 636
Pioneering advertising 636
Differential competitive
    advantage 637

Comparative advertising 637
Co-operative advertising 638
Vertical co-operative advertising 638
Advertising allowance 638
Horizontal co-operative
    advertising 638
Advertising campaign 641
Attention 644
Influence 644
Appeal 645
Execution 645
Copy 646
Illustration 646
Layout 646
Advertising media 647

Cost per thousand (CPM) 648
Fragmentation 649
Direct tests 656
Indirect tests 656
Advertising recall 656
Pretests 657
Advertising agency 657
Sales promotion 658
Trade promotion 658
Consumer promotion 658
Public relations 664
Publicity 665

Questions and Problems

1. Businesses in different industries demonstrate quite different patterns in their advertising expenditures. Some are heavy advertisers on television, while others use no television at all. Some advertise heavily in daily newspapers, while others rely on magazines. Some firms, such as those in the consumer products field, spend as much as 15 percent of sales on advertising, while others, including many industrial marketers, spend less than 1 percent. How do you account for such variations in advertising expenditures?

2. Which advertising medium would you recommend as best for each of these products?

   a. Park benches.

   b. Pantyhose.

   c. Tax preparation service.

   d. A Web-based bookseller.

   e. Funeral services.

   f. Toys for young children.

   g. Plastic clothespins.

   h. Internet-based investment services.

   i. Pet grooming services

3. Many grocery product and chocolate bar manufacturers earmark a good portion of their advertising budgets for use in magazines. Is this a wise choice of media for these firms? Explain.

4. Why do department stores use newspapers more than local radio stations as an advertising medium?

5. Why is it worthwhile to pretest advertisements before they appear in the media? How could a test market be used to pretest an ad? (You may want to refresh your memory with a review of test marketing in Chapter 8.)

6. What procedures can a firm use to determine the level of sales that resulted from a direct-mail ad? How would you determine whether any sales were cannibalized?

7. If a manufacturing firm hires an advertising agency, should it close its own advertising department? Should it consider any changes?

8. Scan a current issue of a major national home and garden magazine and note the sales promotion tools that appear in advertisements in that magazine. Which one do you consider to be particularly effective?

9. Is sales promotion effective for selling expensive consumer products such as houses, automobiles, or cruise trips? Is your answer the same for expensive business products?

10. Explain how sales promotion might be used to offset weak personal selling in retail stores.

11. Can a well-implemented company Web site help to offset weak or inconsistent selling in a company's retail outlets?

12. Describe a recent public relations event in your community. How did it benefit the sponsor?

13. How does publicity differ from advertising?

14. Bring to class an article from a daily newspaper that appears to be the result of a firm's publicity efforts. Summarize the points made in the article that may benefit the firm. Could the same benefits be obtained through advertising?

15. Give a recent example of a company or other organization with which you are familiar that encountered unfavourable publicity. How well do you feel the organization handled the situation? What public relations or publicity tools did it use?

Hands-On Marketing

1. Bring to class four print ads or describe four radio or television ads that illustrate at least four of the specific advertising objectives outlined early in the chapter. As an alternative, find and describe two ads for the same brand that appear to be directed at different objectives.

2. Visit a supermarket, drugstore, or hardware store, and make a list of all the sales promotion tools that you observe. Describe how each one relates to the sales promotion objectives described in the chapter. Which are particularly effective, and why?

Case 6-1

GLOBALSTUDENT.COM

Jason and Krista Trask beamed as they read the May 3, 2000, *Globe and Mail* article "Internet startup offers a leaning experience." The young entrepreneurs were pleased to have received national attention for their start-up Internet venture. "I am confident in our vision," declared Krista. "I know we can develop a site that will serve the needs of all students from preschoolers to graduate students in North America and eventually the rest of the Internet connected world." Globalstudent.com is not just a Web site, but a lifestyle for the student community. The Web property is intended to be a starting place or "one-stop shop" for students of all ages around the world to study, research, communicate, and experience the academic and real world. The Web community has five basic sub-divisions: Primary; Elementary; Junior High; Senior High; and Post-secondary. "We plan to launch the High School and Post-secondary sections of the site in August 2000, the Junior High section in January of 2001 and the Primary and Elementary sections in August 2001," stated Jason. "What we need immediately is a comprehensive marketing strategy to demonstrate how we will attract high school and post-secondary students to our site and encourage them to return. We must clearly define how our service will be positioned in the market and the site's competitive advantages. To raise the needed $2 million slice of capital, which will allow the company to hire additional management and secure partnerships, we must demonstrate that we can secure a revenue stream. Investors will want details on how we plan to generate revenue." With the launch of the first section of the site only months away, the two Internet entrepreneurs had to get their marketing strategy on paper quickly.

Background

Jason and Krista were confident that they understood the needs of high school and post-secondary students. They had both recently graduated from Memorial University of Newfoundland with business degrees and had run an Internet-based company MUNWorld.com while they were students at the university. They launched the MUNWorld Web site in September 1997 to meet the needs of Memorial's student population by selling used textbooks and providing information about student jobs and social activities. The MUNWorld Web site was created and operated by Jason and Krista, who also sold advertising.

MUNWorld.com was launched to target students of Memorial University of Newfoundland's St. John's campus, a potential market of approximately ten thousand students. With limited promotional effort, MUNWorld.com reached approximately 50 percent of the potential market within three months of the launch date. Advertisers were solicited and the service appealed to both advertisers and users. MUNWorld developed a loyal following of students within Memorial University; students liked MUNWorld so much that many of them linked to the site from their personal sites. The following summarizes visits to MUNWorld.com for the period April 24, 1999 to May 24, 1999:

| Unique visitors | 4,595 | Average page views/visit | 6.67 |
| Total visits | 9,024 | Average time/visit | 3.7 minutes |

Globalstudent.com was an offspring of MUNWorld. It was the experience of the two Internet entrepreneurs with MUNWorld that was instrumental in identifying the potential within the student market. Jason and Krista knew that if MUNWorld could be so successful in delivering a specific targeted user group (Memorial University students) to advertisers, they could do the same for the 75 million students (at least 37 million online) in North America. See Tables 1 and 2 for historic data on the North American student market.

TABLE 1: Total Student Population, Canada and United States

Categories	Total Student Population		
	Canada	USA	Total
K – 3 (ages 4–8)	1,412,450	19,739,600	21,152,050
4 – 6 (ages 9–11)	1,412,200	11,574,600	12,786,800
7 – 9 (ages 12–14)	1,212,200	11,574,600	12,786,800
10 – 12 (ages 15–17)	1,196,200	11,732,400	12,928,600
College (ages 18–29)	549,062	14,261,781	14,810,843
University (ages 18–29)	822,722	—	822,722
Total	6,605,134	69,010,981	75,616,115

Source: Statistics Canada, Full-time and Part-time students, 1996. U.S. Bureau of the Census, December 28, 1998.

TABLE 2: Total Student Population with Internet Access, Canada and United States

Categories	Total Student Population With Internet Acess		
	Canada	USA	Total
K – 3 (ages 4–8)	437,860	8,737,688	9,175,548
4 – 6 (ages 9–11)	437,860	6,378,284	6,816,144
7 – 9 (ages 12–14)	715,198	6,018,792	6,733,990
10 – 12 (ages 15–17)	705,758	6,100,848	6,806,606
College (ages 18–29)	285,512	7,416,126	7,701,638
University (ages 18–29)	427,841)	—	427,841
Total	3,010,029	34,651,738	37,661,767

Source: Statistic Canada, Full-time and Part-time students, 1996. U.S. Bureau of the Census, December 28, 1998.

Jason and Krista also realized that there was potential outside the North American market. The number of Internet users around the world was constantly growing. The *Computer Industry Almanac* reported in 1999 that by the year 2002, 490 million people around the world would have Internet connections, that is 79.4 per 1,000 people worldwide. The top fifteen countries would account for nearly 82 percent of the worldwide Internet users (including business, education, and home Internet users). The *Computer Industry Almanac* also reported that in the year 2000, there would be twenty-five countries where over 10 percent of the population would be Internet users.

The two largest growth sectors on the Internet, according to Jupiter Communications, were kids and teens. Jason and Krista were very interested in this younger student market and planned to launch Junior High, Elementary, and Primary sections of the Web site to meet the needs of this segment. See Table 3 for information on the projected growth of kids and teens connected to the Internet. By 2002, Jupiter predicted teens will account for $1.2 billion and kids will account for $100 million of e-commerce dollars spent.

TABLE 3: Kids and Teens on the Internet, 1998 and 2002

	Kids and Teens on the Internet		
	1998	2002	% Increase
Kids	8.6 million	21.9 million	155
Teens	8.4 million	16.6 million	97

Source: Juptier Communications, 1999.
Note: Kids are ages 5–12. Teens are ages 13–18.

Globalstudent.com

Globalstudent.com was designed as a vertically integrated site dedicated to the student market. The concept of the Web site was an online community for students of all ages. The immediate focus of the site was the North American student market, but the long term goal was to meet the needs of students around the world. Globalstudent.com was designed to provide students with a vast number of free services to meet both their academic and entertainment needs. Such services included free e-mail and Web page account, chat, and online concerts. An educational search engine designed specifically for students doing research was also included. Students would be able to look for places to rent and could buy or sell used textbooks. Jason and Krista also planned to allow students to shop online using an e-commerce platform offered to retailers and manufacturers.

The Trasks hoped that Globalstudent.com's wide variety of services would make it the first site that students would visit for their online needs. They planned for Globalstudent.com to go beyond the norm and provide dynamic local content through its OrganizeIT™ technology. Through the use of this proprietary technology, users of the site would have access to information specific to their particular region and also have the ability to personalize the site, allowing them to receive only information they desired. Globalstudent.com's proprietary technology organized information for users based on their interests, location, and information requirements. The personalization process allowed the users to include information from their own or friends' Web sites, enabling a new dynamic of local content produced by a Web community that they lived in, knew of, and were part of.

Trading on the fact that students are constantly seeking opportunities to express themselves, Globalstudent.com was designed to facilitate this process and act as an intermediary. Through Globalstudent.com's proprietary content-organization technology (OrganizeIT™), students who aspired to be journalists, authors, photographers, and reporters had a unique venue to publish their work. In fall 2000 when the High School and Post-secondary segments of the Web site will be launched, registered students could establish a dynamic start page that included the content they choose to receive from students around the world or across the street. For example, a student could get an update on local sports scores from a student sports reporter, find out about local student business issues from a Junior Achievement member, or read a short story from a local creative writer.

Competition

Jason and Krista identified a number of direct competitors to Globalstudent.com. These competitors included:

1. Student.com
2. Funschool.com
3. Collegeclub.com
4. Studyabroad.com
5. Zapme.com
6. Gradeschool.com
7. Gocollege.com
8. Globalschoolhouse.com
9. Homeworkcentral.com
10. Studyweb.com

The Trasks concluded that none of the competitors had identical product breadth or depth to the Globalstudent.com Web site. To help develop their marketing strategy, what they needed was a detailed competitive analysis. This evaluation would reveal each competitor's strengths and weaknesses, as well as the site's differential and competitive advantages.

Jason and Krista were most concerned with the direct competition for the High School and Post-secondary sections of the site in the short term. However, they recognized that indirect competition existed from non-Internet based competitors who targeted students and from Internet-based competitors who did not necessarily target students, for example Yahoo! and Excite. They were certain these indirect competitors could not be ignored.

The Internet entrepreneurs were confident that at present there were no companies serving the entire student market as proposed by Globalstudent.com Inc. They were also confident that Globalstudent.com appeared to be the only site trying to fulfill both academic and social needs of students over an extended period of a student's life. While this demonstrated that Globalstudent.com was different, it did not ensure that the company would have sustainable competitive advantages. The Trasks realized their strategy must outline their sustainable advantages if they were to attract the needed investment and facilitate the long-term growth of the company.

Revenue

In the short term, Globalstudent.com Inc. had two main revenue streams: advertising and e-commerce. Interest in Internet advertising in 1998 showed a continued confidence in the advertising medium, according to an IAB Internet Advertising Revenue Report. This same report indicated that in the United States annual growth rates for Internet advertising far surpassed other media with a rate of 111.8 percent in 1998. In addition to advertising, Globalstudent.com planned to collect a transaction fee for allowing local retailers and manufacturers to set up an e-store using an e-commerce platform provided on the site.

There were a number of options available for advertising on the Internet. These include, but are not limited to, the following:

- Banner advertising
- Button advertising
- Customized advertising
- Run of site or fixed placement
- Sponsorship of content and/or events
- Advertorials, integrated features
- Product placement/sampling
- Contests and promotions
- Co-branded pages

The eAdvertising Report published by eMarketer revealed that banners accounted for 52 percent of all online ads placed in 1998, with sponsorships taking in 40 percent. The report predicted a shift in advertising dollars away from banners toward sponsorships. Sponsorships offered better targeting capabilities by allowing sponsors to integrate themselves within the content and services offered on the site.

In addition to the move toward sponsorships, leading marketers created a core interactive experience on their Web sites that pushed home the brand image one-to-one. This trend was labelled e-branding by *Advertising Age*. Globalstudent.com developed a proprietary technology called CustomAd™, which accomplished this exciting new form of advertising. With its interactive possibilities, the Web puts the onus on the marketer to build relationships with potential customers. The branding power of a site is based on its ability to engage users in repeated interactions. Potential customers must return again and again. Globalstudent.com Inc.'s CustomAd™ accomplished this by dynamically creating and targeting each advertisement to a specific individual.

Globalstudent.com's CustomAd™ allowed advertisers to produce personalized advertisements for each and every individual that viewed the ad. Through Globalstudent.com's ability to accumulate personal information about its users, CustomAd™ can personalize each ad to appeal to the exact personal profile of each user as specified by the advertising client. This was accomplished by loading all of the advertising client's products, spokespeople, promotions, and related content into the CustomAd™ technology. The client then identified the characteristics of the user being targeted and the CustomAD™ technology dynamically matched it to Globalstudent.com users.

Decision

Krista and Jason reviewed the fundamental elements of an effective marketing strategy that they had learned in their business degrees. "In order to obtain a clearer picture of our present situation we must define our goals and review the information on our markets, competitors and company," declared Jason. In the next two weeks we must have our marketing strategy on paper. This information will be critical to attract needed investment and successfully launch the High School and Post-secondary segments of the Web site in August 2000.

Copyright © 2000, Donna M. Stapleton. This case was prepared by Donna M. Stapleton, assistant professor of marketing at Memorial University of Newfoundland. The support of Jason and Krista Trask is gratefully acknowledged.

Questions

1. Describe the target market for the High School and Post-secondary segments of the Web site. How big is this market in North America? What share of market do you believe Globalstudent.com should aim to attract in its first year? How can Jason and Krista attract this market and drive users to the site? What can they do to encourage users to return again and again?

2. How should Globalstudent.com be positioned? How can Jason and Krista communicate this positioning strategy?

3. Complete a competitive analysis for the direct competitors of the High School and Post-secondary segments of the site. What are Globalstudent.com site's competitive advantages? Are these competitive advantages sustainable? Why or why not?

4. Explain how Jason and Krista can use each of the Internet advertising options identified in the case to generate revenue? What type of clients should be targeted to advertise on the site?

5. What types of retailers and manufacturers would be interested in the e-commerce opportunity on the site? Can Jason and Krista partner with existing e-stores to benefit Globalstudent.com? How might these partnerships work?

6. What are some additional ideas Jason and Krista can use to generate revenue in the short and long term?

7. Do you believe investors will be interested in supporting Globalstudent.com Inc.? Why or why not?

Case 6-2

ROYAL BANK OF CANADA (PART 1)

On July 20, 2000, RT Capital Management Inc., the pension investment arm of the Royal Bank of Canada, the country's largest bank, agreed to a package of terms set out by the Ontario Securities Commission, which included a series of stiff penalties and a $3 million fine for stock manipulation. RT Capital Management admitted that its employees manipulated stocks and that its senior managers and directors had not been adequately policing employee activities.

The Ontario Securities Commission (OSC) establishes and administers, in part and with the Toronto Stock Exchange, the regulatory framework in Ontario for the public reporting of financial information as well as the buying and selling of financial instruments (stocks, bonds, mutual funds and others). It also monitors the behaviour of buyers and sellers in the financial services market to see that regulations are complied with. The Commission had been investigating RT Capital for a year prior to making public its findings and entering into an agreement with the pension investment firm. RT Capital and the Royal Bank, by admitting that its employees had acted to manipulate stock prices and agreeing to the fines and other sanctions, thereby avoided a public trial where the details of its activities would be aired over an extended period of time, resulting in much more public damage to the RT and Royal Bank brand images.

Nine of RT Capital's portfolio managers, equity traders, and directors, including its president and chairman, were implicated in a scheme which artificially boosted the stock prices of twenty-six companies during eight days between October 1998 and March 1999. In addition to the fine, sanctions ranged from a one-month suspension to a lifetime ban on trading. The Royal Bank must also pay for the costs of the OSC investigation — $150,000.

In this instance, the price manipulation affected, most directly, the clients of RT Capital Management. The practice that was used to manipulate prices is called "high closing" or "juicing." The use of the prohibited activity is alleged to be well known and twenty cases of its use have been identified and dealt with by fines and suspensions by both the Toronto Stock Exchange and the Vancouver Stock Exchange between 1985 and 2000. It occurs when individual traders inflate, through the artificial buying and selling of shares, the end of day closing price for a stock. This activity misrepresents a stock's performance and value on or near key dates.

Since clients pay RT a regular fee for managing their funds based on the value of funds managed, the result is artificially higher fees to the clients based on artificially inflated values. Thus RT makes more in fees and looks as if it manages funds more effectively than if the practice had not been used. RT's manipulation of the prices of the stocks of the twenty-six companies boosted the value of these stocks in the RT portfolio (belonging to their clients) by $34 million. In other words, RT collected commissions on an extra $34 million that they did not legitimately earn. At the same time, the "high closing" also boosted the price of the stocks in the twenty-six companies outside the RT portfolio by a market value of $413 million.

RT clients, over seven hundred in total, are Canadian companies, governments, and other organizations who have pension or insurance funds (originally comprised of their own contributions as well as those of their employees or members). These groups need to have these funds invested and professionally managed in order to earn returns sufficient to cover the costs of paying the pensions of retired employees. Among the clients are Alcan Aluminum, Hudson's Bay Company, the Cities of Winnipeg and Toronto, the University of Western Ontario, Air Canada, Noranda, and the Provincial Government of Newfoundland. Also directly involved are a number of pension and investment consultants who advise their clients on which firms to make use of to manage their pension funds.

As the news of the results of the investigation by the OSC and admissions by the Royal Bank and RT Capital spread throughout the financial communities and the public, there appeared various reactions. Observers noted that clients of RT appear to be reacting in one or more ways:

- some have stopped transferring any new funds to the accounts managed by RT;
- others have decided that regardless of the price and fee manipulation, they are satisfied with the way their funds were being managed;
- still others are planning to withdraw their funds from RT management and move them to a competitor since they refuse to accept what has occurred;
- a number have demanded meetings with RT personnel to obtain specifics concerning how their business has been handled and what changes are planned;
- many are watching and waiting to see what will occur in terms of changes in RT's methods of operation and the recruitment of new personnel to replace those who have left or been banned from trading.

Commentators on financial markets as well as financial consultants have also adopted a number of positions. The views range from one extreme to another. "This happens all the time, no big fuss — not a serious infraction of the rules, not much money was involved." Others say: "This is the biggest scandal to hit financial markets in many years and will destroy buyers' confidence in funds managers of all types as well as brokers, all at a time when more and more people are turning to discount brokers or computer trading on their own and the industry is in danger of shrinking." This polarity of positions leaves room for concern about behavioural expectations within the industry. It is clear that ethical behaviour on the part of sellers is at issue as is the ability and willingness of buyers to have trust and confidence in the sellers.

The Royal Bank made two strategic moves as the news of the stock manipulation broke. The first was to take out advertisements in a number of national newspapers containing a very public and unprecedented apology from the president of the Royal Bank, John Cleghorn. The second was to appoint Michael Wilson, a former federal Minister of Finance and highly respected and experienced member of the financial community, as the new head of RT Capital. Mr. Wilson had been a very high profile member of government for several years and is sure to receive considerable media attention as he assumes this role.

Mr. Wilson must begin by determining the magnitude of the damage done to RT as well as to the Royal Bank of Canada, and some say the financial community in general. He must then determine what must be done to implement change within RT so that clients are assured and have trust and confidence in the fact that the financial services they are purchasing are of superior quality, fairly priced, and efficiently and ethically delivered.

Pertinent Web Sites

www.royalbank.com/rtcap
www.royalbank.ca
www.osc.gov.on.ca
www.tsc.com

Questions

1. Why would a regulatory body such as the OSC or the TSC make such an agreement with RT Capital instead of conducting a public trial and investigation of the events in question?

2. What public relations action, if any, should Mr. Wilson, RT Capital and/or the Royal Bank take at this time? What should be the objectives of such actions?

3. Which interest groups or "communities" are involved or should be involved in the issue inherent in this situation? What is the nature of their interest — purely ethical, a combination of ethical and competitive threat, or purely competitive and marketing oriented?

4. What kinds of messages and media, over what time frames, should be considered so as to deal with any issues that must be handled from a public relations perspective?

Sources: Dawn Walton, "Royal shifts into damage control," *Globe and Mail*, July 21, 2000, pp. B1, B4; Keith McArthur and Caroline Alphonso, "Reaction to resignations ranges from confidence to concern," ibid; Roma Luciw, "TSE mulls regulation overhaul," ibid, p. B4; Mathew Ingram, "RT Capital settlement is an abject failure," ibid; Guy Dixon and Caroline Alphonso, "Managers batten down hatches on policy, practices," ibid, p. B5; Theresa Tedesco, "RT settles scandal,' *Financial Post*, July 21, 2000, pp. C1, C5; Peter Fitzpatrick, "Wilson moves up to rebuild image at RT Capital," ibid, p. C4; Dawn Walton, "$3-million fine to fund education," *The Globe and Mail*, July 22, 2000, p. B4; Caroline Alphonso, "RT Capital advised to repair image, be open with customers," ibid.

Case 6-3

DRYEL: DO-IT-YOURSELF DRY CLEANING

In 1999, the retail dry cleaning industry in Canada was facing a new competitor. Procter & Gamble had just launched Dryel, a home dry cleaning kit that was described in product advertising as "a revolutionary new way to *clean and freshen* your 'Dry Clean Only' clothes *in your dryer*!" This isn't the first threat to challenge the established dry cleaning business in recent years. Canada's seven thousand retail dry cleaning establishments, which ring up annual sales of approximately $1.2 billion, had already been dealing with a down turn in business since the mid-1990s when Canadians started wearing more casual clothing to work, thereby reducing the need for dry cleaning. In addition, the industry in North America has come under some criticism from environmentalists who have pointed to the possible health hazards associated with the chemicals used in the dry cleaning process.

In mid-1999, Procter & Gamble took direct aim at the $13 billion North American dry cleaning business with the launch of Dryel. The product had been in test market in Columbus, Ohio for the past year and had met with some market acceptance. It was now being rolled out to the North American market with supporting advertising claims that the dry cleaning industry considered misleading.

Dryel is described by Procter & Gamble as a fabric care system that works in a home clothes dryer. The principal focus of media advertising supporting the launch was that the product allows consumers to care for their "Dry Clean Only" garments at home. It comes in a kit that sells in Canada for $16.99 and allows the consumer to do four dryer loads of home cleaning — a total of 16 garments. Each kit contains an instruction pamphlet, a bottle of stain remover, four absorbent pads, four pre-moistened, dryer-activated cloths, and a reusable Dryel bag.

The home dry cleaner first checks the garments to be cleaned for spots and applies the Dryel stain remover to the affected areas, using the absorbent pads. Then one to four garments are placed in the Dryel bag with a single pre-moistened cloth. The bag is put in the home clothes dryer at medium to high heat for 30 minutes, at which time the garments can be removed and hung to allow wrinkles to fall out. Instructions do indicate that garments may require some ironing. The cloth is then thrown away and the bag may be reused up to twenty times. Procter & Gamble warns that the Dryel system should not be used for leather, suede, or fur garments — indicating that these should be dry cleaned by a professional who specializes in their care.

The launch of Dryel was but one component in a new product development strategy of Procter & Gamble. The company had made a commitment to launch more new products and to get them to market faster than they had been able to do in the past. This was designed to inject some competitive edge in a company that had become famous for brands such as Pampers, Crest, and Tide, but is considered by some to have become complacent in recent years, slow to react to consumer trends and competitive innovations. With a US$1.2 billion research and development budget and seven thousand scientists committed to new product development, the company expects to launch many more new products in the coming years. In so doing, the company was branching out somewhat from its traditional lines of business and creating not only new products but entire new categories.

In addition to Dryel, P&G launched in 1999 its new home spray product, Febreze, designed to freshen and deodorize clothing and other fabrics. Swiffer, an electrostatic mop with a disposable cloth intended for dusting dry surfaces, and a new line of Oil of Olay cosmetics, were the other additions to the P&G lineup in Canada. To support the launch, P&G committed an advertising and promotion budget of $60 million for the first year.

In keeping with Procter & Gamble's new commitment to bring products to market faster, Dryel was launched in the North American market after less than eighteen months in test market, as compared with as long as five years in test market for innovations in the past before they were considered ready for national rollout. The test market had been conducted in Columbus, Ohio, where results tended to indicate that sales by conventional dry cleaners had dropped slightly during the test. During the test, P&G employed such marketing tactics as placing the corporate brand on the front of the package, and merchandising the product in department stores. It was supported by an array of advertising in conventional media, including radio, TV, print and outdoor. Demonstrations were held in women's clothing departments of Columbus-area stores, and direct mail coupons and sampling was used.

About 150,000 Columbus households had bought Dryel during the test period. Research during the test indicated that about half of those who had used Dryel regularly indicated that they had purchased at least one new "dry clean only" clothing item and three-quarters said they wear their dry clean only clothing more often.

Test results were sufficiently promising that P&G decided to launch Dryel in the U.S. and Canada in mid-1999 after a test market period that was short by P&G standards. The launch in Canada was supported by a budget that allowed for the same types of advertising and promotion that had been used in the test market. In addition, P&G were successful in receiving the Woolmark and Good Housekeeping seals of approval. In 2000, Good Housekeeping also awarded the product one of their "Good Buy" awards. The company set a sales target of $150 million for the four new products.

The reaction of the retail dry cleaning industry to the introduction of Dryel was mixed. While some dry cleaners experienced no noticeable change in their volume of business, and even suggested that the new product's availability has the potential to actually increase their business, others were not so sure. Not all dry cleaners were negative toward the new product. One British Columbia dry cleaner, Charlotte Morton, who also happens to be director of the B.C. Fabricare Association, thinks Dryel is a good product for travelling, and concludes that it does a fair job of getting stains out. She is one who thinks it may have the potential to increase her business by encouraging some customers to actually buy more dry clean only clothing.

Many professional dry cleaners accused Procter & Gamble of misleading advertising. The International Fabricare Institute in the U.S. even filed a letter of complaint with the Federal Trade Commission, alleging that P&G had made false and deceptive claims in advising consumers to disregard "dry clean only" label instructions.

Procter & Gamble countered that it has never portrayed Dryel as a substitute for dry cleaning. Company spokesperson Win Sakdinan indicated that Dryel marketing is not intended to suggest that the product is a substitute for professional care, but a quick, convenient, and economical way for consumers to extend the wearing time of garments between trips to the dry cleaner. He suggests that the product works best on small stains such as coffee, ink and makeup, and on eliminating odours.

One Toronto-area dry cleaner, Shan Lakhani, general manager of Parkers Custom Clothing Care which operates nine outlets in Toronto, was so angered by what he considers to be Dryel's misleading advertising that he issued a press release warning that the product does not restore creases or remove oil-based stains. He indicates that some of his customers had asked his company to remove stains from clothing that had been treated with Dryel.

It was not only the dry cleaning industry that reacted negatively to the introduction of Dryel; the media also got in on the act. The CBC television program, *Marketplace*, engaged the services of Edith Strasser, a professor of fabric science in the fashion management department of George Brown College to evaluate the product. Professor Strasser's conclusion was that Dryel partially removed some stains, but for the most part stains still remained after the Dryel procedure. The garments did look and feel fresher, but the stains remained. She concluded "I guess for stains as deep as that you're better off to go to a professional dry cleaner, so this is not a replacement for dry cleaning, no. It is OK to freshen things a bit, but for real dry cleaning and any stains, it has to go to the dry cleaners."

The CBC children's program. *Street Cents*, also concluded that Dryel did not remove stains, but rather made clothing "stink like an air freshener." It relegated the product to its "Pit."

Meanwhile, by September 2000, Procter & Gamble was rethinking somewhat its marketing strategy for Dryel, by designing in-store demonstrations to teach customers how to use the product after research showed that many customers who had bought the product had never tried it at home.

Pertinent Web Site
www.dryel.com

Questions

1.   Discuss the consumer psychology associated with dry cleaning? What does a customer look for in dry cleaning and in a dry cleaner? How does a customer know when an item is "clean"? Why do only 20 percent of Canadians use dry cleaners?

2.   What customer needs does Dryel address? How does Dryel create value for the customer? To whom will Dryel likely appeal? How will customers evaluate its performance and the value it creates?

3.   How should Procter & Gamble respond to the charges levelled against Dryel by the dry cleaning industry and by the media?

4.   How should Canadian dry cleaners respond at the customer level to the introduction of Dryel?

Sources: Emily Nelson, "Rehab takes toll on Procter & Gamble," *The Globe and Mail*, September 1, 2000, p. M2; *CBC Marketplace*, "Putting Dryel to the Test," November 2, 1999; Marina Strauss, "Dry cleaners riled by product spin," *The Globe and Mail*, January 21, 2000, p. M1; "Procter and Gamble to lay out new streamlined strategy," *Financial Post*, June 5, 1999, p. D9; "Then latest in breakthrough products?" *Canadian Grocer*, vol. 113, no. 6, June 1999, p. 11; Paul Brent, "Procter & Gamble turns over new leaf; launches four products," *Financial Post*, May 18, 1999, p. C4; Maedhavi Acharya, "Here's the dirt: Dry cleaning comes home," *Toronto Star*, May 18, 1999, p. C4;

Part seven

Managing the Marketing Effort

Evaluating a company's marketing performance, reviewing the role of marketing in society, and considering where marketing is heading in the future.

Up to this point, we have dealt separately with how a firm selects its target markets and then develops and manages the elements of its marketing strategy for those markets. In the first part of Chapter 21, we bring those separate areas together as we present an overview of an organization's marketing plan and a discussion of implementation and evaluation. This discussion follows from the strategic planning stage introduced in Chapter 3. Then, we review the current position of marketing in our society, examine how various organizations have responded to the changing face of marketing, and consider where marketing is headed in the future.

Chapter Twenty-One

Marketing: Its Performance and Its Future

In this chapter, we discuss the implementation and evaluation of a marketing program. **Implementation** is the operational stage — the stage during which an organization attempts to carry out its strategic plan. At the end of an operating period (or even during the period), management should conduct an **evaluation** of the organization's performance. This stage involves determining how well the organization is achieving the goals set in its strategic planning.

We also address a number of criticisms of marketing and responses to these criticisms. Then we conclude our discussion of marketing by looking into the crystal ball and considering some prospects for the future that are certain to provide the inspiration for responses such as those illustrated in the opening pages of this chapter.

After studying this chapter, you should have an understanding of:

◆ The role of implementation in the management process.

◆ Postsale service and its contribution to customer satisfaction.

◆ A societal perspective for evaluating marketing performance.

◆ Some criticisms of marketing.

◆ Consumer, government, and business responses to consumer discontent.

◆ The ethical responsibilities of marketers.

◆ Trends influencing future marketing activity.

◆ Some strategic adjustments necessary to cope with change.

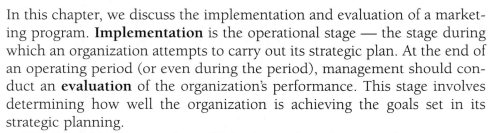

Changing With the Times

All organizations, large and small, businesses and not-for-profits, manufacturers and retailers, must continue to change if they are to keep up to date with the changes that are going on around them, and if they are to remain relevant and attractive to the customers and clients they serve. An excellent example of a changing marketplace and the demands it is placing on companies that operate therein is the North American automobile industry.

For many years now the "Big Three" — General Motors, Ford Motor Company, and Daimler Chrysler have battled to regain dominance of the North American car market. They have recovered much ground but the battle is far from over as more foreign manufacturers enter this market such as Korean producers Daewoo and Kia. No longer content to offer entry-level vehicles, many of the foreign companies now compete in all vehicle classes from SUV to high-end luxury.

But, while increasing model competition has been the most obvious concern, it's not been the only cause for concern. Other, more subtle changes have been bringing about demands that require the Big Three to change completely the way they do business.

The implications for product design, distribution, and customer service have been dramatic. Perhaps the greatest impact has been that of technology. Perhaps the most surprising change has been that these rivals have determined that they have more to gain than lose by working together to harness the potential the Internet promises their industry.

This unprecedented move will be watched closely to see if these manufacturers can successfully develop and operate a completely integrated marketing model utilizing Internet technology. If they can create an Internet supply chain that produces seamless links from the suppliers to its final consumers, they will have revolutionized auto marketing. Such success would serve as a model for countless other industries in transforming the Internet from a concept with great business potential to a reality.

Technology has long been the buzzword in the auto industry from sharing data (EDI) to just-in-time delivery and despite the considerable efficiencies and improvements that have resulted, there is still much that can be accomplished.

Despite evolving efficiencies in this industry, it can still be impossible for a dealer to find available the product a customer requests despite an average of US$60 million of assembled inventory at any given point in time for each of these companies. This means a customer often settles for a car that he or she does not really want, decides on another brand, or

submits an order and yet another vehicle is produced requiring the customer to wait about two months for the special-ordered car! This leaves yet one more car on a lot somewhere to be discounted at a later date. Despite many efforts to tinker with the process, this is as good as it gets!

Ultimately, the consumer will be able to configure his or her exact specifications on the Internet. With that final click of the mouse, information will go to all the suppliers that provide each component, the factory that will assemble it, the finance unit will be notified to underwrite it, and the dealer who will deliver it. As well, this information is available for market research and future model designs. The goal is a completely integrated effort that will bring the industry as close to a one-on-one marketing system as is currently possible.

A lot has to change before it will become this easy to serve the consumer's needs. While the beginnings have been laid, many fundamentals in the industry will have to move into the information age. Cars must continue to become easier to build through the development of module or component systems; all carmakers, suppliers, and consumers would have to be linked through the Internet, and shipping must become more efficient.

As discussed earlier in this text, both General Motors and Ford have established online business-to-business supply networks and will move the ordering of all parts to the Internet by the end of 2001. These provide a link between the manufacturer, suppliers, and dealers. In early 2000 a bombshell was dropped when it was announced that these two makers would join with Daimler Chrysler to form another company similar in concept to GM's TradeXchange and Ford's AutoXchange. It will be operated independently from the automakers and other car companies will be invited to join the system.

What is it the Internet has to offer that has these companies developing such unprecedented friendships? Well, each firm has about thirty thousand suppliers, translating to over US$80 billion a year in goods and services for each company. Going online with these transactions can save money in two ways. Reverse auctions mean decreasing bids thereby reducing component costs, and consolidating purchases secures better prices. Ford estimates that it will be able to save US$8 billion through this new supply chain. Further, the efficiency of Internet transactions reduces processing time and costs. This reduction in administration and paper trails could result in an additional $1 billion in savings a year.

Charging users a service fee for using the system can also generate revenue. This has been estimated to generate $1 to $3 billion in the first year alone. As more and more consumers utilize the Internet, the need for inventory on dealers' lots would be reduced considerably and fewer units would be sold at discounted prices. Consumers will be providing high quality marketing information, receiving products that are better matched to their wants, and those that would have had to special order units will get their cars sooner as the system is developed.

The move by these manufacturers to the Internet ensures that all others will join, either this network or independently, or otherwise risk considerable competitive disadvantage. The consolidation of the three companies to one system will encourage suppliers to deal with this network and reduce concerns of having to operate on multiple channels. It also brings closer the ultimate vision of the industry's future. Suppliers will also be able to utilize the system to make purchases and sell excess inventory.

Dealers feel threatened as until now Web inquiries have been passed on to local dealers. The establishment of this infrastructure has caused dealers to be wary that their roles will be decreased in the near future. Some observers predict a time when cars will be custom-designed and purchased on the Web by consumers who will know the price of every component in advance. Haggling and negotiating will no longer exist. The entire process will be routinely conducted through a series of mouse clicks. The role of dealers may be little more than to provide test-drives and serve as a point of delivery.

Initially, consumers may benefit from the firm's ability to reduce costs through reduced or static pricing. But how will they react to broader Internet applications? How many will buy over the Internet? Will consumers add options such as e-mail, satellite-linked phones, navigation systems, and Web access from the car, along with the $10 to $30 monthly fees they will require? Consumers have shown little interest in establishing relationships with dealers, yet most do find comfort in the fact that if something goes wrong with such an expensive and complicated product, that the seller is nearby.

Will the auto industry move into cyberspace? It seems certain that it will, although there will be many hurdles. First the industry must make the Internet an effective and efficient supply chain. This will also involve dealing with the ramifications of such a move for suppliers and labour unions in response to assembly changes. It's difficult to tell at this stage if there will be any big winners, but those that sit on the sidelines while the rest of the supply chain goes online will most assuredly end up as the losers.

It cannot be predicted with assurance where technology will ultimately lead auto manufacturers, but it is clear that today's technology, and that which will evolve from it, will be an integral component of every facet of auto marketing in the future. Also, that its use in such an industry will serve to ensure that it is adopted by many other industries.[1]

Implementation in Marketing Management

There should be a close relationship among planning, implementation, and evaluation. Without strategic planning, a company's operational activities — its implementation tactics — can go off in any direction, like an unguided missile. Good planning cannot overcome poor implementation. But effective implementation often can overcome poor planning.

For example, Holt Renfrew & Company (www.holtrenfrew.com) has implemented a strong push to reposition itself with younger, more professionally-oriented consumer segments thereby shaking off its image of catering to the gray-haired elite and fur-clad dowager set. This has included greatly increasing the selection of private-label products offered. It has also developed a concierge program to serve as "an integrated lifestyles solution" for the time-starved customer. The service can make travel plans, arrange event tickets, hire a babysitter, and even arrange for personal shopping. To assist in putting this strategy in place, the company uses its Club Select loyalty program, which rewards buyers who use the Holt Renfrew charge card. The retailer has added direct mail to its arsenal of tools as well as redesigning and renaming its magazine/catalogue — now simply called *Holt's*. There are no longer official ads in the publication, but instead product presentations prepared especially for this showcase. Editorial content is included with the intent to entertain and inform. Without traditional advertising, the magazine has shrunk to fewer than one hundred pages compared to over two hundred pages in the old format. Holt Renfrew has stepped up in-store events and subscribes to the view that retail is entertainment. To expand its e-presence, the company has also teamed up with other e-retailers, such as Indigo (www.indigo.ca) to offer exclusive discounts over the Net. Stores also feature "comfort zones" to take time out from a hectic schedule to rest or make phone calls.[2]

Implementation comprises three activities:

1. *Organizing the marketing effort.* Once a company has developed its strategic marketing plan, an early activity is to organize the people who will implement it. The relationship between marketing and the other functional divisions of the firm must be defined. Then, within the marketing department, management must design an organization that will implement both strategies and tactics.

2. *Staffing the organization.* For plans to produce an intended result, an organization needs skilled, dedicated people to carry them out well. Thus, selection of people is very important. Organizations are beginning to rediscover the importance of the people who make up the firm.

    A sales manager's success depends greatly on the people whom the manager selects. The success of relationship marketing programs rests substantially on the sales force as the key implementers of strategies and tactics.

3. *Directing the execution of marketing plans.* In this third phase of implementation, revenues are generated. To do so, management needs to direct the work of the people who have been selected and organized as the company's marketing team. Success in this phase depends on four important aspects of managing employees — delegation, co-ordination, motivation, and communication.

Marketing at Work 21-1

Changing Minds to Rebuild Business: What it Takes to Implement

When you do business in a hard-nosed way, and everybody knows it, and your potential clients don't appreciate it, you have to change how you do business, how you implement. And that's what happened to one of Canada's biggest building contractors, the Ellis-Don company.

Two years ago the construction industry finally came out of a prolonged slump that had begun in the early 1990s. Before the recession in building, the London, Ontario-based company had over $850 million in projects ranging from work at Canary Wharf in the U.K. to the Canada Pavilion for Expo '86 in Vancouver to the Toronto Skydome. But when things turned difficult, those who wanted to survive also got tough. Ellis-Don initiated a hard-nosed system of lump-sum tenders for work. Whereas before there had been growing collaboration between builders and clients, relationships turned adversarial as builders and clients tried to cut costs. While implementing in this fashion carries you through the hard times, for Ellis-Don it meant that when industry conditions improved, it was viewed by potential clients as capable but hard to do business with, egotistical, and hard on subcontractors. Having this kind of brand image is fine — as long as that's what clients want and need.

As the building business recovered, it became clear to Ellis-Don president Geoff Smith that the needs of clients had changed. During the tough times, and in order to cut costs, many had downsized and eliminated their own specialists and experts. Clients now wanted different kinds of help from con-

tractors. But the people at Ellis-Don had just spent 8–10 years being tough just to keep going and now they weren't picking up on the changes in the market. Geoff Smith and Toronto area marketing manager Lynda Stewart believed that the firm had to change its psychology — its implementation style. Ellis-Don wanted to be seen not as a hard-nosed company but one that is professional, is populated with capable listeners who consider client priorities, and who treat subcontractors like customers.

To get this done, a series of programs termed "Client First" were developed. The first step was to ensure that employees understood the changes that were taking place in the market and how these affected them. A seminar series was developed and employees ranging from construction superintendents to inside workers gladly attended.

Session topics ranged from etiquette — learning how to handle situations correctly — to thinking styles — helping technical people understand how others approach problems. Mr. Smith also decided to gradually make the company employee-owned and developed a program for giving out company shares (45 percent of the new shares) to long term workers so that the idea of a productive career would replace the hard driving "train and then leave" approach of the past.

Two years of "client first" oriented implementation has been noticed: Ellis-Don is now seen as not the old-era lean and mean contractor but as customer-focused. And while Mr. Smith accepts that construction will always have its ups and downs, one thing that he says won't happen in lean times is the cutting out of training, career development, and communication.

Source: Adapted from Margot Gibb-Clark, "Ellis-Don rebuilds how it does business," *The Globe and Mail*, May 1, 2000, p. M1.

Organizing for Implementation

Organizational structures are receiving increasing attention in companies around the globe as management recognizes that yesterday's structures may hinder operations in today's dynamic environment. Satisfying customers profitably requires talking to them — and listening carefully to what they have to say. Teamwork across functions such as marketing and production is also essential. Traditional organizational structures, however, isolate different functions and have many managerial layers between customers and decision-makers. Recognizing this, large organizations such as the "Big Three" North American automakers, have made significant organizational changes in recent years.

In a very real sense, traditional vertical structures are being replaced by horizontal organizations.[3] Several specific trends are noteworthy:

◆ *Fewer organizational levels.* The intent is to facilitate communication among executives who develop the strategic plans, the employees who have continuing contact with the market, and the firm's customers.

◆ *Employee empowerment.* Granting more authority to middle-level executives in decentralized locations can stimulate innovation and generate faster responses to market shifts. Empowering customer-contact personnel can boost both customer satisfaction and repeat business. With that in mind, the Ritz-Carlton hotel chain allows any employee who hears that a customer has a problem to spend up to $2,000 trying to rectify that problem for the guest.[4]

◆ *Cross-functional teams.* By having personnel from various departments work on a project, not only are barriers among functions broken down, but the best combination of expertise and experience can be focused on the assignment. Empowering cross-functional teams is a recommended approach for developing new products, particularly in high technology industries.[5]

These trends show that firms today demand an organizational flexibility to respond quickly in a dynamic, information-driven marketing environment characterized by diversity and turbulence. Undoubtedly, new organizational structures will continue to emerge in response to changing environments.

🖋 *Postsale Follow-Through*

warranty
An assurance given to buyers that they will be compensated in case the product does not perform up to reasonable expectations.

express warranty
A statement in written or spoken words regarding restitution from seller to customer if the seller's product does not perform up to reasonable expectations.

implied warranty
An intended but unstated assurance regarding restitution from seller to customer if the seller's product does not perform up to reasonable expectations.

product-liability claim
A legal action alleging that an illness, accident, or death resulted from the named product because it was harmful, faulty, or inadequately labelled.

As already stated, marketing does not end when a sale is made. Some specific elements of a marketing program are implemented largely after a sale is made: Customer satisfaction as well as future revenues require that a company provide its customers with suitable warranties and other desired postsale services. Thus we will now consider important aspects of each of these marketing activities.

WARRANTIES The purpose of a **warranty**, which we use interchangeably with *guarantee*, is to assure buyers they will be compensated if the product does not perform up to reasonable expectations. In North America, companies decide on the terms and length of their product warranties. In contrast, the fifteen countries comprising the European Union agreed jointly that the length of guarantees must be at least two years.

Years ago, courts seemed to recognize only an **express warranty** — one stated in written or spoken words. Usually this form of reassurance was quite limited in its coverage and seemed mainly to protect the seller from buyers' claims. As a result, the following caution was appropriate: "Caveat emptor," which means, "Let the buyer beware."

But times change! Consumer complaints led to governmental campaigns to protect the consumer in many areas, including product warranties. Courts and government agencies have broadened the scope of warranty coverage by recognizing **implied warranty**. This means a warranty was *intended*, although not actually stated, by the seller. Furthermore, producers are being held responsible, even when the sales contract is between the retailer and the consumer.

PRODUCT LIABILITY A legal action asserting that an illness, accident, or death resulted from a specific product because it was harmful, faulty, or inadequately labelled is called **product liability**. Basically, liability results from one or more of three problems:

a flaw in the product design, a defect in production, or a deficiency in warning the customer about proper use and potentially harmful misuse of the product.

Many product liability claims involving entire categories of goods have been filed in the past ten or more years. Courts in the U.S. have been notorious for awarding large amounts in damages to consumer claimants. Canadian courts have been much more conservative in their approach. The real issue is that firms assure that products are properly tested in realistic use situations, that they know how products are perceived, how they are used, and what information and safeguards consumers need in order to not come to harm.

BENEFITS VERSUS COSTS Warranties can be costly if numerous buyers must be compensated when a product fails or is not satisfying. On the other hand, deficient warranties and warning labels that do not protect companies from product-liability claims can also be very expensive.

Rather than considering only costs, some organizations see marketing benefits in their warranties. Many sellers, for example, use their warranties as promotional devices to stimulate first-time and repeat purchases by reducing consumers' risks. With this in mind, more companies are making their warranties understandable and comprehensive — and, therefore, customer-friendly. Others are extending the length of the warranty period for their products. In 2000, Honda Canada (www.honda.ca) offered a five year/100,000 kilometre "No Nonsense Warranty" on its vehicles. As well, further periods are offered on specific components of vehicles. The company believes its coverage remains a "benchmark in customer protection and owner satisfaction."[6]

It is common practice among manufacturers, retailers, and especially service firms to offer a full refund of the purchase price to a dissatisfied buyer. For decades, L.L. Bean (www.llbean.com), which sells outdoors clothing and related gear through catalogues and now online, has offered an unconditional guarantee: "If at any time you are not completely satisfied, return the product for a full refund or exchange." Occasionally, a customer may abuse a full-refund guarantee (by returning a worn-out jacket, for example), but the benefits in terms of avoiding customer dissatisfaction and building customer loyalty are compelling. Such a promise, and the resultant reputation it develops, allows consumers to feel much more at ease with that retailer, thereby increasing overall sales by an amount that far exceeds the costs of occasional abuses.

It is evident that customer-friendly warranties are vital in the online environment. Remember that an Internet-only retailer really can only rely on their "brand" for their reputation and in this medium issues around efficient shipping, guarantees and return policies are the primary basis of this "brand." According to one study, offering a money-back guarantee is the biggest step an Internet merchant can take in order to reduce the risk that consumers associate with online shopping. In mid-1999, after numerous fulfilment problems in prior months, Shopping.com (altavista.shopping.com) tried to improve its image by instituting a "125 percent satisfaction guaranteed" program, meaning that any disgruntled customer would be refunded the full purchase price plus an added 25 percent. Such assurances go a long way toward reassuring potential customers that they are not taking any risk doing business with this retailer or service provider.

Honda warranty periods for components.

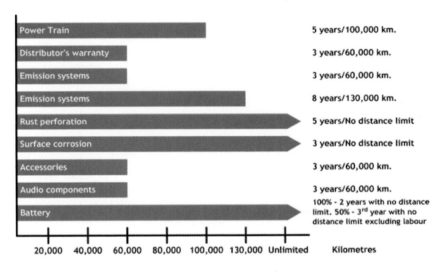

HONDA 2000 Warranty Coverage

The Honda Five Year/100,000 Km No Nonsense Warranty set a new industry standard when it was introduced. Today, it continues to be a benchmark in customer protection and owner satisfaction.

The warranty information you'll find in this section covers all new Honda automobiles manufactured by Honda Motor Company Ltd., sold by authorized Honda automobile dealers within Canada, and normally operated within Canada.

In addition to the Honda Five Year/100,000 Km No Nonsense Warranty, you and your new Honda are also protected by an additional series of warranties for such items as emission controls, body corrosion and more.

For specific details, check the warranty booklet that came with your Honda, or call 1-888-9HONDA9 or the Honda dealer nearest you.

Honda Elevates Your Comfort Quotient

Power Train	5 years/100,000 km.
Distributor's warranty	3 years/60,000 km.
Emission systems	3 years/60,000 km.
Emission systems	8 years/130,000 km.
Rust perforation	5 years/No distance limit
Surface corrosion	3 years/No distance limit
Accessories	3 years/60,000 km.
Audio components	3 years/60,000 km.
Battery	100% - 2 years with no distance limit. 50% - 3rd year with no distance limit excluding labour

20,000 40,000 60,000 80,000 100,000 130,000 Unlimited   **Kilometres**

Note: The owner of the vehicle is responsible to report to an authorized Honda dealer in Canada any items which they feel are defective, and request warranty coverage, if applicable, within the terms of the warranty. The vehicle must be made available to the dealer for warranty repairs within the warranty period.

 *Postsale Service*

postsale activity or service
The final stage of the selling process, including delivery, financing, installation, routine maintenance, employee training, billing, and other areas important to customer satisfaction.

Many companies have to provide **postsale service**, notably maintenance and repairs, to fulfil the terms of their warranties. Other firms offer postsale services to gain a differential advantage over competitors, or at least to fully satisfy their customers. Some businesses use postsale services to augment their revenues. For instance, retailers of appliances and high-tech equipment place great emphasis on offering complete range of service during the initial warranty period allowing them to offer for sale extended service contracts. Although these come with a fee, many such products are otherwise expensive to repair, require on-site repairs, and are too specialized for the layman to repair. Sears (www.sears.ca) has long offered these contracts on all their appliance and electronic purchases. The store's reputation for quick and expert service allows them to generate much additional revenue from sales of such contracts. Future Shop (www.futureshop.ca) and Staples/Business Depot (www.staples.ca) feature separate service counters and staff for service queries as well as offer extended service contracts for their electronics and computer equipment.

With the huge increase in complex products coming to market, increasingly demanding and vocal consumers, and now the Internet environment, postsale service has become essential. There are distinctive challenges, however, in attaining both efficiency and effectiveness when providing such services.

MERCHANDISE RETURNS Occasionally, some customers want or need to return their purchases. Thus a firm needs to consider how stringent or generous its conditions for accepting merchandise returns should be. Stringent conditions may curtail costs but are unlikely to gain favour with customers; the opposite is true for generous conditions.

Merchants that sell through an Internet site and also operate retail stores, such as HMV (www.hmv.ca), Eddie Bauer (www.eddiebauer.ca), etc, or wholesale branches face the decision of whether or not to accept returns of Internet purchases at the physical outlets. Most retailers either accept returns at their stores or are preparing to do so. If a firm prohibits its bricks-and-mortar outlets from accepting returns of online purchases, it forfeits a built-in advantage it has over online only competitors. Companies that only sell online are discovering that making the return process convenient for customers is a special challenge. Typically, customers are asked to send the returns to a warehouse or office operated by the company or to a separate business that handles fulfilment of orders for the online firm. Based on its studies, a research agency recommended that one of the top three ways of improving online service is to establish a simple return process. But that is often easier said than done.[7]

COMPLAINT HANDLING The most common complaints among consumers, as determined by one study, are deficient product quality, deceptive sales methods, and poor repair work. Consumers become even more frustrated if they cannot voice their complaints and get their problems solved. According to research, "A majority of consumers are dissatisfied with the way their complaints are resolved."[8] Ignored or mishandled complaints can have dire consequences with respect to lost business and negative word-of-mouth communication.

Prompt, effective handling of complaints can increase or, if necessary, restore a customer's confidence in a firm, regardless of whether it operates in physical space or cyberspace. Holiday Inn posts its 800 number in each room, in case guests aren't satisfied by a call to the front desk. A toll-free line for complaints apparently is a wise move. Research indicates that about 85 percent of phoned-in complaints are satisfied in a single call; less than 35 percent of complaints conveyed by e-mail or another electronic means are resolved so readily.[9]

Postsale follow-through, like other more visible elements of the marketing mix, can be either a differential advantage or a disadvantage for an organization. Thus the various forms of follow-through certainly should be on the list of matters managers need to constantly heed.

Evaluating Marketing Performance

Soon after a firm's plans have been set in operation, the process of evaluation should begin. Without evaluation, management cannot tell whether a plan is working and what factors are contributing to its success or failure. Evaluation logically follows planning and implementation. A circular relationship exists, as illustrated in Figure 21-1. Plans are made, they are put into action, the results of those actions are evaluated, and new plans are prepared on the basis of this evaluation.

Previously we discussed evaluation as it relates to individual parts of a marketing program — the product-planning process, the performance of the sales force, and the effectiveness of the advertising program, for instance. Now let's look at the evaluation of the total marketing effort.

The Marketing Audit: A Total Evaluation Program

A **marketing audit** is an essential element in a total evaluation program. An audit implies a review and evaluation of some activity. Thus, a marketing audit is a comprehensive review and evaluation of the marketing function in an organization — its philosophy, environment, goals, strategies, organizational structure, human and financial resources, and performance.

It's true that a marketing audit involves evaluation. But it is much more than that. In advocating the value of marketing audits in the banking industry, one writer stressed, "Simply stated, a strategic marketing plan should only be written after completion of an intensive, objective, marketing audit."[10]

A complete marketing audit is an extensive and difficult project. That's why it is conducted infrequently — perhaps every two or three years. However, a company should not delay a marketing audit until a major crisis arises.

The rewards of a marketing audit can be great. Management can identify problem areas in marketing. By reviewing its strategies, the firm is likely to keep abreast of its changing marketing environment. Successes can also be analyzed so that the company can capitalize on its strong points. The audit can spot lack of co-ordination in the marketing program, outdated strategies, or unrealistic goals. Furthermore, an audit should anticipate future situations. It is intended for "prognosis as well as diagnosis.... It is the practice of preventive as well as curative marketing medicine."[11]

Misdirected Marketing Effort

One of the benefits of evaluation is that it helps correct **misdirected** (or misplaced) **marketing effort**.

THE 80–20 PRINCIPLE In most firms, a large proportion of the total orders, customers, territories, or products accounts for only a small share of total sales or profit. Conversely, a small proportion produces a large share of sales or profit. This relationship has been characterized as the **80–20 principle**. That is, 80 percent of the orders, customers, territories, or products contribute only 20 percent of sales or profit. On the other hand, 20 percent of these selling units account for 80 percent of the volume or profit. We use the 80–20 figure simply to highlight the misplacement of marketing effort. In reality, of course, the percentage split varies from one situation to another.

REASONS FOR MISDIRECTED MARKETING EFFORT Frequently, executives cannot uncover their misdirected effort because they lack sufficient information. The **iceberg principle** is an analogy that illustrates this situation. Only a small part

marketing audit A comprehensive review and evaluation of the marketing function in an organization — its philosophy, environment, goals, strategies, organizational structure, human and financial resources, and performance.

80–20 principle A situation in which a large proportion of a company's marketing units (products, territories, customers) accounts for a small share of the company's volume or profit, and vice versa.

iceberg principle A concept related to performance evaluation stating that the summary data (tip of the iceberg) regarding an activity may hide significant variations among segments of this activity.

FIGURE 21-1 The Circular Relationship among Management Tasks

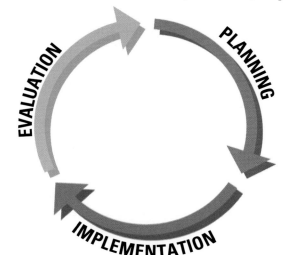

of an iceberg is visible above the surface of the water, and the submerged 90 percent is the dangerous part. The figures representing total sales or total costs on an operating statement are like the visible part of an iceberg. The detailed figures representing sales, costs, and other performance measures for each territory or product correspond to the dangerous submerged segment.

Total sales or cost figures are too general to be useful in evaluation; in fact, they often are misleading. A company may show satisfactory overall sales and profit figures. But when these totals are subdivided by territory or products, serious weaknesses often are discovered. A manufacturer of audio equipment showed an overall annual increase of 12 percent in sales and 9 percent in net profit on one product line one year. But management wasn't satisfied with this "tip of the iceberg." When it analyzed the figures more closely, it found that the sales change within territories ranged from an increase of 19 percent to a decrease of 3 percent. In some territories, profit increased as much as 14 percent, and in others it was down 20 percent.

A more basic cause of misplaced marketing effort is that executives must make decisions based on inadequate knowledge of the exact nature of marketing costs. In other words, management often lacks knowledge of: (a) the disproportionate spread of marketing effort; (b) reliable standards for determining what should be spent on marketing; and (c) what results should be expected from these expenditures.

As an illustration, a company may spend $250,000 more on advertising this year than last year. But management ordinarily cannot state what the resultant increase in sales volume or profit should be. Nor do the executives know what would have happened if they had spent the same amount on (a) new-product development, (b) management training seminars for sales staff or intermediaries, or (c) some other aspect of the marketing program.

🖋 *Evaluating Marketing*

Before we can begin to appraise marketing, we have to agree on a **basis for evaluating performance** — what the objective of marketing should be. In our discussion of the marketing concept, we said that an organization's objective is to determine consumers' wants and satisfy them. Thus, from the point of view of the individual organization, if the firm's target market is satisfied and the organization's objectives are being met, then the marketing effort can be judged successful.

However, this standard makes no distinction between organizations whose behaviour is detrimental to society and whose activities are socially acceptable. Firms that pollute the environment or stimulate demand for harmful products or services would qualify as good marketers right along with firms that behave responsibly. Therefore, we must take a broader, societal view that incorporates the best interests of others as well as the desires of a particular target market and the objectives of the marketer to satisfy that market. Marketing must balance the needs and wants of consumers, the objectives of the organization, and the welfare of society.

Marketing cannot, and certainly does not, exist within a vacuum. Practically speaking, consideration must be given to the cost-effectiveness of marketing efforts. In other words, how much does marketing contribute to the revenue of the firm or to the coffers of the owners — the shareholders? Corporate performance is evaluated as a means to measure the performance of management and the decisions they have made. Various means are employed, but one method is through what is called shareholder value. Have the operations of the firm over a particular period increased the value of the organization for its shareholders? Unfortunately, these are often taken as short-term measurements when many marketing efforts take some time to yield results.

The principal objective of management is the creation of shareholder value. By this measure the firm is assessed according to easily measured financial indicators. However marketing results can sometimes be less easily measured. Marketing is about developing customer relationships. Organizations must recognize that relationships are required to establish long-term shareholder value through accumulative effects that provide future streams of value. Such intangibles are difficult to measure in the short term, yet customer relationships must be assessed for the long-term health of the firm.

Relationships, like marketing, requires an understanding of what the customer wants, how to do it, and where the firm is strong and where it is weak. Measures include customer value, service quality, and customer satisfaction. To develop a sustainable stream of shareholder value a wider group of stakeholders should be considered aside from shareholders. These include employees, suppliers, and customers.

Real shareholder value is created by guaranteeing the long-term viability and growth of the company. Value creation, therefore, is intimately tied to customer loyalty. Loyal customers deliver a stream of revenues as long as they are satisfied. Satisfaction drives customer relationships. Relationships are aided and influenced through well-planned and integrated marketing efforts.[12]

There is evidence all around us of the interrelationship of these three criteria. If a product does not meet the needs of consumers or if a firm is unable to provide the level of service customers want, the consumer will not buy that product or service. The business world is littered with companies that have gone out of business because they were unable to satisfy their customers. Likewise, if a firm behaves in a fashion that is viewed by consumers or the public to be detrimental to society, government will likely intervene, as it does in regulating the advertising of alcohol, tobacco, and other products judged to be potentially damaging to the health and safety of consumers. Finally, companies regularly change advertising and promotional campaigns as their organizational objectives change.

Criticisms of Marketing

Criticisms of marketing focus on actions (or inaction) that relate to the balance between organizational objectives and the wants of customers and/or the well-being of society. These issues can be categorized as follows:

◆ *Exploitation.* Marketers are sometimes accused of taking unfair advantage of a consumer or of a situation. Examples of exploitation are price gouging during a shortage and misleading consumers with false or incomplete information. These behaviours are clearly in conflict with marketing's goal of long-term customer satisfaction.

◆ *Inefficiency.* Some critics feel that marketing uses more resources than necessary. Accusations include ineffective promotional activity, unnecessary distribution functions, and excessive numbers of brands in many product categories. Inefficiency results in higher costs to organizations, higher prices to consumers, and a waste of society's resources.

◆ *Stimulating unwholesome demand.* A number of marketers have been accused of encouraging consumers or businesses to purchase products that are harmful in some way to the individual or the organization. For example, debate has raged throughout the Western world for the past twenty-five years or more concerning the marketing of cigarettes. The issue tends to revolve around the fact that tobacco is a legal product; although there are regulations in most provinces and cities that prohibit the sale of tobacco products to teens and children. Though the marketing of such products may meet the needs of some consumers and satisfy the objectives of organizations that produce and sell them, the marketing of tobacco products is controversial because society generally agrees that the product is detrimental to the health of Canadians.

◆   *Inappropriate values.* Related to the concept of unwholesome demand is that of the promotion of inappropriate values. The use of sexual imagery has often been criticized in advertising as well the association of alcohol consumption and tobacco products linked with images of the "good life." This refers to images of "successful" or "popular" individuals that infer to viewers that the product has a role in delivering such desirable attributes.

◆   *Illegal behaviour.* Laws are passed to protect individuals, organizations, and society in general. Marketers are expected to abide by these laws, even when violating a law may benefit consumers or an organization. Price collusion, for instance, is detrimental to competitors of the colluding firms. Therefore, since the behaviour is unfair to others in society, it is unacceptable.

◆   *Poor service.* Some of the most vocal criticisms of marketing in recent years have been reserved for the way service is delivered to customers when they come into contact with marketing organizations, particularly at the retail level.

   Service has many dimensions — it is a form of product that is comprised of activities, benefits, satisfactions, and outcomes. The quality of delivery of each of these greatly impacts the quality of the product received. There is no doubt that some companies and organizations have made great strides and have developed well-deserved reputations for providing superior service; others have not.

   Customer expectations with regard to how they want to be treated have increased, and many organizations have simply not stepped up to the challenge. The result is considerable consumer dissatisfaction with service. The problem is that many firms and employees do not realize this. The physical service or product provided, the attitude projected, and the efforts of these individuals all combine to represent the quality of service that a consumer receives.

◆   *Reliance on technology.* The use of database marketing and direct mail systems has led many firms to believe that an effective and appropriate marketing program simply pops out of a computer tailored to the organization's needs. This is not the case. Efforts at relationship marketing have been jeopardized by this blind allegiance to technology. It has led to the use of meaningless information to design meaningless marketing programs and waste company resources. This has contributed to the image of direct mail programs as "junk mail" through solicitation without sensitivity to the consumer's needs.

◆   *Short-term goals.* Within the firm marketing decisions may be determined ultimately outside of the marketing department. Short-term sales and budget projections may shape what resources are available for marketing efforts. This may be at the cost of the long-term equity of the brand and of the provision of superior service to customers. Some managers feel marketing efforts are extraneous and that whatever funds are left over can be put forth for marketing. In response to a drop in sales some managers will "compensate" with a drop in marketing expenditure — if sales have already dropped can less marketing and promotion effort improve the situation?

UNDERSTANDING THE CRITICISMS To evaluate criticisms against marketing, we must understand what actually is being criticized. Is the object of the complaint ultimately the economic system? An entire industry? A particular firm? If the criticism applies to a firm, is the marketing department or some other department the culprit?

The free-enterprise system encourages competition, and government regulatory bodies for many years have judged competition by the number of competitors in an industry. Thus when we complain about the number of toothpaste or cereal brands on the market, we are really criticizing the system. Within a particular firm, a faulty product may result from production mistakes, not from marketing problems. Clearly, a failure in manufacturing does not make consumers' complaints less valid. The point is that marketing is not to blame for every business mistake.

This possible confusion raises a very important question that has been implicit in several sections of this book — What exactly is "marketing"? Or, more correctly, what are the boundaries around the "marketing" function in an organization? We observed in Chapter 1 that the single most important objective of marketing is customer satisfaction. But a customer may become dissatisfied with a company for a variety of reasons, many of which have nothing to do directly with what would historically be considered the responsibility of the marketing function within a company.

If the marketing department in an organization actually "owns the customer," that is, has responsibility for customer satisfaction, then it is essential that it works closely with other departments within the organization. Also, this points out the need for other components of the firm to be "marketing oriented." That is, they must have an appreciation for the fact that their functions have as much potential to influence long-term customer satisfaction and dissatisfaction as do those things that are traditionally considered to be the responsibility of marketing.

We also need to consider the sources of criticism directed at marketing. Some critics are well intentioned and well informed. They point out real weaknesses or errors needing correction, such as deceptive packaging, misleading advertising, and irresponsible pricing. But some critics are simply ill informed. They do not understand the functions associated with distribution or are not aware of the costs of producing and selling a product. As a result, though their criticisms may have popular appeal, they cannot withstand careful scrutiny. There are other critics whose views do not reflect the sentiments of society. Nevertheless, they vociferously criticize behaviour they find objectionable to serve their own interests. Some of the protests against the use of advertising in political campaigns is an example. We must examine criticism carefully to separate the legitimate from the erroneous and self-serving.

Responses to Marketing Issues

Efforts to address the issues that arise from marketing activity have come from consumers, the government, and business organizations. In the following paragraphs we discuss some of these **responses to marketing issues**.

Consumer Responses

One response to marketing misdeeds, both actual and alleged, has come from consumer activists. The term **consumerism** was popularized just over thirty years ago when, in response to increasing consumer protests against a variety of business practices, Canada became the first country in the world to establish a government department at the federal level to be responsible for the rights of consumers. The emphasis has been on protecting consumers from harmful products and from false and misleading advertising.

Today, governments are increasingly hard-pressed to meet the increasing demands being placed on public finances and consumer protection programs in some provinces and at the federal level have experienced budget cuts. At the federal level, the Department of Consumer and Corporate Affairs was disbanded in the 90s, as its function was assumed within Industry Canada. These developments were not only a result of government budget cuts, but also reflected the fact that consumers are now being protected in other ways. Many businesses and industry associations have adopted voluntary codes of behaviour to self-regulate their dealings and as legislation had been put in place at the federal and provincial level.

Government Responses

Interest in consumer issues is not likely to disappear. The main reason for this forecast is that today it is politically popular to support various consumer, social, and environmental causes. All the provinces enacted legislation and put consumer protection programs in place.

A significant number of these laws were designed to protect the consumer's "right to safety" — especially in situations where consumers cannot judge for themselves the risk involved in the purchase and use of particular products. Legislation such as the Food and Drugs Act regulates and controls the manufacture, distribution, and sale of food, drugs, and cosmetic products. The Hazardous Products Act establishes standards for the manufacture of consumer products designed for household, garden, personal, recreational, or child use.

One controversial area of product safety legislation is the paternalistic type of law that is intended to protect the consumer, whether or not he or she wants that protection. Thus, it is mandatory to equip automobiles with seat belts, and it is illegal to operate an automobile unless the seat belts are fastened. In many cities, it is required that bicycle riders wear helmets. In effect, somebody else is forcing a consumer to accept what the other person feels is in the consumer's best interests — truly a new and broadening approach to consumer legislation.

Another series of laws and government programs supports the consumer's "right to be informed." These measures help in such areas as reducing confusion and deception in packaging and labelling, identifying the ingredients and nutritional content in food products, advising consumers of the length of life of certain packaged food products, providing instructions and assistance in the care of various textile products, and determining the true rate of interest.

Business Responses

An increasing number of businesses are making substantive responses to consumer problems. Here are a few examples:

◆ *Better communications with and information for consumers.* Toll-free 1-800 phone numbers now appear on the packages of many manufacturers or in their advertising. Increasingly, advertisers are including their Web site addresses in advertisements and are encouraging consumers to contact them via e-mail. Manufacturers' instruction manuals on the use and care of their products are more detailed and easier to read. In many instances, package labels are more informative than they were in the past. Many companies also have installed call-centre operations that are staffed twenty-four hours a day and allow consumers to call with questions or problems using the company's 1-800 toll-free number. The vast majority of larger companies now have Web sites that contain much more information than was available to the public in the past and in a much more accessible form.

◆ *Product improvements.* More marketers are making a concerted effort to incorporate feedback from consumers in the designs of their products. As a result of consumer input or complaints, many companies have made improvements in their products. For example, detergent manufacturers have produced concentrated products that are more environmentally safe and scent-free products that contain no perfumes that may irritate people with allergies.

◆ *Service quality measurement.* Many companies have realized that it is becoming increasingly difficult to gain a competitive advantage through product design and that the key to success is to offer the customer the best possible service. Realizing also that they need feedback so that they know how well they are doing, many have developed and introduced programs that allow them to measure consumers' perceptions of the level of service they are receiving.

◆ *More carefully prepared advertising.* Many advertisers are extremely cautious in approving ads prepared by their advertising agencies, in sharp contrast to past practices. Advertisers are involving their legal departments in the approval process.

◆ *Customer service departments.* A growing number of companies have established departments to handle consumer inquiries and complaints. In addition to dealing with complaints, customer service departments also gauge consumer tastes, act as sounding boards for new ideas, and often gain feedback on new products.

Some trade associations see themselves as defenders of their respective industry or profession. In that capacity, they try to moderate government anti-business legislation through lobbying and head off criticism with arguments to justify almost any behaviour. More enlightened associations have recognized the necessity for responsible corporate behaviour. Such associations reflect those marketers that have been responsive to changes in the social fabric and marketplace that makes up Canada. Though they still engage in lobbying, these groups actively respond to consumer problems by setting industry ethical standards, conducting consumer education, and promoting research among association members.

ethics
The rules and standards of moral behaviour that are generally accepted by a society.

Ethics and Marketing

Ethics are standards of conduct. To act in an ethical fashion is to conform to an accepted standard of moral behaviour. Undoubtedly, virtually all people prefer to act ethically. It is easy to be ethical when no hardship is involved — when a person is winning and life is going well. The test comes when things are not going so well — when pressures build up. These pressures arise in all walks of life, and marketing is no exception.

Marketing executives face the challenge of balancing the best interests of consumers, the organization, and society into a workable guide for their daily activities. In any situation, they must be able to distinguish what is ethical from what is unethical and act accordingly, regardless of the possible consequences. However, there are many circumstances in which what constitutes ethical behaviour is far from straightforward.[13]

Setting Ethical Guidelines

Many organizations have formal codes of ethics that identify specific acts (bribery, accepting gifts) as unethical and describe the standards employees are expected to live up to. A large percentage of major corporations have ethics codes, as do many smaller businesses. These guidelines lessen the chance that an employee will knowingly or unknowingly violate a company's standards. In addition, ethics codes strengthen a company's hand in dealing with customers or prospects that encourage unethical behaviour. For young or inexperienced managers, these codes can be valuable guides, helping them to resist pressure to compromise personal ethics in order to move up in the firm.

However, every decision cannot be taken out of the hands of the manager. Furthermore, determining what is right and what is wrong can be extremely difficult. When faced with an ethical problem, honest answers to the following questions help to indicate which route a manager could follow:

◆ Would I do this to a friend?

◆ Would I be willing to have this done to me?

◆ Would I be embarrassed if this action were publicized nationally?

Socially Responsible Behaviour

social responsibility
The commitment on the part of a company to improving the well-being of society.

Ethical behaviour goes beyond avoiding wrongdoing. The ethical marketer recognizes that the position he or she holds in society carries with it certain obligations. This **social responsibility** involves improving the well-being of society. Besides obeying the law and meeting the normal and reasonable expectations of the public, socially responsible organizations and individuals lead the way in setting standards of business and community performance. Some companies encourage their employees to join volunteer groups and will pay the fees for staff to join service clubs that get involved in community projects. Many companies donate money raised from the sale of certain items to charitable organizations. Avon Canada (www.avon.ca) has raised over $5.2 million for breast cancer research through the sale of Avon Flame pink pens and other Flame items.[14] Ford is a sponsor of the "Run For The Cure" and promotes the cause through its site. Such companies wisely choose social causes that may best identify with core or expanding target groups of consumers.

Protecting the Customer's Right to Privacy

One of the most troublesome issues facing marketers relates to behaviour that threatens the customer's right to privacy. This is especially important today because more and more companies are collecting information on customers from a number of sources and storing the data on databases to be used for marketing purposes. Some consumers object to businesses having the information in the first place and to their use of it to sell them things. The point is that the technology is available today to permit the integration of

Many companies support worthy social causes.

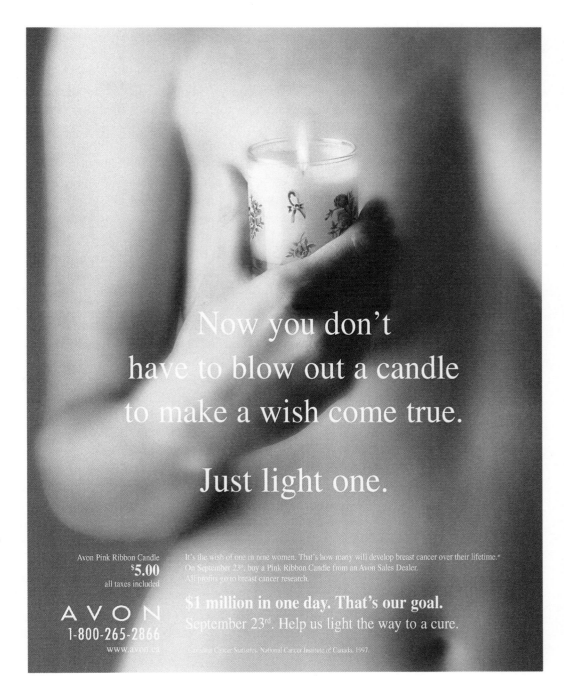

databases, making it possible to obtain information about the characteristics of consumers and their households and to match that information with data about purchases, credit card usage, and other consumption behaviour.

Nowhere is the issue of privacy more pertinent than in the area of telemarketing. As the use of the telephone has increased to contact people in their homes for the purpose of marketing products and services, so too has the public outcry against such practices. Many members of the public object to being telephoned at home. Consequently, they have turned to installing answering machines or a call management service provided by their telephone company that will allow them to screen calls, or they have paid for unlisted telephone numbers.

The direct marketing industry has taken steps to police itself with regard to offering protection to consumers against invasion of privacy. The industry association, the Canadian Direct Marketing Association (www.cdma.org), has adopted a code of standards that regulates its members, who account for about 80 percent of all direct marketers in Canada.

As discussed previously in the text, regulation of the Internet has begun. This has started with the privacy legislation Bill C-6 that took full effect January 1, 2001. This was the first step toward holding site operators accountable for the protection of information they collect from visitors to their sites. The foundation for this legislation rests on the Canadian Standards Association's Moral Code and provides for three levels of consent regarding personal information collected by site operators who may attempt to use the information for purposes other than that for which it was collected.[15]

Advertising and Social Responsibility

The issue of the social responsibility of marketing is also often related to the advertising that businesses present to their target consumers. For example, Benetton (www.benetton.com), the international Italian-owned clothing manufacturer and retailer, has in recent years employed rather controversial approaches in its advertising. Some consumers in many countries have been shocked by the content of Benetton ads.

Advertising is also criticized for the way in which certain groups in society are presented or for the effect that it may have on them. There has been considerable objection, for example, to the portrayal of ultra-thin young models in fashion advertising for such brands as Calvin Klein and Club Monaco. Critics suggest that such advertising promotes the view that thinness is glamorous and may contribute to eating disorders.[16] Similar public discussion surrounds such issues as whether or not manufacturers of prescription drugs should be allowed to advertise them to prospective consumers. Birth control pills stirred up controversy in 2000 when new product Alesse® (Wyeth-Ayerst Canada Inc.) was advertised on MuchMusic. Such ads are prohibited from giving both the name of the drug and its purpose in the same commercial. Two different commercials were run within a few moments of each other providing both pieces of information — some wondered if this was a violation of existing legislation.[17] When Seagram Company Limited moved to begin advertising its liquor products on television in the United States, it set off a controversy involving government officials, health advocates, and rival liquor manufacturers.[18]

Much advertising that appears in the mass media is controversial for a number of reasons. What is often interesting to observe is that the most violent criticism and the most strident demands for the removal of the offending advertising often come from people who are clearly not in the advertiser's intended target consumer segment.

The Future for Marketing

Let's move now to consider what lies ahead for marketing. It can be seen that in recent times the scope of marketing has been broadening to include everything that affects the consumer. It is possible to infer that this trend will continue as the technology that reaches into our homes becomes more pervasive and as competition in the marketplace continues to intensify.

In the future, in order to be more effective and efficient, and to increase levels of customer satisfaction, what do marketers need to know and what do they need to do?

Marketing at Work 21-2

Strategic Philanthropy Pays Back

Philanthropic donations have long been a major component of corporate Canada's marketing and communications budgets. These donations, however, were often made anonymously, or with low-profile support, to whichever charity happened to catch the CEO's fancy. Times have changed and corporations now realize that they have to approach their charitable undertakings far more strategically, as part of their overall image-building and reputation-management efforts.

Public relations professionals, whether internal or external to the organization, help companies develop philanthropic programs that match their corporate culture and values. For example, Edelman Canada conducted research with employees and customers of the Hudson's Bay Company (HBC) to determine where their interests lay and where HBC should focus its contributions.

Not surprising, as The Bay's customer base is predominantly female, women's health emerged as a top-priority issue. Meanwhile, customers and employees of Zellers, HBC's family-oriented chain, wanted to focus on children. As a result, The Bay became national title sponsor of the Heart & Stroke Walk for Mothers and Daughters, while Zellers lent support to the Kids Help Phone and continues its relationship with the Canadian Cystic Fibrosis Foundation.

The growing interest in what is being termed strategic philanthropy is due in part to research results that have shown that consumers will support companies that give back to the communities in which they operate.

To this end, companies have to take ownership of the causes they support — essentially branding the issues just as they would products or services. This must be done cautiously, however, so that a company is not seen to be emphasizing its own role at the expense of promoting the cause itself.

A company must also be careful not to spread itself too thin. By focusing on fewer projects a company is better able to make the most of each one. In order for the charitable donation, or investment, to pay back, the initiative must be leveraged many times over.

This may seem a little cold but corporate Canada now wants some recognition for the millions of dollars it donates to worthy causes each year. The good news for the recipients of these donations is that corporations are investing more, and are also becoming more accountable to the public as they associate themselves more prominently with the causes they support. As corporations' interest in leveraging their philanthropy grows, so too should their contribution. Today the total of corporate Canada's donations account for a mere 2 percent of the demand for charitable dollars in Canada.

Source: Adapted from Wendy Cuthbert, "Charity as PR tool," *Strategy*, April 12, 1999, p. B8.

Changes in the Marketing Environment

Many trends bear watching. We discussed many aspects of the external environment in Chapter 2. In this section, we focus on the implications for marketing of four areas: demographic changes, shifts in values, the impact of technology, and the growth of information.

CONSUMER DEMOGRAPHICS Changes in demographics — the population's age distribution, income, education, ethnic composition, and household structure — all affect marketers' activities. For example, the population is getting older, and senior citizens are the fastest-growing age group. This shift creates expanded marketing opportunities in such areas as travel and tourism and health and medical care. Another demographic change is the greater ethnic diversity in Canada's cities, resulting primarily from increases in the level of immigration from Asia and other areas. These groups are large enough to attract the attention of marketers, but they present interesting challenges.[19]

What do demographic changes tell us? They indicate that some markets will practically disappear and new ones will emerge. Marketers must remain abreast of these developments and adjust their strategies accordingly.

VALUES Values, the widely held beliefs in a society, change slowly. When they do, however, the impact on existing institutions and the opportunities for innovative marketers can be great. Value shifts often accompany demographic changes. As the Canadian population gets older and changes in other ways, we can expect some adjustments in values. For example, we are seeing:

◆ *Broadened perspectives.* Some forecasters see a shift away from a self-orientation to an "other-orientation." For example, volunteerism is on the upswing. Indications are that people may be disturbed by the materialism of the early 1990s, a period in which self-gratification governed many choices.

◆ *Increased skepticism.* Education is at its highest level ever. Consumers have more confidence in their ability to make judgments and are less willing to accept unsubstantiated claims. Authority is subject to challenge. Consumers demand information and are willing to question traditions. The concerns of Canadians with regard to cuts in social programs, including health care and education, are causing considerable skepticism about the leadership of elected officials.

◆ *Balanced lifestyles.* From a society that focused on work to produce a richer lifestyle, we are moving to a society that wants to balance work and leisure to enjoy a lifestyle. This will mean an increasing concern with wellness in the form of nutrition and exercise, the allocation of more time to home, family, and leisure, and a desire to become involved in activities viewed as worthwhile and fulfilling. Younger Canadians, in particular, appear not to be driven to succeed nearly as much as were their parents.

What do these changes mean for marketing? We are likely to see all-increasing emphasis on quality over quantity in consumption and a more careful evaluation of the value of product features that seem to add more to style than substance. One area in which values are evident is a heightened interest in the future quality of life. International concern over the dissipation of the atmosphere's ozone layer, the disappearance of rainforests, increases in acid rain, and the "greenhouse effect" is obvious. Other environmental issues of interest to consumers are waste disposal and landfills, air and water pollution, and biodegradability.

◆ *Heightened interest in entertainment.* All signs during the past decade pointed toward a lifestyle that had consumers focusing more on activities within the home. Stressful jobs and time constraints had led people to seek a place where they could relax in comfort and security. Consumers were spending more on their homes and on products that made their homes enjoyable. But, by the late 1990s, Canadians were again emerging from their homes and spending more than ever on out-of-home entertainment, including movies, plays, opera, and concerts.

◆ *Demands for good service.* The success of businesses such as Four Seasons Hotels and Bell Canada makes it clear that consumers reward good service. It is also apparent that many firms recognize this opportunity. Recognizing the need to offer good service is often easier than finding and training employees to provide it. A major challenge for organizations in the future will be to design and implement systems that provide consumers with high-calibre service. There is every evidence that the offering of superior customer service represents a strategic competitive advantage for successful companies.[20]

TECHNOLOGY There can be little doubt that marketing has been revolutionized in recent years because of the impact of technology. The development of advanced technology has been so rapid that it has created both opportunities and problems that have serious implications for how marketing is carried out within just about every organization. The developments in technology are so vast that we can only provide a brief overview here, but we will touch on a number of key areas where marketing has been affected.

◆ *Internet marketing.* One opportunity that is obvious from the advances in technology of recent years is the use of the Internet to market products and services to prospective customers around the world. Virtually every major company and many smaller ones have created Web sites, and many of these are designed to sell things.

◆ *Fragmentation and customization of the electronic media.* Technology is revolutionizing the media to which consumers are exposed. Not only are there many more television stations, but there are numerous ways for consumers to access entertainment and educational programming. The result is a mind-boggling array of alternatives, most of them delivered through electronic media and on the Internet.

◆ *Impact on service delivery.* Technology has had a very definite impact on the delivery of customer service. On the one hand, some would argue that the introduction of such technology as automated banking machines, interactive voice-response telephone systems, and call-management software has created an impenetrable barrier between some companies and their customers. This suggests that, at a time when companies are generally interested in establishing close relationships with customers, there is a very real danger that technology will get in the way of a company being able to establish personal relationships. On the other hand, this is a very good example of the "two-edged sword" nature of technology. At the same time that technology seems to be getting in the way of service delivery, there are many examples of how technology actually facilitates service delivery.

◆ *Customer monitoring.* Technology has made it possible for companies to get to know their customers far better than has ever been the case in the past. Supermarket scanners and other forms of technology essentially observe the purchase patterns and behaviour of customers and maintain a running record of what has been purchased, where, and when. The result is the comprehensive databases that we will discuss in the next section.

USE OF CUSTOMER INFORMATION Marketers have the ability to pinpoint trends and individual customers as never before. Using scanner data that produces detailed purchase behaviour on a store-by-store basis, Statistics Canada gathers data that provide demographic information down to the city block, and a variety of other sources such as warranty registration cards, contest entries, and rebate requests, firms can build detailed customer and prospect profiles. With this information, they are able to design products and assortments tailored specifically to a customer's needs. Consider the case of Black's Photo Corporation. In the past, the company would make a decision on where to locate a new store primarily "by the seat of its pants." Using a software program from Toronto-based Compusearch Micromarketing (www.compusearch.ca), Black's combines demographic and marketing data with mapping and topographical software to provide detailed information on the market potential of certain areas. The software can provide the following: census data, consumer spending per household in more than eight hundred purchase categories, ownership data on household facilities and equipment, vehicle registrations, business activity in the area, and Compusearch's population and age-group projections ten years ahead. The result is that much of the guesswork is taken out of marketing decisions such as store location.[21]

Knowing more about the market has led to **market fragmentation** and to **niche marketing** — the identification of smaller and smaller market segments. There was a time when a packaged-goods manufacturer could develop a quality product, advertise it nationally using the national media, stock retailers' shelves, and have a reasonable chance of success. But the situation has changed. Marketers can no longer expect large numbers of consumers to compromise their needs and wants and buy standardized products. Rather, they must tailor goods and services to meet the needs of small market segments. The strategy of niche marketing significantly complicates the marketer's job. One version of a product is replaced by several. Different ads must be produced, and new media must be found to reach different consumers. Retailers must choose among many product variations, not all of which can be stocked. The added variety complicates inventory management, distribution, and personal selling.

There are no indications that the trend to niche marketing will end. In fact, with more sophisticated electronic data-collection methods being developed and the diversity of the population increasing, all indications point to even greater fragmentation in the future. The reaching of smaller and smaller market segments is facilitated largely through advances in technology that make it possible to design a unique marketing program to address the needs of individual customers.

Strategic Marketing Adjustments

One common response to change is simply to react as it occurs. However, realizing that change is always occurring, marketers should initiate strategic proactive efforts to improve performance. Six are described in this section.

INSTILLING A MARKET-DRIVEN ORIENTATION Describing the marketing concept and implementing it in an organization are two different things. The concept — combining a customer orientation with co-ordinated marketing and the organization's goals — certainly has intuitive appeal, yet many organizations seem unable to practise it consistently. Despite the fact that marketing has been taught in college and university business schools for over fifty years, the effective implementation of marketing is the exception rather than the rule. What does practising the marketing concept require?

◆ *The marketing concept involves a philosophy of business that focuses on the customer's needs.* However, when faced with the choice of putting the customer first or meeting their own needs, some employees often find it difficult to give the customer priority. Instilling this orientation requires top-management commitment. Lip service is not sufficient. Employees must see management putting the customer first.

◆ *There must be a reward system that encourages a customer orientation.* Employees must be empowered to make decisions that recognize the importance of customers and be publicly rewarded for those decisions.

◆ *Organizations must stay in close contact with the market.* This means having detailed, accurate market knowledge. Consumers are becoming less and less willing to compromise to satisfy their desires. Marketers must develop more marketing programs for smaller markets. In consumer marketing, this means conducting research on a continuous basis. In business-to-business marketing, it may mean creating new

---

market fragmentation
The identification of smaller and smaller market segments.

niche marketing
A strategy in which goods and services are tailored to meet the needs of small market segments.

structures. Progressive research firms have helped their clients by developing research programs to measure the quality of service being delivered and to examine the state of customer relationships with service companies.

◆ *Offer consumers the best value possible.* Many companies have realized that offering discounts and "specials" does little to build long-term customer loyalty and have instead turned to low everyday prices. The concept of adding value is of such importance that we will return to it later in this chapter.

◆ *Listen to the customer.* Successful companies no longer assume that they know what their customers want. Consequently, many are doing more marketing research than they have in the past. They have also learned that they can do nothing to improve the service to customers unless they know when customers are having problems or concerns.

◆ *All exchange partners, not just customers, must be satisfied.* Exchange partners of an organization include its customers, suppliers, intermediaries, owners, regulators, and anyone else with whom it interacts. If suppliers, for example, feel their exchanges with an organization are unsatisfactory, they will not do everything in their power to ensure that the needs of end customers will be met. The same is true of employees. Essential to satisfying final customers are strong, positive relationships among all the parties who contribute to bringing a product or service to market.

ADOPTING A GLOBAL ORIENTATION To be successful in the future, marketers must adopt a global orientation toward markets, products, and marketing activity. In the past, most firms could be successful by focusing on the domestic market and outperforming local rivals. However, that has changed. Now firms, both large and small, are going where the markets are the most attractive.

The cliche that we live in a "small world" is a reality for marketers. Virtually instantaneous communications has greatly increased global awareness. Economic, social, and political developments on one side of the world have an impact everywhere else. On the evening television news we are as likely to hear about developments on the Japanese stock market as we are about activity on Bay Street.

Despite problems, the trend toward global marketing will accelerate. The lure of millions of consumers, combined with an improved understanding of the markets and marketing practices necessary to be successful, will increase the attractiveness of such opportunities.

The rise of e-commerce has made it possible to conduct business across the globe without ever leaving the home office. Internet technology has made every marketplace an international market. Consumers and businesses can now obtain information, place, and receive orders from across the continent as easily as from across the province. Potential clients and competitors can be from anywhere around the globe.

UNDERSTANDING THE CONCEPT OF VALUE AND ITS RELATIONSHIP TO CUSTOMER NEEDS One of the most talked-about but least understood concepts in marketing is value. We hear a great deal in marketing circles about adding value for customers. Presumably, this involves adding something over and above what the customer would normally get in order to make the offering more attractive than that of a competitor. What is often overlooked is the fact that, in order to add value, we must have a very good understanding of what it is that customers value in the first place. Few companies have invested sufficiently in research to be able to answer the question: What do customers value?

Marketing at Work 21-3

Irwin Tries to Play with the Big Kids

Irwin Toys is Canada's leading toy manufacturer, with annual sales of more than $120 million. The company is a major player in the Canadian market, but isn't well known internationally, or even in the United States. This poses an enormous challenge as Irwin tries to grow its business.

Historically, Irwin has marketed and distributed its products in Canada, but this market now provides little opportunity for growth. Irwin has therefore set its sights on the international market, and hopes to become a major force alongside Hasbro and Mattel. By expanding globally, Irwin will have access to bigger and better licensed properties, and can spread its marketing and product development costs over more markets.

George Irwin, President of Irwin Toys, intends to grow the company's worldwide sales to $300 million over the next five years. The company's global marketing plan depends heavily on winning marketing licences for movies or cartoon series. Not the biggest and most expensive properties, however, Irwin would prefer to establish itself by developing a series of medium-sized brands.

One element of Irwin's global strategy is to empower its subsidiaries and licensees to tailor their marketing strategies to their own markets. This is critical as markets will often differ on key factors such as peak toy-buying seasons. In Canada, for example, toys are often launched in September during the back-to-school period and sales build toward the Christmas season. Conversely, Australia's heavy toy-buying occurs during the winter break in July.

The company will also make use of the Internet by offering sneak previews of new products on popular toy sites. This will help build interest and generate important feedback prior to product launches.

According to David Leibowitz, a toy analyst with Burnham Securities in New York, Irwin is heading in the right direction but will need a lot of marketing savvy to break through and take share away from Hasbro and Mattel. Its intention to expand globally is a good strategy, but how it plays out remains to be seen.

Source: Adapted from Craig Saunders, "Irwin playing on global front," *Strategy*, July 17, 2000, p. 1.

This issue of adding value is very closely related to the concept of customer needs, as discussed above and in Chapter 1. Customers will value what allows them to better meet their needs. Thus, to add value for our clients, we must be able to understand their needs.

EMPHASIZING QUALITY AND CUSTOMER SATISFACTION The emphasis on quality in products and services that is sweeping business today requires a rethinking of the role of marketing and even of what marketing means. In fact, there may be some justification in arguing that marketing and quality really refer to the same thing — efforts to produce satisfied customers. They both refer to intrinsic values in organizations that are customer-focused: an attitude, an orientation toward doing whatever is necessary to satisfy the customer. Some companies have gone so far as to dismantle their marketing departments, instead assigning responsibility for customer relationships and satisfaction to senior strategy-makers and to the plants and field staff who actually make and deliver the products and services.[22]

DESIGNING ENVIRONMENTALLY SOUND STRATEGIES Quality applies to more than making products that work better or longer. A broader issue is the general quality of everyday life and the way we treat the environment. In the past, commitments to single-issue efforts (for example, making a product biodegradable or eliminating chlorofluorocarbons) were enough to win consumer approval. However, in the future, environmental acceptance will be based on a product's entire life cycle, from design through disposal.

Firms will be forced to move away from looking for an exploitable or advertisable feature to making environmental concerns an integral part of the business system. This will require a new way of thinking about consumption. One example is to make products so that the materials, components, and packages can be used longer and reused either in part or whole, a process called **reconsumption**.[23] Forms of reconsumption include:

◆ *Refilling.* Rather than discarding a container when it is empty, if it is properly designed, it can be refilled. Over thirty million laser-printer cartridges are used and disposed of every year. Accutone has designed its cartridges so that they can be refilled.

◆ *Repairing.* With proper maintenance, products can be used longer. Thus, rather than waiting to act until after a product fails, SKF (www.skf.se), a Swedish bearing manufacturer, has developed a series of preventive support services and diagnostic techniques that its customers can use to greatly lengthen the life of its bearings.

◆ *Restoring.* Some products can be returned to their original condition by replacing parts and reconditioning others. BMW and Mercedes are now restoring damaged auto parts that in the past were simply discarded.

◆ *Reusing.* Packaging material is often discarded long before it is unusable. Lego, the Danish toy manufacturer, delivers its products to retailers in large, durable boxes that are returned to Lego for reuse.

The key to making reconsumption work is developing methods of manufacturing and marketing that make it profitable. This isn't easy. McDonald's has recently invested nearly 60 percent of its R&D budget in attempting to develop a soluble plastic for packaging. It also requires new ways of thinking. For years, manufacturers have focused on ways of assembling things efficiently. Now the focus must switch to developing technologies for separating materials. For example, finding a method to remove the ink from newspaper economically will be crucial to its recycling.

Quality in many forms clearly is critical to customer satisfaction and therefore must have a high priority with management. The challenge for managers will be to identify or develop systems that can be successfully implemented and sustained within the existing business culture.

BUILDING RELATIONSHIPS One of the most important aspects of the current new way of looking at marketing is the emphasis that many companies now have on the development of relationships with customers. There is a growing appreciation for the fact that it costs a company a great deal more to attract a new customer than it does to keep an existing customer happy. Therefore, we have seen a change in emphasis away from getting customers and toward keeping customers. In fact, some authors have suggested that in the future marketers must pay increasing attention to the "four Rs" of marketing: relationships, retention, referrals, and recovery.[24] In this new way of thinking, marketers will stress building relationships with customers who will generate long-term profits for the company, developing strategies that will keep them satisfied so that they will stay with the company, and creating strategies that will deal with recovering from problems and mistakes when they occur. As the following box reflects, there is a considerable difference between this new way of looking at marketing and what has been practised in the past.

Old Marketing Model	New Marketing Model
• Focus on the product.	• Focus on process for serving customers.
• Define the target group.	• Feed and nourish the relationship.
• Set brand objectives.	• Extend respect and value to customers.
• Opportunity comes from analysis.	• Opportunity comes from synergy.
• Focus on brand benefit.	• Develop and refresh relevance.
• Create strategic advertising.	• Open the doors for dialogue.
• Operate against a brand plan.	• Improvise to sustain the relationship.
• Driven by a marketing group.	• A pervasive interdisciplinary attitude.

Source: John Dalla Costa, "Towards a Model Relationship," *Marketing*, June 27, 1994, p. 12. Reprinted with permission.

One final issue that should be addressed concerns the type of relationship that a company should establish with its customers. There are some who believe that having a customer's name in a database and sending him or her regular mailings constitutes a relationship. But a genuine relationship that will last a long time requires the company to demonstrate a sincere interest in the customer and in his or her well-being — not really different from those factors that contribute to relationships between people.[25]

Summary

The management process in marketing is the planning, implementation, and evaluation of the marketing effort in an organization. Implementation is the stage in which an organization attempts to carry out its strategic planning. Strategic planning is virtually useless if it is not implemented effectively.

Implementation includes three activities — organizing, staffing, and operating. In organizing, the company first should co-ordinate all marketing activities into one department whose top executive reports directly to the president.

The evaluation stage in the management process involves measuring performance results against predetermined goals. Evaluation enables management to determine the effectiveness of its implementation and to plan corrective action where necessary. A marketing audit is a key element in a total marketing evaluation program. Most companies are victims of at least some misdirected marketing effort. That is, the 80–20 and iceberg principles are at work in most firms because marketing costs are expended in relation to the number of marketing units (territories, products, customers), rather than to their profit potential. Too many companies do not know how much they should be spending for marketing activities, or what results they should get from these expenditures.

A firm's marketing performance should be appraised from a broad, societal perspective. Thus, evaluating an organization's marketing efforts must consider how well it satisfies the wants of its target customers, meets its own needs, and serves the best interests of society.

Marketing has been criticized for being exploitative, inefficient, and illegal, and for stimulating unwholesome demand. Many criticisms of marketing are valid. However, the offensive behaviour is confined to a small minority of all marketers, and some of the criticism is based on issues that are more complicated than they first appear.

Consumer responses to marketing problems have included protests, political activism, and support of special-interest groups. Conditions that provide an impetus for widespread consumerism — sensitivity to social and environmental concerns, and the willingness to become actively involved — are present today. Government at the federal, provincial, and local levels enforces consumer-protection legislation. Businesses have responded to criticism by improving communications, providing more and better information, upgrading products, and producing more sensitive advertising.

Many organizations have established codes of conduct to help employees behave ethically. However, it is not possible to have a rule for every situation. Managers can use a form of cost-benefit analysis to evaluate the ethics of alternatives. Another method of judging the ethics of a particular act is to ask three questions: Would I do this to a friend? Would I be willing to have this done to me? Would I be embarrassed if this action were publicized nationally? Besides being morally correct, ethical behaviour by organizations can restore public confidence, avoid government regulation, retain the power granted by society, and protect the image of the organization.

Prospects for the future of marketing are reflected in projected changes in consumer demographics, shifts in values, and the expansion of information. Marketers will react to these and other changes, but they will also have to make some basic strategic adjustments to compete in the 21st century. Among the needed adjustments are instilling a market-driven orientation, adopting a global orientation, better understanding of key concepts like value, emphasizing quality and satisfaction, and retaining customers by building relationships.

Key Terms and Concepts

Implementation 682	Postsale service 689	Basis for evaluating	Ethics 697
Evaluation 682	Marketing audit 691	performance 692	Social responsibility 698
Warranty 687	Misdirected marketing effort 691	Responses to marketing	Market fragmentation 704
Express warranty 687	80–20 principle 691	issues 695	Niche marketing 704
Implied warranty 687	Iceberg principle 691	Consumerism 696	Reconsumption 707
Product liability 687			

Questions and Problems

1. "Good implementation in an organization can overcome poor planning, but good planning cannot overcome poor implementation." Explain, using examples.

2. Give examples of how advertising and personal selling activities might be co-ordinated in a company's marketing department.

3. Can all the criticisms of marketing be dismissed on the basis of critics' being poorly informed or acting in their own interest?

4. Some people believe there are too many fast-food outlets in their communities. Suggest a method for reducing the number of these outlets.

5. What are the social and economic justifications for "paternalistic" laws such as seat-belt regulations and warnings on cigarette packages and alcoholic beverage containers?

6. Discuss some ethical implications of the fact that many companies today are able to obtain considerable volumes of data about consumers and what they buy, and other information that some consumers may wish to keep confidential. What are reasonable boundaries on the use of such information for marketing purposes?

7. Describe a firm whose behaviour toward its customers reflects, in your opinion, the adoption of a customer-focused strategy.

8. Within the overall college and university student segment, describe a smaller or fragmented market segment that you believe exists.

9. Describe how you interact with a business or other organization with which you feel you have a positive relationship.

Hands-On Marketing

1. Interview a marketing executive to find out how the total marketing performance is evaluated in his or her company. As part of your report, include your appraisal of this company's evaluation program.

2. Ask the managers of three firms in the same industry:

   a. What foreseeable developments will have the greatest impact on marketing in their industry over the next five years?

   b. How they think the industry should respond to the developments?

Case 7-1

ROYAL BANK OF CANADA (PART 2)

On July 20, 2000, RT Capital Management Inc., the pension investment arm of the Royal Bank of Canada, the country's largest banking institution, agreed to a package of terms set out by the Ontario Securities Commission (OSC), which included a series of stiff penalties and a $3 million fine for stock price manipulation. RT Capital Management admitted that its employees manipulated stocks and that its senior managers and directors did not adequately police stock trading activities. (Please refer to Part 1 of this case in Part Six, Case 6-2 for background details of the situation in general and with reference to selected public relations issues.)

The Royal Bank made two very public moves as news of the stock manipulation broke. The first was to take out advertisements in a number of national newspapers containing a very public and unprecedented apology from Royal Bank president, John Cleghorn. The second was to appoint Michael Wilson, a former federal Minister of Finance and a highly respected and experienced member of the financial community, as the new head of RT Capital.

Mr. Wilson's first task has been to attempt to determine the magnitude of the damage done to RT Capital as well as the Royal Bank, and what some fear is damage to the financial community in general. He must then determine what must be done to implement change within RT so that clients are assured and have trust and confidence in the fact that the financial services they are purchasing are of superior quality, fairly priced, and efficiently and ethically delivered.

As a result of the agreement between the OSC and RT, and aside from the fines, RT has agreed to appoint a consulting firm to audit its trade monitoring procedures and to review its trades from the highly-publicized "juicing" scandal whereby traders manipulated the close-of-day stock prices of particular companies held by their clients. By artificially inflating these prices, and the value of these companies, RT Capital collected additional commissions on stock portfolios of $34 million. Deloitte & Touche's task, as consultant, is to assess RT's existing policies and procedures to determine whether or not they provide the legal and ethical value-added financial services which clients are entitled to. In effect, the service provision system will be reviewed to assure that what must be provided by regulation and should be provided according to the company's own policies is and can be provided.

The Royal Bank has already conceded that control procedures were too lax and that management as well as service staff ignored operating rules. In other words, the safeguards that "consumers" believe are in place in this industry, and that provide these investors with a sense of order, security, and trust were not adhered to and were not followed by those responsible for doing so. This has left many wondering what types of practices are actually being followed day-to-day within firms such as this. New policies will have to be developed and implemented and behaviour monitored and audited to assure they are being followed.

Some observers of the situation believe that Mr. Wilson's top priority should be to personally contact each client, discuss their concerns, and begin to develop a new sense of trust. At that time the company had approximately seven hundred clients. It is felt that many clients are somewhat nervous about their situation, perhaps not so much in economic terms but more in ethical and even social terms. Various customer responses are believed to exist and the company may learn how to better react to the events if they receive input from a wide circle of clients. Observers suggest that he should provide clients with the complete report that the accounting firm Deloitte & Touche has been hired to prepare — an assessment of policies and procedures as part of the agreed settlement. Also, some suggest that Wilson should be open about what occurred and indicate the company's approach to correcting matters before major changes, other than those mandated by the OSC, have actually been implemented. They further suggest that when details are developed these should be communicated quickly.

Some feel that the matter of gaining new business may prove to be a more difficult matter than just showing good dollar-return performance. Even if RT is able to show, in the next few periods, that they can produce at least their previous average rate of return, this may not be an important enough decision criterion for some current or potential clients. If a financial officer or consultant from any organization were to recommend that it move its funds to RT after all the negative publicity, senior officers and members of a board of directors might be loath to approve such a move. After all, there are other competitors, untainted, who will be more than pleased to provide the needed investment and management services and a similar rate of return or performance.

The firm has lost executives in key positions, some traders have been banned from trading for various periods of time and there are questions about the morale and potential productivity of the ninety-two remaining staff members. Some observers suggest that those who have departed be rapidly replaced so that the task of team re-building can begin rapidly. Others suggest that making rapid changes would make current clients nervous about what is taking place. Bringing in key senior people is a delicate task at best and fraught with potential difficulties in the current situation. Those within RT as well as clients and consultants must be satisfied that appropriate and real changes can occur. Some management and pension consultants feel that re-orienting the RT organizational culture may take months and years to resolve before clients will feel completely comfortable and have confidence in being fairly treated and equitably. It has been pointed out that some funds management and insurance firms believe that compensating traders on bases other than the performance of the funds they work with helps prevent rule-breaking and allows for better client service.

Copyright © 2000. This case was written by Montrose S. Sommers and Peter Dunne and is intended to stimulate class discussion of a marketing problem and not to illustrate either effective or ineffective handling of this problem.

Pertinent Web Sites

www.royalbank.com/rtcap
www.royalbank.ca
www.osc.gov.on.ca
www.tsc.com

Questions

1. What should be Mr. Wilson's priorities in terms of re-establishing client trust?

2. What policy issues should be addressed in order to develop the service producing system that would satisfy current clients and appeal to new ones?

3. What should be done with regard to existing staff that remains with the company and that will now be expected to help bring the company through this crisis? How should the company deal with morale and retraining issues? Do issues exist around team building and the corporate culture that need to be addressed?

4. What considerations and precautions should be addressed with regard to replacing senior and trading staff?

5. As discussed in both parts of this case, learning customers' responses to these events is important to formulating an appropriate corporate response. We learned in the first part of the case that customers had a variety of responses to learning what had happened within RT Capital. What should the company do in light of this variety of responses?

6. Critics and observers have publicly stated that among other things, the company should adopt a policy to share all details and outcomes of its auditor's reports dealing with the events surrounding the scandal. RT previously managed to avoid this "airing out" of details by making an agreement with the OSC and thereby avoiding a public trial. How should they respond to these public demands? Should they concede?

Sources: Dawn Walton, "Royal shifts into damage control,' *The Globe and Mail*, July 21, 2000, pp. B1, B4; Keith McArthur and Caroline Alphonso, "Reaction to resignations ranges from confidence to concern," ibid; Roma Luciw, "TSE mulls regulation overhaul," ibid, p. B4; Mathew Ingram, "RT Capital settlement is an abject failure," ibid; Guy Dixon and Caroline Alphonso, "Managers batten down hatches on policy, practices," ibid, p. B5; Theresa Tedesco, "RT settles scandal,' *Financial Post*, July 21, 2000, p. C1, C5; Peter Fitzpatrick, "Wilson moves up to rebuild image at RT Capital," Ibid., p. C4; Dawn Walton, "$3-million fine to fund education,' *The Globe and Mail*, July 22, 2000, p. B4; Caroline Alphonso, "RT Capital advised to repair image, be open with customers," ibid.

Notes and References

CHAPTER 1

1. Geraldine Williams, "High Performance Marketing: An Interview With Nike's Philip Knight," *Harvard Business Review*," July–August 1992, p. 92.
2. "Meet the New Consumer," *Fortune*, Autumn–Winter, 1993, pp. 7-8.
3. James G. Barnes, Peter A. Dunne, and William J. Glynn, "Self-service and Technology: Unanticipated and Unintended Effects on Customer Relationships," in Teresa A. Swartz and Dawn Iacobucci, eds., *Handbook of Services Marketing and Management* (Thousand Oaks, CA.: Sage Publications, 2000), pp. 89–101.
4. James L. Heskett, Thomas O. Jones, Gary W. Loveman, W. Earl Sasser Jr., and Leonard A. Schlesinger, "Putting the Service–Profit Chain to Work," *Harvard Business Review*, March–April 1994, pp. 164–174.
5. Frederick F. Reichheld, "Loyalty-Based Management," *Harvard Business Review*, March–April 1993, pp. 64–73.
6. Robert Johnson, "In the Chips," *The Wall Street Journal*, March 22, 1991, p. B1.
7. Tyler Hamilton, "The Mobile Concierge," *The Globe and Mail*, March 30, 2000, p. T1.
8. For a complete discussion of ethics in marketing, see Gene R. Lazniak and Patrick Murphy, *Ethical Marketing Decisions: The Higher Road* (New York: Allyn & Bacon, 1993).
9. Shona McKay, "The Year of Living Holistically," *Report on Business Magazine*, April 2000, pp. 55–68.
10. Richard Schoenberger, "Is Strategy Strategic? Impact of Total Quality Management on Strategy," *Academy of Management Executive*, August 1992, pp. 80–87.
11. Elizabeth Church, "Survivors Get It Right," *The Globe and Mail*, May 9, 1997, p. B9.

CHAPTER 2

1. Chapters, Inc. corporate Web site, 2000. Contains primarily corporate and media informa-tion, but will link to its retail sites, www.chaptersinc.com.
2. Chapters Online's retail sites, 2000. Chapters Online, Inc. retails its products through two sites: www.chapters.ca is the primary retail site, while www.chaptersglobe.com fea-tures news articles from *The Globe and Mail* newspaper. Purchases may also be made from this URL.
3. Marina Strauss, "The e-book finds its mark," *The Globe and Mail*, March 2, 2000, p. T1.
4. For a detailed review of the demographics of the baby boomers and how demo-graphics influence buying behaviour, see David K. Foot with Daniel Stoffman, *Boom, Bust & Echo 2000: Profiting from the Demographic Shift in the New Millennium* (Toronto: Macfarlane, Walter & Ross, 1998).
5. Data obtained from Statistics Canada Web site, www.statcan.ca, 2000.
6. Cyndee Miller, "X-ers Know They're a Target Market, and They Hate That," *Marketing News*, vol. 27, no. 25, December 6, 1993, p. 2.
7. David K. Foot with Daniel Stoffman, *Boom, Bust & Echo 2000: Profiting from the Demographic Shift in the New Millennium* (Toronto: Macfarlane, Walter & Ross, 1998).
8. David K. Foot with Daniel Stoffman, *Boom, Bust & Echo* (Toronto: Macfarlane, Walter & Ross, 1996).
9. Astrid Van Den Broek, "Not So Tough A Sell," *Marketing Magazine*, July 19/26, 1999, p. 18.
10. January 2000 the inflation rate for Canada was reported as 2.3 percent by Statistics Canada, www.statcan.ca.
11. Milton Parissis and Michael Helfinger, "Ethnic Shoppers Share Certain Values," *Marketing*, January 11, 1993, p. 16.
12. Chad Skelton, "School Junk Hot Dogs, Hamburgers," *The Globe and Mail*, June 23, 1997, p. A6.
13. Keith McArthur, "Canadians Put Environment First," *The Globe and Mail*, June 23, 1997, p. A4.
14. www.e-com.ic.gc.ca, 2000. This is a site sponsored by Industry Canada. Industry Canada sites provide informa-tion regarding industry statistics for Canada. This particular site provides infor-mation on the expanding e-retail industry in this country.
15. IBM, "Internet Ascending," Advertising Supplement, *The Globe and Mail on Business*, November 1996, p. 105.
16. Ontario Transportation Capital Corporation, "Ontario Transportation Minister Registers for a Highway 407 Transponder," Press Release, Canada NewsWire, May 30, 1997, www.newswire.ca/releases/May1997/30/c6645.html.
17. www.e-com.ic.gc.ca.
18. Sympatico, "Why Should a Business go Online?" Sponsored Supplement, *Strategy*, May 26, 1997, p. 8.
19. The terms *middleman* and *intermediary* may be used interchangeably. We have chosen to use intermediaries throughout this book.
20. From "Internal Marketing: A Relationships, Value-Creation View," by Peter A. Dunne and James G. Barnes, to be pub-lished in *Internal Marketing: Directions for Management*, by Barbara R. Lewis and Richard J. Varey, London: Routledge, 2000.

CHAPTER 3

1. Adapted from Liza Finlay, "Mom Power," *Marketing Magazine*, July19/26, 1999, p. 17 and Lesley Daw, "Female-Friendly Ford," *Marketing Magazine*, August 17, 1998, pp. 21–22.
2. Derek Abell, "Strategic Windows," *Journal of Marketing*, July 1978, pp. 21–26.
3. *Pulse of the Middle Market* — 1990 (New York: BDO Seidman, 1990), pp. 12–13.
4. Shawna Steinberg, "Oh, Canada in the Spotlight," *Marketing Magazine*, November 2, 1998, pp.10–11.
5. Chris Daniels, "Zellers Strives to be Truly Canadian," *Marketing Magazine*, October 19, 1998, p. 2.
6. Douglas Ajram, "Happy Kids Make Happy Moms," *Marketing Magazine*, January 25, 1999, p. 24.
7. Chris Daniels, "Canadian Tire Mulls Money Changes," *Marketing Magazine*, March 13, 2000, p. 3.
8. Marina Strauss, "Fewer Players in Retail Sector: Study," *The Globe and Mail*, March 30, 2000, p. B4.
9. Malcolm H. B. McDonald, "Ten Barriers to Marketing Planning," *The Journal of Business and Industrial Marketing*, Winter 1992, p. 15.
10. Edward DiMingo, "The Fine Art of Positioning," *The Journal of Business Strategy*, March/April 1988, pp. 34–38.
11. Suein L. Hwang, "Its Big Brands Long Taunted as Fatty, CPC Tries A More 'Wholesome' Approach," *The Wall Street Journal*, April 20, 1992, pp. B1, B4.
12. "Buckley's Efforts Gets Quirky," *Marketing Magazine*, November 22, 1999, p.1.
13. Differential advantage in the context of services industries is examined in G. Bharadwj, P. J. Varadarajan, and John Fahy, "Sustainable Competitive Advantages in Service Industries," *Journal of Marketing*, October 1993, pp. 83–99.
14. Frank Gibney, Jr. and Belinda Luscombe, "The Redesigning of America," *Time*, March 20, 2000, p. 44.
15. An excellent source of infor-mation on how various companies prepare their marketing plans is Howard Sutton, *The Marketing Plan* (New York: The Conference Board, 1990).
16. *The Experience Curve Reviewed, IV. The Growth Share Matrix of the Product Portfolio* (Boston: Boston Consulting Group, 1973).
17. Bruce Orwall, "Disney Plans to Narrow Portal Focus," *The Wall Street Journal*, January 28, 2000, p. A3.
18. First proposed by H. Igor Ansoff, "Strategies for Diversification," *Harvard Business Review*, September–October 1957, pp. 113–124; see also Ansoff, *The New*

Corporate Strategy (New York: John Wiley and Sons, 1988), pp. 82–85.

19. Helena Katz, "How A Bankrupt Ski Resort Became #1 in the East," *Marketing Magazine*, November 2, 1988, pp. 22–23.

20. Norma Reveler, "Moo-ving Some Merchandise," *Marketing Magazine*, April 12, 1999, pp. 21, 24.

CHAPTER 4

1. Brian Dunn, "So Hip It Sells," *Marketing Magazine*, June 14, 1999, p. 16.

2. "Degree Spots Stress Stress," *Marketing Magazine*, February 28, 2000, p. 3.

3. Jan Field, "Ice with Edge," *Marketing Magazine*, February 7, 2000, p. 17.

4. Shawna Cohen, "Energizing Elixirs," *Marketing Magazine*, April 3, 2000, pp. 12–13.

5. "Panasonic Beefs Up Audio Ads," *Marketing Magazine*, May 18, 1998, p. 1.

6. "Sony Aims at Young Market," *Marketing Magazine*, July 13, 1998, p. 2.

7. "Million-Dollar Mag," *Marketing Magazine*, August 17, 1998, p. 4.

8. Lara Mills, "Coke May Move Towards Localizing," *Marketing Magazine*, February 7, 2000, p. 3.

9. "Levi's Axes Personal Pairs Program," *Marketing Magazine*, June 7, 1999, p. 2.

10. "Clearly Tries Making Today's News," *Marketing Magazine*, March 13, 2000, p. 1.

11. For Canadian statistics including current and projected population figures, visit the Statistics Canada Web site at www.statcan.ca.

12. For an interesting and detailed discussion on the use of geo-demographic clustering, see the December 1993 issue of *Research PLUS*, a magazine published by the Market Research Society, London, England.

13. *Market Research Handbook*, Statistics Canada, cat. no. 63-224. For additional information on the market represented by seniors in Canada, see *A Portrait of Seniors in Canada* (Ottawa: Statistics Canada, 1998) cat. no. 89-519.

14. For additional information on the market represented by children in Canada, see *A Portrait of Children in Canada* (Ottawa: Statistics Canada, 1998), cat. no. 89-520.

15. Elena Cherney, "Air Canada Bows to Kids' 'Pester Power'," *Montreal Gazette*, March 20, 1996, p. F1.

16. Douglas Ajram, "Happy Kids Make Happy Moms," *Marketing Magazine*, January 25, 1999, p. 24.

17. Holly Quan, "Bums into Seats," *Marketing Magazine*, October 19, 1998, pp. 12–13.

18. Fawzia Sheikh, "Swiss Chalet Targets Younger Crowd," *Marketing Magazine*, August 2, 1999, p. 2.

19. Stephanie Whittaker, "The Gen Next Card," *Marketing Magazine*, May 31, 1999, p. 14.

20. Jennifer Lewington, "Universities Give Recruitment Old College Try," *The Globe and Mail*, July 4, 1997, p. A1.

21. David K. Foot with Daniel Stoffman, *Boom, Bust & Echo 2000: Profiting from the Demographic Shift in the New Millennium* (Toronto: Macfarlane, Walter & Ross, 1998).

22. Andrew Trimble, "Feeding the Seniors' Market: A Food Company is Developing A New Niche," *The Toronto Star*, March 31, 1997, p. E3; Judy Creighton, "Gadgets for Seniors," *Winnipeg Free Press*, November 17, 1995, p. D3.

23. For an additional perspective on the changing segmentation of the women's market, see Michael Adams, *Sex in the Snow: Canadian Social Values at the End of the Millennium* (Toronto: Penguin, 1997).

24. For a view of the family life cycle that reflects the growing number of single adults, with or without dependent children, see Patrick E. Murphy and William A. Staples, "A Modernized Family Life Cycle," *Journal of Consumer Research*, June 1979, pp. 12–22. Also *New Trends in the Family: Demographic Facts and Features* (Ottawa: Statistics Canada, 1999) cat. no. 91-535E occasional.

25. *Vancouver Sun*, September 29, 1995, p. C2.

26. Eve Lazarus, "Supermarket Chain Caters to Asian Shoppers," *Marketing News*, February 24, 1997, p. 2.

CHAPTER 5

1. Patrick Allossery, "Molson Gets Canadian," *National Post*, April 10, 2000, p. C5. Also Jonathon Gatehouse, "With Glowing Hearts We See Thee Advertise," *National Post*, April 12, 2000, pp. A1, A2.

2. Greg Goldin, "When Brand is Grand," *World Business*, November/December 1996, pp. 19–23. Also Anita Lahey, "The Total Brand Experience," *Marketing Magazine*, March 27, 2000, pp. 13–14.

3. Jan Field, "Ice With Edge," *Marketing Magazine*, February 7, 1999, p. 17.

4. Lynn R. Kahle, Sharon E. Beatty, and Pamela Homer, "Alternative Measurement Approaches to Consumer Values: The List of Values (LOV) and Values and Lifestyles (VAL)," *Journal of Consumer Research*, December 1986, pp. 405–409. See also Wagner Kamakura and Thomas Novak, "Value-System Segmentation: Exploring the Meaning of LOV," *Journal of Consumer Research*, June 1992, pp. 119-132.

5. For a more complete discussion of VALS and VALS2, see William L. Wilkie, *Consumer Behavior*, 2nd ed. (New York: John Wiley & Sons, 1990).

6. For a discussion of the concept of benefit segmentation, see Russell J. Haley, "Benefit Segmentation — 20 Years Later," *Journal of Consumer Marketing*, vol.1, no. 2, 1983, pp. 5–13. See also Y. Datta, "Market Segmentation: An Integrated Framework," *Long Range Planning*, December 1996, pp. 797–811.

7. Allanna Sullivan, "Mobil Bets Drivers Pick Cappuccino Over Low Prices," *The Wall Street Journal*, January 30, 1995, p. B1. For information regarding Mobil Speedpass consult the company's Web site at www.exxon.mobil.com.

8. Home page, " The Artful Cookie," 2000, www.vaxxine.com/cookie/.

9. Jonathon Kay, "Caring Company Shields Loved Ones From Illicit Affairs," *National Post*, March 2, 2000, p. A15.

10. Richard Tomkins, "Shaking Out The Last Dollop of Growth," *Financial Times*, June 12, 1999, p. 7.

11. Shawna Cohen, "Holt Tries New Marketing Fashion," *Marketing Magazine*, February 21, 2000, p. 2.

12. "Gerber Launches New Baby Products," *The Telegram*, March 9, 2000, p. 41, reprinted with permission from Associated Press.

13. For a thorough discussion of the modern Canadian consumer and emerging consumer behaviour trends, see Shirley Roberts, *Harness The Future* (Toronto: John Wiley & Sons, 1998).

14. Mark Maremont, "They're All Screaming for Haagan-Dazs," *Business Week*, October 14, 1991, p. 121.

15. Shawna Cohen, "Energizing Elixirs," *Marketing Magazine*, April 3, 2000, pp. 12–13.

16. Eve Lazarus, "Going For Gross to Attract the Kids," *Marketing Magazine*, February 14, 2000, p. 4.

17. Ann Kerr, "Service is the Inn Thing as Prices Hit Floor," *The Globe and Mail*, September 14, 1993, p. C2.

18. Steven E. Prokesch, "Competing On Customer Service: An Interview With British Airway's Sir Colin Marshall," *Harvard Business Review*, November/December 1995, pp. 101–112.

19. Mel Duvall, "Leap of Faith," *Calgary Herald*, July 15, 1996, p. C1.

20. Astrid Van Den Broerk, "Targeting Yourself," *Marketing Magazine*, August 2, 1999, pp. 9–10.

21. Astrid Van Den Broerk, "Yellow Label Tea Is A Hit In Canada," *Marketing Magazine*, July 19, 1999, p. 3.

22. "Nike Slides into Snowboarding," *Marketing Magazine*, January 25, 1999, p. 1.

23. Lara Mills, "Doc Martens Stepping Out to Reach an Older Market," *Marketing Magazine*, October 23, 1995, p. 2. Also, the Air Wair home page, 2000, www.drmartens. com.

24. Eve Lazarus, "Sun-Rype Aims to Build Snack-Food Brands," *Marketing Online*, www.marketingmag.ca.

25. "Corby Uncorks Four New Coolers," *Marketing Magazine*, January 3, 2000, p. 1.

26. James Walker, "Designer Fries Find Niche," *The Financial Post*, September 3, 1996, p. 8. Also, David Carr, "Luring Audiences Back to the

Cinema," *Marketing Magazine*, January 18, 1999, p. 12.

27. Evra Taylor, "A Well Brewed Sales Strategy," *Marketing Magazine*, October 25, 1999, pp. 24–25.

28. Selkirk Tangiers home page, 2000, www.selkirk-tangiers.com/.

29. Toronto Dominion Bank home page, 2000, www.tdbank.ca/.

30. Allan J. Magrath, "Niche Marketing: Finding a Safe, Warm Cave," *Sales and Marketing Management in Canada*, May 1987, p. 40. The reader is also referred to Robert E. Linneman and John L. Stanton Jr., "Mining For Niches," *Business Horizons*, May/June 1992, pp. 43–51.

31. Philip Demont, "CBCI Telecom Inc., *Financial Post*, December 11, 1996, p. 27.

32. Alex Taylor III, "Porsche Slices Up Its Buyers," *Fortune*, January 16, 1995, p. 24.

33. Danny Kucharsky, "Buffing Up Birks," *Marketing Magazine*, October 25, 1999, pp. 17–18.

34. James Pollack, "Pharma Plus Pushes New Health Store Formats," *Marketing Magazine*, September 23, 1996, p. 4.

35. Fawzia Sheikh, "Zellers Unveils Plan to Fight Wal-Mart," *Marketing Magazine*, June 18, 1998, p. 2.

36. Fawzia Sheikh, "Retailers Try to Redefine Casual Days," *Marketing Magazine*, May 3, 1999, p. 4.

37. Cyndee Miller, "Food Producers Appeal to Fat-Free Crowd," *Marketing News*, August 14, 1995, p. 3.

38. Shawna Cohen, "One-Stop Shopping For Dinner," *Marketing Magazine*, February 1, 1999, pp. 10, 12.

39. For more detail on the use of test markets and simulated test markets, see James G. Barnes, *Research for Marketing Decision Making* (Toronto: McGraw-Hill Ryerson, 1991), pp. 516–522.

CHAPTER 6

1. Adapted from the Bugaboos. com Web site, April 11, 2000.

2. "Scratch and Save at Chapters," *Marketing Magazine*, January 24, 1999, p. 9.

3. Tyler Hamilton, "Retailers Merge Clicks and Bricks," *The Globe and Mail*, October 14, 1999, pp. T1, T2.

4. Danny Kucharsky, "Log-ons & Lace," *Marketing Magazine*, January 24, 1999, pp. 14–15.

5. R. Craig Endicott, "Advertising Fact Book," *Advertising Age*, January 6, 1992, p. S-11.

6. Clyde Kluckhohn, *Culture and Behaviour* (New York: Free Press, 1962), p. 26.

7. "The Marketing Report on Multicultural Marketing," *Marketing Magazine*, September 14, 1998, pp. 15–25.

8. For statistical information regarding languages spoken in Canada see the Statistics Canada Web site at www.stat-can.ca. The information reported is based upon the most recent 1996 Canadian census data.

9. For more information see, Dwight Thomas, "Culture and Consumption Behavior in English and French Canada," in Bent Stidsen, ed., *Marketing in the 70s and Beyond* (Edmonton: Marketing Division, 1975), pp. 255–261. Also, Francois Vary, "Quebec Consumer has Unique Buying Habits," *Marketing Magazine*, March 23, 1992, p. 28, and Louise Gagnon's, "Eaton's Quebec Ads Target Hip Shoppers," *Marketing Magazine* (June 16, 1997) and "Price Cuts Escalate Beer Battle," *Marketing Magazine* (June 30, 1997) at www.marketingmag.ca.

10. Astrid Van Den Broek, "Speaking the Same Language," *Marketing Magazine*, June 21, 1999, p. 13.

11. Stephen Ferley, Tony S. Lea, and Barry Watson, "A Comparison of U.S. and Canadian Consumers," *Journal of Advertising Research*, vol. 35, no. 5, Sept/Oct. 1999, pp. 55–65.

12. Eve Lazarus, "The Bay 'Micro-Marketing' to Asians," *Marketing Magazine*, October 14, 1996, p. 5.

13. Mikala Folb, "Marketers Awaken to Ethnic Magazines," *Marketing Magazine*, July 15, 1996.

14. For more Asian market information see Fairchild Television Web site at www.ftv.com.

15. For more information see Richard P. Coleman, "The Continuing Significance of Social Class to Marketing," *Journal of Consumer Research*, vol. 10, no. 3, December 1983, pp. 265–280.

16. Julie Look, "Understanding Tween Culture," *Marketing Magazine*, August 2, 1999, p. 16.

17. Anita Lahey, "Bauer Gets A Boost at World Cup of Hockey," *Marketing Magazine*, September 2, 1996, p. 2.

18. See Elihu Katz and Paul Lazarsfeld, *Personal Influence* (New York: Free Press, 1955) especially p. 325.

19. Sara Curtis, "Radio Show Targets Children 8 to 12," *Marketing Magazine*, October 7, 1996, p. 3.

20. Mikala Folb, "Totally Girl," *Marketing Magazine*, January 4/11, 1999, pp. 10, 12.

21. A. H. Maslow, *Motivation and Personality* (New York: Harper & Row, 1954), pp. 80–106.

22. Steven Reiss and Susan M. Havercamp, "Toward a Comprehensive Assessment of Fundamental Motivation: Factor Structure of the Reiss Profile," *Psychological Assessment*, June 1998, pp. 97–106.

23. Other schools of thought on learning, principally the cognitive approach and gestalt learning, are discussed in books on consumer behaviour. See David Louden and Albert J. Della Bitta, *Consumer Behavior*, 3rd ed. (New York: McGraw-Hill, 1988).

24. For an analytical review of self-concept studies, the research problems connected with these studies, and a comprehensive bibliography, see M. Joseph Sirgy, "Self-Concept in Consumer Behaviour: A Critical Review," *Journal of Consumer Research*, December 1982, pp. 287–300.

25. Andrew Poon and Dawn Walton, "Tables Turning on Fast Food," *The Globe and Mail*, July 5, 1997, pp. B1, B3.

26. For a listing of Canadian companies found on Sympatico, check the Internet address, maplesquare. sympatico.ca.

CHAPTER 7

1. Adapted from the Nortel Networks Web site, March 22, 2000 and Nortel's television advertisements.

2. Statistics Canada, *Market Research Handbook*, catalogue 63-224 (Ottawa, 1999).

3. *1996 Annual Report*, Safeway.

4. Statistics Canada, *Market Research Handbook*, catalogue 63-224 (Ottawa, 1999).

5. "Ranking Governments Top Supplier," *Summit*, November, 1998, pp. 7–11.

6. Robert Parkins, "Bestseller," *Summit*, November 1998, p. 11.

7. Amy Barrett, "Internet Capital's Young Turks," *Business Week*, November 1, 1999, p. EB64+. and Matt Hicks, "A Matter of Trust: B2B e-commerce is booming, but sites need to build trust by setting ground rules," *PC Week*, October 25, 1999, pp. 67–68.

8. Earl D. Honeycutt, Theresa B. Flaherty, and Ken Benassi, "Marketing Industrial Products on the Internet," *Industrial Marketing Management*, January 1998, pp. 63–72.

9. Jeanette J. Arbuthnot, "Identifying Ethical Problems Confronting Small Retail Buyers," *Journal of Business Ethics*, May 1997, pp. 745–755.

10. Sang-Lin Han, David Wilson, and Shirlish P. Dant, "Buyer-Seller Relationships Today," *Industrial Marketing Management*, November 1993, pp. 331–338.

11. "Xerox Multinational Supplier Quality Survey," *Purchasing*, January 1995, p. 112.

12. Background on relationship building is described in F. Robert Dwyer, Paul H. Schurr, and Sejo Oh, "Developing Buyer-Seller Relationships," *Journal of Marketing*, April 1987, pp. 11–27. See also Patricia Doney and Joseph Cannon, "An Examination of the Nature of Trust in Buyer–Seller Relationships," *Journal of Marketing*, April 1997, pp. 31–51.

13. An interesting description of value imaging, the psychological influences on business buying behaviour, can be found in Paul Sherlock, "The Irrationality of 'Rational' Business Buying Decisions," *Marketing Management*, Spring 1992, pp. 8–15.

14. Robert D. McWilliams, Earl Naumann, and Stan Scott, "Determining Buying Center Size," *Industrial Marketing Management*, February 1992, pp. 43–49.

15. Ken Yamada, "Apple to Unveil Mail Order Catalog

and Sell Directly to Big Companies," *The Wall Street Journal*, September 17, 1992, p. B7.

16. For examples of benefit segmentation as used in the business market, see Mark L. Bennion, Jr., "Segmentation and Positioning in a Basic Industry," *Industrial Marketing Management*, February, 1987, pp. 9–18. Also Cornelius A. de Kluyver and David B. Whitlark, "Benefit Segmentation for Industrial Products," *Industrial Marketing Management*, November 1986, pp. 273–286.

17. For an excellent discussion on industrial market segmentation, see Richard E. Plank, "A Critical Review of Industrial Market Segmentation," *Industrial Marketing Management*, May 1985, pp. 75–91. Also, a detailed coverage of the topic is contained in Thomas V. Bonoma and Benson P. Shapiro, *Segmenting the Industrial Market* (Lexington, MA: Lexington Books, 1983).

CHAPTER 8

1. Adapted from Shawns Steinberg, "Have Allowance Will Transform Economy," *Canadian Business*, March 13, 1998, pp. 59–71; Mikala Folb, "Totally Girl," *Marketing Magazine*, January 4/11, 1999, pp. 11, 12; Julie Look, "Understanding Tween Culture," *Marketing Magazine*, August 2, 1999, p. 16. Julie McCann, "Trendspotting," *Marketing Magazine*, October 11, 1999, pp. 11, 12.

2. John Gray, "Levi's Inhabits Planet of the Cats," *Strategy*, March 27, 2000, p. 20.

3. Lesley Daw, "Success Insurance," *Marketing Magazine*, June 30, 1997, p. 21.

4. In "New Marketing Research Definition Approved," *Marketing News*, January 2, 1987, p. 1, the American Marketing Association defined marketing research as follows: "Marketing research links the consumer, customer, and public to the marketer through information — information used to identify and define marketing opportunities and problems; generate, refine, and evaluate marketing actions; monitor marketing performance; and improve

understanding of marketing as a process. Marketing research specifies the information required to address these issues; designs the methods for collecting information; manages and implements the data collection process; analyzes the results; and communicates the findings and their implications."

5. Eva E. Kiess-Moser and James G. Barnes, "Emerging Trends in Marketing Research: The Link with Customer Satisfaction," Ottawa: The Conference Board of Canada, Report 82-92, 1992.

6. For an overview of the development of marketing information systems, see Kimball P. Marshall and Stephen M. LaMotte, "Marketing Information Systems: A Marriage of Systems Analysis and Marketing Management," *Journal of Applied Business Research*, vol. 8, no. 3, 1992, pp. 61–73.

7. Tim Stevens, "Can You Relate? Information Technology Applied to Sales, Marketing, and Customer Service is Powering Stronger Customer Relationships," *Industry Week*, vol. 248, no. 5, March 1, 1999, pp. 26, 27.

8. Gordon Arnaut, "The Best Is Still To Come, Data Base Analysts Say," *The Globe and Mail*, December 17, 1996, p. B29; Terence Belford, "Air Mile Collectors Yield Wealth of Data," *The Globe and Mail*, December 17, 1996, p. B28.

9. Laurie Hays, "Using Computers to Divine Who Might Buy a Gas Grill," *The Wall Street Journal*, August 8, 1994, p. B1.

10. A two-part article exploring the process of and prospects of data mining is Peter R. Peacock, "Data Mining in Marketing: Part 1," *Marketing Management*, Winter 1998, pp. 8–18 and Peter R. Peacock, "Data Mining in Marketing: Part 2," *Marketing Management*, Spring 1999, pp. 14–25.

11. John Verity, "Coaxing Meaning Out of Raw Data," *Business Week*, February 3, 1997, pp. 134–138.

12. Maurice Simms, "Retailers Pin Hope on Marketing Skill," *The Globe and Mail*, February 15, 1994, p. B28; Douglas Arjam,

"Happy Kids Make Happy Moms," *Marketing Magazine*, January 25, 1999, p. 24.

13. Mark Lurie, "Direct Mail Success Takes Sharp Aim," *The Globe and Mail*, December 17, 1996, p. B29.

14. Deborah Wilson, "Banks Face Task of Assuring Clients They're Served, Not Shadowed," *The Globe and Mail*, December 17, 1996, p. B27.

15. Thomas C. Boyd, Timothy C. Krehbiel, and James M. Stearns, "The Impact of Technology on Marketing Research," *The Journal of Marketing Management*, Spring/Summer 1998, pp. 24–34.

16. Robert O'Harrow, Jr., "Buying Patterns Turn Into Directed Marketing," *The Washington Post* as reported in The Idaho Statesman, January 1, 1999, p. D3.

17. For a more detailed discussion of scanner panels and single-source data, see James G. Barnes, *Research for Marketing Decision Making* (Toronto: McGraw-Hill Ryerson, 1991), pp. 137–140.

18. Scott Evans, "Tomes Have Changed," *Strategy*, June 7, 1999, p. 26.

19. For a discussion of the representativeness of the sample in mall-intercept surveys, compared with other approaches to data collection, see Alan J. Bush and A. Parasuraman, "Mall Intercept Versus Telephone Interviewing Environment," *Journal of Advertising Research*, vol. 25, no. 2, April/May 1985, pp. 36–43; and Thomas D. Dupont, "Do Frequent Mall Shoppers Distort Mall-Intercept Survey Results?" *Journal of Advertising Research*, vol. 27, August/September 1987, pp. 45–51.

20. John M. Scheb, "Do-It-Yourself Sampling Proves Cost Effective," *Marketing News*, April 13, 1998, p. 12.

21. A.J. Faria and John R. Dickinson, "Mail Survey Response, Speed, and Cost," *Industrial Marketing Management*, February 1992, pp. 51–60.

22. Brad Edmondson, "The Wild Bunch: Online Surveys and Focus Groups Might Solve the Toughest Problems in Market Research," *American

Demographics*, June 1997, pp. 10–15.

23. Sandra Mingail, "Net Surveys Accurate to Within 0% and 100%," *The Financial Post*, January 26, 2000, p. E7.

24. For additional detail on the use of the individual depth interview and the focus group interview, see James G. Barnes, *Research for Marketing Decision Making* (Toronto: McGraw-Hill Ryerson, 1991), chapter 12; Richard A. Krueger, *Focus Groups*, 2nd ed. (Beverly Hills, CA: Sage Publications, 1994).

25. James Heckman, "Turning the Focus Online: Web Snares Ever-More Qualitative Research," *Marketing News*, February 28, 2000, p. 15.

26. Justin Martin, "Ignore Your Customer," *Fortune*, May 1, 1995, pp. 121–126.

27. For a comprehensive description of Internet marketing, see Judy Strauss and Raymond Frost, *Marketing on the Internet*, (Scarborough: Prentice Hall, 1999).

28. Robert O'Harrow, Jr., loc. cit.

29. Robert Everett-Green, "The Great Canadian Hunt for Home-Grown Movies," *The Globe and Mail*, June 13, 1996, p. A13.

30. Howard Schlossberg, "Simulated vs. Traditional Test Marketing," *Marketing News*, October 23, 1989, pp. 1–2, 11.

31. Kathy Gardner Chadwick, "Some Caveats Regarding the Interpretation of Data From 800 Numbers," *Journal of Services Marketing*, Summer 1991, pp. 55–61.

32. Michelle Cook, "Salesforce: A Source of Competitive Intelligence," *Strategy*, August 30, 1999, p. 32.

33. Lara Mills, "Playing hard to get," *Marketing Magazine Online*, April 24, 2000, www.marketingmag.ca.

34. Doss Struse, "Marketing Research's Top 25 Influences," *Marketing Research*, vol. 11, no. 4, Spring 2000, pp. 5–9.

CHAPTER 9

1. Adapted from, in part, *businesswire.com*, February 16, 1999; *ballard.com/bluebox/bw021699*; *National Post*, Internet Edition, April 7, 2000; *ballard.com/viewpress release and ballard.com/view report*, April 17, 2000.

2. Yumiko Ono, "Some Kids Won't Eat the Middle of an Oreo," *The Wall Street Journal*, November 20, 1991, p. B1.

3. Cadillac home page, April 2000, www.cadillac.gmcanada.com; OnStar® home page, April 2000 www.onstar.com; Gerry Malloy, "Techbyte Cadillac OnStar: Star Trek Technology for the Road," *The Globe and Mail*, October 10, 1996, p. E4.

4. For a different classification scheme that provides strategic guidelines for management by relating products and prices, along with a bibliography on product classification, see Patrick E. Murphy and Ben M. Enis, "Classifying Products Strategically," *Journal of Marketing*, July 1986, pp. 24–42. Also see Ernest F. Cooke, "The Relationship between a Product Classification System and Marketing Strategy," *Journal of Midwest Marketing*, Spring 1987, pp. 230–240.

5. Simon Avery, "Cisco Begins Rollout of Device Merging Internet, Phone," *The Financial Post*, April 12, 2000, p. C5.

6. ING Direct Canada home page, April 2000, www.ingdirect.com. ING international home page, April 2000, www.ing.com. Susan Yellin, "Innovation, Acquisition Catapulting to the Top," The Financial Post, February 12, 1997, p. 8.

7. Bernadette Johnson, "Category Profile — The Canadian Salty Snack Market," *Strategy*, May 24, 1999, p. 13.

8. David Todd, "Package Design: Jumping Off the Shelf," *Strategy*, May 26, 1997, p. 29.

9. Brian Dunn, "Taking on Tropicana," *Marketing Magazine*, November 2, 1998, p. 16.

10. Patti Summerfield, "Milk Builds New Image: Parmalat," *Strategy*, June 22, 1998, p.7.

11. "Procter & Gamble Unveils New Tide High Efficiency," *P&G Product News Release*, P&G home page, March 1997, www.pg.com.

12. Derek DeCloet, "Way, Way Too Cool," *Canadian Business*, August 27, 1999, pp. 30–35.

13. Jo Marney, "Too Much of a Good Thing," *Marketing Magazine*, January 24, 2000, p. 21.

14. Eugene Carlson, "Some Forms of Identification Can't Be Handily Faked," *The Wall Street Journal*, September 14, 1993, p. B2.

15. Honda Motor Company home page, April 2000, www.honda.com.

16. The benefits cited are from a study reported in Robert G. Cooper and Elko J. Kleinschmidt, "New Product Processes at Leading Industrial Firms," *Industrial Management*, May 1991, pp. 137–147. For an approach to improve the management of multiple new-product development projects, see Steven C, Wheelwright and Kim B. Clark, "Creating Project Plans to Focus Product Development Stages," *Harvard Business Review*, March–April 1992, p. 70–82.

17. For a report on the criteria used in making "go – no go" decisions in the product-development process, see Ilkka A. Ronkainen, "Criteria Changes Across Product Development Stages," *Industrial Marketing Management*, August 1985, pp. 171–178.

18. "Study: Launching New Products is Worth the Risk," *Marketing News*, January 20, 1992, p. 2.

19. For more on the first two stages, see Linda Rochford, "Generating and Screening New Product Ideas," *Industrial Marketing Management*, November 1991, pp. 287–296.

20. Wendy Cuthbert, "Shoppers Drug Mart Boosts Status With Addition of Quo," *Strategy*, July 5, 1999, p. 30.

21. Andrew Stodart, "The Road More Traveled," *Marketing Magazine Online*, July 19/26, 1999, www.marketingmag.ca.

22. Jo Marney, "Too Much of A Good Thing," *Marketing Magazine*, January 24, 2000, p. 21.

23. For the foundations of diffusion theory of innovation, see Everett M. Rogers, *Diffusion of Innovations*, 3rd ed. (New York: Free Press, 1983).

24. Rogers, op. cit.

25. "Kodak Video Tape Feature Differentiation," Kodak home page, April 2000, www.kodak.com.

26. Harry Cornelius, "Weathervanes and Beacons," *Marketing Magazine Online*, April 3, 2000, www.marketingmag.ca.

27. Various arrangements are discussed in Eric Olsen, Orville Walker, and Robert Reukert, "Organizing for Effective New Product Development," *Journal of Marketing*, January 1995, pp. 48–62.

CHAPTER 10

1. Labatt Breweries home page, April 2000, www.labatt.com and Molson Breweries home page, April 2000, www.iam.com. Also, Patrick Allossery, "Molson Gets Canadian," *National Post*, April 10, 2000, p. C5. Also Jonathon Gatehouse, "With Glowing Hearts We See Thee Advertise," *National Post*, April 12, 2000, pp. A1, A2.

2. Adapted from David A. Aaker and J. Gary Shansby, "Positioning Your Product," *Business Horizons*, May/June 1982, pp. 56–58.

3. Brian Dunn, "Taking on Tropicana," *Marketing Magazine*, November 2, 1998, p. 16.

4. Marina Strauss, "Canada Rated 6th in Quality of Its Manufactured Goods," *The Globe and Mail*, February 10, 1994, p. B6.

5. Jan Field, "Ice With Edge," *Marketing Magazine*, February 7, 2000, p. 17.

6. Richard Gibson, "Haagan-Dazs' New Ice Creams Have Less Fat," *The Wall Street Journal*, January 10, 1997, p. B14.

7. Debra Sykes, "Low-Fat Market Proves Elusive for Fast-Food Chains," *Stores*, July 1996, pp. 50–53.

8. Kathy Tyrer, "Selling Hockey in the Land of La La and Disney," *Marketing Magazine*, November 8, 1993, p. 5.

9. "New Crest Toothpaste, Toothbrush Introduced," news release, May 26, 1997. Proctor and Gamble Inc. home page, April 2000, wwwpg.com.

10. Andrew Stodart, "The Road More Traveled," *Marketing Magazine* Online, July 19/26, 1999, www.marketingmag.ca.

11. Ariane Sains, "Swiss Army Swells Ranks," *Adweek's Marketing Week*, June 4, 1990, p. 24; Kathleen Deveny, "If Swatch Name Sells Watches, Why Not Cars," *The Wall Street Journal*, September 20, 1990, p. B1. Also the Swatch home page, April 2000, wwwswatch.com.

12. Glenn Collins, "The Cola War Is Expected to Heat Up," *The New York Times*, January 25, 1997, pp. 37, 39.

13. James Pollack, "Ikea Puts Focus on Office Furniture," *Marketing Magazine*, November 4, 1996, p. 4.

14. Mikala Folb, "Minwax Makes Decorative Paint Entry," *Marketing Magazine*, October 4, 1996, p. 21.

15. James R. Hagerty, "Gilding the Drill Bit? Hardware Giants Go High-End," *The Wall Street Journal*, July 28, 1998, pp. B1, B7.

16. Marina Strauss, "Holt Renfrew Brands A Strategy," *The Globe and Mail*, March 20, 1997, p. B13.

17. Lee Gomes, "HP to Create a New Subsidiary to Sell Cheap 'Apollo' Brand of Ink-Jet Printers," *The Wall Street Journal*, January 6, 1999, p. B4; also Susan Caminiti, "Will Old Navy Fill The Gap," *Fortune*, March 18, 1996, p. 59.

18. Adam Feuerstein, "Lego Robots Marching on Marin County," *San Francisco Business Times*, June 11, 1999, p.1; also Cora Daniels, "Lego's Star Wars Robot: Another Great Way to Kill Time in Silicon Valley," *Fortune*, June 7, 1999, p. 190.

19. Jo Marney, "Too Much of A Good Thing," *Marketing Magazine*, January 24, 1999, p. 21.

20. "Kraft Buzzing About Honey Cereal," *Marketing Magazine*, August 2, 1999, p. 1.

21. Ernest Beck, "Unilever to Cut More Than 1,000 Brands," *The Wall Street Journal*, September 22, 1999, p. A17.

22. Vijay Vishwanath and Jonathon Mark, "Your Brand's Best Strategy," *Harvard Business Review*, May–June 1997, pp. 123–129.

23. William C. Symonds, "Would You Spend $1.50 for a Razor Blade?" *Business Week*, April 27, 1998, p. 46; also Mark Maremont, "Gillette Finally Reveals the Future, and It Has Three Blades," *The Wall Street Journal*, April 14, 1998, pp. A1, A10.

24. Dean Takahashi, "Intel to Unveil Speedier Chips on

Monday," *The Wall Street Journal*, October 22, 1999, p. B6; also Andy Reinhardt, "Intel Is Taking No Prisoners," *Business Week*, July 12, 1999, p. 38.

25. The criticisms are summarized in Geoffrey L. Gordon, Roger J. Calantone, and C. Anthony di Benedetto, "Mature Markets and Revitalization Strategies: An American Fable," *Business Horizons*, May–June 1991. Alternative life cycles are proposed in Edward D. Popper and Bruce D. Buskirk, "Technology Life Cycles in Industrial Markets," *Industrial Marketing Management*, February 1992, pp. 23–31.

26. Laurence Zuckerman, "The Hand-Held Computer is Introduced Once Again," *The New York Times*, November 18, 1996, p. D8. Also the Hewlett Packard home page, April 2000, www.hp.com.

27. Jo Marney, "That's No Fad; It's A Trend," *Marketing Magazine*, April 17, 2000, p. 32.

28. Kevin Coughlin, " Are CD's Days Numbered? Two New Technologies Join the Battle for the World's Ear," *St. Louis Post — Dispatch*, September 5, 1999, p. E1; Robert A. Starrett, "Burning Down the House: Home Recorders are Here," *E-Media Professional*, May 1999, p. 50.

29. For more on this subject, see Steven P. Schnaars, "When Entering Growth Markets, Are Pioneers Better Than Poachers?' *Business Horizons*, March–April 1986, pp. 27–36.

30. Reiji Yoshida, "Sega Plays Survival Game with Dreamcast," *Japan Times Weekly, International Edition*, December 14–20, 1998, p. 13.

31. Lesley Daw, "How to Market A Milestone," *Marketing Magazine*, March 10, 1997, pp. 10–11.

32. Mikala Folb, "Playskool Beats Bacteria," *Marketing Magazine*, March 17, 1997, p.3.

33. Lesley Daw, "CIGNA Markets Women's Health Insurance," *Marketing Magazine*, March 10, 1997, p. 4.

34. Kodak home page, April 2000, www.kodak.com.

35. Hardy Green, "The Last Word in New Words," *Business Week*, August 30, 1999, p. 6. also the St. Martins Press home page for scholastic publications, April 2000, www.stmartins-scholarly.com.

36. Bill Saporito, "How to Revive a Fading Firm," *Fortune*, March 22, 1993, p. 80.

CHAPTER 11

1. Sarah Smith, "When the Rubbers Hit the Road," *Marketing Magazine*, August 2, 1999, p. 12.

2. GoTo.com (www.goto.com) is an online marketplace that introduces consumers and advertisers. Advertisers bid in an ongoing auction for priority placement in consumer search results. Details reported in the text originate from a press release dated January 27, 2000, www.goto.com/d/about/news/press29.jhtml.

3. Gay Abbate, "Heirs Win $1-Million 'Anne' Fight," *The Globe and Mail*, March 14, 2000, pp. A1, A7.

4. Howard Schlossberg, "Brand Value Can Be Worth More than Physical Assets," *Marketing News*, March 5, 1990, p. 6.

5. Larry Black, "What's in a Name?" *Report on Business Magazine*, November 1989, pp. 98–110.

6. Information regarding the merger of these luxury hotel chains can be found at www.cphotels.com or www.fairmont.com. Details reported in the text come from a press release dated April 19, 1999, www.cphotels.com/cp.asp?loc=corp.

7. Betsy Morris, "The Brand's the Thing," *Fortune*, March 4, 1996, pp.73–86.

8. Elizabeth Nickson, "The American founders of Roots have been accused of branding the wilderness," *The Globe and Mail*, March 23, 2000, www.theglobeandmail.com.

9. For an in-depth discussion of the value of branding, see David Arnold, *The Handbook of Brand Management* (London: Pitman Publishing, 1992).

10. Michael J. Etzel, Bruce J. Walker, and William J. Stanton, "Branding on the Internet," *Marketing*, 12e, (New York: McGraw-Hill, 2001), p. 269.

11. Jamie Beckett, "Inventing a Product Name is Part Science, Part Art," *The Globe and Mail*, October 27, 1992, p. B4.

12. See also, Kim Robertson, "Strategically Desirable Brand Name Characteristics," *The Journal of Product and Brand Management*, Summer 1992, pp. 62–72.

13. Dean Takahashi, "In Pursuit of Pokemon Pirates," *The Wall Street Journal*, November 8, 1999, pp. B1, B4.

14. Kanran Kashani, "A Future for Brands," *Financial Times, Mastering Management* (London: Pitman, 1997), pp. 171–174.

15. For an excellent discussion of the nature and benefits of this strategy, see Donald G. Norris, "Ingredient Branding: A Strategy Option with Multiple Beneficiaries," *The Journal of Consumer Marketing*, Summer 1992, pp. 19–31.

16. Russell Mitchell, "Intel Isn't Taking This lying Down," *Business Week*, September 30, 1991, pp. 32–33.

17. Canada News Wire, "Air Canada and Second Cup Forge New Partnerships from the Grounds Up," press release, February 17, 1997, www.newswire.ca/releases/february1997/17/c3272.html.

18. For a look at the success of Loblaw's private-label business and at the developer of the program, Dave Nichol, see Mark Stevenson, "Global Gourmet," *Canadian Business*, July 1993, pp. 22–23; see also Anne Kingston, *The Edible Man: Dave Nichol, President's Choice and the Making of Popular Taste* (Toronto: Macfarlane, Walter & Ross, 1994).

19. The 1993 study of personal computers was summarized in Kyle Pope, "Computers: They're No Commodity," *The Wall Street Journal*, October 15, 1993, p. B1.

20. George Stalk, Jr. "What's in a Brand? It's the Experience," *The Globe and Mail*, May 23, 1997, p. B11.

21. The $100 billion forecast was made by Destination Products International, as reported in Stephanie Thompson, "The New Private Enterprise," *Brandweek*, May 3, 1999, p. 36.

22. For a discussion of this topic, see Leonard L. Berry, Edwin F. Lefkowith, and Terry Clark, "In Services, What's in a Name?" *Harvard Business Review*, September/October 1988, pp. 38–40. Some of the examples were drawn from this source.

23. "Science of ketchupology hits new heights at Heinz," *Globe and Mail*, April 3, 2000, p. B4.

24. Debbie Galante Block, "CD-ROM Packaging, Present and Future: The Drive Toward Automation and Alternative Casing," *CD-ROM Professional*, October 1996, pp. 69–79.

25. Information on this program can be obtained from Environment Canada's Web site: www.ns.ec.gc.ca/.

26. "Labelling Cooperation Urged," *Marketing News*, May 9, 1994, p. 17.

27. For information related to this Act, the government has set up the Competition Bureau, which can answer any questions. You can write to Industry Canada, 50 Victoria Street, Hull, Que., K1A 0C9, 1-800-248-5358. Industry Canada's Web site is www.ic.gc.ca. All government departments can be reached through www.gc.ca.

28. For further information on any federal acts or regulations, contact the Government of Canada Web page at www.gc.ca.

29. Ann Gibbon, "Smoking's Labelling Perils," *The Globe and Mail*, May 5, 1994, p. B1; and "The Supreme Court of Canada Ruling on the Tobacco Products Control Act," Health Canada, 1997, www.hcsc.ca.main.hc/web/datapcb/communc/home/news/85kb2e.html (December 1995).

30. Frank Gibney and Belinda Luscombe, "The Redesigning of America," *Time*, March 20, 2000, p. 44.

31. For a list of reasons why product quality is so important and for a discussion of the marketing function's role in quality management, see Neil A. Morgan and Nigel F. Piercy, "Market-Led Quality," *Industrial Marketing Management*, May 1992, pp. 111–118.

CHAPTER 12

1. Joan Skogan, "Once Upon A Tims," *Saturday Night*, September 1999, pp. 68–73.

2. Liza Finlay, "Perpetual Promos," *Marketing Magazine*, May 31, 1999, p. 11.

3. Demographic statistics for Canada can be found at the Statistics Canada Web site at www.statcan.ca.

4. Industry statistics can be found at Industry Canada's Web site at www.strategis.ic.gc.ca.

5. "The Flip Side of Flipping Hamburgers," *The Globe and Mail*, April 8, 1996, p. A6.

6. Leonard L. Berry and Terry Clark, "Four Ways to Make Services More Tangible," *Business*, October/December 1986, p. 53. Also see Betsy D. Gelb, "How Marketers of Intangibles Can Raise the Odds for Consumer Satisfaction," *Journal of Services Marketing*, Summer 1987, pp. 11–17.

7. See Elizabeth Church, "Store Owners Struggle with Staffing," *The Globe and Mail*, November 25, 1996, p. B6; and "Service With A Smile," *The Economist*, July 12, 1997, p. 55. For more details on developing service employees, see Leonard L. Berry, *Discovering the Soul of Service* (New York: Free Press, 1999).

8. Paulette Thomas, "Staples Executives Now Aim to Reinvent Dry Cleaning," *The Wall Street Journal*, April 27, 1999, p. B1.

9. Willian R. Papa, "Putting Customers on the Line," *Inc. Technology*, 1997, no.1, pp. 23–24.

10. Helena Katz, "How A Bankrupt Ski Resort Became #1," *Marketing Magazine*, November 2, 1998, p. 22.

11. See for example, Barbara Ettorre, "The Bottom Line on Customer Loyalty," *Management Review*, March 1997, pp. 16–18; and Elizabeth Church, "How to Keep Customers," *The Globe and Mail*, February 27, 1996, p. B14.

12. John Gray, "B.C. Hydro Powering Up for Deregulation," *Strategy*, June 21, 1999, p. 4.

13. James L. Heskett, Thomas O. Jones, Gary W. Loveman, Earl Sasser, Jr. and Leonard A. Schlesinger, "Putting the Service-Profit Chain to Work," *Harvard Business Review*, March–April, 1994, pp. 164–174. Also, Leonard L. Berry, *Discovering the Soul of Service* (New York: Free Press, 1999).

14. See for example, James G. Barnes, "Establishing Relationships: Getting Closer to the Customer May be More Difficult Than You Think," *Irish Marketing Review*, May 1995, pp. 561–570; and James G. Barnes and Daphne Sheaves, "The Fundamentals of Relationships," in Teresa A. Swartz, David E. Bowen, and Stephen W. Brown, eds., *Advances in Services Marketing and Management*, vol. 5 (Greenwich, CT: JAI Press, 1996), pp. 215–245.

15. Lesley Daw, "Saturn Events Pack A Big Loyalty Punch," *Marketing Magazine*, September 14, 1998, p. 2.

16. Jennifer Ralston, "Beyond Pill Pushing," *Marketing Magazine*, March 27, 2000, p. 19.

17. Neal Templin, "For Hotel Guests with Glitches, High-Tech Room Service," *The Wall Street Journal*, August 30, 1999, p. B1.

18. Christopher W. Hart, James J. Heskett, and W. Earl Sasser, Jr., "The Profitable Art of Service Recovery: How Best to Turn Complaining Customers Into Loyal Ones," *Harvard Business Review*, July–August, 1990, pp. 148–156.

19. For a perspective on how technology can interplay with consumer loyalty, see "Editorial: Poor Call-Centre Service Wreaks Havoc on Loyalty," *Strategy*, November 34, 1997, p. 23. Also, Louise Lariviere's, "Two-Timing Consumers Crave Relationships," *Strategy*, July 19, 1999, p. D6.

20. Oren Harari, "Thank Heaven for Complainers," *Management Review*, March 1997, pp. 25–29.

21. For a discussion of the concept of customer value, see Robert B. Woodruff, "Customer Value: The Next Source for Competitive Advantage," *Journal of the Academy of Marketing Science*, vol. 25, no. 2, 1997, pp. 139–153; and A. Parasuraman, "Reflections on Gaining Competitive Advantage Through Customer Value," *Journal of the Academy of Marketing Science*, vol. 25, no. 2, 1997, pp. 154–161.

22. For a model of new-service development, see Eberhard E. Scheuing and Eugene M. Johnson, "A Proposed Model for New Service Development," *The Journal of Services Marketing*, Spring 1989, pp. 25–34. See also, G. Lynn Shostack, "Service Positioning Through Structural Change," *Journal of Marketing*, January 1987, pp. 34–43. For an insight into the process of introducing new services to the business-to-business market, see Ulrike de Brentani, "Success and Failure in New Industrial Services," *Journal of Product Innovation*, vol. 6, 1989, pp. 238–258.

23. Bernadette Johnson, "Free ISP Puts Focus on e-commerce," *Strategy*, March 27, 2000, p. 5.

24. Douglas McArthur, "B&B's Join Cyberspace Bandwagon," *The Globe and Mail*, March 19, 1997, p. C2.

25. "Two Cheers for Loyalty," *The Economist*, January 6, 1996, p. 49; Joseph Marranca, "Zellers Making A Millionaire," *Marketing Magazine*, March 20, 2000, p. 1.

26. Lisa Saunders, "House Calls," *Winnipeg Free Press*, February 6, 1996, p. B1.

27. Leonard Berry, Edwin F. Lefkowith, and Terry Clark, "In Services, What's in A Name?" *Harvard Business Review*, September–October 1988, pp. 28–30. See also, Sak Onkvisit and John J. Shaw, "Service Marketing: Image, Branding, and Competition," *Business Horizons*, January/February 1989, pp. 13–18.

28. Craig Saunders, "Peachtree Invests in Brand-Building," *Strategy*, March 27, 2000, p. 1.

29. For an excellent overview of the subject of service quality, see Leonard L. Berry, *On Great Service: A Framework for Action* (New York: Free Press, 1995). See also Albert Caruana, "The Role of Service Quality and Satisfaction in Customer Loyalty," *Proceedings of the 1999 Summer Educators Conference*, American Marketing Association, 1999, pp. 139–145.

30. V. A. Zeithaml, L. L. Berry, and A. Parasuraman, "The Behavioral Consequences of Service Quality," *Journal of Marketing*, vol. 60, April 1996, p. 31–46. L.L. Berry and A. Parasuraman, "Listening to the Customer — The Concept of a Service-Quality Information System," *Sloan Management Review*, Spring 1997, pp. 65–76.

31. Judith A. Cumby and James G. Barnes, "How Customers Are Made to Feel: the role of affective reactions in driving customer satisfaction," *International Journal of Customer Relationship Management*, vol. 1, no. 1, 1998, pp. 54–63.

32. "People, Not Tricks, Make Customer Service," *The Globe and Mail*, August 1, 1997, p. B8 (reprinted from The Economist).

33. For further reading see, Mary Jo Bitner, Bernard H. Booms, and Mary Stanfield Tetreault, "The Service Encounter: Diagnosing Favorable and Unfavorable Incidents," *Journal of Marketing*, January 1990, pp. 71–84; and Mary Jo Bitner, "Evaluating Service Encounters: The Effects of Physical Surroundings and Employee Responses," *Journal of Marketing*, April 1990, pp. 69–82.

34. James G. Barnes, Peter A. Dunne and William J. Glynn, "Self-Service and Technology: Unanticipated and Unintended Effects on Customer Relationships," in Teresa A. Swartz and Dawn Iacobucci, (eds.), *Handbook of Services Marketing and Management*, Thousand Oaks, CA: Sage Publications, 2000, pp. 89–102.

35. Leonard A. Schlesinger and James L. Heskett, "The Service-driven Service Company," *Harvard Business Review*, September–October 1991, pp. 71–81.

36. James G. Barnes and Judith A. Cumby, " The Cost of Quality in Service-Oriented Companies: Making Better Customer Service Decisions Through Improved Cost Information," *Proceedings of the 23rd Annual Conference of the Atlantic Schools of Business*, Saint John, New Brunswick, November 4–6, 1993, pp. 241–250.

37. Leonard L. Berry, "Improving America's Service," Marketing Management, vol.1, no.3, pp. 28–38. For each of the five fundamental mistakes, the author discusses several

examples, the reasons for the mistakes, and suggests correcting the situation.

CHAPTER 13

1. Adapted from Chris Wood, "Free Music," *MacLean's*, March 20, 2000, pp. 42–46; Patricia Jacobus, "Napster Suit Tests New Copyright Law", *CNET NEWS.com*, April 11, 2000, www.cnet.com; Robert Thompson, "The Napster Revolution," *National Post*, April 15, 2000, p. A3. Ken Yamada, "Shop Talk: Wake Up, Music Industry," *Red Herring Online*, May 2, 2000, www.redherring.com; and Tyler Hamilton, "Metallica, MP3 and 355,000 Pirates," National Post, May 4, 2000, p. A1, A7 and Jon Maules, "Fishwrap: Breaking Up Is Hard To Do," *Red Herring Online*, May 2, 2000, www.redherring.com.

2. Paul Hunt, "Pricing For Profit," *Marketing Magazine Online*, April 26, 1999, www.marketingmag.ca.

3. Simona Chiose, "The Not-So-Compact Price of CDs," *The Globe and Mail*, January 25, 1997, pp. C1, C19.

4. For a thorough review of pricing, see Thomas T. Nagle and Reed K. Holden, "Chapter 4: Customers: Understanding and Influencing the Purchase Decision," *The Strategy and Tactics of Pricing: A Guide To Profitable Decision Making* (Englewood Cliffs, NJ: Prentice-Hall, 1995), pp. 72–114.

5. Kimya Kamshad, "A Price for Every Customer," *The Financial Post*, February 13, 1997, pp. 12–13.

6. Sarah Smith, "Toy Versus Toy," *Marketing Magazine Online*, January 17, 2000, www.marketingmag.ca.

7. For a review of pricing strategies, see Nessim Hanna and H. Robert Dodge, *Pricing: Policies and Procedures* (London: McMillan Press, 1995).

8. David Steinhart, "Priceline Pushed Toward Profit On Strength of Customer Growth," *The Financial Post*, April 25, 2000, p. C3.

9. Jane Coutts, "Drug Price 'Obscene,' Official Says," *The Globe and Mail*, March 26, 1997, p. A5.

10. Lara Mills, "Communication — Beyond Price Wars," *Marketing Magazine*, June 7, 1999, p. 21.

11. Craig Saunders, "Zellers, Wal-Mart Beef Up Brand Offerings," *Strategy*, August 16, 1999, p. 1.

12. Erica Zlomislic, "What Went Wrong? Tip Top Repositions Too Far, Too Fast," *Strategy*, May 25, 1998, p. 1.

13. "Pricing Gets Easier (Sort Of)," *Inc.*, November 1993, p. 124.

14. Micheal J. Morris and Roger Calantone, "Four Components of Effective Pricing," *Industrial Marketing Management*, November 1990, p. 323.

15. Thomas L. Powers, "Break-Even Analysis with Semi-fixed Costs," *Industrial Marketing Management*, February 1987, pp. 25–41.

16. For a discussion of price wars in fast food, see Gayle MacDonald, "High Stakes in Burger Bargains," *The Globe and Mail*, February 28, 1997, p. B11.

17. Dan Koeppel, "Fast Food's New Reality," *Adweek's Marketing Week*, March 30, 1992, pp. 22–23.

18. "Canadians Like Luxury vehicles," *The Telegram*, p. 27. Reprinted with permission from The Canadian press.

19. Bruce Constantineau, "Cartier defies B.C. retail trend," *Vancouver Sun*, March 29, 1997, pp. B1, B9.

20. Shailaja Neelakantan, "A New Generation of Affluent Shoppers is Changing Luxury Spending Patterns," *Brandweek*, April 19, 1999, pp. 66–68.

21. Jack Kohane, " In The Buff," *Marketing Magazine Online*, November 10, 1997, www.marketingmag.ca.

CHAPTER 14

1. Mercata.Com home page, May 13, 2000, www.mercata.com.

2. Eve Lazarus, "Furniture Stores Buck the Price Pitch," *Marketing Magazine Online*, August 9, 1999, www.marketingmag.ca.

3. John Gray, "Bell Banks on Bundling Strategy," *Strategy*, October 11, 1999, p. 13.

4. For a discussion of value pricing, see Thomas T. Nagle and Reed K. Holden, "Chapter 8: Customer Negotiation, Pricing in the Trenches," *The Strategy and Tactics of Pricing*, 2nd ed. (Englewood Cliffs, NJ: Prentice-Hall, 1995).

5. Sinclair Stewart, "Drug Trading Writes Rx for Success," *Strategy*, April 12, 1999, p. 1.

6. Bernadette Johnson, "House of Tools Adds Web Site to Sales Kit," *Strategy*, May 10, 1999, p. D12.

7. Ian Gordon, "Healthy Relationships Require Work," *Strategy*, March 2, 1998, p. DR8.

8. Discussions on relationship pricing are included in Tony Cram, *The Power of Relationship Marketing: Keeping Customers for Life* (London: Pitman Publishing, 1994). Also Leonard L. Berry, "Relationship Marketing," in Adrian Payne, Martin Christopher, Moira Clark, and Helen Peck, *Relationship Marketing for Competitive Advantage: Winning and Keeping Customers* (Oxford: Butterworth-Heinemann, 1996), pp. 65–74.

9. William Echikson, "Aiming at High and Low Markets," *Fortune*, March 22, 1993, p. 89.

10. Information was obtained from the Panasonic U.S. home page, May 13, 2000. www.panasonic.com.

11. Chris Bucholtz, "Putting Talk into Action: Inferno/Java Partnership Seeks to Take Networks to New Places," *Telephony*, April 14, 1998, p. 22.

12. Lara Mills, "Beyond Price Wars," *Marketing Magazine*, June 7, 1999, p. 21.

13. Michael Szego, "Utility Payment Model has Many Applications," *Strategy*, January 21, 2000, p. D6.

14. Paul Hunt, "Pricing for Profit: It's All About Delivering Value for Dollars, Not Just Nickel-and-Diming Your Customers," *Marketing Magazine Online*, April 26, 1999, www.marketingmag.ca.

15. "Buying Time," *Fortune*, September 8, 1997, p. 192.

16. Robert M. Schindler and Lori S. Warren, "Effects of Odd Pricing on Price Recall," *Journal of Business*, June 1989, pp. 165–177; Robert Blattberg and Kenneth Wisniewski, "How Retail Price Promotions Work: Empirical Results," Marketing Working Paper No. 42 (Chicago: University of Chicago, 1987).

17. Gene Kaproski, "The Price is Right," *Marketing Tools*, September 1995, p. 56.

18. Stephanie Whittaker, "Remaking the Grocery Biz," *Marketing Magazine*, February 21, 2000, p. 16.

19. Stephen J. Hoch, Xavier Dreze, and Mary E. Purk, "EDLP, Hi-Lo and Marketing Arithmetic," *Journal of Marketing*, October 1994, pp. 16–27.

20. "Packaged Goods I: Watching Out for No. 1," *Advertising Age*, June 27, 1997, www.adage.com/news_and_features/.

21. Lara Mills, "Cereal Sales Buck Soggy U.S. Trend," *Marketing Magazine Online*, January 18, 1999, www.marketingmag.ca.

22. Thomas T. Nagle, and Reed K. Holden, *The Strategy and Tactics of Pricing: A Guide to Profitable Decision Making* (Englewood Cliffs, NJ: Prentice-Hall, 1995). For an economic analysis of price wars, see Nessim Hanna and H. Robert Dodge, *Pricing: Policies and Procedures* (London: Macmillan, 1995).

CHAPTER 15

1. David Akin, "Focus on Core Business to Apple's Success," *National Post*, April 22, 2000, p. D5.

2. For a discussion of services distribution, see Christopher Lovelock, *Services Marketing*, 3rd ed. (Englewood Cliffs, NJ: Prentice Hall, 1996).

3. Sinclair Stewart, "Auto Makers May Up Marketing Role," *Strategy Online*, January 18, 1999, www.strategymag.ca.

4. The concept of shifting activities, the possibility of manufacturers shifting some functions away from their firms, and the opportunity for small wholesalers to perform added functions to maintain their economic viability are all discussed in Ronald D. Michman, "Managing Structural Changes in Marketing Channels," *The Journal of Business and Industrial Marketing*, Summer/Fall 1990, pp. 5–14.

5. For further discussion, see Frederick E. Webster, Jr.,

Industrial Marketing Strategy, 2nd ed. (New York: John Wiley & Sons, 1998).

6. Mark Evans, "Direct Distribution Gives Dell, Gateway Competitive Edge," *Financial Post*, August 6, 1996; also, "Gateway Uses its Stores to Lure Small Businesses," *The Wall Street Journal*, April 8, 1999, pp. B1, B4.

7. An alternative approach that emphasizes market analysis is presented in Allan J. Magrath and Kenneth G. Hardy, "Six Steps to Distribution Network Design," *Business Horizons*, January–February 1991, pp. 48–52.

8. Marshall Fisher, "What is the Right Supply Chain for Your Product?," *Harvard Business Review*, March–April 1997, pp. 105–116. For more on selecting channels for international markets, especially the decision of whether to use intermediaries, see Saul Klein, "Selection of International Marketing Channels," *Journal of Global Marketing*, vol. 4, 1991, pp. 21–37.

9. Anita Lahey, "The Total Brand Experience," *Marketing Magazine Online*, March 27, 2000, www.marketingmag.ca.

10. "Levi's Plans its Own Stores," *Marketing News*, January 30, 1995, p. 1.

11. "Alberto President Targets Mass Market," *Marketing Magazine*, July 8, 1996, p. 1.

12. "Now There are 2 Great Ways to Shop On-line," *What's New*, L.L. Bean home page, June 16, 1997, www.llbean.com/new/; Christopher McCormick, "L.L. Bean," *Advertising Age's Marketing 100* (1996), June 1996, www.adage.com/news_and_features/ (July 30, 1997).

13. An excellent discussion of distribution channels for business goods and services is found in Michael D. Hutt and Thomas W. Speh, *Business Marketing and Management*, 4th ed. (Ft. Worth, TX: Dryden Press, 1992), pp. 359–392. For a review of emerging issues on business channels, see Al McGrath, "Managing Distribution Channels," *Business Quarterly*, Spring 1996, pp. 57–65.

14. For a discussion of this topic, see Donald H. Light, "A Guide for New Distribution Channel Strategies for Service Firms," *The Journal of Business Strategy*, Summer 1986, pp. 54–64.

15. Rowland T. Moriarty and Ursula Moran, "Managing Hybrid Marketing Systems," *Harvard Business Review*, November–December 1990, pp. 146–155.

16. For extensive discussion of this strategy, see John A. Quelch, "Why Not Exploit Dual Marketing?," *Business Horizons*, January–February 1987, pp. 52–60.

17. For further discussion of the advantages and disadvantages of multiple channels as well as ways to minimize conflict resulting from multiple channels, see Martin Everett, "When There's More Than One Route To The Customer," *Sales and Marketing Management*, August 1990, pp. 48–50.

18. Jim Carroll, "Futures: When Old Partners Become New Competitors," *Marketing Magazine Online*, November 22, 1999, www.marketingmag.ca.

19. Zena Olijnk, "Loblaw Considers Creating Separate Online Division," *National Post*, May 5, 2000, pp. C1, C12.

20. For more on the idea that market considerations should determine a producer's channel structure, see Louis W. Stern and Frederick D. Sturdivant, "Customer-Driven Distribution Systems," *Harvard Business Review*, July–August 1987, pp. 34–41.

21. John Rossant, "Can Maurizio Gucci Bring the Glamour Back?," *Business Week*, February 5, 1990, pp. 83–84.

22. For further discussion of the strategies that either create or offset conflict between manufacturers and retailers, see Allan J. Magrath and Kenneth G. Hardy, "Avoiding the Pitfalls in Managing Distribution Channels," *Business Horizons*, September–October 1987, pp. 29–33.

23. The emerging dominance of gigantic retailers and their dictates to manufacturers are described in Zachary Schiller and Wendy Zellner, "Clout!," *Business Week*, December 21, 1992, pp. 66–69.

24. Allan J. Magrath, "The Hidden Clout of Middlemen," *Journal of Business Strategy*, March/April 1990, pp. 38–41.

25. Greg Keenan, "Parts Makers Face Competitive Challenge," *The Globe and Mail*, July 14, 1997, p. B6.

26. Gayle MacDonald, "Bata Marches to a Loyal Foot Soldier," *The Globe and Mail*, June 26, 1997, p. B12.

27. Don Tapscott, "Online Parts Exchange Heralds New Era," *The Financial Post*, May 5, 2000, p. C7.

28. Garry Marr, "Number of Online Investors Doubles," *National Post*, May 5, 2000, pp. C1, C12.

29. Simon Avery, "Hollywood, Meet the Internet," *The Financial Post*, May 5, 2000, p. C7.

CHAPTER 16

1. Adapted, in part, from Patrick Brethaur, "Middleman Bucks Trend by Embracing the Web," *The Globe and Mail*, June 1997, p. B9; and the Weber Supply home page, April 25, 2000, www.weber-supply.com.

2. David Todd, "Great Canadian Bagel Makes Slow But Sure Gains in Moscow," *Strategy*, February 14, 2000, p. 27.

3. J. William Gurley, "Why Online Distributors — Once Written Off — May Thrive," *Fortune*, September 6, 1999, p. 270.

4. For a discussion on channels of distribution, see James A. Narus and James C. Anderson, "Rethinking Distribution: Adaptive Channels," *Harvard Business Review*, July–August, 1996, pp. 112–120.

5. The term *merchant wholesaler*, or *wholesaler*, is sometimes used synonymously with *wholesaling intermediary*. This is not accurate, however. *Wholesaling intermediary* is the all-inclusive term, covering the major categories of firms engaged in wholesale trade, whereas *wholesaler* is more restrictive applying to only one category, namely, merchant wholesaling intermediaries.

6. Data relevant to this discussion is contained in "Wholesaling and Retailing in Canada, 1996," (Ottawa: Statistics Canada, 1999), cat. no. 63-236-XPB.

7. Lesley Daw, "Look! See Janes Build Frozen-Food Empire," *Marketing Magazine*, March 24, 1997, p. 3; and the Janes Family Foods home page, May 25, 2000, www.janes-familyfoods.com.

8. "Little Ads Can Be Big trouble, Experts Say," *South Bend Tribune*, January 5, 2000, p. D8.

9. Roger Morton, "Pulling Back Can Be The Best Way In," *Transportation and Distribution*, March 1999, pp. 57–58; and the PBB home page, May 25, 2000, www.pbb.com.

10. For a discussion of new directions in warehousing, see Ton Andel, "Get Your Warehouse Out of Storage," *Transportation and Distribution*, May 1997, pp. 84–105.

11. Jim Thomas, "Growing Pains," *Logistics Management and Distribution Report*," November 1998, p. 71.

12. Julia King, "Electronic Procurement Catching On Among Businesses," *Computerworld*, January 10, 2000, p. 41.

13. For a more thorough groundwork in the JIT concept, see Charles R. O'Neal, "Just-in-Time Exchange Relationships in Industrial Markets," *Journal of Marketing*, October 1988, pp. 52–67; and William D. Presutti, Jr., "Just-in-Time Manufacturing and Marketing — Strategic Relationships for Competitive Advantage," *Journal of Business and Industrial Marketing*, Summer 1988, pp. 27–35.

14. Ernest C. Raia, "Journey to World Class (JIT in USA)," *Purchasing*, September 24, 1987, p. 48.

15. Steve McDaniel, Joseph G. Ormsby and Alicia B. Gresham, The Effect of JIT on Distributors," *Industrial Marketing Management*, May 1992, pp. 145–149.

16. Ronald Henkoff, "Delivering The Goods," *Fortune*, November 28, 1994, pp. 64–78.

17. Brian Milligan, "What's it Going to Take to Make it Work?" *Purchasing*, September 2, 1999, pp. 40–44.

18. Susan Avery, "Foxboro's Strategy for PCs and Peripherals Cuts Costs," *Purchasing*, May 20, 1999, p. 87.

19. Wal-Mart's information technology applications, mentioned throughout this book, are excellent examples of an EDI. The retailer has developed a particularly close inventory management relationship with Proctor & Gamble.

20. Penelope Ody, "Sharing Data is Just The Beginning of The Process," *Financial Times*, September 1, 1999, p. 6; and John Verity, "Collaborative Forecasting: Vision Quest," *Computerworld*, November 10, 1997, pp. S12–S14.

21. Michael Lear-Olimpi, "More Than Just Games," *Warehousing Management*, September 1999, pp. 22–30; Robert D. Hof, "What's With All the Warehouses?" *Business Week e.biz*, November 1, 1999, p. EB88.

22. Janet Bamford, "Why Competitors Shop For Ideas at Ikea," *Business Week*, October 9, 1989, p. 88; and Robert D. Hof, loc. cit. November 1, 1999.

23. John Peel, "Saturday Morning Syndrome," *The Economist*, February 26, 2000, p. survey 37.

24. Nick Wingfield, "Iship.com Hopes to Make Shipping Simpler for e-Stores," *The Wall Street Journal*, September 2, 1999, p. B6.

25. For research results indicating that perceptions of different modes of transportation vary across members of the buying centre, see James H. Martin, James M. Daley, and Henry Burdg, "Buying Influences and Perceptions of Transportation Services," *Industrial Marketing Management*, November 1988, pp. 305–314.

26. "Out of The Box at UPS," *Business Week*, January 10, 2000, p. 76; and Douglas A. Blackmon, "Overnight, Everything Changed for FedEx; Can it Reinvent Itself?" *The Wall Street Journal*, November 4, 1999, pp. A1, A16.

CHAPTER 17

1. David Carr, "Luring Audiences Back to the Cinema," *Marketing Magazine Online*, January 18, 1999; Astrid Van Den Broek, "FP Breaks Out of Movie House Mold," *Marketing Magazine Online*, January 17, 2000, www.marketingmag.ca. Also, the Famous Players home page, May 25, 2000, www.famousplayers.com.

2. Statistical information for this chapter was obtained from various Statistics Canada sources, including the *Market Research Handbook*, 1999 Edition, cat. no. 63-224-XPB, *Retail Trade*, December 1999, cat. no. 63-005, and *Wholesaling and Retailing in Canada, 1996*, cat. no. 63-236-XPB. Each edition was published in 1999 and represents the most recent information available at the time of preparation.

3. For an interesting insight into how a small family-owned kitchenware retailer in Calgary operates with an emphasis on personalized service, see Cathryn Motherwell, "Where the Business is Cooking," *The Globe and Mail*, August 24, 1993, p. B28.

4. Dale D. Buss, "New Dynamics For A New Era," *Nation's Business*, June 1999, pp. 45–48.

5. Dan Morse and Jeffrey A. Tannenbaum, "Poll on High Success Rate for Franchises Raises Eyebrows," *The Wall Street Journal*, March 17, 1998, p. B2; "Survey Reports 92 Percent of Franchisees Say They are Successful," *Franchising World*, May/June 1998, pp. 34–36.

6. Lara Mills, "Sears Planning to 'Think Like a Brand'," *Marketing Magazine*, June 30, 1997, p. 2; Marina Strauss, "Where Department Stores Fit in the Retail Future," *The Globe and Mail*, May 29, 1997, p. B15; David Todd, "Sears Woos Women With Uplifting Spots," *Strategy*, June 5, 2000, p. 4.

7. "Advertising Age — 1995 Power 50 — Retail," *Advertising Age Online*, June 19, 1997, www.adage.com; Angela Kryhul, "The Wal-Mart Decade," *Marketing Magazine Online*, December 20/27, 1999, www.marketingmag.ca.

8. David Eggleston, "Zellers Freshens Up Gen Z," *Strategy*, May 22, 2000, p. D3.

9. James Pollack, "Specialists Thrive on High-End Positioning," *Marketing News*, March 10, 1997, p. 3.

10. Sonja Rasula, "Beyond Clothes," *Marketing Magazine*, May 10, 1999, pp. 16–17.

11. Shawna Cohen, "One-Stop Shopping for Dinner," *Marketing Magazine*, February 1, 1999, pp. 10, 12; Jennifer Bain, "Raw Fish and Piano Bars," *The Globe and Mail*, January 29, 2000, p. R15.

12. Cohen, loc. cit.

13. Eve Lazarus, "Chevron Reimages Town Pantry Brand," *Marketing Magazine*, July 12, 1999, p. 2; Brian Dunn, "The King of Bread, Butts, and Beer," *Marketing Magazine*, October 25, 1999, p. 23.

14. Tamsen Tillson, "Edu-tainment Warehouse Planned for Toronto Area," *The Globe and Mail*, September 27, 1994, p. B12; also Deborah King, "Big-Box Trend Seen Continuing for 2000," *The Globe and Mail*, February 15, 2000, p. W2.

15. "Tupperware Pops Up in Unfamiliar Places," *St. Louis Post-Dispatch*, March 7, 1999, p. E8.

16. Catherine Ramano, "Telemarketing Grows Up," *Management Review*, June 1998, pp. 31-36.

17. Calmetta W. Coleman, "Retailers Strive for Shopping Synergy," *The Wall Street Journal*, December 20, 1999, pp. B1, B6; also "Lands' End, Bean Lead Pack," *Daily News Record*, November 3, 1999, p. 12.

18. Statistics Canada, *Vending Machine Operators*, 1997, cat. no. 63-213; Mary Gooderham, "Your Supermarket Knows Who You Are," *The Globe and Mail*, August 17, 1993, pp. A1, A4.

19. "Coke Tests Machine That Adjusts Prices," *St. Louis Post-Dispatch*, October 28, 1999.

20. "So, What's the Connection Between Movies and Underwear Vending Machines?" *Financial Post*, March 15, 2000, p. E5.

21. For more on established retailers going online, see Greg Farrell, "Clicks-and-Mortar World Values Brands," *USA Today*, October 5, 1999, pp. 1B, 2B; Wendy Zellner and Stephanie Anderson Forest, "The Big Guys Go Online," *Business Week*, September 6, 1999, pp. 30–32.

22. Rebecca Quick, "New Study Finds Hope for Internet Retailers," *The Wall Street Journal*, April 18, 2000, p. A2.

23. Eric Reguly, "Dot-Coms Learning What Goes e-Round Comes e-Round," *The Globe and Mail*, May 2, 2000, p. B17.

24. Christine Y. Chen and Greg Lindsay, "The Straight Dope on Web Retailers: Which Ones Passed the Test?" *Fortune*, February 21, 2000, p. 280.

25. Keith McArthur, "Online Sales Transactions Foul Up 28% of the Time: Study," *The Globe and Mail*, March 8, 2000, p. B2; Marilyn Cohen, "E-Problem," *Forbes*, March 20, 2000, p. 322.

26. "E-Marketplaces Boost B2B Trade," from the Forrester Research Web site, May 26, 2000, www.forrester.com.

27. Cristine Lourosa-Ricardo, "Picking the product," *The Wall Street Journal*, November 22, 1999, pp. R8, R10.

28. Positioning based on price and service is discussed in George H. Lucas, Jr., and Larry G. Gresham, "How to Position for Retail Success," *Business*, April–June 1988, pp. 3–13. Positioning that combines all three variables is presented in Laurence H. Wortzel, "Retailing Strategies for Today's Mature Marketplace," *The Journal of Business Strategy*, Spring 1987, pp. 45–56.

29. Douglas Arjam, "Happy Kids Make Happy Moms," *Marketing Magazine*, January 25, 1999, p. 24; also Eggleston, loc. cit.

30. Gayle MacDonald, "Online Shopping Picks Up Steam," *The Globe and Mail*, July 25, 1997, p. B9.

31. Catherine Harris, "Shop till You Drop — from Home," *The Financial Post*, October 26, 1996, p. C5; see also the Flooz.Com home page, www.flooz.com, June 2, 2000.

32. Stephen Brown, "Variations on a Marketing Enigma: The Wheel of Retailing Theory," *The Journal of Marketing Management*, Summer 1996, pp. 63–66.

33. Janet Ginsberg, "Xtreme Retailing," *Business Week*, December 20, 1999, pp. 120–124.

CHAPTER 18

1. Adapted from Billy Adams, "Hey Hey! It's Sydney Spice,"

The Globe and Mail, May 1, 2000, pp. R1, R10 and Christopher Michael, "Popstars: It's not over until the five finalists sing," *National Post*, July 18, 2000, p. B3.

2. Danny Kucharsky, "A Doggone Great Brand," *Marketing Magazine Online*, December 20/27, 1999, www.marketingmag.ca.

3. Craig Saunders, "Shift To Launch Retail Ventures," *Strategy*, January 3, 2000, p. 10.

4. "Guerilla Tactics Gets Panasonic Noticed," *Strategy*, March 27, 2000, p. BMP10.

5. Emily Nelson, "Penney to Launch Free Teen Magazine," *The Wall Street Journal*, April 6, 1999, p. B2.

6. Eniko Campbell and Kathleen Parle, "Less is Really More," *Strategy*, March 13, 2000, p. 34.

7. "What's Hot: Tune In, Turn On Your Customers," *Strategy*, July 19, 1999, p. 5,

8. Larry Ioannou and Joseph Nanni, "Invasion of the Levi's Cats," *Marketing Magazine Online*, May 15, 2000, www.marketingmag.ca.

9. Chris Pritchard, "Advertisers Cautioned by Olympic Scandals," *Marketing Magazine*, April 24, 2000, p. 6.

10. Angela Kryhul, "Fighting Food Fears," *Marketing Magazine*, February 28, 2000, p. 12.

11. Finbarr O'Reilly, "A Hip, Wacky Star is Born," *National Post*, February 2, 2000, pp. B3, B4.

12. This is a condensed version of the definition offered by Don E. Shultz and Heidi F. Shultz, "Transitioning Marketing Communications into the Twenty-First Century," *Journal of Marketing Communications*, March 1998, pp. 9–26.

13. This example is based on information in Bradley Johnson, "Abe Kohnstann: IBM," *Advertising Age*, June 26, 1995 and Sloane Lucas, "One on One," *Brandweek*, September 20, 1999, p. 16.

14. Adapted from Lara Mills, "Coke may Move Towards Localizing," *Marketing Magazine*, February 7, 2000, p. 3. Also, Lara Mills, "Coke is Thinking and Acting Locally," *Marketing Magazine*, March 20, 2000, p. 3.

15. Russ Green, "Making Measuring Simple: Plan Marcomm, Evaluate Criteria," *Advertising Age's Business Marketing*, September 1999, p. 49.

16. Alice Z. Cuneo, "Bridging the Gap," *Advertising Age*, December 13, 1999, p. 22.

17. Virginia Matthews, "Sex That Didn't Sell," *Marketing Magazine Online*, May 10, 1999, www.marketingmag.ca.

18. Marina Strauss, "Adidas Runs With Bailey Despite Trash Talk," *The Globe and Mail*, June 5, 1997, p. B13.

19. Fawzia Sheikh, "Power Premiums, *Marketing Magazine*, August 18/25, 1997, p. S4.

20. "Tiny Lipsticks Sent Direct," *Marketing Magazine*, October 18, 1999, p. 17.

21. Mark DeWolf, "Crystal Springs Pumps Up Collapsible Bottle," *Strategy*, June 23, 1997, p. 4.

22. "Most e-tailers Circling the Drain, Consulting Firm Suggests," *The Globe and Mail*, April 13, 2000, p. B15, reprinted by permission of Associated Press.

23. Adapted from "DEN, Boo: R.I.P.," *National Post Online*, May 21, 2000. A salon.com story reproduced by CP.

24. John Heinzl, "Food Sector Craves Health Pitch," *Report on Business*, November 18, 1998, p. B29.

25. The Misleading Advertising Division of Industry Canada publishes a quarterly review of misleading advertising cases entitled *Misleading Advertising Bulletin*. Individuals interested in receiving this bulletin can have their names placed on the mailing list by contacting Industry Canada.

26. See "Marketer's Guide to Liquor Advertising Regulations," *Marketing Magazine*, August 21/28, 1997, pp. 14–16.

CHAPTER 19

1. Adapted, in part, from Slade Sohmer, "Emerging as a Global Sales Success," *Sales & Marketing Magazine, Internet Edition*, www.salesandmarketing.com, May 8, 2000. Also, "Anderson and Informix Conquer Operational Challenges at Boston Science

Corporation," www.informix.com/informix/success, May 10, 2000.

2. Mark Stevenson, "The Lean, Mean Sales Machine," *Canadian Business*, January 1994, pp. 34, 36.

3. Geoffrey Brewer et al., "1995 Best Sales Force Awards," *Sales & Marketing Management*, October 1995, pp. 52–63.

4. Robert N. McMurray, "The Mystique of Super-Salesmanship," *Harvard Business Review*, March–April 1961, pp. 113–122; Derek A. Newton, *Sales Force Performance and Turnover* (Cambridge, MA: Marketing Science Institute, 1973).

5. Firms that arrange business-to-business auctions include FreeMarkets Online, eSteel, and MetalSite. Visit their Web sites to learn more about how they operate. See also, Sarah Lorge, "Online Bidding Keeps Suppliers In Line," *Sales & Marketing Management*, August 1998, p. 16.

6. Erika Rasmusson, "The 5 Steps to Successful Sales Force Automation," *Sales & Marketing Management*, March 1999, pp. 34–40.

7. To see an example of a Web-based sales force management system designed for small companies, visit www.salesforce.com.

8. Erika Rasmusson, "The 5 Steps to Successful Sales Force Automation," loc. cit.

9. For more on postsale activities, see A. Coskun Samli, Laurence W. Jacobs, and James Wills, "What Presale and Postsale Services Do You Need to Be Competitive?" *Industrial Marketing Management*, February 1992, pp. 33–41.

10. Lesley Daw, "Y' all Come Back Now, Ya Hear?" *Marketing Magazine Online*, February 14, 2000, www.marketingmag.ca.

11. Rekha Balu, "Whirlpool Gets Real With Customers," *Fast Company*, December 1999, pp. 74–76.

12. For a discussion of the importance of recognition in motivating a sales force, see Greg Cochrane, "Recognition Key to Sustaining Staff Passion," *Strategy*, August 18, 1997, pp. 16, 18.

13. See Mark de Wolf, "What Really Motivates the

Salesperson Today," *Strategy*, August 18, 1997, pp. 19, 22. Also, Ann Kerr, "Incentive Travel Buoyed by Economic Recovery," *The Globe and Mail*, September 17, 1996, p. C11.

CHAPTER 20

1. Rocco Rossi, "Suds and Surfing," *Marketing Magazine Online*, January 24, 2000, www.marketingmag.ca; also, the Interbrew Company home page, June 5, 2000, www.interbrew.com, and the Beer.Com home page, June 5, 2000, www.beer.com.

2. Patrick Allossery, "Medium Misses Important Message," *Financial Post*, March 6, 2000, p. C6.

3. Simon Isrealson, "Court Drums Bunny Out of Rival Ad," *The Toronto Star*, November 5, 1995, pp. B1, B10.

4. "Oil of Olay Creams Dove in Court," *The Globe and Mail*, February 24, 1996, p. B6.

5. "Components of Net Advertising Revenues by Medium," *Marketing Magazine Online*, September 13, 1999, www.marketingmag.ca.

6. "Web Advertising in Canada," *Marketing Magazine Online*, September 13, 1999, www.marketingmag.ca.

7. David Eggleston, "SUMmedia Turns Coupon Clippers into Coupon Clickers," Strategy, November 8, 1999, p. D10; also, David Todd, "Savingumoney.com Builds Awareness Offline," *Strategy*, February 28, 2000, p. NP7.

8. David Bosworth, "Lexus Revs Up Biggest DM campaign," *Strategy*, January 28, 1998, p. DR2; also, Lara Mills, "Lexus Plans to Drive Up Utility Market," *Marketing Magazine*, February 23, 1998, p. 3.

9. "Write Your Own Ads, Say Advertisers," *Strategy*, March 13, 2000, p. 6.

10. Doug Sanders, "Advertisers Aim to Fragment TV Audience," *The Globe and Mail*, August 9, 1997, p. C3.

11. Harvey Enchin, "ExpressVu Launches Satellite TV Service," *The Globe and Mail*, September 11, 1997, p. B8.

12. Matthew Fraser, "Welcome to the Information Superhighway," *The Globe and Mail*, September 13, 1997, pp. D1, D2.

13. Janet Callaghan, "Specialties Adopting Smarter Strategies," *Strategy*, June 21, 1999, p. B14.

14. Lina Alles, "Info-Based Channels Pose Buying Challenge," *Strategy*, August 30, 1999, p. 25.

15. Carey Toane, "Teen Internet Use Survey Challenged," *Marketing Magazine*, June 5, 2000, p. 4; also, Bernadette Johnson, "Teen Study Raises Debate," *Strategy*, June 5, 2000, p. 3.

16. "RSVP Award Winner: Financial Services — Wealth Management," *Strategy*, November 22, 1999, p. R32; and David Eggleston, "LaSenza Girl Aims For Right Fit With Tweens," *Strategy*, September 13, 1999, p. D3.

17. Bernadette Johnson, "Westminster Links Direct Mail Back to Internet," *Strategy*, July 19, 1999, p. D5.

18. John Gray, "Advertising Standards to Examine Direct Mail," *Strategy*, June 7, 1999, p. D2.

19. Doug Checkeris, "Leaner, Meaner and Better?" *Marketing Magazine*, November 18, 1996, p. 11.

20. Bernadette Johnson, "Internet Ad Revenues Soaring," *Strategy*, July 19, 1999, p. 6.

21. "Canadian E-tailers Lagging Behind U.S.," *Strategy*, March 13, 2000, p. 6.

22. Mark De Wolf, "Infomercials Get The Thumbs Down," *Strategy*, March 15, 1999, p. D15; also, Sinclair Stewart, "Infomercials to Run on Specialty Channels," *Strategy*, July 19, 1999, p. D1.

23. Mark De Wolf, "Coupon Distributors Improving Their Aim," *Strategy*, May 10, 1999, p. D5.

24. Bernadette Johnson, "Coupon Companies Make Their Way Online," *Strategy*, July 19, 1999, p. D8; also, Raju Mudhar, "Print and Redeem," *Marketing Magazine Online*, November 22, 1999, www.marketingmag.ca.

25. Wayne Mouland, "How to Use Coupons to Get More Trial," *Marketing Magazine Online*, November 22, 1999, www.marketingmag.ca.

26. For additional insight into the nature and management of public relations in Canada, see Jeff Lake, "Managing Your Reputation," *Marketing Magazine*, April 24, 2000, p. 18. Also, a series of special reports on public relations can be found in *Marketing Magazine*, February 21, 2000.

27. Ijeoma Ross, "Reputation is a Depreciable Asset," *The Globe and Mail*, September 11, 1997, p. B17.

CHAPTER 21

1. Kathleen Kerwin, Marcia Stepanek, and David Welch, "At Ford, E-Commerce is Job 1," *Business Week*, February 28, 2000, pp. 74–78; Robert Simison, "GM Retools to Sell Custom Cars Online," *The Wall Street Journal*, February 22, 2000, p. B23; Mary Connelly, "Ford Searches for E-Dollars," *Automotive News*, January 17, 2000, p. 1; Dianne Trommer, "Ford & GM Set to Ride the Internet Highway," *Electronic Buyers' News*, December 6, 1999, p. 88.

2. Shawna Cohen, "Holt's Tries New Marketing Fashion," *Marketing Magazine Online*, February 21, 2000; also "Report on Magazines: Holt's Refines Fashion Ads," *Marketing Magazine Online*, February 28, 2000, www.marketingmag.ca.

3. Seven elements of a horizontal organization are described in John A. Byrne, "The Horizontal Corporation," *Business Week*, December 20, 1993, pp. 76–81.

4. Evelyn Theiss, "Research Shows Good Service is Getting Harder to Find," *St. Louis Post-Dispatch*, June 28, 1999, p. BP22.

5. Avan R. Jassawalla and Hemant C. Sashittal, "Building Collaborative Cross-Functional New Product Teams," *The Academy of Management Executive*, August 1999, p. 50; also Donald Gerwin, "Team Empowerment in New Product Development," *Business Horizons*, July–August 1999, pp. 29.

6. All warranty information regarding Honda products was obtained from the Honda Canada home page, May 25, 2000, www.honda.ca.

7. "Business Bulletin," *The Wall Street Journal*, January 20, 2000, p. A1; also Laurie Grant, "Online Returns a Hassle, Even With a Storefront," *USA Today*, October 28, 1999, p. B3.

8. William Flannery, "Too Many Firms Have Workers Who Think the Customer Isn't Always Right. Training Could Help," *St. Louis Post-Dispatch*, April 18, 1999, p. E1. The quote is from Stephen W. Brown, "Service Recovery Through IT," *Marketing Management*, Fall 1997, p. 25.

9. "Business Bulletin," *The Wall Street Journal*, February 3, 2000, p. A1.

10. Dale Terry, "Does Your Bank's Marketing Size Up?" *Bank Marketing*, January 1995, pp. 55–58.

11. Abe Schuchman, "The Marketing Audit: Its Nature, Purpose and Problems," in *Analyzing and Improving Marketing Performance: "Marketing Audits" in Theory and Practice* (New York: American Management Association, 1959), Management Report no. 32, p. 14. This article is the classic introduction to the marketing audit concept.

12. James G. Barnes, *Genuine Customer Relationships*, New York: McGraw-Hill Companies, 2000, Chapter 8.

13. For a very good overview of the ethical issues involved in marketing and advertising, see Jack Mahoney, "Buyer Beware: Are Marketing and Advertising Always Ethical?" *Financial Post*, December 14/16, 1996, pp. MM10–MM12; reprinted in *Financial Times Mastering Management* (London: Pitman Publishing, 1997), pp. 375–378.

14. John Deverell, "Fundraising Pitch Good for Business, Avon Says," *Toronto Star*, September 26, 1996, p. D3; the Avon Canada home page, June 24, 2000, www.avon.ca.

15. Lara Mills, "Playing Hard to Get," *Marketing Magazine*, April 24, 2000, pp. MD3–4, MD6.

16. Angela Kryhul, "'Waif' Ads under Fire," *Marketing Magazine*, November 22, 1993, p. 2.

17. Andrew Allentuck, "Drug Ads: A Prescription for Trouble?" *The Globe and Mail*, October 29, 1996, p. C7; Shawna Cohen, "The Pill is Controversial Once Again," *Marketing Magazine*, May 15, 2000, p. 3.

18. Sally Goll Beatty and Yumiko Ono, "Seagram Move to TV Stirs Controversy," *The Globe and Mail*, June 12, 1996, p. B8.

19. For a detailed overview of changes in Canada's population, see David K. Foot and Daniel Stoffman, *Boom, Bust & Echo 2000: Profiting From the Demographic Shift in the New Millennium* (Toronto: Macfarlane, Walter & Ross, 1998).

20. Brian McGrory, "Happiness Is a Warm Hotel," *The Globe and Mail*, September 3, 1997, pp. D1, D2.

21. Gerald Levitch, "Mapping the Market," *Marketing Magazine*, February 7, 1994, p. 12.

22. John Dalla Costa, "A Commitment to Quality," *Marketing Magazine*, April 25, 1994, p. 8.

23. Sandra Vandermerwe and Michael Oliff, "Corporate Challenges for an Age of Reconsumption," *Columbia Journal of World Business*, Fall 1991, pp. 23–28.

24. James G. Barnes, "Close to the Customer: But Is It Really a Relationship," *Journal of Marketing Management*, 1994, vol. 10, pp. 561–570.

25. Daphne A. Sheaves and James G. Barnes, "The Fundamentals of Relationships," in Teresa A. Swartz, David E. Bowen, and Stephen W. Brown, eds., *Advances in Services Marketing and Management*, vol. 5 (Greenwich, CT: JAI Press, Inc., 1996); and James G. Barnes, "Closeness, Strength and Satisfaction: Examining the Nature of Relationships between Providers of Financial Services and their Retail Customers," *Psychology and Marketing, Special Issue on Relationship Marketing*, 1997.

APPENDIX

1. Lisa Wright, "Experts Help Avoid 'Cyber Surprises,'" *Toronto Star*, November 12, 1997, p. D1.

Topical Index

Photo Credits

CHAPTER 4
p. 99, Photo by: Paul Rockett. Courtesy of *NUVO* magazine.

CHAPTER 5
p. 123, Photo © 2000, Molson Canada.
p. 135, Modrobes, October 1998. Print advertisement featured in *Resource* Magazine — national university publication.
p. 138, Courtesy of W. Sullivan.
p. 141, McAuslan Brewing Inc. Agency: Kelly & Aylen Marketing Inc.
p. 142, Fido ad prepared by Goodhue & Associates.

CHAPTER 6
p. 153, Bugaboos.com ad provided courtesy of Palmer Jarvis DDB. Photo: Lyon Behar.
p. 170, Photo courtesy of Christine Lomas.

CHAPTER 7
p. 188, Photo is courtesy of Bombardier Recreational Products.
p. 192, Courtesy of Cebra Inc.
p. 204, Developed for the Purchasing Management Association of Canada by Cooper, Spearing & Stone Advertising.

CHAPTER 8
p. 215, Courtesy of *Toronto Star*/Gedeonova.

CHAPTER 9
p. 267, Photo courtesy of Ballard Power System.
p. 269, © 2000 Hertz System, Inc. & Hertz is a registered service mark and trademark of Hertz System, Inc.

CHAPTER 10
p. 297, Photo © 2000, Molson Canada.

CHAPTER 12
p. 351, Photo courtesy of Christine Lomas.
p. 356, Photo courtesy of Peanuts © United Feature Syndicate, Inc.

CHAPTER 13
p. 407, Advertisement courtesy of L'Oreal Canada.

CHAPTER 14
p. 421, Mercata Inc.
p. 423, Creative Director: Len Laycock. Writer: Nigel Yonge.
p. 427, Advertisement courtesy of L'Oreal Canada.

CHAPTER 15
p. 463, Photo courtesy of Alison Derry.
p. 472, Photo courtesy of Canadian Tire.
p. 479, Photo courtesy of Alison Derry.

CHAPTER 16
p. 501, Copyright © eBay Inc. 1995–2000.
p. 501, Photo courtesy of freemarkets.com.
p. 504, © PBB Global Logistics.

CHAPTER 17
p. 524, Photo courtesy of Alison Derry.
p. 539, Photo courtesy of Alison Derry.

CHAPTER 18
p. 579, Photo by Steve Double.
p. 584, Reproduced with permission of www.can.ibm.com, 2000 by International Business Machines Corporation.
p. 584, Reproduced with permission of www.ibm.com, 2000 by International Business Machines Corporation.
p. 584, Reproduced with permission of www.de.ibm.com, 2000 by International Business Machines Corporation.
p. 585, Photo courtesy of Coca-Cola Ltd. and The Coca-Cola Company.

CHAPTER 19
p. 613, Photo courtesy of Canadian Tire.

CHAPTER 20
p. 633, © beer.com

CHAPTER 21
p. 683, Photo courtesy of Christine Lomas.
p. 689, For complete details, see the Honda Owner's Manual.